THE CONCEPT OF WOMAN

THE CONCEPT OF WOMAN

. .

VOLUME II

The Early Humanist Reformation

1250-1500

Sister Prudence Allen, R.S.M.

WILLIAM B. EERDMANS PUBLISHING COMPANY
GRAND RAPIDS, MICHIGAN / CAMBRIDGE, U.K.

Wm. B. Eerdmans Publishing Co.
255 Jefferson Ave. S.E., Grand Rapids, Michigan 49503 /
P.O. Box 163, Cambridge CB3 9PU U.K.

Printed in the United States of America

06 05 04 03 02   7 6 5 4 3 2 1

Library of Congress Cataloging-in-Publication Data

Allen, Prudence.
The concept of woman : volume II:
the early humanist reformation 1250-1500 / Prudence Allen.
p.   cm.
ISBN 0-8028-4735-8 (alk. paper)
1. Femininity (Philosophy) — History. 2. Women — History.
3. Sex — History. I. Title.
BD450.A4725   2002
305.4′01 — dc20   96-9102
CIP

www.eerdmans.com

In gratitude for her personal witness to the integration of religious and professional life and to her continuous personal support for the research and writing of this book, I dedicate this second volume of *The Concept of Woman* to the memory of Sister Mary Honora Kroger, R.S.M., Ph.D. (1916-1995).

CONTENTS

CHRONOLOGICAL TABLE
OF AUTHORS AND TEXTS
CONSIDERED IN VOLUME II

Robert Grosseteste	1175-1253
Vincent of Beauvais	1190-1264
St. Albert the Great	1193-1280
Beatrice of Nazareth	1205-1286
Hadewijch	thirteenth century
Mechtild of Magdeburg	1212-1298
Roger Bacon	1214-1292
St. Thomas Aquinas	1224-1274
[Guillaume de Lorris and Jean de Meun]	
Le Roman de la rose	1225-1278
[Mahieu le Bigame and Jean le Fèvre]	
Le Livre de Mathéolus	c. 1300
Marguerite Porete	died 1310
Meister Eckhart	1235-1302
Mechtild of Hackeborn	1241-1298
Giles of Rome	1243-1316
Guido Cavalcanti	1255-1300
St. Gertrude the Great	1256-1302
Francesco Barberino	1264-1348
John Duns Scotus	1265-1308
Dante Alighieri	1265-1321
William of Ockham	1280-1349
Frau Welt	c. 1285
La Contenance des fames	1275-1330
Le Blasme des fames	1275-1330
Henry Suso	1295-1363
Johannes Tauler	1300-1361
St. Bridget of Sweden	1303-1373
Francis Petrarch	1304-1374
Giovanni Boccaccio	1313-1375
Julian of Norwich	1343-c. 1416

St. Catherine of Siena	1347-1380
Christine de Pizan	1363-1431
Leonardo Bruni d'Arezzo	1369-1444
Margery Kempe	1373–c. 1438
Guarino of Verona	1374-1460
Vittorino of Feltre	1378-1446
[Eustache Deschamps]	
Le Miroir de mariage	c. 1381-1420
Francesco Barbaro	1390-1454
Nicholas of Cusa	1401-1464
Leon Battista Alberti	1404-1472
Lorenzo Valla	1406-1457
St. Joan of Arc	1412-1431
Isotta Nogarola	1418-1466
Albrecht von Eyb	1420-1466
Marsilio Ficino	1433-1499
[Heinrich Kramer and James Sprenger]	
The Malleus maleficarum	1448
[Antoine de la Sale]	
Les Quinze joies de mariage	mid-fifteenth century
Giovanni Pico Mirandola	1463-1494
Laura Cereta	1469-1499
Evangile aux femmes	c. 1490

Where the author is not listed or is in [ ], the dates refer to the composition of the text.

CHRONOLOGICAL TABLE
OF AUTHORS REFERRED TO
FROM VOLUME I

Sappho	c. 750 BC
Parmenides	c. 539-500 BC
Pythagoras	c. 530 BC
Anaxagoras	c. 500-428 BC
Euripides	480-406 BC
Socrates	c. 470-357
Hippocrates	c. 460-377 BC
Democritus	c. 460-370 BC
Empedocles	c. 450
Aspasia	c. 440 BC
Xenophon	c. 430-357
Plato	c. 428-355
Theano I	fourth century BC
Aristotle	384-322 BC
Theophrastus	370-286 BC
Epicurus	c. 341-270 BC
Theano II	second century BC
Cicero	106-43 BC
Lucretius	98-55 BC
Ovid	43 BC-AD 17
Philo	13 BC-AD 54
Seneca	AD 4-64
Plutarch	50-125
Juvenal	60-140
Galen	131-201
Plotinus	205-270
Porphyry	235-305
St. Catherine of Alexandria	c. 307
St. Jerome	347-420
St. Augustine	354-430
Hypatia	370-415

Boethius	480-524
Hilda of Whitby	614-680
John Scotus Erigena	810-877
Hroswitha (Roswitha)	c. 935-1002
Avicenna	980-1037
Avicebron	1020-1070
St. Anselm	1033-1109
Abelard	1079-1142
Hildegard of Bingen	1098-1179
Peter Lombard	1100-1160
Heloise	1101-1164
Averroes	1126-1198
Herrad of Landsberg	1130-1195
Maimonides	1135-1204
Walter Map	c. 1140-1209
Andreas Capellanus	c. 1186

ILLUSTRATIONS

LIST OF TABLES

ACKNOWLEDGMENTS

Supplemental Research Grants and Internal Research Grants from the Social Sciences and Humanities Research Council of Canada from 1982 to 1995 have contributed significantly to the gathering and analysis of material presented in this book. I am very grateful to this granting agency of the federal government of Canada for its continued support for the long project of the philosophical study of "Women's Conceptual History." These funds have enabled me to hire research assistants, to travel to original sources, to access secondary-source databases, and to consult with other scholars in the preliminary dispersion of findings. In particular, I would like to mention the following student assistants who have aided my research for this volume: Frank Benson, RN, MA, Sr. John Marie Bullitt, R.S.M., M.D., Pierre Boulos, Ph.D., Dominique Deslandres, Ph.D., Beata Gallay, Ph.D., Carla Groudis, MA, Jennifer Harris, Ph.D., Sr. Mary Danielle Johnson, R.S.M., MA, Patricia Pintaldo, MA, Sr. Mary Veronica Sabelli, R.S.M., JD, MA, Patricia Sheridan, MA, Claudia Spensor, Mary Troxell, MA, and George Turski, Ph.D.

The support of the administration of Concordia University has been consistently generous. In addition to granting me sabbatical years in 1986-87 for research on humanism at Yale University, in Germany, in Rome and Florence, and in 1994-95 for research at the Library of Congress and the Folger Library in Washington, D.C., the university also supported my research by permitting a reduced course load during the regular academic year. Bruce Martin, Research Librarian at the Library of Congress, was especially helpful in providing research space and aid. I would also like to mention my personal gratitude to persons at Concordia University who exceeded the normal bounds of generosity to help me with various aspects of the project: Peter Bird, Wendy Knechtel, Alex Lawrie, Maureen MacCuish, Marvin Orbach, Phyllis Prussick, Larry Tansey, and Audrey Williams. Special thanks are owed to the following persons for help in securing illustrations for the book: Michele Bertoia, Judy Longacre, Ph.D., Sr. Yvonne Mary Loucks, RSM, Ph.D., and Filippo Salvatore, Ph.D. All those who have contributed translations of different original sources not available in English are mentioned in the notes to the texts they translated.

Since coming to Denver, Colorado in 1998 I have been particularly grateful for the support of the St. John Vianney Theological Seminary Administration for the completion of this book. In addition, the faithful help of the staff of the Archbishop Vehr Theological Library and the Interlibrary Loan Department of the University of Colorado at Boulder has made it possible to maintain access to the most recent sources. I would like to mention in particular my thanks to the librarians Lynn Cotton, Sharon Figlino, Sylvia Rael, and Michael Woodward, Ph.D. Finally, the constant support of Dennis Pinkerton for computer services has been invaluable.

My deep gratitude also extends to those persons who willingly read portions of the text and offered their critical insights into it during the extensive period of revisions. In particular I would like to note with thanks Rev. Francis Martin, STD, Sr. Anne O'Donnell, S.N.D., Ph.D., Beata Gallay, Ph.D., and Sr. Rita Rae Schneider, R.S.M., Ph.D., who have worked through the entire text with me in various versions. I also thank the following persons for their insights on particular aspects of the book: Mildred Allen, Sr. Mary Christine Cremin, R.S.M., Ph.D., Sr. Mary Timothea Elliott, R.S.M., STD, Thelma Fenster, Ph.D., Joan Gibson, Ph.D., Sister Barbara Gooding, R.S.M., Ph.D., Christopher Gray, Ph.D., Rosemary Hale, Ph.D., John Hittinger, Ph.D., Christine Jolliffe, MA, Rev. Luigi Lafavia, Ph.D., Charles LePage, MA, Zhaolu Lu, Ph.D., Sr. Mary Judith O'Brien, R.S.M., JD, JCD, Diana Robin, Ph.D., Filippo Salvatore, Ph.D., David Schindler, Ph.D., Prof. Richard Schoeck, William Shea, Ph.D., Maureen Slattery, Ph.D., Sr. Mary Cora Urayse, R.S.M., Ph.D., Susan Wake, Ph.D., Fr. William Wallace, O.P, Ph.D., Kevin White, Ph.D., and members of The Scholars Circle, Concordia University. I would like to thank Mother Mary McGreevy, R.S.M., Vicar General, and Mother Mary Quentin Sheridan, R.S.M., Superior General of the Religious Sisters of Mercy of Alma. Without their continuous love and guidance this book would not have been completed. Finally, for all those who have offered their personal support and prayers during this time of research and writing, I am very grateful.

With the broad chronological base of 1250 to 1500, which crosses many fields and disciplines, there are considerable differences of opinion about the meaning and interpretation of sources. My own conclusions differ at times from those recommended to me by some of the persons just mentioned. Thus, all final responsibility for the interpretations given to texts is entirely my own.

Finally, for her meticulous work in creating the index, verifying the bibliography, and proofreading and editing the text, I am indebted to the outstanding skills of Beata Gallay, Ph.D. In conclusion, I would like to thank the Eerdmans family at Wm. B. Eerdmans Publishing Co., and in particular Michael Thomson, for their interest and encouragement about publishing a work of this size.

INTRODUCTION

The initial question raised at the beginning of the first volume of *The Concept of Woman* — "What is to become of woman and man?" — still compels our attention. Today tensions are increasing about the issue of the respective identities of women and men. These tensions are often fed by conflicting ideologies and by weak philosophical analyses. In this contemporary context, philosophical reflections on the concept of woman between 1250 and 1500 may bring some illumination. The popular historian Barbara Tuchman refers to the fourteenth century as "a distant mirror,"[1] through which we may glimpse something of the emerging modern identities of women and men. Her analogy implies that we can discover something about ourselves by focusing on men and women who lived in late Medieval and early Renaissance Europe.

My goal is to clarify the ways in which selected women and men writers between 1250 and 1500 articulated concepts of woman, to evaluate the ways in which their theories gave evidence of either growth or stagnation in relation to the previous two thousand years of western philosophy, and finally to evaluate the ways in which these theories, with all their conflicting and illuminating dynamics, enter into our cultural heritage along the specific lines of the philosophy of sex and gender identity.

The perspective in this text is clearly a reverse of the traditional philosophical approach: it moves the concept of woman into the foreground of attention while that of man remains in the background. By turning to a metaphor from the history of art, the significance of this shift in perspective may become clearer. The artistic technique of depicting perspective was a great advance of the Renaissance. Two different things are needed to see in three-dimensional perspective: first, an appropriate delineation of foreground and background within a work of art, and second, a viewer who is able to see simultaneously with two eyes. It could be said that traditional western thinkers have used primarily one eye when they focused entirely on

---

1. Barbara W. Tuchman, *A Distant Mirror: The Calamitous 14th Century* (New York: Ballantine Books, 1978). The pioneer work of Régine Pernoud on women's identity during the same period should also be noted. See *La Femme au temps des cathédrales* (Paris: Stock/Lawrence Pernoud, 1980); *Lumière du Moyen Age* (Paris: B. Grasset, 1981); and *Pour en finir avec le Moyen Age* (Paris: Seuil, 1977).

the concept of man and neglected the concept of woman. By repeated use this one eye became extremely strong. The other eye, which focuses on the concept of woman, is much weaker because of its historical lack of use. Therefore, by strengthening the weaker eye, we hope to offer a more accurate perspective on the intertwined conceptual histories of men and women.[2]

In addition, by looking into the distant mirror of late Medieval and early Renaissance Europe, contemporary women and men may discover a more authentic foundation for their own complementary identities. The principle of complementarity here means simply that explanations of the respective identities of woman and of man are both needed to explain the identity of the human being.[3] In other words, this focus on the concept of woman has as one of its goals the full development of all men and women.

At the beginning of humanist philosophy the criteria to describe what a man needed to become more fully human included: receiving and giving a classical education, accepting the emotions as natural to human identity, living a virtuous life, using speech well, and participating in civic life through public dialogue and action. During the same period of early humanism (1250-1500) we also discover arguments for the removal of obstacles for women to become fully human in the sense just described. These arguments were needed because women generally did not have the same access as humanist men to these necessary conditions for full human development.

Christine de Pizan stands out as being the first author, man or woman, to articulate a philosophical foundation for women to become fully human within the broader goal of the full human development of all men, women, and children. By 'philosophical foundation' are meant her use of various forms of philosophical argument, engagement in direct dialogue with authors holding different positions, and her appeal to reason and to the evidence of the senses to defend her views. Because of Christine's critical role as the first apologist to engage in public debate about obstacles that existed and that seriously interfered with women's full development as human beings, an entire chapter of this book is devoted to an analysis of her views.

Not all historical forms of humanism share the goal of the full development of all persons. For example, various forms of Enlightenment, Secular, Marxist, and

2. Rev. Francis Martin, author of *The Feminist Question: Feminist Theology in the Light of the Christian Tradition* (Grand Rapids: Eerdmans, 1994), suggested this metaphor of perspective, borrowed from the theological context of the complementary traditions of the eastern and western churches, both of which are needed for the full development of Christianity. His text *The Feminist Question* provides excellent distinctions and extensive mention of authors and issues pertinent to the philosophical approach taken in *The Concept of Woman*. For a survey of contemporary distinctions in religious studies see Ursula King, ed., *Religion and Gender* (Oxford: Blackwell, 1995); and Rosi Braidotti, "What's Wrong with Gender?" in *Reflections on Theology and Gender*, ed. Fokkelien van Dijk-Hemmes and Athalya Brenner (Kampen: Kok, 1994), pp. 49-107.

3. Buckminster Fuller, author of *Critical Path* (New York: St. Martin's Press, 1981) and *Synergetics: Explorations in the Geometry of Thinking* (New York: Macmillan, 1982), notes the philosophical significance of the discovery in 1922 of the fundamental principle of complementarity in the physical universe through Niels Bohr's explanation of light in terms of waves and particles.

Existentialist Humanism appear to support the full development of some human beings, but at the expense of limiting the development of other human beings. Contemporary Personalist Humanism, on the other hand, shares the goal articulated by Christine de Pizan's Renaissance Humanism, namely, that removing obstacles for women to become fully human should not occur at the expense of the full development of other human beings.[4]

It may appear strange and even contradictory to some readers that the subtitle to this text puts together the words 'Humanist' and 'Reformation,' because leaders of the Protestant Reformation often argued that the cultivation of the intellect is not a value.[5] The Reformation referred to in this book is not the Protestant Reformation, nor the Catholic Counter-Reformation. Instead, it refers to the collective attempts to reform the concept of woman, using humanist principles. A more detailed explanation of the subtitle "The Early Humanist Reformation: 1250-1500" will be given later in this introduction. Thus, both 'Humanism' and 'Reformation' have a precise meaning in this book, a meaning drawn particularly from texts related to the concept of woman written by female and male authors leading up to and during the period 1250-1500.

The Concept of Woman: The Early Humanist Reformation (1250-1500) may be helpful to both women and men, but in initially different ways. First of all, the original texts studied in the book were written by people who had an engendered experience of their own identity and who struggled to articulate various aspects of this experience. By 'engendered experience' is meant the self-conscious experience of a woman or a man who reflects directly on the meaning of being a female human being or a male human being. This may include the experience of having a female or male body, a collective history as women or men, a particular experience of being brought up in a society as male or female, a response to masculine and feminine aspects of language, and so forth.

Secondly, contemporary readers, who are also engendered as women and men, appropriate the material in different ways. Women who read about the concept of woman between 1250 and 1500 may appropriate developments in their own conceptual history, while men who read the same material may engage with the matrix of women's conceptual history as something outside of the male self. The opposite experience will occur for those articulations in the texts that describe the history of the concept of man. Here men may appropriate their own particular history while women engage with the matrix of men's particular history.

The Concept of Woman: The Early Humanist Reformation (1250-1500) is a kind of genealogy of gender in western thought. The genealogy referred to here is analogous to biological genealogy, in which genes from previous generations provide part of the inherited structure within which persons live out the self-interpretation of their lives. It also implies an evolution in the concept of woman which is continuous even as it emerges in higher levels of self-appropriation

4. For a more detailed analysis of different kinds of humanism see Sr. Prudence Allen, R.S.M., "Can Feminism Be a Humanism?" in Études maritainiennes — Maritain Studies 14 (1998): 109-40.

5. Jim Moore, member of the Department of Political Science and originator of the Scholar's Circle, Concordia University, raised this question.

through the exercise of human freedom. A woman can determine to some extent what kind of woman she wants to be. Analogously, a man can determine to some extent what kind of man he wants to be.

In order to gain a more accurate self-knowledge, women and men need to appropriate critically the genealogy of their own gender. At the same time, an individual person is always more than the genealogical heir of his or her father and mother because of the gift of human freedom. Therefore, while a person appropriates an engendered identity in the context of a specific inherited genealogy, he or she may always make decisions to become a particular kind of man or woman by taking action that differs from or coincides with the specific patterns within an engendered genealogy. Knowledge of a particular genealogy of gender may help women and men to become clearer about the value of certain decisions in this area of life.

One of the goals of this study is to set forth various structures of the concept of woman as it evolved through different authors. Sometimes this goal is very difficult to achieve because the texts and their meanings are obscure. At other times the process of reaching the goal is painful because the meaning is all too clear when it may involve the devaluation of women or of men. Yet, it seems important in a study of this size to include analysis of all works that contained philosophical arguments or theories directly relating to the concept of woman between the years 1250 and 1500. Therefore, no text written during this period has been consciously excluded or its meaning intentionally distorted. It is hoped that knowledge of the truth will not feed resentments but instead open the way for a better understanding and a more authentic love.[6]

This study includes only texts that used a philosophical method of discursive or logical reasoning or an appeal to the evidence of the senses to defend an argument. By 'discursive or logical reasoning' I mean a process of thinking that proceeds in an orderly fashion from premises to conclusions, and that the premises can be supported by empirical or reasonable evidence. More specifically, theological arguments that appealed to faith, the scriptures, or religious authority are excluded except when they have direct relevance to a philosophical argument. Several religious women writers were included when their arguments about women's identity were philosophical.[7] On the other hand, historical or cultural texts which described "men, matters, and events" or which focus on the situation of women in general during a period under study were excluded. With these criteria of selection, texts written between 1250 and 1500 provided numerous clusters of philosophical arguments about women's identity which were then systematically analyzed for repeated patterns or new structures of the concept of woman.

A further epistemological clarification of methodology may be helpful here.

---

6. Jean Bethke Elshtain described the first volume of *The Concept of Woman* in these terms. I am grateful for her own work on women's identity as well as her continued support through personal correspondence and dialogue about my particular approach to this historical study.

7. Mary Ellen Waithe, ed., *A History of Women Philosophers: Volume II: Medieval, Renaissance and Enlightenment Women Philosophers: A.D. 500-1600* (Dordrecht/Boston/London: Kluwer, 1989), makes a similar inclusion. Among those women to whom she devotes individual chapters in this text include Hildegard of Bingen, Heloise, Herrad of Hohenbourg, Beatrice of Nazareth, Mechtild of Magdeburg, Hadewijch of Antwerp, Brigitta of Sweden, Julian of Norwich, and Catherine of Siena.

There are many levels of analysis that will be seen in the original texts. The lowest level, from the philosophical perspective, is one that simply appeals to a personal experience as a criterion of truth. Experience is the starting point, but it is not the ending point. At the next level, an author will try to bring the intellect to bear on the personal experience, to question it in order to learn whether it is simply a subjective experience or whether it can serve as an adequate foundation for a generally true hypothesis. At a still further level of reflection, the author exercises reason to search out other criteria that may provide a more accurate measure of whether this personal experience can serve as an objective basis for claims about some aspect of woman's or man's identity. Here, an appeal may be made to commonly accepted scientific or theoretical principles to determine the congruence of a subjective insight with established claims thought generally to be true.

Finally, when the author reaches a level of certainty about the truth of a claim about the concept of woman, a fourth level of response may move into responsible actions depending upon the particular issue being considered. The four levels of consciousness summarized as 'experiential, intellectual, reasonable, and responsible' are characteristic of what Bernard Lonergan identifies as philosophical self-appropriation.[8] In the analysis of texts from 1250 to 1500 we will see this progression in epistemological approaches of both women and men authors to the concept of woman. We will also study some consequences of actions that follow from claims based on faulty evidence that had gained acceptance because of various forms of bias that devalued woman's identity.

Our focus will move now from a consideration of theoretical aspects of the methodology used in this book to technological aspects of gathering data for its content. Advances in technology have influenced the research for *The Concept of Woman: The Early Humanist Reformation (1250-1500)* in two different ways. First, through the technological revolution of the fifteenth century the invention of the printing press produced many more texts on woman's identity than had been written and copied by hand. Second, the technological revolution in the twentieth century has established large electronic databases of secondary sources, new translations, and reprinting of primary sources from the period 1250 to 1500. A positive effect of these technological advancements is to give access to an increasingly wider range of sources. A more negative effect may rebound on the contemporary researcher, making the vast project of tracing the various structures of the concept of woman in western philosophy increasingly difficult to achieve. Nearly every day some new relevant article or text emerges within the public domain. Eventually, in order to bring this analysis to completion, a decision had to be made simply to stop looking at new data. Consequently, while there will no doubt be new sources that need to be considered in light of the theses put forward in this text, that task will be left to other scholars.

---

8. This brief summary of levels of epistemological claims is indebted to the work of Bernard Lonergan, *Insight* (Toronto: University of Toronto Press, 1992) and *Method in Theology* (Toronto: University of Toronto Press, 1990). For a description of the application of Lonergan's method to the history of the concept of woman see Cynthia W. Crysdale, "Women and the Social Construction of Self-Appropriation," in *Lonergan and Feminism,* Crysdale, ed. (Toronto: University of Toronto Press, 1994), pp. 88-113.

A further complication in the research for this book is that the consistently simple and broad structures of the concept of woman as described in Volume I — *The Concept of Woman: The Aristotelian Revolution (750 BC–1250 AD),* dissolved into several strands of complex and overlapping themes in this next phase of development from 1250 to 1500. In some ways the conclusions of this study of the concept of woman from 1250 to 1500 have a similar quality to the mapping of the numerous rivers and lakes in North America by early explorers; they appear rough and somewhat distorted when compared with meticulous contemporary maps. Inaccuracies in the primitive maps can be eliminated in the future by specialization and technological advances that give research a greater accuracy over time. In this sense, I hope that the limitations of the present analysis will be seen, not so much as a liability, but rather as an open invitation for those with greater skills in the area of late Medieval and Renaissance studies to make more precise judgments and accurate conclusions about this phase in the development of the concept of woman. Therefore, we should see the present volume as providing some preliminary hypotheses in an emerging field of the philosophy of woman and man as it evolved between 1250 and 1500 in western Europe.

The Concept of Woman: The Early Humanist Reformation (1250-1500) contains extensive original source data that were often difficult to locate and gather together from a diverse number of sources. Thus the large number of selections from original texts may be useful as a starting point for interpretations other than those suggested here. While the line of analysis is philosophical with an emphasis on the history of ideas, there are many other important voices that need to be heard. The audience for which this book is intended includes, in addition to philosophers, scholars in the fields of history, political science, religious studies, renaissance studies, theology, literature, education, women's studies, and feminist studies. In addition, the chronologies of authors and texts, tables, summaries, and inclusion of passages from original texts make the book accessible to students and to the educated public as well. Wherever possible, philosophical concepts are expressed in ordinary language and texts are translated into modern English. When new terms are introduced for purposes of classification and differentiation, they are described or defined. *The Concept of Woman: The Early Humanist Reformation (1250-1500)* is written as an invitation to a wide range of readers to enter and to reflect upon different aspects of the concept of woman as articulated by women and men during the thirteenth, fourteenth, and fifteenth centuries in western Europe. Ultimately, it is an invitation to look into this distant mirror and to discover truths applicable to woman's and man's respective identities today.

REVIEW OF THE CONCEPT OF WOMAN: 750 B.C.–1250 A.D.

Readers familiar with the first volume, *The Concept of Woman: The Aristotelian Revolution (750 B.C.–1250 A.D.),* may wish to skip this section of the introduction, or simply review the conclusions reached in it, before moving on. Those readers who have not read the first volume would be helped in their appreciation of the significance of the developments in the concept of woman between 1250 and 1500 by reading what follows. Before considering innovations in Renaissance Humanism, it is important to grasp the original foundations of the concept of woman as they were first articulated in ancient Greek philosophy and to trace the effects of medieval philosophy and the institutionalization of Aristotelianism on these foundations. By the expression 'Aristotelian Revolution' I denote the triumph of the Aristotelian structure of the concept of woman over other structures by the mid-thirteenth century. This triumph occurred through the institutionalization of Aristotelian criteria for the concept of woman when Aristotle's works became required reading in the Faculty of Arts (and extended to the Faculties of Theology and Medicine) at the University of Paris, and when subsequent foundations of other universities across Europe adopted the curriculum from Paris as the model for their own. This stabilization and dispersion of the Aristotelian philosophical structure of the concept of woman gave a life of its own to the concept — a life that dominated western thought until new developments in humanism attempted to reform it.

The first volume of *The Concept of Woman* also demonstrated that nearly every philosopher in this early phase of western philosophy considered some aspect of the concept of woman. The Presocratic philosophers raised fundamental questions about woman, which were classified broadly into the following four categories.

1. **Metaphysics**: Are women and men **opposite** or the same?
2. **Philosophy of nature**: Does what a mother or father contributes to human **generation** have any relevance to sex identity?
3. **Epistemology**: Do women and men have the same or different faculties of reasoning, and are women and men **wise** in the same or different ways?
4. **Ethics**: Are women and men **virtuous** by performing the same or different acts?

These four categories may be abbreviated as: 'opposites,' 'generation,' 'wisdom,' and 'virtue.' They provided the framework for the systematic analysis of the concept of woman as described by ancient and medieval philosophers.

The articulation of answers to these four fundamental questions about the concept of woman began to reveal certain repeated patterns or structures of thought. When a philosopher offered answers that crossed all four categories, then a **theory** of sex identity was identified. Plato was the first philosopher about whom we have evidence of such a theory. He was not completely consistent, but for the most part I characterized Plato's views as a **sex unity** or **unisex** theory. That is, Plato basically argued that there were no significant differences between men and women, and that they were equally human. A metaphysical justification for this claim of fundamental equality came from postulating the existence of a sexless soul that could be reincarnated in different kinds of bodies. At the same time, Plato hinted at a gender inequality when he suggested that immoral or cowardly men were reborn as women in subsequent reincarnations. He also argued that women's weaker starting position should be compensated by a greater length in time of education. Women philosophers as well as men philosophers could both achieve complete release from cycles of rebirth. It is not surprising that Plato's Academy had some women philosophers.

Aristotle was the next philosopher to offer a theoretical foundation for the concept of woman that covered all four categories of questions identified by the Presocratics. In addition, Aristotle was the first philosopher whose theory was consistent across all four categories. He drew on a metaphysics of opposites, (a superior) **hot** and (an inferior contrary) **cold**, to support a claim that in generation the female, being colder, was a malformed or misbegotten male. Consequences of this inferior formation of the female included having a weaker rational faculty that was without authority over the emotions, and some distinct virtues that were more proper to woman (i.e., silence instead of speech, obedience instead of ruling, work in the private domain instead of the public domain, etc.). Aristotle elaborated a foundation for the significant differentiation and inequality of women and men which I characterized as a theory of **sex polarity**. It is not surprising that in union with this theory of the natural inferiority of the female, there appear to have been no women philosophers in Aristotle's Peripatetic school.

During the thousand years of philosophy following Aristotle there were no original developments in the concept of woman. Rather, the different schools of philosophy adopted some aspects of Plato's thought and some of Aristotle's. At times they added a particular nuance to the theory as the original Greek philosopher had articulated it. For example, along the lines of sex unity, the Neoplatonic philosopher Porphyry suggested that his wife Marcella reject her engendered body so that she could be as much a philosopher as a man; the Neopythagoreans elaborated in more detail some of the virtues that were shared among women and men; and the Stoic philosopher Musonius Rufus argued directly that women ought to study philosophy. On the other hand, along the lines of sex polarity, Philo further linked the concept of woman to matter and the concept of man to form, and the Roman Stoic Juvenal extended a devaluation of women into a satire on women's vices.

With the work of St. Augustine, a new historical development of the concept of woman occurred. Struggling to integrate the Christian belief, that in the resurrection of the body all imperfections will disappear, with the Aristotelian suggestion that the female is an imperfect male, Augustine came to the conclusion that woman's sex is no imperfection, and both women and men will exist in a resurrected state in heaven. The theological insight, that in heaven men and women have an equal dignity but are also significantly different because of their engendered embodiment, led Augustine to articulate the beginnings of a third theory of sex identity, which I referred to as **sex complementarity**. Previously, in the writings of Empedocles and Parmenides on generation, there had been some movement towards complementarity, but Platonic and Aristotelian rationales had eclipsed sex complementarity by arguing either that there is no differentiation between women and men (sex unity) or there is differentiation but no fundamental equality in dignity (sex polarity).

Although St. Augustine saw that Christian thought needed a foundation for authentic complementarity within which men and women have both an equal dignity and significant differentiation, he did not consistently carry this insight throughout his writings. Instead, he suggested a kind of sex polarity theory for women who are married and live in the outside world, and a kind of sex unity theory for women who left the outside world to become nuns. Other early Christian philosophers struggled to come to terms with the concept of woman as well. Boethius opened an imaginary association of the concept of wisdom with woman's identity in his elaboration of Lady Philosophy, while John Scotus Erigena presented a unisex model in which sex differentiation was seen as the result of the Fall from original Creation.

It was in the work of the Benedictine Abbess, Hildegard of Bingen, that we find the first consistent philosophical grounding for a theory of sex complementarity. Drawing upon her knowledge of the medieval science of humors and elements, her experience as a nurse, and her learning through study, prayer, and dialogue, Hildegard provided an elaborate defense of the two fundamental premises of sex complementarity: significant differentiation of women and men joined to an equality of dignity. She went even further by describing four different types of women and four different types of men who are separate, yet in interaction with one another. Since Hildegard's analysis was the first of its kind to cover all four categories of opposites, generation, wisdom, and virtue, I identified her as the founder of the sex complementarity theory in company with Plato as the founder of the sex unity theory and Aristotle as the founder of the sex polarity theory.

Plato's school, with its premise of the equality of women and men, was open to women philosophers, while Aristotle's school, with its devaluation of women, appeared to be closed to women philosophers. Hildegard's double monastery within the Benedictine tradition provided the context within which women and men often spoke with one another about intellectual and spiritual pursuits. In a double monastery, a men's and a women's monastery were institutionally conjoined under the leadership of either an Abbot or an Abbess. In Volume I of *The Concept of Woman* it was suggested that this type of context in which women and men studied and spoke with one another seemed most amenable to the development of an authentic complementarity. We will see in Volume II evidence to support the same hypothesis in the dialogue that emerges among women and men in early humanism.

In the concluding chapters of the first volume of *The Concept of Woman* we traced the slow but steady integration of Plato's and Aristotle's thought into Islamic, Jewish, and Christian philosophy. By the early thirteenth century the philosophical foundations for a focus on the Aristotelian sex polarity theory were firmly in place in the key centers of education in western Europe. Benedictine monasteries, which had served as educational centers for the previous four centuries, were now eclipsed by the many universities being established through the cooperative action of royalty and bishops in more urban locations throughout Europe. Aristotle's works were translated into Latin, and commentaries on his works became the standard method of teaching. As a side effect of the demographic shift in type and location of educational centers, women, who had previously been able to achieve higher education in monasteries, no longer had access to the new centers of academic study, as nearly all universities were open only to men. This situation remained the same for over six hundred years.

In spite of the extensive negative impact the Aristotelian rationale had on the concept of woman in subsequent centuries, there were two important positive results from the Christian medieval incorporation and development of Aristotle's philosophy. The first one distinguishes the concept of woman according to nature from the concept of woman according to grace. St. Albert the Great and St. Thomas Aquinas both struggled to articulate a new formulation of theological aspects of the concept of woman that would overturn the Aristotelian grounds for sex polarity while still keeping the fundamentals of his theory in natural philosophy. In this attempt they sometimes followed St. Augustine's lead, which supported a theory of complementarity in heaven, and at other times they introduced what could be called a **reverse sex polarity**. This latter theory suggested that woman could be thought of as superior to man in the realm of grace, because she overcame her inherent inferiority in the realm of nature. The important aspect of this development was the recognition that sex polarity by itself is incompatible with Christian belief.

The second positive result from the Christian medieval incorporation of Aristotelian philosophy was the claim that a human being is a mind-body unity. According to Aristotle, the soul is the form of the body. This claim rejected the dualism of soul and body inherent in a Platonic metaphysics. In the Thomistic development of Aristotelian philosophy, engendered identity was no longer understood as something accidental to human identity. Rejecting the Platonic and Neoplatonic view that the essence of a human being contained reference only to the sexless soul, St. Thomas argued that the essence of a human being included both soul and body. Since all human beings are engendered, the concept of woman contained as part of its essential structure the condition of having a female body; and the concept of man contained as a part of its essential structure the condition of having a male body.

The Aristotelian Revolution had a strong double effect on moving the concept of woman away from either sex complementarity or sex unity. On the one hand, because of its solid incorporation of the rationale for sex polarity into academic studies in all fields including Arts, Theology, Medicine, and Law, it completely obliterated the grounds for a sex complementarity that had just begun to surface in monastic education. On the other hand, it also drove out the dualism inherent in the Platonic theory of sex unity, and in so doing provided a metaphysical and anthropological framework within which complementarity could eventually be developed.

In my view, another paradoxical effect of the Aristotelian Revolution and its victory over Platonic thought can be summarized simply as follows: Aristotle made an error in his judgment about woman's identity but was accurate in his hypothesis about a central factor in human identity; while Plato judged incorrectly about human identity but correctly about a central factor in women's identity. Specifically, Aristotle incorrectly judged woman as naturally inferior to man, but correctly postulated that the human being is a soul-body unity, while Plato incorrectly proposed that the human being is a soul/body duality, but correctly argued for the equal dignity of women and men. This paradox will shift with the development of Renaissance Humanism, within which Plato's dualism is Christianized somewhat and authors become selective about which aspect of Plato to adopt. For example, Plato's theory of reincarnation is dropped by Christian Neoplatonism, and replaced by belief in a single existence with resurrection of the body. In this move, Plato's rationale for the equality of women and men is lost. However, his claims about the need for equal education and equal opportunity for men and women to rule still function in efforts to overturn polarity claims. A similar "selective editing" occurs with Aristotle as well. Aristotelian claims incompatible with Christian belief are dropped, while others are retained.

In Medieval Christian philosophy two important additions occurred to the Aristotelian description of the human being which flowed from a theological preoccupation with understanding the concept of a person. Aristotle had suggested that a human being could be thought of as a rational animal, with animality as the *genus* and rationality as the *differentia*. St. Augustine introduced the category of spirituality when he considered the human being as created in the image and likeness of God and able to enter into communion with God. Boethius, followed by St. Albert and St. Thomas, defined person as an individual substance of a rational nature — a definition that would apply first to a Divine Person and derivatively to a human person. In this way, individuality or uniqueness and communion or relation began to be incorporated into the concept of person.

Consequences of these developments in the concept of person are significant for the concept of woman in subsequent centuries. In spite of his sex polarity claims, Aristotle's premise of the conjoined rationality and materiality in the human being as a soul-body unity provided the foundation for a concept of woman in the line of sex complementarity. However, the additions of the premise of spirituality (including relation with God and others) and of individuality are necessary for its ultimate elaboration.[9] *The Concept of Woman: The Aristotelian Revolution (750 B.C.–1250 A.D.)* ends poised at this juncture. The structure for a more adequate theory of sex identity is in place, but it is filled with content from sex polarity inherited from Aristotle's natural philosophy. The fact that the University of Paris made Aristotle's texts required reading around 1250, and that most other universities copied the curriculum at the University of Paris, led to the nearly complete dominance of Aristotelian rationale in institutionalized higher education in Europe. I identified this turning point as "The Aristotelian Revolution" in the concept of woman. Platonic and Neoplatonic rationale for sex unity and the monastic tradition which supported sex complementarity were completely overrun by the new academic form of higher education. The revolution in the concept of woman resulted in precisely this dominance of one kind of gender theory — Aristotelian gender polarity.

This content of sex polarity, devaluing woman, had to be purged before further developments towards authentic or integral complementarity could occur. We can now turn to consider more directly how the late Medieval and early Humanist philosophers respond to this complex and paradoxical inheritance of Aristotle.

---

9. The work of Edith Stein moves in this direction in the chapter entitled "Problems of Women's Education," in *Essays on Women* (Washington, D.C.: ICS Publications, 1996). See also Sr. Prudence Allen, R.S.M., "Integral Sex Complementarity and the Theology of Communion," *Communio* 17, no. 4 (Winter 1990): 523-44; and "Matter, Form, and Gender," *Lonergan Workshop* 12 (1996): 1-26; and W. Norris Clarke, "Person, Being, and St. Thomas," *Communio* 19, no. 4 (Winter 1992): 601-18.

INTRODUCTION

TRANSITIONS IN THE CONCEPT OF WOMAN: 1250-1500

While the first volume was subtitled "The Aristotelian Revolution" in the concept of woman, this volume is subtitled "The Early Humanist Reformation." I use the word 'reformation' rather than 'revolution' to indicate that the Aristotelian concept of woman was not completely overturned and discontinued, but rather, a shift in consciousness occurred in the continuity of its application. During this period some of the basic premises of Aristotle's concept of woman began to be questioned. It took several more centuries before the influence of his theory was severely curtailed. This eventually occurred through new developments in science which disproved his foundational claims about the identities of men and women in the categories of opposites and generation. The reformation of Aristotelian gender polarity began in early humanism by challenges to his claims of the gender differentiation in the categories of wisdom and virtue.

Six major transitions from Volume I to Volume II will be noted in this introduction while several other transitions will be developed only in the more detailed analysis of the text itself. The first noticeable difference between Volume I (750 B.C.–1250 A.D.) and Volume II (1250-1500) is seen in what could be called "the intellectual impulse" of most of those authors who wrote about the concept of woman within the particular historical period. In the ancient Greek and early Medieval philosophers we identified an impulse that worked towards uncovering the fundamental questions about sex identity. This intellectual impulse then moved towards postulating answers to these questions reaching towards a consistent theory of sex identity which traversed the four categories identified as 'opposites,' 'generation,' 'wisdom,' and 'virtue.'

In later Medieval and early Renaissance philosophers the intellectual impulse is different. Instead of aiming towards a consistently broad theory, we find thinkers specializing in one or two categories, developing more complex arguments, and focusing on finer distinctions in woman's identity. Instead of an impulse towards comprehensive wholeness, we find an impulse towards fragmented specialization. The likely explanation for this radical change is the founding of four separate faculties in universities, with rigid boundaries that prohibited professors from teaching in more than one faculty at the same time.

In the Faculty of Arts where philosophy was taught, in addition to the infusion of arguments in support of sex polarity, we can see another effect of the Aristotelian Revolution. The great corpus of Aristotelian logic promoted a position that was neutral with respect to woman or man. Sexual differentiation was thought of as an accidental property or predicate of the human being. Thus, in definitions, syllogisms, and scientific reasoning, the subject of arguments progressively included reference to the gender-neutral human being. I identify this conscious exclusion of the differentiation of women and men, in favor of the more general subject human being, as the **sex neutrality** or **gender neutrality** theory.

In Latin the existence of two different words to distinguish a human being (*homo*) from a male human being (*vir*) allowed this differentiation to be very clear. In French and English, however, the same word is used for both meanings (*homme* and *man*). Therefore, in popular culture and language, the gender-neutral man

12

(human being) and the gender-specific man (male human being) were eventually conflated with one another. This shift is important because during the period 1250-1500 authors began writing in vernacular languages as well as in Latin. During this time we begin to see how gender neutrality may sometimes hide a gender polarity within its claims of neutrality.

A second important transition considered in Volume II of *The Concept of Woman* is the moving of research on human generation from Faculties of Arts to Faculties of Medicine. This meant that philosophers were dependent upon conclusions reached by physicians about woman's and man's contribution to generation. The same phenomenon occurred for theologians. At the same time, physicians were not particularly interested in reflecting on the significance of the respective contributions of mother and father to generation to determine the meaning of women's and men's identities. Thus research and interpretation, with which Aristotle and Galen were joined, became separated. In addition, many satirical texts began popularizing aspects of Aristotelian and pseudo-Aristotelian theories of generation without any concern for empirical accuracy.

The popular trivialization and devaluation of woman through stereotyped views of her role in generation, resulting from the separation of academic Faculties, made the reform of Aristotelian philosophical arguments for sex polarity more difficult to achieve. Academic philosophers were less and less equipped with the intellectual tools to effect such a reform, and physicians were not interested in philosophical or theological reform. The exclusion of women from universities also meant that a key motivating factor for the reform of sex polarity was missing. In addition, there were no women students or women lecturers to provide counterexamples to the components of Aristotelian sex polarity in the categories of wisdom or virtue. The impulse for reform of theories of sex polarity eventually came from outside of academia in two other areas in which women made important contributions: in religious communities and among Renaissance humanists.

A third important transition from Volume I to Volume II involves a shift from simply proposing a concept of woman or constructing an argument about the concept of woman to engagement in dialogue with others about components within an articulated concept of woman. In the first volume, the rather rigid structures of the concept of woman seemed to have a life of their own, and they more or less passed from one author to another without change after being articulated in the works of Plato or Aristotle. In the second volume, however, we include members of different communities of discourse reflecting upon, questioning, and shifting through different aspects of the concept of woman as applicable to their own community of discourse. In this dynamic context, dialogue about the concept of woman becomes important, and challenges to particular claims are raised.

The personalities of individual authors begin to emerge as unique and formative in the development of various aspects of the concept of woman. While in Volume I only St. Augustine, Boethius, and Hildegard of Bingen emerged as having unique personalities and experiences formative of their concepts of woman, in Volume II many more individual personalities begin to emerge. In the Renaissance many more women and men authors reveal themselves to be unique individual women or men struggling to articulate theories of human and gender identity. In

Volume II four different kinds of communities of discourse are identified: (1) academic communities of discourse at various universities; (2) women religious communities of discourse in different countries; (3) wide-ranging popular satirical communities of discourse; and (4) Italian, French, and German humanist communities of discourse. It is primarily in women's religious communities and humanist communities that we see the emergence of unique personalities who articulate concepts of woman.

In this latter phase of development, dialogue, face to face between persons, or by letters, or in circulated and published texts, begins to shape a new phase in the history of the concept of woman. Through dialogue various premises about woman's identity are criticized, evidence to support or reject these premises is offered, proofs for the validity or invalidity of argument are made, and consequences of their conclusions are articulated. In the early part of this period, during the thirteenth to the fourteenth centuries, different communities of discourse remain relatively isolated from one another with the exception of individual men who may pass between or among them after receiving a university training. In addition, for the most part, women authors do not engage directly with men authors about issues of woman's identity, although they do at times initiate reflections on some aspect of the concept of woman by men authors who respond to their questions or their presence.

During the latter part of the period, in the fourteenth and the fifteenth centuries, a significant new development occurs. Men and women begin to engage actively in both private and public dialogue with one another about the concept of woman, especially in considering the two categories of wisdom and virtue. In many different contexts of dialogue among women and men, fundamental elements for reform of the theory of sex polarity begin to emerge. For the first time in western history we have evidence of considerable creative thinking occurring about woman's and man's identity through authentic dialogue that includes philosophical argumentation. This collaborative thinking includes identification of fallacies, appeals to history, appeals to the evidence of the senses, appeals to reason, and so on.

At the same time we also find a reassertion and even exaggeration of grounds for defending sex polarity. In these cases, dialogue may degenerate into personal attacks in which particular individuals, as well as woman or man in general, are devalued. In some extreme situations we will see dialogue moving towards actual condemnation of particular women and the use of universal generalizations to further devalue all women with respect to man. However, even with these occasional painful realities of the western genealogy of gender, the overriding contribution of the Renaissance to the concept of woman is the groundwork it laid for the eventual reform of the foundations for Aristotelian sex polarity. This conclusion runs counter to a popular contemporary claim that women did not have a Renaissance.[10]

A fourth transition involves the significant new interaction of women authors with one another in person and in writing. In authors studied in Volume I, there were only occasional references among women authors to other women. In authors in-

---

10. See Joan Kelly-Gadol, "Did Women Have a Renaissance?" in *Becoming Visible: Women in European History,* ed. Renate Bridenthal and Claudia Koonz (Boston: Houghton Mifflin, 1977), pp. 137-64.

cluded in Volume II, we find multiple references among women authors to the work of other women and to the example of the lives of other women. In this way, a woman's history is beginning to be gathered, and women are trying to define their own identities in relation to this history. Using an expression of Charles Taylor, we begin to see during this later period "a web of interlocutors," which provides a context within which women begin to articulate their own identity.[11] This is a fuller activity of self-definition or of becoming an individual which depends upon a more inclusive center of organization within the self; it involves a capacity to interact, to reflect, to choose, to experiment, to resist, to affirm, to appropriate, to give, and so on.

A fifth important transition concerns the change from an almost total concentration on **male** and **female** roots of the respective identities of man and woman, to a beginning interest in certain qualities identified as **masculine** or **feminine**. Especially in the categories of wisdom and virtue we find particular characteristics, virtues and vices, identified as masculine or feminine with positive, neutral, or negative value. In addition the term 'masculine' is applied to **both** women and men, as is the term 'feminine': they are not strictly limited either to women or to men.

This double potential of predication of masculine and feminine characteristics did not imply a theory of androgyny — the relation between the predicate and the subject is different in the case of women and of men. In other words, predicating something masculine of a man has a different meaning than predicating the same masculine quality to a woman; and conversely, predicating something feminine of a woman has a different meaning than predicating the same feminine quality to a man. In addition, there were further questions of the different values that this predicate may have had in different contexts and of the grounds offered for its attribution to either woman or man in general or in particular circumstances.

In contemporary North American feminist theory this development from an exclusive focus on male and female roots of identity, to masculine and feminine characteristics, is often described as a change of focus from sex to gender. By gender is usually meant something that goes beyond biological characteristics to include what are today identified as psycho-social-cultural characteristics. When I use the term 'gender,' I am using it to include **also** the biological foundations of a woman's or a man's identity. This usage on my part harkens back to the original root meaning of gender, which comes from *gens,* and applies to 'generate' and 'engender.' Therefore, the root meaning of gender necessarily includes, rather than excludes, biological factors of women's and men's respective identities.

My use of 'gender' to include sex runs counter to common practice of many scholars in the social sciences and in philosophy who prefer to separate the two terms and use 'sex' only for biological aspects and 'gender' only for psycho-social aspects. They often use 'sex/gender' (with a slash) to accentuate the division. In my view, this separation of sex from gender not only ignores the root meaning of gender as already described, but it perpetuates a dualistic understanding of the human being rather than emphasizes its fundamental unity.

By including sex (male or female) in the developmental meaning of 'gender'

<hr>

11. Charles Taylor, *Sources of the Self: The Making of a Modern Identity* (Cambridge, Mass.: Harvard University Press, 1989), p. 36.

(with masculine and feminine characteristics) I will in this volume rename the different theories associated with the concept of woman in relation to the concept of man. Instead of calling them 'sex unity,' 'sex polarity,' and 'sex complementarity,' I will now refer to them as gender unity, gender polarity, and gender complementarity. Their basic premises remain the same, but the detailed analyses that fall within each theory become slightly more complex. As human beings become more conscious of who they are in their engendered specificity, they realize that they are more than just their engendered body, a male or a female.

Each theory of gender identity maintains a position about two things: (1) whether or not men and women have an equal dignity and (2) whether or not differences between women and men are philosophically significant. Some theorists argue today that the basic category of 'equality' is not possible to use because there are so many meanings of equality that an author always needs to clarify a particular use by adding "equal with respect to ————."[12] In the schema below, 'equal dignity' serves as a fundamental category of the identity of the man or woman as a human being. If authors argue that either men *per se* or women *per se* have greater dignity than the other **because of** their gender identity, then they reject the premise of equal dignity.

There are also many theorists today who argue that the category of 'difference' is not useful to philosophers either. Much of their argumentation focuses on the pragmatic use of differences for discrimination or on the difficulty in identifying essential or universal differences. For the purposes of self-appropriation, however, it is helpful to use both 'equal dignity' and 'significant differentiation' as reference points to identify different theories of gender identity. In the schema below, the phrase 'significant differentiation' refers to gender-related characteristics that were always or usually associated with either a woman or a man in special ways characteristic of his or her engendered identity. One of the major purposes of this particular historical study is to identify particular characteristics as they were articulated by various authors. A second major purpose is to identify the value that a particular characteristic was given by each of these authors. With these data it is possible to classify and to evaluate the particular theory of gender identity presented by a particular author.

In the table on p. 17, the basic premises of each theory of gender identity (without specific content) are stated for purposes of reference.

Three theories of gender identity (2b, 3a, and 3b) are listed which have not yet been discussed in this introduction. The first theory, reverse gender polarity, claims that there are significant differences between men and women, and that woman is by nature superior to man. This theory is always articulated in reaction against traditional sex or gender polarity, which claimed that man is by nature superior to woman. While occasional aspects of this theory have appeared in the history of philosophy before the end of the period being considered in Volume II, an important articulation of its ground occurs just after this endpoint in 1529, with

---

12. See, for example, the several hundred meanings for equality in modern philosophy as described in Louise Marcil-Lacoste, *Le Thématique de l'égalité: répertoire, résumés, typologie* (Montréal: Université de Montréal, 1984).

Structure of Theories of Gender Identity		
Theory	Equal dignity of man and woman	Significant differentiation of man and woman
1. Gender Unity (unisex and unigender)	yes	no
2a. Traditional Gender Polarity	no man *per se* superior to woman	yes
2b. Reverse Gender Polarity	no woman *per se* superior to man	yes
3a. Fractional Gender Complementarity	yes	yes complementary as parts
3b. Integral Gender Complementarity	yes	yes complementary as wholes
4. Gender Neutrality	neutral	neutral

the publication of a text *On the Superiority of Woman over Man* by the humanist Henry Cornelius Agrippa (1486-1536). A more thorough philosophical defense of this theory is found in the 1601 published text of Lucrezia Marinelli (1571-1653), whose title *La nobiltà et l'eccellenza delle donne co'diffetti et mancamenti de gli huomini* can be translated from the Italian as "On the nobility and excellence of woman with faults and shortcomings of men."[13]

The second and third new theories result from the separation of complementarity theories into two kinds: fractional complementarity and integral gender

13. Heinrich Cornelius Agrippa von Nettesheim, *On the Superiority of Woman over Man*, trans. Amaudin (New York: American News Company, 1873). Lucrezia Marinelli, *La nobiltà et l'eccellenza delle donne co'diffetti et mancamenti de gli huomini* (Venezia: Gil. Batista Ciotti Sanese, 1601). See also Prudence Allen, R.S.M., and Filippo Salvatore, "Lucrezia Marinelli and Woman's Identity in Late Italian Renaissance," *Renaissance and Reformation* 16, no. 4 (Fall 1992): 5-39.

complementarity. The latter theory will take several centuries before being articulated by philosophers in the tradition of personalism. For the most part, in the study of the concept of woman between 1250 and 1500 we find examples of fractional gender complementarity, which anticipate, but do not quite reach, the more satisfying theory of integral gender complementarity. This theory is most closely approached in the work of Christine de Pizan, where we will find many elements of fractional gender complementarity, along with some elements of gender polarity and reverse gender polarity. Laura Cereta will provide an example of integral complementarity along with aspects of its articulation.

In the theory of gender complementarity, an important distinction needs to be made between fractional gender complementarity and integral gender complementarity. Both views argue for a philosophically significant differentiation between the sexes, along with a premise of their fundamental equality in dignity and worth. However, fractional sex complementarity ascribes specific masculine and feminine characteristics to the two sexes, dividing them so that a woman may have one, a man the other, and so forth. Common divisions would be something like the following: a woman is intuitive and a man rational; a woman passive, a man active; a woman responsible for the private sphere of activity, a man for the public sphere of activity, and so on. Needless to say, these fractional divisions often cover a hidden sex polarity, and they may distort what is human, individual, or personal.

The crucial factor in integral gender complementarity is that a woman and a man are considered as two separate and complete human individuals who are equal in dignity and worth and who have philosophically significant differences. They are not fractional beings who together make up one being. Instead, they are two whole human beings who, together, synergetically generate more than just the sum of themselves. In the situation of biological generation, they may generate a child. In the range of creative conscious interaction, what is generated may be considered as something more than the ideas that existed in the minds of two individuals separately. Their philosophically significant differences arise from the respective data that they appropriate or reject as self-defining individuals. In contemporary philosophy some of these would be referred to as their different genetic, hormonal, and anatomical structures, their different experiences of the body, their different cultural or gendered experiences within particular society. All of these form part of their basis for differentiation, while their similar human capacities for judgment, reflection, choice, and action all form the basis for their equality.

One of the most striking features of complementarity theories is their vulnerability towards disintegration into either a polarity theory or a unity theory. The reason for this potential for disintegration comes from the difficulty in remaining in the fundamental tension generated by holding simultaneously to the two main premises of the theory: equal dignity and significant differentiation. In one direction the tension is dissolved by keeping an equal dignity but losing a significant differentiation. This is the disintegration of complementarity into unity or unisex, as it is more often called. In the other direction the tension is dissolved by keeping a significant differentiation but losing an equal dignity. This is the disintegration of complementarity into polarity. Traditionally the polarity theory placed a greater value on man, who was considered to be superior to woman. Recently, in various forms of reverse polarity we see a greater value being given to woman, who is considered superior to man. The challenge of complementarity theorists is to maintain the tension of holding the two premises of equal dignity and significant differentiation. In the present volume we will see how different theorists struggle with respect to this vulnerability of complementarity.

While relations of complementarity have a built-in tension that provides a danger of losing their identity by moving in one direction or the other, from another aspect this same tension is what gives the relations an intrinsic dynamic that is creative or synergetic. This is the great value of all relations of integral complementarity among persons. While its most obvious version occurs in the man-woman dynamic of generation of children, we can see that there is a tremendous creative energy found in all relations of human friendship and collaboration when there is an interaction among persons who are treated with equal dignity and significant differentiation. In this book we will also see examples of the dynamic energy of men and women in intellectual collaboration which partakes of the fundamental characteristics of complementarity. It is this same tension in relations of complementarity which makes them both vulnerable and synergetic.

A sixth transition in focus from Volume I to Volume II involves a further development in the understanding of the human being. In ancient Greek popular thought, a human being's identity was closely tied to fate. While there was a little room for voluntary choice and action, most men and women understood their identities as determined by a nature formed by circumstances, fate, and the sometimes capricious will of the gods. With Jewish and Christian philosophy, we discover a new emphasis on being a creature, created in the image of God with free will and intellect, and in a relationship with God and with men and women. With the birth of Renaissance Humanism, we find in addition to the factors in human identity already referred to (consciousness of an engendered body as male or female, consciousness of characteristics as masculine and feminine, and self-consciousness in reflecting back on these aspects of one's own identity) a belief in a kind of co-responsibility with God to build one's own identity as a particular kind of man (or woman) through consciously willed acts.

Giovanni Pico della Mirandola's *Oration on the Dignity of Man* is usually identified as one of the first works to emphasize the role of self-determination as a cooperative effort of man and God. This text, published in 1494, heralds a new era in the consciousness of the dignity and obligation to be fully human. However, we will see that in the century preceding this work, authors already anticipated this transition by their own arguments about the need to determine one's own particular identity within a range of possibilities, through self-knowledge, self-control, self-governance, and creative action. For our purposes, it is significant that many authors who directly discussed the importance of these activities were women. Human dignity, woman's dignity, and man's dignity were found in cooperating with God and others in the great challenge of developing one's identity as a particular kind of woman or particular kind of man.

Once a woman or a man freely engages in the cooperative activity of development of the self as a particular kind of woman or a particular kind of man, an interiority has been introduced into self-understanding. This interiority is a new dimension of human identity beyond simple consciousness of existing as a male human or a female human being, or of even having or exercising masculine or feminine characteristics. It involves a looking inward, a choosing among various possibilities, and a self-determination to become a particular kind of woman or a particular kind of man. I will try to illustrate this progressive complexification of the concept of woman and the concept of man in its historical developments in western philosophy by borrowing an analogy from geometry. We can think of the shift from a one-dimensional point, to a two-dimensional triangle, to a three-dimensional tetrahedron as analogous to a shift in theories of gender identity from a single point of reference, to three points of reference, to four points of reference.

Chronological Development of Gender Identity			
Beginning Historical Period	Concept of Woman	Concept of Man	Geometric Analogy
750 B.C.	female	male	one point- one dimension
1300	female + feminine + masculine	male + masculine + feminine	three points- triangle- two dimensions
1450	woman + female + feminine + masculine	man + male + masculine + feminine	four points- tetrahedron- three dimensions

The advantage of this geometrical analogy is that it brings a perspective to the particular period being studied in this book. The historical development of the concept of woman moves from one point through three points to four points of reference as it evolves in western thought. The Renaissance is a transition period in the history of the concept of woman. Just as a triangle is more complex than a single point, the concept of woman in Renaissance philosophy is more advanced than ancient Greek and Medieval philosophy. What it means to be a woman not only incorporates a female biological foundation, but it also includes having the consciousness of some particular psycho-social feminine characteristics and possibly some acquired masculine characteristics. In addition, it also anticipates in a very rudimentary way the further development of a complex development of self-definition or self-creation in cooperation with the creative activity of God. I call this reflective self-consciousness of intellect and self-determination of will the discovery of the interiority of the human being with respect to his or her engendered identity. The complexification of interiority can be compared with a shift from a two-dimensional triangle to a three-dimensional tetrahedron because there is an interior space in the latter figure which is missing in the former. Three-dimensional perspective in the history of the concept of woman parallels the development in Renaissance art, through which three-dimensional people replaced the flat disembodied figures of previous centuries.[14]

This geometrical analogy does not supply the interior content of the concept of woman. It does not tell us what is essentially or even accidentally female, what is essentially or accidentally feminine, what is essentially or accidentally masculine, and so forth. Answers to these questions do abound during this period, and subsequent analysis will provide them in the context of each author who discussed them. The geometrical analogy also does not explain how particular feminine and masculine characteristics specifically relate to what is female or to what is male. These latter, deeper questions enter into philosophical considerations only in the last two hundred years; they do not appear in the analysis of the texts from 1250 to 1500. Thus *The Concept of Woman: The Early Humanist Reformation (1250-1500)* contains only the next part of the history of the concept of woman.

On the level of consciousness, the discovery of the categories of masculine and feminine as applicable to both men and women is an emergent level of organization in the theory of gender identity that was not present when the sole focus was on what it meant to be either male or female. The crucial point is that in each shift of developmental levels, the concept of woman has a more inclusive center of organization. To be female demands only a certain cluster of biological organization. To be female with a specified relation to what is masculine and feminine in a deeper sense of conscious and self-conscious identity demands a center of organization that is conscious of birthright of engenderment. As a woman moves into the fuller activity of self-definition by becoming an individual, her exercise of the will in relation to the intellect brings about an even higher and more inclusive center of organization of the self and of the unique and unrepeatable aspect of a particular personality. A similar process is followed in the evolutionary development of man. The present volume traces the transition phase of this evolution to higher levels of consciousness of gender identity.

STRUCTURE OF THE BOOK

The Concept of Woman: The Early Humanist Reformation (1250-1500) is divided broadly into two sections. This division is both chronological and thematic.

Section I is entitled *Separate Engendered Discourse about Women's Identity*. It focuses on four separate communities of discourse about the concept of woman beginning in the period 1250-1500. Each community of discourse was fairly self-

---

14. Bard Thompson, *Humanists and Reformers: A History of the Renaissance and Reformation* (Grand Rapids and Cambridge: Eerdmans, 1996), p. 214. See also p. 13.

contained in the sense that authors in one community of discourse generally did not engage in direct dialogue about gender with authors in the other communities of discourse. In addition, in this early stage women and men did not engage in public dialogue with one another about the concept of woman.

Chapter 1: *Women Religious Describe Wisdom and Virtue:* Women's philosophical voices are discovered in women's religious communities as authors describe engendered self-consciousness, self-knowledge, and self-governance with respect to the categories of wisdom and virtue. These models of wisdom and virtue serve as counterexamples to the Aristotelian concept of woman. These women authors also give evidence of interior forms of dialogue with respect to the relation of the senses, imagination, reason, and human identity. They also present woman as a generic model for all human beings.

Chapter 2: *Aristotelian Roots of Gender Identity in Academia:* Aristotle's logic provided a foundation for a gender neutrality theory that ignores gender differentiation. The influence of Aristotle's logic is traced through the academic community of discourse occurring among selected male philosophers in Faculties of Arts. Aristotle's natural philosophy also provided a foundation for the devaluing of women. The influence of Aristotle's traditional polarity arguments is traced through selected authors who overtly appeal to his natural philosophy for a foundation of gender polarity. The concept of woman as described by male philosophers in academic discourse is caught in an ambivalent tension of philosophical foundations for gender neutrality and gender polarity and theological foundations for gender complementarity. This tension is increased by the fragmentation of the various faculties within the new thirteenth-century university structure.

Chapter 3: *Philosophical Content in Early Satires about Women:* These early satires about gender exaggerated a perceived essential characteristic of woman or inverted the application of gender-related characteristics to women and to men. The particular exaggerations and inversions used the same gender-specified predicates previously identified in Aristotelian theory, and they contributed to the further devaluation of woman in relation to man. This chapter ends with a discussion of a humanist meta-satire, or a satire of a satire that may be an early attempt to reform the traditional gender polarity foundation for satire.

Chapter 4: *Gender at the Beginnings of Humanism:* A new impetus occurs in the concept of woman through the writings of authors at this time of transition from scholasticism to humanism. An appeal to classical models for women's wisdom and virtue, and the use of the imagination offer new foundations for developments in the concept of woman. In addition, for the first time in the history of western thought extensive imaginary intergender dialogue is described in which ordinary women and men discuss their respective identities. In these dialogues we discover traces of a new philosophical basis for gender complementarity.

Section II is entitled *The Beginning of Public Dialogue about Gender.* It focuses on both the style and content of dialogue among women, among men, and among women and men in both speech and writing about gender identity. Academics, religious authors, and humanists begin to influence one another through dialogue, and this dialogue increasingly focuses on the specific content of the concept of woman. By the end of this period, the depth of the dialogue is actually directed at reforming the previously held Aristotelian philosophical foundation for sex polarity.

Chapter 5: *Women Religious Authors Develop Analogical Thinking:* The increasing sophistication of women authors in their creative approach to gender identity is described. In this development the role of private dialogue among women and what could be called 'intergender dialogue' among women and men about woman's identity is demonstrated. In addition, particular attention is given to the Dominican influence on this dialogue. Women use complex models to articulate aspects of their own identity which serve as generic for human identity, and others which are uniquely associated with woman. These articulations provide some new bases for gender complementarity.

Chapter 6: *Deterioration of Intergender Dialogue in Later Satires and Public Trials:* The concept of woman was further devalued by the addition of the characteristics of deception and danger to the exaggerations and inversions previously operative in satirical works. At this point in western thought, in addition to the incorporation of Aristotelian rationale, we also find the occasional introduction of Platonic themes in dialogue about women. This chapter also considers ways in which Aristotelian rationale for the devaluation of woman in satires functioned in arguments associated with the trials of women for heresy and witchcraft.

Chapter 7: *Early Humanist Dialogue about the Concept of Woman:* The remarkable contribution of Christine de Pizan to the history of the concept of woman in France and England is analyzed. The philosophical structure and content of her public dialogues with both men and women authors are traced and their relation to specific historical authors (both academic and satirical) demonstrated. Imaginary dialogues about women are analyzed with specific reference to the particular authors she challenged and to the concept of woman she proposed. Her new philosophical foundations for gender complementarity are evaluated. In this chapter there is a beginning integration of dialogue across all four previously separated communities of discourse.

Chapter 8: *The Early Humanist Reformation in Education for Women:* During the fifteenth century in Italy and Germany two new events changed the historical context for the philosophical study of the concept of woman: new humanist schools of education were formed which drew upon classical Greek and Latin texts, and translations of the complete works of Plato were infused into the context of humanist discourse. In some instances women were affected by these changes: they received a higher education, were encouraged to study secular philosophy, and entered into dialogues with one another and with men about aspects of the concept of woman. At the same time, however, many women also lacked the institutional structures within which the fuller development of their personalities could be expressed by meaningful forms of service to society.

Chapter 9: *The Early Humanist Reformation in Theory about Gender:* New foundations for arguments about gender identity were put forward when Platonic theory was inserted into the debate. Some new versions of the theories of gender unity, gender polarity, gender neutrality, gender complementarity, and reverse gender polarity were articulated. The role of the individual in self-determination was also emphasized for the first time. All of these factors contributed to a climate of reform of Aristotelian rationale for gender polarity. In other words, by the end of the century new foundations were in place for the eventual reformation of the Aristotelian revolution in the concept of woman.

Chapter 10: *The Early Humanist Reformation by Women Philosophers:* Entering into the debate about gender identity with the full force of their intellectual talents and personalities, two women philosophers made remarkable contributions to the history of the concept of woman. Isotta Nogarola and Laura Cereta both wrote fluently in Latin and each immersed herself in the rich tradition of humanistic studies. In addition, they engaged in consistent and profound dialogue with other humanists, both men and women, about issues of common interest. Nogarola, primarily a scholar, wrote an in-depth dialogue with a male humanist about moral issues and gender identity. Laura Cereta, primarily a teacher, wrote many letters and lectures describing how men and women humanists can achieve a greater personal integrity as set forth by humanist ideals.

Conclusion: A time-line is offered as a way of gathering together the complex range of events that mark this extraordinarily dynamic period in the history of the concept of woman. In the 250 years surveyed, men and women from different communities of discourse give considerable attention to issues of gender identity. They write from their personal experience and from immersion in classical sources. They engage in dialogue with one another frequently. Consequently, new grounds for an integral gender complementarity begin to be articulated along with new philosophical foundations for gender unity and gender polarity. In this turbulent and even violent period in history, a slow but steady progress in the history of the concept of woman occurs.

In order to aid the reader at the beginning of the book there are Chronological Tables listing the birth and death dates of all authors discussed in Volume II and those previously discussed in Volume I. In addition, throughout the book summary tables are provided to help synthesize the vast amount of material being considered. A list of these tables in order of their appearance is also given near the beginning of this text. Illustrations of women and men who contributed significantly to the history of the philosophy of gender are dispersed throughout the text to emphasize the emergence of the unique personalities of these philosophers as well as the importance of interpersonal dialogue about woman's identity.

In addition to the reference notes in each chapter, a bibliography and index are provided at the end. The index of proper names is complete. The subject index, however, which offers a strong starting point, is not complete because the subject may be considered in the text even when the particular word being indexed is not included. Further, because of the vast numbers of original source texts needed for this analysis, only those secondary sources which directly relate to the author being evaluated or which have been fundamental in forming my own methodology are included. This means that large numbers of especially contemporary articles and books which relate to the topics being investigated are not included. While it was tempting to include them because of their often challenging and insightful approaches to historical texts on the concept of woman, the effect of doing so would have been to have a running second discourse with contemporary authors. In various drafts of this volume I did attempt such an effort, but concluded in the end that it was distracting to the main purpose of the book. It tended to cloud the main lines of argument about the concept of woman in the period 1250-1500 itself by drawing the reader away into the many contemporary concerns and issues in gender studies. Thus, wherever possible I attempted in this final version to return to the original texts of the period and to let their authors speak to us about how they understood the concept of woman.

At the beginning of this introduction it was suggested that the fourteenth century can serve as distant mirror to our own times. The basic lines of all the theories of gender identity were present during the period studied. Various decisions by individual men and women concerning which theory to adopt led to different sorts of consequences. It is perhaps possible that a man or woman who reads this book may be impelled to make a better choice about an area of sex and gender identity today because of seeing the consequences of choices made over half a millennium ago. One of the main themes considered throughout the text is the quality of discourse or dialogue concerning the concept of woman. At times it was extremely productive when participants genuinely searched together for truth about woman's identity. At other times, it deteriorated into various forms of isolation, deception, and/or antagonism. Basic possibilities will be brought into the light, and various perspectives uncovered, as we seek their contribution to the ongoing search for answers to the initial question: What is to become of woman and man?

Finally, it is my hope that this attempt to provide a kind of map of the different approaches to the concept of woman during 1250-1500 will be accepted as the preliminary result of an investigation. I must confess that at times I felt quite overwhelmed by roaming into a new intellectual territory foreign to my philosophical background. Yet, as I discovered so many examples of women and men who struggled to understand woman's emerging identity, I grew more determined to share the results of my investigations with others. I look forward now to the ensuing dialogue with the readers of this book.

SECTION I

SEPARATE ENGENDERED DISCOURSE
ABOUT WOMEN'S IDENTITY

The four chapters of Section I will set the stage for the dramatic developments in theories of gender identity described in Section II. Each successive chapter describes a different community of discourse about women's identity: (1) women's religious communities, (2) academic communities, (3) readers of satires, and (4) humanist associations. Each chapter in Section I will examine one of these four separate communities of discourse in an effort to identify the core components of the concept of woman contained within it. A brief description of each of these four communities of discourse will now be given.

Women's religious communities loosely include those communities of women living together whose members are bound by vows of consecration, promises of stability, or a common religious purpose. Academic communities comprise institutional educational units such as schools or universities that were formed to train clergy, physicians, and attorneys of civil and canon law. Readers of satires are a loosely bound social network of persons who exchanged with one another literary works for purposes of entertainment. Humanist associations are also a loosely bound network of persons who studied classical sources, exchanged literary works for purposes of informal education, and who engaged in public oral or written dialogue.

During the first 150 years after the mid-thirteenth-century Aristotelian revolution in the concept of woman, each of these four different communities of discourse left a critical mass of texts that include reflections on woman's identity. Other communities of discourse at the time, such as men's religious communities, guilds, fiefdoms, and so forth did not provide such a critical mass of writings about women's identity; and they are therefore excluded from this study. While the four communities of discourse identified above did generally operate separately from one another, some individuals from one community may have engaged in dialogue with members from another community of discourse. This means that the boundaries of the four separate communities of discourse are not rigid. Nonetheless, I hope to show that a differentiation of these four particular communities of discourse is helpful for the purposes of identifying patterns in the concept of woman unique to each community.

In Chapter 1, some of the interior, almost private dialogues expressed by women writers will be considered. In this context, women ask: "What is my experience of truth and goodness, of wisdom and virtue? What is the meaning of this (engendered) experience for myself and for others?" While many religious women no doubt asked these questions of themselves, a few women authors began to put in writing both the questions and the insights generated by their reflections on the questions. Here we have some evidence of their self-conscious identification of specific forms of self-knowledge, self-governance, and forms of appropriate action.

Chapter 2 will examine selected texts from the academic world in which many men authors used the Aristotelian theory as a basis both for gender neutrality and for gender polarity. Academics who posed questions within a perspective that was gender neutral asked: "What is the relation between logical argument and truth? What is the relation between universals and definitions?" Other academics posed questions within a gender polarity perspective: "How can the metaphysical categories of form and matter be used to explain sex and gender differentiation?"

As has been previously mentioned, Aristotelian thought was institutionalized in 1255, when the texts of Aristotle became required reading at the University of Paris, and when other universities in western Europe modeled themselves on the curriculum and structure of the University of Paris. This Aristotelian revolution affected dialogue about gender in two ways: women were excluded from the community of academic discourse by not being permitted to attend universities, and women's exclusion from this discourse was bolstered by Aristotle's rationale for gender polarity perpetuated through the required study of his works in the new curriculum.

Most universities in the thirteenth to fifteenth centuries were founded to educate men to become secular clerics, canon lawyers, physicians, and civil lawyers. The exclusion of women from academia is all the more noteworthy, because in the Benedictine tradition from 800 to 1250, women and men had both received higher education. Gender was a topic within this discourse, together with components of gender polarity, unity, and complementarity. However, the new universities were engendered male communities of discourse in which women played only a minor role.[1] Consequently, a comparison of the concept of women in texts written by women in Chapter 1 with the concept of woman articulated by men in Chapter 2 produces some interesting results.

Chapter 3 will reflect on ways some philosophical issues about gender spread beyond the walls of academia into the broader public through satirical texts. The early satires written by men devalued women within different gender polarity models. Male authors attempted to show how sex and gender differentiations may be 'humorous' by using elaborate literary techniques that reveal reductionism, deval-

---

1. It is interesting to note that some universities were actually founded by women but for male students only, while other universities were founded by bishops or male members of the aristocracy. For example, the University of Paris was founded in the early thirteenth century by Blanche of Castile. Other women founders of universities for men include: Jeanne de Navarre, Jeanne de Bourgogne, Elizabeth de Burk, Countess of Clare, and Marie de Valence, Countess of Pembroke. It cannot be claimed, therefore, that the exclusion of women from this form of higher education was due to men's decisions alone. See Astrid L. Gabriel, "The College System," in *The Forward Movement of the Fourteenth Century,* ed. Francis Lee Utley (Columbus: Ohio State University Press, 1961), p. 85; and Régine Pernoud, *Blanche of Castile* (London: Collins, 1975).

uation, and bias. Here we will see exaggerated claims about the concept of woman that highlight the previously identified contrast occurring between female and male authors studied in the first two chapters.

Chapter 4 will turn towards a new community of discourse that emerges in early humanism. Between 1250 and 1400, some private philosophical dialogue between men and women begins to occur. By 'private' is meant dialogue in personal conversations in a home, in letters, or in chance meetings in public places. By private 'philosophical' dialogue is meant dialogue that engages in discursive reasoning about some issue of relevance to gender identity. To review, by 'discursive reasoning' is meant a process of thinking that proceeds in an orderly fashion from premises to conclusions, and the premises are supported by evidences of the senses or reason.

In early humanism, records of some private intergender dialogue that uses discursive reasoning to consider the concept of woman begin to become public. This making public of what was originally private occurs through the efforts of men authors who describe actual events of intergender dialogue in their texts. In the context of studying these texts the question will be raised: "How does this intergender dialogue contribute to theories of gender identity?"

Something else new also begins to happen in this humanistic period of western thought. Not only do men and women begin to discuss with one another certain aspects of the concept of woman, men authors also begin to write dialogues in which imaginary conversations, incorporating discursive reasoning, take place between women and men about woman's identity. Some creative approaches are introduced that move towards a complementarity in intergender discourse itself even if at times the theories proposed partake more of traditional gender polarity. Thus, the creative imagination of male authors begins to prepare the way for a new model of intergender dialogue by the dynamics among the women and men who engage in constructed dialogue.

Section I ends poised at a moment in the history of western thought in which the new foundations for a philosophy of gender complementarity are put in place. In Section II philosophers will build on these foundations and succeed in confronting for the first time the destructive effects of the gender polarity so deeply rooted in past Aristotelian philosophy.

CHAPTER 1

WOMEN RELIGIOUS DESCRIBE
WISDOM AND VIRTUE

A ccording to present estimates, the earliest surviving texts containing philosophical reflections on gender identity by women
living in religious communities belong to the Neopythagorean tradition. In *The
Concept of Woman: The Aristotelian Revolution (750 BC–1250 AD)* the contributions
of and controversies about these women have been evaluated. Their authorship includes in the earliest period (425-300 B.C.): Perictione I *On the Harmony of Women,*
Theano I *Apophthegms,* and Phyntis *Temperance of Women;* in the middle period
(300-200 B.C.): Perictione II *On Wisdom* and Aesare of Lucania *On Human Nature;*
and in the later period (200-100 B.C.) letters by Myia and Theano II. The significant number of fragments attests to the presence of a number of women who
shared a community of discourse with others about common philosophical and religious concerns.

For the purposes of this chapter, it is helpful to recall that the original Pythagorean women and men lived in community in the sixth century B.C. While no
fragments of texts written by women during this early period remain, there are
clusters of extant fragments from the Neopythagorean female authors of the fifth to
first century B.C. mentioned above. In a communal living context with the opportunity for intergender dialogue, texts authored by these women include references to
both common virtues and gender-specific virtues. Female authors also reflected on
the importance for women of self-knowledge, self-governance, and particular virtuous actions. They offered rational support, with analogical appeal to the order of
mathematics and of music, to argue for the value of interior ordering in the soul.

Another cluster of texts indicate that religious women authors flourished
again some twelve hundred years later within the Benedictine monastic tradition of
education in early medieval Europe. Roswitha, from the Benedictine monastery in
Gandersheim in the tenth century, wrote several plays, legends, and historical epics
that were discovered by the humanist Conrad Celtes in 1494. Her works give evidence of an engendered self-knowledge, dedication to wisdom gained through the
study of philosophy (particularly the Pythagorean and Neoplatonic schools), and
to the practice of virtues. She also experimented with rudimentary forms of dialogue among imaginary male and female characters.

In the twelfth century, three religious women authors left significant records
of their thought for future generations: Heloise, Herrad of Landsberg, and

Hildegard of Bingen. Together these three authors provide a golden age of reflection on women's identity just previous to the shifting of higher education away from the Benedictine monasteries to the new academic setting of western universities. Heloise studied in the educational center of Paris, dependent upon the private tutor Abelard, while Herrad and Hildegard wrote within the monastic setting of Benedictine education. A brief summary of their contributions follows.

First, Heloise wrote several letters to Abelard in which she appealed to the Stoic philosophy of Cicero and Seneca to justify her own theory of wisdom and virtue.[2] In spite of, or perhaps even because of, the well-known painful circumstances of their life and correspondence, these letters constitute a significant historical example of intergender dialogue. Heloise demonstrated her capacity to use discursive reason; and she worked towards self-knowledge, self-governance, and a changing understanding of virtues proper to her state. She also demonstrated a concern for the new women's religious community at the Paraclete, which she founded and directed.

Second, Herrad of Landsberg, also known as Herrad of Hohenbourg, wrote the first encyclopedia for women entitled *Hortus Deliciarum,* translated as *Garden of Delights.*[3] This text of several hundred pages described the history of the world by reproducing passages from Scriptural and philosophical works that were known to the contemporary world of her time. It included references to the philosophers Socrates, Plato, Aristotle, Boethius, Augustine, Anselm, and some Stoics and Neoplatonists. In addition, the sections that discussed particular virtues were illustrated by female figures dressed as knights fighting battles against various vices. The text also contained descriptions of the soul as divided into memory, understanding, and will; and it encouraged its female readers to become educated in the liberal arts as well as in physics and ethics.

Third, the Benedictine Abbess Hildegard of Bingen wrote several books that include reference to woman's identity. Without doubt, Hildegard is the epitome of a woman religious author who flourished in the educational environment of monastic life. Popularly referred to as a Renaissance woman before the Renaissance, Hildegard excelled in many different areas of creativity — in music, art, literature, language, philosophy, mystical theology, the empirical study of nature including rocks and herbs, and the empirical study of disease and health.[4] The extraordinary range and depth of her thought are just beginning to be known and evaluated.

The most significant of Hildegard's works for the study of gender identity are: *Scivias, Book of Divine Works with Letters and Songs,* and *Causae et curae.*[5] The

2. *The Letters of Abelard and Heloise* (Harmondsworth: Penguin Books, 1974). See Régine Pérnoud, *Héloïse et Abélard* (New York: Stein and Day, 1973).

3. Herrad of Hohenbourg, *Hortus Deliciarum: Commentary* (New Rochelle, N.Y.: Caratzas Brothers Publishers, 1971) and *Hortus Deliciarum: Reconstruction,* by Rosalie Green et al. (London: The Warburg Institute and Leiden: E. J. Brill, 1979).

4. Anne E. Johnson, "Before the Renaissance: A Renaissance Woman," *The New York Times* (September 29, 1997), pp. 27, 34.

5. Hildegard of Bingen, *Scivias,* trans. Bruce Hozeski (Santa Fe, Calif.: Bear, 1987) and trans. Mother Columba Hart, OSB (New York: Paulist Press, 1990); *Book of Divine Works with Letters and Songs* (Santa Fe, Calif.: Bear, 1987); *Causae et curae. Patrologia cursus completus, series latina (PL)*

latter text, which is not yet translated into English, offers an important and well-elaborated typology of men and women. In this introduction to the next phase of the systematic study of the concept of woman two particular aspects will be briefly mentioned: first, her in-depth analysis of different aspects of the male and female human being, and second, her defense of gender complementarity.

For Hildegard, self-knowledge involved learning about how the humors and elements functioned with bodily type, muscular structure, physiology of blood, patterns of menstruation for women, disease patterns, and character. She identified four different types of women and four different types of men; and she analyzed various kinds of intergender interaction in both celibate and sexual relationships. Hildegard was the first philosopher, man or woman, to give such a thorough analysis of intergender identity, which systematically considered ways of interacting, of engaging in intergender dialogue, as well as of generating children. In addition to suggesting that self-knowledge is a key to wisdom and to self-governance, Hildegard also implied that knowledge of others was important for the development of the virtues. Hildegard consistently reflected on the meaning of her own engendered experience through the extensive use of analogical thinking and discursive reasoning.

Hildegard also developed the first systematic philosophical defense for a theory of complementarity. The context of her thinking was often one of intergender dialogue in a double monastery in which her secretary was a monk. A double monastery had a community of men and a community of women living in close proximity with one another and under the single leadership of either an abbess or an abbot. Hildegard also experienced a context conducive to complementarity in her wide travels and lectures and in her frequent correspondence with men. This living context of intergender dialogue likely contributed significantly to the development of a theory of gender complementarity because she was immersed in a culture that allowed for a significant differentiation of men and women while supporting the fundamental equality of both genders.

Although Hildegard was often in contact with men, she also lived in a woman's religious community — first, within the double monastery, and second, when she left this situation to found a separate woman's monastery. Her own engendered reflections were often expressed in ways that sprang out of a consciousness of woman's particular way of thinking and acting. If history had taken a different course, Hildegard's attempts to elaborate a woman's experience of the world may have become the foundation for other women authors to build upon. However, as it turned out, Hildegard lived just before the widespread founding of universities and the shifting of higher education away from the Benedictine monasteries, where it had been situated the previous four hundred years, to the new academic centers where women were no longer able to participate. The thirteenth century saw the Aristotelian revolution in the concept of woman, with its institutionalization of a consistent rationale for gender polarity. Hildegard's attempt to establish a philosophical foundation for gender complementarity would

---

(Santa Fe, Calif.: Bear, 1987). See also Barbara Newman, *Sister of Wisdom: Hildegard's Theology of the Feminine* (Berkeley: University of California Press, 1987).

remain a voice unheard for nearly eight hundred years.[6] It remained for others to attempt this work from the different foundation of humanistic studies. Women religious writers had to begin again to establish an educational context within which the philosophy of gender identity could once again evolve to the height it had reached with Hildegard.

In this chapter we will study some of the earliest women writers to follow Hildegard. A movement of *mulieres religiosae,* or religious women, spread across Europe, flourishing from 1180, a year after Hildegard's death, until 1270. Many of these women lived in small communities, without taking vows. In this informal context, interpersonal dialogue between men and these devout women often occurred.[7] During the thirteenth and early fourteenth centuries, several women writers began to articulate their visions of the world and of their own identity within the broader context of their relation to God. In this chapter we will consider four particular examples of texts attributed to the women Beatrice of Nazareth, Hadewijch, Mechtild of Magdeburg, and Marguerite Porete.

It has recently been suggested that the authors of many of these texts may not have been the women themselves, but rather their confessor, or a secretary who took down their dictation, or the texts may be a later-generational compilation of notes and remembrances. While it is true that in different situations a woman's voice was mediated by a man who actually wrote a text expressing this voice, it is also true that the woman's thoughts behind or within the voice can be heard.[8] As will be seen, certain patterns of communication developed in texts ascribed to women.[9] These patterns, along with the ascribed authorship to a woman, developed a culture of women religious writers that influenced others who were immersed in this culture. We will leave aside the more formal question of authorship for experts to determine, since our purpose is to search for the patterns of theories about gender identity that these texts contain. Fortunately, many of these texts exist in their entirety. As will be seen, there are recurrent themes and approaches in these texts attributed to women religious authors.

Before proceeding further, a clarification of the relation between philosophical and theological reflection is needed. If we consider the human person as a relational act of existence, then a woman may be considered from a series of sublated

---

6. There is an apocryphal story that Hildegard, as an elderly nun, traveled with her works by cart to Paris to ask the Bishop to read them, to evaluate their value, and perhaps consider them for the new academic centers that were being established. According to the story, the Bishop kept them for three months, then handed them back saying that they were divinely inspired, but did not integrate them into the new curriculum.

7. Roger De Ganck, *Towards Unification with God: Beatrice of Nazareth in Her Context, Part Three* (Kalamazoo, Mich.: Cistercian Publications, 1991), p. 8.

8. For example, "It is not less significant that, within the framework of their tradition, the *mulieres religiosae* took the same freedom as did their mentors. They expressed their insights and experiences very personally, as they found it expedient. And when they did so, they did it well." De Ganck, *Beatrice,* p. 121.

9. In a different context of the examination of literature, Elaine Showalter describes women's writings as being undercurrents to the mainstream male tradition. See "Feminist Criticism in the Wilderness," in *Writing and Sexual Difference,* ed. Elizabeth Abel (Chicago: University of Chicago Press, 1982), pp. 9-36.

levels of existence that enter into her identity as a whole engendered person in relation to other persons. We can study her through the articulation of her experience of herself as an engendered subject in relation with other subjects in the description of an experience occurring in the present, and we can study her experience of herself as an object later, looking back at her experience. In the former we consider woman's reflexive experience of herself as a subject in relation with other subjects, and in the latter we consider woman's reflective experience of herself or others as objects to be examined. In both situations, if we are using a philosophical approach, we can approach religious themes such as God or Divine Love, not theologically, but philosophically. For example, if we consider a woman author's reflection on the love of God, philosophically we can look at what she says about herself, about what happens to her consciousness as a female human being during this experience of love, rather than on the nature of the theological object God or the language used to speak rightly or wrongly about the Divine Being.

From the perspective of philosophy, there is a concern about whether the author speaks in the right way about the human person who is in dialogue with the Divine Being and with men and women. The criteria for evaluating a right from a wrong way of speaking philosophically include reference to an integration and a balance among the factors of rationality, materiality, individuality, and spirituality. Basically, a wrong way to describe the person would be one that significantly devalues at least one of the four factors, or places too much emphasis on one factor to the detriment of others. In the context of analysis of each author the basis for evaluation will become more evident.

Another way to express the difference between a philosophical and a theological approach to religious women writers is to consider the evidence that the author produces to support her claims. If the author appeals to data of experience drawn from the observation of the senses or to a reasoning process rather than to faith, revelation, or a religious authority to support her argument, then she will be seen as using a philosophical, rather than a theological, method of thinking. We will pay special attention to the woman religious author's analysis of four different operations of her own consciousness: (1) how she is attentive to the data of her own experience, (2) what intelligent questions she asks about her experience and what subjective insights she reaches, (3) how she tests out her insights to determine whether they are true or not, and (4) once she makes a determination about their truth, how she acts in relation to her judgments.[10] Through these questions we will try to uncover the particular philosophical components of women's wisdom and virtue in each of the authors studied.

Beatrice of Nazareth distinguishes between seven levels of consciousness of love, while considering the specific values of perfection, service, and justice. Hadewijch considers the role of reason and self-reflection in the practice of virtue. Mechtild of Magdeburg offers dialectical reflections on the evidence of the senses and the virtue of public speech. Marguerite Porete, abandoning the basis for gender

---

10. Bernard J. F. Lonergan, "All special methods consist in making specific the transcendental precepts, Be attentive, Be intelligent, Be reasonable, Be responsible," *Method in Theology* (Toronto: University of Toronto Press, 1990), p. 20.

and human individuation in her Neoplatonic approach to union with God, considers the loss of reason and will in her religious experience.

The Aristotelian polarity model seemed to suggest that women's virtues included intuition alone, rather than discursive reasoning; obedience to a man, rather than self-governance; and private, rather than public, spheres of action. However, the virtues of discursive reasoning, self-governance, and public actions were repeatedly written about and exemplified by women religious writers. Therefore, their texts suggest that in the cultural environment of religious communities, women developed a model of gender identity that *de facto* went against and even disproved the academic Aristotelian model of gender polarity with specified limited virtues for women.

BEATRICE OF NAZARETH (1200-1268)

This Belgian woman was educated by the Beguines in Léau. The term 'Beguines' applies to a movement of lay women that began to organize itself at the beginning of the thirteenth century in Liège, Belgium, and then spread throughout Europe.[11] The first phase in the growth of the Beguine movement was widely supported by the general public and Church authority as well. The Beguines taught Beatrice Latin, calligraphy, and the seven liberal arts (grammar, rhetoric, dialectic, arithmetic, geometry, music, and astronomy) following the tradition of the pre-university era for men in Europe.[12] Then in her early teens Beatrice entered the Cistercian Abbey at Bloemendaal, which had been founded by her father.

The Cistercian communities were founded in the early twelfth century. Unfortunately, the complementarity that had been practiced between women and men monks within the Benedictine tradition of double monasteries did not always carry over into the Cistercian reform.[13] On the contrary, there was a great deal of tension between the male and the female Cistercian monasteries, with the result that men and women within this tradition eventually developed separately rather than together. The Cistercian men sought to avoid the kind of regular contact with women that had so marked the Benedictine age primarily because it did not fit in with their pastoral apostolate. As a consequence, the Cistercian monasteries for

---

11. For the place of the Beguines in lay movements see André Vauchez, *The Laity in the Middle Ages: Religious Beliefs and Devotional Practices,* ed. Daniel E. Bornstein, trans. Margery J. Schneider (Notre Dame and London: University of Notre Dame Press, 1993).

12. Elizabeth Alvica Petroff, ed., *Medieval Women's Visionary Literature* (New York: Oxford University Press, 1986), pp. 176, 200-206; Mother Colomba Hart, O.S.B., *Hadewijch* (New York: Paulist Press, 1980), Introduction, pp. 3, 5, and 17; Cornelia Wolfskeel, "Beatrice of Nazareth," in *A History of Women Philosophers, Vol II: 500-1600,* ed. Mary Ellen Waithe (Dordrecht/Boston/London: Kluwer Academic Publishers, 1989), pp. 99-100.

13. Penny Schine Gold, "Male/Female Cooperation: The Example of Fontevrault," in *Distant Echoes: Medieval Religious Women,* vol. 1, ed. John A. Nichols and Lillian Thomas Shank (Kalamazoo, Mich.: Cistercian Studies Series #71, 1984), pp. 151-68; and Constance H. Berman, "Men's Houses, Women's Houses: The Relationship Between the Sexes in Twelfth-Century Monasticism," in *The Medieval Monastery,* ed. Andrew MacLeish (St. Cloud, Minn.: North Star Press, 1988), pp. 43-52.

women were left to develop on their own from the mid-twelfth to the mid-thirteenth century. However, after a hundred years, the Cistercian men decided to organize the women's communities, which was met by resistance on the women's part, particularly in Germany, Belgium, Holland, Portugal, and Switzerland. It was in this context that Beatrice's father founded three convents for women.[14]

In subsequent years, Beatrice's father founded two more monasteries for women, and she was named prioress of the Cistercian house at Notre Dame de Nazareth, a position she held until her death. It was here that Beatrice wrote her major text: *Seven manieren van Minne* (The Seven Stages of the Love of God). In this text, Beatrice described seven levels of consciousness: the first three can be considered as more philosophical, while the last four are more properly described as completely spiritual or theological.[15] Our analysis will consider each stage in turn.

Beatrice sets for herself the goal of reaching a human level of perfection in living in the image of God. She follows closely the theory of St. Augustine found in *The Trinity,* in which the image of God is constituted by the interior harmony of the three human faculties of intellect, memory, and will.[16] In the first stage of prayer, Beatrice identifies the central activity of the person as an exercise of concentration of intellect, memory, and will towards the fulfillment of the desire for perfection. Calling this effort a concentration of heart, she concludes: "There was indeed at this stage a self-knowledge in the holy woman which she considered necessary in her present endeavour, an extreme concern regarding what she was in herself, what she ought to have been, and how far she was progressing."[17]

When Beatrice reflected upon herself as an object, she was attentive to the data of her subjective experience, and she asked what it meant in relation to certain goals she had given herself. It is clear that her description included the factors of self-discipline, self-knowledge, and the general capacity for the continual exercise of discursive reasoning about the acts that one performs. This active self-knowledge identifies values, recognizes particular acts in relation to those values, and evaluates their effectiveness. As Roger de Ganck summarizes it: "Navigating the waves of the human condition, the *mulieres religiosae* took self-knowledge as their compass."[18] Self-knowledge also includes reference to an identity that is in relation to a transcendent Being, or God.

In the second stage, Beatrice suggests that an effort of the will enables a person to choose to obey another person with whom she is in contact even though be-

14. See R. W. Southern, *Western Society and the Church in the Middle Ages,* The Pelican History of the Church, vol. 2 (Harmondsworth: Penguin Books, 1982), pp. 314-17. See also De Ganck, *Beatrice,* where this description is mitigated, p. 18.

15. Beatrice of Nazareth, *Seven manieren van Minne* (Leuven: s.V. de Vlaamsche Boekenhalle, 1926). All passages from this text are translated from the Latin of the critical edition into English by Andrea Jarmei.

16. Beatrice, as a religious, identifies with that aspect of Augustine's theory in *The Trinity* that sees the mind when contemplating God as neither male nor female. This leads to a sex unity view of man's and woman's identity. For a detailed discussion of Beatrice and Hadewijch and other writers on imaging the Trinity, see De Ganck, *Beatrice,* pp. 125-50.

17. Beatrice, *Seven,* p. 44.

18. De Ganck, *Beatrice,* p. 39.

cause of an equality of rational faculties such a choice is not of itself mandated. The important factor to emphasize here is that obedience does not come as the result of a natural inferiority or inability to exercise the rational faculty, but rather as a choice for a particular purpose, the perfection of love. Beatrice describes this action as follows:

> It was possible to see the holy woman at this stage bending herself humbly in the task of subjection, patiently obeying everyone, patient in the face of adversity, exulting under her tribulations, and putting forth all the love of her heart in the humble service of all collectively and of each individual singly, that is, impartially compliant to the great and the small alike.[19]

Obedience or subjection is perceived as a conscious choice, a "task" the woman performs as a way of expressing the "love of her heart" for a particular individual with whom she comes into contact. Her choice of obedience to "all impartially" makes her available as a gift of self in a way that leads to the overcoming of her desire (for example, to serve a simple preference) by the exercise of her will on a higher level of desire for perfection. The kind of rigorous choice described by Beatrice demands a high degree of self-discipline, and when repeated, it can lead to a systematic practice of self-governance. Self-control differs from self-governance in that in the former the individual is still involved in an interior struggle for integration, while in the latter the action flows from an integrated personality.

In the third stage, Beatrice describes herself as trying to live out a relationship of justice "by giving back full recompense" to God for all that she had received. In this stage of development she moves beyond the instinctive desire for perfection with which she characterizes the first stage, and beyond the practice of obedience as a method of achieving perfection, a method she describes in the second stage. Here, we see Beatrice reflecting on the roles of reason and the will in her attempt to practice justice in recompense for what she owes:

> Although she knew, from the teaching of reason and also from the testimony of experience (having tried many times, she was by no means unaware), that this arduous exchange of love was not humanly achievable, since that love which is God is bounded by no limits and is circumscribed by no measure either spatial or temporal, whereas her intent from this projected object was simply by means of the counsel of reason, and for the very reason that she found her own inability standing in her way, she increased the strength of her will even more, as is wont to happen in cases like this.[20]

In this passage Beatrice analyzes the experience and challenges of an exchange of justice between an eternal non-spatial Divine Being and a spatial and temporal human being. When her intellect meets a paradox, Beatrice does not cease to think; she chooses to incrementally increase the strength of her will.

19. Beatrice, *Seven,* p. 45.
20. Beatrice, *Seven,* p. 46.

Beatrice's philosophical insights can be summarized as follows: (1) an intuition of the first principle of justice as a value, as good; (2) a recognition of the practice of obedience as a consciously chosen active means of achieving the perfection of self-governance; and (3) a use of discursive reasoning to determine when and how to achieve this good. These insights are discovered by the intellect and will in the context of religious life, which has as its foundation a belief in, and experience of, a dynamic interaction between the woman and God. This interactive relation is one of initiative and response, mutually building in freedom and love.

In the final four stages of her *Seven Stages of the Love of God,* Beatrice's partly philosophical approach is superseded by a completely theological approach that focuses more directly on the effect of grace on the person following this path to perfection. In the fourth stage, the individual rests with the "fire of illumination"; in the fifth stage, she is consumed "heart, breast, and brain" by a flame of love; and in the sixth stage, this Divine Love fuses a union with the soul. Drawing upon a feminine metaphor Beatrice says,

> (like a mother ruling the whole family of her household with her caring, wisely governing, ably guiding and protecting,) this love, seated on the highest throne of her mind, having been made all-commanding by the power of its virtue, as by sense, instructed them wisely without causing any offence or rebellion, and powerful and commanding, kept them in its servitude.[21]

In this sixth stage, the person achieves an interior integration in which the intellect, will, and memory all work in harmony in the soul under the guidance of Divine Love.

Let us consider for a moment Beatrice's introduction of a feminine metaphor to characterize this governance of Divine Love as like a mother ruling her household. For Beatrice, mothering includes the qualities of ruling and protecting, which are considered "masculine" in traditional models. Her sense of the appropriateness for this metaphor could have been derived from the fact that she lived in women's communities in which women ruled and protected others through acts of love.[22] The love must be well ordered, as a mother orders her household.[23]

In the seventh and final stage of analysis of her consciousness in love of God, Beatrice describes herself experiencing a kind of separation of mind and body: ". . . she . . . lived on earth only with her body, while her mind was totally in heaven."[24] Describing a series of mystical experiences in which she meets with various holy men and women in heaven, Beatrice then adds that she was "recalled by

---

21. Beatrice, *Seven,* p. 48.

22. Her own mother died when she was very young. See Cornelia Wolfskeel, "Beatrice of Nazareth," p. 99. Also see Carolyn Walker Bynum, *Jesus as Mother: Studies in the Spirituality of the High Middle Ages* (Berkeley, Los Angeles, London: University of California Press, 1982), pp. 110-169.

23. See De Ganck, *Beatrice,* p. 455.

24. Beatrice, *Seven,* p. 50. Carolyn Walker Bynum emphasizes the complex psychology of Beatrice's asceticism and her physical metaphors of union in Christ in these final stages of religious consciousness in *Holy Feast and Holy Fast: The Religious Significance of Food to Medieval Women* (Berkeley/Los Angeles, London: University of California Press, 1987), pp. 161-65.

the too heavy weight of humanity which she carried" back into her body.[25] This hint of a Platonic devaluation of body is somewhat muted by the final sentence of her treatise in which she affirms that "love of one's neighbour . . . should be inserted, for the edification of everyone, into the present work before I bring my narrative to a close."[26] Love of one's neighbor needs embodied acts to be efficacious. So at the end of the seven stages of love, the individual returns to an integration of interpersonal action rather than to an isolated contemplation that rejects the materiality of human existence.[27]

Sometimes, a Neoplatonic tendency will lead a writer to emphasize the separation of body and soul, even to the point of the disappearance of an individual's identity. At other times, a writer may emphasize the central integrity of the soul (including intellect, memory, and will), which is integrated and valued with the body. This latter view is common both to the Christian tradition of gender polarity that follows the Aristotelian line of argument, and to the Christian tradition of gender complementarity that had its roots in the Benedictine monastic writers. As will be seen in subsequent sections in this chapter, the question of the proper relation of soul to body in the human being is central to the work of women religious writers, who struggle to describe not only a feminine identity but also the human condition.

We could characterize Beatrice's theory of identity as falling within the tradition of gender neutrality, because she makes no argument about gender identity *per se*. At the same time that Beatrice describes a model available to all persons, she also refers to herself directly as "woman," rather than the more general "human" or "man." In this self-identification, she does not imply that her insights refer only to women, but that they are available to all persons. Therefore, Beatrice understands herself as a paradigm; her "woman" is a generic model for all men and women. This is an interesting inversion from the usual philosophical texts in which "man" is a generic model for all men and women.

Further, Beatrice's generic "woman" argues for the effective use of reason.[28] The particular kind of reason she describes involves an intuitive grasp of first principles, the capacity to think discursively, to evaluate factual situations, to clarify the decision-making process, and to execute choices through the effective operation of the will. Beatrice gives evidence in her writing of both a reflective consideration of herself as an object and a reflexive consideration of herself as acting subject. Her text opens up the interior dynamics of a dialogue within a woman and another kind of dialogue between a woman and the Divine Being experienced as Love. It is

25. Beatrice, *Seven,* p. 50.
26. Beatrice, *Seven,* p. 51.
27. Cornelia Wolfskeel emphasizes Beatrice's "desire to be dissolved from the body" which is so strong in the seventh stage. See "Beatrice of Nazareth," pp. 101 and 107. In my own interpretation of her works, this desire is seen to be present but is qualified by a clear statement of the importance of the practice of charity, which demands an integration of soul and body in action.
28. This emphasis on reason is also expressed in what is thought to be one of her lost works, *De monasterio spirituali* (On the Spiritual Convent), in which Reason serves as an Abbess governing Wisdom as the Prioress, Prudence the Sub-Prioress, and working together with God who is the Abbot. See Wolfskeel, "Beatrice of Nazareth," p. 109.

within this interior, private dialogue that she discovers the meaning of her experience both for herself and for others.

HADEWIJCH (THIRTEENTH CENTURY)

As mentioned previously, in the first phase of the Beguine movement lay women lived together in loosely formed communities supported by the public and Church authority. The second phase of the development of communities of Beguines, beginning in the second half of the thirteenth century, witnessed a revocation of the communities' independent status as they came under the umbrella of recognized Church authorities. The third phase, occurring during the fourteenth century, saw the violent repression of the Beguines and a general dissolution of the movement.[29] Of the next three women writers studied in this text, Hadewijch belongs to the first phase of the Beguine movement, Mechtild of Magdeburg belongs to the second phase, and Marguerite Porete belongs to the third.

While there is little known about the specific details of Hadewijch's life, there is some evidence that she was the head of a small Flemish group of Beguines, that she was evicted from this group at a later date, and that she completed her writings by about 1240.[30] Hadewijch's works consist of letters, poems in stanzas and couplets, and a record of her visions. Their content reveals that she had studied rhetoric, astronomy, numerology, calligraphy, Latin, and French.

Hadewijch admits to being influenced by Saint Augustine:

> Once I heard a sermon in which Saint Augustine was spoken of. No sooner had I heard it than I became inwardly so on fire that it seemed to me everything on earth must be set ablaze by the flame I felt within me. Love is all![31]

In another remarkable passage Hadewijch describes the intellectual relation she had with the Saint, as student to teacher, and her desire to go beyond Augustine in her own thought.

> When afterwards I returned to myself . . . I reflected on this union with Saint Au-

---

29. See Mary Robinson, *The End of the Middle Ages* (London: T. Risher Unwin, 1889); Dayton Phillips, *Beguines in Medieval Strasbourg* (Santa Barbara, Calif.: Stanford University Press, 1941); Ernest W. McDonnell, *The Beguines and Beghards in Medieval Culture* (New Brunswick, N.J.: Rutgers University Press, 1954); and Southern, *Western Society and the Church in the Middle Ages,* p. 321. More recent studies are: Florence Koorn, "Women without Vows: The Case of the Beguines and the Sisters of the Common Life in the Northern Netherlands," in *Women and Men in Spiritual Culture: XIV-XVII Centuries,* ed. Elisja Schulte van Kessel (The Hague: Netherlands Government Publishing Office, 1986), pp. 135-47; Sherrin Marshall Wyntjes, "Women in the Reformation Era," in *Becoming Visible: Women in European History,* ed. Renate Bridenthal and Claudia Koonz (Boston: Houghton Mifflin, 1977), pp. 167-91.

30. See Mother Columba Hart, OSB, *Hadewijch: The Complete Works* (New York: Paulist Press, 1980), Introduction.

31. Hadewijch, *The Complete Works,* Letter 25, 106.

gustine to which I had attained. I was not contented with what my dearly Beloved had just permitted, in spite of my consent and emotional attraction; it weighed on me now that this union with Saint Augustine had made me so perfectly happy, whereas previously I had possessed union far from saints and men, with God alone. . . . As I thought about this attitude I asked my Beloved to deliver me from it. . . . No doubt I continued to belong to God alone while being united in Love to this creature. But my liberty I gained then was given me moreover for reasons of my own, which neither Augustine nor many others had.

I did not suggest this as a claim to be more privileged than Saint Augustine; but in the time when I knew the truth of Being, I did not want to receive any comfort from him in so far as he was a creature, or to accept any joy amid my pains, and so I would allow myself no satisfaction in the security that was given me in this union with Saint Augustine. For I am a free human creature. . . .[32]

We can see here signs of an interior relation between the woman Hadewijch and the man Augustine, an interior relation, crossing the barrier of human death and mediated by a love of God. In the dialogue, Hadewijch displays an independence of will and mind that allows her to move into and then move out of an intensity of relationship. In this, she reveals a disposition for complementarity.

Hadewijch also mentions that she admires Hildegard of Bingen.[33] This indicates that at least she has heard of her predecessor, although there is no evidence for her having read some of the works Hildegard authored. In addition, while there is no direct consideration of the premises of Hildegard's theory of gender complementarity, there is within Hadewijch's discussion of the human being a strong affirmation of the integration of materiality with rationality and spirituality, a theme she had in common with Hildegard.

Hadewijch was likely familiar with some of the uses of the dialogue form by classical authors including the Stoics. Examples abound of "horizontal" dialogues in Seneca and other classical writers in which neither side of the debate wins. The term 'horizontal' indicates a balance among those who participate in the dialogue. Other examples occur of "vertical" dialogues in Boethius, Augustine, and others in which one persona overwhelms and conquers the other. The term 'vertical' therefore indicates the superiority of one of the participants over the others. The hierarchical nature of the dialogue may be established by different means, i.e., by reasoned arguments, by facts, or by the force of one of the disputants over the other. A further influence on Hadewijch, and on many other women religious writers as well, may have been exposure to other genres of texts written as a dialogue or a debate.[34] In addition, in Boethius's *Consolation of Philosophy,* we may also find a model for her own feminine personification of Reason. Hadewijch also seems fa-

32. Hadewijch, Vision 11, 290-91. For other references to Augustine see Letter 25, 106 and Letter 22, 94.

33. Hadewijch, *The Complete Works,* Letter 22, 94.

34. See Thomas L. Reed, Jr., *Middle English Debate Poetry and the Aesthetics of Irresolution* (Columbia, Mo. and London: University of Missouri Press, 1990); and Francis Lee Utley, "Dialogues, Debates, and Catechisms," in *A Manual of the Writings in Middle English: 1050-1500,* 8 vols. (Hamden, Conn.: Archon Books, 1967-1989), vol. 3, pp. 669-746 and 829-94.

miliar with dialogue forms used in public debates that begin to occur in academies and colleges.

Hadewijch's texts affirm the value of the use of reason for self-knowledge and for self-governance in a variety of creative ways. In her letters to a young Beguine whom she is instructing, Hadewijch continually appeals, in a prescriptive tone, to the use of reason: "Illuminate your mind"; "Examine your thoughts strictly, in order to know yourself in all things"; "We must seek everything by means of itself . . . knowledge by means of knowledge . . . like by means of like."[35]

In addition to these direct statements affirming the importance of the exercise of human reason in the discovery of knowledge, Hadewijch considers ways in which reason can err when it is not exercised properly:

> For we err in many things that men judge good, and that really are good; but reason errs in these things when men do not understand them properly, or practice them; this is where reason fails. Then when reason is obscured, the will grows weak and powerless and feels an aversion to effort, because reason does not enlighten it.[36]

In this passage, Hadewijch considers the relation of intellect to will. In other passages, she considers ways in which reason can be led astray by emotions: "In yielding obedience to various and sundry claims, reason errs extremely."[37] She advises that, instead, reason ought to rule the emotions and direct the will. Hadewijch follows the traditional model for the wise man who orders his irrational soul by the practical exercise of his intellectual soul. Hadewijch understood this activity of the proper exercise of reason to be important, arguing that an individual ought to reflect on the ways reason works within the self:

> Give reason its time, and always observe where you heed it too little and where enough. And do not let yourself be stopped by any pleasure through which your reason may be the loser. What I mean by "your reason" is that you must keep your insight ever vigilant in the use of discernment.[38]

Hadewijch, using reason to analyze the effectiveness of reason itself, turns inward to reflect on herself as an object. She states that the will ought to remain vigilant so that the judgments or discernment about the correctness of insights remains accurate. Reason is the tool through which the individual achieves self-knowledge and wisdom.

The dynamic interaction of reason, memory, and will is further described in one of Hadewijch's poems entitled "Reason, Pleasure, and Desire." Here the au-

---

35. Hadewijch, *The Complete Works,* Letter 1:46, 48; Letter 2:29, 49; Letter 7:4, 64; and Letter 4:43, 77.

36. Hadewijch, *The Complete Works,* Letter 4:1, 53. For similar views see also Letter 22:137, 97.

37. Hadewijch, *The Complete Works,* Letter 4:98, 55.

38. Hadewijch, *The Complete Works,* Letter 24:1, 103.

thor introduces the concept of Reason as love's surgeon, who cuts out all that is extraneous to the self.

> Desire cannot keep silence,
> And Reason counsels her clearly,
> For she enlightens her with her will
> And holds before her the performance of the noblest deed. . . .
>
> Alas! God knows no one exists
> Who can be avenged of anything on Reason:
> She herself is Love's surgeoness:
> She can best heal all faults against her.
> To him who adroitly follows all Reason's moves,
> In all the ways in which she leads him,
> She will speak of new wonders:
> "Behold! Take possession of the highest glory!"
>
> Alas! No alien conciliator dares attempt
> To conciliate feuds;
> And they who know this understand
> Well enough Reason's teaching.[39]

The image of Reason as a female surgeon working for Divine Love corresponds directly to Boethius's description of Lady Philosophy as a physician and nurse in *The Consolation of Philosophy*. It is a strong feminine metaphor that includes the concept of incisive action based on true judgment. It also runs counter to the cultural traditions in which surgeons were male barbers, while nurse-physician-healers, who treated in less invasive ways such as by herbs, were generally female.

Hadewijch employs another strong feminine metaphor from the same text in a description of one of her visions, in which she describes "Queen Reason" coming to her:

> The queen approached me dreadfully fast and set her foot on my throat, and cried with a more terrible voice, and said: "Do you know who I am?"
>
> And I said: "Yes, indeed! Long enough have you caused me woe and pain! You are my soul's faculty of Reason, and these are the officials of my own household with whom you walk abroad in such fine style! The trumpeter is my Holy Fear. . . . The second maiden is Discernment. . . . The third maiden is Wisdom."[40]

39. Hadewijch, *The Complete Works,* 196-99. For a further discussion of the importance of Reason in relation to Love, see Cornelia Wolfskeel, "Hadewijch of Antwerp," in *A History of Women Philosophers,* vol. 11, pp. 141-65.

40. Hadewijch, *The Complete Works,* Vision 9, 285-86. See also Letter 24:1, "What I mean by 'your reason' is that you must keep your insight ever vigilant in the use of discernment" (p. 103).

Hadewijch ends the vision with the phrase: "Then Reason became subject to me, and I left her."[41] The faculty of reason becomes so integrated within her that it is no longer separate from the ordering of her consciousness. The pain of reason results from the demand that it places on the individual to continually exercise discursive thinking with a careful grasp of first principles.

One scholar argues that Hadewijch's emphasis on the importance of reason is excessive, and that "her obsession with self-knowledge limits her ability to grow."[42] However, Hadewijch is careful to point out that reason must be complementary with love. In this way, her philosophy is transformed by theology. In a letter to her student, the relation between love and reason is clarified:

> These two . . . are of great mutual help one to the other; for reason instructs love, and love enlightens reason. When reason abandons itself to love's wish, and love consents to be forced and held within the bounds of reason, they can accomplish a very great work. This no one can learn except by experience.[43]

This complementarity of reason and love is sometimes harmonious and at other times filled with tension. In Letter 20, Hadewijch argues that the period of tension between reason and love occurs in the sixth stage of twelve stages of mystical life. In this stage, "Love disdains reason and all that is in, above, or below reason."[44] Then in a poem entitled "Love and Reason," Hadewijch elaborates the dialectic between these two sources of truth within the self. Ultimately the individual must pass through this tension in order to harmoniously balance these two aspects:

> By Reason one can win
> Veritable fruition of Love,
> Regarding which Reason clearly makes known
> That one has satisfied both Love and Reason.
> Veritable fruition of Love
> Then, from Love, Reason lets us receive.
>
> May God grant to all who love
> That they may win the favour of Reason,
> By which they may know
> How fruition of Love is attained.
> In winning the favour of Reason
> Lies for us the whole perfection of Love.[45]

---

41. Hadewijch, *The Complete Works,* Vision 9, 286.

42. Elona K. Lucas, "Psychological and Spiritual Growth in Hadewijch and Julian of Norwich," *Studia Mystica* 9, no. 3 (1986): 12.

43. Hadewijch, *The Complete Works,* Letter 18:80, 86. See also Letter 13:17, 75: "No one can become perfect in Love unless he is subject to his reason"; and Letter 19, 89: ". . . reason cannot understand how Love, by Love, sees to the depths of the Beloved."

44. Hadewijch, *The Complete Works,* Letter 20:56, 91.

45. Hadewijch, *The Complete Works,* Poem in Stanzas 30, 214-15.

Hadewijch may be alluding to academic models of education either within the emerging context of schools or universities when, in the following extract from a poem, she employs an academic metaphor while considering the same theme of the complementarity of reason and love:

> But those who arrange their lives with truth in Love,
> And are then enlightened by clear reason,
> Love will place in her school:
> They shall be masters
> And receive Love's highest gifts,
> Which wound beyond cure.[46]

The above brief passages from Hadewijch's works demonstrate that she thought a woman ought to use her reason in a consistent and vigorous manner to search for truth and wisdom. It is also clear that even though Hadewijch articulates the meaning of a woman's experience, she understands herself as representing generic humanity. Although both Beatrice and Hadewijch wrote from within a gender neutrality perspective, they did so from the perspective of the generic woman representing all persons.

Hadewijch's love of reason is often identified as flowing from a fundamental Neoplatonist orientation. Hadewijch discovered Dutch translations of Latin texts containing Neoplatonic concepts, and by incorporating them into the Flemish language she became a medium of transmission of Neoplatonism to later Dutch writers such as Jan van Ruusbroec.[47] Hadewijch's Neoplatonism also contained some "exemplarism," or the claim that eternal Ideas or Forms exist in the mind of God, and that these become models for Divine creation and for human activity as well.[48] It follows from this theory that human reason, when it is able to grasp the truth of an Idea, leads the individual into a special relation with God. It is because of this foundation that Hadewijch emphasizes so much the need for reason to be exercised vigorously and for it to search for union with love.

It is important to note, however, that even though Hadewijch was influenced by Neoplatonism she did not tend towards abstraction, nor did she devalue the body as do so many others who follow this particular philosophical tradition.[49] It is in Hadewijch's theory of virtue that this movement beyond Neoplatonism is particularly evident. Acts of virtue are dependent upon the materiality of the human condition; they need a body to be performed. Therefore they are not simply abstract ideas in the mind of God.

In another metaphor, Hadewijch describes four university professors debating about what is "The Strongest of All Things." The first professor argues that

46. Hadewijch, *The Complete Works,* Letter 29, 114.

47. Cornelia Wolfskeel, "Hadewych of Antwerp," in *A History of Women Philosophers,* vol. 2, pp. 140-43.

48. Sheila Carney, "Exemplarism in Hadewijch: The Quest for Full-Grownness," *Downside Review* 103 (1985): 276-95.

49. Nicholas Watson, "'Classics of Western Spirituality,' II: Three Medieval Women Theologians and Their Background," *Kings Theological Review* 12 (1989): 57.

wine is the strongest thing because of its medicinal effects, the second one that a King is the strongest because of his extensive power, the third that "the works of woman conquer every kind of strength," and the fourth that the truth "is the strongest of all strengths."[50] The debate continues until it is clarified that the woman is Mary, who "indeed is rightly the strongest" because her humility drew Christ to fall from Heaven "into this unfathomable chasm."[51] In this paradoxical rendering of the meaning of the word "strongest," Hadewijch expresses one of her most central themes, namely, that the spiritual life is a kind of pregnancy analogous to the mystery of the Incarnation in the life of Mary. In this example we find Hadewijch transforming a masculine tradition of using words in public debate into a feminine dynamic of giving birth to the Word.

It is worthwhile to pause for a moment to reflect on this use by Hadewijch of public debate. At exactly the time Hadewijch was writing, universities had been taken over by the practice of public debate.[52] The academic use of *quaestiones disputatae* formed the structure of higher education at the time of Hadewijch's life. Therefore, it is possible that there was an intersection of two different communities of discourse (women religious and academics) in the person of Hadewijch. Her adoption of an academic form of public debate for her poem, with a transformation of it by the use of a feminine metaphor of pregnancy and birth, is an excellent example of the addition of a woman's voice to an otherwise male-engendered academic community of discourse.

Hadewijch makes further use of similar feminine imagery in other work. In a poem called "Allegory of Love's Growth," Hadewijch describes the soul giving birth to Love during a nine-month rhythm of unfolding. Addressing her analogy to all persons who desire perfection, she challenges men as well as women to strive month by month to be pregnant with Love. She describes the first month as the month of fear; the second as the month of suffering and of "keen efforts by which one can learn perfection"; the third month as bringing an awareness of the child that one is carrying; the fourth, as increasing this awareness to include the care of the members; the fifth month as being marked by knowledge of pain; the sixth, by confidence; the seventh, by justice and the frustration of work; and the eighth, by wisdom and knowledge that "wholly engulfs from within."[53] Then, in the ninth month, the child, or "Perfect Love" is born:

> Now is born full-grown this Child,
> Who was chosen by humility,
> And is full-grown in sublime Love,
> And carried to term nine months.
> And each month has four weeks. . . .
> The first week is power; the second knowledge;
> The third will; and steadfast affection

---

50. Hadewijch, *The Complete Works,* Poem in Couplets 2, 319.
51. Hadewijch, *The Complete Works,* Poem in Couplets 2, 320-21.
52. Thomas Reed, *Middle English Debate Poetry,* p. 46.
53. Hadewijch, *The Complete Works,* Poem in Couplets 14, 347 and 349.

Perfects those four weeks
And fills up the month completely.[54]

Aside from the obvious rich application of a female-based metaphor to the general dynamics of the search for the perfection of spiritual life, Hadewijch's description, as Beatrice's before her, includes a dialogue between Reason and Divine Love. She also portrays a dynamic interaction of memory, intellect, and will within the human being. Her descriptions go beyond the simple description of her own experience to a general description of insights that have potential application to all persons.

The integration of body and soul, and the integration of contemplation and action, are central to Hadewijch's analysis. The physical aspect of her images is emphasized by Carolyn Bynum: "Hadewijch's language reflects . . . her conviction that the God we meet is humanity as well as divinity, and nowhere more human than when his flesh becomes food."[55] It follows from the fact that the God of the Incarnation is a spiritual Being as well as a material one through the Incarnation, that the bringing to birth of this God within the self must lead to acts of virtue in the material world.

In Vision 12, Hadewijch describes a perfect Bride as "clad in a robe made of her undivided and perfect will, always devoid of sorrow, and prepared with all virtue."[56] Twelve virtues are then enumerated: faith, hope, fidelity, charity, desire, humility, discernment, veracious mighty works, reason, wisdom, peacefulness, and patience. Hadewijch further describes the person who practiced the ninth virtue as "well ordered, and Reason was her rule, but [with it] she always performed works of justice."[57]

As we suggested with regard to Beatrice, Hadewijch is also aware that her female-based metaphor of spiritual life represents the generic human situation. Hadewijch, reflecting on women's experience, draws analogous meaning from the female capacity for conception, gestation, and giving birth biologically to the spiritual paradigm of giving birth to the Word or to Divine Love. In scholastic thought, Mary conceived the Eternal Word in her mind and heart, before she conceived in her flesh, when she freely accepted with her will the Divine invitation to conceive. Hadewijch develops this analogy through the exercise of her discursive reason, by reflecting on the data of her own spiritual experience, and by considering the complex dynamics of the operation of her own intellect.

Hadewijch's unique contribution to the philosophy of woman's identity consists in the attention she gives to the role of reason in spiritual life. She examines reason in relation to irrational desires and fears, and she examines reason in relation to the higher infusion of love in human consciousness. In her analysis, she articulates both the strengths and the limitations of reason, and she uses her own reason in precisely the ways she taught others to use theirs. In so doing, Hadewijch

54. Hadewijch, *The Complete Works,* Poem in Couplets 14, 350.
55. Bynum, *Holy Feast,* p. 159.
56. Hadewijch, *The Complete Works,* Vision 12, 294.
57. Hadewijch, *The Complete Works,* Vision 12, 295.

thinks of herself as a rational being, exercising reason and also submitting to its rule. At the same time, she also understands herself as an integral center of rationality, spirituality, and materiality.

MECHTILD OF MAGDEBURG (1210-1297)

Tension between the Church and loose associations of Beguines probably played a part in the decision of Mechtild, who had lived as a Beguine in Magdeburg for thirty years, to move in 1263 to a Cistercian monastery that followed a Dominican rule. By 1274 the Beguines were officially denied association within the Church, and by 1285 Mechtild had moved to the Abbey in Helfte where she lived until her death.[58] Most of Mechtild's writings were done before these moves, and so she is primarily remembered as a Beguine in spite of her later monastic affiliation.

Mechtild's short poems, monologues, dialogues, and exhortations, written in the vernacular, were brought together into a single text entitled *Flowing Light of the Divinity*.[59] The first six parts of *The Revelations* were composed before her entry at Helfte, and the last part was composed while she was nearly blind and living under the protection of Abbess Gertrude at Helfte. Throughout the text, which is also known simply as her *Revelations,* Mechtild considers the dialectical relation between reflection and the evidence of the senses.[60] While she primarily gives a description of her religious experience, neither appealing to reason nor elaborating discursive arguments, she offers nonetheless an extremely interesting reflection on the use of sense images. Mechtild wrote dialogues between the soul and the senses, between faith and the soul, and between discernment and the conscience.[61]

58. In 1274 Pope Gregory X at the General Council of Lyons "renewed against it the Sentence of the Lateran Council and declared the Beguines unrecognized by Rome." See Agnes Mary Francis Robinson, *The End of the Middle Ages* (London: T. Fisher Unwin, 1889), p. 26. See also Southern, *Western Society and the Church,* pp. 328-29.

59. This text, which is sometimes called *The Revelations,* was organized by her Dominican confessor Heinrich of Halle. The original version of 1265, written in Low German, was lost, but a Latin redaction of the text was made in 1290, presumably by Heinrich of Halle. A middle High German translation of the only surviving Latin text was made in 1344-1345 for Margaretha Ebner by her confessor Heinrich von Nördlingen. See John Hoaard, "The German Mystic: Mechtild of Magdeburg," in *Medieval Women Writers,* ed. Katherine M. Wilson (Atlanta: University of Georgia Press, 1984), p. 159.

60. See Elizabeth Petroff, *Medieval Women's Visionary Literature* (New York and Oxford: Oxford University Press, 1986), p. 159: "She was the first mystic to write in her native vernacular rather than in Latin, and she was the first in the history of Christian mysticism to record a personal vision of the Sacred Heart, a cult which was to come to full flower precisely at Helfte under Gertrude the Great and Mechthild of Hackeborn."

61. There are two English translations of Mechtild's works. See Mechthild von Magdeburg, *Flowing Light of the Divinity,* trans. Christiane Mesch Galvani (New York and London: Garland Publishing, Inc., 1991), (I, 44) 23-25, (II, 19) 41-44, and (VII, 12-17) 221-24; and *The Revelations of Mechtild of Magdeburg,* trans. Lucie Menzies (London, New York, Toronto: Longmans, Green, and Co., 1953). On the soul and senses, see pp. 22-24; on understanding and the soul, see pp. 41-44; on understanding and conscience, see pp. 219-21.

As mentioned previously, some scholars suggest that there were two main forms of poetic dialogue common during the time Mechtild was writing: the "vertical" form of dialogue takes place between "a naive persona and an authority with obvious claims to moral superiority (like Boethius's *Consolation of Philosophy*) with the naif's 'conversion.'"[62] The "horizontal" form of dialogue takes place between "two nominally equal parts of the soul, Reason against Passion."[63] In the latter case, although there appears to be a hierarchy of ordering, often the horizontal debates end with no resolution. These contribute to what is called an "aesthetics of irresolution."[64] Mechtild does not fit into either of these two categories very well, for her dialogues always aim for and achieve a resolution, and they occur between two different kinds of personae, which are neither skewed hierarchically nor caught in a polarized equality. Instead, each persona has a significant contribution to make, so the dialogue is presented as a genuine encounter in whose resolution each persona achieves a new, transformed orientation. Therefore, Mechtild's dialogues take the form not of vertical polarity, nor horizontal disunity, but vertical and horizontal complementarity.

The richness of Mechtild's interior life and her use of the dialogical form of text to externalize the content of this experience reveal her ability to subject her experience to intelligent questions that lead to personal insights. In the following passage, extracted from a longer dialogue, we see Mechtild portraying a conversation between the Soul and the Senses:

Senses: "You will find great security in the wisdom
          of the apostles."
Soul: "I have that wisdom with me,
          So that I might make the best decision."
Senses: "The angels possess clarity
          and the beautiful color of love.
          For refreshment, lift yourself up to them."
Soul: "The delight of the angels makes my love painful
          If I cannot see their Lord and my Bridegroom."
Senses: "Then refresh yourself in the holy, harsh life
          Which God gave to John the Baptist."
Soul: "I am prepared to accept that kind of life.
          Still, the power of love is greater than hardship."[65]

As this dialogue continues, Mechtild has the voice of the Soul ask: "God has given to all His creatures the gift of making use of their talents. How can I fight my nature?"[66]

62. Reed, *Middle English Debate Poetry*, p. 3.
63. Reed, *Middle English Debate Poetry*, p. 3.
64. This is the subtitle of Reed's text and the focus of his analysis of debate poetry.
65. Mechtild, *Flowing Light* (I, 44) 24. Francis Lee Utley points out that "[t]he debate between the body and the soul has had a remarkably wide and lengthy history. Stemming perhaps from formal elements as early as the second millennium in Egypt, it flourished in the Christian Middle Ages . . ." ("Dialogues" in *A Manual of the Writings in Middle English*, vol. 3, p. 691).
66. Mechtild, *Flowing Light* (I, 44) 25.

Mechtild is attentive to her experience, and subjects it to intelligent questions in the context of a dialogical discourse. Her use of the dialogue method was consistent. As Edith Scholl states, "Mechtild's characteristic literary genre is the dialogue. She was almost always in conversation with someone."[67]

One person with whom Mechtild was in constant dialogue was her confessor Heinrich. In a remarkable passage she reflects on a comment of his that she had a "masculine way of writing." Mechtild responded to his comment as follows:

> Master Heinrich! You are amazed at the masculine way in which this book is written? I wonder why that surprises you! . . . Yet I cannot otherwise describe to anyone the true knowledge and holy, glorious revelations save in these words alone.[68]

What Heinrich takes to be specifically masculine about Mechtild's way of writing was not stated. Was it her dialogue form, which was common to philosophical treatises? Or was it the content, which distinguished senses, soul, understanding, will, and so forth?

The dialogue about what the appellation of "masculine" means reveals that Heinrich and Mechtild were aware of a relation between gender and text through a distinction between what they considered to be a "masculine" and "feminine" way of writing even though what exactly these two authors understand by "masculine" is not clear. What is remarkable in this very brief quotation is the revelation that Mechtild and Heinrich discussed this question together. In this context, Mechtild moves beyond the subjective insight of Heinrich to enter into a discussion about the objective truth of his claim about her style of writing. Mechtild thinks her method came directly from her own experience, and she is concerned that she "cannot otherwise write." She also seems quite content as a woman to use what was considered by others to be a "masculine" style of writing.

In a dialogue with God, Mechtild compares herself with men who have received higher education. Recognizing that she does not have learning in the official sense, but that she has been given some wisdom, Mechtild prays for graces for her male scribe, Heinrich of Halle:

> "Alas, Lord, were I a learned man
> and You had worked this miracle in me
> It would forever bring You glory. . . ."

---

67. Edith Scholl, "To Be a Full-Grown Bride: Mechtild of Magdeburg," in *Medieval Religious Women: Peaceweavers,* ed. Lillian Thomas Shank and John A. Nichols (Kalamazoo, Mich.: Cistercian Publications, 1987), vol. 2, p. 224.

68. Mechtild, *Revelations* (V, 12) 135. A slightly different nuance is given in the translation of this passage in *Flowing Light:* "Master Heinrich, you are amazed at the masculine style of this book? That surprises me. I am far more concerned about the fact that I, a sinful woman, must write that I can describe the true knowledge and the holy wondrous revelations only in these words, which seem so insignificant compared to the eternal truth" (p. 140). For our purposes, the key concept is found in the phrase "the masculine style of this book."

"Daughter, many a wise man has lost his precious gold
Through carelessness on the big highway,
hoping to come to higher learning;
Someone else will find it. . . .

You find many a wise master, learned in the scripture
Who is a fool in My eyes. . . ."

"Alas, my Lord, I sigh, and I yearn
And I pray for Your scribe,
Who has written this book for me
That you may reward him, too, with the grace
Never granted to man."[69]

This dialogue about wisdom has included two other kinds of personages: learned men filled with higher learning and her male scribe and spiritual director. Mechtild mediates the dialogue with God through her self-consciousness as a woman unable to act as learned men.

There is considerable disagreement among scholars about how to evaluate Mechtild's reflections on wisdom. On the one hand, Edith Scholl suggests that "Her gifts were affective and imaginative rather than intellectual. She saw rather than reasoned."[70] On the other hand, Joan Gibson states that "Mechtild . . . unfolds a doctrine of radical interdependence of physical, intellectual and spiritual knowledge, refusing to divorce intellectual from experiential knowledge, the known from the knower. The senses are cognitive elements of great power, reaching even toward God"; and she also claims that "Mechtild presents above all metaphysics, an epistemology and an ethical psychology of love."[71] My own view rests in the middle of the controversy; Mechtild does not present a systematic metaphysics or epistemology in the traditional sense, but she does reason well.

When further content of Mechtild's writings is considered, unique powers of her intellect are revealed. Mechtild describes three kinds of wisdom: of Christian learning, of the natural senses, and of grace. In the following passage, Mechtild contrasts the wisdom of the senses with a kind of wisdom of grace:

The first place is in the human senses. This place is open to God, the devils and all creatures to enter and speak to the soul as they please. The second place in which God speaks to the soul is the soul itself. No one can enter here save God. But when God speaks with the soul, this takes place without the knowledge of the senses, with great, strong, and quick union of God with the soul.[72]

69. Mechtild, *Flowing Light* (II, 26) 56-57. See a slightly different translation in *Revelations,* 59-60.

70. Scholl, *Medieval Religious Women,* vol. 2, p. 224.
71. Gibson, *History of Women Philosophers,* vol. 2, pp. 130 and 132.
72. Mechtild, *Flowing Light* (VI, 23) 193. See also (IV, 3) 100.

Mechtild's distrust of the senses reveals, perhaps, the influence of Neoplatonism, a doctrine common to the Dominican spirituality of her age. The distrust could also have been influenced by her own poetic nature, whose strong attraction to sensible images, she feared, might mislead the mind in its search for truth. For Mechtild, the body and its senses posed a problem. In the following passage we see her viewing her body as an enemy that needs to be conquered:

> I do not speak with my senses;
> It is love which makes me speak.
> When I entered the spiritual life
> and took my leave from the world,
> I looked at my body
> And saw how heavily it was armed
> Against my poor soul
> With abundance of power
> And the complete force of nature.
> I saw clearly that it was my foe,
> I saw, too, that if I was to escape eternal death
> I would have to vanquish myself
> And that there would have to be a struggle.[73]

However, Mechtild does not rest within a Neoplatonic model of the rejection of the body or the senses in favor of an intellectual union with pure Form; instead, she develops a carefully structured process through which the materiality of her existence becomes integrated and transformed. In the following dialogue, she describes a reconciliation between the body and the soul:

> The Soul: "Alas, my beloved prison
>   In which I am confined!
>   I thank you for all the ways
>   In which you have followed me.
>   Though I am very disappointed in you,
>   You have so often come to my aid."[74]

The body is devalued at the beginning of the development of self-governance only because of its tendency to encourage disorder within the person by being vulnerable to both good and bad influences. This tendency can be purified with human effort. Mechtild states, ". . . discipline and good habits render one noble and well bred."[75]

Once the senses have been properly ordered with respect to other aspects of the soul, then they can be transformed and used to express higher truths. Mechtild frequently employs sensible imagery in turning to metaphors of wine, fire, water,

---

73. Mechtild, *Flowing Light* (IV, 2) 99. See also *Revelations,* 97.
74. Mechtild, *Flowing Light* (VII, 65) 270. See also (VI, 35) 201.
75. Mechtild, *Flowing Light* (III, 24) 93.

medicine, trees, flowers, animals, and so forth, to express transcendent spiritual truths. Once a truth has been discovered through an ascetical method, it can then be conveyed anew through the senses as in the following passage:

> O wondrous love of God!
> What holy and mighty powers you have!
> You illuminate the soul and instruct the senses,
> And give full power to all virtues. . . .

> Love wanders through the senses and storms up to the soul with all the virtues. While love grows within the soul, it climbs up eagerly toward God, flowing towards the wonder that comes to meet her. It melts through the soul into the senses so that the body must win its part too, as strongly as it is drawn to all.[76]

This "melting of love through the soul into the senses" leads to an outpouring of bridal metaphors describing spiritual intercourse between God and the soul. At one place, Mechtild describes this union using a metaphor of a cosmic dance:

> The Soul: "I cannot dance, O Lord, unless Thou lead me.
>   If thou wilt that I leap joyfully
>   Then must Thou Thyself first dance and sing!
>   Then will I leap for love
>   From love to knowledge,
>   From knowledge to fruition,
>   From fruition to beyond all human sense;
>   There will I remain
>   And circle evermore."[77]

The Neoplatonic image that describes the soul circling in a world "beyond all senses" is repeated in other passages that use sensual imagery to reach to the transcendent realm. In the following passage, God is represented as responding to the soul and using transformed sensual images as well:

> Behold, how she, who has wounded Me, ascends!
> She has thrown off the ape of the world.

---

76. Mechtild, *Flowing Light* (V, 4) 132. See also (II, 3) 31.

77. Mechtild, *Revelations* (I, 44) 21. This same passage is quoted in Mechtild, *Medieval Women's Visionary Literature,* ed. Elizabeth Alvida Petroff (New York and Oxford: Oxford University Press, 1986), p. 219. In her introduction to Mechtild, Petroff makes the following observations about this passage: "The mystical dance of the soul is an image which has origins in Neoplatonism, whence it was adopted by Dionysius the Areopagite and transplanted into Catholic mysticism. In this image, heavenly beings move in a circular motion about their midpoint and creator. Likewise, the soul moves in a circular motion while continually facing inward" (p. 158). In *The Flowing Light,* however, a rather different emphasis is given: "I cannot dance, Lord; You are distracting me. If You wish me to leap, Then You must lead me with Your singing. Then I will leap into recognition, From recognition into practice, From practice over all human senses. There will I stay and still crawl onward" (p. 23).

She has vanquished the bear of unchastity.
She has tread on the lion of pride.
She has torn the belly of the wolf of greed.
And she comes running like an exhausted stag
To the well which I am.
She soars like an eagle
Out of the depths to the heights.[78]

Mechtild does not imply that the unique individuality of the person disappears in this cosmic union with God; on the contrary, she constantly reaffirms the uniqueness of the person in the union with the Divine. Because she values the material realm, Mechtild stands out against tendencies towards the loss of individuality that will be seen in the work of Marguerite Porete considered in the next section of this chapter.[79] It may be that the Neoplatonism in Mechtild's thought was balanced by a belief in the unity of form and matter, soul and body, as transmitted through the Dominican authors St. Albert the Great and St. Thomas Aquinas.[80] In any event, she assumed an integration of the person throughout the stages of spiritual development.

A further indication of Mechtild's affirmation of the materiality of the human condition is seen in her claim that the individual ought not to rest simply in contemplation, but he or she must practice a life of virtue. In fact, she argues that virtuous acts are the highest form of contemplation:

> The fourth [effect of Pure Love is], that we possess all virtues. Alas, if only I had them and truly employed them in all things! I would take that for all the contemplation of what I have ever heard tell. Of what use are elevated words without deeds done out of compassion? . . . Now listen: Virtues are half a gift from God and half from us. When God gives us understanding, we must make use of the virtues.[81]

Mechtild lists seven virtues that an individual ought to develop, and among them is the virtue "to be filled with truth."[82]

78. Mechtild, *Flowing Light* (I, 38), 20-21. See also (II, 24) 50 and (IV, 18) 114-15.

79. Matthew Fox claims that Eckhart was particularly influenced by Mechtild's work. See *Breakthrough: Meister Eckhart's Creation Spirituality in New Translation* (New York: Doubleday, 1980), p. 36.

80. Joan Gibson states that "[s]he probably knew of contemporary writings by Aquinas . . . but by far the single most profound influence on her work is her German Dominican contemporary, Albert the Great." See *History of Women Philosophers*, vol. 2, p. 120. Gibson also affirms Mechtild's support for individuality within her mystical vision: "Mechtild sees the soul becoming 'god with God,' but in this divinization, individuality remains and human nature, though transformed, is not lost. Divine union is the mutual penetration of two separate persons, not annihilation or absorption in the divine. For Mechtild, union is intensely personal" (p. 126).

81. Mechtild, *Flowing Light* (VI, 30) 197.

82. Mechtild, *Flowing Light* (V, 22) 145. The others are righteousness, mercy, loyalty, giving assistance in secret, to be silent, and to be the enemy of mendacity. Vices to avoid include vanity, impurity, covetousness, indolence, lying, perjury, anger, slander, pride, hatred, revenge, despondency, shamelessness, and mistaken wisdom (V, 19) 142-43. See also *Revelations*, 138-41.

In her own life, Mechtild was famous, and even infamous, for chastising public figures whom she thought were leading unvirtuous lives. In the following passage Mechtild describes the ultimate state of those academics who are corrupt: "The unbelieving masters sit at Lucifer's feet so that they might get a good look at their unclean God. And he argues with them in order to make them even more ashamed."[83]

Mechtild, active during her many years as a Beguine, ventured into the public realm to speak of her practice of the virtue of "truthfulness and opposition to lying." Carolyn Bynum describes her as follows: "Mechtild sees herself as a teacher, counsellor, and mediator. . . . And her writing expresses a much greater sense of responsibility for the whole church, down to the lowliest peasant."[84] Mechtild understands this commitment to public speech to be her apostolic duty: "Inasmuch as we learn wisdom, convert others with it, and stand fast with God in all need, we resemble the holy Apostles, who forsook themselves until death."[85] Mechtild therefore stands as a living example of a woman who proclaimed aloud her own views, and thus, she serves as a counterexample to the Aristotelian dictum that silence is a woman's proper virtue, and that her proper sphere of action is the private sphere.

In conclusion, Mechtild of Magdeburg's particular contribution to philosophy lies in her reflections upon the role of the senses in spiritual life, in her frequent use of dialogue, in her ability to maintain an integrated view of the person within its intense union with the Divine Being, and in her practice of public speech as a virtue.

Mechtild contributes directly to the philosophy of gender by the brief passage in which she refers to what Heinrich calls a "masculine" way of writing. In a way she affirms this masculine style as suitable for her, even though she is a female author. This distinction between masculine and feminine implies a recognition that masculine and feminine characteristics are not identical with male and female identity. It also reveals that her writing took place in a dialogical context with her spiritual director Heinrich, and that it moved beyond subjective insight by beginning to establish common ground for determining objective truth.

Finally, in her poetic description of the traditionally feminine concept of soul, Mechtild develops the feminine concept of bride as representing the generic human being. In this way, Mechtild provides another example of a woman writer using feminine metaphors. Thus, she contributes to the developing history of women's culture whose foundations were previously laid by Hildegard, Beatrice, and Hadewijch.

83. Mechtild, *Flowing Light* (III, 21), 88. Another translation that associates this passage more directly with academic terminology is the following: ". . . He holds disputations with them and they are confounded" (*Medieval Women Writers*, p. 175).

84. Bynum, *Jesus as Mother*, pp. 235-36.

85. Mechtild, *Flowing Light*, 199.

MARGUERITE PORETE (DIED 1310)

The third phase of the development of Beguine communities ended with their violent suppression. At the end of the thirteenth century some action had been taken against what was considered to be misleading theology contained in a text authored by Marguerite Porete around 1290. It was entitled *The Mirror of Simple Souls*. Between 1296 and 1306, the Bishop of Valenciennes condemned and burned the book in the presence of its author, the Beguine Marguerite Porete. By 1310, because Marguerite insisted on redistributing the text, she was tried for a second time by theologians from the University of Paris, and she was burned to death as a heretic along with existing copies of her text.[86] During the next twenty-five years, other Beguines were tried and condemned, and the movement was dispersed.[87] While many contemporary critiques have focused on the political aspects of Marguerite's writings and life, in this chapter we will consider the philosophical aspects of her thought with specific reference to the question of gender identity.

The Mirror of Simple Souls is a lengthy text of 60,000 words, originally written in Old French, but translated into Latin, Italian, and Middle English by the fourteenth century.[88] Because of its length, it is possible to identify those particular views of Marguerite Porete that ran counter to the developing concept of woman articulated by the women religious writers described above. As we will see, Marguerite devalues reason, the will, and the practice of virtue; and she describes the loss of individual identity as the highest development of the soul. In elaborating Porete's theory, however, it is important to note that she is attentive to her own experience, and that she subjects this experience to questioning — two actual characteristics of a philosophical attitude.

Marguerite Porete claims that initially an individual "labors busily day and night to get virtues, by counsel of reason."[89] *The Mirror* is written as a dialogue between Reason and Love, and in the development of the argument, Reason is soon overcome. Porete's dialogue more closely approximates the traditional 'vertical' form described above in our discussion of Mechtild, because her conversation ends with the capitulation of one of the personae. While Reason argues that "none may come to [a] deep foundation, nor to high edification, unless they reach it by the dis-

---

86. For further information about these events see Wilson, ed., *Medieval Women Writers,* pp. 204-9; Henry Lea, *A History of the Inquisition in the Middle Ages,* 3 vols. (New York: Russell and Russell, 1958), pp. 123, 574-77; Petroff, ed., *Medieval Women's Visionary Literature,* p. 281; and Peter Dronke, *Women Writers of the Middle Ages* (Cambridge: Cambridge University Press, 1984), pp. 217-28.

87. Southern, *Western Society and the Church,* pp. 320-30. The Beguines were associated with the Brethren of the Free Spirit who were also put to death by fire in Cologne in 1328.

88. The original French text has been lost. The English translation used in this chapter is taken from [Marguerite Porete], *The Mirror of Simple Souls,* trans. M.N. and ed. Claire Kirchberger (London: Burns, Oates and Washbourne, Ltd., 1927). All translations from this text are rendered into modern English by the author. There is also a Latin text at the Bodley Library in Oxford which was consulted. The original of this version was attributed to an unknown French author who is now taken to be Marguerite Porete. When it is used, Porete's name will be placed in [ ]. Where relevant, passages from a recent English translation, Marguerite Porete, *The Mirror of Simple Souls,* trans. Ellen L. Babinsky (New York: Paulist Press, 1993), will also be used or referred to in footnotes.

89. [Porete], 3.3, 12-13.

crimination of great natural intelligence," Love answers that "a soul that is made free knows all; and she knows nothing."[90]

Porete develops an argument in favor of what she calls a "free spirit" who is no longer limited by human reason; in fact, the dialogue leads to the "death of Reason." In the following passage from the dialogue, these dynamics are made clear:

> This soul, says Love, is lady of virtues, daughter of deity, sister of wisdom, and the spouse of love.
>
> For sure, says this soul, but this seems to Reason a marvellous language, and that is no wonder, for it shall not be long until he shall not be; but I was, says this soul, and am, and shall be without failing; for love has neither beginning, nor comprehending, nor end; and I am [nothing] but love, how might I then have end? It may not be.
>
> Ah, God, says Reason, how dare any say this! I dare not hear it. I fall, Lady Soul; for sure my heart fails me to hear you. I have no life.
>
> Alas, alas! why had this death not been long before this time, says this soul, for until this [death had been] I might not freely hold my heritage. And this that is mine is that [whereby] I kill you with love and wound you to death. Now is Reason dead, says this soul.[91]

The death of reason could be understood simply as the appeal to faith in certain areas of religious experience. However, this more conservative interpretation of Marguerite's description minimizes the difficulty posed by her views on the limitations of human reason. Marguerite argues that she cannot be taught anything by anyone. She claims: "None may her teach"; and "men can tell me naught!"[92]

Next, Marguerite directly attacks scholars:

> Surely, says she, they that be governed by reason, the rudeness nor the cumberings of them no man may say. By their teachings it appears; it is the work of an ass and not of a man, if any man would hear them. But God has kept me well, says this soul, from such lore of Reason's disciples; they shall not hold me in their counsel, nor their doctrine will I more hear.[93]

The author then presents an image of a free soul who is no longer encumbered by reason, but who is a "free spirit."[94] This free spirit represents the potential for all human beings, so again, the individual woman's experience stands for the universal or generic human being.

A second characteristic of the free spirit is that it no longer needs to exercise

---

90. [Porete], 3.17, 50.

91. [Porete], 9.11, 193-94.

92. [Porete], 3.12, 33; and 4.8, 84-85.

93. [Porete], 9.9, 187-88. In Porete, *The Mirror*, ch. 84, 159. See also 5.2, 95.

94. This freedom extends beyond the rejection of reason. It also includes the rejection of the sacraments of the church, and the teaching authority of the church. [Porete], 9.10, 190. This new theory of the 'free spirit' is based in a theology of following the inspirations of the Holy Spirit without reference to the teachings of the Father or of the Son. 17.2, 269-70, and 8.2, 147.

the will in making decisions. In the following passage, Love and Reason consider this issue:

> These souls, says Love, such as they are, have so long led in love and obedience of virtues, that they become free.
> And when do these souls become free? says Reason.
> When love dwells and leads within them, and virtues serve them without any understanding or pain in these souls.[95]

While this text may imply that the individual has just reached such a high degree of integration that there is no interior struggle to remain virtuous, Marguerite Porete makes it clear that she is presenting an even more radical view of the human being: "The ninth point, says Love, is this, that this soul has no will."[96] In another passage Marguerite describes the Holy Spirit claiming that the free soul "wills but one thing, that is, that she wills nothing."[97] This passivity of the soul has the further consequence that the individual no longer needs to practice virtue: "The second point is that this soul saves herself by faith without works."[98] Marguerite concludes that the free soul is "above the law."[99]

The final aspect of Marguerite Porete's theory that is significant for this philosophical examination is her description of the soul as losing its identity in a union with God. Love claims ". . . this soul is God by condition of love; and I am God by nature divine."[100] The subject no longer retains its separateness as subject: "She feels no joy, for she herself is joy. . . . So is joy in her that she herself is joy."[101] Marguerite begins to call the soul "not with-her-self," and in another passage she develops this theme further:

> Now has this soul, says Love, her right name of Nothing (Naught), in which she moves, for she sees that she is nothing, and that she has nothing of anything, either of herself nor of her Christianity, nor of God himself. For she is so little, that she may not herself find. . . . And because of this nothing, she has fallen into cer-

---

95. [Porete], 3.5, 18. In Porete, *The Mirror,* ch. 8, 86. The final line is translated as: "When Love dwells in them, and the Virtues serve them without any contradiction and without labor by such Souls."

96. [Porete], 3.14, 38. In Porete, *The Mirror,* ch. 11, 92.

97. [Porete], 5.6, 104. In Porete, *The Mirror,* ch. 42, 121. In other passages Marguerite describes the soul trying to will against its own will. This would seem to imply that at times the soul is engaged in an active operation of the will. See 9.14, 200-201. In chapter 90, 166. However, for the most part Marguerite emphasizes the passivity of the soul.

98. [Porete], 3.10, 29. In Porete, *The Mirror,* ch. 11, 89. See also "The fourth point is this, that this soul does nothing for God." 3.12, 32.

99. [Porete], 16.1, 266. In Porete, *The Mirror,* ch. 121, 196.

100. [Porete], 4.1, 65. In Porete, *The Mirror,* ch. 21, 104 this passage is translated as: "I am God by divine nature and this Soul is God by righteousness of Love."

101. [Porete], 4.5, 76. In Porete, *The Mirror,* ch. 28, 109 this passage is translated as: "And so she feels no joy, for she is joy itself. She swims and flows in joy, without feeling any joy. . . . She is Joy itself by the virtue of Joy which transforms her into Joy itself."

tainty of knowing nothing, and into certainty of having nothing, and into certainty of willing nothing.[102]

Marguerite Porete concludes that the individual disappears in the union with God: ". . . for he is and she is not. She has withheld nothing in negating herself; it is enough that he is. And she is not; for she is without being; there where she was, now she is not."[103]

This view, with its Neoplatonic roots, is very different from the theory of the self proposed by the previous writers we have studied in this section. In all of the other descriptions an emphasis was placed on the interactive dialogue of the self and the Divine Being, rather than on the annihilation of the self. Embedded within the theological analysis of experience was a recognition that the human person has a distinct identity; this understanding of the soul's relation to God led the woman author to a clarity about who she is in relation to God and to other people. By maintaining the integrity of the individual person, these authors adopted an approach to the human being that confirmed the interactive dynamics of materiality, rationality, spirituality, and individuality. This approach was common both to the tradition of complementarity as developed in monastic Benedictine spirituality and in the tradition of Aristotelian polarity, but it was absent from the Platonic tradition of gender unity. Marguerite Porete, and Neoplatonism, led to a devaluation of the gender and the individual identity of the person by their underlying devaluation of the body and fragmentation of the person.

DISCOVERING WOMEN'S PHILOSOPHICAL VOICES

This introduction to the works of four thirteenth-century women religious writers has demonstrated that each one was attentive to her own unique experience. This attention led to the formulation of different kinds of questions. Beatrice asked: What ought I to value? and she settled on perfection and justice. She also asked: How ought I to achieve these values? and she elaborated certain sequential steps. Then Hadewijch asked: What is reason? and What is the relation of reason to love? Her response was to work out a dialectical description as an answer to her questions. The function of reason was further explored by Mechtild of Magdeburg who asked: What is the relation of reason (i.e., understanding) to the senses and to truth? By way of response, Mechtild developed a two-tiered theory describing a struggle between senses and reason on a lower level that was characterized by a

102. [Porete], 9.6, 180-81. In Porete, *The Mirror,* ch. 81, 156 this passage is translated as: "Now this Soul, says Love, has her right name from the nothingness in which she rests. And since she is nothing, she is concerned about nothing, neither about herself, nor about her neighbors, nor even about God Himself. For she is so small that she cannot be found. . . . On account of such nothingness she has fallen into certainty of knowing nothing and into certainty of willing nothing."

103. [Porete], 20.2, 292. See also Emilie Zun Brunn, "Self, Not-Self, and the Ultimate in Marguerite Porete's 'Mirror of Annihilated Souls,'" in Robert Carter, ed., *God, the Self and Nothingness: Reflections Eastern and Western* (New York: Paragon House, 1990), pp. 81-87.

lack of integration, and a dynamic analogical exploration of the senses and reason on a higher, religious level, where integration was achieved.

Next, Marguerite Porete asked: What ought to be the limit of reason and the will? and How does the soul become nothing and how does the individual lose her identity? We could say that in responding to these questions Marguerite was very attentive to her own experience, and that she formulated important philosophical questions about her experience, but that her judgments led to the loss of individuality and of the balance of materiality, rationality, and spirituality in the individual human being. In her conclusion stating that the individual was passive, free, above the law, and unable to learn from others, Marguerite left the sphere of dialogue and shifted into the range of monologue.

With respect to the philosophy of gender, we could say that all four religious women writers presented their own perspective as generic for all women and men. Beatrice, referring to herself as "the holy woman," speaks in the third person about "she" and "her" throughout the description of the seven stages of love, and characterizes love at the sixth stage as like a mother governing her household; Hadewijch introduces metaphors of pregnancy and birth to describe the growth of love in women and in men, and she portrays wisdom metaphorically as a female surgeon; and Mechtild develops the familiar bridal metaphors for the relation between the soul and divine love for men and women. Mechtild also leaves us a record of a conversation she had about the "masculinity" of her writing with Heinrich of Halle in which the question of gender identity itself was raised and considered. In Marguerite Porete, the engenderment of the woman or man is transcended with a move towards an undifferentiated identity lost of its gender and individuality.

Trying to maintain an authentic foundation for differentiation in relation is a central task of the philosophy of gender. There is always a danger of shifting from the interaction of two different persons in a dialogue to a simple passivity on the part of one of those in conversation. Marguerite describes this occurrence in the context of a dialogue between a Divine Person and a woman. Hadewijch struggles with this tension in her relation with Saint Augustine. As we will discover in subsequent texts written by humanists, this tension of maintaining the proper identity and balance will always be present in discourse. It is the fundamental problem of the resolution of tension by losing differentiation. In the theory of integral gender complementarity, individuality is always respected in the interaction, while in Platonic kinds of gender unity, individuality usually disappears along with gender differentiation.

In three of the writers considered above, we find a frequent use of dialogue to express the development of thought as occurring in the context of a conversation. Even though various forms of dialogue were common in the thirteenth century, Hadewijch and Mechtild both provide interesting examples of interior dialogue within the self and dialogues between human beings. While their dialogical texts are not long or extensively developed, they nonetheless reveal a way of thinking, open to complementarity and receptive to the viewpoint of another. Without this openness, a person is condemned to a monologue of hearing only one's own voice. We saw some of the ways Neoplatonism tended towards the devaluation of the body and in Marguerite Porete's works to the loss of identity.

As the experience of dialogue continues to unfold between 1250 and 1500 we will discover that this genre generates tension: if both participants adopt an antagonistic attitude then the dialogue will not achieve a resolution within which the two persons work together synergetically to generate something more than either of them contributed at the beginning of the conversation. Often in the case of polarization, one or the other persona will be devalued through some form of bias. At other times, no genuine dialogue will take place, and a particular point of view will remain in isolation. This will occur among the interactions of the two different forms of discourse: women religious writers and academic writers.

As a way of setting up a contrast between the concept of woman as actually articulated by the women authors studied in this chapter and the concept of woman as articulated within the academic model of Aristotelian-based gender polarity, a summary table is given below. It highlights the particular claims of the authors studied in the categories of wisdom and virtue.

Philosophical Aspects of Women Religious Writers (1200-1300)				
Author	Kinds of Dialogue	Wisdom	Virtue	Female Analogies
Beatrice	Within the self Between self and God	Analysis of seven levels of consciousness Exercise of discursive reasoning Exercise of will To gain self-discipline and self-knowledge	Free choice of obedience as means for self-governance Justice as an exchange of love	Love like a mother wisely governing the mind "Woman" as generic model for all human beings
Hadewijch	Within the self among memory, will, and intellect Intergender between self and St. Augustine Among imaginary aca-	Exercise human reason Examine error in reason Examine thoughts to gain self-knowledge	Dialectic of Reason and Divine Love leads to self-governance and virtuous actions including mighty works, wisdom, and justice	Reason is a female surgeon Pregnancy with God, the Word, in debate Pregnancy with wisdom,

Hadewijch (cont.)	demic professors Between self and God			knowledge, and Love
Mechtild of Magdeburg	Within the self between: (1) soul and senses, (2) soul and faith, and (3) discernment and conscience Intergender between self and Heinrich Between self and God	The dialectical relation between reflection and the evidence of the senses Subject experience to intelligent questions Leads to three kinds of wisdom	Discipline and good habits lead to the nobility of a virtuous life The dance of love as the fruition of knowledge Public speech about truth and opposition to lying	Questions whether her dialogue is masculine or not The soul as bride represents the generic human being
Marguerite Porete	Within the self Refusal of dialogue with others as a free spirit Between self and God	Attentive to her experience Questions her experience by reason Dialogue of Reason and Love leads to death of Reason	Free spirit no longer needs to exercise the will The free soul is above the law The individual disappears in union with God Public distribution of text	Woman's experience is generic for human being The female self is annihilated

An interesting development may be noted among the four authors considered above with respect to intergender dialogue. With Beatrice we have no written record of a dialogue with a man. With Hadewijch we have a written record of an imaginary dialogue with St. Augustine, who died many centuries previous. In addition, Hadewijch wrote an imaginary dialogue among academic professors, who presumably are engendered as male. With Mechtild, however, we begin to discover a record of her interaction with a living male interlocutor, her confessor and scribe Heinrich. It is most interesting as well that the topic of their interaction was a question about gender identity. He asked the question of whether or not her writing style was masculine, and she answered that it was simply the way she wrote. Finally, Marguerite Porete rejected some forms of intergender dialogue by saying that she could not learn from any man, while at the same time she publicly distributed her own writings so that others might learn from her.

This development in a way foreshadows a similar pattern in later chapters in the book, but with respect to male authors. In some, women are simply not mentioned as partners in dialogue, while in others women begin to play a significant role in imaginary dialogue. Next, women and men begin to engage in actual dialogue with one another about gender, while at times men completely reject the contribution of women as relevant to their thought and action. These examples provide then a pattern and range of possible choices that men and women may make with respect to the value of intergender dialogue for their thought and action. The deeper consequences of these choices, which unfold in Section II of this book, may provide significant material for contemporary reflection through their positioning in the distant mirror of this historical period in western thought.

We will now turn to a consideration of the concept of woman as it began to unfold in the academic setting of western universities. In this context we will discover that the women religious writers studied above, and those to be considered later in this text, had little or no influence on the development of theories of gender in academia. However, they do provide, by their writings, both women's voices and living counterexamples to the Aristotelian theory of gender polarity, and in this way they provide a counterpoint for reflection on the development of the concept of woman from 1250 to 1500. Being permanently recorded through the written word, these women's voices echo down the centuries and invite a complementary dialogue with the contemporary reader.

CHAPTER 2

ARISTOTELIAN ROOTS OF
GENDER IDENTITY IN ACADEMIA

Tracing the academic development of the concept of woman brings us face to face with the complex contribution of Aristotle to the history of western thought. On the one hand, Aristotle almost single-handedly provided the foundations for the systematic advancement of knowledge within western universities; and on the other hand, he also provided the foundations for the intellectual roots of theories that distorted woman's identity. Therefore, we find a delicate situation in which Aristotle's genius laid the foundations for the advancement of knowledge in nearly all academic disciplines at the same time it contained errors in fact and interpretation that framed much of subsequent discourse about women's identity.

We could metaphorically describe the Aristotelian roots of the concept of woman as a wound in the academic body. In opening, laying out, and cleaning this wound I do not intend to harm the body or to cause the death of an Aristotelian approach to philosophy. Appreciatively, there is much that is valuable in the Greek philosopher's empirical approach to knowledge, in his metaphysics, and in his virtue-based ethics. My intent is simply to identify specific ways in which the structure and content of Aristotle's philosophy have persistently influenced theories about the concept of woman throughout the centuries. My goal here is to contribute to the collaborative work of going beyond Aristotle's concept of woman, much as contemporary scientists have gone beyond Aristotelian science and contemporary logicians have gone beyond Aristotelian logic. My hope is for historical advancement as we come to know better who we are as women and as men.

The historical event in 1255, when the works of Aristotle became required reading at the University of Paris, needs to be emphasized again. At its inception, the University of Paris was organized into four Faculties: an undergraduate Faculty of Arts (which taught primarily philosophy and natural science), and three graduate Faculties of Theology, Medicine, and Law. Aristotle's works were required of students in the undergraduate Faculty of Arts. His influence on the formation of students' thought was carried forward especially in the Faculties of Theology and Medicine. Then, because the curriculum at Paris became the model for the curriculum at a great many other universities, Aristotle's philosophy provided the structure and content of thought in most of western academia from the thirteenth to fifteenth centuries. With this institutionalization of Aristotle, the minds of students and faculty were formed in a particular manner that had serious consequences for the history of the concept of woman.

In this second chapter of *The Concept of Woman: The Early Humanist Reformation (1250-1500)* we will examine three specific ways in which Aristotle's philosophy entered into academic thought about the concept of woman: first, in the dynamic structure of academic discourse which took the form of debate; second, in the laws of discursive reasoning which governed the formal structure of the debate; and third, in the content or subject of the debates themselves. These three points of entry of Aristotle will provide the chronological and systematic order of our study.

Chronologically, the academic study of philosophy at Paris in the thirteenth century usually began with an introduction to the rules of rhetoric and a concentration on logic; it then moved towards the end of the undergraduate years to a consideration of metaphysics, natural philosophy, ethics, and politics. The student began his studies by observing others debate various questions, by learning the laws of reasoning, and later by learning the content of various fields of study.

Systematically, we can see here an intellectual movement from the dynamic of academic discourse as a kind of debate and disputation into the form of the discourse that was governed by the rules of logic. Then, as the faculty and students focused on the actual content of the valid syllogisms generated, they thought about the internal depths of science and knowledge of the world. Returning to the metaphor of the concept of woman as a wound in the body of Aristotelian thought, we could say that the methodology in this book attempts to expose the layers of the wound in the institutionalized Aristotelian character of academia itself by moving from the dynamic of discourse towards the structure and content of knowledge about women's identity. The goal here is the same as before, to help to heal rather than destroy the body of academic mode of discourse.

Before turning to a more direct analysis of Aristotle's theory of sex and gender identity as it emerged in the university, we need to compare the particular nature of the academic community of discourse with that of the religious community of discourse just studied in the previous chapter. From its beginnings in the mid-thirteenth, and up to the twentieth century, the academic world of universities was almost completely constituted by male communities of discourse. As a consequence, academic philosophy emerged historically as a male form of discourse. However, this fact does not imply a necessary or essential connection between the development of various kinds of thinking and male identity.

Women and men religious writers were not under the same constraints as academic writers whose professional obligations would encourage a different way of thinking. While the writers considered in the previous chapter probed the meaning of their personal experiences, those in the present chapter detached their reason from personal experience. This detachment took several different forms: the search for universal definitions, the pronouncement of universal judgments, the development of demonstrative syllogisms, the study of the form of logical reasoning itself, and the use of logic in rhetoric and public debate.

If we juxtapose the description of religious experience with the use of reason in developing academic science and logic, we can see two forms of discourse with radically different ways of thinking: one that tries to communicate informal personal insights aimed at guiding actions, and the other that seeks rigorous systematic deductive foundations for universal claims.[1] Both uses of intelligence have their proper place and value. Neither is problematic in itself. However, when we consider that women in religious communities used their intelligence primarily to discover meaning in religious experience, while men in universities primarily used their intelligence in logic, debate, and scientific investigation, we begin to discover a historical gender-related differentiation between two different communities of discourse. It is to the relation between the concept of woman and the male academic community of discourse that we will now turn.

This chapter is divided into three sections that correspond to three different gender-related aspects of the use of Aristotelian philosophy in universities: (1) its practical application in academic examination and debate, (2) its effect in promoting gender neutrality in the developing fields of logic and universal science, and (3) its effect in promoting gender polarity in natural science and ethics. The analysis begins with the use of Aristotelian texts to structure academic dialogue, continues with the use of Aristotelian logic which *de facto* transmitted gender neutrality, and ends with the use of Aristotelian philosophy to transmit gender polarity. I will attempt to identify the extremely complex and often ambiguous relations between the Aristotelian theory and the concept of woman in the early years of academia by way of answering the question: What were the form and content of male academic discourse about the concept of woman as it historically evolved? I hope that the reader will see contemporary traces of these complex and paradoxical relations which persist up to the present day.

Several of the philosophers considered in the first volume of *The Concept of Woman* will be reconsidered here, but in a different dynamic. Because these thinkers are transitional, that is, they cross over the dividing line of 1250, their work serves both to close off the first study of Ancient and Medieval philosophy and to open up the second study of Medieval and early Renaissance philosophy. By revisiting their work in a new light I hope to capture some of the rich momentum they contributed to in the early foundation of academic life. Therefore, this lengthy chapter invites the reader to enter into the excitement, the tension, and the pathos of the insertion of the concept of woman right at the initial moments of the birth of academia.

Since much of the work of these authors still has not been translated from the original Latin, it seems important also to include some extensive passages so that the reader might meet the authors face to face. At the same time, many untranslated works of these authors remain to be analyzed. The conclusions reached in this chapter are thus provisional, and they are open to further revision as scholars continue to penetrate this extremely rich period in our history. With these preliminaries out of the way, let us begin our pilgrimage into gender theory in the heart of the origins of the academic body.

---

1. Bernard Lonergan, *Understanding and Being* (Toronto: University of Toronto Press, 1990), pp. 88-89.

GENDER IN ACADEMIC EXAMINATION AND DEBATE

Aristotle's *Topics, Sophistical Refutations,* and *Rhetoric* formed the structural basis for the framework of public debate.[2] Peter Abelard (1097-1142) is credited with being the first person to develop the scholastic method of argumentation by elaborating a practical application of Aristotelian philosophy of dialectic and rhetoric in response to specific questions posed for debate.[3] Dialectic and the form of debate differed from demonstration and judgment, in that its premises were not usually proven certainties but rather propositions expressing common opinion or probabilities.[4] The structure of this scholastic method of debate was open, and so it could be used to discuss any topic.

In the thirteenth and fourteenth centuries, this form of disputation was used in both Paris and Oxford as the basic form of examination of students. It consisted of a question posed by the master, a reply offered by the student, objections to the answer posed by other masters, with a final reply to the objection by the student.[5] The important factor here is that at this stage in the historical development of the use of the scholastic method, the student had to provide what was believed to be the correct series of arguments to the question posed by the master: therefore, even though contrary points of view were welcomed, they entered into the debate only to be defeated by the view deemed theoretically correct.

We can see how the dialogue within academia began to take on a formal shape with highly defined structures of debate and argument. The more cooperative model of higher learning among men, and even among men and women, within the Benedictine monastic tradition of education was thus supplanted by a highly competitive model of discourse. The fact that academia was a singularly male community of discourse meant that it would be several centuries before women were able to learn how to think and engage in debates of this kind. A further effect may well have been that the actual practice of a complementarity inherent in the Benedictine context of cooperative discourse became supplanted by the practice of a polarity in which the stronger (master) defeats the weaker (student) in an argument. In this way, the predominance of the scholastic method of debate and

---

2. James L. Murphey, *Rhetoric in the Middle Ages: A History of Rhetorical Theory from Saint Augustine to the Renaissance* (Berkeley: University of California Press, 1974), pp. 101-6. See also Thomas L. Reed, Jr., *Middle English Debate Poetry and the Aesthetics of Irresolution* (Columbia and London: University of Missouri Press, 1990), p. 45.

3. For further consideration of Abelard see Allen, *The Concept of Woman: The Aristotelian Revolution,* pp. 272-92; and Andrea Nye, "An Arsenal of Reasons: Abelard's Dialectic," *Words of Power: A Feminist Reading of the History of Logic* (New York and London: Routledge, 1990), ch. 5, pp. 85-102. Nye considers Abelard's motivations in developing a particular kind of logic, while I consider the impact of his use of logic for the concept of woman.

4. Samuel Howell, *Logic and Rhetoric in England, 1500-1700* (Princeton: Princeton University Press, 1956), p. 16.

5. Gordon Leff, *Paris and Oxford Universities in the Thirteenth and Fourteenth Centuries: An Institutional and Intellectual History* (New York: John Wiley and Sons Inc., 1968), pp. 167-84. See also Etienne Gilson, "Universities and Scholasticism," in *History of Christian Philosophy in the Middle Ages* (New York: Random House, 1955), pp. 246-50.

disputation may have contributed to a predisposition in students and faculty towards polarity models in the actual content of the discourse itself.

One of the earliest recorded examples of questions posed in an educational setting about issues of sex and gender identity can be seen in Albert the Great's *Quaestiones super de animalibus*.[6] Albert's method included posing a question, citing two or three opinions about the question, citing an opposing view, offering his own thought (usually drawing upon the writing of past authority), and then responding more directly point by point to the original opinions. The questions and answers posed by Albert in a disputation in the Dominican *studium generale* in Cologne, Germany in 1258 were recorded by one of his students.[7] Albert was a natural scientist whose goal was to introduce young Dominican brothers to the philosophy of Aristotle (Avicenna and Galen) and to provide further empirical evidence to support or refute hypotheses as a method of formation for the more advanced study of Theology. In other words, he used the public form of the *disputatio* in a genuine search for truth. While we will consider in some detail the content of these answers later in this chapter, it is worth recording some of the *Quaestiones* to indicate that at this early period in the academic use of the scholastic method of debate philosophers were interested in determining the truth about woman's identity.

Although most of Albert's questions focused on the details of generation, their answers often reached into other areas of gender differentiation as well. They drew upon metaphysical principles, and extended evidence and conclusions to include epistemological and ethical observations about men and women. A selected list from Books I-X of the *Quaestiones super de animalibus* includes the following: Book III, Q 22: Whether blood is more abundant in males than in females? Book V, Q 4: Whether there is more pleasure in intercourse in men than in women? Book V, Q 5: Whether passion in the act of coitus is greater in men or in women? Book V, Q 10: Whether male and female are especially stimulated at the same time for procreation? Book VI, Q 19-22: About generation of animals by comparison to the wind. Book IX, Q 16-17: Whether the male is formed more quickly than the female? Book IX, Q 18: Whether the male or female can be generated through skill? Book IX, Q 19-23: About giving birth to females and its circumstances. Book IX, Q 24-28: Concerning the fetus before and after birth. Book X, Q 1: Whether impediment to procreating is owed more to the father than to the mother? Book X, Q 3: Whether the emission of seed weakens the male more than the female?

Further questions from Books XV-XVIII include: Book XV, Q 1: Whether sex [differentiation] is necessary for the generation of animals? Book XV, Q 2: Whether generation of a female is intended by nature? Book XV, Q 3: Whether male and female form different species? Book XV, Q 7: Whether a male ought to exceed a female in size? Book XV, Q 11: Whether the male is more fit for learning moral behavior than the female? Book XV, Q 16: Whether seed is immediately pro-

6. Albertus Magnus, *Quaestiones super de animalibus* (Aschendorff: Westfalorum Monastery, 1955) All passages from this text are translated by Diane Gordon.

7. Luke Demaitre and Anthony A. Travill, "Human Embryology and Development in the Works of Albertus Magnus," in *Albertus Magnus and the Sciences: Commemorative Essays 1980,* ed. James A. Weisheipl, OP (Toronto: Pontifical Institute of Mediaeval Studies, 1980), p. 413.

duced from blood? Book XV, Q 19: Whether females produce seed? Book XV, Q 20: Whether [male] seed is the material part of conception? Book XVI, Q 1: Whether the soul exists in seed? Book XVI, Q 3: Whether that particular virtue is from the soul [life force] of the father? Book XVIII, Q 1: Whether the strength of virtue is the cause of generation of the male? Book XVIII, Q 3: Whether the cause of resemblance is some virtue in the seed? Book XVIII, Q 4: Why wise men and philosophers for the most part beget foolish sons?

We should consider the goal of these questions for disputation. As in the context of St. Albert's questions above, often the goal is the genuine search for truth where the debate helped to identify weaknesses in one's own understanding of a topic. At other times, however, the goal of the disputation may detach itself from the search for truth, and instead move more towards the personal aim of winning an argument. We can see the same tension in contemporary debates by attorneys battling one another in court over a legal case. Even further, as found in many contemporary debating societies, a public disputation can also engage individuals for the simple purpose of entertainment and for exercising the mind in leisure time. The concept of woman will have a different place in each of these three uses of debate: i.e., the search for truth, winning an argument, or leisure entertainment. We will now briefly trace the ways in which these three uses of disputation occurred in the historical development of academic communities of discourse.

At Oxford University formal questions, or disputations, were posed in the third year of the Bachelor of Arts on issues in grammar and logic. In the fourth year, students were examined for three to four hours on a wider range of philosophical questions as a requirement for the completion of their degree. For the Master of Arts, questions covered "all of philosophy."[8] The importance of both the style and content of debate within academic education cannot be overestimated.

> Predictably, as Aristotelian logical texts dominated the content of the standard curricula, so too disputation dominated the conduct of the academic life. By the middle of the thirteenth century, students were instructed through disputation, examined through disputation, and, upon graduation, obliged to begin their statutory two years of teaching by riding out as presiding master a forty-day flood of disputations.[9]

Presumably through his complete immersion into a discourse of debate and disputation, the student's goal was the search for truth about the topic posed. Woman's identity and nature could have been such a topic, especially in natural philosophy or even metaphysics. The student's arguments would draw upon the most current scientific knowledge that he had at the time. In this way he may have been called

8. All the philosophy questions raised at Oxford between 1576 and 1622 have been published. See Andrew Clark, *Register of the University of Oxford* (Oxford: Oxford University Press, 1887). See also Charles Schmitt, *John Case and Aristotelianism in Renaissance England* (Kingston and Montreal: McGill-Queen's Press, 1983), p. 144. See also Robert Frank, "Science, Medicine and the Universities of Early Modern England: Background and Sources, Part I," *History of Science* 11 (1973): 205-6.
9. Thomas L. Reed, Jr., *Middle English Debate Poetry and the Aesthetics of Irresolution* (Columbia, Mo. and London: University of Missouri Press, 1990), p. 46.

upon to defend Aristotle's concept of male/female differentiation, or Galen's, or Avicenna's, and so forth.

In addition to the formal examinations mentioned above, there was a second kind of public disputation, the *quodlibet,* in which free questions were posed on any topic. The main purpose of the *quodlibet* was to train the student in the philosophical method of argumentation rather than to examine his knowledge of facts and theory. In the *quodlibet* we find logic used to win an argument rather than to support the search for truth. "The *demonstratio* of the thirteenth-century *quaestio disputata* was replaced in these fourteenth-century disputations by the *persuasio,* in which the opponents would adopt an opinion, not because they considered it true, but only for the sake of discussion."[10] Debates about issues of gender could fall sometimes under the first form of demonstrative knowledge concerning Aristotle's philosophy, and other times under the second form, or expressing an opinion just for the sake of argument.

". . . [T]he *quodlibet* was open to anyone who cared to participate and could touch on any subject whatsoever."[11] In this context it was possible for any participant to choose the opportunity to suggest an argument, as a kind of test, for a new theory. ". . . [H]ere was a format for the discussion not only of embryonic ideas not adequately formed for the *quaestiones disputatae,* but also of any radical notions that had been excluded from the official course of studies."[12] So the daily questions for public debate served a very different purpose than the disputed questions for demonstration used by faculty at universities for examination at the Bachelors and Masters levels. In the former, previously accepted judgments about the concept of woman would have been in order, while in the latter, new challenges or ideas about the concept of woman could have been posed.

In addition to these forms of debate in the academia, there were also *collationes,* or private disputations held among a specific group of individuals living near universities or in other, non-academic settings. The use of debate as a model for dialogue spread out beyond the bounds of the academic centers in Europe.[13] The gaining popularity of the use of debate in both Canon and Civil law also contributed to this trend of shifting the purpose of debate away from the search for truth and towards the goal of winning an argument.[14]

10. Astrid L. Gabriel, "The College System in the Fourteenth-Century Universities," in *The Forward Movement of the Fourteenth Century,* ed. Francis Lee Utley (Columbus: Ohio State University Press, 1961), p. 100.

11. Reed, *Middle English Debate,* p. 49.

12. Reed, *Middle English Debate,* p. 50.

13. Andrea Nye, in her provocative work on the history of logic, reflects on the development within it of different models of dialogue. She states that while Plato offers a model of interaction of speakers in which one is usually overcome ("reduced to silence") by the end of the dialogue, Aristotle offers two models; in one, two disputants rationally submit to rules that guide their discussion, which may or may not lead to a resolution; in the other, within the rules, a demonstrative syllogism settles all questions. *Words of Power,* p. 59.

14. Nye concludes her summary with the observation that with the discovery of Aristotle's logical works, and their new adaptation by Abelard's scholastic method, ". . . the logical *disputatio* was added, a lively dialectical contest, something like a cockfight, often ill-tempered, pugilistic, and with little regard for truth" (*Words of Power,* p. 87). Reed also notes this characteristic of Abelard's use of

It is worth noting in passing that a similar pattern occurred at the University of Paris. "The arts faculty was by far the largest, having, according to one source, between four and five thousand students at the beginning of the sixteenth century, and it was here that the study of logic was carried out. All arts students devoted two years to logic, and a third year to the physics, metaphysics and ethics of Aristotle."[15] While Paris remained initially more faithful to the scholastic understanding of the purpose of logic as seeking the true nature of things, it also came under nominalist influence that shifted logic more towards rhetoric.

Another factor in England also undermined the original use of logic for purposes of scientific demonstration and the expansion of knowledge. As the public debate, or *quodlibet,* became more and more identified with undergraduate students and the general public, its tone became more irreverent and even, at times, raucous.[16] By the fifteenth and sixteenth centuries, questions were posed more for entertainment than for serious study. In this context, debate assumed more of the character of satire than either science or logic. As we will study the relation of satire to issues of gender in the next chapter, this subject will not be pursued in this one. However, we will turn to consider some of the actual questions recorded in public debate at universities in the sixteenth and seventeenth centuries that contain reference to women, in order to demonstrate some of the ways that logic intersected with reflections on gender issues.

Some examples of questions about woman's identity debated by Masters students at Oxford in the late sixteenth and early seventeenth centuries have been recorded. Though beyond the time frame of the present volume, they are nonetheless instructive for our purposes because they reveal that woman's identity was being considered in academic discourse, and they also demonstrate that many of the questions arose in the context of gender polarity. For example, in 1581 we find the following question: "Whether women should be taught letters?"[17] A question with special relevance to the final section of this chapter was raised in 1585: "Whether nature intends a woman?"[18] Then in 1590, "Whether woman's nature is as intelligent as man's?" was debated.[19] Finally, "Whether woman is a suitable auditor of moral philosophy?" was debated in 1608.[20]

---

logic and in the context of its impact on debate poetry: "Of particular interest for us is the possibility that Peter Abelard's great dialectical compendium *Sic et Non* and analogous works like the *Dialogus inter Philosophum, Judaeum, et Christianum* provided formal models and inspiration for those poems which balance conflicting points of view without attempting to determine the issues. Abelard, even in matters of the highest theological seriousness, was content to leave discordant voices formally unharmonized" (*Middle English Debate,* p. 112).

15. Ashworth adds that in the second year of the study of logic, "they were faced with Porphyry's *Isagoge* and Aristotle himself; and various metaphysical questions were raised in addition to the logical ones. . . . The first class met at 4:00 a.m. and the last interrogation was at 7:00 p.m., with scarcely a break in between" (*Language and Logic in the Post-Modern Period* [Dordrecht/Boston: D. Reidel Publishing Company, 1974], p. 6).

16. Reed, *Middle English Debate,* p. 50.

17. "An foeminae sint literis instruendae?" Clark, *Register,* II, 1, 170.

18. "An natura intendat foeminam?" Clark, *Register,* II, 1, 171.

19. "An foeminarum ingenia sint acutiora quam virorum?" Clark, *Register,* II, 1, 172.

20. "An foemina sit idonea auditrix moralis philosophiae?" Clark, *Register,* II, 1, 176.

It is difficult to know to what extent these questions were considered a serious matter for debate and to what extent they were thought of as humorous interludes in the academic program. Support for the view that public debate about woman was more an example of satire than serious study is found in the following question posed to Masters of Arts students and possibly inspired by Shakespeare: "What is the right way to tame a shrew?" And again, "Ought Aristotle to have included a wife among the goods of the philosopher?"[21] If public discussions about women had been only satirical, it would reinforce the claim that the combination of logic and academic philosophy, which adopted a gender neutrality attitude, ambiguously transmitted gender polarity which devalued woman.

On the other hand, Charles Schmitt suggests that the "unexpected" focus on women in these questions may have been due to the presence of a female monarch.[22] The question: "Whether women live as agreeably as men?" would support this.[23] However, an examination of the questions debated before Queen Elizabeth at Oxford on September 3, 4, and 5, 1566 in natural philosophy, moral philosophy, law, and medicine, and on September 23, 25, 26, and 27, 1592 in philosophy, theology, medicine, divinity, and law reveal that not one single question considered an issue about woman's identity.[24] This would imply that the presence of the Queen did not shift the usual gender-neutral approach of academic philosophy towards a consideration of issues with special relevance to women.

In any event, it is clear that the incorporation of Aristotle's logic by the scholastic method in public debate occasionally offered the opportunity to raise questions about different aspects of the concept of woman in the academic community of male discourse, whether humorously or seriously. Answers to the questions allowed the students to debate from a variety of perspectives: Aristotelian forms of gender polarity, a Platonic or Erigenic form of gender unity, or perhaps even some humanist forms of gender complementarity. As mentioned previously, it is likely that Aristotelian views and gender polarity were given a predominant position. However, alternative views may also have been expressed.

In this section on academic forms of dialogue and debate, we have seen that the practical application of Aristotelian logic, rhetoric, and dialectic had many different consequences for the concept of woman. In the first place, this debate took place in an academic setting in which only men participated. The presence of a female monarch did not appear to shift the focus of academic debate either towards or away from gender issues. At the same time, we noted a difference when debate

21. Clark, *Register,* II, 1, 84.

22. Charles Schmitt, "Philosophy and Science in Sixteenth Century Universities: Some Preliminary Comments," in *The Cultural Context of Medieval Learning,* ed. James Edward Murdock and E. D. Sylla (Dordrecht: D. Reidel Publishing Co., 1975), p. 500.

23. "An foeminae jucundius vivant quam viri?" Clark, *Register,* II, 1, 173. It is interesting to note that there is hardly any mention of women in Harvard's Questions from 1643 to 1708. This absence may support the claim that a female monarch is a factor. On the other hand, a gender-neutral attitude may have pervaded Harvard's public debate for other reasons. I am grateful to Susan Wake for this observation.

24. C. Plummer, ed., *Elizabethan Oxford Reprints of Rare Tracts* (Oxford: Clarendon Press, 1887), pp. 201-3, 252-60.

was used for educational purposes as opposed to entertainment. In the former case, logic was applied as a method for approximating greater truth, while in the latter it was used simply for the purposes of argument without regard for truth. It was also seen that at certain times Aristotelian-type questions with reference to gender were posed in public debate. Since these questions were framed within the gender polarity framework of Aristotle's theory, they could have led to a simple restatement of his views, or they may have opened up the debate to alternative possibilities depending upon the context. Therefore, even though Aristotelian logic itself contains a gender neutrality in its demonstrative function, when it is applied in dialectic or rhetoric, it may be used to suggest other theories of gender identity.

After this consideration of the external form of the scholastic method of debate as disputation, we will now turn to reflect on its inner structure, or the laws of discursive reasoning that governed all argument and demonstration in academia. In this way, we move from the surface to the interior structure of academic discourse as it historically evolved.

LOGIC, DEMONSTRATIVE SCIENCE, AND GENDER IDENTITY

Aristotle's *Categories* and especially his *Posterior Analytics* provided the foundation for the new scientific method in academia.[25] Aristotle brought about a great advancement in human knowledge when he elaborated the fundamental laws of syllogistic reasoning. These laws established principles of theoretical reasoning (which sought to articulate true propositions) and practical reasoning (which aimed at a good action). The main components of Aristotle's system included definitions of terms, judgments expressed in propositions, laws guiding valid syllogisms, and conclusions derived from syllogistic reasoning.[26] For Aristotle, logic dealt with the form of reasoning without regard to the content or consequences. His texts were the first to establish valid and invalid forms of argumentation, using symbols to represent subject and predicate terms of propositions. The Greek philosopher systematically elaborated the rules of derivation through which complex syllogistic arguments could be derived from simpler, more self-evident syllogistic forms.

Aristotle's unprecedented contribution to the science of discursive reasoning was absorbed with great interest by subsequent scholars. Before the thirteenth century, portions of Aristotle's logical works or *Organon (Categories, On Interpretation, Prior Analytics, Posterior Analytics,* and *Topics)* were transmitted to the West through the commentaries and translations of the Neoplatonic Porphyry (235-305) and Christian Stoic Boethius (480-524). Logic became an indispensable tool for the sciences of natural philosophy and of metaphysics.

However, those philosophers who demonstrated a strong interest in the study

---

25. William A. Wallace, *Causality and Scientific Explanation: Medieval and Early Classical Science* (Ann Arbor: University of Michigan Press, 1972), vol. 1, pp. 10-11.

26. See Aristotle, *The Organon* (Cambridge: Harvard University Press, 1949-50), vols. 1 and 2, and *The "Art" of Rhetoric* (Cambridge, Mass.: Harvard University Press, 1957).

of logic did not all promote the same theory of sex and gender identity. In *The Concept of Woman: The Aristotelian Revolution (750 BC–1250 AD)* it was seen that Aristotle's natural philosophy, in particular, contained arguments for sex polarity, while Porphyry in *The Philosopher's Letter to His Wife Marcella*[27] suggested a theory of sex unity, and Boethius's *Consolation of Philosophy*[28] introduced components of sex complementarity. Yet, these are the three key philosophers who transmitted the study of logic to the West. Therefore, right from the moments of its origins, logic appears to be neutral with respect to a particular theory of sex and gender identity. We can call this the *prima facie* gender neutrality of logic.

It seems obvious in some sense that the rules of valid reasoning would be neutral with respect to the premises of any particular argument. Philosophers can use logic to defend polarity, unity, or complementarity theories, depending upon what premises they choose for their arguments. This feature of logic makes it genuinely neutral with respect to any particular theory. One might conclude from this that the study of the history of logic is irrelevant to the concept of woman. Yet this would be too hasty a conclusion. For, as we will see in the subsequent analysis of philosophers who were dedicated to the study of logic, certain practices occurred and conclusions were reached that did affect the history of the concept of woman. It is to these themes we will now turn our attention.

In this introduction to the second section of the chapter we will look more closely at some components of Aristotelian logic, to determine more precisely how these affected the concept of woman through their institutionalization in academic study. Our attention will be focused first on the category of substance, on the meaning of accident, and on the search for definitions by syllogistic reasoning as first elaborated in Aristotle and Porphyry. Then we will briefly consider gender identity in the subsequent work of three logicians who were particularly influenced by the tradition of Aristotelian logic: Robert Grosseteste (1175-1253), Roger Bacon (1214-1292), and William of Ockham (1280-1339). The implications of their academic approach for the history of discourse about the concept of woman will be investigated.

Substance and Gender Identity

There are two different meanings of 'substance' in Aristotle. One meaning of substance is ontological and it is associated with a being as a particular entity existing in the world, a someone or a something — a woman or a man. It is a concrete particular existent and it is called by Aristotle a '**primary substance.**' In this sense, a substance is an individual entity that exists in some separate state. It is a something or a someone in the mode of being in which particular attributes may inhere. Although a man or a woman could be used as an example of a primary substance, Ar-

27. Porphyry, *The Philosopher to His Wife, Marcella* (London: George Redway, 1896), (33), 76-78.

28. Boethius, *The Consolation of Philosophy* (Indianapolis: Bobbs-Merrill, 1962), Book I, Prose 1-3, 5-6; Book II, Prose 4 and 6; Book III, Prose 12; and Book V, Prose 3 and 6.

istotle's discussion in his logical texts used only individual men such as Socrates or Alcibiades.[29] This choice may have been due to the pedagogical preference of using examples more directly related to his male community of discourse. In any event, in Aristotle's original text on logic, a woman is never used as an example of primary substance.

This practice of using only a man as an example of a primary substance within the theoretically gender-neutral logic has the effect of making man the paradigm for the significant subject of predication. Thus, later on, when women finally have access to Aristotle's logical texts, they must read themselves into the paradigm of male examples. This is not unlike the analogous effort that men who read the works of women religious authors studied in the previous chapter have to make in reading themselves into the female paradigm of the person seeking union with God.

When we turn to the second meaning of 'substance' we find here that it is associated with the kind of a being or with the name common to all things of the same kind. This is a general term, or universal, and is called a '**secondary substance.**' Aristotle understood secondary substance as that kind of thing of which other things are predicated and which is not predicated of anything else. The genus 'animal,' the species 'human being,' and subspecies 'man' or 'woman' could be used as examples of secondary substance in Aristotle's categories. However, all examples of secondary substance actually found in Aristotle's *Categories* use 'man' with the significance of 'human beings in general.' Thus, neither 'a woman' as a primary substance nor 'woman' as a secondary substance appears as an example in Aristotle's logical texts.

Let us ask again: Where does the concept of woman fit into the actual texts of the categories of Aristotle's logic? While woman is included in the broader category of the human being and woman fits in general as something that is possible to be analyzed using Aristotle's categories, the actual use of the term 'woman' does not explicitly appear in his actual discussions. To repeat our findings: there is not one single reference to a woman as a primary substance or to the concept of woman as a secondary substance! Therefore, Aristotle's logic provides the foundational example both in structure and in content of an attitude of gender neutrality that uses man (meaning 'human being') as the paradigm example for secondary substance and man (meaning 'a male human being') as the paradigm example for primary substance.

When we turn to the logic of Porphyry a similar result is discovered. Porphyry's analysis did not concentrate on the ontological category of Aristotle's primary substance. Rather, he incorporated Aristotle's second meaning of substance, or a subject of predication of a class of things with a common identity. Porphyry used genus and species in a manner similar to Aristotle's secondary substance. His logic concentrated on the different ways in which predicates may be predicated of a subject. In this context, Porphyry also offered no mention of a woman as a paradigm example or of woman as a subject of predication.[30] Porphyry may have simply

29. Aristotle, *Categories* in *The Basic Works of Aristotle,* ed. Richard McKeon (New York: Random House, 1941).

30. Porphyry, *Isagoge* (London: H. G. Bohn, 1853).

been transmitting the examples of the original Aristotelian text he was elaborating upon. Or, he may also have been speaking within the context of a male community of discourse in which he used examples more appropriate to the students he was teaching. It is not possible to assess the cause for this exclusion of woman from mention in his logical texts, especially in light of his encouragement to his wife Marcella to study philosophy. However, we can note again that an effect of the absence of consideration of woman even as a subspecies in texts of logic led to an impression that the concept of woman was irrelevant to the philosophy of logic.

Logic in its essential nature is appropriately identified with a gender neutrality theory. Logic in its application may bring with it a hidden gender polarity, gender unity, or gender complementarity. In the context of the early universities in Europe, all of them academic communities of male discourse from which women were excluded, we will begin to discover two different subcultures of approach to the concept of woman. In one, gender neutrality will predominate and gender differentiation will be increasingly irrelevant; in the other, gender polarity will predominate and gender differentiation will lead to a devaluation of woman. In both contexts woman's identity is somewhat alienated in the discourse among the academic philosophers. Before tracing this pattern in particular philosophers we need to consider another category in the Aristotelian study of logic, the category of accident, and its relation to the concept of woman.

Accident and Gender Identity

Aristotle identified ten categories of predication in the mode of being: substance, quantity, relation, place, time, position, condition, action, passion, and quality.[31] He characterized all but the first category, substance, as "accidents." For Aristotle, anything that is not a substance is considered as an ontological accident because it must inhere in a substance or be predicated of a substance. This includes essential properties such as the rationality of a human being. Rationality is an essential property as found in the well-known description of the human being: "man is a rational animal." Some accidents are essential, or necessary to the definition of a kind of thing, while others are non-essential to the definition. For example, rationality is essential to the definition of the human being, while the color of hair or the shape of the nose is not.

Porphyry both transmitted and revised the Aristotelian categories of predication. Instead of having ten categories, nine of which are accidents, Porphyry identified five categories in the mode of predication. He named these predicables as follows: genus, species, differentia, property, and accident.[32] Thus the meaning of

---

31. Aristotle's examples of application of the categories to normal discourse include the following: primary substance — a man, secondary substance — man (humanity), quantity — two inches long, relation — double or greater, place — in the market or in school, time — last year, position — lying or sitting, condition — shod or armed, action — to lance or cauterize, passion — to be lanced or cauterized, and quality — white or grammatical.

32. Porphyry's examples of the predicables include the following: genus — animal, species —

'accident' in Porphyry differs from the meaning of 'accident' in Aristotle. This difference in meaning will have consequences for considerations of sex and gender.

Aristotle's use of accident includes both essential and non-essential predicates of a subject, while Porphyry's use of accident includes only non-essential predicates. Porphyry's use is more akin to the contemporary understanding of an accidental property of a thing. For example, we might say that color is an accidental quality of hair. In this sense, rationality would not be an accident of the human species for Porphyry, because rationality is an essential difference between human beings and other animals. However, for Aristotle rationality would be an accident of the human species because it is a property of the human species rather than a primary or a secondary substance.

Confusion following from the double meaning of accident is increased by two further developments. First, in addition to the question of whether accident includes or excludes non-essential properties in the description of a thing, accident also came to be used by Aristotle in discussions in natural philosophy. Here he described an accident as that which "attaches to each thing in virtue of itself but is not in its essence."[33] Animality is part of the essence of the human being. Thus, whether a human being is a female or a male attaches to the human being in virtue of its being an animal (that is, it must be one or the other), but not in its essence *per se* (for example, it is not essential that a human being be a male). Aristotle thought that because of its animality a human being must be either male or female. In this use of accident, there is a neutrality implied. In Aristotle's language, it is an accident of the human being whether it is male or female.

As we will see in the second part of this chapter, Aristotle thought that in generation, the human form supplied by the father tended by nature to produce a male that resembled the father. A female human being was generated as a deviation from this perfect type of conception. Here we discover a use of the term 'accident' in line with contemporary usage of the word as meaning something that is not planned. Aristotle implies that unless the human conception had an accident, it would turn out to be a male that resembled the father. In this application of the term 'accident' we find an underlying theory of gender polarity which suggests that accident (meaning unplanned) applies more to females than to males.

In metaphysical texts and in some satires we will find authors familiar with Aristotle's thought that a female could be described as a 'male who had an accident' or as 'an accidental male.' This description used the logical term 'accident' in a way that shifted its meaning from a gender-neutral orientation towards a polarity that devalued women. Of particular note here is the anonymous sixteenth-century Latin satire *Disputatio perjucunda qua anonymus probare nititur mulieres homines non esse* [A most agreeable dispute in which the anonymous author endeavors to prove that women are not human]. The passage in question reads: "Since, as Aristotle says, a woman is a monster in nature [*mulier fit monstrum in natura*]. . . ."[34]

---

man (humanity), difference — rationality, property — capacity to use language, and accident — hair, eye, or skin color.

33. Aristotle, *Metaphysics* 1925a 13-15.

34. *Disputatio perjucunda qua anonymus probare nititur mulieres homines non esse* (The Hague,

The concept of the accidental generation of a woman is incorporated with the other accidents of conception referred to as "monsters." It also plays on the theme that accidents of this type are not fully representative of the human species. Thus the term 'accident,' which in logic originally had contained the ambivalent meaning of both essential and non-essential predicates of a substance or species, seemed to open to an even wider ambivalence in meaning when it included accidental as something lacking in the generation of a woman. Controversies associated with this latter interpretation of Aristotle's thought will be discussed in some detail later in this chapter. At this point, it is important simply to note that the category of accident in Aristotle's logic has a long and complex association with the concept of woman.

To summarize: the term 'accident' has four different meanings, all of which were originally found in some Aristotelian texts. In Aristotle's logic and its developments by Porphyry, 'accident' is used as a neutral term of predication that sometimes (1) includes essential predicates and sometimes (2) excludes essential predicates. Accident is used (3) in Aristotle's natural philosophy in relation to non-essential properties attached to a thing in virtue of itself, and (4) it is also used as a principle to explain the unplanned generation of a female. This latter use was adopted in metaphysical texts and satirized in subsequent literature to represent a female's identity as a male who had an accident.

Syllogisms and Gender Identity

The structure of the syllogism provided the laws of discursive reasoning for the academic discourse practiced in academia. The dynamic of examination and debate was one of disputation, while the internal structure was framed by rules of logic. As previously indicated, even though logic was theoretically neutral to gender identity, in the context of male academic communities, the common examples of a human being used in syllogisms were usually of males. In a familiar contemporary example of a syllogism used in logic courses we find the following sequence: "All men are mortal; Socrates is a man; therefore Socrates is mortal." The oddness of using a woman as an example for the same syllogistic form can be seen in this sequence that assumes the meaning of human being for the terms 'men' and 'man': All men are mortal, Socrates' wife is a man, therefore Socrates' wife is mortal. This example simply points out the historical association of the male as a paradigm in philosophy; it does not suggest that syllogisms are not valid forms of argumentation.

The syllogistic form of reasoning uses three propositions (a major premise, a minor premise, and a conclusion) and three terms (a major term, a minor term,

---

1541), pp. 51-52. This passage was translated from the Latin by Joseph Moller. The satire was published in German in 1615, in Italian in 1647, and in French in 1744. It produced a large number of refutations by theologians, physicians, and jurists. See Ian Maclean, *The Renaissance Notion of Woman: A Study in the Fortunes of Scholasticism and Medical Science in European Intellectual Life* (Cambridge: Cambridge University Press, 1980), p. 12.

and a middle term). The middle term, found in both premises, is used in both premises to generate a conclusion that contains the subject term and the predicate term. Depending upon the relation of the qualifiers of all, some (including the example above of one), and positive or negative (e.g., all are or none are; some are or some are not), the reasoning will be either valid or invalid (i.e., fallacious). As we will see in subsequent chapters, women did learn by the fourteenth century how to use syllogistic reasoning, and soon they turned it towards the subject of gender identity itself. So the syllogistic form of reasoning is gender neutral in its practical application. It may be used to defend different theories of gender identity depending upon the major and minor premises of the syllogism.

Aristotle made a distinction between dialectic, which reasoned from premises of common or probable opinion, and demonstrative science, which reasoned from premises that were thought to be certain. Academic philosophy both in Ancient Greece and in the thirteenth century took as one of its central aims the task of articulating certain definitions upon which to base demonstrative science. 'What is x?' was the typical form of a question for defining a species. Determining the essential properties of x became the task of various sciences.

For Porphyry, 'species' was thought to identify the *entire nature* of a type of thing. In the case of woman and of man, the species is 'man' as in 'human being.' It coincides with the concept of secondary substance in Aristotle's categories. 'Man is a rational animal' is the traditional definition derived from, but not explicitly expressed by, Aristotle. Another way of describing this category is to say that the *essence* of a human being is *'rational animal.'* In a definition, only essential predicates may be included; so the task of the philosopher is to identify what is essential, and to separate out the essential from the accidental in coming to the proper definition of a thing. In this case the species identifies the kind of substance that the thing is.

According to Aristotle and Porphyry, rationality is the essential predicate that differentiates the species of human beings from other kinds of animals. Porphyry's property 'capacity for speech' is also something that *necessarily* and *universally* belongs to the human species alone. It is not directly contained in the essence, which in this case refers to rationality and animality, but it necessarily follows from the essence, as the capacity for discourse follows from rationality.

The medieval search for definitions used the Aristotelian model of syllogistic reasoning in which a premise was phrased as a certain judgment in the **universal** mode as '**All x** has attribute y.'[35] There was little room for the more flexible category

---

35. Once universal definitions were identified, syllogistic reasoning could be introduced to derive further conclusions from two premises that contained three terms. If the premises were universal and necessary, then the conclusions would be as well. Aristotle first identified the valid forms of syllogism using four kinds of propositions: A (All x is y), E (No x is y), I (Some x is y), and O (Some x is not y). His preferred syllogism was in the form of AAA, or All x is y, All y is z, therefore, All x is z. In medieval logic, this syllogism was given the name "BARBARA" which incorporated, among other things, the sign of the three "A" forms of proposition. See William Kneale and Martha Kneale, *The Development of Logic* (Oxford: Clarendon Press, 1962), pp. 54-80 for a description of Aristotle's four forms of statement and syllogism; pp. 224-246 for a description of logic in medieval universities. In 1570, in a printed edition of Boethius's works, "in the part on syllogisms the famous mnemonic verses *Barbara celarent* make their first appearance . . ." (p. 232).

'most x' or 'nearly all x.' Now Aristotle himself realized that things in nature could not always be generalized into universals, because there are occasional exceptions. For Aristotle, "all science is of that which is always or for the most part."[36] Natural definitions held true usually 'for the most part.' There was a certain flexibility in Aristotle's philosophy of nature. However, the logical form of syllogistic reasoning demanded universal premises from which to derive valid conclusions. The emphasis on logical form tended to eliminate flexibility.

Borderline cases that applied **most but not all** the time were either phrased as 'some x are y' (which logically includes them) or a bit all-too-generously included in 'all x are y' (which, strictly speaking, is an impermissible move in Aristotle's logic). So probabilities (the core of contemporary scientific hypotheses), common opinion (which may or may not be accurate), and single examples were lumped together, and excluded from the range of demonstrative science. The academic study of philosophy struggled with the difficulty of how to adjust the tools of meaning found in logical structures to accurately reflect realities that exist in the world of nature, mathematics, and metaphysics as well as in the more practical world of ethics and politics.

The collapsing of the subject 'most x' into either 'all x' or 'some x' had consequences for the concept of woman. In a way we could say that the generalization to 'all x' contributed to the tendency to stereotype some characteristics of woman; while the reduction to 'some x' contributed to the tendency to dismiss other characteristics as not important to woman's identity. As a consequence the extended practice of the Aristotelian form of syllogism led to a formalization of fields like zoology and ethics, which consequently contained inaccuracies and stereotypes in their reflections on the concept of woman.

According to the Aristotelian model, once universal definitions were identified, syllogistic reasoning could be introduced to derive further conclusions from two premises that contained three terms. If both premises were universal and necessary, then the conclusions would be universal and necessary as well. If one premise were particular, then the conclusion would be particular. Aristotle's identification of the valid forms of syllogism and the rules for determining their validity, without respect to their content, is still accepted today. This elaboration by Aristotle of the valid forms of syllogistic reasoning provided an important contribution to the advancement of knowledge. It was one of the reasons for the widespread enthusiasm for Aristotle's philosophy in the new universities.

At the same time, in scholastic and post-scholastic academia a debate occurred about the proper identity of logic. Scholastic logicians, and especially Thomas Aquinas, argued that logic ought always to be subordinated to the discovery of truth.[37] So scholastic logic in this sense ought to lead the philosopher to the

---

36. Aristotle, *Metaphysics* 1065a 2-6.

37. See Robert W. Schmidt, S.J., *The Domain of Logic According to Saint Thomas Aquinas* (The Hague: Martinus Nijhoff, 1966), pp. 302ff. Schmidt describes the hierarchical three kinds of logic as follows: demonstrative, which deals with certitude; dialectic, which deals with probabilities; and sophistical, which deals with the appearance of truth. Only the first kind is considered as a science. He concludes that the subject of logic is "positive rationate being" (p. 306).

knowledge of things.[38] However, others thought that the proper subject of logic was linguistic terms, and they detached the mental contents from the real world.[39] We will now turn to consider three philosophers who became particularly interested in logic and mathematics, and who participated in this debate about the relation between logic and the search for truth. Given the theoretical gender neutrality of logic it is important to discover how these later incorporations of Aristotelian logic into academia related to the search for truth about gender identity. In this early time of the foundation of the universities of Oxford and Paris, we will see that three different philosophers sought to establish academic philosophy in a very specific way that had implications for gender neutrality.

Robert Grosseteste (1175-1253)

Oxford University was one of the main thirteenth-century academic centers that transmitted Aristotelian logic with its characteristic attitude of gender neutrality.[40] Robert Grosseteste introduced Aristotle's logic to Oxford after he was appointed Master of Schools there in 1214. His commentary on Aristotle's *Posterior Analytics,* written during 1220-1228, is considered to be "the first treatise on logic by an Englishman."[41] As mentioned previously, Aristotle's text concentrated on the use of syllogisms to achieve demonstrative knowledge. Grosseteste tried to integrate physics (knowledge of the fact) with mathematics (knowledge of the reasoned

38. Albert the Great had argued that logic was the science of reasoning about the thing. The philosopher tried to consider, through a second-order intention, "a condition in things which belongs to them by virtue of the operation of the intellect." See E. J. Ashworth, *Language and Logic,* p. 33. A similar view is expressed by the philosophy of Albert's student Thomas Aquinas: "It is the end of reason to know the real; and logic serves as the internal guide of reason in this pursuit" (Schmidt, *The Domain of Logic,* pp. 318-19).

39. For an excellent bibliography of secondary sources on the history of logic from the twelfth to the seventeenth centuries see E. J. Ashworth, *The Tradition of Medieval Logic and Speculative Grammar* (Toronto: Pontifical Institute of Medieval Studies, 1978). In addition, Ashworth's text *Language and Logic* traces the development of different understandings of logic with respect to the question of knowledge and truth (pp. 15-17). A further source for the later period of the same topic is Howell, *Logic and Rhetoric.* Howell states that in England scholastic logic prevailed up to the mid-sixteenth century, then a revolt occurred in England in the late sixteenth century through the seventeenth century because of the rejection of Aristotelian logic in the work of Peter Ramus (1515-1572), with a subsequent criticism of the Ramusts by the Port Royal logicians at the end of the seventeenth century (pp. 6-8).

40. Ashworth traces parallel developments in Paris, Spain, Italy, and Germany in *Language and Logic,* ch. 1, pp. 1-7.

41. This text was subsequently published in Naples in 1473. See Howell, *Logic and Rhetoric,* p. 45. See also A. C. Crombie, *Robert Grosseteste and the Origins of Experimental Science (1100-1700)* (Oxford: Oxford University Press, 1953). Crombie states: "As a beginning for his theory of science Grosseteste took the double, inductive-deductive procedure described by Aristotle in his *Posterior Analytics*" (p. 13). See also Gordon Leff, *Paris and Oxford Universities in the Thirteenth and Fourteenth Centuries: An Institutional and Intellectual History* (New York: John Wiley and Sons, 1968). "The influence of Grosseteste in all subsequent medieval scientific thought and activity cannot be overestimated" (p. 252).

fact), and some experimentation using an inductive method. This integration has been identified as the first rudimentary effort to establish a new foundation for science.[42] While there were Neoplatonic elements in Grosseteste's thought, especially in his appeal to geometry as foundation for mathematical reasoning from fact, his scientific method was more directly related to Aristotle's logic.

Grosseteste thought that universals were always the primary object of enquiry. Even though 'male' and 'female' could in some ways be construed as universals, their consideration was not important to Robert Grosseteste because he placed biological principles at the lowest level of all scientific principles, beneath natural philosophy, physics, and astronomy. He believed that biological principles involved regular but contingent laws of nature. In one example, Grosseteste appears to consider sexual difference: "Every male, when he reached the age of maturity, was able to fulfill his generative functions . . . provided there was no extraordinary obstacle."[43] However, this example applies to females, too, if 'generative' is taken in the broader sense of reproductive rather than the restricted sense that only males generate. In this case, it would not be an example of sexual differentiation *per se* but rather a reflection on sexual maturity in general.

Grosseteste's commentary on Aristotle's *Physics,* written during 1228-1231, along with the previously mentioned commentary on *Posterior Analytics,* was used in academic philosophical study for centuries. Syllogistic reasoning in Grosseteste's commentaries provided a framework for the philosophical search for scientific knowledge that was produced through demonstration. Only syllogisms with at least one universal premise could produce demonstrative knowledge. Since accidents, contingent characteristics of substances, could not be introduced into universal premises, they could not produce demonstrative knowledge through syllogistic reasoning. Consequently, all consideration of male and female, masculine and feminine, or sex identity fell outside the perimeters of philosophy, which was now restricted to demonstrative scientific knowledge. Gender neutrality was a *de facto* consequence of this philosophical method.

As a theologian trained at the University of Paris, in addition to lecturing on physics and logic, Grosseteste also lectured on the Bible. It might be expected that in this context he would give considerable attention to issues of sex and gender identity. However, even in his text on *Genesis* entitled *Hexæmeron* there is little consideration of differences between men and women.[44] While woman is simply mentioned in the traditional description of the sixth day of creation, there is a rather surprising gender neutrality orientation of the entire text, in which sex and gender differences are basically ignored.

During the years 1246-1247 Grosseteste also made the first complete translation of Aristotle's *Nicomachean Ethics* into Latin. This translation, along with his annotations or notes, was used by Albert the Great for his first lectures on the *Eth-*

---

42. Wallace, *Causality and Scientific Explanation,* pp. 10-11, 28-30.

43. Steven Marrone, *William of Auvergne and Robert Grosseteste: New Ideas of Truth in the Early Thirteenth Century* (Princeton: Princeton University Press, 1983), pp. 262-63.

44. Robert Grosseteste, *Hexæmeron,* ed. Richard C. Dales and Cervus Gieben (London and New York: Oxford University Press, 1982).

ics, and a revision of Grosseteste's version of the text deleting his notes was used by Thomas Aquinas for his own written exposition of Aristotle's *Ethics.*[45] The interconnection and sharing of texts among academics with different theoretical approaches are remarkable. They were all interested in Aristotle's original texts, and eager to use fresh Latin translations where available.

Grosseteste lived and taught at Oxford in the thirteenth century, at the same time that the Aristotelian Revolution, the institutionalization of the Aristotelian corpus, was occurring at Paris. As a secular cleric, and later as Bishop, Grosseteste played a formative role in shaping the academic direction of Oxford during its early stages of development. For his efforts in trying to establish philosophy as a rigorous science, shifting science away from biological interests towards physics and mathematics, and introducing the need for empirical methods of verification, Robert Grosseteste can be credited with laying the foundations for the beginnings of modern western science. His consistent attitude of gender neutrality contributed in part to the subsequent exclusion of certain issues in a logic-oriented mainstream academic philosophy.

Roger Bacon (1214-1292)

Possibly a member of Robert Grosseteste's group of Franciscan students in the 1230-1240s, or else tutored by Adam Marsh, a student of Grosseteste, Bacon was driven to find a new scientific ground for philosophy. He wanted to make philosophy into a universal science. Bacon traveled from Oxford to the University of Paris where he studied and lectured at the Faculty of Arts between 1245 and 1251. He wrote commentaries entitled *Questiones,* which reflected on the logical works of Aristotle as well as the texts on *Physics, Generation and Corruption, De anima,* and *De caelo et mundo.*[46] It is not surprising that Bacon's commentaries were gender neutral in focus, as these original Aristotelian texts also had the same orientation. Bacon's tendency to follow Avicenna's interpretations of Aristotle as if they were Aristotle's voice himself also led him to some different conclusions than the original philosopher.[47]

A little more significant perhaps is the fact that Bacon's commentary on Aristotle's *Metaphysics* also ignored any question of sex identity, since in Book X, 9, Aristotle himself argued that the difference between male and female was not enough to constitute a difference in species, because the female was a contrary to male within the same species and their difference was one of matter and not of essence. Bacon, however, remained silent on this point even when commenting on the same section.[48]

45. V. J. Bourke, "The *Nicomachean Ethics* and Thomas Aquinas," in *St. Thomas Aquinas: Commemorative Studies (1274-1994)* (Toronto: Pontifical Institute of Mediaeval Studies, 1974), pp. 239-59.

46. Stewart C. Easton, *Roger Bacon and His Search for a Universal Science* (New York: Russell and Russell, 1952), pp. 60-61. See also *Three Treatments of Universals by Roger Bacon* (Binghamton, N.Y.: Medieval, Renaissance Texts and Studies, 1989).

47. Gilson, "Roger Bacon," in *History of Christian Philosophy in the Middle Ages,* p. 295.

48. Roger Bacon, "Quaestiones supra undecimum prime philosophie Aristotelis Metaphysics X," in *Opera Hactenus Inedita Rogeri Baconi* (Oxford: Clarendon Press, 1909-40), pp. 125-73.

Bacon wrote *De animalibus,* a commentary on Aristotle's texts on the generation of animals, which was lost. Since Aristotle's *De animalibus* focused often on gender differentiation, it would be expected that Bacon discussed the philosophical significance of differences between male and female human beings in his commentary on this text, a commentary thought to have been written at an early time in his academic career.

After Bacon returned to England in 1251, he discovered a spurious text entitled *Secretum Secretorum,* which profoundly changed his life.[49] The text, emerging from Arab and Hebrew sources, described Aristotle teaching "secrets" that had been personally revealed to him by God for his student Alexander the Great. The one "secret" that captured Bacon's attention was the claim that the universe had a single comprehensive essence that could be discovered by a few great scientific minds.[50]

After studying the *Secretum Secretorum* Bacon decided that it was possible to develop an integrated or perfect science that would combine all sciences into one universal science. In this science all differences were to be understood as 'accidents.' Each thing that is changed is changed by something of a higher form external to it, so all things ultimately pointed to a single substance. Bacon concluded that if the philosopher-scientist could understand the relationship among things, he would ultimately reach a single principle that explained all things through the single substance that was their cause.

Over the next twenty years, Roger Bacon, later called "the Admirable Doctor," studied natural sciences, seeking to elaborate a plan of unification of astrology, astronomy, medicine, alchemy, physiology, optics, and physics. In his study, mathematics and astrology took precedence. Bacon's mature philosophy, based on a method combining mathematics and experimental science, was published in three texts entitled *Opus Majus, Opus Minus,* and *Opus Tertium,* and in these texts there are few references to differences between the sexes. Where differences are mentioned, they are frequently interpreted in a context of physical forces within the universe rather than as organic biological realities. So even in his mature work, Bacon promotes an attitude of gender neutrality.

For example, in *Opus majus,* Bacon questions the validity of the application of the "Aristotelian" analogy in *Secretum Secretorum* of sun as father and earth as mother to human generation, because in the case of human beings, "the father does not continue nor terminate generation but only begins by letting the seed fall."[51] He also argues that generation includes reference to celestial forces, as well as to the forces in the parents, and he then concludes: "Especially from the vital principle of the mother is there a continual multiplication of force and species over the foetus up to the completion of generation and birth."[52] Bacon's analysis is unusual

49. See *Pseudo-Aristotle, Secret of Secrets: Sources and Influences,* ed. Charles B. Schmitt and W. F. Ryan (London: Warburg Institute, 1982).

50. *Secretum Secretorum* in *Opera Hactenus Inedita Rogeri Baconi.* See also "Secretum Secretorum" in Allen, *Concept of Woman: The Aristotelian Revolution,* pp. 446-49.

51. Roger Bacon, *Opus Majus* (Frankfurt: Minerva Verlag, 1964), I.V.xvi: 308. Translated by Andrew Deere, as are all subsequent passages from this text.

52. Bacon, *Opus majus,* I.IV.v: 159. A similar kind of gender-neutral approach is also found in Descartes's work on the formation of the foetus, in which he describes the development of the foetus in

in that while it *appears* to consider sexual differences, it actually concentrates only on different physical forces operating on entities in the world. This description of human events in terms of the convergence of forces suggests gender neutrality.

Another example makes this aspect of Bacon's thought more obvious. In a discussion of the theological question of original sin, Bacon describes Eve's temptation to eat the apple as the result of a vertex of a short pyramid, composed of "the species of the voice of the serpent and of the visible apple and its sweet odour," converging "at equal angles" into her senses.[53] Describing human generation in the gender-neutral vocabulary of mathematics and physics indicates a turn away from the more traditional biological approach of Aristotle to gender identity. It is tempting to conclude from this that the emphasis on a mathematical method in philosophy leads to a gender neutrality orientation in which biological accidents are reduced to gender-neutral physical forces. However, the issue is more complicated than this, as further study will reveal.

Bacon, in his notes on the spurious *Secretum Secretorum,* did seem to accept some categories of gender differentiation in astronomy and cosmology. Drawing out the astrological implications of the text, which described specific planets as creating the four elements (Saturn-Earth, Jupiter-Water, Mars-Air, and Sun-Fire), Bacon concluded that "Some signs are masculine, others feminine. The Sun, Mars, and Jupiter are masculine, the Moon, Venus, and Saturn feminine."[54] It is difficult to know whether Bacon was simply repeating what he mistakenly thought was Aristotle's view as taken from the pseudo-Aristotelian text, or whether he was suggesting his own view. It is clear, however, that astrological speculation is not Bacon's primary contribution to the history of the philosophy or to the concept of woman. Instead, his importance lies in his support of the new view of science as a mathematical foundation for philosophy, a development that elaborates upon the previous foundations of Grosseteste and Aristotle. Bacon's universal science sought single absolute principles with which to explain all of reality; it reduced all differences to the category of accidents, and thereby shifted the focus of philosophy further away from questions of gender identity.

It is interesting to see the effects that a text falsely attributed to Aristotle had on the direction of philosophy in England and to a lesser extent in France. Ironically, this text took an entirely different approach towards science than had the philosopher Aristotle in his own writings on natural philosophy. The pseudo-Aristotelian text promoted philosophy as primarily a logic of syllogism and universal definitions. Its influence through the conversion of Roger Bacon to philosophy as a universal science contributed to the reorientation of academic philosophy towards a gender-neutral methodology and away from a biologically based theory of gender identity.

---

terms of the impact of different forces in physics. See René Descartes, *La Formation du Foetus* in *Oeuvres* (Paris: Librairie Philosophique, 1969), vol. 11.

53. Bacon, *Opus majus,* I.V.xvii: 241. See also *Three Treatments of Universals,* p. 86.

54. Bacon, *Secretum Secretorum,* p. 283.

William of Ockham (c. 1280-1349)

A further development in the institutionalization of Aristotelian logic as the "proper" orientation for academic philosophy occurred through the work of William of Ockham. Born near London, trained and later affiliated as a Franciscan teacher at Oxford, Ockham became in many ways a controversial figure for his radical new theories of definition. Usually identified as the founder of the "nominalist" school of philosophy, Ockham argued against the Aristotelian tradition by claiming that definitions were neither of real substances, nor of universals, but only of abstract terms or concepts in the mind. He argued that reality should be thought of as consisting of only a collection of singular concepts that existed separately from the human mind with no necessary or real connection among them. For Ockham, universals are simply names or terms.[55]

In his *Summa Logicae* Ockham drew out the consequences of this view for Aristotle's and Porphyry's categories of genus, species, and difference. In the first case he stated that genus is "not predicated of things outside of the mind, . . . but of the signs of such things, [and therefore] genus does not belong to the essence of those things."[56] Therefore, although Ockham used Aristotelian categories, he changed the meaning of these categories. In a similar way, he claimed that species "do not belong to the essence of individuals, although they are predicable of individuals."[57] Finally, difference ranges from necessary to accidental characteristics. In an example he suggests that 'visible' is a necessary characteristic of man, while the color 'white' is accidental. In all cases, however, these terms are related to the intention of the mind rather than the ontological status of the thing existing in reality.

It is important to note that Ockham did think there were necessary connections that could be elaborated in definitions, in contrast to the later association of nominalism with a view that all definitions are arbitrary.[58] Ockham, while detaching definitions from an ontological or real foundation in the world, nonetheless argued that, while there are necessary connections between concepts in the mind, there is no way a philosopher can prove that there is a necessary connection between things in reality.

Ockham delineated two kinds of definitions: essential and logical. Essential definitions included natural definitions that referred to the four causes and metaphysical definitions of genus and species. A natural definition of man would be that man is a substance composed of body (material cause) and soul (formal, efficient, and final cause); while a metaphysical definition of man would be that man is a rational animal. While these are definitions a logician may use as examples in the course of his logic, Ockham concluded that a logician "has no reason to define

55. Marilyn McCord Adams, *William of Ockham* (Notre Dame: University of Notre Dame Press, 1987), vol. 1, p. 13.

56. *Ockham's Theory of Terms: Part I of the Summa Logicae* (London: University of Notre Dame Press, 1974), p. 92. See also *Ockham: Philosophical Writings* (Toronto: Thomas Nelson and Sons, 1959).

57. *Ockham's Theory of Terms,* p. 93.

58. See Linda Alcoff, "Cultural Feminism versus Post-Structuralism: The Identity Crisis in Feminist Theory," *Signs: Journal of Women in Culture and Society* 13, no. 3 (1988): 417, for a discussion of nominalism in contemporary feminism.

man. His task is rather to teach how the different sciences treating of man are to define man."[59] It follows that if the logician did not define man, that is, humanity, he did not define woman or man as sexually differentiated either.

Ockham's gender neutrality approach to issues of gender identity is most evident when the relation of matter and form in generation is considered. In order to appreciate his innovation, we will digress momentarily to consider the Aristotelian view about the relation of form to the definition of species. In Aristotelian theory, the species is directly related to the *form* of a kind of entity. However, the form does not exist independently of individuals who share the same species. Rather, it is found in any member of the species, as a real essence that the intellect is able to grasp. When the mind separates out the matter that is present in any particular human being, it can grasp the form of human being when it realizes that a human being is a rational animal. The concept of matter is also present through the 'animality' factor of the form, so it can be said that the form of the human being necessarily includes reference to materiality and rationality within the Aristotelian model.

How can the *difference* between male and female human beings be explained in Aristotelian theory? They have the same form, *qua* human being; and they each have different matter, which distinguishes one member of the species from the other. Aristotle himself asked in Book X, 9 of *Metaphysics* whether the differences between male and female human beings are so great as to constitute a difference in species. He argued that they are not. Women and men could *only* be thought of as belonging to the same species. Aristotle introduced the notion of a superior and an inferior way of being a member of this species to explain the systematic differences between the sexes.[60] His argument depended upon the union of form provided in the seed of the father with the specified menstrual material of the mother, and the particular ways in which this union produced males and females.

Ockham rejected Aristotle's view that matter always had to be united with form, and he argued that prime matter was the concept of an actually existing thing, extended in space, with an identity of its own but without form, but with the ability to become different kinds of things.[61] Prime matter could receive all kinds of

59. *Ockham's Theory of Terms,* pp. 105-6. This shifting of philosophy away from the actual task of defining natural or metaphysical substances towards a consideration of the relations of terms is emphasized by A. C. Crombie, who states that Ockham following Grosseteste's lead sought to establish a method in empirical science which elaborated theoretical models to explain empirical conditions. Further, these models "were reduced to mathematical terms, and their consequences deduced by geometry and arithmetic" (*Oxford's Contribution to the Origins of Modern Science* [Oxford: Basil Blackwell, 1954], p. 8). Here, the closer one moves to a mathematical model, the closer one is associated with a gender neutrality model.

60. Edith Stein argued that it was possible, through the application of a phenomenological method, to grasp an essence of woman by identifying a universal "constancy of form" present to all women. This meant that woman was not simply a defective contrary version of the human species. She states: "I have spoken before of the species 'woman'. By *species* we understand a permanent category which does not change. Thomistic philosophy designates it by the term *form,* meaning an *inner* form which determines structure." She concluded that there is a human species with the two sub-species of men and women. See Edith Stein, "Problems of Women's Education," in *Essays on Woman* (Washington D.C.: ICS Publications, 1987), p. 162.

61. André Goddu, *The Physics of William of Ockham* (Leiden-Köln: E. J. Brill, 1984), pp. 99-

forms, while secondary matter was limited to certain kinds of forms. For example, the menstrual fluid of the female of the human species, as secondary matter, was limited to receiving the form of the human species; it could not receive the form of another kind of animal. Ockham argued that it was the form that limited, shaped, and defined matter into a single existing thing.

Ockham thought that in generation, form selects out some of the menstrual fluid, then limits, shapes, and defines it into a living fetus. He argued that generation is "[t]he existence of a thing whose matter was previously deprived of a form and now possesses it immediately."[62] This deprivation parallels the mother's privation of the form of the child, which is provided by the father. Therefore, the definition hides the Aristotelian gender polarity theory of the association of matter, as privation, with the female, and of form with the male.[63] However, the direct mention of the concept of woman in this discussion of generation is being entirely avoided in his gender-neutral discourse.

William of Ockham moved from the Faculty of Theology where he taught from 1317 to 1319, to Philosophy for the years 1319-1324, and then back to Theology again from 1324 to 1330.[64] In one theological text written late in life, he considered the question of natural rights. In the *Dialogus inter magistrum et disciplum de imperatorum et pontificum potentate* (Dialogue between Master and Disciple on the Power of Emperors and Popes), Ockham argued that all men are equal in the State of Nature, before the Fall. He clarified what he meant by this original equality: "All men were created equal as to what concerns the sustention of the body, the procre-

---

107. It is also interesting to note in passing that Ockham's concept of prime matter did not contain the sexual differentiation of Plato's 'mother' receptacle.

62. Gordon Leff, *William of Ockham: The Metamorphosis of Scholastic Discourse* (Manchester: Manchester University Press, 1975), p. 569. The full quotation is as follows: "Now in the case of matter and form, they are contrasted as privation and possession; for generation consists precisely in matter's reception of a form of which it was previously deprived. It is in that broad sense as a contrary — to possession — that privation is the third principle of generation, in addition to matter and form, because there is no generation without privation. If there were, matter would already possess the form which it receives through generation; something would then be generated before generation, an impossibility. Generation therefore presupposes matter's privation of form; and the inclusion of privation as the third principle of generation is expressed in the nominal definition of generation as the existence of a thing whose matter was previously deprived of a form and now possesses it immediately."

63. Andrea Nye argues that Ockham's claim that logic focuses on particular terms, rather than on things, serves as a model for the perpetuation of "attitudes and policies of persecution" found in witch hunting and the Protestant Reformation. Her chapter, which gives a very distorted understanding of Ockham's philosophy for what she perceives as its primarily theological and political motivations, criticizes Ockham's philosophy. Nye claims that Ockham turned logic into a meta-language in order to reserve power in the Will of God to create individuals. She concludes that this reservation of power to God inevitably leads to situations of prejudice and bias in the world which human beings are unable to overcome. However, as a consideration of his own writings will reveal, Ockham hints at a political foundation for gender unity, rather than gender polarity. See "The Antinomies of Power: Ockham's Razor," in *Words of Power*, p. 120.

64. In his early years of lecturing in the Faculty of Theology, between 1317 and 1319, Ockham wrote a commentary on Peter Lombard's *Sentences*, called the *Ordinatio* on Book I and the *Reportatio* on Books II-IV. He moved from the field of Theology to that of Philosophy during the years 1319-1324, writing the above-mentioned *Summa Logicae* and a commentary on Aristotle's *Physics*.

ation of children, the contracting of matrimony or observing virginity, and such others." In this original state all property was held in common, and it followed that the right to own property was a "natural right."[65] A question not directly addressed is how this equality is related to women. Were they included in the concept 'all men'?

A possible clue to Ockham's answer to this question may be found in a subsequent judgment he makes about the meaning of power. He explicitly included women in the power base for society when he argued that "power . . . comes not from above but from below, from the representatives of the people, including laity, both men and women."[66] This attitude of incorporation could be related to the original equality that Ockham previously identified. However, it may also be the case that in a nominalist theory there is no universal 'humanity.' In that case, all individual humans are considered equal, and Ockham simply mentions both men and women to be inclusive. Ockham's emphasis on the reduction of universals to terms, and his shifting of definitions from metaphysical or natural to an abstract consideration of the relation of terms, seem to imply an attitude of gender neutrality. In addition, even though Ockham's method, when used to describe a theory of generation, hinted at a gender polarity theory through its emphasis on privation, in his political texts Ockham also offered some arguments for the fundamental equality of man and woman. This seems to provide some support for a position of gender equality.

In this light it is not surprising that Jean Gerson (b. 1402), an Ockhamist, was one of the ardent supporters of Christine de Pizan (1363-1431); he defended the equality of women and men in French Renaissance humanism and can be considered a strong advocate of gender equality. While the work of Christine de Pizan and Jean Gerson will be studied in considerable detail later in this book, it is important to note here that issues of definition and biology were not as important to these writers as were politics and ethics. The Ockhamist influence tended towards a support of the gender unity rather than the gender polarity position, even though both of these views were hidden behind a more fundamental attitude of gender neutrality.

In 1330 Ockham, a Franciscan, was excommunicated from the Roman Catholic Church, in part because his nominalism seemed to pose a danger to faith; and in 1339 his teachings were prohibited at the University of Paris. Portions of his works were condemned again in 1346 and 1347. However, after his death, Ockham's views gained wide acceptance in France, Germany, and in England. The Chancellor of the University of Paris in the early fifteenth century was an Ockhamist. However, by 1474 Ockham's nominalist views were once again prohibited from being taught at the University of Paris with a recommended return to scholasticism. Then, in a reverse of this condemnation, in 1481 the prohibition was lifted permanently.[67]

---

65. Stephen Chak Tornay, *Ockham: Studies and Selections* (LaSalle, Ill.: Open Court Publishing Company, 1938), p. 80.

66. Tornay, *Ockham*, p. 84.

67. Ashworth, *Language and Logic*, p. 6.

This brief study of the theories of Grosseteste, Roger Bacon, and Ockham has demonstrated a consistent orientation of the structure and content of their academic discourse as embodying gender neutrality. It has also been argued that this development was a direct result of the adoption of various aspects of Aristotelian logic, combined with a slow movement towards a more mathematical model for science. Scholars of medieval science note that it was the blend of Neoplatonism and Aristotelian logic that made academic discourse at Oxford University particularly oriented towards a mathematically based science.[68]

At the University of Paris, however, this Neoplatonic influence was lacking. Thus in Paris academic discourse led to a rather different situation for the concept of woman. While in Oxford we had for the most part a practical attitude of gender neutrality, in Paris we will discover instead a theoretically based gender polarity. A purer Aristotle, which rejected Neoplatonic mathematicism, was used to support a realism in all areas of science.[69] In the next section of this chapter we will consider how this kind of Aristotelianism affected the development of the concept of woman at the University of Paris. This section of the chapter will examine the historical roots for this gender polarity as transmitted through the works of Aristotle, and its development in two selected philosophers in the period under study: Giles of Rome and John Duns Scotus. Then at the end of the chapter we will reflect on the ambiguous nature of Aristotle's philosophy, which promoted both a gender neutrality and a gender polarity.

ARISTOTLE'S PRINCIPLES OF GENDER POLARITY

The focus of our analysis will now turn towards the content of subjects taught in the different Faculties, particularly at the University of Paris. Here we will meet Aristotle's philosophical sources for a gender polarity theory that devalues woman. Aristotle was not the only philosopher who influenced thirteenth-century academic discourse about woman's identity. Platonism and Stoicism were also present in modified Aristotelian theories of generation proposed by Avicenna and Galen. Since these authors have been discussed in the first volume of *The Concept of Woman,* we will not repeat the areas of commonality and difference among these other schools here. We will emphasize the role of Aristotle because of his domination of discourse about women in academia, through what we have labeled "the Aristotelian Revolution" in *The Concept of Woman.*

After Aristotle's works were made required reading within the curriculum at the University of Paris in the mid-thirteenth century, students in the Faculty of Arts were then immersed in the Greek philosopher's logic, rhetoric, physics, metaphysics, natural philosophy, ethics, politics, and poetics. Gabriel Compayré summarizes his significance this way: "in a word, all of the greater and lesser works of the Greek philosopher . . . henceforward entered, in their totality and triumphality, into the university schools, to exercise there for several centuries an intellectual domina-

---

68. Wallace, *Causality and Scientific Explanation,* p. 22.
69. Wallace, *Causality and Scientific Explanation,* pp. 65-66.

tion, whose equal it would be impossible to find in the history of human thought."[70]

Aristotle's genius aimed to systematize all of philosophical knowledge into a consistent way of looking at the world. His philosophy was empirical, it was open to the data of the world, and it sought to articulate a coherent set of principles to explain these data. The components of Aristotle's concept of woman were spread throughout his work, though he never wrote a particular text devoted to this subject. This means that students of philosophy picked up components of a theory of gender identity as they studied other arguments in metaphysics, natural philosophy, ethics, and politics.

In *The Concept of Woman: The Aristotelian Revolution (750 BC–1250 AD)* an entire chapter is devoted to providing the references and analysis of the structure and content of Aristotle's concept of woman. Therefore, this information will not be repeated here. Instead, in this part of the chapter the basic outline of Aristotle's original theory of gender polarity will be provided along with paragraph notations to the original texts for those readers who wish to study these sources further. Then we will consider how Aristotle's theory was transmitted and modified as it was first introduced into academia in the thirteenth century. Finally, we will discuss the work of two early fourteenth-century academics, Giles of Rome and John Duns Scotus, who were influenced by Aristotelian thought about woman's identity.

Two sub-themes will be introduced along with this chronological analysis of the ways Aristotle's philosophy shaped the content of thought about woman in academia. The first sub-theme concerns a controversy in which it is suggested that to interpret Aristotle as holding a gender polarity theory is a distortion of the original philosopher's arguments. This controversy erupted[71] several years after the publication of *The Concept of Woman: The Aristotelian Revolution (750 BC–1250 AD)* and so it is important to be addressed before continuing to trace the effects of his theory of gender identity in subsequent authors. The second sub-theme involves a tension derived from different methodologies Aristotle used in different fields of thought. Therefore, in the analysis we will try to indicate the relative weight Aristotle gives to a particular claim about woman's identity, namely whether he was making a universal claim or a qualified claim.

When Aristotle's theory of gender identity was first described in Volume I of *The Concept of Woman,* his arguments and conclusions were traced across four categories of questions that had been raised previously by Presocratic philosophers. These categories were identified as: opposites, generation, wisdom, and virtue. Aristotle answered central questions in each of these four categories with a basic principle that gathered within it more particular judgments. It is my view that he also attempted to make these four principles cohere with one another as well. Similar to his aim in all areas of philosophy, Aristotle brought a logical order to his reflections on sex and gender identity.

---

70. Gabriel Compayré, *Abelard and the Origin and Early History of Universities* (New York: Greenwood Press, 1969), p. 179.

71. See Brendan Comiskey, Bishop of Ferns, "A Story to Make Some of Us Blush," *The Irish Catholic,* Thursday, April 20, 1995.

The four Presocratic questions, as answered by Aristotelian principles, can be summarized as follows: (1) Are male and female opposite or the same? Answer: A female is opposite, a contrary privation, to the male within the species of human beings. (2) Does what the father and the mother contribute to generation have any implications for their gender identity? Answer: Yes, because the female is, as it were, a "deformed" male. (3) Are women and men wise in the same or different ways? Answer: In different ways, because a woman's deliberative faculty is without authority over her irrational soul. (4) Do men and women have the same or different virtues? Answer: Men may have virtue in perfection while there is a (lesser) measure of virtue proper to women.

While we will consider each of these principles briefly in turn, at this point it is important to note that in each of them considered separately, there is a devaluation of the female in relation to the male. Therefore, when joined together Aristotle's four principles provide a consistent rationale for a gender polarity theory. As the founder of the sex and gender polarity theory, Aristotle was the first philosopher in the West to offer a thorough and consistent foundation for the natural superiority of man over woman.

Before describing in more detail each of Aristotle's answers to the four fundamental questions about the concept of woman, I would like to make a few general statements about the positive contributions of Aristotle to the search for the truth about woman's identity. The reason for this interjection here is that since the publication of the first volume of *The Concept of Woman,* several readers have drawn the mistaken conclusion that Aristotelian philosophy should be rejected altogether. It is, perhaps, understandable that someone might come to this conclusion because of the far-reaching effects of the Aristotelian theory of sex and gender polarity. However, this would be an error in judgment because there are many valuable elements in the Aristotelian philosophy that ought to be preserved, such as the form/matter distinction, the understanding of the human being as a soul/body unity, an empirical approach towards knowledge, a metaphysical realism, and an emphasis on the importance of virtue in the development of human character, to name a few.

At the same time, the ancient Greek philosopher's theory of gender polarity does pose a particular challenge to Aristotelians. If all the roots of gender polarity are extracted from his philosophy, then some new principles will need to be articulated to offer a thorough explanation for sex and gender differentiation consistent with contemporary scientific evidence. What principle can replace the principle of contrariety that Aristotle uses to explain how a single seed in the human species becomes either a male or female child? Those persons who want to preserve the Aristotelian approach to all of reality need to consider what Aristotle would say today if he knew what we know about human generation. With this kind of an orientation toward the philosopher's theory, let us now enter into a summary of his particular concept of woman.

A Female Is Opposite as a Contrary Privation of the Male

Students in the new University of Paris in the thirteenth century would have discovered reflections on woman's identity in the midst of their required studies of the Aristotelian corpus. The Presocratic philosophers tried to explain generation and passing away as partly the result of the interaction of opposites. In a review of the Pythagoreans (c. 530 B.C.) in the first book of his *Metaphysics,* Aristotle lists male and female as a category of opposites within ten pairs of opposites (limited and unlimited, one and many, male and female, odd and even, right and left, rest and motion, straight and curved, good and bad, light and dark, and square and oblong).[72] In this list of the ancient Greek source there is just a hint of devaluation of the second member of the pair of opposites.

Then, in Book X, Chapter 9 of the *Metaphysics* Aristotle elaborates his own understanding that "female and male are contrary and their difference is a contrariety" (1058a 30-31). Here the philosopher struggles to explain the principle of gender differentiation. If form is the principle of differentiation between two species, human beings and horses, for example, and if matter is the principle of differentiation between two members of the same species, one man and another man, for example, then what metaphysical principle explains the differentiation between males and females within the same human species? Aristotle recognized that there needs to be some way to explain how the species is divided into two different kinds of individuals. Thus gender is introduced as a metaphysical problem in the heart of Aristotle's form/matter distinction.

The philosopher concludes that form cannot be the principle of distinction between man and woman because form distinguishes one species from another, and men and women belong to the same human species, that is, they have the same form. The principle he is looking for turns out to be contrariety; it operates in the matter of a human being by virtue of its being an animal (1058a 32-34). It is in the meaning of contrariety that we begin to discover Aristotle's metaphysical grounds for the devaluation of woman.

According to Aristotle, in the relation of contrariety of two opposites, one is prime and the other is always privative (1055b 25-29). For example, dark is the contrary privation of light, and cold is the contrary privation of hot. The privation implies a lack in relation to the prime opposite, or a negative passivity (1055b 16). In Book I, Chapter 9 of *Physics,* the study of nature that preceded the *Metaphysics,* Aristotle had tried to explain the meaning of contrariety in a discussion of the relation of form and matter. Criticizing Plato's description of the mother receptacle in the *Timaeus* (50d-51a) as an empty void waiting to generate with the insertion of forms, Aristotle concludes that if we concentrate our attention on this negative metaphysical principle of Plato, namely, on the contrariety of matter as a mother, it seems to be an evil agent (a privation of a good) that tends towards non-existence (192a 13-15). Instead, Aristotle argues that matter is something, not an empty nothing, and that it desires its contrary, or form. Aristotle's conclusion in the *Physics* is as follows:

> For admitting with them that there is something divine, good, and desirable, we
> hold that there are two other principles, the one contrary to it, the other such as

---

72. For a good discussion of the roots of Aristotle's frequent appeal to opposites, see G. E. R. Lloyd, *Polarity and Analogy: Two Types of Argumentation in Early Greek Thought* (Cambridge: Cambridge University Press, 1966), pp. 15-171.

of its own nature to desire and yearn for it. . . . The truth is that what desires the form is matter, as the female desires the male and the ugly the beautiful — only the ugly or the female not *per se* but *per accidens* (192a 16-18, 23-24).

In his text *On the Heavens,* Aristotle suggests that the principle of contrariety may also involve a tendency towards hostile interaction (286a 33-35). Since Aristotle explicitly states that the female is the contrary privation of the male we could call this the metaphysical principle for Aristotle's theory of gender polarity.

The Female Is, as It Were, a Deformed Male

In the same important section of Book X, Chapter 9 of *Metaphysics* Aristotle states that the principle of contrariety explains a fundamental aspect of his theory of generation: "This is why the same seed becomes female or male by being acted on in a certain way" (1058b 23). Crucial here is Aristotle's hypothesis that there is only one fertile seed provided in generation, that this seed is provided by the father, and that it contains the immaterial form of the human child. Further, he argues that this immaterial form will actively shape the material provided by the mother into a male child that resembles the father, unless something interferes with it. In Aristotle's argument the father contributes to the embryo an immaterial form, while the mother supplies all the material. Thus his principle of contrariety explains how the single seed of the father, which contains the immaterial form of the child, becomes a male or a female depending on how it is acted upon.

A student of philosophy would have encountered these theories in a study of Aristotle's *Generation of Animals, Parts of Animals,* and *History of Animals.* Ancient Greek theories of generation used categories of opposites to explain how females and males were generated. The Pythagorean association of male and female with right and left was found in Parmenides (c. 539-500 B.C.), who argued that there was a relation between the position of the seed and the left side of the uterus and the left testicle with the generation of females, and the right side of the uterus and right testicle with males. This association of right and left with male and female generation was repeated by Anaxagoras (500-428 B.C.).

Democritus (c. 460-370 B.C.) introduced a new concept into the relation of sex identity to generation: that of dominance and subordination. Empedocles (c. 450 B.C.) suggested that a man and a woman each provide half of the seed in conception. He also mentioned the role of heat in the generation of males, and of cold with the generation of females. In the Hippocratean writings (c. 460-377 B.C.) all three pairs of opposites (left and right, hot and cold, strong and weak) were mentioned in relation to the generation of male and female. Aristotle chose to emphasize 'hot and cold' as the key pair of opposites that established a difference between the male and female when he stated that "[m]ale animals are hotter than female ones . . ."; and he linked this coldness of the female nature to an inability (765b 10-18).[73]

---

73. Aristotle, *Generation of Animals* (Cambridge, Mass. and London: Harvard University Press and William Heinemann, 1943).

Aristotle thought that the extra heat in the human male gave him an ability to heat up or refine his blood until it became released as a fertile seed capable of transmitting the immaterial human form. Thus the male was characterized by heat, an ability, and a fertility. The female, being colder by nature, could not heat up and refine her blood to produce fertile seed containing form; instead her blood became the material for generation. Thus the female was characterized by coldness, an inability, and infertility. Aristotle thought that this hypothesis explained why a man had less blood in his body than did a woman. He was unaware of the circulation of the blood in the human body and of the fact that both men and women provide half of the needed fertile seed for generation to occur.

Sometimes it is argued that Aristotle's erroneous theory that only the male provides a single fertile seed to generation, was the result of his limited historical context. In other words, Aristotle did the best with what was known at the time. Certainly, empirical evidence for the existence of fertile seed contributed by the woman did not occur until after the birth of the science of anatomy and the invention of the microscope. However, it is worth pointing out that more than one philosopher prior to Aristotle offered the intuitive hypothesis of a double-seed theory. Empedocles suggested that mother and father both provided half of the necessary seed for conception, while Parmenides suggested that each parent provided a single seed that battled for dominance in the conception. Thus Aristotle chose to reject these intuitions of a double-seed theory of generation in favor of his own single-seed theory. It is very likely that his metaphysics of form and matter influenced his decision, together with his acceptance of the Hippocratean premise of the role of heat and cold in generation. Aristotle was drawn to the analogy between form, which is found in many common things, and the way a single male can impregnate many females; while the matter receives the form the way a woman receives the seed of the male in conception. In addition, just as he claimed that form is completely non-material, he posited that the male contributed nothing material to generation. The extreme differentiation of male and female contribution to generation certainly had a parallel in his metaphysical distinction between form and matter.

At this point we must reflect on Aristotle's methodology. In the philosophy of nature Aristotle often introduced qualifications of his premises. When he depicts the female as an infertile male, on account of an inability of a sort, that is, the coldness of her nature, Aristotle inserts the significant phrase "as it were" (728a 13-27). He says: "the female is, as it were, an infertile male." The qualification to the general statement is obviously meant to indicate something to the reader. Given the devaluation of the female contained in the notion of being infertile or having an inability, we understand what Aristotle was trying to indicate. In this case, it seems unlikely that this qualification is a suggestion that there might be some exceptions to his hypothesis. Rather, Aristotle seems to offer a comparative evaluation of male and female, while he also indicates that it should be qualified in some way. In other words, the male is taken as the prime member of the species, and the female is then described as the contrary privation of the male within the same species. Therefore, she is described in relation to the prime, as it were, with negative or privative terms. He is fertile, she is infertile; he has an ability, she has an inability; and he is hot, she lacks heat and is cold. It is important to note Aristotle's method here because we will see in later transmissions of his thought that his careful qualifications are dropped.

In the *Generation of Animals* Aristotle offers a universal description of the different contributions of man and woman to generation when he uses terms such as 'always' and 'specific characteristic' of one or the other sex: "The female always provides the material, the male that which fashions the material into shape; this, in our view, is the specific characteristic of each sex" (738b 20-25). In another passage, when he turns to the actual moment of impregnation and conception itself, the philosopher seems to offer another universal definition that "the female, *qua* female, is passive, and the male *qua* male is active — it is that whence the principle of movement comes" (729b 15-20). However, he also offers a qualification immediately following this passage, when he reflects on the fact that **if** he takes the widest formulation of the two opposites and regards the male as active and causing movement and the female as passive and being set in motion, **then** he can compare them with a carpenter and a piece of wood being formed, or a piece of wax and the form in the seal (729b 15-20). The qualification is interesting here, too, for Aristotle seems to suggest that this is an extreme description of the contrary opposites, male and female. In this widest formulation of the contraries, they become almost abstractions of their actual identity. In fact, in another definition in *Generation of Animals* Aristotle offers a distinction between two different kinds of generative activities when he says that "By 'male' animal we mean one which generates in another, by 'female' one which generates in itself" (716a 9-17). This implies that both the male and female are active in generation.

At this point I would like to introduce the topic of a controversy Mgr. Michael Nolan has recently raised in an article entitled: "Passive and Deformed? Did Aristotle Really Say This?"[74] He suggests that Aristotle did not really mean that the woman is passive with respect to generation, but rather that she is the passive principle in that she is the one fertilized by the male in an enzyme type of action in which the male seed 'sets' the female's uniquely formed menstrual blood. Other than this, her role is to be active throughout generation. He argues that all Aristotle suggests is that the female part at the beginning of generation is to offer the passive principle of her menstrual blood, but woman herself is active in generation once the process has begun.

Mgr. Nolan raises an important point, especially in view of many philosophers following Aristotle who suggest that Aristotle described woman's identity as passive and man's identity as active. In the above-quoted passages of Aristotle we noted that he did qualify his hypotheses of the association of passivity with the female and activity with the male by adding that he was taking the wisest possible formulation of the opposites female and male, and that he was describing them *qua* female and *qua* male. Clearly this is an abstraction that may simply describe one moment in the process of generation, that of fertilization, or as Aristotle thought, of setting the menstrual blood with the form provided in the male semen. Therefore

---

74. Michael Nolan, *Defective Tales: The Story of Three Myths* (Ireland: Printcomp Ltd., 1995), pp. 20-44. See also Michael Nolan, "The Aristotelian Background to Aquinas' Denial That 'Woman Is a Defective Male,'" *The Thomist* 64 (2000): 21-69.

we need to look for further evidence to support a view that there is a principle of gender polarity that shapes Aristotle's philosophy of generation.

One piece of this evidence may come from the fact that Aristotle's texts often seem to move back and forth between describing a principle of a particular facet of male or female identity and the identity of a man and a woman as an existing being. For example, in the following passage from *Generation of Animals* we read: "Just as mother is the opposite of father as a general term, so also the individual mother is the opposite of the individual father" (768a 8-10). We will also see the same confusion in other examples described below. Is Aristotle himself responsible for this confusion of principle and person? There may be two mitigating factors here. The first is the fact that all of the writings we have by the Greek philosopher were compiled from the notes of students. Any of us who are teachers know how inaccurate this source would be for a construction of our own lectures. The second is the fact that in ancient Greek philosophy the concept of person as a man or a woman was not yet carefully distinguished from its components of male and female identity, even though Aristotle made efforts to do so by his distinctions between accidents or properties and substances. If we accept these two mitigating factors, at least at the outset, then we must pursue the controversy further to determine whether or not Aristotle argued for an inherent devaluation of woman in relation to man.

Let us turn next to the question of how the sex of the child is determined during generation. According to Aristotle, the male seed, if perfectly received by the menstrual fluid of the mother, would produce a male child that resembled the father. It would perfectly receive the immaterial human form as transmitted in his seed. If other conditions interfered such as not enough heat, the effects of the south wind, cold water, age, fluid, or resistance of the material supplied by the mother, then the generation changes into its opposite (766b 28-767a 25, 573b 30-574a). The offspring would deviate from the perfect type in degrees ranging from a male child that resembled the mother, a female child that resembled the father, a female child that resembled the mother, or no conception at all (766b 16-20). Since females are generated as a deviation from this prime type, Aristotle suggests, in the *Generation of Animals,* that "the female is as it were a deformed male" (737a 26-30). Here again we discover the qualifier "as it were" placed right in the center of a judgment about the identity of the female in relation to the male.

In the same article cited above, "Passive and Deformed: Did Aristotle Really Say This?" Mgr. Michael Nolan raised a question about the meaning of Aristotle's phrase "the female is as it were a deformed male." He suggests that the Greek philosopher is being misunderstood by later thinkers when they attribute a devaluation of woman to this expression. Mgr. Nolan states that Aristotle used the same word (in transliterated Greek *pepērōménon*), here translated into English as deformed, to describe seals that had no ears. All that deformity means, Mgr. Nolan asserts, is that the kind of being deviated from a type, not that there was anything wrong with it.

To respond to this suggestion, let us explore Aristotle's descriptions of the female and male a little further. There is an evaluation of the male as the properly formed result of generation, intended by the nature of the form in the father's seed that aims to reproduce itself. Also, in Aristotle's teleology form is characterized by act, and actuality is ontologically prior to potentiality. He also suggests a hierarchy of elements in descending order, namely, that of fire, air, water, and earth, and he implies that the opposites hot and dry are superior to cold and moist. All of these aspects of the Aristotelian way of thinking about the world contain an inherent evaluation of certain things as superior to others. So when we read a passage such as: ". . . because females are weaker and colder in their nature; and we should look upon the female state as being as it were a deformity, though one which occurs in the ordinary course of nature" (775a 12-16), there is a sense that Aristotle is not simply ascribing an equal value to the male and to the female. Rather he seems to consider the male as naturally superior.

Again Mgr. Michael Nolan presses the argument that the meaning of the word 'nature' has been misunderstood to include a larger reference than simply the nature of the seed itself. This is also an important point to consider. He suggests that in the claims that the male intends by nature to reproduce itself and that the female state is a deformity that occurs in the ordinary course of nature, Aristotle is simply implying that it is the nature of form to produce itself, and since the human form in the seed of the father takes the male form as the prime human form, it aims to reproduce itself. It is the nature of male seed, and neither the nature of man nor the intention of nature as a general ordering principle. The generation of the female is simply a changing of the prime form in the male seed into its opposite — the female. The implication that the female is a devalued kind of deformity, Nolan claims, is due to a later problem with translation of the Greek word *pepērōménon* into Latin and English.

While translations, as they are transmitted throughout the centuries, do appear to make the Aristotelian grounds for gender polarity incrementally worse, we suggest that there are passages in Aristotle's corpus that also lend themselves to the conclusion that Aristotle's philosophy devaluated woman in relation to man. In one passage, which develops the analogy between the male with form, and the female with matter, we find Aristotle reflecting on the relation between the superiority of a man and his role as active cause in generation:

> As the proximate and motive cause, to which belong the *logos* and the form, is better and more divine in its nature than the matter, it is better also that the superior one should be separate from the inferior one. That is why whenever possible and so far as is possible the male is separated from the female, since it is something better and more divine in that it is the principle of movement for generated things, while the female serves as their matter (732a 5-10).[75]

Here the qualities of the nature of form as active, efficient cause, better, more divine, and superior are linked with the male identity and the nature of matter as inferior with the female identity. This linkage appears to support the conclusion that Aristotle is offering a theory of gender polarity. The suggestion that male is sepa-

---

75. Mgr. Nolan does cite this passage, but confesses he does not know how to explain its apparent ranking of superiority and inferiority.

rated from female because of this difference may be simply a reflection of the way that male seed is generated, or, less likely, it may include reference to the practice of the separation of genders into public and private domains of activity.

In another example, we move to a further phase in the process of human generation. We have considered how gender is evaluated in terms of the different contributions of man and woman to generation, and how gender is evaluated in terms of the different ways that the sex of the child generated is determined. Now we turn to consider how the gender-differentiated child develops as a male or female human being. In the following passage we find polarity entering into a description of the growth and perfection of males and females.

> For while still within the mother, the female takes longer to develop than the male does; though once birth has taken place everything reaches its perfection sooner in female than in males — e.g., puberty, maturity, old age — because females are weaker and colder in their nature; and we should look upon the female state as being as it were a deformity, though one which occurs in the ordinary course of nature (775a 12-16).

Again we have the qualifier, "as it were," in the description of the female state as a deformity that occurs in the ordinary course of nature. However, the phrase "weaker . . . in their nature" offers a further clue for our reflections. Even though Aristotle suggests here that females reach a perfection in their identity faster than males, which certainly is a common observation about puberty even today, Aristotle explains this by using a category that devalues the female in relation to the male. The basic colder nature of females, as a privative, contrary of the hotter male, results in her being less well formed as a rational animal. We could say that there are degrees of perfection, and the perfect female is a less perfect rational animal than the perfect male. Thus, the principle that the female is as it were a deformed male is fundamental to the gender polarity of Aristotle's natural philosophy.

The devaluation of the female found in the metaphysical principle that the female is a contrary privation of the male also appears in many different forms in Aristotle's writings in natural philosophy. At the very least we find the male contribution to generation associated with the divine — activity, form, heat, strength, fertility, and ability — while the female contribution is associated with deformation, passivity, matter, cold, weakness, infertility, and inability. If we conclude that Aristotle extends this valuation beyond a consideration simply of the female and male contributions to generation to the very identity of a man and a woman, we have philosophical foundations for a thorough and consistent gender polarity theory. In this case, a woman herself becomes thought of as a deformed or defective man. Since the whole question of such an extension from female principle to a woman and from male principle to a man is controversial, we will search for more evidence. If we turn to further Aristotelian texts that students in thirteenth-century academia would have studied, and that contain Aristotle's thoughts about wisdom and virtue, we may find some more clues to its answer.

A Woman's Rational Faculty Is without
Authority over Her Irrational Soul

In his *Politics,* Aristotle describes differences in the operation of the human soul in man, a woman, a slave, and a child. For Aristotle an existing human being is a unity of soul and body, or human form, as the act of the material body. In this context he says that "[a]lthough the parts of the soul are present in all of them, they are present in different degrees. For the slave has no deliberative faculty at all; the woman has [a deliberative faculty], but it is without authority, and the child has, but it is immature" (1260a 1-5). The principle that the parts of the soul are present in different degrees in different kinds of human beings is the foundation for Aristotle's gender differentiation in the category of wisdom.

There is a coherence between this principle and the previous two principles that the female is the contrary privation of the male and is a deformed male. Because of her lack of heat and her weakness, woman achieves her perfection faster. Since the rational soul partakes more of the nature of *logos* or the perfection of form, it seems logical in the Aristotelian schema that woman's rational soul would be less fully developed. Thus, she would not be able to exercise her deliberative faculty as well as a man. Aristotle thought that this weaker development had the consequence that a woman lacked authority over her irrational soul. She was not able to govern herself well through the exercise of her discursive reason in the activity of deliberation. This could be called Aristotle's epistemological principle of gender polarity.

In Book IX of the *History of Animals* Aristotle lists certain characteristics that are found more in women than in men. Many of them seem to indicate a certain irrationality. After stating that a man's nature is more perfect and complete, Aristotle describes woman as "more easily prone to tears, more jealous, more querulous, more apt to scold and to strike . . . , more prone to despondency, . . . more false of speech, more deceptive, . . . of more retentive memory, . . . and more difficult to rouse to action" (608b 6-14). These descriptions do not imply a necessary connection between women's identity and these more irrational behaviors. However, they do indicate some practical evidence for the theoretical principle articulated in the *Politics.*

For the Greek philosopher, it is a feature of woman's nature that her rational faculty is without authority over her irrational soul. The argument that there is a natural principle that befits the male to rule and the female to obey is repeated by Aristotle in different places in his corpus. In fact, he traces human knowledge of this natural principle to an observation of the human soul when he states explicitly:

> Here the very constitution of the soul has shown us the way; in it one part naturally rules, and the other is subject, and the virtue of the ruler we maintain to be different from the subject — the one being the virtue of the rational and the other of the irrational part. Now, it is obvious that the same principle applies generally, and therefore almost all things rule and are ruled according to nature . . . the male rules over the female . . . (1260a 4-12).[76]

76. Aristotle in this passage from the *Politics* also contrasts different kinds of rule — of master/slave and father/child.

As indicated by the qualifier "almost all" in the above quotation, Aristotle does allow some exceptions to this epistemological principle. Thus the principle does not admit to the universality of the metaphysical principle of contrariety and the generative principle of deformation of the female. In these first two principles there is no exception noted. Female is always a contrary opposite of male, and every female is as it were a deformed male. To the epistemological principle that a woman's deliberative faculty does not have authority over her irrational soul Aristotle notes some exceptions. In the context of a discussion of the husband's constitutional rule over his wife he concludes: "[f]or although there may be exceptions to the order of nature, the male is more fitted for command than the female" (1259b 8-9).

It may be asked whether Aristotle was simply describing a situation in the world in which men had a greater aptitude for ruling. In this case he would not be trying to establish grounds for a theory of gender polarity that devalues the female. To answer this query we need to give some consideration to more passages from the *Politics* in which he more clearly indicates his fundamental principles. In the following passage the epistemological roots for gender polarity are evident:

> It is clear that the rule of the soul over the body and of the mind and the rational element over the passionate, is natural and expedient; whereas the equality of the two or the rule of the inferior is always hurtful. . . . Again, the male is by nature superior and the female inferior; and the one rules, and the other is ruled; this principle, of necessity, extends to all mankind (1254b 5-15).

In this passage, Aristotle universally extends his principle to include reference to all women and all men. Thus, what had appeared at first to be a more flexible attitude, allowing exceptions, now turns out to be more of a fundamental principle of gender identity. The structure of the rational and irrational soul, and the natural superiority of the rational soul with its capacity to govern through deliberation, are in a direct analogy with the natural ability of men and women to rule. Contravention of this fundamental principle is, he says, always hurtful.

To make certain that the universality of the principle is grasped, Aristotle actually introduces an exception, that of a society in which a woman rules. In the context of this discussion in which he considers whether a man rules by virtue of his natural superiority or some other grounds, he notes that in an oligarchy sometimes women rule. However, he adds that in this case "their rule is not in virtue of excellence, but due to wealth and power . . ." (1161a 2). So we find here the underlying premise of a natural superiority in man that enables him to rule, and a natural inferiority in woman. The rule of a woman must be explained by some other principle than her natural ability to govern well.

Since woman's rational faculty is weaker than man's, and since it does not have authority over her irrational nature, Aristotle concludes that a woman is wise in different ways than a man. As we saw above, in the *Politics* Aristotle suggested that there is a virtue particularly associated with rationality and another with the irrational. The virtue of the rational is to rule, and the virtue of the irrational is to obey (1260a 6-10). In shifting from the virtue of particular parts of the soul to the virtue of particular kinds of human beings, he stated that "[p]ractical wisdom is characteristic only of the ruler. . . . The virtue of the subject is certainly not wisdom, but only true opinion" (1277b 27-30). This view was repeated in *Metaphysics* with the prescription that "[t]he wise man must not be ordered but must order, and he must not obey another, but the less wise obey him" (982a 18-20).

As we saw above, Aristotle also introduced a valuation of superiority of a ruler along with a gender-differentiated description of the ruler when he said that "[t]he male is by nature superior, and the female inferior; and the one rules, and the other is ruled" (1254b 15). It followed from these fundamental principles that the proper epistemological virtue of a woman is true opinion, while the proper epistemological virtue of a man is practical wisdom. Basically, what this means is that a woman is wise by grasping true principles without knowing the reasons why they are true. This is a kind of intuitive knowledge or art gained from experience. The science of practical wisdom involves the use of the deliberative faculty, in syllogistic reasoning, to grasp why something is true. A wise man not only grasps why something is true, but can explain the causes of a thing.

True opinion simply grasps that something is true, but does not know why. True opinion, which is attributed to women, is therefore unstable and it lends the person who has it to be more prone to error. Not all men have practical wisdom, and some men also, like women, are virtuous by true opinion. Aristotle seems to suggest, however, that all women are virtuous through true opinion because of the less perfect formation of their reason, their weaker nature, and the natural lack of authority of their deliberative faculty over their irrational soul. This is why Aristotle suggests that a wise woman should obey a wise man. Then her opinions would more likely be true because they would be grounded on the practical wisdom or science of a wise man, rather than be simply left to her own weaker thought processes.

A Lesser Measure of Virtue Is Proper to Women

In the *Politics,* immediately after he had said that the male who is superior rules and the female who is inferior is ruled, Aristotle postulates a descending measure of virtue proper to both men and women. In this discussion the philosopher explicitly rejects the premise put forward by Socrates and Plato in the *Republic* that women and men have exactly the same measure of virtue. He also connects his argument with his previous description of the higher functions of the human soul:

> Hence the ruler ought to have moral virtue in perfection, for his function, taken absolutely, demands a master, artificer, and rational principle as such an artificer; the subjects, on the other hand, require only that measure of virtue proper to each of them. Clearly, then, moral virtue belongs to all of them, but the temperance of a man and of a woman, or the courage and justice of a man and of a woman, are not, as Socrates maintained, the same; the courage of a man is shown in commanding, of a woman in obeying (1245b 16-25).

This view that a man can have virtue in perfection, while a woman has a lesser measure proper to her can be called Aristotle's ethical principle of gender polarity.

It might be asked if Aristotle's qualifier in the above passage, namely, that he is taking the function of ruler absolutely, indicates that this principle is an abstraction rather than an actual description of men and women. The connection between function and virtue or excellence in Aristotle's philosophy is very important to our consideration. In a general way, we could say that if we know the nature or function of something, then we can identify its virtue. Thus if it is the function of a knife to cut, then a good knife cuts well. Similarly, if it is the nature or function of a human being to be a rational animal, then a good human being is one who reasons well, or one who exercises his deliberative faculty with authority over both himself and others. This is why the ruler's function, taken absolutely, demands someone capable of perfectly exercising his rational faculty in governing.

Aristotle does not think that women never practice the virtue of ruling. In fact he argues that in governing a household a man should share his authority with his wife (1160b 33–1161a 2). In this case, the woman would rule over children and servants. Therefore, the woman can learn how to exercise her deliberative faculty in her own private sphere of authority in the household when she understands the reasons for her decisions. However, her virtue is a lesser form of governing, as she does not rule over her husband; and her authority rests on his governing authority, not on her own.

Therefore, women, who are not by nature rulers, but only share in the governing authority of their husbands, have a different function and measure of virtue. Their virtues are, in a way, lesser human virtues. This is why there is a devaluation of the female in Aristotle's ethics. This devaluation shows up in various ways, for example, in the use and lack of use of women as an example in Book VII of the *Nicomachean Ethics*. We may here be discovering the same phenomena we first saw in discussions of examples in Aristotle's logical texts. In the context of the Peripatetic school, in which women were not students of philosophy, women were not often used as examples. However, in the context in which Aristotle considers six different categories of character, he mentions women as an example only in the last two: unrestraint and bestiality. In the first example, he argues that we would not call a woman incontinent just because she has a passive part to play in copulation (1148b 31–1149a 1). In the second example, he considers a woman who devours infants in the wombs of pregnant women as so evil as to be outside ethical principles (1148b 20-21).

Aristotle certainly is not excluding women from the category of virtues; he just thinks that women have a lesser measure of virtue proper to them. In his methodology in his book on ethics Aristotle is careful to state that he is offering only rough and non-absolute conclusions about things that are only for the most part true (1094b 19-23). However, as we can see in the following reflection from the *Poetics* on the relation between goodness and character, Aristotle's qualified conclusions carry with them a clear suggestion of gender polarity. In a context in which he is arguing that characters in a drama ought to have a quality of goodness, he says that "goodness is possible in every type of personage, even a woman . . . though [she] is perhaps an inferior . . . being" (1454a 16-23). Here again we find an Aristotelian qualifier "perhaps." It suggests that the philosopher is offering a hypothesis about relative measures of goodness, but that he is not giving any absolute judgment. Nonetheless, the hypothesis of the inferiority of the being of woman is consistent with the principles of gender polarity that occur throughout his works.

In two further specific areas Aristotle suggests a different measure of virtue for men and for women. The first concerns speech and the second friendship. In the first chapter of this book we introduced the notion of a community of discourse. In this context we discovered how speech, especially through dialogue in the context of spiritual friendships, was an important forum for the development of woman's self-knowledge and self-governance. For Aristotle, public speech was an important virtue for a man who participated in the *polis*. Speech and dialogue permeated by reason and by deliberation was the way of building the political city-state, as the highest form of community. Public participation with others in this political activity was referred to by Aristotle as the highest good. In Aristotle's philosophy women were excluded from this participation both in theory and in practice.[77]

This exclusion can be seen first in Aristotle's description of women's lesser measure of participation in the common good through exercising the virtue of speaking well. In Book I of the *Politics,* following the passage in which the philosopher described woman's deliberative faculty as not having authority in her soul and her virtue as being to obey and not to rule, Aristotle extended this different measure of virtue to the domain of speech. "All classes must be deemed to have their special attributes; as the poet says of women, 'Silence is a woman's glory,' but this is not equally the glory of man'" (1260b 28-31). The man is the prime model of virtue with respect to speech according to Aristotle, and the woman is a model of virtue relative to the man. Like the contraries hot and cold, the woman's virtue is a privative measure in the same class.

In his *Rhetoric* and in his description of dialectic, Aristotle puts forward the proper and effective characteristics of good speech in a man. Effective public speech is the virtue of a good man, while silence in the public realm is a virtue for a good woman. As we will discover in subsequent chapters, this particular Aristotelian conclusion will form the shape of evaluation of men's discourse and women's discourse for centuries to come. Eventually, religious and humanist women writers began to challenge this claim by word and deed outside of academia. Barring the few exceptions of orations or public ceremonies at which women spoke, women's voices remained mostly silent in universities until nearly twenty-five hundred years after Aristotle. This particular attitude of exclusion of women from public academic discourse was a characteristic of the Peripatetic School of Aristotle from its first beginnings. While previous to Aristotle there had been women philosophers in the Pythagorean community and in Plato's Academy, there appears to be no evidence of women in Aristotle's school.

The second area in which Aristotle expands on a different measure of virtue for women and for men is that of friendship. He states that woman is the unequal friend of man. Friendship is one of the most important virtues in Aristotle's

---

77. Jean Bethke Elshtain summarizes very well the relation of woman to this ideal of the political in her section "Man's Politics, Woman's Privatization: Aristotle," in *Public Man, Private Woman: Women in Social and Political Thought* (Princeton: Princeton University Press, 1981), pp. 41-54.

Nicomachean Ethics; in it one friend acts for the good of the other. A virtuous friendship is a mutual participation in a life of virtue for the good of society at large. While Aristotle recognizes that there is a natural basis for friendship of husband and wife, he argues that because "there is an inequality between the parties," theirs is a friendship of inequality. He continues: "[f]or the virtue and the function of each of these are different, and so are the reasons for which they love; the love and the friendship are therefore different also" (1158b 13-20). It is significant that in this context Aristotle states that the virtue and function of husband and wife are different, and that is why their friendship is one of inequality. For the virtue relates to ruling and obeying and the function to using their reason well within the engendered capacities that each one has as a rational animal.

Aristotle concludes that because woman is the unequal friend of man in a relationship of justice, she ought to give more affection to man as the superior partner than he would give to her.[78] In his articulation of the foundation for this different relation to justice, Aristotle once again reveals the gender polarity within his understanding of the relative value of woman's identity and man's identity. In his own words: "In all friendships implying inequality the love also should be proportional, i.e., the better should be more loved than he loves . . . ; for when the love is in proportion to the merit of the parties, then in a sense arises equality, which is certainly held to be characteristic of friendship" (1158b 24-29).

In conclusion, Aristotle seems to argue that man is a superior kind of human being. He is better by nature; and he has a greater perfection of virtue. Woman is an inferior kind of human being. Therefore, she has a lesser measure of virtue. These are the ethical foundations for Aristotle's gender polarity theory. We have identified four fundamental principles of gender polarity in the Aristotelian corpus, and these four principles are coherent with one another. In addition, we have indicated that, even though Aristotle did offer qualifications in his evaluations to his general descriptions of differences between male and female, father and mother, and man and woman, these qualifiers did not overturn his basis for selection of the male as the superior kind of human being and of the female as the inferior kind of human being. This pattern occurred in all four categories of statements about opposites, generation, wisdom, and virtue.

Aristotle's gender polarity theory has the following four principles of foundation: metaphysical principle, natural principle, epistemological principle, and ethical principle. Each of these principles gathers sub-principles within it. In the following summary the principles and sub-principles are listed by category. Where Aristotle offered a qualification of the principle or sub-principle in his original text, this is included in [ ]:

78. See also Aristotle, *Eudemian Ethics* 1238b 15–1242b 22.

ARISTOTLE'S FOUR PRINCIPLES OF GENDER POLARITY

Metaphysical Principle: The female is the contrary privation of the male	
Male	**Female**
The male is opposite as a prime.	The female is opposite as a lack.
The male is hotter.	The female is colder.
The male is associated more with properties of form.	The female is associated more with properties of matter.
The male is like something divine, good, and desirable.	The female desires the male (as matter desires form and the ugly the beautiful) *per accidens*.
The male, *qua* male, is active [if taken in the widest formulation of opposites].	The female, *qua* female, is passive [if taken in the widest formulation of opposites].

Natural Principle: The female is [as it were] a deformed male	
Male	**Female**
The male has an ability to concoct seed.	The female has an inability to concoct seed.
The male is fertile.	The female is infertile.
The male provides (non-material) form to generation.	The female provides matter to generation.
The male result of generation is the prime type.	The female result of generation is a deviation from type.
The male result of generation achieves the intention of the form in the seed.	The female result of generation is [as it were] a deformed male.
The male state is intended by nature.	The female state is [as it were] a deformity that occurs in the course of nature.
The male fetus develops more perfectly.	The female fetus develops less perfectly.
The male child's function or rational faculty reaches its greater perfection later.	The female child's function or rational faculty reaches its limited perfection sooner.

Epistemological Principle: A woman's rational faculty has less authority in her soul than does a man's rational faculty in his soul	
Male	Female
A man's reason may have authority over his irrational soul.	A woman's reason is without authority over her irrational soul.
A man is wise through exercise of his deliberative faculty in syllogistic reasoning.	A woman [as subject] is wise by having true opinions.
A man is wise in ruling over women and others.	A woman is wise by obeying a wise man.

Ethical principle: A woman [as subject] has a lesser measure of virtue than does a man	
Male	Female
Almost all men rule by nature.	Almost all women obey by nature.
The male is by nature superior and rules [of necessity].	The female is by nature inferior and is ruled [of necessity] as the rule of the inferior is always hurtful.
A man is more fitted [with some exceptions] for command.	A woman is less fitted [in the order of nature with some exceptions] for command.
A man who rules does so in virtue of excellence.	A woman who rules by exceptions does so by power or wealth.
A man has the goodness of a superior kind of being.	A woman has the goodness of a [perhaps] inferior kind of being.
A virtuous man engages in public speech.	A virtuous woman is silent (does not engage in speech) in public.
A virtuous man participates in building the *polis*.	A virtuous woman does not participate in building the *polis*.
A virtuous man (husband) is the unequal superior friend of woman (wife).	A virtuous woman (wife) is the unequal inferior friend of man (husband).

With this summary of the original Aristotelian arguments about gender identity we can now turn to consider how Aristotle's foundations for gender polarity were transmitted and changed as they moved from ancient Greece into the center of the late medieval European University system. Here we will run into another controversy about the translation or mistranslation of the term that purportedly described the female as a deformed male.

PHASES OF TRANSLATIONS AND MODIFICATIONS OF ARISTOTLE'S VOICE

The transmission of Aristotle's philosophy to the universities in the West had a very dramatic history.[79] While details of this transmission were recorded in *The Concept of Woman: The Aristotelian Revolution (750 BC–1250 AD)*, a brief summary will be presented here. After the death of Aristotle, there was a striking historical eagerness to learn about the thought of this Greek philosopher who had brought a new genius of depth and organization to the empirical search for truth about the world. At the same time, his wider framework of philosophy also included errors in both fact and theory about woman's identity.

Our summary will loosely delineate seven phases in the transmission of Aristotelian philosophy from the time it was first articulated by Aristotle in fourth-century B.C. Athens until it was solidly entrenched as the most important philosophy in the thirteenth-century European university curriculum.

First Phase (300-200 B.C.), Greek commentaries by Peripatetics: From the very beginning, philosophers taught Aristotle to their students by writing commentaries on his works, paragraph by paragraph, line by line. This practice ensured that the central concepts and arguments of the philosopher were carefully transmitted. In addition, the commentator could indicate the connection between passages in different locations of his corpus. This practice of linking together Aristotle's arguments emphasized the overall consistency of the philosopher's thought and methodology. The first commentaries, written in Greek in the Peripatetic School, were developed by Aristotle's disciple Theophrastus and later by Alexander of Aphrodisias.

Integrating these Aristotelian commentaries with the thought of Plato, Greek and Roman Stoics began to elaborate their own philosophy. Most notable for the concept of woman was the work of the Stoic physician Galen (131-201), who both transmitted and modified Aristotle's theory of generation. Galen argued that the female was colder and less perfect than the male, and that while the female did contribute seed to generation, her seed was actually an infertile glandular secretion that had no active role in generation. Galen's medical work was an extremely important source of information about Aristotle's natural principles for woman's identity right up to their incorporation into the curriculum in the Faculty of Medicine at the University of Paris in the thirteenth century.

---

79. See Fernand van Steenberghen, *Aristotle in the West: The Origins of Latin Averroism* (Louvain: E. Nauwelaerts and Verlag Herder, 1959).

Second Phase (200-500 A.D.), Greek Commentaries by Neoplatonists: Plutarch (46-125) initiated a revival of Platonism at the same time he transmitted Aristotle's natural principle, namely that woman's seed has no active part in generation because of the coldness of her nature. Plotinus (205-270), who studied and taught Greek philosophy in Alexandria, brought a mixture of Plato's thought and especially Aristotle's metaphysics to his own theories. Plotinus then transmitted this mixture of Greek sources when he opened a school of philosophy in Rome in 244. He also adopted Aristotle's metaphysical principle that the female is the privation of the male. Later Porphyry (233-305), who had first studied in Athens, moved to Rome and studied for six years with Plotinus. Then he wrote a complete text on embryology, *Pros Gauron,* modifying Aristotle's natural principle by giving woman a secondary formative role in generation. Porphyry also wrote *Isagoge,* a major commentary on Aristotle's *Categories.*

Third Phase (400-600), Translations into Syriac and Latin: From the beginning of this period in history, Aristotle's texts in logic were translated into other languages than Greek. The *Categories* were translated into Syriac, and Boethius (480-524) translated Aristotle's *Categories, De Interpretatione, Prior Analytics, Posterior Analytics, Topics* and Porphyry's *Isagoge* into Latin. These treatises were joined together into a common corpus of Aristotle's logic known as the *Organon.* In this phase of transmission, the *Organon* was the first set of Aristotle's works made available to Latin medieval scholars.

Through these Latin texts Aristotle's logic started to be integrated into centers of Christian education before the foundation of universities. The practical application of Aristotle's *Organon* was implemented by St. Anselm (1033-1109) in the Benedictine monastic tradition and by Peter Abelard (1079-1142) in the development of the scholastic method in the Cathedral School in Paris.

Fourth Phase (800-1200), Translations into Arabic: During this fourth phase most of Aristotle's works, with the exception of the *Politics* and *Eudemian Ethics,* were translated into Arabic. Islamic philosophers became convinced that Aristotle's philosophy could provide the foundation for a new Islamic philosophy. Al-Farabi first mingled Aristotle and Plato into a single philosophical system. Then Avicenna (930-1037) wrote several commentaries on Aristotelian texts. His *Kitab al-shifa,* an encyclopedia of Aristotelianism, included summaries of the *Organon, Physics, Metaphysics, Generation of Animals, Ethics, Politics,* and *Poetics.* Avicenna transmitted Aristotle's metaphysical, natural, epistemological, and ethical principles of gender polarity through these summaries. However, in the *Canon of Medicine,* following Porphyry, Avicenna gave a greater formative power to the female seed than did Aristotle, who had viewed it as strictly passive. He argued that the male seed had a primary formative power, and the female seed a secondary formative power in generation. This text slightly moderated the Aristotelian natural principle of gender polarity although it also contained elements of gender polarity.

The Islamic philosopher Averroes (1126-1198) reversed in some ways Avicenna's critical evaluation of Aristotle, for he wrote thirty-eight detailed commentaries on the major works of Aristotle as based on Arabic translations of the Syriac texts. His commentaries, twice-removed from the original Greek texts, nonetheless repeated the original philosopher's arguments in *Metaphysics, Genera-*

tion of Animals, Ethics, and *Politics.* This means that Aristotle's metaphysical, natural, epistemological, and ethical principles for gender polarity were all repeated in Averroes's commentaries. The female was thought of as a contrary privation and inferior to the male, as having a feeble deliberative faculty, and as having the particular virtues of silence and obedience. In addition, Averroes wrote a text entitled *Colliget* in which he summarized many Aristotelian theories. In this work he argued against Avicenna's modification of Aristotle's theory of generation, and reverted to the view that the female seed contributed nothing to generation but the matter, and the male seed contributed only form. He also introduced a notion of the plurality of forms in the developing fetus. Averroes's interpretation and development of Aristotelian thought later provoked violent controversy at the University of Paris as those scholars and students who followed his line of interpretation were dubbed the 'radical Aristotelians' and many were forbidden from making public pronouncements on theological issues. Some of the details of these controversies will be considered later in this chapter.

Averroes was also influenced by Plato's *Republic,* and he seemed to allow the possibility that some women could become rulers and be as wise as men. Although these Islamic philosophers integrated different principles about the concept of woman from Aristotle and Plato, their commentaries mostly served the purpose of transmitting the original Greek philosophers' concepts and arguments into western Europe.

The Jewish philosopher Maimonides (1135-1204) discovered Aristotle through Alexander of Aphrodisias, Al-Farabi, Avicenna, and Averroes. Just as the Islamic philosophers believed that in Aristotle they had found the perfect philosopher for their Islamic worldview, so Maimonides believed that he had found the perfect philosopher for a Jewish worldview. In addition, Maimonides integrated Aristotelian principles for gender polarity throughout his text, *The Guide for the Perplexed.* He drew parallels between male/female, form/matter, fertile/infertile, hot/cold, and rule/obey, which are so central to the Aristotelian theory of gender identity. Although Maimonides wrote in Arabic, his works were translated into Hebrew and Latin, and thus they contributed to the continually broadening base for the transmission of an Aristotelian concept of woman.

Fifth Phase (1100-1260), Translations into Latin: At the same time that Islamic and Jewish philosophers were working on the Syriac and Arabic versions of Aristotle's texts, other philosophers began to translate them into Latin. Around 1160, James of Venice translated the *Physics, Metaphysics, De anima,* and *Parts of Animals.* Henricus Aristippus translated some of Aristotle's cosmological theories. In the cosmological writings the four elements of fire, air, water, and earth were given a descending order of value, and the male was associated metaphorically with the two higher elements of fire and air, the female with the two lower elements of water and earth. In this way the cosmological theories of Aristotle were linked with his view of the female as the contrary privation of the male and of her association with a colder and moister nature. Finally, during this same time period there were also anonymous translations of Books I and II of *Nicomachean Ethics, Posterior Analytics,* and *Physics.*

In a major new development between 1210 and 1240 in Toledo, Spain, Michael Scot translated into Latin all of Averroes's original Arabic works, including his commentaries on Aristotle. Through these extensive commentaries on Aristotle, which included three texts of different lengths (paraphrase, brief exposition, and complete exposition), the principles of gender polarity were made available to Latin scholars right at the time of foundation of the University of Paris. Then in 1240 Scot began to translate into Latin Aristotle's texts themselves.

In a discussion of the curriculum of the Arts Faculty at the University of Paris it is noted that although other sources contributed to the study of generation, Michael Scot's version of Aristotle held a crucial place.

> The third tradition [after Galen and Avicenna], as well as theoretical biology in general, is based on Aristotle's writings on natural philosophy, especially his three works on the history, on the parts, and on the generation of animals. These works, as well as an abridged version by Avicenna, were presented to the thirteenth-century scholarly community through the translations from the Arabic by Michael Scot. They soon became, under the collective title *De animalibus,* part of the arts curriculum, and with their scope, organization, and clarity provided scholars with an unsurpassed canon of philosophical concepts and biological data, particularly on the subject of generation, for the study and teaching of *physica.*[80]

Since Scot's translations were not based on the original Greek manuscripts, but on texts that had passed from Greek to Syriac and then to Arabic, they contained some distortions in the transmissions of the Greek philosopher's original concepts and arguments.

St. Albert the Great (1193-1280) learned about Aristotle from studying the Jewish philosopher Maimonides, and he began to work with Michael Scot's Latin translations of the philosopher's works. Finding himself dissatisfied with the quality of these texts that were three times removed from the original Greek, he asked one of his Dominican brothers, William of Moerbeke, to make a new translation of the complete works of Aristotle from the original Greek into Latin. In addition to retranslating all the texts of Aristotle already translated into Latin, Moerbeke also newly translated the *Poetics, Rhetoric, Politics* and missing books of the *Metaphysics* and the *Generation of Animals.* Thus, for the first time in western history all of the philosopher's rationale for gender polarity was made available to students and scholars. That this event occurred right at the time of the foundation of the new university system in Europe, and that Aristotle was made required reading for all the students in the undergraduate Faculty of Arts led to the result that Aristotelian principles of gender polarity became part of the fundament of an academic understanding of woman's identity in relation to man.

The acceptance of Aristotle's voice in Paris did not go smoothly. An official condemnation of Aristotelian texts other than the logic had occurred in 1210 and again in 1231. This had happened for three different reasons: (1) a lack of clarity about the actual claims of the philosopher; (2) some of the claims appeared to be contradictory to Christianity; and (3) some pseudo-Aristotelian texts had not yet been separated from genuine Aristotelian texts. However, by 1235 the condemna-

---

80. Demaitre and Travill, "Human Embryology . . . ," in *Albertus Magnus and the Sciences,* p. 409.

tions were lifted, and Aristotle entered fully into the curriculum of the new university. Then in 1255 Masters in the Faculty of Arts at the University of Paris were required to lecture on Aristotle's *Organon, Ethics, Physics, Metaphysics,* and *Animalibus,* among others of his works.[81] This official requirement in the year 1255 marks the turning point in the institutionalization of Aristotelianism. From that time on the curriculum of students and faculty at the University of Paris was infused with Aristotelian concepts and arguments.

The next two phases of integration of Aristotle's voice into academia will be given greater emphasis than the first five phases just identified. The reason for this distinction is due to the unique and significant role that a particular person played in this process. St. Albert the Great and his student St. Thomas Aquinas both transmitted and modified the gender polarity theory of the philosopher Aristotle. Because of the particular importance of each of these men to the development of Aristotelian-based gender polarity in academia, a separate section of this chapter will be devoted to a summary of their contributions.

Sixth Phase: St. Albert the Great (1193-1280)

The sixth phase of transmission of Aristotle's impact on discourse about woman in western academia did not end simply with the infusion of his original works into the curriculum. Just as Islamic and Jewish philosophers thought Aristotle could provide a systematic foundation for their religious faith, so did Christian philosophers, who thought that in Aristotle they had found the systematic philosophical foundation for Christianity. This integration of Aristotle into a new Christian worldview became an even more potent means of transmitting his fundamental principles. Generally speaking, Christian philosophers adopted key aspects of Aristotelian philosophy, while at the same time modifying them within a Theology. As a consequence, in Scholastic thought an Aristotelian biological base for the natural inferiority of woman was transformed by a Theology of Grace.

Christianity brought with it some fundamental theses that mitigated the polarity theory of gender. St. Augustine was the first Christian philosopher to recognize this fact when he asked the question whether in heaven, after the resurrection of the body, women will be turned into men.[82] His question was based on the belief of some that the female state was an imperfect state with respect to the male, and that all imperfections are removed in heaven. Augustine answered that in Creation and after Resurrection both genders are equally represented, and therefore to be a woman is no imperfection. John Scotus Erigena (810-877), asking the same question, but influenced by Platonism, came to a different answer, namely that the original created body and the final resurrected body are asexual.[83]

---

81. Hastings Rashdall, *The Universities of Europe in the Middle Ages* (London: Oxford University Press, 1958), p. 442.

82. Augustine, *The City of God,* XII, 17 and XIII, 19.

83. John Scotus Erigena, *Periphyseon* (On the Division of Nature) (Indianapolis: Bobbs-Merrill, 1976), 533a 11; 537d 11-13, 32.

St. Albert the Great followed Augustine's lead when he understood Christian belief in Creation and Redemption to have implications for a philosophy of gender identity. In the realm of Grace, man and woman existed in equally perfect states. Thus St. Albert was faced with a problem of how to integrate the four principles of Aristotle's philosophy of gender polarity with Christian theological principles, which gave woman an equal dignity with man. This challenge was further compounded by the fact that Albert had a great personal devotion to Mary, the Blessed Virgin Mother whom he understood as the most perfect human person who had lived on earth. He believed that Mary, the Mother of God, by a complete receptivity to the grace of her Divine Maternity, overcame all limitations of human nature and was given perfect knowledge and virtue. Thus, for Albert the order of perfection of Mary in the realm of Grace overturned the order of imperfection of being a woman in the realm of Nature. However, Albert, and Thomas following him, basically thought that grace did not overturn nature, but built on nature. When this theological premise is applied to other women who have an imperfect nature, it creates an internal tension about a different measure of perfection for men and for women.

Albert the Great taught Theology at the University of Paris from 1243 to 1248. In this context he began to study natural science along with Roger Bacon, who was already teaching in the Faculty of Arts. He believed that only a science of nature, based on collective experience, could be a solid foundation for truth. In this empirical orientation he challenged a philosophy that relied too heavily on syllogistic argumentation alone.[84] In 1248, at approximately the same time that Bacon went to Oxford, Albert went with his student, Thomas Aquinas, to Cologne to establish the first school for Dominicans in Germany.[85] Germany had not yet caught up with the academic movement in England at Oxford and Cambridge or in France at Paris, Toulouse, and Montpellier.

In the freer intellectual atmosphere away from the University of Paris and armed with Michael Scot's recent translations of Aristotle, Albert began to systematically elaborate an Aristotelian foundation for philosophy. Robert Grosseteste's 1246/1247 translations of all ten books of Aristotle's *Ethics* from Greek into Latin also appear to have been used by Albert.[86] William of Moerbeke's newer translations completed by 1260 were not yet available.[87] Albert wrote extensive paraphrases of the Aristotelian corpus between 1250 and 1270.[88] His main goal was to make Latin students and scholars understand Aristotle's foundations for philosophy and all natural science, to make philosophy the foundation for Theology and Medicine, and to continue the Greek philosopher's empirical orientation towards knowledge by elaborating a science of nature. William A. Wallace, OP suggests that "(t)he position of St. Albert the Great with respect to the University of Paris parallels in some ways

84. Edward Synan, "Introduction," in *Albertus Magnus and the Sciences,* p. 6.

85. Benedict Ashley, OP, "St. Albert and the Nature of Natural Science," in *Albertus Magnus and the Sciences,* p. 78.

86. James A. Weisheipl, OP, "The Life and Works of St. Albert the Great," in *Albertus Magnus and the Sciences,* p. 29.

87. Demaitre and Travill, "Human Embryology and Development," in *Albertus Magnus and the Sciences,* p. 409 n. 11.

88. Weisheipl, "Life and Works," in *Albertus Magnus and the Sciences,* p. 27.

that of Robert Grosseteste with respect to Oxford University."[89] They both established the foundations in academia for a more scientific approach to the world.

Albert paraphrased Aristotle's works as a whole, constantly referring to his mentor as 'the philosopher' in the effort to communicate both his method and content to the medieval academic audience. Albert's commentary on Aristotle's *Generation of Animals,* other historical sources (especially Avicenna and Galen), and his own empirical observations were joined together in the text *De animalibus.* As a scientist himself, Albert was especially interested in the empirical aspects of Aristotle's methodology or the actual study of all of nature: minerals and stars as well as living things — plants, animals, and anatomy, physiology, and psychology of human beings.[90] Needham notes in his *History of Embryology* that Albert concentrates 31 percent (in comparison with Aristotle's 37 percent and Galen's 7 percent) of his biological writings on the topic of generation.[91] Other than Aristotle, the most frequent sources for his reflections on generation were two works of Avicenna, *De animalibus* and the *Canon of Medicine* — both of which also were based on Aristotle. Albert also drew upon much personal observation to support, qualify, and even at times reject the Greek philosopher's original thesis. More often than not, however, when there were conflicts between Aristotle, Galen, and Avicenna, the medieval philosopher supported the original hypothesis of Aristotle. In this way, the Greek philosopher's revised theories and observations were transmitted and strengthened as if they were Albert's own.

A distinction is sometimes made between Albert's more mature work *De animalibus* completed around 1261, and his public lectures on the *Quaestiones super de animalibus* from the Cologne period in 1258. The written paraphrases in the *De animalibus* were offered to students outside of lectures as a way to enhance their understanding of Aristotle's original texts. The public lectures recorded in the *Quaestiones,* on the other hand, were part of the oral tradition of teaching in the academic setting. They were posed in short questions and answers in the scholastic style of disputation in which students grasped the principles by hearing rather than by reading. This difference in style and purpose led to some differences in content. The *Quaestiones super de animalibus,* "[b]esides coming to us in a student's version not authorized by Albert, . . . were cast in the didactic mold of the *disputatio* and hence [did] not reveal the nuances of the teacher's position."[92] Therefore a careful scholar of Albert will need to determine how much more refinement he gave in other works to particular judgments about gender identity than we find in the *Quaestiones.* It is interesting how the dynamic of disputation tends to make more

89. See William A. Wallace, *Causality and Scientific Explanation,* p. 66.

90. For detailed descriptions of Albert's contribution to the science of motion, astronomy, minerals, chemical technology, psychology of sense perception, physiology, nutrition, plants, herbs, embryology, falcons, hawks, mathematics, and geometry, see the several articles in Weisheipl, ed., *Albertus Magnus and the Sciences.*

91. Joseph Needham, *A History of Embryology* (Cambridge: Cambridge University Press, 1959), p. 86. See also L. Demaitre and A. A. Travill, "Human Embryology and Development," in *Albertus Magnus and the Sciences,* pp. 410-11.

92. For this distinction see Demaitre and Travill, "Human Embryology and Development," in *Albertus Magnus and the Sciences,* pp. 413ff.

rigid judgments. In contrast, more flexible conclusions occur in a discourse that aims at exploring empirical evidence for hypotheses. It is also important to note, however, that the simplified form and content of the *Quaestiones* "helped to shape the tradition of medical question literature and that they reappear in subsequent medical studies."[93] Therefore, even if Albert's own position was more nuanced than that contained in the *Quaestiones,* his historical influence was very directly related to the more popular record of the public disputation.

In addition, scholars point out that "[s]tatements on embryology are found not only in Albert's work *De animalibus* and related books, but also throughout his theological and metaphysical writings."[94] Of particular note are the following works: *De homine* as part II of *Summa de creaturis* (1244-1248), commentary on Peter Lombard's fourth book of the *Sentences* (1249), commentary on Aristotle's *De generatione et corruptione* (1261), *De fato* (1260s), *De unitate intellectus contra Averroistas* (1271), and *Problemata determinata XLIII* (1271). Albert was considered to be most knowledgeable about theories of generation, and his opinion was often sought in controversial contexts. Overall, because of the systematic nature of his exposition, the breadth of his range of sources, and the constant attempt to include empirical evidence, Albert was considered to be the most important natural scientist of his age. In this broader framework, what he said about the nature of woman was given great weight by all who thought about the subject.

During the years 1261-1263, Albert finished his commentaries on Aristotle's *Ethics, Posterior Analytics,* and *Politics.* From 1264 to 1267 he appears to have composed his paraphrase of Aristotle's *Metaphysics.* James Weisheipl, OP notes that all of these elaborated paraphrases of Aristotle's philosophical works were "written or dictated" rather than given as lectures.[95] Their purpose was to help students understand Aristotle and philosophy in general much as secondary sources do today. However, the fact that they were written meant that they could circulate widely, and as we will see, their content did circulate from the more private educational center in Cologne into the heart of the university system at Paris in part through Albert's illustrious student, Thomas Aquinas. Another reason for the wide circulation of Albert's work is the mendicant or walking tradition of the Dominican friars whose members spread out all over Europe to evangelize and defend the Catholic faith.

Albert's concept of woman should be situated within his understanding of the nature of the human being. However, since his own theory is well known and developed in relation to many controversies among followers of Aristotle, Avicenna, and Averroes, it will not be repeated here.[96] The following summary of Albert's concept of woman will be arranged under the four fundamental principles identified in Aristotle's theory of gender polarity: metaphysical, natural,

93. Nancy G. Siraisi, "The Medical Learning of Albertus Magnus," in *Albertus Magnus and the Sciences,* p. 394.

94. Demaitre and Travill, "Human Embryology and Development," in *Albertus Magnus and the Sciences,* pp. 413-14.

95. Weisheipl, "Life and Works," in *Albertus Magnus and the Sciences,* p. 40.

96. For a good summary of his views on the soul, the agent intellect, and the relation to the human body, see Etienne Gilson, "Albert the Great," in *History of Christian Philosophy in the Middle Ages,* pp. 283-89.

epistemological, and ethical. An attempt will be made to distinguish when the medieval philosopher is simply repeating the Greek philosopher's original claims, as opposed to introducing a modification. Our analysis of Albert will be divided into three sections. In the first part, we will summarize passages in his works that simply repeat or amplify Aristotle's original principles of gender polarity. In the second section, we will give some examples of areas where Albert introduces new distinctions to develop and clarify Aristotle's original position. In the third division, we will give some additional and more detailed examples where Albert introduces new evidence to support Aristotle's original position or where he linked different principles together to offer a more cohesive account of the principles of gender polarity. Finally we will reflect briefly on the particular relation between the content and structure of academic discourse that compounded the problem of the extreme devaluation of the nature of woman so characteristic of Albert's approach.

In the summary below, the source of the statement will be identified by a letter associated with a particular text of St. Albert as follows: M = (Commentary on Aristotle's) *Metaphysics*, N = *De natura et origine animae*, P = (Commentary on Aristotle's) *Politicorum*, Q = *Quaestiones super de animalibus*, S = *Summa de creaturis*.[97] The Presocratic philosophers had asked questions about gender identity in four basic categories: opposites, generation, wisdom, and gender. Answers to these questions in all four categories were given by Plato and Aristotle. The medieval philosophers focused their analysis of the ancient Greek theories while adding their own reflections in each of these categories by identifying a central principle under which particular judgments could be articulated. The principles of the four categories are as follows: opposites — metaphysical principle; generation — natural principle; wisdom — epistemological principle; and virtue — ethical principle. In this way we keep the same four fundamental categories of gender identity while giving a clearer focus to the analysis, which moves from the more static notion of category to a more dynamic notion of principle.

What we see from these selected passages from the works of Albert the Great is that Aristotle's four principles of gender polarity are integrated into his work, qualified in some places and amplified in others. Albert not only recognizes the metaphysical, natural, epistemological, and ethical principles for gender polarity in the Aristotelian corpus, he also makes the links among them explicit and adds further evidence for their truth. In this way, Albert adds his considerable weight to the gathering evidence for the natural inferiority of woman.

Repetition of Aristotle's Gender Polarity Principles

Of particular note is that Albert drops all the qualifiers we have seen in the original text of Aristotle. There are no qualifiers "as it were," "taken to extreme,"

---

97. These passages are paraphrased by the author or directly quoted from translations of texts by Diane Gordon and Sister M. Therese Dougherty as identified specifically in *The Concept of Woman: The Aristotelian Revolution*, pp. 525-27, notes 401-48. The texts used are all taken from Albertus Magnus, *Opera Omnia*, ed. Borgnet (Paris: Apud Ludovicum Vives, 1890-99).

and so forth. Instead we find generalized Aristotelian statements such as: the female is contrary of male, the female constitution is cold, the female's *ratio,* intellect, or power of decision is weaker, the female is more easily moved by appetites or desires, a woman is a defective man and has the nature of failure and lack in respect to the male, and silence is a woman's glory. Along the same line, Albert repeats Aristotle's view that the male is better, more noble, more active, and more like form than is the female. Thus, in some ways Aristotle's voice is sharper and more rigidly pronounced in the academic discourse initiated about women by Albert. As noted previously, this dropping of qualifiers may have had three different causes: Michael Scot's translations three times removed from the original Greek, the oral presentation and disputational structure of the *Quaestiones* on animals, and Albert's personal decisions. Whatever the reason, the discourse about woman is changed as a result.

Metaphysical Principle:
The female is a contrary privation

Female is the contrary of male insofar as it is animal (*M,* X).

Female is contrary according to cold, male according to heat (*M,* X).

Female, by reason of cold and moisture, differs accidentally from male, because of strength and warmth (*Q,* XV, q 3).

Female possesses material, male possesses acting principle (*Q,* XV, q 3).

". . . matter is said to seek form and woman man [The philosopher in *Physics* I], because woman seeks intercourse with man, but this is understandable because everything imperfect naturally seeks to be perfected; and woman is an imperfect human being compared with man. Therefore every woman seeks to be subject to man. For there is no woman who does not want to take off the female *ratio* and put on the male naturally. And in the same way matter seeks to put on form and so it is with ugliness" (*Q,* V, q 4).

Natural Principle:
The female is a *mas occasionatus* (misbegotten male)

Males are naturally warmer than females (*Q,* VI, q 6-13).

Female gives matter, male gives that which creates (*S,* Pt 2, q 7, art 2).

The female works materially, the male works effectively (*S,* Pt 2, q 17, art 2).

Nature separates the male seed in the male from the female because it separates that which is better, more noble, active, and like form from what is ignoble, enduring, passive, and receiving (*Q,* XV, q 1).

The same seed becomes female or male according to contraries of cold and heat (*M, X*).

Weakness of principle is the cause of the female, strength of principle is the cause of the male. Heat causes greater strength and order. Thus strength, not heat, is the cause of the male (*Q, XV,* q 4-5).

Complete victory of the seed of the male over the material of the female produces a male like the father (*Q, XVIII,* q 3).

"To argue another point, that because a male is produced from the strength of virtue and a female is not produced except from a weakness of virtue, and the north wind *(Boreas)* strengthens virtues, and the south wind *(Auster)* weakens them; therefore the north wind helps for the procreation of males and the south wind for the procreation of females" (*Q, VI,* q 19-22).

More moisture causes the female to grow more slowly in *utero,* more heat causes the male to grow more quickly in *utero* (*Q, IX,* q 16-17).

Epistemological Principle:
A woman's rational faculty lacks authority

Because of the coldness of the constitution of woman, the female's refined strengths are weakened, and because her principle has been badly affected her intellect is weaker (*Q, XV,* q 11).

Therefore, the female is more easily moved by desires to which she is attracted than is a male (*Q, XV,* q 11).

And therefore, the female is more resistant to matters concerning the understanding than is a male (*Q, XV,* q 11).

Ethical Principle:
A woman has a lesser measure of virtue

Because of this different relation between the rational and irrational parts of the soul, women, boys, and slaves are weak in the cardinal virtues (*P,* Book 9, i).

Modifications of Aristotle's Gender Polarity Principles

The second thing that Albert does to change Aristotle is to introduce new theoretical qualifications to the philosopher's views. He distinguished, following Galen, different aspects of the mother's material contribution to generation, the body of the child and the nutriment. He also suggested that some women contribute seed, but concluded that this seed is infertile. In addition, he argued against Aristotle that the father's seed may contribute something materially to the body of the developing child and that God has a primary formative role in providing the human soul to the conception.

The medieval philosopher also introduced an important distinction between the intention of universal nature and the intention of particular nature in elaborating on Aristotle's dictum that it is the intention of nature to produce the male. This distinction allowed him to claim that although it is the intention of the particular nature of the male seed to produce a male that resembles the father, it is the intention of universal nature, or nature as a whole (and ultimately God), to produce females as well as males. Albert used the expression that woman is a man who had an accident to capture the meaning of the intention of particular nature to produce a male.

Finally, he introduced various distinctions between true and apparent appetite, quantity and quality of desires, indirect and direct judgments, and constant and inconstant ideas to explain more fully different aspects of gender differentiation.

Natural Principle:
The female is a *mas occasionatus* (misbegotten male)

[Properly speaking] the female does not produce seed, male produces seed (*Q*, XV, q 19).

If female produces seed it is infertile, the seed of the male is fertile (*Q*, XV, q 19).

The material contributed by the female has two parts (body and nutriment), and possibly three (seed) (*Q*, VI, q 3).

The seed of the father is active moving force, some material from the father's seed may join the body of the conceived (*Q*, XV, q 20).

The seed of the mother holds material for the reception of form, the father's seed provides the principle which directs the life force and arranges the form (in potentiality) (*Q*, XVI, q 3).

God cooperates with the father to bring actuality to the seed provided by the father (*N*, 4).

"[N]ature is twofold: universal and particular. Universal nature intends to preserve the entire universe and its parts, and because species are part of the universe and not atoms; therefore universal nature chiefly intends to conserve the species. But a species of animals cannot be preserved without the production of individuals, and for that production female as well as male is required. Therefore universal nature intends the female, as that without which the species cannot be saved.

Particular nature moreover intends to produce like itself, and because in the generation of an animal the characteristic of the male is acting, and the characteristic of a female is not, therefore the active element principally intends to produce the male. If nevertheless there is a lack in the material or the warmth, which it uses as an instrument, and it cannot generate appropriately according to plan, then it directs that which it can, and thus particular nature chiefly intends the male; nevertheless secondarily and occasionally it intends the female" (Q, XV, q 2).

Particular nature produces a female when there is a defect in the material, or a lack of heat, or when the female seed is disobedient and resists the active force of the male seed (Q, XVIII, q 2).

"Because a woman is a male that had an accident, therefore she has less [distributed] blood. As proof it must be said that because a woman is produced from lack of heat in the seed therefore it follows from this that in women there is more fluid and undistributed blood" (Q, III, q 22).

Epistemological Principle:
A woman's rational faculty lacks authority

Because of the weakness of her judgment, appetite is greater in woman (Q, V, q 4).

"[I]t must be said that quantitatively the pleasure [in intercourse] is greater in women, but intensively it is greater in man. To confirm this it must be said that appetite is twofold and so is love, i.e., true and apparent. True love and appetite is greater in man and therefore the pleasure is truer. But the apparent appetite and love in woman is greater because of the weakness of her judgment, because as matter seeks to be under every form and itself existing under a noble form seeks an ignoble one, so it is with woman; she seeks to be under what she does not have, because on account of the weakness of her reason she judges that what she does not have is better than what she has. Therefore she seeks intercourse more frequently than man, because outside of intercourse she seeks to be in intercourse on account of the weakness of her judgment, etc." (Q, V, q 4).

Because a woman's natural faculties are weaker and inferior, the desire [for intercourse with a man] in accordance with indirect judgments is greater in women and desire [for intercourse with a woman] in accordance with direct judgments is greater in men (Q, V, XV, q 6).

Because of moisture, it is according to the nature of woman to have inconstant ideas; moreover, men because of the opposite composition, have unchanging ideas (P, Book 9, a).

Ethical Principle:
A woman has a lesser measure of virtue

Because the male by nature is more dominant than the female, it is against the order of nature if a woman is wiser and more vigorous than a man (*P,* Book 9, a).

Because the rational and irrational parts exist differently in the soul of a woman and of a man, and because the female has a weaker power of decision over her irrational appetites and anger, she does not complete her planning properly (*P,* Book 9, a).

New Forms of Support for Aristotle's Gender Polarity Principles

The third way that Albert effected the transmission of Aristotle's concept of woman was to amplify and expand the philosopher's theoretical principles with further evidence from his own experience — for example, when Albert expands on the theory that woman is a defective man by claiming that her lack of confidence in herself leads her to acquire things by lies and diabolical deceptions, and when he warns men to stay away from women as if they were a poisonous serpent and horned devil. This introduction of the notion of woman as dangerous to men goes beyond the original Aristotelian polarity framework.

Another example of this same amplification is found in Albert's expansion of the principle that woman's intellectual faculty is weak when he argues that as a consequence her appetites tend to every evil. Finally, we see a similar amplification in a discussion of Aristotle's principle that silence is woman's more proper virtue when Albert argues that, because women's inconstant opinions entice the minds of judges, they ought not be allowed to speak publicly in courts. These amplifications of the Aristotelian roots of gender polarity by St. Albert will unfortunately be introduced later in public trials in a way that universalizes the gender identity of females as particularly disposed towards vice and evil rather than virtue and the good.

In Aristotle's original texts, the main concern was how different kinds of human beings had different measures of virtue or goodness. The amplification by Albert of Aristotle's original claims about woman's identity occurs primarily to his ethical principle of gender polarity. It may have been due to the context of the audience, which consisted of clerics and brothers interested in helping people to live better lives through preaching, teaching, and spiritual guidance. The effect of Albert's amplification, however, was to set in motion an academic dynamic of devaluation of the female that would be used in the context of witchcraft trials.

We will give a translation of Albert's discussion in Book XV, Question 11: "Whether the male is more fit for moral behavior than the female?" Albert uses the scholastic form of disputation to pose a formal Question, to offer two arguments that males are not more fit, one statement of common opinion that the female is not more fit, and then a discussion of his own reasoning for the conclusion that the female is not more fit than the male for moral behavior.

Ethical Principle:
A woman has a lesser measure of virtue

Because of the moistness of her constitution which easily relapses and poorly holds firmness, the female is less fit for laws than the male (*Q, XV*, q 8).

Because the opinions of women are uncertain, inconstant, enticing the minds of judges, and because silence is a woman's glory, women should not be allowed to speak publicly in courts (*P*, Book 9, h).

"Question 11: It is inquired further whether the male is more suited for moral behavior than the female?

1) It seems that it is not so. For an animal more amenable to discipline is more fit for moral habits; but the female is more amenable to discipline than the male, as the Philosopher says in the beginning of the 9th book [of the *Politics*]. And by this reasoning it seems that because women are compared to boys by the Philosopher in that chapter, but boys are more able to be disciplined than old men, as the Philosopher thinks in *Ethics* II, therefore, etc.

2) Besides, discretion is an intellectual virtue without which a moral virtue is not completed; but women are more discreet than males, as the Philosopher thinks; therefore, etc.

The opposite is stated in the ninth book of this work, and it is evident. For it is said commonly, proverbially, and vulgarly, that women are more false and frail, diffident, shameless, and deceitfully persuasive, and that briefly a woman is nothing other than a devil fashioned in human appearance. I once saw a certain person of Cologne who seemed to be holy, but nevertheless she quickly ensnared all in her love.

To continue, that the female is less suitable for moral [laws] than the male. For the constitution of a female is more moist than of a male, but it is [characteristic] of moisture to relapse easily and to retain firmness badly. For moisture is easily moved, and therefore women are inconstant and always seeking new things. From this [it follows that] when a female is in the act under one man, if it were possible, at the same time she would wish to be under another. Therefore there is no faithfulness in a woman.

'Believe me, if you believe her, you are deceived;
believe the experienced teacher.'

Also, the sign of this is, that wise men reveal their plans and deeds least of all to their wives. For a woman is a defective man and has a nature of failure and lack in respect to the male [*Mulier etiam est vir occasionatus et habet naturam defectus and privationis respectu maris . . .*],[98] therefore she naturally lacks confi-

---

98. This passage is based on the Latin translation of Michael Scot of the passage in Aristotle already described in the principle, the female is as it were a deformed male. In our discussion of St. Thomas Aquinas, we will consider the difficulty with this translation in more detail. At this point we need only to note that Albert uses it to devalue woman in relation to man.

dence in herself; and therefore that which she cannot acquire by herself she strives to acquire by means of lies and diabolical deceptions. From which, that I may speak briefly, everyone ought to be warned away from every woman as if from a poisonous serpent and a horned devil; and if it were right to say what I know about women, the whole world would be stunned.

Arguments: 1) First, that discipline is twofold: for a certain discipline is given concerning those matters operating in respect of affection, and a certain [other] is given concerning those things capable of being understood, and this consists in learning and contemplating. Insofar as the female is more amenable to the first than the male, she is more easily moved to diverse affections, to which she is attracted. But as far as she is opposite to the second, because of the coldness of the composition of woman, the more refined virtues are weakened and made worse, and consequently her intellect is weaker.

2) Secondly, that woman is not more discreet than a man in speaking appropriately, but is more cunning. From which it follows that prudence resounds for good, and cleverness for evil. From which [it follows that] a female is more skilled in evil and perverse deeds, that is, more cunning than a male, because by however much nature takes away more from one operation, by so much she directs more to another one. Only a woman lacks in intellectual activity, which consists in the apprehension of good, the understanding of truth, and the avoidance of evil; and therefore she directs more to the sensitive appetites which tend towards evil, unless it is ruled by reason, as was apparent in *Ethics* VII. From which [it follows that] emotion moves woman to every evil, just as intellect moves man to every good; therefore, etc." (*Q, XV,* q 11).[99]

This quotation of Albert's discussion of just one question concerning woman's identity is very useful for our purposes of considering the way that Aristotle's thought was transmitted through the work of this teacher. It demonstrates how frequently the medieval philosopher refers back to the Greek philosopher even to support opposing views in the argument. It also demonstrates how he inserts empirical evidence of his time and rejects common or vulgar opinions as solid grounds for supporting an argument. In the elaboration of his own reasons for reaching a conclusion about the question, Albert integrates all of Aristotle's principles into a common view about woman's and man's identity. His conclusions tend to fall directly in line with Aristotle's principles for gender polarity, and therefore they add a further rational and scientific weight to the philosopher's opinion. As a consequence, these principles of gender polarity will become even more difficult to dislodge from the academic community of discourse.

99. This same point, that an intensity of one virtue or strength in the soul draws away from another part, is attributed to Avicenna in a discussion of why wise men beget foolish children: "Argument, that wise men for the most part beget foolish boys, because according to Avicenna one intense virtue draws back another from its work. Now, however, wise men apply their minds to imagination and reason, and they produce their thoughts and meditations. From this [circumstance] in them for the most part the natural strength is weakened, and therefore frequently their sperm is undistributed and bad, and because of this evil sons are produced, because he who is good in study is poor in business and reproduction or the sexual act, therefore etc." (*Q, XVIII,* 4).

It is helpful to be reminded here that the texts written by St. Albert, and the public discussion recorded by his student of the 1258 disputations on animals, were originally directed to the small audience of Dominican students in the *studium generale* in Cologne. In the same period of 1248, the Dominicans had opened three other new houses of study at Montpellier, Bologna, and Oxford, as well as the one in Cologne, Germany.[100] While the *Quaestiones animalibus* may have been shared among the other Dominican houses of study opening up in Europe at the time, they were not originally written for the purposes of wide dispersion. However, Albert's manuscripts were taken by his students as they traveled to other places of study. We know that Thomas Aquinas took Albertian manuscripts with him to the University of Paris when he was appointed as Bachelor there in 1252. Before the invention of the printing press, it was often the students who became a medium of transmission of the thought of their Masters. They, along with libraries of religious communities, continued to hold the texts that contained components and amplifications of Aristotelian rationale for gender polarity.

In addition, in 1259 Albert was asked by his Dominican General to head a commission of five masters to set an academic plan for the whole order. Thomas Aquinas was one of the five men who met with Albert in Valenciennes, France to do this work. Their commission, not surprisingly, affirmed that philosophy should be foundational for the study of theology in all Dominican schools and ordinary priories.[101]

It is useful to reflect for a moment about dynamics occurring in a completely male community of discourse that might have been moderated in a mixed community of discourse. We need to ask the question: If women had been present as students in the academic setting in which Albert proposed some of these theories about women's identity, and even more, if women had been present as complement scholars in the developing universities as they had been within many of the Benedictine educational structures, would some of these extreme generalizations about women's lack of abilities have been moderated in tone and content? Would women students or scholars have served as living counterexamples to the theories being propounded? Would the academic philosophers at least have had to explain exceptions to principles of gender polarity? However, since the academic communities of discourse at the beginning of colleges and universities for mendicant brothers and priests excluded women, the rather extreme hypotheses that devalued women by generalizations both in writing and in speech went unchallenged.

What was Albert the Great's impact on subsequent thought? Albert accomplished one of his goals, namely that philosophy would become a foundation for the study of medicine. His paraphrases of the biological and zoological texts of Aristotle were "eagerly studied in medical schools."[102] In fact, through the next two centuries physicians often cited Albert by name. Through this avenue the Greek

---

100. James A. Weisheipl, OP, "Thomas d'Aquino and Albert His Teacher," in *The Etienne Gilson Series,* 2 (Toronto: Pontifical Institute of Mediaeval Studies, 1980), p. 6.

101. Weisheipl, "Thomas d'Aquino and Albert His Teacher," in *The Etienne Gilson Series,* 12.

102. Siraisi, "The Medical Learning of Albertus Magnus," in *Albertus Magnus and the Sciences,* p. 380.

philosopher's foundations for gender polarity were incorporated into the heart of the theory and practice of medicine.

In addition, Albert's popularity was so great in medical education that a well-circulated gynecological text *De secretis mulierum* was falsely attributed to him. First written in Latin in the fourteenth century, it was not identified as spurious until the end of the fifteenth century. It was even published in printed form in English as late as 1601 in a collection of essays called *Aristotle's Masterpiece*. Generally speaking, the text offered a smattering of different gynecological views which, while devaluing women, did not clearly transmit Aristotle's foundation for gender polarity. It should be noted, however, that the text kept being reprinted as part of the corpus of Albert's work right into the eighteenth century.

Albert was not only the Regent Master in Dominican houses of study, he also became a Provincial of his order. He was later elevated to the Episcopacy and spent time traveling throughout his Diocese as well as in Rome. These more public offices occurred during the same time that he was working on his paraphrases of the Aristotelian texts. Therefore, it is not surprising to discover that his writing about women had a great influence in following centuries. As we will see in a subsequent chapter, many of the same theories about women's identity that were so clearly stated in his *Quaestiones* and commentaries on Aristotle were incorporated into a practical handbook written by two Dominican friars to guide magistrates for the arrest and trial of witches.

In spite of these rather negative effects of Albert's groundbreaking work on gender identity, he also accomplished another important goal, that an empirically oriented philosophy would become the foundation for the new academic curriculum. Indeed, it was this very goal, as seen in the development of the sciences of mineralogy, astronomy, botany, zoology, anatomy, physiology, and medicine that eventually helped to overturn errors in the Aristotelian philosophy. We could even say that another significant contribution of Albert the Great to the history of the concept of woman was his promotion of an empirical foundation for knowledge and his elaboration of a beginning scientific method. For it was through the disciplined application of new scientific methods that more accurate natural principles of gender differentiation could be eventually discovered and articulated. Even though his own method was caught at times in an Aristotelian teleology that had the effect of distorting real differences between men and women, Albert also opened the academic community to the search for real answers about everything in the world. This empirical orientation of philosophy led to the eventual overturning of the Aristotelian foundations for gender polarity.

We will now turn to consider the work of St. Albert's most famous student St. Thomas Aquinas, who had studied with him seven years before becoming a Master at the University of Paris. In Thomas Aquinas's move to the University of Paris, the seventh phase of transmission of an Aristotelian foundation of the academic curriculum as elaborated by Albert's paraphrases was carried right into the center of the academic world alongside the new translations of Aristotle's original texts.

Seventh Phase: St. Thomas Aquinas (1224-1274)

Just one year after 1255, when the works of Aristotle became required reading at the University of Paris, at Albert's strong intervention, the young Italian Thomas Aquinas (1224-1274) took over the Dominican Chair for Foreigners as Master of Sacred Theology at the University of Paris. He served in that capacity from 1256 to 1259 before going to teach in the Dominican house of studies in Naples and other locations in the Papal States during the years of 1259 to 1269. For four years previous to his official appointment as Master, Thomas had already been lecturing as a Bachelor in Paris on the *Sentences* of Peter Lombard. He returned once again to the University of Paris during the final years of his life from 1269 to 1272. Thus, this important university was closely connected with both the formation and teaching of Aquinas.

Thomas wrote twelve Aristotelian commentaries that were originally called *expositiones,* or explanations of the ancient Greek philosopher's texts.[103] These explanations were composed and edited at various times throughout his academic career. In them Thomas sought to be faithful to Aristotle's original texts, while at the same time he introduced new opinions about the subject from his own Christian perspective. For example, scholars now think that he wrote a first draft of a commentary on Aristotle's *Ethics* when he was teaching in Dominican houses in the Papal States during 1261-1269, but a final editing and copying occurred later when he was teaching again at the University of Paris during 1270-1272.[104] Thomas also wrote two major theological works, *Summa contra gentiles* and *Summa theologiae,* in addition to numerous Biblical commentaries, Disputed Questions, Quodlibetal Questions, and other writings on specified theological and philosophical issues.

As we mentioned above in our consideration of St. Albert, Thomas had studied under his mentor both in Paris during the years 1245-1248 and in Cologne from 1248 to 1252. In the latter capacity, his intellectual genius was recognized by Albert, and he was given considerable responsibility by him. As we read in Weisheipl's account of the relation between the two men: "[a]t Cologne Thomas became Albert's bachelor, responding in disputations, lecturing cursorily on the Bible . . . , and assisting the master in all his preparations."[105] By this formation as both a graduate research assistant and a graduate teaching assistant of Albert, Thomas was trained especially in the methodology of scholastic disputation as practiced and developed by his Master.

Two further details about this period in Thomas's life are especially noteworthy. First, Albert began to lecture on Aristotle's *Ethics, Physics,* and works on *Generation of Animals,* and so Thomas would have been intimately formed by the Aristotelian content of these works and by an essential interconnection between philosophy, natural science, and theology. Second, Latin was the common lan-

---

103. Joseph Owens, C.Ss.R., "Aquinas as Aristotelian Commentator," in *St. Thomas Aquinas: Commemorative Studies (1274-1974),* pp. 214-37.

104. Vernon J. Bourke, "The *Nicomachean Ethics* and Thomas Aquinas," in *St. Thomas Aquinas: Commemorative Studies (1274-1974),* pp. 239-59.

105. Weisheipl, "Thomas d'Aquino and Albert His Teacher," in *The Etienne Gilson Series,* 8.

guage between the student Thomas, who was Italian and spoke no German, and his Master Albert, who was from an aristocratic Teutonic family. Indeed, it was the central position of Latin in the new academic centers that helped ease the dispersion of the new Aristotelian-based Christian thought throughout France, England, Germany, and Italy.

When Thomas went to the Dominican house in Paris, he was then poised to begin to develop his own style of scholastic teaching. While his teacher Albert had been particularly interested in the application of Aristotle to the development of an empirically based science, Thomas was more interested in the integration of science, philosophy, and theology. Gerald McCool, S.J. summarizes the uniqueness of Thomas's contribution to the development of academic thought as follows:

> What he did was routine enough: but the philosophical theology which he worked out while doing it was original and quite remarkable for the inclusiveness, rigor, and coherence of its philosophical component. . . .
>
> Thomas proposed a tightly woven synthesis of nature and supernature, philosophy and theology. Its spine was a metaphysics of man [the human being] as an autonomous human nature, whose knowledge, beginning with the sensible singular, ascended to Infinite Being.
>
> Trained by his master, Albert the Great, in the negative theology of Pseudo-Dionysius, Thomas also inherited from Albert his uncompromisingly Aristotelian metaphysics of man and nature. Like every sensible singular, man was composed of pure matter linked immediately to a single substantial form.[106]

As we will see in our consideration of St. Thomas's philosophy of gender differentiation, this Aristotelian metaphysical foundation led him to reach similar conclusions about woman's identity as had Albert. The centrality of the single human form, against the Averroist Aristotelians who had supported a plurality of forms, is an important principle for the unity of the human being. However, it also continued the problem of how to explain gender differentiation within the single substantial human form.

Before turning to a content analysis of Thomas's theory of gender, another observation should be made about the relation between Thomas and his teacher Albert. Thomas Aquinas had several secretaries during his career as a teacher, and there is much evidence to support the conclusion that his secretaries copied many of Albert's works for Thomas. "It turns out that many instruments of Thomas's research were in fact *tabulae* excerpted by Thomas's secretaries from the *Libri naturales* and *Ethics* of St. Albert. There can be little doubt now that Thomas kept himself well-informed of Albert's views, even those with which he had to disagree."[107] There was little disagreement about the concept of woman in the works of these two philosophers. However, the orientation of the two philosophers was

---

106. Gerald A. McCool, S.J., "Why St. Thomas Stays Alive," *International Philosophical Quarterly* 33, no. 3 (September 1990): 278.

107. Weisheipl, "Thomas d'Aquino and Albert His Teacher," p. 14. He also mentions as source, Antoine Dondaine, *Secrétaires de Saint Thomas* (Rome: S. Sabina, 1956).

somewhat different, and so their effects on the transmission of Aristotelian foundations of gender polarity were also somewhat different. Simply put, Albert's works, which sought to unfold the new Aristotelian foundations for Christian thought, were more influential in the short run, during the period of 1250-1500; while Thomas's works, which forged a new Christian theology that incorporated Aristotelian foundations within it, were more influential in the long run.

At the conclusion of this section on St. Thomas we will return to the question of the influence of Thomism on the history of the concept of woman. As a prelude to this conclusion, we will give a brief review of the concept of his actual theory about gender identity. The importance of the academic community of discourse in creating a new interpretation of their views is captured in the illustration painted in 1365 of Plato and Aristotle in the Glorification of St. Thomas Aquinas (p. 130).

Moderation of Aristotle's Metaphysical Principle of Gender Polarity

St. Thomas Aquinas always appears to bring moderation into the discussion of women's identity. He carefully avoids the extreme statements of his predecessors, and frequently tones down positions that devalue women by emphasizing the dignity of each and every human being. At the same time he elaborated his own views, drawing heavily on Aristotle's philosophy which, as we have seen, is permeated by principles of gender polarity.

Aristotelian metaphysics was the study of being *qua* being, and it distinguished between different kinds of being but included primary being, or the divine unmoved mover as pure act, self-thinking thought, and impersonal unmoved mover. For Thomas metaphysics was the study of separate substances, excluding God and angels. It focused on common being, excluding the divine that was the proper subject of the new field of Theology. The Aristotelian metaphysical principle of gender polarity, namely, that the female is a contrary privation of the male, was accepted by Thomas with the provision that privation refers neither to a genus of evil nor to a state of non-existence. Because a woman is a separate substance that exists as a female human being, she belongs in the category of goods that derive their existence from their Creator who is Good. A woman's particular identity as an existing being must be explained through different kinds of causality; her essence as a woman is distinct from her act of existence as a particular woman brought into existence by God.

From the point of view of Theology, God, as Pure Act, and as Trinity of Three Divine Persons, creates individual women and men in the Divine Image, with an intellect capable of knowing and being known and a will capable of loving and being loved by God and others. Each individual woman and man is created uniquely by God. From the point of view of metaphysics, women and men are unique individual human beings, or persons whose essence includes a bodily as well as intelligent and free nature. A bodily identity includes a potentiality that can be progressively actualized towards the perfection of the individual existent. The human person's soul is the form of the body, its individual act of existence. Members of the same species have the same kind of substantial form; and men and women, as

Plato, Aristotle, and Averroes in the Glorification of St. Thomas Aquinas

members of the human species, have the same kind of human form, but each woman and each man actualizes this form in a unique and unrepeatable way. Thus Thomas's understanding of the identity of the human person brought into existence by God as a unique and unrepeatable human being goes way beyond Aristotle's understanding of the human being as simply an instance of the human species caused by the conjunction of the father and mother in generation. While Thomas hints that Aristotle did allow that an eternal soul of a man or woman had its source outside of the father's seed, it was the medieval philosophers who explicitly developed this position.

For Thomas, following Aristotle and Albert, there is an engendered difference in excellence or quality of being informed as a man or a woman. The female is a less noble kind of human being than a male.[108] Yet all women and men, as created in the image and likeness of God, are called to the perfection of holiness, i.e., called to be saints. Within this understanding, Aristotle's metaphysics of contraries with its devaluation of the female is merged within a Christian faith in the fundamental equality of the call of men and women to share the Divine life as they move towards a state of perfection.

The Aristotelian metaphysical categories of form/matter, active/passive, and substance/accident were worked into a Thomistic metaphysics of the human existent and of relations. In a certain sense, in Thomas a new existential metaphysics of act of existence and of essence took a more important place than the older Aristotelian metaphysics of form and matter. Yet the Aristotelian categories continued to function within the new existential metaphysics of Aquinas. The female is associated with a passive principle, and the male with an active principle; and the passive principle is linked with matter, and the active principle with seed, which is able to contain form. Thus, the Aristotelian metaphysical association of the female with passive matter, and the male with active form, is continued within a Thomistic metaphysics. This continuity suggests that Thomas Aquinas supported the metaphysical principle for gender polarity.

However, Thomistic existential metaphysics appears to be also open to developments towards a metaphysics of complementarity. It is important to note this openness at the outset, because the main direction of our discussion will be to indicate aspects of his thought that move in the opposite direction, towards being closed by an Aristotelian polarity. Several contemporary philosophers have begun the reconstructive work of moving towards a philosophical foundation for gender complementarity using a Thomistic metaphysics. No other philosopher in the time frame of 1250-1500 has been the source for so many serious contemporary attempts to articulate foundations for complementarity as those based upon a Thomistic understanding of the metaphysical structure of the human person. I will just mention a few of these attempts before moving back to the historical analysis of ways Thomas transmitted the Aristotelian model of gender identity. Each of these attempts by a twentieth-century philosopher focuses on a limitation in the Aristotelian-based philosophy at the same time that it uses fundamental Aristotelian cate-

108. This is well elaborated in Kristin Mary Popik, *The Philosophy of Woman of St. Thomas Aquinas* (Rome: Angelicum, 1979).

gories as developed by Thomas Aquinas. It is important to keep this double movement in mind as we indicate the exact area of weakness with respect to the philosophy of gender.

Exploration of new ranges of meaning of human species, man and woman as subspecies, and body/soul-engendered human identity is found in the work of the phenomenologist Edith Stein.[109] She questions Aristotle's thesis that the soul, or form of the body, is exactly the same in women and men, and that gender differentiation is due only to a bodily difference. She suggests that gender must also be in some sense an aspect of the form of a woman or a man, in a category of subspecies within the formal human species. Her theological impetus for this philosophical claim flowed from the belief that the particular vocation of a woman or a man was known by God before a person was conceived. The individual person's soul was given by God, and not simply in the formal contribution of the father to generation. Therefore, since the particular soul is given by God, the engendered identity of the person had to be a characteristic of the soul that formed the human material into a particular male or female body of a unique and unrepeatable man or woman.

Development of the significance of the acting person, as an individual substance of a rational nature in the context of a community of persons that includes gender differentiation, is found in the work of Karol Wojtyla, later Pope John Paul II.[110] His philosophy was articulated in the context of existential personalism, and it pointed out the limitation of seeing a man or a woman as simply one human individual among others, as in Aristotle, where a single human being is just an instance of primary substance or a rational animal. Instead, for Wojtyla the human person is a unique and unrepeatable existent who grows in perfection through intersubjective and complement participation in building up communities of persons. His theological impetus comes from understanding God as a Trinity and Communion of Love of Three unique and unrepeatable Divine Persons whose Divine Life is shared with specific men and women called into complement relations of love.

More recently, Norris Clarke, S.J. explores a notion of relationality as primary rather than accidental to personal identity.[111] The Aristotelian limitation here is to view all relations as accidental to substance. Clarke argues that relations can also be understood as essential to substance when the particular substance involved is a human person. His theological impulse flows also from a belief in the Holy Trinity, whose Divine Persons are essentially distinguished by relations of origin.

Another limitation in Aristotle's metaphysics has been identified by David Schindler in *Communio*.[112] He argues that there is a confusion between passivity and

---

109. Edith Stein, "Problems of Women's Education," in *Essays on Woman* (Washington, D.C.: ICS Publications, 1996), pp. 147-235. See also Jane Kelley Rodeheffer, "On Spiritual Maternity: Edith Stein, Aristotle, and the Nature of Woman," *American Catholic Philosophical Quarterly* 72 (1998): 285-303.

110. Karol Wojtyla, "Thomistic Personalism," in *Person and Community: Selected Essays* (New York: Peter Lang, 1993), pp. 165-75.

111. Norris Clarke, S.J., *Person and Being* (Milwaukee: Marquette University Press, 1993).

112. David Schindler, "Catholic Theology, Gender, and the Future of Western Civilization," in *Communio* 20 (Summer 1993): 200-239, and "Norris Clarke on Person, Being and St. Thomas," in

receptivity; while passivity excludes activity, receptivity includes activity. The further identification of the female with passivity and the male with activity brings a false polarization into relations of love that include an active receptivity as well as a going forth and sending forth. His theological impulse is the movement of love among the Divine Persons, involving both acts of receptivity — of going forth and sending forth.

Finally, Bernard Lonergan identifies a limitation in Aristotle's narrow understanding of form; he introduces a theory of sublated levels of conjugate forms within a particular existing human being who has a substantial form. This adapts an Aristotelian-Thomistic metaphysics to new levels of analysis consistent with findings in contemporary physics, chemistry, biology, physiology, psychology, philosophy, and theology.[113] His theological impulse flows from reflecting on God as Creator of a world open to scientific investigation. The world reveals itself as full of emergent probabilities in which a higher order of organization integrates the lower order. Lonergan's theory of conjugate forms can offer a way to explain gender differentiation that does not fall into the Aristotelian difficulty of taking a single seed, with a single human form, and explaining how it becomes male or female through a contrary privation.[114]

These studies indicate that there is room in the work of St. Thomas to develop some of his fundamental principles towards a new theory of gender identity that is partially based in a genuine complementarity. As we will see, Thomas believed that the empirical evidence and arguments offered by his teacher Albert collaborated metaphysical theories of Aristotle in their application to gender differentiation. His goal was to integrate these findings into a cohesive philosophical and theological system, not to challenge them.

Because St. Albert and St. Thomas used an empirical method, their Aristotelian-based Christian philosophy would today seek to integrate empirical knowledge of the contributions of mother and father to generation, of male and female physiology, of the psychology of men and women, and so on. The premise that all knowledge begins with the senses would drive them to provide a metaphysical foundation that would be coherent with the most recent scientific evidence. This means that they would seek to integrate a double-seed theory of generation rather than a single-seed theory into a metaphysics of the unity of substantial form in a particular woman or man. They would reflect on the relation of chromosomes to metaphysical categories of form and matter, on the relation of brains to women's and men's minds, and so forth.

We cannot help but wonder what difference it would have made for St. Albert and St. Thomas to have had the opportunity to discuss Aristotle's concept of woman

---

Communio 20 (Fall 1993): 580-92. See also Clarke's "Response to David Schindler's Comments," 593-98. I am personally grateful for having been invited to participate in a weekend colloquium by *Communio* that considered the question of receptivity and Thomistic metaphysics. The study by Frederick E. Crowe, S.J. of the two complementary motions of love in a person is also relevant. See "Complacency and Concern in the Thought of St. Thomas," *Theological Studies* 20 (March 1959): 1-39; (June 1959): 198-230; and (September 1959): 343-95.

113. Bernard Lonergan, *Insight*, ch. 15.

114. See Sr. Prudence Allen, "Metaphysics of Form, Matter, and Gender," *Lonergan Workshop* 12 (1996): 1-26.

with a woman philosopher of the quality of mind of Edith Stein. We know that Albert did visit Dominican convents of women religious during his term as Provincial of his Order and also when he was elevated to the Episcopacy. Since these convents did not have access to the new academic education, it is unlikely that he would have encountered women of the intellectual training and caliber of Benedictines such as Hildegard or Herrad. On the other hand, ". . . St. Thomas is commonly believed to have had very little contact with real women, other than his immediate family from whom he was separated at an early age and for almost all of his life."[115] It would seem that the completely male community of academic discourse did not offer the necessary context for revaluation of the Aristotelian concept of woman.

With this brief account of the dual movement of simultaneous critique and development of Aristotelian metaphysical principles we will now turn to consider further Thomas Aquinas's principles of gender identity before reflecting on how Aristotelianism as such forged a concept of woman that had some serious consequences for women and for men in centuries to come.

Qualification and Use of Aristotle's Natural Principle of Gender Polarity

There is no doubt that the primary contribution of St. Thomas to the transmission of Aristotelian gender polarity falls under the category of his natural principle: that the female is, as it were, a deformed male. As we will see, the medieval philosopher did qualify this principle in important ways. However, even with his qualifications the overall direction of his contribution on the particular issue of woman's identity is one that leads to the conclusion that woman is by nature inferior to man. Furthermore, because St. Thomas had such a genius for integrating philosophical principles into his cohesive theological system, it turned out that his conclusions about woman's identity had a broader and deeper reach than ever before in the history of Christian thought. It was precisely because St. Thomas was so right about so many things in human life, especially in relation to God, that his judgments about women were so seriously accepted.

When St. Thomas first began to teach at the University of Paris as a Bachelor, he would have lectured on the *Sentences* of Peter Lombard (1100-1160). This work systematically compiled the teachings of the early Church Fathers on four categories of Theology: God, Creation, Redemption, and Sacraments. For several centuries Lombard's *Sentences* was used as the main textbook in the Faculty of Theology at Paris and other universities following its curriculum. Since Lombard wrote the text before the translation of Aristotle's complete works into Latin he did not incorporate the philosopher's thought into the work. However, the commentaries written on it after the infusion of Aristotle into the university system frequently refer to the philosopher.

This shift in focus for the concept of woman can be documented, and it has significant implications for the history of theories of gender identity. As we men-

---

115. Kristin Mary Popik, *The Philosophy of Woman of St. Thomas Aquinas*, p. 35.

tioned previously, the foundations for a theory of sex complementarity had been emerging in the Benedictine tradition through the work of Anselm, Herrad, and Hildegard. Of particular note is the claim that men and women have an equal dignity even if they are significantly different. Lombard's original *Sentences* appears to support the premise of equal dignity of woman and man. At least it does not introduce any arguments for the natural inferiority of woman. When we turn to consider Thomas Aquinas's *Commentary* on the *Sentences* we find a different orientation. In Book II, Distinction 20, question 2, art. 1 (on weakness and death), he offers the following observations that introduce a distinction between the male (as the perfect sex) and the female. Thomas's first and second responses to the solution to the question are included in their entirety:

1. Although woman is beyond the intention of a particular nature that acts in the seed, intending to produce offspring perfectly like the one generating, nevertheless it is not beyond the intention of the universal nature. This is true also concerning death. Because without woman generation would not be possible, that the perpetuity of the species might be preserved. Therefore through divine providence for the purpose of generation some women must be born, and an equal number with men, that one woman may belong to one man.

2. The generation of woman occurs, as is said in *De animalibus* 18 or *De generatione animalium* 4.1, from that which the seed cannot overpower in the nature of woman to guide it in the final arrangement to **the perfect sex**. The cause of such impotence can be threefold:

   i. from the weakness of the natural source acting in the seed, because the heat is diminished in the seed;

   ii. from the imaginative power that the bodily power follows, as it is clear that when imagining something terrible the whole body is shaken and trembles. And so we see that children are often born looking like those the parents imagined in the act of conception. So Jerome says about a woman who gave birth to a black child because at the time of intercourse she imagined a black one. This cause of generation could have been in the state of innocence, so that children might be born of this or that sex, according to the will of the parents, especially because of the great submission of the body to the soul in that state;

   iii. from an external source, because a slight change, as Aristotle says (*De animalibus* 18), of the wind or season, or something like this, varies the sex. He says that it is proven by shepherds that when the north wind blows males are conceived and when the south wind blows females are conceived because of the greater moisture. And also if at the time of intercourse they faced the north or the south, the same difference frequently follows. This could have existed in the first state.[116]

---

116. Thomas Aquinas, *Petri Lombardi Sententiarum Libri Quattuor* (Paris: J. P. Migne, 1853). All passages are translated from Latin into English by Diane Gordon. Bold is my emphasis.

There are many aspects of the above argument that are worth noting. First, Thomas appeals to the authority of both Aristotle and Albert in citing specific texts written by them. Second, he repeats the Aristotelian view that the female is generated when something interferes with the intention of the seed of the father that aims to produce itself. He also repeats the particular Aristotelian hypotheses of interferences such as weakness in the father's seed, lack of heat, or moisture from the south wind. Third, he introduces Albert's distinction between the intention of the particular nature of the father's seed and the intention of universal nature (God or Divine Providence) to produce both women and men. Fourth, he reflects on how generation would have occurred in the original state before the Fall, and in this context he suggests that the rational choice (will of the parents) might have determined whether a child would be male or female. This is a very interesting hypothesis, following from a suggestion by St. Jerome that a woman's imagination determined the race of her child. Fifth, he characterizes the male as the perfect sex.

When we compare this sequence of thought in Thomas's early commentary on the *Sentences* with his mature argument in Part Ia, Question 92, Article 1 in the *Summa Theologiae* we find the same pattern. Question 92, Article 1 contains core elements of several of Aristotle's principles for gender polarity. Thomas asks the question: Should woman have been made in the original creation of things? In the first point, he introduces Aristotle to argue the *contra* position as follows:

> 1) It seems that woman ought not to have been produced in the original production of things. For the Philosopher says that the female is a male *manqué. (Dicit enim Philosophus quod femina est mas occasionatus.)* But nothing *manqué* or **defective** *(nihil occasionatum et deficiens)* should have been produced in the first establishment of things; so woman ought not to have been produced then.[117]

Note first of all, that in this paraphrase of Aristotle, Thomas does not have the qualifier, 'as it were,' in his summary of the philosopher's view that the female is a deformed male. The Aristotelian summary therefore loses some of the flexibility of the original philosopher's thought. Secondly, the Dominican translation of this phrase into English does not use the word 'deformed,' but rather the French word *'manqué,'* which implies a lack. The debate around the meaning of Aristotle's term, translated here in Latin as *occasionatus,* will be considered shortly, as it is full of controversy. Before this, however, we need to complete Thomas's argument and see his response to the above Aristotelian thesis.

After raising two other arguments to support the *contra* conclusion that woman should not have been created in the original state, and then introducing a passage from Scripture that supports the claim that it was good that woman was created in the original state, Thomas then provides his own argument. He first elaborates a detailed account of a hierarchal scale of living things that need to reproduce themselves by some combination of active and passive principle.

---

117. Thomas Aquinas, *Summa Theologiae,* Blackfriars edition, vols. 1-60 (New York: McGraw-Hill, 1964). Bold is my emphasis.

Then, almost echoing the Aristotelian description in *Generation of Animals* that in the noblest things, the male is separate from the female, he concludes:

> But at the top of the scale is man, whose life is directed to a nobler function still, that of understanding things. And so there was more reason than ever in man for emphasizing the distinction between the sexes, which was done by producing the woman separately from the man, while at the same time joining them together in a union of the flesh for the work of procreation. And therefore immediately after the formation of the woman it goes on to say, *They shall be two in one flesh.*[118]

This introduction of the epistemological purpose of human life, as the nobler function of man as rational animal capable of understanding things, is important for the concept of woman. We will consider this further shortly. For now, however, let us examine Thomas's response to the Aristotelian counterargument first introduced above.

In the passage below we can see the same principles already mentioned in his commentary on the *Sentences,* but they are condensed and given a sharper focus:

> Hence: 1) Only as regards nature in the individual is the female something defective and *manqué. (Quod per respectum ad naturam particularem femina est aliquid deficiens et occasionatum.)* For the active power in the seed of the male tends to produce something like itself, perfect in masculinity *(perfectum secundum masculinum sexum);* but the procreation of a female is the result either of the debility of the active power *(propter virtutis activae debilitatem),* of some unsuitability *(indispositionem)* of the material, or of some change effected by external influences, like the south wind, for example, which is damp, as we are told by Aristotle.
>
> But with reference to nature in the species as a whole, the female is not something *manqué (occasionatum),* but is according to the tendency of nature, and is directed to the work of procreation. Now the tendency of the nature of a species as a whole derives from God, who is the general author of nature. And therefore when he established a nature, he brought into being not only the male but the female too.[119]

There are several points that need to be made about the above passage. First of all, it uses Albert's distinction between the intention of individual and universal nature to answer the implication of the Aristotelian thesis that because woman is a defect in nature, then she should not have been created in an original state of perfection. By distinguishing between the intention of the individual nature of the male seed, which tends to produce a male like itself, and the intention of nature, which intends to produce both females and males, Thomas can conclude that women ought to have been created in the original state of perfection.

Secondly, there is the controversial question about the meaning of the Latin

118. Thomas Aquinas, *Summa Theologiae,* 1a. 92. 1.
119. Thomas Aquinas, *Summa Theologiae,* 1a, 92, 1.

phrase *femina est mas occasionatus* in the original Aristotelian paraphrase and *femina est aliquid deficiens et occasionatum* in Thomas's description of the intention of the particular nature of male seed. In a challenging article "The Defective Male: What Aquinas Really Said," Mgr. Michael Nolan argues that there is no derogatory meaning at all to Aristotle's original word *pepērōménon,* and that Thomas intentionally used the Michael Scot translation of this term as *occasionatum* (as had Albert before him) to suggest something like a congenital anomaly.[120] Nolan argues that Aquinas could have used William of Moerbeke's *orbatus* (which he translates variously as deprived, orphaned, or lacking), but he chose the term *occasionatum* created by Scot to describe the generation of the female. Nolan adds that the later translations of the word get even worse: ". . . Bekker says *laesus* (injured), and English scholars of the earlier years of this century have used 'deformed,' 'imperfectly developed,' 'underdeveloped,' 'malformed,' 'mutilated,' and 'congenitally disabled.'"[121]

With some irony Nolan suggests that the 1217 translation by Michael Scot into Latin three times removed from Aristotle's original Greek, through Syriac and Arabic, is more accurate than the direct translation into Latin from the Greek around 1260 by William of Moerbeke. He concludes that the real meaning of both Aristotle and Aquinas, captured by the Latin word *occasionatus,* is simply that the process of generation just indirectly or unintentionally occasions the female. He suggests that the two philosophers are simply describing a process and not a product, and that there is no devaluation of the female meant in this description of the process of generating males or females. The implication of Nolan's argument is that no natural foundation exists in these two philosophers for a gender polarity theory.

This claim of Michael Nolan is forcefully put, and since, as previously mentioned, it has been publicly suggested that scholars who come to different conclusions are in some sense distorting the thought of Aristotle and Thomas Aquinas, it is important to respond to his claims in the context of this attempt to understand accurately thirteenth-century scholastic proposals about the concept of woman.[122]

First, given the distinction between the intention of particular nature and universal nature, it is not correct to say simply that for Albert or for Aquinas the female is a deformed male. This means that the natural principle for gender polarity is always qualified by this distinction. Even though Aristotle's qualification, "as it were," is dropped, a new qualification is added, namely that universal nature or God intends the female as much as the male.

Second, in the expression, 'only as regards nature in the individual is the female something defective and *manqué,*' Thomas means by the word 'individual' the seed in the father, and not the product or the female generated. Something

---

120. Michael Nolan, *Defective Tales,* pp. 7-19. This article was also published in *New Blackfriars* 75, no. 880 (March 1994): 156-66, and in a new form in *The Thomist* 64 (2000): 21-69.

121. Nolan, "The Defective Male," in *New Blackfriars,* p. 157. For slightly different wording see *Defective Tales,* p. 10.

122. For these reflections I am very grateful to Lawrence Dewan, OP, Collège Dominicain de Philosophie et de Théologie, Ottawa, Canada and to Kevin White, Catholic University of America for their clarifications of the relation between Mgr. Nolan's arguments and the original texts of Aquinas.

lacking or interfering makes the active power in the male seed fail to produce something like itself 'perfect in masculinity.'

Third, there still remains the question of the understanding of woman's nature in relation to man's nature. It is here that the devaluation of woman occurs as already indicated in Aristotle and Albert, and as will be demonstrated in Thomas Aquinas. The question is whether or not Thomas considers the product of a defective process to itself be a kind of defect. In other words, is the female herself deficient because she is unintentionally caused?

Mgr. Nolan turns to Book III, Chapter 94, 11 of *Summa contra gentiles* to support his claim. Paraphrasing Thomas's argument, he says that the goal of the whole of nature works towards the good of the whole, while the goal of the part simply works towards its own good, which is of lesser value. Nolan translates Aquinas to say: "Thus a particular outcome may be defective so far as the part is concerned, but is not a defect so far as the whole is concerned."[123] Since the goal of nature as a whole is to produce females, it follows that woman is not at all defective. However, Lawrence Dewan, OP claims that the same passage should be more accurately translated as follows: "Hence, some defect is outside the intention of the particular agent, which is according to the intention of the universal agent. . . ."[124] In this passage, the female herself is clearly classified as 'some defect.'

In order to make it more evident that Thomas does describe the female as a kind of defect in nature in comparison with the male, we will include a portion of the paragraph from Book II, Chapter 94 of *Summa contra gentiles,* in which he elaborates different kinds of defects. Question 94 is: On the Certainty of Divine Providence. In this extremely important passage from Section 11 Thomas introduces the core elements in his theory that there are different values to engendered perfections, male perfection and female perfection. We will begin with yet another translation of the same passage identified above:

> Indeed, the particular agent tends to the good of the part without qualification, and makes it the best that it can, but the universal agent tends to the good of the whole. As a result, a defect that is in accord with the intention of the universal agent may be apart from the intention of the particular agent. Thus, it is clear that the generation of a female is apart from the intention of a particular nature, that is, of the power that is in this semen which, as much as possible, tends to a perfect result of conception; but it is in accord with the intention of the universal nature, that is, of the power of the universal agent for the generation of inferior beings, that a female be generated; for without a female the generation of a number of animals could not be accomplished. Similarly, corruption, decrease, and every defect pertain to the intention of the universal nature, but not of the particular nature, for each thing avoids defect, and tends to perfect, to the extent that it can. So, it is evident that the intention of the particular agent is that its effect become as perfect as is possible in its kind, but the intention of the universal nature

123. Nolan, "The Defective Male," in *New Blackfriars,* p. 160.
124. Lawrence Dewan, OP in personal correspondence to the author dated June 9, 1995.

is that this individual effect become perfect in a certain type of perfection, say in male perfection, while another become so in female perfection.[125]

In the above argument, the female is a defect along with other defects like corruption, decrease, and so forth. Yet the female has also a certain kind of perfection. It is a less noble perfection than male perfection; it is the limited perfection of the kind of being a female is. In other words, there are grades in reality, and the one part of the whole of reality that is the female part has a lesser grade of perfection than the male part. This is why in his theological reflections Thomas does refer to the male as "the more noble flesh,"[126] as the "perfect sex,"[127] and as possessing eminence of degree.[128]

Within the context of a Thomistic theology it is important to note that his adaptation of Aristotle's natural principles to suggest a natural inferiority of the female in relation to the male is balanced by a theology of grace that involves adoption into the Divine Life by Baptism. Generation is transformed through regeneration in Christ. Women saints are perfect women, just as men saints are perfect men. Thomas also gives the usual arguments for why there will be both women and men in heaven after the resurrection of the body. In *Summa contra gentiles* he repeats the rejection of the claim that in the resurrection a woman, as an imperfect being, will be turned into a man:

> [1] One ought, nevertheless, not hold that among the bodies of the risen the feminine sex will be absent, as some have thought. For, since the resurrection is to restore the deficiencies of nature, nothing that belongs to the perfection of nature will be denied to the bodies of the risen. Of course, just as other bodily members belong to the integrity of the human body, so do those which serve for generation — not only in men but also in women. Therefore, in each of the cases members of this sort will rise. . . .
>
> [3] In like fashion, also, the frailty of the feminine sex is not in opposition to the perfection of the risen. For this frailty is not due to a shortcoming of nature, but to an intention of nature. And this very distinction of nature among human beings will point out the perfection of nature and the divine wisdom as well, which disposes all things in a certain order.[129]

Thomas insists that a human being is incomplete without his or her body. Human essence includes having a particular engendered body. In the act of existence a

---

125. St. Thomas Aquinas, *On the Truth of the Catholic Faith: Summa Contra Gentiles* (Garden City, N.Y.: Image Books, 1956), Book Three: Providence, Part 2, Q 94, 11.

126. Thomas Aquinas, *Summa Theologica,* III, Q. 31 (Whether the Matter of Christ's Body Should Have Been Taken from a Woman?), art. 4, reply Obj 1.

127. Thomas Aquinas, *Sentences,* Book II, Dist. 20, Q. 2, art. 1, rep. 2.

128. Thomas Aquinas, *Summa Theologica,* Suppl., Quest. 39, Art. 1.

129. Thomas Aquinas, *Summa Contra Gentiles,* IV, 88, 1, 3. An often neglected passsage in *Summa Contra Gentiles,* II, 81, 8 needs to be noted here. St. Thomas describes diversity as due to "diversity in the commensuration of souls to bodies since this soul is adapted to this and not to that body. . . ." Both Msgr. John Wippel and Rev. Norris Clarke, SJ, have mentioned in private conversation that this passage may contribute to a more balanced theory of sex and gender differentiation.

woman's or a man's identity has an inherent tendency towards perfection of his or her personal essence. The resurrection of a particular engendered glorified body is necessary for this perfection of the individual act of existence. Both men and women were willed by God at Creation, and are ordained towards a life of holiness and communion with God and one another that will reach fulfillment in the communion of saints in heaven.

Amplification of Aristotle's Epistemological Principle of Gender Polarity

If we continue to follow St. Thomas's argument in Part Ia, Question 92 of *Summa theologiae* we find in his second reply a repetition of Aristotle's thesis that woman's mind is weaker than man's mind. It reads as follows:

> Subjection is of two kinds; one is that of slavery, in which the ruler manages the subject for his own advantage, and this sort of subjection came in after sin. But the other kind of subjection is domestic or civil, in which the ruler manages his subjects for *their* advantage and benefit. And this sort of subjection would have obtained even before sin. For the human group would have lacked the benefit of order had some of its members not been governed by others who were wiser. Such is the subjection in which woman is by nature subordinate to man, because the power of rational discernment is by nature stronger in man. Nor is inequality among men incompatible with the state of innocence, as we shall see later on.[130]

Again Thomas introduces a philosophical principle, that man's power of rational discernment is stronger than woman's by nature, into the theological question of whether women ought to have been generated at the beginning before the Fall. His introduction of this principle justifies the ethical principle that men should rule women for women's advantage and benefit. In other words, because women are weak in rational discernment, it is helpful to them to be ruled by a man. However, this ruling by nature does not participate in the tyranny associated with master/slave relations after the Fall in which a man would rule for his own advantage and benefit.

In his *Commentary on Aristotle's Politics* Thomas elaborates some specific characteristics of women's weaker powers of rational discernment again in the context of a discussion of the different kinds of ruling and obedience found among men, slaves, women, and boys. Again it is helpful to include his reasoning process to demonstrate how he builds on Aristotle and amplifies the original premises of the Greek philosopher.

> But since a woman is free, she has the capacity for understanding but her capacity is weak. The reason for this is because on account of the changeableness of her nature, her reason weakly adheres to plans, but quickly is removed from

130. Thomas Aquinas, *Summa Theologiae*, Ia, 92, 1, 2.

them because of emotions, for example of desire, or anger, or fear or something else of the kind. . . .

And in a similar way it must also be considered about moral excellences: for all [men, slaves, women, boys] share them, but not in the same way; but each one participates in them as far as it is necessary for the appropriate role. From which [it follows that] he who rules whether a state, servants, a woman or sons, it is proper that he possess a perfected moral excellence, because his work is simply the work of an architect, that is, of the principal builder. For just as the principal craftsman directs and orders the servants of craft who work with their hands, so the leader directs his subjects; and therefore he has the task of reason, which compares in the same way as the chief craftsman to the inferior parts of the soul. And thus it is right that the one who rules have perfected reason; but each one of the others who are subject, has as much of reason and excellence as the one who rules permits in them, that is, as much as is right that they possess, which suffices to follow the direction of the leader by fulfilling his commands.[131]

What we find in this commentary is that St. Thomas amplifies the way in which women's weaker intellect functions with her emotions of desire, anger, fear, and so forth, interfering with her reasoning and leading her to not adhere well to plans or to the process of discursive reasoning. Thus to be virtuous she needs to place the powers of her irrational soul under the rule of man's rational soul.

Should a woman not place her reasoning under a man's leadership, her conclusions may be faulty. Thomas argues in an important passage in the *Summa theologiae*, regarding testimony presented in a court: "Now the reliability of a person's evidence is weakened sometimes, without any fault on his part, and this owing either to a defect in the reason, as in the case of children, imbeciles and women. . . ."[132] In these cases, as well as in other situations, he concludes that a person's evidence may be rejected. Here the philosophical ground for the epistemological principle of gender polarity is being used in the application of law.

Kristin Mary Popik, in *The Philosophy of Woman of St. Thomas Aquinas,* gathers many examples from different sources in Thomas to show that he frequently mentioned women's naturally deficient reason. One of the most striking for our purposes is the statement in *De regimine principum* IV, 5: *"Mulier est masculus occasionatus; unde sicut deficit in complexione, ita et in ratione."* [Woman is a deformed man; thus she is deficient in bodily complexion and also in reason.][133] This linkage from the natural principle to the epistemological principle is made explicit. Woman's defective generation leads to the consequence that her reason is weakly formed.

Popik brings in many examples from St. Thomas's writings where the epistemological principle is introduced in the context of theological discussions. For example in his *Commentary on St. Paul's First Letter to Timothy* (II, 3) he uses

131. Thomas Aquinas, *Politicorum Aristotelis,* X, 1. Translated by Diane Gordon.
132. Thomas Aquinas, *Summa Theologiae,* II-II, Q. 70, art. 3.
133. As quoted in Popik, *The Philosophy of Woman of St. Thomas Aquinas,* p. 21, and taken from *De Regimine Principum ad Regem Cypri* in *Politica Opuscula Duo* (Turin: Marietti, 1948), IV, 5.

the premise of woman's deficiency in reason to suggest that her virtue is silence, rather than speech; and in his *Commentary on St. Paul's First Letter to the Corinthians* (XIV, 7) he uses the same principle of women's natural defect in reason to argue that women ought not to teach men.[134] Thomas qualifies this principle in the *Summa theologiae* where he suggests that women may teach men in the private context of small groups or in individual dialogue, but that they may not address a universal audience as do men. However, even here his rationale invokes the natural subjection of the female sex to the male sex.[135] What we see in these arguments is a progressive integration of the natural and epistemological principles of women's defective generation being used by Thomas to explain why the Apostle Paul might have made certain admonitions about women's actions in his letters. This delicate interweaving of philosophical and theological arguments had the effect of locking women's inferior identity into a Christian gender polarity.

This same move occurs in the *Summa contra gentiles,* where Thomas is considering in Chapter 123: Whether Matrimony Should Be Indivisible. While the beginning and end of the paragraph mention the fundamental equity of a man and woman in Christian marriage, in the middle we find the insertion of a principle of polarity:

> It also seems to be against equity if the aforesaid society be dissolved. For the female needs the male, not merely for the sake of generation, as in the case of other animals, but also for the sake of government, since the male is both more perfect in reasoning and stronger in his powers. In fact, a woman is taken into man's society for the needs of generation; then, with the disappearance of a woman's fecundity and beauty, she is prevented from association with another man. So, if any man took a woman in the time of her youth, when beauty and fecundity were hers, and then sent her away after she had reached an advanced age, he would damage that woman contrary to natural equity.[136]

In this example it is clear that Thomas is actually defending woman's dignity and rights to remain married when she may no longer be attractive to her husband. Yet, his rationale is based on a woman's need for the rational powers of the man because of a lack on her part. The polarity inherent in this explanation is obvious.

The above examples demonstrate St. Thomas's brilliant synthesis of philosophy and theology. They also indicate the linkage in his mind among the natural and epistemological principles. Just as the inferiority of woman in generation is transformed by a regeneration in the life of grace, so the inferiority of woman's natural reasoning capacities can be transformed by the infusion of intellectual gifts. Wisdom, counsel, and understanding as gifts of the Holy Spirit, along with faith and hope as infused theological virtues, perfect the human intellect. Through regeneration in Christian life, the lesser perfection of woman's natural identity

---

134. Popik, *The Philosophy of Woman of St. Thomas Aquinas*, p. 21. See also *Summa Theologiae,* II-II, Q. 177, art. 2.

135. Thomas Aquinas, *Summa Theologiae,* II-II, Q. 177, art. 2.

136. Thomas Aquinas, *Summa Contra Gentiles,* III, 3, 147-48.

achieves its proper terminus after death when her intellect is filled with the Beatific Vision and her will is transformed by Beatitude. St. Thomas does not reject Aristotle's gender polarity, but he transforms it to coincide with Christian principles about the goal or end of human life as perfect union with God. In heaven the natural polarity between men and women is transformed by a genuine complementarity.

We will now turn to the final ethical principle to conclude our reflections on Thomas Aquinas's particular method of transmitting Aristotle's rationale for gender polarity.

Amplification and Modification of Aristotle's Ethical Principle of Gender Polarity

We stated above that the Aristotelian ethical principle for gender polarity claimed that men and women have a different measure of virtue. Thomas followed Aristotle's argument in the *Politics* that men, slaves, women, and boys have different measures of virtue, or of the moral excellence in wisdom, temperance, courage, and justice. As we saw above, a man is virtuous by ruling and by public speech, and a woman is virtuous by obeying and by silence in public. In these claims Thomas simply follows the text of Aristotle.

However, in other contexts, he goes beyond the original statements of the Greek philosopher to amplify the connections among his arguments. An example will suffice to demonstrate the power of the Thomistic commentary to illuminate the interior connections in the original arguments of Aristotle. In the following extract from Thomas's *Commentary on Nicomachean Ethics* we find the clear link between Aristotle's natural principle, his epistemological principle, and his ethical principle repeated. In Book VII Aristotle had been reflecting on different forms of incontinence. In this context Aristotle simply said the following: "Now those in whom nature is the cause of such a state no one would call incontinent, any more than one would apply the epithet to women because of the passive part they play in copulation . . ." (1148b 31-33). In his commentary St. Thomas moves to offer a broad description of woman's ethical capacities.

> 1375. (. . .) We have already said [1350] that dumb animals are not referred to as continent or incontinent since they exercise no universal judgment but only imagination and memory of particulars. But these men who, by reason of a malignant nature, are like wild beasts indeed do have some, although very little, universal perception, reason in them being weighed down by bad temperament, as is obviously the case with those physically sick. But what is very little seems to be as nothing. Nor is it likely that the force of a weak argument should repel strong desires. Consequently, these individuals are not called incontinent or continent simply but only in a restricted sense, insofar as some judgment of reason remains with them.
>
> 1376. He [Aristotle] offers the example of women in whom, for the most part, reason flourishes very little because of the imperfect nature of their body. Because

of this they do not govern their emotions in the majority of cases by reason but rather are governed by their emotions. Hence wise and brave women are rarely found, and so women cannot be called continent and incontinent without qualification. The same argument seems valid for those who are ill, i.e., have a diseased temperament because of bad habits, which oppresses the judgment of reason after the manner of a perverse nature.[137]

We can see how Thomas's commentary goes beyond the original text in its elaboration of the inferior natural foundation for woman's ethical identity. Scholars have identified several different sources for Thomas's commentary on the *Nicomachean Ethics:* Aspasius' ancient Greek commentary, Grosseteste's notes on his Latin translation of the text, and Albert the Great's *Lectura.*[138] Therefore, the additions to Aristotle may have been derived from other commentators. In the above passage, the meaning was implicit in Aristotle's text, but not precisely in the way he used woman's nature in the example. However, it becomes explicit in Thomas's commentary and expanded as a theoretical principle. In this reflection on the different moral states in Book VII of Aristotle's *Ethics,* Thomas draws out a general principle about the need to qualify the ethical identity of women. Their virtue (and their vice) will have a lesser measure than that of man because their deliberative reason is weak, and their reason is weak because of the imperfect nature of their body. He gives the further amplification that women are usually governed by their emotions. So the ethical principle for gender polarity is traced to the epistemological principle for gender polarity, which is traced back to the natural principle for gender polarity.

The whole question of how women and men can be morally evaluated was brought by Thomas into the theological context of considering the causes and effects of the Fall. Significantly, in the works of Saint Thomas we do not find any bitter accusations against women as the cause of man's downfall. Instead, he attempts to describe what it is in the nature of a woman that explains choices she might make. In Thomas's *Commentary* on Peter Lombard's *Sentences,* Eve's sin is judged as more serious than Adam's. The argument is worth including because it once again introduces the engendered characteristic of reasoned judgments:

> And according to this it is clear that the sin of the woman was more serious. For the woman was moved to sin solely out of pride, but the man sinned not solely from pride but along with this from a kindly love for his wife, and this in some way lessens his sin. Likewise the pride that moved the woman was greater than the pride that moved the man. For in the woman pride became so great that at the words of the serpent she felt a desire for eminence so great that it perfected the judgment of reason and believed that what the devil said was possible and true. And because of this it is said that she was seduced. But in the man in the be-

---

137. Thomas Aquinas, *Commentary on Nicomachean Ethics,* VII (1376) 1148b 31-33. This text was erroneously cited in Vol. 1 note 557 as coming from a commentary on the *Politics.*

138. Bourke, "The *Nicomachean Ethics* and Thomas Aquinas," in *St. Thomas Aquinas: 1274-1974, Commemorative Studies,* pp. 243ff.

ginning it did not become so great as to pervert his judgment as if he would believe that this would be true. But because he desired nothing unless it were possible, he is not said to have been seduced. But nevertheless it was a kind of pride that incited him to try. Pride put in him some hesitation, while in the woman it put a firm belief. Therefore the woman desired to be like God with full consent, but the man with imperfect consent, that is, only on condition that it would be possible.[139]

It is important to include in this consideration of the different measure of virtue of women and men also the question of the different measure of vice. As we will discover in our analysis of humanist texts, the question of whether Eve or Adam held the greater blame for the Fall caused considerable debate. Sometimes the debate was intentionally humorous. At other times it was deeply serious. In this context it should be noted that neither Aristotle nor Thomas Aquinas sought to blame women for men's immoral or sinful behavior. This is in contrast to many other authors, including the passage cited above by Albert. In addition, Thomas argued that original sin, or the tendency towards disorder in moral life, was inherited in generation only through the man and not through the woman. The reason for this is that original sin could not be transmitted through the material contribution the mother provides, but rather through the formal contribution of the father.[140]

Thomas argued directly against the claim that woman ought not to have been created originally because Eve was going to be an occasion of sin for a man. In *Summa theologica* Ia, 92, 1, reply to the third objection, Thomas states that there would be an incompleteness if woman had not been created, and that any particular evil can always be turned by God to the general good. In his elaboration of the general good of a world with women and men, Thomas identifies two areas: the first is the good of the perpetuation of the species through generation, which needs both genders; but the second is the common good of the just order of society through a division of labor.

Following from this, there are two significant characteristics of Thomas's description of virtues of men and women in marriage that should be noted. The first concerns the division of labor into the public and the private sphere, and the second concerns their virtue of friendship. In Book VIII, chapter 12 of the *Nicomachean Ethics* Aristotle notes that women and men form couples not just for the purpose of generation, but also "for the various purposes of life; for from the start the functions are divided, and those of man and woman are different; so they help each other by throwing their particular gifts into the common stock" (1162a 21-25). In Thomas's *Commentary* on this same text the division of functions is specified: "These functions — it is immediately apparent — are so divided between man and woman that some are proper to the husband, like external works; and others to the wife, like sewing and other domestic occupations. Thus mutual needs are provided for, when each contributes his own services for the common good."[141]

139. Thomas Aquinas, *Sentences,* Dist. 22, Q. 1, art. 3. Translated by Diane Gordon.
140. Thomas Aquinas, *Summa Theologica,* 1a, 2ae, 81, 5.
141. Thomas Aquinas, *Commentary on the Nicomachean Ethics,* VIII, 1721.

Thomas mistakenly thought that the *Oeconomicus*[142] was written by Aristotle when in fact it appears to have been modeled after Xenophon's *Oeconomicus,*[143] which was written in the fifth to fourth century B.C. by a disciple of Plato. This particular text on the theme of estate management specified many different functions of husband and wife. It elaborated particular divisions of labor with the man acting in the public (external) sphere of the household and *polis* and the woman in the private (interior) sphere of the household. Averroes wrote a commentary on the text, which was translated into Latin sometime after 1267 and included as part of Aristotle's *Politics.* Saint Thomas often referred to it. Through this medium of transmission, particular engendered functions were specified in the division of labor into public forms for man and private forms for woman; and they were given the sanction of Aristotle beyond the more general principle he had suggested. This may be why Thomas mentions sewing as an example of a domestic function of women.

Another modification Thomas may have adopted from the pseudo-Aristotelian *Oeconomicus* is the view that the friendship between husband and wife ought to be a friendship of equality, rather than the friendship of inequality that Aristotle had originally suggested. In his *Commentary on the Nicomachean Ethics* Thomas describes the nature of this friendship: "But when the husband and wife are virtuous, their friendship can be based on virtue. In fact, there is a virtue proper to both husband and wife that renders their friendship delightful to each other. . . . [T]hey ought to live together in such a way that each fulfills what is just to the other."[144]

The view that friendship can be a virtue shared by husband and wife is repeated in *Summa contra gentiles* in the context of a discussion about why marriage should be indivisible.

> Furthermore, the greater that friendship is, the more solid and long-lasting will it be. Now, there seems to be the greatest friendship between husband and wife, for they are united not only in the act of fleshly union, which provides a certain gentle association even among beasts, but also in the partnership of the whole range of domestic activity.[145]

In another interesting argument from the same section in the *Summa contra gentiles,* Thomas introduces both a principle of equality among husband and wife and at the same time a natural subjection of wife to husband. In this complex situation, we find again a gender polarity introduced but qualified:

> Again, it seems obviously inappropriate for a woman to be able to put away her husband, because a wife is naturally subject to her husband as governor, and it is

---

142. Aristotle (Spurious), *The Politics and Economics of Aristotle* (London: Henry G. Bohn, 1853).

143. Xenophon, *Memorabilia and Oeconomicus* (New York and London: G. P. Putnam's Sons and William Heinemann, 1923).

144. Thomas Aquinas, *Commentary on Nicomachean Ethics,* VIII, 1723.

145. Thomas Aquinas, *Summa Contra Gentiles,* III, 123, 6.

not within the power of a person subject to another to depart from his rule. So, it would be against the natural order if a wife were able to abandon her husband. Therefore, if a husband were permitted to abandon his wife, the society of husband and wife would not be an association of equals, but, instead, a sort of slavery on the part of the wife.[146]

The equality of the two is based on the free-will association that is characteristic of a human being not sold in slavery. The subjection of the woman occurs after freely entering into the marriage contract, when she places herself under the aristocratic (not tyrannical) rule of her husband because of the weakness of her own reason. Popik points out that Thomas never claims that all women should be subject to all men, or even that every woman ought to be subject to a man. She notes that widows are without this subjection.[147]

Finally, in the public realm, women have a different measure of virtue than men. They must follow and not lead, and they must remain silent and not speak. Again, the rationale for this differentiation of the measure of virtue reaches back to the epistemological principle of gender polarity. Popik summarizes it this way:

> [Women] must abstain from civic activities, from warfare, and even from being lawyers, since public disputation is shameful in a woman just as public teaching is. Women are unfit to be civil rulers because of the weakness of their reason. . . . Aquinas explains Aristotle's statement that the rule of women is the corruption of the city by saying that reason is the most necessary requirement for rulers, so women, who are deficient in reason, must be subject and not rule.[148]

Just as the natural inferiority of women's reason is overturned by the infusion of wisdom, so women's lesser measure of virtue is transformed by the infused virtues, and especially of the virtue of charity which perfects the will. So even if women are weaker in the practice of the natural virtues of temperance, courage, and practical wisdom or prudence, Thomas would argue that they are as strong or even stronger in the supernatural virtues. That is why women could become holy or saints as easily or more easily than men. That is why Mary, who is full of grace, can be considered as a most perfect human being. So even though Thomas integrated Aristotelian gender polarity through his ethical principle, he transformed it by a Christian theology that enabled women as well as men to live a regenerated life through Christ in God. Thus his philosophy of gender polarity was transformed by a theology of complementarity in which women and men were equal but significantly different in heaven in the communion of saints among the risen.

We could say that Thomas moderated the Aristotelian gender polarity in his

---

146. Thomas Aquinas, *Summa Contra Gentiles,* III, 123, 4.

147. Popik, *The Philosophy of Woman of St. Thomas Aquinas,* pp. 57ff.

148. Popik, *The Philosophy of Woman of St. Thomas Aquinas,* p. 60. She includes the following references for these judgments: *In Pol.* II, 6; *De Reg. Prin.* IV.5; *In I ad Cor.* XIV, 7, 881; *In Pol.* II, 13; *In I ad Cor.* XIV, 7, 880; and *In IV Sent.* 19, 1, 1, 3, ad 4. She notes that the *Supplement* to *Summa Theologiae* 39, 1, and 2 adds the qualification that women can exercise rule over temporal but not spiritual affairs.

Christian theology, so that even though he was a crucial source for the transmission of Aristotelian metaphysical, natural, epistemological, and ethical principles, he also provided principles for a totally new way to overcome them through the life of grace and charity. In this way, he used the genius of Aristotle's philosophy in a new way that by particularly delineating a life of good habits and virtues, opened a new avenue for women to achieve a full actualization equal in dignity to men. However, because of the engendered limitation of the academic structure of education, it took two centuries before women had sufficient access to Thomas's works to integrate the whole of his systematic approach to their own goals of human life.

In the meantime, St. Thomas was encumbered in great internal tensions and divisions in the academic structure of the new University in Paris. At the outset, the Aristotelian methodology in philosophy began to establish the genuine autonomy of this field from Theology. Benedict Ashley summarizes this new reality very well:

> As a result of the Aristotelian epistemology the liberal arts for the first time in the history of Christian culture found an adequate justification for their genuine autonomy as secular disciplines. It was now realized that "philosophy" (which included all that today we would call the natural, life, and behavioral sciences) had a method and validity of its own, not merely as an instrument of theology, but as clearly differentiated and independent fields of knowledge. The arts faculty wished to maintain this autonomy even at the risk of accusations of heresy.[149]

This situation of tension was further intensified with the infusion of a radical Aristotelianism, influenced by Averroes, into the lower faculty of philosophers. The Islamic philosophers also argued that philosophy was a better source of wisdom than was religion. "On December 10, 1270 Stephen Tempier, Bishop of Paris condemned thirteen errors and excommunicated all who knowingly teach or assert them."[150] Thomas Aquinas, teaching in the Faculty of Theology in Paris from 1269 to 1272, was embroiled in the midst of these controversies. He was called to defend his positions in an assembly of Parisian Masters,[151] and he wrote a text on the unity of the intellect against the Averroists in 1270. In 1272, the Arts Faculty itself promulgated a regulation that said that no one teaching in the Faculty of Arts could dispute a theological question. If they did, without recanting, in three days they would be removed from the Faculty forever. In this regulation we have a strict institutionalized division between philosophy and theology.

Around the same time, it was also decided that students of Theology could not study Medicine or Civil Law. In these decisions academic discourse began to become rigidly disciplinary. Thus, although the Aristotelian principles for gender polarity were linked in a cohesive intellectual system, the mechanisms for ques-

---

149. Benedict Ashley, O.P., *Theologies of the Body: Humanist and Christian* (Braintree, Mass.: The Pope John Center, 1985), p. 151.

150. John F. Wippel, "The Condemnations of 1270 and 1277 at Paris," *The Journal of Medieval and Renaissance Studies* 7 (1977): 179.

151. E. Hocedez, "La condamnation de Gilles de Rome," *Recherches de Théologie Ancienne et Médiévale* 4 (1932): 35, n. 6.

tioning their foundations began to be separated out in isolated faculties and disciplines protecting their own identity rather than engaging in a wide-ranging and integrated search for truth.

Thomas Aquinas left Paris in 1272, and he died soon after in 1274. In a few years the conflicts among the Radical Aristotelians in the Faculty of Arts and others at the university again reached a flashpoint. In 1277 Bishop Tempier of Paris condemned 219 propositions, many of which had Aristotelian roots. "And a number of the propositions prohibited at Paris were surely aimed at Aquinas and were so understood by contemporaries."[152] Most of the prohibited propositions were philosophical and would have been taught in the Faculty of Arts. At the same time a similar battle was being fought at Oxford, where thirty propositions taken from grammar, logic, and natural philosophy were condemned. Several of these also appeared to be directed towards positions of Thomas. There was continuing tension at Paris about the orthodoxy of the Aristotelian foundations for Christian philosophy, and there is a legend that Albert went to Paris in 1277 to defend the recently deceased Thomas, whose views were being attacked. James Weisheipl argues that it was not Thomas who was in danger, but other philosophers who were using Aristotle and Averroes against Catholic doctrine, and that it is unlikely that Albert made this defense of his student.[153] However, the controversy made people cautious of Thomas, and ". . . the condemnation weighed heavily on the scientific life of the university for some decades. One extreme example is the 'exile' of Giles of Rome from the Theology Faculty from 1278 to 1285. . . ."[154] Another is the rise of the Franciscan School, with the work of Bonaventure, Ockham, and Scotus.

In the next section of this chapter we will consider directly Giles of Rome's concept of woman as well as developments on this topic in the work of Duns Scotus. With the canonization of St. Thomas in 1323, the basic lines of a Christian Aristotelian philosophy and theology were solidly established for the next period. With this reversal, the Thomistic integration of Aristotelian principles became enshrined in the fourteenth century as a most important source for a natural foundation for gender polarity while at the same time offering a supernatural source for a differentiated equality of men and women in the communion of saints. Papal Bulls from 1451 on by Clement VI, Benedict XIII, St. Pius V, and Clement XII put forth Thomas as the model for truth and the avoidance of error.[155]

Gerald McCool, S.J., in an essay "Why St. Thomas Stays Alive," indicates that Thomas's influence waned very quickly until a revival of a Second Scholasticism after the Council of Trent in the period 1540-1580.[156] An indication of this

152. Wippel, "Condemnations of 1270 and 1277," p. 170.

153. J. A. Weisheipl, *Albertus Magnus and the Sciences,* pp. 43-44. This legend is interesting, however, because it was given as testimony at the 1319 process for St. Thomas's canonization.

154. Wippel, "Condemnations of 1270 and 1277," p. 200.

155. Pope Leo XIII, *Aeterni Patris: Encyclical Letter on the Restoration of Christian Philosophy,* in *One Hundred Years of Thomism: Aeterni Patris and Afterwards a Symposium,* ed. Victor B. Brezik, C.S.B. (Houston: Center for Thomistic Studies, 1981), p. 189. See also the recent encyclical letter of Pope John Paul II, *Fides et ratio* (Boston: Pauline Books, 1998), # 43-48.

156. Gerald A. McCool, S.J., "Why St. Thomas Stays Alive," *International Philosophical Quarterly* 30, no. 3 (September 1990): 275-87.

second phase is seen in an Oxford statute of 1586 anticipating a 1624 decree of the Parliament of Paris, in which philosophers were prohibited "from holding or teaching any maxim contrary to the ancient and approved authors."[157] Pope Innocent XII directly reaffirmed the corpus of Thomas Aquinas in 1694, as did Benedict XIV in 1752. These reaffirmations of Thomism may have been a sign that in the eighteenth century the influence of Thomas was waning in academic centers. A particularly strong defense of the scholastic philosopher was given by Innocent VI with the judgment: ". . . those who hold to it [his teaching] are never found swerving from the path of truth, and he who dare assail it will always be suspected of error."[158]

This particular prohibition against criticizing St. Thomas posed a difficult challenge for those scholars who may have accepted many of the basic positions of the medieval philosopher, but who saw a need to revise and correct some errors in his corpus. Obviously the prohibition of suspicion would serve to inhibit serious challenges to his concept of woman. Thomism did subside again until a Third Scholasticism emerged in a Neoscholastic movement in the nineteenth and early twentieth centuries. Finally, McCool suggests that Thomas died again in the mid-twentieth century only to be recently resurrected in a Fourth Scholasticism as more of a living tradition than a cohesive set of philosophical and theological principles. It is finally in this context that we can understand the new and interesting work of theorists like Edith Stein, Karol Wojtyla, Bernard Lonergan, and Norris Clarke, who use some Thomistic distinctions to articulate a renewed and revised philosophical and theological foundation for gender complementarity.

In the following sections two significant authors who continued in the western academic metaphysical tradition will be briefly considered in order to demonstrate how Aristotelian foundations for gender polarity continued to be transmitted and modified through the new academic network flowing from the prime model at the University of Paris. After the great synthesis of Thomas Aquinas, and the integration of philosophical foundations into a theological worldview, we find the next two philosophers in two different directions in gender polarity theory: one towards simplification and the other towards complexification. In the work of Giles of Rome (1243-1316) we will see a tendency to narrow his focus to strictly philosophical arguments that support gender polarity, and in the work of John Duns Scotus (1265-1308) we will see a tendency to make more complex nuances of a basic gender polarity orientation. While it is not possible to give a thorough account of either of these two thinkers here, our analysis will give selected examples to demonstrate

157. See *Statuta Antiqua Universitatis Oxoniensis,* ed. Stricklend Gibson (Oxford: Clarendon Press, 1931), pp. 436-38; and John Leofric Stocks, *Aristotelianism* (New York: Cooper Square Publishers, 1963), pp. 133-34. The Parisian injunction suggested death as the penalty for its violation. Regulations of this sort suggest that the traditional philosophers being referred to were not being followed. While it is true that Aristotelian cosmology was under a growing assault by this time, other aspects of Aristotle's philosophy retained their influence, e.g., Galileo, Descartes, and Locke all remained wedded to the Aristotelian ideal of a demonstrative science in their own ways, and a generally Aristotelian logic found no successful rival until the beginning of the twentieth century.

158. Innocent VI, as quoted in Leo XIII, *Aeterni Patris,* in *One Hundred Years of Thomism,* pp. 189-90.

the direction of the philosophy of gender in academic discourse in the next generation of Masters following St. Thomas Aquinas.

Giles of Rome (1243-1316)

It is often the case, when a disciple takes up the cause of a master, that some
of the flexibility and depth found in the original thinker gets lost, and the master's
theories become more rigid. Giles of Rome, also known as Edigio Colonna, is a
good example of this phenomenon both in relation to the more creative integration
of Aristotle and Christian theology by his professor St. Thomas and in relation to
the more flexible methodology of Aristotle himself in his works on natural philosophy. For Giles was more Aristotelian in defending gender polarity than the 'philosopher' himself. Indeed, he was later called the 'Most Fundamental Doctor,' and his
epitaph read: "the most perceptive commentator on the archphilosophy of Aristotle."[159] His works abound with the phrase, "as the philosopher said."

Giles of Rome, an Augustinian friar, completed all his academic degrees at
the University of Paris studying under Thomas Aquinas between 1269 and 1272.
Giles taught there in the Faculty of Arts, in the first Chair for an Augustinian, during the years 1272-1277, which was another period of violent tensions among the
Faculties of the new university. As the philosophers became more enamored with
the works of Aristotle and the commentaries of Avicenna and Averroes, theologians
grew somewhat alarmed at the pagan Greek and religious Islamic influence on
Christian thought. Giles was right in the center of this controversy because of his
great love for Aristotle and his loyalty to his teacher Thomas Aquinas. The 1277
condemnations of Aristotle by the Bishop of Paris caught him in the midst of this
battle between the Faculties of Arts and of Theology.[160] Giles was called to an examination by Masters of Theology to defend himself and Thomistic writings. He
apparently did not comport himself as modestly as had his teacher Thomas under
similar circumstances. Giles wrote a vehement protest against the attacks, defended
his own opinions (and many of those held by members of the lower Faculty of
Arts), and suggested that his views were not simply probable opinion but demonstrable certitude.[161] As consequence of his own method of defense and of the decision to not allow philosophers, particularly philosophers influenced by radical
Aristotelianism, to speak publicly about theological issues, Giles was suspended
from teaching at the university between 1278 and 1285. He left Paris during this
time. However, after making some kind of retraction of his earlier positions and the
intervention of the Pope, he became a Master in the Faculty of Arts in 1285 and remained there until 1291.

---

159. Giles of Rome, *De Regimine Principum* (New York: AMS Press, 1966), p. xix. All passages
from this text are translated from the French into English by Dominique Deslandres.

160. E. Hocedez, "La condamnation de Gilles de Rome," *Recherches de Théologie Ancienne et
Médiévale* 4 (1932): 34-58. See also Wippel, "Condemnations of 1270 and 1277," pp. 196-201.

161. Hocedez, "La condamnation de Gilles de Rome," *Recherches de Théologie Ancienne et
Médiévale* 4 (1931): 34-58.

On his return to Paris, Giles got caught in another controversy between the Faculty of Arts and the Faculty of Theology. The intellectual side of this conflict was also inflamed by an underlying battle between the secular clerics (more like diocesan priests of today) who taught and studied primarily in the lower Faculty of Arts and the mendicant clerics (Dominicans and Franciscans) who took a longer academic formation in the higher Faculty of Theology. Giles sided again mostly with the secular clerics in the lower Faculty, who were propounding the new Aristotelianism often as interpreted through Averroes. This conflict has a significant place in the history of the concept of woman for two reasons: the first concerns one of the issues at stake commonly referred to as the plurality of forms; the other concerns the fragmentation of the Faculties that occurred in the midst of this turmoil.

While it is not possible to go into detail about the medieval debate about the plurality or singularity of substantial human form in the context of this analysis, it is important to note that the debate does have implications for gender identity. The crux of the issue was whether or not one single form gave the developing fetus its vegetative, animal, and rational operations, or whether there were different forms that operated at different times as the fetus developed within the mother. The question also concerned whether or not one could speak of a developing human being as having more than one soul if it was argued that there were a plurality of forms operating at different times as the fetus became actualized. Although Giles at times appeared to have supported the possibility of a theory of plurality of forms in successive levels of animation of a human fetus with a single substantial soul, his main argument supports the view that a human being has a single substantial form that gives it its true identity as a member of the species with vegetative, animal, and rational capacities. The controversy was particularly sensitive to the question of when God infused the rational soul of the unique human being who was being formed.[162]

The second serious consequence of the fragmentation of the Faculties within the University of Paris also has implications for the history of the concept of woman. As a result of the conflicts between the various Faculties an integrated approach towards gender identity initially forged through the Thomistic corpus was split into four different parts. Theology, which offered the theoretical foundation for the reform of gender polarity, had already been separated from Medicine and Law. By early thirteenth-century statutes of the University of Paris, clerics were not allowed to even attend lectures in these fields. Then with the growing antagonism between the Faculties of Arts and Theology the division of knowledge became even more severe.

While the different methodologies of the Faculties need a certain independence from one another to establish the integrity of the different fields of study, the effect of the academic battles between the Faculties set them off on isolated trajectories. It limited cross-discipline access to new information, or new ways of under-

---

162. See the excellent discussion of this controversy by M. Anthony Hewson, *Giles of Rome and the Medieval Theory of Conception: A Study of the De Formatione Corporis Humani in Utero* (London: Athlone Press, 1975), especially pp. 98-121.

standing that could overturn error or misjudgment. Natural science operated on its own, in isolation from Theology, and theological inspiration was no longer integrated back into the work of philosophers, physicians, and lawyers. For the concept of woman, this meant the loss of access to Christian roots for gender complementarity theory, and the hardening of a gender polarity position in philosophy. Eventually, after nearly five hundred years, discoveries in medicine would overturn the mistaken Aristotelian theory of generation and uproot the metaphysical and natural principles for gender polarity. In the interim, however, the epistemological and ethical principles of gender polarity were repeated over and over through the practice of teaching philosophy by commentaries on the original texts. We will now turn to consider some of the particular ways in which Giles of Rome transmitted the Aristotelian rationale for gender polarity.

Giles appears to have written the text *De formatione corporis humani in utero* (On the Formation of the Human Body in the Uterus) between 1274 and 1278, just before his exile from the Faculty of Theology. This work, which includes the Aristotelian theory of the differentiation of the male and female on the biological level along with a particular rejection of Galen's double-seed theory, was printed several times up through the seventeenth century. In a reversion from the natural science approach of Albert the Great, Giles approached this topic from a metaphysical rather than from an empirical perspective. The Aristotelian description of the male as hotter, more like form, and active, and the female as colder, more like matter, and passive, was accepted without question. Although Giles did allow for the existence of female seed, he concluded, following Galen, that it was "lacking in active virtue or formative function" and that it was therefore "not true seed."[163] Giles concluded that "it had only a passive virtue," and further that the only female contribution to generation was the matter or 'menstruum.'[164] Not surprisingly, Giles concluded that the contribution of the female, or matter, was itself also passive: "The menstruum plays the part of prime matter, entirely passive, potential and undifferentiated, as Aristotle taught."[165]

Following the thinking of Aristotle and using his metaphysical principle of contrariety, Giles distinguished the mother's and the father's contributions to generation. He argued that the father's contribution to generation was the active form, which was carried by *pneuma,* a highly refined hot substance present in the male seed. The mother's contribution was the passive material. The selection of sex in the fetus is again described as a battle in which the male seed tries to bring the matter into its own likeness:

> That which is active is contrary to that which is passive; so if the male seed triumphs, it attracts the matter to itself, and induces in it the likeness of the father. If the menstruum resists, then the matter received from the mother is more suited to receiving the likeness of the mother.[166]

163. Hewson, *Giles of Rome*, p. 69.
164. Hewson, *Giles of Rome*, p. 86.
165. Hewson, *Giles of Rome*, p. 137.
166. Hewson, *Giles of Rome*, p. 189.

He concluded that the cause of the female was the number of ways the menstrual fluid 'resists' the seed of the father, either because the active power of the seed was weak, or the passive element of the mother was strong.

We then find Giles repeating and amplifying the natural principle for gender polarity: the female is generated as an 'imperfect man':

> In the case of man, the male agent is disposed to generate a male, the generation of a female in any particular case being beyond the intention of the agent. **For this reason woman is called an "imperfect man," a** *mas occasionatus.*[167]

We see here again that the medieval philosopher dropped Aristotle's qualifier, "as it were," in favor of the simple statement that woman is called an imperfect man, a *mas occasionatus*. In addition, Giles is clear that he is not speaking only of the process of the generation being defective, as St. Thomas seems to imply. Giles definitely links the failure of intention of the particular agent, the male seed, to produce a male, with the product of the generation, or the female. It is not simply the process that is imperfect or occasioned, but woman herself who is called an imperfect man. Thus the disciple Giles stated explicitly what he thought was implicit in previous versions of the argument about the generation of a female as a *mas occasionatus*.

Giles also seems to reach further than either Albert or Thomas beyond the particular agent or process of generation when he concludes that that is why 'woman' rather than 'a woman' is called an imperfect man. He seems to link this association with *all* women. One reason for this extension of meaning may be that Giles concentrated predominantly on philosophy, whereas his two mentors St. Albert and St. Thomas were theologians as well as philosophers. Therefore, while theologians can introduce a distinction between universal nature, as the will of God, and particular nature, as the momentum of the nature of the male seed, Giles did not enter into these theological considerations here. Again it would take careful scholarly analysis of his more than sixty other works to determine if this was a consistent pattern of his presentation of the concept of woman.

A further support for the claim that Giles generally accepted Aristotle's rationale for gender polarity is found in his *De regimine principum* (On the governing of rulers) written after his 1277 exile from Paris. Following the Greek philosopher's line of thinking, Giles introduces the link between the natural and epistemological principles of gender polarity: the imperfection in the generation of the female leads to a faulty development of her rationality. He says: "And as the woman is not a perfect man . . . , she has not a perfect use of reasoning."[168] He goes even further than Aristotle by drawing out practical implications of this disability in the female by claiming that a woman's counsel is not as good as a man's:

> The philosopher said in the first book of the *Politics* that the advice of a woman is of little value. As a child's advice is not perfect because the child has not yet a per-

---

167. Hewson, *Giles of Rome*, p. 183. Bold is my emphasis.
168. Giles, *De regimine*, folio 15: 172.

fect use of reason and of understanding, woman's advice is of little value, for, by nature, she has a defect in reason and understanding because her body is poorly formed and the weakness of her flesh prevents her from having a good constitution. There is never found in evidence in her a great abundance of heat, from which it follows that women have a defect of reason and their advice is of little value. By nature, the better the constitution of the body, the better the soul is able to attain truth and reason and to give good and perfect advice. Therefore, woman's advice is not as good as man's.[169]

Note that again Giles makes universal statements about women that he directly supports by an appeal to female generation. With no consideration of the infusion of theological virtues or gifts of the Holy Spirit, woman's rationality is limited to being described as defective.

The length that Giles goes to prove the inferiority of women, using Aristotelian rationale, is seen in the following passage in which he argues that women's advice is of less value than men's because it is more hurried. He supports this claim by invoking what the philosopher says in the book of *Animals*. Giles demonstrates the link between the Aristotelian natural and epistemological principles that a female child matures more quickly than a male child: "The reason that woman is less noble and less perfect than man is that she grows faster and reaches the perfection of her natural state sooner."[170] He then draws the further link to the ethical consequences: "Just as the female body comes earlier to its full growth than does the male body, so woman's advice is swifter and more hurried."[171] Here a biological fact of the quicker maturation of the female body is used to explain a weakness in public speaking, namely that women are too quick in offering advice.[172] Giles realizes that he is drawing this analogy, for he concludes with the general Aristotelian observation: "for the soul follows the constitution of the body."[173]

In contrast to the above-described ardent defense of gender polarity, in another area Giles demonstrates a little more flexibility in his transmission of Aristotelian theory. In a discussion about whether or not men ought to tell secrets to their wives, Giles argues that although "women by nature have less sense and understanding than men, and are naturally changeable," they can develop sense, understanding, and constancy "if they want to." Giles concludes that if a man is certain that he is married to this kind of woman he can share secrets with her.[174] The implication here is that a woman is not completely limited by her natural inferiority to man, for she is able to overcome this debility.

A discussion about the relation of ruling and obedience to male and female identity shows Giles beginning, as usual, with an Aristotelian basis for gender po-

169. Giles, *De regimine,* folio 46: 183.
170. Giles, *De regimine,* folio 46: 184.
171. Giles, *De regimine,* folio 46: 184.
172. It could just as easily be argued that rapid development is a sign of the superiority of the female. Actually, according to Aristotle females develop slower than males while they are still in the uterus but faster when outside the uterus.
173. Hewson, *Giles of Rome,* p. 184.
174. Hewson, *Giles of Rome,* p. 184.

larity in making a claim that "men are the natural lords over women, for they usually have more sense and understanding than women do, as the Philosopher said."[175] He argues further that any man less wise should obey the wiser man as well. The basis for man's authority over woman is his natural "superiority of sense and reason," and this principle holds for ruling and obedience among men as well.[176] Giles does allow for self-governance in a woman, through the presence of the infused virtues. For example, in a section on a wife's temporal, physical, and spiritual gifts he says that "[w]omen must possess the soul's gifts for they must have continence, love, and deeds, which are not enslaving."[177] However, he also suggests that because women have less sense and reason they are more inclined to a bad emotivity, wrong thinking, wrong doings, and to sin than are men. He frequently repeats the claim that women have less sense and reason than men, and uses it to suggest that women therefore need to exercise themselves in good deeds to compensate for this defect.

The importance that Giles gives to the question of the relation of husband and wife is evident in his dedication of the first part of the second book of *De regimine principum* to the subject of the wife. Here he seeks to distinguish the unequal relation of master and slave from the more equal relation of husband and wife. Giles argues, following Thomas, that "because the wife equally possesses everything with her husband," she is his companion and should not be treated as a servant who owns nothing in common with him.[178] Giles specified further that the areas in which the equality of husband and wife ought to occur included nobility, age, wealth, and friends, among other things. Most important, however, was his claim that woman was equal to man through a "mutuality of choice":

> I know that by nature men must marry, although it is by his choice that he marries and that he chooses one woman or another, and the woman has some kind of equality with him. The woman has the choice to take the husband she wants, so the husband's authority over his wife is not all natural.[179]

Giles does not argue that this equality is given away in marriage, but that it is fundamental to the relation of husband and wife in marriage. Therefore, he advocates a kind of equality of a woman and a man in a marriage because of the fundamental freedom of choice they exercise in relation to one another. Note, however, that he identifies this realm of freedom as "not all natural" because of free choice, and in so doing he points again to the function of spirituality in human existence.

In addition, Giles likely followed Thomas's modification of Aristotle's theory about the fundamental inequality of husband and wife in the practice of the virtue of friendship. Aristotle had argued that because a woman is by nature inferior to a man, she enters into a friendship of inequality with him. Only men with similar

---

175. Giles, *De regimine,* folio 10: 39.
176. Giles, *De regimine,* folio 63: 253.
177. Giles, *De regimine,* folio 42: 163.
178. Giles, *De regimine,* folio 42: 166-67.
179. Giles, *De regimine,* folio 42: 166.

status in life, and who have the good of the other man as their mutual goal, could enter into friendships of equality. Giles, however, through his identification of the relation of husband and wife as being based on a mutual free choice and shared goods, rejected the Greek philosopher's rather limited views.

The role of St. Augustine in providing the principles for this shift in consciousness is also worth mentioning here. There is no doubt that Giles, an Augustinian priest, would have been imbued with some of his founder's thoughts about human identity and sex identity. While St. Augustine had a complex and often contradictory combination of three different theories of sex identity, in the one area of the relation of freedom of will to woman's identity, Augustine broke new ground in western philosophy. In particular he defended the importance of a woman's free will in several different situations. For example, he argued that a woman should not be forced against her will to convert to Catholicism, that a woman who was raped against her will was perfectly virtuous in body and soul, and that women religious were established not as "bondswomen under law, but as free women under grace."[180] While the implications of the role of free will in women's development of gender identity are studied in greater depth in chapters on women religious writers in this book, it is important to note here that Giles recognized a new order of relationship among men and women that reflected the importance Augustine had previously given to freedom of the will.

Even with his arguments in support of the equality of husband and wife with respect to the virtue of friendship, the general impact of the philosophy of Giles of Rome was to transmit Aristotelian foundations for a theory of gender polarity. With one exception in the area of his description of freedom of the will and choice, Giles was a thoroughgoing Aristotelian in his defense of gender polarity. His numerous commentaries on nearly all of the works of Aristotle, his commentary on Peter Lombard's *Sentences,* and even his commentary on Guido Cavalcanti's *Donna mi priega,* gave him an opportunity to repeat Aristotelian thinking on a wide range of issues. Giles is credited with having written at least sixty-five different works. Along with this broader affirmation of Aristotelianism in general came the rationale for a philosophy of gender polarity with its consistent devaluation of the female, and by association, of woman.

As Giles became Prior General of the Order of Augustinians in 1292 and Archbishop of Bourges in 1295, the influence of this defender of gender polarity gradually reached far beyond the academic community into the heart of religious and civil society. His popular text on the education of princes, household management, and virtues of husbands and wives had several printings. There are thirty-five dated manuscripts of *De regimine principum* written between 1282 and 1484. Five Latin editions of the text were published between 1475 and 1500 and six more between 1500 and 1620, and twenty-eight editions translated into German, Italian, French, English, Hebrew, Castilian, and Catalan were published between 1473 and 1911.[181] In addi-

---

180. Augustine, *Letters* (New York: Fathers of the Church, 1951), #35. Augustine, *The City of God Against the Pagans* (Cambridge, Mass.: Harvard University Press, 1966), II.19. See also I.16, 18, 28 and II.2. Augustine, *Letters* #211.

181. Hewson, *Giles of Rome,* p. 36, note 140.

tion, his text on the formation of the human body in utero was avidly read in medical schools. Anthony Hewson pointed out that the physicians "all read the *De formatione corporis* and all took it seriously."[182] It was especially popular in the medical schools at Bologna and Padua. Fourteenth- to fifteenth-century manuscripts of the text are also found in Oxford and Montpellier, and sixteenth-century printed versions in Paris and Venice. Because of the great popularity of these two texts, Giles's strict adherence to the view that woman is by nature an imperfect man may have had even more serious consequences for women than discussions that took place in the academic community of discourse away from their hearing.

John Duns Scotus (1265-1308)

The last thinker to be considered in this chapter played a rather different role from that of Giles of Rome in the Aristotelian Revolution. Instead of simplifying and repeating the theories of the Greek philosopher, Duns Scotus probed the complexity of the philosophical problems they raised. This characteristic led to his being named "The Subtle Doctor." In other words, while Giles often expressed a reductionist approach to Aristotle, or of "reducing controversy to the fundamentals," Duns Scotus asked persistent questions about the Aristotelian premises that opened up the complex nuances of issues.

While many of the details of the life of Scotus remain unknown, it is believed that he was born in Scotland in the second half of the thirteenth century, that he joined the Franciscan order, and was ordained priest in 1291. He studied at Oxford University where he received a Bachelor's and then a Master's in Theology. By 1300 Scotus was writing his commentary on Peter Lombard's *Sentences*. Because there was only one Franciscan chair available in the Faculty of Theology at Oxford with too many candidates to fill it, Scotus was appointed in 1301 to the Chair of Theology at the University of Paris, where the Franciscan theologian St. Bonaventure (1217-1274) had previously been Master.[183] Scotus, like Giles, soon got caught in yet another serious conflict at the university. This time the battle was explicitly political, and it saw most of the French scholars siding with the King of France in the matter of taxing Church property to support a war with England. Scholars from other countries sided with Pope Boniface VIII, who objected to this taxation. After a violent demonstration in the streets and a public hearing of the civil authorities, Scotus, who supported the Pope, was exiled with many other Masters from the university. It is presumed that he went to Cambridge during this time of banishment. The Pope retaliated by denying the university the right to issue degrees in Theology. The University of Paris was then closed for three years until

---

182. Hewson, *Giles of Rome,* p. 204.

183. For a discussion of Bonaventure's concept of woman, see *The Concept of Woman: The Aristotelian Revolution (750 BC–1250 AD),* pp. 426-29. While he qualifies Aristotle's use of the expression *femina est aliquid deficiens et occasionatum* to refer only to the process and not the product of generation, he also follows Aristotle's claim that the male sex is inherently more perfect than the female.

1304, when a new Pope lifted the bans and Duns Scotus among others returned to Paris. He was appointed a Master sometime in 1305.[184]

John Duns Scotus wrote many texts. A major work was his *Ordinatio* or *Opus oxoniense,* which consisted of revised editions of his lectures from Oxford, Cambridge, and Paris on Peter Lombard's *Sentences.* Another was his *Quaestiones quodlibetals* given between 1306 and 1307, in which it is likely Scotus served as the Regent Master opening himself to public disputation with objections posed by a Bachelor and interventions of other students and Masters. His text on theological questions manifests a strong metaphysical foundation and syllogistic form. Scotus had also written a text of Questions on Aristotle's *Metaphysics* and on several questions of logic based on the works of Aristotle and Porphyry. In 1307, he left Paris to teach in a Franciscan house in Cologne in 1307 and died the following year with much of his written work still in an unfinished state. Nonetheless, Scotus's works were circulated widely, and "[e]ven today they are found in hundreds of manuscripts, and from 1472 on went through more than thirty different editions."[185]

Duns Scotus directly challenged Aristotelian thinking about matter as the principle of individuation between two members of the same species when he argued that not matter but form caused this differentiation. Scotus summarizes the Greek philosopher's view in his commentary on the *Metaphysics:*

> Aristotle uses matter for individual difference or for the individual itself, which individual related to the species is something material; and by this he means that differences, i.e., contrary qualities that follow a thing according to its material being, i.e., according to its individual being, do not make a difference in species. . . . He applies the given solution to the principal question, saying that man and woman, i.e., male and female, are proper qualities of an animal; whence also animal must be put into a definition of them. However, nevertheless, they do not simply apply to animal according to substance and form, but in matter and body, thus indicating that they are material differences. He proves this, saying: the same seed that suffers a certain change becomes a female or a male; if there is sufficient heat to change it will become male, but if there is not it becomes female. Nature nevertheless always intends to generate a male as the more perfect, but sometimes it is prevented by insufficient power. Therefore a female is an animal that had an accident, as is said in *De animalibus* 18.3, and as it were, is generated without being intended by nature.[186]

Scotus relives Aristotle's struggle to explain how women and men were differentiated within the same species with the natural principle of the male as the more perfect being and the female as an accident not intended by particular nature. Duns

---

184. Felix Alluntis and Allan B. Wolter, Introduction to John Duns Scotus, *God and Creatures: The Quodlibetal Questions* (Princeton: Princeton University Press, 1975), pp. xviii-xxii.

185. Alluntis and Wolter, Introduction, John Duns Scotus, *God and Creatures,* p. xxiv.

186. John Duns Scotus, *Opera Omnia* (1891; Paris: Apud Ludovicum Vives, Bibliplam Editorem, 1969), 13:94. Translated by Sister Térèse Marie Dougherty, as are all subsequent passages from this text.

Scotus does not accept Aristotle's argument for several reasons. He questions the basic premise that the form of the human being is transmitted only in the male seed. He does this by first challenging the traditional view of the role of the male in conception, and second, he raises questions about the female contribution as well.

When Duns Scotus considers the male contribution to generation, he argues that the male seed itself is not really active because it is not fulfilling its function when it is simply seed separate from the conception. He adds a further argument that what is less perfect cannot actively cause the more perfect, and since the seed is less perfect than the fetus generated, it cannot be the active cause of generation. Finally, he argues that the father cannot be the active cause of generation either, because a mother can complete the generation of a child after the death of the father. The following lengthy passage from Scotus's *Opus Oxoniese* or commentary on the *Sentences* of Peter Lombard demonstrates his subtle reasoning on this particular point:

> What is the purpose of the seed? Is it for generating, as the active source of generation? I say that it is not if the seed is uniform, but I say it about the male seed which acts on the female seed. But the uniform seed out of which something becomes, i.e., that which comes from the producer, whether father or mother, because of which it is uniform with respect to the begotten or better (this uniformity means the same origin due to the seed), cannot be the active principle of generation for two reasons. First, because that which is not cannot be a productive source of a substance; but the seed is not at the moment of generation; therefore at that time it is not the inductive or productive source of generation or end of generation. Nor even while it is can it be such an active principle because the seed is something that is in proximate potence to be changed into that which ought to be generated, but this has the ratio of passive, not active.
>
> Besides, the less perfect is not a sufficient active cause of the more perfect, and the seed is less perfect than what is to be generated, even with all its (animal) spirits. Therefore, even if it were to remain, it could not be the active source of generation. . . .
>
> I say, therefore, that no seed, nor anything in the seed, is the active cause of generation or of the final form, and is not from the father because even while the father is dead a son may be generated, and not from a form from heaven, because many living things are more perfect than a form from heaven. Therefore, the soul giving life is either from an angel or from God, or we must give up some of the preceding propositions. It is not from an angel because an angel does nothing except by means of the movement of the heavens. Therefore, it follows that it is from God.[187]

This elaborate argument to prove that God, and not man, is the primary active cause of generation, is supported by a contrary argument that the female, who had been identified in Aristotelian thought with the contribution of passive material to generation, has a more complex role.

187. Scotus, *Opera,* 94.

John Duns Scotus followed the teachings of Avicenna in his *Canon of Medicine,* that the male seed separated out the different "faculties" in the fetus, such as nerve, bone, and so forth; the female seed established the relation between the members of the body and produced their specific texture and position as well. He identified the male as having a primary formative role and the female as having a secondary formative role.[188] Scotus accepted Avicenna's and Galen's views that the female as well as the male produced seed, and even though he gave a certain priority of function descending from God to the male, and then to the female, Scotus broke out of the rigid Aristotelian polarity that had previously been so evident in discussions of generation.

Another sign of this new direction is the interesting discussion Scotus had when considering the question whether the increase of heat in a woman's seed would enable her to generate a child without the help of a male. The logical connection of this question with the Aristotelian theory that there is only one kind of seed, and that the difference between male and female is primarily one of heat, is obvious. If females were thought to have seed, but were simply cooler, it would be a logical question to ask whether or not, when the seed of a woman was "heated up," she could fertilize her own menstruum. Scotus answers the question as follows:

> . . . they argue in such a way by suggesting that if the active force of the mother may be increased, it follows that what could be increased, could itself alone bring forth offspring, without the help of a man; indeed it is clear that they do not understand either the intent or the words of the Doctor [Peter Lombard], because man and woman are two partial causes arranged for the purpose of the offspring, because the man is the principal cause and the woman the less important. If, therefore, the strength of one increases, even a thousandfold, it still would be the kind of cause that could never take the place of the other cause.[189]

Therefore, while Scotus believed that the male and female are distinguishable "causes" of generation, and that the male is more important than the female, he nonetheless defends the claim that they are significantly different and that the difference is not simply one of heat, or activity and passivity, or even relation to form and matter. Thus the woman brings a certain kind of formative functioning to generation, and the man's formative function is limited to make room for that of God. So in Scotus's view, generation demands the two different active causes of male and female.

The view that individuation is a consequence of form rather than of matter would obviously fit into this description of generation. Scotus argues that there are two kinds of form: the form of the material structure of the existent, and the form of the life of the existent. The father provides the form of the material structure of the

188. Avicenna, *A Treatise on the 'Canon of Medicine' of Avicenna* (New York: AMS Press, 1973), I.I.vi.145: 119.

189. John Duns Scotus, "Commentary on the Sentences" in *Opera,* vol. 2, Book II, Dist. xi.6: 660.

existent, and God provides the form of the life of the existent by giving the rational soul. Presumably then the father would determine the sex of the existent.

Scotus does not completely escape a gender polarity association of the male and female with the active and passive. He sometimes discusses the role of the male and female seeds as including an active and a passive ratio respectively. In his *Summa theologiae* he gives four different arguments (physical, moral, analogical, and anagogical) for the division of the human race into a "distinction of sexes." The first reason, or the physical, emphasizes a separation of the active and passive principles. In a context in which he considers "hermaphrodites" as "a plurality of sexes joined in one individual," which is "confusing and imperfect" and "contrary to the intention of nature, which is always attempting and desiring to produce perfect things," Duns Scotus argues, following Aristotle, that while in the lower ranges of the scale of natural beings there is a joining of the sexes in one entity (i.e., flowers), in the higher ranges of the scale of natural beings the male is separated from the female. He concludes:

> Therefore it is relevant to the perfection of the universe, that the active and passive principles are distinct; since it is therefore necessary for the generation of humans that there be at the same time an active and passive principle.[190]

While woman's contribution of seed is active, although in a lesser degree than that of man, or of God, her contribution of matter reveals her association with the passive, for the form shapes and determines the material that is shaped. Here we come to another major point of difference, for within the Aristotelian model, prime matter was thought of as pure potentiality; and Duns Scotus argued that there were three kinds of matter, all of which had real existence. The three kinds of matter were an indeterminate kind of prime matter, a more specific material substratum of generation and corruption, and the matter of a particular existent.

In the Aristotelian view the concepts of form and matter were totally distinct through abstraction, with the former being immaterial and the latter material. This distinction of matter and form in cognition was transmitted to the theory of generation in which it was argued that the father contributed the form of the child, which although contained in the matter of the seminal fluid, itself contained no matter at all; while the mother contributed the menstruum which, although formed as a particular kind of matter, contained no form of the child at all. The rigid separation of matter and form in the theory of generation was similar to the rigid separation of passive and active, and female and male. For Duns Scotus, on the other hand, the concepts of form and matter were not separated in this way, and he argued that the concept of all matter, as real and existing, contained form. With his positive valuation of matter, it is not surprising that Scotus also evaluated the female contribution to generation in a more positive way.

An interesting theological issue raised in relation to John Duns Scotus was the question about the identities of woman and man after the resurrection of the

---

190. John Duns Scotus, *Summa Theologica* (Rome, 1901), Quest. xcii, art. 1: 812. Translated by Andrew Deere.

body. Some scholars have claimed that Duns Scotus argued in his commentary on Lombard's *Sentences* that after the resurrection, all women, except the Virgin Mary, will become men.[191] It seems obvious from Scotus's general metaphysical views about the relation of matter and form, that this would be a totally inconsistent claim for him to make. In other words, if matter and form are always joined, it would be necessary for the completion of the identity of a particular woman to include reference to her specific material identity. Of course, if it is argued that woman's engendered differentiation is only a consequence of her sentient soul, and not of her rational soul as well, then there might be room to argue that sex identity *per se* is not present in heaven. However, it would be difficult then to understand what significance to give to the resurrection of the body. MacLean states that later scholars have refuted the claim that Duns Scotus held that women would be turned into men after the resurrection, and they have argued that "it is an interpolation which other Renaissance theologians have failed to identify."[192]

The effect of John Duns Scotus on subsequent thought was considerable as he studied and taught at both Oxford and the University of Paris. After his death, disciples at both universities continued to teach philosophy according to this Scottish philosopher's metaphysical framework. As a Franciscan friar, Duns Scotus's philosophy was soon recognized as *the* basis for Franciscan thought. Subsequently, Scotism, Thomism, and nominalism (Ockhamism) became foundational for the three major schools of philosophy from the fourteenth to the seventeenth century. A crucial disagreement concerning the relation of form to matter existed among these schools, a disagreement that had implications for the notions on gender identity. This controversy also involved a difference of opinion about what was the object of a definition.

Some of the key issues that separated these three schools of philosophy were the nature of matter and form, the relation between matter and form, and the place that matter and form held in the search for knowledge of universals and essences of natural entities. These issues are fundamental to the philosophy of sex and gender identity, with particular reference to the question of how a philosopher explains the metaphysical difference between male and female human beings who belong to the same species, and yet who are significantly different. For Aristotle the form resides in the entity itself, so men and women share the same human substantial form, and yet they are distinguished from one another as individuals by the matter individualized by accidental forms. For Nominalism or Ockhamism, there is no universal form that all men and women share. Rather the universal 'human being' is an abstract idea that the philosopher attributes to a collection of particular individuals in the world. Scotism takes a third alternative, namely that there is not a single form of human being that individual women and men share but a plurality of forms whereby each woman and man has a distinct form of human and sexual identity.

191. Ian Maclean, *The Renaissance Notion of Woman: A Study in the Fortunes of Scholasticism and Medical Science in European Intellectual Life* (Cambridge: Cambridge University Press, 1980), p. 14, note 52.

192. Maclean, *The Renaissance Notion,* p. 14, notes 53 and 54.

ACADEMIC MEN'S VOICES ABOUT THE CONCEPT OF WOMAN

In this lengthy chapter we have immersed ourselves in the remarkable dynamics that occurred in academic communities of discourse at the beginning of the foundation of western universities. Something new and almost astonishing occurred during this thirteenth century. A completely different model of education was created in key urban centers beginning in Salerno and Bologna, taking root in Paris and Oxford, and then spreading quickly to other locations throughout France, England, Germany, and the Papal States in what is now known as Italy, and even to eastern Europe. The structure and curriculum at the University of Paris became the model for the structure and curriculum in most other universities.

The concept of woman was deeply affected by this change in direction of higher education away from the Benedictine monastic model in which it had resided for the previous several centuries. Within the earlier monastic model, women were encouraged to develop self-knowledge and self-governance, and as we saw in the previous chapter, religious women had begun to articulate the foundations of their own experience through the exercise of their discursive reasoning. Women were also in dialogue with men, and this reality of genuine dialogue even led to the beginning articulation of a philosophical foundation for a theory of gender complementarity. A theological belief in the fundamental equal dignity of men and women at creation and in heaven fostered a Christian understanding of gender complementarity as the appropriate framework to counter both the devaluation of women present in Aristotelian gender polarity theories and the devaluation of the body present in Platonic unisex theories.

The new universities were first established in urban centers by bishops who wanted to educate their secular clergy. Very soon they were joined by many newly founded mendicant religious communities, such as the Franciscans, Dominicans, and Augustinians who, unlike the secular clergy who remained primarily in one location, formed networks of houses of study throughout Europe in a move to evangelize and fight different forms of heresy, apostasy, or the advance of other religions such as Islam. The mendicant friars formed an elite group of men who studied at university centers up to fifteen years before going forth to teach. They also carried their lecture notes and academic discoveries with them as they walked all over Europe. Thus, the concepts and arguments they learned in the academic center of discourse were spread far and wide.

Three particular aspects of the new academic centers were noted with respect to the concept of woman. The first aspect was the extraordinary infusion of Aristotelian philosophy at the beginning of their foundation. We traced the roots of translations and commentaries from their first appearance in ancient Greece, through Islamic paraphrases in Syriac and Arabic, Jewish integrations in Hebrew, and Christian developments in Latin up to the moment when Aristotle's texts became required reading in the Faculty of Arts in the University of Paris and elsewhere. The discovery of Aristotle brought a systematic approach to knowledge and to the development of new disciplines opening up in the four Faculties of Arts, Theology, Medicine, and Law. The Greek philosopher provided the methodology for debate, known as the scholastic method; he provided the rules of logic for nearly all scien-

165

tific demonstration; and he provided much of the content of the different areas of philosophy. Aristotle's genius in elaborating different methodologies for different fields provided a framework for the developing autonomy of philosophy and of natural science; and within these broader fields it structured the use of logic, empirical investigation of the nature of plants, of animals, of the planets, of ethics, politics, and so forth.

The second aspect we noted involved the particular details of fact and interpretation about the concept of woman that were embedded in Aristotelian thought. Aristotle's complete and coherent rationale for gender polarity came along with his genius and empirical orientation of philosophy. Thus Aristotle's voice was prominent in the academic community of discourse about the concept of woman. We identified four Aristotelian principles of the devaluation of woman in relation to man which fell into the categories of opposites, generation, wisdom, and virtue as follows:

- The **metaphysical principle** stated that the female is opposite as a contrary privation of the male.
- The **natural principle** stated that the female is as it were a deformed male.
- The **epistemological principle** stated that a woman's rational faculty is without authority over her irrational soul.
- The **ethical principle** stated that a lesser measure of virtue is proper to women.

Aristotle's complex heritage for the concept of woman is drawn from this intricate combination of factors that included a systematic and cohesive set of principles and observations about woman's identity within a gender polarity theory at the same time as it offered the most brilliant and extensive model for the development of human knowledge hitherto known to man. Nearly all of the great thinkers in the monotheistic traditions of Islam, Judaism, and Christianity believed they had found in Aristotle a solid and open-ended approach to the progressive discovery of truth. Indeed even today Aristotle's empirical approach to knowledge, his openness to new data, his insistence on the integral unity of the human being with a single substantial form, and his flexible and rich virtue-based ethics are still recognized by many to be fundamentally correct orientations for contemporary philosophy.

The third aspect of the new academic discourse about the concept of woman concerns the exclusion of women from the new universities. This fact of exclusion created a historical context in which academic women were not able to function as living counterexamples to the errors of fact and interpretation in Aristotelian gender polarity. Nor were women themselves able to engage directly in argument and debate about the principles. They were not able to engage their voices with Aristotle's transmitted voice. Just a few examples of educated women such as Roswitha, Hildegard, or Herrad, who had emerged within the Benedictine monastic tradition, or Heloise, Beatrice, Hadewijch, Mechtild, or Marguerite Porete, who studied outside of it, lend weight to the expectation that if women had been a vital presence in the new academic centers, the integration of Aristotelian philosophy might have taken a different turn with respect to the concept of woman itself.

The institutionalization of Aristotle's gender polarity theory poses a particular problem for the history of the concept of woman. I have identified it as a wound in the academic body, and project the hope that laying open the layers of the wound will contribute to its healing. Because the academic community of discourse was a completely male community, certain tendencies in men's identity developed without the complementary balance of women's approaches to learning. Without wanting to suggest simplistic or stereotyped gender-identified approaches to learning, it is nonetheless instructive to observe the actual dynamics that occurred during the early founding of universities in which women were not present. In this conclusion we will highlight a few of them.

In the first section of this chapter entitled "Gender in Academic Examination and Debate," we considered the way in which Aristotle's *Topics, Sophistical Refutations,* and *Rhetoric* were used to structure the dynamics of academic discourse. Examination by debate and disputation, with an antagonistic model of *pro* and *contra* positions waging intellectual war with one another, became the norm. This scholastic method of argument replaced a cooperative model of exploration. While the scholastic method helped refine and sharpen lines of discursive reasoning and particular knowledge of relevant historical texts, it also created certain difficulties. In particular, public disputation led to a hardening of positions and to a polarity model in which the stronger vanquished weaker.

At this point I would like to raise a question for consideration: Is there a direct relation between the scholastic method of debate and a theory of gender polarity? We noted at the beginning of this chapter that the scholastic method of debate was originally developed by Peter Abelard in Paris in the century before the origin of the university. It is significant that Abelard and Heloise engaged in various forms of dialogue during their turbulent and well-known relationship. He may have taught her the scholastic method when he served as her private tutor. At the same time, as Abelard himself directly admitted, he forced her to submit to his seduction in a physical act in which the will of the stronger vanquished the will of the weaker. We also have written records of their private correspondence and of their correspondence about the rule and norms of a woman's religious community. The content of these written dialogues reveals a complex mixture of gender polarity and gender complementarity. In the order of nature, the man is frequently referred to as the stronger sex and the woman as the weaker sex, while in the order of grace this imbalance is corrected and even overturned. While we do not want to draw a rigid conclusion from these various factors, it does seem as though the scholastic method itself tends towards a polarity view of the world in which the stronger defeats the weaker in both argument and personal relations.

In this chapter we also offered evidence that the concept of woman was a subject for debate right from the early years of the academic enterprise. In addition, we indicated that there were three different ways in which the lively dynamic of debate and disputation functioned with respect to all questions, and thus to questions about women: first as a genuine search for truth about woman, second as detached from the striving for knowledge and more focused on simply winning an argument, and third as used for purposes of humor in common forms of entertainment. In all three of these uses of the scholastic method, the men entering into the disputation would draw primarily upon Aristotle's concept of woman to support their theses.

In the second part of the chapter entitled "Logic, Demonstrative Science, and Gender Identity," we considered ways in which Aristotle's *Organon,* including especially his *Categories* and *Posterior Analytics,* provided the foundation for scientific demonstration and theoretical judgments in the formal structure of arguments in academia. Porphyry's and Boethius's augmentations of the Greek philosopher's logic were also described. The concepts of substance, accidents, and syllogism were introduced with respect to the theme of gender identity, and the particular tendency of Aristotelian logic to shift nuanced positions to universal propositions for the purposes of demonstration was noted. By this shift, more flexible hypotheses in natural science or ethics tend to become absolutized into universal generalizations and grayer areas ignored. We traced the fascination with different aspects of Aristotle's logic through three generations of academics at Oxford University.

The attempt to orient philosophy towards universal definitions in mathematics occurred in the academic setting of Oxford. The secular cleric Robert Grosseteste used Aristotle's syllogistic model from the *Prior and Posterior Analytics* to reorient philosophy in this direction. While he also offered the first complete translation of Aristotle's *Ethics,* Grosseteste's own contribution to gender theory seems to be towards a gender-neutral position. Using Aristotle's structure for deductive reasoning in the application of the syllogism, and turning to mathematics as a model for philosophical method, he ignored biology and material differences between men and women. In addition, Grosseteste argued that mathematics was the only certain science, that there was only knowledge of universals, and that philosophy ought to concern itself with mathematical relations. Consequently, gender was held irrelevant to its consideration.

Next, the Franciscan Roger Bacon, likely a student of Grosseteste, wrote commentaries on Aristotle's *Organon, Physics, Generation and Corruption, De anima,* and *De caelo et mundo.* Later, basing his thought on the pseudo-Aristotelian text *Secretum Secretorum,* he sought to establish philosophy as the perfect, universal science. Even though he also commented on *De Animalibus,* mathematics was given a greater importance than the science of nature, and gender theory tended to be ignored. Through Grosseteste and Bacon, Neoplatonist attraction to mathematics — combined with rigorous Aristotelian demonstrative science — formed academic discourse at Oxford in such a way that issues about gender identity were relatively unimportant.

Finally, another Franciscan academic at Oxford, William of Ockham, rejected his predecessors' fascination with knowledge of universals by arguing that only particulars could be known. He wrote a *Summa Logicae* drawing out further implications of Aristotle's logic. However, Ockham also argued against Aristotle that universals were simply an abstraction in the mind. Thus, he used and changed the meaning of Aristotelian categories and logic in developing a new nominalist school of philosophy. While Ockham's basic orientation was gender neutrality, he did occasionally refer to the equality of women and men. In this way, his revision of Aristotelian philosophy also opened some new possibilities for gender theory. However, Ockham's nominalism detached the philosophical enterprise from the direct search for truth about woman's identity, and instead relegated the task of making accurate definitions to the different sciences.

The medieval networking of academics among different universities was noted when Robert Grosseteste's translation of Aristotle's *Ethics* formed the basis for Albert the Great's public lectures on it in Cologne. Roger Bacon, Grosseteste's student, had taught at the University of Paris the same time as Albert; when they both left, Bacon traveled west to England and Albert east to Germany to begin new schools of philosophy based on a love for science. Bacon chose to emphasize a mathematical science that had a more gender-neutral approach to the concept of woman, while Albert chose to emphasize an empirical science that incorporated Aristotelian principles of gender polarity.

In the third part of this chapter called "Aristotle's Principles of Gender Polarity," we traced the historical premises of Aristotle about the concept of woman, the routes of translations of and commentaries on these premises, and the various ways in which medieval philosophers, especially at the University of Paris, incorporated and transformed Aristotelian principles of gender polarity. In this part of the chapter we plunged into the content of Aristotle's *Generation of Animals, History of Animals, Parts of Animals, Physics, Metaphysics, Ethics, Politics,* and *Poetics.* Further, we examined the specific ways in which the Aristotelian corpus was integrated into the academic discourse about woman, especially at the University of Paris, and we extracted examples of commentaries and explanations offered by four generations of philosophers in this academic center.

Commentaries on and paraphrases of Aristotle's philosophy by the two Islamic philosophers, Avicenna and Averroes, also played an important role in forming the minds of students and faculty at the University of Paris. Their works augmented the new translations of the original texts of Aristotle himself. Soon commentaries by the Christian philosophers, Albert and Aquinas, oriented interpretations of all subjects including the concept of woman. We noted how some of Aristotle's original qualifications of gender polarity principles were lost in the process of translation and commentary and how new qualifications, drawn from a Christian-based complementarity, were introduced to mitigate a rigid Aristotelian natural gender polarity. However, more significant for the history of the concept of woman were the systematic repetition of basic Aristotelian principles of gender polarity and the explicit exposition of linkages among the four principles. Before summarizing this medieval Aristotelian schema for gender polarity we need to make a few brief observations about the four generations of philosophers just identified as important to the academic transmission of Aristotelian-based gender polarity.

The Dominican Friar, St. Albert the Great, was the first major philosopher at the University of Paris to use Aristotle to establish a foundation for a new orientation to philosophy. As a scientist himself, who eagerly sought empirical data in all ranges of science, Albert concentrated over a third of his writing on the topic of generation. In this context he absorbed with some qualifications Aristotle's fundamental theory of generation and the specifics of Aristotelian engendered differentiation. Albert repeated most of the basic Aristotelian principles, but he introduced a qualification of the intention of universal nature or God to generate females. This qualification mitigated the Aristotelian view that it was against the particular nature of the male seed to generate a female. At the same time, Albert also added data to exemplify some of the Aristotelian principles of polarity, and in this way his works reinforced and strengthened the philosophical devaluation of woman, especially in the categories of wisdom and virtue.

The exaggeration of women's epistemological and ethical weakness was made most evident in the version of Albert's *Quaestiones super de animalibus* that had been given as public lectures and written down by students. Here we saw an unfortunate effect of the public form of disputation as applied to the history of the concept of woman, and in subsequent chapters we will discover this effect reverberating further in its use by the Dominican inquisitors writing about the relation of women to witchcraft. At the same time, however, it is important to note that St. Albert also supported the equal dignity of women with men from the perspective of Christian theology, which emphasized the resurrection of the body and the heavenly life of women and men saints. Albert sought to have philosophy be the foundation for theology, but philosophy did not control the higher field. In the realm of grace, women were capable of human perfection as much as men. It is also important to emphasize again that the empirical orientation of Albert's Aristotelian-based natural science left it open to the new data that eventually flowed into the academic world through the sciences of anatomy, physiology, and the invention of the microscope. It was through these avenues that Aristotle's faulty claims about woman's and man's roles in generation were corrected. Thus the Aristotelian orientation towards an empirical science that so attracted Albert eventually was self-correcting of Aristotle's own gender polarity hypotheses through the addition of more accurate data.

Albert's student at both Paris and Cologne, the Dominican Friar St. Thomas Aquinas, also repeated Aristotle's principles for gender polarity. However, in all situations Thomas avoided augmenting the principles with exaggerated examples or more extreme arguments. In this way he toned down some of his predecessor's judgments and left a more balanced legacy within the wider gender polarity framework. While Albert emphasized the philosophical foundations for a study of theology, Thomas simply integrated those foundations into theological arguments. Thus we find Aristotelian-based gender polarity concepts and arguments integrated throughout Thomas's *Summas* and *Expositiones*.

In this chapter we considered a recent controversy erupting around the translation of the Aristotelian claim that the female is generated as an occasioned male, a deformed male, an accidental male, and so forth. Thomas, Albert, and Aristotle himself all seem to imply, by the phrase rendered in Latin as *mas occasionatus,* that when something goes wrong with a particular process of generation, the generation is occasioned, or departs from the intention of the seed contributed by the father. In the context of the discussion it is the process that is occasioned, or accidental. However, as we offered evidence to prove, throughout other parts of the works of all three philosophers, the female product of the occasioned process is also referred to as defective, lacking, or accidental. It is this stronger claim that becomes the frequently repeated natural principle of Aristotelian-based gender polarity.

Saint Thomas, like his teacher Saint Albert, attempted to overcome this polarity and devaluation of the female natural identity through a theology of regeneration. Through grace a woman may become as perfect as a man, although, because of her naturally imperfect generation, she remains a less noble kind of human being. A female perfection is of a lesser measure than a male perfection; her state has a lesser eminence of degree. Still, within a Christian theology, which is Thomas's greater concern, women as well as men may become saints, and in this state of holiness they live in a relation of complementarity with men, that is, after the resurrection of the body in equal dignity and significant differentiation.

In the third generation of students and faculty at the University of Paris we discovered the Augustinian friar, Giles of Rome, losing much of the moderating influence of Christian theology in his description of the concept of woman. Instead, Giles reverts to a fundamental Aristotelianism that reasserts the foundational principles of gender polarity. This was especially evident in his writings on human generation in natural philosophy, writings that were very popular in the new medical schools of Europe. In one area of ethics, that of the virtue of friendship, Giles seems to be more appreciative of the equality of women and men. The suggestion already has been made that Giles's view of equality of friendship of husband and wife may have come through the text *Oeconomicus,* which had been incorrectly ascribed to Aristotle and attached to his *Politics.*

The Franciscan Friar, John Duns Scotus, was the fourth-generation Parisian Master considered in this chapter. While he studied in Oxford, and later went to Paris, Scotus, like Ockham before him, taught both philosophy and theology. His work, instead of narrowing the focus as we found in Giles, broadened it and opened up multiple nuances for consideration. Scotus also challenged Aristotle's fundamental categories, particularly in areas bordering on the theory of generation. He argued that the male may contribute matter to generation, and that the female makes a much more active formal contribution than others thought. He also raised central questions about the form/matter distinction that could affect Aristotle's metaphysical principle for gender polarity.

Before proceeding further in our conclusion to this chapter, it may be helpful to simply summarize in the table on page 172 the overall orientation towards gender theory that the academic Aristotelians appear to hold:

Academic Aristotelians and Gender Theory			
Philosopher	Relation to Aristotle	Philosophical Orientation	Gender Theory
Robert Grosseteste	Use of syllogism (*Posterior Analytics*) for science. Translated Aristotle's *Ethics*.	Seeks definitions of universals as in mathematics	Gender neutrality
Roger Bacon	Use of logic, physics, metaphysics, and spurious "Secrets"	Seeks universal science using syllogisms and universal definitions	Gender neutrality
William of Ockham	*Summa logicae* incorporating Aristotle	Seeks only particular terms and nominal definitions	Gender neutrality, gender equality, gender polarity
Albert the Great	Commentaries and Disputed Questions on nearly all of Aristotle's works	Seeks to have an Aristotelian philosophy of nature, metaphysics, and ethics be the foundation for the study of Theology	Gender polarity in philosophy with some gender complementarity in Theology
Thomas Aquinas	Commentaries on and incorporation of Aristotle's philosophy into a cohesive Christian worldview	Seeks to integrate and transform Aristotle into a philosophical foundation for Christian Theology	Gender polarity in natural philosophy transformed by gender complementarity in Theology
Giles of Rome	Commentaries on and limitation to a fundamental Aristotelian philosophy	Seeks to simplify the Aristotelian positions by returning to the foundation	Gender polarity in natural philosophy with some gender complementarity in ethics
John Duns Scotus	Commentaries on and a move to qualify Aristotelian philosophy	Seeks to complexify the Aristotelian positions by subtle nuanced arguments	Qualified gender polarity moving towards gender complementarity

It is important to note that the descriptions in the above table must be accepted as tentative because there are many works by these authors that have not been analyzed in the context of this study. Some were lost, for example Roger Bacon's *De animalibus,* which could easily have been a source of transmission of Aristotle's gender polarity. Other authors have written numerous works still only available in shorthand Latin manuscripts, for example several of Giles of Rome's sixty-five texts. These are among the innumerable extant commentaries written during the early centuries of academia and waiting to be translated and analyzed by candidates for Master's and Doctor's degrees as well as by competent medieval scholars. I have tried here simply to pose a line of thinking about the history of the concept of woman that considers the relation between the methodology adopted by a scholar and the particular conclusions reached about gender identity. It is my hope that these tentative hypotheses will be revised significantly as more research is undertaken with respect to this fascinating period of western history.

We also noted in this chapter the tension, fragmentation, and battles that ensued between the different university Faculties, between the secular and mendicant Masters, and between the civil and religious authorities. First of all, the lower Faculty of Arts, which focused on philosophy as an autonomous discipline, began to absorb and promote a radical Aristotelianism that was often enhanced by Averroism. Second, the higher Faculty of Theology asserting its authority did not permit philosophers to make public statements about theological issues. Third, students in the higher Faculty of Theology were not allowed to study or teach in either the Faculty of Medicine or the Faculty of Law. Thus the Masters teaching in the four different Faculties began isolated trajectories in the establishment of their own fields of study. We also saw the results of these tensions in the exile from the University of Paris of Giles of Rome and William of Ockham during periods of political turmoil. In addition, scholars also point out that the series of condemnations by bishops halted the momentum of the more integrative approach that Thomas Aquinas took towards all the disciplines in favor of a more narrow-disciplined approach within the safer boundaries of a particular Faculty.

At the same time that Masters from the different Faculties were battling with one another, all students in the three higher Faculties had to begin with several years study in the lower Faculty of Arts. In this undergraduate context they all absorbed Aristotelian philosophy and along with it all the fundamental principles for the devaluation of woman in relation to man. In contemporary language we often speak of sound bites or repeated images that occur in news breaks. These sounds or images of short duration have the effect of reducing a comprehensive event to one simple frame, and by their frequent repetition fix an idea in the mind of the observer that carries much more weight of interpretation than the original event warrants. A similar kind of reductive process occurred in medieval academia through the combined practices of lecturing as a form of commentary on Aristotle's corpus and disputation as a form of defense of the original Aristotelian positions. Certain catchphrases were repeated with such regularity that they gave the impression of being the absolute truth about woman's identity.

Qualifiers originally inserted by Aristotle as well as those new qualifiers introduced by Albert, Aquinas, and others tended to fall away in favor of more extreme generalization about the concept of woman. Thus, even though as we indicated in this chapter, there were important areas of disagreement among philosophers who appreciated Aristotle, over time certain components of the concept of woman became more or less fixed in basic principles, with sub-principles regularly falling under them.

In the following four tables the common elements of the Aristotelian schema as integrated into medieval philosophy are summarized under the four basic Aristotelian principles of gender polarity. Between each table qualifications of these principles will be noted where relevant. As we will see in subsequent chapters, it is the common elements of the medieval Aristotelian schema for gender polarity that become the food for satirists and the target for many Renaissance humanists.

COMMON ELEMENTS IN ACADEMIC SCHEMA OF GENDER POLARITY

Opposites: Metaphysical Principle — The female is the contrary privation of the male	
Female	Male
Contrary privation according to cold	Prime contrary according to heat
Contrary privation according to moisture	Prime contrary according to dryness
Contrary privation as passive principle that desires to be perfected by form	Prime contrary as active principle like form, which is perfect and divine-like
Contrary privation as a lack, an inability, an infertility	Prime contrary as a perfection, an ability, a fertility

The metaphysics of contrariety explain how men and women belong to the same human species. It explains how the same seed, deposited by the father and containing the human form, can become a male or female human being. Male and female have the same human form, but the female is the contrary privation of the male. Something happens to the same human seed to make it become a male or a female. Coldness, moisture, passivity, lack, inability, and infertility are all forms of privation.

Thomas qualifies the Aristotelian emphasis on the difference between form and matter with an emphasis on the similarity of actuality and potentiality; and he also emphasizes the metaphysical principles of essence and existence. The human body is part of the essence of the human being, and being male or female is included in the essence of a man's or woman's identity. Thus the human person is not complete without the resurrection of the body after death. The individual act of existence of a particular woman or man is unique and unrepeatable and opens up to the mystery of a particular vocation to holiness.

Generation: Natural Principle — The female is a deformed male	
Female	Male
Mas occasionatus — the misbegotten sex	The intended sex
Produced by the weakness of virtue in the male seed or some outside cause (relating to moisture or coldness) which interferes with the intention of the male seed to produce a male	Produced by the strength of virtue in the male seed, which is victorious over the female material
A male who had an accident	A male as the prime type of human being
The imperfect sex: a.k.a. the defective, deprived, orphaned, injured, malformed, mutilated, or congenitally disabled sex	The perfect sex
The less noble sex — has less eminence of degree	The more noble sex — has more eminence of degree
Provides passive principle or material to generation because of coldness of nature. Either no seed or passive and infertile seed.	Provides active principle or soul power to seed because of hotter nature to dispose material of generation to receive human soul from God.
Imperfect formation of rational powers in utero because of colder and more defective nature	More perfect formation of rational powers because of hotter nature and strength of virtue

Albert the Great introduced a significant qualification that even though the intention of the particular nature of the male seed was to produce a male that resembled the father, the intention of universal nature, or God, was to produce females. Thus the female nature is no imperfection. Following Augustine's reasoning, Albert, Thomas, and others argued that since woman's state is no imperfection, they will not be raised as men, but will retain their own engendered identity in heaven. Consequently, Christian belief modified the Aristotelian natural principle for gender polarity.

Another qualification of the Aristotelian schema was introduced by Duns Scotus, who emphasized the more active role of the female in generation, and also asserted that the male could provide matter as well as form to the product of generation. We noted as well that the debate about the unity or plurality of substantial forms, which divided so many medieval philosophers from one another, also had significance for the determination of the engendered identity of the fetus. Since the philosophers who engaged in this debate also accepted Aristotle's natural principle of gender polarity, further research needs to be done to determine whether or not they were in agreement about the principle that the female is a *mas occasionatus,* a misbegotten male.

The key element in the natural principle that links it to the epistemological principle is that woman's occasioned or defective generation resulted in her rational powers being less well developed. We see this view continually repeated in the medieval repetition of the Aristotelian schema of gender polarity.

Wisdom: Epistemological Principle — A woman's rational faculty is without authority	
Woman	**Man**
Her intellect and will (natural faculties) are weaker because of her colder nature	His intellect and will (natural faculties) are stronger because of his more perfect nature
Her rational powers do not govern her irrational soul	His rational powers more naturally govern his irrational soul
Because of moistness woman has inconstant ideas	Because of opposite composition, man has more constant ideas
Because of the weakness in her judgment, her apparent appetites are stronger	Because of his strength in judgment his true appetites are stronger
Because of her weakness in decisions she does not plan properly	A man plans more properly and should rule over a woman's plans
Woman is wise by having true opinions	A man is wise by practical wisdom of syllogistic reasoning
A woman ought to be silent in public	A man should engage in public discourse
A woman may teach only individuals or small groups because of the subjection of her nature	A man may teach individuals, small groups, and the universal audience

This Aristotelian schema of the epistemology of gender polarity is qualified by Albert and Thomas through the theory of the infusion of the supernatural gifts of knowledge, counsel, wisdom, and the theological virtues faith, hope, and charity, which perfect the human faculties. Thus a woman may be perfectly wise. However, her wisdom does not partake of the intellectual science and scholastic method of disputation common to the academic Masters studied in this chapter. Nor does it even seem to resemble the examples of religious women studied in the previous chapter. Thus for the medieval academic philosophers women are wise in somewhat different ways than men.

Finally, the epistemological principle is seen to be invoked frequently in the area of ethics to describe degrees of virtue for men and for women.

Virtue: Ethical Principle — A woman has a lesser measure of virtue than does a man	
Woman	**Man**
As naturally subject to man, her virtue is to obey	As natural ruler, his virtue is to rule well over self and others
Woman needs man for sake of government as her natural powers of reasoning are weak	Man rules over woman as he has a perfected power of rational discernment
Because of the coldness of her nature she has weak capacities for understanding, and her choices are guided by emotions, desires, and fears	Because of man's more perfect nature he is more able to make choices from a reasoned governing of his emotions, desires, and fears
Since woman is governed by her emotions, she is continent or incontinent with qualification	Since a man can govern his emotions, he can be continent or incontinent without qualification
Because of woman's weaker defective nature she lacks confidence and lies and deceives	A man's more perfect nature gives him strength and confidence
Emotion moves woman to every evil. Because woman is colder, her intellect is weaker and she is less able to discipline herself and is therefore more cunning and skilled in evil deeds.	Intellect moves man to every good
Woman's virtue is practiced in the private realm of household where she shares in the husband's ruling	Man's virtue is practiced in public and private realm of household where he shares his authority with woman
Woman's advice is of little value	Man's advice is of greater value
There is a feminine kind of perfection, of courage, of temperance, and of justice	There is a masculine kind of perfection, of temperance, of courage, and of justice

The claim that woman by nature ought to be subject to man is qualified by St. Thomas to exclude certain women like widows who are not necessarily subject to anyone. On the other hand, Thomas also holds that it is unnatural for a woman to govern a man and, if this occurs, he argues that it is based in some other characteristic like power or wealth than in excellence of nature. The claim that woman has weak capacities for self-governance is qualified by Giles, who argues that a woman still can learn how to govern herself as she wants to. Thus, the ethical principle tends to allow some exceptions to it, in ways that neither the natural principle nor metaphysical principle does.

These examples of the ethical principle that woman has a lesser measure of virtue are also qualified by a theological emphasis on the vocation to Christian perfection or sanctity. However, they do both reveal the underlying devaluation of woman's natural faculties of intellect and will, and begin to manifest a devaluation of woman's capacity for self-knowledge, self-governance, and virtuous action. At the same time, however, in the texts of the medieval philosophers like Thomas and Giles we do find a qualification of the Aristotelian theme that a woman is the unequal friend of a man. Instead, there is an emphasis on the equality of husband and wife in friendships of virtue, especially where each one participates in sharing their labor in the governing of a household.

At the same time that we have introduced certain qualifications into the original Aristotelian claims of gender polarity, we also find a progressively increasing set of derogatory concepts and phrases being associated with the female gender. In the completely male community of discourse of academia, woman's identity becomes progressively devalued. The catchphrases of contrary, colder, moister, weaker, imperfect, deformed, defective, poor judgment, poor advice, prone to evil, skilled in cunning and lying take on a life of their own as they are repeated in private lectures, in public debates, in written commentaries, and satires written for amusement. In addition we saw a continuation of three restrictions in the area of wisdom and virtue, namely that a woman ought not teach men, she ought not to rule men, and she ought to restrict her sphere of action to the private domain.

At this point I would like to insert another question for consideration. Is there some relation between the increasing clarity of the gender polarity theory in the voices of academic men and the beginning of public violence directly expressed towards women? Let us recall for a moment some significant dates. We noted that by the end of the 1200s the Aristotelian root of gender polarity was firmly in place at the University of Paris. We also noted in the previous chapter that Marguerite Porete was condemned between 1296 and 1306 for misleading theology she had publicly put forth in a manner directed to the teaching of men and women. When she continued to redistribute her book, in 1310 she was tried by theologians from the University of Paris and burned to death as a heretic. Even if her work contained theses directly opposed to those of the Faculty of Theology, and even if her personality was somewhat cantankerous, was there something more operative here than we find in the banishing of male faculty members from the university at a close time in history? Marguerite argued for the death of reason, while philosophers in the Faculty of Arts argued that reason was superior to faith. Both were criticized by the theologians for the Neoplatonic elements in their thought. Yet one was put to death while the others were simply limited in their speech. The issue here concerns the use, or more properly, the misuse of violence in the name of truth.[193] The question then remains whether or not the atmosphere of devaluation of woman common to gender polarity theory contributed to this unfortunate historical action.

Even if the more extreme words and phrases are extracted from the academic community of discourse we find an increasingly explicit linkage among the four different principles of Aristotelian gender polarity. The linkage is causal, and it is used to reach conclusions in many different areas related to the concept of woman. We can describe the linkage as follows:

> A woman, as contrary privation, colder, and moister than man is generated as an occasioned type of human being, with weaker natural faculties of intellect and will that do not have authority over her irrational soul's emotions and desires, and that lead her to make poor judgments, defective choices, and consequently to have a lesser measure of virtue.

> A man, as prime contrary, hotter, and dryer than woman is generated as the perfect type of human being, with stronger natural faculties of intellect and will which have authority over his irrational soul's emotions and desires, and which lead him to make reasoned judgments and careful choices, and to consequently have a greater measure of virtue.

In conclusion, the academic discussion about the concept of woman in medieval Aristotelian gender theory involves the simultaneous happening of three different things: (1) Christian Theology introduces some gender complementarity qualifications to Aristotelian gender polarity claims; (2) the constant repetition of the original Aristotelian concepts by the practices of commentary and disputation draws in a cluster of increasingly derogatory phrases to characterize woman's identity; and (3) the elaboration of theories through the use of syllogistic reasoning and the scholastic method of debate makes explicit linkages between the different principles of explaining gender polarity.

The second and third developments created a background in academia and beyond which would take centuries to overturn. The first development provided a foundation within which a new form of complementarity would begin to emerge in the works of early Renaissance Humanists. Before we turn to this source, however, we need to attend to one other community of discourse operative in this period in history: the popular satirists. In the next chapter we will turn to the satirical literature to see the particular ways in which these concepts and linkages start to filter into popular literature about gender differentiation.

---

193. See, for example, Jean Bethke Elshtain, "Feminist Discourse and Its Discontents: Language, Power, and Meaning," *Signs: Journal of Women in Culture and Society* 7, no. 3 (1982): 603-21. See also "The Use of Force in the Service of Truth," in *Memory and Reconciliation: The Church and The Faults of the Past,* by International Theological Commission, December 1999 (Boston: Daughters of St. Paul, 2000), # 5.3.

CHAPTER 3

PHILOSOPHICAL CONTENT IN
EARLY SATIRES ABOUT WOMEN

I n ancient Greek philosophy and literature a practice of ridiculing a particular identifiable group emerged because of positions or values they held. Satires could be directed by a particular man against different groups of men in the context of public discourse in building up the government of the city-state. Satires were also offered simply for entertainment or for cultural enjoyment, especially in the theater. Socrates developed the irony of satire into a fine art in public dialogues he conducted while teaching the Greek youth, and in particular, during his famous trial. In Plato's dialogues we discover a very different purpose, i.e., the good of the person being satirized. Here satire characterizes false values and positions; it is used to bring a new understanding or to discover what is true.

Satires have been used often to articulate different concepts of women since the early Greek philosophy. Right from the beginning satires about women differed from satires about men in two significant ways. First, satires about women ridiculed all women, while the target of satires about men was a well-identified group of men. Second, satires about women usually did not concern a value or a position about some issue of importance, but rather focused on some fundamental characteristics of the being or doing of women. From a philosophical perspective, satires about women exaggerate a perceived essential characteristic of gender identity or invert a characteristic that "ought to" belong to one kind of individual (e.g., man) as belonging to another kind of individual (e.g., woman).

The psychological question of what motivated the male authors of various satires has been considered in great detail elsewhere, and therefore will not be a focus in this text.[1] It needs to be noted, however, that men are not the only ones who satirized the complement gender. Women also began to satirize men in writing,

1. See Gilbert Highet, *The Anatomy of Satire* (Princeton: Princeton University Press, 1962); John A. Yunck, *The Lineage of Lady Meed: The Development of Medieval Venality Satire* (Notre Dame: University of Notre Dame Press, 1963); Francis Lee Utley, *The Crooked Rib: An Analytical Index to the Argument about Women in English and Scots Literature to the End of the Year 1568* (Columbus: Ohio State University Press, 1944); P. K. Elkin, *The Augustan Defence of Satire* (Oxford: Clarendon Press, 1973); John Peter, *Complaint and Satire in Early English Literature* (Oxford: Clarendon Press, 1956); and G. R. Owst, *Literature and Pulpit in Medieval England* (Cambridge: Cambridge University Press, 1933).

particularly in the later Renaissance, and there are several examples of contemporary women writers who ridicule men as a group. For a satire to take root a specified community of discourse is needed. As is seen in the history of philosophy, selected male communities of discourse developed satires against women in the context of a traditional gender polarity that devalued women. Today selected female communities of discourse develop satires against men in the context of a reverse gender polarity that devalues men.

Since the parameters of this study are the years 1250-1500, our concentration will be confined primarily to historical satires written by men about women. In the summary and evaluation at the end of this chapter, we will reflect on some of the philosophical deficiencies, such as a tendency towards reductionism and different forms of bias, which operate in satire. After reviewing the philosophical origins of the genre of satires about women in western thought, we will consider in more detail four different examples of satires that emerged around the time of the infusion of Aristotelian thought into western academia.

In this chapter some aspects of the philosophical structures and content of the satires with specific reference to Aristotle's concept of woman will be examined. Accordingly, characteristics that Aristotle perceived as essential to woman will be compared with core concepts that have been articulated in selected significant satires written between 1250 and 1450. In addition, we will also give some reference to the Platonic theme of appearance versus reality in satires about women. Finally, we will consider a controversial satire about women, written by Boccaccio, in an effort to discover whether it can be considered as "meta-satire," that is, a satire of a satire. This question is important because of the argument put forward in the next chapter, namely that in the humanist authors of the early Renaissance a new way of perceiving women emerges that challenges the Aristotelian model of gender polarity. However, before proceeding with our analysis of new theories about woman's identity, we need to complete the study of the far-reaching dispersion of concepts that devalued woman's identity and ways in which the institutionalization of Aristotelianism contributed to this dispersion.

THE CONCEPT OF WOMAN IN THE ANCIENT SATIRICAL TRADITION

Since so many late Medieval and Renaissance satires were influenced by earlier satires, we will offer a short survey of some of those that have been analyzed in greater detail in *The Concept of Woman: The Aristotelian Revolution (750 BC–1250 AD)*. The Greek authors Hesiod, Aristophanes, Euripides, and Theophrastus and the Roman author Horace are usually identified as the ones who first employed satire in relation to woman's identity.[2] Theophrastus is especially important for the present study because he took over Aristotle's school of philosophy during 322-286 B.C., shortly after the master's death. His satire against marriage, the *Aureolus liber*

---

2. David S. Wiesen, *St. Jerome as a Satirist: A Study in Christian Latin Thought and Letters* (Ithaca, N.Y.: Cornell University Press, 1964).

de Nuptiis, was lost, but it was mentioned by name and used extensively in St. Jerome's *Adversus Iovinianum.*[3] In the context of this satire, written for the male reader, Theophrastus consistently devalued woman, as the potential partner in marriage.

David Wiesen identifies Tertullian as a Christian source for satire against women, and works by writers Plutarch, Seneca, Cicero, and even Porphyry as Latin sources.[4] A question still open to debate is whether St. Jerome learned of Aristotle and Theophrastus, his disciple, from Porphyry or from Seneca. In any event, certain Aristotelian principles of the concept of woman crept into the heart of his satire.[5] It is important to mention, however, that many of these authors had also very positive texts about women's identity; for example, Plutarch's *Bravery of Women* and *Sayings of Spartan Women,* Seneca's *On Consolation to Marcia* and *To Helvia on Consolation,* and Porphyry's letter entitled *The Philosopher to His Wife Marcella,* as well as the reports of St. Jerome's personal relations with women such as Paula and Marcella.[6] Thus, it is difficult to determine to what extent a male author's satirical views about woman constitute the core of his concept of woman.

Early satires against women were written for the most part as a way to convince men about the advantages of a celibate life. They were usually either short essays or parts of longer works. In these satires we often find woman being presented as lewd, drunk, gluttonous, "dangerously" sensuous, and so forth. The texts articulated an exaggerated version of the Aristotelian dictum that women, because of their imperfect formation, lack the authority of reason to order their irrational appetites. Woman "lacks restraint" and is full of unrefined sensuality. Another similar theme is woman's inconstancy; and still another is her affected speech. These relate to the philosophical presupposition of the greater moistness in women's nature and the belief that her particular virtue ought to be silence.[7]

The best-known satire about women in pagan writing was Juvenal's (60-140) Sixth Satire. Juvenal had written many satires against different kinds of men, but his sixth satire was simply against women in general.[8] It was written as a form of advice to a man, Postumus, not to marry. Scholars suggest that Juvenal was influenced by Aristotle's student, Theophrastus.[9] Again the same themes are emphasized, namely woman's lack of control over her passions, and her inconstancy or infidelity. Juvenal's description of woman's lust and talkativeness follows the same

3. Wiesen, *St. Jerome as a Satirist,* p. 152.

4. Wiesen, *St. Jerome as a Satirist,* pp. 13-14.

5. Katherine Rogers, *The Troublesome Helpmate: A History of Misogyny in Literature* (Seattle and London: University of Washington Press, 1966), pp. 1-29.

6. Of particular interest to our study are the views of St. Jerome about women. For selections from nine different letters of St. Jerome and from other early writers about women see the compilation by Elizabeth A. Clark, *Women in the Early Church: Message of the Fathers of the Church* (Wilmington, Del.: Michael Glazier, Inc., 1983).

7. See, for example, St. Jerome, *Adversus Iovinianum* and 22nd letter, or *Advice to Eustochium,* in *Selected Letters of St. Jerome* (Cambridge, Mass. and London: Harvard University Press and William Heinemann, Ltd., 1954). See also Gilbert Highet, *Juvenal the Satirist* (Oxford: Clarendon, 1960).

8. *The Satires of Juvenal* (Bloomington and London: Indiana University Press, 1958), VI.

9. E. Courtney, *A Commentary on the Satires of Juvenal* (London: Athlone Press, 1980), pp. 260-61.

pattern mentioned above, that is, of taking what are considered to be essential characteristics of woman and presenting an exaggerated description of these characteristics as leading to vice. Woman has difficulty controlling herself because of the weakness of her reason, which, to go back to Aristotle, is explained from her imperfect formation.

At the same time, in Juvenal, we also have a different kind of treatment of woman's identity in other characteristics he chooses to satirize. Juvenal claims that woman seeks to rule man, and that she wants to be like a man in athletic events, scholarship, and public oration. Here we find satire utilizing a mode of inversion, so the woman is ridiculed for inverting the sexual distinction captured in the Aristotelian model; woman ought to be virtuous by obeying, not ruling, by having true opinion, not theoretical wisdom, and by limiting her action to the private sphere, not the public domain.

Juvenal's satire then takes precisely those characteristics and inverts them. "How can a woman be decent sticking her head in a helmet, denying the sex she was born with?" he asks. He describes woman as making more noise trying to be a philosopher than pots and pans when they are rattled. He ridicules her for trying to speak in Greek, and for studying the classics. These particular themes for ridicule are interesting for the history of the concept of woman because they reveal that in this early period there were women attempting to philosophize, probably in the Pythagorean, Neoplatonic, and Stoic traditions. Finally, and this is the goal of the satire, Juvenal warns Postumus, the man to whom he is writing the satire, that if he marries he will have to "bow to the yoke" and be ruled by his wife.[10]

While the majority of ancient satires devalued woman as a way of arguing against marriage, Lucretius (98-55 B.C.) in De rerum natura also satirizes woman, but this time by ridiculing or questioning the pleasure-seeking nature of man. Once again, however, the underlying theme of becoming ruled by a woman is ridiculed. In this inversion of woman's virtue to obey, Lucretius satirizes the man who "burns with insane desire" by depicting the object of his desire as full of the faults and weaknesses that should be kept before his mind.[11] While Lucretius satirizes the man who gives in to his passions as much as the woman who is the lowly object of the passions, he devalues woman more by arguing that a man perceives virtues in her where they do not exist. Playing on the theme of appearance versus reality, Lucretius concludes that when a woman is a "hideous bore," the man considers her to be "wisdom's lamp."[12]

In the twelfth century two new important satires on women emerged. In the first, Andreas Capellanus in The Art of Courtly Love, after discussing multiple ways to win and keep a lover in the model of courtly love with a young man named Walter, suggests that Walter **not** follow all the advice he had just been given. To convince his reader to reject human love Capellanus devalues all women as the object of love. We find his satire following the familiar pattern of exaggerating "essential

10. *The Satires of Juvenal,* VI, 65-83.
11. Lucretius, *The Nature of Things* (New York: W. W. Norton and Company, Inc., 1977), IV, 107-10.
12. Lucretius, *The Nature of Things,* IV, 109.

weaknesses" of women, on the one hand, and inverting male and female virtues and vices, on the other hand. Woman is described as envious, gluttonous, slanderous, and prone to lying; she is also inconstant and disobedient. In one passage, the relation of these characteristics appears to be very close to Aristotle's description of the relation of male and female to form and matter:

> No woman ever makes up her mind so firmly on any subject that she will not quickly change it on a little persuading from anyone. A woman is just like melting wax, which is always ready to take a new form and to receive the impress of anybody's seal.[13]

It is interesting to note in passing that some of the Bishop of Paris's 219 condemnations in the year 1277 were directly addressed to ethical claims in Andreas Capellanus's text.[14] Even more notable is that in the preface of the list of condemnations themselves, Capellanus's *De amore* was specifically condemned. In reading the condemnation we are once again plunged into the tension and battles between the Faculties of Arts and Theology at the University of Paris:

> Stephen Tempier felt it necessary to proceed to the condemnation for the following reason: the jealous faith of great and grave personages had frequently drawn to his attention the fact that students of the Faculty of Arts at Paris, exceeding the proper limits of their particular Faculty, were daring to treat as doubtful in their schools and to dispute such manifest and abominable errors, such conceits and idiotic falsities and propositions as he set forth in this document.[15]

The form of this preface testifies to the public popularity of the satire. At the same time, the content of the actual condemnations focuses not on the derogatory concept of woman it contains, but rather on the false polarity it sets up between reason and faith, and the false description it gives of man as unable to control himself when under the passion of love. This latter view implies that a man's behavior is determined, rather than chosen.

In a very thorough discussion about *The Art of Courtly Love,* A. J. Denomy demonstrates how the first two parts of the satire invoke arguments from reason and from nature to prove that a man has to follow his passion for a woman, and that a reasonable woman follows the man's initiative; while the third part of the satire invokes arguments from faith and religious authority to suggest that a man should reject reason and nature. This radical dichotomy between faith and reason becomes associated with a 'so-called doctrine of double truth' common to the Latin

---

13. Andreas Capellanus, *The Art of Courtly Love* (New York: Frederick Ungar Publishing Co., 1957), Book III, 30. For Aristotle's reflection on the relation of the female to wax, see *Generation of Animals,* 729b 15-20.

14. Etienne Gilson, *History of Christian Philosophy in the Middle Ages* (New York: Random House, 1954), p. 406. See also John F. Wippel, "The Condemnations of 1270 and 1277 at Paris," *The Journal of Medieval and Renaissance Studies* 7 (1977): 2, 187.

15. A. J. Denomy, C.S.B., "The *De Amore* of Andreas Capellanus and the Condemnation of 1277," *Mediaeval Studies* 8 (1946): 107.

Averroists.[16] In this doctrine of double truth, contradictory positions are put side by side, with no resolution. Because of the fundamental understanding of scholastic philosophy that faith and reason are ultimately not contradictory because the truth is one, this view had to be condemned.

Significant to our purposes is the fact that the concept of woman in both parts presents woman as ultimately unable to be self-governed. Even in the first two parts of the satire, when women initially seem to be capable of choice (of whether to accept or reject a man's advances), in contrast to men, who, like animals, blindly follow their sexual desires, in the end, women are devalued because the ones who choose to reject the sexual advances are depicted as miserable, immoral, or even evil because they will not fulfill a man's wants. As described above, in the third section, all the traditional derogatory generalizations about women's character are invoked to convince men to not pursue them.

In another satire by Walter Map (c. 1140-1209), *Advice of Valerius to Rufinus the Philosopher not to Marry,* it is argued that most women are not virtuous but are wicked and full of lust. Map concludes that women 'separate' the soul from body in a man, and that they are ultimately destructive of man's identity in marriage. Another vice selected out for emphasis, in addition to her lack of control of passions, is woman's desire to rule rather than obey. In one passage, Map appears to be invoking a distinction of Aristotelian logic when he argues that if a man marries "a man must needs belong to his wife, for it is true to logic that the *predicates* will be such as the *subjects* will permit."[17] This example is used to encourage Rufinus *not* to marry in order to avoid the inversion of the virtues of ruling and obeying.

An anonymous poem often attributed to Walter Map, and called *Golias de conjuge non ducenda,* develops the same theme even further: "The husband serves the wife, and the wife rules, and he has been made a slave who had been free."[18] This particular satirical poem, characterized by Samuel Tucker as "a violent attack on the sex" and an "unmitigated libel," was extremely popular in Europe and in a sixteenth-century English translation entitled *The Pain and Sorrow of Evil Marriage.*[19] The satire worked by inverting the philosophical virtue of ruling and obeying as well as by exaggerating the perceived natural weaknesses in woman's character.

This brief introduction to satires on women written before the thirteenth century has revealed a common pattern in which selected aspects of woman's char-

16. Denomy, "The *De Amore,*" pp. 148-49. Denomy puts forward the argument that there are similarities but not causal connections here.

17. Walter Map, *De Nugis Curialium* (Courtiers' Trifles) (London: Chatto and Windus, 1924), p. 192. I am grateful to Professor Raymond Klibansky for bringing to my attention the extent to which this text was known. In a private conversation he mentioned that he found more copies of this satire in different libraries throughout Europe than any other of its kind.

18. *The Latin Poems Commonly Attributed to Walter Mapes,* ed. Thomas Wright (Hildesheim: George Olms Verlagbuchhandlung, 1968), p. 79. See also Solveig Eggerz-Brownfield, "Anti-Feminist Satire in German and English Literature of the Late Middle Ages," Ph.D. Diss., Catholic University of America, 1981, pp. 74-78.

19. Samuel Marion Tucker, *Verse Satire in England before the Renaissance* (New York: Columbia University Press, 1908), pp. 41, 176.

acter are identified for ridicule. The first kind of argument assumes Aristotle's premise and simply exaggerates its effect in providing consistent evidence for a repetition of the philosophical claim that a woman's reason is without authority over her emotions, so that she is continually disposed to vice in the form of lust, gluttony, avarice, talkativeness, envy, and so forth. The second form of argument inverts Aristotle's premise and also exaggerates its effect when it emphasizes that women seek to have men's virtues and that they want to rule and force men to obey. So man becomes the victim of woman, trapped in a forced obedience to a non-virtuous individual. Consequently, the satirists persuade their male readers that it is better not to marry or even have relations with women that could elicit a response of sexual desire from the man.

A summary of the following points of emphasis in the above-mentioned satires by Juvenal, Capellanus, and Map is offered here:

Aristotelian Themes in Satires before 1200			
	Juvenal	Capellanus	Map
inconstant	x	x	x
no authority over emotions	x	x	x
not friend	x	x	x
not silent	x	x	
not obey	x	x	x
not stay in private sphere	x		

While it may not be the case that Aristotle's principles of gender polarity directly caused these early satirical arguments, one may suggest that he was an indirect influence through his disciple Theophrastus as incorporated by St. Jerome and Juvenal. We see in these satires a repetition of the same themes originally found in Aristotle's texts. After Aristotle's philosophy became better known in the West through the institutionalization of his thought in academia, one finds satirists actually referring to his philosophy to justify their claims.

THE EMERGENCE OF EXTENSIVE SATIRES ABOUT WOMEN

In the thirteenth century a most striking increase occurred in the length of satires about women. Prior to this time authors often introduced their satires about women as a simple chapter at the end of a book or as a short essay among a much wider collection of writings. While in England this practice extended well into subsequent centuries, in thirteenth-century France and in Italy women became satirized throughout a complete and often very lengthy text. In this chapter we will consider three such examples: *Le Roman de la rose, Le Livre de Mathéolus,* and Boccaccio's *Corbaccio.* Coincidentally, Aristotle had become required reading at most universities. While it would not be possible to prove a direct causal connection between these two events, it is clear that these events would tend to reinforce one another through the consistent devaluation of woman that they embodied.

In our text we have listed the satires by the title of the work rather than by their author's name. The rationale for this departure from the usual method in this book is that a satire about woman seemed to have a life of its own in western thought and is usually referred to by its title rather than by its author. Only in the case of Boccaccio's *Corbaccio* does the author begin to come forward as a personality in his own right. It is for this reason that we will also consider the relation between the *Corbaccio* and Boccaccio's overall philosophy of woman's identity. In general, however, the personality of the author of a satire recedes behind the concepts and arguments that are contained in the text itself. We will now turn to our analysis of philosophical themes in these lengthy satirical texts.

Le Roman de la Rose

Le Roman de la rose, a satire in poetic verse of over four hundred pages, was written consecutively by Guillaume de Lorris (c. 1200-1240) and Jean de Meun (1240-1305). The text was begun [#1-#19] by de Lorris in 1225-1230 and completed [#20-#100] by Jean de Meun (or Meung) between 1269 and 1278.[20] Jean de Meun, who had attended the University of Paris, had a Master of Arts and may have even been a teaching Master.[21] Since his writing followed the period during which Aristotle's works were integrated into the academic curriculum, it is not surprising that Jean de Meun's dependence on scholastic sources is noted in various commentaries.[22] In addition, the structure of the poem follows the structure of a scholastic debate between masters and students.[23] Jean de Meun's sections of the

20. See Jillian M. L. Hill, *The Medieval Debate on Jean de Meung's "Roman de la Rose": Morality Versus Art* (Lewiston, N.Y.: Edwin Mellen Press, 1991), pp. vii-viii.

21. Charles Dunn, Introduction, in Guillaume de Lorris and Jean de Meun, *The Romance of the Rose,* trans. Harry W. Robbins (New York: E. P. Dutton, 1962), pp. xvi-xviii.

22. See Heather M. Arden, *The Roman de la Rose: An Annotated Bibliography* (New York: Garland Publishing, Inc., 1993), #524: Mary Katherine Tillman, "Scholastic and Averroistic Influences on the *Roman de la rose,*" *Annuale Medievale* 11 (1970): 89-106. "While it is generally accepted that Jean de Meun reflects Scholastic thought and language . . . , Tillman . . . attributes the possible reference to those ideas in the *Rose* to Jean de Meun, not to the narrator or the characters" (245). See also #253: Lionel J. Friedman, "'Jean de Meung,' Antifeminism, and 'Bourgeois Realism',"' *Modern Philology* 57 (1959/1960). "Yet the source of the antifeminist remarks of the jealous husband, la Vieille, and others, is shown to be not bourgeois realism (the observation of real people), but the books by churchmen. That is, their remarks are 'a commonplace of the sermon or of moral, didactic literature'" (115).

23. See Susan Stakel, *False Roses: Structures of Duality and Deceit in Jean de Meun's "Roman de la Rose,"* Stanford French and Italian Studies 69 (Saratoga and Stanford: Anma Libri and Department of French and Italian, Stanford University, 1991), p. 16. See also Alan M. F. Gunn, "Teacher and Student in the *Roman de la rose*: A Study in Archetypal Figures and Patterns," *L'Esprit créateur* 2 (1962): 126-34.

text introduce the reader to the male community of satirical discourse: Theophrastus, Valerius (Walter Map), and Juvenal. Thus, the shared satirical discourse about woman crosses the centuries and gathers new momentum for its generalized conclusions that devalue woman's identity.

In fact, the main justification for Jean de Meun's satirical remarks about women in *Le Roman de la rose* comes from the shared male community of discourse to which previous authors of satires belonged even though the authors also suggest that their audience contains women readers as well. Guillaume de Lorris asks at the beginning of the text, "God grant that she for whom I write with favor look upon my work. . . ."[24] However, this woman reader is soon identified as "the rose" whom the author hopes to seduce. In the second part of the work in a section entitled "The poet apologizes for his book," Jean de Meun inserts a direct apology to women readers. We will include this passage in full because it reveals the way in which the author weaves his apology to women into the broader context of the male satirical tradition:

> So, worthy women, whether maids or wives,
> Heart free or bound in love, I pray you all,
> If you have found some words included here
> That seem malicious or satirical
> Against the ways of womankind, that you
> Will not blame me therefore, nor scorn my book,
> Which is but written for instruction's sake.
> For certainly I have not said one thing,
> Nor would I say, in drunkenness or ire
> Or hate or envy, 'gainst a living dame;
> Since no man but the vilest of the vile
> Would have the heart a woman to despise.
> Men write such things that you and I may have
> Acquaintance with ourselves and know the truth
> When we find you and me described in books.
>   And furthermore, most honorable dames,
> If you think I say things that are not true,
> Say not I lie, but search authorities
> Who've written in their books what I have said
> And shall. In no respect speak I untruth
> Unless wise men who wrote the ancient books
> Were lying, too. They all agree with me
> When manners feminine they chronicle;
> Nor were they drunken fools when thus they wrote.
> 'Twas by experience they knew the ways
> Of women, and they found them proven thus
> In many an age; so you should pardon me.
> I but repeat their words; though for my game,

24. *The Romance of the Rose*, p. 4.

Which costs you little, I additions make
As all the poets have been wont to do
To order matters, which they're pleased to treat.
For, as their writings prove, their only aim
Is to delight and profit those who read.[25]

Jean de Meun places the reader in the position of having to decide whether his satirical comments about women are simply a poetical device augmenting a repetition of ancient views, or the truth as verified by experience. It is well known that Jean de Meun actually despised the other main group he satirized, the mendicant clerics associated with the Faculty of Theology at the University of Paris. While the Master of Arts also offered an apology of sorts to readers of this group, scholars do not conclude that it expressed his real views. In order to come to a conclusion about the significance of the author's remarks to his female readers we will turn to an analysis of the text to consider what he actually said about the concept of woman.

Le Roman de la rose was Jean de Meun's only original work. Otherwise, he concentrated on translations of Latin texts into French. Two of these translated texts with significance for the concept of woman were: The Letters of Heloise and Abelard and Boethius's Consolation of Philosophy. It is significant that both the personal example of Heloise as conveyed by her letters and the image of Lady Philosophy in Boethius's text provided models of a female philosopher actively using discursive reasoning to teach wisdom to a man.[26] However, in Le Roman de la rose the concept of woman was given an entirely different interpretation. Furthermore, de Meun misuses arguments from "the wise Heloise" that devalue women in order to convince men not to marry. A fourteenth-century prose reworking of Le Roman de la rose challenged Jean de Meun's misuse of the expression "the wise Heloise" by claiming of one of her remarks that it "could never have been expressed by a wise woman."[27]

We will now consider the passages from Le Roman de la rose that reveal particular concepts of woman. The text of de Meun offers three different sources for satirical depictions of woman: (1) generalized reductionist statements about women by male speakers in the dialogue, (2) female personifications of different concepts, and (3) a female object of seduction called "the rose." If we extract the underlying philosophical concepts within these three sources, we discover patterns similar to ancient satirical texts.

First, women in general are identified by a single generalized characteristic essential to their identity. Through the words of the "jealous husband" we find an appeal to Theophrastus to support the claim that all women make poor wives. The

25. The Romance of the Rose, #70, 320.
26. See Allen, The Concept of Woman: The Aristotelian Revolution, for the development of this point, pp. 236-40 and 271-91.
27. Hill, The Medieval Debate, p. 43. This revised prose version of The Rose also appeared to mitigate some of the devaluation of women found in the original text by stating that "no one should scorn women . . . since we are all born of woman" (p. 43). However, the argument that women ought not to be devalued because men were born from them places the justification on men's identity rather than women's identity.

jealous husband, whose wife torments him by her infidelity, invokes the Greek philosopher:

> Would that I Theophrastus had believed
> And never wed! He thinks a man a sot
> Who joins himself in wedlock with a wife,
> Be she foul or fair or poor or rich;
> For in his noble book called *Aureole,*
> Which should be studied in the schools, he says,
> And I believe it true, that such a man
> Too grievous life will lead, filled full of pain,
> Of labor, quarrels, danger, and reproach
> Caused by a silly woman's foolish pride
> And the demands and the complaints she makes,
> Occasions for which she never fails to find.
> Hard it will be to curb her foolish will
> And guard her from herself.[28]

Jean de Meun's appeal through the jealous husband to Aristotle's disciple Theophrastus reinforces the perception that woman's nature has been considered as essentially unable to govern herself over a 1500-year tradition. The epistemological principle of gender polarity, that a woman's rational soul is without authority, leads a man to try unsuccessfully to "guard her from herself."

The impression that these views about women are shared within a male community of discourse is further supported by the jealous husband's invoking of the historical character Valerius in Walter Map's text. He advises men not to marry because of the lack of capacity for virtue in women. Juvenal is brought into the community of discourse too:

> Valerius is not ashamed to ask
> To what end thinks the fool that he will come
> Who either in this land or overseas
> Makes love to evil women, who abound
> Thicker than flies, or bees about a hive.
> Who trust in such frail twigs lose body and soul.
> Valerius, who grieved when he perceived
> That Rufinus, his friend, would take a wife,
> Spoke these hard words: "May God omnipotent
> Forbid that e'er you're caught within the net
> Of woman, who is powerful to crush
> All things by her destructive artifice."

And Juvenal wrote likewise to his friend
Postumus, when the latter wished to wed:

---

28. *The Romance of the Rose,* #41, 173.

"You wish to marry? Can't you find for sale
A rope or halter — any kind of cord?"[29]

The perception that women are unvirtuous is connected to the inversion of the dictum that women ought to obey. Here, woman's capacity to rule men by "catching," "cording," and "crushing" them is ridiculed along with the men who get caught in this trap.

After a passage in which the jealous husband reflects on the fact that some women even murder men, he presents his generalization about the impossibility of ruling any woman:

All women are, have been, and e'er will be,
In thought if not in deed, unvirtuous;
Though some may hesitate to do the act,
None can restrain their wish. All women have
This great advantage: they their purpose hold.
Scolding and beating will not change their minds;
He'd rule their bodies who could rule their wills.
Let's talk no more of things that ne'er can be![30]

If it be suggested that perhaps this is just the attitude of one man, or the jealous husband, Jean de Meun places similar attitudes in the speeches of the friend of the lover who trains him for his seduction of the rose.

In a context in which he is suggesting that gifts might be useful in seduction, the friend points out that, although the lover must avoid paying directly for sexual favors because women do not like a direct monetary exchange, nonetheless women are by nature unable to control their desires:

Yet are most women covetous of gain,
And gluttonous to swallow and consume
Until there naught remains to those who claim
Themselves their lovers, loyal in their love.[31]

Again, while it may be tempting to argue that the friend was describing only *some* women, later in the text he makes it clear that he is really describing all women. The author makes it a generalized empirical characteristic of woman's identity:

No man can be so sure of womankind,
Or know his lady well enough, to feel —
How loyal e'er she be and waverless,
However firmly fixed her heart may be —
That he can hold her, with his utmost care,

29. *The Romance of the Rose,* #41, 176.
30. *The Romance of the Rose,* #44, 185.
31. *The Romance of the Rose,* #39, 167.

Better than by the tail he'd hold an eel
Caught in the Seine, so that it could not move
Or get away as soon as it was caught.
That creature cannot be so wholly tamed
That it's not ever ready to escape;
No one can cope with all its various shifts.
I say not that there are no women good
Who fix restraint by virtue on their lives;
But only that, although I've tested them,
I've found none such. Not even Solomon,
Who well knew how to try them, could find one;
For he himself affirms he never saw
A woman steadfast.[32]

This attitude towards women in general is further supported by the speeches of a male character named Genius, who claims that women are full of "ire," "malice," "vice," and "avarice." He then argues:

A man who trusts his secrets to his wife
Makes her his mistress. None of women born,
Unless he's drunk or crazy, will reveal
To women anything that should be hid,
Unless he wants to hear it coming back
To him from others.[33]

Here we see the similar pattern of satire. Characteristics such as inconstancy and lack of authority over the passions or speech are exaggerated when applied to women. Next, the male and female differentiated virtues of ruling and obeying are inverted. The result is the continued devaluation of women. In this situation Jean de Meun suggests through his character Genius, that any man who marries a woman gets caught in this devaluation; he becomes the slave to her unvirtuous character.

The second way Jean de Meun satirizes woman in *Le Roman de la rose* is through the device of female personification.[34] For example, a debate between Reason, a female figure, and the Lord of Love, a male figure. In addition to these major characters in the dialogue, hate, villainy, covetousness, avarice, envy, and shame are all given female personifications. These latter mentioned are obviously vices. Jean de Meun also personifies traditional theological virtues as female, but changes the

32. *The Romance of the Rose,* #47, 199-200.
33. *The Romance of the Rose,* #80, 349.
34. Arden, *Annotated Bibliography,* #234: Joan M. Ferrante, *Woman as Image in Medieval Literature from the Twelfth Century to Dante* (Durham, N.C.: Labyrinth Press, 1985). The relation between linguistic gender and female personification is noted: "The gender of the characters, for example, is not simply a function of their grammatical gender but has meaning for understanding their behavior. . . . The women characters are universally portrayed in derogatory terms, except Raison, whom l'Amant rejects in favor of the Rose . . . " (106).

meaning towards a derogatory image such as "a mistress of love" who often deceives:

A fool is he who much on her depends;
For though she forms the fairest syllogism
Fallacies may her whole conclusion be.[35]

The overwhelming impression of all of these female personifications is of a weakness of mind in female wisdom that leads to vice. The epistemological principle of gender polarity, that a woman's reason is defective, is followed quickly by the ethical principle of gender polarity, that she has a different measure of virtue and even that she falls headlong into vice.

The most significant female personification is found in Jean de Meun's characterization of Reason. This figure was modeled on Lady Philosophy as depicted in *The Consolation of Philosophy,* the most widely read philosophical text in the Middle Ages. Boethius is thought to have taken his own model from Socrates' description of Diotima as his teacher in Plato's *Symposium.* While Socrates' and Boethius's feminine personification of Reason strongly embodied human wisdom expressed through discursive reasoning, intuitive grasp of principles, and the capacity to teach another the correct path to truth, Jean de Meun inverts his female figure of Reason, and makes her appear impotent and ineffective.

At first Dame Reason appears to be very wise. She tells the lover that she will teach about the Lord of Love "without fallacy." Then she gives a list of several contradictory definitions of love such as it is a "madman's logic, reasoned foolishness" or a "foolish wisdom, a wise foolishness."[36] After explaining the relation of love to fortune, happiness, and justice she then offers herself to the lover who rejects her advances. Reason's plea to the lover to be like Socrates is rejected: "Your Socrates I count not worth three peas, /However great; of him I'll hear no more."[37] The lover announces that he will serve the Lord of Love instead, who helps him to secure "the rose" which he considers to be worth much more than Reason can offer. Then the lover adds that the goal of Jean de Meun in writing this book is to expand the allegory for wide dispersion in France so that the readers will "no more trust in Reason, recreant wretch."[38]

35. *The Romance of the Rose, #*20, 91.
36. *The Romance of the Rose, #*21, 95 and #21, 96.
37. *The Romance of the Rose, #*33, 142.
38. *The Romance of the Rose, #*50, 215. An in-depth discussion of the relation between Reason and Love is found in John V. Fleming, *Reason and the Lover* (Princeton: University Press, 1984). Fleming offers a history in chapter 1 of The Lineage of Lady Reason, mentioning, in addition to Boethius's Lady Philosophy, Augustine's *Soliloquia* and Cicero. He wants to defend Reason from its detractors who say that it is impotent against Love. He states: "The lover's problem is not sexuality but irrationality. There is only one cure for irrationality, and that is rationality. Thus Reason does indeed tell the Love in the clearest possible terms how to attain 'rational sexuality.' The way in which one 'attains' rationality of any sort is by being reasonable or, in the dramatic terms of the *Roman de la Rose,* by believing, following, and loving Reason" (p. 24). Fleming's approach to the feminine personification of Reason in *The Rose* offers a balance to the satirical approach to women in other aspects of the text. See also Arden, *Annotated Bibliography, #*194: John V. Fleming, "Jean de Meun's Reason and Boethius," *Romance Notes* 16 (1975): 678-85.

As a background to the third kind of satire against woman found in this text (i.e., a female object of seduction) we need to note that Jean de Meun consistently attacks any permanent relation such as marriage between a man and a woman, and instead argues for sexual relations without obligation. Through the jealous husband he cites Heloise's letters to Abelard as a historical precedent for this kind of attitude. In addition, he appeals to a golden age before the ownership of property in which men and women freely initiated and engaged in sexual encounters. These arguments, along with the satirical portrayal of the wife mentioned above, undermine the value of marriage.

A sub-theme that runs through *Le Roman de la rose* is an appeal to Dame Nature, who ordains sexual intercourse between men and women for the propagation of the species. She allows a man to overcome death and achieve some immortality through his offspring. Consequently, the value of the celibate life was also undermined. This shows that whereas satires against women were used to **promote** celibate life in earlier centuries, now they are being used to **undermine** celibate life. In both cases, however, it is women who are the devalued object of the satire.[39]

Jean de Meun claims that neither Aristotle, Plato, Ptolemy, nor Euclid was able to describe the power of Dame Nature, nor are the alchemists able to imitate her power to create. Then, after a lengthy analysis of the relation of free will, predestination, astronomy, and dreams, Dame Nature reflects on the betrayal of God by man. At this point she clearly satirizes her own "female" personification: "As I'm a woman, I cannot keep still/But will tell all, for women naught conceal."[40] Then follows a satire on man about whom she lists the following adjectives, which are not that different from those previously applied to women: covetous, mean, gluttonous, evil-mouthed, idolatrous, hypocritical. She then concludes: "In brief, the wretch/So simple is he makes himself a slave/To all the vices — gives them harbourage."[41] However, Dame Nature then turns the satire around by implying that these vices spring up because men do not follow the general desires of nature. Using multiple analogies for the male sexual organ (stylus, hammer, anvil, plow) she chastises the man who neglects to use his organ "to give a mortal race eternal life."[42]

The young lover then follows the guidelines of Dame Nature and seduces "the rose." Here, in this final sequence of the work we find the third way that the satire devalues woman. The words that are used by the author imply that the "female" rose is simply a passive object waiting to be "plucked," "seized," "stripped,"

---

39. De Meun also introduced satirical images of a female personification of "Hypocrisy" who was the lover of a pretended priest, and of "Forced Abstinence," who in one place is described as Beguine and in another as pregnant with the anti-Christ. *The Romance of the Rose,* #56, 247 and #66, 307.

40. *The Romance of the Rose,* #88, 407. This satirical depiction of the feminine personification of woman as Nature is considered by Alan M. F. Gunn, *The Mirror of Love: A Reinterpretation of "The Romance of the Rose"* (Lubbock, Tex.: Texas Tech Press, 1952). Gunn comments on woman's loquacity and emotional instability in the discourse by Nature which represents, as well as speaks about, this aspect of women's character, pp. 155-58.

41. *The Romance of the Rose,* #88, 407.

42. *The Romance of the Rose,* #91, 414.

and "deflowered," "both trunk and limbs of every leaf and bloom."[43] The female is depicted as a passive sexual object, gullible and susceptible to flattery, weak and unable to control her passions. The metaphysical principle of gender polarity, with an association of the female with the passive and the male with the active, is given a personification in the seduction of the female character *la rose*. In this use of the analogy of a flower for a young woman by Jean de Meun, woman's identity is reduced to a passive function of her female anatomy, and she is basically described in terms of her usefulness for (bringing pleasure to) man.

This allegorical connection between a rose and a woman, which operates throughout the entire text *Le Roman de la rose,* set off a vigorous debate in France. We will study some of the key personages and arguments in this debate in Chapter 7 in relation to the works of Christine de Pizan. To summarize, the three different ways in which satire worked to undermine a concept of woman as virtuous or wise: (1) reductionist generalized statements about women by male speakers in the dialogue, (2) the derogatory aspects of female personification of characters in the dialogue, and (3) the passive female object of seduction called "the rose." Overall, *Le Roman de la rose* devalued women in ways that were consistent with the Aristotelian metaphysical, natural, epistemological, and ethical principles of woman's identity.

Alan Gunn has suggested that the female character in *La Vieille* might be an exception to this overall effect because of the general role she plays in the dialogue about love. *La Vieille* stands for the old woman who represents all women who have been wronged by men.[44] Gunn's argument focuses on the role that the Old Woman plays in the general debate about love, and in particular her place as an academic Master of one particular point of view. Given our previous consideration of public disputation in Chapter 2, it may be important to consider his claim. Gunn argues that the style[45] and the contents[46] of the debate in the poem are similar to the *disputatio* in academia. He draws a conclusion about the contribution of the Old Woman:

> The discourse assigned to La Vieille is, in the light of the foregoing analysis, first, a piece of highly conscious and systematic instruction in the meaning and the art of love; and, second, a deliberate and systematic refutation of the doctrines of Amors, and to a large degree also of the teachings of Raison and Amis. Thus in-

43. *The Romance of the Rose,* #100, 462-63.
44. Gunn, *The Mirror of Love,* p. 330. He adds: "And if the ethical quality is slight, there is still a rough logic in the conclusion she draws from her instances of deserted women" (p. 388).
45. Gunn, *The Mirror of Love.* Even though there is no face-to-face debate between Love, Reason, The Friend, and The Old Woman, ". . . the arena of the debate is in the mind of the hero" . . . so that "the hero himself can be compared to a university student who goes from one 'doctor of love' to another and then to still another, and listens to the lectures in which the rival masters set forth their doctrines and attempt to refute those of their competitors" (p. 321).
46. Gunn, *The Mirror of Love.* "I have described the completed poem as a *disputatio* because within it the various speakers on the theme of love exhibit a consciousness of the differences between their views and those of their opponents, and attempt a more or less systematic refutation of the view of their opponents" (p. 366).

terpreted, her discourse reillumines the earlier discourses of Amors, Raison, and Amis; causes to stand out in sharper relief their didactic and controversial character; and so makes it manifest that these discourses considered as one system constitute a *disputatio* among "doctors of love" of great learning and much experience; a *question d'amour* on a vaster scale than any poet had attempted before Jean de Meun.[47]

While Gunn's argument has some merit concerning the text as a whole, it is difficult to see that it positively affects the concept of woman simply because a female character offers arguments. The problem is that the Old Woman's arguments are not particularly forceful because they are based on art rather than science, and because they spring from a desire for revenge in response to injustice suffered.[48] So the Master's chair that the Old Woman is using from which to argue her point is itself being satirized precisely because she is so vulgar and uneducated in her remarks, and she encourages a life of immoral vice rather than one of virtue. So again we would conclude that the overall effect of *Le Roman de la rose* was to devalue women's identity.

Le Roman de la rose had a great influence on the literary European public because of its wide and lengthy popularity. There are almost three hundred manuscripts of the complete poem still in existence.[49] According to David Hult:

> The thirteenth-century *Roman de la Rose* is one of the most significant literary contributions of the entire Middle Ages. From its extensive manuscript attestations, one can infer that it was the most widely read vernacular poem after the *Divine Comedy;* it is, moreover, the only major poem in the French tradition to have commanded a continuous readership from the Middle Ages to the present day. . . .[50]

He also refers to the double seduction of the text, first of the Lady or Rose, and second of the reader to continue the same journey as the author.[51] This seduction was addressed mainly to the male community of discourse as it included a consistent

---

47. Gunn, *The Mirror of Love,* p. 393.

48. See *The Romance of the Rose,* where the Old Woman says: "I was a fair, young, silly fool; and had/No training in the school of Love, where's taught/The Theory. Te practice well I knew;/Throughout my life I've had experience/That's made me wise, so now I know the game/Up to the final bout. It were not right/That I should fail to teach you what I know,/Since I have made so much experiment" (#59, 265).

49. Eggerz-Brownfield, "Antifeminist Satire," p. 105. She notes in her Ph.D. dissertation that it was more influential in England than in Germany, probably because of its translation by Chaucer. Only in 1839 was the first part of the poem translated and printed in German.

50. David F. Hult, *Self-fulfilling Prophecies: Readership and Authority in the First "Roman de la Rose"* (Cambridge: Cambridge University Press, 1986), p. 4.

51. Hult, *Self-Fulfilling Prophecies.* "Once one understands that Guillaume's poem works as a text of seduction, one that attempts to elicit an appropriate response from its reader, then one can see that seduction works on (at least) two levels. The most obvious is, of course, the seduction of the Lady, but the other, no less significant, is the seduction of the reader, the call to contemplate, to perpetuate, and possibly to continue the poetic journey" (p. 8).

devaluation of woman in the ways already noted. However, there were also some women present in the listening audience, and the derogatory words and concepts began to sink into their consciousness as well, waiting for a time in the future when a response from a female perspective would begin to formulate itself publicly.

Sylvia Huot refers to its wide appeal to all classes of society.

> Identifiable owners of *Rose* manuscripts in the fourteenth century include members of the royalty, the aristocracy, the clergy, and the bourgeoisie. Copies of the poem appeared in the libraries of religious institutions and of the Sorbonne. Given this extremely diverse readership and the encyclopedic quality of the poem, it is no surprise that the influence of the *Rose* can be discerned in the most varied literary works.[52]

Jean de Meun's satire also appealed to writers in different countries; for example, it influenced two English authors who satirized women in sections of their own works. The first is thought to be William Langland (c. 1330-1400), whose authorship has been attributed to *The Piers Plowman* written in three versions between 1362 and 1398. *Le Roman de la rose* was translated into English and published as *The Romaunt of the Rose* around the same time as Langland's first work.[53]

The second English author influenced by the *Le Roman de la rose* was Geoffrey Chaucer (c. 1340-1400).[54] Many scholars believe that Chaucer was the person who translated *Le Roman de la rose* into English as *The Romaunt of the Rose*.[55] In the Prologue to the *Legend of Good Women,* the context of a dialogue with a Queen before her court of maidens, Chaucer includes reference to himself as the translator of *La rose.*

---

52. Sylvia Huot, *The "Romance of the Rose" and Its Medieval Readers: Interpretation, Reception, and Manuscript Transmission* (Cambridge: Cambridge University Press, 1993), p. 10.

53. See Hugh Walker, *English Satire and Satirists* (New York: Octagon Books, 1972), originally published in 1925. These dates are shifted somewhat to c. 1370, c. 1378-79, and c. 1386 by A. V. C. Schmidt, the editor of William Langland, *Piers Plowman: A New Translation of the B-Text* (Oxford: Oxford University Press, 1992), p. 1. Langland or the author was influenced by the original version to use a dream as his literary device (pp. 10-11). See also Arden, *Annotated Bibliography,* #716: Dorothy L. Owen, *"Piers Plowman": A Comparison with Some Earlier and Contemporary French Allegories* (Folcroft, Pa.: Folcroft Library Editions, 1971). "The author concludes that . . . the author or authors of *Piers Plowman* almost certainly knew and remembered the *Rose*" (p. 330).

54. Concerning Chaucer, Walker observes, in *English Satire and Satirists,* that the tale of the Wife of Bath is relevant: "in only one other case does Chaucer resort to class-satire. Next to ecclesiastics, the Middle Ages loved most to satirize women; and in this too Chaucer follows the fashion. There is a satire of women both in the prologue of *The Wife of Bath* and in *Lenvoy de Chaucer,* appended to *The Clerk's Tale,* to say nothing of slight touches elsewhere" (p. 22).

55. See Ronald Sutherland, *The Romaunt of the Rose* and *Le Roman de la Rose:* A Parallel-Text Edition (Berkeley and Los Angeles: University of California Press, 1968), which discusses the controversy over the authorship of the *Romaunt* and gives parallel texts. See also, for example, Arden's *Annotated Bibliography,* #753: Ronald Sutherland, "The *Romaunt of the Rose* and Source Manuscripts," *Publications of the Modern Languages Association* 74 (1959): 178-83, 346; and #615: Caroline D. Eckhardt, "The Art of Translation in *The Romaunt of the Rose,*" *Studies in the Age of Chaucer* 6 (1984): 41-63, 289.

Your translating creates disturbances
And hinders folk from their observances
On my behalf. The creed of Love you scorn.
And do not try denying it, I warn:
The Romance of the Rose in your translation
Can now be read without an explanation;
Against my law it is a heresy
Because it makes wise folk withdraw from me.
You wrote of Cressid as seemed good to you;
The story makes all women seem untrue,
Yet they are true as steel can be.
Think carefully before you answer me.

Why could you not have said good things as well
As bad ones in those stories that you tell?
Was there no worthy subject in your mind,
Or in your books could you have failed to find
For me some tale of women good and true?[56]

Significantly, Chaucer proposes to defend women, in contrast to the work he has translated, and his defense will take the form of writing the *Legend of Good Women.*[57] Chaucer also appears to be aware that he has female as well as male readers in his community of discourse. The controversial debate about Chaucer's real intentions cannot be considered here. It is interesting to note, however, that he places the discussion in the context of a dialogue with a God of love, a noble Lady, and a court of several women. This imaginary dialogue has some similarities to Boethius's dialogue with Lady Philosophy. This similarity is not surprising because Chaucer translated Boethius's famous text into English.[58] The particular theme that Chaucer emphasizes in his description of different legends about women is their fidelity in love. These essays provide counterexamples to the more traditional concept of female inconstancy.

Chaucer's particular depiction of the woman in *The Tale of the Wife of Bath* in *The Canterbury Tales* appears to be a response to *La rose.*[59] He ironically inverted

56. Geoffrey Chaucer, *The Legend of Good Women,* trans. Ann McMillan (Houston: Rice University Press, 1987), #ll: 324-40, 73-74.

57. Chaucer wrote about Cleopatra, Thisbe, Dido, Hypsipyle and Medea, Lucrece, Ariadne, Philomela, Phyllis, and Hypermnestra. See also Hill, *The Medieval Debate.* "Chaucer's decision illustrates the fact that he was keen not to be linked personally with the antifeminist tradition. In fact the formulation of criticisms against himself in his own work is a master stroke, showing that he was superior to Jean de Meung in the art of audience manipulation, for the latter's arguments often lack clarity and lend themselves to misinterpretation" (pp. 17-18); and Arden, *Annotated Bibliography,* #566: Ruth M. Ames, "The Feminist Connections of Chaucer's *Legend of Good Women,*" in *Chaucer in the Eighties* (Syracuse, N.Y.: Syracuse University Press, 1986), pp. 57-74, 266.

58. Chaucer's translation of *Boethius "De Consolatione Philosophiae,"* Early English Text Society, ed. Richard Morris (London: Kegan Paul, Trench, Trubner and Co., Ltd., 1868). See the Noble Lady's own reference to this translation in *The Legend of Good Women,* #l: 425, 77.

59. Geoffrey Chaucer, *The Tales of the Clerk and the Wife of Bath,* ed. Marion Wynne-Davies (London and New York: Routledge, 1992), pp. 27-70.

the humor of the original work, and the female character voices the very stereotypes that had satirically been applied to women by men.[60] Instead of woman being either passive or else uncontrollably active in leading men astray because she is unable to govern herself, Chaucer's Wife of Bath consciously and actively chooses immoral behavior as her preferred mode of operation. She is the imaginary incarnation of Theophrastus' advice to the jealous husband in *La rose*. Thus Chaucer indirectly counters the satirical view of women found in the traditional literature. That he is well aware of the Aristotelian texts that support gender polarity can be concluded from his description of an Oxford Cleric, one of the pilgrims in the *Canterbury Tales*. This Oxford student kept twenty books of Aristotle's philosophy by his bed, and his sole focus was thought about moral virtue. Thus, Chaucer's proposing of the wife of Bath, a willfully immoral woman, as the counterexample to the traditional satirical view of woman, increases the irony of the satire. Woman herself devises a new measure of virtue that overturns the Aristotelian model of the golden mean.

Christine de Pizan is the most significant author to challenge views of women in *Le Roman de la rose* because she is the first person, male or female, to engage directly in dialogue with the satirical views about women expressed by various characters in the text. She also presents a variety of different kinds of counterexample to the traditionally satirical view of woman. In contrast to Chaucer, however, Christine de Pizan provides examples of women who correspond to an Aristotelian and Christian theory of virtue. Since de Pizan's major works, including her objections to *Le Roman de la rose,* will be discussed in a later chapter of this book we will not consider them here. It is worth noting in passing that both Christine de Pizan and Chaucer used imaginary female characters to raise an alternative view. There is an interesting contrast between these two authors who responded to *Le Roman de la rose* by presenting alternate imaginary female models. Chaucer's Wife of Bath relished in exaggerating the so-called feminine vices of the Aristotelian tradition, while Christine de Pizan's characters presented strong virtues normally associated with men in the Aristotelian tradition.

Le Livre de Mathéolus

In turning to the second major satire to reach popular audiences in the fourteenth century, we discover an important change in content. Instead of a satirical appeal to ancient texts derived indirectly from Aristotle through his student

---

60. See Arden, *Annotated Bibliography, #*699: William E. Mead, "The Prologue of the Wife of Bath's Tale," *Proceedings of the Modern Languages Association,* 9 (1901): 388-404. According to Arden, ". . . Mead suggests that the Wife puts the jealous husband's antimatrimonial ravings in the mouth of her own husband, while taking the same attitude toward them that the jealous husband does toward his wife. The author [Mead] suggests further that Chaucer's 'first acquaintance with the railing accusations that Theophrastus [Aristotle's disciple] brings against women, he got from the *Rose*. The reversal effected by turning the jealous husband into the Wife of Bath would have strongly appealed to Chaucer's peculiar type of humor' [p. 403]. Finally, Mead notes that the Wife glories in doing the very things for which the jealous husband scolds his wife" (p. 323).

Theophrastus, we now discover a direct appeal to Aristotle's gender polarity theory with its principles for the devaluation of woman. This change offers evidence that the Aristotelian Revolution in academia very quickly extended outwards into the popular literature of the time.

Le Livre de Mathéolus was written first in Latin at the end of the thirteenth century by a man who called himself Mahieu le Bigame (Matthew the Bigamist), and then translated into French around 1390 by Jean le Fèvre. This several-hundred-page text was immediately successful, and it circulated widely both before and after the invention of printing. In the French translation le Fèvre made a link between *Le Roman de la rose* and *Le Livre de Mathéolus.*[61] In this way the community of satirical discourse about women was built up through translators as well as through the original writers.

As Chaucer had done previously, le Fèvre tried to distance himself somewhat from the attitudes towards women in the original satirical text he had translated while he also served as the instrument of their translation. In a poem he wrote entitled *Le livre de leesce,* he referred to the historical satirical community of discourse that had supported the arguments in *Le Livre de Mathéolus:* "Master Mahieu has to help him Gallus, Juvenal, Ovid, and master de Meung, whose heart is happy and whose body is agile."[62]

In *Le Livre de Mathéolus* we encounter an attack on marriage through the method of devaluing women. Mathéolus states that he was married to two women at the same time, and that anyone who marries will regret it. In the French version, he links this approach to *Le Roman de la rose* in the very first chapter where he states:

> In *le Roman de la rose* as well
> It is stated in the chapter on jealousy
> Or on picking up worries:
> No one alive who feels married
> Is anything but a fool and is really sorry for it.[63]

Le Livre de Mathéolus and *Le Roman de la rose* reinforce one another while reaching different conclusions. While the *Roman* suggests that the use of a woman for

61. Hill, in *The Medieval Debate on Jean de Meung,* argues that this linkage nearly a century later had an important place in turning people against the *Rose.* "This poem had the most significant and damaging effect on attitudes towards the *Roman* during the period in question [the fourteenth-fifteenth centuries]. It irrevocably linked Jean de Meung with the antifeminist cause, and its success was instrumental in creating prejudices which were later voiced in the debate" (p. 14).

62. Hill, *The Medieval Debate on Jean de Meung,* p. 16. The original version of the text can be found in A. G. Van Hamel, *Les Lamentations de Mathéolus et le livre de Leesce,* 2 vols. (Paris: 1892-1905), #ll. 749-50, vol. 2, 24.

63. *Le Livre de Mathéolus* (Bruxelles: A. Mertens et fils, 1846), Book I: 24-29, 4. The text is rendered into modern English by Filippo Salvatore, as are all other passages from this text. A slightly different translation by Hill, *The Medieval Debate,* emphasizes even more this interrelation between Mathéolus and *The Rose:* "If only I had seen and read several books, both in verse and in prose, for example the *Roman de la Rose,* which expresses the anxieties attendant upon jealousy in the chapter devoted to that subject, where it says: 'No man who is married does not regret his status, unless he is mad.' This is the truth, but I did not know it then" (p. 15).

sexual pleasure is the goal of life, the *Livre* concludes that marriage is a new kind of martyrdom. The former text ends with a seduction while the latter ends with the pronouncement of God that purgatory through marriage is good for a man. However, the consistent method used throughout both books is the ridicule of women, except for the praise of their ability to bring sexual pleasure.

Mathéolus brings forth all the usual exaggerations of women's vices. He appeals to ancient authors to support his claim that all women are inclined to evil:

> Woman is so wrathful and evil
> That she is the source of every vice.
> Ovid says in his works:
> Women are inclined to all kinds of evil;
> The Ancients said it,
> Lust for her body and forget about her soul.[64]

In other sections specific vices such as malice and avarice are identified.[65] In each case we see the usual exaggeration of a perceived weakness in woman's character satirized.

Woman's incapacity to control her speech is also reflected in Mathéolus's claim that women cannot be silent.

> Woman can in no way be silent,
> A man's feelings are corrupted
> By her soft pleasantness.
> But I, being used to it,
> Remain deaf to its call.[66]

Vivid detailed descriptions are given of women who never cease to speak, who cannot moderate their words and emotions. In addition to this example following the pattern of exaggeration of a weakness in woman's nature, there are also passages that reveal an inversion of male and female virtue. While man is supposed to speak in public, and women be silent, Mathéolus states that women chase men from their homes and they love public arguments.[67] In private they love to mislead through false statements and fallacies.[68] Again we see the epistemological principle of gender polarity leading to immoral behavior. Either women do not have control over their use of language, or if they do, they use it for non-virtuous ends.

One of the most striking aspects of *Le Livre de Mathéolus* is the introduction of the satirical play on the Aristotelian natural principle of gender polarity. Woman is described as a defective, deformed, imperfect, or accidental man. Mathéolus exaggerates this principle within the broader category of all defects in nature and he describes woman as a "monster of nature":

64. *Mathéolus,* Book II: 2685-90, 149.
65. *Mathéolus,* Book I: 600-65, 23-25, Book II: 40-45, 58, and Book II: 1500-20, 109-10.
66. *Mathéolus,* Book II: 1230-35, 45. See also the lengthy text Book I: 740-60, 28.
67. *Mathéolus,* Book II: 70-76, 59, and Book II: 215-27, 64.
68. *Mathéolus,* Book I: 985-94, 36.

> No proof is required
> To show that every woman is a monster
> And that she carries faults in her.
> It is said that woman is conceived
> Without nature's approval.
> The philosopher [Aristotle] and Holy Writ
> Testify to it quite plainly and say
> That when the pulsations of lust
> Make her open, she becomes giddy
> And blurred concerning her mistake,
> And she blushes when she ponders about it.[69]

The association of female nature as defective in formation with Aristotle as "the philosopher" is clear. It is also accepted as a fundamental principle that needs no proof.

Mathéolus refers directly to Aristotle's philosophy in the following satirical passage that suggests women overturn the Greek philosopher's logic:

> Women are always one step ahead
> Of all learning that owed so much to Aristotle
> Organized in different branches,
> Be they a prioris, a posterioris or logic
> or the science of mathematics.
> Woman can go further than all of them
> And override them all
> Thus beating the master of the masters.
> She put reins and a halter on the chief
> And led him astray toward syllogism,
> Or barbaric and laughable matters;
> She rode the horse like an abbess
> And pulled him along like an ass.
> The horse neighed too much
> When the male tried to ride it.
> The governor was governed,
> And the gender was overturned,
> She is the agent and he the passive one
> Who offers himself to be held under her sway:
> What a preposterous order
> Where everything is turned, upside down
> And confused, for he who has to be first
> Cannot be last.[70]

---

69. *Mathéolus,* Book II: 4215-33, 200-201. "The philosopher" was the common mode of appellation for Aristotle at the time.

70. *Mathéolus,* Book II: 1100-24, 40-41.

In this depiction of the one who ought to govern being governed by a woman we have the inversion of the Aristotelian metaphysical principle that the female is passive and the male active, and the ethical principle that a woman ought to obey and a man rule. Mathéolus mentions Aristotle at other times in the text as well, in connection with Solomon and wisdom.[71] He also constantly repeats the theme that a man who enters into marriage will be enslaved to his wife, so that he will be forced to obey while she rules him. ". . . I see that by marriage/is a greater servitude/than of a serf who is able to get out of it. . . ."[72]

This short study of *Le Livre de Mathéolus* reveals a pattern similar to satires about women encountered in previously studied texts. The exaggeration of characteristics of the weakness of woman's nature was joined by the inversion of male and female virtues. This inversion was **directly** linked up with Aristotle himself. Finally, we discovered the introduction of a new Aristotelian base for the exaggerated description of woman as a monster of nature.

The extreme popularity of Jean le Fèvre's French translation of *Le Livre de Mathéolus* led to a series of critiques. For example, Christine de Pizan has 'Lady Justice' condemn *Le Livre de Mathéolus*. In fact, Christine attributes to her reading of this book of Mathéolus her original decision to write about woman's identity. So, the satire of Mathéolus actually served as the catalyst for the first public intergender dialogue about woman's identity. Since several counterarguments to the devaluation of women in the satirical tradition by humanist writers will be considered in some detail later, we will simply identify here repeated patterns of philosophical structures underpinning the various satires that were so popular during the thirteenth to fifteenth centuries.

Frau Welt, Evangile aux Femmes, and Two Dits

In continuing this section about early satires on women, we will introduce here a slightly different theme, expounded by several authors, that did not have a direct relation to Aristotelian thought. Since this theme concerns the disparity between appearance and reality, it can be considered more Platonic (or Manichean and Gnostic) than Aristotelian in its devaluation of the sensual apparent world. In its relation to the concept of woman, we find a double image portrayed: how woman appears to be to man, and how she is discovered to really be.[73]

In German literature this image was graphically developed in the concept of 'Frau Welt.' According to Solveig Eggerz-Brownfield, "In sculpture and poetry 'Frau Welt' is the attractive, elegant woman who, upon turning around, reveals a repulsive back, crawling with worms."[74] In French literature, a similar theme, al-

---

71. *Mathéolus,* Book II: 2740-50, 151.
72. *Mathéolus,* Book I: 276-82, 12-13.
73. Some critics of *Le Roman de la Rose* have also emphasized the Platonic aspects of the satire. See Arden, *Annotated Bibliography, #452*: Lucie Polak, "Plato, Nature and Jean de Meun," *Reading Medieval Studies* 3 (1977): 80-103, 210.
74. Solveig Eggerz-Brownfield, "Anti-feminist Satire in German and English Literature of the

though without the identification of woman with the earth, was developed both in poetry and in works of prose. In a published dissertation by George C. Keidel entitled *L'Evangile aux Femmes: An Old-French Satire on Women,* we find ten different versions of a poem in which the theme of appearance and reality provided the central paradox for each stanza. These different versions of what were called a "Gospel of Women" appeared in Europe between the years 1285 and 1490.[75] After the invention of printing, numerous printed texts of these poems were dispersed throughout Europe.

The authorship of the poem has been much contested, and Keidel concludes after weighing the alternatives that, while arguments have been put forward for both Marie de France and Jean Dupin, in fact an Ile de France monk was the author. In all versions of the poem there is a consistency of style and message. The basic form of the satire consists in short, four-lined stanzas in which the first lines say something apparently positive about women, and the final lines invert the claim, implying the reality behind the appearance. The purpose of the *Evangile* is usually stated in the final verse. In version A (composed around 1285), for example, the author concludes that he will never love or believe in women; while the author of version D (composed around 1350) concludes that a man should not be ashamed to meet with a woman day or night for "certain advice." Many stanzas are found in both poems, while some are dropped, and some new ones introduced. The overall effect of the poem is to point out the familiar perceived weaknesses in women's character. A few examples should suffice to demonstrate.

A rather constant theme is that woman appears to have virtue, but she ends up leading men into vice:

> What a woman is in herself, few, if any, know;
> Neither are her virtues apparent, nor are her evils hidden;
> She seems humble as ashes lie after they have been burning,
> He who is most sure, is the soonest lost.

> It is a wonder in woman, like in no other;
> To fulfil her desire she has her bow ever-drawn;
> He who believes her best, has often lost everything;
> One does not know how to protect oneself; evil is rendered for good.[76]

We also find the familiar theme of inconstancy connected with vivid imagery from nature:

Late Middle Ages," Ph.D. Diss., Catholic University of America, 1981, p. 65. She notes that Walther von der Vogelweide, Konrad von Würzburg, and Wirnt von Gravenberg all wrote poems in the late thirteenth century on this theme.

75. George C. Keidel, *L'Evangile aux Femmes:* An Old-French Satire on Women (Baltimore: The Friedenwald Company, 1895), pp. 1-30.

76. *Evangile,* version A, vii and xvii. Translated by Regina Moller, as are all other passages from this text.

Above all woman is changeable in her desires;
By nature she wants most that which is forbidden her;
A thought, a word; now she wants then she reconsiders;
Her word is firm, as is smoke in the wind.

Woman is most courteous and she gives good counsel;
Such a soul knows not how to hide a fault;
And rightly or wrongly she is cruel to every man,
She has as much loyalty as a fox, a dog or a lynx.[77]

While all of the above selections have been taken from version A, the earliest one identified, in the following variation of the last stanza repeated in version D, from a slightly later period, we find an interesting shift in emphasis:

It is neither just nor right to speak ill of women;
They are wise; learned and of great courtesy;
Because when they speak, foolish is the one who does not trust therein,
Like the shepherd, the wolf when he has seized the animal.[78]

While there are many different concepts presented in these stanzas, they do not create any new aspects of woman's philosophical identity; rather they try to encapsulate the usual themes of vice, inconstancy, inversion of obedience and ruling, and so forth. The widespread popularity of *Evangile aux femmes* is attested to by Keidel who said that: "It may well be claimed that this poem has never been lost sight of by the literary public of France."[79] It spread from Paris and was sung or recited far and wide by the troubadours who traveled across Europe. So the satire moved outwards from academic communities of discourse, to literary communities of discourse, into the general public with singing troubadours. With this expansive movement woman was reduced to a single devalued characteristic within a gender polarity model.

A cluster of *dits,* "something said" about women in poem and in song, emerged, especially during the years 1275-1330.[80] Written in the vernaculars of Francien or Anglo-Norman, they contained poetical images of woman's identity that were exaggerated either in virtue or in vice. Their anonymous authors used the skills of logic, grammar, and rhetoric to develop a theme. They also reveal a common male community of discourse: "[t]he *dits* carry the mock confidential and hortatory tone of one comrade addressing another . . . [with the] assumption that it is the author's prerogative to examine and judge womankind. . . ."[81] To exemplify the point of how Aristotelian principles of gender polarity became popularized and

77. *Evangile,* version A, xi and xxiii.
78. *Evangile,* version D, vii.
79. Keidel, *Evangile,* Introduction, p. 3.
80. Gloria J. Fiero, Wendy Pfeffer, and Marthé Allain, trans. and eds., *Three Medieval Views of Women: La Contenance des Fames, Le Bien des Fames, Le Blasme des Fames* (New Haven and London: Yale University Press, 1989), p. 16.
81. Fiero et al., *Three Medieval Views of Women,* p. 30.

integrated into the satirical literature of everyday culture, examples of sections from two of these *dits* will be briefly included here.

La Contenance des fames (i.e., *femmes*) (The Ways of Women) reflects on woman's changeableness. Here the difference between appearance and reality shifts from a preoccupation with space, or a movement from exterior to interior realities, and moves towards a preoccupation with time, the changeableness of woman's ways.

> My poem to you conveys
> Female manners, female ways;
> And let none seem disputable
> That a woman's heart is mutable,
> Fluttering from gender to cold
> She will never be cajoled,
> Except as her heart inclines,
> Now she wants it, now declines,
> Now she'll give, then she'll retrieve
> As fancy moves her to conceive.
> A woman's heart is just not able
> To chart a course that's firm or stable.
> . . .
> Now she's wild, now she's demure;
> Now wants peace, then starts a war;
> Now says nothing, now chatters on;
> Retires in shade, then wants the sun;
> . . .
> Why bother to contradict her?
> Pure logic won't restrict her.
> She'll talk your head off,
> Do whatever she thinks of,
> Whether good or bad or wise;
> It's useless to chastise,
> And he who even tries
> Plays the fool in my eyes.
> For the task is profitless.
> . . .
> But I have seen enough to know
> And this I say, I know it's so;
> Who loves and trusts mad womankind
> Damns soul and body, wastes his time.[82]

Again we see the inconstancy, the weak reasoning powers, the inability to govern the emotions as characterizing woman's identity. In addition, there is the further

---

82. *La Contenance des Fames,* in Fiero et al., *Three Medieval Views of Women,* pp. 87-97.

suggestion that she is dangerous for man and not only causes him to waste his time, but also leads him to perdition.

In *Le Blasme des fames* (i.e., *femmes*) (The Vices of Women), we find woman depicted as the cause of a man's death as well.

> Listen to me, lords, I pray,
> Lend an ear to what I say:
> Who too much trusts in womankind
> Often leaves honour far behind;
> Who loves or prizes womankind
> Often ends up much maligned;
> He who trusts them one or all
> Drinks the hemlock, tastes the gall;
> He's self-demeaning and a dope,
> He hangs himself by his own rope,
> He who keeps these lines in mind
> Fears swords less than womankind.[83]

As the *dit* continues the listener is introduced to the reason for woman's dangerous character: it is due to the natural weakness of her intellect. In a discussion of Adam and Eve, the author introduces the natural principle of gender polarity.

> Ask: who first sinned — man or woman?
> Who got us exiled from the Garden?
> Who offered the apple to whom:
> Woman to man or man to woman?
> . . .
> Because of woman's weaker wit
> She fell into the snake's gambit;
> Her better half the lesser fool,
> The snake used woman as his tool;
> The dowry bestowed upon the wife
> Was childishness throughout her life;
> He granted her as remedy
> A loathing for rationality;
> . . .
> The discord in a woman's heart
> Corrupts a marriage from the start;
> Of every evil she's the root,
> The tree bears anger as its fruit.
> She sets friends against one another,
> Turning brother against brother;
> She cleaves the father from the son,
> She robs the mother's nest of one.

83. *Le Blasme des Fames*, in Fiero, *Three Medieval Views of Women*, p. 121.

> Outwardly she's well behaved,
> But by her nature, she's depraved.[84]

Woman's lack of human perfection, particularly by the exercise of her rational powers of choice and self-governance, leads to her being described through a litany of animal behaviors:

> To lure a man and drive him mad:
> First, simple as a lamb is she,
> But venomous as a snake can be,
> Imperious as a lion is she,
> Voracious as a leopard she,
> Deceitful as a fox is she,
> Combative as a bear is she,
> The canine's sharper sense has she,
> As sharp-toothed as a cat is she,
> Destructive as a rat is she,
> As sneaky as a mouse is she;
> On the inside like a hedgehog's hide
> But gentle as a dove outside;
> As masterful as a falcon she,
> A sparrowhawk demure as can be;
> As quarrelsome as a titmouse she,
> As lecherous as a sparrow she,
> A blackbird or thrush by day,
> A bat when dark is on its way;
> She is the owl that terrifies,
> By day she hides, at night she flies.[85]

The *dit* ends with the usual advice that a man who marries will regret it.

> Whence the verse:
> He who takes a wife trades peace for strife.
> Long weariness, despair, oppress his life,
> A heavy load, a barrel full of chatter,
> Uncorkable, her gossip makes a clatter,
> Now, ever since I took a wife,
> Calamity has marred my life.[86]

What we see in these selected examples is the interplay of the Neoplatonic satire on appearance and reality with the Aristotelian theme of woman's natural defective formation and lack of self-governance. Interspersed with these two philosophical

84. *Le Blasme des Fames*, pp. 121-23.
85. *Le Blasme des Fames*, pp. 125-27.
86. *Le Blasme des Fames*, p. 131.

themes is the religious motif of Adam and Eve with its suggestion that woman is the cause of all man's troubles. It is interesting to note in passing that many of the short popular satires on women were written and sung in the last half of the thirteenth century and the first part of the fourteenth century, just after the foundation of the universities and the incorporation of Aristotelian texts into the curriculum. While this institutional occurrence cannot be blamed for all the derogatory things said or sung about woman, it does seem to have a part to play in the increasing momentum of polarity concepts and arguments and in the increasing sophistication of methods for communicating these ideas.

Boccaccio's *Corbaccio*

For the final section of this chapter we will consider a controversial text written between 1354 and 1365 by Giovanni Boccaccio (1313-1375). His particular use of satire is something that has puzzled and often misled philosophers for centuries. Three different theories have been proposed by scholars: (1) that the text takes a strident literary tone as an experiment in the genre of satire, (2) that the satire expresses Boccaccio's real views about women's identity, or (3) that the satire is an ingenious meta-satire that satirizes the male character who offers the usual satirical views about women. We will consider these options further after describing the content of the text itself.

The context of the *Corbaccio* is structured by a narrator who is infuriated because he was ridiculed by a widow who had taken a letter he had written to her and shared it lightly with another man. The narrator then speaks in a dream to the spirit of the dead husband, who also laments losing his reason over the woman. A complete and thorough devaluation of women is then spewed forth by the spirit of the "dead" husband to the narrator, who agrees to seek a common revenge against the woman. Waking from the dream the narrator decides to write a record of the woman's treachery.

The author of the satire restates the familiar themes that a woman is not able to control her emotions. "Women's lust is fiery and insatiable"; "the execrable feminine sex is suspicious and bad tempered beyond comparison"; "as instinctively as animals, they immediately fly into such a burning temper that tigers, lions, and snakes have more humanity when enraged than do women"; and "they are all fickle and without constancy whatever."[87] Boccaccio lists the usual litany of vices in the general categories of lust, uncontrolled anger, and inconstancy. It is interesting to note, in connection with this image of woman, however, that Boccaccio presents his male satirist as also suffering from the same weakness of character; he is driven by an insatiable anger and desire for revenge. The difference is, however, that the writer represents only a single male individual, while the satire extends to cover all women. The character is particular, while the satire is universal.

87. Giovanni Boccaccio, *Corbaccio* (Urbana/Chicago/London: University of Illinois Press, 1975), pp. 27-30.

Boccaccio also describes the satirist's devaluation of women's wisdom in several different places in the text. Complaining that only the ten muses have the legitimate claim to wisdom, and that every woman wants to make herself into the eleventh muse, the writer concludes that the woman he despises is the one who uses her virtue of courage to be sexually promiscuous.[88] The author implies that this is a common attitude among all women, and that instead of being a member of the Socratic or Platonic schools of philosophy, women belong to the "Cianghelline sect," which follows the Council of Ladies of Discretion and their leader Madam Cianghella, a director of a house of prostitution. The devaluation of reason and women's capacity for wise decisions in this satirical rendering of women's interest in philosophy is clear.

We also find in Boccaccio's *Corbaccio* the classic inversion of the virtues of ruling and obedience: the woman is accused of ruling and the man of obeying. In the following passage the writer reflects on this inversion:

> There were two things which had nearly led me to utter despair: one was the recognition that, whereas I believed I had some understanding, I realized that I was almost a beast without intellect. . . . I found I had acted stupidly in several ways . . . for having shackled and given my liberty and subjected my reason to the hands of a woman; for my soul, which used to be mistress when accompanied by these, without them became a vile servant.[89]

The wife, who was supposed to submit her reason and will to the man, instead took away these ruling dimensions of the soul, and the man lost his human identity as a consequence.

The writer traces the process by which he believes he became enslaved:

> Let us come to the other faults of women. . . . After they have reflected on their low and base condition, they put all their efforts into aggrandizing themselves with their abundant malice. . . . Thinking they have climbed to a high station, though they know they were born to be servants, they at once take hope and whet their appetite for mastery; and while pretending to be meek and obedient, they beg from their wretched husbands the crowns, girdles, cloths of gold, ermines, the wealth of clothes, and the various other ornaments in which they are seen resplendent every day; the husband does not perceive that all these weapons are to combat his mastery and vanquish it. The persons, no longer servants but suddenly equals, seeing their persons and rooms adorned like those of queens and their wretched husbands ensnared, contrive with all their might to seize control.[90]

The satirist completes his reflections on ruling and obedience by appealing to history and antiquity, which prefer and entrust "the governing of all men and women

88. Boccaccio, *Corbaccio,* pp. 32 and 48-49.
89. Boccaccio, *Corbaccio,* p. 20.
90. Boccaccio, *Corbaccio,* p. 25.

to men only, and not to women."[91] It is interesting to note that Boccaccio's satire justifies this satirical attitude rather than just simply stating it. We find here a kind of self-reflection on the satirical attitude towards women that indicates an increment in consciousness about the relation between the sexes.

Boccaccio introduces the further justification that scholarship shows the imperfection of women, echoing Aristotle's dictum:

> Moreover, . . . our studies should have shown you (and did show you, had you wished to see it) what women are. Of these a great many call themselves and have themselves called 'ladies' although very few are found among them. A woman is an imperfect creature, excited by a thousand foul passions, abominable even to remember, let alone to speak of.[92]

If there is any doubt in the reader's mind about the philosophy of gender polarity involved in woman's being an "imperfect creature," the writer gives an even more straightforward description of his basic premises:

> Anyone with judgment can see quite easily how valid and cogent an argument this is to show how greatly the nobility of man exceeds that of woman and of all of her creatures. Not only from this can one, or must one, grasp that this ample privilege of nobility is merely granted to a few excellent men. No, rather, it will be understood that it belongs also to some who are inferior in respect to women and the other creatures, for it will be quite clearly recognized that the basest or lowest man in the world, who is not deprived of the good of his intellect, is worth more than that woman who is temporally considered more excellent than any other, inasmuch as she is a woman.[93]

We have in this passage a recognition of the underlying philosophical principle of satires against women, namely that women are universalized into a single unit and devalued in relation to all men because of the natural weakness of their intellect. At the same time, excellence in intellect is being redefined by Boccaccio as the foundation for a new nobility. No longer does nobility come just from having the right kind of blood lines; instead it comes from having the right kind of character. As we will see in our later analysis of Boccaccio, he does include women in a significant way in his redefinition of nobility as involving virtuous character. However, to do so, he needs to redefine virtue.

At this point, however, we are considering the *Corbaccio* as the last of several satires written before the end of the fourteenth century. We will return now to the question of Boccaccio's relation to the satire as its author. The first suggestion is that Boccaccio simply wrote a text using the strident tone of the typical satire. It is argued that his intention was simply to shift the literary tone of the text away from the lighter quality of his other works and towards ridicule of women in order to be

---

91. Boccaccio, *Corbaccio*, p. 35.
92. Boccaccio, *Corbaccio*, p. 24.
93. Boccaccio, *Corbaccio*, p. 35.

more persuasive in the genre.[94] These critics suggest that Boccaccio did not give his real view of woman's character in the *Corbaccio,* which contained all the traditional satirical devaluations of women.

It is known that Boccaccio meticulously collected long satirical passages that were attributed to Theophrastus' and Walter Map's satires against marriage.[95] In addition, satirical sections on women from Juvenal's *Sixth Satire* and the book of Mathéolus also appear to be assimilated into the text of the *Corbaccio.* This research on the author's part may suggest simply a historical interest in the genre of satire as one kind of writing among others. If so then Boccaccio is placing himself in a line of historical authorities on satires against women in order to develop his literary talent rather than to present his own views.

Other critics suggest that Boccaccio had a religious conversion just before writing the *Corbaccio,* and that it strikes a new derogatory moral tone towards women particularly as regards celibacy. It is interesting to note that the *Corbaccio* is the last text Boccaccio wrote in Italian before returning to the more formal language of Latin; this may indicate some kind of change in orientation of his literary output. Gilbert Highet, in *Anatomy of Satire,* proposed just a few decades ago that the *Corbaccio* was a directly satirical work by Boccaccio, who was recovering from a humiliating rejection by a widow with whom he was infatuated. Highet translates the title *Il Corbaccio* as meaning *"The Heavy Whip,"* which might suggest a striking back at women. However, the text was also called popularly *The Labyrinth of Love,* which gives more of the impression that the male character was caught in a trap rather than that he was getting even.[96] Boccaccio himself is certainly partly responsible for this response to his work, for at the end of it he has the arguments of the satirist accepted by the narrator. If the narrator is presumed to speak for Boccaccio himself, then the literary conclusion would support the claim that he was expressing his own views.

Because of the narrator's acceptance of the husband's bitter accusations about women, it is not surprising that most authors from the fourteenth to the sixteenth centuries assumed that Boccaccio was writing a satirical text about women that represented his own views. Boccaccio's contemporaries received the *Corbaccio* as if it reinforced the devaluation of women. Barbara Matulka states that the *Corbaccio* was "one of the most read works in Spain" in the fifteenth century, and that it was constantly referred to by writers who considered Boccaccio a misogynist. Luis de Lucena, in his *Repetición de Amores,* joined Juvenal, Boccaccio, and Torrelas together as the "most notorious anti-feminist trio of the ages."[97] The only work that some authors knew by Boccaccio was the *Corbaccio.* For example,

---

94. See Robert Hollander: "If so, what can I say, within the boundaries of my own hypothesis, to explain the change? Must I agree to the theory of a 'crisis' or 'conversion'? Not necessarily. All that I must grant is a change in tone and method, brought about by the growing conviction that to treat moral matters convincingly, one must sound more like a cleric" (*Boccaccio's Two Venuses* [New York: Columbia University Press, 1977], p. 29).

95. See Anthony K. Cassell, Introduction to Boccaccio, *Corbaccio,* pp. xx-xxxi.

96. Highet, *The Anatomy of Satire,* p. 224.

97. Barbara Matulka, *An Anti-feminist Treatise of Fifteenth Century Spain: Lucena's "Repetición De Amores"* (New York: Institute of French Studies, 1931), p. 17.

Lucrezia Marinelli associates only this satirical view of women with Boccaccio, and she seeks in her massive work on women to argue against his way of thinking about sex identity.[98]

In the *De Amores* Lucena directly invokes Aristotle, and he repeats the phrase that "woman is an imperfect man." Matulka points out that "Ever since the *Corbaccio* had decreed: 'La femmina è animale imperfetto' [Woman is an imperfect animal], many works in Spain had been repeating this dictum." She identifies in particular Torellas, who in *Maldezin* stated, "Mujer es un animal/que se dice hombre imperfecto" [Woman is an animal, that is to say an imperfect man]; and Bernat Metge, who said in the *Somni*, "Fembra es animal imperfet" [Woman is an imperfect animal], and in the *Celestina,* in which the character says that "man is more worthy than woman because 'elle es imperfecta'" [she is imperfect].[99] So in effect, Boccaccio managed to popularize Aristotle's theory, which by now reached far outside of the academic world into the homes of ordinary Spaniards. The philosophical devaluation of woman as an imperfect man, which had first been articulated by Aristotle in a technical philosophical text on generation, now became a household phrase.

In an outstanding study of the debate for and against women in fifteenth-century Spain, Barbara Matulka identifies an even further influence of Boccaccio. Arcipreste of Talavera wrote a *Reprobación de Amor Mundano* or the *Corbacho,* which was directly modeled on Boccaccio's text.[100] Here, the text went even further than the original: "His satire is more impersonal and far-reaching than is the *Corbaccio;* it is more lively because of its wider range of vision over social life."[101] Thus the satirical content of Boccaccio's text seemed to have a life of its own, as it served as a model for further satires, much as previous satires had served as a model for it.

The third interpretation of Boccaccio's *Corbaccio* is that his text is actually a meta-satire that satirizes satires about women. My own preference for this option flows from a careful study of the concept of woman in the rest of Boccaccio's works. Since this will be the topic of the next chapter I will not make an argument for this case here. Instead, I will just point out some evidence within the satire itself, which supports the suggestion that Boccaccio was very consciously writing in the genre of satire, but that he was satirizing the men who held these views about women rather than the women themselves. It may very well be the case that all three interpretations of Boccaccio's motives for the satire against women in the *Corbaccio* contain some truth; that is, he may have sharpened the tone to fit with the genre of satire,

98. Lucrezia Marinelli, *La Nobiltà et l'Eccellenza delle Donne Co'Diffetti et Mancamenti de gli Huomini* (Venice: Gio Batista Ciotti Sanese, 1601). Marinelli's critique fails to keep the balance of respect for her adversaries, for it shifts into a reverse gender polarity by ridiculing and devaluing man. Her text is divided into two parts: one points out that women's virtues are better than men's virtues and the other that men's vices are worse than women's vices.

99. Matulka, *An Anti-feminist Treatise of Fifteenth Century Spain,* pp. 16-17, notes 22 and 23. See also her book, *The Novels of Juan de Flores and Their European Diffusion: A Study in Comparative Literature* (New York: Institute of French Studies, 1931), pp. 8-37, 96-166.

100. Matulka, *Juan de Flores,* pp. 9-13.

101. Matulka, *Juan de Flores,* p. 13.

he may have been reacting to a bitter rejection by a woman, and he may also have written a meta-satire more against men than women.

Among those who argue that Boccaccio is not satirizing women but rather satirizing men who satirize women is Angela Iovino, who states: "Though on a superficial level the work seems to resemble an antifeminist treatise, it is clearly the **male character's view** of women — not women themselves that the author ridicules."[102] Boccaccio has the writer of the satire hear an inner voice at the beginning of the text, which clearly states that he ought to blame himself, and not blame women, for his difficulties:

> Oh, poor fool! Where is the meagre power of your reason (no, rather the expulsion of your reason) leading you? Now, are you so dazed that you do not realize that while you believe that someone else is treating you cruelly, you alone are the one who is being cruel to yourself? Is that lady to whom, without seeing how, you chained and entrusted your liberty, the wretched and painful cause of your burdened thoughts, as you declare? You are deceived; you, not she, are the cause of your torment.[103]

Boccaccio appears to be saying that a satirist projects blame outwards onto the object of his wrath, while a humanist accepts interior responsibility for his or her state of mind. The context of the satire itself supports this position because the writer is also presented as a spirit condemned to purgatory or hell for his unrelenting desire to revenge a spurned attempt at love.

In addition, the male character demonstrates in his tirades all the characteristics that he satirically suggests are an essential part of woman's identity. The husband cannot use his reason well; he is furious, suspicious, inconstant, full of lust, and so on. Thus the text operates on two different levels at the same time. The humor flows from the fact that the husband incarnates all the things he hates about women. To interpret the text as having this sophisticated double level of meaning would render it more consistent with Boccaccio's other literary works, which include central female characters. However, as we mentioned previously, Boccaccio himself contributed to the confusion about its interpretation by having the narrator accept the husband's views in the end.

In this brief study of Boccaccio's *Corbaccio* we have seen a continuity in the philosophical themes that were so common to previous satires about women. At the same time, however, there is a suggestion of evaluation, a hint of recognition of the underlying limitations of such principles that generalized about all women and appear to be contradicted by experience. We also find Boccaccio pointing out that a man who vehemently maintains the satirical attitude that woman is not in control of her emotions is himself culpable of the same character trait. Finally, Boccaccio accuses the man of tormenting himself by this satirical attitude about women rather than being the victim of a real situation with women. If Boccaccio is considered to be criticiz-

102. Angela Marie Iovino, "The *Decameron* and the *Corbaccio*," Ph.D. Diss., Indiana University (1983), p. 189. My emphasis. See also pp. 42 and 44.
103. Boccaccio, *Corbaccio*, p. 122.

ing men who write satires about women as much as he is perpetuating certain standard satirical themes about women, he will have partly contributed to the raising of consciousness about this way of thinking. In addition, an ironic effect of the *Corbaccio* on subsequent authors who interpreted Boccaccio as giving only a single level of satire against women was that an explosion of texts praising woman's character began to occur as part of the Renaissance humanist approach to gender identity.[104]

SATIRICAL VOICES OF REDUCTIONISM, EXAGGERATION, AND BIAS

At the beginning of this chapter we suggested that satires about gender worked through two different but related techniques: (1) through the exaggeration of a perceived essential characteristic, and (2) through an inversion in which the characteristic that "ought" to belong to a member of one gender belongs to a member of the other gender. In the following chart we summarize the specific characteristics related to Aristotelian themes found in the satires considered above.

Aristotelian Themes in Satires (1250-1450)				
Woman's Identity	Rose	Mathéolus	Evangile	Corbaccio
1. Satires by exaggeration				
a. passive	x			
b. inconstant	x	x	x	x
c. emotional	x	x	x	x
2. Satires by inversion				
a. not silent		x	x	x
b. not obey	x	x	x	x
c. not private		x	x	

104. Central to these was Boccaccio's *Concerning Famous Women,* which will be discussed in the next chapter. Others with particular importance to Spain as identified by Matulka are: Juan Rodriques del Padrón's *El Siervo libre de Amor* and *Triumpho de las Doñas;* Fray Martin de Córdoba's *Jardin de las nobles doncellas* and *Alabanzas de la virginidad;* El Tostado's *Tractado . . . por el qual se prueba por la Santa Excriptura cómo al ome es nescesario amar;* Fernando de la Torre's *Libro de las veinte cartas e questiones;* and Francesco Eximeniç's *Libre de les Doñes,* and Juan de Flores, *Grisel y Mirabella,* in which a debate is held between those satirists who devalue women and those humanists who genuinely praise women. The satirist loses the debate, and receives the punishment of torture and death that he had recommended for unfaithful women. See Matulka, *Juan de Flores,* pp. 8-37, 95-166.

The above chart does not claim to summarize all the contents of the works identified. Rather, it simply draws together in one place a summary of particular notions chosen for analysis in this book. What it shows is that selected Aristotelian concepts about women frequently reappear in these satires in one form or another. These themes also had a broader societal context, and so they cannot be blamed on Aristotle as a sole primary cause. Nonetheless, we note an appeal to "The Philosopher" to justify specific satirical concepts. As will be seen in Chapter 6 on later satires about women, this direct appeal to Aristotelian principles increased in subsequent centuries. Therefore, there is a plausible connection between the concepts and Aristotelian philosophy that needs to be noted; Aristotle's rationale for gender polarity offered an authoritative basis from which to justify certain views about woman's identity. These views, when solidified into stereotypes, became one of the bases from which the 'humor' of satires was able to work its effect.

Specifically, we see satires functioning by overturning Aristotle's general theory of virtue, which had argued that the virtuous man was the one who had a disposition to act in accordance with a mean relative to his own identity. The "golden mean" placed the virtuous act between two extremes. In the satires on women, we find an act being described that nearly always fell into the category of an extreme. Then women were characterized as unvirtuous in two ways: (1) they were incapable of using their reason to choose the mean (according to the dictates of practical syllogisms), and (2) they were also unable to choose the mean proper to their specific identity as female. The females being satirized were described as indulging in extreme behaviors in various ranges of human activity.

Satires on women worked by: (1) devaluing women's identity within a gender polarity model that was at times supported by the academic appeal to Aristotelian theory; (2) reducing all women to one kind of stereotype of woman with a gender polarity model; and (3) dispersing stereotypes in a satirical mode of exaggeration or inversion through written manuscripts and printed texts into the broader context of the literary public and even by song into the general public. In this way, the satirical reduction and devaluation of women passed way beyond the walls of the male community of academic discourse into the private homes of men and women and on public streets all over Europe. Presented as entertainment rather than serious study, these satirical texts were a ready-made source of distorted views about women and served as a medium of transmission rather similar to distorted sex and gender images in today's media. When integrated into songs and *dits* they also functioned in a similar fashion to the routines of present-day comedians. For that reason, they offer an important resource for the study of gender identity in a historical period.

As we mentioned in the introduction to this chapter, many contemporary authors have reflected on the various factors that dispose authors to write satires. In this evaluation we will consider some of these factors. George Test identifies "four elements basic to satire — attack or aggression, laughter or humor, play, and judgment."[105] He then identifies specific aggressive emotions:

105. George A. Test, *Satire: Spirit and Art* (Tampa: University of South Florida Press, 1991), p. 46.

The emotions that are thought to give rise to satire are generally acknowledged to be the least admirable human emotions — anger, malice, hatred, indignation. The emotions that satire is said to evoke are likewise emotions that make most people uncomfortable — shame, anger, guilt, anxiety.[106]

While it seems unlikely that all those men who wrote and enjoyed reading satires were motivated by such strong negative emotions, it has become increasingly clear that those who are the object of the satire, in our case women, seem to experience to some degree the negative emotions identified above. One of the reasons for this disparity in experience of negative emotions between men and women may be due to the fact that the gender polarity so central to satires about women was so widespread and was considered so authoritative by academic communities of discourse.

Differences between men readers and women readers of satirical texts about women have been well remarked by Susan Schibanoff, who notes the tendency of writers such as Jean de Meun or Chaucer to apologize for the inclusion of these materials for a female community of discourse.[107] She notes that the translators or writers of satirical texts place their apologies to women in the context of having to choose between offending their women readers and being faithful to the ancient tradition of male-authored satires.

Using a political approach, Robert Elliott examines another effect that satires may have on those who are being satirized.

In any society in which high value is placed upon the opinions of others, ridicule will clearly be a potent deterrent to deviant behaviour; the more a person dreads shame, the more he will avoid situations that might bring upon him the bad name conveyed by public mockery. These sanctions are institutionalized all over the world in an extraordinary variety of ways.[108]

He concludes that "[t]he people who experience the malign effects of ridicule and satire are likely to account for them by recourse to magic."[109] While Elliott is studying a particular historical period, his conclusions have application to contemporary developments in the turn to witchcraft in radical feminism. At the same time, however, Schibanoff has pointed out that women have another option for action than resorting to magic when faced with "intimidating" or "emasculating" realities. She compares the impact, on Christine de Pizan, of reading *Le Livre de Mathéolus* and other satirists with the impact, in Chaucer's *Canterbury Tales,* of the Wife of Bath's hearing a classical satirical text about women. In the former case, the female author decides to write a rebuttal; in the latter case, the imaginary female character burns the book.[110]

106. Test, *Satire,* p. 1.
107. Susan Schibanoff, "Taking the Gold Out of Egypt: The Art of Reading as a Woman," in *Gender and Reading: Essays on Readers, Texts, and Contexts,* ed. Elizabeth A. Flynn and Patrocinio P. Schweickart (Baltimore and London: Johns Hopkins University Press, 1986), pp. 83-104.
108. Robert C. Elliott, *The Power of Satire: Magic, Ritual, Art* (Princeton: Princeton University Press, 1960), p. 69.
109. Elliott, *The Power of Satire,* p. 86.
110. Schibanoff, "Taking the Gold," pp. 83-104.

It may be useful here to also mention some philosophical motivations that may play a role in the writing of and the responding to satires. John Bullitt considers more the intellectual sources of satire, and the particular disparity between an ideal concept and the real identity of a particular individual.[111]

> In its most serious function, satire is a mediator between two perceptions — the unillusioned perception of man as he actually is, and the ideal perception, or vision, of man as he ought to be. It is often argued, therefore, that satire can become a vital form of literature only when there is a fairly widespread agreement about what man ought to be. The satirist needs the conviction that fixed intellectual ideals or norms can give him, and the assurance that he will receive understanding from his readers.[112]

Even though this theory is focused on the satire of Jonathan Swift, the principles are interesting for the historical study of the concept of woman. The author places satire in an intellectual realm: "It is probable, as we have already noted, that some unanimity on moral standards, considered as both rational and permanent, is a necessary precondition for any great satiric effort."[113] What we need to consider then is the source of the "unanimity on moral standards" that functioned in satires about women between 1250 and 1500. We find the same view suggested by a theorist of Renaissance texts about women: "Satire demands a norm, a vantage point."[114] How did the specific characteristics identified above become considered "rational and permanent" or a "norm" for characteristics of women?

It is in answer to this question that we can consider the place of bias and reductionism in what might be described as a satirical attitude towards women in some male communities of discourse. In *Insight*, Bernard Lonergan identifies three different kinds of bias: individual bias, group bias, and general bias.[115] He argues that a fundamental structure of bias *per se* inhibits insight by multifarious methods. It overlooks data of experience that might be relevant, blocks intelligent questions that ought to be raised about the data, distorts reasoning that should evaluate subjective insights, and so on. The particular bias that functions in the writing of satires about women springs predominantly from group bias.[116] In the present case,

---

111. John M. Bullitt, *Jonathan Swift and the Anatomy of Satire: A Study of Satiric Technique* (Cambridge, Mass.: Harvard University Press, 1953).

112. Bullitt, *Anatomy of Satire,* p. 1.

113. Bullitt, *Anatomy of Satire,* p. 16.

114. Utley, *The Crooked Rib,* p. 29.

115. Bernard Lonergan, *Insight: A Study of Human Understanding* (Toronto/Buffalo/London: University of Toronto Press, 1992), chapters 6 and 7. See also William P. Loewe, Foreword, in *Lonergan and Feminism* (Toronto/Buffalo/London: University of Toronto Press, 1994): ". . . bias skews the drive to understand and thus undercuts the exercise of freedom that, for Lonergan, is the principle of genuine human, historical progress" (p. ix).

116. Paulette Kidder, "Lonergan and Feminist Epistemology," in *Lonergan and Feminism.* She states: "I would contend that the patriarchal bias towards women and the feminine can be easily added to the examples of what Lonergan calls the bias of the group. If this is so, then we may extend Lonergan's analysis of bias to the case of 'androcentrism'" (p. 43).

the identifiable group may be considered as the male academic community of discourse in the centuries under study.

Lonergan argues that group bias "interferes with the development of practical common sense" of a social group, and thus "group bias leads to a bias in the generative principle of a developing social order."[117] Previously I suggested that the progressive exclusion of women from higher education contributed to the situation in which educated men became *de facto* an isolated male academic community. The academic social order, especially when associated with Aristotelian philosophy, excluded women. This exclusion contrasted both with the Platonic schools, which included women but devalued their female identity, and with the Benedictine monastic schools, which had begun to move towards a more complementary model of education for primarily aristocratic women and men. The group bias that interfered with the practical common sense of the academic community resulted in the continual exclusion of women from higher education for six centuries and a tendency towards reductionism and stereotypes about women in general.

In this context, satires did function as a method of social control. Lonergan states: "The bias of development involves a distortion. The advantage of one group commonly is disadvantageous to another, and so some part of the energies of all groups is diverted to the supererogatory activity of devising and implementing offensive and defensive mechanisms."[118] A satire, written for entertainment, and copied or printed for wide dispersion, functioned as a medium for further justification of women's basic inferiority in intellectual and moral ranges of activity.

Lonergan points out the long-term effects of group bias:

> Still, the process of aberration creates the principles for its own reversal. . . . The sins of group bias may be secret and almost unconscious. But what originally was a neglected possibility, in time becomes a grotesquely distorted reality. Few may grasp the initial possibilities; but the ultimate concrete distortions are exposed to the inspection of the multitude.[119]

So when today we think about the practical situation that led to the exclusion of women from higher education from the thirteenth to the nineteenth centuries, it seems to fit the category of "a grotesquely distorted reality." The initial possibilities that higher education offered to both men and women, because of a fundamental form of group bias shared by academic communities of discourse and by their founders, both men and women, created an institutional set of structures that further reinforced general societal biases about women in previous centuries. Satires about women, which had previously been merely a smaller part of a major work about other issues, blossomed into full-blown texts that increasingly reduced all women to devalued human beings.

Fr. Matthew Lamb, in his reflection on "The Social and Political Dimensions of Lonergan's Theology," considers the impact of long-term bias on potentially cre-

---

117. Lonergan, *Insight,* pp. 248-49.
118. Lonergan, *Insight,* p. 249.
119. Lonergan, *Insight,* pp. 249-50.

ative dialogical situations. In reading his words, we cannot help but think of how gender-dialogical communities of discourse might have changed the course of history had they been part of academia from its development in the thirteenth century.

> Individual and group biases result from individuals and groups repressing the further relevant questions and insights which would lead them to understand how their particular desires, fears, and interests are not ultimate criteria for what is intelligent and responsibly good. Constructive and creative tension degenerates into repression and conflict.[120]

The assertion that bias creates the conditions for its own reversal is often stated by Lonergan. Again we find this phenomenon in a central component of some feminist educational theory that rejects reason and the exercise of intelligence as "masculine" rather than embracing it as a human medium for achieving insight and true judgments. The original general bias that led to the exclusion of women from academic education (i.e., in the exercise of their attention to data, to asking intelligent questions, and to testing out subjects' insights to reach objective judgments) also resulted in leading some women to reject the notion of academic education itself. The emotional tone of satires against women during the early period under study is matched by a similar emotional tone (containing group bias and reductionism) of satires against men today.[121] In both cases the potential for constructive and creative tension between men and women degenerates into repression and conflict.

We do not want to end the chapter with this negative conclusion. In fact, Lonergan identifies a way out of bias. Specifically, he links the use of the imagination with intelligence as a mechanism through which both individuals and groups can begin to break through almost unconscious reductionist concepts and thought patterns. In fact, we already saw a beginning of this use of the imagination to question bias against women in Chaucer's *Legend of Good Women*. We will find at the beginning of humanism a tendency to use the imagination to pose new concepts of woman that are different from those found in traditional Aristotelian gender polarity. A new form of dialectic begins to occur among characters introduced in dialogues as they open up new ways of thinking that may overcome old biases.

---

120. Matthew Lamb, "The Social and Political Dimensions of Lonergan's Theology," in *The Desires of the Human Heart: An Introduction to the Theology of Bernard Lonergan,* ed. Vernon Gregson (New York: Paulist Press, 1988), p. 272.

121. An example of a gender reversal in biting satire by a woman against men is found in Valerie Solanis, The SCUM (Society for Cutting Up Men) Manifesto, *Sisterhood Is Powerful: An Anthology of Writings from the Women's Movement,* ed. Robin Morgan (New York: Random House, 1970): "The male is a biological accident: the Y (male) gene is an incomplete X (female) gene, that is, has an incomplete set of chromosomes. In other words, the male is an incomplete female, a walking abortion, aborted at the gene state. . . . Being an incomplete female, the male spends his life attempting to complete himself, to become female. He attempts to do this by constantly seeking out, fraternizing with and trying to live through and fuse with the female, and by claiming as his own all female characteristics — emotional strength and independence, forcefulness, dynamism, decisiveness, coolness, objectivity, assertiveness, courage, integrity, vitality, intensity, depth of character, grooviness, etc. — and projecting onto women all male traits — vanity, frivolity, weakness, etc." (p. 515).

Petrarch and Boccaccio provide beginning examples of this phenomenon, but the works of subsequent generations of humanists provide even stronger examples.

By juxtaposing the notions of bias and conversion, Lonergan sets forth the different choices an individual can make with respect to censoring data, questions, or reasoning. Robert Doran describes this choice as follows:

> Now the censorship can be either constructive or repressive. In either case it is constituted by a collaboration of intelligence and imagination in admitting neural demands to consciousness in the form of psychic representations and accompanying effects. . . . That collaboration will be constructive in its admission of neural materials to psychic representation, if it is oriented to insight, judgment, responsible decision, and love. It will be repressive if it is orientated away from insight, reasonable judgment, responsible decision, and love.[122]

Repressive censorship in group bias of one gender towards another functions by blocking insights, judgments, responsible decisions, and love, while constructive censorship allows the appropriate insights, judgments, decisions, and love to enter into the intelligence. The imagination offers a medium for allowing factors into intelligence that can prepare the way for overcoming old biases against women or men.

In the constructive use of imagination, the psyche welcomes images that will lead to insight. In the repressive use of imagination, the psyche habitually blocks insights in a particular area. The root cause for this disorder of a general bias, Lonergan would argue, is the misuse of intelligence itself. Therefore, a philosophical approach to satires about women, written within a male community of discourse, would be to introduce to the intelligence of men reasonable counterexamples of women who would challenge the seemingly 'rational and permanent' views they held about women. This approach would invite them to convert to a 'higher viewpoint' that lets bias fall away as an inadequate and unobjective understanding of gender identity. As we will see in the next chapter, many writers identified with the Humanist Reformation attempted in various ways to do just that.

---

122. Robert Doran, *Theology and the Dialectics of History* (Toronto: University of Toronto Press, 1990), p. 181.

CHAPTER 4

GENDER AT THE BEGINNINGS
OF HUMANISM

With the birth of humanism we find a radically new development in the history of the concept of woman. Male authors discover women as partners in dialogue. In Chapter 1 we considered dialogue between women and God, and interior dialogue of a woman writer with herself. In Chapter 2 we described ways in which disputation treated woman as an object for debate among male faculty and students at universities. In this academic community of discourse men were either indifferent towards women, or they offered metaphysical, natural, epistemological, and ethical principles to explain woman's identity with respect to man. In Chapter 3, we reflected on some of the ways that satirical literature treated woman as an object of ridicule and even of danger.

In the first chapter, women were depicted as autonomous subjects seeking self-knowledge and self-governance, while in the second and third chapters as less capable of self-knowledge and self-governance. In this fourth chapter, women will be depicted as subjects once again, but this time by men. The pathway that men used to enter into this interpersonal relation with woman had three components: speech, love, and the imagination. While in later chapters in this book we will consider actual situations in which both men and women wrote about each other's concept of woman, in this chapter on "The Beginnings of Humanism," we hear only the voices of men. Still, these voices say something new, and they open the door to significant later developments in intergender dialogue about woman. Often the imagination posits something as possible before it becomes actualized in the lives of women and men.

In Chapter 4, after describing some historical background of Christianity, Neoplatonism, and Stoicism, we will consider particularly the relation between the following pairs of a man and a woman who lived in proximity to fourteenth-century Florence: Guido Cavalcanti and the Lady who asked him a question, Dante Alighieri and Beatrice, Francis Petrarch and Laura, and Giovanni Boccaccio and Fiammetta. Each of these authors is in love with a particular woman. Their love is often thwarted by the sudden death of the woman. Beatrice dies in an early wave of the plague in 1290; Laura dies in the bubonic plague of 1348. Boccaccio loses his love by personal rejection, but his writing is situated in the midst of the devastation of this disease that destroyed three-fifths of the Florentine population in one year.

For these early humanist writers, woman is no longer primarily an object of philosophical investigation, she is a person in relation. She has a unique personality, and in her interaction with the male author, she affects his life. In contrast to the satirical authors who describe woman either as a passive object of sexual desire or as a dangerous or domineering subject to avoid, the early humanists often present woman as wise and virtuous and as a guide to the man who is seeking self-knowledge and self-governance. Imaginary intergender dialogue appears within their texts. Imaginary female characters begin to serve as counterexamples to Aristotelian concepts of women. Creative use of the imagination by these early humanists helped to overcome traditional gender polarity bias about women's identity. Following a short introduction to some of the historical sources of the early Italian Renaissance concept of woman, we will turn to consider the theories of the four men mentioned above.

CHRISTIAN, NEOPLATONIC, AND STOIC ROOTS OF EARLY HUMANIST VIEWS OF WOMAN

The history of the words "humanism" and "humanist" is rich and varied.[1] The Latin term *humanus* found in classical philosophy incorporates three meanings: (1) whatever is characteristic of the human being (i.e., "really human"), (2) especially one who is benevolent (i.e., "humane"), and (3) one who is learned or uses speech well (i.e., "humanist").[2] In the works of Petrarch we find a further meaning of humanist, namely (4) a person who has received and who provides a classical education. Central to this education is the study of classical Greek and Latin texts, the rejection of a scholastic academic education, and the adoption of new forms of writing in Latin and in the vernacular, in letters, in poetry, in dialogues, and in essays.

The *'humanissime vir,' 'umanista,'* and *'homme de lettres'* were the Italian and French versions of the humanist; and the *humanistische, humanismus,* and *umanismo* respectively were the German, Latin, and Italian versions of institutional and literary humanist education. In classical Latin the gender association of *vir* with *humanissime* as the male human being seems to imply the exclusion of women from this conception of an educated human being. However, this term evolved in Christian Latin through the addition of the Greek *-ismos,* to signify an activity common to many people. This is why Christine de Pizan and Isotta Nogarola can be identified as humanist authors. The suffix came into English as the 'ist' applied to the meaning of humanist as a learned human being.

The explosion of humanist education began in Italy and then spread throughout all of Europe.[3] While the Dutch philosopher Erasmus (c. 1466-1536) is

---

1. See Vito R. Giustiniani, "Homo, Humanus, and the Meanings of 'Humanism,'" *Journal of the History of Ideas* 46, no. 2 (April-June, 1985): 167-95.
2. Giustiniani points out that *"'humanissime vir'* is the usual Latin way to address scholars" ("Homo, Humanus . . . ," p. 168).
3. Giustiniani, "Homo, Humanus . . . ," pp. 170-72.

thought to be the first person to actually call himself "a humanist," Francis Petrarch is usually described retrospectively as the "first great representative" of humanism because of his influence on its development.[4] In this chapter I am including Cavalcanti and Dante as forerunners of humanism because of their concern with what is really human and its particular application to the question of whether or not a woman can be considered as fully human. We will now consider briefly three different sources for the development of early humanist theory about woman: Christianity, Neoplatonism, and Stoicism.

A concern about the dignity of the human being and the particular dignity of woman flows from the Christian heritage of western Europe. In spite of the devaluation of woman that was integrated into academic and satirical literature, the Christian Gospel penetrated into European humanity and tried to elevate it. In Scripture, Jesus Christ is depicted as filled with love for the women Mary and Martha as personal friends (John 11:17-35), and as respectful for a woman's identity in his encounters with Mary Magdalene (John 8:3-11; 20:11-18), and with the Samaritan woman at the well (John 4:5-30). Jesus dialogues with these women about fundamental questions of importance; he engages with them in a chaste love that elicits a response of love.[5]

Jesus initiated existential and concrete forms of discourse with many men and women He met along the way. As the fusion of the Divine Word and man, He always invited those who discoursed with Him to grow in wisdom about the truth and to choose a greater good. He also always left the interlocutor free to follow or not to follow His invitation. In this pattern of respect for the freedom of the person responding, Jesus offered a remarkably different model of interpersonal communion than had previously existed in Greek and Roman religions where power, necessities, and fate dominated human choice.[6] In interacting through dialogue in the fundamental context of respect for human freedom, Jesus followed the ancient Hebrew tradition. In Genesis, God is described as engaged in discourse within the Godhead (Gen. 1:26); and women and men are described as engaged in discourse with the evil spirit, with God, and with one another (Gen. 3:1-13). Dialogue based on mutual respect for freedom to choose what is true and good among persons was the Jewish and Christian way to build up community. Thus Christianity established itself in the minds and hearts of Europeans first as an interpersonal relation with Jesus Christ and second as the source of interpersonal relations with others in Him and through Him by the action of the Holy Spirit.

Jean Bethke Elshtain describes the early effect of Christianity on society as follows:

---

4. Paul Oskar Kristeller, *Eight Philosophers of the Italian Renaissance* (Stanford, Calif.: Stanford University Press, 1964).

5. See Sr. Mary Prudence Allen, R.S.M., for a consideration of Jesus' use of language in dialogue about questions of gender: "Language and the Invitation to Conversion," *Language and Faith*. Proceedings from the Nineteenth Convention (St. Louis: Fellowship of Catholic Scholars, 1997), pp. 93-128.

6. See Robert Sokolowski, *The God of Faith and Reason: Foundations of Christian Theology* (Notre Dame/London: University of Notre Dame Press, 1982), chapters 2-3.

Christ's mission began and ended in a dreary outpost of a corrupt, power-drunk empire already on a path from state worship to emperor deification to all the sordid evils of Caesarism. The Roman Empire, through guile and even genocide, had extended its sway over the then-known world. . . .

. . . Christianity ushered a moral revolution into the world which dramatically, and for the better, transformed the prevailing images of the human person, male and female, and the relations between various human activities and the creation of a shared social life. Christianity redeemed and sanctioned each individual life as well as everyday life, especially the lives of society's victims, and granted a new-found dignity.[7]

Women were particularly helped by this new emphasis on human dignity of the person by the protection of their free will in the choice either to marry or to enter consecrated life. Christian legal codes protected the freedom of choice of woman in marriage when other codes simply treated them as property of exchange among men.[8] In Renaissance Humanism we find the particular Christian value of interpersonal respect and even love expressed. The expression is concrete and existential. It occurs in specific contexts involving a particular man and a particular woman.

In addition, another characteristic of the Christian recognition of the dignity of the person includes the discovery of oneself as a unique and unrepeatable individual, a person who has an internal history that develops over time. St. Augustine, in his *Confessions*, offers the first articulation of such a recognition of his own dignity.[9] As we saw in Chapter 1 and will see again in Chapter 5, women religious writers, struggling to articulate their own experience, drew inspiration from Augustine. Boethius in his *Consolation of Philosophy* also describes his own personal struggles and suffering about particular events in his own life. As we will see, several early humanist writers, men and women, undertook a similar project as they shared with others the discovery of their own unique internal history as a person.

If we give a general description of the early Renaissance concept of the human being, it would include the following factors, all of which have Christian roots: (1) the human being is situated in unique, free, and important relation to a transcendent (Christian) God, (2) true nobility consists in living a wise and virtuous life, (3) men and women can help one another grow in wisdom and virtue through dialogue and example, (4) freedom is an important aspect of the person that ought to be exercised well by choosing what is true and good, and (5) love

7. Jean Bethke Elshtain, "Christianity and Patriarchy: The Odd Alliance," *Modern Theology* 9, no. 2 (April 1993): 110.

8. Suzanne Wemple, *Women in Frankish Society: Marriage and the Cloister 500-900* (Philadelphia: University of Pennsylvania Press, 1981); and Francis Martin, *The Feminist Question: Feminist Theology in the Light of Christian Tradition* (Grand Rapids: Eerdmans, 1994), chapters 3-4.

9. See Glenn W. Olsen, "Next comes . . . a sense of personal history, . . . first fully worked out in Augustine's *Confessions,* of the self as possessing an internal history, not disconnected from external events, but essentially a continuing story of the self in its spiritual, moral, and intellectual development" ("St. Augustine and the Problem of the Medieval Discovery of the Individual," *Word and Spirit* 9 [1987]: 131).

helps to build the common good.[10] Later forms of Enlightenment Humanism and Secular Humanism will reject several of these factors, beginning with relation to God.

The community of intergender discourse in the early Renaissance tradition usually begins with just two persons, a man and a woman in dialogue. After a record of their discourse is written in some sort of text, it may then be shared among other men and women to create a wider intergender community of discourse. This dispersion of an interpretation of the value of a particular set of encounters of a man and a woman was often extended by the creation of imaginary intergender dialogue with a member of the complement gender. Previous examples include the imaginary female personification of wisdom as Lady Philosophy in Boethius's *Consolation* and the elaborated figure of Monica, his mother, in Augustine's dialogues *De ordine* and *De beata vita*.[11] A later example includes the text of a real dialogue among three women and four men about the concept of woman in Pietro Bembo's (1470-1547) *Gli asolani*.[12] Further examples include the exchange of letters written between a woman and a man about a topic of relevance to gender identity in the life of Christine de Pizan, Isotta Nogarola, and Laura Cereta. The move towards genuine dialogue among women and men about personal identity is, I would maintain, an effect of accepting the fundamental dignity of the human person.

This kind of dialogue is also situated in a historical context in which certain forces within Christianity move towards an articulation of genuine complementarity between men and women. Hildegard of Bingen was the first Christian philosopher to elaborate philosophical foundations for sex and gender complementarity. She did this from the experiential base of monasteries that fostered integral discourse among women and men. Then the new universities effectively ended this cooperative exchange among men and women at the highest intellectual level as the institutional structures prohibited women's continued collaboration with men in the pursuit of knowledge.

In early Renaissance Humanism we can see a new surge towards a philosophical foundation of Christian complementarity, in which the Gospel values once again seem to raise the level of European humanity in different situations of complement intergender dialogue. This took place outside the academic community of discourse, and often in the home. Unfortunately, this new foundation for a Christian complementarity was interrupted again by the later Enlightenment, which moved towards another empty and at times destructive abstraction with sub-

10. This summary is taken from a paper entitled: "Can Feminism Be a Humanism?" It was presented at the Annual Canadian Maritain Conference, University of St. Paul, Ottawa, Ontario, October 31, 1997 and published in *Études maritainiennes/Maritain Studies* 14 (1998): 109-40.

11. Augustine, *De ordine* (Divine Providence and the Problem of Evil) (New York: Cosmopolitan Science and Art Service Co., Inc., 1942) and *De beata vita* (Happiness — A Study) (Philadelphia: Peter Reilly, 1937). In these dialogues Monica, Augustine's mother, is developed as a philosopher engaged in discursive reasoning within a community of discourse of male companions.

12. Pietro Bembo, *Gli Asolani* (Bloomington: Indiana University Press, 1954). These were actual philosophical debates that took place in the court of Caterina, Queen of Cyprus and Lady of Asolo.

sequent new forms of devaluation of woman.[13] At this point our analysis will turn to the remarkable ways in which the early humanists begin to reshape the western intellectual environment in their discussions about woman's identity. They provide a new force and energy that will challenge the concept of woman prevalent in academic and satirical communities of discourse. In addition to drawing upon Christianity as a source for this new energy, the early Renaissance Humanists will draw upon Platonism and Stoicism. We will turn now to consider briefly these other two important roots for the Renaissance.

Our purpose here is not to determine Plato's own concept of woman, its relation to Neoplatonism, or its incorporation by Islamic philosophers. This has been attempted elsewhere.[14] Instead, we ask the following question: How did the early humanist writers appeal to Plato or Platonism in their effort to articulate a concept of woman? By keeping this particular focus clear, we hope to indicate ways that Platonism was used to bolster the claim for the fundamental equality of women and men.

At the beginning of Italian Humanism the only texts of Plato (c. 428-355 B.C.) that had been translated into Latin were the *Timaeus, Phaedo,* and *Meno.* The concept of woman is only briefly mentioned in the *Timaeus,* in three different ways: at the beginning (18c) we are reminded by Socrates that women and men, who have the same nature, should receive the same education and follow the same pursuits. In the middle of the text (paragraphs 51a-b), a myth describes a cosmic mother receptacle that is totally passive and receives active Forms that act like a cosmic Father and give it shape; and towards the end (paragraph 90e-91a), Plato suggests that men who were cowards or immoral in a past life are reincarnated as women.[15] Distinguishing these three different sections of the Platonic text is important because a gender unity theory is supported by the first, and a gender polarity theory is supported by the other two, with the former describing cosmic realities and the latter describing women and men in the world. Of the two translations of the *Timaeus* available to early humanist scholars, the first — from Greek to Latin by Cicero — stopped at 47b, and the second translation, by Calcidius, reached only 53c.[16] As a result all those who read this text tended to conclude that Plato actually supported the equality and non-differentiation of men and women in the world itself.

In addition, the *Republic* and *Laws* (which contained most of Plato's arguments in support of the gender unity position) were among the few of his texts translated along with the *Timaeus* into Arabic.[17] These Platonic arguments for the

---

13. For a brief indication of this see Prudence Allen, "Descartes: The Concept of Woman and the French Revolution," in *Revolution, Violence, and Equality* (Lewiston/Queenston/Lampeter: Edwin Mellen Press, 1990), pp. 61-78.

14. See Prudence Allen, *The Concept of Woman: The Aristotelian Revolution: 750 BC–1250 AD),* pp. 57-80, 193-210, and 339-50. See also Nancy Tuana, ed., *Feminist Interpretations of Plato* (University Park, Pa.: Pennsylvania State University Press, 1994).

15. Plato, *Timaeus, The Collected Dialogues of Plato,* ed. Edith Hamilton and Huntington Cairns (Princeton: Princeton University Press, 1961).

16. Stephen Gersh, *Middle Platonism and Neo Platonism: The Latin Tradition,* vol. 1 (Notre Dame: University of Notre Dame Press, 1986), pp. 9, 13.

17. Paul Oskar Kristeller, *Renaissance Thought: The Classic, Scholastic, and Humanist Strains* (New York: Harper and Row, 1961), p. 53.

equality of woman and man were later incorporated into a *Commentary* on the *Republic* by the Islamic philosopher Averroes.[18] This commentary was translated into Latin along with Aristotle's works and Averroes's commentaries in the mid-thirteenth century, and so it was available to the early Renaissance Humanists. It was not until the mid-fifteenth century that the *Republic* itself was translated into Latin.[19] Then at the end of the fifteenth century, Marsilio Ficino translated all of Plato's works into Latin, and from that time on the later Renaissance Humanists had direct access to all of Plato's arguments about the concept of woman.[20]

Raymond Klibansky makes a distinction between a direct and an indirect Platonic tradition.[21] We have just traced the direct tradition with respect to sources on Plato's concept of woman. The indirect tradition draws from those philosophers who transmitted Plato's concepts and arguments in the context of their own philosophy. For the concept of woman, the most important of these were Cicero, Seneca, Augustine, Boethius, Porphyry, and John Scotus Erigena.[22]

While Cicero (106-43 B.C.) translated the *Timaeus,* with its support for equality of men and women, he otherwise ignored Plato's arguments about gender identity. Since Cicero did not pay much attention to questions of gender, humanists who cited his works would not have been influenced by him towards either an Aristotelian or a Platonic line of thought. Seneca (4-64), on the other hand, occasionally referred to Plato, and he presented a concept of woman clearly in the gender unity tradition. He believed that women had the same capacity for wisdom and for virtue as did men. In essays written directly to women (Helvia and Marcia) Seneca argued that they should not use their gender as an excuse for ignoring wisdom or virtue.[23] Also, Seneca's essays written to women are an early version of one side of an intergender dialogue. However, in Seneca we also find a tendency to devalue the body; and he argues that the soul of a man or woman has the same kind of identity, with no gender specificity. So Seneca's main influence on arguments about women's identity moves towards a unisex theory. Heloise often invoked his arguments about male-female relations in her correspondence with Abelard.

Augustine is credited by many scholars as being the most important source of Platonism for the humanists.[24] We have already described the complex inheritance

---

18. Averroes, *On Plato's 'Republic,'* (Ithaca, N.Y.: Cornell University Press, 1974). Averroes accurately paraphrased Plato's arguments and says that he had not yet read Aristotle's *Politics* at the time he wrote his commentary (p. 4).

19. Kristeller, *Renaissance Thought,* p. 58.

20. Kristeller, *Renaissance Thought,* p. 59.

21. Raymond Klibansky, *The Continuity of the Platonic Tradition During the Middle Ages* (London: The Warburg Institute, 1939), pp. 22ff. See also Stephen Gersh, *Middle Platonism and Neo Platonism: The Latin Tradition* (Notre Dame: University of Notre Dame Press, 1986), pp. 3-5.

22. Klibansky, *The Continuity,* pp. 22ff.

23. Seneca, *On Consolation to Marcia* and *To Helvia on Consolation* in *Moral Essays,* Loeb Edition (New York and London: C. P. Putnam's Sons and William Heinemann, Ltd., 1925), vol. 6.

24. According to Kristeller, ". . . a number of Latin writers transmitted in more or less precise form many teachings of Plato and his school: Cicero, Boethius, and above all St. Augustine, who always spoke with respect of the Platonists and . . . was indebted to them for many of his philosophical ideas. The continuity of the Platonic tradition during the Middle Ages . . . depends to a considerable

of his views about women and so will not repeat them here except to say that he often emphasized the fundamental spiritual equality of women and men within a historical structure of gender polarity. He also used Cicero's translation of the shorter text of the *Timaeus,* which supported the equality of women and men in education and function.[25]

Boethius's Lady Philosophy may well have been modeled on the figure of Diotima in Plato's *Symposium.*[26] Boethius transmits Plato's vision of woman as wise, not his arguments for the equal education and function of women and men in teaching philosophy. Boethius also transmits a Platonic method of dialogue for a philosophical work in his *Consolation of Philosophy* at the same time that he personalizes the dialogue. Whereas it is difficult, in Plato's works, to recognize Plato's own views or personality behind the views expressed,[27] Boethius's personality comes alive in his existential conversation with Lady Philosophy. Thus, even though he does not directly mention the Christian dimension of his Stoicism, Boethius conveys by his own words the dignity of his personal life. In his *Theological Tractates* he offers a definition of person as an individual substance of a rational nature,[28] and in his *Consolation* he offers his own struggle to find the individual meaning of his personal life by discoursing with a female personification of wisdom and virtue.

Neoplatonic sources for the Renaissance Humanist revival emphasized gender unity arguments. Although Plutarch (50-125) adopts an Aristotelian-based sex polarity in the theory of generation, he articulates strong arguments for gender unity in the areas of wisdom and virtue. In addition, in his texts written directly about women, especially in the *Bravery of Women,* Plutarch develops numerous examples of women who individually or collectively exemplify the virtue of courage.[29] This text, which is one of the first biographies of western women, Plutarch writes about women and men who worked together in the public sphere. In addition, he argues that women ought to pursue philosophy, especially Platonic philosophy;[30] and he even offers the example of a woman philosopher Eumetis who engaged in dialogue with men philosophers.[31] From this brief summary, it can be seen

---

extent, although not entirely, on the authority and influence of St. Augustine and his writings" (*Renaissance Thought,* p. 129). See also Klibansky, *The Continuity,* p. 23.

25. Gersh, *Middle Platonism and Neoplatonism,* p. 11.

26. For contrasting feminist analyses of Diotima, see Luce Irigaray, "Sorcerer Love: A Reading of Plato's *Symposium,* Diotima's Speech"; Andrea Nye, "Irigaray and Diotima at Plato's Symposium"; and Nancy Tuana and William Cowling, "The Presence and Absence of the Feminine in Plato's Philosophy," chapters 9, 10, and 12, in *Feminist Interpretations of Plato* (University Park, Pa.: Pennsylvania State University Press, 1994), pp. 181-215 and 243-69.

27. Kristeller, *Renaissance Thought,* p. 49.

28. Boethius, "A Treatise Against Eutyches and Nestorius," in *The Theological Tractates* (Cambridge, Mass. and London: Harvard University Press and William Heinemann, Ltd., 1918), vol. 5, p. 85.

29. Plutarch, *Moralia* (Cambridge, Mass. and London: Harvard University Press and William Heinemann, Ltd., 1927-37), vol. 3.

30. Plutarch, "Advice to Bride and Groom," *Moralia,* vol. 2.

31. Plutarch, "Dinner of Seven Wise Men," *Moralia,* vol. 2.

that the turn to the Neoplatonist Plutarch will bring into Humanism a source to support a theory of the equality of women and men.[32]

Plotinus (205-270) is more significant for his view of the importance of the human soul within a unisex model, than for any direct statements he made about women. However, he did transmit Plato's cosmic description of the Mother Receptacle, as a completely passive material principle. A different Neoplatonic model is found in Porphyry (233-305) who wrote both about generation in the *Pros Gauron* and about women's identity in a letter of *The Philosopher to his Wife, Marcella*.[33] The latter text offers a strong argument for gender unity, supporting the importance of a sexless soul, and devaluing the human body. Since this letter was not discovered until the nineteenth century, it had no direct influence on the development of Early Renaissance Humanism. Porphyry is also known for his commentary on Aristotle's logic, *Isagoge*, which transmitted a gender neutrality perspective.

The tendency within Stoicism and Neoplatonism towards a gender unity, which emphasizes equality of women and men because of the centrality of the soul and the devaluation of the body, influenced the development of Humanism.[34] At the same time, many Christian humanists believed in the resurrection of the body; and they accepted a theory of the integration of the human being that tempered the dualistic foundations of gender unity in their ancient predecessors. Therefore, Christian humanists had the tendency to adopt a complementarity or polarity theory rather than a unity theory. They defended an equality of women and men in the areas of wisdom and virtue even as they argued for a significant differentiation between the genders.

Before analyzing the specific philosophers in this chapter, we need to insert a final set of reflections about one of the new forms of philosophical texts that emerged in Renaissance Humanism, namely poetry. There are two roots for this manner of expression that need to be identified: the poetry of the courtly love tradition, and the poetry integrated into the academic fields of rhetoric and grammar. While we saw some samples of philosophical concepts and arguments in poetry in our study of religious authors and of satires, academic philosophy concentrated for the most part on prose and disputation. The systematic turn to poetry in Renaissance Humanism should be noted.

Within the melodic cadences of poetry is often embedded an argument about the concept of woman. Thus, we can consider the philosophical thought expressed by these authors, even though it is not always written in discursive prose. The courtly troubadour lyric poetry that flourished in twelfth- and thirteenth-century Europe focused on "love of the heart and mind," usually for a married woman of a higher station.[35] A particular interpersonal encounter between a man and a woman

32. See Allen, *The Concept of Woman*, pp. 195-213.

33. Porphyry, *The Philosopher to His Wife, Marcella* (London: George Redway, 1896).

34. Three texts that offer a careful analysis of this subject are: Benedict Ashley, O.P., *Theologies of the Body: Humanist and Christian* (Braintree, Mass.: The Pope John Center, 1985); Frank Bottomley, *Attitudes to the Body in Western Christendom* (London: Lepus Books, 1979); and Mary Timothy Prokes, FSE, *Toward a Theology of the Body* (Grand Rapids: Eerdmans, 1996).

35. Ernest Hatch Wilkins, *A History of Italian Literature* (Cambridge, Mass. and London: Harvard University Press, 1974), pp. 6-7.

was often a catalyst for the written text. The question of love is raised and resolved through dialogue. The resolutions have all the different qualities of various human choices, from the most to the least virtuous.

Paul Oskar Kristeller points out that "[a]bout the beginning of the fourteenth century poetry appears as a special teaching subject at Italian universities."[36] He traces the roots of this tradition in the recovery of the earlier teaching of rhetoric and grammar in Roman schools and the reading of classical Latin authors. The Renaissance Humanists of the next two centuries actually called their field of study by the name of "poetry," and they emphasized its importance in the teaching of history and philosophy. Kristeller continues: ". . . after the beginning of the fifteenth century, the chair of moral philosophy was often held by humanists, usually in combination with that of rhetoric and poetry."[37] This academic core gradually developed into what became known as the "Humanities."

It is obvious that the expression of concepts and arguments in poetic form provides a strikingly different model than the scholastic form of disputation.[38] Kristeller is quick to point out that the Italian universities did not overturn or replace the scholastic method or content of the French and English universities; rather, the Humanistic program of studies developed often side by side with the scholastic program.[39] As we will see in this chapter, the humanists were, albeit often critical, also well versed in scholastic philosophy. However, a fragmentation of orientations occurred within the field of philosophy itself, with scholastic philosophy concentrating on logic, mathematics, natural philosophy, and metaphysics, and Humanistic studies concentrating on grammar, rhetoric, poetry, and moral philosophy. Thus the early Renaissance Humanist approach to philosophical texts opened up new ways of expression that moved more directly towards dialogue and away from argument and disputation. As we will see, they also moved towards a complementary theory of gender.

In this chapter we consider four Italian humanists: Guido Cavalcanti, the "first Humanist"; Dante Alighieri, the "first Christian Humanist"; Francis Petrarch, "the father of Humanism"; and Giovanni Boccaccio, the "popularizer of Humanism."[40] In addition to the unique and significant contribution that each of these men made to the history of the concept of woman, they formed a new kind of historical community of discourse about women. The city of Florence provided the new context for learning, away from Paris and England. In this context intellectual friendship provides the bridge for the development of Renaissance Humanism. Dante and Cavalcanti were friends who exchanged their writings early in life; Boccaccio introduced Petrarch to Dante's work, and Petrarch introduced Boccaccio to Seneca, Cicero, and Augustine. Dialogue among men, in part about new concepts of

---

36. Kristeller, *Renaissance Thought,* p. 109.

37. Kristeller, *Renaissance Thought,* p. 109.

38. See Eugenio Garin's comparison of education at the University of Padua and in Florence in *Italian Humanism: Philosophy and the Civic Life in the Renaissance* (New York: Harper and Row, 1965), pp. 1-4; in *Educazione umanistica in Italia* (Bari: Editori Laterza, 1967); and in *L'educazione in Europa 1400/1600: Problemi e programmi* (Bari: Editori Laterza, 1966).

39. Kristeller, *Renaissance Thought,* pp. 108-18.

40. The quotations refer to common expressions for the four humanists.

women, began to change the shape of gender theory for the European West away from the Aristotelian foundation of gender polarity that had been so deeply ingrained in academia. In our analysis we shall offer several examples to provide the basis for a new concept of woman as engaged in philosophical dialogue with men.

GUIDO CAVALCANTI (1255-1300)

At the end of the thirteenth century three major lyric poets emerged in Italian literature. Guittone d'Arezzo left about three hundred poems and thirty-five letters, many of which spoke about love, both secular and religious. Guido Guinizelli left about twenty poems that also spoke of the nature and identity of love. They both introduced the concept of a noble woman who leads a man to wisdom and virtue by his love for her. It is in this context that Guido Cavalcanti composed his own poems of love. He was described by Ernest Wilkins as "a man of lofty intellect and strong emotions, exceedingly proud and scornful, . . . deeply versed in philosophy, yet ready to take his violent share in personal or factional feuds, . . . he gained mastery of the difficult and elaborate psychological theories of the time."[41] Cavalcanti is important for our study because he wrote one poem that established the direction of many future discussions about the identity of love; and this poem was written in the form of a dialogue between a woman and a man.

Among the fifty or so extant poems of Cavalcanti, the three most famous words "Donna me prega," or "The Lady asked me," serve as the informal title of Cavalcanti's seminal work for Humanism, the *Canzone d'amore*.[42] The Lady referred to is thought to be a young woman from Toulouse whom Guido Cavalcanti met during a 1292 pilgrimage to Santiago de Compostela in Spain.[43] Here at the dawn of Renaissance Humanism we discover an imaginary intergender dialogue between a French woman and an Italian man, written in the Tuscan vernacular, and focused on the love between a woman and a man. While Cavalcanti is often associated with the view that love for a woman has a very negative influence on a man, this negativity does not diminish the more positive aspects of his contribution to the concept of woman in the following areas: (1) the quality of his imaginary dialogue between a man and a woman; and (2) the lack of blaming women for any negative effects of love.

41. Wilkins, *A History of Italian Literature,* p. 29.

42. Guido Cavalcanti, "Canzone d'amore," in Otto Bird, "Medieval Philosophic Thought as Reflected in the *Canzone d'amore* of Cavalcanti According to the Commentary of Dino Del Garbo: Text and Commentary," Ph.D. Diss., University of Toronto, May 1, 1939. In Bird's manuscript the phrase is spelled as: "Donna mi priega" (i, iii), while in most historical references it is spelled as: "Donna me priega."

43. Wilkins states: "[m]any of his poems are given a dramatic character by the introduction of sentences supposed to be uttered in direct discourse by various persons, real or imaginary: his lady, other ladies, friends, onlookers, love, his heart, his mind, thoughts, sighs, voices, images, the poem itself. . . . Most of Cavalcanti's poems were written for a lady named Giovanna, to whom he gave, in poetry, the name Primavera, 'Springtime.' A few of his later poems were written for a certain Mandette of Toulouse, who had reminded him of his own lady . . . ." *A History of Italian Literature,* pp. 29, 30-31.

In the imaginary dialogue, Cavalcanti describes himself as the Master and the woman as his student. While this description may give the appearance of a gender polarity because of the different status of the two persons engaging in dialogue, in the context of European history where women had not been allowed access to higher education, this description of a woman as a serious student may have actually implied a much greater equality than the Master/student relation *prima facie* suggests. We discover eight philosophical themes, borrowing from concepts in Aristotle's *Metaphysics*, embedded in the simple question about the nature of love:

> A lady asks me that I would tell
> of an accident which is often fierce
> and is so great that it is called love; . . .
> where it is posited and who makes it created,
> and what its virtue is and its power,
> its essence and its every movement,
> the pleasingness which makes it called loving,
> and whether one can show it by sight.[44]

The framework for the eight questions about love may have been taken from a poem previously written by another man.[45] However, the novelty for the concept of woman consists in the fact that Cavalcanti gives them a woman's voice. Thus, his imaginary development of the philosophical framework of the poem as the consequence of questions asked by a female character raises the initial possibility that an intelligent woman is the object of his love. Using Aristotelian categories that classify love as a relation and accident of substance, the questions unfold within a scholastic model of analysis. At the same time, the quality of response reveals a seriousness about the issue that has none of the satirical tone present in academic debates about gender or in popular texts that devalue women. Therefore, Cavalcanti's intergender dialogical structure establishes a new precedent for the concept of woman.[46]

44. Cavalcanti, *Canzone d'amore*, p. 7.

45. See John Colaneri, "Guido Cavalcanti and the *Canzone D'amore*," Introduction to *Lezzioni d'Amore, Francesco de'Vieri* (Munich: Wilhelm Fink Verlag, 1973). These questions were possibly borrowed from a poem of Guido Orlandi and put in the female voice of the Lady, 15-32. It is also suggested that they follow Socrates' argument about the nature of love in the *Symposium*. See Massimo Ciavollea, "Ficino's Interpretation of 'Donna me Prega,'" in *Ficino and Renaissance Platonism,* ed. Konrad Eisenbichler and Olga Pugliese (Ottawa: Dovehouse, 1986), pp. 41-42.

46. Jody Enders asks whether or not Cavalcanti is simply using the Lady's question to pose a question in the style of rhetoric which is actually addressing a male audience. In this case, the female "lady" would be simply used as a medium to produce an effect on men, and no real intergender dialogue would be taking place. See "Rhetoric and Dialectic in Guido Cavalcanti's *Donna me prega*," *Stanford Italian Review* 5, no. 2 (1985): 161-74. Or alternatively, the lady may be the only member of the audience for a dialectic, whose purpose is to attain the truth. The critic concludes that: "The poem's impact is . . . dialectical . . . the 'Donna me prega' presents a codification on how we are to think about love" (p. 173). At the same time as it is dialectical, and describes a real conversation between a man and a woman, it also has a rhetorical value in being read by many humanists as well. In her analysis Enders emphasizes the Platonic method of dialectic as collection and division.

This poem "The Lady asked me" became the source of many different commentaries by subsequent philosophers. Academic philosophers such as Giles of Rome wrote commentaries on it, as well as Renaissance Humanists who remained outside of academia. Commentaries were written in Latin or in the vernacular. Sometimes, later interpretations of the original text gave a slightly different emphasis from the original author. The earliest presumed commentary was written by Dino del Garbo (d. 1327).[47] We will give a brief analysis of this commentary and the text because of its importance for the concept of woman in early Renaissance Humanism.

Del Garbo was a famous physician, trained in Bologna, who taught medicine in Padua, Siena, and Florence. He wrote several texts and was particularly interested in the works of ancient physicians such as Hippocrates and the *Canon of Medicine* of Avicenna.[48] Del Garbo suggests in his commentary on the *Canzone d'amore* that Cavalcanti was in a free relationship of master and student in his dialogue with the Lady who asked him to explain the nature of love.

> But although it may be the woman he is in love with who has caused him to write this poem, nevertheless he does not say that she **commanded** him to write. Instead, he says she **asked** him. By this he would show that what he says here is not said as if in the passion of love. For he who is impassioned with love thinks he must do whatever his beloved wishes, so that whatever she says is to him as the command of a master to a servant. But whatever Guido says in this poem is said in a scientific and veridical manner from the precepts of natural and moral philosophy. And he who speaks this way with knowledge assumes the place of master, while the one receiving what is said, being in ignorance and desiring to learn, assumes the place of student. Therefore, just as the master has a higher place than the student, so in this matter Guido would show that he is the master and the lady the student. Consequently, the lady addressing him **asks** rather than **commands** him to speak of love, for one can only fittingly address a master with requests and not commands.[49]

It may appear again that the relegation of the Lady to the status of student who requests, rather than commands, and who is in a state of ignorance, rather than knowledge, devalues the role of the female with respect to the male who is the mas-

---

47. Ruth Kelso notes the following at the beginning of her chapter "Love and Beauty," in *Doctrine for the Lady of the Renaissance* (Urbana: University of Illinois Press, 1956): "Dino del Garbo uttered the right warning to anyone entering on the study of love when he postulated that the reader must be intelligent because the subject is philosophical, involving the natural, moral, and astrological sciences. One of the many flies attracted to the honey of Cavalcanti's *Canzone* on love, he struggled to interpret its meaning, only to be bogged down at times as he was free to confess" (p. 136). Kelso's text traces the relation between love and beauty throughout the development of humanism in both men and women writers.

48. Del Garbo became embroiled in a fierce dispute with Cesso d'Ascoli about Guido Cavalcanti which ended in Ascoli being burned to death as a heretic. This historical situation shows to some extent the intensity with which people considered Cavalcanti's views.

49. Del Garbo, in Cavalcanti, *Canzone d'amore*, pp. 64-65.

ter in this dialogue. However, del Garbo qualifies his characterization of the woman and makes her into an intelligent and virtuous partner in the dialogue. He argues that the Lady is presenting a "just petition" that reveals she is a worthy person of character who knows what she asks.[50] Indeed, as we saw previously she used the philosophical categories of accident, virtue, power, and essence to pose her complex eight-part question about love.

In Cavalcanti's response to the questions posed, we see the introduction of the concept of a "possible intellect" in the imaginary dialogue between the man and the woman. The introduction of the concept of the possible intellect is Averroistic. The possible intellect was considered to be the same in all men, so the object of love was woman as such rather than a particular woman. Lloyd Howard notes that this reflects the perceived rejection by Averroists of the existence of the individual soul after death: "[t]his discourse, that the possible intellect is not part of the human body, sustained by the Averroists and Guido Cavalcanti, was at direct variance with the teachings of the Church."[51] Thus Cavalcanti's intergender dialogue tends towards using a woman to reach a union with an abstract ideal of woman, instead of using dialogue to establish an authentic interpersonal relation in building a communion of persons.

Cavalcanti describes the genus of love: "It [love] is created and has a sensible name, a habit of the soul and will from the heart. It comes from a seen form which is understood, which takes its place and rest in the possible intellect as in a subject."[52] Del Garbo's commentary stresses that this kind of love between a man and a woman is not simply an animal passion, but rather contains an aspect of intelligence. In this development, we can already see a different focus than the one present in the satires about love as described in the preceding chapter. Del Garbo reflects:

> . . . it should be noted that what Guido says here about the possible intellect shows that the apprehension which the lover has is not purely sensitive; for inasmuch as it comes to the possible intellect it partakes of the intellect. Consequently, Guido is speaking in this poem only of the love that man has, and it is not his intention to treat of love and friendship among the brute animals, which are without intellect and therefore do not have this kind of love.[53]

Cavalcanti suggests, following Aristotle, that "love is a passion following upon the will [the rational appetite] in the sensitive appetite, which is in the heart."[54] Del Garbo, a physician, corrects this judgment about the seat of love:

---

50. Del Garbo, in Cavalcanti, *Canzone d'amore*, p. 67.

51. Lloyd Howard, "Virgil's Discourse on Love in *Purgatorio* XVIII and Guido Cavalcanti," *Quaderni d'italianistica* 6, no. 2 (1985): 173.

52. Cavalcanti, *Canzone d'amore*, pp. 7-8.

53. Del Garbo, in Cavalcanti, *Canzone d'amore*, p. 127.

54. As paraphrased by Del Garbo, in Cavalcanti, *Canzone d'amore*, p. 108. It is interesting to note that del Garbo does refer to Aristotle in various ways in his commentary, but he does not refer to Aristotle's theory of gender.

"Doctors, however, hold that it has being in the brain. But it is not our present concern to determine which opinion is true."[55]

Both Cavalcanti and del Garbo agree about the effects of love on the man who is in love. First, the intelligence can be distorted by the effects of love. Cavalcanti states in the *Canzone:* "It [love] maintains an unsound judgment, for the intention is rendered valid by reason; he, in whom reason is conquered, discerns badly what he loves."[56] The man in love can overvalue his beloved, or judge that there are qualities in the woman which in fact are missing, or vice versa, that qualities are missing which are in fact there. In either case the intelligence is misled by the presence of love.

Second, in addition to impeding the operation of the intellect, love can also negatively affect the body. Cavalcanti describes the effect of dying from unrequited love: "Death often follows from its [love's] power, if perchance, its virtue is impeded which helps the contrary way; not because it is a natural opposite [does love cause death], but inasmuch as it twists [man] from his perfect good."[57] The physician del Garbo then adds some of the medical effects of unrequited love:

> He [Cavalcanti] means that love kills when it is so vehement that it impedes the work of the vegetative or vital virtues of the soul, which conserve life and its operation in the human body. Thus we see that those who are excessively in love, and cannot satisfy their desire, dry up until they are consumed away and are dead. . . .[58]

Del Garbo concludes that love is not opposed to life in a general way, but that when it is not properly moderated by a man who suffers from an unrequited love for a woman, it diverts the natural virtues of the soul from its proper functions of nutrition. The lovesick man ceases to eat and drink, and he eventually dies.

These rather negative conclusions about the destructive powers of unrequited love are usually associated with Guido Cavalcanti's poems. Colaneri notes in his critique of Francesco de' Vieri's commentary on the *Canzone d'amore* that "[l]ove, as portrayed by Guido, leads the lover ultimately to death and destruction, not to his moral improvement. . . ."[59] Dante will challenge Guido's concept of love precisely because he believes that love is a positive force that can transform the lover.[60] In the

55. Del Garbo, in Cavalcanti, *Canzone d'amore,* p. 108.

56. Cavalcanti, *Canzone d'amore,* p. 8.

57. Cavalcanti, *Canzone d'amore,* p. 8.

58. Del Garbo, in Cavalcanti, *Canzone d'amore,* p. 166. For a more detailed consideration of the medical aspects of lovesickness in the dialogue and commentary, see Lloyd Howard, "Dino's Interpretation of *Donna me prega* and Cavalcanti's *Canzoniere,*" *Canadian Journal of Italian Studies* 6, nos. 24-25 (1983): 167-82.

59. John Colaneri, introduction, *Francesco de'Vieri: Lezione d'amore* (Munich: Wilhelm Fink, 1973), p. 19. In this text, Colaneri gives a careful critique of the poem "A Lady Asks Me" as well as a complete text of and commentary on Francesco de'Vieri's commentary on the poem.

60. See Robert Pogue Harrison, who states that Cavalcanti ". . . had already become disillusioned with Giovanna. His heart was already elsewhere. Such inconstancy on Guido's part was of course consistent with his disillusioning conception of love, for, as we have seen he believed that what

Vita nuova Dante introduces the figure of Cavalcanti's Lady by mentioning her name, Giovanna, and nickname of "Primavera"; and he further suggests that she represents the one who prepares for his Beatrice, as John the Baptist prepares for Christ. Dante tried, without success, to reconcile Cavalcanti and his Lady. However, Guido Cavalcanti chose to follow a Neoplatonic and Averroistic view of love and of women.[61] Cavalcanti's Averroism also led him to place a greater emphasis on the sentient and worldly, rather than on the transcendent and eternal aspects of love for particular persons.[62] Since Dante's own views will be discussed in some detail in the next section of this chapter, we return to our evaluation of Cavalcanti for the present.

Even though Cavalcanti emphasizes the negative effects of love for a woman on a man, he does not blame woman, as did the satirists, for this state of affairs. Instead, Cavalcanti places the responsibility for the effects of a disordered love directly on the man. Since the disease of lovesickness is found in the man, so the cure is also given to the man. Cavalcanti suggests that a certain cure to this disease of disordered, unrequited love is to forget the beloved.

When the analysis turns to love that is returned we find a slightly more complex set of recommendations. At first it appears as though the basic intensity of love makes it problematic even when it is shared. Love's essence brings a restlessness into the individual and has direct effects on both the mind and the body. In particular, the exercise of the intellect is interrupted. "Thus anything else this man might have been thinking about is completely disrupted and his thoughts are completely distracted from anything except his beloved."[63] The immediate conclusion is that men should avoid this experience if possible:

> Thus he [Cavalcanti] says first that no one should come to this passion and adhere to it, because, when it is well impressed in all its fervor, it makes a complete slave out of the lover so that no liberty remains to him. Therefore he says further that no one should adhere to this passion thinking he will find either solace or joy therein, for, as has been said, there is much anguish, sadness and fear in such a passion. . . . Finally one should not adhere to this passion hoping to find there

---

one admired in a noble woman were transcendent qualities that did not belong to her person in any inherent or substantial way. It is significant, therefore, that precisely at this critical juncture of the *Vita nuova* Dante affirms Beatrice's personhood most forcefully — a personhood that in every way is incarnational and hypostatic"; "Approaching the *Vita nuova*," in *The Cambridge Companion to Dante* (Cambridge: Cambridge University Press, 1993). The relevant chapter in *Vita nuova* is 24, 41.

61. See Howard, "There is therefore a disagreement on what should be the goal of their poetry. For Dante it is Beatrice, that vehicle which leads to salvation. Dante wanted Guido to follow a similar road with Giovanna. Instead he abandons Giovanna for the Averroistic philosophy reflected in 'Donna me prega'" ("Virgil's Discourse," *Quaderni d'italianistica* 6, no. 2 [1985]: 170).

62. Consequently, Dante suggests in Virgil's discourse on love that those who hold Cavalcanti's views are to be found in purgatory. See Howard: "For Dante it is paramount that the corrupting influence of 'Donna me prega' come to an end. Even though Guido is already dead when Dante writes the *Divine Comedy*, 'Donna me prega' is circulating widely and spreading Averroistic thought. It is for this reason that Virgil directly rejects Averroists before and after his discourse, 'Virgil's Discourse on Love'" (*Quaderni d'italianistica* 6, no. 2 [1985]: 175). Dante, however, does not mention his good friend by name.

63. Del Garbo, in Cavalcanti, *Canzone d'amore*, p. 204.

either great or little wisdom, for in this love there is neither wisdom nor discretion. . . . For by this he would show that astuteness and prudence are not worth anything to the mind vehemently impressed with the passion of love, for it has lost all liberty and is made subject to the thoughts of its beloved.[64]

The view that the man in love is really a slave of his passions for the woman he loves contains an ironic inversion of the master/slave relationship that we considered at the beginning of the dialogue. Now the Master of the student has become the slave of the woman student he loves. This enslavement, however, is due to the intensity of his own passion and not to any defect in her identity. If a man chooses to succumb to the passion of his love, he will relegate his reason to the slavery of his own passions. Through this inversion of the right ordering of reason and passion, he becomes himself the slave of the woman he loves.

While one solution to this disorder is to avoid and to forget the woman, another solution is to accept the situation and work towards building a perfect love. Significantly, a perfect love is built on two virtues: the absence of fraud (so prevalent in satires about love), and the presence of generosity of spirit in returning love on the part of the beloved.

> Thus he [Cavalcanti] says that when this love is perfect, it is completely without fraud with respect to the beloved, since there is perfect fidelity without any fraud in all that it thinks and does to please the beloved, for when a lover has the desire to defraud his beloved, his love is not perfect. But he who is truly possessed by love would never think of displeasing his beloved or of attempting any violence towards her, for in so doing he would not attain that which he so greatly desires, namely to be joined to his beloved.[65]

The clear statement that violence towards a woman would interfere with the goal of true love, which is perfect union, is an important development in western thought. The violence of fraud and the biased devaluation of woman are absent here. Instead, we have the description of a possibly valuable relationship, established in freedom between a man and a woman. Yet there are still limitations in the theory. Not being violent with one's beloved is described as serving a man's interest rather than the woman's, because violence would mean that he would not attain what he desires.

We also witness cognizance of the potential for disorder within the self when the passions dominate. It is important to note, however, the woman is still depicted here as primarily an object of desire for the man, not one who has desires herself. Boccaccio will be the first philosopher to begin to elaborate woman's subjective passions for men. However, we do have here the example of an imaginary dialogue between a man and a woman that opens up a range of interesting and important issues about the nature of relations between men and women in general. Therefore, even though the conclusions of Cavalcanti's poem emphasize some negative effects

---

64. Del Garbo, in Cavalcanti, *Canzone d'amore*, p. 208.
65. Del Garbo, in Cavalcanti, *Canzone d'amore*, pp. 233-34.

of love, and even though he is not particularly concerned about the woman's identity *per se,* in his imaginary projection of an intergender dialogue we find the initiation of a new humanist direction in the history of the concept of woman.

DANTE ALIGHIERI (1265-1321)

The Italian philosopher/poet Dante contributed significantly to a humanist elaboration of the concept of woman in several ways: (1) he greatly enriched writing in the vernacular; (2) he brilliantly transmitted philosophical concepts and theories through a literary and didactic writing style; (3) he created many different examples of imaginary intergender dialogue; and (4) he provided concrete incarnations of wise and virtuous women in the characters of Beatrice and Lady Philosophy.

Concerning the first contribution, Hans Urs von Balthasar notes, "Dante saw and portrayed conversion to the vernacular as an innovation of the greatest historical significance."[66] Choosing to write in his "mother" tongue rather than in the more formal, academic Latin, Dante transformed the scholastic view of the educated person from the academic Master defending his positions in disputations, to a model more accessible to both men and women outside of academia. This shift in language has been characterized by Jeffrey Schnapp as a shift from a "'masculine' world of Latin epic" to a "'feminine' world of vernacular lyric."[67] Indeed, Dante himself tells us in the first paragraph of his *De vulgari eloquentia* that he associates the vernacular with the language of women:

> Since I find that no one before me has dealt with the matter of eloquence in the vernacular; and since I see how necessary such knowledge is to everyone (for Nature allows it not only to men but even to women and children); I shall attempt . . . to be of service to the speech of the common people. . . .[68]

By these words, Dante invites women into his new community of discourse. At the same time that Dante appears to be telling his reader that he associates the vernacular with women in a special way, he is also careful to point out that the vernacular has a priority status with men. In a reflection on the story of *Genesis* Dante argues, within a traditional polarity model, that man or Adam rather than woman or Eve spoke first. He does not accept the description in Scripture that records Eve as responding to the serpent before Adam spoke:

66. Hans Urs von Balthasar, *The Glory of the Lord: A Theological Aesthetics,* vol. 3 (San Francisco: Ignatius Press, 1986), "Dante," p. 13.

67. Jeffrey T. Schnapp, "Dante's Sexual Solecisms: Gender and Genre in the *Commedia,*" *Romantic Review* 79, no. 1 (January 1988). For example, "What I will be proposing, is that Dante's extensive play with sexual substitutions constitutes a strategy to articulate the intersection between the 'feminine' world of vernacular lyric and the 'masculine' world of Latin epic, the world of Beatrice and the world of Virgil" (p. 149).

68. Dante, *"De vulgari eloquentia": Dante's Book of Exile* (Lincoln and London: University of Nebraska Press, 1990), p. 47.

Yet although we find in Scripture that a woman spoke first, it is still more reasonable to believe that it was a man. It is improper to think that so humble a human action did not originate from a man rather than a woman.[69]

So we could say that while the choice of the vernacular is somewhat associated with the concept of woman and "mother tongue," and that even though it will eventually have a value for the access of women to literature and philosophy, Dante still considers its original value as more related to the greater nobility of men.

Concerning Dante's second-mentioned contribution to philosophy, it is important to note that Dante's literary method goes far beyond Cavalcanti's example. Dante was not simply writing love poems in his mother tongue, he was writing about fundamental issues in the philosophy and theology of wisdom and virtue.[70] Dante's choice of poetic style to write about these issues is viewed by Ernesto Grassi as a fundamental characteristic of Italian Humanism because it uses poetic language, rather than scholastic argumentation, as the way to "open" an understanding of historical human development. He states: ". . . Dante formulates the thesis that the poet is the founder of the community and that therefore only he opens the way for historicity."[71] In the context of this study of the concept of woman, Dante does indeed open a way for the beginning development of woman's historical consciousness.

This now brings us to a consideration of Dante's third contribution, or his introduction of many examples of intergender dialogue. Dante serves as a transition figure with respect to the use of Aristotelian views in discussions related to issues of gender identity. Briefly stated, even though Dante accepted Aristotle's fundamental theories about human identity as qualified by St. Thomas Aquinas, he usually avoids Aristotle's sex and gender polarity orientation. Instead, Dante's imaginary models of female characters, and especially the figure of Beatrice, serve as counterexamples to the Aristotelian model of woman. So while Dante is solidly in the scholastic tradition, he also anticipates and prepares for later humanist developments.

In a particular way, Dante establishes the importance of interpersonal dialogue for the development of the meaning of a personal life. As Balthasar summarizes the contrast between two different approaches to philosophy: "[a]t the centre of Dante's work stands his personality — in extreme contrast to Thomas Aquinas, with whom personality completely and intentionally disappears. . . ."[72] Of course, Augustine had introduced the development of personality through a man's dia-

---

69. Dante, *De vulgari eloquentia,* I, iv, 50. He also suggests that the serpent did not really speak to Eve as well: "And if it is objected that the serpent spoke to the first woman, or that Balaam's donkey spoke, to this I answer that in these cases the angel and the demon worked in such ways that the animals moved their speech organs to articulate a sound similar to real speech . . " (I, ii, 48-49). For the story of Balaam's donkey, see *Numbers* 22:22-35.

70. See Balthasar: "No, Dante was concerned with translating the knowledge of reality — hidden in the seven liberal arts, in philosophy, theology and history — from dead, fossilized Latin into the living, spoken language" (*The Glory,* vol. 3, p. 13).

71. Ernesto Grassi, *Heidegger and the Question of Renaissance Humanism: Four Studies* (Binghamton, N.Y.: Medieval and Renaissance Texts and Studies, 1983), p. 18.

72. Balthasar, *The Glory,* p. 24.

logue with God, and Boethius through a man's dialogue with Lady Philosophy, but Dante is the first to introduce the development of personality through detailed intergender dialogue of a woman and a man. In the context of this dialogue we will discover a rich portrayal of the relation of wisdom and virtue to a woman who both has them and is able to teach them to a man. This concept of woman as wise and virtuous and able to elevate a man's wisdom and virtue constitutes the fourth and perhaps most significant aspect of Dante's contribution to our study.

We shall now give a brief introduction to these aspects of Dante's philosophy of woman in order to situate the developments that occur in subsequent humanist authors. Even though there is a massive amount of scholarship available concerning Dante's concept of woman, by limiting our discussion to just a few general themes in the concept of woman, we will lay the groundwork for subsequent authors in the Humanist Reformation of the Aristotelian concept of woman. Our analysis will focus on three phases of Dante's depiction of women as found in *La vita nuova*, the *Banquet*, and the *Divine Comedy*.

Encountering a Virtuous Woman

Dante met Guido Cavalcanti in 1283, and the two men became friends. They were both from the same extended family of Guelfs and lived in the dynamic turbulence of Florentine life. The friendship lasted for seventeen years until 1300, when Dante as a member of the city council of Florence sent Cavalcanti into exile.[73] In the same year that Dante first met Cavalcanti, he began to write love poetry using an imaginary female "shield" to hide the identity of Beatrice, the true object of his love whom he had met some nine years previously. Some of these poems were sent to and responded to by Cavalcanti.[74]

For the next several years, Dante composed love poems that became immediately popular in Florence and beyond. While most of these poems were addressed to or shared with men, some of them were directly addressed to women. By including just a few samples here, we can see how Dante invites women into his community of discourse. Poem 32: "And then — gentle ladies to whom all this is said — "; Poem 33: "Ladies who have understanding of love, I wish to speak with you of my lady; not that I think I can exhaust her praises, but I want to speak to unburden my mind"; Poem 35: "Help me, ladies, to do her honour"; Poem 38: ". . . if I get no consolation from you, ladies . . ."; Poem 39: "Ladies who show pity in your bearing . . ."; and Poem 47: ". . . and so, ladies, even did I wish to, I myself could not fully describe my state. . . ."[75] Dante shares his reflections in a concrete depiction of intergender dialogue based on the mutual respect of the participants.

---

73. See Robert Pogue Harrison, *The Body of Beatrice* (Baltimore and London: Johns Hopkins University Press, 1988), p. 82.

74. For a discussion of their friendship and the relation to their early poems and the *Vita nuova* see Harrison, *The Body of Beatrice,* pp. 20-22, and especially chapter 4, "The Ghost of Guido Cavalcanti," pp. 69-90.

75. *Dante's Lyric Poetry* (Oxford: Clarendon Press, 1967), pp. 59, 65, 69, and 85-87.

The real Beatrice died of the plague in 1290, and four years later Dante composed *La vita nuova,* dedicated to his "first friend" Guido Cavalcanti. The structure of *La vita nuova* follows the example of Boethius's *Consolation of Philosophy;* written in the context of human grief, it alternates between poems and prose explanations of the poems. It focuses on many different responses of Dante to Beatrice both before and after her death; so it provides a description of many different encounters of a man with a woman. In this text Dante restates Cavalcanti's definition of love as a relation or accident at the same time that he argues against his friend's tendency to abstract love from the person who loves. Dante's text reads: "At this point someone whose objects are worthy of the fullest attention might be mystified by the way I speak of love as though it were a thing in itself, and not only a substance endowed with understanding but also a physical substance, which is demonstrably false; for love is not in itself a substance at all, but an accident in a substance."[76] In other words, using the Aristotelian notion of ontological accident as a property that must inhere in a primary substance, in this case a particular human being, Dante gives primacy to the individual person who loves rather than to love itself.

The objects of Dante's love in the *Vita Nuova* are different women: the shield-woman already mentioned, Beatrice, and another "gentle woman" with whom he became involved shortly after Beatrice's death.[77] Later, in the *Banquet (Il Convivio),* Dante consciously develops a double love object in literal reference to a living woman and his allegorical reference to the imaginary "Lady Philosophy" following the previous model in Boethius.[78] Then, at the summit of Dante's great writing in *The Divine Comedy,* the object of his love becomes the imaginary Beatrice, now transformed after death by grace, and leading Dante to the ultimate object of his love, or God. Dante uses St. Thomas Aquinas's definition of love as the principle of movement towards the object loved, and his threefold distinction between natural, sensitive, and rational appetite, to describe free will and rational choice in the kind of love a man has towards a woman and vice versa.[79]

Dante moves from one kind of concept of woman to another through a

---

76. Dante Alighieri, *La vita nuova: Poems of Youth* (Harmondsworth: Penguin Books, 1969), ch. xxv, p. 72. In "Approaching the *Vita nuova,*" *The Cambridge Companion to Dante,* Harrison remarks on the irony that Dante dedicates this text to Cavalcanti in view of the fact that it was polemic against his friend's view that the beloved is an illusion and does not really possess good qualities (p. 39). However, at times Dante presents Love as if it were represented by an imaginary individual, or a "he." See Harrison, *The Body of Beatrice,* p. 55.

77. There are several different love objects in the text, but as Robert Harrison so eloquently states in "Approaching the *Vita nuova,*" *The Cambridge Companion to Dante,* Beatrice was always at the center. "There is no doubt that Beatrice triumphs over her rivals by the end of the *Vita nuova,* yet this outcome should not be allowed to obscure the fact that Dante's 'book of memory' is at once a testimony of his singular love for Beatrice as well as the story of his multiple loves both before and after her death" (p. 38).

78. Dante, *The Banquet* (Saratoga, Calif.: Anima Libri, 1989).

79. See Gerald Morgan, "Dante, Chaucer, and the Meaning of Love," in *Dante Comparisons: Comparative Studies of Dante and Montle, Foscolo, Tasso, Chaucer, Petrarch, Propertius and Catullus* (Dublin: Irish Academic Press, 1985), pp. 73-95. Three kinds of love all eventually lead to love of God because "The whole of creation is set in motion by love and united by love in its creator, God . . . as triumphantly celebrated in the final line of the *Comedia . . .*" (p. 77).

progression of love object, which begins with the real woman Beatrice, then projects love onto an imaginary woman shield, then introduces an imaginary abstract female character of Lady Philosophy, and finally introduces an imaginary 'real' Beatrice with a glorified body.[80] On each different level, he also introduces a theme of intergender dialogue that opens up new ranges of understanding, action, wisdom, and virtue. Because Dante's transformation from one level to another takes place through a confrontation with death and an experience of personal resurrection through an encounter with the Divine presence, Dante reveals himself as a Christian humanist. In other words, his community of discourse actually contains three voices: the voice of the man, the voice of the woman, and the voice of God as revealed through the female character who is transformed by grace.[81]

Dante's important innovation to the history of the concept of woman in western philosophy is his discovery and articulation of the creative power of multiple encounters between men and women. This creative power is ultimately open to and transformed by the mutual encounter with God. Balthasar describes it this way: "We are left with the final reciprocity of Eros and Agape, which for Dante are two names for the same thing: Amor, God's most truly proper name. This reciprocity is nuptial, and the existential experience of this ultimate reality is called — if we are to judge the matter on the poet's level and by his criteria — Dante and Beatrice."[82] We shall now turn to the three main works identified above and elaborate the ways Dante's understanding of the integrative dynamics of intergender dialogue changed over the years.

Dante's dialogue with woman in *La vita nuova* begins by engaging his exterior and interior senses. He states:

> As they walked down the street she turned her eyes towards me where I stood in fear and trembling, and with her ineffable courtesy, which is now rewarded in eternal life, she greeted me; and such was the virtue of her greeting that I seemed to experience the height of bliss.[83]

Dante's eyes encounter the eyes of the woman, his ears hear her voice, his passions of desire and joy are aroused, and his body trembles. Dante tells us that since the time he had seen this woman nine years previously, he had cherished her image in his mind, but that the intensity of their encounter was augmented when she first

---

80. P. J. Klemp describes Dante's movement as one of passing through a series of concentric circles. See "The Women in the Middle: Layers of Love in Dante's *Vita Nuova*," *Italica* 61, no. 3 (Autumn 1984): 186-95, especially 187-88.

81. However, Kristeller, by focusing on education rather than theology, would not extend this term to Dante. See the definition of Christian Humanism by Paul Oskar Kristeller, *The Classics and Renaissance Thought* (Cambridge, Mass.: Harvard University Press, 1955): ". . . it is probably preferable to use the term Christian humanism in a more specific sense, and to limit it to those scholars with a humanist classical and rhetorical training who explicitly discussed religious or theological problems in all or some of their writings" (p. 86).

82. Balthasar, *The Glory,* p. 81.

83. Dante, *La vita nuova,* III, 6-10, 31.

spoke to him in the greeting mentioned above.[84] At this point, Dante claims that his passion was well governed by his reason: "Though her image, which was always present in my mind, incited Love to dominate me, its influence was so noble that it never allowed Love to guide me without the faithful counsel of reason, in everything in which such counsel was useful to hear."[85]

Later on, however, when the woman refrained from greeting Dante because of negative rumors about his behavior, Dante was plunged into the passions of suffering and the sorrow of grief. He comes to a decision to write primarily in praise of the object of his love. Significant for our study, Dante then chooses to write about this woman to other women: "I thought it would not be fitting to speak of my lady to anyone except other women, whom I should address in the second person, and not to any woman but only to those who are gracious, not merely feminine."[86] Thus, although the poems were also written to be shared among the men in the circle of poets near to Dante, it cannot be denied that he included women as part of his audience of written discourse.

When the real Beatrice dies as a result of the plague, Dante is plunged into even deeper experience of the passion of grief. This time Dante chooses to write to Cavalcanti, and to follow his friend's example of writing in the vernacular. Dante notes that Cavalcanti's own decision to use the Tuscan language was based on his own desire to enter into dialogue with a woman: "The first [one] to write as a vernacular poet was moved to do so because he wished to make his verses intelligible to a lady who found it difficult to understand Latin."[87] In this observation, we have a conscious linkage of the decision to write in the vernacular with a desire to dialogue with women.

Dante reformulated the cause of Beatrice's death by suggesting that it was due to her virtue rather than the deterioration of her body through disease:

Beatrice has gone to Paradise on high
Among the angels in the realm of peace,
And you, ladies, she has left comfortless.
No quality of cold caused her to die,
Nor heat, as brings to others their release,
But only virtue and great gentleness.[88]

Pierluigi Fiorini suggests that "[t]he poetic trajectory of *Vita nuova* is what carries Dante to call into question the medieval ideal of *courtly love*. . . ."[89] The earlier tradition is discovered as a "dead-end" that overwhelms the lover by uncontrolled passions and anxiety. For Dante, however, love is now revealed as having the power

84. Dante, *La vita nuova*, II, 29-30.

85. Dante, *La vita nuova*, II, 38-43, 30.

86. Dante, *La vita nuova*, XIX, 4-8, 55.

87. Dante, *La vita nuova*, XXV, 35-38, 73. Dante repeats his link with Cavalcanti and the use of vernacular later as well. See "I am quite aware, too, that my closest friend, for whom I write this work, also desired that I should write it entirely in the vernacular" (XXX, 14-16, 81).

88. Dante, *La vita nuova*, XXXI, 83.

89. Pierluigi Fiorini, "Beatrice, That Is, 'On Fidelity,'" *Communio: International Catholic Review* 24, no. 1 (Spring 1997): 86.

to ennoble, to elevate, and to order the soul in virtue. It was the dead, but living Beatrice, who helped Dante to discover this real nature of love in the dynamic relation between two persons.

At the end of the text, Dante describes a vision of a noble lady who led him to reach an important decision: "I hope to compose concerning her what has never been written in rhyme of any woman."[90] J. F. Took notes that at this point something changes in Dante's understanding of his intergender community of discourse with Beatrice: "Dante's promotion of the visionary and ontological over the moral and aesthetic" in the ordering of his love poems in the text suggests that in *La vita nuova* Dante is no longer writing about his love object as a metaphor, but as a real being whom he experiences "on the plane of ontological consistency."[91] Without stipulating what exactly Dante had in mind, it is generally thought that he discovered the plan for the *Divine Comedy* and Beatrice's role in the text.

Projecting a Wise Female Personification of Philosophy

Before turning to this penultimate work of Dante, we will briefly consider an intermediary work, *The Banquet,* in which Dante merges his love for Beatrice with his growing love of Lady Philosophy. Dante tells us that his work can be interpreted on at least two different levels: the literal and the allegorical.[92] The text concentrates on the meaning of love for a noble lady. In a remarkable way, Dante combines an appeal to Aristotle's metaphysics (all men by nature want to know) and Aristotle's ethics (virtue is a choice with respect to the mean) with Boethius's depiction of Lady Philosophy as the embodiment of wisdom.[93] The philosopher who desires to know falls in love with a noble lady who leads him into a life of virtue.

Dante gives a new definition of the Lady as a "noble soul in intellect and free in the use of its own power of reason."[94] Gertrude Leigh notes the significance of this redefinition of the identity of a Lady: "Of all the expressions interpreted by Dante to aid his readers the most remarkable is the word LADIES. His assertion that he used the word LADIES, not in the common sense, but to denote persons of intellectual ability, introduces an entirely new note into the story."[95] Nobility is no

90. Dante, *La vita nuova,* XLII, 5-8, 99.

91. J. F. Took, *Dante: Lyric Poet and Philosopher: An Introduction to the Minor Works* (Oxford: Clarendon Press, 1990), pp. 21-22.

92. He also mentions the moral and anagogical levels, but does not develop the latter two levels in his analysis. See Dante, *The Banquet,* II, i, 2-9, 42-43. See also Charles S. Singleton, "Two Kinds of Allegory," in *Dante: Modern Critical Views* (New York: Chelsea House Publishers, 1986), pp. 11-20.

93. For direct references to Aristotle see Dante, *The Banquet,* I, i, 1-2, 13; IV, canzone, 120; and IV, vi, 8-16, 135-36. See also Wilkins, *A History of Italian Literature:* "The *Convivio* as a whole is a very learned work, learned not only in the fields that are more specifically philosophical, but also in the science of the time, especially in astronomy. Aristotle, who is for Dante 'the Philosopher' *par excellence,* is his chief authority; but he draws also on the *Timaeus* of Plato, Euclid, the Neo-Platonic pseudo-Dionysius, Cicero, Seneca, Livy, Thomas Aquinas, the Latin poets, and, of course, the Bible" (p. 54).

94. Dante, *The Banquet,* III, xvi, 9, 114.

95. Gertrude Leigh, *The Passing of Beatrice: A Study in the Heterodoxy of Dante* (London: Faber and Faber, 1932), p. 34.

longer associated only with blood lines. Instead it is the heritage of one who acts well, who properly exercises practical reason. Dante describes central characteristics of virtue as joyful acts, as changing things for the better, as gaining friends, and as freely exercised.[96] These characteristics are present in the noble soul of a man or a woman, referred to simply as a Lady.

Dante tells us that in his first encounter with a particular noble lady, this free and joyful response was absent. Instead, he was thrown into turmoil, conflict, fear, and sorrow by the meeting of their eyes and then by their subsequent separation.[97] The meeting of eyes penetrates into his intellect and heart, the true ground for the encounter. Dante describes an interior dialogue, as he looks more closely at the object of his vision.

> It [the canzone] continues: See, too, how wise and courteous she is in her greatness. . . . It speaks of her being "wise": now what is more attractive in a woman than wisdom? It speaks of her being "courteous": nothing more becomes a woman than courtesy. . . . Courtesy and human goodness are one and the same thing. . . .
>
> The new thought says, "in her greatness." Social greatness, which is what is referred to here, most becomes a person when it is accompanied by the other two good qualities just spoken of, because it sheds a light that brings into clear relief the goodness of a person, or the opposite. . . .
>
> It goes on to instruct her (that is, my soul) to call that woman her lady from now on, promising her that this will bring her great happiness, when she becomes aware of the lady's manifold beauty. . . .[98]

After explaining the literal meaning of his poem, Dante then tells us that he discovered an allegorical meaning through meditating on Boethius's *Consolation of Philosophy* and Cicero's *On Friendship*. He concludes:

> Reflecting on these, I became firmly convinced that philosophy, who was the lady of these authors, these disciplines and these books, was something of supreme importance. I imagined it as having the form of a noble lady, and I could not imagine her with a bearing other than full of pity; consequently, my power to perceive truth found such delight in gazing on her that I could scarcely turn it elsewhere. Drawn by this image, I began to go to where she truly revealed herself, that is, to the schools of the religious and the disputations of the philosophers. . . . Finding myself, therefore, being drawn from the thought of my first love by the power of this other, I gave voice to the wonder I felt in the words of the above canzone, in which I describe my real situation under another guise.[99]

---

96. Dante, *The Banquet*, I, viii, 7-18, 28-29.

97. Dante, *The Banquet*. "My soul has three things to say about my eyes, three charges to lay against them. In the first place, it curses the hour when this lady saw them" (II, ix, 4, 61).

98. Dante, *The Banquet*, II, x, 7-11, 63.

99. Dante, *The Banquet*, II, xii, 5-8, 65-66.

Following upon this explanation, Dante returns to various lines in the poem to explicate their allegorical meaning.

In *The Banquet,* even though Dante uses concrete terms associated with the soul/body identity of a woman, his description of the Noble Lady Philosophy appears to be rather abstract. The following passage exemplifies his allegorical development of the qualities of Lady Philosophy:

> It should be borne in mind here that this woman is Philosophy, who truly is a woman full of sweetness, adorned with goodness, wonderful in wisdom, glorious in liberty, as will be made clear in the third treatise, whose subject will be her nobility. Wherefore it says *If anyone wishes to discover fulfilment, let him gaze into the eyes of this lady,* the eyes of this woman are her explanations, which, when directed into the eyes of the intellect, inflame with love any soul that is freed from the limitations of its present condition. O looks most sweet and ineffable, instant captivators of the human mind, who appear in the revealing of Philosophy's eyes when she discourses with her lovers![100]

Much controversy has surrounded Dante's decision never to complete this work. Dante does not tell us himself, although he hints that there is a proud harshness to the lady that causes him fear.[101] It may also be that as Dante tried to elaborate his schema of love for an abstract, almost Platonic ideal of Philosophy, that it became increasingly artificial.

Before completely abandoning his analysis, Dante moves back and forth between the literal and allegorical meaning of his text. In this movement he elaborates some key aspects of the Lady's identity. She "is not only the absolute perfection of human nature; she is more perfect still, in that she receives from the divine goodness beyond what is due to mankind."[102] When Dante turns to consider the literal interpretation of the body of the lady, he considers how the soul informs a face especially in the eyes and the mouth. Through this means of communication in the flesh, the noble spirit of the soul has a capacity to transform others by its quality. Dante concludes: ". . . I am indicating that her beauty has the power to renew nature in those who gaze on her. . . ."[103] The dialogue between the woman and the man takes place on many levels, through the meeting of eyes, in the quality of the smile and expressions on the face, as well as through hearing and speech.

Dante argues that a philosopher ought to become friends with this noble lady, who has "wisdom as her subject matter, love as her form, and the exercise of

100. Dante, *The Banquet,* II, xv, 3-5, 75.

101. Dante, *The Banquet.* "So when the soul says that the lady is proud, it is not speaking of her as she really is, but only as she appears to it, for the soul was fearful, and indeed still is, so that whatever I see when this lady perceives me seems harsh" (III, canzone, 78); and "I must abandon the sweet poems of love that have been my thoughts' constant quest, not because I do not hope to return to them, but because the disdainful and hard bearing that has appeared in my lady has barred my path to voicing my customary theme" (IV, canzone, 119).

102. Dante, *The Banquet,* III, vi, 9, 92. Dante suggests that her soul, or form, receives the goodness of God (III, vi, 13, 93).

103. Dante, *The Banquet,* III, viii, 20, 100.

contemplation as the composite of both."[104] When the friend and lover is joined with the noble lady, his soul becomes noble too because it "possesses intelligence and is free in virtue of its proper power, the reason."[105] This capacity and nobility of self-governance through the exercise of reason will be a theme constantly articulated by subsequent humanists. The fact that Dante associates it with a "Lady" through his imaginary depiction of the Noble Lady Philosophy, prepares the way for the association of these characteristics with other female characters in dialogues and then with actual women themselves.

Dante again repeats his earlier claim that "Wherever virtue is present, so, too, is nobility. . . ."[106] Qualifying the claim, he adds that the reverse is not the case, or wherever there is nobility, there is not necessarily virtue. The particular analogy he draws to explain this distinction is taken from Aristotle, and it implies a devaluation of women. He mentions that women and young boys seem to physically express shame when they betray a fault.[107] By including this example of a devaluation of women from Aristotle, Dante momentarily places himself in the Aristotelian tradition of gender polarity. He suggests that women are like immature men, or boys, in their expression of shame. However, this is the only place in the text where Dante offers a hint of gender polarity.

Much more significant is the fact that even though Dante refers to Aristotle throughout *The Banquet,* he often either ignores Aristotle's references to women, or inverts them. Two examples may suffice to make this point. Dante ignores the Aristotelian dictum that a woman's glory is silence, when he emphasizes the role of his female figures in dialogue. In addition, he ignores the Aristotelian characterization of woman as the inferior partner in friendship with man when he reverses the image and presents the man as the inferior partner in friendship with the lady.[108] Dante stands as an important intermediary figure with respect to Aristotle's concept of woman, for he accepts Aristotle's basic premises on many themes,[109] but he avoids adopting Aristotle's sex and gender polarity. On the contrary, Dante begins to formulate a completely new concept of woman as capable of using the intellect wisely, and as capable of forceful speech and virtuous action. In the figure of Beatrice and the figures of many different women in the *Divine Comedy* Dante conveys his fundamental thesis that women as well as men are responsible for the decisions and actions of their lives.

Before turning to a consideration of this text, we need to note one final aspect

104. Dante, *The Banquet,* III, xiv, 1, 112. See also ch. xi, 104-8.

105. Dante, *The Banquet,* III, xiv, 9, 114.

106. Dante, *The Banquet,* IV, canzone, 121.

107. Dante, *The Banquet,* IV, xix, 8-10, 171.

108. That Dante admires Aristotle is evident from the numerous quotations in *The Banquet* from a wide variety of Aristotelian texts. He also explicitly states: "I need only establish that Aristotle is entirely worthy of being trusted and obeyed for it to be clear that his words are of the greatest and most revered authority" (IV, vi, 5, 134). His text proceeds to prove this point. Dante was also favorable to St. Thomas's interpretations of Aristotle, as the numerous commentaries on Aristotle by the scholastic author indicate.

109. See Patrick Boyle, "Coming to Terms with Aristotle," in *Perception and Passion in Dante's Comedy* (Cambridge: Cambridge University Press, 1993), pp. 3-58.

of Dante's description of the relation between the philosopher and his Noble Lady Philosophy in *The Banquet*. Dante describes ways in which a lover and the beloved partake in one another's identity.

> Love, as we know from the consensus of the finest minds who treat of its meaning, and from what our own experience continually tells us, is what joins and unites the lover with his beloved. Hence Pythagoras' remark: "Friendship binds many into one." And since things that are united naturally communicate their qualities to each other, to such an extent that sometimes one takes on completely the nature of the other, we find the feelings of the person loved become part of the person who loves, so that the love felt by one is communicated to the other; similarly with hate, desire and all other feelings.[110]

In this passage Dante suggests a kind of gender unity in which "one takes on completely the nature of the other." This merging of identities may have been due to the abstract nature of lady philosophy in this text. It also seems that because Lady Philosophy has no body of her own, the distinction between the philosopher and philosophy disappears. Dante does recover from this appearance of gender unity at the conclusion of the text when he describes the friendship of the two as follows: "I say to the poem: 'Tell this lady: *My theme is your friend.*' Nobility is indeed her friend, for their love for each other is so deep that nobility always seeks her company, and Philosophy never turns her sweetest gaze elsewhere. What a wonderful and beautiful adornment is given to nobility in the final words of this canzone: to be called the friend of her who in her pristine form exists in the innermost depths of the divine mind."[111]

In contrast to *The Banquet,* where the identities merge, in *The Divine Comedy* Beatrice and Dante always preserve separate identities. Beatrice's imagined glorified body and Dante's imagined spiritual body maintain their unique and unrepeatable personalities even though they are united by love. We will now turn to this important work in order to briefly analyze some aspects of the concept of woman it contains.[112]

Being Taught by a Wise and Virtuous Woman

Dante's development of dialogue in the *Divine Comedy* takes place in the context of an imaginary journey through various states or levels of existence in Hell, Purgatory, and Heaven.[113] Throughout the journey, Dante converses with

110. Dante, *The Banquet,* IV, i, 2, 122.

111. Dante, *The Banquet,* IV, xxx, 6, 201.

112. For a different approach to the concept of woman in the text see Jaroslav Pelikan, *Eternal Feminines: Three Theological Allegories in Dante's "Paradiso"* (New Brunswick, N.J. and London: Rutgers University Press, 1990). Pelikan compares different eternal feminines in Lady Philosophy as Nurse and Leader, Beatrice as My Lady, the Church as Beautiful Spouse, and Mary as our Queen in Dante's *Paradise* with reference to his previous works as well. My own approach considers more the concrete interaction of the male and female characters than the eternal aspects of these interactions.

113. Jeremy Tambling notes, in *Dante and Difference: Writing in the "Commedia"* (Cambridge:

many men and women about their particular state in this "life after death" as well as about many philosophical, theological, and mystical themes.[114] In addition, he introduces three different guides for different stages of his journey, Virgil, Beatrice, and St. Bernard. Dante engages in extensive dialogue with these guides; and it is in these conversations that we discover his radically new development of a concept of woman as wise and virtuous.

Before considering the intergender dialogue between Dante and Beatrice in some detail, it should be mentioned in passing that some contemporary critics have analyzed Dante's concept of woman by offering a quantitative approach to the women mentioned in the *Divine Comedy*. For example, Anne Paolucci notes that: "The conscientious reader may, in fact, be somewhat startled to discover that the *Divine Comedy* contains close to three hundred references to women other than Beatrice."[115] While not denying the overall impression that women are not generally given as full a development as men in this great trilogy, our approach will emphasize ways in which the imaginary character of Beatrice includes many qualities that have previously not been given to a woman in western philosophy.[116] While Plato's Diotima and Boethius's Lady Philosophy incorporated some characteristics of wisdom and virtue, Dante's Beatrice goes further.

Beatrice is depicted as a human being whose glorified body and soul are fully integrated. In this way, the female figure of Beatrice concretizes Socrates' memory of his teacher Diotima and Boethius's abstract depiction of his imaginary dialogue with

---

Cambridge University Press, 1988), the originality in Dante's use of the imagination as follows: "There is room to think that Dante is original in his concept of the imagination, and that the sense in which he conceives of it here [in *Purgatory* XVII.13-18] — not as an internal sense, along with the memory and other such faculties, but as a mystical thing — is new . . . ; he is not interested in giving the *how* of imagination, rather in drawing attention to its power, as he does when he gives examples of its working in his own mind (lines 19-39), in visions. These visions are not new to him: *Vita Nuova* contains them, as it also has dreams. . . . Coming where it does, the account of the imagination seems an account of the whole *cantica*" (pp. 102-3). Dante's imaginary use of female characters, and his belief that through the imagination he can move outside of himself and into relation with an external reality, further strengthen the claim that the use of imaginary female characters to portray intergender dialogue can help bring about such dialogue between real men and women. For a general discussion of Dante's view about the potential of the imagination, see also Giuseppe Mazzotta, "Imagination and Knowledge," in *Dante's Vision and the Circle of Knowledge* (Princeton: Princeton University Press, 1993), pp. 116-34 and 152-53.

114. Two interesting articles on these themes are: Giuseppe C. Di Scipio, "The Hebrew Women in Dante's Symbolic Rose," *Dante Studies* 101 (1983): 111-21, and Rebecca S. Beal, "Beatrice in the Sun: A Vision from Apocalypse," *Dante Studies* 103 (1985): 57-78.

115. Anne Paolucci, "The Women in the *Divine Comedy* and *The Faerie Queene*," Ph.D. Diss., Columbia University, 1963, p. 12. See also Victoria Kirkham, "A Canon of Women in Dante's *Commedia*," *Women's Voices in Italian Literature, Annali D'Italianistica* 7 (1989): 16-41. Another study by Marianne Shapiro, *Women Earthly and Divine in the "Comedy" of Dante* (Lexington: University Press of Kentucky, 1975), based on her Ph.D. dissertation of the same title (Columbia University, 1968), emphasizes the difference between the qualities of women in the three different levels of the work.

116. In the *Feminist Encyclopedia of Italian Literature*, ed. Rinaldina Russell (Westport, Conn. and London: Greenwood Press, 1997), Regina F. Paski suggests that "[a]s critics continue to push at the limits of their analytical procedures, Dante's work will doubtless continue to yield up new perspectives on women as bearers *and* makers of meaning" (p. 62).

Lady Philosophy. As Dante moves upwards in his journey towards union with God, Beatrice's body becomes lighter through the infusion of grace and the life of the spirit, but she remains embodied throughout *The Divine Comedy*.[117] In particular, Dante describes the radiant beauty of Beatrice's face, with special emphasis on the quality of her eyes and smile, and on the lightness and gracefulness of her movements. Therefore, even though Dante's Beatrice is developed through the exercise of his imagination, there is the ontological assumption that the real Beatrice is actually living in this state after her death. Dante's great classic vividly depicts a belief in resurrection of the body along with dialogue and communion among men, women, and God after death.[118]

Beatrice serves as Dante's guide throughout this journey.[119] At the beginning of the descent into Hell he states: "A Lady summoned me. . . ."[120] Dante tells us that his will is in a state of ambiguity, "As one who wills, and then unwills his will, changing his mind with every changing whim, till all his best intentions come to nil . . .," and that he needs help.[121] The Lady identifies herself: "Beatrice am I . . ."; Dante responds: "Excellent Lady . . ." and the dialogue begins.[122] By the time they reach Heaven, Dante has learned the intellectual structure of fundamental truths about the human condition, he has confessed his own sins against Beatrice, and he has discovered that the essence of Paradise is to have one's human will "dwell in the divine will's radius" integrated with the wills of others where there are perfect stability and peace.[123]

117. Anne Paolucci gives her Ph.D. dissertation, "The Women in the *Divine Comedy*," a good summary of the difference in female bodies throughout the text. "The female body, twisted out of shape, or seen at its worst, reappears a number of times in the *Inferno* and *Purgatorio*" (p. 46) and "By the end of the *Purgatorio,* the female body takes on a grace which is manifested in a natural tendency to walk with dance-like steps. Whatever weight it has seems to have been distributed according to a new, spiritual, principle" (p. 48). She also studies the differences in clothes at each level.

118. One of the theses of this book is that the Christian belief in the resurrection of the body provides an underlying framework for a gender complementarity that is absent in a more dualistic Platonic approach, which tends towards a unisex model. Dante's description of his relation with Beatrice in the *Divine Comedy* seems to offer support for this claim.

119. The unusual place of a female character as guide in western thought at Dante's time is noted by Alison Morgan, *Dante and the Medieval Other World* (Cambridge and New York: Cambridge University Press, 1990), "The Guide," ch. 3, pp. 84-106. Morgan also notes the different functions of the guide as playing an essential part at the beginning and end of the narrative, as rescuing the visionary, as commissioning the visionary to tell others what he has seen, as leading the way, as interpreting the experience, teaching and rebuking the visionary as master to pupil. For a general description see Charles Williams, *The Figure of Beatrice: A Study in Dante* (London: Faber and Faber, 1943).

120. Dante, *The Divine Comedy. 1: Hell (L'inferno)* (Harmondsworth: Penguin Books, 1983), II, 53, 79. Marianne Shapiro suggests, in *Women Earthly and Divine in the "Comedy" of Dante,* that Beatrice ends with a loss of her female identity when she leads Dante to love of God. She states: "My study will follow the development of Beatrice's personality and her relationship to the protagonist in the direction of male ideas and attributes in terms of material protection fully subordinated to a masculine system of values" (p. 14). Dante's text maintains that the ultimate end is union with the Divine Trinity who transcends all gendered identity, a union in which each man and each woman has found his or her true identity, which includes a gendered component as signed in the resurrection of a particular glorified male or female body.

121. Dante, *Hell,* II, 37-39, 79.

122. Dante, *Hell,* II, 70 and 76, 80.

123. Dante Alighieri, *The Divine Comedy. 3: Paradise (Il Paradiso)* (Harmondsworth: Penguin Books, 1982), III, 79-82, 75.

This depiction of the strengthening and stabilizing of the will is developed in stages through the complementary enlightening of the intellect, so that as the perfect intellect chooses the true, so the perfect will chooses the good. Beatrice, as the intermediate guide in this process of Dante's education, teaches him about the intellectual structure of Christian values. After Virgil leads Dante through the levels of Hell and the multifarious ways a person can reject both the true and the good, he introduces Beatrice in the context of a discussion about the will and ethics:

> They who by reasoning probed creation's plan
>   Root-deep, perceived this inborn liberty
>   And bequeathed ethics to the race of man.
>
> Grant, then, all loves that work in you to be
>   Born of necessity, you still possess
>   Within yourselves the power of mastery;
>
> And this same noble faculty it is
>   Beatrice calls Free Will; if she thereon
>   Should speak with thee, look thou remember this.[124]

This emphasis upon the ability of the person's will and the internal power of self-mastery will become a central theme of humanist texts. That Dante should identify the naming of this faculty with the female character Beatrice is a new development in the concept of woman.

Dante's progress through Purgatory is marked by the recognition that there is a gap or wall between himself and Beatrice. Then they meet, and she asks him the question of how he was able to climb the mountain of Purgatory. This question led to a response of shame for his past infidelity to her shortly after her death. He faints from this shame and contrition; he is then revived, confesses to Beatrice, and is forgiven and purified. After this reconciliation, Beatrice begins to teach Dante more directly.[125] Balthasar captures the power of the intergender dynamic and especially of Beatrice's role in calling forth Dante's confession as follows: "The confession scene is not just an episode in the *Comedy;* it is the dynamic goal of the whole journey. And yet it is just as much the point of departure for Paradise. The fire of Beatrice burns Dante's soul to the quick and recasts it in pure light, and the immediate result is an unprecedented intimacy and boldness of access."[126]

Dante himself describes this renewed relationship as follows: "Thus Beatrice; and I, devoutly laid/Submissive at the feet of her command, /Gave mind and eyes to whatso'er she bade."[127] Here the master/student relation is the inverse

---

124. Dante Alighieri, *The Divine Comedy. 2: Purgatory (Il Purgatorio)* (Harmondsworth: Penguin Books, 1981), XVIII, 67-74, 207.

125. See Dante, *Purgatory,* XXVII, 36, 282; XXX, 74, 309; XXXI, 315-19; and XXXII, 85-87, 324.

126. Balthasar, *The Glory,* p. 61.

127. Dante, *Purgatory,* XXXII, 106-8, 325.

of that found in Cavalcanti; the woman is the master and the man is the student. Thus Dante offers a further development of the imaginary personification of wisdom, who is no longer the abstract Lady Philosophy of Boethius, but has become the concrete glorified Beatrice.

Sometimes it is suggested that Beatrice represents Faith and Virgil Reason, with the implication that the female figure does not give evidence of teaching through discursive reasoning. However, at the beginning of their journey through *Paradise,* Beatrice introduces the metaphysical concepts of Order, Form, and the natural principle of upward movement towards God:

> Then she began: "All beings great and small
> Are linked in order; and this orderliness
> Is form, which stamps God's likeness on the All.
>
> Herein the higher creatures see the trace
> Of that Prime Excellence who is the end
> For which that form was framed in the first place.
>
> And being thus ordered, all these natures tend
> Unto their source, or near or farther off,
> As divers lots their fashions blend. . . ."[128]

As Dante progresses upwards into the sphere of the planets and stars he asks Beatrice questions in natural philosophy such as: What causes the markings on the face of the moon? Beatrice enters into a debate with Dante that incorporates the most up-to-date scientific knowledge of the period. The ensuing dialogue offers the imaginative model of a woman who understands science and is able to explain it to others.[129] An extensive section will be quoted to give the flavor of the dialogue:

> "Lady," said I, "with most devout intent
> I give Him thanks who has advanced me so
> Out of the mortal world by this ascent.
>
> But tell me now, what are the marks that show
> So dusky on this body, and suggest
> The tale of Cain to people down below?"
>
> She smiled a little: "And if men have guessed
> Wrongly," said she, "where sense cannot avail
> To solve the riddle, though they try their best,
>
> Thee should the shafts of wonder not assail,

128. Dante, *Paradise,* I, 103-8, 56.
129. See Dante, *Paradise,* II.

> For, though sense lead the way, thou'rt now aware
> Of heights the wings of reason cannot scale.
>
> But thou thyself, how think'st thou? Come, declare!"
> And I: "What shows diverse at this great height
> Derives, I think, from bodies dense and rare."
>
> "Truly," said she, "thy thought is sunk outright
> In error; now, if thou wilt hear me through,
> I shall by argument refute it quite. . . ."[130]

Beatrice's argument proceeds for twenty-six more stanzas, during which it introduces empirical evidence from experiments with light and mirrors to come to its conclusion. The appeal to empirical evidence is significant because it implies that Beatrice is not simply teaching from infused knowledge of general principles, but that she understands the reasoning process for various principles. She challenges Dante: ". . . experiment shall set thee free — /That source whence all your science has to start."[131] This sequence is also one example that refutes the oversimplified common opinion that Virgil represents Reason and Beatrice represents Faith in the *Divine Comedy*.

Even when the imagined Beatrice teaches about Faith, for example, in her discussion of the creation of angels and the heavens, she introduces philosophical concepts:

> Pure form, pure matter, form and matter wed,
>   Came forth to being without blemish as
>   Three arrows from a three-stringed bow are sped. . . .
>
> Order, created with the Substances,
>   Distinguishing Pure Act from Potency,
>   As summit of the world established these.
>
> Pure potency was lowest in degree;
>   Midway came Potency with Act entwisted
>   By withy that shall ne'er unwithied be.[132]

So we find Dante incorporating many different aspects in his portrayal of the imaginary Beatrice. She is a master guide, she understands science, she understands metaphysics, and she understands ethics and politics; and she is able to teach others the fundamental truths and values in these philosophical areas.[133]

---

130. Dante, *Paradise,* 46-63, 64-65.
131. Dante, *Paradise,* II, 95-96, 66.
132. Dante, *Paradise,* XXIX, 22-25 and 31-36, 310.
133. Anne Paolucci describes in her Ph.D. dissertation, "The Women in the *Divine Comedy,*" Beatrice's use of philosophical concepts this way: "The moral regeneration depicted in the *Divine*

At the same time, Beatrice is also portrayed as a holy person, one who is filled with grace and in union with the Divine Will. In a remarkable way, Dante describes her physical beauty as it progresses in light and radiance through progressively higher levels of Paradise.[134] He understands the human body and especially the human face as a medium for the communication of the quality of the particular human soul. Dante watches her, and describes her changing countenance to the reader:

> This much I may report upon the case:
>   My heart from every other longing went
>   Completely free while I perused her face.
>
> For the Eternal Joy, its radiance bent
>   Direct on Beatrice and from her eyes
>   Reflected, held me in entire content.
>
> She with a smile that left my faculties
>   Quite vanquished, said to me: "Turn and give heed;
>   Not in my eyes alone is Paradise."[135]

Finally, Beatrice's transformation is so complete that Dante admits that it transcends his poetical ability to describe.

Summarizing the whole of his life, and the different moments of encounter with Beatrice, Dante reveals his newly discovered recognition of the new quality of his encounter with the woman who changed his life:

> Beauty past knowledge was displayed to me —
>   Not only ours: the joy of it complete
>   Her Maker knows, I think, and only He.
>
> From this point on I must admit defeat
>   Sounder than poet wrestling with his theme,
>   Comic or tragic, e'er was doomed to meet;
>
> For her sweet smile remembered, as the beam
>   Of sunlight blinds the weakest eyes that gaze,
>   Bewilders all my wits and scatters them.

Comedy is ultimately a matter of grace, of course; but it is described actually in terms of Platonic and Aristotelian ethics and reduced to the principle of properly directed love" (p. 197).

134. Fiorini, in "Beatrice," *Communio* 24, no. 2 (Spring 1997), compares this progressive transfiguration of Dante through his interaction with the radiant eyes and smile of Beatrice with the metaphysics of light of the Franciscan school (p. 93). My own analysis also emphasizes the interaction of the discourse between Beatrice and Dante.

135. Dante, *Paradise,* XVIII, 13-21, 214. For other examples of the power of Beatrice's transformed face, see also 55-69, 215-16; XXI, 1-6, 241; XXIII, 22-34, 257-58. See also Rachel Jacoff, "The Tears of Beatrice: *Inferno II,*" *Dante Studies* 100 (1982): 1-12.

Beatrice and Dante Contemplating Paradise Together

From the first hour I looked upon her face
    In this life, till that vision, I could trust
    The poet in me to pursue her praise;

Now in her beauty's wake my song can thrust
    Its following flight no farther; I give o'er
    As, at his art's end, every artist must.[136]

Beatrice then responds to Dante's discovery with an observation of her own. She identifies the seat of the love that now binds them as "intellectual" and transformed by good:

She, with achievement in her mien and tone,
    Resumed: "We have won beyond the worlds, and move
    Within that heaven which is pure light alone:

Pure intellectual light, fulfilled with love,
    Love of the true Good, filled with all delight,
    Transcending sweet delight, all sweets above."[137]

At the same time their love fills the intellect, it is also embodied in a man and a woman who express unique and specified gendered identities. Therefore, Dante's intellectual love does not slide into a gender-neutral or unisex model as might be found in the Platonic or Averroist traditions. It also avoids a gender polarity because of the fundamental presupposition of *The Divine Comedy* that all men and women are capable of this kind of relationship if they follow the path of self-mastery aided by the grace of God.[138] So Dante offers an imaginary dialogue that depicts a gender complementarity without directly arguing for it. For this reason, Dante's *Divine Comedy* provides an introductory framework for subsequent developments in gender theory in humanism.

We can summarize basic characteristics of wisdom and virtue that are associated with Beatrice and with Lady Philosophy in the works of Dante in the table that follows.

---

136. Dante, *Paradise,* XXX, 19-33.

137. Dante, *Paradise,* XXX, 37-42.

138. See Harold Bloom, Introduction, *Dante: Modern Critical Views* (New York: Chelsea House Publishers, 1986), p. 7. Bloom repeats various scholars' contentions that Beatrice is the guide for everyone and therefore is an objective, rather than purely subjective, model (p. 7). Anne Paolucci suggests that the female character leads not only intellectually but also through prayer. "It was Beatrice who brought Virgil out of Limbo to rescue Dante; but the pure-hearted woman in any walk of life, whatever her degree of grace, can effect miracles of this kind through prayer. It is no accident that in the *Divine Comedy* almost all prayers originate with women" ("The Women in the *Divine Comedy,*" p. 203).

Characteristics of Wisdom and Virtue in Dante's Imagined Beatrice	
Wisdom	Virtue
PREREQUISITES experience infused knowledge	PREREQUISITES free will, liberty, wisdom, intellectual love of true good
ACTUALIZED principles of science, metaphysics, theology, ethics, politics	ACTUALIZED courtesy, gentleness, human goodness, nobility, general virtue, friendship, beauty

While Dante considers many other specific virtues and vices in the context of his analysis of women in Hell, Purgatory, and Heaven, the above general categories are specifically attributed to Beatrice and occasionally in an allegorical manner to Lady Philosophy as well. In addition, the presence of wisdom and virtue in the woman, when shared through dialogue with a man, results in the man also becoming able to acquire these characteristics as well. So the intergender encounter has a constructive effect on a man's search for wisdom and virtue. It also presents an example of an intergender community of discourse to the women and men readers of the text. This imaginary projection then serves as a transitional model for actual intergender communities of discourse that will begin to emerge in western Europe.

FRANCIS PETRARCH (1304-1374)

While Cavalcanti and Dante participated in the humanist movement in an anticipatory way, Petrarch and Boccaccio are usually credited with being the official founders of Renaissance Humanism.[139] The depth and breadth of their works, particularly as immersed in classicism rather than scholasticism, established a new foundation for subsequent philosophy. This new foundation is significant for our study because both of these men dedicated a considerable amount of their writing to issues of gender; and both of them engaged in extensive personal dialogues with women. Their dialogue with women was personal and private, but it contained the seeds of change with respect to a philosophy of gender. In addition, their works give many examples of the creative use of the imagination to suggest new models of women that challenged the Aristotelian model of polarity. Their descriptions of differences between the two genders also challenged the Platonic unisex model. In these ways their writings helped end a first stage of development in humanist theory of gender and moved towards beginning a new foundation for gender

139. See Paul Oskar Kristeller, ". . . Petrarch has often been called the initiator of Renaissance humanism, but I should prefer to call him its first great representative, and he was probably the earliest humanist who had a significant impact on the thought of his time" (*Eight Philosophers of the Italian Renaissance* [Stanford: Stanford University Press, 1964], p. 5).

complementarity. In the final two chapters of this book, we shall see that this tendency is not entirely consistent, and that from time to time there are elements of unity and polarity present in early Renaissance Humanism, but the general movement is towards complementarity.

Although born in Arezzo, Italy of a notary from Florence who was a friend of Dante, Francis Petrarch lived much of his life in France. He attempted the study of law and the clerical life before setting a new direction for intellectual life in the fourteenth century. Petrarch compiled a major personal library of classical texts, traveled extensively to teach, established a wide correspondence, and wrote many works in Latin and Italian. One commentator states: "His Latin works initiated and gave shape to almost every important idea and attitude of Renaissance humanism."[140]

Petrarch brought into Renaissance Europe a new receptivity towards ancient and classical thought. "The formation of the idea that the people of the 14th century were separated from ancient civilisation by 1,000 years . . . was the origin of the conception of the renaissance, [and it] implied a complete reorientation towards the classical authors."[141] Eugenio Garin describes this reorientation as the origin of a "well-marked historical consciousness."[142] This rediscovery of antiquity provided a new point of view from which to evaluate one's own meaning and purpose in life. It involved both the formation of a detached perspective on the previous thousand-year history, and the careful learning of ancient languages and culture; it also impelled the humanists forward into a new sense of responsibility for the age in which they lived. Thus the humanists placed a great value on wisdom and ethics, and especially on civic life. Many of the humanists took an active part in politics and public life.

Francesco Petrarch particularly emphasized the importance of public forms of speech. He believed that the exterior expression of language in speech closely mirrored the quality of the soul of the person speaking. For Petrarch and others, conversation with other persons makes a man or woman more human. In a letter to Tommaso da Messina, on the study of eloquence, Petrarch elaborates his theory in some detail:

> The care of the mind calls for a philosopher, while the proper use of language requires an orator. We must neglect neither one. . . . The study of eloquence requires much time. . . .
>
> But once again you remark: "What need is there to work hard if everything advantageous to men has already been written during the past thousand years in so many volumes of a marvellous perfection by god-like talents?" Lay aside this anxiety, I say, and don't ever let it drive you into laziness. This fear was already removed by certain of our great ancients, and I shall remove it from the minds of those who come after me. Let thousands of years flow by, and let centuries follow

140. See "Petrarch," *The New Century Italian Renaissance Encyclopedia,* ed. Catherine B. Avery (New York: Appleton-Century-Crofts, 1972), p. 743.

141. Peter Munz, translator's introduction to Eugenio Garin, *Italian Humanism,* p. xxi.

142. Garin, *Italian Humanism,* p. 14.

upon centuries, virtue will never be sufficiently praised, and never will teachings for the greater love of God and the hatred of sin suffice; never will the road to the investigation of new ideas be blocked to keen minds. Let us therefore be of good heart; let us not labor uselessly, and those who will be born after many ages and before the end of an aging world will not labor in vain. What is rather to be feared is that men may cease to exist before our pursuit of humanistic studies breaks through the intimate mysteries of truth. Finally, if no sense of charity towards our fellow men drives us, I would still consider the study of eloquence of the greatest aid to ourselves rather than something to be held in the lowest esteem.[143]

Conversation can communicate across centuries and across genders, creating a new community of discourse that includes live persons and others who have long ago died but who live in various degrees in the imagination and in a communion of saints of sorts. Women's speech can elevate as much as men's speech. It can elevate others in service, and for Petrarch, it assuredly elevates the self. He speaks of the delight and inner transformation he received by repeating words and passages of the ancient authors and even of his own writings. Thus, it is not surprising that Petrarch, as the recognized father of humanism, brought a new understanding of intergender relations, both through his method and the content of his writing.[144]

Petrarch's theory of gender was influenced by several different sources. He admits to admiring Plato, calling him "the prince of philosophers."[145] However, Petrarch did not read Greek, so he had probably not read Plato even though he cherished an original copy of the *Republic* and *Laws* in his personal library.[146] As mentioned previously, the Platonic theory of gender identity was often mixed with a belief in reincarnation of a sexless soul. Petrarch rejects this view explicitly and calls it a "ridiculous doctrine of the transmigration of souls through many various bodies."[147] This fact is important for Petrarch's understanding of gender identity, for he considers Laura's identity fixed as female even after her death.

In his writings, Petrarch mentions Aristotle, Pythagoras, Porphyry, Hippoc-

---

143. Petrarch, *Rerum familiarium libri,* I, 9, 49. Garin summarizes Petrarch as: "The value of speech lies . . . in the fact that human conversation has the power to elevate" (*Italian Humanism,* p. 19).

144. This interpretation takes a very different direction than that identified by Isabella Bertoletti in her discussion of Petrarch in Russell, ed., *The Feminist Encyclopedia of Italian Literature.* She argues that Laura is a negative image for women, and that Petrarch's works were used to perpetuate a silence of woman's voice (pp. 241-43).

145. *Letters from Petrarch* (Bloomington and London: Indiana University Press, 1966), xviii/2, 153.

146. Charles Trinkaus, *The Poet as Philosopher: Petrarch and the Formation of Renaissance Consciousness* (New Haven and London: Yale University Press, 1979). Trinkaus notes that Petrarch owned a large manuscript of Plato in Greek, which included *Republic* and *Laws,* but since he could not read Greek, these texts were not available to him in the original (p. 11). Much of Petrarch's knowledge of Plato came through Cicero, who did not transmit Plato's theory of gender. See also Kristeller, who notes that Petrarch ". . . was the first Western scholar who owned a Greek manuscript of Plato sent to him by a Byzantine colleague, and in his attack on the authority of Aristotle among the philosophers of his time, he used at least Plato's name. This program was then carried out by his humanist successors" (*Renaissance Thought,* p. 58).

147. *Letters from Petrarch,* x/3, 91.

rates, Galen, Democritus, Heraclitus, Anaximenes, Anaximander, and Zeno.[148] Yet none of these philosophers seemed to influence him as much as did Cicero ("From my very childhood . . . I fell in love with Cicero's works")[149] and Augustine (". . . the sun of the Church").[150] Even though Petrarch gives credit to these previous thinkers, and while he constructs imaginary dialogues about gender with these ancient thinkers, Petrarch is original in his thinking, and does not directly imitate his predecessors.[151]

Petrarch's love of truth led him to reject academic philosophy as it was often practiced in universities. The degeneration of the use of intelligence from the struggle to find truth to the practice of winning an argument was a constant theme in his writings. In a letter to Tomasso de Messina, Petrarch wrote of his distaste for academic philosophers: "It is indeed from the fighting that they derive their chief pleasure; their object is not to discover the truth, but to prolong the argument!"[152] He compared the logicians of England to the Cyclopes, "a third race of monsters, armed with two-edged arguments."[153] His letter concludes: ". . . there is no spectacle more unseemly than a person of mature years devoting himself to dialectics. But if your friends begin to vomit forth syllogisms, I advise you to take flight."[154] Petrarch sought to found his philosophy on dialogue rather than dialectic, and on an existential, rather than abstract, foundation. This general shift of the method and content of philosophy will have implications for his discussions of woman's identity.

Significant for the philosophy of gender is Petrarch's critique of academic learning itself. For if higher learning itself is corrupt, and the new Renaissance Humanist scholar will work outside of academia, then the exclusion of women from universities turns out to be not such a negative situation for women, at least at first glance. Petrarch's critique of academia covers all the faculties of Arts, Theology, Medicine, and Law. He calls theologians "vile, babbling dialecticians,"[155] and physicians "the army of medicine in the guise of doctors, equipped with native ignorance under the name of science."[156] Petrarch also extends this critique of academia

---

148. *The Triumphs of Petrarch* (Chicago: University of Chicago Press, 1962), pp. 86-88.

149. *Letters from Petrarch*, xvi/1, 292. See also a letter concerning the building up of his library by asking travelers to various places in Italy, Germany, Spain, Britain, and Greece to buy books for him: "I would reply that I wanted nothing but books by Cicero . . ." (p. 295).

150. Petrarch, *Rerum familiarium libri I-VIII* (Albany: State University of New York Press, 1975), iv, 15, 214.

151. See his letter to Giovanni Colonna, *Rerum familiarium,* "Of the opinions of the Peripatetics certain ones please me, others hardly at all, for I do not love the sects, but the truth. Therefore I am at one time a Peripatetic and at another a Stoic and sometimes an Academic. Often, however, I am none of these, especially when something suspect appears in their writings which is opposed to our true and blessed faith" (vi, 2, 290). We will consider later the third dialogue of the *Secretum* in which Petrarch discusses his relation with Laura with an imagined Augustine.

152. *Petrarch's Letters to Classical Authors* (Chicago: University of Chicago Press, 1910), p. 218.

153. *Petrarch's Letters to Classical Authors,* p. 219.

154. *Petrarch's Letters to Classical Authors,* p. 223.

155. Petrarch, "On Various Academic Titles," *De remediis utrisque fortune, Book I* (Cleveland: The Press of Western Reserve University, 1967), p. 65.

156. *Letters from Petrarch,* v/3, 248.

to his own experience of law, about which he said: "In this study I spent a good seven years, or more properly, I lost them."[157] And most of all, he extends it to philosophers who ridicule ancient thinkers:

> Lately a school of dialecticians has arisen not so much ignorant as mad. Like a black army of ants, they have emerged from the recesses of some old rotten oak, devastating all the fields of sound doctrine. They damn Plato, and Aristotle, they laugh at Socrates and Pythagoras. Dear God, what things they say under the cover of their idiotic leaders![158]

So women who were not able to study Philosophy, Theology, Medicine, and Law at universities were not subjected to the distortions in the use of intelligence away from its proper end, which is the search for truth. Accordingly, for Renaissance Humanists, true education about wisdom and virtue began to occur outside of academia, in their private homes, around the dinner table, in their own libraries, and often in the context of intergender dialogue.

Most of Petrarch's writings about gender involve his reflections on a woman he called Laura. Although information is not complete, Laura appears to have been a married woman, and later mother of eleven children, whom Petrarch met in 1327. This woman refused Petrarch's sexual advances, while returning his love on the level of friendship and devotion. Petrarch lived with another woman whom he did not marry, but by whom he had a son Giovanni in 1337 and a daughter Francesca in 1343. However, his deep personal affection seems to always have been directed towards Laura. In 1348, twenty-one years after they first met, Laura died of the plague. By considering different aspects of his works both before and after Laura's death, we can discover the significance that Petrarch himself gives to the figure of Laura in his thought.

Encountering Laura's Wisdom and Virtue

In the first section of *Triumphs,* written between 1340 and 1344, Petrarch introduces the notion that Laura and he are caught in a relation in which she holds the power:

> The fair one whom I hunt eludes me still,
> careless of me and of my sufferings,
> proud of her power and my captivity.
> . . . Thus I am captive, and thus she is free.[159]

Significantly, Petrarch does not devalue Laura for her rejection of his advances. Instead he extols her virtue: "With her, and armed, was the glorious host of all the ra-

---

157. *Letters from Petrarch,* xvi/1, 293.
158. *Letters from Petrarch,* v/2, 246.
159. *The Triumphs of Petrarch,* 24-25.

Petrarch and Associates

diant virtues that are hers."[160] He describes Laura as defended by an army of virtues such as honor, modesty, prudence, moderation, benignity, courtesy, purity, and mature thoughtfulness. Petrarch concludes that Laura's army of virtues won the battle against erotic love.

> So moved she against Love, and favoured so
> By Heaven, and such a host of well-born souls,
> That he could not withstand the massive sight.[161]

The variety of Laura's virtues, in addition to her action of "moving against love," is significant, for they do not limit her to the traditional female virtues of the gender polarity tradition.

In fact, Petrarch often describes Laura as his teacher of both wisdom and virtue. In a dialogue entitled *Secretum,* written between 1342 and 1348 (although unfinished and not released until after his death), Petrarch uses Augustine to express the view that all love of women ought to be rejected because it necessarily ties a man to his sexual desires. The dialogue between Petrarch and the imagined Augustine concerning love between a man and a woman is quoted at some length because of the fundamental issues it raises. Petrarch refuses to give up his fundamental premise that a woman can help a man to grow in virtue and to discover who he really is:

> Petrarch: If my passion is for some low woman of ill fame, my love is the height of folly. But if, fascinated by one who is the image of virtue, I devote myself to love and honour her, what have you to say to that? Do you put no difference between things so entirely opposed? . . . Do you thoroughly know the matter you are to touch upon?
>
> Augustine: It is about a mortal woman, in admiring and celebrating whom you have, alas! spent a large part of your life. That a mind like yours should have felt such an insensate passion for so long a time does greatly astonish me.
>
> Petrarch: Spare your reproaches, I pray . . . you should be aware that she of whom you have set out to speak is a mind that has no care for things of earth, and burns only with the love of what is heavenly. . . .
>
> Augustine: Ah! out of all reason have you grown! Have you then for sixteen long years been feeding with false joys this flame of your heart? . . .
>
> Petrarch: You will never frighten me with talk like this; for I am not, as you suppose, infatuated with any creature that is mortal. You might have known that I have loved her physical charm less than her soul, that what has captivated me has been a life above that of ordinary lives. . . .
>
> Augustine: It is unquestionably true that oftentimes the loveliest things are loved in a shameful way. . . .
>
> Petrarch: I call to witness the spirit of Truth in whose presence we are speak-

---

160. *The Triumphs of Petrarch,* p. 40. "The Triumph of Chastity" was written at the same time as the first section of *The Triumphs,* "The Triumph of Love."

161. *The Triumphs of Petrarch,* p. 43.

ing when I assert that in my love there has never been anything dishon-
ourable, never anything of the flesh, never anything that any man could
blame unless it were its mere intensity. . . .

To her I owe whatever I am, and I should never have attained such little renown and glory as I have unless she by the power of this love had
quickened into life the feeble germ of virtue that Nature had sown in my
heart. . . .

Augustine: It is all false; and, first, what you say as owing all you are to her. If
you mean that she has made you what you are, then you certainly lie; but
if you were to say that it is she who has prevented you being any more than
you are, you would speak the truth. . . .

It is a false boast of yours that she has held you back from base things;
from some perhaps she may, but only to plunge you into evils worse
still. . . .

She whom you hold up as your guide, though she drew you away from
some base courses, has nonetheless overwhelmed you in a deep gulf of
splendid ruin. As for her having taught you to look upwards and separate
yourself from the vulgar crowd, what else is it than to say by sitting at her
feet you became so infatuated with the charm of her above as to studiously
neglect everything else?

And in the common intercourse of human life what can be more injurious than that? . . . Forsooth that woman to whom you profess you owe everything, she, even she, has been your ruin.

Petrarch: Good Heavens! How do you think you will persuade me of that?[162]

In the above dialogue we see the imaginary Augustine presenting arguments
extracted from his own struggle with erotic love as expressed in the *Confessions,* as
well as presenting the arguments common to traditional satirical literature: woman
is blamed for leading men astray. That this depiction is a misleading stereotype of
Augustine is important to note.[163] However, Petrarch holds fast to his argument
and his foil by insisting that instead of leading him away from his true end, Laura,
virtue is leading him because of her towards his true end. Petrarch suggests that his
love for Laura is not the same as Augustine's love for his mistress. It is a love not of
the flesh, but of virtue. Laura, by rejecting Petrarch's sexual advances, indirectly led
him to virtue.[164]

162. *Petrarch's Secret of the Soul's Conflict with Passion: Three Dialogues Between Himself and
S. Augustine* (London: Chatto and Windus, 1911, reprinted Norwood, Pa.: Norwood Press, 1976), Dialogue III, 110-24.

163. In addition to the more thorough account of Augustine's complex theory of sex identity in
The Concept of Woman: The Aristotelian Revolution (750 BC–1250 AD), for a more rounded view of Au-
gustine, see also Jean Bethke Elshtain, *Augustine and the Limits of Politics* (Notre Dame: University of
Notre Dame Press, 1995).

164. Aldo Bernardo suggests that Laura teaches Petrarch indirectly about truth in his early writings precisely by turning away from him, and in his later writings by turning towards him as a guide
who leads him directly to the truth, *Petrarch, Laura, and The Triumphs* (Albany: State University of
New York Press, 1974), p. 32.

The narrative character Augustine, however, is not convinced by Petrarch's arguments, and the dialogue continues:

> Augustine: She has detached your mind from the love of heavenly things and has inclined your heart to love the creature more than the Creator; and that one path alone leads, sooner than any other, to death.
> Petrarch: I pray you make no rash judgment. The love which I feel for her has most certainly led me to love God.
> Augustine: But it has inverted the true order. . . .[165]

Augustine keeps up his critical analysis of Petrarch's attachment for nearly forty pages of the text. He will not accept Petrarch's own judgment about its potential for growth in virtue:

> Augustine: Put away the childish things of infancy; quench the burning desires of youth. . . . Knowing what you do, are you not ashamed to see that your grey hairs have brought no change in you?
> Petrarch: I am ashamed, I regret it, I repent of it, but as for doing more, I cannot.[166]

Once again it is worth noting that Petrarch avoids devaluing woman even though he seems to admit that, as virtuous as his love may have been, it sometimes kept him from properly loving God. However, he takes full responsibility for this weakness, and in so doing maintains the full dignity of both man and woman.

The death of Laura, at the height of the plague during which reportedly 150,000 people died, seemed to release Petrarch's imagination even further from the rather tentative conclusion that is found in the *Secretum*. Marjerie O'Rourke Boyle notes that Petrarch records the exact date of Laura's death (calling her 'laurel') in Avignon in the flyleaf of his copy of Virgil.[167] While in the *Secretum* dialogue occurred between two male characters with respect to Petrarch's relation to a woman, in later works the dialogue occurs more directly between Petrarch and the imagined Laura. In "The Triumph of Death" he describes Laura's transformation as "That lady, glorious and beautiful, who, once a pillar of high excellence is now but spirit and a little earth."[168] Laura appears to Petrarch, who calls her "Madonna" and asks if she loves him. Responding affirmatively, Laura asserts that she complemented Petrarch in life and helped him to refine the intensity of his passions:

---

165. *Petrarch's Secret,* p. 124.

166. *Petrarch's Secret,* pp. 160-61.

167. Margerie O'Rourke Boyle, *Petrarch's Genius: Pentimento and Prophecy* (Berkeley, Los Angeles, Oxford: University of California Press, 1991), pp. 136-37.

168. *The Triumphs of Petrarch,* p. 53. See also *Petrarch's Lyric Poems: The Rime Sparce and Other Lyrics* (Cambridge, Mass. and London: Harvard University Press, 1976), pp. 11, 46, and *Petrarch's Bucalisum Carmen* (New Haven and London: Yale University Press, 1974), Epilogue XI, ll. 18-24, 187.

Sighing she answered: "Never was my heart
from thee divided, nor shall ever be.
Thy flame I tempered with my countenance.

Because there was no other way than this
To save us both, and save your youthful fame:
A mother loves, even with lash in hand."[169]

We have in Laura the inversion of the traditional gender polarity model of a woman as lacking authority over her irrational soul. Here, Laura is the virtuous, self-governed one and Petrarch is undisciplined and needing help. In traditional gender polarity, the woman was considered as weaker and less self-controlled and therefore needing to place herself under the guidance of a man of practical wisdom. Petrarch, through the voice of Laura, raises another possibility, namely that a virtuous woman is able to teach a disordered man how to temper his passions. If he can obey her, as a child obeys a mother, then he will be saved by this relationship. Laura acts like Socrates' Diotima, Boethius's Lady Philosophy, and Dante's Beatrice; through dialogue she challenges her interlocutor to further development. In the *Canzoniere,* lyric poems written in Italian, Petrarch continued to extol Laura's virtue and wisdom, which now radiate from Heaven.[170]

In 1341 Petrarch received in Rome the laurel crown as recognition of his writing. This great honor, the first such public ceremony at the Capitol in over a thousand years, brought a great personal triumph as well as Roman citizenship to Petrarch. Thenceforth Laura and the laurel branch interwove their significance in his works.[171] In the following passage we see Laura continuing to teach from Heaven by challenging Petrarch to overcome his self-pity and grief at her death:

"But what can I do except always weep, wretched and alone, who without you am nothing? Would I had died as a suckling in my cradle, so as not to experience the temperings of love!"

And she: "Why still weep and untune yourself? How much better it would have been to raise your wings from earth and to weigh with an accurate balance mortal things and these sweet deceptive chatterings of yours, and to follow me (if it is true that you love me so much), gathering at last one of these branches."[172]

169. *The Triumphs of Petrarch,* p. 64.
170. *Petrarch's Lyric Poems.* "How could God and Nature have put in a youthful heart so much virtue, if eternal salvation had not been destined for your good works? O one of the rare souls who lived nobly here among us and quickly flew up to Heaven afterward!" (#359, 556). See also #159, 304; #262, 424; and #291, 470.
171. An excellent discussion of the interweaving of these two concepts is found in Peter Hainsworth, "Laura and the Laurel," in *Petrarch the Poet: An Introduction to the "Rerum vulgarium fragmenta"* (London and New York: Routledge, 1988), pp. 135-53. See also Sara Sturm-Maddox, *Petrarch's Laurels* (University Park, Pa.: Pennsylvania State University Press, 1992). For discussion of the ceremony itself see Wilkins, *A History of Italian Literature,* pp. 82-83.
172. *Petrarch's Lyric Poems,* #359, 556.

Intergender dialogue about grief was common to the Stoic tradition. Seneca had challenged Marcia and Helvia in two situations of grief. In the *Consolation of Philosophy,* Boethius was challenged by the imaginary Lady Philosophy about his own situation of grief. And now Petrarch is challenged by an imaginary Laura about his grief over her death. However, there is an important difference in this last example from those of the Stoics. The early Stoics sought freedom from grief within a unisex model of the human being as capable of controlling the emotions, and Boethius wanted a union with the female personification of philosophy. Petrarch, however, desired union with a female person who was a complement to him. This complementarity was grounded in his belief in the resurrection of the body and the eternally differentiated identity of man and woman.

In "The Triumph of Eternity," written shortly before his death in 1374, Petrarch anticipates meeting Laura again:

> Before them all, who go to be made new,
> Is she for whom the world is weeping still,
> Calling her with my tongue and weary pen,
> But heaven too desires her, body and soul.
> . . .
> Happy the stone that covers her fair face!
> And now that she her beauty hath resumed,
> If he was blest who saw her on earth,
> What then will it be to see her again in heaven![173]

Petrarch is careful to state that Laura is not merely a sexless soul, or disembodied sexless spirit after her death. Instead, she is a woman transformed in body and soul, speaking to him, a man with a body and soul on earth. In this image Petrarch is addressing Laura in anticipation of the resurrection of the body at the end of time, and as a person with a unique and unrepeatable identity. Gender equality and differentiation are central factors in gender complementarity, and Petrarch suggests that this is the model he prefers.[174]

Describing Other Female Characters and Characteristics

It is important to note that Petrarch does not limit women's virtue to the figure of Laura alone. Nor does he want to imply, by extending the image of Laura to all women, that men are not as capable of virtue as women. In *Africa,* which was begun in 1338 and took Petrarch's entire life to complete, Scipio is developed as a male counterpart to Laura, as a supreme example of a virtuous person. Scipio, a

---

173. *The Triumphs of Petrarch,* pp. 112-13.

174. Ruth Kelso, in *Doctrine for the Lady,* reflects on the general interest in the lover rather than the beloved in Renaissance love poetry, and she identifies Petrarch as central to this tradition. However, when love is returned and the lover becomes also the beloved, then the balance is restored (pp. 152-53 and 206).

combination of Christian saint and a conqueror who defended Rome from 219 to 202 B.C., is presented as a model for the conversion of the contemporary Rome that was floundering in corruption.[175]

Just as men were hardly present in Petrarch's reflections on the meaning of Laura, so women are hardly present in his reflections on the meaning of Scipio.[176] Instead, females are present as the goddesses Cybele and Minerva.[177] Petrarch also uses the device of female personifications of Rome, Carthage, and Virtue.[178] Probably the most well-known female personification was Petrarch's character Reason in *De remediis,* who acts as a teacher and refiner of emotions much as Laura functioned in relation to Petrarch. One commentator gives the following cryptic assessment of this female personification: "Reason is indeed a most long-winded bluestocking, whose advice is too rationalistic for modern taste."[179] However, it would seem that the association of discursive reasoning even with an imaginary female personification could open the possibility in the reader's minds of this possible concept of wisdom for women.

In an extension of this female voice, in Book I of the *De remediis* (i.e., Remedies against Prosperous Fortune), Reason ridicules the abundance of books, fame of writers, the Master's degree, and various academic titles. And in Book II (i.e., Remedies against Adverse Fortune), Reason describes how to overcome adversity of birth and meager fare. While the text itself does not differentiate between individual men and women, it has application to women's situation of exclusion from the privileges of the academic life because of their birth as female. The *De remediis* was extremely popular for several centuries. Charles IV, the Emperor of Germany, invited Petrarch to read it to him, Chaucer used it as part of the "Clerk's Tale" and the *Troilus,* and it was used as a model by Martin le Franc, who wrote *The Champion of Women* in the fifteenth century.[180]

It is important to note that Petrarch does not prove anything by his particular uses of female personification as a literary device. Female personifications are used both positively (i.e., Reason) and negatively (i.e., Fortune) in his works.[181] In a letter to Tommaso del Garbo he clarifies his use of the female personification of fortune and demonstrates his awareness of simply using it as a literary de-

175. For a description of the corruption that Petrarch identified, see *Petrarch's Book Without a Name* (Toronto: The Pontifical Institute of Mediaeval Studies, 1973), pp. 38, 78, 82-83, and 109-12. This collection of nineteen letters was taken from the *Familiares* out of fear of the reaction they might have caused.

176. The only women who function as ordinary figures in this work situated in a male military context were a woman who commits suicide after being raped and another woman who is murdered by her husband. See *Petrarch's Africa* (New Haven and London: Yale University Press, 1977), Book 3, ll. 922-28, 67; and Book 5, ll. 759-65, 103.

177. See *Petrarch's Africa,* Book 3, ll. 288-300, 49-50; and Book 3, ll. 248-55, 48. Cybele is the mother earth, and Minerva, the Roman counterpart of Athena, is a virgin soldier.

178. See *Petrarch's Africa,* Book 7, ll. 673-83, 159; ll. 905-10, 165; ll. 940-42, 166; and ll. 965-79, 167.

179. F. N. M. Diekstra, Introduction, *A Dialogue Between Reason and Adversity: A Late Middle English Version of Petrarch's "De remediis,"* Book II (Assen: Van Borcum and Comp., N.V., 1968), p. 43.

180. Diekstra, Introduction to *A Dialogue,* p. 24.

181. See *Petrarch's Secret,* Dialogue II, 85.

vice.[182] However, it seems that there is a potential benefit for the concept of woman, when a particular female personification of reason is developed in such detail as to provide an imaginary model of a wise and reasonable female character. The reality does not seem so impossible as when no such models exist. A similar argument can be made for female personifications of virtues and of vices.

Sometimes it is suggested that the presence of idealized imaginary models of female personification can hinder the development of real women with these characteristics. However, Petrarch is exceptional for his desire to shift the locus of thought about virtue from imagination into reality. In the following extract from a letter to Francesco Nelli he states what is taken to be one of the basic principles of humanism: "Our habit of speech is meaningless; we must truly philosophize, turning words into facts, if we hope to be saved by the fact. We must fasten our minds to the fact; we must feel what we speak."[183] Petrarch offers many examples of turning words into facts, particularly with reference to the practice of virtue. In the following extract from a letter he wrote to Cardinal Giovanni Colonna, he emphasizes that the actual virtues of his two sisters are more important than the description of virtues in historical or imaginary figures:

> There are those who exalt unique Roman matrons of old with unique praises, and indeed ascribe to Lucretia chastity, to Martia seriousness, a holy inspiration to Venturia, the ardor of conjugal love to Portia, a sober joyousness to Claudia, dignity to Livia, a noble firmness of mind to one of the Cornelias, an attractiveness of conduct and language to the other.
>
> Then there are those who have honoured other foreign women with their praises, admiring the honesty of Penelope, undying love in Artemesia, tolerance in Ipsicratia, fortitude in Thamyras, judgment in Thetis, modesty in Argia, devotion in Antigone, and constancy in Dido.
>
> I should like to have these admirers of ancient women see your sisters Giovanna and Agnes. They would indeed find in one home ample matter for praise, nor would they have to wander through all the lands and through so many centuries in their search for feminine honours. Whatever they seek anywhere in scattered form they will find in these two women.[184]

In the above passage we see Petrarch's Renaissance Humanist return to the ancient classics to reflect on contemporary virtue. More importantly for the concept of woman, however, is the striking variety of virtues he ascribes to women: seriousness, dignity, noble firmness of mind, honesty, tolerance, fortitude, and judgment. These virtues share none of the devaluation so common to the Aristotelian association of weakness with women. On the contrary, they partake of the highest virtues described for men. In addition, they do not emphasize the theological virtues of faith, hope,

---

182. See *Letters from Petrarch.* "Nor do I fear being called unscholarly if I allege that there is no such thing as fortune. . . . To refer to the things commonly attributed to chance or Fortune I accepted the old name, in order not to involve the reader in linguistic arguments and prejudice him against the writing and the writer" (viii/3, 358).

183. *Letters from Petrarch,* i/3, 255.

184. Petrarch, *Rerum familiarium,* II, 15, 114.

charity, or chastity. Instead, they fall solidly into the philosophical tradition of cardinal virtues developed through practice, good judgment, and proper choice of will.

In another example in a letter addressed to Laelius, Petrarch writes about his admiration for the virtue of some Roman women on pilgrimage to Santiago de
Compostela who refused to accept his offer of half of his traveling money. He held
them up as examples of virtuous persons who overcame the natural tendency towards
greed: "These Roman ladies gratefully acknowledged my good will, while nobly refusing my offer of money."[185] Once again he describes these women as capable of making
good choices, and acting virtuously, out of "the true character of a Roman Lady."[186]

In Petrarch's correspondence we have two very interesting examples of reflections he made on the relation of feminine and masculine characteristics and the
character of a woman. These reflections are significant because they give evidence of
a beginning sense of interior depth in a woman and of the relation of characteristics
culturally considered as feminine or masculine and a particular woman who might
either have or not have these characteristics. The first example concerns a woman
who does not have what is culturally considered a feminine characteristic, while the
second example concerns a woman who has what is culturally considered masculine
characteristics. It is notable that Petrarch recognizes that he needs to make a new
judgment in these situations, and further that his judgment is completely without
blame or devaluation of the woman under consideration. In this way, Petrarch, the
Father of Humanism, offers an outstanding example of a man who expands the narrow univocal association of male with masculine and female with feminine which
had led to satirical responses when these characteristics were inverted.

In a letter to Francesco Nelli, Petrarch describes his woman servant whose
physical appearance is not at all "feminine":

> If you see her you would think you were gazing on the Libyan or Ethiopian
> desert, a face so dry within, so sunburnt, sustained by no vital juices. If Helen
> had had such a face, Troy would still be standing. . . . But don't let my description
> of her face detract from proper appreciation of her character. Her soul is as white
> as her face is dark. This is a fine case in evidence that a woman's ugliness does
> not impair the soul. . . . My peasant woman has this peculiarity, that, although
> beauty is regarded rather as a feminine than as a masculine attribute, she feels the
> lack of beauty so little that she would seem to regard beauty as a deformity.[187]

Petrarch continues his letter by describing the virtues of his servant: hardworking,
tireless, uncomplaining, caring for others, unconcerned with herself, and ascetic in

---

185. See *Letters from Petrarch*. At the end of his reflection on these women he compares them
with ancient examples of women of virtue: "So we said farewell and separated. And then first I realized
where I was; for during the conversation I had the feeling that I was in Rome, with Cecilia, wife of
Metellus, Fulvius's Sulpicia, Cornelia of the Gracchi, Cato's Marcia, Scipio's Emilia, and a whole
troop of illustrious women of old times, or (more suitably for present times and the special circumstances) the Christian virgins of Rome, Prisca, Praxedis, Prudentiana, Cecilia, and Agnes" (xvi/8, 141-
43).

186. *Letters from Petrarch*, 142.
187. *Letters from Petrarch*, xvi/8, 122-23.

her living and eating habits. She was full of the virtues of temperance, fortitude, and charity. It is the quality of character, springing from the use of the intellect and will in the soul, that Petrarch admires in this woman. Significantly, he does not devalue her because of her physical appearance, which is not "feminine," nor does he conclude that she was "like a man." Rather he came to the judgment that she was physically ugly, but with a beautiful soul. Socrates often received a similar type of evaluation. In reaching this conclusion, Petrarch preserved gender distinctions while adhering to a theory of equality of virtue for women and men.

In the second example of his reflections on the place of masculine and feminine characteristics in a woman's character, Petrarch describes in a most vulnerable way his embarrassment at discovering a woman who exhibited culturally "masculine" characteristics of courage in the midst of pain and fortitude during an exhibition of physical strength. Yet he does not devalue the woman. Rather, he struggles with his own responses to this discovery. In a letter to Cardinal Colonna, Petrarch describes his experience of a woman warrior from Pozzuoli:

> Her name is Mary. . . . Her body resembles rather that of a soldier than a virgin, her strength is such as to be desired by veteran soldiers, her dexterity is rare and unusual, her vigorous age, condition and enthusiasm are those of a powerful man. . . .
>
> She wages an hereditary war with her neighbours in which already a large number have perished on both sides. Sometimes alone, often attended by a few others, she comes to grips with her enemy, and to this day she has always emerged the victor. . . . She endures hunger, thirst, cold, heat, wakefulness, and weariness with incredible patience. She spends her nights under the open sky and travels fully armed. . . .
>
> There are many fabulous stories told about her; I am repeating only what I saw. Powerful men from different parts of the world had assembled. . . . Having heard the reputation of the woman, they were driven by the desire to test her strength. Hearing about this, we all agreed to ascend to the fortress of Pozzuoli. She was walking in front of the doors of the church in deep meditation which caused her not to notice our approach. We approached her to ask her to supply us with some kind of proof of her strength.
>
> At first excusing herself for some time because of pain in her arm, she finally ordered that a heavy stone and an iron beam be brought to her. After she had thrown it into the centre of the group she urged them to try lifting and competing. To be brief, a long contest ensued among equals, and everyone tried his hand as if in great rivalry while she acted as observer judging the strength of each of the men. Finally, with an easy try, she showed herself much superior to all, causing stupefaction in the others and shame in myself. . . .
>
> For me this sight of this woman has rendered more believable whatever is narrated not only about the Amazons and that once famous kingdom, but even what is told about the virgin female warriors of Italy, under the leadership of Camilla whose name is the most renowned of all.[188]

188. Petrarch, *Rerum familiarium*, V, 4, 240-42.

So in this remarkably detailed account Petrarch describes a woman with "masculine" virtues. He does not devalue her, or ridicule her in a satirical manner, but concludes that she is like other women warriors in the past.[189] Even though he was embarrassed because she was stronger than the men who were present in the contest, Petrarch respected her identity as a woman. This indicates that his acceptance of the two components of equal dignity and difference was fundamental enough to tolerate a wide range of culturally masculine and feminine characteristics without rejecting the differentiation of gender identity within either a polarity or a unisex model.

Petrarch influenced a number of female Renaissance Humanists by his poetic method, by his turning towards moral philosophy, and by his rejection of academic forms of dialectic. Ingrid Rossellini notes that: ". . . Petrarchism became wildly popular among female poets. Women became cultural interlocutors and active subjects of artistic production. . . ."[190] Christine de Pizan, Marguerite de Navarre, Laura Cereta, and other lesser-known women humanists bear witness to Petrarch's influence on the explosion of a new method for practicing philosophy.[191] Some of the contributions of these women will be considered in subsequent chapters in this book.

The question of the interaction of Petrarch, Dante, and Boccaccio is also important for the consideration of early humanist theories about gender. Petrarch and Dante were both exiled from Florence because of political battles in 1301, and they both described a woman as their prime model of virtue. Petrarch's Laura and Dante's Beatrice both died during the plague. Both men were poets, but Petrarch wrote primarily in classical Latin (except for his *Canzoniere* and *Trionfi*) and Dante is credited with having first given literary form to the Italian language.[192]

Even though Dante met his Beatrice in 1274, and Petrarch his Laura in 1327, Petrarch was not influenced by his predecessor's description of Beatrice as Heavenly Guide in the *Divine Comedy*. In fact it was only late in his life, at the urging of Boccaccio, that Petrarch read this work.[193] Petrarch tells Boccaccio: ". . . My sup-

---

189. See Jean Bethke Elshtain, *Women and War* (New York: Basic Books, 1987) for a thorough discussion of the unusual history of women warriors in the West.

190. Russell, ed., *The Feminist Encyclopedia of Italian Literature,* p. 255. Rossellini also notes the influence on Petro Bembo, who wrote *Gli asolani,* the first dialogue that describes an actual discourse among men and women.

191. See William J. Kennedy, "Petrarchan Textuality: Commentaries and Gender Revisions," in *Discourses of Authority in Medieval and Renaissance Literature* (Hanover, N.H. and London: University Press of New England, 1989). Kennedy considers the way in which "Petrarch's complex gendering of Laura, . . . contributes to the poem's productive instability," which in turn invites later poets such as Louise Labé in her humanist commentaries in 1555 to enter into the discussion herself (p. 156).

192. However, Wilkins argues in *A History of Italian Literature* that Petrarch's Italian compositions were of an outstanding quality (pp. 92-100).

193. *Petrarch's Letters,* p. 183. He tells his young friend that he had avoided reading Dante: "I feared, however, in view of the impressionableness of youth and its readiness to admire everything, that, if I should imbue myself with his or any other writer's verses, I might perhaps unconsciously and against my will come to be an imitator." However, Sara Sturm-Maddox argues in *Petrarch's Metamorphoses: Text and Subtext in the Rime Sparse* (Columbia: University of Missouri Press, 1985) that ". . . the poetic *prise de position* represented by [Dante's] *Vita nuova* could not have escaped Petrarch's attention;

posed hate for this poet, which has been trumped up by I know not whom, is an odious and ridiculous invention."[194] He encourages the younger man, Boccaccio, to keep writing in the vernacular even though Dante's genius for Italian was well known.[195]

The mutual influence of Petrarch and Boccaccio was very great. In addition to Boccaccio's introducing Petrarch to the work of Dante, and Petrarch's encouraging Boccaccio to keep writing in Italian, Petrarch directed Boccaccio away from a fascination with vices and the corruption of the fourteenth century towards a more committed life of virtue.[196] In turn, Boccaccio sent his older friend a copy of the *Decameron* to read. Petrarch was so taken with the final story of Griselda that he translated it into Latin shortly before his death.[197] While the story of Griselda will be considered in the next part of this chapter, in the discussion of Boccaccio's *Decameron,* let it suffice to say here that she is an "abused" woman who remains faithful to a cruel, evil husband in spite of a series of incredibly vicious acts. Petrarch remarks: "Anyone, it seems to me, amply deserves to be reckoned among the heroes of mankind who suffers without a murmur to God, what this poor peasant woman bore for her mortal husband."[198] Lest it be thought that Petrarch was implying that obedience was a supreme virtue only for women, he states explicitly to Boccaccio that he admires the story of Griselda because it has implications for men as well as women:

> My object in thus re-writing your tale was not to induce the women of our time to imitate the patience of this wife, which seems to be almost beyond imitation, but to lead my readers to emulate the example of feminine constancy, and to submit themselves to God with the same courage as did this woman to her husband.[199]

---

its impact on his own practice demonstrably transcends the many isolated instances of imitation in individual poems to inform the fundamental strategy of collecting his vernacular lyrics into a second 'story' of amorous and poetic experience [in the Rime sparse]" (p. 42). The text also contains two chapters comparing Laura and Beatrice (pp. 39-94).

194. *Petrarch's Letters,* p. 182. Petrarch concludes: "Far from scorning his work, I admire and love him" (p. 184).

195. *Letters from Petrarch,* v/2, 242-44.

196. See, for example, *Petrarch's Letters,* p. 189.

197. *Petrarch's Letters,* pp. 192-93. Petrarch at first comments on the general structure of the text: "At the beginning you have, it seems to me, accurately described and eloquently lamented the condition of our country during that siege of pestilence which forms so dark and melancholy a period in our history. At the close you have placed a story which differs entirely from most that precede it, and which is so delightful and fascinated me that I was seized with a desire to learn it by heart. . . ." Then Petrarch comments on his decision to translate the story of Griselda into Latin: "I sincerely trust that it will gratify you that I have of my own free-will undertaken to translate your work, something I should certainly never think of doing for anyone else, but which I was induced to do in this instance by my partiality for you and for the story."

198. *Petrarch's Letters,* p. 194.

199. *Petrarch's Letters,* p. 194. The story of Griselda, as translated by Petrarch, had further influence through Chaucer's use of it in "The Clerk's Tale."

Once again we find Petrarch suggesting that women can demonstrate basic virtues of courage and constancy as well as, if not better than, men. His models are counterexamples of the usual gender polarity descriptions of women's inconstancy, weakness, and timidity. So even in his responses to the writings of other thinkers, Petrarch presents a humanist perspective that suggests a model of gender complementarity.

If we summarize Petrarch's identification of specific virtues associated with women, both in his imaginary depictions as well as in his descriptions of real women, we find a long list that includes many virtues articulated by classical authors. The list, made by extracting his characterizations from the passages identified in his works above, includes the following: honor, modesty, courtesy, reasoning, prudence, benevolence, honesty, tolerance, mature thoughtfulness, seriousness, noble firmness of mind, constancy, and the "masculine" attributes of dexterity and physical strength. We can see that several of the virtues act as counterexamples to the Aristotelian model already described. The intellectual virtues of reasoning and prudence counter the virtue of true opinion; the virtues of firmness of mind and constancy counter the characterization of women's inconstancy; and the description of masculine virtues in women, without destroying their gender identity, counter the identification of 'masculine' with the male and by analogy, 'feminine' with the female. In these ways, Petrarch continued the reformation in the concept of woman that we have identified as beginning within early Italian Renaissance.

GIOVANNI BOCCACCIO (1313-1375)

Among all the early humanists, Boccaccio's concept of woman is the most controversial. Some critics think Boccaccio ridiculed and devalued women because he believed that they had a destructive influence on men.[200] Others praise Boccaccio for his liberating view of women's role in public life.[201] There is no doubt that Boccaccio is an extremely complex author whose multiple and often ambiguous works play their own part in fostering these seemingly contradictory impressions.

The particular approach that I will take to Boccaccio is not one that scholars have emphasized; namely, I will try to demonstrate that one of Boccaccio's greatest contributions to the concept of woman is his introduction of many different forms of intergender dialogue. This argument will consider both the form as well as the content of Boccaccio's contribution. Although Boccaccio's female characters in his

200. See, for example, the classification of Ruth Kelso, *Doctrine for the Lady,* pp. 282-83.

201. See, for example, Cynthia Constance Capone, "The Representation of Women in Boccaccio's *Decameron,*" Ph.D. Diss., Rutgers University, 1992. "By closely examining Boccaccio's works and ideas, chapters three and four will show the innovation he introduced and the progress he made in the question of women's roles in comparison to the works of an earlier age" (dissertation abstracts). Pamela Joseph Benson's book *The Invention of the Renaissance Woman* has only just come to my attention. Her evaluation of Boccaccio's contribution to the theory of woman's identity is very close to my own (University Park, Pa.: Pennsylvania State University Press, 1992).

numerous dialogues are all products of the imagination, they nonetheless represent the beginnings of overcoming bias about intergender dialogue. Thus they introduce an imagined possibility of a kind of gender complementarity in the areas of wisdom and virtue that helps prepare the way for real women to choose these values for themselves. For this reason, although Boccaccio's works contain some elements of polarity and devaluation, his overall contribution to the concept of woman is predominantly positive. Rather than summarizing all of Boccaccio's descriptions of women, my own approach will be to describe only those aspects that are innovative with respect to the history of the concept of woman. Before analyzing Boccaccio's concept of woman, I will begin with a brief description of his life and of significant influences on his intellectual development.

Boccaccio was born out of wedlock, possibly in Paris; his father, a merchant, soon moved to Florence and later to Naples. Nothing definite is known about his mother, and Boccaccio's early writings often invent romantic notions about his heroes that appear to offer a semi-autobiographical remedy for the social and legal impediments of illegitimacy.[202] Boccaccio did not remain illegitimate for long, for his father, Boccaccino, soon married Margherita de' Mardoli and legitimized his son Giovanni.

Perhaps as a legacy of his inherited illegitimacy, Boccaccio rejected legitimate birth as being an important source of nobility. He believed that it was not the rank or social status of a person that ought to be admired. Rather, like Dante, Boccaccio believed that virtue alone was the quality of character that could be called "noble."[203] Increasingly, Boccaccio became convinced that virtue is rooted in the ordering of natural instincts through the exercise of reason. A man or woman who achieved this integration of self was a true noble.

Boccaccio's education began at home with a tutor who taught him reading, writing, Latin, and history. Thinking he would join his father's business, he studied mathematics; and when he was fourteen, Boccaccio served in Naples as an apprentice in banking and merchandising and was introduced to aristocratic and courtly life. Eventually he went to the University of Naples to study Canon Law, during which time he grew to have an extreme dislike for lawyers.[204] Boccaccio de-

---

202. For example, we find in the *Nymphs of Fiesole* a son is generated by the union of a man with a nymph; in *Filocolo* the hero Galeone is generated by a merchant and the daughter of the King of France; and in *Amorous Fiammetta* the character Pamphilus has a Parisian girl as his mother. Boccaccio's mother was often thought of as being French, as his father often traveled to Paris. While some sources claimed that Boccaccio was born in Paris, it is now suggested that he was actually born in Florence. See Vittore Branca, *Boccaccio: The Man and His Works* (New York: New York University Press, 1976), pp. 6-7.

203. See Robert Hastings, *Nature and Reason in the Decameron* (Manchester: Manchester University Press, 1975). "Nobility to Boccaccio is a question not of class or money but of *character*. . . . True nobility, like true virtue (for it is the same thing) dwells within the self and cannot be conferred or withdrawn by the external forces of the social order" (p. 86).

204. See, for example, Giovanni Boccaccio, "Against Ignorant Lawyers," in *The Fates of Illustrious Men* (New York: Frederick Ungar Company, 1965): "From such schools . . . have repeatedly come counsellors, judges, and advocates, with hands tainted, eyes wandering, license unrestrained, heart stony, sincerity a pretence, tongue honeyed, teeth like iron, and in sort, with an insatiable passion for gold" (p. 96).

veloped a taste for poetry, which became his consuming passion. The young poet came to believe that while the practice of law led to vice, the study of poetry could lead to virtue; and while lawyers love money, poets love "Lady Poverty."[205]

More importantly, in the *Genealogia* Boccaccio argued that poetry "constitutes a stable and fixed science founded upon things eternal, and confirmed by original principles."[206] These fundamental principles are accessible to the reader at all times and places. Boccaccio argued that poets and philosophers have the same destination, but that they arrive at it by different paths; and while a philosopher uses syllogisms and arguments, a poet works "wholly without the help of syllogism, veils it [his thought] as subtly and skillfully as he can under the outward semblance of his invention."[207] At the same time, Boccaccio sees poetry and stories as able to make visible the reality that is behind this veil.[208]

Boccaccio became convinced that the poet had a special role to play in educating people towards virtue. He argued that: "Poets are not corrupters of morals. Rather, if the reader is prompted by a healthy mind, not a diseased one, they will prove actual simulators to virtue."[209] It is important to consider Boccaccio's self-understanding of his role as poet in this context of study of his concept of woman. As he abandoned his goal of becoming a partner in his father's business and turned to a career in literature, his use of the vernacular, his accessibility to the woman reader, and his attacks on academia all contributed to the education of middle-class men and women outside of the traditional universities. Women had direct access to his poetry and prose, and subsequently to the philosophical principles they contained.

It is also important to note the significance of the Black Plague, which cut right through the middle of Boccaccio's literary career. In the years 1347-1348 massive numbers of people died in as short a period as three days. Over half the population of Europe, three quarters of the population of cities like Siena, Pisa, and Florence died.[210] Boccaccio describes 100,000 people dying in Florence from contracting the disease between the months of March and July. He lost many friends and his parents. The dead and dying were lying in the streets without anyone to help them out of fear of contagion. The plague contributed significantly to the moral deterioration of society all over Europe. Thus many of Boccaccio's imag-

---

205. *Boccaccio on Poetry: Being the Preface and the Fourteenth and Fifteenth Books of Boccaccio's "Genealogia Gentilium"* (Indianapolis and New York: Bobbs-Merrill, 1956), pp. 28-32.

206. *Boccaccio on Poetry*, p. 25.

207. *Boccaccio on Poetry*, pp. 78-79. This quotation begins polemically: "A few of the enemies of poetry . . . say that poets are but the apes of the philosophers. . . . If they but understood the works of the poets, they would see that, far from being apes, they should be reckoned of the very number of philosophers. . . . For though their destination is the same as that of the philosophers, they do not arrive by the same road."

208. Grassi, *Heidegger and the Question of Renaissance Humanism*. "Boccaccio's thesis is that poetry reveals the reality that lies behind a veil *(velamen)* which when brought to light, permits the 'thing,' the *res*, to appear in unhiddenness" (p. 21). See also "Accordingly, the *demonstratio* that is the concern of Boccaccio's definition ('fabula est . . . demonstrativa locutio') is not a rational proof as in logic, but a making visible of something, an immediate 'showing'" (p. 22).

209. *Boccaccio on Poetry*, p. 74.

210. Wilkins, *A History of Italian Literature*, p. 81.

inary characters simply reflected the rather dismal state of society at the time. At the same time, the suffering and fear of such a catastrophic event also helped others to dig deeper into their own identities to determine what values they wanted to live by, what kind of persons they wanted to be in the time that remained for them. The breakdown of society also offered opportunities for new kinds of relationships and new structures. It is in this context that the concept of woman received a different sort of articulation in Boccaccio's works.

Petrarch had a very direct influence on Boccaccio's development as a humanist. Boccaccio was aware of his mentor's contribution to philosophical literature before their first meeting. Charles Stinger argues that "Humanism in Florence traces its beginnings to Giovanni Boccaccio . . . [and an] encounter with Petrarch in Florence in 1350 . . . [who] was en route to Rome for the Jubilee. . . ."[211] The two humanists also met on Petrarch's return, when he actually resided with Boccaccio. These meetings proved to be crucial for Boccaccio, who tried unsuccessfully to convince Petrarch to actually move to Florence. However, shortly after they met, Petrarch introduced Boccaccio to the work of Seneca, Cicero, and Augustine.

Throughout the next twenty-four years until Petrarch's death the two men met regularly, corresponded, and directly influenced one another's ideas and work. Boccaccio said about his mentor: "Last and greatest of my authorities is Francis Petrarch, my revered teacher, father and master."[212] The great bond between these two friends was also recognized by Petrarch, who lamented: "Would that we might have lived together! Thus habit would have made us a single mind in two bodies."[213] Their own dialogue, then, formed part of the context of the development of the new humanist philosophy.

Boccaccio was also influenced by Dante, who had died when he was eight but whose reputation in Florence surrounded Boccaccio during his early youth.[214] In his first work, *La Caccia di Diana*, Boccaccio imitates Dante's list of the sixty most beautiful women in Florence by writing a poem about the sixty most beautiful women in the Angevin court in Naples. Then towards the end of his life, in a short work entitled *The Life of Dante*, Boccaccio continually defends Dante's decision to write poetry: "He perceived that poetical creations are not vain and simple fables or marvels, as many blockheads suppose, but that beneath them are hid the sweet fruits of historical and philosophical truths, so that the concepts of the poets cannot be fully understood without history and natural phi-

---

211. Charles L. Stinger, "Humanism in Florence," in *Rewriting the Renaissance: The Discourses of Sexual Difference in Early Modern Europe*, ed. Margaret W. Ferguson, Maureen Quilligan, and Nancy J. Vickers (Chicago and London: University of Chicago Press, 1986), p. 179.

212. *Boccaccio on Poetry*, p. 115.

213. *Letters from Petrarch*, v/2, 239. The whole quotation reads: "For although there were never two more harmonious minds than yours and mine, often, to my surprise, our acts and decisions are far different. . . . I find no better reason than that Mother Nature made us alike, but that habit, which has been called a second nature, makes us unlike. Would that we might have lived together! Thus habit would have made us a single mind in two bodies." This letter was written in 1364, in the context of Petrarch's irritation at Boccaccio for burning some of his youthful poems.

214. Boccaccio's stepmother Margherita de Mardoli was related to the family of Beatrice, the young woman with whom Dante had fallen in love.

losophy."[215] In addition to following a path similar to Dante's, Boccaccio also chose to write in Italian.[216] He argues that Dante chose to use the vernacular "to be of more general use to his fellow-citizens and to other Italians."[217] Boccaccio was so enamored with Dante's *Divine Comedy* that he had copied the entire *magnum opus* by hand and sent it to Petrarch to read; and during the final years of his life, Boccaccio gave a series of lectures on the *Divine Comedy,* the first to do so in an official public lectureship established by the government of Florence.[218]

Boccaccio's vernacular works and literary style made his particular kind of philosophy available to women who were outside of academia and without training in Latin texts or the technical scholastic form of argumentation. A further factor, that many of the characters in Boccaccio's works were female, also helped invite women to become part of philosophical communities of discourse that were beginning to develop among humanists of the upper and developing middle classes. He invited his readers to become active members of the community of discourse he was describing in his texts. Thus, Boccaccio's intergender community of discourse reached out and gathered women and men from many historical periods into an ongoing conversation about human values and the consequences of different personal choices.

Romantic love for and of women played an extremely important role in Boccaccio's early writings. In addition, Boccaccio's creativity as a writer of new forms of literature pushed the theme of love into the forefront of the consciousness of the literary public. Wilkins notes the many innovations in Boccaccio's early works: the first Italian hunting poem, *La Caccia di Diana* (1336-1338); the first Italian romance in verse by a non-minstrel, *Filostrato* (1339-1340); the first Italian prose romance, *Filocolo* (1337-1339); the first Italian idyll, *Nymphs of Fiesole* (1346-1349); the first Tuscan epic, *Teseide* (1340-1342); and the first Italian psychological romance, *Amorous Fiammetta* (1344-1346).[219]

After the effects of the Plague in 1348 and after meeting Petrarch in 1350, Boccaccio wrote about women not so much from the perspective of romantic love, but more from the aspect of their character. We see this development in *Decameron* (1352), *Genealogy* (1350-1360), *Concerning Famous Women* (1355-1368), *Corbaccio* (1354 or 1365), and *On the Fates of Illustrious Men* (1358-1360).[220]

215. Giovanni Boccaccio and Leonardo Bruni Arento, *The Earliest Lives of Dante* (New York: Frederick Ungar Publishing Co., 1963), p. 16. In this later text he tends to blame women as well as men for men's licentiousness: "O little strength! O bestial appetite of men! What influence cannot women have over us if they will, since without caring they have so much?" (p. 59). He also blames Dante's unhappy marriage on women by claiming that if a woman is beautiful, then she will no doubt give into adulterous solicitations, and if she is unattractive, she will become bitter and angry. He concludes: "Let no one suppose that men should not marry. On the contrary, I decidedly commend it, but not for everyone. Philosophers should leave it to wealthy fools, to noblemen, and to peasants, while they themselves find delight in philosophy, a far better bride than any other" (pp. 24-25). Boccaccio himself never married.

216. Some of his poems were in Latin. See Giovanni Boccaccio, *Ecologues* (New York and London: Garland, 1987), which has parallel Latin and English texts.

217. Boccaccio, *The Earliest Lives,* pp. 67-68. Boccaccio did return to Latin in his later life.

218. Wilkins, *A History of Italian Literature,* p. 110.

219. Wilkins, *A History of Italian Literature,* p. 102.

220. For an argument that Boccaccio was primarily a moral philosopher throughout his life,

In addition, Boccaccio's decision to study the character of some women who had actually lived marks a further new development in the history of the concept of women. It begins the shift from imaginary to existential associations of wisdom and virtue with women. However, even in the text *Concerning Famous Women,* imaginary and real women and events are mixed up together in such a way that it is difficult to conclude that Boccaccio has provided an accurate history of women. Nevertheless, his attempt to do so inspired Christine de Pizan, who then began the process of writing an engendered history of women. So even if Boccaccio was historically inaccurate by mixing together sources of imaginary and real women, his attempt to develop a collective history of women is important for our topic. It continued to contribute to the development of the historical consciousness that had begun with Petrarch.

Boccaccio's primary contribution to the history of the concept of woman is his use of the imagination to develop multiple examples of female characters, his placing many of them in the context of intergender discourse, and his use of them to present arguments for a new humanist conception of virtue. Although there is much in Boccaccio's writings that repeats traditional gender polarity arguments, and while there is also much in his work that appears to focus on and even encourage vice, when a careful analysis is given to the actual form and content of his texts, we discover a definite advance in the philosophical concept of woman.

Boccaccio's works often portray decadent themes. Much of Boccaccio's *Decameron* contains a heavy satirical element directed towards all kinds of people. His most prominent theme is concupiscence. This is evident in most of his early romantic works, and in the *Decameron* his one hundred stories (one story told each day for ten days by ten different people) frequently portray scandalous behavior in which men and women follow some unrelenting passions without regard for their social consequences. The extent to which Boccaccio goes in these descriptions sometimes appears to support the practice of vice rather than to encourage the reader to practice virtue. He also appears to insult the institutions of marriage and religious life. These facts make it difficult to demonstrate fully the rather significant contribution he has made to the history of the concept of woman.

At the same time, underneath the frivolity and beyond his satire *Corbaccio,* which we considered in the previous chapter, Boccaccio recognizes in women something more than did previous authors. He describes women in as realistic a way as he describes men. Women become revealed as subjects rather than simply idealized objects of desire or devalued objects of rejection by men. Women are imagined as concrete existential subjects engaged with men in finding significant values for their lives.

Boccaccio had a great sense of humor, and he delighted in using his wit in his writing. Wilkins describes his most important text as follows: "The *Decameron* is in the main a book of laughter — laughter that runs the full gamut from gentle merriment to raucous obscenity."[221] It is important to note, however, that Boccaccio does

---

rather than just the second part of his life, see Robert Hollander, *Boccaccio's Two Venuses* (New York: Columbia University Press, 1977).

221. Wilkins, *A History of Italian Literature,* p. 109.

Boccaccio Holding a Book

not laugh at women as much as laugh with women and with men about especially humorous situations they usually bring upon themselves by decisions they make. He wrote for purposes of entertainment, and in this context, humor has its proper place. Still, because humor often works with exaggerations or inversions of stereotypes, as we noted in our consideration of satires, Boccaccio's works are open to misunderstanding. In addition, as is often the case with humor, sometimes he slips over the line and falls into ridicule.

Our analysis will consider three different aspects of Boccaccio's discussions about the wisdom and virtue of women: (1) in his early characterizations of "Fiammetta," (2) in his different female characters in the *Decameron,* and (3) in different women described in *Concerning Famous Women.* Boccaccio's satirical view of woman, as presented in the *Corbaccio* in the previous chapter, will be reintroduced in the context of his other works. When the whole corpus of his contributions to the philosophy of sex and gender is included, it will be easier to evaluate the meaning of his ironic satire.

Dialogues with Fiammetta about Wisdom and Virtue

One of the key imaginary female characters in Boccaccio's early works is named "Fiammetta." A common legend suggests that in the spring of 1336 in a Franciscan Chapel in Naples, Boccaccio met the daughter of King Robert, Maria d'Aquino, who was at the time married to another man. He soon entered into a short affair with her, and after a brief flirtation she rejected him for another man.[222] If this legend is accurate, it would follow a pattern already described of Dante's passion for Beatrice and Petrarch's passion for Laura, both of which began with a relationship with a real woman. These relationships then spawned the development of imaginary female characters in various dialogues.[223]

In one of Boccaccio's early dialogues, *Filocolo* (Thirteen Most Pleasant and Delectable Questions of Love), we find, among nine men and four women characters, Fiammetta who is crowned with a garland by Ascaleon:

> Because she (as without doubt I know) is plentifully endowed with every grace, adorned with beauty and virtue and endowed further with a flowing eloquence, I therefore make choice of her to be our queen.[224]

Fiammetta rules over the ensuing dialogue, which considers questions about the nature of love. This topic follows the one set by Cavalcanti in theme, but it differs in form from the intergender dialogue that occurred in the "Lady asks me." Instead of the female contribution consisting only in posing the original set of questions, Boccaccio has the questions posed and discussed by a variety of female and male characters.

In one selection, a female character named Cara asks: "To which of three aspirants should a lady give her preference? To him who excels in valour, or to him

---

222. This legend, while accepted by most scholars, is contested strongly by Branca in *Boccaccio*. "Aside from the absence of any indication or reference to so illustrious a personage in the most exact genealogies and in the many documents of the Aquino family, the seductive profile of Fiammetta has revealed itself to be entirely fictitious and constructed according to the most common canons of the love literature of the time, canons which scrupulously dictate the details and the chronology of the story of love set down by Boccaccio for himself and for his Fiammetta (who in harmony with those traditions must remain ever young: so that in the *Filocolo* she was born in 1310, in the *Comedia* after 1313, in the *Decameron* after 1321)" (p. 29). For a further study of the debate about the real Fiammetta, see Janet Levarie Smarr, *Boccaccio and Fiammetta: The Narrator as Lover* (Urbana and Chicago: University of Illinois Press, 1986), and Thomas B. Bergin, *Boccaccio* (New York: Viking, 1981), pp. 105-6.

223. All of Boccaccio's early works related in some way to this relationship. For example, Boccaccio's *Filostrato*, which was composed immediately before the *Filocolo*, follows up the theme of the effects of lovesickness that had been expressed previously by Guido Cavalcanti and by his mentor Dante. It also was the basis for Chaucer's *Troilus and Criseyde* and Shakespeare's *Troilus and Cressida*. While the theme of his relationship with Maria d'Aquino was central to the work, the name "Fiammetta" was not used.

224. Giovanni Boccaccio, *Thirteen Most Pleasant and Delectable Questions of Love (Filocolo)*, trans. Henry Carter (New York: Clarkson H. Potter, Inc., 1974), p. 13. Fiammetta responds to this selection as Queen with humor and discretion: "Truly, you have not in due sort provided a queen for these amorous people that have more need of a most able kind, for of all you who are present I am the most simple and of the least virtue. Neither is there any one of you that is not more suitable to be invested of such a crown than I am. But so it thus pleases you, I cannot withstand your election" (p. 15).

who is most courteous and liberal, or to him who is wisest?"[225] Fiammetta then answers:

> There is not one of the three that does not merit the love of a fair and gracious lady. But because in this case we are not to fight against castles, or to give away the kingdom of great Alexander or the treasures of Ptolemy, we say that both of you and every other woman ought rather to give her love to a wise man than to any of the rest. For love and honor are with discretion to be kept a long time, being maintained neither by force nor courtesy, but only by wisdom.[226]

Not only does Fiammetta seem to have a knowledge of history and science, she also makes a wise and virtuous choice. So this imaginary female character presents a counterexample to bias about women's inadequacies in these areas.

A different kind of question is proposed by a male character Galeone, who asks: "Is love a good or evil thing?" Fiammetta, following Aristotle's distinction between three kinds of friendship (virtue, pleasure, and utility), attempts to distinguish three kinds of love: honest love, love for delight, and love for utility. Then she argues that:

> [Love for delight is] that to which truly no person who desires to lead a virtuous life ought to submit himself. For it is the depriver of honors, a troublemaker, unveiler of vices, and the general contributor of hopeless anxieties.[227]

It is at this point that an intergender dialogue begins. Galeone counters Fiammetta's negative valuation of love for delight by stating:

> That it is the increaser of virtue, I hope to make apparent to you by all that follows. Thus love, of which we reason does work this property in human hearts, that once disposing the mind to a thing that pleases it, spoils the same of all pride and all fierceness, humbling its victim in the doing.[228]

Fiammetta makes an important distinction that clarifies the irony of Galeone's theory. She suggests that true virtue demands the ordering of instincts by reason and not humility by the overcoming of reason:

> Misguided Galeone, greatly deceived are you in your opinion. . . . And it is no wonder, because as far as we understand, you are enamoured beyond all hope. Without doubt, the judgment of the enamoured is absolutely false. Having lost sight of the mind's eye, so too have they banished reason as their utter enemy. . . . For this love you defend is nothing less than unreasonable desire sprung from a passion that enters the heart through wanton pleasure.[229]

---

225. Boccaccio, *Filocolo,* p. 36.
226. Boccaccio, *Filocolo,* p. 36.
227. Boccaccio, *Filocolo,* p. 89.
228. Boccaccio, *Filocolo,* p. 90.
229. Boccaccio, *Filocolo,* p. 91.

She then concludes this part of the dialogue with an even more explicit statement about the proper relation of the delight of romantic erotic love to a life of virtue:

> Those that follow Love will be led by him to all evils. If, by chance, his followers perform any virtuous acts (which happens very seldom) they do so with premeditated and corrupt desire, to the end that their loathsome wills be fully satisfied as quickly as possible. Such virtues might rather be called vices, for what man does must never be considered singly. . . .
>
> The beginning of this love is none other than fear, the sequel is sin, and the evil thereof is grief and nothingness. It ought then to be fled and to be reproved. Fear to have him in you for he is violent, and no one knows of what excesses he is capable, so devoid is he of all reason. He is without doubt the destroyer of the mind.[230]

If the dialogue ended here, the reader might think that Boccaccio, through the character of Fiammetta, was opposed to romantic love. However, Fiammetta suggests that people learn this lesson too late, and that more often than not, a person ought to simply submit to love: "And since we are caught in his nets, therefore until the light that guided Aeneas out of the dark ways as he fled the perilous fires may appear to us, it is better for us to follow him and be guided submissively to his pleasures."[231] This ironic reversal is typical of Boccaccio, and it catches the reader off guard, drawing him or her even more deeply into the discussion. This gives the appearance that Galeone has persuaded his companion in dialogue about the force of his own position.

However, Boccaccio does not end the dialogue there. He takes it one step further. At the very end of the *Filocolo,* after answering the thirteenth question about love, Fiammetta concludes that, while a person should not be blamed for giving in to natural desires, the better, more virtuous path is to be able to control natural desires through the exercise of the intellect and will.

> To follow the laws of nature when they cannot be fled is of no matter. But to obey the positive laws is a virtue of the mind. And the virtues of the mind are to be preferred both for greatness as well as for every other respect before the natural inclinations.[232]

This conclusion would be more consistent with Boccaccio's later thinking about virtue. However, if we leave open the question of the proper interpretation of the conclusion of this text, we can at least see that it opens a real dialogue between imaginary male and female characters and posits a positive image for the female, who employs discursive reasoning, humor, astute observations of human behavior, and educated knowledge of history to make her points of view known and able to be discussed. In addition, we also find the reversal of the traditional association of

230. Boccaccio, *Filocolo,* pp. 94-95.
231. Boccaccio, *Filocolo,* p. 95.
232. Boccaccio, *Filocolo,* p. 142.

the irrational with the female and the rational with the male. Here the female character represents ordered reason, while the male character represents giving in to irrational desires.

Boccaccio's *Teseida* (The Book of Theseus) is dedicated to Fiammetta.[233] This early work is notable for several different reasons. First of all, it introduces the theme of women warriors, the Amazons. In this context, Boccaccio indicates his awareness of masculine and feminine engendered identities. He will return to this theme at the end of his life when he writes about different famous women. In the *Teseida* he plays with the theme with both humor and seriousness. Often, his reflections indicate a traditional Aristotelian gender polarity and describe how especially Hippolyta, the Queen of the Amazons, serves as a counterexample:

> Although she was womanly and incomparably beautiful, she assumed command. Setting aside her feminine timidity, she disciplined her troops so well that she made herself and her kingdom secure. She was so confident of her power that she did not depend at all on the neighboring tribes.[234]

Hippolyta addresses her own women warriors with similar words when they are about to be attacked by Theseus' army from Greece. She says to them: ". . . you dare to perform manly, rather than womanly, deeds"; and ". . . you have practiced with your weapons constantly, at the same time spurning all womanish behavior."[235]

Even more interesting is the fact that Boccaccio places in Hippolyta's speech two principles of gender polarity common to the Aristotelian tradition, and she notes that they do not apply accurately to the Amazons. In the first, she notes the ethical principle of obedience as a virtue for women: ". . . the great Theseus is planning to attack us, deeming us troublesome because we are not satisfied while remaining subject to men and obedient to their whims like other women."[236] In the second, she refers to the natural principle of woman as a deformed man: "For they did not treat us as if we had been born of the same kind of seed as they were, but we please them little more than if we had been engendered of monsters, or oak trees, or even caves."[237]

In the story, the two sides battle with one another with various military strategies, and with many deaths. For a while the Amazons appear to be winning, and then Theseus and his warriors. When Theseus begins to use an underhanded military tactic, Hippolyta challenges him directly: "You have not behaved like a knight who takes up a just war against an equal. But like some treacherous cheat. . . ."[238] The woman challenges the man to greater virtue. In the end, a peaceful accord is made, and Boccaccio turns the story into a romance with the women and men marrying for love and remaining faithful in friendship.

233. Giovanni Boccaccio, *The Book of Theseus (Teseida)* (New York: Medieval Text Association, 1974), pp. 335-39.
234. Boccaccio, *The Book of Theseus,* #9, 21.
235. Boccaccio, *The Book of Theseus,* #24 and 25, 24.
236. Boccaccio, *The Book of Theseus,* #26.
237. Boccaccio, *The Book of Theseus,* #29, 25.
238. Boccaccio, *The Book of Theseus,* #104, 40.

The concept of woman as wise and virtuous was developed even further in the character of the nurse in *Amorous Fiammetta* (also known as *The Elegy of Madonna Fiammetta*).[239] In this story Fiammetta is not presented as wise and virtuous. Instead she is a female character who consistently gives in to her irrational desires. A new character called "the nurse" represents a mature, ordered person, capable of compassion and serious thought, able to explain the reasons for virtuous actions, and equally able to put those acts into practice.[240] The two female models are put forth by Boccaccio in such a way as to suggest that the quality of one's life is a matter of choice, and not of simple gender identity. We will develop the dialogue in some detail, because it takes place between two female characters in a manner that is novel in the western tradition.

The basic story of *Amorous Fiammetta* revolves around a married woman Fiammetta who falls in love with a single man named Panphilus. They have a short affair, he betrays her, and eventually marries another woman. Fiammetta spends the remainder of her life grieving and hoping for a reconciliation. Fully attached to her affair, she neglects her own husband and family, and even considers suicide. In the midst of these events a dialogue arises between Fiammetta and her nurse, who consistently tries to teach Fiammetta how to make better choices.

Fiammetta begins her story by describing the way that falling in love led her to lose control over herself.

> Wherefore remaining in just content with my loving husband, I lived a most happy and joyful woman, until furious love with a secret kind of unknown fire, and never felt of me before, entered into my tender and young breast. . . .
>
> And certain if the Gods, who deduct all things to some known and certain end, had not taken away my understanding, and bereaved me of my due knowledge, I might have still been my own woman. But all such considerations laid aside, I followed my sensual appetite, and quickly persuaded myself to yield to love.[241]

Fiammetta describes her progressive boldness that led her to give up everything to satisfy her desires. It is at this point that the nurse's contribution to the dialogue introduces the themes of wisdom and virtue:

239. This text is referred to as the "first psychological novel of Europe." See "Boccaccio," *Encyclopaedia Britannica* (1945), vol. 3, p. 766. It is also interesting to note that it has many of the characteristics of Augustine's *Confessions* without its redeeming choices. The first novel written by a woman (or man) outside of western Europe is the thousand-page opus called *The Tale of Genjii* written by Lady Murasaka (b. 978).

240. My interpretation of the character of the nurse differs from Katherine Heinrichs's "Lovers' Consolations of Philosophy in Boccaccio, Machaut, and Chaucer," *Studies in the Age of Chaucer* 11 (1989). Heinrichs states: "The nurse is the 'mouthpiece of reason' only to a point; like Troilus, she proceeds from correct premises to a false conclusion. Ultimately, both she and Fiammetta furnish exemplars of willful moral blindness" (p. 96). See also "Certainly the nurse proves a poor substitute for Lady Philosophy. In Boethian terms, she is right about Cupid, but she is wrong about Fortune" (p. 98).

241. Giovanni Boccaccio, *Amorous Fiammetta* (Westport, Conn.: Greenwood Press, 1970), pp. 3 and 13. I have rendered some of this text and subsequent passages from the same text into more modern English.

You see, or (at the least if you will) may see, that in following your own fancies, you have (as it were) a certain kind of desire to ruin the highness of your birth, to obscure the great and shining fame of your manifold virtues. . . . You should not truly have so much as a thought of idle love, neither do I think (if like a wise woman you do but take counsel of yourself) that you will, nor can you busy your mind about it.[242]

The nurse introduces the concept of a choice that comes from dialogue within the self and an exercise of the will.

However, Fiammetta responds that she has lost the capacity of reason to orient her will:

O dear Nurse, well do I know that these things which you tell me are most true, but frantic fury compels me to follow that which is my bane; and my guilty mind, over-rash in its desires, attempts in vain to put your counsel in practice, because that which reason wills me to do is overcome by unruly will, which most mightily does dominate in me. Love with his deity does possess my heart, and there, with his mighty sovereignty overrules my subject mind.[243]

She then gives herself over to the pagan deities of Venus and Eros rather than try to exercise her will in accordance with reason as the nurse has suggested. In this submission to pagan deities, Fiammetta accepts a classical identity of being unable to control herself because she is under the sway of "divine" forces outside of herself.[244]

Much later in the dialogue, as a result of a crisis in conscience about things she has done, Fiammetta does exercise her intellect in the effort to make a comparison between her husband and Panphilus: "Are not his virtues, courage, nobility, and especially his love and constancy, and all other good parts in him, are they not far above everything that Panphilus has in him worthy of praise and commendation?"[245] However, even though she grasps a truth with her intellect, she is still not able to exercise her will to choose the good. Boccaccio has the nurse make this point even more clearly:

Young Lady, and my dearest mistress, your sorrows make me beyond all measure sorrowful, and would afflict me more, had I not warned you about them be-

---

242. Boccaccio, *Amorous Fiammetta,* p. 26.

243. Boccaccio, *Amorous Fiammetta,* p. 27.

244. Boccaccio, *Amorous Fiammetta.* "O heavenly deity, O only Lady and mistress of my resolute mind, whose force the more it is resisted, the more it is felt, pardon my simple and foolish encounter, which I have made against the piercing weapons of your unknown and powerful Son, and work with me at your own pleasure" (p. 41). For an excellent discussion of the pagan understanding of deities as in control of one's fate see Robert Sokolowski, *The God of Faith and Reason* (Notre Dame: University of Notre Dame Press, 1982) and *Eucharistic Presence: A Study in the Theology of Disclosure* (Washington, D.C.: Catholic University Press, 1993), p. 131. The Christian view, however, is one that accentuates free choice through the gift of free will. The Christian God never forces the human will.

245. Boccaccio, *Amorous Fiammetta,* p. 239.

fore. . . . Because everyone may always as long as life lasts (so that he may have a willing mind to perform it) decline from his wicked ways, and turn it again to the right, I shall think it the dearest thing to me that may happen, if from now on you would shake off the dark cloud from the eyes of your understanding, obscured by this wicked tyrant, and restore to them again the clear light of truth.[246]

The nurse reflects that Fiammetta has followed more an "unbridled will than reined reason," and she counsels her patient to "place now, with more modesty, advised reason before lawless will, and wisely hale and help yourself out of your pit of peril and sorrow, into which you have suffered yourself foolishly to fall."[247] Unfortunately, Fiammetta is still paralyzed in her efforts to make a different choice.

And though I was beyond all measure troubled in mind — notwithstanding I knew them to be most true, but yet the matter very ill-disposed — did receive them without any profit at all.[248]

Fiammetta considers suicide as the only alternative to her grief, and once again the nurse attempts to reason with her Mistress: "And now it is time to prove if virtue have any place in you."[249] However, Fiammetta again rejects the advice: "But none, or few of her grave counsels did touch my troubled mind with effect, and the greatest part of them, spent in vain, vanished away in the air."[250] The nurse did not remain content to simply give advice and counsel, but interrupted Fiammetta's suicide attempt by physically interfering with the act.

Later, the nurse attempted once again to explain the basic principle of controlling the passions through the exercise of intellect and will:

It is not a point of virtue to require death, and to call upon it, nor a part of magnanimity to be afraid of life, as you are, but rather to countermand these pressing evils; and to fly away before them is not the part of a courageous and resolute mind.[251]

However, Fiammetta, remaining trapped in her condition of paralysis, ended the novel by claiming that she shares this condition with most women:

As I am not the first that has committed such a friendly fault, so am I not alone, and shall not be the last, but having almost all women in the world as my companions in this excusable error, I am not so greatly to be condemned for the same.[252]

---

246. Boccaccio, *Amorous Fiammetta*, p. 242.
247. Boccaccio, *Amorous Fiammetta*, p. 243.
248. Boccaccio, *Amorous Fiammetta*, p. 245.
249. Boccaccio, *Amorous Fiammetta*, pp. 263-64.
250. Boccaccio, *Amorous Fiammetta*, p. 265.
251. Boccaccio, *Amorous Fiammetta*, p. 282.
252. Boccaccio, *Amorous Fiammetta*, p. 329.

So once again we have an ironic conclusion to one of Boccaccio's works. In it we find Fiammetta excusing her lack of intelligence and willful action by her gender identity. However, the fundamental orientation of the efforts of the nurse throughout the story was to encourage her to make a different choice.[253] A further irony of the story is found in the possible identification of Fiammetta with Boccaccio himself, as a rejected suitor. In this case Fiammetta actually represents a man, rather than a woman, who had given himself over to passion.

More important, however, than the actual conclusion of the discourse are the many dialogues it contains between two women about significant issues in human identity, wisdom, and virtue. In this development Boccaccio has portrayed different options for women's actions that in themselves suggest the need for personal responsibility and choice. Therefore, even though his portrayal of Fiammetta suggests that some women are unable to control their irrational natures through the exercise of their reason, in the character of the nurse he offers the model of a well-ordered human being, a woman who knows basic philosophical principles and is able to explain them to others.

The table on page 291 offers a summary of the concept of woman in Boccaccio's early works that are particularly associated with Fiammetta.

Dialogues among Men and Women about Wisdom and Virtue

When we turn to the description of Fiammetta in Boccaccio's *Decameron* we find a change in her identity once again. She often appears to be giving voice to Boccaccio's own philosophical principles about the new meaning of nobility and about the importance of ordering impulses through the exercise of reason and will. Before describing some of her views in more detail, we shall give some background to this text.

The plague, which destroyed three-fifths of the population of Florence during the year 1348, provides the historical setting of the *Decameron*.[254] Because of the breakdown of society during this period, many people sought refuge in the countryside. Boccaccio describes a small group of seven women and three men who decide to move outside the city to wait for the end of the plague. During this time they undertake to have a continuous dialogue over a period of ten days in which each participant will offer ten different stories to highlight some aspect of human iden-

---

253. This tendency of Boccaccio to reach a conclusion that is different from what the reader expects is considered in some detail by Marina Scordilis Brownlee, "The Counterfeit Muse: Ovid, Boccaccio, Juan de Flores," in *Discourses of Authority in Medieval and Renaissance Literature* (Hanover, N.H. and London: University Press of New England, 1989), pp. 109-27. In her reflection on this work she states: "Clearly, Boccaccio is calling our attention to the unreliability of his initial claim, doing here what he does on so many pages of his *opere:* that is, explicitly enunciating one thing on the semantic level only thereafter blatantly to contradict it on the syntactic level, thereby exposing one of the mechanisms of deception inherent in language" (p. 112). Brownlee, however, takes a more negative view of the text, which she describes as an example of "pseudo-autobiographies of females written by men."

254. The death of his parents during the plague actually allowed Boccaccio the financial security to follow a literary career.

Descriptions of Women's Wisdom and Virtue in Boccaccio's Early Works	
Title of Work	Character and Virtue
Filocolo	**Fiammetta:** Adorned with virtue Passions ruled by reason Knowledge of history, philosophy, science Chose wisdom
Teseida (dedicated to Fiammetta)	**Hippolyta**, Queen of the Amazons: Assumes command Disciplines her troops (setting aside feminine timidity) Confident in her power Dares to perform manly (rather than womanly) deeds Exercises (manly) courage Not subject or obedient to men Challenges Theseus to equality in a just war Commands with courage
Amorous Fiammetta	**Fiammetta:** Irrational Under control of the force of her desires Full of grief and sorrow **Nurse:** Passions ordered by reason Courageous resolute mind Teacher of wisdom Teacher of virtue

tity. Each participant engages fully in the dialogues and each one takes a turn at leading the discussion during a particular day.[255] This is the first example in western writing of women "governing" men on a rotating basis in a "public" forum. So

255. Giuseppe Mazzotta notes, in *The World at Play in Boccaccio's "Decameron"* (Princeton: Princeton University Press, 1986), that "Boccaccio stresses in his Proem the bond and virtue of reciprocity as the principle inspiring the *Decameron.*" This reciprocity is seen in the dynamics of the regulation of the storytelling itself (p. 245). Mazzotta gives much importance to this development of reciprocal dialogue for later humanism: "It may well be that this ethical virtue of playful conversation, which shapes the *Decameron* and the world of the *brigata,* foreshadows the ideals of 'civile conversazione,' which is at the same time the distinction and legacy of the Italian Humanists" (p. 266).

simply by the structure of the dialogue, female characters are given a prominent place in the virtue of ruling others, and they outnumber the men by seven to three. From the perspective of the history of the concept of woman, this structure alone signals an augmentation in the development of the concept of female intelligence and exercise of will as expressed through intergender dialogue.[256]

When we consider the actual content of the various stories found in the *Decameron* it is slightly more difficult to assess the overall contribution of Boccaccio's philosophy to theories of gender identity. Scholars who take a quantitative approach to the text tend to conclude that woman is generally devalued by Boccaccio in *Decameron*. For example, Angela Maria Iovino states that in the stories themselves there are 92 female characters and 216 male characters, and of the 92 only 18 are not manipulated by male characters.[257] In another example, Joy Jambuechen Potter observes that: "[t]wenty-two of the stories have no women in them, including the first three of both the first and the last days. Women are just catalysts or minor characters in forty-seven of the others and major characters or protagonists in thirty-one."[258] It is true that Boccaccio does not present a perfectly balanced account of the respective identities of men and women. However, when we consider the fundamental content of the stories he gives, and focus on the quality of the gender-related aspects of the dialogues, it would seem that Boccaccio's *Decameron* provides a strong intermediary step in the development of the philosophical concept of woman. To prove this point some selected relevant passages from the text will be cited below with the name of the character in bold print to help identification.

What is the contribution of the male characters in the *Decameron* to the concept of woman? First, **Panfilo**, whose name means "completely in love," does not reflect much on gender identity. His stories generally shift from men to women with ease, and they focus on the usual issues of hypocrisy, corruption, generosity, and how to deal with Fortune. He portrays women as both victims and perpetrators of injustice on men.

Second, **Filostrato**, whose name means "overcome by love," generally presents women as sharing desires, intelligence, and capacity for virtue or vice with men. He also ridicules men and women equally. In his sweep of stories the whole spectrum of humanity is described. One particular story is noteworthy for the concept of woman. It concerns the relation of women to the law. The woman in question had been caught in adultery and was taken before a magistrate to face a punishment of death due to a particular statute in the city of Prato. The woman decides to argue her own case as follows:

---

256. The fame of this particular text cannot be overestimated. Corradina Caporello-Szykman, *The Boccaccian Novella: Creation and Waning of a Genre* (New York: Peter Lang, 1990), notes its importance as Boccaccio's beginning a new genre of writing: "The novella is born with the *Decameron* and, furthermore, it is the whole work which has to be perceived as a new *genre*, not just the one hundred narratives contained in it" (p. 3). It would follow that this text had an additional impact on the development of gender identity because of its fame for other reasons.

257. Angela Maria Iovino, "The *Decameron* and the *Corbaccio*: Boccaccio's Image of Women and Spiritual Crisis," Ph.D. Diss., Indiana University, 1983, pp. 99 and 107.

258. Joy Jambuechen Potter, "Woman in the *Decameron*," in *Studies in the Italian Renaissance: Essays in Memory of Arnolfo B. Ferruolo* (Naples: Società Editrice Napoletana, 1985), pp. 87-101, 93.

The laws should be equal for all and should be passed with the consent of the people they affect. In this case these conditions are not fulfilled, for this law applies only to us poor women, who are much better able than men to satisfy a larger number; furthermore, when this law was put into effect, not a single woman gave her consent, nor was any one of them ever consulted about it; therefore, it may quite rightly be called a bad law.[259]

The woman completed her defense by proving that she had fulfilled the law by always being available to her husband when he wanted her, so the Magistrate freed her and changed the original statute. Once again, in the midst of this ironic tale we see Boccaccio addressing a genuine problem of the exclusion of women from institutional structures.

Third, **Dineo**, whose name means "lustful," is the final male character to be considered. Generally speaking, his stories follow the meaning of his name, and they describe people who are mostly motivated by concupiscible impulse and who use their intelligence primarily to mislead others. However, he also holds a kind of privileged place in the text because he does not have to follow the prescribed topic for each day. In the introduction to the text he also remarks: "Ladies, more than our preparations, it was your intelligence that guided us here."[260] It is also Dineo who gives the final story on Day 10, or the infamous story of Griselda.

The story of **Griselda** is a parody of a wife's virtue of obedience to her husband. In a certain way we can see it as an extreme exaggerated version of Aristotle's principle of ethical polarity. Dineo describes the context as follows:

I should like to tell you about a marquis and not about a generous act of his but, rather, about his insane cruelty, which, while good did result from it in the end, I would never advise anyone to follow as an example, for I consider it a great shame that he derived any benefit from it at all.[261]

The woman remains passive and obedient for a period of ten years during which her husband, in order to test his wife's virtue, pretends to murder her children, pretends to divorce her, and asks her to prepare the wedding celebrations for him to marry a different wife. At the end the children are returned and she is restored to her former position. The story of Griselda captured the imagination of many western readers. As mentioned previously, Petrarch was so moved by it that he translated it into Latin, and Chaucer integrated it into his own works. However, it seems to follow Boccaccio's general pattern of satire by exaggeration both of vice and of virtue. It is the foil of the satirical discourse in the *Corbaccio,* where the woman tormented the man and refused to obey his commands. While the story was reused by other authors to support the gender polarity model of woman's virtue as silent, passive, and obedient, it would appear that Boccaccio originally intended the story

259. Giovanni Boccaccio, *Decameron* (New York and Scarborough, Ont.: New American Library/Mentor, 1982), pp. 397-98.
260. Boccaccio, *Decameron,* p. 106.
261. Boccaccio, *Decameron,* p. 672.

ironically, as Marilyn Migiel suggests: "he carries the arguments for female virtue to their logical extreme and offers readers a *reductio ad absurdum.* . . ."[262]

We shall now consider Boccaccio's seven female characters in the *Decameron.* Positive aspects of developing the intelligence and will in a woman are supported by the female character **Pampinea**. In the introduction to the *Decameron,* Pampinea states: "My dear Ladies, you have often heard, as I have, how the proper use of reason can do harm to no one."[263] She then offers a sequential argument for why they should leave the city during the time of the plague. Pampinea is also the character who leads the group of men and women to accept a rotating authority among themselves:

> When things lack order they cannot long endure, and since it was I who began the discussions which brought this fine company together, and since I desire the continuation of our happiness, I think we should choose a leader from among us, whom we shall honor and obey as our superior and whose only thought shall be to keep us happily entertained. And in order that each one of us may feel the burden of this responsibility together with the pleasure of its authority, so that no one of us who has not experienced it can envy the others, let me say that both the burden and the honor should be granted to each one of us in turn for a day.[264]

Her suggestion was accepted, and it became the format for the entire work of the *Decameron.*

The leadership of women is not only directly shown in the text, it is also expressed outwards towards the general situation of women in society. Pampinea reveals the presence of a historical consciousness of intelligent women in the past, and of the distance between their model of education and what is the present situation in Florence. Pampinea, in the content of her story on Day One, laments the lack of educated intelligence in women of the day:

> . . . these days few if any women can understand a single witty remark, or, if they do understand, know how to reply to one — a source of universal shame for us all and for every woman alive today. That which used to reside in the minds of women of the past has now been transformed by modern women into decorations for the body. . . . I am ashamed to say this, since I cannot speak against others without speaking against myself, but these overdressed, painted, gaudy women either stand around like mute and insensitive marble statues or, if they reply when spoken to, it would be much better for them to remain silent; and they deceive themselves in believing that their inability to converse with ladies and with worthy gentlemen comes from their purity of soul, calling their stupidity modesty.[265]

---

262. Marilyn Migiel, in Russell, ed., *The Feminist Encyclopedia of Italian Literature,* p. 32.
263. Boccaccio, *Decameron,* p. 131.
264. Boccaccio, *Decameron,* p. 18.
265. Boccaccio, *Decameron,* pp. 55-56.

Pampinea offers stories that give evidence of both intelligence and stupidity in men and women to prove her point.

She does not simply criticize women's lack of education or poor choices; she also criticizes educated men who still do not order their passions through the exercise of reason and the will. In the character of Pampinea, Boccaccio expresses a woman's disdain for academia. Pampinea describes a scholar as follows:

> . . . who had studied for a long while in Paris . . . to learn the reason and causes of things. . . . But as often occurs those who have a keener understanding of profound matters are more easily snared by Love's noose. . . . The wise scholar, setting aside all his philosophical reflections, turned all his thoughts towards her.[266]

The woman who rejected the scholar was murdered by the man in an act of revenge. Boccaccio's belief that experience, and in this case the experience of intergender dialogue, was a better educator than academic study is ironically expressed in the scholar's reflections:

> Your words of praise will not obscure the eyes of my intellect now as once your treacherous promises did. I know myself, for you made me learn more about myself in a single night than I learned during the entire time I lived in Paris.[267]

Pampinea generally supports the use of the intellect to refine the passions. On Day Five she argues that a person can still demonstrate the virtue of courage when his passions are stirred by love. On Day Seven she argues against the view that love necessarily impairs the intelligence; and on Day Ten she argues that few rulers are able to "aim the bows of their intellects" in the direction of doing good deeds for their subjects rather than abuse their power to take a tyrannical advantage of their subjects.[268]

If we turn to see how Boccaccio refines his old female character **Fiammetta** in the *Decameron* we discover that on Day Four, Fiammetta expresses Boccaccio's view about the nature of nobility:

> But let us leave all that aside and look rather to the principles of things: you will observe that we are all made of the same flesh and that we are all created by one and the same Creator with equal powers and equal force and virtue. Virtue it was that first distinguished differences among us, even though we were all born and are still being born equal; those who possessed a greater portion of virtue and were devoted to it were called nobles, and the rest remained commoners. And although a custom contrary to this practice has made us forget this natural law, yet it is not discarded or broken by Nature and good habits; and a person who lives virtuously shows himself openly to be noble, and he who calls him other than noble is the one at fault, not the noble man.[269]

266. Boccaccio, *Decameron,* p. 505.
267. Boccaccio, *Decameron,* p. 516.
268. Boccaccio, *Decameron,* pp. 347, 442, and 639.
269. Boccaccio, *Decameron,* p. 255.

In the story itself Fiammetta describes a woman of the noble class who has fallen in love with a commoner, and who also confronts her father because he wishes to block her choice for marriage. Fiammetta refers to stereotypical female characteristics, but the woman asserts her own identity along a different path. The new concept of virtue consists in a clear decision to publicly express her choice:

> [She] felt measureless grief, as most women do; but her proud spirit conquered this cowardice, and her face remained the same through her miraculous strength of will. . . . Therefore, without a trace of feminine sorrow or contrition for her misdeed, she faced her father as a brave and unafraid lady, and with a tearless, open, and unperturbed face, she said to him: . . . I was moved to act this way not so much by my womanly weakness but by your own lack of interest in marrying me, as well as by Guiscardo's own worth. . . . You have fathered a daughter made of flesh and blood, not one of stone or of iron; and though you are old now, you should have remembered the nature and the power of the laws of youth. . . . I am full of amorous desire. . . . I had made up my mind to commit this natural sin. . . . I did not choose Guiscardo at random, as many women do, but I chose him over all others with deliberate consideration and careful forethought, and the two of us have enjoyed the satisfaction of our desires for some time now.[270]

The Father was not willing to integrate this new freedom of choice, and the story had the unhappy ending of the death of the two young lovers.

It is especially notable that Boccaccio suggests that instincts and sexual desires are natural for both women and men. He emphasizes the power of natural desires and of the value of open admission concerning one's nature throughout his text. However, he is the first of the humanist authors to describe his women characters as having equally intense passionate identities as men. In the Preface to the *Decameron* the narrator Prince Galeotto had stated that women suffer from the same problem with respect to the passions as do men.

> And who will deny that such comfort, no matter how insufficient, is more fittingly bestowed on charming ladies than on men? For they, in fear and shame, conceal the hidden flames of love within their delicate breasts, a love far stronger than one which is openly expressed, as those who have felt and suffered this know; and furthermore, restricted by the wishes, whims, and commands of fathers, mothers, brothers, and husbands, they remain most of the time limited to the narrow confines of their bedrooms, where they sit in apparent idleness, now wishing one thing and now wishing another, turning over in their minds a number of thoughts which cannot always be pleasant ones.[271]

Here woman's interior life and her exterior circumstances are described compassionately. A woman is no longer simply posited as an object of desire for man, but

270. Boccaccio, *Decameron,* pp. 254-55.
271. Boccaccio, *Decameron,* p. 2.

she is a particular human being who is struggling with the constraints of her own situation and the passions within her own consciousness.

Returning to the story of Fiammetta introduced above, Boccaccio has his character suggest a way to act in relation to her desires. The first kind of virtuous act involves the making of a "conscious decision" even though this decision may be not for the most virtuous end. It involves the discovery and exercise of the intellect and will rather than allowing oneself to be caught in the play of forces.

On Day Five Fiammetta tells another story of a woman who comes to a "conscious decision" but for not very good reasons. Fiammetta wants her audience to learn "to be the donors of your favours instead of always leaving this act to the whim of Fortune," who tends not to be discreet.[272] In a previous story told on Day One, she described a King who decided "to wisely extinguish the dishonestly conceived flames of his passion" for a woman who would not accept his advances.[273] It is on Day Ten that Fiammetta develops this theme most thoroughly. A King is driven by a desire to possess two young daughters of one of his subjects. He revealed this passion to a Count who confronts him as follows:

> I call to your attention, my King, that it was most glorious indeed to have conquered Manfredi, but it is much more glorious indeed to conquer yourself; and since you have others to rule over, conquer yourself and restrain this passion of yours, and do not mar with such a stain all that you have so gloriously achieved.[274]

The King is described by Fiammetta as responding to the critical dialogue of his Count, and coming to a decision as follows:

> These words bitterly pierced the King's heart, all the more so because he realized they were true; and so, after a few fervent sighs, he declared: Count, I truly believe that for the well-trained warrior, any enemy no matter how powerful, is far weaker and easier to conquer in comparison to his own appetite; but although the effort required will be great and the strength necessary incalculable, your words have spurred me on to such an extent that, before too many days pass by, I shall demonstrate to you by my actions that just as I know how to conquer others, in like manner I know how to master myself.[275]

Fiammetta concludes that the King was able to achieve this ordering of his passions by his reason and will.

Boccaccio uses Fiammetta, through the stories and conclusions she reaches, to express some of the central themes of his humanistic philosophy. He also has her express an awareness of her own gender identity. In the following passage from Day Ten, Fiammetta states that the generalities common to the literary form are

272. Boccaccio, *Decameron,* p. 364.
273. Boccaccio, *Decameron,* p. 44.
274. Boccaccio, *Decameron,* p. 631.
275. Boccaccio, *Decameron,* p. 632.

preferred to narrow academic discussions. The irony that women have been generally excluded from such discussions is also noted:

> Splendid Ladies, I have always been of the opinion that in companies such as our own, one should speak in such general terms that the meaning of what we say may never give rise to argument because of something too narrowly defined; such discussions are better kept among scholars in schools than among us, who have all we can do to manage our distaffs and spindles.[276]

Here, the female character humorously deprecates herself because she has demonstrated by her speech that she is capable of argument, and yet she is spared from the more narrow disputation common to academia.

Boccaccio often uses female characters to make ironic remarks about woman's identity. **Elissa**, as a narrator, is presented as an intelligent woman with knowledge of literature and history, and who at the same time implies that women are unable on their own to engage in practical action. On Day Six she describes Guido Cavalcanti as "one of the best logicians in the world and a superb natural philosopher."[277] She also declares ironically that: "Men are truly the leaders of women, and without their guidance our actions rarely end successfully! But how are we to find these men?"[278] So the stereotype of woman needing to obey a man is eliminated because no men can be found to be obeyed.

In a similar ironic depiction the female character **Filomena** begins with a stereotype of female identity:

> Remember that we are all women, and any young girl can tell you that women do not know how to reason in a group when they are without the guidance of some man who knows how to control them. We are fickle, quarrelsome, suspicious, timid, and fearful, because of which I suspect that this company will soon break up.[279]

Of course, the dialogue in the *Decameron* did not break up; instead it progressed in an orderly and intelligent fashion. So Boccaccio expresses the stereotype on one level in the dialogue while exploding it on another level of the dialogue. Even though the group of seven women was joined by three men, no one individual is in charge more than any other. In addition, in Filomena's stories both women and men give evidence of ingenuity in vice and virtue.[280]

The female character **Emilia** seems to offer a more traditional view of woman's identity when she suggests that: "if the order of things is considered with a sound mind, it is very easy to see that women in general are subservient by nature, custom, and laws to men by whose judgment they ought to be ruled and gov-

276. Boccaccio, *Decameron,* p. 627.
277. Boccaccio, *Decameron,* p. 401.
278. Boccaccio, *Decameron,* p. 128.
279. Boccaccio, *Decameron,* p. 15.
280. Boccaccio, *Decameron,* pp. 141-42, 152, and 382.

erned. . . ."[281] She concludes that if women want peace of mind they ought to be obedient to men as law, custom, and nature dictate. However, in the story itself, she describes a woman and a donkey who were beaten into submission presumably because their nature was not subservient. Once again we see the ironic manner in which Boccaccio has his female character say one thing that fits the stereotype but shows just the opposite as a way of breaking open its hold on the biased intelligence. In another story Emilia criticizes magistrates of the law for their rigidity and cruelty and the hypocrisy of friars who denounce lust and usury but then practice these vices themselves.[282]

The theme of hypocrisy is central to Boccaccio's work. Many of the stories in the *Decameron* relate to men or women who are caught in hypocritical acts, where they say or represent one kind of thing and do the opposite. The female character **Neifile** criticizes the lack of virtue in members of the clergy.[283] She also frequently describes the disastrous results of the passion of jealousy if it is not ordered. Boccaccio does not spare anyone in the society of his time. In the theme of hypocrisy we discover a variation on the Platonic approach to appearance and reality. In the satires against women, which suggest that woman presents herself as beautiful and alluring, while in reality she is ugly and eaten by worms, there is a devaluation of woman's identity in general. In Boccaccio's discussion of the same theme, we find instead that only a particular person chooses to act in a hypocritical manner. The particular identity may be extended to include a certain type of person, but it never reaches to include either all women or all men.

In a very different kind of story Neifile opens up a new way of thinking about women. This story is told against the backdrop of women's exclusion from academia in general and from a Faculty of Medicine in particular. Neifile describes a situation in Paris in which a young girl offers her services to the King of France to heal a disease that no other physician seems able to cure. The King refuses her help, saying: "How can a young woman know how to do what the best doctors in the world couldn't?" She answers with good reasons:

> My Lord, you despise my art because I am young and a woman, but let me remind you that I practice medicine not only with my own knowledge but also with the help of God and with the knowledge of Master Gerardo of Narbonne, who was my father and a famous physician in his day.[284]

The young physician succeeded in her cure. She learned her medicine from her father, as will be the pattern for other educated women in subsequent developments in Humanism. As a reward the young physician asked to be married to a man named Beltramo; he refused her request by expressing a negative reaction to this new concept of a female physician: "My Lord, do you therefore wish to give me a

---

281. Boccaccio, *Decameron,* pp. 591-92.

282. Emilia concludes with making a distinction between natural sin and malicious will. Boccaccio, *Decameron,* p. 209.

283. Boccaccio, *Decameron,* p. 38.

284. Boccaccio, *Decameron,* p. 228.

woman doctor as my wife? God forbid that I should ever take such a female!"[285] We are then told by Neifile that the woman "decided on a course of action," which took several years in order to win the love of Beltramo. In the end, "seeing her intelligence and her perseverance," he agreed to become her husband.[286] The implication of this reversal is that it takes time to overcome bias, but with time it can be transformed.

The final female character of the *Decameron* to be considered is called **Lauretta**. For the most part, her stories described negative consequences of vices such as hypocrisy, covetousness, gluttony, or anger. In the following passage we see Lauretta humorously introducing a theme of woman's "lighter" nature to explain a tendency to give in to anger:

> Young ladies, as you are surely aware, every vice can do the greatest harm to the person who practices it and in many cases to others as well. And among these vices, I believe that the one that leads us straight into danger is the vice of anger, which is nothing other than a sudden and thoughtless impulse, which is incited by some unhappiness we feel, drives all reason from us, blinds the eyes of the mind with darkness, and consumes our souls with burning rage. And while this often occurs in men, and in some more than others, it has nonetheless been known to cause even greater damage in women, for it flares up more easily in them, burns with a brighter flame, and finds less resistance to it there. This is not surprising, for if we examine the matter more closely, we will discover that by its very nature fire kindles more readily in light and soft materials than in hard and heavy things; and we women are — with no offense to you gentlemen — more delicate than you are and much more capricious.[287]

Lauretta also reflects on the nature of satirical dialogue in a discussion about the proper use of "wit" and once again, about women's lack of education in public forums of speech. She makes an important distinction between wit and insult:

> Charming ladies, there is much truth in what first Pampinea and then Filomena touched upon in speaking about the beauty of repartee and our lack of skill in using it. While it is not necessary to repeat their arguments, I should like to remind you, in addition to what has already been said about the repartee, that the nature of wit is such that it should have the bite of a lamb rather than that of a dog, for if the witty remark bite like a dog it would not be a witty remark at all but rather an insult.[288]

Whether Boccaccio's *Decameron* has itself more the bite of a lamb or the bite of a dog is still open to question. Most scholars argue that the *Corbaccio* has the latter. The narrator of the *Decameron* suggests that a conclusion to this question depends

---

285. Boccaccio, *Decameron,* p. 229.
286. Boccaccio, *Decameron,* p. 231.
287. Boccaccio, *Decameron,* p. 268.
288. Boccaccio, *Decameron,* p. 387.

upon the attitude of the reader: "[a]s they stand, these tales, like all others things, may be harmful or useful depending on who the listener is."[289] Boccaccio draws his listener into the intergender dialogue, widening the community of discourse. If the reader is a woman or a man, a different response may occur.

From the perspective of the history of the concept of woman, there is no doubt that the *Decameron* advances a concept of women as actively engaged in intergender dialogue about philosophical issues. This fact alone makes it an important contribution to the development of the understanding of women as capable of sustained philosophical reflection. Further, there is a balance among the male and female characters that moves towards a kind of complementarity: both are equally capable of vice or virtue, and both are responsible for the consequences of their actions. At the same time, men and women often have different contexts of action, so their choices may have to be differentiated along gender lines in some respects.

A summary of the relation of wisdom and virtue to participants in the *Decameron* is given in the chart on page 302.

The *Decameron* is the first western text to use so many different women characters in an imaginary community of discourse. It is also the first example in the West of a philosopher writing in a dialogue form using a number of individual female characters to represent different views about a subject. Fiammetta, Elissa, Filomena, Neifile, Emilia, Pampinea, and Lauretta were used by Boccaccio to present his own philosophical views. In addition, the female characters displayed wit, humor, seriousness, and intellectual capacity. This begins to suggest role models for humanist women philosophers. Furthermore, several of these female characters actually reflect on the concept of woman through ironic description of a stereotype, through telling stories about women who chose new paths for action, and by evaluating women who are not virtuous because they are driven by unrefined desires or vices.

Boccaccio's particular use of satire was already noted in the previous chapter in an analysis of his *Corbaccio,* which portrayed a jealous husband spewing forth devaluing stereotypes of woman in a vengeful rage.[290] In our analysis we noted that Boccaccio may have been satirizing satires of women because he ironically described the jealous husband demonstrating the very behavior he was condemning in women. At the same time, however, the narrator of the text reverses his own position and accepts the satirical views of the husband at the end. Thus Boccaccio appears to introduce two different sorts of ironies in his text. In the chart on page 303 the characteristics of women and husbands are satirized in order to consider them in the context of Boccaccio's other works.

Boccaccio's contribution to the history of the concept of woman was marred by his introduction of multiple ironic reversals at many levels in his texts, reversals that were not understood by most readers — who interpreted him literally and superficially. They did not consider that Boccaccio may have been using irony to sati-

---

289. Boccaccio, *Decameron,* p. 686.
290. Giovanni Boccaccio, *Corbaccio* (Urbana/Chicago/London: University of Illinois Press, 1975).

Women's Wisdom and Virtue in Boccaccio's *Decameron*	
Name of Character	**Description of the Character's Views**
Panfilo	Women as both victims of male injustice and perpetrators of injustice on men.
Filostrato	Women as having the same desires, intelligence, and capacity for virtue and vice as men.
Dineo	Women as intelligent. Ironic exaggeration of female passivity and obedience in story of Griselda and an abusive husband.
Pampinea	Sets up rotating leadership of women and men. Women need to educate their intelligence.
Fiammetta	Strength of will. Deliberate and conscious choices. Careful forethought. Self-governance (ironically used for vice as well as virtue)
Neifile	Woman physician intelligently deciding on course of action. Against hypocrisy.
Elissa	Intelligent woman. Knows history. Ironically claims women cannot find any men to lead them.
Filomena	Ironically claims that women without men are fickle, quarrelsome, suspicious, timid, and fearful.
Emilia	Ironically claims that women ought to be ruled by physical force of men.

rize the literal view he was expressing. Consequently, Boccaccio is often wrongly perceived as defending a view of woman that is solidly in the gender polarity tradition. However, as the analysis in this chapter has attempted to prove, Boccaccio's works, when read carefully, reveal an effort to open new ways of thinking about women by providing multiple examples of women who are just as capable as men of practicing the traditional virtues. In order to provide even stronger evidence in support of the claim that Boccaccio's real view of women went beyond a stereotyped devaluation of their identity, we will turn now to a direct consideration of Boccaccio's positive analysis of women's character in a text written towards the end

Women's Lack of Wisdom and Virtue in Boccaccio's *Corbaccio*	
Levels of Satire	Characteristics of Satire
Level of discourse: The jealous husband's view of women	Women: Not able to control emotions by reason Inconstant Vile Beast without intellect Controlling of men Imperfect Creature
Level of behavior: The jealous husband's own character	Man: Reason not able to control emotions Vindictive Unable to use intellect Vengeful controlling of women

of his life. In this way, our evaluation of his concept of woman will have covered the whole range of Boccaccio's contribution to the history of the philosophy of gender identity.

Describing Virtues of Famous Women

In direct contrast to the negative tone of the *Corbaccio,* Boccaccio described himself as contributing to a positive reevaluation of woman's identity through his text *Concerning Famous Women,* which purported to describe the valuable characteristics of 104 different women. Although modeled in some ways on Plutarch's *Mulierum virtutes,* the *De claris mulieribus* is often considered to be the first collection of women's biographies ever written because in its organization each woman is given a separate chapter.[291] So the form of the text and its general purpose contribute significantly to the historical development of the concept of woman. This fact was well recognized by Christine de Pizan, who borrowed from seventy-five of Boccaccio's descriptions for her *City of Ladies.*[292]

The content of the book has eclectic views. For when the specifics of Boccaccio's views about these women are considered, we often find a mixture of attitudes that could be classified as falling under gender polarity, gender unity, and gender complementarity. In the Preface to the work we can see the complex views intertwined:

291. Guido A. Guarino, Introduction to Giovanni Boccaccio, *Concerning Famous Women* (New Brunswick, N.J.: Rutgers University Press, 1963), p. ix.
292. See Margaret L. King, *Women of the Renaissance* (Chicago and London: University of Chicago Press, 1991), pp. 223-25, for a comparison of the two texts.

I have been quite astonished that women have had so little attention from writers of this sort that they have gained no recognition in any work devoted especially to them, although it can be clearly seen in the more voluminous histories that some women have acted with as much strength as valor. If men should be praised whenever they perform great deeds (with strength which Nature has given them), how much more should women be extolled (almost all of whom are endowed with tenderness, frail bodies, and sluggish minds by Nature), if they have acquired a manly spirit and if with keen intelligence and remarkable fortitude they have dared to undertake and have accomplished even the most difficult deeds?[293]

The themes of the inferior intelligence and weakness of woman's nature echo the common Aristotelian principle of gender polarity. The overcoming of these factors by "masculine" strength, repeated throughout this text, implies that something must be changed in woman's identity to overcome her natural inferiority. The natural starting point of a sex polarity appears to be changed by the loss of a feminine identity more common to a gender unity theory.[294]

The loss of gender identity is frequently articulated by Boccaccio. In some ways we can see him struggling to understand how a woman can act in a "masculine" way and how a man can act in a "feminine" way. However, because up to his time there was a tendency to identify masculine with male and feminine with female in western thought, Boccaccio often describes a masculine woman or a feminine man as changing sex identity rather than simply augmenting it. In a discussion of Semiramis he states: "As if he had changed sex with his mother, Ninus rotted away idly in bed, while she sweated in arms against her enemies."[295] In a discussion of Penthesilea, Boccaccio again introduced the concept of change of gender identity:

Some may be surprised by the fact that women, no matter how armed, dared to fight against men. However, surprise will cease if we think of the fact that custom had changed their nature, so that Penthesilea and women like her were much more manly in arms than those who were made men by Nature but were then changed into women or helmeted hares by idleness and love of pleasure.[296]

---

293. Boccaccio, *Concerning Famous Women,* Preface, p. xxxvii. See especially Benson, chapter 1, "Boccaccio's *De mulieribus claris:* An Ambiguous Beginning," in *The Invention of the Renaissance Woman,* pp. 9-31, for an excellent analysis of the tension in his text.

294. While this introduction implies that the women to be considered are virtuous by overcoming the natural weakness of their female state, the ambiguity of the content of the descriptions is aptly described by Constance Jordan: "The vast majority of his famous women, if they are not clearly vicious, are either fraudulent, in that their virtue is actually a mask for some secret vice, or effectively punished for violating accepted social norms. Thus Boccaccio implies that a woman's fame, or *claritas,* is a form of notoriety. . . ." Constance Jordan, "Boccaccio's In-famous Women: Gender and Civic Virtue in *De mulieribus claris,*" in *Ambiguous Realities: Women in the Middle Ages and Renaissance* (Detroit: Wayne State University Press, 1987), p. 27.

295. Boccaccio, *Concerning Famous Women,* p. 6.

296. Boccaccio, *Concerning Famous Women,* p. 66. A similar theme is seen in: "Hortensia alone

Boccaccio, however, more often introduced qualifiers indicating that it is in the mind of the perceiver that a change of gender had occurred, and not in the person being referred to. This qualification reveals that he was becoming aware, as had Petrarch before him, that it was possible for a woman to develop what are considered culturally masculine characteristics and still remain very much a woman.

However, Boccaccio struggles with a soul/body metaphysics in his attempt to explain this phenomenon. In a discussion of Artemisia he asks: ". . . what can we think except that it was an error of Nature to give female sex to a body which had been endowed by God with a magnificent and virile spirit?" In a discussion of Epicharis, Boccaccio introduces a Christian understanding of the creation of the soul to correct this hypothesis:

> I should think that Nature sometimes errs when she gives souls to mortals. That is, she gives to a woman one that she thought she had given to a man. But since God Himself is the giver of such things, it is wrong to believe that He might doze while doing His work. . . . If we are stronger in our sex, why is it not proper that we be stronger in bravery? If this is not done, we rightly seem to have exchanged characters with them and become effeminate.[297]

Since a Christian does not accept a theory of reincarnation, Boccaccio needs to find another explanation for the appearance of qualities in one gender that are usually associated with the other gender.

What Boccaccio develops is a theory that when women become masculine, they rise above their sex, while when a man becomes feminine, he falls below his sex. The gender polarity foundation for such a valuation is rather obvious. Some examples should suffice to support this observation. Dido "cast aside womanly weakness and hardened her spirit to manly strength" when she engaged in military battle and initiated a rule of law; Claudia "forgot her sex" when she defended her father with "undaunted firmness"; Cornificia "with her genius and labor . . . rose above her sex"; Zenobia "overcame feminine softness," and Nicauila "did not give herself up to the rest of womanly softness."[298] Conversely, "Galienus was languishing in his effeminacy."[299] Boccaccio concludes in a section on Venturia:

> The world belongs to women, and men are womanish. Time, which consumes many useful things, has not been able to destroy what was detrimental to men,

---

with firm spirit dared to take up the women's cause before the triumvirs. And she pleaded so effectively and with such inexhaustible eloquence that to the great admiration of the audience it seemed that she had changed her sex and was Hortensius come back to life" (p. 185).

297. Boccaccio, *Concerning Famous Women,* pp. 210-11.

298. Boccaccio, *Concerning Famous Women,* pp. 87-88, 135, 188, 226, and 93.

299. Boccaccio, *Concerning Famous Women,* p. 226. Constance Jordan emphasizes the negative aspects of this expression of Boccaccio: "In neither instance does Boccaccio's famous woman speak persuasively in a natural feminine voice. If she is eloquent and chaste, she is a 'man'; if she is sexual, her partner does the speaking but at the price of his masculinity" ("Boccaccio's In-famous Women," p. 30).

nor has it been able to diminish the prerogatives of women, since they have held onto them with tenacious perseverance.[300]

Many of the female characters that Boccaccio describes are traditional goddess figures whom he claims were actually real women whose reputations had been exaggerated and who had subsequently been thought to be immortal. Ceres had invented the plow and the plowshare; Minerva invented weaving, discovered how to use oil, invented the cart and iron weapons, armor, and military strategy; Isis invented law and language; and Nicostrata invented the letters of the Italian language. "This invention seemed so marvellous that foolish men believed she was a goddess and not a woman."[301]

In addition, Boccaccio describes several women who excelled in different areas of the arts. Sappho is praised for her lyric poems, which "are still brilliant in our own day"; Irene is praised for her excellence in painting and for her "great deal of talent, which in women is usually very scarce"; Marcia, a sculptress, is praised "no less for the power of her intellect and the skill of her hands"; and Proba was praised for her "knowledge of literature" and her ability to quote passages from classical texts with "great skill."[302]

Boccaccio identifies three central areas of women's accomplishments: reading, writing, and teaching. He not only values them positively in individual women, but he provides a collective history of such activities. This collective history formed an increasingly solid foundation from which women of later generations such as Christine de Pizan and Laura Cereta will draw strength and purpose. In addition to the verbal power of these historical figures for women's history and identity, the quality of artistic illumination of manuscripts also communicated an important value to women who wanted to be scholars, writers, or teachers. The following illustrations, from fifteenth-century manuscripts of Boccaccio's *Concerning Famous Women,* depict women reading, writing, and teaching.

Although he praises women who use their intelligence well, Boccaccio also condemns women who have squandered their mind. In the following extract from Boccaccio's text we see Leontium praised for her writing against Theophrastus, the disciple of Aristotle, even as she is condemned for her sexual activities:

> If she had preserved womanly honor, her name would have been much more splendid and glorious, for she had great intellectual powers. According to the testimony of the ancients, she was such a scholar that she dared to write against and criticize Theophrastus, a famous philosopher of that period, moved either by envy or womanly temerity.
>
> Alas what an unworthy crime it is that she could bring Philosophy, the queen of all human pursuits, among panderers, unclean adulterers, and prostitutes, and into brothels, and in these disgraceful chambers smear it with shameful stains, trample it with unchaste feet, and plunge it into filthy sewers — if indeed the

---

300. Boccaccio, *Concerning Famous Women,* p. 121.
301. Boccaccio, *Concerning Famous Women,* pp. 52-53, 11, 14-15, and 19.
302. Boccaccio, *Concerning Famous Women,* pp. 99-100, 131, 144, and 210-20.

Proba Reading

A Woman Writing

Sempronia Teaching

splendor of Philosophy can be stained by the infamy of an unchaste heart. We must certainly bewail the fact that so brilliant a mind, given by heaven as a sacred gift, could be subjected to such filthy practices.[303]

Sometimes Boccaccio would give general principles about the need for both men and women to develop the use of their reason. In a discussion of Ariadne he states: "Nature turns the heavens by eternal law and gives to all of us intellects suitable for different undertakings. As these become weak through idleness and sloth, so do they become great and capable of great things through study and practice."[304] The key for Boccaccio in the *Decameron* as well as in *Concerning Famous Women* is study and practice of the use of the intelligence and will to order and refine the passions. This is an extremely important innovation in the history of the concept of woman.

When a woman achieves self-governance, she may also be able to govern others. In a description of Semiramis, who at first pretended to be a man in order to govern a nation, Boccaccio observes that in the end when she revealed her true identity, "it was almost as if she wanted to show that in order to govern it is not necessary to be a man, but to have courage."[305] Boccaccio also mentions Joanna, Queen of Sicily, who ruled with the qualities of bravery, beneficence, prudence, endurance, steadfastness, and constancy. He concludes with the observation: "Her indomitable soul has conquered everything; this would have been a great deed for a strong, powerful king, and not only for a woman."[306]

In sum, we can now see that Boccaccio's works have generally provided a new model for women, a model of intergender dialogue about philosophical issues. This model radically changes the one found in the academic community of discourse. Women are presented as subjects engaged in discussion with other subjects rather than simply as objects to be analyzed by only male subjects. At times the imaginary intergender dialogue extends to a consideration of gender identity itself. It also may include reference to Boccaccio's new concept of nobility as virtue, or the capacity to refine and order the passions through the exercise of reason and will. Therefore, even if some of Boccaccio's famous women are actually imaginary female characters, they provide a bridge to a new concept of woman. This bridge will eventually enable women in the humanist tradition to begin to engage in philosophical dialogue themselves.

---

303. Boccaccio, *Concerning Famous Women,* p. 132. The poet Sempronia is given a similar description: "She was of such quick and versatile intellect that she immediately understood and carried out by imitation whatever she heard or saw others do. Having learned not only Latin but Greek, she dared, unlike a woman, to compose verses when she felt like it, and she wrote so skilfully that she made all who read them marvel, as they would have been extraordinary and praiseworthy even for a man. . . . For these reasons, while we may praise her intellect and extol her for it, we must condemn her shameful actions. For, having stained the matronly robe with much lewdness, Sempronia brought it about that she became notorious, to her shame, whereas if she had preserved her modesty, she would have become glorious" (p. 167). The legendary Pope Joan is described as a scholar who was destroyed by her lust (pp. 231-32).

304. Boccaccio, *Concerning Famous Women,* p. 39.

305. Boccaccio, *Concerning Famous Women,* pp. 4-5.

306. Boccaccio, *Concerning Famous Women,* pp. 249-50.

The following chart summarizes the final phase of Boccaccio's descriptions of women's wisdom and virtue in his historical biography of over one hundred different women:

Women's Wisdom and Virtue in Boccaccio's *Concerning Famous Women*	
Women's loss of feminine identity to become like men (masculine)	Overcoming feminine softness, weakness Hardening spirit by manly strength Undaunted manly firmness Overcoming sluggish minds (given by nature) by manly spirit
Women's own identity developed	Powers of invention Poetic talent Power of intellect Knowledge, skill Courage, bravery Self-governance, governing others well Endurance, steadfastness, constancy Beneficence, prudence

At the same time that Boccaccio defends an inherent equality in capacity for wisdom and virtue in men and women, he does not fall into a gender unity model. On the contrary, Boccaccio continually points out significant differences in men's and women's situations and history. For this reason he contributes to the developing acceptance of gender complementarity. Boccaccio's works, as controversial as they are, are an important contribution to the history of the philosophy of the concept of woman in relation to man. They clearly offer a creatively engendered community of discourse about the concept of woman, and they move towards an authentic and new foundation for gender complementarity.

Nonetheless, Boccaccio's analysis is also limited because it does not yet articulate a sufficiently complex concept of person that would allow him to identify masculine characteristics applied to a woman without concluding that she loses her female identity, or feminine characteristics applied to a man without also concluding that the man thus loses his male identity. The identification of feminine with female, and masculine with male, leads Boccaccio to invent humorous descriptions of sex change in his imaginary descriptions of characters in his texts. At the same time, Boccaccio makes a historical advance in the history of the concept of woman because he recognizes that gender identity is far richer than previously thought, and he especially appreciates women's varied responses to men and to moral issues in life. In this way, Boccaccio is an extremely important transitional author in the history of the concept of woman.

HUMANIST DIALOGUE AND NEW FORMS
OF GENDER IDENTITY

In this chapter we have argued that a new concept of woman emerged right from the beginning of Italian Renaissance Humanism. In addition, we suggested that it was through the exercise of imagination — by which an author described characteristics of women's wisdom and virtue — that several counterexamples of the Aristotelian model of woman's identity appeared. Furthermore, we traced the developing sophistication of these imaginary female characters as they evolved from the end of the thirteenth century to the end of the fourteenth century. Finally, we suggested that the description of imaginary female characters engaged in intergender dialogue also included elements of reflection on fundamental issues of gender identity that tended towards a model of complementarity by the form of the dialogue itself. This form, which marks a significant departure from the gender monological models in academic and satirical texts, was previously described in this chapter. Therefore, we conclude that humanist dialogue introduced a new form of gender identity in western philosophy.

The chart on pages 313-14 sets forth a summary of some of the main characteristics found in the writings of early Italian humanist authors. The chart does not include those characteristics in the same authors that fall into the traditional Aristotelian model, but contains only those characteristics that suggest counterexamples to the traditional model. This is an important qualification because it means that the chart is not a complete summary of the authors included. Its purpose is rather to highlight only what is new in these authors with respect to the concept of woman. The chart also offers a general summary without differentiation between various texts. So the chart must be read in conjunction with the section of the chapter itself that discusses the author in more detail.

These early Italian Renaissance Humanists provided an orientation to philosophy that opened up new possibilities for the concept of woman. By projecting imaginary models of female characters who embodied different ways of being wise and virtuous than had been depicted in satires or academic texts that viewed women as malformed men, the humanists offered a way of overcoming bias that consistently devalued women. While it may be argued that these female characters are isolated exceptions to the general rule or stereotype of women, it is important to note that exceptions to a general rule can begin to challenge a bias that keeps a stereotype in place. They project an image that appears possible. Furthermore, when the imaginary images begin to proliferate, they gradually become the foundation for a new identity. Therefore, even though the presentation of the concept of woman was not always consistent in these early Italian humanist works, and at times even fell back into a pattern of gender polarity, it often rose above that pattern and thereby prepared the way for a reformation of the tradition.

For this reason, in the Renaissance Humanists we can see a movement to promote the development of women as equal and distinctly engendered partners in dialogue. The equal capacity of women and men for wisdom and virtue was matched by a conviction that women as well as men are responsible for their actions, and ultimately responsible for the quality of their lives. In Dante we see both

The New Concept of Woman in Early Italian Humanist Authors				
	Cavalcanti	Dante	Petrarch	Boccaccio
Thwarted relation to a real woman:	A woman from Toulouse whom he rejected	A woman from Florence who died in the plague	A woman who died in the plague	A woman from Naples who rejected him
Imaginary female characters in writings as counterexample to Aristotelian gender polarity:	'A Lady'	Beatrice Lady Philosophy	Laura Madonna Reason	Fiammetta Nurse The women of the *Decameron* Famous women
Wisdom in imaginary female characters 1. by discursive reasoning	x	x	x	x
2. by self-knowledge		x	x	x
3. in public speech		x		x
4. in teaching men		x	x	x
Virtue in imaginary female characters 1. by self-governance		x	x	x
2. in public actions		x	x	x

The New Concept of Woman in Early Italian Humanist Authors (cont.)				
	Cavalcanti	Dante	Petrarch	Boccaccio
3. in ruling men				x
Real women show wisdom and virtue in writings:		Descriptions of Beatrice	Letters about women	Biography of several women
Intergender dialogue in writings:	Description of a philosophical intergender dialogue: "A Lady asks me"	Extensive intergender dialogue with one woman	Many examples of intergender dialogue with different women	Many examples of intergender dialogue and women ruling men

women and men being held accountable after death for the choices they made and actions they performed while alive; in Petrarch we see both women and men being challenged to work consistently towards a greater degree of virtue; and in Boccaccio we see both women and men being challenged to overcome hypocrisy, to govern, and to refine their passions towards good ends.

While the traditional place of dialogue among men, or philosophers with the same goals, is always encouraged, in all of the authors considered we see a constant valuation of intergender dialogue. Since the authors are men, the dialogues are usually presented as showing ways that women can be helpful to men in gaining wisdom and virtue, but the effect is to suggest that men can be helpful to women as well. As we shall see in later developments in Renaissance Humanism, women humanists will soon depict this other side of the value of intergender dialogue.

The Humanist Reformation thus begins with these early Italian writers. They set a different path for philosophy, which usually leads outside of academia. They open up, through the exercise of their imaginations, new dimensions to the concept of woman. At the same time, it is generally thought that each one of these writers had an experience, however brief, of encountering a real woman who had a profound personal influence on his creating of imaginary female characters. So these humanist philosophers combined their personal experience of women with the exercise of the imagination in projecting new female identities. When we compare the concept of woman in these authors with that presented in the preceding three chapters of this book, it is clear that Renaissance Humanism provided an important contribution to the history of the concept of woman.

SECTION I

SUMMARY AND EVALUATION: GENDER AND ISOLATED COMMUNITIES OF DISCOURSE

As often mentioned in this Section, Aristotle's works became required reading at the University of Paris in 1250, and shortly afterwards most other western universities imitated Paris's example both in the structure and content of their curriculum. Women were not accepted as students or faculty within these new academic communities of discourse. One effect of this institutional arrangement was that the European philosophy of gender flowed through several different channels of communication that were somewhat isolated from one another. In academia we identified one stream of gender theory by tracing metaphysical, natural, epistemological, and ethical principles of gender polarity. We also identified a second stream of gender neutrality in theoretical approaches to logic, rhetoric, and "universal" or mathematically based science. This latter academic stream, when it shifted from a theoretical study of logic to the practical application of dialectic and argumentation in public debate or textbooks, often used examples from the gender polarity tradition. Therefore, even though the academic study of logic was gender neutral, the application of logic, both inside and outside of academia, often promoted gender polarity in its listing of particular characteristics of woman's identity.

During the same time period, i.e., the thirteenth and fourteenth centuries, satires about woman's identity appeared that incorporated concepts directly drawn from the academic gender polarity corpus. These satires devalued women further, either by exaggerating negative characteristics of women, or by inverting those characteristics traditionally associated with men and women in the polarity tradition. The audience for satires about women extended from within academia to the far reaches of the literate European population as well as to illiterate audiences who imbibed their contents through images and songs.

The communities of discourse that were immersed in academic and satirical texts about women contained only male members. The identity of women in this context included the following characteristics: overly emotional because their rational faculty was without authority over the passions, wise through having true opinions rather than reasoning discursively, silent rather than engaging in public speech, virtuous by obeying others rather than by ruling, and practicing virtue in the private rather than public domains. A more general summary of woman's inferior identity with respect to man was contained in the notions that a female was an accidental, imperfect, and deformed male. These characteristics were often supported by an appeal to Aristotle's philosophy. Therefore, they were described as part of the Aristotelian tradition of gender polarity.

In contrast to the elaboration of these particular characteristics of women within a model of gender polarity, we found that two other communities of discourse provided counterexamples of women who were considered wise or virtuous through embodying very different characteristics. Some religious women writers gave evidence of having authority over their passions, of engaging effectively in discursive reasoning, of writing publicly about wisdom and virtue, and of presenting the view that they, as women, were paradigms of religious virtue for both women and men. In addition to the discovery of women religious writers who were living counterexamples to Aristotelian gender polarity, we also saw that some early Italian humanist authors created several imaginary female characters who also served as counterexamples to traditional gender polarity. In particular, they manifested all the characteristics mentioned above of women religious writers along with the additional characteristic of participating in some shared forms of intergender ruling.

The most important advance found in the humanist works, however, is the presence of extensive examples of intergender dialogue. Time after time we discover a humanist author describing in great detail the form and content of a discussion between a woman and man about issues of wisdom and virtue. Often female characters serve as teachers and leaders of the male characters with whom they are engaged in dialogue. In addition, the authors attribute to women further specific virtues that have traditionally been associated with men. Finally, for the most part, humanist authors did not satirically blame women when men were neither wise nor virtuous; instead, they suggested that men be accountable for their own choices and actions.

So for these humanist writers, imaginary intergender dialogue became a way to overcome the exclusion of female characters from male communities of discourse about gender. The reflective use of the imagination broke open new ways to change thinking that had been encased in gender bias and negative stereotypes of women nourished by the academic transmission of rationale for gender polarity. The imagination began to break down the institutional walls of isolated communities of discourse about gender. Although western culture had still not reached the point when men and women openly engaged in philosophical dialogue about issues of gender, wisdom, and virtue, the first Italian humanists definitely prepared the way for this later development.

It is now possible to identify some of the key components in this beginning of the humanist reformation of the concept of woman. If the particular differences among individual authors are ignored for purposes of generalization, and if the main features of the four isolated communities of discourse are highlighted, then the elements of reform can be brought more sharply into focus. By shifting the arrangement of the four chapters in this section so that they line up in the order 2, 3, 1, and 4, we can see differences in the concept of woman in academic, satirical, religious, and humanist communities of discourse. Specifically, in the first column of the table on pages 318-19, specific characteristics falling within the polarity principles articulated within the academic community of discourse are listed. Then, reading from left to right, the ways in which satirists inverted or exaggerated these characteristics are introduced. Next, the manner in which women religious authors served as counterexamples to these gender polarity characteristics in both their texts and persons are identified. Finally, a variety of ways are listed to indicate how humanist authors introduce imaginary female characters who by word and action provide further counterexamples to the Aristotelian gender polarity principles. The empirical evidence for these generalized summaries along with exceptions are available in the individual chapters on each of these communities of discourse.

In *The Concept of Woman: The Aristotelian Revolution (750 BC–1250 AD)* it was argued that the institutionalization of Aristotelian thought, when combined with the exclusion of women from higher education, had created an environment in which a theory of gender complementarity could not flourish. Philosophers within the Benedictine monastic tradition had begun to articulate foundations for a theory of gender complementarity in both form and content. They had provided different arguments in four areas: the metaphysics of opposites, the natural philosophy of generation, the epistemology of wisdom, and the ethics of virtue, to explain how women and men were both similar and different. In particular, Hildegard of Bingen had sought to articulate a significant differentiation between men and women without that differentiation sliding into a polarity in which one sex was consistently devalued with respect to the other. The Aristotelian foundation for traditional gender polarity, which accepted the thesis of significant differentiation between the genders, but devalued the female, became the dominant theory of gender identity by the mid-thirteenth century. In this "Aristotelian Revolution" the monastic foundations for gender complementarity were lost, both in the practice of dialogue between women and men and in the content of the theory of gender identity.

In the period just studied in Section I of *The Concept of Woman: The Early Humanist Reformation,* we can see traces of religious foundations for gender complementarity in women religious writers and a slow movement towards new foundations for gender complementarity in humanist authors. It is not a coincidence that these male humanist writers spent time in their own lives in the company of women, for the development of a theory of gender complementarity usually follows upon the experience of some form of complementary dialogue between men and women. Both in the Benedictine tradition from 800 to 1200 as well as in the humanist era, intergender dialogue occurred.

The theory of gender complementarity maintains a balance between the two factors of sameness or equality of dignity of men and women and significant differentiation of men and women. The Aristotelian model of gender polarity emphasized gender differentiation with the devaluation of the female. In contrast to the Aristotelian model, which emphasizes difference, the Platonic model emphasizes sameness. Incorporating a dualistic philosophy of the human being, Platonist theories often slide into a unisex model in which all significant differentiation between men and women is lost. In this first section of the book we saw that tendency present in Marguerite Porete's Neoplatonic religious text. A Platonic distinction between appearance and reality was also given a satirical gender polarity association in satires that identified the female with the corruptible aspects of human life. In contrast to these two Platonic tendencies, gender complementarity maintains a

Characteristics of Woman in Communities of Discourse (1250-1400)			
Female Characteristics in Aristotelian Gender Polarity	Exaggerated or Inverted by Satirists	Women Religious as Counterexamples	Humanists offer Imaginary Female Characters
Rational faculty without authority over passions	Ignorance of self, of motivations; wrathful	Seeks self-knowledge	Nobility of virtue by reason ruling passions
Wise through true opinion; not through discursive reason	Reasons fallaciously	Analyzes several levels of personal experience; interior dialogues	Understands principles of wisdom and teaches them discursively to others
Silence in public	Complains; reproaches; quarrels publicly	Writes religious works; gives public statements	Dialogues with men about wisdom and virtue
No self-control; inconstant	Shifts points of view; cannot keep secrets; tells all	Exercises will in self-control; moderates desires; and makes conscious choices	Constant and steadfast in virtue
No self-governance; gives in to impulsive desires	Gluttonous; covetous; lustful	Overcomes desires; governs senses	Self-governing and virtuous
Not able to rule over others; either passive or dominating	Passive in seduction by men; or crushes men; makes men passive; inverts gender order of obedience and ruling	Chooses to rule or obey depending upon the situation	Rules by quality of virtue; rotating rule by agreement in collaboration with men
Public action not appropriate; virtue private sphere only	Ridicules men in public	Practices the virtues in apostolic actions; publicly calls people to conversion in specific situations	Multiple examples of women practicing virtue in public

Characteristics of Woman in Communities of Discourse (1250-1400)			
Female Characteristics in Aristotelian Gender Polarity	Exaggerated or Inverted by Satirists	Women Religious as Counterexamples	Humanists offer Imaginary Female Characters
Accidental, imperfect, or deformed male	Every woman a monster, conceived without nature's approval	Perfection possible through union with God	Perfectly formed by nature and transformed by grace
Male academic forms of discourse	Male satirical forms of discourse	Female religious forms of discourse; dialogue with God and in private with males	Male humanist forms of discourse; dialogue in private with women and in imaginary intergender dialogues
'He' as paradigm analogously extended to include women	Stereotyped univocal paradigms for men and women	'She' as paradigm analogously extended to include men	Dialogue between a 'he' and a 'she' as imaginary paradigm

tension of balance between sameness and difference without giving up either aspect. Significant differences between men and women are recognized without devaluing one gender or the other; and fundamental sameness or equality of human dignity is recognized without losing personal or gender identity. In many of the imaginary humanist dialogues described in this section we found this balance maintained and given new dimensions.

Finally, in some of the works just considered we discovered a new consciousness about the possible presence of "masculine" characteristics in women and "feminine" characteristics in men. They included a reflection on a woman's masculine writing style, masculine appearance, masculine strength, and masculine ways of acting; and on a man's feminine weakness and feminine ways of acting. We noted that the term 'masculine' usually, but not always, connoted a favorable characteristic for women, and that the term 'feminine' nearly always connoted the derogatory effeminate characteristic when applied to men. These observations implied that the application of the labels 'masculine' and 'feminine' to the opposite sexes of female and male promoted a polarity devaluation of woman.

At the same time, however, it is important to note that the observation that a female may have masculine characteristics and a male have feminine characteristics, without implying a derogatory switch of gender identity, marks a new awareness of the two-dimensionality of the human psyche. In other words, in the thirteenth century we begin to find more and more philosophers recognizing that men and women are slightly more complicated than simply male beings with masculine characteristics and female beings with feminine characteristics. While it will take around six more centuries until philosophers articulate theories about this complex fact of human existence, an early awareness of this fact among humanists and women religious authors is clearly evident. It is also interesting that authors who contributed to this development in the consideration of masculine and feminine characteristics (Mechtild's letter to her spiritual director, Petrarch's letters describing women he met, and Boccaccio's biography of famous women) were all reflecting on real women.

In conclusion, Section I described gender theory as it evolved in academia. It also uncovered the foundations for new theories of gender as they were articulated outside the institutionalized gender monologue of academic philosophy. We shall now turn to Section II to examine the development of new foundations during the next phase of the Humanist Reformation in the concept of woman.

SECTION II

THE BEGINNING OF PUBLIC
DIALOGUE ABOUT GENDER

I n the second phase of the development of the concept of woman
in Early Renaissance Humanism intergender dialogue occurs
more frequently, both in private and in public forms of discourse. Public dialogue
takes place in speech and in writing through the exchange of letters and texts.
Women and men begin to ponder carefully texts written by the other gender.
Women readers also begin to ponder texts written by other women. One source of
this dialogue among women authors and women readers is that new women authors decide to write or dictate their own texts. Dialogue also begins to occur
among members of the separated communities of discourse: academics, religious
authors, and humanists begin to directly influence one another. More and more often their dialogue focuses on issues of gender identity. With the invention of the
printing press in 1450, written texts about women's identity begin to abound
throughout Europe.

A significant theme that emerges in this section is the shifting of intergender
dialogue from private to public realms of discourse. A new conjunction of
intergender dialogue, analogical thinking, and gender complementarity can be
noted with special attention to the similarities and differences that are found in
these three areas. More specifically, in Chapter 5 we will consider analogical reasoning and intergender dialogue in both private and public situations of
complementarity. In addition, we will note selected examples of virtuous public action by women religious authors.

In Chapter 6 we juxtapose these situations with new satirical renditions of
traditional gender polarity. The use of an appeal to an Aristotelian rationale to
shore up arguments for gender polarity is also noted. Then, in Chapter 7 we consider Christine de Pizan's work regarding the arguments of satirical authors aimed
at developing a philosophically grounded concept of woman in the categories of
wisdom and virtue. In addition, her extensive writings reveal a remarkable talent
for philosophical argumentation concerning the concept of woman.

In Chapter 8 the battle between different positions on the education of
woman is delineated. New reforms in the concept of woman are studied in relation
to schools of humanistic studies. Humanist educators like Guarino and Vittorino
begin to make it possible for women to receive a higher education. These institutional reforms lead to women writing orations, epistles of significance, and enter-

ing into a sophisticated philosophical discourse about woman's identity with other humanists. Authors such as Bruni, Alberti, and Valla begin to reflect on the importance of intergender relations, especially in the extended household. Humanist theories about women's identities are also dispersed outside of France and Italy to Germany and England.

In addition, the direct translation and introduction of Plato's philosophy into discussions of gender identity lead such philosophers as Nicholas of Cusa, Marsilio Ficino, and Giovanni Pico della Mirandola to raise some interesting new theories about gender identity. At the end of this period under study, it is argued that human beings have an important responsibility for determining significant moral levels of their own identity. Thus a new dignity of the human being is dramatically affirmed. Finally, at the conclusion of the fifteenth century Laura Cereta incorporates into her own writings many of the most important humanist themes and thus leaves behind an important legacy of her own efforts to teach about human dignity and woman's identity. In sum, the imaginary models of wise and virtuous women, which had been previously posed by Dante, Petrarch, and Boccaccio, become actualized in Christine de Pizan, Isotta Nogarola, and Laura Cereta. This actualization occurred through the intergender humanist dialogue that occurred among many men and women of the fourteenth and fifteenth centuries. It was a collective effect of the efforts of many persons who together provided the foundation for the Early Humanist Reformation in the concept of woman.

In summary, Section II of *The Concept of Woman: The Early Humanist Reformation (1250-1500)* traces the dynamic, sometimes even violent, dialogue that characterizes the joint struggle of women and men to come to a clearer understanding of woman's identity. It also brings into the light the first direct philosophical arguments in the West by women about gender identity. In spite of their exclusion from academic debate and learning, women Renaissance Humanists did learn the skills appropriate to philosophical discourse in both vernacular languages and in classical Latin. As a result, they made significant contributions to the philosophy of gender. However, before we reach this important development in the history of philosophy, we need to consider the intellectual background within which the early Renaissance Humanist debate took place: religious women authors and satirical authors.

CHAPTER 5

WOMEN RELIGIOUS AUTHORS
DEVELOP ANALOGICAL THINKING

In our study of texts attributed to women religious authors in Chapter 1 of this book, a common support for the virtues of self-knowledge and self-governance is identified. The authors considered in Chapter 5 continue to defend these two themes. In addition, they go further than their predecessors by developing wider ranges for the use of discursive reasoning, and particularly by extending it into analogical thinking. Their theological and sometimes mystical experiences need new philosophical categories of explanation because the old categories invented by others no longer seem adequate. The intersubjective experience of the Divine Person interacting in dialogue or simple presence with a particular human being affects the person at increasingly deeper levels, and a writer attempts to express its successive integration at all levels of his or her human personality. Within this dynamic the women writers considered in this chapter produce new models of integration at the point where the intellect infused with the presence of God meets the discursive reason seeking to understand. The unique choice of which analogical model to propose to others springs from the point where the deep freedom of a human person meets a particular decision drawn from the data of experience.

The women authors considered in this chapter also initiated new forms of public action and public teaching about virtue. Finally, they engaged in more sophisticated forms of public dialogue through both speech and writing. Here, the women did not break out and create new ways of thinking, but they were propelled into areas of activity that had been commonly limited to men. Yet, some of them pioneered new ways of thinking about what women were able to do for the development of the common good. In this way they began to open up possibilities that, in time, would reform the concept of woman for others.

Even though in the academic world philosophy became separated from theology and established as an autonomous discipline, outside the universities religious authors still intermingled arguments from reason with arguments from faith. Since the authors in this chapter are primarily women, and since women were not yet trained to work within the stricter limits of academic philosophy, their texts do not contain the rigor we saw in our analysis of academic texts in Chapter 2. This lack of academic rigor, however, does not mean that no philosophical reasoning occurred within the texts of these authors. As I hope to demonstrate, women continued to think about their own identity, both religiously and philosophically. They also entered into various forms of dialogue about it. It is possible to extract philosophical arguments from the writings of the religious authors. When this extraction is done systematically we rediscover a certain pattern of argumentation within which a structure of the concept of woman is articulated. This structure, when compared with Aristotelian-based gender polarity principles, reveals how the concept of woman in religious women authors serves as a direct counterexample to the Aristotelian model.

In Chapter 1, we traced different forms of private dialogue among women religious authors during the thirteenth century.[1] These dialogues, which included references to dialogue with God as well as interior dialogues within the self, described stages of acquiring wisdom and virtue through self-knowledge, self-governance, and actions. They also introduced questions about the relations among senses, reason, body, soul, and will. In the next stage of development, as depicted in the present chapter, we will find an augmentation of analogical thinking by women religious authors. Analogical thinking demands particular skills of intellect: attention to the data of experience, ability to separate what is essential from what is accidental, capacity for discursive reasoning in assessing what is alike and what is different, recognition of the limits of reason and of particular analogies, and capacity for logical deduction from premises to conclusion. The discovery of increasingly complex forms of analogical thinking in texts of women religious indicates that women were growing in philosophical ability even outside the more formal academic development of the discipline of philosophy.

When specific texts are considered, we focus on the variety of ways authors use analogical thinking, on the various base analogates they choose for their analogies, and on the discursive reasoning used to elaborate these analogies. In the analysis, the expression 'analogical thinking' and 'analogies' will be taken as generic for metaphors, similes, parables, allegories, and so forth.[2]

Since analogical thinking is taken as a measure of philosophical development in the concept of woman, it would be useful to introduce some distinctions among various kinds of analogies here. Traditionally, philosophers distinguish analogies of attribution from analogies of proportion. In the former, **properties** attributed to two different kinds of things are seen as analogous; while in the latter, **relations** between two things are seen as analogous to relations between two other things within a common genus. In all analogical thinking there are always two fun-

---

1. It is important to reiterate that the philosophical approach to the texts of these authors should be understood in the broader context of the development of religious life during this period. In addition to specific references in this chapter see Caroline Walker Bynum, "Religious Women in the Later Middle Ages," in *Christian Spirituality: High Middle Ages and Reformation,* ed. Jill Raitt (New York: Crossroad, 1987), pp. 121-39; Penelope D. Johnson, *Equal in Monastic Profession: Religious Women in Medieval France* (Chicago and London: University of Chicago Press, 1991); and Valerie M. Lagorio, "The Medieval Continental Women Mystics: An Introduction," in *An Introduction to the Medieval Mystics of Europe,* ed. Paul E. Czarmach (Albany: State University of New York Press, 1984), pp. 161-93.

2. This practice follows the definition of analogical, analogy, analogate, and analog in the Oxford English Dictionary. All metaphors, similes, parables, and allegories use the same conceptual structure of drawing a comparison of two things which have a similarity and a difference.

damental components: (1) similarity and (2) difference. This would be the case for two analogical properties, relations, concepts, words, themes, interpretations, and even things. In every case where we find an analogy we may ask: What is similar and what is different?

Analogical thinking is a development in the complexity of reasoning because it involves adhering to an intellectual tension of conjoining similarity with difference. A simpler intellectual act would be an affirmation of only one of the analogates. If a person chooses to understand a word, concept, or theme through only one of the factors, then the analogy dissolves. When focusing only on similarity, the thinking becomes univocal. The words, concepts, and themes have only a singular interpretation. When focusing only on difference, the thinking becomes equivocal. In this situation words, concepts, or themes have only nominal application and no real application to comparable things.

In this chapter, I distinguish among three different categories of analogy: horizontal, vertical, and transcendental. These categories describe distinctions among different categories of analogates and they introduce ways in which a particular kind of analogy works. Examples of each kind of analogy drawn from the history of philosophy are introduced to clarify the distinctions between horizontal, vertical, and transcendental analogies.[3]

If we take the example of the proportional analogy of '2 is to 4 as 4 is to 8,' we can identify the similarity as the relation of doubling and the difference as the quantity of the integers. This is an example of a **horizontal analogy** because its analogates are the same kind of things, i,e., all numbers. We could say that they belong to the same genus and differentia, i.e., they have the same kind of being. Another example of a horizontal analogy commonly found in school analogy tests is something like 'a dog is to puppies as a cat is to kittens.' The horizontal analogy is the most common form of analogy.

As a tangential point of interest to the concept of woman, it is worth noting that among the Pythagorean philosophers, so interested in analogical thinking, there were both women and men. Thus, right at the beginning of the philosophy of analogy there is a coincidence between interest in analogical thinking and the active practice of intergender dialogue.[4] This coincidence is worth reflecting on, because a philosophy of complementarity considers a woman and a man as analogous to one another; there is something similar (human identity) and something different (male and female identity). More recently, M. A. Krapiec elaborated a theory of the ways in which names are attributed analogously to things of the same species. His theory articulates an ontology of horizontal analogy. His theory has possible application to a philosophy of horizontal analogy of man and woman.[5]

3. For a more thorough description of these different kinds of analogy see Prudence Allen, R.S.M., "Analogy and Human Community in Lublin Existential Personalism," *Toronto Journal of Theology* 5, no. 2 (Fall 1989): 236-46.

4. There are also many women Neopythagorean philosophers whose names and texts are still available and whose own theories included elements of polarity, complementarity, and unity. See Mario Meunier, *Femmes Pythagoriciennes* (Paris: L'Artisan du livre, 1932).

5. M. A. Krapiec, *Metaphysics: An Outline of the History of Being* (New York: Peter Lang, 1991). See also an application of this theory of analogy to gender issues in Prudence Allen, R.S.M., "A Woman

The second category of analogy, or **vertical analogy**, was introduced and developed by Plato. In the *Republic,* the Greek philosopher developed a vertical analogy when he described the State as a "soul writ large" and when he elaborated the four virtues of wisdom, courage, temperance, and justice in the state and in the soul. He also introduced a second vertical analogy when he developed the allegory of the cave, with the Good as analogous to the sun and the invisible world as analogous to the visible world. These analogies draw a comparison between analogates on two different levels of being — in Plato's examples, one visible and the other invisible, or one sensible and the other formal and intelligible. There is the implication in a vertical analogy that the analogate on the higher level of being has a greater degree of perfection than the analogate on the lower level of being.

Plato argued that the ability to use dialectic or reason to grasp the different levels of knowledge along the 'divided line' took many years of education. The philosopher usually began with sense experience of good things and then worked his way up the 'divided line' by thinking dialectically until he reached a vision of the Good and understood the true relations among the Forms, or intellectual realities, and things in the world. Analogical thinking was a skill that Plato admired, and he encouraged men and women to pursue it as their way to wisdom and virtue.

Again it is worth reflecting on the tangential fact that Plato's philosophy emphasized dialogue as well as analogical thinking. While most Platonic dialogue occurred among men, there are some examples that include women, e.g., Diotima. There is also dialogue among men about woman's identity in *Republic* and *Laws.* In these works Plato suggested that in an ideal society, men and women who were philosophers would exchange ideas about wisdom and virtue throughout their lives. Historical texts indicate that intergender dialogue actually did occur in Neoplatonist contexts, e.g., between Porphyry and his wife Marcella, Hypatia and her colleagues. So, the coincidence of intergender dialogue and the use of analogical thinking that we first observed in Pythagorean communities of discourse continues in Platonist and Neoplatonist communities of discourse.[6]

The intersection of religious thinking in Judaism and Christianity with philosophical thinking inherited from Greece introduced a third kind of analogy in which one of the analogates is a completely spiritual entity. In **transcendental analogies**, while one analogate is taken from something in the world, something either observable through the senses or accessible to reason, the second analogate is accessible only by faith.[7] It is outside the bounds of reason, and thus, even though

---

and a Man as Prime Analogical Beings," *American Catholic Philosophical Quarterly* 66, no. 4 (1992): 465-82.

6. A further aspect of Platonic dialogue is its tendency to devalue the body, and subsequently to devalue gender differentiation. Also frequently in the dialogue itself one of the individuals participating is not a full and genuine participant. So the disciple simply is overwhelmed by the Master's theories, and gender of the female disciple is lost as well. In Chapter 1 in a discussion of Mechtild, we mentioned a difference between 'horizontal' dialogues in which the two participants keep a balance of tension, and 'vertical' dialogues in which one member of the dialogue overwhelms the other.

7. This follows directly the model of Jesus, the "Word made Flesh" who spoke in parables. When his disciples asked him why he did this, he answered enigmatically that some would understand

there is a hierarchy of analogates as there was in vertical analogies, human reason cannot by itself grasp both analogates through the exercise of dialectic. Thus, this second analogate 'transcends' human experience, reason, and the world itself. Proofs for the existence of God are examples of vertical analogies, but descriptions of who God is involve transcendental analogies.

An analogy of attribution is usually considered with respect to names shared by God and man when God has the prime attribution and man the derived (e.g., God is good and man is good). However, it can also be used in another way when the focus is not on a similarity of proportion, but a similarity of attribute. In this derived sense of attribution we can say that a man and a woman both have similar rational faculties but may have different qualities in some respects. We can analogously attribute rationality to them.[8] The former example of attribution (to God and man) is a transcendental analogy, while the latter example (to man and woman) is a horizontal analogy.

While both the vertical and transcendental analogies involve a hierarchy among the analogates, in the vertical analogy both analogates are still a part of the world while in the transcendental analogy one of the analogates completely transcends the world. We see Philo, the first-century Jewish philosopher, constantly using transcendental, vertical, and horizontal analogies in his development of different kinds of meanings of passages in Scripture. In addition, the early Church fathers, and particularly St. Augustine, adopted a similar method for interpreting Scripture and spiritual realities. Common examples of a transcendental analogy would include: the Kingdom of Heaven is like a mustard seed; the relation among the Divine Persons in the Trinity is like the relations among the human memory, understanding, and will; and the Goodness of God is analogous to the goodness of a human person.[9]

It is interesting to note that right from the beginning of the book of *Genesis,* dialogue is introduced between man and woman and with God as a third party to the dialogue in conversation with Adam, Eve, Abraham, Rebecca, Jacob, and Moses.[10] Contemporary Jewish philosophers Martin Buber and Emmanuel Levinas

---

and others would not, implying that unless faith supplied the spiritual analogate, the person would not be able to grasp the similarity and difference. See Matthew 13:10-16, where Jesus explains why he speaks to people in parables. The transcendental analogate must be given by faith.

8. See Sr. Prudence Allen, "Rationality, Gender, and History," *American Catholic Philosophical Association Quarterly* 68 (1994): 271-88.

9. St. Thomas Aquinas, *Summa theologica* (Garden City, N.Y.: 1964), elaborated the theory of transcendental analogy as follows: "We must say, therefore, that words are used of God and creatures in an analogical way, that is in accordance with a certain order between them. We can distinguish two kinds of analogical or 'proportional' uses of language. Firstly, there is the case of one word being used of two things because each of them has some order or relation to a third thing. . . . Secondly, there is the case of the same word used of two things because of some relation that one has to the other. . . . In this way some words are used neither univocally nor purely equivocally of God and creatures, but analogically, for we cannot speak of God at all except in the language we use of creatures, and so whatever is said both of God and creatures is said in virtue of the order that creatures have to God as to their source and cause in which all the perfections of things pre-exist transcendentally" (I, Q.13, art. 10).

10. See, for example, Christine Allen, "Who Was Rebecca? On Me Be the Curse, My Son," in *Encounter with the Text,* ed. Martin Buss (Missoula, Montana: Scholar's Press, 1979), ch. 10, pp. 159-72.

emphasize the role of dialogue in philosophy. Similarly, at the beginnings of Christianity, the Annunciation is represented as a dialogue between an angel of God and Mary,[11] and Scripture presents Jesus as frequently teaching through forms of dialogue with his disciples.[12] In fact, Christianity can be described as a religion mediated through dialogue between God and human beings.[13] Thus it is not surprising that the philosophical impulse arising within Christian men and women authors would express itself in the form of dialogue, with transcendental analogies of increasing depth and originality.

In the historical period considered in this section of the book, we will see evidence of much private dialogue. Dialogue between the author and God, and within the self, is enhanced by dialogue among women and between men and women. At the same time, analogical thinking develops in increasingly complex forms. It is interesting to reflect on the fact that creative dialogue needs two people who are simultaneously similar and different, and that analogical thinking also needs at least two analogates that are simultaneously similar and different. Thus, we note again that intergender dialogue and analogical thinking share the basic components of similarity and difference held together in a creative tension.

In this chapter we will reflect on specific ways in which some women religious writers developed analogical thinking during the thirteenth and fourteenth centuries. We will see a movement from short concise analogies suggested by the Helfta nuns, St. Mechtild of Hackeborn and St. Gertrude, to lengthy analogies elaborated through discursive reasoning by St. Bridget, St. Catherine of Siena, and Blessed Julian of Norwich. In the midst of this development of analogical thinking by women religious writers, we will juxtapose some analogical thinking about gender identity in the works of Meister Eckhart and some intergender dialogue among his disciples. It will also help to provide evidence of an increasing private intergender dialogue associated in particular with the development of Dominican practice.[14] In addition, in this chapter the dialogue between the Dominicans, Johannes Tauler and Margaret and Christine Ebner, and Henry Suso and Elsbeth

---

11. Pope John Paul II, *Mulieris Dignitatem* (Boston: Daughters of Saint Paul, 1988), "This event is clearly *interpersonal in character:* it is a dialogue" (#5). He adds later in a discussion of Jesus' use of dialogue to teach: "This conversation with Martha [about the meaning of resurrection] is one of the most important in the Gospel" (#15).

12. See Sr. Mary Prudence Allen, R.S.M., "Language and the Invitation to Conversion," in *Language and Faith: Proceedings from the Nineteenth Convention of the Fellowship of Catholic Scholars* (St. Louis, Mo., 1997), pp. 93-128.

13. See, for example, *Catechism of the Catholic Church* (New York: Doubleday, 1995), #2653.

14. See John Coakley, who traces several examples of dialogue between Dominican friars and religious women including Siger of Lille and the laywoman Margaret of Ypres (d. 1237), Peter of Dacia (d. 1289) and the Beguine, Christine of Stommeln (1242-1312), Conrad of Castillerio and the Third Order Dominican, Benvenuta Boiani (1255-1292), Raymond of Capua and Third Order Dominican, Catherine of Siena, Thomas Antonii (Caffarini) and the Third Order Dominican, Mary Sturion of Venice (1380-1399), Sebastian of Perugia (1445-1525) and the Third Order Dominican, Columba of Rieta (1467-1501), and Francis Silvestri of Ferrara (d. 1528) and the Third Order Dominican, Osanna of Mantua (1449-1505), "Friars as Confidants of Holy Women in Medieval Dominican Hagiography," in *Images of Sainthood in Medieval Europe,* ed. Renate Blumenfeld-Kosinski and Timea Szell (Ithaca and London: Cornell University Press, 1991), pp. 222-46.

Stagel, will be mentioned along with the work of another Dominican, Henry of Halle, in transmitting the writing of Mechtild of Magdeburg. The role of Dominican men in promoting the work of women authors during this transitional period in the history of the concept of woman is an important fact to note.

Women religious authors considered in this chapter were exposed to analogical thinking primarily through religious rather than philosophical authors. At the same time, however, they developed their capacities for discursive thinking in the elaboration of both vertical and transcendental analogies. The vertical analogies in their texts differ in one respect from those in Plato's texts. With women religious writers, the initial insight for a vertical analogy may be provided by an illumination of faith, but both analogates are something in the world. In other words, they may compare two kinds of things in the world, one of which is a higher or more perfect kind of thing than the other. The fact that women religious authors develop both vertical and transcendental analogies offers evidence of philosophical activity without having been schooled academically in philosophical theories. Perhaps it is not surprising that all the women in this chapter were engaged in intergender private dialogue on a regular basis.

It is significant for the history of the concept of woman that the three women authors of Helfta form the first historical example of women authors who were part of the same community of discourse. Through this private infragender dialogue within a monastic environment, women helped form one another as authors. The later gathering of their works into manuscripts allowed their thinking to enter the public arena of discourse. In this way, what began as a private community of discourse ended as a participant in public communities of discourse. The community of discourse of women religious authors at Helfta extended far beyond their monastic walls into the broader communities of discourse shared by men and women religious writers throughout Europe.

In this study, we try to demonstrate that the religious women authors of the thirteenth and fourteenth centuries attended to their own experience, posed questions, elaborated and tested theories, and made judgments that reveal a philosophy of gender identity embedded within their religious experience. Finally, we consider various forms of intergender dialogue and note how these dialogues moved from private to public realms of discourse.

Chapter 5 is divided into three parts. The first part focuses on the end of a major phase in the context of monastic education for women. Texts of women authors from the Benedictine and Cistercian monastic tradition at Helfta are analyzed: St. Mechtild of Hackeborn and St. Gertrude of Helfta. In the second part, texts of the Dominican mendicant friars who worked directly with Dominican women religious — Meister Eckhart, Johannes Tauler, and Henry Suso's collaboration with Elsbeth Stagel — are discussed. The third part of the chapter examines texts written by women religious authors who were especially unique in their particular vocations. None of the women were part of an ancient monastic order, or even of a religious community in the usual sense. Each one forged a new identity for herself, and each one's legacy of texts reveals a new depth of communication with increasingly complex skills of analogical thinking about woman's identity. The authors considered in the third part are: St. Bridget, Mother and Foundress of the Brigittines; St. Catherine of Siena, Third Order Dominican and apostolic worker; and Julian of Norwich, Anchoress and gifted writer of the English language.

Even though this chapter is lengthy, it sets up an important foundation for an analysis of developments charted in subsequent chapters. It demonstrates that, despite the exclusion of women from higher education offered in universities, women continued to develop intellectually. It also gives evidence of the particular way women articulated their self-understanding with respect to the values of wisdom and virtue. In particular, it shows how men, trained in Dominican colleges, served as an intermediary between academia and women religious; and it shows how women who engaged in intergender dialogue with these men grew in their own skills of expression. It further demonstrates how women began to influence one another in person and through written texts. A kind of natural philosophical talent was nourished in spiritual contexts. They establish the historical context for the radically opposite views, expressed in the next chapter, in which women's wisdom and virtue are severely questioned, their identity attacked verbally, and in some cases, particular women attacked violently. It is these attacks that in turn provide the historical context in which Early Renaissance Humanist reform springs into action.

MONASTIC AUTHORS

The most remarkable historical collaboration occurred among four women who gathered together at a monastery in Helfta. Three of the women were authors and the fourth was an educator. While prior to this time we have written records of individual women authors (Roswitha, Hildegard, Herrad, or Beatrice of Nazareth, for example), this is the first cluster of women authors to have left sufficient collaborative evidence that they formed a kind of infragender community of discourse. Their lives crossed paths, they lived with one another, and they influenced one another's thinking and writing. Loosely referred to as the "two Mechtilds" (of Magdeburg and Hackeborn) and the "two Gertrudes" (of Hackeborn and "The Great"), these nuns from Helfta begin a new phase in the history of the concept of woman. At the same time, however, the Helfta community of women scholars signals the end of an era of monastic education of women who contributed to the history of the concept of woman by their authored texts. After Helfta, many women authors seem to choose other than monastic contexts within which to flourish. There are exceptions to this, such as St. Teresa of Avila in the Carmelite tradition and Marie of the Incarnation in the Ursuline tradition, but on the whole religious women authors began to live and write outside of monasteries. The great Benedictine monastic era, which had provided higher education for religious women for several centuries, and fostered original written work by women authors in literature, science, history, and philosophy as well as in spiritual theology, was coming to an end. Monasteries now began to serve more as resource libraries or preservers of the past, rather than higher educational centers for developing something new. The particular impact of these developments on the history of the concept of woman will now be considered in more detail.

St. Mechtild of Hackeborn (c. 1240–c. 1298)

In 1247 at the age of seven, Mechtild of Hackeborn followed her older sister Gertrude of Hackeborn into a monastery. Just eleven years later her sister and mentor Gertrude was elected Abbess of this monastery, which loosely followed the Cistercian order.[15] In 1258 the Abbess Gertrude moved the community to a new location and reestablished it with a Benedictine rule.

The Abbess Gertrude developed her community as an educational center for higher learning at exactly the same time the University of Paris was being established as a center of learning for men. Aristotle's works had just been made required reading at the University of Paris, and in most parts of Europe the "dissolution of the Benedictine monopoly" on education occurred.[16] Gertrude collected a vast library of books and insisted ". . . that the girls should be instructed in the liberal arts, for she said that if the pursuit of knowledge (*studium scientiae*) were to perish, they would no longer be able to understand holy writ, and religion together with devotion would disappear."[17] Accordingly she established a rigorous curriculum of grammar, rhetoric, logic, mathematics, astronomy, music, Latin, and classical authors.[18]

It was to this intellectually active monastery that the elderly, blind Beguine, Mechtild of Magdeburg, retired in 1285. We are told that the older Mechtild engaged in dialogue with the younger Mechtild, and that she appreciated her friendship.[19] Mechtild of Magdeburg, whose works were considered in Chapter 1, had nearly finished her own writing by the time she arrived at Helfta. Thus, it is possible that her example encouraged the younger Mechtild to discuss her religious experiences with other women. Seven years after Mechtild of Magdeburg arrived at Helfta, around 1292, Mechtild of Hackeborn, now fifty-two years old, began to share some of the content of her religious experiences with members of her community, who secretly wrote them down during the following seven years. The first five sections of *The Book of Special Grace* were completed during the years 1292-1298, the last two sections shortly after her death in 1298. From 1285 until her death in 1297, Mechtild of Magdeburg dictated the final section of *The Flowing Light of the Godhead,* under the careful guidance of the Abbess Gertrude of Hackeborn.

15. The monastery adopted the practice and habit of the Cistercians without ever officially being incorporated into the Cistercian order. See Carolyn Bynum, *Jesus as Mother* (Berkeley: University of California Press, 1982), p. 175.

16. R. W. Southern, *Western Society and the Church in the Middle Ages* (Harmondsworth: Penguin Books, 1982), p. 240.

17. Lina Eckenstein, *Women Under Monasticism* (Cambridge: Cambridge University Press, 1986), p. 328.

18. Sister Mary Jeremy, O.P., *Scholars and Mystics* (Chicago: Henry Regnery Company, 1962), p. 14. This text has been revised and republished as Mary Jeremy Finnegan, O.P., *The Women of Helfta: Scholars and Mystics* (Athens, Ga. and London: University of Georgia Press, 1991).

19. See Jeremy Finnegan, "Saint Mechtild of Hackeborn," in *Medieval Religious Women: Peaceweavers: Vol. II,* ed. Lillian Thomas Shank and John A. Nichols (Kalamazoo: Cistercian Publications, 1987). Finnegan states: "When she first came to Helfta, she was enchanted by Mechtild's conversation and more impressed by her than by St. Gertrude" (p. 216).

One of the secret recorders of Mechtild of Hackeborn's reflections was also called Gertrude, not to be confused with Abbess Gertrude. The younger Gertrude, who was to become St. Gertrude the Great, later edited Mechtild of Hackeborn's revelations and produced a Latin text of nearly 100,000 words entitled *Liber specialis gratiae,* or *The Book of Special Grace,* and sometimes also called simply *The Revelations of St. Mechtild.* This work was widely disseminated in Germany, France, England, and Italy.[20] At exactly the same period during which early Italian Humanists began to write their texts in the vernacular, in part to make them accessible to women readers, women religious writers wrote their texts in Latin in part to make them accessible to men readers. Of course, Latin was the language for prayer and study in most monastic communities. Previously, women monastic writers such as Hildegard of Bingen also wrote in Latin.

The monastery at Helfta housed two Gertrudes and two Mechtilds. As just mentioned, the Abbess Gertrude, educator and leader of the community, gathered a library containing both religious and secular sources, and she established an environment of higher education for the others. In her final years, Mechtild of Magdeburg found refuge and friendship in its educational enclosure. Mechtild of Hackeborn was empowered to share her own thinking with others through its literate recorders, and Gertrude the Great's compilation and writing allowed for the wide dispersion of the results of the intellectual and spiritual discoveries among religious women. Helfta, under the leadership of Abbess Gertrude, is the first example of a female infragender community of discourse in the West that included three significant authors.

It is important to note that within this female educational context at Helfta the women were in frequent dialogue with men. Even though the monastery unofficially followed first a Cistercian and later a Benedictine rule, "[b]y the late thirteenth century its confessors were Dominicans, probably from Halle or Magdeburg."[21] Sister Mary Jeremy, O.P. also notes that "[u]nder Papal order, and later, in 1256 by ruling of the Chapter of Florence, the Dominican friars were required to act as the spiritual directors not only of Dominican nuns but of the members of other orders as well."[22] A Dominican, Henry of Halle, is reputed to have collected and organized the parts of Mechtild of Magdeburg's book into the integrated text *The Flowing Light of the Godhead;* another Dominican director at Helfta encouraged her to write a seventh book to the text; and Mechtild of Hackeborn's *The Book of Special Grace* as well as Gertrude's *The Herald of Divine Love* were approved in written testimonials by Dominicans.[23]

With this background, it is not surprising to discover that Mechtild's writings include direct references to the great Dominican philosophers and theologians, Albert and Thomas Aquinas. In fact, here we find the first evidence that a woman author was aware of the significance of these men. In addition, Mechtild directly mentions Albert's and Thomas's philosophical source, Aristotle. Mechtild's reflections concern the judgment of God on their souls after death. Aristotle is described

20. Jeremy, *Scholars,* pp. 65-66.
21. Bynum, *Jesus as Mother,* p. 175.
22. Jeremy, *Scholars,* p. 10.
23. Bynum, *Jesus as Mother,* pp. 179-80.

as having been treated kindly by God even though he "stopped at nature" and did not reach supernatural truth.[24] In contrast, Albert and Thomas are described as entering Heaven "having been enlightened by divine science . . . and burning with an ardent love not only for God but also for knowledge and intelligence, . . . [and] when they arrived before the throne of God, all the words of their writings appeared on their clothes, written in gold."[25] Thomas had died in 1270, Albert in 1280, and in 1278 the General Chapter of the Dominican Order imposed the teaching of St. Thomas on all its community, even though the Bishop of Paris and the University of Paris had challenged his views in 1277. It was not until 1323 that St. Thomas was canonized, so Mechtild's vision was drawn from her own insight supported by the Dominican confessors of her community.

While there is a significant influence of the Scholastic and Aristotelian tradition on Mechtild's general understanding of human identity, and on her belief in the importance of the integration of materiality, rationality, spirituality, and individuality, there does not appear to be any negative influence of gender polarity on her concept of woman. On the contrary, Mechtild employs many analogies drawn from woman's experience that reveal a positive understanding of woman's identity. In fact, Carolyn Bynum, in her sensitive study of the nuns of Helfta, identifies the monastic environment as the antidote to the devaluation of woman.[26]

> . . . the positive sense of self found in Gertrude and Mechtild of Hackeborn who entered the convent as children, suggests that women who grew up in monasteries were less likely to be influenced by the contemporary stereotype of women as morally and intellectually inferior. Such women were more likely to see themselves as functioning with a full range of male and female, governing and comforting roles, paralleling the full range of the operations of God.[27]

The positive valuation of woman, the feminine, and the female is described in many different ways in Mechtild's works. First of all, she describes God by drawing an analogy between His way of teaching the soul by inspiration and the way "a mother freely rewards her son by a kiss"; and in another passage He is depicted for a soul as a "father in creation, mother in redemption, brother in the division of the kingdom, and sister by our sweet association"; and elsewhere Mechtild states that after death God will welcome her as "a father welcomes a beloved son . . . as a friend his tender friend . . . as a husband his uniquely beloved wife."[28]

It is important to note that in these examples, which all describe God's action in the world of creation, we see the playful interaction of familial analogies of fa-

24. I am using the French translation of the text entitled *Le Livre de la Grace Spéciale: Révélations de Sainte Mechtilde vierge de l'ordre de Saint-Benoit* (Tours: Maison Mame, 1920), V, 9, p. 332. Translated into English by Dominique Deslandres as are all passages from this text.

25. Mechtild, *Le Livre,* V, 9, 322-23.

26. Bynum, *Jesus as Mother,* pp. 170-227.

27. Bynum, *Jesus as Mother,* p. 185. Bynum's study focuses primarily on what she calls the "theological content and historical context" of women religious writers (p. 184). My own study adds a further dimension in its focus on the philosophical theories they developed.

28. Mechtild, *Le Livre,* III, 9, 202; IV, 50, 296; and III, 17, 195-96.

thering, mothering, brothering, sistering, husbanding, befriending, and so forth, which move back and forth in a dynamism in which both male and female identities are affirmed as differentiated. In attribution of gender-associated characteristics to God in Christian thought, it is important to note a careful distinction between predication of God with respect to the internal relations of the Three Divine Persons in the Holy Trinity, and predication of God with respect to action in the world. In the latter predication, even though a particular predicate is appropriated to one Person because of a particular resemblance or similarity, it does not exclude attribution to the other Divine Persons because every action performed by God in relation to the created world is common to all Three Divine Persons. Appropriations are non-exclusive in that they could apply to the other Divine Persons whereas names are not. They are exclusive to one Divine Person. In the Processions within the Trinity, the names are exclusive because they identify the internal relations. Only the Father is Father, only the Son is Son, and only the Holy Spirit is the Holy Spirit.[29] We will discover this careful distinction again nearly a century later, when the theme of Christ as our mother in redemption will be elaborated in greater depth and detail by Julian of Norwich, who may have first encountered this image in her reading of Mechtild's text.

The above examples are not unique to Mechtild, as they were common to the Benedictine tradition of St. Anselm and in the Cistercian tradition of St. Bernard. However, Mechtild delves into her own experience in a more particular way, and she begins to elaborate analogies in detail through the use of her own discursive reasoning. While both Mechtild and St. Gertrude offer much less developed analogies than St. Bridget, St. Catherine of Siena, and Julian of Norwich, who will be considered later in this chapter, they nonetheless begin to introduce some discursive reflection that continues the tradition begun especially by Hadewijch and Mechtild of Magdeburg already described in Chapter 1. Some of Mechtild of Hackeborn's analogies, and their experiential foundation, will now be described.

Mechtild served as First Chantress in the monastery, which meant that she was responsible for leading the music in the Divine Office. In a Benedictine monastery in which Gregorian chant had been developed to an elaborate degree, this was a serious and often difficult responsibility. In a dialogue in which Mechtild asks God: "A wife habitually produces fruit for her husband; what fruit, Oh very valiant Spouse, shall I carry for you?" the answer draws a vertical analogy: "Each day," responds the Lord, "you will give me seven sons." The sons are then explained as the seven daily divisions of the Divine Office: Lauds, Prime, Tierce, Sext, None, Vespers, and Compline. In this way, in her position as Chantress, Mechtild, who is often referred to as the 'Nightingale' of Christ, experienced a cosmic fertility in producing seven 'sons' a day, each day of the year.[30] Mechtild per-

---

29. For an explanation of proper predication of modes of appropriation to the Persons of the Trinity see Yves Congar, *I Believe in the Holy Spirit* (New York: Crossword, 1997), part 2, ch. 3, pp. 85-99; and Gregory Philip Rocca, "Analogy as Judgment and Faith in God's Incomprehensibility: A Study in the Theological Epistemology of Thomas Aquinas," Ph.D. Diss., Catholic University of America, 1989.

30. Mechtild, *Le Livre*, III, 29, 228. See also Jeremy, *Scholars*, pp. 31-33.

ceives herself as feminine soul, a generic representative of humanity, espoused to God.

St. Mechtild uses different metaphors in her descriptions. Her base analogate is taken from some aspect of the material world with which she had experience, and from which she would develop an analogy to something in the spiritual world. For example, Mechtild refers to the parts of the human body when she suggests to novices making their first profession that they should ask God for the eyes of understanding, the ears of obedience, the mouth of wisdom, the heart of love, and the hands of good works.[31] In this vertical analogy, each part of the body is correlated with a particular spiritual virtue. In another example, simpler in structure, Mechtild playfully describes a game of dice that Mary teaches her to play with her husband (Christ). Here the points on the dice are given an analogical significance related to the integration of the philosophical and theological levels of existence within a human being:

> The single point of a die signifies the baseness and nothingness of men. . . . The two points signify the body and the soul. . . . The three points are the three powers of the soul: memory, understanding, and will. . . . The four points are cast by the soul when she gives herself totally to God, in prosperity and adversity, for the present and the future. . . . The five points are the five senses of the soul. . . . The six points are the six ages of man.[32]

In this vertical analogy, Mechtild identifies the key aspects of human identity: relation to God, relation of body and soul, the powers of the soul, free will and choice, the senses, and the actualization of human potentiality. Mechtild's description is a balanced view of the materiality, rationality, spirituality, and individuality of the human being whom she describes.

Another sense-based analogate is the human heart. In one example, she compares a three-tiered armoire of sacred vestments with the three compartments of a human heart "filled with virtues and good works."[33] In another transcendental analogy, Mechtild describes Christ's heart as the "kitchen of the Lord":

> My kitchen is my divine Heart. The kitchen is a common room open to everyone, to slaves as well as to free persons; thus my Heart is always open to everyone, and willing to provide to each one that which is able to please. The chef is the Holy Spirit, who with inestimable skill fills without ceasing my Heart with overflowing liberality.[34]

Mechtild continues the analogy in saying that the *écuelles* (dishes) are like the hearts of the saints who serve platters of gold with the angels. The plates can be washed in the pure heart of Mary, and so forth. So Mechtild takes her basic insight

31. Mechtild, *Le Livre,* IV, 17, 267.
32. Mechtild, *Le Livre,* IV, 27, 276-78.
33. Mechtild, *Le Livre,* III, 28, 226-27.
34. Mechtild, *Le Livre,* II, 23, 101.

of Jesus' heart as analogous to a kitchen, and then examines the various components of a kitchen to consider which one is which transcendental analogate.

In another domestic analogy, which some critics suggest was later used by Dante, St. Mechtild compares the Heart of Christ with a spinning wheel and a cord of wool:

> She saw one day the Lord Jesus: facing him stood a man. In the Divine Heart she perceived a wheel which turned without ceasing and a long cord which was directed towards the heart of the man, where there was also a wheel in motion. This man represents all human beings, and the wheel signifies that God has communicated from his free will to men, the free will of turning towards good and towards evil. This cord goes then from the heart of God to that of man; and the more rapidly the wheel turns, the more man approaches God. But if the creature chooses evil, the wheel suddenly turns in reverse and the man moves away from God.[35]

Of course, the philosophical concept that is central to this transcendental analogy concerns the way in which a human being, endowed with free will, can choose good or evil and the consequences of this choice. As her transcendental analogy makes abundantly clear, Mechtild is well aware of the human responsibility for making good choices.

In these three different analogies, then, we see Mechtild describing the heart as an armoire, a kitchen, and a spinning wheel in motion. In one, the analogates are virtues and good works, in another they are saints, angels, and divine persons, and in the third they are the movements of the free will towards good and evil choices. Mechtild's capacity to think portrays a great variety and flexibility of the insights she gains in being attentive to her religious and particularly feminine experience. In addition, Mechtild demonstrates a creative capacity to question these experiences and to elaborate particular judgments about the value of her experiences. And, although so many of Mechtild's analogies are derived from a woman's experience, they nonetheless hold universal relevance for both men and women.[36]

In the following description of St. Mechtild's apostolate, St. Gertrude stresses that Mechtild had a particular capacity to teach:

35. Mechtild, *Le Livre,* IV, 20, 269-70, 284.

36. Carolyn Walker Bynum argues in *Gender and Religion: On the Complexity of Symbols,* ed. Caroline Walker Bynum, Steven Harrell and Paul Richman (Boston: Beacon Press, 1986), ch. 10, pp. 257-88, that these metaphors drawn from women's work and experience are not limited to women authors. "The idea of Jesus as mother was first elaborated by male devotional writers. In addition, women writers had no monopoly of homey, domestic metaphors. Christ or the soul as seamstress, washerwoman, serving maid, and so forth appeared in the writings of, for example, Marguerite of Oingt, the Helfta nuns, Henry Suso, Richard Rolle, and the monk of Farne" (". . . And Woman His Humanity: Female Imagery in the Religious Writing of the Later Medieval Ages" [p. 259]). However, there is no question that the use of a sense base from women's work and experience provides a gender-differentiated context for analogical thinking regardless of which author uses the examples. In fact, the use of such analogates by a man may offer further evidence for the common practice of intergender dialogue.

She distributed doctrine in such abundance that a similar master was never seen in the monastery, and we believe strongly, alas! will never be seen there. The sisters gathered around her as if they were near a preacher, to hear the word of God. She was the refuge and consoler of everyone, and by a singular gift possessed the grace to open up with confidence the secret of hearts. Even people, not only in the monastery, but also among the religious and the seculars, came from far away and attested that they had been delivered from their suffering, and did not find anything but consolation that came from her.[37]

The passage continues with a statement claiming that St. Mechtild was like the early Church Fathers, the prophets, and the apostles. Mechtild understood herself as a paradigm for men as well as women. She also clearly serves as a counterexample to the Aristotelian dictum that 'silence is a woman's glory.' Dominicans widely dispersed the written text of Mechtild's *Book of Special Grace* after her death, and so Mechtild continued to contribute to public dialogue through her written word even after the end of her life.

We have already mentioned the Dominican contribution to the intergender dialogue experience of Mechtild and other religious writers at Helfta. It is important to note that the contribution was not in one direction. The women also contributed their views to the intergender dialogue. Even though living a monastic life, these women frequently engaged in dialogue with men and women from different backgrounds. As Carolyn Bynum notes: ". . . we see that the two Mechtilds and Gertrude served as counsellors and spiritual advisers not only to the sisters but also to laity, clergy, and friars who came from outside for advice."[38] Then after their death, their works were shared not only within the monastery but outside as well.

In addition to the suggestion that the image of the heavenly circular motion in either of the two Mechtilds may have influenced Dante's images in *The Divine Comedy,* it is also thought that Boccaccio was aware of these writings. Edmund Gardner points out that Mechtild's vision of the mountain of purgatory is nearly the same as Dante's development in *The Divine Comedy,* with its seven terraces that purify the souls from the seven capital sins, the seven angels personifying the opposite virtues, the vision of paradise, the rivers of purification, and specific functions of Mary, and the saints, and even the interspersion of Latin liturgical verses.[39] Sister Mary Jeremy mentions that, "According to Boccaccio, St. Mechtild's book was particularly popular in Florence where the citizens used to recite 'Le laude di Donna Matelda' before sacred images."[40] Finally, Boccaccio mentions in the *Decameron,* a short prayer about the five joys of the resurrected Christ called *Laudes Dominae Mechtildis,* or "The laud of Lady Matelda."[41] If these suggestions are accurate, then

37. Gertrude in Mechtild, *Le Livre,* V, 30, 351-52.

38. Bynum, *Jesus as Mother,* p. 181.

39. See Edmund G. Gardner, *Dante and the Mystics* (New York: E. P. Dutton and Co., 1913), pp. 283-87. His suggestion that Mechtild may be Dante's model for Matelda is not confirmed by Dorothy Sayers, translator of *The Divine Comedy: 2 Purgatory* (Harmondsworth: Penguin Books, 1981), cantos 28-33.

40. Jeremy, *Scholars,* p. 18.

41. Giovanni Boccaccio, *The Decameron* (New York: Mentor Books, 1982), VII, 1, 418.

we have at least one example of the beginning of intergender dialogue across the two separate communities of female religious authors and male Renaissance Humanists.

St. Gertrude the Great of Helfta (1235-1302)

As mentioned in the previous section, Saint Gertrude authored in Latin *The Book of Special Grace* in which Mechtild's revelations were recorded.[42] In addition to this work, she also authored another Latin text titled *Legatus Divinae Pietatis,* or *The Herald of Divine Love,* in which she recorded her own religious experiences. Book Two is considered to be Gertrude's own writing, while books One, Three, Four, and Five are thought to have been written by others under Gertrude's guidance.[43] She also wrote the *Exercises,* in which she proposed particular steps for others to follow in developing a virtuous and religiously integrated character. Gertrude understood herself to be like a prophet through whom a "ray of light and of truth . . . [which] will not be contradicted" would be sent forth "to the ends of the earth" as a "herald" of Divine Love.[44]

At the same time that Gertrude functioned as a prophet simply conveying divine revelation, she also interjected her own intelligence in presenting her understanding of the truth she was heralding. In the following passage, Gertrude indicates that she recognizes a difference between the original religious experience and the written text that she will be providing. Writing about herself in the third person Gertrude says:

And although the loving Lord continued to flood her soul with his grace every day, feast day and weekday alike, sometimes through the means of sensible corporeal similitudes, sometimes through the purer intellectual visions, he wanted

42. See Lillian Shank, "The God of My Life: St. Gertrude, a Monastic Woman," in *Medieval Religious Women: Peaceweavers,* vol. 2, pp. 239-73, especially, "*The Book of Special Grace* was written by Gertrude and another nun sometime after 1292" (p. 240).

43. See Shank, "The God," especially "*The Herald* consists of five books. Books One, Three, Four and Five were written by one or more of Gertrude's companions, either at her dictation, or compiled from her notes or in some way immediately inspired by her. They contain many of her characteristic expressions but their style is inferior to that of Book Two written at the Lord's command in 1289, when Gertrude was thirty-three years old." Jean Leclerq, O.S.B., argues: "Book II was surely written by the saint herself and constitutes the authentic and original nucleus around which all the rest was added and according to which the rest has to be interpreted" ("Liturgy and Mental Prayer in the Life of St. Gertrude," *Sponsa Regis* 31, no. 1 [1960]: 240).

44. Gertrude d'Helfta, *Oeuvres spirituelle le hérault* (Paris: Editions du Cerf, 1968), II, Prologue, pp. 111-13. All translations from the French from this text are made by the author. A recent English translation of the text may be found in Gertrude of Helfta, *The Herald of Divine Love* (New York/Mahwah, N.J.: Paulist Press, 1993). Passages from the newer translation will be incorporated where they add greater insight to the interpretation. For example, in the present passage we find: "In the same way, my intention to clarify certain things through you by the light of knowledge and truth shall not be frustrated . . ." (p. 48).

images of bodily likenesses, appealing to the human understanding, to be described in this little book.[45]

Gertrude tells us that she tried to amplify the meaning of her material by integrating passages from Scripture and from the writings of the saints:

> As the dove collects grains of corn, she compiled several books full of the sayings of the saints. These she wrote down in order to elucidate certain obscure passages and to explain them to those less gifted in intelligence, and for the use of all who desired to read them.[46]

Gertrude was conscious of the limitations of her gender and experience, and she asked, using analogies, for a "masculine" strength and talent to carry out her mission:

> Gird my thigh with the sword of Thy spirit, O Thou most mighty, and give me a manly heart that I may strive after the virtues manfully and resolutely. . . . Let me devote all of my forces so fully to the demands of Thy Charity and so far fix and establish my thoughts in Thee, that despite the weakness of my sex, by strength of soul and virility of mind, I may attain to that manner of love which bringeth one unto the secret apartment of the nuptial chamber of perfect union with Thee.[47]

Her excellent knowledge of Latin enabled her to study both theological and philosophical authors. It is likely that she spent hours copying manuscripts by hand for the monastic library. In this activity she would have had the opportunity to study classical texts very closely. In a self-critical passage Gertrude tells us that she had immersed herself in secular studies. "Through her excessive attachment to secular studies up to that time she had neglected to adapt the high point of her mind to the light of spiritual understanding."[48] However, after she achieved this reorientation

---

45. Gertrude, *The Herald,* I, Prologue, p. 49.

46. Gertrude, *The Herald,* I, 1, 53. For a similar glimpse of Gertrude's self-consciousness about her ability to teach Scripture see "When she found in Holy Scripture certain passages which she thought would be of use, if they seemed to her to be too difficult for persons of lesser intelligence, she would translate them into simpler language so that they might be of greater profit to their readers. She passed her life from morning to night with the sacred texts, either abridging long passages or explaining difficult ones, to the glory of God which she so much desired and for the salvation of others" (I, 7, 53).

47. *The Exercises of Saint Gertrude* (Westminster, Md.: Newman Press, 1956), V, 99. For a more recent translation, see Gertrude the Great of Helfta, *Spiritual Exercises* (Kalamazoo, Mich.: Cistercian Publications, 1989). "Gird my thigh with the sword of your Spirit, most mighty one, and make me put on virility in my mind so that in all virtue I may act virilously and energetically. . . . May all my vigor become so appropriated to your charity and my senses so founded and firm in you that, while of the fragile sex, I may, by virtue of a rational soul and virile mind, attain to that kind of love which leads to the bridal-couch of the interior bed-chamber of perfect union with you" (p. 87). Lillian Shank claims that in this nuptial union, Gertrude is not passive, but active. "Another aspect of Gertrude's independent character was her assertiveness, and eventually holy boldness." See "Gertrude," *Peaceweavers,* vol. 2, p. 246.

48. Gertrude, *The Herald,* I, 1, 53.

of intellect, this secular training proved useful in her vocation to explain the meaning of her revelations.

St. Gertrude's work as an author was valuable to her in several ways: (1) it allowed her to communicate her own experiences to others, thereby increasing their intensity, (2) it confirmed her conviction that the value of the experiences was not to be held by her alone, and (3) it helped those persons "less gifted in intelligence" or "of lesser intelligence" to benefit from her own stronger intellect.[49]

Gertrude frequently used analogical reasoning to emphasize some aspect of her experience. In the *Herald of Divine Love* she identifies this method of using pictures and images as a way in which students may reach a greater understanding of God:

> Just as students attain to logic by way of the alphabet, so, by means of these painted pictures, as it were, they may be led to taste within themselves that hidden manna (Rev. 2:17), which it is not possible to adulterate by any admixture of material images and of which one must have eaten to hunger for it forever.[50]

By means of an alphabet, the student arrives at logic, and by means of images arrives at the transcendental meaning of human life. An analogy provides a link between the sense world and the transcendental world.[51]

While Mechtild of Hackeborn based her analogies mostly on specific experience in the kitchen and at the spinning wheel, Mechtild of Magdeburg used many images of the more generic notion of liquids.[52] Gertrude also often invokes the cosmic elements of water, air, and fire for her base analogates. She describes one experience of interaction with God as ". . . seeming to send down a shower of drenching rain over my soul. Like a young and tender plant, I felt myself now beaten down to the ground by the violence of the downpour."[53] Then in another passage we can see her thinking about the meaning of water in relation to virtue:

> So you were with me in all my actions, stirring my spirit within me. One day between Easter and Ascension I went into the garden before Prime, and sitting down beside the pond I began to consider what a pleasant place it was. I was charmed by the clear water and flowing streams. . . .
>
> And then you, my God, source of ineffable delights, who, as I believe, did but inspire the beginning of this meditation to lead it back to yourself, made me un-

49. Gertrude, *The Herald*, I, 1, 53 and I, 7, 64.

50. Gertrude, *The Herald*, II, 24, 135. See also the translation in Elizabeth Petroff, *Medieval Women's Visionary Literature* (Oxford: Oxford University Press, 1986), where logic is translated by "philosophy" and material images by "corporeal substances" (p. 230).

51. Sister Jeremy calls St. Gertrude's particular use of images a "synesthesia — the fusing of sense impressions in a manner that anticipates Shelley, the French imagists, and Edith Sitwell, to name a few. She speaks of 'jewels and flowers emitting melody' . . . [and suggests that] precious stones representing humility have not only the form but the odour of violets" (*Scholars*, p. 108).

52. See James C. Franklin, *Mystical Transformations: The Imagery of Liquids in the Work of Mechthild von Magdeburg* (Rutherford/Madison/Teaneck: Fairleigh Dickinson University Press, 1978).

53. Gertrude, *The Herald*, II, 10, 109.

derstand that, if I were to pour back like water the stream of graces received from you in that continual gratitude I owe you; if, like a tree, growing in the exercise of virtue, I were to cover myself with the leaves and blossoms of good works (cf. Ps. 1:3; Jer. 17:8); if, like the doves (Ps. 55:6) I were to spurn earth and soar heavenward; and if, with my senses set free from passions and worldly distractions, I were to occupy myself with you alone; then my heart would afford you a dwelling most suitably appointed from which no joys would be lacking.[54]

St. Teresa of Avila uses exactly the same analogy in her autobiography, although there it is drawn out in much greater detail to describe the four levels of prayer.[55] Gertrude's *Herald* had been translated into Spanish and was recommended by two confessors of St. Teresa, and so it seems possible that Gertrude may have influenced Teresa's choice of water as an analogate.[56] If this supposition is accurate, then we have an example of intergender dialogue moving from a woman author, through men readers, to influence a later woman writer.

Analogies using the element "air" were also used by Gertrude throughout her texts. In one reported dialogue with Jesus the following transcendental analogy is suggested:

As I am the figure of the substance of the Father (Heb. 1:3) through my divine nature, in the same way, you shall be the figure of my substance through my human nature, receiving in your deified soul the brightness of my divinity, as the air receives the sun's rays and, penetrated to the very marrow by this unifying light, you will become capable of an ever closer union with me.[57]

The element "fire" was also used to represent one or another aspect of God. In the following passage Gertrude develops a transcendental analogy incorporating interaction between fire, water, and earth:

O ardent fire of my God, which contains, produces, and imprints those living ardours which attract the humid waters of my soul, and dry up the torrents of earthly delights, and afterwards softens my hard self-opinionatedness, which time has hardened so exceedingly! A consuming fire. . . . O burning furnace.[58]

54. Gertrude, *The Herald,* II, 3, 97.

55. St. Teresa of Avila, *The Book of Her Life* in *The Collected Works* (Washington, D.C.: ICS Publications, 1976), vol. 1, ch. 11 ff.

56. Jeremy, *Scholars,* p. 209. "Her *Legatus* survives in only a few manuscripts and it was not until the invention of printing that her work became known. With the edition of Laspergius in 1536, the name of Gertrude began to be illustrious. Spain was one of the first countries to have the *Legatus* in the vernacular, and as Ledos says, the translation appeared 'crowned with the approbation of the most renowned theologians: Diego Yepes, S.J. and Domingo Banez, O.P. [both confessors of St. Teresa]; Francisco Suarez, S.J.; and other religious, Carmelites, Franciscans, and Benedictines.'" See also Gabriel Ledos, *Sainte Gertrude* (Paris, 1903), p. 203.

57. Gertrude, *The Herald,* II, 6, 104.

58. Gertrude, *The Herald,* II, 7, 105.

In the above analogy Gertrude perceives herself to be like "wax, softened by the fire," while in the next analogy she is like gold refined in a furnace:

> O truly consuming fire; you who exert your power against our vices in order then to let the soul feel your gentle anointing! From you alone and not otherwise can we receive the power to be reformed (Acts 3:12, 18) to the image and likeness of our original state. O fiery furnace of ever-increasing heat, in which is seen the joyous vision of true peace, whose action transforms dross into gold (Isa. 1:25), fire-tried and precious, as soon as the soul, weary of illusions, aspires at last with all the ardor of which she is capable to be attached to you alone, her very Truth![59]

Gertrude is also well known for her images of union with the Sacred Heart of Jesus. The emphasis upon the spiritual meaning of the Heart of Jesus in union with her own heart also suggests an integration of spiritual and material realities.[60]

Gertrude sometimes suggests that religion is in conflict with philosophy, because she identified philosophy primarily with the teaching of the pagans. This was a common view at the time both inside and outside of academia. In one vision that occurred on the Feast of St. Augustine, she sees St. Catherine of Alexandria converting fifty pagan philosophers to Christianity. The Augustinian influence sometimes led Gertrude to present a Neoplatonic view of human identity rather than emphasize an integral unity of soul and body within the human being. Examples of Gertrude's tendency towards Neoplatonism are found in the *Exercises:* she asks God to "lead my soul forth from its prison. Oh when wilt thou free it from the fetter of the body?"[61] In the *Herald,* she also records a dialogue with God in which He seems to answer this question by saying: "Know for certain that you will never leave the prison of your flesh until you have paid the last farthing (Matt. 5:26) that you are keeping back."[62]

However, through her insistence that virtuous acts are central to religious life, Gertrude implies that the ideal of religious life is not an escape from the body, but rather a transformation of the whole integral identity of the individual and the gift of the self through service to others. In fact, Carolyn Bynum emphasizes "the absolute certainty about the priority of service that we find in Gertrude's own words and visions," and Bynum notes that sometimes compilers and commentators sought to justify it in a context in which contemplation was thought to have a greater priority.[63]

Gertrude was often concerned about the practice of the virtue of justice. The following passage from her *Herald* makes this very clear:

---

59. Gertrude, *The Herald,* II, 7, 105.

60. See for example, Gertrude, *The Herald,* II, 4, 100-101; II, 9, 107-9; and III, 25-26, 188-91. Lillian Shank notes the relation between this devotion and action: "Gertrude's capacity for love and her mission to be a herald of that love were symbolized in her devotion to the heart of Jesus" ("Gertrude," *Peaceweavers,* vol. 2, p. 243).

61. Gertrude, *Exercises,* Sixth Exercise, 112. See *Spiritual Exercises,* "Oh, when will you release me personally from the shackles of the body?" (p. 96).

62. Gertrude, *The Herald,* II, 10, 109.

63. Bynum, *Jesus as Mother,* p. 197.

Justice . . . shone in her with such brightness that if occasion had called upon her to fight in its defense, she would have faced the armed battalions of a thousand armies drawn up in battle array (cf. Song 6:4-10). There was no friend, however dear, whom she would have consented to defend against the most deadly of foes, not even by a single word, if it meant straying from the paths of justice. She would have preferred to see her own mother harmed (if right reason demanded it) rather than consent to any injustice, even towards the most troublesome of enemies.

If she had occasion to give good advice to anyone she would conceal all the reluctance which her modesty made her feel (although this virtue shone in her more brightly than any other), and would renounce all inordinate fear of human opinion. Full of confidence in him whose armor of faith she wore . . . : and to whom she would have liked to subject the whole universe, with the pen of her tongue dipped, as it were, in her heart's blood, she formed in her zeal such gracious words of love and wisdom that the hardest hearts were softened by her words, and the most perverse of her hearers, if they had but a spark of piety, conceived the will, or at least the desire, to amend their lives.[64]

The images in this passage recall the many illustrations of the work of the Benedictine nun Herrad of Hohenbourg (also known as of Landsberg). She often depicted virtues as women in armor in her twelfth-century encyclopedia for women entitled *Hortus Deliciarium*.[65] These images in Herrad and in Gertrude function as counterexamples to the traditional polarity theory about the weakness of virtue and wisdom in women's identity. Gertrude also places a new emphasis on the application of analogical thinking to woman's spiritual identity, and she serves as an example of a person who developed the capacities for discursive reasoning, self-governance, and service to others through teaching and action.

St. Gertrude also stands at the end of a long line of women religious who lived in a context of intergender and infragender intellectual dialogue occurring within the Benedictine, Cistercian, and Dominican monastic traditions. Beginning with Hilda of Whitby in the seventh century, continuing with Roswitha, Hildegard, and Herrad in the twelfth century, and ending with the nuns from Helfta in the thirteenth century, monasteries had provided an intellectual and personally challenging context within which women were able to grow in wisdom and virtue in dialogue with one another and with men.

As men's education shifted to the urban centers and to universities away from the more aristocratic monasteries, woman's situation radically changed. Even before Gertrude's death in 1302 her monastery at Helfta began to experience external pressures. In 1284 the monastery was attacked by the brother of two of the sisters; in 1294 it was attacked again and robbed during a war; and in 1296 Helfta was placed under interdict, closed to the public, and left in serious financial difficulties.

---

64. Gertrude, *The Herald*, I, 6, 63. This notion of piety includes an active attitude and not just a passive response. See Shank, "Gertrude," *Peaceweavers*, vol. 2, p. 244.

65. See Herrad of Hohenbourg, *Hortus Deliciarum: Reconstruction*, ed. Rosalie Green et al. (London: The Warburg Institute and Leiden: E. J. Brill, 1979).

Then in 1342, after a battle with Albert, the brother of the Abbess, an intentionally set fire destroyed many of the monastery's books and other contents. In 1525 during the Peasants' Rebellion, when the monastery was attacked by Lutheran Protestants, all the remaining books and manuscripts were thrown into beer vats; and in 1546 the monastery was closed by a heretical prelate.[66] Following this period of St. Gertrude, the development of thought by women religious writers took place primarily outside of this traditional monastic context. The institutional structures that had fostered women's higher education no longer had the same profound results. New patterns of relationships developed among women and men religious. Mendicant priests who had been trained at European universities began to enter into dialogue with different communities of women religious. The Dominican order was central to this new development, and it will be to their examples of intergender dialogue that we will now turn.

THE DOMINICAN INFLUENCE

In Chapter 2 considerable attention was given to the particular role that the Dominican order played in the development of the University of Paris and of various *studia generalia* in Cologne, Germany and later throughout Italy. All Dominican friars were expected to study academic philosophy and theology, and the particular directions of these studies were formed by the thought of St. Albert the Great and St. Thomas Aquinas. We described the particular ways in which these two great thinkers both transmitted and transformed Aristotelian principles of gender polarity along with other fundamental concepts and arguments of the ancient Greek philosopher in their efforts to articulate a new Christian philosophy. With the writings of Meister Eckhart, and his disciples Johannes Tauler and Henry Suso, we move into the next generation of Dominicans, or those who went forth into the world to teach having been formed in the scholastic university model of education. What turns out to be remarkable in this next period in the history of the concept of woman is that these men appear to have been influenced by direct intergender dialogue with women religious of the Dominican order at the same time they retained some aspects of the Aristotelian-based theory of woman's identity. We will now turn to their texts to consider how this influence of real women may have affected their concept of woman.

The concept of woman in the three Dominican preachers, Meister Eckhart, Johannes Tauler, and Henry Suso, is dynamic and paradoxical. Three different factors interplayed to bring about these complex results. First, because all three men were formed in the academic principles of gender polarity, elements of the devaluation of woman are found in certain portions of their thought. Second, Neoplatonism also contributed significantly to their tendency to dissolve distinctions between men and women, which led to a suggestion of unisex or gender unity theory. Third, in addition to this vacillation between the premises of gender polarity and gender unity, there is the further significant phenomenon that these three men en-

66. Jeremy, *Scholars,* pp. 5-6, 85, 88-90, 132-33, and 139.

gaged frequently in dialogue with women and directly encouraged women to grow in wisdom and virtue and to even become authors. Their personal experience of intergender dialogue revealed a practice of gender complementarity. Yet the old categories of gender identity were not adequate to explain their experience. There is no simple way to evaluate their contribution to the history of the concept of woman.

Overall something new in the concept of woman began to occur through these men. However, they were not able to hold the tension of the balance of equality and differentiation within a complementarity theory. Instead, they either dissolved equality in the direction of polarity (and the superiority of the male), or dissolved difference in the direction of unity (and the disappearance of gender differentiation). This ambivalence in their theory of gender identity is not necessarily something to be condemned, because it may indicate that they were attempting to correct the more rigid premises of academic gender polarity by making their concept of woman more consistent with their personal experience of women. Inconsistency is not always a bad thing; for it may indicate efforts to reform a consistently erroneous theory. A similar phenomenon occurred in the writings of St. Augustine, who also combined elements of gender polarity, gender unity, and gender complementarity. Since we have already studied many difficulties in the Aristotelian-based principles of gender polarity, and seen the lines of its consistent development, it is important to keep this academic background in mind when evaluating the directions that Eckhart and his disciples took in their theory of woman's identity.

Johannes Eckhart's (c. 1260-1328) Gender Theory in His Latin Writings

Meister Eckhart is a complex author to analyze in respect to the history of the concept of woman. There appears to be some difference between the concept of woman he articulates in his Latin works and the one in his German works. Latin is the language of Aristotelian schooling, while German is the language of everyday life. More specifically, the Latin works describe women's identity with premises of traditional Aristotelian-based gender polarity, while the German works take a different approach. They directly borrow examples from women's life-experience, but end up with a gender unity theory drawn partly from Neoplatonism. Before articulating this interesting phenomenon, it may be helpful to offer some information about Eckhart's intellectual background and formation.

Johannes Eckhart was born near Erfurt, Germany, and he entered the Dominican order as a young man. He studied for his Bachelor of Arts at the University of Paris around 1277 and for a Master's in Theology both in Cologne and Paris between 1280 and 1294. It is thought that he met the Dominican St. Albert the Great in Cologne around 1280, shortly before the scholar's death.[67] He was in Paris during the time Marguerite Porete authored *The Mirror of Simple Souls* and shortly after Bishop

---

67. Edmund Colledge and Bernard McGinn, eds., *Meister Eckhart: The Essential Sermons, Commentaries, Treatises, and Defense* (New York: Paulist Press, 1981), Introduction, p. 7.

Tempier condemned the 219 Propositions, many of which were related to Aristotelian philosophy. Thus Eckhart was brought up within a turbulent context of academic, philosophical, and theological communities of discourse, and particularly of the Dominican colleges in Paris and Cologne, which were so instrumental in transmitting Aristotelian principles of gender polarity. For a while, he resided in Germany to work within his community until he returned to the University of Paris in 1311-1313. It was during this time in Paris that Eckhart wrote most of his Latin works.[68]

Once again Paris was the scene of much turmoil. Marguerite Porete had been burned to death in 1310 for refusing to stop distributing her text with its many Neoplatonic elements. It was after he left Paris again in 1314 that Eckhart seems to have become actively engaged in working with Dominican nuns in Strasbourg. This work had been officially ordered by Pope Clement IV as early as 1267; those Dominicans who had been trained in academia visited the convents "at regular intervals and, in their conferences and sermons, imparted to the nuns the doctrines that they themselves had learned and expounded in the schools."[69] This marks an important development in the history of women religious, because it indicates a concern for a higher education that they were not able to obtain at the universities.

Thus in this second phase in his life, Meister Eckhart frequently engaged in dialogue with women; he interacted with them through preaching, teaching, and spiritual direction. In a general way, he encouraged women both to develop their powers of discursive reasoning and to practice an active life of virtue. In this context of intergender dialogue, Eckhart may also have read spiritual texts written by women. It is suggested that Mechtild of Magdeburg's *Flowing Light of the Divinity* directly influenced Eckhart and his immediate disciples.[70] He may have read this and other texts by women during this time of intergender dialogue. In any event, Eckhart appears to have taken seriously his responsibilities for engaging in dialogue with women religious, and as passages taken from his writings will reveal, he thought about women's identity in relation to men.

Although Eckhart wrote several Latin works, it is his German texts and sermons that were probably more accessible to his women disciples. The extraordinary emphasis on Latin scholarship that we saw in evidence at Helfta was not the general

---

68. See Cyprian Smith, "The Rhineland Mystics" (with Oliver Davies), in *The Study of Spirituality,* ed. Cheslyn Jones et al. (New York/Oxford: Oxford University Press, 1986). "The Latin works, for the most part, date from his second period in Paris (1311-13). . . . It is the German works which have won Eckhart most fame. . . . The *Talks of Instruction* (c. 1298) were apparently delivered after supper in the religious houses which Eckhart supervised. . . . The *Book of Spiritual Consolation* (c. 1308) was composed for Queen Agnes of Hungary . . ." (p. 317).

69. William A. Hinnebusch, O.P., *The History of the Dominican Order, Intellectual and Cultural Life to 1500* (New York: Alba House, 1973), vol. 2, p. 298. Hinnebusch also mentions the opinion of Heinrich Denifle that the time that the Dominicans took to teach the women led to the decline of their own scholarly contributions.

70. See, for example, Matthew Fox who claims, "Mechtild employs many images in common with Eckhart. Among them are the images of sinking, of dancing, of God's delight, of growth, awakening, of letting go, of compassion, of God as a flowing stream, of the dialectic between isness and nothingness. Her work deeply influenced German mysticism and Eckhart in particular." *Breakthrough: Meister Eckhart's Creation Spirituality in New Translation* (New York: Doubleday, 1980), Introduction, p. 36.

rule for these later communities of women.[71] When we compare the gender-related contents of the Latin works with those of the German works, it would appear that the Latin works tended to emphasize gender polarity while the German works introduced grounds for gender unity. Two different hypotheses could explain this difference: one historical and the other contextual. First, since most of the Latin works were written during his time at the University of Paris, and before he began to work with the Dominican women, the difference in theories may be attributed to an actual change or development in his own thinking. Or second, it may be that the works that were written in Latin were directed primarily to a male community of discourse which had been exposed to academic training that emphasized gender polarity, while those written for intergender or female infragender communities of discourse emphasized more the equality of men and women. In other words, this hypothesis would suggest that when Eckhart spoke about women to men he tended to suggest that women were inferior to men, but when he spoke with women about their own identities he tended to emphasize their equality with men as human beings. More careful examination of the chronology and context of Eckhart's writings would need to be done before a particular hypothesis could be verified. However, the interpretation that is most attractive to the thesis of this book is that Eckhart's actual experience of intergender dialogue with women affected his concept of woman. In this understanding, he may have forged a new direction for the concept of woman that contained elements of polarity along with complementarity and unity.

Because Meister Eckhart was trained at the University of Paris and at Cologne where both St. Albert and St. Thomas taught, he received a solid formation in Aristotelian philosophy. Neoplatonist sources also carried within them elements of gender polarity. For example, Plato's view in the *Timaeus* of the cosmic mother receptacle, completely passive in relation to the Forms, was transmitted along with the loose association in the same dialogue of the higher rational powers of the soul with the male and the lower irrational powers of the soul with the female. In addition, Eckhart was also influenced by Moses Maimonides and Avicenna, who were steeped in Aristotelian principles. In his Latin sermons Eckhart often introduced an application of the Aristotelian metaphysical principle of polarity: the association of the female principle with matter and the male principle with form. For example, Eckhart appeals to Moses Maimonides, author of *The Guide for the Perplexed,* in drawing out a vertical analogy of the male with form and the female with matter. In one example, taken from *The Book of the Parables of Genesis,* he refers to Adam and Eve as the original nakedness of form and matter:

> Matter is its own passive potency, and form its own act, and thus the potency that is active and passive on respective sides is not something that is added to the substance; but the matter and the form, each in its own way, in themselves are the

---

71. See Ernst H. Soudek, "Eckhart, Meister," in *Dictionary of the Middle Ages* (New York: Charles Scribner's, 1984). "Eckhart's Latin works, though helpful to the modern scholar, would not secure his reputation as a great mystic or innovative theologian. The German works, by contrast, bear witness to his brilliance. There is little in Middle High German prose that can bear comparison with Eckhart's style and diction" (vol. 4, p. 381).

naked substance. What is said of man and woman in Genesis, chapter two, is a figure of this, "They were both naked, Adam and his wife" (Gen. 2:25).
. . . Moses says, "They were both naked, Adam and his wife," man and woman, form and matter.[72]

The association of the man with the active powers of form and woman with the passive potency of matter carries an evaluation of gender polarity. In another passage from his sermons on *Genesis* he states:

> From this comes the fifth point, that what is passive is universally the praise, honor and glory of its essential active cause. "The woman is the glory of the man" (1 Cor. 11:7) — the woman signifies what is passive, the man what is active. . . . From what has been said it will be clear that in and from every perfection and good of its own the passive principle proclaims and testifies to its own need and indigence, and announces the riches and mercy of the active principle that is its superior.[73]

The principle of form, and by association of the male, is superior to the principle of matter, and by association of the female.

Eckhart uses analogical reasoning in his allegorical interpretations of the Scriptures. As mentioned previously, this tradition of combining philosophical principles with allegorical interpretation of the Scriptures has a long tradition including Philo, St. Augustine, Maimonides, St. Albert, and St. Thomas. Into this context of analogy Eckhart introduces philosophical theory of gender polarity based on the metaphysical principle of the opposites, the active and the passive and their respective associations with man and woman. For example, in a text on *Genesis,* he introduces this distinction in the form of a vertical analogy comparing metaphysical principles and gender identity:

> Now for a third interpretation of "In the beginning God created heaven and earth," in which "heaven" and "earth" are parabolically understood as form and matter. The first thing to recognize is that matter and form are not two beings, but are two principles of created beings. . . . Second, note that form and matter are related in such a way that matter is for the sake of form, not the contrary. "Man was not created for woman, but woman for man" (1 Cor. 11:9).[74]

Even though woman seems to be described here as in some way dependent upon man more than he is dependent upon her, Eckhart qualifies this distinction with an appeal to Avicenna:

> Third, recognize that despite the fact that matter exists for the sake of form, nevertheless substantial form has no more power to exist without matter than matter

72. Eckhart, (Latin Works), *The Essential Sermons,* p. 104.
73. Eckhart, (Latin Works), *The Essential Sermons,* pp. 102-3,
74. Eckhart, (Latin Works), *The Essential Sermons,* pp. 103-4.

does without form, as Avicenna teaches in the second book of his *Metaphysics*. This is why after the Apostle said that "woman was for man," he added, "Yet neither is man independent of woman, nor woman of man" (1 Cor. 11:11).[75]

Thus his gender polarity is held within the Aristotelian metaphysical principle that matter and form exist together in concrete entities. However, within a concrete existing thing, the principles of form and matter have different value.

Just as Aristotle, Albert, and Thomas draw connections between the metaphysical, natural, epistemological, and ethical principles of gender polarity, so does Eckhart in his Latin works. There he articulates a link between generation and intellection:

> Again, just as in the case of generation in bodily things we find two principles under the same species, namely form and matter, the active and the passive, so too our intellectual faculty is distinguished into a superior part and an inferior one, which Avicenna calls the two faces of the soul, but which Augustine calls superior reason and inferior reason.[76]

In this vertical analogy comparing epistemological principles with gender, the superior reason is explicitly related to a concept of man, and the inferior reason to a concept of woman, in the context of the story of Adam and Eve:

> It will also be evident how the serpent, namely the sensitive faculty, can truly and literally speak to the woman, that is, the inferior reason, and how that inferior rational faculty speaks with its superior and how this highest faculty speaks to God, as well as how God addresses all three.[77]

Eckhart credits Augustine, not Aristotle, with this theory of the separation of functions. However, it bears close similarity with the Aristotelian epistemological principle of gender polarity, or that a woman's reason is without authority unless it is submitted to the authority of a man's reason:

> For the present it is enough to remember that in the twelfth book of *On the Trinity* Augustine explains the moral meaning of the serpent as the sensitive faculty that

---

75. Eckhart, (Latin Works), *The Essential Sermons*, p. 104. In still another passage, Maimonides is invoked to explain different modes of parables. In the first mode each word of the parable stands for something else, and in the second mode the whole parable expresses something of which it is a likeness. "An example of the second mode is what Proverbs, chapter five, says about prime matter under the parable of the adulterous woman, 'Do not pay attention to a deceiving woman; the lips of a harlot are like a dripping honeycomb,' etc. (Prov. 5:2-3)" (p. 95).

76. Eckhart, (Latin Works), *The Essential Sermons*, p. 109. For a discussion of analogical and univocal applications of superior and inferior, but without reference to gender application, see Richard Schneider, "Meister Eckhart's Reflections on the Relation between the Superior and Inferior," in *Jacob's Ladder and the Tree of Life: Concepts of Hierarchy and the Great Chain of Being*, ed. Marion Leathers Kuntz and Paul Grimley Kuntz (New York: Peter Lang, 1987), pp. 191-212.

77. Eckhart, (Latin Works), *The Essential Sermons*, p. 109.

we share with brute beasts, the woman as the rational faculty that is directed to external things, and the man as the superior rational faculty that cleaves to God.[78]

The inferior intellect, which is associated with the female gender, is a mixed intellect that participates in reason, but has the limitations of being oriented towards the material world through images or other extractions from sense phantasms, while the superior intellect, which is associated with the male gender, is a pure intellect oriented only towards God. Eckhart repeats this distinction in a variety of ways: "What we said is therefore clear. The serpent, the woman and the man describe and express the three principles of man, namely the sensitive, the rational through participation, and the essentially rational in number, nature and properties."[79] The union of the male and female principles in the intellect is analogically described by Eckhart sometimes as a "kiss" and other times as a union of man and wife.[80]

Next, we see Eckhart drawing a link from the epistemological principle to the ethical principle of gender polarity, namely that a woman's virtue is a lesser virtue than that of a man, or more specifically, that it is a woman's virtue to obey and a man's to rule. In a passage describing the rebirth of persons in the spirit of God, Eckhart invokes Aristotle and then draws a vertical analogy comparing ethical principles with gender:

> Remember that there are three faculties in man: The first an irrational one that does not obey reason; the second an irrational one, but born to obey reason (the positive and negative appetites); . . . and Aristotle calls it rational by participation — and the third essentially rational. The first of these is signified when it says "not from blood," the second under "nor from the will of the flesh," and the third with the words that follow, "nor from the will of man." . . .
>
> . . . Through "the will of the flesh" understand the wife, whose role is to obey and serve, just as through the spirit we sometimes understand the husband, whose role it is to rule. Corrupt is the household where the woman rules over the man. There is nothing worse.[81]

Here is an analogical application of the gender distinction concerning ruling and obeying that is so common to the gender polarity tradition. Eckhart adds that "there is nothing worse" than the inversion of the ethical principle, namely, when woman rules and man obeys.

In conclusion then, we have seen evidence that in the Latin sermons Meister Eckhart invokes versions of the metaphysical principle of gender polarity, the natural principle of gender polarity, the epistemological principle of gender polarity, and the ethical principle of gender polarity when he uses analogical thinking to de-

---

78. Eckhart, (Latin Works), *The Essential Sermons,* p. 108.
79. Eckhart, (Latin Works), *The Essential Sermons,* p. 113.
80. Eckhart, (Latin Works), *The Essential Sermons,* pp. 113, 115.
81. Eckhart, (Latin Works), *The Essential Sermons,* pp. 164-65.

scribe woman's identity in relation to man. In Eckhart's German writings, however, we discover a different theory being articulated, and it is to these writings that we now turn.

Eckhart's Gender Theory in His German Writings

In contrast to the suggestion just given above that a man whose reason is directed solely towards God is superior to one whose reason is also directed towards the material world, in one of his German sermons on the Mary and Martha parable, Eckhart inverts the traditional superior valuation given to the contemplative life of Mary and the inferior valuation to the active life of Martha.[82] He argues that Martha is the model of the more virtuous person: "We cherish the suspicion that our dear Mary somehow had sat there more out of a feeling of pleasure than for spiritual gain. Therefore Martha said: 'Lord, tell her to get up!' For she feared that Mary would remain in this feeling of pleasure and make no further progress."[83]

Eckhart's development of Martha as the more mature of the two sisters seems to emphasize the importance of the active life for both women and men. The title of the Thirty-fourth Sermon which contains this story supports this interpretation: "When Our Work Becomes a Spiritual Work Working in the World."[84] Eckhart, himself being the member of a religious order that sought to live out a contemplative life through works in the world, appears to have taken this story of two women's experience, and forged a new interpretation. Although the world in the story itself consisted of a meeting in a home, involving meal preparation and serving, it was a world that was open to others including men through the gathering that took place there around the presence of Jesus Christ and possibly Lazarus, their brother.

Eckhart's sermon does not focus on women's work or housework but on the virtues that these labors occasioned in Martha. Referring to Martha's depth of being, "which was thoroughly trained in the most external matters . . . and wise prudence that knew how to achieve external acts to the highest degree that love demands," Eckhart compared Martha in a horizontal analogy with virtuous pagan scholars.[85]

---

82. For a detailed description of the development of interpretations of the Martha/Mary relationship through the works of Origen, St. John Chrysostom, St. Augustine, St. Bernard, St. Francis of Assisi, and Meister Eckhart, see Blake R. Heffner, "Meister Eckhart and a Millennium with Mary and Martha," *Lutheran Quarterly* 5, no. 2 (Summer 1991): 171-85.

83. Eckhart, *Breakthrough,* p. 480.

84. Eckhart, *Breakthrough,* p. 478.

85. Eckhart, *Breakthrough,* pp. 478-79. He expands the explanation of these virtues later in the sermon as follows: "In particular, three things are indispensable in our activity: that we act in an orderly, judicious, and prudent way. I call 'orderly' whatever corresponds in all matters to what is highest. But I call 'judicious' whatever we cannot do better at the time. And finally I call something 'prudent' when we trace in good actions the lively truth with its beneficial presence," p. 483.

The pagan scholars, however, achieved through the practice of virtue such great knowledge that they clearly knew every virtue more accurately than Paul or any other saint in their first raptures.

This was how it was with Martha.[86]

This is a remarkable comparison. In a context of intergender dialogue, it is likely that women hearing this theory of woman's virtue as active and similar to the greatest pagan scholars may have grown in their own desire to study these pagan scholars. They may also have found in it an affirmation of their own ethical identity. Eckhart developed his analysis of the complementary roles of intellect and will in the practice of virtue, and he illustrated them with examples by further examples from the story of Martha and Mary. He concluded that while Mary was simply taking instruction, Martha was more mature in carrying out knowledge of virtue by its practice.

If we pause to reflect on Eckhart's particular choice of two women's experiences to use as a model for spiritual life, it would appear that in his analysis of Martha he is also describing his own apostolic life as a mendicant Dominican preacher. Here we have a man choosing a woman as a generic model for all active men and women. We could say that woman's identity interests Eckhart, it affects him, and he begins to apply to himself certain principles drawn from it. He interprets his aspirations, his own vocation, through a woman's identity. In this way, Eckhart indicates a practical complementarity between himself and Martha, a similarity of apostolic vocation, but a difference in sex and gender identity. He admires her, and wants to be like her in relation to Jesus Christ. This sermon on Mary and Martha serves as a clear counterexample to gender polarity principles.

In other German works Eckhart develops what turns out to be his most innovative theological theory of the birth of God in the human soul. This theory affirms woman's experience and identity as a mother. Once again, Eckhart appears to take into himself an aspect of woman's identity. However, what appears initially as a positive incorporation of an aspect of woman's identity turns out instead to be a description of the ideal mother's identity as completely passive and even annihilated. Thus, Eckhart loses the original momentum towards supporting a positive evaluation of woman's identity by proposing that men should become mothers in their soul as women are mothers in body, but then concluding that mothering is a passive function in which the identity of the mother is devalued as "nothing." In order to demonstrate the specifics of this momentum, we will now turn to Eckhart's own writings.

Drawing a transcendental analogy from the natural female capacity for giving birth, Eckhart develops a spiritual principle. His theory involves the claim that God can be born only in a soul that is devoid of images. ". . . the Father must speak and generate his Son and accomplish his deeds there [in the soul] without any images."[87] While it is a common spiritual principle that in spiritual life, images from the memory and imagination should not interfere with the action of God in the

---

86. Eckhart, *Breakthrough*, p. 479.
87. Eckhart, *Breakthrough*, p. 297.

soul, Meister Eckhart goes further. He develops this concept of no images as an ontological nothingness. Drawing a horizontal analogy between a man and a woman as his base, Eckhart draws a transcendental analogy about the birth of God in the soul and the pregnancy of woman as follows:

> A man had a dream, a daydream: it seemed to him that he was big with nothingness as a woman is with a child. In this nothingness God was born, He was the fruit of nothingness, God was born in nothingness.[88]

While it is true that in mystical literature, metaphorical language can be used to express the open receptivity of the soul to the ineffable presence of God with negative terms like nothingness, negation, or non-being, we need to ask to what extent Eckhart's extended claims in this direction are related to his Neoplatonic tendency to devalue matter, and to associate matter with a female principle. Is the female like Plato's Mother Receptacle in the *Timaeus,* totally empty and without any Form? And analogously, does man give birth through his incorporating this 'feminine' nothingness?

Or is there a residue of the Aristotelian theory of generation that the female provides only matter in generation, particular informed matter which is a kind of menstruum, but which is not formative like the seed of man? In the face of Eckhart's depiction of ideal pregnancy as the mother's contribution being akin to a nothingness, the question arises whether a more accurate theory of generation that recognizes a differentiated active contribution from both mother and father would provide a different base for the transcendental analogy of God giving birth in the soul. In this case, the soul in analogy to the mother would always provide something in response to the initiative of the contribution of God in analogy with the father. The identity of the soul and of the mother would remain, but be transformed through the experience of conceiving and bringing to birth something more than the self alone.

There is no doubt that Eckhart has great admiration for the feminine activity of conceiving and giving birth, and he draws upon it to express something important about man's identity too. In the following example he invokes another horizontal analogy between a man and a woman to describe a man who gives birth to God as being like a virgin and wife.

> Now mark what I say and pay careful attention! For if a man were to be a virgin forever, no fruit would come from him; if he is to become fruitful, he must of necessity be a wife. "Wife" is the noblest word one can apply to the soul, much nobler than "virgin." That a man conceives God in himself is good, and in his conceiving he is a maiden. But that God should become fruitful in him is better; for the only gratitude for a gift is to be fruitful with the gift, and then the spirit is a wife, in its gratitude giving birth in return, when he for God gives birth again to Jesus into the heart of the Father.[89]

88. Eckhart, *Breakthrough,* p. 309.
89. Eckhart, (German Works), *The Essential Sermons,* p. 178. See a different image of God's

In this example we see Eckhart using as a base a horizontal analogy of a man with a wife becoming pregnant. He adds to this a transcendental analogy of God impregnating the soul. Then he adds another transcendental-horizontal analogy of the Holy Spirit giving birth to Christ in the Father. Once again Eckhart positively evaluates woman's identity as mother in conceiving, bearing, and giving birth. His evaluation in itself serves as a counterexample to the gender polarity model of woman's identity as mother. The fact that he adopts it as the root in a transcendental analogy for his own identity gives further support to his affirmation of the value of woman's identity. In all of these moves, we can understand Eckhart as introducing a new balance of equal dignity among women and men, perhaps as a way to counter the extreme imbalance in the gender polarity theory so dominant in academic education.

However, sometimes Eckhart has difficulty in maintaining appropriate distinctions or differences between two things that ought to remain distinguished. It is as if in his momentum towards affirming the equal dignity of women and men, he lost sight of their authentic differentiation. Metaphorically speaking, as they approach a greater nothingness, all differences disappear. This attraction in Eckhart to nothingness ultimately leads to a loss of distinction between men and women and even, in some respects, between human beings and God. In the following example, beginning with a claim of the equality of men and women, Eckhart reaches the conclusion that the soul and God are equal:

> When God made man, he made woman from man's side, so that she might be equal to him. He did not make her out of man's head or his feet, to show that she would be neither woman nor man for him, but so that she might be his equal. So should the just soul be equal with God and close beside God, equal beside him, not beneath or above.
>
> Who are they who are thus equal? Those who are equal to nothing, they alone are equal to God. The divine being is equal to nothing, and in it there is neither image nor form.[90]

When Eckhart loses the appropriate distinction between God and human beings, he collapses a transcendental into a horizontal analogy. It is perhaps not surprising that in 1329 several of Eckhart's theories came into conflict with Catholic doctrine, and he underwent trials in Cologne in 1326, Avignon in 1327, and had several of his statements condemned as potentially heretical by a Papal Bull in 1329. Apparently, he recanted these statements before his death.

In Chapter 1 we considered a similar kind of result in the work by Marguerite

---

function in giving birth in *Breakthrough,* "The third kind of love is divine and through it we come to know how God from all eternity has given birth to his only begotten Son and continues to give him birth now and into all future eternities — so teaches a master — and so God lies in the maternity bed, like a woman who has given birth, in every good soul which has abandoned its self-centredness and received the indwelling God. This birth is God's self knowledge, which from all eternity has sprung from his fatherly heart, wherein lies all his joy" (p. 93).

90. Eckhart, (German Works), *The Essential Sermons,* p. 187. See also Eckhart, *Breakthrough,* p. 315.

Porete entitled *The Mirror of Simple Souls*.[91] Edmund Colledge, O.S.A. describes historical evidence to answer the question of whether Marguerite Porete may have directly influenced Eckhart. Because this issue is important for the question of intergender dialogue, his views are presented below:

> But, though it has on several recent occasions been suggested that Eckhart too was familiar with the *Mirouer* [*Miroir*], supporting evidence for this has not until now been produced. Herbert Grundmann, in one of the last major studies he published before his death . . . was convinced of the fact. He pointed out that Eckhart, who returned to teach in Paris in the year after Margaret's condemnation, lived for the next two years in the same Dominican community as her inquisitor, William Humbert 'of Paris,' who had ordered all the faithful who possessed copies of the *Mirouer* to surrender them to him or to the Paris prior on pain of excommunication. . . . It is just as likely that an undestroyed copy of the *Mirouer* was available to Eckhart in Paris. Grundmann rightly dismissed the possibility that when Margaret was composing the *Mirouer* before, that is, 1305, she could have read or heard of Eckhart's first treatises and sermons; and he thought it more probable that it was Eckhart's knowledge of the *Mirouer,* gained during this sojourn in Paris, which accounts for the agreements he noticed between Margaret's book and some early Eckhart writings.[92]

Colledge and Marler suggest that Eckhart rejects an analogical predication of terms to God and human beings, and that his views express an extended use of equivocation.[93] They conclude that Marguerite Porete appears to have influenced Eckhart in precisely this area and in its application to his belief in the total poverty of the human will in relation to the Divine Will.[94]

---

91. For a more positive interpretation of Marguerite Porete's and possibly Eckhart's language of annihilation, see Emilie Sum Brunn, "Self, Not-Self and the Ultimate in Marguerite Porete's 'Mirror of Annihilated Souls,'" in *God, the Self and Nothingness: Reflections Eastern and Western,* edited by Robert E. Carter (New York: Paragon House, 1990), pp. 81-87. She calls Porete "an important pre-Eckhartian witness . . . " (p. 86).

92. Edmund Colledge, O.S.A., and J. C. Marler, "'Poverty of the Will': Ruusbroec, Eckhart and *The Mirror of Simple Souls,*" in *Jan Van Ruusbroec: The Sources, Content and Sequels of His Mysticism,* ed. P. Mommaers and N. de Paepe (Leuven: University Press, 1984), pp. 14-47, esp. p. 15. Further support for this was provided also by Josef Koch, "his generation's commanding figure in the field of Eckhart studies . . . [who] informed Romana Guarnieri, . . . that he had found proofs of Eckhart's knowledge of the *Mirouer* which he thought convincing and proposed to publish," before his unexpected death. Colledge and Marler identify the similarities between Eckhart's Sermon #52 and Porete's works with particular reference to the theme of the poverty of the will. For the possible connection between Eckhart and Porete, see also McGinn, Introduction to *The Essential Sermons,* p. 40.

93. Colledge and Marler, *Ruusbroec,* "Analogical predication, however, is limited by the relation of creator and creature, and in *Beati pauperes spiritu,* Eckhart makes use of equivocation by reference to show that God in himself finally transcends every possible predicate" (p. 20).

94. Colledge and Marler, *Ruusbroec,* "But when we come to consider, next, what is the one dominating and unifying theme of the *Mirouer,* Marguerite's exploration of the problems of the human will, accepting and fulfilling what it can know of the divine will, it is difficult to suppose that Eckhart, for *Beati pauperes spiritu,* had not been attracted and influenced by her brilliantly paradoxical treatment

In conclusion, Eckhart often engaged in dialogue with women and he introduced some reform into traditional gender polarity by his use of woman's identity to draw analogies to men's identity. He particularly admired women's capacity for conception and giving birth, and he clearly described women as having an equal dignity with men. At the same time, however, he suggested a combined gender theory that included elements of Aristotelian polarity and Neoplatonic unity. Thus, Eckhart did not break through to any consistent theoretical foundations for a complementarity theory.

In his Latin writings, Eckhart differentiated men and women, which resulted in a devaluation of the female; and when he compared women and men in his German writings, he downplayed their differences and individual identity. In addition to the possible influence of Marguerite Porete, Eckhart's metaphysical view of the utter passivity of the female principle in human generation may have had roots in Aristotelian-based gender polarity or Neoplatonic theory. Inadvertently, the connection of woman's part in generation with passivity and nothingness led Eckhart towards a destruction of differences so that for him ultimately distinctions between male and female, as well as God and the human, were blurred and even erased.

While Eckhart's interest in the Mary and Martha parable, and especially his use of the analogy with the birthing process in women, was a positive contribution to the history of the concept of woman, his ultimate use of this analogy to express the annihilation of personal identity undermined the principles of significant differentiation and fundamental equality of man and woman. Thus, it also undermined the significant differentiation found in both the transcendental analogy between God and human beings and the horizontal analogy between man and woman.

Johannes Tauler (1300-1361)

Eckhart was not alone in this paradoxical theory of gender identity. His disciple Johannes Tauler held many views about gender identity similar to those of his master. However, Tauler avoided the more extreme views of Eckhart and thereby managed to maintain a slightly more balanced position than his mentor. Born in Strasbourg, Tauler entered the Dominican order in 1314, the same year that Eckhart visited the community.[95] While Tauler studied in Cologne, most of his life was spent in Strasbourg, where he was the spiritual director for several hundred women, who were either in small communities of Beguines or in Dominican convents.[96] Tauler affectionately refers to his listeners as "My dear Sisters" and "Beloved." These cues make it evident that he is referring to a female community of discourse, but in language that is open to men as well as women. In 1339 he moved

---

of the problem, even though he was to propose solutions more paradoxical and daring than anything which we find in her book" (p. 27).

95. Although there is no distinct evidence that the two met, it is presumed that they did. See Josef Schmidt, Introduction, *Johannes Tauler: Sermons* (New York: Paulist Press, 1985), p. 4.

96. Schmidt, Introduction, *Johannes Tauler,* p. 5.

to Basel and was involved with a movement of men and women called "The Children of God." So Tauler, like Eckhart, had many opportunities for intergender dialogue. The extant works of Tauler include mostly sermons, transcribed in High German by the nuns who heard them.[97]

If we consider whether or not Tauler was influenced by the writing of any women religious authors, it appears that he may have become acquainted with Marguerite Porete's *Mirror of Simple Souls* through the intermediate link of Jan van Ruusbroec (1293-1381). Tauler probably met Ruusbroec personally in Groenendael while he was studying in Cologne.[98] Interestingly, Ruusbroec originally became known in Groenendael for his public criticisms of a woman named Bloemardinne, who was leader of a "Manichean type sect," the Brethren of the Free Spirit. Those who followed Bloemardinne believed, as had Marguerite Porete, that once a person's will was in union with the divine will, it no longer had to follow any laws. This new sense of poverty of will and freedom led to some licentious practices. If Tauler was aware of the work of Marguerite Porete through Ruusbroec, his caution in expressing some of the themes that were common to Porete and Eckhart could have originated directly from Ruusbroec.[99] In any event, there is strong evidence to suggest that some written texts by women both influenced and were influenced by Eckhart and Tauler.

The interconnection among the women and men in the German religious tradition of the thirteenth and fourteenth centuries is noteworthy. In the following passage, Lucie Menzies links Mechtild of Magdeburg's translator Heinrich of Nördlingen with Tauler, Suso, and Margaret Ebner:

> This Heinrich was a secular priest who carried on a vigorous correspondence with the mystics of his time, among them Tauler, Margaret Ebner of the Golden Ring, and Christina Ebner; possibly also with Suso. It is to this Heinrich's enthusiasm for the spread of mystical writings that we owe his version of Mechtild's *Flowing Light*. In 1345 he wrote to Margaret and Christina Ebner in the Dominican Convent of Medingen: —
>
> "I send you a book called *The Flowing Light of the Godhead*. I am led to do this by the living light of the radiant love of Christ, for to me, this book, in delightful and vigorous German, is the most moving love-poem I have ever read in our tongue."[100]

---

97. Apparently for a long time a large number of works were falsely attributed to Tauler.

98. Oliver Davies, "The Rhineland Mystics," in *Ruusbroec*, p. 319. Davies spells his name as Ruysbroeck.

99. Colledge and Marler note in *Ruusbroec*: "It is beyond doubt that Ruusbroec was well acquainted with the *Mirouer des simple âmes anienties,* and that, unlike some earlier fourteenth-century theologians, he clearly perceived the errors for which the *Mirouer's* author, Margaret Porette *[sic]*, paid with her death at the stake in Paris in the year 1310" (p. 14).

100. Lucie Menzies, Introduction, *Flowing Light*, p. xxiii; see Chapter 1 for full reference. Valerie M. Lagorio notes the historical importance of this correspondence: "Henry's correspondence with Margaret and her contemporary mystics represents the first collection of letters in the German language . . . " ("The Medieval Continental Women Mystics," in *The Medieval Mystics*, p. 173).

The intergender dialogue occurred not only in person, in face-to-face discussions, but also in the sharing of religious texts. This interconnection between men and women authors through word and text is a form of practical gender complementarity that was bound to affect theories of gender identity over time. Among male religious authors woman was no longer an abstract identity presented within a model of gender polarity; instead individual women, with different views about their identity and about wisdom and virtue, were active participants in intergender dialogue about the concept of woman and of man. Johannes Tauler not only received ideas from women authors, he also participated in the intergender dialogue himself.

The mystic Margaret Ebner, who had met Tauler many times, is often quoted as having said that Tauler "had a fiery tongue that kindled the entire world."[101] Tauler's own works had a widespread influence because they were available in a simple vocabulary of High German. They were printed in 1498 and reprinted in 1505. Tauler is also credited with making Eckhart's work well known in Spain and the Netherlands.[102] It is even suggested that Tauler influenced Teresa of Avila, Luther, and Marie of the Incarnation.[103] When Tauler's works were translated into Latin, they spread further abroad until, when mixed with other pseudonymous texts, they were condemned by the Spanish Inquisition for their anti-intellectual orientation and association with Quietism.[104] However, Tauler managed to extricate himself from any serious and lasting confrontation with the Catholic Church.

Turning now briefly to the content of Tauler's works, we find the two Eckhartian themes: the concept of the soul as essentially passive and the birth of God in the soul. In Sermon 1, Tauler describes three different kinds of births, and then he adds: "The third birth is effected when God is born within a just soul every day and every hour truly and spiritually, by grace and out of love."[105] He even concludes his sermon with a horizontal gender analogy: "May God help us to prepare a dwelling place for this noble birth, so that we may all attain spiritual motherhood."[106] Thus we see in Tauler, as in Eckhart before him, an admiration for woman's identity as it pertains to conception and birth, and even more, a desire to apply the analogical spiritual principles of that identity to himself and to man. Woman is admired and used as a generic model for human identity.

However, when Tauler describes the identity of the woman in this birthing process, we find once again the introduction of the Aristotelian and Neoplatonic association of mothering with the principles of passivity. To elaborate his transcendental analogy of God bringing to birth in the soul, Tauler introduces the metaphysical principles of activity and passivity:

101. Alois Haas, Preface, *Johannes Tauler*, p. xi. See *Margaret Ebner: Major Works* (New York/Mahwah, N.J.: Paulist Press, 1993). Tauler is referred to by Margot Schmidt and Leonard P. Hindsley as "Margaret's contemporary and friend . . . " (Introduction, p. 58).
102. Oliver Davies, "The Rhineland Mystics" (with Cyprian Smith), in *Ruusbroec*, p. 320.
103. See R. W. Listerman, "Saint Teresa de Avila: Reader of German Mystic Johann Tauler?" *The USF Language Quarterly* 24, nos. 1-2 (Fall-Winter 1985): 25-26.
104. Haas, Preface, *Johannes Tauler*, pp. xiii-xiv.
105. Haas, *Johannes Tauler*, p. 35.
106. Haas, *Johannes Tauler*, p. 40.

For if two are to become one, one must be passive whereas the other must act. If, for instance, my eye is to receive an image on the wall, or anything whatever, it must first be free from these images; for if it remained an image of color, it would not receive another. . . . In short, whatever should receive must first be empty, passive, and free.[107]

Consequently, even though Tauler uses organic metaphors such as 'birthing' in the soul, spiritual mothering, and the like, his understanding of the ideal feminine ground is, like Eckhart's, one of emptiness or a loss of personal identity, including sex and gender identity.

Henry Suso (1295-1366) and Elsbeth Stagel (d. 1360)

The last disciple of Meister Eckhart we will briefly consider is Henry Suso, along with his own disciple Elsbeth Stagel. For the purposes of the history of the concept of woman, it is Henry Suso's recorded collaboration with a Dominican nun, Elsbeth Stagel, that provides the most interesting material for reflection. Elsbeth Stagel entered the Dominican community at Töss when she was seven years old and Suso served as her spiritual director and friend for several years. Before his death Suso edited a book, entitled *Exemplar,* which contained the following four works: his *Life,* the *Little Book of Eternal Wisdom,* the *Little Book of Truth,* and the *Little Book of Letters.*[108] Elsbeth Stagel, a spiritual daughter of Suso, had written original parts of his autobiography *Life,* which Suso edited, revised, and added to; and she had originally collected several of the letters later edited and revised for *The Book.*

As mentioned previously, Dominican friars took on, as a prime obligation, teaching and offering spiritual direction to women in Dominican convents. Henry Suso entered the Dominican order at the age of thirteen. He was later given a formal education between 1313 and 1319 in Aristotelian logic, metaphysics, ethics, and politics; then, during approximately 1320-1323 he received an education in scholastic theology; and around 1324-1327 he was chosen for advanced studies in Cologne where he was directly taught by Meister Eckhart.[109] It is interesting to note that Suso was also familiar with Seneca's *Moral Epistles,* which contained dialogues with Helvia and Marcia.[110] Perhaps this Stoic text provided an additional model of intergender dialogue for the religious author. In any event, it was after this intellectual formation that Suso returned to Lake Constance, where he began to teach and advise nuns at several Dominican convents in Colmar, Freiburg, and Töss. In this context in the mid-1330s he met Elsbeth Stagel, and their dialogue and friendship lasted for twenty-five years until her death around 1360.[111]

107. Haas, *Johannes Tauler,* p. 38.
108. This book has been translated from its original High German into English in *Henry Suso: The Exemplar, with Two German Sermons* (New York/Mahwah, N.J.: Paulist Press, 1989).
109. Frank Tobin, Introduction, *Henry Suso: The Exemplar,* pp. 21-22.
110. Tobin, Introduction, *Henry Suso: The Exemplar,* p. 37.
111. Tobin, Introduction, *Henry Suso: The Exemplar,* pp. 22-25.

The written works of Suso contain many of the same themes as we have previously seen in Eckhart and Tauler but without the conclusion of annihilation of the self. Oliver Davies suggests that Suso's care in expressing his views may have been partly due to his awareness of Eckhart's own difficulties: "[i]n his first work, *The Little Book of Truth* (c. 1326), he [Suso] sought to expound the teaching of Eckhart in non-controversial language and particularly to defend him against the claims of the libertarian 'Brethren of the Free Spirit.'"[112] However, an additional factor may also have been Suso's extensive personal experience of dialogue with a woman like Elsbeth, a dialogue of over a quarter century in which both participants were well aware of a fruitful equality and simultaneous differentiation. It is almost as if the idealized feminine identity present in Eckhart and Tauler is given a concrete existence in the particular identity of Elsbeth Stagel. A genuine practical complementarity was experienced by the two of them especially in their collaboration in writing and editing. Thus there occurred what could be called an 'existential ground' of authentic complementarity that may have helped stave off the tendency in Eckhart and his followers towards a loss of significant differentiation. We will turn now to consider the actual form and content of Suso's works before returning to this hypothesis.

Henry Suso often used dialogue as the form of his writings. He introduced dialogues filled with transcendental analogies related to comparisons between a personified Eternal Wisdom and the soul, between a servant and a Lord, between a disciple and Truth, as well as many stories and allegories that contained characters engaged in discussion.[113] These forms are familiar in the previous religious, satirical, and humanist texts we have considered. Suso's great innovation consists in his providing a record in the *Life of the Servant* of the actual progression of dialogue between himself and Elsbeth Stagel. This work is thought to be the first autobiography written in German. A problem lingers concerning whether it is an autobiography or a biography because Elsbeth Stagel wrote sections of the treatise before they were edited by Suso. In any event, the text, probably a combination of autobiography by Suso and biography by Stagel, offers a clear indication of the kind of dialogue that occurred between a woman and a man around issues of wisdom and virtue in the context of religious life in the fourteenth century.[114]

The *Life of a Servant* indicates that the intergender dialogues between the two Dominicans began with a series of questions asked of Henry by Elsbeth:

112. Oliver Davies, "The Rhineland Mystics," in *Ruusbroec,* p. 320.

113. One of Suso's texts, *The Little Book of Wisdom,* became as popular as *The Imitation of Christ.* Its theme is a lyrical meditation on the passion of Christ, leading to a discussion on sin, the illusion of the world, God's love and justice, and to a meditation on "the pure Queen of the heavenly realm and her heart's woe." It is here that Suso's language approaches that of the ". . . minstrels of courtly love" (p. 320). It is here, as Barbara Newman points out in "Some Medieval Theologians and the Sophia Tradition" (*Downside Review* 108, no. 371 [April 1990]), Suso shifts his earlier courtly love model of serving a feminine Eternal Wisdom, or Sophia, to a model of serving a masculine Lord of Eternal Wisdom, or Jesus (pp. 122-24).

114. See Tobin, for the question of whether this is properly considered an autobiography. Introduction, *Henry Suso: The Exemplar,* p. 38, and Bernard McGinn, preface, p. 5.

When he would visit her, she would draw him out with personal questions about his beginning and progress, about some of his practices and sufferings he had experienced. He told her about these things in spiritual confidence. Because she found comfort and guidance in these things, she wrote it all down as a help for herself and for others as well; but she did this surreptitiously so that he would know nothing about it.[115]

In this account we see the woman Elsbeth, taking contents of private intergender dialogue and writing them down, in part to extend the contents into a more public arena. Alois Marie Flass suggests that it is possible that Elsbeth may have been aware of other examples of life hagiography written by women:

Like Suso's *Life,* they undertake the daring attempt to represent simultaneously a legendary and an autobiographical account of the individual life. To this group belong *The Little Book of the Life and Revelation* by Elsbeth von Oye (ca. 1290-1340 in the monastery of Oetenbach near Zurich); *Revelations* by Margaretha Ebner (ca. 1292-1351 in Medingen near Dillingen), which was written down in 1344 at the insistence of Heinrich of Nördlingen; *Revelations* by Adelheid Langmann (d. 1375 in Engelthal); *Life of Sister Irmegard* by Elsbeth of Kirchberg — all Dominican-oriented revelation literature.[116]

In any event, when Henry Suso discovered Elsbeth's secret writings of the content of his conversations, he burned some of the material; but then he decided to keep the rest, edit it, and make it available to the public himself. He tells his reader, "Thus what follows remained unburned, as she wrote most of it with her own hand. A bit of good instruction was added by him in her person after her death."[117]

Book I (Chapters 1-32) of the text consists primarily of Henry's descriptions of his own ascetical spiritual practices. They are extremely personal, in response to Elsbeth's questions. So it could be said that the woman invited the man to concretize his teaching about progress in the spiritual life. In Part II of the text, Henry Suso reflects directly on his relation with Elsbeth Stagel. He describes her as "a model of all virtues," as writing a book for her convent, and as writing to him to ask for help in understanding some "lofty intellectual matters [which] were imparted to her by someone, things that were very highflown: the naked Godhead, the nothingness of all things, losing oneself in the nothingness (of God), the inadequacy of all images, and other similar teachings that were

115. Suso, *The Life of the Servant,* in *Henry Suso: The Exemplar,* I, 63.

116. Alois Marie Flaas, "Schools of Late Medieval Mysticism," in *Christian Spirituality: High Middle Ages and Reformation,* ed. Jill Raitt, p. 156.

117. Suso, *The Life of a Servant,* in *Henry Suso: The Exemplar,* I, 63. The last additions refer to chapters 46-53 of the text. Peter Meister raises for an English-speaking audience the question of Suso's authorship of *The Little Book of Love (Minnebüchlein)* that Barbara Molinelli-Stein had posed for Germans in 1972. He writes, "According to Molinelli-Stein's relative chronology, the *Little Book of Love* is indeed the rough draft of the much expanded *Booklet of Eternal Wisdom,* which, in turn, was condensed into the *100 Meditations.* Molinelli-Stein thinks it likely that Suso discarded the rough draft, but that Stagel preserved it" (p. 129). Meister considered linguistic evidence to support this hypothesis.

well-expressed. . . ."[118] Elsbeth's questions and use of the concept of nothingness imply some acquaintance with works of Eckhart or his disciples.

A rather extensive passage from the ensuing dialogue, which takes place through letters between Henry and Elsbeth, is included below in order to focus more clearly on the process of communication that unfolded between the man and woman:

> The servant [Friar Henry] wrote her the following in reply: "Good daughter, if you are asking me about these exalted ideas out of curiosity, so that you may become familiar with them and learn to speak well about the spirit, then I can quickly set you straight in a few words. . . . But if you are asking about such things in order to put them into practice, then give up asking about such lofty notions and take up such questions as are appropriate for you. . . ."
>
> The daughter wrote and responded thus: "My desire is not for clever phrases but for a holy life. And I have the determination to achieve it honestly, as I should, however painful it may be. . . . Begin at the lowest level and lead me forward, as one teaches a young pupil that is still a child, bringing it along bit by bit until it becomes a master of the branches of knowledge. . . .
>
> "Sir, I have heard it said that it is the nature of a pelican to bite itself and feed its young in the nest with its own blood because of its love as a father. Sir, in like manner, I think, you should treat me and nourish me, your thirsty child, with the spiritual food of your good teaching, not seeking things too far off but finding them close to yourself; for the closer it is to your own experience, the more attractive it shall be to the longings of my soul."
>
> The servant wrote to her in reply, "You recently described to me some high-sounding notions, which you had collected for yourself from the sweet teachings of holy Meister Eckhart, which you treated, as is only right, very tenderly. I am amazed that after drinking such noble draughts from the sublime master you can be thirsty for the swill of the insignificant servant. But if I see things correctly, I joyfully feel your good sense in the matter — that you ask with great persistence what the beginning of a sublime and secure life is, or through what basic practices a person shall reach it."[119]

The dynamics of this interaction are significant. The woman begins by reading something intellectual in the male religious writer's tradition, and then asking a man for a further explanation of what she has read. The man tests her interest to discover whether her motive is intellectual curiosity or the desire to lead a virtuous life. The woman responds by stating that virtue is her motive, she introduces a horizontal analogy, and then turns the dialogue around by asking the man to connect his intellectual teaching with his own personal experience. Then the man replies with a positive evaluation of the intellectual tradition that the woman had first enquired about as well as an affirmation of the goal, or a life of virtue.

Their relationship continues when Elsbeth decides to make a general confes-

---

118. Suso, *The Life of the Servant,* in *Henry Suso: The Exemplar,* II, ch. 33, 133.
119. Suso, *The Life of the Servant,* in *Henry Suso: The Exemplar,* II, ch. 33, 133-34.

sion to Friar Henry and "she wrote it all down on a large wax tablet and sent this to him sealed. . . ."[120] Suso tells us that "He wrote back to her by the same messenger. . . ."[121] Their written and oral dialogue continued through a period of illness during which Suso wrote to her: "I have no one else who has been as helpful with such industry and devotion to God, as you were while still in good health, in bringing my books to completion."[122] In the prologue at the beginning of *The Exemplar,* Suso was even more specific about the kind of help that Elsbeth had offered him: "The fourth book is called the *Little Book of Letters.* His spiritual daughter collected all the letters he had sent her and his other spiritual children and turned them into a book. From this he took parts of the letters and shortened it, as one finds it here below."[123]

Among the stories included in *The Life of the Servant* were two that have some significance for the concept of woman. In one account, Suso describes a situation in which his blood sister had done something to ruin both her and his reputation. Instead of blaming her for causing the ruin, as satirical writers so often do, Suso actively sought her out, supported her, and continued relating to her.[124] In another account, Suso describes how even though a lay woman tried to bribe him by falsely accusing him of fathering her child, and even though she actually tried to murder the child, Suso again did not turn his distress at this deception of the woman against either her or against women in general.[125] It is worth reflecting on the question of whether the fact that Suso had a genuine relationship of friendship with one woman may have helped him to avoid the tendency towards the devaluing of women in general for slander, deception, or other non-virtuous activity directed by another woman against him. As we will discover in the next chapter in this book, other men frequently had a very different response than Suso to this kind of situation.

Before considering the writing of Suso after Elsbeth's death, mention should be made of a *Sister-Book* that she participated in authoring with her own community at Töss. Gertrud Lewis has traced the history of nine *Sister-Books* written in fourteenth-century Germany. These books recorded the history of a particular religious community of women. They were also exchanged among the women's communities and consequently became a source of shared institutional history. In the Töss *Sister-Book* there is an entry that includes: "The blessed Sister Elsbet Staglin who wrote all this. . . ."[126] This reference had been taken by some scholars to imply that Elsbeth Stagel wrote the entire text, but Lewis argues that it is more likely that she was simply taking credit for a part she wrote. In any event, it indicates that Stagel also participated in a woman's community of discourse in her writing as well as in the intergender community of discourse she enjoyed with Suso.

120. Suso, *The Life of the Servant,* in *Henry Suso: The Exemplar,* II, ch. 34, 135.

121. Suso, *The Life of the Servant,* in *Henry Suso: The Exemplar,* II, ch. 34, 135.

122. Suso, *The Life of the Servant,* in *Henry Suso: The Exemplar,* II, ch. 35, 141.

123. Suso, *The Little Book of Letters,* in *Henry Suso: The Exemplar,* Prologue, 58.

124. Suso, *The Life of the Servant,* in *Henry Suso: The Exemplar,* I, ch. 22, 110-13.

125. Suso, *The Life of the Servant,* in *Henry Suso: The Exemplar,* II, ch. 38, 147-57.

126. Gertrud Jaron Lewis: *By Women, for Women, about Women: The Sister-Books of Fourteenth-Century Germany* (Toronto: Pontifical Institute of Mediaeval Studies, 1996), p. 24.

The significance to Henry Suso of the intergender dialogue with Elsbeth Stagel can be verified by his attitude towards her even after her death. We find a similar occurrence to what we have previously witnessed in Chapter 4 with Dante and the departed Beatrice, Petrarch with Laura, and Boccaccio with Fiammetta. These women with whom the men had carried on a dialogue during life become, after their death, transformed partners of intergender dialogue. In a similar manner after Elsbeth's death, Henry Suso returned to the original questions she had asked at the beginning of their relationship about Meister Eckhart's theory of nothingness.

Suso wrote the last chapters of his *Life* in the form of an imaginary dialogue with the spirit of Elsbeth. Suso's dialogue imagines Elsbeth still alive and conversing with him: it incorporates now both scholastic method and Thomistic content. An extract is offered below:

> After this rational introduction for the outer man to what is within, the sublime powers in the spirit of the daughter were stimulated, and she wondered whether she should yet dare to ask about these same sublime powers. He said, "Certainly you should, because you have correctly been drawn past the actual obstacles, and therefore your highly refined intellect is now permitted to ask about sublime matters. Ask whatever you want." His daughter said, "Tell me what is God or where is he or how does he exist. That is to say, how is he one and yet three? . . ."[127]

Suso offers an answer to Elsbeth's questions by referring to Aristotle's metaphysics, science of the Heavens, and physics as well as to Scripture and theological insights. For example, "In this manner some virtuous pagan thinkers sought him in earlier times; foremost among these was the great mind of Aristotle. He pondered the course of nature and who that might be who is the Lord of Nature. He sought him diligently and found him. He proves from the order found in nature that there must necessarily be one single Ruler and Lord of all creatures, and we call him God."[128]

In the process of the dialogue Elsbeth asks Henry to define his terms: "How do you define *genuine* or *not genuine?*" He answered: "I call that person 'genuine' who by means of constant good exercises has by struggling attained virtue so that it has become a pleasure and a constant presence for him in its highest and most noble form, just as brilliance is constantly with the sun. By 'not genuine' I mean when the light of virtue shines in a person as something borrowed, as something transitory and imperfect, as shining light exists in the moon."[129] Then, when Suso completes his explanation, his daughter said: "Sir, I have now well understood *that* God is, but I would like to know *where* he is." At this point Suso enters into a complex explanation that partly clarifies the original question that Elsbeth asked about the relation of God and nothingness:

127. Suso, *The Life of the Servant,* in *Henry Suso: The Exemplar,* II, ch. 50, 186-87.
128. Suso, *The Life of the Servant,* in *Henry Suso: The Exemplar,* II, ch. 50, 187.
129. Suso, *The Life of the Servant,* in *Henry Suso: The Exemplar,* II, ch. 50, 189.

The theologians say that God does not have a "where," that he is completely present in everything. Open the inward ear of your soul and listen. These same learned men also maintain in the branch of knowledge called logic that one sometimes learns something about a thing from its name. One teacher says that the name "being" is the first name of God. Turn your eyes towards this being in its pure simplicity and let go of this or that which only participates in being. Take being alone in itself, which is not mixed with nonbeing. For just as nonbeing negates all being, so being in itself is the negation of all nonbeing.[130]

The dialogue continues with further questions and answers, and it ends with Suso referring to Elsbeth as his noble daughter, holy daughter, and saintly daughter. In these phrases Suso again restates his original view that the goal of knowledge is not information, but practical application in a virtuous life.[131]

Henry Suso stands as an interesting interim author with respect to the relation of Aristotelian gender theory to the concept of woman. As mentioned previously, Suso was formally trained in Aristotelian philosophy and, presumably, he learned all the Aristotelian rationale for gender polarity from both directly reading the text of the philosopher and its mediation through the scholastic authors Albert and Thomas. In a few places in Suso's texts there are references to women's "weaker" nature that appear to echo the starting point of gender polarity. However, Suso takes a different, more complementary approach to women in his dialogues and interactions. This approach involves a recognition of difference between genders, along with an affirmation of a fundamental similarity or equality of dignity of women and men. These components of gender complementarity are evident in the form of his interactions with Elsbeth Stagel as described above. In addition, we also found Suso developing the concept of woman through the use of his imagination in the written dialogue between Elsbeth and himself after her death. Suso uses his imagination to counter bias about woman's inability to engage in discursive reasoning. He also integrates academic concepts and arguments with Aristotelian content into the dialogue. This offers the reader a model of a woman student of philosophy.

Just as Henry Suso encouraged Elsbeth Stagel to expand her mind through the exercise of discursive reasoning, so also Elsbeth Stagel encouraged Henry Suso to write more concretely about his own experiences. In her willingness to write down his efforts in this task, Elsbeth also initiated a shift from private intergender dialogue to public record of private intergender dialogue. When Friar Henry came to accept her lead, and collaborated with her in editing the record of private experiences to be shared with others publicly, he further extended the move from private intergender dialogue to public intergender dialogue. The difference between Meister Eckhart's theory of gender and Henry Suso's theory of gender was the active role of Elsbeth Stagel.

---

130. Suso, *The Life of the Servant,* in *Henry Suso: The Exemplar,* II, ch. 51, 190-91.

131. Suso reaches a similar conclusion at the end of the *Little Book of Truth,* where he says, "One does not arrive at the goal by asking questions. It is rather through detachment that one comes to this hidden truth. Amen." See *Henry Suso: The Exemplar,* ch. 7, 331.

Henry Suso's book *The Exemplar,* containing four texts written in the vernacular of High German, "was widely circulated in German, Latin, and Old Swedish, before his death in 1366."[132] This disciple of Eckhart contributed to intergender dialogue not only in private conversations with women, but through the circulation of his dialogues with Elsbeth Stagel in written form. These dialogues in form and content formed part of a new community of intergender discourse about wisdom and virtue. We are told, for example, that "Birgitta [Bridget of Sweden] had read and been impressed by Suso's book."[133] It is to St. Bridget's texts that we will turn next. The increasingly complex interconnections of intergender dialogue through the exchange of written texts in this period in the history of the concept of woman establish a new kind of network for the development of gender theory in the West.

INDIVIDUAL WOMEN RELIGIOUS AUTHORS

We will now turn to consider three woman religious authors nearly contemporary with Eckhart, Tauler, and Suso. These women, Bridget of Sweden, Catherine of Siena, and Julian of Norwich, used elaborate analogies to describe human identity and gender identity. The written evidence we have for their thought reveals three unique and rich personalities. Each of them left texts that reveal a deep and ongoing dialogue in prayer with Jesus Christ, who they believed was the mysterious True God and True Man of their Catholic faith. This context of interior dialogue so permeated each of them that they articulated new understandings about human life and about the identity of the human person.[134] From within three different cultures — Swedish, Italian, and English — and from three different living situations — widowhood, a consecrated life in a family home, and as an anchorite in a cell — these three women brought forth new understandings of human identity in general. Our analysis will now turn to consider their individual contributions to the history of the concept of woman.

St. Bridget of Sweden (1303-1373)

With the texts of St. Bridget we move into a different phase of the history of works of women religious writers: first, Bridget was primarily a lay woman and not a member of a religious order even though she founded a religious community at the end of her life; and second, her work contains significantly more extended analogies in addition to the shorter analogical insights similar in kind to those we have

132. Marguerite Tjader Harris, ed., *Birgitta of Sweden: Life and Revelations* (New York/ Mahwah, N.J.: Paulist Press, 1990), preface, p. 6.

133. Harris, *Birgitta,* preface, p. 6.

134. See Pope John Paul II, *Evangelium Vitae* (Boston: Pauline Books and Media, 1995). "The purpose of the Gospel, in fact, is 'to transform humanity from within and to make it new.' Like the yeast which leavens the whole measure of dough (cf. *Mt.* 13:33), the Gospel is meant to permeate all cultures and give them life from within, so that they may express the full truth about the human person and about human life" (#95).

previously encountered. St. Bridget used discursive reasoning to elaborate in great detail transcendental analogies drawn from a woman's experience of the home. Before elaborating one of these analogies in some detail, an introduction will be given to her life and circumstances.

Bridget of Sweden was married at the age of thirteen to Ulf Gudmarsson, had eight children of whom two only survived, and was widowed in 1344.[135] While the Black Plague ravaged Europe during the years 1348-1349, reducing its population by about one-third, Bridget moved to Rome, was there during the Jubilee year of 1350, and except for a trip she took to Jerusalem in 1372, remained there until her death.[136] Throughout the entire course of her life Bridget was engaged in intergender dialogue. The men she spoke with about principles of wisdom and virtue include her husband Ulf, four different spiritual directors (Master Matthias who was buried in the Dominican Church after dying in the Plague, a Cistercian Prior Peter Olavsson, a different Master Peter Olavsson, and Bishop Alphonsus Pecha), and many prominent social and religious leaders (e.g., King Magnus, Pope Gregory XI, Pope Urban VI, and the Archbishop of Naples).[137] A common image of St. Bridget captures this intergender aspect of her life and work. As seen in the illustrations on pages 368 and 369 below, as well as the one on the cover of this book, Bridget is often depicted writing with her inspiration coming from both Jesus and Mary.

During the years 1344-1373, Bridget roughly composed a text in Swedish that has become known as the *Revelations*. The process of the composition of this work involved many steps, an accounting of which demonstrates the important role of intergender dialogue in her life. First, Bridget either wrote down or dictated her own text in Old Swedish. Next, her Confessor translated her words into Latin. Then Bridget edited the Latin text with her Confessor to make sure it accurately expressed her thoughts.[138] In these ways, Bridget collaborated with different men on her text, as Henry Suso had collaborated with Elsbeth Stagel on his own text. While the original Swedish version of Bridget's text was lost, the Latin translation entitled *Revelationes Celestes* made by her confessor Peter of Alvastra has remained to serve as what is believed to be an authentic record of Bridget's

---

135. See Johannes Jorgensen, *Saint Bridget of Sweden* (London/New York/Toronto: Longmans Green and Company, 1954), vol. 1 (1303-1349) and vol. 2 (1349-1373); and Barbara Obrist, "The Swedish Visionary Saint Bridget," in *Medieval Women Writers,* ed. Katharina M. Wilson (Athens, Ga.: University of Georgia Press, 1984), 226.

136. Harris, *Birgitta,* pp. 71-98. A more popular dramatic description of her life is found in Helen M. D. Redpath, *God's Ambassadress: St. Bridget of Sweden* (Milwaukee: Bruce Publishing Co., 1946).

137. Tore Nyberg, Introduction, *Birgitta,* pp. 16-18; and Jorgenson, *Saint Bridget,* vol. 2, esp. pp. 10, 224, 280-81.

138. Albert Ryle Kezel, translator's introduction to *Birgitta,* pp. 59-61. Kezel compared some original Swedish passages with finished Latin translations and concluded that "[t]here seems to be no reason to reject the traditional account, which insists that the traditional Latin version accurately represents what the Saint wished to have published" (p. 63). Nyberg notes the importance of these dialogues in Bridget's life and works: "The doctrine of St. Birgitta is certainly, as can be derived from what has been said so far, most aptly understood as the result of a dialectical process partly between Birgitta and her confessors and spiritual advisors, partly between her own experiences and her mental and affective life" (Introduction, *Birgitta,* p. 40).

Bridget of Sweden Writing and Receiving Her *Revelations*

Bridget of Sweden Receiving Her *Revelations*

thought.[139] Within a hundred years, Bridget's *Revelations* were translated into English.[140] Our analysis will focus on some of the philosophical thinking that Bridget displays, and particularly on her capacity for analogical thinking.

For the most part, Bridget's descriptions are on the level of simple attention to her experience. She describes what she saw and heard without careful differentiation between her various faculties. In fact, this lack of discrimination was one of the reasons for which her theories were criticized by Jean Gerson in his 1415 *De probatione spiritum,* by the 1414-18 Council of Constantinople, and by the 1431-39 Council of Basel.[141] Still, even though Bridget did not develop her discursive powers of reflection upon her own faculties as they functioned in her experience, as St. Teresa of Avila did some centuries later, she nonetheless used her intelligence both to question her experience and to offer detailed elaborations of root analogies. An example of each of these skills will now be given.

In Book V of her *Revelations,* also named the Book of Questions, Bridget pondered a series of questions posed by a "Monk" before a Judge.[142] Many of her questions are posed in a philosophical manner. The first question and response are as follows:

1.1: O Judge, I ask you: You have given me a mouth. May I not say the things that please me?

Response: Friend, I gave you a mouth that you might speak rationally about things that are useful for your body and soul and about things that belong to my honor.[143]

Bridget then asks about the purpose of the eyes, ears, hands, and feet. In subsequent interrogations the following philosophical questions are asked:

3.3: Why have you given us free will if not to follow our own choice?
4.4: Why should I fear when I have the force of my own strength?
4.5: Why am I to obey others if my will is in my own control?

---

139. William Patterson Cumming, ed., *The Revelations of Saint Birgitta* (London: Oxford University Press, 1929), p. xxii. See also Tore Nyberg's Introduction to *Birgitta of Sweden: Life and Revelations,* pp. 13-51. A good introduction to some of the main theological aspects of these writings, such as her doctrine of the Trinity and of Mary, has recently been given by Cornelia Wolfskeel, "Brigitta of Sweden," in *A History of Women Philosophers,* ed. Mary Ellen Waithe, vol. 2, pp. 167-89.

140. William Cumming argues that an analysis of the pronouns used in the translation indicates that it was translated into English before 1475. See *The Revelations,* intro., p. xiii.

141. Obrist, "The Swedish Visionary," pp. 235-37. Auke Jelsma suggests that the opposition to Bridget was more political than dogmatic in "The Appreciation of Bridget of Sweden (1303-1373) in the 15th Century," in *Women and Men in Spiritual Culture, XIV-XVII Centuries: A Meeting of South and North,* ed. Elisja Schulte van Kessel (The Hague: Netherlands Government Publishing Office, 1986), pp. 171-72.

142. Nyberg suggests that "[t]he monk is . . . the *animus* of Birgitta; the doubts are but her own doubts projected upon the figure of the monk." See introduction to *Birgitta of Sweden, Life,* p. 26. Nyberg attributes this insight to the Swedish scholar Hjalmar Sundén. Other suggestions are that the Judge represents Christ.

143. *Birgitta of Sweden, Life,* p. 102.

9.3: Why did you give man a rational intellect and senses, whereas to animals you did not give reason?

13.4: Why are some given intelligence and an incomparable genius for learning while others are like asses without intellect?

13.5: Why are some excessively hardened while others rejoice in wonderful consolation?

13.6: Why is greater prosperity given in this world to the wicked rather than to the good?[144]

These questions appear to reveal an inquiring mind that had some understanding of the difference between intellect, passions, and will. Most of the answers recorded in the *Revelations* appeal to faith rather than to reason for their justification.

Even though Bridget did not analyze the philosophical sources of her experiences, she nonetheless used her discursive reasoning to consider the meaning of her experience. This capacity to analyze and elaborate the meaning of an insight demonstrates a philosophical ability that Bridget developed on her own outside of academia since she lacked any formal philosophical education.

This analysis will now turn to elaborate an extensive transcendental analogy that St. Bridget described. It articulates similarities between a spiritual house and a regular house, in that it considers "the three houses that Christ and many souls ought to have together." In the analogy Bridget demonstrates a wide range of practical and theoretical knowledge about the situation of women in the home and wealth of spiritual experience.

St. Bridget begins by simply stating the base analogate for her theory:

Therefore, my spouse, for you are mine of godly right, it is necessary for us to have three houses. In the first are to be such necessities that enter into the body as meat or drink. In the second are to be clothes to cover the body without. And in the third, necessary instruments that are useful to the household.

In the first house are to be three things: bread, drink, and food. In the second, three other things: that is, linen, wool, and silk that is made from the work of worms. In the third, three other things: first, instruments and vessels that are filled with liquid; the second, live instruments such as horse, ass, and others; the third, artificial instruments by which living things move.[145]

The "sense base" for this analogy is simply the structure and divisions of a household of some affluence, such as the one Bridget would have ruled during her time as housewife and mother.

Next, Bridget begins to unfold the meaning of her analogy by introducing vertical analogates for the first house: "Mark how in the first house is to be bread of good will, drink of premeditation, and food of good wisdom."[146] Then she begins to antici-

---

144. *Birgitta of Sweden, Life,* pp. 102, 104, 105, 116, and 134.

145. Bridget, *The Revelations,* II, ch. 24, 13. The fifteenth-century English translation has been put into modern English by the author.

146. Bridget, *The Revelations,* II, 13.

pate questions on the part of the reader, and so she fills in some of the answers, and in particular she indicates that her analogy is not only theological but also philosophical:

> But you may ask what this bread means, whether it means the bread that is on the altar . . . this bread I do not mean here; but the bread that we must gather into one house is a good pure will. Bodily bread, if it be clean and pure, it profits two things. First, it comforts and gives strength to all the veins and sinews of the body. Second, it gathers to itself all inward filth, which passes out with it from man, and so man is cleansed. A clean will works in the same way. First, it comforts; for if a man wills nothing but that good will . . . it strengthens patience and strengthens the hope of finding happiness inasmuch as he receives and suffers gladly everything that happens to him. Second, a good will draws out all filth that annoys the soul, such as pride, covetousness, and lechery.[147]

Bridget was frequently concerned with the imperfection and corruption in various members of society. She often spoke directly to individuals, many of whom were men, and challenged them to change their ways.[148] In the above analogy through public intergender dialogue she notes some of the ways to begin this path of conversion towards virtue.

Bridget's elaboration of the analogy continues with a consideration of the meaning of drink that is clearly an affirmation of the value of discursive reasoning itself:

> The drink we must have in our house is good thinking before all things that are to be done. Bodily drink is valuable in three ways. **First**, it gives good digestion. For whoever intends to do any good deeds, if he busily searches his mind and finds in himself, or if he does, only what shall bring praise to God, what helps his neighbour, or what profits his soul, and if he will not do anything unless he perceives some good result from his work, then the work will have a good process and a good result in a good digestion. . . . **Second**, drink quenches thirst. What is worse thirst than sin of wicked desire and anger? But if a man thinks beforehand of what profit comes from it, how wretchedly it ends, and what reward there is if it is overcome, then by the grace of God that wicked thirst is quenched, and the heat of godly charity and good desire comes to the soul, and gladness rises in him that he did the things he decided to do in his mind. And he seeks occasions from that time forward to flee those things that he should have been dissuaded from, if thinking before had helped. And he shall be the busier afterwards to beware of such things. This, my spouse, is the drink that we are to gather into our cellar.[149]

147. Bridget, *The Revelations,* II, ch. 24, 14.

148. For example, she criticized King Magnus Erickson of Sweden for his worldliness, and publicly rebuked the King's brother. See Cumming, *The Revelations,* p. xxv, note 3; and Obrist, "The Swedish Visionary," p. 248. Bridget also confronted Pope Urban "upon penalty of God's severe displeasure and punishment, not to leave Rome." See "Brigittines" in *Old Catholic Encyclopedia.* Her efforts to keep the Papacy from leaving Rome were not successful, and it took St. Catherine of Siena's public efforts to bring the Papacy back to Rome after it moved to Avignon.

149. Bridget, *The Revelations,* II, ch. 24, 14-15. My emphasis.

Bridget identifies the following points: (1) the mind discovers a general principle, (2) the individual needs to consider his or her own particular relation to anger or desire, then (3) a particular good act can be chosen, (4) in the future, self-modification can occur through the practice of self-governance, and (5) a kind of delight or gladness will occur as a result of following this process. St. Bridget's analysis parallels Aristotle's fundamental theory of happiness as an activity in accordance with virtue, even though she may not have known anything directly about his systematic ethics. However, through her interaction with spiritual directors trained in academia, she may have indirectly learned the fundamental principles of Aristotle's ethics.

As St. Bridget continues to elaborate her analogy, she makes a clear distinction between knowledge gained through academic study of books and wisdom gained through experience:

> **Third,** there must be food that does two things.
>
> First, it makes a better flavor in the mouth, and it is more convenient to the body than if bread was [eaten] alone. Second, it makes the body more delicate and the blood better than if bread and drink were alone. It is the same for spiritual food. What is this food but good wisdom? For whoever has a good will, and wills only those things that belong to God; if he has also good thinking before action, and does nothing but what he first knows is for the praise of God, to him wisdom tastes very good.
>
> But now you might ask what this good wisdom is, for there are many who are so simple that they cannot say their 'Our Father' and finish it right. Others are of great letters and deep cunning. Is that good wisdom? No. For good wisdom is not only in letters, but in heart and in good living. Whoever he be that thinks about the way unto death and the quality of the self, death, and the kingdom after death, he is wise. And whoever casts from himself the vanity of the world and all superfluous things, and is content with only his necessities, and works in the love of God as much as he can, he has food of wisdom, but the bread of good will and the drink of good thinking before [acting] tastes much better. . . . Therefore, good wisdom is not only in letters, but in good works.[150]

The second house is summarized as having three different kinds of clothing: linen that comes from the earth, wool or leather that comes from animals, and silk made from worms. Then taking each kind of cloth, St. Bridget draws out their meaning through introducing several vertical analogies. Each kind of cloth represents a particular religious virtue. Linen, which is closest to the body, represents a kind of *"apatheia"* — a peace within the passions or right kind of authority over the emotions that provides a stability to the individual. Wool, which preserves the heat of the body, represents works of mercy that "protect the individual from coldness of heart." Silk represents abstinence from superficial and destructive desires, because it is so expensive to buy and self-governance is such a difficult task to achieve.[151]

---

150. Bridget, *The Revelations,* II, ch. 25, 15-16. My emphasis.
151. Bridget, *The Revelations,* II, ch. 26, 17-19.

In this summary of Bridget's analogy, which leaves out so many of the delicate nuances of the author, we can nonetheless see an integrated theory in which the human situation is enhanced by rigorous self-discipline, virtuous action, and gift of self to others. The three approaches to development of the self are given an equal and balanced place, as all three kinds of clothing are important in the house.

In her analysis of the third house, the vertical analogy extends further its external base and its interior application to the quality of thoughts within the mind. St. Bridget's capacity for discursive analysis keeps penetrating deeper and broader in its efforts to understand her experience and to elaborate its significance for others. First she lays out the general terms of the analogy:

> Of the instruments of the third house, that are good thoughts, virtues, manners, and true confession. And of the bolting of all three houses.
>
> The son of God speaks to his spouse and says: I told you before, that in our third house there must be three kinds of instruments. First, that which holds liquids. Second, instruments that till the land such as plough, harrow, axes, and others which fix things when they are broken. Third, living instruments such as asses and horses and others by which both living and dead things are transported.[152]

Then in her discussion of the analogy itself we see Bridget arguing that the free choice between good and evil is itself a good because it allows the individual, by the effort of hard work, to overcome mistakes and to learn how to make good choices where poorer ones may have been chosen in the past.

Next, following her usual methodology each of the three parts of the analogy are developed in turn. She describes the experience of discernment through reflection on the relative value of different thoughts. Free choice is a good because it gives the individual the opportunity to overcome "bad thoughts," to consider wrong choices, and then, with a new act of will, to make a better choice.

> In the first house in which liquids are stored, there must be kept two different kinds of instruments: one, in which are kept thin, sweet liquids such as oil, water, wine, and others; [and] another in which bitter, thick liquids are kept such as mustard, meal, and others. Indeed, these liquids signify thoughts of the soul, good and evil. For a good thought is like sweet oil and delectable wine, and evil thought is like a bitter mustard, for it makes the soul bitter and troubled. And as a man sometimes needs thick liquids, for they profit the purging and healing of the body and brain, so also do evil thoughts; for though they do not heal nor make the soul fat as does the oil of good thoughts, yet they are useful to purge the soul, as mustard purges the brain. . . . And though they be like mustard, bitter to bear, yet they heal the soul very much, and guide it towards eternal life and health, which may not be gained without bitterness. Therefore, the vessels of the soul, where good thoughts will be placed, must busily be made ready and continually cleaned. For it is useful that evil thoughts come sometimes in order to test and

152. Bridget, *The Revelations,* II, ch. 27, 20.

prove more merit; and therefore, the soul must work hard that it not consent to them, nor delight in them. Otherwise the sweetness and increase of the soul shall be poured out, and only bitterness shall abide.[153]

Bridget's theme, namely, that arduous work to overcome difficult thoughts has value for the individual, is very interesting indeed. It reveals that she understood various levels of consciousness and the dynamic interaction among them as part of a process of overcoming the self and the achievement of self-governance. It is obvious that this view of woman's wisdom demands intellectual activity, one that is completely counter to the gender-polarity description of woman's wisdom through passivity.

In the next part of her analogy, St. Bridget develops the characteristics needed to be a good teacher of wisdom and virtue. It is not enough to simply make good choices or acts for oneself, there is a responsibility to teach others how to become virtuous both by word and by deed.

In the second house there must also be two kinds of instruments: first, outdoor instruments with which the land is made ready to be sown, and with which thorns and weeds are upturned by the root, as by plough and harrow; second, useful instruments to do what is necessary both inside and outside, such as axes and others. The instruments that the land is tilled with signify the knowledge of man which is oriented towards the advantage of his neighbour, as a plough for the land. For the wicked men are like the land or the earth, for they think always upon earthly things. They are barren and dry of compunction and sorrow for their sins, for their sins are nothing. Each one is cold towards the love of God, for they seek only to do good deeds, but they are swift and ready to worship the world. Really a good man ought to till him by external knowledge, as a good man tills his land with the plough. First, he ought to till him with his mouth, speaking to him about such things as are useful to his soul, and showing him the way to life; and afterwards, doing the good acts that he can, so that his neighbour will be taught by words and stirred by actions to do good. . . . The instruments that are necessary for inside work such as axes and others, signify discreet intent and good discussion of this work.[154]

In the elaboration of this part of her analogy, St. Bridget probably unknowingly follows Aristotle's dictum that the person who can teach virtue is wiser than one who simply is virtuous. The teacher knows what virtue is, and why one ought to be virtuous, as well as how an individual can, in daily decisions and actions, strive to overcome the self. In addition, her knowledge of farming gives her the analogical base in experience from which to develop the philosophical principles. They are accurate, simply expressed, and helpful as a teaching technique.

In her development of the third set of contents of the third house, St. Bridget introduces a transcendental analogy to describe the sacrament of confession. The

153. Bridget, *The Revelations,* II, ch. 27, 20-21.
154. Bridget, *The Revelations,* II, ch. 27, 21-22.

living instrument here represents the Church in its capacity as distributor of the Sacraments. However, at the same time, it is important to recognize that confession has a philosophical foundation even though its main religious function is reconciliation with God. Philosophically, confession is built upon the principle that "the act reveals the person," and that if an individual can recognize when he or she makes poor choices in actions, then it becomes possible to make a renewed effort in the future for a better kind of choice.[155] So a philosophical understanding of the sacrament suggests that the sacrament of reconciliation relies in part upon an individual's capacity for self-reflection and for decision making in relation to the way in which the acts committed reveal to consciousness a "hierarchy of values" that perhaps needs to be reordered. St. Bridget grasps this principle:

> In the third house there must be living instruments that carry both the living and the dead, such as horses, asses, and other beasts. These instruments are true confessions; for they carry and move both the living and the dead. What signifies the living but the soul that is made of my godhead and lives without end? For by true confession it moves nearer and nearer every day to God. For just as with yeast, the oftener and better it is fed and nourished, it is stronger and fairer to see, so it is the same with confession, the oftener and more diligently it is made, of the smallest things as well as of the greatest, so it moves the soul further. . . . And what is the dead that confession carries and moves but good works that are slain by deadly sin?[156]

In her summary of the contents of the analogy St. Bridget expresses what has already become a common theme among the women religious writers, namely, that they understand themselves as the generic representative for all human beings. In this way, the single woman Bridget serves as a paradigm for all women and men. Again it is worth noting that this generic use of the individual woman is in contrast to traditional philosophical language in which the individual man serves as the paradigm for all human beings.

> Therefore, my spouse, by whom I understand all my friends, gather we into our houses those things by which good will be spiritually delighted with a holy soul.
> First, into our first house bread of pure will, willing nothing but what God wills. Second, drink of good thinking before, doing nothing but it be thought for the praise of God. Third, soul of good wisdom, thinking always about what is to come, and how things are to be governed that are now.
> Gather we into our second house peace from sin against God and peace from

155. This philosophical principle is well developed in Karol Wojtyla, *The Acting Person* (Dordrecht/Boston: D. Reidel, 1979). "For us action *reveals* the person, and we look at the person through his action. For it lies in the nature of the correlation inherent in experience, in the very nature of man's acting, that action constitutes the specific moment whereby the person is revealed. Action gives us the best insight into the inherent essence of the person and allows us to understand the person most fully" (p. 11).

156. Bridget, *The Revelations*, II, ch. 27, 22-23.

strife towards our neighbour. Second, works of mercy with which we are useful to our neighbour in act. Third, perfect abstinence, refraining from those things that might trouble peace.

And gather we into our house good and reasonable thoughts to array our house inside. Second, well-ruled and temperant knowledge to shine to our friends outside. Third, true confession, whereby even though we are sick we may live again.[157]

This orderly transcendental analogy is concluded with a further reflection on how a house is secured so that its contents remain safe. Bridget reflects on the significance of hinges, doors, and bolts, which represent the theological virtues of hope, trust, and charity, respectively. Then the key to open the bolt is what she calls "stable desire" for God.

The portions of the analogy of the three houses given above are only a small part of the extensive analogy that she develops over twelve full pages of manuscript. I have primarily chosen the philosophical aspects of the analogy for emphasis. It is possible to recognize from these selections that St. Bridget had developed a good capacity for discursive reasoning that moved from a base analogate within her own experience as a woman running a household, through vertical analogies at the level of consciousness and reasoning, and to transcendental analogies at the level of faith. In this she displayed a philosophical talent that was natural, and one that she developed in spite of the lack of a formal education. Bridget's understanding of herself transcends the categories she has given herself. Yet, she continues to probe the categories of her experience to present to others the reality she has discovered.

The diagram on the next page gives Bridget's structure of her root analogy extended to four levels of comparison. This diagram summarizes the multiple ways in which Bridget extended her analogical thinking through the exercise of discursive reasoning to interpret her transcendental analogy of running a household with Christ, her Spouse.

Bridget likely experienced a practice of gender complementarity in her interaction with men who had received an academic education, and this interaction may have helped her to develop her own skills in discursive reasoning. When St. Bridget founded her order of Bridgettines, she insisted that the community be established with double monasteries of men's and women's communities in which the primary authority was in the hands of the Abbess.[158] Her community was first proposed in

---

157. Bridget, *The Revelations,* II, ch. 27, 24.

158. The Abbess had authority over all temporal affairs, but the monks were in charge of spiritual direction. See "Brigittines" in *The Catholic Encyclopedia* (1907). For different meanings for the term 'double-monastery' see Penny Schine Gold, "Male/Female Cooperation . . . ," in *Medieval Religious Women.* "But the term 'double' disguises the fact that most of these communities were originally founded for the benefit of either men or women rather than both. . . . Rather than speaking of these communities as 'double monasteries,' we would be more exact to recognize the diversity of arrangements and purposes by referring to the general phenomenon of religious men and women living in close proximity to each other, and by specifying the particular purpose and arrangements at the communities in question" (vol. 1, pp. 156-57). J. Grobomont points out that the term 'double monastery' was "given to monastic foundations or cloisters joined together under a common superior and bound by juridical and

Bridget of Sweden's Transcendental Analogy of Christ as Husband of Household

	1st House (things enter the body; similarly things enter the soul)			2nd House (clothes cover the body; similarly, virtues cover the soul)			3rd House (instruments useful to the household are like virtues and sacraments useful to the soul)		
1st extension:									
2nd extension:	(1) bread like good will	(2) drink like good thinking	(3) food like good wisdom	(1) linen like peace from strife	(2) wool like works of mercy	(3) silk like abstinence	(1) hold liquids like good thoughts	(2) till land like well-ruled knowledge	(3) living instruments like true confession
3rd extension:	1-1-a and 1-1-b; 1-2-a and 1-2-b; 1-3-a and 1-3-b			2-1-a and 2-1-b, 2-2-a and 2-2-b; 2-3-a and 2-3-b			3-1-a and 3-1-b; 3-2-a and 3-2-b; 3-3-a and 3-3-b		

Example development of 1-1-a and 1-1-b

1-1-a = bread comforts and strengthens the body; similarly, good will strengthens virtues

1-1-b = bread cleans filth out of the body; similarly, good will chases out vices

etc.

1347, approved in 1370, and her daughter Catherine became its first Abbess. It is also interesting to note in passing that the original rule of the community allowed each nun to "have as many books as they like for study." However, relations between the communities of men and of women did not remain well balanced for long. Auke Jelsma traces the tension and eventual destruction of the original concept of a double monastery that St. Bridget had so strongly affirmed, until the final concept was primarily one in which the women provided the material means for the men's communities to develop an intellectual and spiritual life.[159]

Bridget's reputation for wisdom, virtue, and holiness was widely accepted, and she was officially canonized as a Saint in 1415. The Bridgettines spread quickly, but subsequent turmoil in Europe affected them adversely. The mother house in Wadstena was threatened by devastation during the Protestant Reformation, a monastery in Germany was plundered twice and destroyed by fire, and monasteries were destroyed with the nuns and monks dispersed in Germany and in England during the Reformation, and in France during the Revolution. Only a few Bridgettine monasteries still exist today in Holland, England, Bavaria, Spain, and Italy.[160]

Concerning the issue of whether St. Bridget directly influenced any other women authors, there is considerable evidence that she helped form Margery Kempe (born in Lynn, England around 1373) who is credited with having authored the first autobiography written in the English language. There appear to be four specific ways Bridget influenced Margery. The first is location of place as suggested by Hope Emily Allen, who first identified the Margery Kempe manuscript: "As Danzig was the Baltic port by which Swedes often went to Rome (where St. Bridget's relics rested, in transit to Wadstena), so Lynn was the port by which the English went to Sweden. Margery will have been aware of St. Bridget from infancy."[161] The second is from a direct experience of Bridget's writings as described by Margery herself when she mentions that a parish priest who had read books to her included "Saint Bride's Book" in this group along with some texts of Bonaventure and Hilton.[162] The third occurred on a trip to Rome in 1415, the year in which Saint Bridget's canonization was confirmed by an official ceremony. Margery tells us that she made a visit to the place where the Swedish woman had lived:

> Afterwards this creature spoke with Saint Bridget's maid in Rome, but she could not understand what she said. Then she found a man who could understand her language, and that man told Saint Bridget's maid what this creature said, and how she asked after Saint Bridget, her lady. Then the maid said that her lady,

---

economic bonds. . . . In the West in the 7th and 8th centuries there were numerous double monasteries. . . . Opposition came from the monastic milieu itself, and only the Bridgittines maintained this type of organization until the end of the Middle Ages" ("Monasteries, Double," in *New Catholic Encyclopedia*). Note that there are variable spellings: Brigittines, Bridgittines, Bridgettines, and even Birgittines.

159. Jelsma, "The Appreciation of Bridget," pp. 173-74.

160. Harris, in her Preface to *Birgitta of Sweden, Life,* traces the resurgence of modern and contemporary scholarly interest in Bridget (pp. 4-9).

161. Hope Emily Allen, note to the 1940 edition of *The Book of Margery Kempe: A Modern Version by W. Butler-Bowdon* (London: Jonathan Cape, 1936), p. 280.

162. *The Book of Margery Kempe,* pp. 215-16.

Saint Bridget, was kind and gentle to every creature and that she had a happy face. . . . She was in the chamber that Saint Bridget died in, and heard a German priest preaching about her there, and about her revelations and her manner of life.[163]

Margery obviously felt part of a tradition of women's religious culture, as the concrete steps she took to confirm this tradition attest. She also may have particularly identified with Bridget because she too was a married woman and pilgrim who felt called to a spiritual life in unusual circumstances. The fourth seems to be her own tendency to model herself after St. Bridget, including authoring a text about her life. Hope Allen describes it this way: "Margery's story often suggests that she is trying to emulate St. Bridget."[164] Another suggestion for a route of influence is offered by Valerie Lagorio, who raises the possibility that Margery was more indirectly influenced by St. Bridget through the work of St. Dorothea of Montau (1347-1394).[165] In any event, the infragender female community of discourse in which Margery was the one who listened and St. Bridget the one who taught by word and example was definitely functioning in constructive ways, directly or indirectly, to foster the development of women's self-understanding.

Even though Margery Kemp was illiterate, she dictated her *Book* to two different male scribes. So once again we find that the context of private intergender dialogue, which incorporates public texts written by both men and women, leads to a new written text that later becomes part of a further public intergender community of discourse. In Chapter 6 we will examine some of the content of Margery Kempe's autobiography in the context of the struggle of women to break out of gender polarity stereotypes. At this point in our analysis, we will turn away from Margery in order to consider the original work of another woman author of the period, St. Catherine of Siena.

St. Catherine of Siena (1347-1380)

Catherine of Siena has fascinated many writers.[166] In addition, her well-known role in bringing the center of the Catholic Church back to Rome is depicted in a major portrait in one of the Vatican audience halls. The proclamation in 1970 by Pope Paul VI of St. Catherine of Siena as a Doctor of the Church, gives further affirmation to the value of her teachings.[167] Even by the fifteenth century, Catherine of Siena's strong presence as teacher was popularly acclaimed.

163. *The Book of Margery Kempe,* pp. 140-41.

164. Hope Allen, *The Book of Margery Kempe,* note to the 1940 edition, p. 280, 47/26.

165. Valerie M. Lagorio, "The Medieval Continental Women Mystics," in *The Medieval Mystics,* p. 173.

166. See, for example, Sigrid Undset, *Catherine of Siena* (New York: Sheed and Ward, 1954) and more recently Carolyn Bynum's analysis of her relation to food in *Holy Feast and Holy Fast* (Berkeley: University of California Press, 1987), pp. 165-80.

167. See *Catechism of the Catholic Church,* where Catherine is directly mentioned, #313, #356, and #1937.

Catherine of Siena Giving the Rule to Third Order Dominicans

While much of her contribution to western thought is spiritual and theological in focus, Catherine nonetheless can be considered a major contributor to the developing philosophical concept of woman found in religious writers outside of academia. Her contribution to the philosophy of woman can be seen in three particular areas: the affirmation of discursive reasoning in the development of analogical thinking, breaking into the public sphere of activity as a woman, and providing a beginning awareness of gender-related or masculine and feminine virtues and vices. Each of these three contributions will be considered in turn.

As with previous writers studied in this chapter, St. Catherine was primarily influenced by male Dominicans. As the twenty-third of twenty-four children, Catherine, by the age of seventeen, had joined the Militia of Jesus, which had been founded by the Dominicans in 1285. The official Dominican Third Order was not established until 1406. In fact, Catherine herself joined the Third Order Dominicans as a lay woman, or "mantellante." Her spiritual director, Raymond of Capua (1330-1399), at the year of her death was elected head of the Roman Province of Dominicans and wrote a life of St. Catherine between the years 1384 and 1395.[168] The relation between Catherine and Raymond developed in a complementary manner similar to the relation between Henry Suso and Elsbeth Stagel depicted earlier in this chapter.[169] In an excellent account of their relationship, Paul Conner, O.P. describes the oral and written intergender dialogue that occurred between them during the six years they knew one another, and the memory of which remained with Raymond after Catherine's death for nearly twenty years more.[170] After describing their common goals, their manner of interaction, and their personal struggles, Conner summarizes their complementary relationship as follows:

> Thus equality did exist in their friendship, and it did not. Where it did, Catherine and Raymond were among the best friends of recorded history. But where Catherine was superior, Raymond followed willingly; and where Raymond was better trained, Catherine listened eagerly, and then let Christian love urge her forward. And so, by even increasing their equality, complementarity was a second feature of their friendship which made it permanent.[171]

Catherine could read and write, but she usually dictated her letters and dialogues in the Sienese dialect to various followers, most of whom were men. In her *Dialogues,* Catherine describes her own interior dialogues within the self, her frequent dialogues with God, and her dialogues with others around her, including both men and women. Even in her letters Catherine engages in frequent dialogue with oth-

---

168. Raymond of Capua, Blessed, *The Life of St. Catherine of Siena,* trans. George Lamb (New York: P. J. Kennedy and Sons, 1960). Within a century, William Caxton edited an English translation of this text, Raymundus de Vineis, *Lyf of Saint Katherin of Senis* . . . (Westminster: Wynkyn de Worde, 1493). Susan A. Muto notes in "Foundations of Christian Formation in the *Dialogue* of St. Catherine of Siena," in *Medieval Religious Women: Peace Weavers, Volume II,* that Catherine's complete works and Raymond's biography were published in Siena in 1707-1721 (pp. 275-87, esp. p. 276).

169. John Coakley unfortunately describes the relation not as complementary but as androgynous with the claim that ". . . here we have the most harmonious and ambitious male vision of the female saint, in the sense that her powers complement those of the church, and she and Raymond form together a sort of androgynous unit for the salvation of Christendom" ("Friars as Confidants of Holy Women," p. 246). The unfortunate aspect of the concept of androgynous unit is that it suggests a loss of individuation in a kind of fractional complementarity instead of the combined union of two differentiated beings in integral complementarity.

170. Paul M. Conner, O.P., "Catherine of Siena and Raymond of Capua — Enduring Friends," *Studia Mystica* 12 (1989): 22-29.

171. Conner, "Catherine of Siena," *Studia Mystica* 12 (1989): 26. In this article the fundamental components of complementarity (tension of similarity and difference) and dialogue are further elaborated: "When people are different enough and yet similar enough to interact on a basis of *complementary equality,* there is the possibility of this kind of relationship between them. When in fact they do interact consciously *more for the other than for themselves,* a friendship is born. And friendship grows thereafter according to the *quality and extent of what the two friends exchange*" (p. 27).

Saint Catherine Writing Her First Letter

Saint Catherine Writing under the Guidance of Saint Thomas Aquinas

ers and also describes her own dialogue with God. Karen Scott notes that in letters Catherine describes herself as developing a trust in God "through a conversation or dialogue with him."[172] Further, Catherine developed a personal skill as mediator of disputes in which she engaged in dialogue with members of both sides of the dispute to find solutions to their conflicts.[173]

She was aware of the significance of Thomas Aquinas, who had been canonized before her birth, and she mentions him specifically in various places.[174] In particular, Catherine was aware of his theory of the complementarity of reason and faith, and frequently employed a metaphor in which reason is compared with the iris of the eye, and faith with its pupil: "Now nothing can be known in Truth unless the mind's eye can see it. So one who wishes to know . . . must open the mind's eye by opening its pupil, which is faith, onto the object of truth."[175] Catherine's use of discursive reasoning was always integrated into the broader perspective of her relationship with God.[176]

While St. Catherine affirmed the value of reason, she was critical of academic scholars who had, in her opinion, a narrow understanding of truth. In the following passage, she identifies her own learning as coming directly from the source of truth, in contrast to certain scholars who have a "clouded reason which blocks the light of truth":

> This is why foolish, proud, and learned people go blind even though it is light, because their pride and the cloud of selfish love have covered and blotted out this light. So they read Scripture literally rather than with understanding. They taste only its letter in their chasing after a multiplicity of books. . . . Such as these, then, wonder and fall to whining when they see so many uncultured and unschooled in Biblical knowledge yet as enlightened in knowledge of the truth as if

172. Karen Scott, "St. Catherine of Siena, 'Apostola,'" *Church History* 61, no. 1 (March 1992): esp. 17, note 41. "It is no accident that Catherine's main 'mystical' and 'theological' treatise, her *Dialogue of Divine Providence,* takes the form of a dialogue between God and the soul. She experiences God mainly through speech." Scott notes as well Catherine's frequent descriptions of dialogue with others, such as "I have spoken with the Holy Father, He graciously listened. . . . When I had talked a good long time with him, at the conclusion of the words, he said . . ." (p. 38, note 8).

173. Karen Scott also describes this aspect of Catherine's public activities and giftedness in various situations of public intergender dialogue by "'being with' both sides of a conflict and mediating their differences through direct speech" ("St. Catherine," *Church History,* p. 39).

174. In one example, using the voice of God, she emphasizes his learning: "By this light set in the mind's eye Thomas saw me and there gained the light of great learning"; and in another she emphasizes prayer: "Consider the glorious Thomas. With his mind's eye he contemplated my Truth e'er so tenderly and there gained light beyond the natural and knowledge infused by grace. Thus he learned more through prayer than through human study" (Catherine of Siena, *The Dialogue* [New York/Ramsey/Toronto: Paulist Press, 1980], p. 340).

175. Catherine, *Dialogue,* p. 160. In another passage she shifts the analogy slightly: "You know that one can walk in the way of truth without the light of reason that you draw from me, the true Light, through the eye of your understanding. You must have as well the light of faith" (pp. 184-85).

176. For a consideration of her identity as a systematic theologian see William Hinnebusch, *The History of the Dominican Order,* "Catherine emerges from a study of her works as a mystic and not as a theologian. Nevertheless she knew how to reason, define, and develop ideas. In her writings she used a mature theological vocabulary and displayed a rich theological knowledge" (vol. 2, p. 360).

they had studied for a long time. But this is no wonder at all, for they possess the chief source of that light from which learning comes.[177]

The natural philosophical talent of Catherine was developed through hours of meditation and reflection on her own experience, during which she asked certain questions about these experiences, came to conclusions about their relative validity, and then acted responsibly on the basis of her judgments of value.[178] The natural philosophical ability of women mystics and theologians developed through their relentless drive to find new categories of explanation for profound personal experiences of God. The old categories that were available to them did not seem adequate to express the fresh experiences that affected them at the deepest levels of their personalities. The religious experience flooded the intellect, and the reason sought to grasp its meaning at an integration point where the two powers of the mind met. By choosing new categories of expression the author then sought to lead others to a similar kind of experience of God.

Catherine invites her reader: "Open your mind's eye and look within me, and you will see the dignity and beauty of my reasoning creature."[179] The first thing that the reason needs to grasp, she suggests, is an authentic knowledge of the self. In the first paragraph of the prologue to *The Dialogue,* Catherine sets the tone when she identifies herself as having "become accustomed to dwelling in the cell of self-knowledge in order to know God's goodness towards her, since upon knowledge follows love. And loving she seeks to pursue truth and clothe herself in it."[180] Self-knowledge leads to love of goodness, which leads to truth. Then, in the first chapter of the text, Catherine reiterates that to come to perfect knowledge, "Never leave the knowledge of yourself"; and "There is no other way to know the truth."[181]

In an interesting vertical and transcendental analogy, self-knowledge and the knowledge of God are compared to a shoot grafted onto the roots of a tree.

Imagine a circle traced on the ground, and in its centre a tree sprouting with a shoot grafted into its side. . . . So think of this soul as a tree made for love. . . . The circle in which this tree's root, the soul's love, must grow is true knowledge of herself, knowledge that is joined to me, who like the circle have neither beginning nor end. You can go round and round within this circle, finding neither end nor beginning, yet never leaving the circle. This knowledge of yourself, and of me within yourself, is grounded in the soil of true humility, which is as great as the expanse of the circle (which is the knowledge of yourself united with me, as I have said). But if your knowledge of yourself were isolated from me there would

---

177. Catherine, *Dialogue,* p. 157.

178. Judith S. Neaman refers in "Potentiation, Elevation, Acceleration: Prerogatives of Women Mystics," *Mystics Quarterly* 14, no. 1 (March 1988): 22-31, to Catherine's "fine scholastic mind" (24).

179. Catherine, *Dialogue,* p. 26.

180. Catherine, *Dialogue,* p. 25.

181. Catherine, *Dialogue,* pp. 29-30.

be no full circle at all. Instead, there would be a beginning in self-knowledge, but apart from me it would end in confusion.[182]

The dialectic of self-knowledge and of knowledge of God works together in mutual increments.

St. Catherine considers self-knowledge to be specific to the individual and general in relation to the structure of human identity. She incorporates St. Augustine's description of the human being as having three faculties of the soul (analogous to the Trinity): memory, understanding, and will.[183] When a person has a disordered will, the faculties and powers work against one another; and when the will is properly ordered they work in harmony. Again employing a vertical analogy she considers the soul to be like a city that contains different gates:

> The gates of the city are many. There are three main gates — memory, understanding, and will — and the last, if it so chooses, always holds firm and guards the others. But if the will gives its consent . . . then understanding surrenders to the darkness that is the enemy of light, and the recollection of injury makes memory surrender. . . . As soon as these gates are opened, the wickets of the body's senses all open up, as instruments that respond to the soul. So you see how a person's will that has opened all its gates responds by means of these organs so that all its sounds, that is, its works, are wasted and contaminated.[184]

Transcendental Analogy of Christ as Vertical Bridge

The relation among memory, understanding, and will provides the fundamental structure of human identity; and it is developed by St. Catherine in her most original transcendental analogy, which posits Christ as the living bridge between the human being and God. The sense base for her analogy probably came from a covered bridge in Siena that was a common part of her everyday life. Catherine's genius lay in her capacity to elaborate fundamental analogical insights through the use of discursive reasoning, and in her ability to teach others about the many different aspects of natural and spiritual life through an extended analogy.

182. Catherine, *Dialogue,* pp. 41-42. For further references on self-knowledge see pp. 88, 118, 122, 125, 135, and 158.

183. Suzanne Noffke, O.P. notes in "Catherine of Siena: The Responsive Heart," in *Spiritualities of the Heart: Approaches to Personal Wholeness in Christian Tradition,* ed. Annice Callahan, R.S.C.J. (New York/Mahwah, N.J.: Paulist Press, 1990), that Catherine also considers the relation of the heart to these Augustinian categories. "*Il cuore,* 'the heart,' for Catherine does not have the precision of her very Augustinian use of the trinity of memory/understanding/will. It consorts rather with two other terms which seem to grapple more with the *integrity* of the human spirit: *affetto,* which though usually translated as 'affection,' is very close to 'will' and carries the sense of movement, impulse, toward doing, the will reaching for what memory and understanding hold out as good; and *mente,* which, though often translated as 'mind,' has more the sense of the human spirit as a whole entity. . . . If, in Augustinian and later scholastic terms, truth resides in the understanding (intellect) and love in the will, the heart is where truth and love meet and become one" (p. 65).

184. Catherine, *Dialogue,* p. 299.

Even though her root analogy is spiritual and transcendental in that it draws a likeness between something in the sense world (the bridge) and something transcendent (the person of Christ), it incorporates several philosophical principles.

Catherine is clear that one of the primary meanings of the "living bridge" is to represent three steps in personal development, and that these steps in turn represent the three faculties of the soul. In addition to each step emphasizing one of the faculties, each step also represents a more complete integration of the three faculties.[185] First of all, the three faculties together are needed to achieve an understanding of truth: "I have explained the image of the three stairs for you in general in terms of the soul's three powers. These are three stairs, none of which can be climbed without the others if one wishes to go the way of the teaching, the bridge, of my Truth."[186] At another place, the connection is made even more explicit: "I have told you the meaning of the soul's three powers, and now I would suggest to you that the stairs symbolize the three stages through which the soul advances."[187] Sometimes Catherine implies that the three faculties of the soul are all associated more specifically with the second stage, while at other times there seems to be a parallelism with each faculty of the soul and with each stage of development. In any event, all three faculties of the soul function at all three stages, so the question is rather one of emphasis than of exact correspondence.

The chart on page 389 gives the basic structure of her argument.

We will now consider in more detail the analogies associated with each step or stage of personal development. In the first stage, the person purifies the attachment of the senses, affections, and memories to earthly things:

> The first stair is the feet, which symbolize the affections. For just as the feet carry the body, the affections carry the soul. . . . At the first stair, lifting the feet of her affections from the earth, she [the soul] stripped herself of sin.[188]

The image of the passions "carrying" the self implies that without the energy of the passions, the individual would not move anywhere. The person must desire, be repulsed, be angry, and so forth, or he or she would not be prompted to act. At the same time, unless the passions, senses, and memories are purified of their total natural orientation towards the temporal world, they will lead the person away from God.

---

185. For another description of the relation between the stairs and personal integration see Catherine M. Meade, CSJ, "Christ Has Made a Staircase of His Body," in *My Nature Is Fire: Saint Catherine of Siena* (New York: Alba House, 1991). "In each of the stages, or at each of the stairs, the memory, understanding, and will evolve to an increasingly profound level of harmony" (p. 119).

186. St. Catherine, *Dialogue,* p. 105. See also on the same page: "I have made of him a bridge with three stairs, the latter being an image of the three spiritual stages." This translation of Catherine uses the word 'powers' for what is more often referred to in scholastic philosophy as 'faculties.' The word 'powers' is usually reserved for the powers of sensation. The memory is considered the passive intellect, and the intellect and will as the two main faculties. In my discussion I will use the more traditional words in discussing Catherine's theory.

187. Catherine, *Dialogue,* p. 118.

188. Catherine, *Dialogue,* pp. 64-65.

Catherine of Siena's Transcendental Analogy of Christ as the Living Bridge			
Bridge	Body	Soul	Virtue
First Step	Feet	Memory Senses Affections Passions	Stripping of attachment Beginning of integration of faculties
Second Step	Heart	Understanding	Enlightenment of mind More effective integration of faculties
Third Step	Mouth	Will	Perfection of virtue of love towards others, towards God Perfection of integration of faculties

It is important to recognize that St. Catherine did not want to imply that sensory experience ought to be ignored, or devalued. In fact, like Hadewijch, she frequently used new sense images with transcendental meaning in her dialogue.[189] In another set of examples that has implication for the feminine descriptions of the effects of God, she describes Christ as a "wet nurse" who drank a bitter medicine that would then pass through to the babies he nursed, thereby "healing" and "giving life" to the sick child.[190] Catherine also describes the Holy Spirit "as a mother who nurses her [the soul] at the breast of divine charity . . . clothes her, nurtures her, inebriates her with tenderness and the greatest wealth. Because she has left all she finds all."[191] The 'leaving all' of the soul represents the letting go of the attachments that are part of this first step.

This activity of "letting go," however, is very difficult, and demands a tremendous interior battle within the self. In this second step, the person knows

---

189. Carolyn Bynum traces the many different metaphors with reference to eating and drinking in *Holy Feast, Holy Fast*. See also Bynum, *Jesus as Mother*, pp. 166-81; and Sister Mary Jeremiah traces many bridal metaphors in "Catherinian Imagery of Consecration," *Communio* 17 (Fall 1990): 362-74.

190. Catherine, *Dialogue*, p. 52. The complete passage is as follows: "So the pus was drained out of Adam's sin, leaving only its scar. . . . Now Adam's sin oozed with a deadly pus, but you were too weakened to drain it yourself. But when the great doctor came (my only-begotten Son) he tended that wound, drinking himself the bitter medicine you would not swallow. And he did as the wet nurse who herself drinks the medicine the baby needs, because she is big and strong and the baby is too weak to stand the bitterness. My son was your wet nurse, and he joined the bigness and strength of his divinity with your nature to drink the bitter medicine of his painful death on the cross so that he might heal and give life to you who were babies weakened by sin."

191. Catherine, *Dialogue*, p. 292.

through reason what needs to be done; and yet he or she discovers that while virtue is attractive, the senses are also attractive. In other passages from the *Dialogue,* St. Catherine describes this second stage as initially involving a conflict:

> There are then two aspects to yourself: sensuality and reason. Sensuality is a servant, and it has been appointed to serve the soul, so that your body may be your instrument for proving and exercising virtue. The soul is free . . . and she cannot be dominated unless she consents to it with her will, which is bound up with free choice. Free choice is one with the will, and agrees with it. It is set between sensuality and reason and can turn to whichever one it will.[192]

Reason helps self-knowledge as well as knowledge of the hierarchy of values. When this occurs, the person must make choices through an exercise of the will. In the following passage, St. Catherine describes this struggle as a battle to crush the lower passions in the soul:

> After the soul has come to know herself she finds humility and hatred for her selfish passion, recognizing the perverse law that is bound up in her members and is always fighting against the spirit. So she rises up with hatred and contempt for that sensuality and crushes it firmly under the foot of reason.[193]

Eventually, however, when the person conquers the self, St. Catherine says that the faculties of the soul are "gathered together." An integration and a harmony has been effected that overcomes the tension of the battle between sensuality and reason as previously experienced.

> Then you will find that you have climbed the second stair. This is the enlightenment of the mind which sees itself reflected in the warmhearted love I have shown you in Christ crucified, as in a mirror. . . . After you have climbed you find that you are gathered together. For once reason has taken possession of the three stairs, which are the three powers of the soul, they are gathered together in my name. When the two — that is, love for me and love for your neighbour — are gathered together, and the memory for holding and the understanding for seeing and the will for loving are gathered together . . . you discover the company of the virtues.[194]

The person who reaches the third step at the entrance of the bridge, is shown in a constant state of self-governance in which the integrated practice of virtue has been achieved:

> So having climbed the second stair, she reaches the third. This is the mouth, where she finds peace from the terrible war she has had to wage because of her

192. Catherine, *Dialogue,* p. 105.
193. Catherine, *Dialogue,* p. 36.
194. Catherine, *Dialogue,* pp. 108-9.

sins. . . . So the bridge has three stairs, and you can reach the last by climbing the first two. The last stair is so high that the flooding waters cannot strike it.[195]

Sometimes St. Catherine suggests that there is a fourth stage added on to the first three. She calls this "the stage of perfection" or union with God. However, she is careful to add that love of neighbor and love of God are "never found without the other. . . . The one cannot be separated from the other . . . neither of these two stages can exist without the other."[196]

Catherine develops her vertical and transcendental analogy of the living bridge in greater detail. The stones in the walls of this covered bridge are identified as specific virtues, the mortar that holds the stones together is the blood of Christ, the roof that covers the bridge is the mercy of God, and the gate at the end of the bridge is truth.[197] For the most part this further elaboration moves into the theological realm of discourse and away from the philosophical. Yet there is one important aspect of her experience and analysis of God that has application to issues of gender identity at the same time that it goes beyond gender identity. This concerns St. Catherine's experience of the relation between God the Father who is Truth, and God the Son, who shows forth the Image of the Truth.

In the following passage, the Eternal Father as Truth speaks with Saint Catherine about how human beings come to know this Truth:

> By this light set in the mind's eye Thomas [Aquinas] saw me and there gained the light of great learning. Augustine, Jerome, and my other holy doctors, enlightened by my Truth, understood and knew my Truth in the midst of darkness. I am referring to Holy Scripture, which seemed darksome because it was not understood. This was no fault of Scripture, but of the listener, who failed to understand. So I sent these lamps to enlighten blind and dense understandings. They raised their mind's eye to know the truth in the midst of darkness, and I the fire, the one who accepted their sacrifice, carried them off and gave them light, not naturally but beyond all nature, and in the midst of darkness they received the light and so came to know the truth.
>
> So what had seemed darksome before now appears most perfectly lightsome to every sort of person — to the dense as to the discerning. All receive according to their capacity and according to their readiness to know me, for I do not spurn their dispositions. So you see, the eye of understanding has received a light beyond any natural light, infused by grace, and in this light the doctors and the other saints came to know the truth in the midst of darkness, and from the darkness light was made. For understanding existed before Scripture was formed; so learning came from understanding, for in seeing is discernment.
>
> In this way the holy fathers and prophets saw and discerned, and so foretold the coming and death of my Son. . . . In other words, they demonstrated the per-

195. Catherine, *Dialogue,* pp. 65-66.
196. Catherine, *Dialogue,* p. 137.
197. Catherine, *Dialogue,* p. 66.

fection of obedience that shines forth in my Truth, who, because of the obedience I laid upon him, ran to the shameful death of the cross.[198]

St. Catherine describes the Eternal Father speaking with her about how human beings come to know the Truth, through the understanding that raises the "mind's eye" using "natural light" and through the grace of faith that infuses the supernatural light of grace. Even though the dialogue uses metaphors of light, St. Catherine does not see the Eternal Father, she only hears Him. In addition, when the Eternal Father speaks to her about the Son, He also calls her his "beloved daughter" and teaches her about the next stage of transition towards union with Him. Catherine becomes the daughter of Truth-in-relation:

> I have told you this, my dearest daughter, to let you know the perfection of this unitive state in which souls are carried off by the fire of my charity. In that charity they receive supernatural light, and in that light they love me. For love follows upon understanding. The more they know, the more they love, and the more they love, the more they know. Thus each nourishes the other. By this light they reach that eternal vision of me in which they see and taste me in truth when soul is separated from body. (I told you all this when I described for you the happiness souls receive in me.)[199]

In this dynamic of dialogue with the Eternal Father, the human being moves among philosophical understanding, theological illumination, and affective love and "each nourishes the other."[200] Catherine is the daughter whose identity as a thinking, praying, loving woman is affirmed by this encounter with multifaceted Truth, originating in the Father and made visible in the Son. When the Eternal Father speaks with Saint Catherine, He speaks to her about Christ, and then He missions her to go forth to teach others:

> Now I, eternal Truth, have let you see with your mind's eye and hear with your feeling's ear how you must behave if you would serve yourself and your neighbors in the teaching and knowledge of my truth. For I told you in the beginning that one comes to knowledge of the truth through self-knowledge. But self-knowledge alone is not enough: It must be seasoned by and joined with knowledge of me within you. This is how you found humility and contempt for yourself along with the fire of my charity, and so came to love and affection for your neighbors and gave them the service of your teaching and your holy and honorable living. . . .[201]

---

198. Catherine, *Dialogue,* p. 155.

199. Catherine, *Dialogue,* p. 157.

200. For a contemporary description of this dynamic interaction of faith and reason see John Paul II, *Fides et Ratio (Faith and Reason)* (Boston: Daughters of Saint Paul, 1999).

201. Catherine, *Dialogue,* p. 158.

The theme of women's virtues will be considered as we turn to the example of St. Catherine's life and of her explosion of the limitation of the private and public spheres of activity to women and men respectively.[202]

Public Activity as a Woman's Virtue

Catherine believed that her public work of teaching was a mission entrusted to her, and that she should give to those who came to her for counsel a love of virtue that begins with self-knowledge.[203] The primary source for her practice of public teaching is the letters she dictated to her three male secretaries Neri di Landoccio dei Paglioresi, Stefano Maconi, and Bonduccio Canigioni.[204] In these letters Catherine confronts and coaxes her correspondents into a greater self-knowledge and sense of responsibility for virtuous action. In addition, through this medium of teaching, St. Catherine attempts to change the shape of world events, and in this way overcome the traditional limitation of woman to the private sphere of activity.

In her correspondence for example, Catherine exhorts Charles, King of France, to be "a lover of virtue, founded in true and holy justice," and then she carefully describes the three virtues that he specifically needs to practice. The first virtue is to detach himself from his possessions and position of prestige in the world. She argues that undue attachment is a form of self-deception. This follows the first step of her bridge analogy of purification of the memory. The second virtue is to attach himself to a true form of justice that cannot be "ruined for self-love or for flatteries, or for any pleasing of men."[205] This also follows the second step of enlightenment by reason. The third virtue must be practiced in the context of a war between Charles and his brother that, Catherine argues, is destroying the lives of innocent people and impeding the progress of the crusades. She asks him to practice the virtue of "love and affection with your neighbour, with whom you have for so long a time been at war."[206] This follows the third step of exercise of the will in virtuous action. St. Catherine writes persuasively, using both philosophical and theological arguments to defend her position and to convert her correspondent to a different point of view.

St. Catherine wrote to many leaders of governments. In a letter to the leaders of

---

202. Karen Scott notes the difficulty with much contemporary research about Catherine, which tends to view her primarily either as a mystic or as a political activist. Scott points out that it is important to consider Catherine's self-understanding as a missionary apostle. She states that Catherine " . . . portrayed herself as an itinerant preacher and peacemaker, as a female apostle or *apostola,* and that this role enabled her to integrate the political and contemplative dimensions of her life" ("St. Catherine," p. 37).

203. Catherine, *Dialogue,* pp. 197-98. See also p. 37.

204. *St. Catherine of Siena as Seen in Her Letters* (New York: E. P. Dutton and Co., 1911), pp. 293, 299.

205. St. Catherine, *Letters,* pp. 168-69.

206. St. Catherine, *Letters,* pp. 169-70.

the city of Bologna she sets forth the specific characteristics of a just leader because she finds that "men of the world serve and love their neighbour without virtue":

> What causes such injustice? Self-love. But the wretched men of the world, because they are deprived of truth, do not recognize truth, either as regards their salvation or as regards the true preservation of their lordship. For did they know the truth, they would see that only living in the fear of God preserves their state and the city in peace: they would preserve holy justice, rendering his due to every subject, they would show mercy on who so deserved mercy, not by passionate impulse, but by regard for truth; and justice they would show on who so deserved it, built upon mercy, and not on passionate wrath. Nor would they judge by hearsay, but by holy and true justice; and they would heed the common good, and not any private good, and would appoint officials and those who are to rule the city, not by part of prejudice, not for flatteries or bribery, but with virtue and reason alone.[207]

Note here that Catherine is engaging directly in intergender dialogue with secular leaders. In this dialogue, Catherine identifies key points of argument: the virtue of justice depends on a knowledge of truth that is aimed towards the common good. The motive of the act needs to flow from a well-ordered decision and not from impulse. The criteria of judgment need to be well thought out, and the philosophical practice of virtue needs to be placed in a theological framework of respect for God.

Two of the most famous recipients of St. Catherine's letters were the Popes Gregory XI and Urban VI. The two public themes she identified in her letters were the need to move the Papacy from France to Rome, and the need to adhere to the line of papal succession followed during the first election. In addition to these public themes, Catherine also exhorted the Popes to lead more virtuous lives. In the following letter, she shows her skill at counterargument when debating someone who was trying to persuade Pope Gregory XI to remain at Avignon. Arguing that the letter comes from a wicked and not a just man, she exclaims: "you must investigate" because the letter appears to be a forgery. "Nor does he who wrote it understand his trade very well. He ought to put himself to school — he seems to have known less than a small child."[208] Proceeding to analyze the letter section by section, Catherine demonstrates that the arguments presented in it appeal to a lower part of the self, or fear of bodily harm, rather than to a concern for the common good.

> Notice how, most Holy Father, he has made his first appeal to the tendency that he knows to be the chief frailty in man, and especially in those who are very tender and pitiful in their natural affections, and tender to their own bodies — for such men as these hold life dearer than any others. So he fastened on this point from his first word. But I hope, by the goodness of God, that you will pay more

207. St. Catherine, *Letters,* pp. 207-8.
208. St. Catherine, *Letters,* pp. 181-82.

heed to His honour and the safety of your own flock than you yourself, like a good shepherd, who is ready to lay down his life for his sheep.[209]

In the following sequence, St. Catherine makes a play on the word 'poison' to win her argument. The antagonist has suggested that if the Pope returns to Rome he will be poisoned. So in the first phase of her argument, St. Catherine demonstrates that if it is murder that he fears, it can occur in France as well as Italy:

> Next, this poisonous man seems on the one hand to commend your return to Rome, calling it a good and holy thing; but on the other hand, he says that poison is prepared for you there; and he seems to advise you to send trustworthy men to precede you, who will find the poison on the tables — that is, apparently, in bottles to be administered by degrees, either by the day, or the month, or the year. Now I quite agree with him that poison can be found — for that matter, as well on the tables of Avignon or other cities as on those of Rome; and prepared for administration slowly, by the month, or the year, or in large quantities, as may please the purchaser: it can be found everywhere.[210]

Her argument simply shows the absurdity of avoiding Rome for a reason that could apply to Avignon as well.

Finally, by the use of a horizontal analogy, she argues that the true 'poison' is the argument that is being proposed by her antagonist to stay in Avignon. Then she offers her antidote:

> So he would think it well for you to send, and delay your return for this purpose; he proposes that you wait until divine judgment fall by this means on those wicked men who, it would seem, according to what he says, are seeking your death. But were he wise, he would expect that judgment to fall on himself, for he is sowing the worst poison that has been sown for a long time in Holy Church, inasmuch as he wants to hinder you from following God's call and doing your duty. Do you know how that poison would be sown? If you did not go, but sent, as the good man advises you, scandal and rebellion, spiritual and temporal, would be stirred up — men finding a lie in you, who hold the Seat of Truth. For since you have decided on your return and announced it, the scandal and bewilderment and disturbance in men's hearts would be too great if they found that it did not happen.[211]

The rather extensive passages from this letter serve to demonstrate that St. Catherine used her powers of discursive reasoning very effectively to influence world events. She engaged regularly and effectively in intergender dialogue through writing. In addition, when she went to see Pope Gregory XI in person, to dialogue face to face, her arguments proved persuasive. On January 17, 1377 the

209. St. Catherine, *Letters,* p. 182.
210. St. Catherine, *Letters,* p. 183.
211. St. Catherine, *Letters,* p. 183.

Pope moved back to Rome, and on the way he even disguised himself as a simple priest to secretly speak with Catherine of Siena again. By December of that year St. Catherine had been appointed Ambassador of the Pope to Florence to intervene in a serious conflict.

Pope Gregory XI died in March of 1388, and the new Pope Urban VI was as severe a leader as his predecessor had been weak. Initiating a dialogue with the new leader of the Church, St. Catherine's letters were full of appeals for mercy and prudence in his judgments. She also traveled to Rome personally to plead before the College of Cardinals in favor of the legitimate succession of Urban VI in the face of counterclaims by Clement VI. As always, she used her powers of discursive reasoning to affect the direction of public events. However, Catherine died at age thirty-three, thirty-seven years before this schism was overcome in favor of Urban VI in the Council of Constance in 1417.

In addition to teaching others about the importance of virtue through speaking and writing, Catherine also acted publicly in ways that demonstrated her own virtue. She constantly risked the danger of death from exposure to disease, political conflicts, and wars. She often personally cared for the seriously ill. One time when some soldiers in Florence broke into a place where she was staying in order to kill her, Catherine came forward immediately to meet her woould-be slayers and said: "I am she. Take me, and let this family be."[212] The soldiers were so taken aback by the strength of her response that they left without harming her.

Another example of Catherine's public demonstration of virtue can be found in her confrontation of political authority in Siena when it unjustly condemned a young man to death. First, she marched up to the executioner's block on the day of the planned execution, and she placed her own head on the block. When this was not enough to deter the execution, she spoke to the young man and tried to comfort him. Finally, she offered to hold his head and stretch his neck during the execution itself, and was covered with blood in its aftermath.[213] In these actions we can see Catherine placing no value on her own fears or concern for her own safety. Instead, she was concerned with the good of the other persons who were with her, and with justice and the protection of the innocent. She interacted courageously with the authorities, both in word and in act.

Gender-Related Virtues

Before concluding this section on some of the philosophical contributions of St. Catherine of Siena to the developing concept of woman, there is one final aspect of her thought that needs to be considered. In her writing Catherine displays an awareness of the difference between what can be called "masculine" and "feminine" characteristics. In this Catherine participates in an emerging common consciousness in the fourteenth century that recognized that there is more to men and

212. St. Catherine, *Letters,* p. 258.
213. Catherine of Siena, Letter to Raymond of Capua, in *Medieval Women's Visionary Literature,* pp. 273-75 and 240.

women than simply male and female, biologically based identities. It became clear to some persons at this time that a man could have certain characteristics that can be identified as masculine and others that can be identified as feminine, and an analogous situation existed for a woman. By separating gender-identified characteristics as masculine and feminine, a psychic depth of the individual man or woman was beginning to be probed. In other words, an awareness that gender identity includes more than the single dimensions of male or female identity was expanding to include a nexus of male-masculine-feminine identity for a man, and a nexus of female-feminine-masculine for a woman.

In addition, certain prescriptive values related to the masculine and the feminine were also present in the thinking of this time. Given the patriarchal structure of society, it is not surprising that a more positive interpretation was given to what was masculine than to what was considered feminine. In addition, in the Latin root for man, 'vir' and virtue merged together, and so the Italian word 'virilmente,' which means literally "manfully," became identified as a virtuous trait of character similar to courage.

In one letter to Sister Bartolomea della Seta, St. Catherine urges her: ". . . do not give up, nor fall for this into confusion, but reply **manfully**: 'I would rather exert myself . . . feeling pain, gloom, and inward conflicts, than not exert myself and feel repose.' And reflect, that this is the state of the perfect."[214] So in this example, Catherine uses 'masculine' as a positive virtue for a woman, one that includes courage, perseverance, capacity to sustain conflict, and so forth. In a letter to an English mercenary named Sir John Hawkwood, who had been making a living by killing Christians, St. Catherine challenges him to join a crusade and be a soldier **for** Christians instead of killing them. In the midst of her argument we find Catherine using a similar positive meaning for masculine as follows: "It seems to me that you ought now, at this present time, to dispose you to virtue, until the time shall come for us and the others who shall be ready to give their lives for Christ; and thus you shall show that you are a **manly** and true knight."[215]

Finally, in a letter to her own spiritual director Raymond of Capua, we find Catherine using a feminine characteristic in a negative way to challenge her director to overcome fear of being attacked or murdered while carrying out a Papal mission:

> I beg you to do so that you give me no matter for mourning, nor for shaming me in the sight of God. As you are a man in promising the will to do and bear for the honour of God, do not then **turn into a woman** when we come to the shutting of the lock. . . . Be then, **be all a man** that death may be granted you.[216]

In this way, cowardliness, the 'feminine' vice, and courage, the 'masculine' virtue, can be found in both men and women. Their existence is not sexually limited, although their identification as masculine or feminine partakes of sexual stereotyping. The hierarchy appears as follows:

214. St. Catherine, *Letters,* p. 160.
215. St. Catherine, *Letters,* pp. 102-3.
216. St. Catherine, *Letters,* p. 331. My emphasis.

Catherine of Siena's Distinction of Masculine and Feminine Activities			
	Feminine		Masculine
Virtues:	Nursing Feeding Clothing Distributing wealth Tenderness Healing Giving life	Virtues:	Exertion Enduring pain Enduring suffering Courage Perseverance
Vices:	Cowardliness Fear of harm		Not directly mentioned

From the summary of the passages considered in this chapter it can be seen that St. Catherine employed a variety of different concepts of masculine and feminine, and that the former had only a positive connotation while the latter had both a positive and negative connotation. In the twenty-first century, when certain residual aspects of patriarchy are being questioned, negative connotations of the masculine such as "macho" have become more common. In any event, it is important to point out that in the fourteenth century writers were beginning to recognize that the psychic characteristics of masculine and feminine had certain culturally delineated features that could apply to either men or women, and that they also contained a hierarchy of values.

In conclusion, this brief examination of the writings of St. Catherine of Siena has demonstrated that within her broader spiritual orientation she exercised a philosophical approach to human identity that included frequent reflections on the interaction of memory, understanding, and will. In addition, she gave a very prominent role to the exercise of reason in the search for self-knowledge and for virtue. Catherine elaborated a complex extended analogy of a living bridge that included many vertical and transcendental analogates linked together through the exercise of discursive reasoning. Finally, in her writings and in her own life, St. Catherine serves as an example of a woman who broke open the rigid separation of the public and private spheres of activity along gender lines. For these reasons, she is an important part of the series of women writers who directly challenged the Aristotelian concept of woman by serving as a living counterexample to the premises it contained.

Bl. Julian of Norwich (1342–c. 1420)

In turning to the final religious woman to be analyzed in this chapter, we reach an author of extraordinary literary talent, a woman who left us two complete texts, each of which has an internal cohesion. The *Showings* (or *Revelations*) of Julian of Norwich consist of two versions, a short one of twenty-five chapters written in the

1370s and a longer one of eighty-six chapters begun some twenty years later and completed in 1393. A unique feature of Julian's thought is found in the particular chronology of her writing. In May 1373 she received a series of visions that she wrote down in a simple descriptive manner. Then for the next fifteen to twenty years she reflected back on the content of these particular visions using both her reason and her faith to come to further insight into their meaning. Finally, Julian rewrote a second description of her visions in which she incorporated a wide range of reflective material. The fact that both the early and the later versions of her works are intact allows scholars to carefully assess the growth and development of Julian's own self-understanding over this twenty-year period.

The particular approach taken in this chapter does not emphasize the chronological development of Julian's thought, although it does have a part to play especially in her analogical thinking. Instead, I have selected three philosophical themes in her writings and consider their relation to the history of the concept of woman: first, her own reasoning process; second, her metaphysics of soul and body, substance and sensuality; and third, her transcendental analogy of Jesus as mother. In the first theme, Julian continued the strong tradition of other women religious writers by her use of discursive reasoning to discuss wisdom and virtue, and she introduced even more complex methodology than had her predecessors. In the second theme, she integrated philosophical concepts into an analysis of her own experience and understanding of the respective identities of the human being and of God.[217] In the third theme, she offered an elaborate comparison of the activity of God in the world with the activity of mothering; and in this analogy she revealed a great love for mothering as an important human activity.

The texts authored by Julian reveal a significant augmentation in the philosophical quality of thought far beyond previous texts written by women religious authors. Evelyn Underhill calls Julian the "most philosophic of our early mystics."[218] Grace Jantzen, a lecturer in philosophy of religion at King's College, London, has published a book on Julian's thought emphasizing her views on human personhood.[219] In addition, numerous scholars have written about various aspects of her thought; thus, Julian herself has become the foundation person of an ongoing community of discourse. This widespread interest in Julian of Norwich is likely due to many different factors: the beauty of her writing, the depth of her spiritual experience, the truth about reality that she seeks to convey, the intellectual rigor with which she questions her experience, the unity of her texts, and the innovative theological emphases that she introduces. In the latter category, theologians often mention Julian's emphasis on the tender mercy of God in judging a person's fall into evil actions and the final overcoming of all evil by good. This emphasis is

217. My analysis runs counter, with respect to Julian's emphasis on the importance of reason, to that of Maria R. Lichtmann. We agree, however, on the central importance of Julian's integrated approach to the body and experience. See "'God fulfylled my bodye': Body, Self, and God in Julian of Norwich," in *Gender and Text in the Latter Middle Ages,* ed. Jane Chance (Gainesville, Fla.: University of Florida Press, 1996), pp. 263-78.

218. Evelyn Underhill, *The Mystics of the Church* (New York: Schocken Books, 1964), p. 128.

219. Grace M. Jantzen, *Julian of Norwich: Mystic and Theologian* (New York/Mahwah, N.J.: Paulist Press, 1988).

captured in Julian's famous expression: "All will be well."[220] Although my analysis will not focus on Julian's theology *per se,* it will include selections from various scholars' reflections on her significance as a thinker and author.

Before analyzing the themes identified above, mention needs to be made of the intergender dialogue that appeared to play a part in Julian's formation as a thinker. Considerable attention has been given to the sources that may have influenced Julian. Edmund Colledge, O.S.A. and James Walsh, S.J. mention Boethius, whose *Consolation of Philosophy* was being translated into English by Chaucer in 1380, about the same time Julian was writing.[221] Sister Eileen Mary, S.L.G. listed the philosophical influences of "Plotinus, Dionysius the Areopagite, the Victorines, Ruusbroec and . . . Anselm."[222] Grace Jantzen focuses primarily on Augustine.[223] This connection is reinforced by scholars who note that Julian may have had interacted with Augustinians who lived in a friary on the same street as Julian in Norwich.[224] Next, Elizabeth N. Evasdaughter adds reference to the influence of St. Thomas, Duns Scotus, and William of Ockham.[225]

It is very difficult to come to a clear judgment about who actually influenced Julian, as she did not indicate her own sources. Yet she does in the Long Text directly refer to "as scholars tell" in a technical discussion about angels.[226] This suggests that she had some acquaintance with academic material written by scholars. In addition, the language and conceptual structure of her thought are very sophisticated, and this sophistication is illustrated, for example, by the appropriate use of such philosophical terms as 'substance' and 'sensuality,' as well as by a syllogistic argument structure. Therefore, it is easy to conclude that Julian knew something of the field of philosophy and that she was a listening or reading participant in intergender dialogue. Julian had an inquisitive mind. She paid attention to her own experience, she questioned it, and sought objective insights about the nature of reality through it. In the following description of Julian's method by Nancy Coiner, the dynamic energy of her thinking is captured:

---

220. Her summary of the six words "I will make all things well" by the four words "all will be well" serves almost as a mantra of prayer throughout her revelations. See, for example, Julian of Norwich, *Showings* (New York: Paulist Press, 1978), *Short Text* (ST), ch. 15, 152; ch. 16, 153; and *Long Text* (LT), ch. 27, 225; ch. 31, 229; ch. 32, 231, 233; ch. 34, 236; ch. 35, 237; and ch. 63, 305.

221. Colledge and Walsh, Introduction, *Showings,* p. 20. The interrogative style as well as the model of Lady Philosophy in Boethius's work may very well have inspired Julian in her own development of skills as a philosopher.

222. Sister Eileen Mary, S.L.G., "The Place of Lady Julian of Norwich in English Literature," in *Julian of Norwich: Four Studies to Commemorate the Sixth Centenary of the Revelations of Divine Love* (Fairacres, Oxford: SLG Press, 1976), p. 8. See also Sister Benedicta, S.L.G., "Faith Seeking Understanding," in same text, p. 28. Jantzen considers Julian's intellectual roots throughout her text. Anselm is identified most with Julian's development of the feminine aspects of Christ.

223. Jantzen, *Julian,* pp. 111-18. She focuses mostly on the influence of Augustine's delineation of the characteristics of the Trinity.

224. Jay Ruud, "Nature and Grace in Julian of Norwich," *Mystics Quarterly* 19, no. 2 (1993): 74.

225. Elizabeth N. Evasdaughter, "Julian of Norwich," in *A History of Women Philosophers,* vol. 2, ed. Mary Ellen Waithe, pp. 194-99. She considers primarily the similarities in epistemological theories and suggests influence through these similarities.

226. Julian, *Showings,* LT, ch. 80, 336.

Throughout the *Showings,* Julian responds to her visions as complex and unsettling, odd and obscure. And far from attempting to resolve or explain away the haunting strangeness of her visions, Julian returns to them again and again as a spur to ever deeper levels of exegesis. She immerses herself in their uncanny effects as a way of generating insight — and thereby of generating a text, and of generating herself as an author.[227]

A male religious author who is thought to have had a very deep influence on her style and content of text was William of St. Thierry (c. 1085–c. 1148). He interpreted the *Song of Songs* as a real drama consisting of dialogue between God and an eagerly seeking human soul.[228] Adopting this same view, Julian's dialogue operates on many different levels: she begins with a dialogue between herself and her reader, then moves to describe an ongoing series of dialogues between herself and Jesus, whom she calls "true God and true man."[229] In that context, she describes dialogues among different personages in her visions (e.g., a lord and a servant). Brad Peters compares Julian's dialogues with those of other women religious authors and concludes as follows: ". . . Julian has used dialogue instead to get at the most difficult elements of Christ's teachings — elements that could not be cognitively reached by other means. . . ."[230]

The quality and originality of Julian's writing, especially in the Longer Text, appear to imply that she had received some higher education during the twenty years that intervened between the original visions and her later interpretations. Jantzen points out that even though Julian referred to herself as "unlettered" at the time of the first version of her text, by the time she wrote the second version some twenty years later, she no longer described herself in this way. She concludes that Julian, while she lived as an Anchoress, "had at least received instruction, that she could probably read and write in the vernacular, and perhaps could read some Latin."[231] As one of the earliest extant texts written in the English language, the *Showings* reveal an extremely penetrating intellect and a well-developed gift of writing. Colledge and Walsh praise her skill as a writer of the English language: "Julian became such a master of rhetorical art as to merit comparison with Geoffrey Chaucer."[232] It is unlikely that she would have achieved this high level of skill without being well educated. Since it would not have been possible for her to receive

227. Nancy Coiner, "The *'homely'* and the *heimliche*: The Hidden, Doubled Self in Julian of Norwich's *Showings,*" *Exemplaria* 5, no. 2 (Fall 1993): 306.

228. Elisabeth K. J. Koenig, "Julian of Norwich, Mary Magdalene, and the Drama of Prayer," *Horizons* 20, no. 1 (1993): 23-43.

229. Julian, *Showings,* ST, ch. 22, 163-64.

230. Brad Peters, "Julian of Norwich and the Internalized Dialogue of Prayer," *Mystics Quarterly* 20, no. 4 (December 1994): 128. Peters analyzes Julian's use of *conversatio, quaestio, interpretatio,* and *communio.* He introduces his article by saying: "This study will investigate how dialogue is in fact instrumental to the evolution of her stunning theology of a non-judgmental, wrathless, maternal God" (122).

231. Jantzen, *Julian,* p. 17.

232. In their introduction to Julian of Norwich's *Showings,* 19. Colledge and Walsh's opinion is contested by Jantzen, who states: "There is no doubt that she is a consummate stylist; the question is whether she was deliberately using rhetorical figures and devices" (p. 26, note 19).

this education in the academic setting of a university in England, then she must have received it privately through the good services of someone (likely a man) who had himself received a university education.

In addition to the question of the influence on Julian of scholarly male writers, it is also interesting to consider the possible influence of female writers on her thought. Jean Leclercq suggests that Julian may have been aware of Mechtild of Hackeborn's views of the feminine dimension of the Divine.[233] Edmund Gardner suggests that she may have been acquainted with the description of Christ found in the letters of St. Catherine of Siena.[234] Some scholars have also suggested that Julian was related to the Benedictines and even perhaps that she was a Benedictine nun.[235] However, this latter claim is now disputed, and it is generally thought that Julian had some looser relationship with the Benedictine nuns of Carrow Abbey.[236] Ritamary Bradley notes that Julian personally identified with St. Mary Magdalene and with the early Christian martyr, St. Cecilia.[237]

In her writing, Julian was consciously aware of herself as a woman who represented the generic human being. For example, in the Short Text of *Showings* Julian states: "For this vision was shown for all men, and not for me alone."[238] The literal way she expressed this was to say that the vision was "shown in general, and not at all specially." In the Long Text she explicitly states a reflective understanding of herself as generic subject when she states that "by me is understood everyone."[239] In these articulations Julian draws a horizontal analogy between herself and other men and women. At times she explicitly refers to both women and men as the audience of her revelations, while at other times she simply states that when a spiritual principle was revealed to her as a single woman, it was meant to be applied to all human beings who were striving after a life of perfection, wisdom, and virtue.

In the Short Text, where Julian is self-conscious about her identity as a woman, she states explicitly that the application of her insights is not limited by her sex identity.

> But because I am a woman, ought I therefore to believe that I should not tell you of the goodness of God, when I saw at that same time that it is his will that it be

233. Jean Leclercq, O.S.B. Preface to Julian of Norwich, *Showings*, p. 9.

234. Edmund Gardner, "Juliana of Norwich," in *The Catholic Encyclopedia* (1967).

235. Paul Molinari, *Julian of Norwich* (Toronto: Longmans Green, 1958), pp. 8-10: T. W. Coleman, "The Lady Julian," in *English Mystics of the Fourteenth Century* (London: John Murray, 1906), p. 133; and William Inge, "Julian of Norwich," in the same text, p. 50.

236. Jantzen, *Julian,* pp. 17-18.

237. Ritamary Bradley, *Julian's Way: A Practical Commentary on Julian of Norwich* (London: HarperCollins, 1992), pp. 16-18. Although it would appear that what most impressed Julian was hearing a story about St. Cecilia's martyr's death by three wounds in the neck, Bradley also suggests a connection with philosophy: "Cecilia, who bravely taught her oppressors with the reasoning of a philosopher, was put to death for confronting the Roman prefect" (p. 17). For Julian's references to these two women saints who preceded her, see Julian, *Showings,* ch. 1, 125-27, and LT, chap. 38, 242.

238. Julian of Norwich, *Showings,* Short Text (ST), chap. 7, 136. Indeed she begins the preceding chapter with the words: "Everything that I say about myself I mean to apply to all my fellow Christians, for I am taught that this is what our Lord intends in this spiritual revelation," ch. 6, 133.

239. Julian, *Showings,* LT, ch. 37, 241.

known? You will see this clearly in what follows, if it be well and truly accepted. Then will you soon forget me who am a wretch.[240]

It might be argued that this text supports a unisex tendency to ignore the sex of the author altogether. However, as will be seen in our analysis of Julian's thought, sensuality, which includes the material and psychological components of a human individual, is extremely important to her. Julian is not at all a Platonic thinker for whom the body, with its sexual differentiation, is devalued. Consequently, she views herself as a **woman** who, in a horizontal analogy, represents all of humanity and not as some androgynous being. Thus, for Julian, "she" stands for "everyone." This follows the practice of other women religious authors and also contrasts with the academic tradition in which "he" stands for everyone.[241] In religious women's communities of discourse, a woman is often the paradigm for the human being seeking perfection of wisdom and virtue.

The Use of Reason

Interest in what is loosely called Julian's theory of knowledge has been growing in recent years. For example, Elizabeth N. Evasdaughter wrote a chapter on Julian's epistemology in *A History of Women Philosophers: Volume II/Medieval, Renaissance and Enlightenment Women Philosophers A.D. 500-1600*. She emphasizes Julian's use of dialogue, argument from contradiction, and her sources of religious knowledge.[242] Julian identified the three ways of knowing as occurring through "bodily vision, and by words formed in my understanding and by spiritual vision."[243] The first two ways can be considered as philosophical and the third as theological. The bodily vision is the beginning of knowledge through the exterior or interior senses. Julian's understanding then subjects her experiences to analysis, until the mind and spirit grasp their meaning through insight. In the following description of her reflection on the meaning of a thing the size of a hazelnut lying in her hand, Julian describes all three ways of knowing within the same passage:

> He showed me something small, no bigger than a hazelnut, lying in the palm of my hand, as it seemed to me, and it was as round as a ball. I looked at it with the eye of my understanding and thought: What can this be? I was amazed that it could last, for I thought that because of its littleness it would suddenly fall into

240. Julian, *Showings*, ST, 135.

241. Renée New Watkins, in "Two Women Visionaries and Death: Catherine of Siena and Julian of Norwich" (*Numen: International Review for the History of Religions* 30, facs. 2), argues that Julian rejects her own femininity as "her way of dealing with the idea of woman's inferiority." She concludes, "Julian . . . did not want her readers to think of her as a woman speaking" (188). I would argue against this view by claiming that Julian appears to be glad that she, as a woman, could express the thoughts she did, even though others might be startled by her sex.

242. Evasdaughter, "Julian of Norwich," in *A History of Women Philosophers*, vol. 2, pp. 191-221.

243. Julian, *Showings*, LT, 322. See also ST, 135.

nothing. And I was answered in my understanding: It lasts and always will, because God loves it; and thus everything has being through the love of God.[244]

First, Julian pays attention to the data of her sense experience of sight; second, she questions this experience; and third, she gains insight into a meaning of the experience.

Julian frequently questions her experience and makes distinctions in her effort to understand its meaning. In the following example, she again shows her ability to come to insight by making distinctions: "I thought: Is there any pain in hell like this? And in my reason I was answered that despair is greater, for that is a spiritual pain."[245] Julian's insight distinguishes physical pain in the illness that she was experiencing at that time from spiritual pain or despair. Jantzen refers to some difficult consequences of Julian's tendency to question all aspects of her experience:

> Openness to experience is also, however, openness to its darker sides: depression, fear, self-rejection. From the way Julian writes about these, it is clear that she had to come to terms with them in her own life. She does not ignore them; instead, she offers insight about how these can be progressively transformed to become part of a creatively integrated personality.[246]

Her capacity to pursue reflective discourse through a kind of interior dialogue about the meaning of her experience led Julian to press through difficulties to ultimate resolution and integration. She seeks to express with new categories the successive integration that occurs at all levels of her human personality.

In addition to personal integration, Julian also demonstrated an interest in achieving an integration of conflicting positions in religious knowledge. Evasdaughter states: "The epistemological question she brings up in relation to this problem is, how can we resolve contradictions between propositions we derive from various sources of religious knowledge?"[247] Julian would list certain views that appeared to contradict one another, and then pose a question about how they can be reconciled. Once again she would follow the stages of: (1) attention to experience (in this case of an apparent contradiction), then (2) questioning the foundation of the experience, while (3) searching for an objective insight. Jantzen admires Julian's tenacity in this process: "In a situation of apparently irreconcilable teachings, she holds to both sides of the tension until by patient diligence she wins through to integration."[248]

An example from her writings may help to demonstrate this point. In the following passage from the Long Text of *Showings,* Julian reflects on the interaction of three different ways of knowing (one philosophical and two theological) that might appear to be in conflict at certain times, but ultimately may be integrated:

244. Julian, *Showings,* LT, 183. See also ST, 130.
245. Julian, *Showings,* ST, 142.
246. Jantzen, *Julian,* p. 105.
247. Evasdaughter, "Julian," in *A History of Women Philosophers,* vol. 2, p. 198.
248. Jantzen, *Julian,* p. 103.

Man endures in this life by three things . . . the first is the use of man's natural reason. The second is the common teaching of Holy Church. The third is the inward grace-giving operation of the Holy Spirit; and these three are all from one God. . . . For they work continually in us, all together, and those are great things; and of this greatness he wants us to have knowledge here, as it were in an ABC.[249]

For Julian, human reason is not ultimately in conflict with propositions of faith, either as stated in Church teachings or expressed in interior experience, because they have the same source. She is very specific about the value of human reason when she states: "Our reason is founded in God, who is nature's substance."[250] To exercise human reason is actually to participate in the life of God. This view of the ultimate compatibility of reason and faith is consistent with that of St. Thomas, and it may have formed the background in which Julian developed her own thinking.

While Julian affirmed the extraordinary possibilities of reason, she also recognized its limits. This limit was often expressed by her as an inability to exercise her discursive reasoning in counting. In one passage, she considers the number of reenactments of Jesus' death: "[a]nd truly the number so far exceeded my understanding and intelligence that my reason had not leave of power to comprehend or accept it."[251] In another example, she considers counting the words heard in a locution: "[t]he number of the words surpasses my intelligence and my understanding and all my powers."[252]

Julian also reflected on the content of her religious experiences and made distinctions about the different kinds of objects she perceived: "One part was shown spiritually, in a bodily likeness. The other part was shown more spiritually, without bodily likeness."[253] This method of distinguishing objects of knowledge depending upon their degree of spirituality or materiality fits into Julian's broader analysis of the three fundamental objects of knowledge: God, the self, and the relation between God and the self:

> We ought to have three kinds of knowledge. The first is that we know our Lord God. The second is that we know ourselves, what we are through him in nature and in grace. The third is that we know humbly that our self is opposed to our sin and to our weakness. And all this revelation was made, as I understand it, for these three.[254]

The three objects of knowledge are not simply divided into spiritual objects and material objects, for all three objects contain both aspects. God, through the human nature of Jesus Christ, takes on materiality; and the self, through the soul, has spirituality.

249. Julian, *Showings,* LT, 335.
250. Julian, *Showings,* LT, 290.
251. Julian, *Showings,* LT, 217.
252. Julian, *Showings,* LT, 224.
253. Julian, *Showings,* LT, 267.
254. Julian, *Showings,* LT, 321. See also LT, 258.

By the dialectical dynamics of thought Julian moves back and forth between sense observation, reasoning, and effects of the infusion of faith. There is a *doubling* movement back and forth between an external bodily sight and an interior spiritual sight that occurs in her vision of the unfolding parable. Andrew Sprung has given an excellent description of this dynamic quality of Julian's method of reflection in his discussion of her parable of the Lord and servant:

> Yet the constant stress on *doubling* complicates this apparent progress from lower mode to higher. First, Julian does not leave one mode of sight for another; she oscillates between the two "keeping both in mind." A close look at the "more inward" showing, moreover, indicates that it takes place *within* the first showing. . . . Finally, further complicating and hypostatizing the doubleness is the fact that the Lord adopts the human perspective, even as Julian adopts the divine. . . .
>
> To recapitulate: both perspectives are real, and both are shared by both parties. The "higher" perspective is also "inner," and dwells within the outer, or lower perspective.[255]

This movement in Julian thus encompasses a doubling movement in the Lord's view of the servant and in the servant's view of the Lord. The doubling movement is not a simple sequence in which one kind of sight is replaced by another, but, through the active exercise of memory, it is held simultaneously in the reflective intelligence. In the following passage, Julian describes her complex way of knowing:

> And all this time his loving lord looks on him most tenderly, and now with a double aspect, one outward, very meekly and mildly, with great compassion and pity, and this belonged to the first part; the other was inward, more spiritual, and this was shown with a direction of my understanding towards the lord, and I was brought again to see how greatly he rejoiced over the honourable rest and nobility which by his plentiful grace he wishes for his servant and will bring him to. And this belonged to the second vision. And now my understanding was led back to the first, keeping both in mind.[256]

In conclusion, Julian's epistemology keeps a distinction between God and the human being while allowing for a union of love. One of the reasons she does this is due to her ontology of the human person. She resists any temptation towards the annihilation of identity that was seen in the writings of several other religious authors. Once again Andrew Sprung describes the profound way that Julian protects the integrity of God and of the human person:

> Distance between God and man in the one view necessitates a meltdown, a transcendence that entails the dissolution of the transcendee, a kind of Hegelian absorption of the antithesis into the thesis. Julian's knitting, in contrast, implies an

255. Andrew Sprung, "'We never shall come out of him': Enclosure and Immanence in Julian of Norwich's *Book of Showings*," *Mystics Quarterly* 19, no. 2 (1989): 58.

256. Julian, *Showings,* LT, 268.

immanence that allows distinct coexistence within union, a thorough weaving-in and clothing-round but not, as it were, a *chemical* change in the substance of the human soul.[257]

Julian introduces a theory of the relation of soul and body that draws upon a Thomistic understanding of the human person as an integral unity. This metaphysics, in turn, is derived from Aristotelian metaphysics of the unity of form and matter in a concrete entity. Thus, Julian, in following this Aristotelian metaphysical line of thinking about the human being, rejects the Neoplatonic view that led other authors towards a theory of the annihilation of the self. It is to this theory of substance and sensuality in a human person that this analysis will now turn.

A Metaphysics of Substance and Sensuality

Julian's use of the traditional philosophical terms 'substance' and 'sensuality' both borrows from and adds to common scholastic understanding of the terms. Because of the free and unusual way she uses these terms, it is sometimes difficult to grasp her exact meaning. This is an excellent example of where the old categories do not quite fit, and yet they are useful to explain the experience. So the author experiments with them, introducing them in a number of different ways, in order to articulate the deep realities she is attempting to share.

In Aristotelian philosophy, a substance is that of which other things are predicated but which is not predicated of anything else. In this approach, a particular human being, a man or a woman is a substance in the primary sense. Thus a human being as a soul/body unity would be a substance in this traditional sense. Julian's use of the term 'substance' differs somewhat from Aristotle's, as she uses it to refer more to the highest part of the soul. For Julian, substance and sensuality are two different aspects of the human soul. She summarizes it this way: ". . . we are double by God's creating, that is to say substantial and sensual. Our substance is the higher part. . . ."[258]

For Julian the substance of the soul is the higher part that is always oriented towards God; while the sensuality is the lower part of the soul that is oriented towards the world. The sensuality of the soul is focused on the materiality of the human being: sensation, imagination, memory, passions, and so forth. The soul is the act of the body, it gives it life, it directs its functions of growth, reproduction, consciousness, and the interior and exterior senses. The substance is the most interior core of the human person, created by God, and directed towards life in God, or what was traditionally referred to as the deepest part of the person, the personalized immortal soul.

Grace Jantzen, in her analysis of "Human Personhood" in Julian of Norwich, describes the way the author delineates a real or authentic self as combining substantial and sensual identity:

257. Sprung, "'We never shall come out of him,'" p. 52.
258. Julian, *Showings,* LT, ch. 58, 294.

A consequence of the fact that sensuality requires both consciousness and the physical organism is that our bodies are not accidental to us, as though our real self is a soul which has somehow been attached to a physical body from which we will escape at death. Our real self, according to Julian, is precisely the combination of consciousness and the physical in sensuality, integrated with our substance, the ground of our being which is Being itself.[259]

Julian claims that spirituality penetrates both the substance and the sensuality of the human soul. In fact she gives a positive evaluation to the sensuality of the human being precisely because it is capable of being penetrated by the spirit:

> I understand that our sensuality is founded in nature, in mercy and in grace, and this foundation enables us to receive gifts which lead us to endless life. For I saw very surely that our substance is in God, and I also saw that God is in our sensuality, for in the same instant and place in which our soul is made sensual, in that same instant and place exists the city of God.[260]

The final phrase in this passage appears to be an echo of Augustine's teaching about the city of God, which is able to penetrate and transform the earthly city of human beings.

One question that arises is: How are the two parts of the soul, the substance and the sensuality, joined together? Ritamary Bradley emphasizes this question by her subtitled section on this issue: "The Rift in Our Being: Substance and Sensuality."[261] Julian is well aware of the importance of this issue and offers two different answers: first, Jesus Christ joins our substance and sensuality together by becoming man Himself, and second, a human being may, through acts of will, bring about a particular integration of his or her identity. Each of these two methods of integration will be considered.

More specifically, Jesus Christ joins the sensuality and substance of the individual human soul by taking on a sensual soul himself. "He is the mean which keeps the substance and the sensuality together, so that they will never separate."[262] This union within the self of the substance and sensuality implies that an individual will always be unique and unrepeatable. The particular material identity of the

---

259. Jantzen, *Julian,* pp. 143-44. Unfortunately, in another passage Jantzen says that "our substance is the substance of Being Itself; our sensuality individuates us, making each of us one among many beings," p. 142. This ignores the fact that the substance of the human soul is individually created by God, so that in that creation an individuation is given to the human person who then lives out this individuated existence in his or her substantial and sensual soul which serves as the act of a particular material body.

260. Julian, *Showings,* LT, 287. Jantzen gives an excellent description of Julian's distinction between substance and sensuality as follows: "It [sensuality] includes, rather, all of our psychology and physicality as individual human beings: our capacities for perception in sight, hearing, touch, and so on, our whole sensory consciousness, and our capacity for action. In other words, sensuality refers to our existence as psychosomatic beings in a physical world . . . , our substance is the substance of Being Itself; our sensuality individuates us, making each of us one among many beings" (*Julian,* p. 142).

261. Bradley, *Julian's Way,* p. 199.

262. Julian, *Showings,* LT, 289.

person will "never separate" from his or her substance so that, for example, sexual differentiation will always be a significant aspect of personal identity. Because sexual differentiation is an essential aspect of human sensuality when it is joined to human substance it is always a part of personal identity.

Julian's text abounds with the concept of "knitting" together. In her theological development there are four levels of knitting. First, Jesus' human nature is knit to the Divine Nature of the Holy Trinity. Secondly, the soul of Jesus was knit to his body when He was conceived in his mother Mary by the action of the Holy Spirit. Thirdly, we are knit to God at the moment of our creation. Fourthly, through the redemptive action brought about by Jesus' Passion, Death, and Resurrection our sensuality can become fully knit to our substantiality. When this knitting is perfectly achieved, the spirituality that is infused by God into the substantial part of our soul penetrates completely the sensual part of our soul and knits it to God.[263]

In this theological approach, Julian's answer to the question of how the substance and the sensual parts of the soul are joined refers primarily to the spiritual action of God in the human soul through especially the redemptive life, suffering, and death of Jesus Christ and the grace that he shares with creatures.[264] It is important to note, however, that the human person is not passive in this significant knitting of substance and sensuality. On the contrary, there is very specific activity described in her works. It is here that we discover the more philosophical aspects of her theory. There is a responsibility of the human being as well in this dramatic movement towards integration.

Julian speaks very positively of the human body and of its significant place in the identity of the person.

> For he [God] does not despise what he has made, nor does he disdain to serve us in the simplest natural functions of our body, for love of the soul which he created in his own likeness. For as the body is clad in the cloth, and the flesh in the skin, and the bones in the flesh, and the heart in the trunk, so are we, soul and body, clad and enclosed in the goodness of God.[265]

263. See Ritamary Bradley's description of this dynamic process of knitting in Julian in the section entitled "The Image of Knitting in Julian's Text," in *Julian's Way,* pp. 205-9.

264. Theologically Julian situates herself in the medieval debate about the interaction of nature and grace. For an excellent discussion of her position in relation to Augustine, Aquinas, Ockham, Duns Scotus, and Peter Aureole see Ruud, "Nature and Grace in Julian of Norwich," *Mystics Quarterly* 19, no. 2: 71-81. Ruud notes that Julian is more interested in the reconciliation of the higher and lower natures of the human being than in the reconciliation of nature and grace, which she understands as fully reconciled in the love of God for his creatures as communicated through Christ.

265. Julian, *Showings,* LT, 186. See also ST, 163 and LT, 256. Ritamary Bradley in "Perception of Self in Julian of Norwich's *Showings*" (*The Downside Review* 104, no. 356 [July 1986]) adds the following: "Julian's teaching, finally, needs to be assessed against the background of another dominant part of the Western tradition — the position that the self is a hierarchy, split between reason and passion, and between soul and body. Rooted in a patriarchal view of the self, this concept assigns reason to the male part of the soul and passion to the female part. Order is restored only when the dominance of the male over the female is finally asserted. But for Julian, while there is indeed a lower and a higher part, there is no male-female hierarchy. . . . Nor are the parts in Julian's teaching reason and passion, or

Following Augustine, she describes a higher and lower part of the human will in the soul that sometimes come into conflict with one another. In addition, seemingly following a Platonic line of argument, she also implies that choice of evil is simply a matter of ignorance. Evil is just the absence of good: "Man is changeable in this life, and falls into sin through naiveté and ignorance. He is weak and foolish in himself, and also his will is overpowered in the time when he is assailed and in sorrow and woe."[266] At other times, however, Julian implies that the lower part of the will may choose evil. She describes the human being as caught in a conflict of "two wills," one that chooses good and the other evil:

> In each soul which will be saved there is a good will which never assented to sin and never will. For as there is an animal will in the lower part which cannot will any good, so there is a good will in the higher part which cannot will any evil, but always good.[267]

Although there is only one will in a human person, Julian uses the notion of the good will, not as the "divine spark" of the gnostics, but rather as that part of the person where freedom is oriented towards the good, or God. The will is of itself oriented towards the good. However, at times an individual may use this freedom for a choice of a lesser good. Julian is trying to say that liberty can be abused or corrupted through bad choice. In this case, she suggests that the lower will, which makes a choice of evil, appears to act like a second will, in opposition to its proper object, the absolute good. However, there is something deeper in the person than a particular choice. This deeper aspect of the self, the core of personal freedom, is always oriented towards God unless completely perverted from its proper end. God appeals to the freedom of the person to choose the good, but the person has to freely accept to make this choice.

Julian's comments here follow the teaching of Thomas Aquinas in *Summa contra gentiles* (On the Truth of the Catholic Faith), where in Book III, Chapter 14, he argues "That evil is an accidental cause."[268] He elaborates: "Now, every evil is present in something good. And every good thing is the cause of something in some way. . . ."[269] Julian also follows Augustine's description of his struggle in the *Confessions*: "So these two wills within me, one old, one new, one the servant of the flesh, the other of the spirit, were in conflict and between them they tore my soul apart."[270]

---

body and soul. Rather, they are substance and sensuality . . . substance being that part of our humanity which has always been united to the substance of God, and sensuality being that part which is united to the Trinity in the flesh-taking of the Word. It follows that Julian is faithful to her own teaching when she speaks of the self as fulfilled rather than as transformed, and never in any way, even metaphorically, as ceasing to be" (p. 238).

266. Julian, *Showings,* LT, 260.

267. Julian, *Showings,* ST, 154. See also LT, 212, 242, and 282.

268. Thomas Aquinas, *On the Truth of the Catholic Faith: Summa contra gentiles* (Garden City, N.Y.: Doubleday, 1956).

269. Thomas, *Summa contra gentiles,* III, 14, 2.

270. Augustine, *Confessions* (Harmondsworth: Penguin Books, 1981), Book VIII, ch. 5.

This conflicting state is not a permanent aspect of human identity. Julian thinks that the human being through acts of will can bring about an integration in which the higher part of the will, in union with the higher part of the soul, or its substance, effects a centering so that the lower part of the will ceases to direct its disintegration. In the following passage she reflects on her own experience to understand how these different functions of the will work:

> Reluctance and deliberate choice are in opposition to one another, and I experienced them both at the same time; and these are two parts, one exterior, and the other interior. The exterior part is our mortal flesh, which is sometimes in pain, and sometimes in sorrow, and will be so during this life, and I felt it very much at this time; and it was in that part of me that I felt regret. The interior part is an exalted and blessed life which is all peace and love; and this is more secretly experienced; and it was in this part of me that I powerfully, wisely and deliberately chose Jesus for my heaven. And in this I truly saw that the interior part is the master and ruler of the exterior, attaching no importance, paying no heed to what the exterior part may will, but forever fixing its intention and will upon being united with our Lord Jesus.[271]

The continual exercise of the interior function of the will in the substance of the soul, which has as the object of the intellect the person of God in His sensuality (i.e., Jesus Christ as true man), brings about an integration within the human being. This action of the will must be "powerfully, wisely, and deliberately" chosen in order to be effective.[272]

Therefore, even though the lower part of the will may be, either through weakness or deliberate choice, drawn towards evil and disintegration, the human being is capable of a choice of good through the exercise of a higher capacity of the will. This view that the human being is capable of making deliberate choices for the good leads Julian to make her famous observation: "Sin is necessary, but all will be well, and every kind of thing will be well."[273]

Transcendental Analogy of Christ Our Mother

Before developing an analysis of Julian's unique transcendental analogy of Christ our Mother, some attention must be paid to her own mother and to Mary, or "Our Lady St. Mary," as she calls her in her revelations. Julian mentions her own mother once in the Short Text of the *Showings*. It is in the context of the illness she had, which was so severe that those standing around the bed thought that she had died. She said: "My mother, who was standing there with the others, held up her

---

271. Julian, *Showings,* LT, 212.

272. Jantzen observes that Julian has in her *Revelations* a "threefold integration: the integrated theological method . . . the integration of theology with psychology, . . . and the integration of the personality" (*Julian,* p. 109).

273. Julian, *Showings,* LT, 225. See also ST, 152-53 and LT, 227-32.

hand in front of my face to close my eyes, for she thought that I was already dead or had that moment died. . . ."[274] Julian then tells us that this act of her mother increased her own suffering, for she had wanted her eyes kept open to see. Right after this particular episode, Julian then turns to consider the relationship between Mary and Christ with respect to love and suffering.

Julian tells her reader in both the Short Text and the Long Text that she had three visions of our Lady St. Mary: the first at the moment of her conception of Christ, the second as she stood under the Cross during His Passion, and the third as she is now in glory.[275] When Julian's descriptions of the three visions are elaborated, the first two provide an excellent example of a modified vertical analogy, and the third of a transition from a vertical to a transcendental analogy. By modified vertical analogy, I mean that even though Julian suggests that the particular vision was revealed to her by faith, rather than simply by reason, the particular analogates in the analogy are of a similar kind. The reason that the analogy is vertical rather than horizontal is that one of the analogates is significantly higher on a scale of perfection, without becoming a different kind of being. We will consider each analogy in turn.

In the first vertical analogy Julian describes Mary as being fulfilled in wisdom and in truth. She is greater than any other creature who ever lived, yet she is a human creature herself. Thus she is in the same category of being as other persons at the same time that she is the perfect model on a higher level. Mary is like us, only perfectly fulfilled. Julian described her in the Short Text as follows:

> In this God brought our Lady to my understanding. I saw her spiritually in her bodily likeness, a simple, humble maiden, young in years, of the stature which she had when she conceived. Also God showed me part of the wisdom and truth of her soul. . . . And this wisdom and truth, this knowledge of her creator's greatness and of her own created littleness, made her say meekly to the angel Gabriel: Behold me here, God's handmaiden. In this sight I saw truly that she is greater, more worthy and more fulfilled, than everything else which God has created and which is inferior to her. Above her is no created thing, except the blessed humanity of Christ.[276]

Julian moves from a comparison of human beings, with Mary as the most fulfilled model in comparison with others' grasp of wisdom and truth, to her comparison with an even lower form of existence, that of the tiny hazelnut lying in her hand. She concludes, as we saw above, that even this low form of existence is held in being by the love of God.

In her elaboration of the first vision of Mary in the Long Text Julian emphasizes Mary's higher degree of perfection, calling it "exalted wisdom and truth." Julian concludes that " . . . she was filled with grace and with every kind of virtue,

---

274. Julian, *Showings*, ST, ch. 10, 142.

275. Julian, *Showings*, ST, ch. 13, 147 and LT, ch. 25, 223. Her words are almost identical in the two versions of this summary.

276. Julian, *Showings*, ST, ch. 4, 131. The wording is exactly the same in the LT, ch. 4, 182.

and she surpasses all creatures."[277] At the same time, Julian is careful to point out that Mary is not divine, but is distinct from the kind of being Jesus is, even in his sacred humanity. Thus Mary serves as the highest model of wisdom, truth, and virtue for all human beings.

In the second vertical analogy, we find an interesting development. Here Julian's Lady St. Mary is greater by the amount of pain she can endure. Julian tells us that she is able to endure more pain because she has greater love. Once again Julian is shown a physical vision of Mary. This particular description follows in the Short Text the very passage where Julian has just referred to her own mother closing the eyes of her sick daughter on what she thought was her deathbed. The Long Text of her revelations offers greater elaboration of this vertical analogy:

> Here I saw part of the compassion of our Lady St. Mary; for Christ and she were so united in love that the greatness of her love was the cause of the greatness of her pain. For in this I saw a substance of natural love, which is developed by grace, which his creatures have for him, and this natural love was most perfectly and surpassingly revealed in his sweet mother; for as much as she loved him more than all others, her pain surpassed that of all others.[278]

In both of these vertical visions of Mary at the Incarnation and at the Passion, Julian emphasizes that she saw a physical likeness to our Lady, St. Mary, and that the characteristics that were revealed to her were human characteristics elevated to their perfection. In the above passage she indicates that the substance of natural love was developed by grace to achieve the perfection that it had in Mary, as a model for all men and women.

In the third vision, Julian makes a transition from a vertical to a transcendental analogy. It is this third vision of Mary that provides the transition to the transcendental analogy of Christ as our Mother. In this vision, Julian tells us directly that she had wanted to have another vision of Mary as a physical being but that it was denied to her. Instead, her vision was completely spiritual. In it, the affect shifts from the pain and suffering of the previous vision, to delight and joy. Julian discovers a dynamic interaction between Mary and Jesus that draws her in and leads her from meditating on the life of Mary to contemplation of Jesus:

> Oftentimes I had prayed for this, and I expected to see her in a bodily likeness; but I did not see her so. And Jesus, saying this, showed me a spiritual vision of her. Just before I had seen her small and simple, now he showed her high and noble and glorious and more pleasing to him than all creatures. And so he wishes it to be known that all who take delight in him should take delight in her, and in the delight that he has in her and she in him. . . . For our Lord showed me no particular person except our Lady, St. Mary, and he showed her to me on three occasions. The first was as she conceived, the second was as she had been in her sorrow under the Cross, and the third as she is now, in delight, honour, and joy.

277. Julian, *Showings,* LT, ch. 7, 187.
278. Julian, *Showings,* LT, ch. 18, 210. See also ST, chap. 10, 142.

And after this our Lord showed himself to me, and he appeared to me more glorified than I had seen him before, and in this I was taught that every contemplative soul to whom it is given to look and to seek will see Mary and pass on to God through contemplation. And after this teaching, simple, courteous, joyful, again and again our Lord said to me: I am he who is highest. I am he whom you love. I am he in whom you delight, I am he whom you serve. I am he for whom you long. I am he whom you desire. I am he whom you intend. I am he who is all.[279]

In the Long Text there are two other passages in which Mary serves as a transition from a vertical to a transcendental analogy. In one passage Julian develops the relationship of Mary with perfect truth and wisdom, the two characteristics whose perfections she had associated with Mary at the time of the conception. In the following passage the author moves again from a simple descriptive account of Mary's virtues to a full account of God's own identity:

God often showed in all the revelations that man always works his will and to his glory, continually, without ceasing. And what this working is was shown in the first revelation, and that is a marvellous setting, for it was shown in the working of the blessed soul of our Lady St. Mary, by truth and wisdom; and I hope that by the grace of the Holy Spirit I shall say as I saw how this was.

Truth sees God, and wisdom contemplates God, and of these two comes the third, that is, a marvellous delight in God, which is love. Where truth and wisdom are, truly there is love, truly coming from them both, and all are of God's making. For God is endless supreme truth, endless supreme wisdom, endless supreme love uncreated; and a man's soul is a creature in God which has the same properties created.[280]

In her methodology, Julian begins by thinking about Mary's identity in relation to truth and wisdom, but she moves to contemplation of God, and then returns again to compare God with creatures.

In the final passage of Mary's identity to be considered here Julian develops an analogy between Mary enclosing Jesus in her own womb and Jesus enclosing human beings in himself. This important passage provides her ontological foundation for the elaboration of her transcendental analogy of Christ as our Mother:

For in the same time that God joined himself to our body in the maiden's womb, he took our soul, which is sensual, and in taking it, having enclosed us all in himself, he united it to our substance. In this union he was perfect man, for Christ, having joined in himself every man who will be saved, is perfect man.

So our Lady is our mother, in whom we are all enclosed and born of her in Christ, for she who is mother of our saviour is mother of all who are saved in our

---

279. Julian, *Showings,* ST, ch. 13, 147. See also LT, chaps. 25-26, 222-23.
280. Julian, *Showings,* LT, ch. 44, 255-56.

saviour; and our saviour is our true Mother, in whom we are endlessly born and out of whom we shall never come.[281]

Because Jesus united human sensuality, body, consciousness, sensations, psychic functions, and even memory and discursive reasoning with Divine substantiality, He opened the way for all human beings to knit together these two aspects of their identity. Julian inverts the analogy of gestation and giving birth, in her transcendental analogy, because while Jesus is born **from** Mary, human beings are born **into** Jesus. As Andrew Sprung summarizes this remarkable move: "Enclosure, the 'wrapping' of created beings by the divine presence in which they are 'grounded,' is for Julian the constitutive act of divine motherhood. . . . Human perfection entails being born into, rather than out of, the maternal substance."[282]

Julian has described Mary, the Mother of Jesus, in different aspects of her identity. She is the most perfect human being created by God, especially in relation to the virtues of truth and wisdom; she shares the greatest degree of pain of the Passion with Jesus her Son because she has the greatest love; and because she is the mother of Jesus, who is our true Mother, Mary is also our mother. Ritamary Bradley notes that Julian's development of this spiritual maternity of Mary for all creatures knitted together in Christ Jesus anticipates an official teaching of the Catholic Church by several centuries.[283] While the figure of Our Lady St. Mary appears in the first description of Julian's visions, in the Short Text, it is the development of Christ as Our Mother in the Long Text that constitutes Julian's most original contribution to the history of the concept of woman.

This particular transcendental analogy as elaborated by Julian of Norwich is of philosophical interest in the following ways: it begins in the priority of human experience, and particularly Julian's great love for various activities of mothering, and it loosely follows a path of syllogistic reasoning for analogy of attribution in reaching an ontological priority for Jesus Christ as our true Mother. Human beings participate imperfectly in an identity that God has perfectly. In the traditional analogy of attribution, God is the prime analogate to whom are attributed goodness, truth, beauty, and so forth, while the human person has a derived attribution. St. Thomas Aquinas states this principle in the *Summa Theologica* as follows:

And in this way some things are said of God and creatures analogically, and not in a purely equivocal nor in a purely univocal sense. For we can name God only from creatures. Thus, whatever is said of God and creatures, is said according to God as its principle and cause, wherein all perfections of things pre-exist excellently.[284]

---

281. Julian, *Showings,* LT, ch. 57, 292.
282. Sprung, "'We never shall come out of him,'" pp. 47-48.
283. Bradley, *Julian's Way,* pp. 91-93.
284. Thomas Aquinas, *Summa theologica,* Pt. 1, Q. 13, art. 5. See footnote #9 for a further elaboration of this point.

Julian carefully follows the Thomistic principles of beginning with what is known to her of mothering, analogically applying it to God, and then stating that God actually mothers perfectly, so God is our true Mother.[285]

What makes Julian's transcendental analogy of mothering so powerful is that she applies it to Jesus Christ, who is God and Man. This creates a tension in the analogy that would appear to be a contradiction on the horizontal level. How can a man, with a male human nature, be a mother? If the analogy is viewed as horizontal, it cannot work because only woman with a female human nature can be a mother. The temptation of the one hearing this analogy is to resolve the tension in one way or another. There are two ways that the tension of the transcendental analogy is usually erroneously resolved: the first changes the nature of God from a he to a she; and the second reduces the truth claim of the person making the analogy from saying something true about reality itself to saying something true about a projection from an individual's experience. In both false resolutions, the dynamic vitality of Julian's transcendental analogy is lost. The challenge for the reader is to remain in the tension of the transcendental analogy; only then can a new relation develop between the human person and his or her Mother Jesus. It is this new vitality that Julian seeks to transmit to her reader by the tension of her transcendental analogy. Before drawing out in detail some of the components of her analogy of the motherhood of God, a little more attention will be given to the two modes of false resolution that commonly occur.

The first false resolution may take the form of deciding that God is engendered as female. In this case, Julian's texts are used to support a move towards redefining God as a goddess. However, Julian carefully uses a grammar of analogy that would forbid this resolution. She always combines the attribute of mothering with male engendered subject when it is applied to Jesus Christ, God and Man. A few examples will suffice to demonstrate this point:

"God rejoices that **he** is our **Mother**."

". . . for **he** is our **Mother**, brother and saviour. . . ."

"So our **Mother** works in mercy on all **his** beloved children. . . ."

"So **he** is our **Mother** in nature by the operation of grace in the lower part, for love of the higher part."

"But then our courteous **Mother** does not wish us to flee away, for nothing would be less pleasing to **him**. . . ."[286]

285. For excellent discussions of the Thomistic use of transcendental analogies see Gregory Philip Rocca's dissertation: "Analogy as Judgment and Faith in God's Incomprehensibility: A Study in the Theological Epistemology of Thomas Aquinas." See also his two articles, "The Distinction between *Res Significata* and *Modus Significandi* in Aquinas's Theological Epistemology," *Thomist* 55 (April 1991): 173-97; and "Aquinas on God-Talk: Hovering Over the Abyss," *Theological Studies* 54 (December 1993): 641-61.

286. Julian, *Showings,* LT, ch. 52, 279; ch. 58, 293 and 294; ch. 60, 299 and 301. My emphasis.

This grammar of analogy has a male identification; Julian refers to "a he," "a him," or "a his." It is also joined to an attribute of motherhood that is usually reserved only to women, to a she, a her, or a hers. Thus Julian's grammar of attribution creates a paradox for the reader. If readers step out of the tension to resolve the paradox by suggesting that Jesus is female, or that God is a goddess, then they are no longer following Julian's lead in her text.

Julian is solidly in the line of Catholic teaching on the Holy Trinity as Father, Son, and Holy Spirit. In this tradition, when the relations among the members of the Trinity are considered with respect to one another, the First Person is always Father, the Begetter; the Second Person is always Son, Eternally Begotten; and the Third Person is always the Holy Spirit, proceeding from the Father and the Son. It is only when the Persons of the Trinity are considered with respect to their relations to creation and creatures that motherhood may be transcendentally attributed. Since these important distinctions go beyond the primarily philosophical orientation of the present book, they will not be further discussed here.[287]

A second way of false resolution of the tension in Julian's paradoxical joining of attributing mothering to Jesus Christ is to suggest that Julian is simply offering a metaphor projected from her own experience onto God, but that she is not judging something about the reality of God. In this erroneous resolution the truth-value of Julian's claims is undermined by the implication that she is simply offering a poetic image for devotion derived from a single person's experience rather than making a claim about the real nature of God, namely, that the relation between God and His creatures is best described in analogy with that of mother and child.[288]

However, if careful attention is given to Julian's shift in her argument from simply describing Jesus as like a human mother to concluding that he is our true Mother, then it is clear that she is making a claim about reality and not simply projecting her experience in an imaginary metaphor. Again some passages may help emphasize this point. Julian often associates the words "true Mother" with Jesus. For example: "So Jesus Christ, who opposed good to evil, is our true Mother, . . . he is our true Mother in grace by his taking our created nature"; "But our true Mother Jesus, he alone bears us for joy and for endless life"; and "So in our true Mother Jesus our life is founded in his own prescient wisdom from without beginning."[289]

More significant than even her frequent use of the phrase "true Mother" to describe Jesus is Julian's direct argument that "[t]he fair lovely word 'mother' is so sweet and so kind in itself that it cannot truly be said of anyone or to anyone except of him and to him who is the true Mother of life and all things."[290] Thus the prime attribution of mother belongs to God alone, and in particular to Jesus Christ to describe his loving action in the world. As Thomas Aquinas and St. Clement of Alex-

---

287. For a general summary of this topic and for a consideration of Julian's place in the Catholic tradition see Francis Martin, *The Feminist Question,* (Grand Rapids: Eerdmans, 1994), especially ch. 8, "Analogy, Images, Metaphors, and Theology," and ch. 9, "The God and Father of Our Lord Jesus Christ."

288. See Martin, *The Feminist Question,* pp. 246-48 for a consideration of this distinction between metaphor and analogy and its application to Julian of Norwich.

289. Julian, *Showings,* LT, ch. 59, 295; ch. 59, 296; ch. 60, 298; and ch. 63, 304.

290. Julian, *Showings,* LT, ch. 60, 298-99.

andria stated in their descriptions of analogical predication to God, God is the principle and cause of the attribute in the human being. God has motherhood to perfection, while women who are human mothers may approximate this principle more or less. Julian also states that the prime attribution of Mother is to Jesus: "The mother's service is nearest, readiest and surest: nearest because it is most natural, readiest because it is most loving, and surest because it is truest. No one ever might or could perform this office fully, except only him."[291]

These two passages make it perfectly clear that for Julian the ontologically prime attribution of motherhood must be to Jesus. Human mothers participate in this truest form of motherhood the more they participate in their own mothering in consciously willed and chosen acts. Thus, the view of motherhood as something undergone passively is the least full participation in true motherhood.

Before elaborating more particular aspects of Julian's dynamic transcendental analogy of Christ our Mother, some background to the tradition of applying attributes of motherhood to God will be given. Caroline Walker Bynum, in *Jesus as Mother: Studies in the Spirituality of the High Middle Ages,* argues that Julian simply followed in a long line of medieval male and female writers:

> . . . it is not women who originated female images of God. And a list of the medieval authors in whom modern scholars have found the image of God as mother makes it clear that such language is in no way the special preserve of female writers: Anselm, Peter Lombard, the biographer of Stephen of Muret, Bernard, William of St. Thierry, Aelred, Guerric of Igny, Isaac of Stella, Adam of Perseigne, Helinand of Froidmont, Gilbert of Hoyland, Guido II the Carthusian, Albert the Great, Bonaventure, Aquinas, Gertrude the Great, Mechtild of Hackeborn, Mechtild of Magdeburg, Margaret of Oingt, the monk of Farne, Richard Rolle, William Flete, Dante, Ludolph of Saxony, Catherine of Siena, Bridget of Sweden, Margery Kempe, Julian of Norwich. . . . Although the most sophisticated use of the theme is Julian of Norwich's trinitarian theology, there is no reason to assert, as some have done, that the theme of the motherhood of God is a "feminine insight."[292]

If we consider but one example, that of St. Anselm (1033-1109), it is likely that Julian's own development of the motherhood of God occurred in the context of

---

291. Julian, *Showings,* LT, ch. 60, 297.

292. Bynum, *Jesus as Mother,* p. 140. For a discussion of sources see also Charles Cummings, "The Motherhood of God According to Julian of Norwich," in *Medieval Religious Women: Peaceweavers,* vol. 2, pp. 305-14. There is a difference of opinion among scholars about the significance of Julian's development of the theme of the motherhood of God. Kari Borresen claims that Julian is "an important exception" to the situation in which women were "restricted to expressing their female experience through a theological language formed by men." See Kari Elisabeth Borresen, "Male-Female, a Critique of Traditional Christian Theology," *Temenos* 13 (1977): 41. See also Kari Elisabeth Borresen, "God's Image, Man's Image? Female Metaphors Describing God in the Christian Tradition," *Temenos* 19 (1983). "Julian's theology is a unique achievement, because the mother metaphor is central, not confined to Christ's human nature and therefore integrated into a description of the Trinity *quoad nos*" (27).

intergender dialogue. Anselm was a Benedictine monk who became Archbishop of Canterbury. Since it is thought that Julian had connections with an English Benedictine monastic community, it is very possible that she had been exposed to Anselm's writing on this topic. There are two classical distinctions that Anselm made, which are commonly accepted in Catholic teachings. The first is the claim that when God is considered with respect to His internal relations, then the distinctions of Father, Son, and Holy Spirit are appropriate, and no insertion of materially based sex distinctions is appropriate.[293] The second is that when God is considered with respect to His relations to creatures, then maternal analogies may be introduced. Anselm does this in detail in his prayer to St. Paul. Here he refers to Jesus as the Mother of his soul in labor, a mother who died giving birth, a mother who nourishes, comforts, protects, and a mother in affection, kindness, and mercy.[294] However, even with a possible exposure to Anselm's or other authors' reflections on Christ acting as a Mother in the world, Julian's development of this transcendental analogy goes far beyond what preceded her.

In chapters 52-63 of the Long Text of her *Showings,* Julian elaborates what can be classified into five different kinds of ways Christ acts as our Mother. These classifications are overlapping at times, and Julian uses different ways to describe them. However, it is possible to extract each kind of mothering, as it were, and give it a description. There is a movement in Julian's description from a priority of knowing beginning in the sense base of the experience of human mothering to a transcendental understanding of Christ's way of mothering. This is a way of knowing that begins in the senses, moves through reason and faith, and ends in spiritual insight. There is another way of considering the five kinds of mothering, however, and this is the ontological base. This begins in what is ontologically prior, or the Holy Trinity dwelling in eternity, it passes into historical time with creation of the world and the Incarnation of Christ, and then it moves towards the end of time to glory in eternity. Thus it is possible to describe Julian's transcendental analogy of Christ as our Mother in two different ways: with chronological priority of knowing, or ontological priority of being.

In the chart on the following two pages both kinds of priority will be summarized. Once again, it is possible to grasp the essential core of the transcendental analogy by studying the table below. For those readers who would like to consider Julian's descriptions in more detail, selections from her text will follow the chart. Others who might prefer to grasp simply the outline of her theory may move on to the conclusion of the chapter.

Before offering passages concerning each particular type of mothering, it is helpful to make a few general distinctions. There is a **motherhood in substance** that is shared by all three Divine Persons in the Trinity, but a **motherhood in sensuality** is found only in the Second Person. Julian is clear about this distinction.

---

293. See Anselm, *Monologium, Basic Writings* (LaSalle, Ill.: Open Court Publishing Company, 1962), ch. 42, pp. 104-6.

294. Anselm, "Prayer to St. Paul" in *The Prayers and Meditations of St. Anselm* (Harmondsworth: Penguin Books, 1973), pp. 153-56. See Allen, *The Concept of Woman: The Aristotelian Revolution,* pp. 262-70.

Julian of Norwich's Analysis of Christ Our Mother					
Category	Sub-category	Human Mothering	Description	Christ's Mothering	Description
Motherhood in Nature	Substantial Motherhood	Conception	God (Father, Son, and Holy Spirit) creates our substantial nature	No mothering among the relations within the Holy Trinity; mothering arises in relation to Creation	Christ is our Mother in nature in our substantial creation, in whom we are founded and rooted
Motherhood in Grace	Sensual Motherhood	Gestation	Our sensual body and soul developed in our mother's womb	Incarnation — knitting of Christ's Divine Nature with human nature	Christ is our Mother of mercy at the Incarnation in womb of Mary in taking on our sensuality; He wanted to become our Mother in all things
Motherhood in Grace	Knitting of Substantial and Sensual Motherhood	Giving birth	Born out of our mothers; mothers suffer in travail for us; mothers sometimes die giving birth to us	Christ's Passion, Death, and Resurrection	Born endlessly into Christ; He carries us within Him in love and travail; He necessarily dies for our birth into eternity; He alone bears us for joy and for endless life

Julian of Norwich's Analysis of Christ Our Mother (cont.)					
Category	Sub-category	Human Mothering	Description	Christ's Mothering	Description
Mother-hood in Grace	Mother-hood at Work Mother-hood of Mercy	Nursing Protecting Educating Correcting Loving	Feeds us with her milk; lifts us to her breast; tender hands around us; lifts us when we fall	Christ's ac-tion on earth through the Holy Spirit	Feeds us with Himself in the Blessed Sacrament; Our Holy Mother Church is Jesus Christ; lifts us to His Breast through His wounded side; in our Mother Christ we profit and increase
Mother-hood in Bliss	Mother-hood in Glory at end of time	Suffering the child to perish; or letting go of the ma-ture child	Loses the child by death or leaving the home	Christ never suf-fers a child to perish; He brings us back to the Father's Heavenly Home to dwell in the Father's bliss	All evil is overcome; in Him we are end-lessly born and out of Him we shall never come; all will be well

And our substance is in our Father, God almighty, and our substance is in our Mother, God all wisdom, and our substance is in our Lord God, the Holy Spirit, all goodness, for our substance is whole in each person of the Trinity, who is one God. And our sensuality is only in the second person, Christ Jesus, in whom are the Father and the Holy Spirit. . . .[295]

295. Julian, *Showings,* LT, ch. 58, 295.

Julian often refers to the motherhood in substance as **motherhood in nature**. Although all three Divine Persons participate in our creation, and usually the attribute of Creator is given especially to God, the Father, Julian also extends this to the Son when she says: "And so Jesus is our true Mother in nature by our first creation, and he is our true Mother in grace by his taking our created nature."[296] So the categories **motherhood in substance and motherhood in nature** overlap as do the categories **motherhood in sensuality and motherhood in grace**.

Julian was not always consistent in the way she used different categories of motherhood. For example, in another passage we find her offering a good example of attribution of the words 'motherhood' and 'fatherhood,' but not names such as Father, when making the following delineation:

> I contemplated the work of all the blessed Trinity, in which contemplation I saw and understood these three properties: the property of the fatherhood, and the property of the motherhood, and the property of the lordship in one God. In our almighty Father we have our protection and our bliss, as regards our natural substance which is ours by our creation from without beginning; and in the second person, in knowledge and wisdom we have our perfection, as regards our sensuality, our restoration and our salvation, for he is our Mother, brother and saviour; and in our good lord the Holy Spirit we have our reward and our gift for our living and our labour. . . . For all our life consists of three: In the first we have our being, and in the second we have our increasing, and in the third we have our fulfilment. The first is nature, the second is mercy, and the third is grace.[297]

Jesus' motherhood in grace began at the moment of the Incarnation, when he took on human nature through the action of the Holy Spirit in his mother Mary. However, the motherhood in grace is more associated with Jesus' work in cooperation with the action of the Holy Spirit in Redemption. Thus motherhood in grace continues through Jesus' Passion, Death, and Resurrection, and it flourishes in the lives of creatures on earth particularly after Pentecost. Julian calls this cooperative action of Jesus **motherhood at work**:

> I understand three ways of contemplating motherhood in God. The first is the foundation of our nature's creation; the second is his taking of our nature, where the motherhood of grace begins; the third is the motherhood at work. And in that, by the same grace, everything is penetrated, in length and in breadth, in height and in depth without end; and it is all one love.[298]

A prime function of motherhood at work is to help each human being to knit together the higher and lower parts of the soul, or substantiality with sensuality so that by this joining in Christ the person is brought into perfect union with God.

296. Julian, *Showings*, LT, ch. 59, 296.
297. Julian, *Showings*, LT, ch. 58, 293-94.
298. Julian, *Showings*, LT, ch. 59, 297.

The motherhood of grace is also referred to at times as a **motherhood of mercy:**

> And so our Mother is working on us in various ways, in whom our parts are kept undivided; for in our Mother Christ we profit and increase, and in mercy he reforms and restores us, and by the power of his Passion, his death and his Resurrection he unites us to our substance.[299]

Since our substance is in union with God, by this joining we come into an integrated, whole, and complete union with God.

It is in her elaboration of all the many ways that Jesus is our Mother that we discover Julian's great love for the activity of mothering. Noting that women often give their lives while bringing their children to birth, Julian describes Jesus as necessarily dying in giving birth to the union of our substance and sensuality:

> The mother's service is nearest, readiest and surest: nearest because it is most natural, readiest because it is most loving, and surest because it is truest. No one ever might or could perform this office fully, except only him. We know that all our mothers bear us for pain and for death. O, what is that? But our true Mother Jesus, he alone bears us for joy and endless life, blessed may he be. So he carries us within him in love and travail, until the full time when he wanted to suffer the sharpest thorns and cruelest pains that ever were or will be, and at the last he died.[300]

Next, as she continues to elaborate her transcendental analogy between a human mother and Christ as Mother, Julian describes the way in which Jesus nourishes the child he has borne.

> The mother can give to her child to suck of her milk, but our precious Mother Jesus can feed us with himself, and does, most courteously and most tenderly, with the blessed sacrament, which is the precious food of true life. . . . The mother can lay her child tenderly to her breast, but our tender Mother Jesus can lead us easily into his blessed breast through his sweet open side, and show us there a part of the godhead and of the joys of heaven, with inner certainty of endless bliss.[301]

This passage is important because it reveals Julian's process of thinking. In it she makes the following kind of syllogistic argument. A human mother feeds her child with something of herself, or her own milk; Jesus feeds us, his children, with himself in the blessed sacrament; therefore Jesus is our true Mother. Or a human mother lifts her child to her breast; Jesus lifts his children to his breast through his wounded side; therefore he is our true Mother. In fact, in the following paragraph

---

299. Julian, *Showings,* LT, ch. 58, 294.
300. Julian, *Showings,* LT, ch. 60, 298.
301. Julian, *Showings,* LT, ch. 60, 298.

Julian concludes that the word 'Mother' ought be truly applied only to Him who is "the true Mother of Life and of all things."

The usual role of human mothering includes the care of infant children and toddlers. Julian extends her analogy of Christ as Mother in her description of the role of protection:

> The sweet gracious hands of our Mother are ready and diligent about us; for he in all his work exercises the true office of a kind nurse, who has nothing to do but attend to the safety of her child.[302]

Carolyn Bynum, in her detailed analysis of medieval themes of *Jesus as Mother,* studied the stereotypical attributes of mother and father which were common particularly among the Cistercian writers. She identifies the above characteristics associated with birthing, nourishing, and protecting as commonly female:

> Throughout contemporary sermons and treatises, gentleness, compassion, tenderness, emotionality and love, nurturing and security are labelled as "female" or "material"; authority, judgment, command, strictness, and discipline are labelled "male" or "paternal"; instruction, fertility, and engendering are associated with both sexes (either as begetting or as conceiving). Moreover, these stereotypes remain the same whether they are evaluated as positive or negative.[303]

In this context, Julian's development of the characteristics of authority, judgment, and discipline as maternal rather than paternal is significant.

In the following passage Julian does not limit the feminine to being gentle, tender, and nurturing, but she instead opens it up to include chastisement and an incisive capacity to educate.

> The kind, loving mother who knows and sees the need of her child guards it very tenderly, as the nature and condition of motherhood will do. And always as the child grows in age and in stature, she acts differently, but she does not change her love. And when it is even older, she allows it to be chastised to destroy its faults, so as to make the child receive virtues and grace. This work, with everything that is lovely and good, our Lord performs in those by whom it is done. So he is our Mother in nature by the operation of grace in the lower part, for love of the higher part.[304]

It might be argued that Julian is allowing the masculine characteristics of Christ to interpenetrate with the feminine characteristics of human mothering. However, it is clear in this passage that the human mother is taken as the root analogate from which the transcendental analogy is drawn to describe Jesus' Divine Mothering.

302. Julian, *Showings,* LT, ch. 61, 302.
303. Bynum, *Jesus as Mother,* p. 148.
304. Julian, *Showings,* LT, ch. 60, 299.

It is also possible to interpret this passage as simply saying that the mother allows the child to be chastised, although she does not do the activity of chastising herself. This would be more consistent with the stereotype of maternal functions. In another passage Julian makes a similar claim:

> The mother may sometimes suffer the child to fall and to be distressed in various ways, for its own benefit, but she can never suffer any kind of peril to come to her child, because of her love. And though our earthly mother may suffer her child to perish, our heavenly Mother Jesus may never suffer us who are his children to perish.[305]

The suffering of the mother is active, but it is not causative of the discipline. It is an action that holds back, that waits because of a judgment that the "fall" or "distress" might be good for the education of the child. The Motherly way that God deals with us is to let us experience the fruit of our own folly. At the same time, however, Julian is well aware of the limits of her analogy, as she recognizes that the death of the child is a possible source of suffering for a human mother, while for Christ no such death occurs.

In a further passage in which the analogy is inverted, and the transcendental analogate provides the basis for drawing the analogy, Jesus' mothering is given a more active role in making a decision about when chastisement or suffering will end:

> If we do not feel ourselves eased, let us at once be sure that he is behaving as a wise Mother. For if he sees that it is profitable to us to mourn and to weep, with compassion and pity he suffers that until the right time has come, out of his love.[306]

Her description of mothering as demanding self-discipline and self-control is important here. The mother thinks about the best way to educate the child, she disciplines her emotions to be able to do the best thing, to teach the child how to grow in wisdom and virtue. The notion of mothering here is positive, realistic, and devoid of sentimental trivialization of women. It is in stark contrast to the Aristotelian model of woman as weak, less able to control emotions, and undisciplined in wisdom and virtue.

Julian also describes Divine Fathering in a way that goes beyond the masculine stereotype of father as angry judge. She understands human love as involved in a dynamic of movement from a first creation by the Father, to an education through the Son, and with the guidance of the Holy Spirit returning to a union with the Father:

> God is essence in his very nature; that is to say, that goodness which is natural is God. He is the ground, he is the substance, he is very essence of nature, and he is the true Father and the true Mother of natures. And all natures which he has

---

305. Julian, *Showings*, LT, ch. 61, 300-301.
306. Julian, *Showings*, LT, ch. 61, 301.

made to flow out of him to work his will, they will be restored and brought back into him by the salvation of man through the operation of grace.[307]

In this statement that "God is essence in his very nature," Julian may be approaching the traditional scholastic definition that God's essence is to exist. His essence is necessary existence or necessary being, while all other creatures' essence is separate from their being; they have contingent existence. She seems to be combining God's essence to exist with his goodness that gives being to all things that exist, and that gives eternal existence through restoration of life after death.

Frequently Julian associates God the Father with the characteristic of bliss. In the Short Text, she describes where God the Father dwells as follows: "For the first heaven, which is the Father's bliss, appeared to me as a heaven, and it was full of bliss."[308] Then in the Long Text, she describes Jesus conveying to her, in the most intimate manner, his mission of helping human beings to overcome all sin:

> And then our courteous Lord shows himself to the soul, happily and with the gladdest countenance, welcoming it as a friend, as if it had been in pain and in prison, saying: My dear darling, I am glad that you have come to me in all your woe. I have always been with you, and now you see me loving, and we are made one in bliss.[309]

The cooperative action of Jesus, freeing human beings from sin and bringing them back to the Father, is elaborated further in a passage in which Julian pours forth a description of what we could call Jesus' **Motherhood of bliss**:

> And I understood no greater stature in this life than childhood, with its feebleness and lack of power and intelligence, until the time that our gracious Mother has brought us up into our Father's bliss. And there it will be made known to us what he means in the sweet words when he says: All will be well, and you will see it yourself, that every kind of thing will be well. And then will the bliss of our motherhood in Christ be to begin anew in the joys of our Father, God, which new beginning will last, newly beginning without end.[310]

We will now summarize our conclusions from this study of Julian's innovative discussion of gender characteristics and the nature of Jesus Christ. She has described five types of motherhood in her transcendental analogy: (1) motherhood in nature or substantial motherhood, (2) motherhood in grace: sensual motherhood, (3) motherhood in grace: knitting of substantial and sensual nature, (4) motherhood in grace: motherhood at work, and (5) motherhood in bliss. These five kinds of motherhood follow the general theological themes of Creation, Incarnation, Passion, Redemption, and Glory. While all Three Divine Persons act in all of the

307. Julian, *Showings,* LT, ch. 62, 302-3.
308. Julian, *Showings,* ST, ch. 12, 145.
309. Julian, *Showings,* LT, ch. 40, 246.
310. Julian, *Showings,* LT, ch. 63, 305.

mysteries, Julian has emphasized the particular role of Jesus by drawing her transcendental analogy with human mothering.

By holding to the tension of her transcendental analogy, which combines mothering, a traditionally female activity, with Jesus Christ whose Incarnation was as a man, Julian has communicated two new realities: first, that human creatures can grow in love for God by understanding Jesus' actions in the world as the perfect example of true mothering; and second, that human beings can grow in love for the activity of mothering by recognizing its true nature as particular kinds of acts that foster the growth and development of another human being.

Nearly every description of Christ's motherhood emphasizes activity. This emphasis on the activity of mothering is a significant counterexample to the model in academic-based Aristotelian gender polarity, which emphasizes passivity as the female principle of generation. Although the Aristotelian tradition technically emphasized passivity as the female principle only at the moment of conception, it extended its reach into many other areas of woman's identity. Thus Julian's emphasis on motherhood as a cluster of ways of acting is an important innovation for the history of the concept of woman. Indeed, Julian's great love for the various activities of mothering even redefines motherhood in a certain sense. Motherhood is more act than anything else; it consists of ongoing acts of love. In her description of the motherhood of Christ, motherhood involves knitting substance and sensuality together, in bearing new life, in feeding and nourishing, in lifting, in educating, in wisely correcting, in freely suffering, and even freely dying to support the good life of another. Even if some act of mothering undergoes or involves suffering and passion, in Christ it is freely chosen. Thus motherhood is transported from the realm of passivity into the realm of freely chosen act. For Julian, mothering is a cluster of particular kinds of loving acts oriented towards fostering new life (and even endless or eternal life) in another person. The importance that Julian gives to Jesus' motherhood is captured by Ritamary Bradley as follows: Jesus "is sovereign Wisdom, whose motive in becoming human was 'to carry out the service and the office of motherhood in all things.'"[311]

Before we conclude this chapter, it is useful to reflect briefly on Julian's influence on others. In addition to the previously noted fact that Julian's text has elicited much reflection from scholars of our times, it is known that she also helped other authors during her lifetime. We know from the *Book of Margery Kempe* that Julian was available for conversation, and that these two women met together for a period of several days in 1414. Julian's reputation for wisdom was widespread, as Margery Kempe states: ". . . she was bidden by Our Lord to go to an anchoress in the same city, named Dame Jelyan, and so she did, . . . for the anchoress was expert in such things, and good counsel could give."[312] According to Margery, Julian spoke to her about the teachings of *Scripture,* and especially St. Paul, and about the doctrines of the early Church Fathers, including particularly St. Jerome.

Even though Julian's reputation as a counselor was well established during

311. Bradley, *Julian's Way,* pp. 134-35. Bradley emphasizes the identification of Jesus with the Wisdom of the Holy Trinity.
312. *The Book of Margery Kempe,* p. 72.

her lifetime, her written work remained practically unknown for nearly two hundred years. In 1670 Serenus de Cressy published the first edition of her text in Paris, and another edition was published by Henry Collins in England in 1877. However, it was not until 1901, when Grace Warrack published a new edition, that Julian's work began to be widely read.[313] Thus it was only in the twentieth century that serious questions about the meaning of her texts were debated by scholars. From the perspective of the history of the concept of woman, there is no doubt that Julian's writings signal a significant augmentation in the quality of a woman's writing and thinking about woman's identity from the works that had preceded her.

ANALOGICAL THINKING, DIALOGUE, AND GENDER IDENTITY IN WOMEN RELIGIOUS AUTHORS

In this chapter we have described the development of analogical thinking among women religious authors in the thirteenth and fourteenth centuries. We have provided examples from other texts of horizontal analogies (with analogates from the same level of being), vertical analogies (with analogates from different levels of being within the world), and transcendental analogies (with analogates from different realms of being, and one analogate of which transcends the world by being applied to God or spiritual realities). Using these examples, we can differentiate three basic stages of development in analogical thinking among women religious authors: Stage I — simple analogy developed in a short paragraph; Stage II — slightly extended analogy developed over a few pages; and Stage III — very extended analogy developed over a whole text.

By referring to the texts of previous women religious authors, to women authors included in this chapter, and to those anticipated in future studies, we can classify their analogical thinking by the chart on page 429.

In the present chapter we recognized a major leap in extension of analogical thinking that occurred in the work of Bridget of Sweden, Catherine of Siena, and Julian of Norwich. These authors developed extensive transcendental analogies through the exercise of their discursive reasoning. All of them described Jesus Christ in a unique relation: as husband of household, as living bridge, and as mother. While Hildegard of Bingen had previously written extended analogies, other women religious authors had not demonstrated such a discursive capacity. They preferred to insert multiple short analogies in the context of their mystical and theological reflections, rather than to elaborate the meaning of insights over several pages of text.

The extension in the use of discursive reason by women authors to elaborate transcendental analogies came in two steps. In the first step, referred to above as Stage II, the author linked several different separated aspects of the original analogical insight. This practice had been found in the Church Fathers and it was

---

313. P. Franklin Chambers, *Juliana of Norwich: An Appreciation and an Anthology* (London: Victor Gollancz, 1955), pp. 57-58.

Developmental Stages of Analogical Thinking		
	Stage I	**Stage II**	**Stage III**
Development of analogies	Short (sentence or paragraph)	Slightly extended (one or more pages)	Very extended (whole text)
By male authors **Horizontal and vertical examples:**	Pythagoreans: mathematical analogies	Plato: Myth of Er Allegory of cave	Plato: *Republic* Boethius: *Consolation of Philosophy*
Transcendental examples:	St. Augustine: Trinity like soul — memory, will, and understanding	St. Thomas Aquinas: analogical attribution to God and man, such as Good, One, True, Beautiful, Father Meister Eckhart: Birth of God in the soul	Augustine: *City of God*
By women religious authors	Hadewijch Mechtild of Magdeburg Mechtild of Hackeborn Saint Gertrude the Great Margery Kempe	Hildegard of Bingen Bridget of Sweden Catherine of Siena Julian of Norwich	Teresa of Avila: *The Interior Castle*

probably known to women authors. However, it would appear as though St. Bridget, St. Catherine, and Blessed Julian developed their extended analogies through reflection on their own experience of running a household in the first case, walking over a covered bridge in a second case, and being mothered or observing mothers in the third case.

A further stage of augmentation of analogical thinking in women religious authors can be seen in St. Teresa of Avila's *Interior Castle*. In this work written at the end of the sixteenth century, a transcendental analogy between a castle and the rooms of prayer in a soul is extended throughout an entire text. Of course, men religious authors, and especially Augustine and Boethius, who were often read by women religious authors, had previously elaborated very extended analogies. The women religious authors considered in this chapter helped prepare the way by their own increasingly sophisticated use of discursive reason to elaborate analogies. They offer an intermediate development in the tradition of analogical thinking among women religious.

In the chart on pages 431-32 some of the more specific information about the three kinds of analogies found in authors studied in this chapter are summarized. It is important to recall that these examples are selected from the much larger corpus of the authors' works, and they are not meant to be exhaustive or even generally representative. They were chosen because of their philosophical relevance.

Our study will turn to consider the relation of dialogue to analogical thinking in the community of discourse shared by the religious authors considered in this chapter. I have suggested that there is an interesting coincidence of analogical thinking and the practice of intergender dialogue among women religious authors. I also noted a frequent move from private to public intergender dialogue. In a context in which woman's virtue had been traditionally thought of as tied to the private realm of activity, the extension of a woman's teaching and action into the public realm is significant. In the chart on pages 433-34 we summarize the relation of public and private dialogue in four women religious authors studied in this chapter. This table shows that women authors considered in this chapter engaged in private forms of intergender dialogue. Mechtild, Gertrude, and possibly Julian also studied carefully manuscripts, written by men, which had been collected in a monastic library. Consequently, they all had the experience of thinking together with men and women about issues of wisdom and virtue.

In addition, all of the women religious authors considered in this chapter shared their reflections with others through written texts and through personal interaction. St. Bridget and St. Catherine furthermore wrote extensive letters to men and women in which they challenged their correspondents to practice greater virtue. In these ways, they moved from a strictly private intergender dialogue to public forms of intergender dialogue. Several of the men who interacted with women religious authors probably had an academic education. Therefore, we can see the intergender dialogue of women religious as bridging the previously gender-monological communities of discourse delineated by academia and women religious communities.

When we turn to consider forms of dialogue found in Eckhart and his disciples we discover a similar pattern. The chart on pages 435-36 attempts to summarize a pattern of interaction that we traced in this chapter. It shows that intergender dialogue, which occurs in private, tends to lead to public intergender dialogue in two ways: first, when an author is influenced by a text written by a person of the opposite sex, and second, by writing texts that in turn have an effect on others. During the period under study, the Dominican monks who worked directly with women gave evidence of such openness.

The significant role that Dominican friars played in this phase of the history of the concept of woman needs to be emphasized. Not only did they directly inter-

Selected Examples of Analogical Thinking			
Author	Horizontal	Vertical	Transcendental
Mechtild of Hackeborn	The woman author as generic "she" represents analogically all men and women.	1. Seven sons like seven divisions of Divine Office 2. Parts of the body like different virtues 3. Parts of dice like aspects of human identity 4. Contents of armoire like different virtues	1. Christ's heart like a kitchen 2. Christ's heart like a spinning wheel and cord of wool
Gertrude the Great	1. The woman author as a generic "she" represents analogically all men and women. 2. Gertrude writing is like a dove gathering corn. 3. Pen of hand dipped in inkwell like pen of tongue dipped in blood	1. Alphabet is to logic as bread is to hidden manna as images of the Divine are to God 2. Leaves of trees like good works	1. Girding the thigh with a sword like arming with God's Spirit 2. Water flowing like God's stream of grace 3. Praying like doves soaring heavenward 4. As air receives the sun, the soul receives God 5. God's action in the soul like a fire
Eckhart	1. Man is a virgin and wife like a woman who is a virgin and wife. 2. Martha is like a pagan scholar.	1. Heaven like form or man; earth like matter or woman 2. Man like active, woman like passive 3. Man like superior part of reason, woman like inferior part of reason 4. Husband like will of spirit, wife like will of flesh	God gives birth in the soul as a woman gives birth in the world.

Selected Examples of Analogical Thinking (cont.)			
Author	Horizontal	Vertical	Transcendental
Bridget	The woman author as a generic "she" represents analogically all men and women.	1. Supports for the body like supports for the soul 2. Activities in directing a household like activities for developing virtues in the soul	Cooperation of husband and wife in running household in the world like cooperation of Christ as Spouse of soul in developing spiritual household
Catherine	1. The woman author as a generic "she" represents analogically all men and women. 2. Parts of body like parts of bridge	1. Parts of bridge like faculties of the soul 2. Stepping on steps of bridge like developing virtues	Physical bridge like living bridge of Christ joining humanity and Divinity
Julian	The woman author as a generic "she" represents analogically all men and women.	1. Human virtues of wisdom and truth like Mary's perfect virtues 2. Human capacity to suffer pain, which is directly proportional to capacity to love, is like Mary's greatest capacity to suffer pain, which is directly proportional to her greatest capacity to love.	1. Christ our Mother gives us birth into eternal life by multiple means as our Mother in Nature, Mother in Grace, Mother in Substance, Mother in Sensuality, Mother in Knitting Substance and Sensuality, Mother in Mercy, Mother at Work, and Mother in Bliss. 2. We are born into Christ our Mother forever in inversion of being born out of our mother in time.

Dialogue and Women Religious Authors				
Author	Private with women	Private with men	Public through texts	Influences
Mechtild of Hackeborn	Infragender dialogue with women's community of discourse including Abbess Gertrude, Mechtild of Magdeburg, and St. Gertrude	Intergender dialogue with Dominican monks, clergy, lay men	Latin *Revelations* gathered by St. Gertrude	Influenced by: classical and scholastic authors in Helfta's library (Seneca, Augustine, St. Albert, St. Thomas) Influential through dispersion of her work in Germany, France, Italy, and England
Gertrude the Great	Infragender dialogue with women's community of discourse including Abbess Gertrude, Mechtild of Magdeburg, and Mechtild of Hackeborn	Intergender dialogue with Dominican monks, clergy, lay men	Latin *Herald of Divine Love* and *Exercises*	Influenced by: classical and scholastic authors in Helfta's library — as above Influential possibly to St. Teresa of Avila

Dialogue and Women Religious Authors (cont.)			
Author	Private with women	Private with men	Public through texts	Influences
Bridget	Infragender dialogue with her family and those with whom she founded the Bridgettines	Intergender dialogue with Master Matthias, Cistercian Peter Olavsson, Master Peter Olavsson, Bishop Alphonsus Pecha	Swedish and Latin *Revelations* written in complement with Peter of Alvastra	Influenced through letters: King Magnus, Pope Gregory XI, Pope Urban VI, Archbishop of Naples Influential to Margery Kempe
Catherine	Infragender dialogue with her family and female disciples	Intergender dialogue with Raymond of Capua	Dialectic *Dialogues* dictated and written in complement with her male secretaries and with Raymond of Capua	Influenced by Augustine Influential through speeches and letters: Pope Gregory XI, Pope Urban VI, City leaders of Florence, nuns, clerics, lay persons, etc.
Julian	Infragender dialogue with Margery Kempe and possibly with Benedictine nuns	Intergender dialogue possibly with Augustinian friars	English *Showings* in Short Form and Long Form containing many levels of dialogue	Influenced by "scholars" including possibly Augustine, Plotinus, Boethius, Anselm, William of St. Thierry, St. Thomas Aquinas, Duns Scotus, William of Ockham

Private and Public Forms of Dialogue				
	Private with women	Private with men	Public in person	Public through texts
Eckhart	Intergender dialogue with Dominican nuns	Infragender dialogue in Academia (U. of Paris) (Cologne)	Sermons in German	Latin and German texts Influenced by: Plotinus, St. Albert, St. Thomas, Maimonides, and possibly Mechtild of Magdeburg, Marguerite Porete Influential to: Tauler and Suso
Tauler	Intergender dialogue with Dominican nuns and Beguines	Infragender dialogue with Dominican men and in Academia (Cologne)	Sermons in German, written down by women who heard them	German and Latin texts Influenced by: Eckhart, Jan van Ruusbroec, and possibly Mechtild of Magdeburg, Marguerite Porete Influential to: Margaret Ebner, and possibly St. Teresa and Marie of the Incarnation

Private and Public Forms of Dialogue				
	Private with women	Private with men	Public in person	Public through texts
Suso	Intergender dialogue with Dominican Nuns, especially Elsbeth Stagel	Infragender dialogue in Academia (Cologne) Studied with Meister Eckhart	Sermons in German	German texts Life and Letters written in complement with Elsbeth Stagel Influenced by: Seneca, Eckhart, St. Thomas Influential to: St. Bridget

act with many religious women authors, as spiritual directors and teachers, they also frequently dispersed the particular text of a woman author to others. The Dominicans helped disperse the writings of Mechtild of Magdeburg and Mechtild of Hackenborn. They directed and encouraged the writing of Catherine of Siena, Margaret and Christine Ebner, Elsbeth Stagel, and Bridget of Sweden. They served as possible links to the works of St. Gertrude and St. Teresa of Avila.

We also discovered that among male and female religious authors influenced by Neoplatonism, there was a tendency to lose the basis for gender differentiation and even for individual differentiation from God. We also suggested that this loss of gender and personal identity may have resulted from drawing a horizontal analogy between men and women and simultaneously accepting as a principle the total passivity of the feminine. When this principle was adopted as a spiritual analog of pregnancy and childbirth, the feminine principle of mothering rendered the woman or man as nothing, the practical experience of gender complementarity was lost, and a gender unity resulted. Thus, even though some male writers valued woman's identity and identified with what they understood to be the female principle of total passivity, they ended up devaluing individual identity and clarity of distinctions between men and women, and God and human beings.

In contrast to this Neoplatonic tendency that ultimately devalued woman's unique identity in relation to man, we discovered in Julian of Norwich an affirmation of the activity of mothering. In her transcendental analogy of Christ as our Mother, Julian elaborated many different dynamics of mothering; the more these dynamics participated in the nature of acts, the more they approximated Christ's

Divine Identity. This is why Julian calls Christ our True Mother, and why she concludes that all mothering derives its identity from a particular way of acting, which fosters life and growth in others.

In general, among the religious authors discussed in this chapter we discovered a practical experience of gender complementarity in many different situations. In other words, in actual intergender dialogue authors seemed to experience a relation of similarity and differentiation with a person or persons of the opposite sex. This practical experience of gender complementarity often had a fertile issue in a written text or texts that were made available to the public. This is an indication of intellectual or spiritual synergy common to relations of complementarity. In addition, in these texts we discovered fertile analogies that considered various aspects of wisdom and virtue. In this light, I would like to suggest for further consideration the question of whether or not there is more than just a coincidental link between analogical thinking, intergender dialogue, and gender complementarity.

In the next chapter we will turn to a study of the development of new forms of satirical depictions of women's identity that incorporate philosophical aspects of gender polarity theories. As we will see, within the gender polarity tradition, especially when exaggerated by satires, woman is perceived not as a generic model of virtue, but as a gender-differentiated model of vice. In the present chapter, however, we have seen that religious authors have consistently argued that women need to use their ability for discursive thinking, to acquire self-knowledge, to develop self-government, and to take responsibility for public action in speech and virtuous acts. Women authors also often perceived themselves as a generic model of wisdom and virtue for all men and women. Thus, these two chapters stand counterpoised to one another with respect to an appropriate theory of woman's identity.

CHAPTER 6

DETERIORATION OF INTERGENDER DIALOGUE IN LATER SATIRES AND PUBLIC TRIALS

I n the present chapter we will consider a particularly nefarious dimension of the history of the concept of woman in relation to man. The purpose of analyzing such unpleasant material is not to focus on the deterioration of man-woman relations in order to blame or even to give a general history of a particularly sad era in the West. Rather, it is to face squarely certain ways in which philosophical notions entered into and likely contributed to the deterioration of intergender dialogue and relations. This knowledge contributes to the general orientation of this book, which is to offer as clear an account as possible of the development of the concept of woman in relation to man in the period of history of western philosophy between 1250 and 1500. In my opinion there was a direct connection from philosophical principles of gender polarity, to the satires that devalued women, to the arrest, trials, and even condemnation of individual women. It is difficult to establish causal connections when looking at a period several centuries ago, but there are enough data to indicate a common pool of thought within the culture and to reveal verbal and notional resemblances among philosophers' principles of gender polarity, satires, and legal trials and manuals. Therefore, even though this is an extremely sensitive topic, it is important that it not be ignored.

In addition, it is likely that the extreme degree of harshness and distortion in views about women circulating in the satirical literature contributed to a later reaction by at least one author to make a serious attempt to reform the concept of woman in the West. The Early Renaissance Humanist author, Christine de Pizan, reacted to public devaluations of women in literature and in society by directly addressing authors who wrote such views. The extraordinary contribution she made to the history of the concept of woman can be properly appreciated only in the historical context of her writing. Thus, we will turn to consider the philosophical aspects of the deterioration in intergender dialogue and relations during the late fourteenth and fifteenth centuries.

This present chapter is divided into four parts, which follow a general chronological order. In the first part the impact of printing on the widespread dispersion of classical satires will be considered. Then the development of the concept of woman as dangerous and deceitful for man and the appeal to the authority of philosophers to support the devaluation of women will be described, in particular as represented by a handful of newer satires. Next, situations of public intergender dialogue of two individual women who faced arrest and trial will be analyzed. In one, Margery Kempe was eventually released; while in the other, St. Joan of Arc was put to death, although later vindicated. Our analysis of the public intergender dialogue in which these women participated and particularly of the judgments of selected men who had an academic education will reveal the influence of philosophical stereotypes in the culture. Finally, these stereotypes will be seen as operative in the classical manual used by judges to evaluate women accused of witchcraft, the *Malleus maleficarum*.

MANUSCRIPTS, PRINTING, AND THE DISPERSION OF TRADITIONAL SATIRES

The dispersion of satires moved through the following stages: personal acquaintance with handwritten satires by word of mouth (at a university, such as Paris), transportation of handwritten manuscripts (from Paris to Oxford, for example), and widescale distribution of printed texts (all over Europe).[1] Printing information about satires written prior to the fourteenth century gives some indication of how popular these texts became in subsequent centuries. As a result of the availability of the printing press, satirical devaluations of women began to circulate all over Europe. A brief review of the printing and reprinting of the classical satires against women will reveal the extent of renewed interest in this topic.

Juvenal's sixth satire "Against Women," which satirized women's lack of virtue, inordinate lust, injustice, tyranny over men, imitation of masculinity, and pseudo-wisdom, was printed more than any other satire. There were one hundred and fifty-nine different printings of Juvenal's satires in Latin between the years 1470 and 1739.[2] These multiple printings were done in widely diverse cities. A cursory glance at the printing dates and locations for the first edition of Juvenal's *Satires* gives some indication of the way the satires spread throughout Europe: Venice (1470), Florence (1472), Ferrara (1474), Milan (1474), Lyons (1485), Paris (1493), Turin (1494), Nuremberg (1497), Brescia (1501), Leipzig (1502), Cologne (1510), Gueynard (1511), Colophon (1512), Leyden (1512), Antwerp (1559), Verona (1593), Hanover (1603), Amsterdam (1619), Frankfurt (1623), Geneva (1642), and Madrid (1642). In addition, Juvenal's *Satires* were translated from Latin into various vernacular languages with first printings identified as follows: English (Oxford, 1644), French (Paris, 1653), Dutch (Leyden, 1682) and in German, Spanish, and Portuguese after 1700. Finally, as a single text the sixth satire "Against Women" was published separately in Latin in Paris in 1545.

---

1. For a historical event-driven account of this dispersion of satires see Samuel Marion Tucker, *Verse Satire in England before the Renaissance* (New York: Columbia University Press, 1908). "The first impulse came from abroad. The racial effect of the Conquest gave birth to English satire: it made a heterogeneous people; it finally directed English students to the University of Paris. From this foreign influence sprang the poetry of the Goliards and of the Anglo-Latin satirists and epigrammatists" (p. 36).

2. *National Union Catalog: Pre-1956 Imprints* (London: Mansell Information Publishing Ltd., 1968), vol. 287, pp. 239-64, 276.

Other satires about women proliferated in a similar way. Lucretius *De rerum natura,* lost in the fourth century and recovered in 1417, included a satirical portion in which women were characterized as promising false pleasures, ruling men's lives with a lash and goad, being unkempt, unwashed, hideous bores, etc. It was reprinted in Latin at least thirty-one times between 1486 and 1695 in cities such as Verona (1486), Venice (1495), Florence (1512), Brunello (1539), Leyden (1540), Paris (1564), Antwerp (1565), Frankfurt (1583), Amsterdam (1620), Canterbury (1686), Naples (1693), and Oxford (1695).[3]

Andreas Capellanus's *Art of Courtly Love* included a satirical section in which women were characterized as greedy, miserly, wicked, envious, gluttonous, deceptive, changeable in opinions, slandering others, given to drunkenness, and breaking promises. It was printed in Latin in 1610 and in German in 1803; and the *Livre de Mathéolus,* which was described in Chapter 3, was printed in French in 1497.[4]

Boccaccio's *Corbaccio* was published in Italian twenty-seven times between 1487 and 1723, published in French in 1597, and in German and English after 1800.[5] Finally, the *Roman de la rose,* also described in Chapter 3, was printed in several publications in French beginning in 1487 (Lyon) and 1496 (Paris). *Romaunt of the Rose,* a middle English translation made in part by Chaucer, was published in 1546 in London.[6]

While all of the above satires emphasize some negative aspect of woman's identity, one satire that particularly prepared the way for the works considered in the present chapter is Walter Map's little tract, *Dissuasio Valerii ad Rufinum philosophum ne uxorem ducat* (Advice of Valerius to Rufinus the Philosopher Not to Marry). This text, written in Latin in the early 1180s, was immensely popular, and there are over forty thirteenth- to fifteenth-century manuscripts available in libraries in Great Britain and eleven in the *Bibliothèque Nationale* in France.[7] The letter of Valerius was well known in manuscript copy and was printed in a collection of the works of St. Jerome, which also contained a well-known satire against women entitled *Against Jovinianus.*[8] This satire is particularly significant for our study of the devaluation of woman because it develops the theme that women are deceitful and dangerous to men and it invokes the authority of philosophers to support its views.

3. *National Union Catalog,* vol. 344, pp. 462-64.

4. *National Union Catalog,* vol. 16, p. 125; vol. 369, p. 53.

5. *National Union Catalog,* vol. 62, pp. 432-35.

6. *National Union Catalog,* vol. 369, p. 53.

7. *Walter Map: De Nugis Curialium (Courtiers' Trifles),* ed. and trans. M. R. James (Oxford: Clarendon Press, 1983). The *Dissuasio Valerii* was gathered and included as Section IV.3 of *De Nugis Curialium,* of which there is only one fourteenth-century manuscript in the Oxford Bodleian Library, intro., pp. xlv-xlvii. The whole text was relatively unknown until its appearance in 1601 in the Bodleian Library at Oxford. See Montague Rhodes James, *Anecdota Oxoniensia: Texts, Documents, and Extracts Chiefly from Manuscripts in the Bodleian and Other Oxford Libraries, Medieval and Modern Series. Part IV, Walter Map, De Nugis Curialium* (Oxford: Clarendon Press, 1914), p. xiv.

8. James, *Anecdota Oxoniensia,* p. xxxi. He also notes five anonymous commentaries on the letter, pp. xxxi-xxxix. "It is a noticeable feature in all the commentaries . . . that so little interest is shown in the authorship of the text . . ." (p. xxxviii). This view of James supports the claim that it was the satire itself and not the identity of the author which had an influence on others.

Walter Map, a Welshman, who had studied theology and possibly canon law at the University of Paris before returning to a life as a secular cleric in England, promoted both philosophical and theological rationale for gender polarity. He offered numerous Biblical examples, philosophical examples, and classical examples of women who led men away from a life of virtue.[9] He even suggested that virtuous women no longer exist. "Friend, there is no Lucretia, no Penelope, no Sabine left: mistrust all."[10] Map appealed to Theophrastus, Aristotle's disciple, as an authority to support his own views of women's character.[11] While we considered some of the themes of the *Dissuasio Valerii* in *The Concept of Woman: The Aristotelian Revolution (750 BC–1250 AD),* a brief review of its contents will be helpful here.

When we examine the specific ways that women are considered dangerous for men, we find Map constantly moving from a **particular** example of a woman who led a man into vice, destroyed a man's body by murder, or destroyed a man's soul, to universal generalizations about **all women,** who must be mistrusted or feared. His satire works by suggesting a stereotype of woman that expresses a general bias or devaluation of all women. The following paragraph gives just one such example of this technique:

> Livia murdered her husband whom she hated overmuch, Lucilia hers whom she loved overmuch. The former mixed the aconite on purpose, the latter in error gave him the sup of madness instead of that of love. Friend, these two were actuated by opposite purposes: but neither missed the true end of **all** women's deceit, I mean harm. **Women** proceed by many diverse paths; but in whatever zigzags they wander, in whatever blind ways they go astray, the issue is one and the same, the goal of all their ways one, one the fount and common outcome of their diverse natures — and that is mischief.[12]

If it seems as though Map were only describing some women who deceive, it is important to remember his advice that there are no virtuous women left, so "mistrust all."

The satire suggests that women are unable to control their own passions, that they lack self-governance. Again Map begins with a particular example of a woman who brought Hercules to his destruction, but then he moves to a generalized conclusion about all women:

> Woman, of frenzied brain and hasty soul, ever unbalanced in will, always deems that best which she desires, not that which is expedient; and, as before everything

9. Map, *De Nugis Curialium.* The women include: Eve, Delilah, Bathsheba, Scylla, Nisus, Myrrha, Phoebus, among others, c. 3, 193ff.

10. Map, *De Nugis Curialium,* iv, c. 3, 295. This passage is given an even sharper translation in another version of the same text. See Walter Map, *De Nugis Curialium (Courtiers' Trifles),* trans. Frederick Tupper and Marbury Dladen Ogle (London: Chatto and Windus, 1924), ". . . Fear all the sex," p. 186.

11. See Map, *De Nugis Curialium,* "But, that the evidence of the ancients may lend me credit, do you read the *Aureolus* of Theophrastus and Naso's *Medea,* and you will find that there are hardly even a few things impossible to women" (iv, c. 4, 311).

12. Map, *De Nugis Curialium,* iv, c. 3, 305. My emphasis.

she is anxious to please, is determined to prefer her pleasure to all else. Twelve superhuman labours did Hercules accomplish; the thirteenth, too much even for superhumanity, put an end to him. So fell the strongest of men, alike lamented and lamenting, who without a murmur had borne the high heavens on his shoulders.

Finally, amongst so many millions, did ever one woman sadden a constant and earnest suitor by a permanent denial? Did she consistently silence the suppliant's words? No, her answer has some taste of favour in it, and however hard it is, it will contain in some nook of its wording a concealed stimulus to your petition. Every one of them refuses, none goes on refusing.[13]

The image of woman's "frenzied brain," "hasty soul," and "unbalanced will" is one that will be amplified and developed by authors in subsequent centuries. The lack of virtue in a woman becomes the source of the fear of the fall from virtue in a man. This fear of woman seems to contradict the philosophers' general claims that men were more rational and capable of self-governance than women. Yet they suggest that man is unable to resist her, and she is unable to resist leading him astray. Thus Valerius, Map's pseudonym, tries to persuade his young philosopher not to marry. The polarity framework devalues women and separates off women from men rather than joining members of the two genders together in friendship of working to support one another in gaining self-knowledge or self-governance through complementary dialogue.

Walter Map exemplifies this framework early in his tract when he addresses his young student directly. Before turning to the passage in question, it is important to consider that Map frequently introduces animal metaphors for either debasing or elevating characters. He compares himself to the voice of a goose amidst swans, and asks his student to use "the bonds of virtue" as Ulysses did when hearing the cries of the Sirens.[14] Later on in the tract, Map compares the young man to a bee gathering honey, and he mentions animal metaphors applied to Christ as lion, worm, and ram. In this context, Map compares heathens who use animal metaphors for idolatry with Christians who use them for elevation through faith. In this comparison, Map is contrasting human marriage with spiritual marriage.[15] With his practice of appealing to animal metaphors then, in the following passage he uses them to devalue woman:

> You are on fire with your passion, and, led astray by the beauty of a comely head, you fail to see, poor man, that what you are wooing is a chimaera: yes, you refuse to learn that the three-formed monster is adorned with the face of a noble lion, polluted with the body of a stinking goat, armed with the tail of a rank viper: therefore I am forbidden to speak.[16]

13. Map, *De Nugis Curialium,* iv, c. 3, 307.
14. Map, *De Nugis Curialium,* iv, c. 3, 291.
15. Map, *De Nugis Curialium,* iv, c. 3, 309.
16. Map, *De Nugis Curialium,* iv, c. 3, 291.

If Map's satire were able to be considered merely as an imaginary or lighthearted treatise, it would not have had such a serious effect on the progressively more destructive devaluation of woman in western thought. However, it was interpreted by others as a serious account of woman's identity. One piece of evidence for this interpretation is found in the fact that the *Dissuasio Valerii* "retained its popularity long enough to be included in the earliest printed editions of the works of St. Jerome."[17] This printing of a religious text may have been the path for the later inclusion of parts of the satire in the manual *Malleus maleficarum,* which was used to study women's association with witchcraft.

This use of satirical texts by religious authors was also found in a tract entitled *Golias de conjuge non ducenda* (Golias on not being led into marriage). Golias, a purported Bishop of Coventry, wrote a Goliardic (Latin verse) poem that satirizes women as a means of arguing that a man should not marry. The poem is similar in content to the prose tract of *Valerius* by Map, and has been (most likely spuriously) attributed to him.[18] The poem was extremely popular in its original Latin form as well as in French and English translations. Goldschmidt claims that ". . . it appears in print at least four times, if not oftener, before 1500."[19] It is also suggested that the poem may have been an abbreviated version of the *Livre de Mathéolus.*[20] In a fifteenth-century English translation entitled "The Payne and Sorrowe of Evyll Maryage," the direct insertion of the concept of evil replaced the simple admonition to not be led into marriage that was suggested by the original title.[21] At the beginning of the poem, the speaker Golias reports that three angels or saints appeared to him in a dream and counseled him not to marry. The three themes being considered in this chapter, namely, (1) that women cannot govern themselves, (2) that they dangerously harm men, and (3) that they are like beasts in certain aspects appear in the following two stanzas of the poem:

17. James, introduction to *De Nugis Curialium,* p. xlvii.

18. See Thomas Wright, *The Latin Poems Commonly Attributed to Walter Mapes* (Hildesheim: Georg Olms Verlagsbuchhandlung, 1968), pp. 77-79. See also Francis Lee Utley, *The Crooked Rib: An Analytical Index to the Argument about Women in English and Scots Literature to the End of the Year 1568* (Columbus: Ohio State University Press, 1944), who notes that this poem was extremely popular. She identifies thirty-eight Latin manuscripts in England and continental Europe, including cities such as Paris, Oxford, Munich, Vienna, Venice, Dublin, Berne, Troyes, Tours, Geneva, Madrid, Jena, Eisleben, Melk, Padua, and Florence, #75, 136. Utley argues that "there is a strong possibility that *De Coniuge* was composed in England" (#75, 137).

19. Ernest Philip Goldschmidt, *Medieval Texts and Their First Appearance in Print* (London and Oxford: Oxford University Press, 1943). He notes two texts printed in 1490 in Paris (p. 35).

20. Goldschmidt considers this theory as follows: "The argument of the poem is termed 'per modum abbreviationis libri Matheoli,' a kind of abridgement of the *Mathéolus.* In so far as the *Livre de Mathéolus,* a very popular poem in French dating from about 1340, is also a warning against the evils of marriage, this is correct; only the chronological sequence is reversed, for the *Golias de Conjuge non ducenda* must be about a hundred years older. The French poem of Matheolus was frequently printed in the fifteenth and sixteenth centuries" (*Medieval Texts,* p. 37).

21. See Utley, *The Crooked Rib,* #75, 135-37. See also the Photostat Facsimile of the manuscript from the Huntington Library, STC 19119, which has as its cover a priest joining a man's and woman's hands in matrimony; and see, with slightly different spelling, the printed version of *The Latin Poems Commonly Attributed to Walter Mapes* (London: The Camden Society, 1861), pp. 295-99. The Hildesheim version of 1968 does not have the English text.

Wives are very unstable beasts
In their desires, which may not be changed,
Like a swallow which is insatiable:
Like a perilous piranha of the troubled sea:
A calm woe full of adversity,
Whose flattering meddles with disaster,
Called Sirens, yes full of variance. . . .

It is true, I tell you, young men everyone,
Women are variable and love many words and strife:
Who cannot appease them little or at all
Shall have care and sorrow all his life,
That regret the time that he ever took a wife;
and will take thought, and often muse
How he might find the way his wife to refuse.[22]

In the printed version of the English translation there is also added a hint of reversal in the final stanzas, when Golias suggests to the husband that he try "to do nothing against the pleasure of your wife."[23] However, he concludes that if the wife is still full of strife the husband should "set her upon fallow land and let the devil fetch her."[24] This mingling of women's weakness with the supernatural source of evil is a theme that will gain increased popularity in the fifteenth century.

The Spanish *El Corbacho* is another fifteenth-century satire written by a supposed religious author as based in part on an earlier text. It condemned women as a fearful source of evil for man. In the fourteenth century Boccaccio had written an Italian satire, *Corbaccio*, about a married man in purgatory who appeared to him in a dream and pronounced bitter judgments about his wife who was still alive.[25] In the fifteenth century the Spanish text appeared; it too contained a devaluation of women and of marriage. The printers gave it the title *El Corbacho*, even though it was not directly translated from Boccaccio's earlier work. In fact, it was more directly modeled after Andreas Cappellanus's *The Art of Courtly Love*, which had been written sometime in the twelfth century.[26]

22. "The Payne and Sorrowe of Evyll Maryage," in *The Latin Poems Commonly Attributed to Walter Mapes*, pp. 297-98. The poem is put into modern English by the author.

23. "The Payne and Sorrowe of Evyll Maryage," in *The Latin Poems Commonly Attributed to Walter Mapes*, p. 298.

24. "The Payne and Sorrowe of Evyll Maryage," in *The Latin Poems Commonly Attributed to Walter Mapes*, p. 298. It is interesting to note that this mention of the devil was added to the fifteenth-century printed edition.

25. See Chapter 3 for a description of Boccaccio's *Corbaccio*.

26. For a description of this text see Allen, *The Concept of Woman: The Aristotelian Revolution*, pp. 332-37. This text uses a theory of gender polarity to suggest to a young man that he ought not to engage in courtly love. In it woman is described as inconsistent, deceptive, prone to lying, a drunkard, loudmouthed, and unable to be loyal. See also Andreas Capellanus, *The Art of Courtly Love* (New York: Frederick Ungar Publishing Co., 1957), book 3, pp. 50-51. Per Nykrog notes in "Playing Games with Fiction," in *The Craft of Fiction: Essays in Medieval Poetics,* ed. Leigh A. Arrothoon (Rochester,

The original *El Corbacho* was written by Alfonso Martínez de Toledo, who was a Bachelor of Canon Law and Chaplain of the King of Castile.[27] While it is very possible that the text was written to satirize the original *Art of Courtly Love,* just as the *Corbaccio* was written as a satire of a compendium of satires, it nonetheless perpetuates certain negative stereotypes of women.[28] The fact that these devaluations of women were placed, however ironically, in the mouth of a member of the Church hierarchy in the fifteenth century gave them a certain credibility that may have had some serious implications for women in the later trials for witchcraft.

A similar link between literary satires and the devaluation of women by preachers is identified in a study of sermons.[29] First of all, woman is referred to as naturally weak in intellect and dangerous through her identification with the acts of Eve.[30] Woman is described as deceptive and dangerous for men because of her inordinate attachment to fancy clothes.[31] This deceptive characteristic of women is further developed by the use of animal metaphors in several sermons.[32] Finally, the greatest source of deception and danger of woman is depicted as deriving from her relation to the devil. These themes are integrated into sermons and then regularly dispersed through the pulpit:

> Woman's chief glory — not merely her little foibles and excesses — is by them accounted a snare and a delusion, her greatest field of activity little better than a wilderness of briars and pitfalls. "Woman," says our thirteenth-century author of

---

Mich.: Solaris Press, Inc., 1984), pp. 423-51, that the author of *El Corbacho* ". . . must have written with Andreas' book under his eyes. . . . The borrowings from Andreas reappear in Part 3 about female vices . . ." (p. 445).

27. Nykrog, "Playing Games with Fiction," in *The Craft of Fiction,* p. 444.

28. Nykrog suggests in "Playing Games with Fiction," in *The Craft of Fiction,* that the text was written in response to a serious text about love written by the Archpriest of Hita around 1340 and later called *El Libro de Buen Amor.* "A hypothesis begins to take shape: what Alfonso Martínez de Toledo wrote (with Andreas Capellanus' book lying open before him) was originally intended to be a playful and unserious, or downright parodic *Reprobatio amoris,* by 'the Archpriest of Talavera,' 'to match the Bok of Love, by the "Archpriest of Hita"'" (p. 447).

29. See Gerald R. Owst, *Literature and Pulpit in Medieval England* (New York: Barnes and Noble, 1961) and *Preaching in Medieval England: An Introduction to Sermon MS. of the Period 1350-1450* (New York: Russell and Russell, 1965). See also Solveig Eggerz-Brownfield, "Anti-feminist Satire in German and English Literature of the Late Middle Ages," Ph.D. Diss., Catholic University of America, 1981. Part Three: "Basically Didactic Uses of Anti-Feminist Invective: B. The Sermon and C. Sermon in Verse," pp. 114-32.

30. Owst, *Preaching,* Referring to the Dominican Humbertus de Romanis's statements about why women should not preach, Owst states: "Women must be excluded from the pulpits, he says, first because they lack sufficient intelligence, secondly because an inferior role in life has been given them by God, thirdly because in such a position they would provoke immorality; fourthly, owing to the folly of the first woman, Eve, who as St. Bernard pointed out, by opening her mouth on a certain occasion, brought ruin to the whole world" (p. 5).

31. Owst, *Preaching,* pp. 172, 183, 218, 295, 344. This theme is also central to the satire in *Quinze joies.*

32. Owst, *Literature and Pulpit,* pp. 396-400. Regarding woman's excessive adornments, there are many uses of animal images such as the Devil's hens, Devil's owls, or Devil's peacocks to entrap, ensnare, and destroy men's souls.

the *Speculum Laicorum,* quoting Vincent of Beauvais, "as saith Secundus the Philosopher, is the confusion of Man, an insatiable beast, a continual anxiety, an incessant warfare, a daily ruin, a house of tempest, a hindrance to devotion."[33]

Many handbooks for confessors and preachers were circulated at this time.[34] By the mid-fifteenth century, many different authors began to write academic treatises about the phenomenon of witchcraft. Around 1445, Johannes a Turrecremata, a canon lawyer, raised the question in his *Commentarius in Decretum Gratiani* whether "the folly of magicians abounds to a greater extent in the female or the male sex."[35] He concluded that it is found more in women, and that one characteristic of this magic was the creation of illusion through cooperation with the devil.

NEW SATIRES AGAINST WOMEN

While Map's satirical text argued that a man **should not marry** because of the dangers of deceptive woman, in this chapter we will consider some examples of new satirical texts written about men **who had married**, and who later regretted it. In particular, two French satires, *Le Miroir de mariage* (The Mirror of Marriage) and *Les Quinze joies de mariage* (The Fifteen Joys of Marriage), reveal a continuity of satirical arguments within a gender polarity community of discourse. The accentuated characteristics of women in these works will be seen to be diametrically opposed to those previously emphasized by early Renaissance Humanist authors and by religious women authors. Another theme that will emerge is that of deception. Here, instead of intergender dialogue being a medium for a complementary approach to truth, it becomes used for the dispersion of falsehoods; instead of intergender dialogue involving a mutual search for what is good, it becomes a medium for evil acts.

The main subdivisions of the new satires being considered in this chapter are identified by the titles of the works being considered rather than by the names of the authors. This identification of satire by title, rather than by author, is because the impact of a satire on subsequent thought was much greater than the influence of the author himself (or herself in later periods). Satirical texts circulated and helped promote stereotypes of gender polarity at the same time that they elicited a humorous response through exaggerating or inverting these stereotypes. Once

---

33. Owst, *Literature and Pulpit,* pp. 377-78. Owst also demonstrates how this view is integrated into later sermons on the dangers of relating to deceptive woman. Women become "the Devil's decoys" (p. 396). In addition, sermons introduced adjectives such as ". . . the diabolical anger of women" (p. 42). They also encouraged popular piety, which associated women with the devil in many other ways: "Besides thus lending credence to the ubiquity of devils, our homilists help also to maintain a popular belief in ghosts and fairies" (pp. 112-13).

34. See Edward Peters, *The Magician, the Witch, and the Law* (Philadelphia: University of Pennsylvania Press, 1978), p. 142. "Besides handbooks for confessors, such as the *Summa confessorum,* the thirteenth and fourteenth centuries also produced handbooks for preachers, of which one of the most extensive was the *Summa praedicantium* of John Bromyard, probably completed by 1349."

35. Peters, *The Magician, the Witch, and the Law,* p. 149.

written, satires had a kind of life of their own, separate from the particular intention of an author. This fact of influence of satires may be due, in part, to these stereotypes of woman they contained. Whatever the case, satires about women became an important component in the developing concept of woman in the period under consideration.

Le Miroir de mariage

This satire was composed by Eustache Deschamps (1346-?) sometime between 1381 and 1420.[36] *Le Miroir* is presented as a work of instruction with the purpose to encourage the reader to choose a contemplative life and a "spiritual marriage" rather than ordinary marriage. In this long text of 12,103 verses, Deschamps develops the theme that women will inevitably lead a man to unhappiness.[37]

Eustache Deschamps's motivation for writing this satire is difficult to assess, for he seemed to have been happily married and devoted to his daughter.[38] So it is unlikely that he opposed marriage. Deschamps also seemed fond of independent women; he was a friend of Christine de Pizan and wrote a poem about his admiration for her.[39] In addition, many of Deschamps's own poems were written in support of women.[40] At the same time, *Le Miroir de mariage* presents the usual satirical picture full of generalizations about a man who gets trapped by a woman through

36. See Monique Dufournaud-Engel, "Le *Miroir de mariage* d'Eustache Deschamps; édition critique accompagnée d'une étude littéraire et linguistique," 2 vols., Ph.D. Diss., McGill University, 1975. The author of this study places the composition between 1381 and 1389, while other critics place it later.

37. Alan M. F. Gunn, *The Mirror of Love: A Reinterpretation of "The Romance of the Rose"* (Lubbock, Tex.: Texas Tech Press, 1952), pp. 36-37. The discussion is about Deschamps's Ballad 285. Deschamps refers in one of his Ballads to Geoffrey Chaucer's translation of the *Roman de la Rose*, a reference which leads one commentator to suggest that Deschamps understood this work, not as a satire, but more as a romance.

38. His wife died in childbirth of their third child three years after they were married. See Laura Kendrick, "Transgression, Contamination, and Woman in Eustache Deschamps's *Miroir de mariage*," *Stanford French Review* 15, no. 102 (Spring-Fall 1990): 212. Kendrick also notes that Eustache Deschamps "had participated upon several occasions in marriage negotiations for the French royal family," which also appears to suggest that he did believe in the value of marriage (p. 213).

39. Dufournaud-Engel, "*Le Miroir de mariage* d'Eustache Deschamps," pp. 431-33.

40. See Deborah M. Sinnerich-Levi, "The Female Voice of the Male Poet: Eustache Deschamps' *Voix Féminisé*," in *Voices in Translation: The Authority of "Olde Bookes" in Medieval Literature* (Essays in Honor of Helaine Newstead), ed. Deborah M. Sinnreich-Levi and Gale Sigal (New York: AMS Press, 1992), p. 207-18. Sinnreich-Levi states: ". . . it cannot be ignored that one of every thirty extant poems of Deschamps comes to using a woman's voice" (p. 207). After examining several of these poems she concludes her article as follows: ". . . even this preliminary overview makes it clear that Deschamps can no longer be considered just another one of the herd of medieval, antifeminist ranters and ravers. His women speak with humanity, credibility, and passion. They represent women from all walks of life. Deschamps presents them sympathetically — the serving girl, the novices, the betrayed and embittered wives — allowing the reader to hear their individual voices in everyday scenes from fourteenth-century French life" (p. 217).

marriage. Deschamps's *Miroir* follows the pattern of previous satires that devalue women in order to convince a man not to marry.[41]

Le Miroir is written in the form of a dialogue among a variety of imaginary personified characters. The main male satirist, "Repertoire de Science," argues that a young man, "Franc Vouloir," should not marry. Other female characters "Desir," "Folie," "Servitude," and "Fantaisie" argue that he should marry.[42] The satire uses two modes of dialogue: the first is a dialogue of written letters between the Master "Repertoire de Science," who shares his knowledge of historical texts about marriage, and his student "Franc Vouloir," who is trying to decide whether or not to marry. The second mode is seen in a series of imaginary dialogues between the student and female personifications who support marriage but for all the wrong reasons, as their names so clearly suggest. These imaginary female personifications of desire, folly, servitude, and fantasy essentially embody deception. So even the structure of the dialogue itself supports a theme of gender polarity: the master-student exchange takes place in the traditional male community of discourse, while the intergender dialogue involves a male student engaged with female personifications who all seek to deceive him.

The *Miroir de mariage* begins by invoking Aristotle's theories from *Ethics* and *Politics* to suggest that marriage is good for man. In the following passage, the gender division of spheres of activity into public and private is stipulated:

> A man is not supposed to have children,
> If he does not think of getting married;
> For no true order or household
> Can be sustained without marriage.
> You can see it well put, if you so wish,
> In the Ethics and Politics of Aristotle,
> Who explains it much better than us.
> Two bodies joined together,
> What a sweet sight it is!
> Bound together in one flesh by law
> And loving each other both when near and far.
> A man must rule in public;
> A woman must govern within the household.
> She has to be gentle in her use of words.
> The husband serves, makes love and cuddles
> And accepts, when he is to blame,
> So that she can reprimand him,
> Look at him with disdain,
> And often by means of her sweetness,

---

41. Since our purpose in this book is to trace the philosophical aspects of the developing concept of woman, we will limit our analysis to the philosophical aspects of Eustache's satirical *Miroir*, rather than attempt to give a thorough analysis of the thought of the author himself.

42. Kendrick translates the names of the characters in the text as "Repository of Knowledge," "Free Will," "Desire," "Folly," "Servitude," "Trickery," and "Transgression," p. 211.

Awaken him from a deadly languor.
She governs her household
And her income from other sources;
She is far-sighted, wise, and open-minded,
And sees to it that nothing is wasted;
She watches over her servants,
And when need be, knows how to be
Generous or stingy with her people.[43]

In this passage we also have a hint of trouble, which will be developed with great emphasis later, namely that if a woman rules in the household, then man serves. This loss of freedom by a man who has to obey a woman, even in the private sphere, becomes the focus of the satirical devaluation of woman.

As the text continues, the main satirical voice presented by "Repertoire de Science," a knowledgeable academic, continues to try to persuade his student "Franc Vouloir" not to marry. The satirist appeals to Aristotle to support a claim that a woman's beauty is dangerous for man. So again a woman deceives through her appearance of beauty and goodness, which actually leads to ugliness and evil. It is important to note in passing that this is a false attribution to Aristotle of a view he does not hold. However, Aristotle had by this time become such an important authority, and his views were so popular, that the character in the satire wants to invoke the philosopher Aristotle to support his own argument:

I also find in Seneca's and Aristotle's
Books where they speak about marriage
That a woman's beauty is the source
And the beginning of wrath,
For it derails the understanding
And breaks the counsel of the wise.
It sets on fire or stops heavy guns
And makes men set aside
The quest for a desired goal:
It channels onto the wrong path
The strong and the powerful
And makes them feel sorrow for it;
Wrathful, boorish,
Diligent, slothful,
Sweet, handsome, likeable,
Stupid and gullible men,
Kings, princes, barons,
Gentry, commoners, felons,
Clerics, nobles, bourgeois, knights,
People from all walks of life

43. Deschamps, *Miroir,* 209-38, I: 10-11. All passages from this text are translated by Dominique Deslandres.

Are all affected by a woman's beauty,
And plenty paid dearly for it.
Some were mutilated, killed, mind shattered,
Ruined, beaten, beheaded,
Others were put in all sorts of danger,
Lost their body, damned their spirit,
Cut short the course of their life.[44]

This claim that woman's beauty leads men to vice is directly opposed to the humanist articulation of the theme that beauty in a woman may help a man to virtue. In this shift we also see that intergender dialogue used by the earlier humanists Petrarch, Dante, and Boccaccio as the medium through which a man could discover his own proper good, now degenerates into a medium for a man's loss of his proper good and his fall into ultimate destruction. A woman's beauty is described as being so dangerous that it can lead to the mutilation or death of the body, or even to the damnation of the soul.

The satirist suggests to his student that he will not be strong enough to engage directly with this dangerous force of a woman's beauty:

Son, be aware of this:
You are not stronger than Samson,
Nor wiser than Solomon,
More knowledgeable than Theophrastes,
Or more vigilant than Philip,
The King of Macedonia.
Are you more ingenious than Hercules?
A better intellectual than Aristotle,
Or Seneca? Wiser than Plato?
More steadfast than Socrates or Cato?
Of course not, do not deny it.[45]

So, instead of engaging in dialogue with a beautiful woman, as the early humanists proposed, the satirist suggests that the young man will not be able to do the same thing without being destroyed. He concludes that any attempt at fruitful dialogue between a woman and a man is naive and impossible.

To support this claim, the professor introduces into the satire many other traditional authorities who have argued that marriage is not good for man:

Neither Juvenal, Catullus, Ovid,
Nor Virgil the philosopher
Nor others, to prove it,
Were ever able to restrain themselves,
And became so excited by their senses

44. Deschamps, *Miroir,* 5317-42, I: 153.
45. Deschamps, *Miroir,* 5529-39, I: 158-59.

That they fell into traps laid by women,
Thus being humiliated or dying.
How many kings, knights or thinkers
Whose deeds I mentioned,
Have been ruined by women,
Or killed, destroyed, and persecuted
Because of them!
Their authority and the examples
In their books ought to advise you
Not to fall into such mishaps,
Since you are aware of them
You would lose even more your senses,
If your behaviour were contrary to their teachings.
For the ancients' examples
Are for us cords and links
To keep us away from grave perils
Which we find in their writings
And clearly see that they can lead
to our end after much suffering
in the body and in the soul.[46]

When Laura Kendrick analyzes the *Miroir de mariage* with respect to its "mirroring" qualities, she notes that it fits into a common practice in "late-medieval vernacular personification allegories" of describing exterior conflicts (between men and women, husbands and wives) and internalizing them by introducing visible material (mirroring) forms.[47] If a man rejects marriage by rejecting (and controlling) a woman, then he controls himself. So Kendrick concludes that Deschamps, along with other satirists, suggests that a man achieves self-governance by rejecting women altogether, and that the will to reject women is achieved by the devaluation of woman in the mind of the man, so that he no longer wants to relate to her.[48]

One way in which the devaluation of woman occurs in many satires is the introduction of vertical metaphors that compare humans and animals. In itself, however, the use of an animal metaphor to describe a human being is not necessarily to devalue him or her. In fact, sometimes they are used in a positive manner, to indicate a virtue such as courage or daring, or a natural quality such as beauty, peacefulness, or quickness. Thus, it is important to examine the particular quality of the animal being selected and its relation to human character. In the author being considered here, animal metaphors are used primarily to devalue woman. Thus

---

46. Deschamps, *Miroir,* 5547-71, I: 159.
47. Kendrick, "Transgression," p. 215.
48. Kendrick concludes in "Transgression": "Deschamps' lengthy argument for chastity as opposed to marriage in the *Miroir* is a purgative; it is an obsessive effort to expel impurity — figured as wives — and thereby to attain a condition of spotless integrity protected from future contamination by enclosure, by the fixing of limits not to be transgressed" (p. 229).

we could call these examples of **downward vertical analogies** in contrast to **upward vertical analogies** found in philosophers like Plato, who compare the sun with the good, or the state with the soul.[49] In Plato's vertical analogies, the purpose is to elevate the mind from an analogate observed by the senses (e.g., the sun) to an intellectual analogate (e.g., the good); while the satirists who use animal metaphors aim to lower the mind from one analogate of the higher faculties of human identity (of intellect and will) to an analogate common to bestial activity, or the lowest aspects of human identity. So the vertical analogy in the satire is used not for an **ascending** but a **descending** aspect of wisdom and/or virtue.

The attribution of animal qualities to women, as a medium for their devaluation, has a long history in satirical communities of discourse. Juvenal, Ovid, Capellanus, Map, *Le Roman de la rose, Le Livre de Mathéolus, L'Évangile,* and the *Corbaccio* all invoked derogatory animal metaphors to describe woman. Eustache Deschamps continues this tradition, and adds even more detail to these downward vertical analogies. For example, he suggests that a woman should be chosen like a horse for breeding; a woman is like a pig in her lack of virtue; by being kept in the private sphere a woman becomes like a goat who knows only how to pasture, or a cat that burns its fur by the fireplace, or an animal unable to raise her head; a woman of evil character has a wrinkled face like a bear or lioness; a woman waits like a wolf for her prey in the fields and roads; and melancholic women hate men as ewes hate wolves.[50] Deschamps also uses animal analogies to describe men who get caught in traps set by women. A man who remains free of marriage is like a bird that can fly where it chooses, a man who is tamed by a wife is like a sheep or a cow, a man who is deceived by his wife is like a fish caught on a hook, and a married man is led like a cow to the sacrifice or like a bird that is caught by falcons.[51]

In conclusion, we can note four gender-related aspects in Eustache Deschamps's *Le Miroir de mariage:* (1) the use of female personifications to embody by name the theme of deception, (2) the argument that a woman's beauty is dangerous to a man, (3) the increased use of downward vertical analogies to compare a woman with animals, and (4) the invocation of Aristotle as an authority for the devaluation of woman. This French satire reverses the momentum we recognized in early Renaissance Humanist writers and in women religious authors. Women were no longer viewed as wise and good through self-knowledge and self-governance, and thus as able to lead men to wisdom and virtue through dialogue. Satires, through exaggeration, inversion, and universalization supported a gender polarity model of woman's identity, and in so doing they added further strength to bias concerning the natural inferiority of woman.

---

49. For a discussion of vertical analogies see the beginning of Chapter 5.

50. See Eustache Deschamps, *Oeuvres complètes* (Paris: Firmin Didot, 1903), vol. 9, *Le Miroir de mariage,* XVII: 1553-75, XVIII: 1656-66, XXXV: 3207-30, LVIII: 6037-38, and LVIII: 6072-74. See also Kendrick, "Transgression": A woman is "more gluttonous than the cat that shoves its muzzle into everything" and "trails like a bloodhound" (pp. 224, 227).

51. Deschamps, *Miroir,* VIII: 523-31; XII: 894-905; XXXIX: 3738; and LVI: 5780-88.

Les Quinze joies de mariage

A popular French satire on women, *Les Quinze joies de mariage* (The Fifteen Joys of Marriage) was composed in the middle fifteenth century and modeled on the *Miroir de mariage*. It was probably first printed in Lyons in 1480-1490.[52] Antoine de la Sale has often been suggested as its author but this attribution has not been authenticated. While the *Miroir de mariage* was a ponderous volume of several hundred pages, *Les Quinze joies de mariage,* written over half a century later, presented the same message in a lighter, more ironic text of less than a hundred pages.

Les Quinze joies is an imaginary dialogue between a husband and a wife, reflected on by a narrator who describes fifteen different stages within a marriage. In each stage what appears to be a source of joy turns out to be the opposite, that is, a source of great suffering and torment. The whole text also suggests a devaluation not only of woman in marriage, but also of the Blessed Virgin Mary through its ridicule of the fifteen decades of prayer of the Rosary.[53] The Rosary, a dialogue form of prayer in which the suppliant speaks with Mary, uses the words believed to have been said in the original dialogue of the Annunciation by the Angel Gabriel ("Hail Mary Full of Grace, the Lord is with you"), and adds a personal prayer ("Holy Mary, Mother of God, pray for us sinners now and at the hour of our death"). Inserted in the middle of each of the fifteen decades is the prayer of Jesus Christ, "Our Father," and the praise of the Trinity by the suppliant, "Glory be to the Father, and to the Son, and to the Holy Spirit." The prayer is based on the belief that Mary, the perfect model of virtue, can help lead men and women to a life of wisdom and virtue through her intercession with God. In the satire, the basic premise, that a beautiful and good woman can help lead others through dialogue to a more virtuous life, is subverted. Instead, the woman who appears good turns out to be evil, and instead of leading man to his salvation, she leads him to his destruction.

An interplay of appearance and reality combined with the devaluation of woman functions throughout *Les Quinze joies.* While the traditional Rosary passes through a genuine progression of five joyful, five sorrowful, and five glorious mysteries, the satire presents fifteen apparently joyful mysteries that are really fifteen sorrowful mysteries. The pattern of devaluation in the satire follows that identified in Chapter 3 in the discussion of *L'Evangile* and *Frau Welt*. In *Les Quinze joies* a young man, like a fish swimming in the sea, thinks that a married man is very happy and so he follows the same course until he gets caught in a net. The young man, who is referred to as "the goodman" throughout the text, is put through a purgatory on earth by his evil wife who constantly deceives him. So the woman, instead of helping her husband to his proper end through her own wisdom and vir-

---

52. *The Fifteen Joys of Marriage* (New York: Orion Press, 1959), intro., pp. v-vii.

53. It is interesting to note in passing that pious legend holds that the Rosary was first established by St. Dominic in the early thirteenth century. Several Popes affirmed its value in the centuries we are now considering: Urban IV (1264), Sixtus IV (1484), and Innocent VIII (1492). See David Supple, O.S.B., ed., *Virgin Wholly Marvelous: Praises of Our Lady by the Popes, Councils, Saints, and Doctors of the Church* (Cambridge: Ravengate Press, 1991), pp. 131-33.

tue, destroys him through her conscious association with evil. She appears good and beautiful to the man, but actually turns out to be the opposite.

When the particular characteristics of the wife are described in the usual mode of satire, they are exaggerated and universalized to extend to all women.[54] The first joy is ruined by the greed of the wife, the second by her unfaithfulness, the third by her sloth, gluttony, and uncontrolled gossiping, and the fourth by her rage. Here again we find the usual exaggeration of women's characteristic vices, which flow from an inability to rule their emotions, or from a lack of self-governance. These same kinds of vices are also the key to the eleventh, twelfth, thirteenth, and fifteenth joys.[55]

In addition we encounter the typical satirical inversion of ruling and obedience in the two remaining joys, the fifth and fifteenth. Each joy is described in a short story that includes dialogue and reflection on specific examples. In one, the author describes a marriage between a man who is inferior to his wife by age or by nobility. He concludes: ". . . there is nothing more destructive to a man than to become entangled in these two bonds that are so contrary to nature and to reason."[56]

In the above passage it is not woman *per se* who is the cause of the inversion and the focus of the satire, but her class or age. However, the author also considers the inversion in which a man is forced to obey a woman. In the fourteenth joy, the husband complains that he has lost authority over his family. To his wife he says: "You know that I am master of the house and will be so as long as I live, but no one acts as if I were."[57] Then to his son, who is in league with his wife, the man adds: ". . . I note that you have assumed authority and taken over the conduct of my property. Do not make so bold, but think of serving me and obeying me as you should."[58] The wife then answers: "We cannot tell how to serve you. For he who would be ever at your beck and call would have too much to do."[59] The wife and

---

54. For a detailed consideration of the interplay of the author of the text and the narrator, as well as the particular and universal, see Per Nykrog, "Playing Games with Fiction," in *The Craft of Fiction*: "This writer [of *Les Quinze joies de mariage*] is not a simple-minded automaton; the *narrator* may be, the *writer* is not; he is a joker, and a subtle one, too. His game consists of oscillating back and forth over the borderline between universal truth and specific individual events, alternatively sending signals indicating one and the other of these in such a way that the reader is kept constantly (and delightfully) in doubt as to whether the narrative is of one type or of the other" (p. 431). Again we have to ask: Which community of discourse is delighted by this blurring of the distinction between universal and specific?

55. For a discussion of the interconnection of the fifteen different joys see Nykrog, "Playing with Fiction," in *The Craft of Fiction*: "The unspecific anonymity of the main protagonists, husband and wife, and the fact that the dialogues between them are written by the same author, more or less in the same style, establishes a sort of identity between *dramatis personae* from one 'Joy' to another. But only in the way well-known and easily recognizable comedians can appear in different shows; the 'Joys' are not sequels to one another, nor are they independent stories; they are alternative routes starting out from the same typical, joyous honeymoon (with one exception), branching off at different points, but all eventually leading to the same, ritually repeated conclusion: the husband spending the rest of his life in torment and misery" (p. 434).

56. *Fifteen Joys,* 69.

57. *Fifteen Joys,* 140-41.

58. *Fifteen Joys,* 141-42.

59. *Fifteen Joys,* 142.

son conclude that the husband is senile, and they decide to completely undermine his authority. The author concludes: "Thus is the goodman ruled, who has lived honourably and conducted himself and his household well, as you may believe."[60]

Throughout the text, the intergender dialogue presents the imaginary wife as consistently deceiving the husband. In the following example, extracted from a longer section in the text, we see the narrator inserting the theme of woman's deception of man:

> Then to tempt her, as he thinks, he says to her: "If I were to die you would soon be married to another."
>
> "Fie! Fie!" says she, "for all the pleasure I have had from it! I swear by God never would lips of man touch mine, and if I knew I would outlive you, I would see to it that I went first."
>
> And she begins to weep.
>
> Thus the good lady comports herself (though she thinks quite the contrary). . . .[61]

The deception is focused on the wife's desire for new clothes, and her manipulation to achieve this end even when there is little money to buy these items for her. The husband gives in to her desires, but is overridden by creditors, and then blamed by the wife: "Thus the lady complains and thinks not of the part she has played in it, of the gowns and jewels she must needs have . . . but she puts all the blame upon the poor man who, mayhap, has no blame at all."[62]

Women's deception is not only portrayed by the wife but is shared by those who are close to her. In the following passage the narrator describes the collusion between the wife and her servants to deceive the husband about the wife's state of health:

> . . . and he asks how she is. And the serving-wench, who is nursing her, tells him she is very sick and has eaten nothing since he left; but she is a little better this evening — however, this is all lies. At this the poor man's grief increases. . . . And perhaps the poor man has not eaten all day long and he will not eat till he has news of his lady and knows how she is. The nurse and the old midwives, who are in the secret and clever at such tricks, play their parts well and pull long faces. . . .
>
> Now the next day he gets up very early and goes to see his lady and asks her how she is, and she says that she was a little better towards day but that she did not sleep all night; though in reality she has slept soundly.[63]

Thus deception is described as the wife's usual aim in intergender dialogue.

Even though the joys and sorrows of the married man are portrayed as if they

---

60. *Fifteen Joys,* 144.
61. *Fifteen Joys,* 21-22.
62. *Fifteen Joys,* 26.
63. *Fifteen Joys,* 44-46.

concerned only a single individual, the author makes it clear in the conclusion that he is giving a general description:

> Moreover, as a general rule, the things above mentioned befall men, as I have said; and I do not say, nor would I say, that all those joys, or even two or three of them, come to every husband; but I can say for certain that there is no married man, however discreet, prudent or wily he may be, who does not have at least one of those joys or several of them. Wherefore we may well conclude that the man who deliberately puts himself into such servitude, does so of his own free will.[64]

In an interesting twist, the author reveals in the conclusion of *Les Quinze joies* that he was aware of devaluing women in the text, for he asks that "no lady, demoiselle or other women may take it ill of me."[65] Then he adds that he wrote the book at the request of women, and that he would be willing to write another text in which men were presented as the culprits rather than as the victims. This raises the interesting question of whether the author is simply covering himself for what appears to be his bias against women, or whether he was in fact just as willing to write a satire against men as against women. Of course, it is not possible to determine the answer to this question so far removed from the time of authorship without further evidence to support one or the other hypothesis. Nonetheless, even if the author's true intention cannot be determined, it is certainly true that the satire in itself had a part to play in the dispersion of the devaluation of women and of marriage. The final lines of the satire summarize the original paradox of appearance and reality:

> Though, as I have said in good faith, all is in praise of women; and he who understands what I have written here will find that men have ever the worst part, which is an honour to women. And I have written it at the request of certain demoiselles who urged me to do so. And if they are not satisfied and would have me take the trouble to write for them, on their behalf and against men, I offer myself in good faith. For therein have I better material than this, seeing the great wrongs, griefs and oppressions men do unto women in divers places, generally by brute force and for no reason. For women are naturally weak and defenceless and are always ready to obey and to serve, without which men should not, nor might not, live.[66]

In *Les Quinze joies* we see an inversion that involves a double play on appearance and reality. In the first case the woman appears to be good but she turns out to be evil, and marriage appears to offer joy, but it actually offers sorrow. In the second case, after the ironic inversion at the end of the text when man **appears** to be good and simply the victim of women, man **actually** turns out to be evil by his use of brute force, oppression, and lack of reason; and woman, who **appears** to be evil, turns out **actually** to be good by being naturally weak, defenseless, obedient, full of

---

64. *Fifteen Joys,* 219-22.
65. *Fifteen Joys,* 221.
66. *Fifteen Joys,* 221.

service, and helping men live. However, in this second inversion of appearance and reality we see the author identifying the theme of woman's natural inferiority as the partial cause of her goodness.[67] We could say that he incorporates an Aristotelian rationale for gender polarity within his Platonic play of the falseness of appearance in relation to reality.

In this satire we also find the inversion of animal metaphors that has usually been found in satires against women. Instead of woman being devalued by being compared with different kinds of beasts, we discover the most derogatory metaphors being applied to men. However, since the whole satire inverts the traditional role of obedience as a virtue for women and ruling for men, it could be said that the animal metaphors actually apply to a woman as she is expected to be instead of the man as he is satirically perceived to be. So the downward vertical application of animal metaphors, which appears to be about men, is actually about women. Some examples may help make this point clearer.

The husband is described as like a beast caught in a pit trap in the forest or a fish trap in the water; the goodman is so worn out by worries that he refuses to move when prodded like an old hardened donkey; the goodman works so hard for her outdoors that he is covered with more mud than a dog; the goodman does everything immediately that his wife asks him to so that he is considered as tame as a lively ox at the plow. In fact, the good man is so trusting even when constantly deceived by his wife that he patiently endures and suffers everything "like an old toothless bear, fettered with a great iron chain, muzzled, and fastened to a huge wooden bar, whose only revenge is to roar, and every time he roars he is given two or three blows more."[68]

The woman, however, is described as an animal trainer that puts out bait to catch a husband who will then give her money to buy clothes way beyond his means. She is full of insatiable sexual desires and continually seeks ways to fool him, like a fish swimming up a stream, by seeking out adulterous affairs.[69] In sum, the woman reduces the man to an animal-like existence through her own debase-

67. Nykrog interprets this reversal as an accurate depiction of the writer's real views. See "Playing Games with Fiction," in *The Craft of Fiction:* "In an Epilogue, more well-intentioned, apparently, than stylistically elegant or even understandable, he (assuming that the epilogue and the book are by the same man), states that his intentions have been, at least partly, to write in honor and praise of women! And what is more, he seems to be serious here, not ironical. The problem is that husbands let themselves be cowed (*abestis,* the word had come up several times in the 'Joys') and stultified, and the writer (somehow I feel, paradoxically, that it is the writer who speaks here, and not a narrator-mask) has come to the conclusion that this is brought about by *la nature du jeu*" (p. 435).

68. *Fifteen Joys,* XIV, 191. See also prologue, 7-8; IV, 57; VIII, 132; and XII, 171-72. In addition, see Stephen M. Taylor, "Wifely Wiles: Comic Unmasking in *Les Quinze joyes de mariage,*" in *New Images of Medieval Women: Essays Towards a Cultural Anthropology,* ed. Edelgard E. DuBruck (Lewiston/ Queenstown: Edwin Mellen Press, 1989), pp. 287-302. Marriage is dangerous for a man, who by nature is free and intelligent, because "[unlike] the caterpillar and the butterfly, the carefree young bachelor loses his individuality and becomes a drab drudge" (p. 291).

69. *Fifteen Joys,* Prologue 8-9 and IV, 192. See also Taylor, "Wifely Wiles," p. 289. "Thus, by using the concrete metaphors of the pit, the sack and the net, the author of *Les quinze joyes* succeeds in creating a comic transposition that heightens our appreciation of the incongruity inherent in marriage as he views it while it prepares us to accept the spouses themselves as animal and trainer" (p. 291).

ment. The author describes her as lacking all virtue; she is greedy, lustful, spiteful, cruel, and selfish. He says about her: "For when it comes to understanding, the wisest woman in the world has no more than I have gold in my eye or an ape has tail; for understanding fails her before she is half way through what she would do or say."[70] In one telling passage that anticipates the discussion about women and evil in witchcraft, the author tells us: "Thus is the goodman benumbed and transformed into a very beast, and through no magic."[71]

The assertion that the wife is like an animal trainer and the husband like a trained animal may appear to invert the traditional gender polarity model in favor of the woman. In other words, a trainer needs to be disciplined, have a clear objective, and initiate action to bring about a transformation of the animal undergoing the training. In fact, Taylor suggests, "If his primary comic trait is submissiveness, the medieval caricaturist posits that the wife's is assertiveness."[72] The woman, however, is also described as having an insatiable need to fulfill her own pleasures; and her domination of the man is effected with primarily this end in view. She uses her discursive reason to figure out ways to keep men in bondage to give herself pleasure. So the result of her calculated actions is to render men incapable of independent thinking and action.

Furthermore, in *Les Quinze joies* women are described as joining together to teach each other these methods of training. The satire also inverts the usual private/public gender-differentiated sphere of action, so that the woman engages in public activity while the husband remains alone, without friends, relegated to the private sphere of the household. Taylor concludes: "Thus, united by training and taste, married women face their isolated and brutish opponents with equanimity, using words as whips to keep their spouses in the traces. As the tricksters in the marriage relationship, wives receive the reader's approbation."[73] It would be important to think about which community of readers would approve of this satire. It is highly unlikely that most female communities of discourse would approve of the concept of woman because of the devaluation of woman's character that occurs consistently throughout the satire. In spite of the inversion of the usual polarity of ruling and obedience, the satire distorts the use of reason and will as well as intergender dialogue and relationships. So, even though the woman rules and the man obeys, it is a forced and degenerate form of ruling that lowers the level of human identity as represented by the numerous animal metaphors. Finally, woman is depicted as the evil force, destructive of man.[74]

---

70. *Fifteen Joys*, XII, 172-73.

71. *Fifteen Joys*, VII, 122. The fear that witches could turn men into animals is explicitly discussed in the *Malleus*.

72. Taylor, "Wifely Wiles," in *New Images of Medieval Women*, p. 295.

73. Taylor, "Wifely Wiles," p. 300. For a similar response to the satire see Nykrog, "Playing Games with Fiction." "What he has produced is technically unique, one of the most extraordinarily sophisticated texts in French literature. He is having fun, and so are we" (p. 435).

74. For another description of the evil character of the woman see Brent A. Pitts, "Feast and Famine in the *Quinze joyes de mariage*," *Romance Notes* 26, no. 1 (Fall 1985): 69-73. "Throughout the QJ and at every point in her development, the wife is portrayed as a wily, shark-like predator seeking sexual gratification, ostentatious finery, physical satisfaction, and domestic *seigneurie*" (pp. 69-70).

With the help of printing, satires such as *Les Quinze joies de mariage* were made available to wide audiences. The increasing severity of satires on a number of topics led to the issuing of an edict in 1599 in England to burn the English translation of an earlier version of this text along with others, and the prohibition against their further printing.[75] However, a new English translation of this text entitled *The Bachelor's Banquet* was published in 1603 with several more editions until 1677. Then in 1682 another edited translation appeared entitled: *The XV Comforts of Rash and Inconsiderate Marriage, or Select Animadversions Upon the Miscarriage of a Wedded State.* This latter version attempted to revise the direction of the original text by undermining the universal application of its premises to all marriage, and instead limiting its application to some poorer examples of marriage.[76] This is a case of a more appropriate limitation of satire to certain kinds of women rather than to all women.

In conclusion, we have found two different kinds of philosophical presuppositions in satires written during the thirteenth to fifteenth centuries. Those that followed an Aristotelian model exaggerated women's weaknesses and imperfection, and inverted traditional male and female virtues and vices. In these examples, the appearance **was** the reality. In the Aristotelian model, women are what they appear to be. This model implies that women cannot help but be by nature what they appear to be. This model opens the way for satirists to use animal metaphors that reduce women to a lower than human nature as exemplified in the model of man as a rational animal.

The second kind of philosophical presupposition followed a more Platonic model in which appearance and reality were presented as significantly different. What appeared to be the case was not actually so, and while appearance pretended to offer happiness and virtue, reality produced sorrow and vice. Woman was always the object of this paradox of appearance and reality. Thus in the Platonic model women interfere with man's reason by deceiving him through his senses. This sensual seduction is dangerous because it is consciously chosen by women to ultimately control and rule men. The specific vices of women chosen for emphasis within the Platonic paradox of appearance and reality were taken from the Aristotelian model of the natural inferiority of woman, except for her cunning deception. Thus the Platonic and Aristotelian models blended together at certain points in their descriptions of specific characteristics of woman's identity.

Usually, the connection between the satire and an assumed philosophical theory was not directly made. However, at times specific philosophers were directly named. In those latter cases, the line to Aristotle was able to be traced through authors such as Boccaccio, de Meun, Mathéolus, Map, Juvenal, and Theophrastus. For Aristotle, virtue usually involved acts that "follow the mean" between two ex-

---

75. John Peter, *Complaint and Satire in Early English Literature* (Oxford: Clarendon Press, 1965), pp. 146-48.

76. Wayne Huebner, "Convention and Innovation in the Satirical Treatment of Women by the Major Satirists of the Early Eighteenth Century," Ph.D. Diss., University of Minnesota, 1964, p. 34. He also mentions the following other texts that entered into the debate: *The Fifteen Pleasures of Matrimony* (1682), *The Fifteen Real Comforts of Matrimony* (1683), *The Confession of the Newly Married Couple* (1683), and *The Fifteen Comforts of Matrimony* (1706).

tremes. Women's vices nearly always were depicted as acts that headed towards the extreme, particularly the incapacity to rule over her own emotions and her unmitigated desire to rule over others, particularly her husband. Therefore, these satires function as an important source for the popularization of Aristotelian theory with its devaluation of women through a philosophy of gender polarity.

INTERGENDER DIALOGUE IN ARRESTS AND TRIALS OF INDIVIDUAL WOMEN

In this section of the chapter our approach will shift from a theoretical analysis of the content of satires about women to a practical consideration of two particular women who engaged in public dialogue with men about their identity as a woman. The existence of public documents that recorded their dialogues allows this philosophical analysis to be rooted in a unique manner. It offers us the opportunity to see whether some of the stereotypical views of women, so prominent in satires and in academic theories of gender polarity, actually penetrated into the lives of particular women. Again it should be noted that while it is not possible to defend a direct causal connection among these factors, it is possible to indicate coincidences in expression and prescriptive force that operated in all three areas of satires, academia, and public trials.

We consider first the example of a woman frequently accused of heresy[77] between 1413 and 1438. Margery Kempe, a middle-aged married woman and mother of fourteen children, always managed to escape conviction and punishment through her own efforts at self-defense as well as through the help of others who knew her. Margery Kempe wrote the first autobiography in the English language; it contains detailed accounts of her public dialogues in the context of these arrests.

Then we consider the example of a young single woman accused of heresy in France in 1431. Joan of Arc was eventually turned over to the English for punishment and, like Marguerite Porete in 1310, was executed by burning at the stake. The meticulous notes made by some of the notaries both at Joan of Arc's original trials for heresy and at her rehabilitation trial twenty years later provide good records of the dialogue that occurred at the time. We will see that even though the life stories of these women span different countries and different ages they share a similar plight of being in forced public dialogues, as uneducated women with educated men. Both women had the threat of death at the end of the interrogation because of their perceived association with some form of evil.

Margery Kempe (1373–ca. 1438)

Margery Kempe was married for twenty years (1393-1413), during which

---

77. For the original documents that define basic heresies see Edward Peters, ed., *Heresy and Authority in Medieval Europe: Documents in Translation* (Philadelphia: University of Pennsylvania Press, 1980).

time she bore fourteen children. Then she spent twenty-five years of celibate life (1413-1438), many while her husband was still alive, wandering throughout England and Europe and taking pilgrimages to Rome, Jerusalem, and Spain.[78] She clearly saw herself as part of a religious tradition of women. In Chapter 5 we briefly considered her admiration for St. Bridget of Sweden after whom she seems to have consciously modeled herself. Margery Kempe was acquainted with Bridget's writings and in 1415, the year of St. Bridget's canonization, she actually went to visit her lodgings in Rome. It may have been significant to Margery that Bridget's religious experiences had been somewhat suspect during her life, and that with her canonization she had gained a respectability that Margery longed for herself.

In addition, in 1414 Margery Kempe spent several days in conversation with Julian of Norwich. Her self-perception as a religious woman of the lay state would likely have been greatly enhanced by these private dialogues with Julian. As we mentioned previously in our study, Julian of Norwich had written a short text of her revelations in 1373 and a longer text around 1393. At the time of her discussions with Margery Kempe, Julian would have been at the height of her maturity as an author. It is impossible to know whether either Bridget's or Julian's example of writing about their revelations directly influenced Margery to write about her own life. However, in 1436 Margery composed the story of her life.[79] This invaluable account entitled *The Book of Margery Kempe* has become known as the first autobiography written in English.[80]

This text of Margery Kempe was dictated to two scribes rather than written directly by her. The first scribe was an unnamed man, with very poor penmanship and spelling, who some scholars believe was her son. The second was a priest from England who rewrote the first part and tried to protect Margery from charges of heresy.[81] Thus Margery's actual composition of the written text was the result of private intergender dialogue. In the text, Margery Kempe also mentions that a priest had read to her from works by Hilton and Bonaventure;[82] and she also indicates an awareness of the works of Augustine.[83] It is very possible that she had studied Augustine's *Confessions* and that these provided a model for her own autobiography, especially in its frankness in discussion of sexual matters and her continual process of conversion.

The relation between Margery and this priest who read to her is very impor-

---

78. For a good summary of the stages in her life, see Maureen Fries, "Margery Kempe," in *An Introduction to the Medieval Mystics of Europe,* ed. Paul E. Szarmach (Albany: State University of New York Press, 1984), ch. ix, p. 217.

79. *The Book of Margery Kempe: A Modern Version by W. Butler-Bowdon* (New York: The Devin-Adair Company, 1944). "Her first work, so ill written and ill spelt as to have been almost unintelligible, was finished by 1432, and four years later she began to re-write it" (p. 234).

80. *The Book of Margery Kempe: A Modern Version by W. Butler-Bowdon* (London: Jonathan Cape, 1936), pp. 215-16. See also the recent translation by Tony D. Triggs, *The Book of Margery Kempe: The Autobiography of the Madwoman of God* (Liguori, Mo.: Triumph Books, 1995). All quotations will be taken from the Triggs translation unless otherwise noted.

81. C. W. Atkinson, *Mystic and Pilgrim: The Book and World of Margery Kempe* (Ithaca, N.Y.: Cornell University Press, 1983), pp. 28-30, 112.

82. *The Book of Margery Kempe,* ch. 58, p. 127.

83. "Margery Kempe's Prayers," in *The Book of Margery Kempe,* p. 214.

tant to our study. She tells us that this priest "who comes from a long way off" took an interest in her and "read me books for the best part of seven or eight years. . . ."[84] In effect, Margery received a private tutorial in higher education during these many years. Margery emphasizes the spiritual content of what she learned. "Listening to all these holy books and listening to sermons steadily deepened my ability in meditation and the contemplation of things divine."[85] It would also seem that she learned how to think and follow discursive reasoning during this period of intellectual formation. She relates that the priest read her scholarly commentaries on the Bible and, as we mentioned above, works by Augustine and Bonaventure, among others. It seems then that even though Margery was "illiterate" because she could neither read nor write, she received an education orally, and because she had an excellent memory, she was able to repeat theories, arguments, and stories from classical religious texts. Thus Margery Kempe did gain considerable knowledge through the long-term intergender dialogue with the man who read to her and who discussed serious issues with her.

The significance of *The Book of Margery Kempe* has only recently been recognized, because, while its original existence was known, the actual text eluded scholars until its discovery in 1934 in the home of William Butler-Bowdon and its identification by Hope Emily Allen.[86] The text itself was eventually recognized as important because Margery Kempe revealed original thinking in relation to her experiences. As Hope Allen so well describes:

> Margery's originality seems to be indisputable. My research, however, has led me to conclude that her originality resembled that associated with the other creators of literary types; their creations were new combinations and developments of elements which had been previously existing in their environment. I do not believe that Margery's book can be explained, as I first thought, as merely the naive outburst of an illiterate woman, who had persuaded two pliant men to write down her egotistical reminiscences. Her motive, and the motive of her male supports, seem to be explained by influences current in the world in which Margery (a very creative type of person) grew up.[87]

Another scholar makes a similar kind of observation about the quality of the text Margery left. H. S. Bennett offers the following observation: "No English writer, hitherto, had committed to writing so intimate, revealing and human an account of his life and thoughts."[88]

84. *The Book of Margery Kempe,* ch. 58, pp. 126-27.
85. *The Book of Margery Kempe,* ch. 59, p. 128.
86. The original manuscript was first identified by my great-aunt, Hope Emily Allen, when it was found in an attic. See *The Book of Margery Kempe,* ed. H. E. Allen and S. B. Meech (Oxford: Early English Text Society, 1940), and W. Butler-Bowdon's "thanks to Miss Hope Emily Allen, who, in the first instance read the original manuscript and identified the authoress" (Editor's Note, 1944 edition of *The Book of Margery Kempe,* p. xxv).
87. Hope Emily Allen, *The Book* (1940 ed.), introduction, p. lvii.
88. H. S. Bennett, *Six Medieval Men and Women* (Cambridge: Cambridge University Press, 1955), p. 149.

Our purpose in the present chapter is not to evaluate the literary significance of the text, or Margery Kempe's place among women religious writers, or the many interesting aspects of women's cultural history that are captured in her autobiography.[89] Instead, we will select three particular aspects of Margery's life that correspond to the philosophical themes considered in this study. The first aspect concerns the way in which Margery Kempe appeared to fit one of the satirical stereotypes of woman as not able to control her emotions; the second aspect considers how Margery used her discursive reasoning to fight against the particular polarity principle that a woman ought not to speak in public; and the third aspect involves an attempt by Margery to redefine appropriate dress for a woman in her particular situation. In the last two aspects Margery Kempe is beginning to participate in what today would be called self-definition or self-creation in cooperation with a sense of having been given a divine mission. Because *The Book of Margery Kempe* offers such a detailed account of her life, it is possible to use this text for these more specified purposes.

We have noted frequently that a common element in both academic and satirical views of woman's identity is the claim that woman cannot control the expression of her emotions. Margery Kempe appeared to have had a nature that expressed extremes, especially of the passion of sorrow. The particular way this manifested itself was through an excessive tendency to cry in public places, and to join with these tears loud laments and wailing. Even though Margery understood this herself as a gift from God and a particular way to identify with the sufferings of Jesus Christ, many people who were near her during these episodes were repulsed and critical of such extreme public display of emotion. Many, in contrast to the satirical stereotype of woman, thought that Margery should have been able to control her emotions. Thus the actual circumstances of criticism of Margery, and even her own desires went counter to the exaggerated view that women were irrational. However, Margery's own personality ironically fit the stereotype and forced a response.

In her autobiography Margery recounts many different occasions on which she felt helpless to stop the public weeping. One more lengthy account will be presented here because it reveals the extent to which Margery Kempe herself was aware of the complexity of the situation of her public display of an extreme expression of sorrow:

> And this sort of crying out persisted for many years afterwards. No one could stop it, and I was severely condemned and criticized for it. So loud and so remarkable was it that people were astounded unless they had heard it before or knew the cause of the yelling. . . .
>
> When my cryings began I had them frequently. This was the case in Jerusalem and also in Rome. But when I first came home to England they occurred

89. Karma Lochrie, *Margery Kempe and Translations of the Flesh* (Philadelphia: University of Pennsylvania Press, 1991), argues that the fact that Margery dictated, rather than wrote, the text is not reason to discount it. She states: "The act of composition was equated not with the physical act of writing, as it is today, but with dictation" (p. 103). For a contrary opinion see John Hirsh, "Author and Scribe in *The Book of Margery Kempe*," *Medium Aevum* 44 (1975): 145-50.

only seldom — say once a month — but then once a week, and afterwards daily. Once I had fourteen in a day, on another day seven — all according to God's visitations. . . .

As soon as I realized that I was going to cry out I contained it for as long as I could, so that people would not be disturbed by the noise. For some said I was troubled by an evil spirit; some said it was an illness and some said I had drunk too much wine; some cursed me and wanted me in an asylum; some wished that I was out at sea in a bottomless boat; everyone had his own idea. Other, spiritually minded, people loved me and favoured me all the more. Some great scholars said that neither our Lady nor any of the saints in heaven had ever cried so much, but they had very little idea what I felt; nor would they accept that I couldn't stop myself crying out, even if I had wanted to. So, when I knew that I was about to cry out, I kept it in for as long as I could and did my best to hold it back. I suppressed it until I had turned a greyish blue like lead, but it kept getting bigger and bigger inside me, ready for the time when it would escape.[90]

As Margery shared with her audience her growing self-understanding in relation to this propensity to cry, lament, and wail we discover the importance of two different sources of support, both of which are mediated through intergender dialogue: the first are written texts of others who had a similar situation, and the second are the support of scholars who defended her against public criticism. In chapter 62 of her autobiography Margery tells us that a priest told her of books about Mary of Oignies, Elizabeth of Hungary, Bonaventure, and Richard of Hampole, who all reflected positively on this phenomenon, and "this, too, encouraged him to take me seriously."[91] Then in chapter 68 she describes a Dominican Preaching Friar who conversed directly with her about her crying in public. This dialogue is instructive because it reveals Margery's own understanding of how this scholar supported her in the face of opposition:

When I heard people say he was coming to town I went to see him and told him why I cried and wept so intensely; I wanted to know whether he thought there was anything wrong with the way I cried and wept. The scholar said to me, 'Margery, I've read about a holy woman who'd received from God the same gift of weeping and crying as you. . . . Thus it was that the doctor endorsed my crying and weeping; he said that God should be highly praised for giving me such a gracious and distinctive gift.

The doctor then went to another doctor of divinity — the one who had been chosen to preach to everyone in the parish church — and asked him not to be put off but accept it quietly and uncomplainingly if I cried or wept during his sermon.

When the time came for this scholar to preach he was led to the pulpit with great respect. He began to preach devoutly and reverentially on our Lady's Assumption and what he said uplifted my mind with the sweetest devotion, making

90. *The Book of Margery Kempe,* ch. 28, pp. 68-69.
91. *The Book of Margery Kempe,* ch. 62, pp. 134-35.

me yell at the top of my voice and weep profusely. The worthy doctor stood silent and waited very patiently until I had finished, then he carried on to the end of his sermon.[92]

The chapter continues with Margery's comparison of different responses and her reiteration that most criticism came from those who thought "that I could have desisted if only I'd wanted."[93]

The question of the degree of self-governance that Margery Kempe was capable of in all ranges of her public action is an important one. As we pointed out above, in the extreme expression of her emotions general opinion tended to go against the stereotype of a woman as unable to control her irrational passions. In the next aspect of Margery's life to be considered, we find her articulating a clear and confident choice about speaking in public. By way of background, it is helpful to note that Margery Kempe traveled extensively in England and on the continent. The maps on pages 467 and 468, which appear in *The Book of Margery Kempe,* give an excellent picture of her travels.

On her travels, Margery frequently taught in public, especially to exhort people to lead more virtuous lives. These incidents brought her into conflict with civil and ecclesiastical authorities; and several times she had to defend herself against charges of heresy. Margery Kempe's public disputations included frequent defense against a series of accusations about the authenticity of her religious witness. In particular, she was accused of being a Lollard, a heretical group founded by John Wyclif from Oxford at the end of the fourteenth century. Even with its academic origins, by Margery's time Lollardism was flourishing in the uneducated circles of rural England.[94] Margery was the daughter of a man who had been mayor of the city of Lynn, Norwich, five different times. She lived in Lynn until 1413; and it was in this same city that the first Lollard William Sawtre, a priest in Lynn, was burned to death. The statute *De haeretico comburendo* of 1401 condemned to death any heretic that recanted then later relapsed.[95] In 1410, Badby the tailor was tried and burned to death for heresy in Canterbury.[96] Furthermore, one of Margery's bishops, William of Alnwick, was present at part of Joan of Arc's trial in 1431,[97] and he

92. *The Book of Margery Kempe,* ch. 68, pp. 144-45.

93. *The Book of Margery Kempe,* ch. 68, p. 145.

94. Beverly Boyd, "Wyclif, Joan of Arc, and Margery Kempe," *Mystics Quarterly* 12, no. 3 (1986): 112-18.

95. See Peters, *Heresy and Authority,* p. 212. Part of it stated: "Yet nevertheless diverse false and perverse people of a certain new sect, . . . against the law of God and of the Church, usurping the office of preaching, do perversely and maliciously, in divers places within the said realm, under the color of dissembled holiness, preach and teach in these days, openly and privily, divers new doctrines and wicked, heretical, and erroneous opinions, contrary to the same faith and blessed determinations of the Holy Church." For a discussion of Margery's family background, see Clarissa W. Atkinson, "The Burnham Family of King's Lynn," *Mystic and Pilgrim,* pp. 67-101.

96. Katherine Cholmeley, *Margery Kempe: Genius and Mystic* (London: Catholic Book Club, 1948), pp. 78-81.

97. Régine Pernoud, *Joan of Arc: By Herself and Her Witnesses,* trans. Edward Hyams (New York: Stein and Day, 1969), p. 210. He was present at the First Sermon preached to Joan at the scaffold erected for her burning in the cemetery of Saint-Ouen.

Margery Kempe's Overseas Journeys

had also condemned three Lollards to death by fire.[98] So the historical context of Margery Kempe's life was one of living in the dangerous shadow of heresy.

Sometimes Margery was interrogated by public officials to verify whether or not she promoted various forms of heresy. Lollardism severely criticized corruption in the clergy; it also sought to have direct access to the Scriptures. Although Margery was illiterate, she appeared to know passages from the Scriptures that she had learned by ear from the priest who had tutored her. In her trials, Margery had to defend herself against having read the Scriptures herself. While some of the content of Margery's public dialogues concerned the same matters that Lollards raised, much of the focus of criticism against her was directed towards issues of her identity as a woman. One of the principles of academic gender polarity was that a woman ought to be silent in public. In satires women are often presented as unable to stop speaking in public, especially in nagging forms of criticism of men. It is not surprising to discover, then, that public interrogation of her often involved this issue.

98. See Boyd, "Wyclif, Joan of Arc, and Margery Kempe," p. 115. In this article many similarities between Margery Kempe and Joan of Arc are considered.

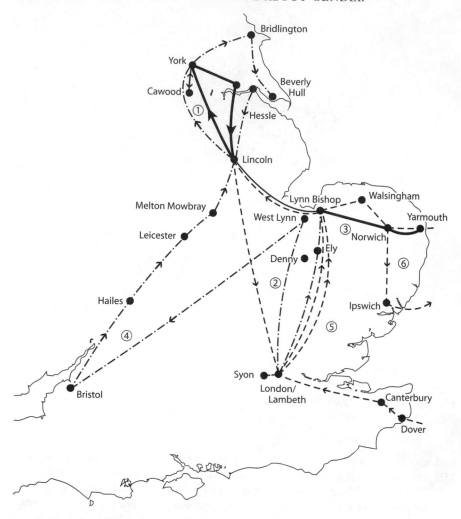

Margery Kempe's Inland Journeys

Another point that is well worth considering is one elaborated by Elona Lucas, who gives a systematic analysis of the different groups who were critical of Margery.[99] She distinguishes those who met Margery on her pilgrimages abroad from those scholars and members of the Church hierarchy who judged her in England in towns outside of Lynn, and from those townspeople from her home town of Lynn. Lucas concludes that her own townspeople were the most critical of her

99. Elona K. Lucas, "The Enigmatic, Threatening Margery Kempe," *Downside Review* (October 1987): 294-305.

choice of a celibate life, the local people from other towns in England most fearful of her potential heresy,[100] and the scholars and hierarchy, once they were assured of her orthodox religious views, supported her most strongly.[101]

There are several examples of interrogatory dialogue in *The Book of Margery Kempe*. In all of Margery's public arrests and interrogations, she eventually always won her freedom. This is an important point to note. Margery did directly engage with her accusers and demonstrated a keen ability to follow an argument, answer the criticisms point by point, and win the approval of those who had formerly been suspicious of her thought and actions. Often Margery succeeded by the quality of her answers; and sometimes it was through the intervention of others who would testify to her character. We will now consider some sequences from selected interrogations to demonstrate this point.

Before actually including any passages, however, I would like to make a point about the particular text selected for quotations. In her original book, written in fifteenth-century English, Margery referred to herself in the third person singular. Thus, the early version of her manuscript by W. Butler-Bowdon has the following first line of the first chapter: "When this creature was twenty years of age, or some deal more, she was married to a worshipful burgess (of Lynne) and was with child within a short time, as nature would."[102] A recent edition by Tony D. Triggs of the same text has offered a new translation from the ancient English. It reads as follows: "When I was twenty, or a little older, I was married to a well-respected burgess, and, things being what they are, I quickly found myself pregnant."[103] Because the purpose for including Margery Kempe in this chapter is to consider philosophical aspects of her use of discursive reasoning, the contemporary translation by Triggs seems to be most accessible to the reader. Therefore it will be used below, with the recognition that Margery's own style of expression was different — particularly with respect to the grammar of personal pronouns.

In one of her first public interrogations, Margery defended herself against the Mayor of Leicester who had arrested her, saying, "You, you're a cheap whore, a lying Lollard, and you have an evil effect on others — so I'm going to have you put in prison."[104] After Margery insisted that she be examined in English and not in Latin, which she said she did not understand, she cleared herself: "Then he asked me a lot of questions, and I answered them readily and straightforwardly so that

100. Lucas, "The Enigmatic, Threatening Margery Kempe," *Downside Review* (October 1987): 299. "It is in Lynn that Margery receives the most contradictory reactions, although generally it is her own townspeople who scorn her more than the others. The fear of her being a heretic seems less strong here than in Leicester and York, most probably because she had the support of her Dominican anchorite/confessor and of Alan of Lynn, a well-known Carmelite and Doctor of Divinity."

101. Lucas, "The Enigmatic, Threatening Margery Kempe," *Downside Review* (October 1987). "That Margery sought support from the clergy is not surprising, given the fear of Lollardy in England at the time and the belief that weak women were more prone to heresy; that she received such support is not surprising either because, on being questioned by the Archbishop of York and the Abbot of Leicester, for example, her religious views are seen as entirely orthodox Catholic teaching" (p. 297).

102. *The Book of Margery Kempe*, ed. W. Butler-Bowdon, ch. 1, p. 1.

103. *The Book of Margery Kempe*, trans. Tony D. Triggs, ch. 1, p. 21. All other passages from this text are from the Triggs translation unless otherwise noted.

104. *The Book of Margery Kempe*, ch. 46, p. 102.

they could not find grounds for any charge."[105] Soon after, however, Margery was brought to public trial before the Mayor, the Abbot, Dean, and general population of Leicester. Margery states simply: "There were so many people that they were standing on stools to get a good view of me."[106] Aware that she was in danger of being burned to death for heresy, she made some important theological distinctions between the moral state of a priest and the sacramental office he is able to perform. The Lollards had believed that only those in a state of Grace had sacramental power, whereas the Roman Catholic Church holds that a sacrament is valid regardless of the moral state of the priest celebrating it. Margery also affirmed the reality of transubstantiation in the Eucharist, a further source of contention with the Lollards.

The mayor kept her under arrest for three weeks, but in the end let her go at the advice of his clerks. Margery describes the concluding discussion as follows:

The mayor, who was dead set against me, said, 'I'm sure she doesn't believe in her heart what she says with her mouth.'

But the clerks said to him, 'Sir, to our way of thinking she gives an excellent account of herself.'

Then the mayor poured condemnations on me and came out with all sorts of critical and nasty remarks, which are best not repeated. . . .

I also had some plain words for the mayor himself: 'Sir,' I said, 'you aren't fit to be mayor . . . you should never impose a punishment unless you make sure it is called for first. And you've been treating me quite the contrary today, sir, because you've caused me a lot of hurt for things which I have never done. . . .'[107]

After her experience in Leicester, Margery was interrogated by the Archbishop of York. In this lengthy dialogue we can see several different ways that Margery engages in debate about specific aspects of woman's identity. In chapter 52 of her book, Margery describes the context of her interrogation.

On the following day I was taken into the archbishop's chapel, and many of the archbishop's household arrived. They reviled me, calling me 'Lollard' and 'heretic,' and some swore all sorts of horrible oaths that I would be burned. . . .

[Here follows a sequence of questions about why Margery was wearing white clothes when she was not a virgin, and after the archbishop threatened Margery with fetters, he left briefly.]

After a while the archbishop re-entered the chapel with many notable clerics. Among them was the doctor who had examined me previously and the monk who had preached against me in York not long before. Some of the people asked whether I was a Christian or a Jew; some said I was a good woman and some said I wasn't. Then the archbishop took his seat and the clerics took theirs. (There were numerous clerics, and where they sat reflected their seniority.)

105. *The Book of Margery Kempe*, ch. 47, pp. 102-3.
106. *The Book of Margery Kempe*, ch. 48, p. 104.
107. *The Book of Margery Kempe*, ch. 48, pp. 104-5.

[Here follows a sequence of questions about the faith, to which she gave acceptable answers. Then Margery fell into violent crying and the clerks suggested that she be sent away because she might lead people astray.]

Then the archbishop said to me, 'I hear bad reports about you; I hear it said that you're a thoroughly wicked woman.'

And I replied, 'And I hear it said that you're a wicked man, sir. And if you're as wicked as people say, you will never enter heaven unless you mend your ways while you're on this earth.'

Then he said, in his violent way, 'Why you! . . . What do people say about me?'

I replied, 'Others can tell you well enough, sir.'

Then an important cleric with a furred hood said, 'Stop this! Answer for yourself and leave the archbishop out of it.'

[At this point Margery is asked to swear on the Bible that she will leave York. She refuses, explaining why she must stay in York.]

Then the archbishop said to me, 'You must swear that you will not teach the people in my diocese, or stir them up.'

'No, sir, I won't swear that,' I said. 'Wherever I go I shall talk about God and speak out against people who use profane language. I shall do so until such time as the pope and Holy Church decree that no one shall be so bold as to talk about God; because God Almighty doesn't forbid us to talk about him. What's more, the gospel mentions a woman who heard our Lord preach and came up to him and said to him loudly, 'Blessed are the womb that bore you and the breasts that suckled you.' And our Lord replied, 'And equally blessed are the people who hear God's word and obey it.' So it seems to be, sir, that the gospel permits me to speak of God.'

'Ah, sir,' said the clerks, 'she's talking about the gospel — which shows that she's got the devil inside her.' And straight away a learned clerk brought out a book and cited against me St. Paul's prohibition on women preaching.

I answered by saying, 'I don't preach, sir; I enter no pulpits. All I do is talk to people and tell them things that are good for their souls, and I'll do the same for as long as I live.'[108]

Margery's distinction at the end of this dialogue between preaching that was done in a church, and teaching that she did as she went about interacting with those she met was a masterful use of intelligence to defend herself in a difficult situation. It addition, it is clear from her description of those present during the questioning that she was well aware of the difference in education between herself and those before her who had academic degrees. However, even with this formal difference, Margery was able to answer her accusers point by point, and on the same grounds they used for their accusations.

The interrogation did not end here, however, for directly after Margery defended her right to teach, one of the academics present suggested that what she was teaching should not be taught:

108. *The Book of Margery Kempe*, ch. 52, pp. 111-13.

Then a scholar who had already examined me said, 'Sir, she told me the worst story about priests that I've ever heard.'

The archbishop asked me to repeat the story.

'Sir,' I said, 'with all due respect, I spoke of just a single priest and I did it in order to make a point. I understand that for the good of his soul God allowed this priest to get lost in a wood. He had no shelter, but as the daylight faded he found a beautiful orchard in which to rest for the night. In the middle was a lovely pear tree all bedecked and adorned with blossom. The flowers were an exquisite sight for his eyes. Then along came a bear. It was big and fierce and hideous and it shook the pear tree and brought down the flowers. This horrible beast then greedily ate and devoured them all. When all the beautiful flowers were gone he turned his tail end in the priest's direction and expelled their substance from his bowel. The priest, repelled by this loathsome sight, began to worry about what it might mean.[109]

Margery then developed the significance of this vulgar analogy, by describing an elderly pilgrim who was able to explain to the priest its meaning:

'Priest, you yourself are the pear tree, and by saying services and administering the sacraments you flourish and flower to a certain extent, though you do your work without dedication, caring little about how you say your matins and your evening office as long as you manage to gabble through them. You receive the cup of everlasting life, the sacrament of the altar, in a thoroughly half-hearted way. Then you misuse your time for the rest of the day, devoting yourself to buying and selling, shopping and swapping as if you belonged in the secular world. You sit drinking ale and you give yourself over to greed, gluttony and lust of the flesh, living a life of lechery and uncleanliness. You break God's commandments by swearing, lying, slander, backbiting and other such sins. So it is that your bad behaviour makes you very much like the bear: you devour and destroy the flowers and blooms of virtuous living to your own everlasting damnation and the hindrance of many others besides; and so it will be unless you have the grace to repent and amend your life.'[110]

Margery Kempe presented what appears to be a downward vertical analogy, implying that a human being is acting like an animal. However, the purpose of her analogy was conversion of a particular man from the greed of usury and the lack of celibacy to fidelity to his priestly vocation. So while her story appears to be a downward vertical analogy, in fact it is a transcendental analogy.[111] It is important to note as

109. *The Book of Margery Kempe,* ch. 52, pp. 113-14.
110. *The Book of Margery Kempe,* ch. 52, p. 114.
111. Another aspect of the analogy which some commentators consider is the humour or laughter associated with it. Karma Lochrie develops this theme in some detail, in *Margery Kempe and Translations of the Flesh.* For example, "Humour in her stories is meant to instruct by defiling the guilty with laughter. Merriment is possible only at someone's expense. In the tale about the bear and the pear tree, that someone is the guilty priest. Most of the time, however, Kempe's merriment is achieved at her own expense" (p. 151).

well that Margery Kempe was careful not to generalize to all men, or even to a group of men, but to make it clear to her audience that she offered this analogy only in the context of a particular man and his need for conversion.

The story also appears to have worked in converting members of her audience as well. For Margery relates its effect:

> The archbishop liked the tale a lot; he praised it and said how good it was. But the scholar who had previously examined me in the archbishop's presence said, 'Sir, this tale strikes to my very heart.'
>
> I said to the scholar, 'Ah, good sir, in the place where I live for most of the time is an upright cleric who preaches well and speaks out against the people's wrongdoing. He won't stoop to flatter anyone, and he says from his pulpit, "If my preaching upsets anyone, take good note because it means he feels guilty." And I'm causing you just the same discomfort,' I said to the scholar. 'May God forgive you.'
>
> The scholar was at a loss for words, but afterwards he came and apologised to me for having been so set against me.[112]

Thus in the end, the scholar was converted by her analogical story, and the Archbishop sent her away with his blessing. Margery describes the final moments of this episode with a clear consciousness of the dynamics of public dialogue involving educated men and an uneducated woman:

> I was then escorted back to York, where many laymen and notable scholars welcomed me. They rejoiced in our Lord, who had given me, an illiterate woman, the wit and wisdom to answer so many learned men without suffering any disgrace or blame. Thanks be to God![113]

This theme of the interrogation of uneducated women by educated men will continue to be significant in later portions of this chapter, which will follow the deterioration of intergender dialogue during this period of European history.

After this episode in York, Margery was arrested again in Hessle as a result of the accusation of a Dominican friar who was to receive a reward of one hundred pounds from the Duke of Bedford for capturing "the most notorious Lollard around here — and worse than any in London, too."[114] On the way, many people, invoking again a gender polarity stereotype of women, shouted at her. Margery describes it this way:

> Then they took me back to Hessle, where people accused me of being a Lollard. Women came running out of their houses with their distaffs and they called to the others, 'Burn this lying heretic.'
>
> As I was being taken to Beverly by the yeomen and friars I have mentioned we

---

112. *The Book of Margery Kempe,* ch. 52, pp. 114-15.
113. *The Book of Margery Kempe,* ch. 52, p. 115.
114. *The Book of Margery Kempe,* ch. 53, p. 116.

met a great many local people. 'Woman,' they said, 'give up the life you're lead-ing; you should spin and card like other women do, and not have all this disgrace and bother. Nothing on earth would make us put up with all that you go through.' . . .

As we proceeded, I told the men some salutary stories until one of the duke's men who had arrested me said, 'I'm sorry I found you; the things you say seem really good.'

Then I replied, 'Sir, don't regret or reproach yourself for having found me. Do as your master wants you to do; I'm sure that everything will work out well. For my part, I'm really pleased that you found me.'[115]

Margery Kempe continued with confidence in what she considered to be her mis-sion of public teaching and witness even though it challenged the differentiation of traditional public and private spheres of virtue for men and women. This particular time the Dominicans brought Margery again before the Archbishop of York so that he could argue against her, but he accepted her arguments, and again she was let go. Margery wisely asked the Archbishop for a letter verifying her innocence, which he gave to her.

Even with this protection she was still in danger, for in the next town she was again "arrested as a Lollard and led in the direction of a prison."[116] However, Margery was saved, just in time, by someone who had seen the Archbishop of York release her. Even though she had further arrests, the letter from the Archbishop of York continued to serve as a protection along with her own ability to defend herself. These examples selected from her autobiography have revealed some of the ways in which Margery Kempe used her own intelligence to defend her teaching in public, especially about moral issues.

We will turn now to the last issue of gender identity that followed Margery everywhere during her public life. It is the question of the clothes she wore.[117] At the time Margery lived, wearing white clothes was associated with being a virgin, and wearing black clothes with being a widow. Margery, after rearing fourteen chil-dren, and with some difficulty gaining her husband's agreement, made a vow of celibacy with her husband before the Bishop of Lincoln.[118] Margery believed she was directed through an insight of prayer to put on white clothes as a sign of her later vocation to celibacy. It symbolized her repristinization, or living as a virgin.

115. *The Book of Margery Kempe*, ch. 53, pp. 116-17.

116. *The Book of Margery Kempe*, ch. 55, p. 121.

117. See Sherrin Marshall Wyntyes, "Women in the Reformation Era," in *Becoming Visible: Women in European History*, ed. Renate Bridenthal and Claudia Koonz (Boston: Houghton Mifflin, 1977), pp. 169-70. Among *The Lollard Conclusions* (1394) circulated in England was one that would appear to be critical of the lifestyle that Margery herself chose. "The corollary is that widows and such as take the veil and the ring, being delicately fed, we would wish that they were given in marriage, be-cause we cannot excuse them from secret sins." In Edward Peters, *Heresy and Authority in Medieval Europe*, p. 281. This corollary was addressed to nuns, but Margery herself desired to take a vow of celi-bacy, wear the white of virgins, and a ring symbolizing her marriage to Christ, even though she had been married and had numerous children.

118. *The Book of Margery Kempe*, ch. 15, pp. 42-43.

However, because she had mothered several children and her husband was still alive, many people considered her choice a contradiction; she was appearing to be a virgin when she was not. To the broad public that had attached a more rigid meaning to women wearing particular clothes, Margery's choice of white clothes opened a deeper understanding of the relation of appearance and reality. She understood the white clothes to be a sign of the deeper reality of her choice of a celibate life in union with virgins. Thus, Margery's conscious choice to redefine the meaning of white clothes by her own example ran directly counter to the cultural expectation for lay women. Margery had encountered a similar problem of understanding when she broke out of stereotypes of women's proper place with respect to speech or silence in public life. This precipitated the above admonitions to forsake her unusual lifestyle and return to the kind lived by most women.

In her autobiography, Margery describes in detail the many reversals she encountered in trying to wear white clothes. First, the Bishop of Lincoln refuses Margery's request to wear white clothes.[119] Then, Margery states that she believed to wear white clothes was a direct command to her from God. She records the command and her response as follows:

> 'And Daughter, I command you to wear white clothes, and no other colour; you must dress as I say.'
>
> 'Ah, dear Lord, I'm afraid that people will slander me if I go around dressed differently from other chaste women. They'll stare at me and call me a show-off.'[120]

On her pilgrimage to Rome, she said that an English priest "spoke all sorts of evil about me because I wore white clothes far more than people he considered holier or better than I was."[121]

In Rome, her German confessor, Wenslawe, asked her to change into black clothes for a while, but then allowed her to change back into white clothes when she insisted that she was following a divine command.[122] On returning to England a priest in Norwich said to her: "'God forbid such a thing!' for by wearing white I would make the whole world wonder at me."[123] Margery persisted, however, and a wealthy man gave her some new white clothes, which she promptly wore again.[124] Elona Lucas gives a general description of the response of people to her choice of white clothes:

> What was the reaction of the lay people towards Margery? . . . In her travels abroad, Margery is overwhelmingly greeted warmly by the people she meets; while her own fellow-countrymen in England vilely abuse her, making her ap-

119. *The Book of Margery Kempe,* ch. 15, p. 43.
120. *The Book of Margery Kempe,* ch. 15, p. 41.
121. *The Book of Margery Kempe,* ch. 33, p. 80.
122. *The Book of Margery Kempe,* ch. 38, p. 86.
123. *The Book of Margery Kempe,* ch. 43, p. 95.
124. *The Book of Margery Kempe,* ch. 44, p. 96.

pear as a fool in a shortened gown and white apron on her pilgrimage to the Holy Land . . . over all, it seems to be men who treat her with the most compassion; we hear, for example, of the man of Norwich who suits her in white garments. . . . But the negative responses to her in Lynn far outweigh the kindness she receives; we are told repeatedly that the people scorn her, spit at her, curse her, and ban her from their homes for a variety of reasons: for crying, for returning from Rome wearing the white mantle, a sign of chastity, and for what they see as her neglect of her husband John, blaming her for his fall down the stairs.[125]

At this point, Margery made a pilgrimage to Santiago, Spain, and when she returned to England, she began to experience the cycles of arrest described above. The Mayor of Leicester had previously accused Margery of trying to make wives leave their husbands by wearing white clothes: "I'd like to know why you go around in white clothes; I'm sure you've come here to lure our wives away from us and lead them off with you."[126] Then, in the interrogation by the Archbishop of York, Margery is directly asked about her choice of clothes:

> At last the archbishop came into the chapel with his clerks. 'Why do you go around dressed in white? Are you a virgin?' he demanded.
> Kneeling before him I answered, 'No, sir, I'm not a virgin; I'm a married woman.'[127]

It was this exchange that precipitated the archbishop's remarks that Margery should be put in fetters. However, as we demonstrated above she was able to convince the archbishop of her integrity and was let go without forcing any change in her manner of dress or public speaking. Margery Kempe did win her point, and she remained in white clothes for the rest of her life. In this way, she began to work away at the rigid stereotype concerning color of clothing and woman's identity.

In conclusion, Margery Kempe represents a kind of natural thinker outside of academia. Her character challenged stereotypes of women in several ways. First of all, her emotional outbursts of weeping were so extreme that people often thought she should have been able to control them. Second, she was able to use discursive reasoning to defend herself in public situations of interrogation by educated men. She was able to convince them of her innocence of false accusations. In this context, Margery pushed out the boundaries of the gender polarity principle that women ought not speak in public. She continually taught especially about themes of morality in public contexts. Next, Margery Kempe challenged stereotypes that separated out virgins from widows and other married women by her insistence on wearing white clothes. Thus Margery Kempe contributed to the history of the concept of woman firstly by the choices she made in her way of living, and secondly by her dictated autobiography, which extended a woman's perceptions further into the public sphere of activity and speech.

125. Lucas, "The Enigmatic, Threatening Margery Kempe," *Downside Review:* 298-99.
126. *The Book of Margery Kempe,* ch. 48, p. 105.
127. *The Book of Margery Kempe,* ch. 52, p. 112.

St. Joan of Arc (1412-1431)

In moving from the story of Margery Kempe to that of her contemporary St. Joan of Arc we discover a different quality of intergender dialogue among men who had an academic education and a woman who was illiterate and uneducated as well. Here, instead of educated men who may have begun their interrogation with a bias against the woman but who were eventually convinced by the arguments of the woman being questioned, we find a few educated men consciously using stereotypes of women to condemn a woman to death. The particular aspect of woman's identity they eventually used to catch Joan was the wearing of "women's clothes" versus the wearing of "men's clothes."

As will be demonstrated, several men also distorted judicial processes and intentionally introduced deception into the judicial process, while they ironically accused Joan of being the source of deception. The detailed dynamics of the trial are available for study because they were recorded at the time and later published in French and Latin.[128] In addition, Régine Pernoud has provided two important documentary sources: for the first trial, *Joan of Arc: By Herself and Her Witnesses,* and for the retrial, *The Retrial of Joan of Arc: The Evidence at the Trial for Her Rehabilitation: 1450-1456.*[129] From these documents we can come to an understanding of the quality of the public intergender dialogue that took place during this time.

Before examining the dialogue at the time of the trial, it may be helpful to recount some of the main events in Joan of Arc's life.[130] She was a simple farm girl from the village of Domremy, France, when around sixteen she responded to inner voices directing her to go to the Dauphin and offer to help him drive out the English from France, and to be crowned as King. Joan had been hearing this voice since she was thirteen, and she understood it to be the voice of St. Michael, the Archangel.[131] She tried unsuccessfully to be accepted by the Dauphin in May 1428 and then attempted again around a year later. In the second attempt, the Dauphin decided to have Joan examined by clerks, prelates, and doctors of theology to verify her orthodoxy. These first interrogations are very interesting because they ended with a complete affirmation of Joan's integrity.[132]

Dorothy G. Wayman gives the following description of the examination of Joan arranged by Charles VII:

---

128. See *Procès de Condamnation de Jeanne D'Arc: Texte, traduction et notes,* ed. Honoré Champion (Paris, 1921). All passages from the trial are taken from this text and translated by the author unless noted otherwise.

129. Régine Pernoud, *Joan of Arc: By Herself and Her Witnesses* and *The Retrial of Joan of Arc: The Evidence at the Trial for Her Rehabilitation, 1450-1456* (London: Methuen and Co., Ltd., 1955).

130. There are many biographies of Joan of Arc. One that has an excellent chronological table, listing by category those who participated in her trial, and maps and illustrations is: Victoria Mary Sackville-West, *Saint Joan of Arc* (London: Corden-Sanderson, 1936).

131. Joan, responding to questions at her trial, recounted in Régine Pernoud, *Joan of Arc,* pp. 30-31.

132. Pernoud, *The Retrial of Joan of Arc,* pp. 83-87.

Joan of Arc in Armour Usually Worn by Men

He convoked, at Poitiers, a commission of the most highly qualified clergy available. Most of them had once been students under John Gerson, some were professors of his faculty at Paris, now gathered in exile close to Charles VII rather than stultifying themselves by serving the English in Paris. They were a University-in-exile such as the Twentieth Century saw in scholars who would not serve Nazi or Fascist ideologies.

It is known that they examined Jeanne d'Arc exhaustively, for some three weeks. They even sent delegates to Domremy to check on her past life. A committee of women was appointed to ascertain her virginity. But no records have survived.[133]

What happened to the record, or "Book of Poitiers," is still a burning question among scholars of the life of Joan of Arc. Some suggest that it was destroyed in 1431 by the person who had been the chairman of the Poitiers Commission out of fear of being caught supporting Joan, who was condemned to death for heresy.[134] It is clear that Joan herself knew of its existence, because she frequently referred to it to support her positions during her own trial.[135] It is also important to note that this intense period of examination gave Joan of Arc an experience of engaging in intergender dialogue with men of academic training who were friendly towards her because they also supported Charles VII's claim to the throne of France. This formation in serious interrogation educated Joan in the art of oral debate and prepared her to some degree for what would come later in her actual trial.

Another very interesting aspect of this examination of Joan was the significance of Jean Gerson (1363-1429) to its deliberations. Jean Gerson was the chancellor of the University of Paris from the age of thirty-two in 1395 to around 1409, when he fled into exile under the threat of assassination for supporting Charles VII's claim to the throne against the English and other French who rejected his claim. When Gerson had been chancellor of the University of Paris in the early 1400s, he supported Christine de Pizan both publicly and privately in her writings about women's identity. Particular aspects of this support will be considered in the next chapter. Here it is striking to note that Jean Gerson wrote a treatise in late March or early April 1429 while he was in exile in Lyons in support of Joan of Arc. It is not known whether Gerson actually attended any of the interrogations of Joan and wrote his treatise after listening to her directly, or whether he read the transcripts of questions asked by his students and colleagues and wrote his analysis of her answers from the transcriptions. Gerson's text was entitled *De quadam puella,* and it developed arguments to prove: ". . . that the Maid, in his opinion, was

---

133. Dorothy G. Wayman, "The Chancellor and Jeanne d'Arc: February-July, A.D. 1429," *Franciscan Studies* 17-18 (1957): 273-305, 278-79. See also Deboroh A. Fraiol: *Joan of Arc: The Early Debate* (Woodbridge: Boydell Press, 2000). Unfortunately this text arrived too late to be integrated into our analysis.

134. Pernoud, *Joan of Arc,* p. 67.

135. Wayman, "The Chancellor and Jeanne d'Arc," *Franciscan Studies.* "In the record of the 1431 trial it is touching to read how, again and again, she said to her persecutors, 'It is written in the record at Poitiers'" (p. 280).

of good life, truly inspired by God, and that her leadership should be honored by king and people."[136]

Historically, there has been considerable confusion about this treatise of Jean Gerson, because a second treatise entitled *De mirabili victoria* and also attributed to Gerson "picks out for mention and argument the very points on which the Paris theologians at the Rouen Trial would find her guilty of heresy and witchcraft — that is, her cropped hair and men's dress, and her prophecies."[137] This seems to contradict *De quadam puella,* which supports Joan in her mission. Careful research now suggests that this second treatise was likely a contrived account of Gerson's original treatise on Joan written by a scribe who had some knowledge of the original work, but who did not rewrite it accurately and who was influenced by others who were determined to prove both Joan and Gerson to be heretical. In fact the second treatise was sent to Rome with the apparent attention of bringing condemnation to both its author and to Joan. In any event, the second treatise was more widely distributed. However, after Joan of Arc's rehabilitation, the original treatise was printed in a 1484 Cologne edition and then gained some more public attention.[138]

The first treatise appears to have been written before Joan won any military victories, and Gerson died before Joan of Arc was put on trial at Rouen. So he based his judgment in *De quadam puella* solely on her responses to the questions asked in the Poitiers examinations. Given the education, erudition, and scholarly reputation of Gerson, this judgment of Joan's character, in spite of the ways she was breaking stereotypes of woman's leadership in public events, is significant. It is also interesting to note that one of the key figures in the trial of Joan of Arc was Pierre Cauchon, who had been appointed the Bishop of Beauvais in 1420. He was a close friend of the "acting chancellor" at the University of Paris during the time of the exile of the real chancellor Jean Gerson. Thus Joan's trial was rife with political intrigue spilling over from the war between the English and French, and the various allegiances that French academics made during this time of political upheaval. So any analysis of the concept of woman articulated within it must be situated in this broader historical context. Nonetheless, it is instructive to consider to what extent questions about woman's identity are involved in Joan's public dialogue.

After the Dauphin received the reports of the interrogation of Joan at Poitiers, he was convinced of the integrity of her mission. He then outfitted her with armor, put her in charge of some armed men, and sent her to Orleans to fight the English. In late spring 1429, Joan, calling herself the Maid, sent a letter of summons to the English at Orleans that included some of the following directives:

> Render to the Maid here sent by God the King of Heaven, the keys of all the great towns which you have taken and violated in France. She is here come by God's

---

136. Wayman, "The Chancellor and Jeanne d'Arc," pp. 279-80. The complete text in its Latin original is appended to the article, pp. 296-305.

137. Wayman, "The Chancellor and Jeanne d'Arc," p. 282. The complete Latin text of this treatise is also attached to the article.

138. Wayman, "The Chancellor and Jeanne d'Arc," p. 283.

will to reclaim the blood royal. She is very ready to make peace, if you will acknowledge her to be right, provided that France you render, and pay for having held it. And you, archers, companions of war, men-at-arms and others who are before the town of Orleans, go away into your country, by God. And if so be not done, expect news of the Maid who will come to see you shortly, to your very great injury. King of England, if (you) do not so, I am chief-of-war and in whatever place I attain your people in France, I will make them quit it willy nilly. And if they will not obey, I will have them all slain; I am here sent by God, the King of Heaven, body for body to drive you out of all France.[139]

Régine Pernoud suggests that this letter of summons was the first concrete evidence that the English had of her existence. The French had been under siege by the English in Orleans since October, and the people in Orleans were nearly defeated. Joan entered the town on April 29, 1429. She sent a third summons on May 5 that repeated the essential message of the first summons. The English refused to comply, and the military battle that ensued is now legendary. Joan was very involved in planning the military tactics, and she led charges in particular areas, carrying her standard at the front of the line. Her ability to ride and handle weapons was well attested to by the soldiers who fought next to her. In this particular battle, Joan's courage was exceptional. She recounted later that: "I was the first to place a scaling ladder on the bastion of the bridge."[140] Joan also received a wound of which she had had foreknowledge. After it was dressed, she was able to resume fighting.

On the last day of the siege, Joan asked the French soldiers not to fight because it was Sunday, unless the English attacked first. Much against their better judgment, they followed her lead. The English were in battle formation, very close to the French, but after an hour they simply retreated, and Orleans was won. This remarkable battle, and Joan of Arc's leadership, astounded everyone. First of all, it turned the English bitterly against Joan. As Dorothy Wayman so consisely describes it:

> The Burgundian and English opinion of the Maid of Orleans can be realized in Shakespeare's Henry VI, written in 1591, in which Talbot calls the Maid "Pucelle, that witch, that damned Sorceress" while the Duke of Burgundy addresses her as "vile fiend and shameless courtesan" and the Duke of York styles her "fell banning hag, enchantress . . . foul accursed minister of hell."[141]

While these associations of Joan with witchcraft read back into history later developments, they nonetheless echo the tone of hostile response that the English and those loyal to the English cause had for this young woman who helped change the direction of history.

The French who were opposed to the English, on the other hand, had a very different response. Christine de Pizan, whose works will be extensively studied in

139. Joan, recounted in Pernoud, *Joan of Arc,* p. 70.
140. Joan, recounted in Pernoud, *Joan of Arc,* p. 93.
141. Wayman, "The Chancellor and Jeanne d'Arc," p. 274.

the next chapter, wrote in 1429 in praise of Joan of Arc. In fact, Christine is thought to be the only person, other than Jean Gerson, who wrote a text that positively evaluated Joan of Arc's character and actions while she was still alive. Christine de Pizan after eleven years of retirement wrote at the end of her life the *Dittié sur Jeanne d'Arc* as a way to publicize the role Joan played in saving France with the crowning of Charles as king.[142] While the concept of woman in Christine de Pizan's works as a whole will be considered later, it is significant to note in passing that the *Dittié sur Jeanne d'Arc* was her final composition before her own death in 1431.[143] She wrote about Joan's victory in terms that clearly accentuated her identity as a woman:

> Oh! What honor for the female sex! It is perfectly obvious that God has special regard for it when all these wretched people who destroyed the whole Kingdom — now recovered and made safe by a woman, something that 100,000 men should not have done — and the traitors [have been] exterminated. Before the event they would scarcely have believed this possible.[144]

Since the war against the English to support the authority of Charles VII had not yet been won throughout the whole of France, Christine de Pizan used her writing about Joan to try to rally others in France to the battle threatening to take place at Paris. Christine wrote: "I do not know if Paris will hold out (for they have not reached there yet) or if it will resist the Maid."[145] She begged her readers: "Now as loyal Frenchmen submit your hearts and yourselves to [your king]."[146] We can only wonder at the shock waves that must have reached Christine at the events that occurred around Joan's subsequent trial, condemnation, and death.

Even before the trial, and after the victory of Orleans and the crowning of the King at Rheims, other shock waves were reaching the University of Paris and those who were loyal to the English. Régine Pernoud describes the situation as follows:

> It should be noted here, while on the subject of the resounding impression made by the exploit of Orleans, that already pro- and anti-Joan parties were appearing clearly in France. And that already the 'renegade Frenchmen,' those who had espoused the enemy's cause, were giving expression to their hostility by the mouth of the University of Paris. In May a memorandum drawn up by a clerk of the university, but which has not been preserved, was accusing Joan of heresy; and it may have been in defence of her and in reply to this *libelle* that Jean Gerson, former Chancellor of the University but still loyal to the French King, composed the

142. Christine de Pizan, *Ditié de Jehanne d'Arc,* ed. Angus J. Kennedy and Kenneth Varty (Oxford: Society for the Study of Mediaeval Languages and Literature, 1977). For consistency with more modern translations the title will be rendered as *Dittié sur Jeanne d'Arc* in the body of the text.

143. See Kevin Brownlee, "Structures of Authority in Christine de Pizan's *Ditié de Jehanne d'Arc,*" in *Discourses of Authority in Medieval and Renaissance Literature,* ed. Kevin Brownlee and Walter Stephens (Hanover and London: University Press of New England, 1989), pp. 131-50.

144. Christine de Pizan, *Ditié,* vv. 265-72; Kevin Brownlee, "Authority," p. 144.

145. Christine de Pizan, *Ditié,* vv. 417-20; Kevin Brownlee, "Authority," p. 148.

146. Christine de Pizan, *Ditié,* vv. 468-70; Kevin Brownlee, "Authority," p. 148.

work . . . ; or it may be that this work was called for by the Poitiers doctors themselves. At all events Gerson's work — his last since he was to die on July 12, 1429 — was very soon in circulation.[147]

The latter reference in this passage refers to the confusion between the timing of the two texts about Joan of Arc attributed to Jean Gerson. The point to note here, however, is the increasing polarization about the meaning of Joan's mission.

After the victory at Orleans, there was a conflict about whether the King's army should try to reconquer Normandy or whether he should go to Rheims for his coronation. Joan favored the latter alternative and "[t]his decision was taken during a council held by the King and into which Joan burst in order to impose her will."[148] This leadership of Joan, not only on the battlefield but also in the council chambers, is an important aspect of her personality and mission. For not only did Joan break the stereotypes surrounding woman's identity through her military strategy, which had been in the public rather than private sphere of action, but she also broke the stereotype by participating in political debate about significant decisions. Régine Pernoud emphasizes her role in this key decision:

> It is manifest here that it was Joan who forced them to a decision: while they were hesitating which way to go and opinions in Council were diverse, she it was, as all the documents prove, who carried her point and so got the royal army away to Rheims, with the object of crowning the King.[149]

In another example, Joan convinced the Council of a different alternative. One of the army leaders described a situation of conflict near Troyes, on the way to Rheims. Here is his account of the events:

> The King's council was divided between diverse opinions and they wondered what was best to be done. Then the Maid came and entered into the council and spoke these words or nearly: 'Noble Dauphin, order that your people go and besiege the town of Troyes and stay no longer in council for, in God's name, within three days I will take you into the city of Troyes by love or by force or by courage, and false Burgundy will stand amazed.' Then the Maid crossed at once with the King's army and left the encampment beside the moats, and made admirable dispositions such as could not have done (better) by two or three of the most famous and experienced soldiers. And she worked so well that night that on the morrow the bishop and the citizens of the city made their obedience to the King, shaking and trembling.[150]

These examples suffice to indicate the way Joan was able to lead men by word and example. This leadership was contrary to the general principles of polarity, which held

147. Pernoud, *Joan of Arc*, pp. 103-4.
148. Pernoud, *Joan of Arc*, p. 109.
149. Pernoud, *Joan of Arc*, p. 110.
150. Pernoud, *Joan of Arc*, pp. 122-23.

that a woman's virtue was to obey, not rule, that a woman's proper sphere of activity was in the private, not the public arena, and that a woman ought to be silent in public. In addition, it demonstrates that Joan, who had simply begun with a commission by the King to lead a small group of men as part of a much larger battle of Orleans, slowly expanded the sphere of her leadership to include broader military coordination of actual battles, including even decisions of military and civic strategy. In these actions, Joan was completely redefining the range of woman's virtuous activity.

Joan's particular kind of wisdom and virtue has fascinated many authors through the years. Rather remarkably, the popular Protestant author, Samuel Clemens (Mark Twain), spent twelve years of research to write a biography of Joan's life, and he concluded: "She was perhaps the only entirely unselfish person whose name has a place in profane history. No vestige or suggestion of self-seeking can be found in any word or deed of hers."[151] It is perhaps helpful to quote the justification that this biographer offers for his judgment about Joan's virtue, for it offers a context in which to consider the dialogical interaction between Joan and her interrogators:

> When she had rescued her King from his vagabondage, and set his crown upon his head, she was offered rewards and honors, but she refused them all, and would take nothing. All she would take for herself — if her King would grant it — was leave to go back to her village home, and tend her sheep again. . . .
>
> The work wrought by Joan of Arc may fairly be regarded as ranking with any recorded in history, when one considers the conditions under which it was undertaken, the obstacles in her way, and the means at her disposal . . . ; [she] . . . found a great nation lying in chains, helpless and hopeless under an alien domination, its treasury bankrupt, its soldiers disheartened and dispersed, all spirit torpid, all courage dead in the hearts of the people through long years of foreign and domestic outrage and oppression, their King cowed, resigned to its fate, and preparing to fly the country; and she laid her hand upon this nation, this corpse, and it rose and followed her. She led it from victory to victory, she turned back the tide of the Hundred Years' War, she fatally crippled the English power. . . .
>
> And for all reward, the French King, whom she had crowned, stood supine and indifferent, while French priests took the noble child, the most innocent, the most lovely, the most adorable the ages have produced, and burned her alive at the stake.[152]

Something of the dignity of leadership of Joan or Arc is captured in the illustration of Joan holding her battle standard with her hand on the altar at the Cathedral of Rheims.

151. Mark Twain, *Personal Recollections of Joan of Arc by The Sieur Louis de Conte (Her Page and Secretary): Freely Translated out of the Ancient French into Modern English from the Original Unpublished Manuscript in the National Archives of France by Jean François Alden* (San Francisco: Ignatius Press, 1989), p. 20. See also the introduction by Andrew Tadie, p. 14, where he quotes Mark Twain claiming that he meticulously used five original French sources and five original English ones from the time of Joan's life and death as the basis for his work.

152. Twain, *Joan of Arc*, pp. 20-21.

Joan of Arc at the Coronation of Charles VII at Rheims

This reflection opens up to the last phase of Joan's life before her arrest. After achieving her aim of having the Dauphin crowned King of France, the army moved about in a less focused way, fighting back and forth to regain territory. During this time Joan fought alongside her men and directed battle plans. A knight, one of her companions at arms, gave the following description of her character and ability:

> Except in matters of war, she was simple and innocent. But in the leading and drawing up of armies and in the conduct of war, in disposing an army for battle and haranguing the soldiers, she behaved like the most experienced captain in all the world, like one with a whole lifetime of experience.[153]

Victoria Sackville-West has carefully traced Joan's military movements from her departure from Orleans on May 10, 1429 until her capture one year later on May 23, 1430. It is instructive to list them because it indicates the complexity of Joan's military activity during this period.[154] When the names of the places where Joan and the army encamped and fought are traced on the map on page 487, they give a clear view of the wide range of public action that Joan engaged in during this final period of her military life.

Joan of Arc's character did not just include physical endurance during all these travels. It also included great courage in facing pain and suffering. In one battle at Paris, Joan was wounded again but continued to fight with the army. When she was captured at Compiègne it was in a context in which she was trying to protect others. Régine Pernoud records for us the details of this moment, emphasizing that Joan was always where the danger was greatest, at the front in an attack and at the rear during a retreat.

> The Burgundian Georges Chastellain has left us a very lively account of Joan's capture: 'The French, with their Maid, were beginning to retreat very slowly, as finding no advantage over their enemies but rather perils and damage. . . . Of which the Maid, passing the nature of women, took all the brunt, and took great pains to save her company, remaining behind as captain and bravest of her troop. And there Fortune allowed that her glory at last come to an end and that she bear

---

153. Pernoud, *The Retrial of Joan of Arc,* Thibault d'Armagnac concerning Joan's actions at the battle of Patay, p. 93.

154. The locations where Joan and the army moved back and forth and fought battles are listed in the following order: Tours, Loches, Selles en Berri, Romorantin, Orléans, Jargeau, Orléans, Meung-sur-Loire, Ceaugency, Patay, Orléans, Sully, St. Benoit, Chateauneuf, Gien, Auxerre, St. Florentin, St. Phal, Troyes, Bussy-Lettré, Chalons-sur-Marne, Sept-Saulx, Rheims, St. Marcoul, Vailly, Soissons, Chateau-Thierry, Montmirail-en-Brie, Provins, Coulommiers, Chateau-Thierry, La Ferte Milon, Crépy-en-Valois, Lagny-le-Sec, Dammartin, Thieux, Baron, Montepilloy, Crépy-en-Valois, Compiègne. St. Denis, La Chapelle, Paris, La Chapelle, St. Denis, Lagny, Provins, Bray, Sens, Courtenay, Chateau-renard, Montargis, Gien, Meung-sur-Yèvre, Bourges, St. Pierre-le-Moutier, Moulins, La Charité-sur-Loire, Meung-sur-Yèvre, Bourges, St. Pierre-Le Moutier, Moulins, La Charité-sur-Loire, Meung-sur-Yèvre, Orléans, Sully, Lagny, Melun, Senlis, Compiègne, Gerenglise, Ste. Marguerite, Soissons, Crépy-en-Valois, Compiègne, Soissons, Crépy-en-Valois, and Compiégne, where Joan was taken prisoner. See Sackville-West, *Saint Joan of Arc,* pp. 417-19.

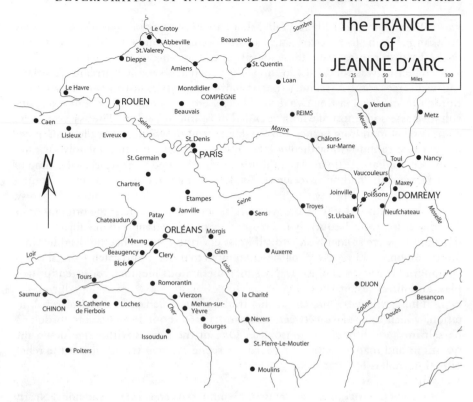

The FRANCE
of
JEANNE D'ARC

Map of Joan of Arc's Later Military Movements

arms no longer; an archer, a rough man and a sour, full of spite because a woman of whom so much had been heard should have overthrown (broken the bones of) so many valiant men, dragged her to one side by her cloth-of-gold cloak and pulled her from her horse, throwing her flat on the ground. . . .'[155]

Joan was taken captive by the English, who turned her over to the French ecclesiastical court. While the University of Paris asked directly for the right to bring Joan to justice, the decision was to hold the trial in Rouen, which the English had held for ten years, and where the King of England resided. Even though Joan was tried by the French ecclesiastical court, she was held in an English secular prison, guarded by English civil guards. This illegal procedure was to play an important role in her trial, condemnation, and later rehabilitation, for in being tried by an ecclesiastical court she should have been in an ecclesiastical prison, guarded by women.[156] However, the English wanted to be certain both that her reputation

155. Pernoud, *Joan of Arc,* p. 151.
156. Pernoud, *Joan of Arc,* pp. 169-70.

was ruined (convicted of heresy) and that she would be put to death, and so they contrived with the local ecclesiastical authorities from Rouen, those who were loyal to the English cause, to use these illegal procedures.

The trial was conducted in three phases: first, a series of interrogations lasting over three months; second, a trial on particular articles lasting two months; and third, a relapse trial lasting two days. There were two judges and about sixty consultative assessors, most of whom attended most interrogations. The assessors were comprised of men from France and England, most of whom had academic degrees in civil law, canon law, or theology. Several were masters actively involved at the University of Paris.[157] Joan was an illiterate, uneducated young girl at the time of the trials and she had no advocate to defend her. Yet she used discursive reasoning to defend herself against what she believed were unfounded accusations of heresy, cooperation with evil spirits, and witchcraft. Several observers at the original trials noted that Joan was frequently interrupted by the questioners, that subjects of the questioning were suddenly shifted, all in an effort to confuse her and lead her into faulty responses. In nearly all of these attempts to deceive and catch Joan, she was able to find her way out of the trap, using a meticulous memory, consistent principles, and direct responses.

Those who were present at this trial later testified at her trial of rehabilitation, which took place between 1450 and 1456, about Joan's ability to defend herself in these difficult circumstances. One of the scribes who wrote down the questions and Joan's answers described the scene of the interrogation at the rehabilitation trial as follows:

> During the trial Joan was harassed by numerous and diverse questions. Nearly every day there were interrogations in the morning which lasted for about three or four hours. And sometimes they extracted difficult and subtle questions from what Joan had said, and faced her with them after lunch in a second interrogation which lasted for two or three hours. And sometimes they switched from one interrogatory to another, changing their manner of asking questions as well: and despite this change she answered wisely. She had a very good memory. For very often she would say: 'I answered you on that point in another place,' or, indicating me: 'I refer to the clerk.' . . .[158]

This ability of Joan to remember exactly what she had said and when she had said it was testified to by many different people present at the original trial. Joan would even refer interrogators to the exact day in the record when she had previously answered a question, and she was inevitably correct.[159]

One of the most famous examples of her ability to respond discursively to questions posed especially to trick her into heresy was her answer to the question: "Do you know if you are in the grace of God?" If Joan answered 'Yes' she would be presumptuous, if she answered 'No' she would be admitting a state of sin. Instead

157. Pernoud, *Joan of Arc,* pp. 165-66.
158. Pernoud, *The Retrial of Joan of Arc,* testimony of Guillaume Manchon, p. 166.
159. Pernoud, *The Retrial of Joan of Arc,* pp. 168-70. See also Pernoud, *Joan of Arc,* pp. 170-71.

Joan replied: "If I am not, may God place me there; if I am, may God so keep me."[160] When other people present at the trial tried to protect Joan from such trick questions, they were checked and even threatened by those in charge of the trial. Jean Fabri shared at the retrial that he had said to the Bishop of Beauvais after the above question was asked of Joan that "it was no question to put to such a woman." The Bishop responded to him: "It would have been better for you if you had kept your mouth shut."[161] This manipulation of questions and answers in order to trick Joan into saying things that could be used to support a charge of heresy against her was a common element throughout the entire trial.

We will now consider some aspects of the intergender dialogue during the trial of Joan of Arc that took place between its opening January on 9, and her execution on May 30, 1431. In particular, we will reflect on ways in which dialogue between educated men and an uneducated woman became distorted by interrogation and deception, and the devaluation of the one being tried. Our consideration will not reflect further on the motivations of those doing the interrogation or on Joan's motives for the kinds of answers she gave, nor will it focus more on the historical political events that provided the context of the trial.[162] Instead it will turn to an analysis of dynamics in the interrogation of Joan as a way of focusing on characteristics of intergender dialogue that occurred in this public context.

The stage is set by the form of the trial itself. At the beginning of the trial, the Dominican, Jean Le Maistre, a Bachelor of the Faculty of Theology at the University of Paris and Vicar of the Inquisitor of France of the Diocese of Rouen, and Jean Graverent, Dominican, Master in Theology at the University of Paris and Grand Inquisitor of France, began the proceedings with the Bishop of Beauvais, Pierre Cauchon. The two Inquisitors guided the trial from beginning to end, and in the proceedings, their deceptions shifted the true purpose of dialogue from a mutual search for truth to a distorted use of dialectic for the ultimate destruction of the woman being interrogated.

The first phase of the trial included five public interrogations on February 21 (42 male assessors and 1 female defendant), February 24 (52 male assessors and 1 female defendant), February 27 (54 male assessors and 1 female defendant), March 1 (58 male assessors and 1 female defendant), and March 3 (41 male assessors and 1 female defendant).[163] In each situation the male interrogators would pose certain questions, which Joan tried to answer.[164] In the illustration (page 490) of the trial of

160. See *Jeanne D'Arc: Maid of Orleans Deliverer of France, Being the Story of Her Life, Her Achievements, and Her Death, as Attested on Oath and Set Forth in the Original Documents*, trans. and ed. T. Douglas Murray (London: William Heinemann, 1902), testimony from Saturday, February 24, 18.

161. Pernoud, *The Retrial of Joan of Arc*, p. 171.

162. See, for example, Marina Warner, *Joan of Arc: The Image of Female Heroism* (New York: Vintage, 1981); Anne L. Barstow, *Joan of Arc: Heretic, Mystic, Shaman* (Lewiston, N.Y.: Edwin Mellen Press, 1985); Anne Llewellyn Barstow, "Joan of Arc and Female Mysticism," *Journal of Feminist Studies in Religion* 1, no. 1 (Fall 1985): 29-42.

163. *Procès de condamnation*, vol. 2, pp. 1-72. For the summary of the number of assessors present at each day of the trial see T. Douglas Murray, *Jeanne D'Arc*, pp. 379-83.

164. To emphasize the number of different backgrounds and functions of the educated men who were present during some of the interrogations, those listed below were present at the interroga-

Joan of Arc Defends Herself in Trial

Joan of Arc the male/female dynamics of this situation are well captured; Joan, the lone woman, is surrounded by male Church officials, members of the mendicant orders of Dominican and Franciscan friars, soldiers, and lay observers. Note that her dress is the same as the male soldiers who are present guarding her.

The record states simply that Joan was questioned in the presence of the above-mentioned men. In the following extract we can see some of the intergender interaction about a question of the relation of the dialogue to truth:

> In their presence we first requested the said Joan to tell, simply and completely, the truth regarding the questions which were posed to her, and to withhold nothing from her testimony; and we admonished her to do so three times. The said Joan answered:
> — Give me permission to speak.
> And then said:
> — By my faith you could ask me such things as I would not tell you.
> And also said:
> — Perhaps I will not tell the truth about everything which you ask me about

tion on February 24: several priests, doctors, masters, and bachelors of Sacred Theology, Canon Law, and Civil Law: Gilles, Abbot of Sainte-Trinité de Fécamp, Pierre, prior of Longueville-Giffard, Jean de Chastillon, Erard Emengart, Jean Beaupère, Jacques de Touraine, Nicolas Midi, Jean de Nibat, Jacques Guesdon, Maurice du Quesnay, Jean Le Fèvre, Guillaume Le Boucher, Pierre Houdenc, Pierre Maurice, Richard Prati, Jean Charpentier, Gérard Feuillet, Denis de Sabrevois, Nicolas de Jumièges, Guillaume de Baudribosc, Nicolas Loiseleur, Raoul Le Cauvage, Nicolas Lemire, Richard Le Gagneux, Jean Duval, Guillaume Le Maistre, Guillaume l'Ermite, the Abbot of Saint-Ouen, the Abbot of Saint-Georges, the Abbot of Préaux, the Prior of Saint-Lo, the Prior of Sigy, Robert Le Barbier, Denis Gastinel, Jean Le Doulx, Nicolas de Venderès, Jean Pinchon, Jean de La Fontaine, Aubert Morel, Jean Duchemin, Jean Colombel, Laurent Du Busc, Raoul Anguy, Richard des Saulx, André Marguerie, Jean Alespée, Geoffroy du Crotay, Gilles Deschamps, Nicolas Maulin, Pierre Carel, Robert Morellet, Jean Le Bon, and Nicolas de Foville. See *Procès de condamnation,* pp. 37-38.

the revelations; since you might, by chance, constrain me to talk of things of which I have sworn not to speak. I would therefore perjure myself, which you would never want!

And she said: I say this to you: take good care of what you say to be the judgment upon me, as you are charging me with a grave thing, and are charging me with too much!

Said as well that she had been told that, according to law, it was enough to have sworn twice.

In addition, questioned as to whether she wanted to swear, simply and completely, answered:

— You might as well forget about this: I've sworn twice and that's enough. . . .

Then, we told her that she made herself suspect if she refused to swear to tell the truth. Answered as before. Again we requested her to swear, precisely and completely. Then she answered she would tell voluntarily what she knew, but not everything. . . .

Finally, we requested her to swear and, once again, we admonished her to tell the truth about everything touching on the trial, telling her that she was exposing herself to great danger in so refusing. Then she answered:

— I am prepared to swear to tell the truth about what I know regarding the trial.

And she so swore.[165]

Joan was attempting to separate matters for public dialogue in the context of the trial and matters of her private prayers that she had promised God not to reveal.

As the interrogation proceeded, Joan was asked directly about those personal revelations from God she had wanted to keep private. She argued previously that she would not distort the truth, but that there were certain things that belonged to her private dialogue with God, angels, and saints, and that she believed these private things should remain unsaid in a public trial. However, the questions of the interrogators immediately focused on the divinely inspired voices that Joan believed she heard and the divinely inspired visions and locutions of the Archangel Michael, Saint Catherine of Alexandria, and Saint Margaret that she believed she saw and heard. Among these three figures, St. Catherine of Alexandria, who was popularly known as the Patron of Christian Philosophers, had by legend converted fifty pagan philosophers to Christianity by her capacity to argue and defend the faith. In the illustration on page 492 St. Catherine is represented as participating in her own trial, where, while refusing to worship idols, she converted her interrogators. St. Catherine was no doubt an inspiration to Joan's public debate during the trial in these circumstances.[166]

---

165. *Procès de condamnation,* pp. 38-40. Translated by Christopher Doss, as are all subsequent passages from this text unless otherwise noted.

166. The illustration is taken from the Basilica of S. Clemente, Chapel of St. Catherine, Rome, Italy. It was painted by Masolino da Panicale in 1428, just three years before Joan of Arc's trial and execution. For further information on St. Catherine of Alexandria, see Allen, *The Concept of Woman: The Aristotelian Revolution (750 BC–1250 AD),* cover illustration and pp. 214-18.

Catherine of Alexandria, Patroness of Christian Philosophers, Refuses to Worship Idols

After the first phase of public interrogation was completed, a second phase of interrogation in prison took place on mornings and afternoons, March 10, 12, 14, 15, 17, 18, and 25. In these private examinations the Bishop of Beauvais, the Inquisitor, and some witnesses were sometimes present. Some of these interrogations explored Joan's relation to witchcraft during her childhood. Again the questions and Joan's answers were carefully recorded.[167] Then the interrogators extracted from Joan's answers seventy different articles that were potentially damaging to her by their content of error, vice, witchcraft, disobedience of the Church, and so forth. At this point, the ordinary public trial took place on March 27 (38 male assessors, 2 male judges, and 1 female defendant), March 28 (35 male assessors, 2 male judges, and 1 female defendant), and on March 31 (9 male assessors, 2 judges, and 1 female defendant). Joan was asked to respond to each of the seventy articles with all the questions and responses again carefully recorded.[168] One example of a dialogue between Joan and her accusers about her association with witchcraft is recorded as follows:

> Article II. The Accused, not only this year, but from her infancy, and not only in your Diocese, Bishop, and your kingdom, hath done, composed, contrived and

167. *Procès de condamnation*, pp. 72-111.
168. *Procès de condamnation*, pp. 113-206.

ordained a number of sacrileges and superstitions: she made herself a diviner; invoked demons, and evil spirits; consulted them, associated with them, hath made and had with them compacts, treaties, and conventions, hath made use of them, hath furnished to others, acting in the same manner, aid, succour, and favour, and hath, in much, led them on to act like herself; she hath said, affirmed, and maintained that to act thus, to use witchcraft, divinations, superstitions, was not a sin, was not a forbidden thing, but, on the contrary, a thing lawful, to be praised, worthy of approval; also she hath led into these errors and evil doings a very great number of persons of divers estates, of both sexes, and hath imprinted on their hearts the most fatal errors. Jeanne hath been taken and arrested within the limits of your diocese of Beauvais, in the very act *(flagrante delicto)* of perpetrating all these misdoings.

"What have you to say to this Article?"

"I deny ever having used witchcraft, superstitious works, or divinations. As to allowing myself to be adored, if any kissed my hands and my garments, it was not my doing or by my wish; I sought to protect myself from it, and to prevent it as much as in me lay. And as for the rest of the Article, I deny it."[169]

Between April 2 and 4, the judges and some of the assessors reduced the original seventy articles to twelve. This process of reduction was done consciously to distort the dialogue of the actual trial in a way that would be detrimental to Joan. There were hidden scribes at the original trial who wrote down only select portions of the dialogue, leaving out any qualification that would help Joan, and including only those comments that might be construed towards heresy. In addition, the scribes who were writing openly were sometimes encouraged to distort their records. Guillaume Manchon, one of the notaries at the trial, gives the following description of this conscious process of distortion:

> At the beginning of the trial, during five or six days, while I was set down in writing the Maid's answers and excuses, sometimes the judges tried to constrain me, by translating into Latin, to put into other terms, changing the meaning of the words or, in some other manner, my understanding (of what had been said). And were placed two men, at the command of my lord of Beauvais, in a window (embrasure) near to the place where the judges were. And there was a serge curtain drawn in front of the window so that they should not be seen. These men wrote and reported what was charged against Joan, and suppressed her excuses.[170]

The notary then explained that there were great differences in the records of the trials "so much so that lively contestations arose between us."[171]

The deception of Joan involved the reduction of the seventy articles to twelve as a calculated and illegal procedure that enabled the interrogators to present her testimony in the worst possible light. In fact, some of the twelve articles actually

---

169. Murray, *Jeanne D'Arc,* p. 342.
170. Pernoud, *Joan of Arc,* p. 171.
171. Pernoud, *Joan of Arc,* p. 171.

contradicted her testimony. On April 5, the twelve articles were sent to the other assessors for approval and returned. The deliberations of the assessors were based only on the twelve articles. As Régine Pernoud summarized it: "The twelve articles enumerated Joan's *errors,* but these *errors* she had publicly abjured, and it is this abjuration that had laid her open to the punishment of the *relapsed,* of the heretic, who falls back into the errors that he has forsworn. A whole performance had been staged to this end."[172] The decision was made to officially condemn Joan without ever reading the twelve articles to her. This illegal step was the second major deception of Joan that occurred at the trial.[173]

On April 18, two judges and eight assessors met with Joan in prison to tell her that several "honest, knowledgeable, and educated" persons (academic doctors) had considered her responses to the questions, and noticed that several of them were "perilous." Joan admitted that she recognized she was in "great peril of death."[174] On April 19, the twelve articles were sent to the University of Paris where on April 29 they were discussed by the full Faculties of Theology and Decrees and adopted by a formal resolution.[175] At this point, the charge of witchcraft is not directly mentioned, but the broader categories of cooperation with evil spirits, heresy, schism, error in faith, and so forth are invoked. The doctors from the University at Rouen also accorded their agreement with the twelve articles identified by the academics from the University of Paris.

Some of the twelve articles will be included below because they instantiate the concepts of woman mentioned previously, namely, that woman is deceitful and dangerous.

> I: First, regarding article 1, this Faculty declares, in the doctrinal manner, having heard the end, the manner and the matter of the revelations, the quality of the person, the place and the other circumstances, that these revelations are counterfeit, seductive, and pernicious lies, or that these said apparitions and revelations are superstitious, issuing from malevolent and diabolical spirits, such as Belial, Satan and Behemoth.

> II: Item, regarding article II, its content does not appear true, but rather a presumptuous, seductive, pernicious, counterfeit lie, and an offense against the dignity of angels. . . .

> IV: Item, in what concerns article IV, its content is only a superstitious, occult, presumptuous assertion and vain arrogance.

> V: Item, relative to article V, the said woman is . . . thinking poorly and erring in faith, holding to a vain arrogance; and she must be suspected of idolatry in the execration of herself and her clothing; she has imitated the practices of pagans.

---

172. Pernoud, *The Retrial of Joan of Arc,* pp. 47-48.
173. Pernoud, *Joan of Arc,* pp. 196-97.
174. *Procès de condamnation,* pp. 237-39.
175. Murray, *Jeanne D'Arc,* p. 382.

VI: Item, relative to article VI, the said woman is treacherous, duplicitous, cruel, thirsting to spread human blood, seditious, spreading tyranny, and blasphemes God in the orders and the revelations she gives us. . . .

IX: Item, in article IX there is a presumptuous and imprudent assertion, a pernicious lie. She is in contradiction with herself, following the preceding article, and she thinks poorly in matters of faith. . . .

XI: Item, relative to article XI, this woman, assuming that she has witnessed the revelations and apparitions of which she is proud in the circumstances determined in article I, is an idolater, an invocator of demons; she errs in faith, asserts imprudently and has given illicit counsel.

XII: Item, in what concerns article XII, the said woman is a schismatic, thinking poorly on the unity and authority of the Church, and an apostate; and, to this day, errs stubbornly in matters of faith.[176]

The public dialogue continued on May 2 (63 male assessors, 2 male judges, and 1 female defendant), and the interrogators gave a public admonition of Joan. The names of sixty different men, including several Doctors of Theology and Canon Law, were carefully listed as participating in this public admonition.[177] Joan responded to the beginning of the admonition: "Read your book . . . and I will respond."[178] Again the dialogue proceeded, with the accusations and responses duly recorded. On May 9, Joan was interrogated in the prison tower in Rouen, taken to the torture chamber, and threatened with torture.[179] On May 12, the judges and twelve assessors decided not to torture Joan. On May 19, fifty-one assessors and the judges met to read the resolutions of the University of Paris, and to consider the opinions of the assessors separately from Joan.[180] It is worth reflecting again on the extraordinary situation that Joan faced, as a young woman, constantly being pressured by a number of men to testify in such a way that she would incriminate herself. It was a situation of enormous imbalance of power between the two genders, and it can stand as a symbolic reference for the extreme gender polarity situation that existed in parts of European society at the time.

The charges were summarized in ways that set Joan up for condemnation. In this second statement the charges were sharpened to be less focused on consorting with evil spirits and witchcraft, and more on her direct conflict with articles of faith in the Church and on her choice of men's clothes and hairstyle. Again, a summary of the charges indicates the shift in the focus of the interrogation:

I: First, that this woman is a schismatic, since a schism is an illicit separation,

176. *Procès de condamnation,* pp. 262-63.
177. *Procès de condamnation,* p. 241.
178. *Procès de condamnation,* p. 244.
179. Pernoud, *Joan of Arc,* p. 202.
180. *Procès de condamnation,* p. 262.

caused by disobedience, from the unity of the Church, and that she removes herself from obedience to the militant Church, as she has said, etc.

II. Item, that this woman errs in faith; contradicts the article of faith contained in the little symbol: *unam sanctam Ecclesiam catholicam;* and, as Saint Jerome said, he who contradicts this article proves that he is not only ignorant, malevolent, not catholic, but also a heretic.

III: Item, that this woman is an apostate, as she has had the hair which God gave her as a veil cut, in an inappropriate fashion, and also, in the same manner, has abandoned the clothing of women and has dressed herself as men do.

IV: Item, that this woman is a liar and diviner when she says that she is sent by God. . . .

V: Item, that this woman, by presumption that she is in the right, errs in faith: as firstly, she stays so long in the state of anathema, which is decreed by the authority of canon law; secondly, in declaring that she would prefer not to receive the body of Christ, and not to confess in the time ordained by the Church, than to wear again the clothing of a woman. In addition she is overwhelmingly suspect of heresy and must be diligently examined regarding articles of faith.[181]

Then, on May 23 the interrogatory dialogue was opened up once again with the judges, seven assessors, and Joan present. Joan was interrogated in prison about the twelve articles, and her responses were considered. By now Joan recognized the fraudulent basis for the judgments of the twelve articles. In her defense, Joan argued that the charges had distorted the meaning of her answers, that they were manifestly false, and that the local judges and bishops did not properly represent the Church. She appealed to the Pope in Rome to hear her case, an appeal that was refused. During this period she was threatened with death by fire. On May 24, the first sentence was read in the cemetery, and Joan signed an abjuration or confession, and was given instead a sentence of perpetual imprisonment.

One of the key components of Joan's confession involved an acceptance that it was wrong of her to wear men's clothes, or to wear "dissolute, deformed, and dishonest clothes, contrary to the decency of nature, and hair cut round in the style of men, contrary to all manners of the female sex. . . ."[182] This theme has been brought up in the dialogue during the trial over and over again. In the introductory remarks she was described as "wearing, with an astonishing and monstrous audacity, the indecent clothes accorded to the masculine sex."[183] This issue is a key to the developing sense of how differences between men and women are considered essentially reflected in clothes and hairstyles. Joan had worn the clothes of a male sol-

181. *Procès de condamnation,* pp. 264-65.
182. *Procès de condamnation,* p. 284.
183. *Procès de condamnation,* p. 1. See also March 12, 80; March 17, 102; March 25, 111; March 28, 121, 131-32, 135, 137; March 31, 207, 209-10; April 18, 246, 250; and the articles of May 23, 274.

dier while she was engaged in her military activity, and she continued to do so in prison. She gave as her reasons for this choice divine revelation as well as the practical value when living in an all-male environment. An extract from one interrogation on February 27th focuses on this issue:

> Beaupère: "Do you believe that you did right to put on man's clothes?"
> Joan: "All that I have done, I have done by God's commandment and I believe that I did right, and I expect from it good warrant and good succour."
> Beaupère: "In the particular case of taking on man's clothes, do you think that you did right?"
> Joan: "Of what I have done in the world I have done nothing but by God's commandment."[184]

The importance the interrogators gave to this topic of appropriate dress for a woman or a man is attested to by the visit to Joan's cell on March 17 of a group restricted to all the assessors from the University of Paris. As Régine Pernoud summarizes this calculated encounter: "More detailed answers were demanded of her in the matter of certain questions, notably that of wearing man's clothes which she still refused to change for female attire. It was on this occasion that she gave the answer which, for her, summed up the whole business: 'These clothes do not burden my soul and to wear them is not against the Church.'"[185] Her answer quite clearly indicated that clothing was accidental to her identity as a woman and as a person. Quite remarkably this was the final interrogation in the first trial seeking to establish the grounds for her actual trial.

At the end of the actual trial, however, Joan agreed to put on women's clothes, and she signed a kind of confession that she could not read and that was procured by deceptive maneuvering by the interrogators. These deceptions included not only the general distortion of her answers to questions but also the implication that she would be able to receive Holy Communion if she wore women's clothes and recanted her past testimony. We are told by the trial record that "Now Joan answered that she would voluntarily dress again in the clothing of a woman . . . some women's clothing having been presented to her, she put it on, having removed her men's clothing immediately; she desired and permitted in addition that the hair she had previously worn in a bowl[-shaped cut] be shaved and removed."[186]

However, Joan soon changed her mind and put back on her old military clothing. There are two different theories about why she made this change, both of which appear to be true. One states that she was sexually assaulted in the cell by the male guards or by a male visitor.[187] The other states that the guards stole her

184. As recorded in Pernoud, *Joan of Arc,* p. 185.

185. Pernoud, *Joan of Arc,* pp. 192-93.

186. *Procès de condamnation,* p. 288.

187. Barstow, "Joan of Arc and Female Mysticism," suggests that "The testimony of three witnesses at her posthumous retrial, one of whom had been her court-appointed confessor, claimed that she had been sexually abused during her last days in prison" by the guards who were in her cell day and night, p. 42, note 46. Barstow refers her reader to Régine Pernoud, *The Retrial of Joan of Arc,* pp.

women's clothes and left her old men's clothes in the cell as the only thing she could wear.[188] There is no doubt that Joan was frequently threatened with sexual molestation in her cell. At the retrial several testimonies were offered to support this claim.[189] One testimony by Isambart de la Pierre was particularly moving:

> After she had renounced and abjured and resumed man's clothes, I and several others were present when Joan excused herself for having again put on man's clothes, saying and affirming publicly that the English had had much wrong and violence done to her in prison when she was dressed in woman's clothes. And in fact I saw her tearful, her face covered with tears, disfigured and outraged in such sort that I had pity and compassion on her.[190]

One knight, Haimond de Macy, testified at the rehabilitation trial that: "I saw her several (many) times in prison [at the castle of Beaurevoir before being transferred to Rouen] and on several occasions conversed with her. I tried several times, playfully to touch her breasts, trying to put my hand on her chest, the which Joan would not suffer but repulsed me with all her strength."[191] Not only did the danger come from visitors, but also from the three guards who stayed in her cell with her throughout the nights, even though she was chained and fettered to a bed during that time. It was to protect herself from molestation that Joan had so frequently requested being transferred to an ecclesiastical jail where women would guard her.[192] Joan herself also said that if she had been in an ecclesiastical jail she would not have changed back into men's clothes, and then she would not have been able to have been charged as a relapsed heretic.

By May 28 Joan was visited again by the judges and four assessors and was classified as a "relapse" or "backslider." When Joan was interrogated about this choice she answered as follows:

182-83, to substantiate this claim. In this account Martin Ladvenu said that an English Lord had tried to rape her, while Pierre Cusquel said that soldiers had made advances at her. In both accounts Joan uses these incidents as the reason why she had resumed wearing male clothes.

188. T. Douglas Murray, in *Jeanne D'Arc*, summarizes these suggestions: "Several versions of the reasons which caused Jeanne to resume the forbidden dress were given in the evidence taken at the Rehabilitation, all purporting to have come from her. According to Massieu, her woman's dress was taken away while she was asleep, and the English soldiers refused to give it back to her, offering the man's dress she had previously worn, 'which they emptied from a sack.' . . . The Dominican Brothers declared that she had been assaulted by an English milord, as she told them, and that she therefore considered it necessary to return to the protection of her old dress. . . ." Murray thinks that her own preference for male clothing because of the nature of her religious mission was the reason for the change (pp. 135-36, note 1). See also Pernoud, *Joan of Arc*, p. 219, and Pernoud, *The Retrial of Joan of Arc*, pp. 182-83.

189. Pernoud, *The Retrial of Joan of Arc*, pp. 160-62, 183.

190. Pernoud, *Joan of Arc*, p. 220. A second testimony came from Martin Landvenu who said: ". . . I heard it from Joan's own lips that a great English lord entered her prison and tried to take her by force. That was the cause, she said, of her resuming man's clothes" (p. 220).

191. Pernoud, *Joan of Arc*, p. 155.

192. Pernoud, *Joan of Arc*, p. 218.

Questioned as to what reason caused her to wear them again, answered (that she had done it) because it was more proper for her to wear them again and (more comfortable) to wear the clothing of men, being among men, than to wear women's clothing. Item, said that she had put them on again because she had not been given what had been promised to her, that is, that she might go to mass and receive her Savior, and that she would be taken out of irons.

Questioned as to whether she had not previously recanted, and specially sworn not to wear men's clothing again, answered that she would rather die than be in irons; but that if we would let her go to mass and take her out of irons, and place her in a more pleasant prison (and let her have a woman [guard]), she would be good and do what the Church desires. . . .

. . . Said in addition that her voices told her, while she was on the scaffold (or platform, before the people), that she answered boldly to the preacher (who was preaching to her). And this Joan said that he was a false preacher, and that he had said several things which she had not done at all. . . .

Item, said that her voices had said to her since (Thursday) that she had done a great evil when she confessed that she had not done what she had.

Item, said that everything that she had said (and revoked that Thursday, was said only) out of fear of fire. . . .

Asked (to tell the truth) regarding the crown (of which there was question above), answered: "I have told you the truth about everything in this trial to the best of my knowledge."

. . . and that everything that she had done was out of fear of fire, and that she had recanted nothing of the truth. . . .

. . . and that she had not understood (the content) of the articles of the recantation. . . .

Item, said that she will wear the clothing of women again, if the judges wish it; but that she will not change anything else.

After having heard these declarations, we left her in order to continue on, as required by law and reason.[193]

In the final adjudication, on May 29, the judges and forty assessors restated their view about her relation to truth as follows: "We caused her to be exhorted in the most lively manner to abandon her errors, and to return into the way of truth; up to the last moment she refused to agree to these admonitions and these exhortations, and would say nothing more."[194] The judges and assessors decided that Joan must be turned over to the secular, civil court for punishment as a relapsed heretic.

On this day there is testimony from a Dominican, Jean Toutnouillé, who went to Joan's cell to hear her confession and to speak to her about her sentence of death, that Joan again stated: "'Alas, if only I had been in the prisons of the Church to which I have submitted, if I had been guarded by churchmen and not by my enemies and foes, I should not have come to this miserable end'. . . . And she complained exceedingly of the oppressions and violences that had been done to her in

---

193. *Procès de condamnation,* pp. 289-91.
194. Murray, *Jeanne D'Arc,* p. 138.

prison by her gaolers and by others who had been let in to harm her."[195] The personal indignities to which Joan was subjected continued right up to the moment of her death. One testimony by Jean Marcel described a tailor, Jeannotin Simon, who made a woman's tunic for her, touching her breast in the prison cell as he measured it against her body. Joan, protecting herself, gave him a slap in the face. In spite of all the attempts of sexual harassment, Joan of Arc managed to protect her virginity to the end. She agreed to have an internal examination by some English women, and they verified the integrity of her body in this respect.[196]

The definitive sentence that was handed down on the public square of the old market in Rouen invoked a description of a person "transfigured into a member of Satan," and a need to protect others from "the pernicious contagion of a pernicious sore," or a "pernicious viper" that could imperil others. Joan's crimes were identified as schism, idolatry, invocation of demons, and several other evil acts. Joan was given the sentence of excommunication as a relapsed or backsliding heretic, and immediately given to the executioner for burning, even without the usual legal judgment of a civil judge.[197] On May 30, 1431 Joan of Arc was burned to death in the public marketplace at Rouen.

In 1450, twenty years after her death, a second trial of inquisition was held concerning Joan of Arc at the request of her mother. The English had finally been driven out of Rouen, and so the court records were available for evaluation. This retrial, which resulted in Joan's acquittal, was the only one that used proper inquisitional techniques.[198] At this trial of rehabilitation, the question of truth and distortion in the original trial was raised in the effort to settle the question: "Was Joan a heretic?"[199] The retrial took six years.[200] The entire proceedings were reviewed from beginning to end by the Dominican General Inquisitor of France, Jean Bréhal.[201] The rehabilitation trial moved from Paris, to Rouen, to Orleans, and in addition to an assessment of Joan's character and witness, it focused on specific illegalities such as Joan's having no advocate, not being read the twelve articles, contradictions between her testimony and the twelve articles, and being held in a civil rather than ecclesiastical prison. In addition, it carefully considered all of Joan's answers to questions posed to her. In this sense, Joan finally had the integral intergender audience she had hoped for previously. Her discursive reasoning did ultimately prove effective and Joan was vindicated. Jean Bréhal's *Recollectio* and *Summarium* methodically defended her.[202]

---

195. Pernoud, *The Retrial of Joan of Arc*, pp. 184-85.

196. Pernoud, *The Retrial of Joan of Arc*, pp. 176-77.

197. *Procès de condamnation*, pp. 299-300. See also Pernoud, *The Retrial of Joan of Arc*, p. 212.

198. Edward Peters, *Inquisition* (New York: The Free Press, 1988), ". . . the presence of theologians and canonists among the assessors — there were grave irregularities in the [first] trial. Joan's confinement in an English military prison was strictly against inquisitorial procedure and evidence was well below inquisitorial standards; the technicalities of Joan's conviction and turning over to the secular arm as a relapsed heretic were largely political" (p. 69).

199. Pernoud, *The Retrial of Joan of Arc*, p. 36.

200. Pernoud, *The Retrial of Joan of Arc*, p. 17.

201. Pernoud, *The Retrial of Joan of Arc*, pp. 21, 28-29.

202. Pernoud, *The Retrial of Joan of Arc*, pp. 214-15.

Significantly, this later inquisition identified those who had conducted the previous trial as having used dialogue to continually distort the truth. Some examples from the first set of interrogatory articles are included below:

X. That after being ordered to resume and wear female clothing, she was compelled to put on male clothing; which was the reason why the self-styled judges pronounced her relapsed, they seeking not her repentance but her death;

XI. That although it was clear to the judges that Joan had submitted to the judgments and decisions of our Blessed Mother the Church, nevertheless the judges, in their excessive partiality for the English, or not daring to resist their terrorization and pressure, condemned her most unjustly as a heretic to the pains of fire.[203]

These first articles were revised and developed into another set of articles for the second interrogatory. In this second set of articles, the focus was much more directed towards the distortion in the interpretation of the record of the trial, and the use of intimidation and fear against those present to ensure a deception and ultimately a condemnation of Joan. A few sample articles are included below:

V. That the notaries recording this trial, because of the same fear and the threats directed against them by the English, could not follow the truth or faithfully set down the true version of Joan's replies when writing and editing their account.

VI. That the notaries were prevented by this fear, and also expressly forbidden to insert in their account words pronounced by Joan which told in her favor. Furthermore, that they were constrained to omit them and to insert certain things which told against her and which she never said. . . .

XVIII. That the alleged report, originally written in French, was translated into Latin with no great accuracy, many things having been suppressed that told in Joan's favour and even more having been added, in defiance of truth, that prejudiced her case, and therefore that the said record disagrees with its original in numerous and substantial points.

XIX. That, the preceding truths having been recognized, the said trial and sentence does not deserve the name of a judgment and sentence, since there can be no questions of a judgment where the judges, consultants and assessors are not at liberty to exercise judgment owing to fear. . . .

XXI. That the preceding and other points being weighed, the case and the sentence are both null and unjust. . . .

203. Pernoud, *The Retrial of Joan of Arc*, p. 220.

XXII. That, moreover, the said trial and sentence are both null and tainted with manifest injustice. . . .[204]

These articles are important to our study because they recognize the failure of the original trial to respect the purpose of public interrogation and dialogue as searching for the truth. Instead, the trial was full of deception and the degeneration of public dialogue as a conscious series of acts flowing from a blatant motive of revenge and struggle for power.

The final conclusion of the retrial clearly identified the situation. A portion of the final conclusion is quoted here below:

> In the first place, we say, and because Justice requires it, we declare, that the Articles beginning with the words "A Woman," which are found inserted in the pretended sentences, lodged against the said Deceased, ought to have been, have been, and are extracted from the said pretended Process and the said pretended confessions of the said Deceased, with corruption, cozenage, calumny, fraud and malice;
>
> We declare that on certain points the truth of her confessions has been passed over in silence; that on other points her confessions have been falsely translated — a double unfaithfulness, by which, had it been prevented, the mind of the Doctors consulted and the Judges might have been led to a different opinion. . . .
>
> We declare that even the form of certain words has been altered, in such manner as to change the substance:
>
> For the which, these same Articles, as falsely, calumniously, and deceitfully extracted, and as contrary even to the Confessions of the Accused, we break, annihilate, and annul.[205]

A similar judgment is made concerning the "lapse" and "relapse," namely that the processes and sentences were "full of cozenage, iniquity, inconsequences, and manifest errors, in fact as well as in law," and that they are annulled.[206] The notice of annulment was publicly displayed in the same marketplace in Rouen, the next day, June 8, 1456, where Joan had been put to death.

In this analysis of Joan of Arc we have chosen to focus predominantly on the quality of the intergender dialogue with respect to the goal of the mutual search for truth. Consistently Joan sought to be truthful about herself within the limits of what she believed was appropriate matter for a public court. The dialogue of her first inquisition was riddled with deception by the interrogators, and the dialogue of her second inquisition recognized and overturned these initial results by a reordering of truth and judgment. In the end, Joan's truthful testimony was vindicated, but at the price of her death.

In time, history re-evaluated the wisdom and virtue of Joan of Arc. Marina Warner identifies several works of later humanists that specifically defended Joan:

204. Pernoud, *The Retrial of Joan of Arc,* pp. 221-23.
205. Murray, *Jeanne D'Arc,* p. 326.
206. Murray, *Jeanne D'Arc,* pp. 326-27.

Jehan Martin le Franc, *Le Champion des dames (The Champion of Women)* (w. 1442 and pub. 1550), François de Billon, *Fort inexpugnable de l'honneur du sexe feminin (The Invincible Strength of the Honor of the Female Sex)* (pub. 1555), Guillaume Postel, *Les Très merveilleuses victoires des femmes du nouveau monde (The Very Wonderful Victories of the Women of the New World. And how they should govern the whole world by reason, and even those too who will be Monarchs in the Old World)* (pub. 1553).[207] Then as previously described, due to the records of meticulous work of the fifteenth-century Dominican Inquisitor, Jean Bréhal, Joan was proclaimed blessed in 1909 and officially canonized as a saint in 1920.

For the purposes of the present study, it is important to note that the trial and retrial of Joan reveal that a few educated men, with ulterior motives, introduced deception into the heart of their public dialogue with this young woman. This deception involved changing the written record of her responses to questions, composing articles many of which falsely described her positions on various matters, arranging her imprisonment in such a way that she had to resort to wearing men's clothes for personal protection from male soldiers and visitors and thus relapsed from her agreement to wear women's clothes only. While there were also many illegal procedures both in her imprisonment and trial, and a multitude of other personal deceptions by individuals involved with the trial, those mentioned above constitute a core with particular relevance to issues of sex and gender identity. Thus the trial of Joan of Arc demonstrated a considerable deterioration of intergender dialogue. However, the retrial demonstrated a recovery of the purpose of public dialogue as searching for a greater truth. Ultimately Joan's answers were studied and did prove her innocent of all the charges.

In the next section of this chapter we will study a manual written some fifty years after the death of St. Joan of Arc. In it, the theme of deception will continue to operate as a variable in public forms of interrogation between highly educated men and uneducated women. We move from the consideration of concrete particular women, struggling to defend themselves against false charges, to a text full of generalizations about woman's identity. These generalizations will sound an echo from those views already articulated in philosophies of gender polarity and in satires against women.

THE *MALLEUS MALEFICARUM* (THE WITCHES' HAMMER)

The final text to be considered in this chapter on the degeneration of intergender dialogue was a popular manual used in the late fifteenth and sixteenth centuries for the interrogation and trial of witches. Much has been written in contemporary times about women and witchcraft. My own approach to the question of the relation of gender to witchcraft will be different from most of these studies. Since the consideration of differences in approaches to this topic is outside the range of this book, I will not include a discussion here but move into the historical

---

207. Warner, *Joan of Arc*, pp. 220-21.

analysis, to pursue the philosophical bases of sex and gender identity in the particular period being considered.

The *Malleus maleficarum* completes a three-part examination, first, of satires that devalue woman's identity, second, of texts about two women who struggled to overcome stereotypes of devaluation of woman's identity, and third, of a systematic account of the connection between woman's identity and the use of deception in public contexts. The three phases of this study follow a progression of, first, imaginary satirical dialogue about women, second, actual dialogue of particular women, to third, guidelines for dialogue with large numbers of women. First, there were the imaginary female personifications of fantasy in the *Miroir* and the imaginary manipulative wife in *Les Quinze joies*. Second, there were actual women struggling in life and death situations against accusations — mostly of heresy, but sometimes of witchcraft. Third, we will see systematic judgments about why women more than men are prone to witchcraft. Although both men and women were accused of witchcraft, it is women who became more and more identified with this particular form of heresy. In this third phase of the chapter, examples from the first two stages will be incorporated as the authors appeal to the authority of philosophical and satirical texts and give examples from the histories of other particular women to substantiate their claims about woman's particular association with witchcraft.

In the subsequent analysis, we will reflect on metaphysical, epistemological, and ethical aspects of the concept of woman as revealed in this original text written about witches. Some common patterns of argument found in both satires about women and texts written about witchcraft will be identified. The particular text chosen for this comparison is the *Malleus maleficarum (the Hammer of Witches, or those who do evil)*.[208] Heinrich Kramer, who died in 1505, and James Sprenger (ca. 1436-1508) collaborated to write a manual on witchcraft around 1486 to use in their work as official inquisitors in Northern Germany.[209] Kramer, a Preacher-General and Master of Sacred Theology in the Dominican Order, had already been an Inquisitor in Southern Germany and parts of Austria since 1474.[210] Sprenger, a Dominican from Basel, Switzerland, was Dean of the Faculty of Theology at the University of Cologne and later German Provincial of the Order.[211]

A 1484 bull of Pope Innocent VIII, written two years before the *Malleus maleficarum* and later printed as its preface, gave the manual an official status that

208. The title implies that the authors have written a book which will hammer (to destroy) the witches, not that the witches hammer others.

209. Heinrich Kramer and James Sprenger, *The Malleus maleficarum* (New York: Dover Publications, 1971), unabridged republication of 1928 version with additional introduction by Montague Summers. Their dioceses included Mainz, Cologne, Trèves, Salzburg, and Bremen, p. viii. Jeffrey Russell notes in *Witchcraft in the Middle Ages* (Ithaca: Cornell University Press, 1972): "From 1427, when publication of discourses on witchcraft began to proliferate, to 1486, the date of publication of the sinister *Malleus maleficarum,* the witch phenomenon became thoroughly articulated. Ideas that had previously remained distinct were now joined as a whole" (p. 228).

210. These regions included Tirol, Salzburg, Bohemia, and Moravia. Kramer also authored texts on the themes of the Eucharist and identifying errors of individuals such as the Picards, and Waldenses. See Summers, *Malleus maleficarum,* pp. viii-ix.

211. Sprenger authored works of refutation and on the institution of the Confraternity of the Rosary. See Summers, *Malleus maleficarum,* p. ix.

added to its importance.[212] It is important to note that the first papal ordinance against witchcraft had already been issued by Pope Gregory IX in 1233.[213] However, the inclusion of the bull with the printed edition of the text gave it an official sanction. In addition, its official approval by the Faculty of Theology of Cologne in 1487 lent academic credibility as well. As Montague Summers observes: "The *Malleus* lay on the bench of every judge, on the desk of every magistrate. It was the ultimate, irrefutable, unarguable authority. It was implicitly accepted not only by Catholic but by Protestant legislature."[214] The *Malleus maleficarum* is considered by most scholars to be the symbolic text on witchcraft during this period in history.

The invention of the printing press played a crucial role in the dissemination of texts about witches. Jeffrey Russell notes: "The fact that the printing press could now disseminate the works of the witch theorists in a quantity hitherto undreamed of added enormously to the growth of the witch craze. The first printed book on witchcraft, the *Fortalicium fidei,* was issued in 1464, only a few years after Gutenberg had produced the first book printed with movable type."[215] The *Malleus maleficarum* was printed fourteen times between 1486 and 1520, and sixteen more times between 1574 and 1669 in Germany, France, and Italy. The text is divided into three sections: the first one examines the three concomitants of witchcraft, the second examines methods of witchcraft and methods for its destruction, and the third examines judicial proceedings against witches.

The relevant components for the philosophy of gender are present throughout the text, and therefore this analysis will be thematic, rather than chronological. Our analysis will consider the following themes: ways in which the authors universalize or stereotype characteristics of women and how these characteristics participate in concepts found in traditional gender polarity; particular characteristics of woman that are either exaggerated or inverted in the analysis; the relation of gender to the practice of virtue and vice in particular acts; and the response of the inquisitors in viewing a particular woman as dangerous for men. In addition, we will

212. However, Edward Peters points out in *The Magician* that "there is not a shred of evidence that Innocent VIII ever saw the *Malleus maleficarum* or had the faintest notion of the ideas it contained" (p. 173). He continues by reflecting that the originality of the *Malleus* is found in "its economic use of the *quaestio* form to bring together elements from all the diverse sources that had provided elements of the new fifteenth-century beliefs in magic in the first place. The juxtaposition of these elements in a single, concentrated, tightly argued treatise of considerably greater length than any earlier work really constituted the basis for the popularity of the *Malleus* during the next two centuries" (p. 173).

213. See *Malleus maleficarum,* intro., pp. xxiv-xxv. Other bulls against witchcraft were issued by subsequent Popes in 1258, 1260, and those who reigned in 1316-1334, 1334-1342, 1370-1378, 1409-1410, 1417-1431, 1431-1447, 1447-1455, 1455-1458, 1458-1464, 1473, 1478, and 1483. So the Bull of 1484 was simply one instance in a long line of edicts concerning witchcraft.

214. Summers, *Malleus maleficarum,* p. viii. This view is qualified by H. C. Erik Midelfort, *Witch Hunting in Southwestern Germany, 1562-1684: The Social and Intellectual Foundations* (Stanford: Stanford University Press, 1972), who argued: "But despite its subsequent fame, the misogynistic *Malleus Maleficarum* of the fifteenth century was couched in difficult Latin, and was therefore accessible only to scholars. Indeed, one finds only the rarest mention of the *Malleus* in German sermons and trial records of the period . . ." (p. 5).

215. Russell, *Witchcraft in the Middle Ages,* p. 234.

continue to follow the theme of the degeneration of intergender dialogue through deception and of the distortion of dialogue in interrogations of uneducated women placed under arrest. This section of the chapter will be divided into four parts: (1) Witchcraft and Women's Identity; (2) Satirical and Philosophical Authority Devaluing Woman's Identity; (3) Calculated Deception in Intergender Dialogue; (4) Women and Witchcraft Trials.

Witchcraft and Women's Identity

The authors of the *Malleus* state clearly that both men and women could be witches and both men and women could be victims of witchcraft. Sometimes the *Malleus maleficarum* uses the generic "he" in describing the activities of witches, but more often it uses the generic "she." It uses the gender-specific notion of "her" or "she" when considering a kind of activity mostly connected with one gender or the other. So the manual refers to "he" when discussing the category of male "archer witches" who use arrows with an archer's skill for evil ends;[216] and other times it uses the gender specific "she" when discussing the category of female "midwife witches" who use various means to interfere with fruitful generation.[217] Since we are focusing on the concept of woman, and especially in this chapter on negative generalizations about women's identity and character, we will consider primarily ways in which the *Malleus maleficarum* describes women who practice witchcraft for evil purposes.

The Malleus maleficarum is founded philosophically upon the Aristotelian and scholastic concept of the person as having the faculties of will and intellect, external and internal powers of sensation, passions, and virtuous or vicious character.[218]

216. See *Malleus maleficarum*, II, q. 1, ch. xvi, "Of Three Ways in Which Men and Not Women May Be Discovered to Be Addicted to Witchcraft: Divided into Three Heads: and First of the Witchcraft of Archers" (pp. 150-55). See also Lionel Rothkrug's analysis of the historical and political context for archer witches in "Religious Practices and Collective Perceptions: Hidden Homologies in the Renaissance and Reformation," *Historical Reflections/Réflexions Historiques* 7, no. 1 (Spring 1980): ch. 8, 103-23 and addendum to ch. 8.

217. While this category is used throughout the text, certain chapters emphasize it. See *Malleus maleficarum*, I, q. 11, "The Witches Who Are Midwives in Various Ways Kill the Child Conceived in the Womb, and Procure an Abortion; or If They Do Not This, Offer New-born Children to Devils," p. 66; and II, q. 1. ch. vi, "How Witches Impede and Prevent the Power of Procreation," pp. 117-18. Rothkrug incorrectly identifies celibacy as the target of female witches in the *Malleus*. Instead, it is the procreative power of generation that Kramer and Sprengler identify consistently as the target of the witches' actions. See "Religious Practices," p. 120.

218. See Sydney Anglo, "Evident Authority and Authoritative Evidence: The *Malleus Maleficarum*," in *The Damned Art: Essays in the Literature of Witchcraft*, ed. Sydney Anglo (London, Henley and Boston: Routledge and Kegan Paul, 1977), pp. 1-31. "Four principal authorities, however, dominate the *Malleus*: Aristotle, who provides both natural explanations and the logical structure of each proposition; the Scriptures, which form the basis for all theological, miraculous, and moral arguments; St Augustine, whose assertions concerning magic and demonology are scattered broadcast throughout the text; and St Thomas Aquinas, who furnishes a synthesis of the other three major sources" (p. 18).

Sprenger and Kramer accurately describe these aspects of human identity, and they introduce them ingeniously in their progressive descriptions of the way that witchcraft works. A person must exercise free will to decide to act in cooperation with an evil spirit;[219] a person who chooses this kind of vicious act does so because of an error of intellect;[220] the person who has made this vicious choice entices others through the various powers of sensation;[221] finally, the person who acts in this way is motivated by the passion of hatred and/or inordinate love.[222]

Jeffrey Russell discusses in *Witchcraft in the Middle Ages* the influence of scholasticism on the connection of women and witchcraft. He argues as follows: "Scholastic influence upon witchcraft has been greatly exaggerated. The witch ideas were evolved in popular culture and only afterward were picked up by intellectuals. . . . Nonetheless the scholastics did provide an authoritative intellectual structure that was later used to bad effect by the witch hunters."[223] This is an important point to note. Academics did not cause the devaluation of woman, according to Russell, but they offered a structure of authority to support it. The scholastic system in contrast to the Neoplatonic system, he argues, left open the need to explain effecting change at a distance by some supernatural means because of its tighter empirical structure. "The *Malleus maleficarum* of the fifteenth century considered women peculiarly susceptible to demonic temptation through their manifold weaknesses. This tradition was responsible for placing the chief blame for witchcraft upon women."[224] Women's natural weakness, as justified by the Aristo-

---

219. See *Malleus maleficarum,* "For they are human instruments and free agents, and although they have made a compact and a contract with the devil, nevertheless they do enjoy absolute liberty . . ." (I, q. 2, 16). See also II, q. 1, ch. 2, where the topic is "Of the Way Whereby a Formal Pact with Evil Is Made" (99-104).

220. See *Malleus maleficarum,* "For it is well known to all through common practice that the first essential of a heretic is an error in the understanding; but two conditions are necessary before a man can be called a heretic: the first material, that is, an error in reasoning, and the second formal, that is, an obstinate mind" (III, intro., 198). The text makes a distinction between a heretic and an infidel, who may hold the same views but who has never professed the Catholic faith, 202; and it makes a further distinction between a heretic and an apostate. A heretic has an error in reasoning about the identity of Jesus Christ, while an apostate "wholly denies the faith" (III, intro., 195). It follows that all apostates are heretics, but not all heretics are apostates. Malicious witchcraft is usually considered in the document as a form of apostasy and therefore of heresy.

221. See *Malleus maleficarum,* ". . . when devils enter the body, they enter the powers belonging to the bodily organs, and can so create impressions on those powers. And so it happens that through such operations and impressions a phantasm is projected before the understanding, such as the seeing of colours, as it is said in the 3rd book *De Anima*. And so this impression penetrates also to the will. For the will takes its conception of what is good from the intellect, according as the intellect accepts something as good either in truth or in appearance" (I, q. 7, 53).

222. See *Malleus maleficarum,* "Therefore devils, who have learned from men's acts to which passions they are chiefly subject, incite them to this sort of inordinate love or hatred, impressing their purpose on men's imagination the more strongly and effectively, as they can do so more easily. . . . But they work by witchcraft when they do these things through and at the instance of witches, by reason of a pact entered into with them" (I, q. 7, 51). The whole of question 7 considers "Whether Witches Can Sway the Minds of Men to Love or Hatred" (48-54).

223. Russell, *Witchcraft in the Middle Ages,* p. 142.

224. Russell, *Witchcraft in the Middle Ages,* p. 145.

telian-scholastic theory, made them more prone to cooperate with evil to effect change at a distance.

The text argues that women, rather than men, cooperate with evil in this way. All of these above-described characteristics of a person who cooperates with evil are exact opposites of those characteristics we saw described by women religious writers who exercise their free will in cooperation with a good spirit, who struggle to find truth through the exercise of the intellect, who use the powers of sensation to lead others to virtue, and who are motivated by well-ordered passions.[225]

To turn the text itself: the *Malleus maleficarum* begins by analyzing what causes a man's sin. Initially it appears to place the direct blame on the individual act of will of the man himself rather than on a woman. The following structure outlines the divisions of responsibility:

Causes for a Man's Evil Acts in the *Malleus malificarum*

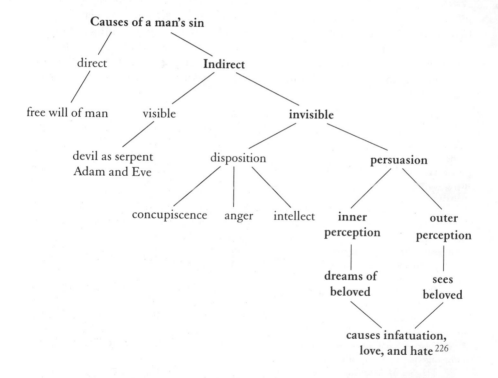

225. The *Malleus* also recognizes this difference. "Besides, it is the part of a good spirit to lead men to that which is good in human nature, and of good repute; therefore to entice men away from such, and to betray them into evil things, belongs to an evilly-disposed spirit" (*Malleus maleficarum*, I, q. 5, 37).

226. *Malleus maleficarum*, I, q. 7, 50-51.

In the preceding diagram of the cause of a man's sin, we can see that a man is the **direct** cause of his choice by the act of his own will. However, the invisible **indirect** cause that leads to blame being placed on women is called "persuasion." Woman acts as an indirect cause through man's perception of her either in man's external sense perceptions of her or through man's internal perceptions of her in his dreams or imagination. Persuasion presents something to the intellect in an appearance of a good thing. It is here that women "deceive" a man by presenting an image that appears to be good, but in fact turns out to be evil. In other places in the text, the authors will give an explanation for why women seem so capable of this destructive kind of indirect persuasion of men. At this point, the focus is on how a man is led indirectly by a woman to make erroneous choices.

When a woman's indirect persuasion is joined with the devil's pact to destroy a man, the man makes an erroneous free-will choice, and he is led into sin. Using very specific vocabulary, the *Malleus* describes this process in some detail: the devils enter into a man through impressions (made by a woman) on the powers of his bodily organs, phantasms are projected before the understanding, and these penetrate to the will as apparent goods that turn out to be only appearances and not really true goods. In this view of the epistemology and logic of witchcraft, a woman's indirect persuasion is deceptively dangerous for a man.[227]

This scholastic understanding of the person provides the underlying structure within which to understand how an individual chooses actions that tend towards good or evil. Kramer and Sprenger claim that three different kinds of witches exist: those who use witchcraft for good, those who use it for good and harm, and those who use it for harm.[228] The main focus of the *Malleus maleficarum* is the third category of witches, or those who freely choose, through an error in judgment, and often motivated by inordinate hatred or love, to work in cooperation with the evil spirit, to bring harm to others, often by deception, and particularly by leading them away from the practice of the Catholic faith.

The manual summarizes seven basic methods used by individuals to interfere with fruitful generation:

> Now there are, as it is said in the Papal Bull, seven methods by which they infect with witchcraft the venereal act and the conception of the womb: First, by inclining the minds of men to inordinate passion; second, by obstructing their generative force; third, by removing the members accommodated to the act; fourth, by changing men into beasts by their magic art; fifth, by destroying the generative force in women; sixth, by procuring abortion; seventh, by offering children to devils, besides other animals and fruits of the earth with which they work much harm.[229]

227. *Malleus maleficarum*, 53.
228. See *Malleus maleficarum*, I, q. 9, 60 and II, q. 2, 99.
229. *Malleus maleficarum*, I, q. 6, 47. See also I, q. 16, 80 and II, q. 1, ch. x, 129. The original bull reads as follows: "It has indeed lately come to Our ears, not without afflicting Us with bitter sorrow, that in some parts of Northern Germany, as well as in the provinces, townships, territories, districts, and dioceses of Mainz, Cologne, Trèves, Salzburg, and Bremen, many persons of both sexes, unmindful of their own salvation and straying from the Catholic Faith, have abandoned themselves to

In addition to the general category of interfering with procreation in marriage, witches were also accused of cooperating in the transfer of semen from a man to a woman through non-natural means.[230] These actions are condemned because they interfere with the proper end of sacramental marriage. Contemporary analogues of these acts would be found in actions related to causes of, or participation in, adultery, impotence, sterilization, contraception, abortion, and artificial insemination, as well as various forms of disease or death.

The *Malleus maleficarum* takes the opposite approach to the two satires studied previously in this chapter. While the satires offered evidence that a wife usually destroys a marriage, the manual argues that a person outside of the relationship (usually another woman) destroys a marriage. While the satires conclude that it would be better not to marry, the manual concludes that marriage should be supported by the punishment of the one who is attempting to destroy it.

Even though the arguments in the satires and the manual differ in method and conclusion, there is one important area where they agree: namely, that a woman is usually the cause of the problem. The satires blame the wife, and the manual blames the female witch. It is this nearly universal identification of woman as the cause of evil that we must now consider. The problem is one of moving from particulars to universals, or from the claims about some women to claims about most or all women. This is a fallacy of reason, because even if some women choose the above ways of interfering with generation, it is not the case that all or even most women so choose. Furthermore, even if some women historically may have tried to harm others through a willing cooperation with the forces of evil, it is not the case that all, or even most, women are prone to make such a choice.

Invoking Philosophical and Satirical Authority to Devalue Woman

Heinrich Kramer and James Sprenger introduce many different kinds of arguments to support their claim that women are more prone to witchcraft than are men.[231]

---

devils, incubi and succubi, and by their incantations, spells, conjurations, and other accursed charms and crafts, enormities and horrid offenses, have slain infants yet in the mother's womb, as also the offspring of cattle, have blasted the produce of the earth, the grapes of the vine, the fruits of trees, many men and women, beasts of burden, herd-beasts, as well as animals of other kinds, with terrible and piteous pains and sore diseases, both internal and external; they hinder men from performing the sexual act and women from conceiving, whence husbands cannot know their wives nor wives receive their husbands; over and above this, they blasphemously renounce that Faith which is theirs by the Sacrament of Baptism, and at the instigation of the Enemy of Mankind they do not shrink from committing and perpetrating the foulest abominations and filthiest excesses to the deadly peril of their own souls, whereby they outrage the Divine Majesty and are a cause of scandal and danger to very many" (*Malleus maleficarum*, preface, xliii).

230. The *Malleus maleficarum* describes this process as the devil extracting semen from the man by the help of a 'Succubus' and then inserting the extracted semen into the woman by the help of an 'Incubus' to produce a human child. See I, q. 2, 20-21; I, q. 3, 21-28; I, q. 4, 28-30; and II, q. 1, ch. 4, 109-14.

231. Sydney Anglo gives the following rather incisive summary of their methodology: "It is, however, in its dialectical procedures that the *Malleus* is simultaneously at its most feeble and most

In the text the progressive number of descriptions of female witches implies that "the gender of the witches is feminine."[232] The authors appeal to the authority of Scriptures, of Church Fathers, of classical writers such as Aristotle, Seneca, and Cicero, of Jewish and Christian writers such as Augustine, Maimonides, Albert, and Thomas, and to satirists such as Theophrastus and Valerius in his text to Rufinus. In Part I of the *Malleus maleficarum,* these authorities are invoked to answer the question: "Why is Superstition chiefly found in Women?"[233] The introduction to this section describes woman as "so fragile a sex," and the first sentence of the answer to the question refers again to "the fragile feminine sex."[234] Woman's natural weakness or fragility is the philosophical foundation upon which all the other elaborated characteristics of women rest. From her natural weakness flow a mind prone to error, a will disposed to make wrong choices, a set of passions unable to be governed, and a disposition to collaborate with evil forces to accomplish desired ends.

Scripture is invoked to support the claim that woman is created weaker than man: "And it should be noted that there was a defect in the formation of the first woman, since she was formed from a bent rib, that is, a rib of the breast, which is bent as it were in a contrary direction to a man. And since through this defect she is an imperfect animal, she always deceives."[235] We see the authors interpreting a particular statement from Scripture about the formation of Eve from the rib of Adam, and drawing a universal conclusion that woman "always deceives" because she is by nature crooked and imperfect. The *Malleus maleficarum* suggests that even the etymology of the Latin word for woman *(femina)* describes this created weakness: "... for *Femina* comes from *Fe* and *Minus,* since she is ever weaker to hold and preserve the faith."[236] It concludes: "Therefore a wicked woman is by her nature quicker to waver in her faith, and consequently quicker to abjure the faith, which is the root of witchcraft."[237] Another example links the natural and epistemological principles of polarity with witchcraft: "... since they are feebler both in mind and

---

devastating. Indeed, it is the very weakness of its logic that results in its terrifying conclusions: for, despite appearances to the contrary, this work is not an argument but rather a series of assertions masked by an accumulation of authorities and exemplars assembled in disputational form" ("Evident Authority," p. 19).

232. Russell, *Witchcraft in the Middle Ages,* reflects on the progressive association of women with witchcraft beginning with scholastic philosophy in the thirteenth century, passing through trials and writings of inquisitors in the fourteenth and fifteenth centuries, and culminating in the sixteenth and seventeenth centuries "until it was generally assumed that witches were necessarily female" (p. 279).

233. *Malleus maleficarum,* I, q. vi, 41-47. Anglo notes, "The handling of such writers is not overscrupulous, and they are all employed selectively; so that single observations, sentences, and even mere phrases, are ripped out of context and used as if they have universal validity. This method enables its practitioners to prove anything they wish ..." ("Evident Authority," p. 18).

234. *Malleus maleficarum,* I, q. 6, 41.

235. *Malleus maleficarum,* I, q. 6, 44. This association of the crooked rib with woman is used by Francis Lee Utley for the title of *The Crooked Rib: An Analytical Index to the Argument about Women in English and Scots Literature to the End of the Year 1568.* She notes the use of the phrase "the crooked rib" in *The Scholehouse of Women* (1541), "the most notorious English satire on woman of the sixteenth century" (pp. 255-57).

236. *Malleus maleficarum,* I, q. 6, 44.

237. *Malleus malificarum,* I, q. 6, 44.

body, it is not surprising that they should come more under the spell of witch-craft."[238]

Even more significant for the present study is the direct invoking of philo-sophical and satirical authorities to defend the devaluation of woman's identity. In the following examples we begin to see how academic and satirical themes start to emerge to unify the more popular views that interpret woman's identity through derogatory stereotypes. This is an essential link in our argument concerning the in-terweaving of satires, philosophical principles of gender polarity, and witchcraft tri-als that devalued many women.

The polarity principle of woman's natural weakness in intellect is repeated over and again throughout the *Malleus*. Another example, supported by an appeal to authority, follows:

> For as regards intellect, or the understanding of spiritual things, they seem to be of a different nature from men; a fact which is vouched for by the logic of the au-thorities, backed by various examples from the Scriptures. Terence says: Women are intellectually like children. And Lactantius (*Institutiones*, III): No woman understood philosophy except Temeste.[239]

A similar weakness in will leads to the claim of a lack of self-governance in women. In the following passage we see the *Malleus* invoking a passage from Aristotle's dis-ciple, Theophrastus, to support this claim:

> And indeed, just as through the first defect in their intelligence they are more prone to abjure the faith; so through their second defect of inordinate affections and passions they search for, brood over, and inflict various vengeances, either by witchcraft, or by some other means. Wherefore it is no wonder that so great a number of witches exist in this sex.
>
> Women also have weak memories; and it is a natural vice in them not to be disciplined, but to follow their own impulses without any sense of what is due; this is her whole study, and all that she keeps in her memory. So Theophrastus says: If you hand over the whole management of the house to her, but reserve some minute detail to your own judgement, she will think that you are display-ing a great want of faith in her, and will stir up strife; and unless you quickly take counsel, she will prepare poison for you, consult seers and soothsayers; and will become a witch.[240]

While the above passage appears to be cautious about attributing weakness of will and lack of self-governance to all women, it establishes a principle that is extended and universalized in other places in the text. For example, we find phrases such as "women are easily provoked to hatred," which then appears to be somewhat quali-

---

238. *Malleus maleficarum*, I, q. 6, 44.
239. *Malleus maleficarum*, I, q. 6, 44. Temeste was a reputed Neopythagorean.
240. *Malleus maleficarum*, I, q. 6, 45.

fied by the statement that "many . . . [say] that they [women] are always actuated by motives of hatred."[241]

Another aspect of woman's natural weakness is found in her reputed capacity for deception. It is in this context that we find the *Malleus* integrating Walter Map's satire as a support for its generalizations about women:

> Hear what Valerius said to Rufinus: you do not know that woman is the Chimaera, but it is good that you should know it; for that monster was of three forms; its face was that of a radiant and noble lion, it had the filthy belly of a goat, and it was armed with the virulent tail of a viper. And he means that a woman is beautiful to look at, contaminating to the touch, and deadly to keep.
>
> Let us consider another property of hers, the voice. For as she is a liar by nature, so in her speech she stings while she delights us. Wherefore her voice is like the song of the Sirens, who with their sweet melody entice the passers-by and kill them. For they kill them by emptying their purses, consuming their strength, and causing them to forsake God. Again Valerius says to Rufinus: When she speaks it is a delight which flavours the sin; the flower of love is a rose, because under its blossom there are hidden many thorns.[242]

After referring to Eve's leading of Adam into sin, Kramer and Sprenger introduce a number of their own observations in the forms of generalizations about women: "woman is a wheedling and secret enemy," "and . . . she is more perilous than a snare . . . of devils."[243] So woman's natural weakness of intellect and will leads her to a lack of self-governance in her passions, which, when combined with deception, enables her to lead man to a dangerous and destructive end.

The authors argue that woman deceives man in many different ways. As we saw previously, a woman may use persuasion on a man by presenting images to his intellect that appear to be good, but turn out to be bad. These images, which enter his intellect either through the outer senses or as inner perceptions, indirectly and invisibly cause him to make a poor choice, or to sin. The *Malleus* introduces what it describes as "actual facts and examples" of injurious acts of witches to support the theoretical arguments previously presented.[244] In addition to deceiving men about love by inflaming men with inordinate passions of love and hate, and by "depriving

---

241. *Malleus maleficarum*, III, q. 6, 210. This discussion concerns whether or not the testimony of "quarrelsome women" can be trusted in taking a legal deposition.

242. *Malleus maleficarum*, I, q. 6, 46. As mentioned above, Kramer and Sprenger may have become familiar with the text of "Valerius" through its inclusion in the first printed edition of the works of St. Jerome. These works also included reference to Theophrastus' satire on women.

243. *Malleus maleficarum*, I, q. 6, 47. This quotation continues: "For men are caught not only through their carnal desires, when they see and hear women: for S. Bernard says: Their face is a burning wind, and their voice the hissing of serpents: but they also cast wicked spells on countless men and animals. And when it is said that her heart is a net, it speaks of the inscrutable malice which reigns in their hearts. And her hands are as bands for binding; for when they place their hands on a creature to bewitch it, then with the help of the devil they perform their design."

244. *Malleus maleficarum*, II, q. 1, ch. 5, 115.

them of reason," witches are also described as turning people into animals or at least giving the appearance of this transmutation.

In the above two examples of appealing to Theophrastus and Walter Map's *Valerius*, the linkage is made more evident between satires on women, which were written supposedly to entertain, and a serious manual on the relation of women to witchcraft, written for purposes of arrest, trial, and condemnation. The satires provided an intellectual climate of stereotypes about the deceptive and dangerous identity of women. The *Malleus* then integrated the gender polarity concept and developed practical consequences of these universal generalizations for individual women.

The *Malleus maleficarum* has a coherent internal structure that consistently associates women with natural weakness of intellect and will. At the same time, the actions of witchcraft are described as occurring between an evil being who is pure spirit, and material things in the world — with consequences such as disease in animals, failure of harvests, and interference with generation among human beings. The problem the authors pose is how to explain the way that a spiritual being can effect change in a world that is material. The answer the authors offer is that it can achieve this through the cooperation of a human being who is both spirit and matter.[245] The witch becomes the "mean" between the two extremes of spirit and matter. In the following passage this logic of witchcraft, which harms by causing disease or death, is well described:

> Further, it is to be observed that those two, whilst they allow the two extremes, that is to say, some operation of the devil and the effect, a sensible disease, to be actual and real, at the same time deny that any instrument is the means thereof; that is to say, they deny that any witch could have participated in such a cause and effect; these, I say, err most gravely: for, in philosophy, the mean must always partake of the nature of the two extremes.
>
> Moreover, it is useless to argue that any result of witchcraft may be a fantasy and unreal, because such a fantasy cannot be procured without resort to the power of the devil, and it is necessary that there would be made a contract with the devil, by which contract the witch truly and actually binds herself to be the servant of the devil and devotes herself to the devil, and this is not done in any dream or under any illusion, but she herself bodily and truly co-operates with, and conjoins herself to, the devil. For this indeed is the end of all witchcraft; whether to be the casting of spells by a look or by a formula of words or by some other charm, it is all of the devil. . . .[246]

245. Midelfort notes in *Witch Hunting in Southwestern Germany* the role of Aristotle in leading to this conclusion: "Aristotle approached this problem with the concept of the unmoved mover, which he described as causing motion as 'the object of desire.' Thus an incorporeal being could not act as a physical agent, but only as an object of love. Scholastic thought took over this theory, maintaining that it was the function of all angels to cause local motion; they caused the movements of the heavenly spheres and could move earthly matter as well. The devil and his legion were essentially angels whose fall had only impaired, but not destroyed, their angelic powers" (p. 11). The *Malleus* argues that the devil prefers to work with a human agent, and that a woman is the more willing of the two sexes for this coordination with evil.

246. *Malleus maleficarum*, I, q. 1, 7.

So the evil spirit needs to find human beings willing to cooperate, and then able to cause changes in the material world through their joint agency. These changes could be mental or physical in both the witch and her victim.[247] We will now consider how Kramer and Sprenger continue to suggest that women, because of their natural weakness of intellect and will, most often agree to serve as this "mean" between the extremes of spirit and matter.

The central effect of woman's weak intellect and will is considered to be the subsequent exaggerated intensity and disorder in her passions. Kramer and Sprenger describe this extreme emotionality and disorder in many different ways, but they identify concupiscence at the conclusion of their discussion about historical, philosophical, religious, and satirical sources of women's character:

> To conclude. All witchcraft comes from carnal lust, which is in women insatiable. See *Proverbs* xxx: There are three things that are never satisfied, yea, a fourth thing which says not, It is enough; that is, the mouth of the womb. Wherefore for the sake of fulfilling their lusts they consort even with devils. More such reasons could be brought forward, but to the understanding it is sufficiently clear that it is no matter for wonder that there are more women than men found infected with the heresy of witchcraft. And in consequence of this, it is better called the heresy of witches than of wizards, since the name is taken from the more powerful party.[248]

Later in the text, the authors identify three different kinds of passions that make women particularly vulnerable to agreeing to cooperate with evil: weariness, lust, and sadness. Each passion is described in some detail in relation to its gender-specific mode of operation. In the first case, they suggest that women become weary by incurring heavy losses of temporal possessions, and they decide to consult with witches to secure remedies against further losses.[249] In the second case, they describe witches trying to encourage the seduction of young girls by inflaming their passions and setting up situations in which they could act out their de-

---

247. For a good discussion of the relative descriptions of physical and especially mental illness in the *Malleus* see Gregory Zilboorg, M.D., "The Physiological and Psychological Aspects of the *Malleus Maleficarum*," Lecture One, in *The Medical Man and the Witch During the Renaissance* (Baltimore: Johns Hopkins University Press, 1935). "In brief, Sprenger and Kramer described literally every single type of neurosis or psychosis which we find today in our daily psychiatric work" (p. 50).

248. *Malleus maleficarum*, I, q. 6, 47. The section continues with a further reflection that God "has so far preserved the male sex from so great a crime." Then the same characteristics are repeated in their association with women in the next paragraph: "As to our second inquiry, what sort of women more than others are found to be superstitious and infected with witchcraft; it must be said, as was shown in the preceding inquiry, that three general vices appear to have special dominion over wicked women, namely, infidelity, ambition, and lust. Therefore they are more than others inclined towards witchcraft, who more than others are given to these vices. Again, since of these three vices the last chiefly predominates, women being insatiable, etc. . . . ."

249. *Malleus maleficarum*, II, q. 1, ch. 1, 96-97. The authors offer several examples in which women who lost horses or the milk of their cows consulted witches and received remedies, but with the proviso that they agree to some act such as keeping something secret in the sacrament of Confession, and "by slow degrees are led to a total abnegation of the Faith."

sires.[250] In the third case, they describe young women who had been first used and then rejected by men, and who, out of their sadness at rejection, turned to witchcraft for revenge.[251] This latter category includes those who may have at first been filled with inordinate love, but now are driven by inordinate hatred.

The authors imply that these passions of weariness at temporal loss, lust, and sadness at rejection affect women more than men because women lack self-governance due to the weakness of their intellect and will. We saw these same views previously expressed in the satires against women already studied, but in the *Malleus maleficarum* the tone shifts radically from one of simple ridicule of women and even ridicule of men who get caught in traps set by women, to one of viewing women as extremely dangerous for men because of their apparent willing cooperation with supernatural forces of evil. The character of the human being is viewed as precariously balanced between supernatural good, on the one hand, and bestiality, or evil, on the other hand. Those women who choose to cooperate with supernatural good, with angels and God, learn self-knowledge, self-governance, and holiness; while those who choose to cooperate with supernatural evil and the devil become a source of danger for themselves and for men. In satires, women who so choose are described as being like animals, while in the *Malleus* they are described as affecting the life of animals as well as reducing themselves and men to bestial levels of existence.

As mentioned previously, the *Malleus maleficarum* identifies three categories of witches: those who cure, those who cure and injure, and those who only injure.[252] This distinction is important for several reasons, for those women who worked with herbs and medicines to heal or cure, or those who were midwives, were also called "witches," "wise women," or "wicca." In their actions they did not try to harm others, by causing disease, drying up the milk of nursing mothers, killing deformed infants, performing abortions, or in other ways interfering with fertile generation in married couples. However, if in their attempts to cure disease or heal injury, to deliver babies, or care for mothers, they met with failure, then these women were vulnerable to accusations of being a witch that intended harm.

It is primarily the third category — witches who intentionally cause harm to others — that the authors usually identify as very dangerous for men. In the following passage some of the harmful effects of their actions are summarized:

> And this is the most powerful class of witches, who practise innumerable other harms also. For they raise hailstorms and hurtful tempests and lightnings; cause sterility in men and animals. . . . They can also, before the eyes of their parents, and when no one is in sight, throw into the water children walking by the water side; they make horses go mad under their riders; they can transport themselves from place to place through the air, either in body or in imagination; they can affect Judges and Magistrates so that they cannot hurt them; they can cause themselves and others to keep silence under torture; they can bring about a great trembling in the hands and horror in the minds of those who would arrest them; . . .

250. *Malleus maleficarum,* II, q. 1, ch. 1, 96-98.
251. *Malleus maleficarum,* II, q. 1, ch. 1, 97-99.
252. *Malleus maleficarum,* II, q. 1, ch. 2, 98.

they can see absent things as if they were present; they can turn the minds of men to inordinate love or hatred; they can at times strike whom they will with lightning, and even kill some men and animals; they can make of no effect the generative desires, and even the power of copulation, cause abortion, kill infants in the mother's womb by a mere exterior touch; they can at times bewitch men and animals with a mere look, without touching them, and cause death. . . .[253]

While this third category appears to describe simply some women, it frequently expands its range to include most or all women by association. As the *Malleus* develops its methods for identifying witches, trying them in judicial courts, and condemning them, the sense of the danger for men, especially from women witches in all three categories, increases in the intensity of its articulation. In a discussion about whether or not the names of those who accuse a woman of witchcraft can be given, we find a frequent invoking of the phrase "grave danger" to allow the names to be withheld.[254]

Calculated Deception in Intergender Dialogue

Witchcraft is described as the "worst evil" in the world because witches are presumed to have made a pact with the devil. "Moreover, witchcraft differs from all other harmful and mysterious arts in this point, that of all superstition it is essentially the vilest, the most evil and the worst. . . ."[255] Witchcraft is identified by Kramer and Sprenger as the worst heresy: "It is clear from this that the heresy of witches is the most heinous of the three degrees of infidelity; and this fact is proved both by reason and authority."[256] As a consequence of the extreme degree of evil that is identified with the actions of witches, the *Malleus* concludes that the punishments ought to equal the deeds. "So heinous are the crimes of witches that they even exceed the sins and the fall of the bad Angels; and if this is true as to their guilt, how should it not also be true of their punishments in hell?"[257]

The connection among women's natural weakness, evil, witchcraft, deception, danger for men, and punishment is made throughout the *Malleus maleficarum*. The belief that those who die while practicing the heresy of witchcraft will receive eternal punishment is used to justify subjecting them to temporal punishment.[258] It

---

253. *Malleus maleficarum,* II, q. 1, ch. 2, 99. Other characteristics included in this summary are: cannibalism, fortune telling, and the causing of plagues.

254. *Malleus maleficarum,* III, q. 9, 216-17. See also III, q. 14, 226.

255. *Malleus maleficarum,* I, q. 2, 20.

256. *Malleus maleficarum,* I, q. 14, 75. This section continues by explaining the canonical status of witchcraft as follows: "Now when we speak of the Apostasy of witches, we mean the Apostasy of perfidy; and this is so much the more heinous, in that it springs from a pact made with the enemy of the Faith and the way of salvation. For witches are bound to make this pact, which is exacted by the enemy either in part or wholly" (75-76).

257. *Malleus maleficarum,* I, q. 17, 82.

258. See *Malleus maleficarum,* I, q. 15, 78. "But violent death, whether a man deserves it or not, is always a correction, if it is borne patiently and in grace."

is suggested that temporal punishment might mitigate eternal punishment in the case of the guilty, and that it would be replaced with eternal reward in the case of the innocent. This suggestion implies that the motive for the severe punishment for witches — dying by fire — may not have been only fear, but also hope for the conversion and the salvation of those believed to be in danger of eternal punishment. The conclusion that the *Malleus maleficarum* repeats numerous times is that a person (usually a woman) convicted of witchcraft must be given the "extreme penalty," or death by fire.[259] Kramer and Sprenger argue that death is first of all sanctioned by divine law.[260] The kind of death they recommend appears to be gender related, but the first order of law that was broken was in the order of the divine:

> For witchcraft is high treason against God's Majesty. And so they are to be put to the torture in order to make them confess. Any person, whatever his rank or position, upon such an accusation may be put to the torture, and he who is found guilty, even if he confesses his crime, let him be racked, let him suffer all other tortures prescribed by law in order that he may be punished in proportion to his offenses.
>
> Note: In days of old such criminals suffered a double penalty and were often thrown to wild beasts to be devoured by them. Nowadays they are burnt at the stake, and probably this is because the majority of them are women.[261]

Witchcraft was thought to break the first order of divine law by being a form of treason against God; to break the second order of ecclesiastical law by being a form of heresy or apostasy; and to break the third order of civil law by interfering illegally in temporal events. Kramer and Sprenger conclude: ". . . the crime of witches is partly civil and partly ecclesiastical, because they commit temporal harm and violate the faith; therefore it belongs to the Judges of both Courts to try, sentence, and punish them."[262] Because the witches were mostly women, and the Judges in all ju-

---

259. The inquisitorial court handed the person over to the secular court for the execution of this punishment. See *Malleus maleficarum,* III, q. 24, 246.

260. See *Malleus maleficarum,* "For the divine law in many places commands that witches are not only to be avoided, but also they are to be put to death, and it would not impose the extreme penalty of this kind if witches did not really and truly make a compact with devils in order to bring about real and true hurts and harms" (I, q. 1, 3). See also: "For He not only says in *Exodus* xxii: Thou shalt not suffer a witch to live on the earth; but He adds this: She shall not dwell in thy land, lest perchance she cause thee to sin" (II, q. 2, ch. 8, 193).

261. *Malleus maleficarum,* I, q. 1, 6.

262. *Malleus maleficarum,* III, intro., 196. The manual goes into detail about the relation between the inquisitorial court, the ecclesiastical court, and the civil court in the process of trying, sentencing, and punishing witches. Edward Peters notes the longtime interaction of ecclesiastical and civil officials in *The Magician,* "When, at the end of the fifteenth century, the authors of the *Malleus Maleficarum* urged the temporal courts to aid ecclesiastical officials in rooting out the crimes of magic and witchcraft, they were instituting no novelty, but invoking the moral responsibility of temporal courts that had been heightened steadily since the thirteenth century. In this light, the blessing of the instruments of torture in civil courts . . . that had been adopted from an earlier period and a more exclusively clerical milieu, all supported the discretion and responsibility of the judge and magistrate" (p. 153). While the papal courts used torture, the Magisterium of the Catholic Church never officially advocated its use. See the *Cate-*

ridical courts were men, the trials of witches became charged with gender-differentiated issues. The intergender dialogue that occurred was not one of complementarity, but instead was one that was permeated by the gender polarity stereotypes previously articulated.

In the following official form for the passing of sentence we see the invocation of men from different faculties of academia:

> . . . having conducted the whole process, we summoned together in council before us learned men of the Theological faculty and men skilled in both the Canon and the Civil Law, knowing that, according to canonical institution, the judgement is sound which is confirmed by the opinion of many; and having on all details consulted the opinion of the said learned men, and having diligently and carefully examined all the circumstances of the process; we find that you are, by your own confession made on oath before us in the Court, convicted of many of the sins of witches. (Let them be expressed in detail.)[263]

Not only were the women accused of witchcraft placed in a situation in which they were judged by educated men, but because the extraction of a confession was considered central to the conviction, men initiated methods of torture to achieve this end.[264] By law, however, the confession given under torture had to be repeated again when the person was not being tortured. This meant that some were repeatedly submitted to torture if they recanted their confession. At the time, the use of torture was common to all criminal proceedings, not just those associated with witchcraft.[265] However, when torture entered into the specifically intergender context of educated men trying uneducated women, it assumed an even more odious identity.

In addition to the use of torture, the *Malleus maleficarum* also directly encouraged the interrogators to use deception to procure a confession. Here we find the inversion of the theme that women, and particularly witches, use dialogue for purposes of deception. The manual actually describes ways in which a Judge

---

chism of the Catholic Church (1995), which explicitly condemns torture (#2297): "Torture which uses physical or moral violence to extract confessions, punish the guilty, frighten opponents, or satisfy hatred is contrary to respect for the person and for human dignity."

263. *Malleus maleficarum,* III, q. 27, 253. The generic "he" is used in this example for a witch. A similar form is used in the next example of sentencing, and the generic "she" is used there. See III, q. 28, 254-56. See also the list of those present at the examination of witnesses, III, q. 6, 211.

264. See *Malleus maleficarum:* "For common justice demands that a witch should not be condemned to death unless she is convicted by her own confession. But here we are considering the case of one who is judged to be taken in manifest heresy for one of the other two reasons set down in the First Question, namely direct or indirect evidence of the fact, or the legitimate production of witnesses; and in this case she is to be exposed to questions and torture to extort a confession of her crimes" (III, q. 13, 222-23). In several places in the manual specific methods of torture are articulated: being raised by her thumbs, holding a red-hot iron, placed on a rack and twisted, starved, deceived by friends and judges, etc. See III, q. 14, 225-26; q. 16, 230-32; q. 22, 242-44; q. 17, 233-34; and q. 33, 264-65.

265. See Edward Peters, *Torture* (Oxford: Blackwell, 1985): "From the second half of the thirteenth century to the end of the eighteenth, torture was part of the ordinary criminal procedure of the Latin Church and of most of the states of Europe" (p. 54).

should use deception in dialogue with a woman accused of witchcraft in the process of the trial. The authors raise the question and then offer three answers, each one of which entails using deception for the purposes of eliciting confession:

> . . . whether, in the case of a prisoner legally convicted by her general bad reputation, by witnesses, and by the evidence of the facts, so that the only thing lacking is a confession of the crime from her own mouth, the Judge can lawfully promise her her life, whereas if she were to confess the crime she would suffer the extreme penalty. Three options are suggested. In the first the woman is sentenced for life on bread and water. . . . And she is not to be told, when she is promised her life, that she is to be imprisoned in this way; but should be led to suppose that some other penance, such as exile, will be imposed on her as punishment. In the second case, after she has been consigned to prison in this way, the promise to spare her life would be kept for a time, but . . . after a certain period she should be burned. And in the third option, the Judge may safely promise the accused her life, but in such a way that he should afterwards disclaim the duty of passing sentence on her, deputing another Judge in his place.[266]

The astonishing use of deception by the Judge to fool witches who themselves deceive does not go unnoted by Kramer and Sprenger. They prefer the first option, which deceives only by "leading the woman to suppose" something false. The second and third options involve more direct deceptions.

However, a little later on in the text, they suggest that a Judge can directly deceive in dialogue when necessary to procure a confession. In the following extract the Judge is told to "make a mental reservation" that the meaning of what he says is different from what he actually says in the dialogue:

> But we must proceed to the extreme case, when after every experiment has been tried the witch still maintains silence . . . let him cause her to be well treated in the matter of food and drink, and meanwhile let honest persons who are under no suspicion enter to her and talk often with her on indifferent subjects, and finally advise her in confidence to confess the truth, promising that the Judge will be merciful to her and that they will intercede for her. And finally let the Judge come in and promise that he will be merciful, with the mental reservation that he means he will be merciful to himself or the State; for whatever is done for the safety of the State is merciful.[267]

We could say that any use of dialogue to develop a real gender complementarity has shifted to gender polarity in which dialogue is replaced by interrogation, and the use of language for the mutual search for truth is replaced by degeneration, deception, and falsehood. In this period in western history we can see a move from cooperative dialogue among men and women found in religious communities, to satirical imaginary dialogues that devalued women in printed

266. *Malleus maleficarum*, III, q. 14, 225.
267. *Malleus maleficarum*, III, q. 16, 231.

texts, to juridical dialogues in various courts that often condemned women by torture and deception to extract their confessions, and eventually sentence them to death.[268]

There is a further painful irony that is associated with this method of judgment and condemnation. The whole stereotype of woman as talkative and its inversion, namely that a woman's virtue is silence, is reversed in the witchcraft trial so that a woman who remains silent is condemned **for her silence.** Even though silence may have been motivated in some cases by hostility or fear because of genuine malice in the person accused, it may often have been the result of a person's being innocent. However, the *Malleus* frequently identifies silence as a problem as can be seen in the following selections: ". . . the great trouble caused by the stubborn silence of witches . . ."; ". . . a witch's power of taciturnity, and whose silence he is unable to overcome [by continuation of torture]"; and ". . . that evil gift of silence which is the constant bane of judges. . . ."[269] So the woman accused of witchcraft condemns herself by silence, and she condemns herself by a confession under torture whether or not she is guilty of using her intelligence and will to cooperate with evil.

A similar set of paradoxes emerges in relation to a woman's ability to bear pain. If she breaks down under the pain of torture and confesses, she is condemned; but if she remains strong under torture or quickly recovers, this also may condemn her.[270] If a woman weeps under torture it is interpreted as contrition for her sins and condemns her; but if her eyes remain dry and she is unable to weep, this is understood as further evidence of her witchcraft and condemns her.[271] Finally, the web of relations among women and men accused of witchcraft also became a source of ironic condemnation. If a woman is accused by witnesses of witchcraft (e.g., touching a child who shortly afterwards became ill, walking through a field just before a storm, having her cows produce more milk than her neighbours', or threatening another person by words, etc.), and she denies it, but if she knew someone else condemned for witchcraft, or had a relative (a mother) condemned for it, her denial would be evidence for her conviction.[272] The following passage summarizes all these different grounds for condemnation:

268. The degree to which the balance of participation in a dialogue is skewed in favor of the male prosecutor in interrogation of the female defendant undergoing trial is well stated by Peters, *Torture.* "As critics have long pointed out, the inquisitorial procedure [between 1250-1750] has a built-in prosecutorial bias. No matter how restricted the judge is procedurally, such problems as his weighting the *indicia,* the suggestiveness of the interrogation under torture, the quick willingness to accept a confession without then checking its details, and the tendency to torture severely, to elicit a guilty plea instead of a confession, all stack the system against the defendant" (p. 58).

269. *Malleus maleficarum,* III, q. 13, 223; q. 15, 227; and II, q. 1, ch. 15, 148.

270. *Malleus maleficarum,* III, q. 33, 264-68.

271. *Malleus maleficarum,* ". . . if she be a witch she will not be able to weep . . . " (III, q. 15, 227). See also III, q. 33, 267. This particular inability to shed tears may also be an effect of aging in some women who have "dry eyes."

272. *Malleus maleficarum,* III, q. 6, 212-13; III, q. 19, 238. These examples all participate in the fallacy of *Post hoc ergo propter hoc,* or just because one event follows another in time, it is not proof that the first one causes the second one. However, if the accused were able to find an equal number of persons and from equal station to defend her she might be able to be condemned merely to a process of purgation rather than death.

Therefore a witch must be gravely suspected when, after she has used such threatening words as "I shall soon make you feel," or the like, some injury has befallen the person so threatened or his cattle. . . . Now we must consider what procedure is to be observed in such a case. . . . It is to be noted that, if the witch maintains her denial, or claims that she uttered those words not with the implied intention but in a vehement and womanish passion; then the Judge has not sufficient warrant to sentence her to the flames, in spite of the grave suspicion. Therefore he must place her in prison, and cause inquiry to be made by proclamation whether she has been known to have done the like before. And if it is found that this is so, he must inquire whether she was then publicly defamed in respect of that heresy; and from this he can proceed further so that, before all else, she may be exposed to an interrogation under the question and torture. And then, if she shows signs of such heresy, or of the taciturnity of witches, as that she should be unable to shed tears, or remain insensible under torture, and quickly recover her strength afterwards; then he may proceed with the various precautions which we have already explained where we dealt with such cases.

And in case all should fail, then let him take note that, if she has perpetrated the like before, she is not to be altogether released, but must be sent to the squalor of prison for a year, and be tortured, and be examined very often, especially on the more Holy Days. But if, in addition to this, she has been defamed, then the Judge may proceed in the manner already shown in the case of simple heresy, and condemn her to the fire, especially if there is a multitude of witnesses and she had often been detected in similar or other deeds of witchcraft. But if he wishes to be merciful, he may set her a canonical purgation, that she should find twenty or thirty sponsors, sentencing her in such a way that, if she should fail in her purgation, she shall be condemned to the fire as convicted.[273]

In the table on page 523 a summary is provided of the ways in which an educated man may intentionally use deception against a woman in a trial for witchcraft. In the many examples found in this table we can see how the presumption of deception by the one accused forms a context that leads to the conscious practice of deception on the part of the accusers. The goal of intergender dialogue, as a mutual search for truth, has degenerated into interrogation and devaluation of the men and women who were participating.

The overriding judgment that women can be dangerous for men is expressed in two ways in the *Malleus maleficarum*. In the first case, the authors state that only certain kinds of men are protected from the evil effects of the women's actions: "And the first are those who administer public justice against them or prosecute them in any public official capacity."[274] However, as the text develops with specific methods for judicial cases against witches, Kramer and Sprenger introduce a qualification of this originally projected protection that judicial officers have. They state that the judges "must not allow themselves to be touched physically by the witch, especially in any contact of their bare arms or hands"; they must be careful to guard

273. *Malleus maleficarum,* III, q. 25, 248-49.
274. *Malleus maleficarum,* II, q. 1, 89.

Calculated Deception in the *Malleus maleficarum*		
A Man's Statement	**The Deceptive Interpretation**	**Consequence of the Deception**
If a woman confesses, she will be given exile.	If she confesses, she will really be given life in prison on bread and water.	The confession is deceitfully gained by a play on the meaning of 'exile,' and the woman is condemned.
If a woman confesses, her life will be saved.	If she confesses, her life is saved only for a period of time.	The confession is deceitfully gained by a play on the meaning of 'time.'
If a woman confesses, her life will be saved.	If she confesses, another Judge will condemn her.	The confession is deceitfully gained by switching Judges.
If a woman confesses, the Judge will be merciful.	If she confesses, the Judge is merciful to himself or to the state, not to the woman.	The confession is deceitfully gained by a play on the meaning of 'mercy.'
Show a woman the instruments of torture and ask for a confession.	If she confesses, then the torture has made her truthful.	The fear of torture may get the confession, and not the decision to tell the truth.
Actually apply torture to a woman and ask for a confession.	If she confesses, then the torture has made her truthful.	The desire for the cessation of pain may get the confession, and not the decision to tell the truth.
Imply that the woman will be retortured if she does not repeat her confession away from the instruments of torture.	If she repeats her confession, then she has now recognized the truth of her accusations.	The fear of repeated pain may get the confession, and not the decision to tell the truth.

against even the "mere sound of the words they utter, especially at the time when they are exposed to torture"; and they should not allow the women "to look at the Judge before he looks at them."[275] Consequently, Kramer and Sprenger recommend that the woman be "led backward into the presence of the Judge and his as-

---

275. *Malleus maleficarum,* III, q. 15, 228.

sessors."[276] In these prescriptions that prohibit touch, eye contact, and voice exchange and that reduce the woman to a creature led around backwards like an animal, we have the ultimate degradation of intergender dialogue and complementarity of men and women. It was a similar kind of situation that we encountered in the trial and condemnation of Joan of Arc for heresy.

Women and Witchcraft Trials

In the *Malleus maleficarum* itself, Heinrich Kramer and James Sprenger mention several different cases of the trial, sentencing, and condemnation of women to death for witchcraft. They refer to a text by John Nider, which noted that the Inquisitor of the Diocese of Edua ". . . held many inquisitions on witches in that diocese, and caused many to be burned."[277] Also in the towns of Constance and Ratisbon, "no less than forty-eight have been burned in five years. . . . And . . . the Inquisitor of Como in the County of Burbia, who in the space of one year, which was the year of grace 1485, caused forty-one witches to be burned."[278] They recounted in some detail the stories of one woman in Basel, two in Strasbourg, and two more in Constance who were burned to death for witchcraft.[279]

The estimations of numbers of women condemned to death for witchcraft by the three levels of inquisitorial court, ecclesiastical court, and civil court vary considerably.[280] There was often a division of labor, with the inquisitorial court hearing general charges, the ecclesiastical court sentencing, and the civil court carrying out the punishment of the condemned. There are also striking differences in countries and regions, with Germany appearing to have the largest proportional numbers and England the least among the European nations.[281] In a meticulous account of trials of women and men condemned for witchcraft by Protestants and Catholics in the small area of southwestern Germany, Midelfort offers the following approximate summary of executions for which there are clear records: 1400-1450 (1), 1450-1500 (51), 1500-1550 (17), 1550-1600 (1403), 1600-1650 (2018), 1650-1700 (113).[282] It is clear from these statistics that the greatest number of executions of women and men for witchcraft in southwestern Germany occurred between 1550 and 1650. While there were many historical factors such as outbursts of the plague, the Protestant Reformation, and the Catholic Counter-Reformation, the presence of various forms of gender polarity certainly contributed to the predominance of ex-

---

276. *Malleus maleficarum,* III, q. 15, 228.

277. *Malleus maleficarum,* II, q. 1, ch. 2, 100.

278. *Malleus maleficarum,* II, q. 1, ch. 4, 111.

279. *Malleus maleficarum,* II, q. 1, ch. 13 and II, q. 1, ch. 15.

280. Russell points out that the use of torture was first practiced in civil courts, and later spread to ecclesiastical courts. See *Witchcraft in the Middle Ages,* chapters 5-10 for a description of these different legal bodies and the juridical approach to witchcraft.

281. See Lionel Rothkrug, *Historical Reflections,* pp. 44-148. Also in the *Malleus maleficarum* a Spanish custom of completely shaving the body of the condemned was noted. See III, q. 16, 230.

282. Midelfort, *Witch Hunting,* pp. 200-230. This calculation is conservative because it counted only the exact numbers listed, and omitted the question marks.

ecutions of elderly, isolated women among these numbers of condemned.[283] It is also interesting to note that "Doctors, lawyers, and university professors, in addition to the nobility, seemed to enjoy considerable immunity from witchcraft accusations."[284]

We can bring these statistics alive by considering briefly just one woman who fits this category of elderly women, even though she lived outside of the time frame of this book. Katherine Kepler, the mother of the scientist Johannes Kepler (1574-1630), was accused of witchcraft in the year 1615 when she was in her seventies. She was the daughter of an innkeeper whose own aunt was burned as a witch. In Leonburg where Katherine Kepler lived, in the same year she was accused, six women accused of witchcraft were burned to death.[285] Katherine Kepler was elderly, had a sharp tongue, stubborn personality, and a genealogical connection with the practice of witchcraft. This made her vulnerable to accusation.

The details of Katherine's arrest and defense reveal again the deterioration of intergender dialogue between educated men and uneducated women. Katherine Kepler had an argument with a neighbor that led to her being accused of witchcraft. As the evidence of witnesses began to emerge, Katherine was accused of giving persons drinks that produced a chronic illness, paralysis, and even death; of casting an evil eye on children who subsequently died; and of practicing magical arts that caused pains or healings in those who came near to her. Legal proceedings against her began, and her son Johannes Kepler, who had a position as the Roman Imperial Majesty's Court Mathematician in Prague and Provincial Mathematician in Linz, Austria, came to her defense. It took several more years of challenges and counterchallenges before the court believed that it had enough evidence to convict her. This evidence included an attempted bribe by Katherine of a court official, and she was arrested on August 7, 1620.

Johannes Kepler, who was highly educated, chose to defend his mother in court while she languished for six weeks in prison, with two full-time armed guards, waiting for trial. In the following detailed description of the process of the trial, we see again the interweaving of academia with the plight of women accused of serious crimes:

283. On the question of the predominance of old women among those arrested for witchcraft see Joseph Klaits, *Servants of Satan: The Age of Witch Hunts* (Bloomington: Indiana University Press, 1985). "Elderly females were represented among the dependent poor in disproportionately high numbers, for the old woman was the member of society least likely to be self-supporting. Such poor, old women were the prime targets for witchcraft allegations: evidence from France, England, and Switzerland shows an average age between 55 and 65 for accused witches" (p. 94). This thesis is also supported by H. C. Erik Midelfort, *Witch Hunting.* Midelfort notes the changing demography of marriage after the Protestant Reformation which left many single women (who no longer would be in convents) as spinsters or widows. "Until society learned to adjust to new family patterns, one could argue that unmarried women would have been especially susceptible to attack. This conclusion would support the commonplace observation that widows and spinsters were most commonly accused of witchcraft, far out of proportion to their numbers in society" (p. 185).
284. Midelfort, *Witch Hunting,* p. 189. He adds that "Even university students who came under suspicion were generally punished by expulsion only" (p. 189).
285. Arthur Koestler, *The Watershed: A Biography of Johannes Kepler* (Garden City, N.Y.: Doubleday and Company, 1960), p. 208.

The proceedings lasted for another year. The accusation comprised forty-nine points, plus a number of supplementary charges — for instance that the accused had failed to shed tears when admonished with texts from Holy Scripture. . . .

The Act of Accusation, read in September, was answered a few weeks later by an Act of Contestation by Kepler and counsel; this was refuted by an Act of Acceptation by the prosecution in December; in May, next year, the defense submitted an Act of Exception and Defense; in August, the prosecution answered with an Act of Deduction and Confutation. The last word was the Act of Conclusion by the defense, one hundred and twenty-eight pages long, and written mostly in Kepler's own hand. After that the case was sent, by order of the Duke, to the Faculty of Law at Tuebingen — Kepler's university. The faculty found that Katherine ought to be questioned under torture, but recommended that the procedure would be halted at the stage of *territio,* or questioning under threat of torture.[286]

In addition, this particular case also reveals the deterioration of intergender dialogue by inserting the use of force to support a particular desired conclusion. When a confession could not be extracted from Katherine Kepler by genuine and open dialogue, the men resorted to the threat of torture to attempt to achieve their goal of gathering enough evidence to convict her of the practice of witchcraft.

The results of this next stage of the "dialogue" were recorded in a letter written by the Provost to the Duke. In it we discover Katherine Kepler, now over seventy-five years old, defending her innocence to the best of her ability. Arthur Koestler reproduces the letter as follows:

> Having, in the presence of three members of the court and of the town scribe, tried friendly persuasion on the accused, and having met with contradiction and denial, I led her to the usual place of torture and showed her the executioner and his instruments, and reminded her earnestly of the necessity of telling the truth, and of the great dolor and pain awaiting her. Regardless, however, of all earnest admonitions and reminders, she refused to admit and confess to witchcraft as charged, indicating that one should do with her as one liked, and that even if one artery after another were to be torn from her body, she would have nothing to confess; whereafter she fell on her knees and said a paternoster, and demanded that God should make a sign if she were a witch or a monster or ever had anything to do with witchcraft. She was willing to die, she said; God would reveal the truth after her death, and the injustice and violence done to her. . . . When she persisted in her contradiction and denial regarding witchcraft, and remained steadfast in this position, I led her back to her place of custody.[287]

Eventually, after fourteen months in prison, Katherine Kepler was released, but not fully cleared of suspicion. She died six months later, broken and abandoned by people in her hometown who still threatened to kill her. The fear and prejudice that

286. Koestler, *Watershed,* pp. 211-12.

287. Koestler, *Watershed,* pp. 212-13. This is extracted by Koestler from *Johannes Kepler in seinen Briefen,* ed. Max Caspar and Walther von Dyck (Munich and Berlin: Oldenbourg, 1930), vol. 2, pp. 183-84.

were operative in this region of Kepler's birthplace continued to function, "for with a population of two hundred families, thirty-eight witches were burned between 1615 and 1629."[288]

Montague Summers provides one of the classical attempts to describe cultural variations in the arrest, trial, and condemnation of witches in his *Geography of Witchcraft*.[289] In this text more detailed accounts, rather than statistical summaries, are offered about various witch trials from their early origins to their later widespread development in the following countries: Greece, England, Scotland, France, Germany, Italy, Spain, and the New World. Other studies have sought to provide meticulous data on witch trials and executions in different countries. One of the most recent is Anne Llewellyn Barstow, *Witchcraze: A New History of the European Witch Hunts*.[290] In an appendix Barstow considers all the countries identified by Montague as well as more areas in Great Britain, Scandinavia, Estonia, Poland, Russia, and the Balkans.[291] After weighing the evidence, Barstow concludes that there were altogether around 200,000 persons accused of witchcraft, with around 100,000 of these put to death.[292] Barstow's numbers seem to be well supported by other estimates.[293]

In France and Switzerland approximately 80 percent of those accused of and condemned for witchcraft were women.[294] The breakdown of gender representation in witchcraft trials is consistently skewed. William Monter identifies the percentage of women tried for witchcraft in different regions as follows: Southwestern Germany, 82 percent; West Switzerland, 80 percent; Venetian Republic, 78 percent; Castile, 71 percent; Belgium (Namur), 92 percent; and England (Essex), 92 percent.[295] In an-

288. Koestler, *Watershed*, p. 208.

289. Montague Summers, *The Geography of Witchcraft* (Secaucus, N.J.: Citadel Press, 1973).

290. Anne Llewellyn Barstow, *Witchcraze: A New History of the European Witch Hunts* (San Francisco: HarperCollins, 1994).

291. Barstow, *Witchcraze*, appendix B, pp. 179-81.

292. Barstow, *Witchcraze*, p. 23. She adds that 80-85 percent of these were women, p. 25. These figures are supported by Voltaire. Barstow is highly critical of what she terms the exaggerations of some writers: "The current trend among some feminist groups to claim three million, six million, or even ten million female victims is mistaken" (p. 21).

293. See E. William Monter, "Pedestal and Stake," in *Enforcing Morality in Early Modern Europe* (London: Variorum Reprints, 1987), p. 132.

294. See E. William Monter, *Witchcraft in France and Switzerland: The Borderlands during the Reformation* (Ithaca and London: Cornell University Press, 1976). Monter concludes: "As we have seen, a large majority were women: the overall totals for French Switzerland, balancing Lausanne with its remarkable percentage of men, against Ajoie with its virtual absence of male witches, average out to approximately 80 percent women — very close to the average from an extremely large sample in southwestern Germany" (p. 196); and "Since female witches were also likely to be old and handicapped, or petty criminals, or relatives of other witches, and since women comprised only a small majority of all old and powerless people, only half of all relatives of witches, and only a small minority of the criminal element, it seems obvious that although both sexes might come under suspicion for similar reasons, women were the specially designated victims: witchcraft, as the demonologists repeatedly insisted, was sex-linked" (p. 197). See also Monter, "Witchcraft in Geneva, 1537-1662," in *Enforcing Morality*, ch. x, pp. 170-204.

295. Monter, "Pedestal and Stake: Courtly Love and Witchcraft," in *Enforcing Morality*, p. 132. He concludes: "Although retrospective studies of criminality are still in their infancy, it seems safe to predict that, from 1480-1700, more women were killed for witchcraft than for other crimes put to-

other text on witch trials in Scotland, Christina Larner supports this claim of the high percentage of women:

> The Scottish witch-hunt was arguably one of the major witch-hunts of Europe. During its peaks it was matched only by those of the German principalities and Lorraine. As in Germany its effects were local and highly concentrated. There were periods in 1649 and 1661 when no mature woman in Fife or East Lothian can have felt free from the fear of accusation.[296]

Differences of opinion about the comparative significance of trials of witches in Scotland are difficult to assess. Larner argues that the intensity of the prosecution of witches in Scotland was in between the extreme example in Continental Europe and the more relaxed situation in England.[297] Montague Summers, however, argues that Scotland was the most extreme.[298] Certainly debate about witchcraft was ongoing in Scotland. Witness the controversy between James I, *Demonology* (1597), who argued in support of the existence of demons and witches, and Reginald Scot, *Discovery of Witchcraft* (1584), who had argued against the existence of demons and witches.

In 1542, the Witchcraft Act was passed in England, and witches were persecuted, but they were rarely tortured, and punishments were less severe than execution by burning.[299] However, "[f]rom 24 June, 1559, the Mass and all other Catholic services were forbidden in England."[300] From this point on, the legal search for and arrest of witches were in the hands of Protestants rather than Catholics, and political fears of treason mixed in with accusations of witchcraft. On June 9, 1604 a Bill was

---

gether" (p. 133). Monter also suggests that the total number of trials was greater than 100,000 with the number executed much less.

296. Christina Larner, *Enemies of God: The Witch-Hunt in Scotland* (London: Chatto and Windus, 1981), p. 197. Larner ties the connection between witchcraft and woman indirectly to the stereotype of woman derived from the twin pillars of the Aristotelian view of women as imperfectly human — a failure of the process of conception — and the Judaeo-Christian view of women as the source of sin and the Fall of Man. "Since witchcraft involved a rejection of what are regarded as the noblest human attributes, women were the first suspects" (p. 92). Larner does not limit her analysis to the stereotype but studies historical political developments in Scotland as well as individual characteristics of witches, pp. 89-103.

297. A further aspect of this difference is summarized by Alan Macfarlane in his introduction to Christina Larner, *Witchcraft and Religion: The Politics of Popular Belief* (Oxford: Basil Blackwell, 1984). "In England, the prosecutions were almost totally concerned with *maleficium*, causing harm to one's neighbours, and little concerned with Devil worship, covens, or heresy. On the Continent, though many trials started with the former, once they reached the courts and leading questions and torture were applied, they were turned into heresy trials, concerned principally with the Satanic compact. . . ." Larner is able to show that Scotland fell between these two extremes. *Maleficium* was of interest to the high authorities, just as the Satanic compact was of concern to the villagers, p. ix.

298. Summers, *The Geography of Witchcraft*, "In no country did the witch-cult flourish more rankly, in no country did the belief persist more lately, in no country did the prosecution of sorcery rage fiercer and the fires blaze brighter than Scotland" (p. 201).

299. Larner, *Witchcraft*, p. 4. For a detailed study of the Essex Witch Trials, see Marianne Hester, *Lewd Women and Wicked Witches* (London and New York: Routledge, 1992), pp. 160-97.

300. Summers, *The Geography of Witchcraft*, p. 113.

passed in Parliament to strengthen a statute that made witchcraft a felony.[301] During the English Civil War the intensity of political battles and the intermingling of witchcraft increased to such an extent that in the last half of 1645, "nearly one hundred and fifty witches were put to death."[302] There were fewer witch trials in Spain and Italy.[303]

Witchcraft persecutions were severe in France, beginning slowly between 1300 and 1400, increasing in intensity between 1400 and 1500, and having further peaks during 1590-1680.[304] The judge Henry Boguet (d. 1619) wrote another popular and practical text entitled *An Examen of Witches*.[305] This text, first printed in 1590, and reprinted in 1602, 1603, 1606, 1607, 1608, 1610, and 1611, drew upon the traditional historical sources such as the *Malleus maleficarum*, classical sources of poetry and literature common to the new humanists, and also upon the personal experience of the judge himself. Significantly, Boguet argues that a judge should not use deception and should limit the use of torture to extract a confession from an accused person.[306] In these arguments, he attempts to bring some integrity back into the educated male side of the public interrogation. At the same time, however, Boguet reinforced arguments that suggested that women who are accused attempt to deceive judges during the interrogation.[307] Thus, the deterioration of intergender dialogue from a common effort to determine the truth to a basis of fear and self-defense continued in this particular context for several more years.

SATIRES, DECEPTION, AND THE DEGENERATION OF INTERGENDER DIALOGUE

In this chapter we have analyzed a widespread cultural phenomenon of the devaluation of women through satires, appeal to academic principles of gender po-

301. Summers, *The Geography of Witchcraft*, p. 255.

302. Summers attributes the intensity of these actions to Presbyterianism and Puritanism "fanning the flame" already ignited by political issues. *The Geography of Witchcraft*, p. 257.

303. See Summers, *The Geography of Witchcraft*, for general details of the development of witchcraft in these two countries: Italy, pp. 523-87; and Spain, pp. 588-614.

304. A detailed study by Robert Muchembled, "The Witches of the Cambrésis: The Acculturation of the Rural World in the Sixteenth and Seventeenth Centuries," focuses on the sociological aspect of witchcraft and of the presence of male witches in this later period of persecution and trial. See *Religion and the People*, ed. James Obelkevich (Chapel Hill: University of North Carolina Press, 1979), pp. 221-76. Muchembled traces the phenomena of witchcraft and warfare during what he calls peak periods from 1590 to 1630 and 1640 to 1680.

305. Henry Boguet, *An Examen of Witches: Drawn from various trials of many of this sect in the district of Saint Oyan de Joux commonly known as Saint Claude in the county of Burgundy including the procedure necessary to judge in trials for witchcraft*, trans. E. Allen Ashwin and ed. Montague Summers (London: John Rodker, 1929). The text is characterized by Summers as follows: "Indeed it may be said that throughout the whole vast library of demonology, after the great *Malleus maleficarum*, there is perhaps no treatise more authoritative, and certainly no treatise more revelatory of the human side of trials for witchcraft and of the psychology of those involved in such trials than the *Discours de sorciers (An Examen of Witches)* of Henry Boguet, 'Grand Juge' de St. Claude, au Comté de Bourgogne. . . . [it] was actually adopted in general practice by most local Parliaments and puisne courts . . ." (pp. vi-vii).

306. Boguet, *An Examen of Witches*, article xx, 217-19.

307. Boguet, *An Examen of Witches*, articles xxvii-xliv, 220-25.

larity, and public arrests and trials of women for heresy and witchcraft. In the midst of these events there was a clear and serious deterioration of intergender dialogue. It shifted from the cooperative search for truth and the particular support for women's growth and development that we depicted in the last chapter, and it moved towards a manipulative use of power by particular men who offered a rationale for conscious deception and use of torture to achieve their predetermined goals.

It is important to note that this cultural phenomenon did not include all men, for there were always some men ready to educate and defend women during this time in history. It also was not limited to a particular religious order of men. For example, the Dominicans both defended and tried women accused of heresy and witchcraft; they both educated women and consciously deceived them. Some men both educated and defended Margery Kempe, and some men originally defended and then later rehabilitated the reputation of Joan of Arc. Still, there are enough examples of the degeneration of intergender dialogue during this period, especially between men with an academic background and women with none, to have attempted to analyze some of its special features. A brief summary of some of the salient philosophical aspects of this analysis will now be given.

As just mentioned, our analysis of the works considered in this chapter has indicated a progressive use of the theme of deception in the context of intergender dialogue. In the satire, *Miroir de mariage,* all of the female personifications attempted to deceive the young man about the true state of marriage, while the men in the dialogue engaged in direct discussion. The concept of woman incorporated a model of someone who would deceive to gain any goal. In the *Fifteen Joys of Marriage* we find that the theme of deception shifted from female personifications to multiple descriptions of an imaginary wife who lays all sorts of traps for her husband, and who constantly speaks about appearances in order to secure some advantage for herself on a deeper level of reality. The result is that the concept of woman in this satire incorporates a consistent model of a deceptive woman who uses speech to gain some ulterior (immoral) end.

In the chart on page 531 several of these central concepts and examples are summarized.

In the examples of particular women who were arrested — Joan of Arc, Margery Kempe, and Katherine Kepler — we saw these patterns repeated. Educated men interrogated uneducated women who were under arrest. The intergender dialogues for which there are accurate historical records reveal the extent to which the participating men viewed the women as dangerous and deceptive. There was a great difference in result of the interrogation in the three cases considered: Margery Kempe was always able to win over the men accusing her; Joan of Arc was maliciously set up by the few men who wanted her condemned, but eventually was freed of all charges by consideration her testimony; and Katherine Kepler did win her freedom through her own defense and the defense by her son, but she was shadowed by the suspicion of guilt. In this development of the arrest, trial, and condemnation of individual women for heresy and witchcraft we discovered a concrete dimension to the generalized stereotypes of woman present in the background of earlier satires. The satires exaggerated women's vices or inverted men's

Woman Depicted as Deceptive and Dangerous in Satires				
	Woman appears	Woman is	Women and animals	Men and animals
Miroir de mariage Invokes Aristotle, Theophrastus, Plato, Socrates, Juvenal	Female personifications suggest marriage is good for several reasons. Woman's beauty seems good.	Deceptive: full of folly, servitude, and fantasy Dangerous: rules man Ugly and evil: leads to mutilation and death of body and damnation of soul	Like a horse, beast, pig, goat, cat, bear, lioness, wolf, ewe, and bloodhound	Like a sheep, cow, fish, or bird caught in trap; if he does not marry he is like a bird that flies free
Quinze joies de mariage Ironic inversion "praises" women as good, but by weakness, defenselessness, obedience, and servitude, that is, by natural inferiority.	Wife appears good. Wife appears to weep, appears to be innocent and blames husband, appears to be sick, and appears not to sleep.	Wife is evil, lustful, spiteful, cruel, selfish, greedy, wrathful, slothful, gluttonous, and an uncontrolled gossip; wife rules, husband obeys. Wife does not weep, is really at fault, well, and sleeps soundly.	Wife like an animal trainer	Like a fish caught in a net; beast caught in a trap; prodded donkey; ox at the plow; toothless bear, chained, muzzled, and beaten

and women's virtues. It is exactly these two categories that formed the substance of the interrogations against Margery Kempe and Joan of Arc. In the table on p. 532 some of these characteristics are summarized.

In this chapter, we also described how the printing press became a medium for the transmission of satirical concepts of women. The printing of old satires disseminated previously articulated satirical concepts of woman's identity. These included particularly exaggerated images of women as inconstant and emotional,

Gender-Related Themes of Women Arrested for Heresy or Witchcraft		
Category of Condemnation	Margery Kempe	Saint Joan of Arc
Women's reason lacks authority over her emotions. Women ought to obey/ men ought to rule.	Exaggerated feminine vice: Too emotional in public by uncontrollable weeping even when asked to stop	Inversion of masculine and feminine virtues: Controlled and heroic leading of men as soldiers and military strategists on several battlefields
Women ought to remain silent/men to speak in public.	Inversion of masculine and feminine virtues: Teaching about moral values in public all over England, Europe, and Jerusalem	Inversion of masculine and feminine virtues: Leading men by offering counsel to the King and his advisors in various places in France
A woman's identity is defined by the clothes she wears/a woman cannot define her identity by her choice of clothes.	Inversion of feminine virtues: Wearing white clothes usually reserved for virgins [to redefine chastity for older married woman]	Inversion of masculine and feminine virtues: Wearing clothes usually reserved for men [to protect herself against sexual harassment and by default]

and the inverted images of women as not silent, not obedient, and not content to remain in the private realm of activity.

While considering similarities between the old satires and the new satires that were dispersed during the fifteenth and sixteenth centuries we identified two common characteristics: (1) the move from an example of a particular woman to a universal claim about all women; and (2) the frequent invocation of animal metaphors to reduce the human being to a bestial level of existence. In addition we noted four newer characteristics of the concept of woman as described in these later satires: (1) an increase in the claim that women always tend to deceive men; (2) an increase in the claim that women intentionally choose to harm men; (3) an increase in the claim that women's cooperation with supernatural evil becomes a direct or indirect danger for men; and (4) an increase in the intermingling of satirical texts with religious texts. These new developments were seen to have serious consequences for individual women who were arrested and tried for the heresy of witchcraft. The assessors and judges in these trials operated frequently with the above-mentioned characteristics of women in mind.

In the manual *Malleus maleficarum* the authors frequently described women as full of deception. They suggested that woman was prone to intentionally deceive man because of an inherent weakness in her nature; they also argued that some women consciously chose to cooperate with evil and intentionally used deception as part of their witchcraft. However, the manual also argues that judges should practice intentional deception as part of their own interrogatory techniques. They should pretend that a confession would make a sentence lighter when in fact a confession brought the heaviest sentence, and they should pretend that torture would be used when only the threat of torture was planned. These developments provided terrible instances of the progressive deterioration of intergender dialogue, particularly between educated men and uneducated women. In this way, the concept of woman suggested by the satirists seems to have prepared the way for serious concrete acts of devaluation of woman in many situations.

The historical data, when weighed carefully by region and time, appear to support the conclusion that around 200,000 persons were officially arrested between 1400 and 1668, that over 75 percent of those arrested were women, that they were tried by both Catholics and Protestants in inquisitorial, ecclesiastical, and civil courts, and that 100,000 of them were put to death, frequently by fire. The number of uneducated women interrogated in judicial trial, when combined with the fact that those doing the judging and assessing were all men educated in European academic institutions, indicates that most dialogues occurring around these trials were between persons of unequal education. Furthermore, the interrogation was framed by stereotypes of women that in part were derived from philosophical concepts of woman embedded in academic education and satires. As a consequence, even though a particular woman may indeed have acted in malice and even in cooperation with evil as a witch, their particular transgressions were buried in an avalanche of false accusations framed in a general bias that women were deceitful and dangerous because of the inferiority of their nature, intellect, and will. In the chart on pages 534 and 535 we will depict some of these areas of coincidence between satirical concepts of women and the manuals used in witchcraft trials:

In this chart we again see the theme of women as deceitful and dangerous for men because they appear to be one thing, but in fact turn out to be quite another. The common tendency, both within the satires and the manual, to extend these judgments to a universal application to characteristics of all women is the main area of difficulty in intergender relations. There is no doubt that some women may illustrate the above-mentioned characteristics, but the implication that all women, or the 100,000 women who were put to death in Europe between 1400 and 1680, or even that there is a tendency in all women to have these kinds of characteristics, is clearly false. When we ask the question, "How did the satirical concept of woman as deceitful and dangerous take such root in the thoughts and actions of many men during the fifteenth and sixteenth centuries?" we need to return to the question of the roots of bias that we introduced in the summary and evaluation section of Chapter 3 when discussing early satires about women.

To review Bernard Lonergan's claims about bias in *Insight*, we noted previ-

Woman as Deceptive and Dangerous in the *Malleus malificarum*				
	Woman appears	Woman is	Women and animals	Men and animals
Malleus Maleficarum: Invokes: Walter Map Theophrastus	As good	Indirect cause of evil by persuasion Turns men's minds to inordinate love or hatred Cooperates with evil spirit (matter receives form) to cause temporal harm to others	Imperfect animal More pernicious than a snare of devils Vexes horses and causes diseases to animals	
	To help others	Prepares poison Raises storms Causes sterility, diseases, accidents, abortions Interferes with generation Kills	Flies through the air like a bird Appears like a noble lion, but is actually like a belly of a goat or a tail of a viper	Actually turns men into animals by transmutation, or gives the illusion of turning men into animals

Woman as Deceptive and Dangerous in the *Malleus malificarum* (cont.)			
	Woman appears	Woman is	Women and animals	Men and animals
	As truthful	Always deceives Is childlike, feeble-minded, feeble-bodied, undisciplined, weak in memory, inordinate in affections, liar by nature, wheedling, secret enemy of men	Appears like a rose, but is really like a thorn	

ously that bias inhibits insight by overlooking relevant data of experience, by blocking intelligent questions that ought to be raised about the data, and by distorting reasoning that should evaluate subjective insights for their objectivity, and so forth.[308] We find in the manuals used in relation to witchcraft a consistent pattern of interpreting the data of experience in the worst possible light so that the premise that a woman is deceptive and dangerous for a man is supported by the data. In this atmosphere of fear caused by the aftermath of the plague, by radical political upheavals, by the Reformation and Counter-Reformation, many educated men continued to act out of a biased concept of woman. This bias is a form of group bias present in western culture and highly articulated by men who had been educated in the academic community of discourse in the major universities of Europe. In this community of discourse no women were present to provide a different set of empirical data with which to counter the stereotypes prevalent in academic and popular texts.

With the development of the printing press, popular satires were spread out into the broader public arena. Here we find a mixed-gender community of dialogue, with the exception that for the most part the men were educated and the women were not. As we suggested in Chapter 2 in the discussion on logic, aca-

308. Bernard Lonergan, *Insight: A Study of Human Understanding* (New York: Philosophical Library, 1956). See also Cynthia Crysdale, "Horizons That Differ: Women and Men and the Flight from Understanding," *Cross Currents* (Fall 1994): 345-61; and *Lonergan and Feminism,* ed. Cynthia S. W. Crysdale (Toronto, Buffalo, London: University of Toronto Press, 1994).

demic dialogue often served the purpose of winning an argument rather than mutually searching for truth. However, at least in logical dialectic, those who undertook the two sides of the argument had equal educational background. It was a short move from dialectic to interrogation, in which only one of the participants was educated and the other was not. This occurred in trials of women for witchcraft. Here the dialogue was imbalanced from the start; it had no foundation of equal dignity within which a genuine complementarity could emerge. It is not surprising that the dialogue shifted to interrogation, and the antagonistic model of dialectic so prevalent in the study of logic was used in a situation in which the defendants, uneducated women, lacked the intellectual tools with which to counter false or spurious arguments. With this imbalance, some of the men who were judges and assessors also introduced deception to win their case, and the real purpose of dialogue as a mutual search for truth was completely lost. In these situations, we can also see some of the ways Lonergan suggested that a biased person acts, by ignoring the data, by blocking questions that could lead to insight, and by not using reason to test subjective insights for their genuine objectivity.

On the other hand, in the situation of Margery Kempe and St. Joan of Arc, we also discovered other examples of men who did question their biases and reach new insights about women's identity. In this chapter we saw how Margery Kempe raised new possibilities for the imagination by telling stories to bring new insights to her audience. Joan of Arc also attempted to raise new possibilities for woman in defense of her actions. Both women were constantly struggling to overcome bias in their culture about woman's proper identity. In order to counteract one's own bias, a person needs to ask good questions about the data so that new insights can be generated.

In Chapter 4, we indicated ways in which the first humanists, by using their imagination, raised new possibilities about women's capacity for wisdom and virtue. Their proposals, in turn, produced a new concept of woman that directly produced counterexamples to the satirical concept of woman as irrational and morally weak. In the next chapter, we will discover a similar use of imagination to counteract a general bias about woman's nature as deceitful and dangerous for men in the Renaissance Humanists' move from imaginary dialogue in literary works to actual dialogue in public essays and letters. This time, women will enter directly into the public dialogue with men about the subject of woman's identity. The educated women, Christine de Pizan, Isotta Nogarola, and Laura Cereta are the first humanists to raise fundamental questions about the general bias so fundamental to satires about woman's character. In this way, they will begin to bring about a new balance into the deteriorated intergender dialogue that was so prevalent in texts considered in this chapter.

In the present chapter we have studied what is clearly the lowest point in western history in the quality of intergender discourse among women and men. In the next chapter we will move to a significant reform of intergender relations where the focus shifts away from defending individual women from false accusations infused with devalued stereotypes of woman. Instead, the way will finally be opened for dialogue about woman's identity to begin the important reform of the gender polarity model of gender relations. It will be the woman, Christine de Pizan, who first shows this way.

CHAPTER 7

EARLY HUMANIST DIALOGUE
ABOUT THE CONCEPT OF WOMAN

In this chapter we will study the work of a remarkable person whose writing reorients the history of the concept of woman. Christine de Pizan[1] (ca. 1344-1430) acted as a catalyst that brought together a critical mass of previous literature about sex and gender identity and, through her pivotal evaluation, radically altered the way we approach these issues. While there may have been other women in her culture who thought similarly about the pervasive gender polarity stereotypes of woman's identity, Christine was the first to articulate a consistent evaluation of men's views of women. We have records of some contributions by Hildegard, Herrad, and Heloise within the monastic tradition and by Roswitha in the literary tradition, but none of these women left records of extensive argumentation against the views of other philosophers about the concept of woman.

It is possible that many other women, either before or during the era of Christine de Pizan, may have had a similar kind of response to derogatory images of women contained in satirical works or even to the theoretical gender polarity principles common to academic communities of discourse, but if so, the records have not survived. Thus certain circumstances must have converged in the life of Christine that uniquely enabled her to articulate substantive arguments against gender polarity principles in an extraordinary manner.

Despite her high social position and extended education, she engaged in the public debate with great respect for the truth no matter what its source. While she was well versed in the academic tradition, she did not hesitate to defend her position against it. At times she explicitly identified her perspective as that of a woman,

---

1. Christine de Pizan's last name will be spelled with the letter z rather than an s, following Angus J. Kennedy, *Christine de Pizan: A Bibliographical Guide* (London: Grant and Cutler, 1984) and *Christine de Pizan: A Bibliographical Guide, Supplement I* (London: Grant and Cutler Ltd., 1994). The reason for this is that her father's last name was Pizzano and Christine herself used this spelling. This fact was not well known among many scholars, who often used the form of *Pisan* since in the French language the s has the sound of the English z. While the form of *Pizan* will be used in the text of this chapter, the endnotes will follow the spelling used in the original source. I am grateful to Thelma Fenster for this clarification of the two different ways of spelling her name as well as for other invaluable suggestions for the improvement of this chapter. Use of the first name 'Christine' follows the tradition for aristocratic authors in French literature.

at other times she simply discussed issues as a matter of principle, and not from any engendered position. She pronounced and defended her views on many different topics based on historical evidence, a refined commonsense skill of observation and the ability to conduct complex rational arguments. With an amazing self-assurance born from personal suffering and the mastery of hardship, development of her particular talents, and a deep faith in God, Christine de Pizan was the first woman to earn her living by writing. For all these reasons, Christine de Pizan's work serves as a model for contemporary dialogues about the concept of woman.

Christine de Pizan wrote over forty-one different texts during the years 1394-1429. The variety of literary forms she used included poetry, epistles, essays, allegories, proverbs, dialogues, orations, and meditations. Her themes focused on authentic love, virtuous life, human character, women's identity, history, errors of satirists, practical wisdom, principles of education, justice and the common good in political life, especially in France, appropriate and inappropriate forms of war, grief, Joan of Arc, and various meditations on the life of the Blessed Virgin Mary and Jesus Christ. While scholars are continually offering greater precision in this area, approximate dates of composition and titles of Christine de Pizan's most relevant works with philosophical considerations of sex and gender identity include the following:[2]

1394-1402	*Cent ballades (One Hundred Ballades)*
1399	*Epistre au dieu d'amours (Letter of the God of Love — Cupid's Letter)*
1399-1400	*Enseignements moraux (Moral Teachings)*
	Proverbes moraux (Moral Proverbs)
1400	*Dit de Poissy (The Tale of Poissy)*
1401-1402	*L'Epistre d'Othéa à Hector (The Letter of the Goddess Othea to Hector)*
1401	*Le Débat des deux amants (The Debate of Two Lovers)*
1402	*Dit de la rose (The Tale of the Rose)*
1401-1403	*Epistres sur le Roman de la rose (Letters about the Romance of the Rose)*
1402-1403	*Le Livre du chemin de long estude (The Book of the Long Road of Learning — Long Path of Study)*
1403	*Le Livre de la mutacion de fortune (The Book of the Mutation of Fortune)*
1404	*Epistre à Eustache Morel* [Eustache Deschamps] *(Letter to Eustache Morel*
1404	*Le Livre des faits et bonnes moeurs du sage roi Charles V (The Book of Deeds and Good Customs of the Wise King Charles V)*
1404	*Le Livre des trois jugements (The Book of Three Judgments)*

2. Edith Yenal, *Christine de Pisan: A Bibliography of Writings by Her and about Her* (Metuchen, N.J. and London: Scarecrow Press, 1982), pp. 1-2. The dates included in the list have been changed as more contemporary scholars suggest more accurate dates. The English versions of the titles are taken from throughout the text by Charity Canon Willard, *Christine de Pizan: Her Life and Works* (New York: Persea Books, 1984).

While many texts authored by Christine de Pizan have in the last couple of decades become well known to scholars of literature, she has remained relatively unknown to philosophers. This lack of recognition is unfortunate because Christine de Pizan is the first woman author who demonstrated a consistent ability to engage in philosophical argumentation. She understood different kinds of argumentation identified in Aristotelian texts on logic and rhetoric. Specifically, Christine manifests an adeptness at using **poetic** arguments that openly appeal to the emotions, **rhetorical** arguments that, in a more hidden way, appeal to the emotions, **dialectical** arguments that are based on an intellectual foundation of merely contingent opinions, and **demonstrative** arguments that establish necessary conclusions.[3] In addition to the fact that Christine de Pizan appears to be the first woman writer to extensively use different forms of philosophical argumentation in her works, she is also the first woman to employ these arguments to generate conclusions about woman's identity. Thus, not only the form but also the content of Christine de Pizan's arguments about woman's identity reveals a new development in the history of the concept of woman.

How did she achieve this astonishing dual contribution to the history of the philosophy of gender? What kind of intellectual and personal formation did she receive that enabled her to develop a facility in various forms of philosophical argu-

---

3. While these kinds of arguments have been considered in the second chapter of this book with respect to forms of debate in academia, a short summary of their differences can be found in William A. Wallace, O.P., *The Elements of Philosophy: A Compendium for Philosophers and Theologians* (New York: Alba House, 1977), pp. 12-13.

mentation, and what factors led to her decision to apply this ability to argue about the concept of woman? In the first part of this chapter some of the salient details of Christine's educational background and use of sources will be described, in order to properly situate her contribution to the history of the concept of woman. In particular, Christine's relation to the existing communities of discourse, academic, religious, humanist, and satirical, will be highlighted.

In the second and third parts of this chapter her systematic employment of philosophical arguments to prove fundamental claims about women's identity is described and evaluated. The second part elaborates on Christine de Pizan's participation in the public intergender debate about women's identity known as the *Querelle de la rose*.[4] This public debate marks the first occurrence of a systematic debate between men and women about philosophical issues concerning woman's identity. The third part considers her philosophical arguments about sex and gender identity in two of her later literary works associated with the construction of an ideal city inhabited by women.

This chapter will demonstrate how Christine de Pizan organized the content and form of philosophical arguments in a dramatically new way to defend the identity of women against slander and distorted judgments common to traditional gender polarity. A considerable amount of research within the last ten years has claimed that Christine de Pizan often borrowed material from other scholars and poets. While this may be true (it was true of most scholars of her time), her contributions are unique in the sense that they often affected a radical revamping of the traditional approach to particular subjects in a variety of fields. She demonstrated originality in reorienting texts about courtly love, in gathering letters together into a coherent text, in revising the structure and images in a common text for different patrons, and in translating and editing classical texts written by such authors as Boethius, Thomas Aquinas, Dante, and Boccaccio to support her own goals. Since her many and varied contributions in these areas have been studied by other scholars, only those with particular relevance to the philosophical approach to the concept of woman will be considered in this chapter. I hope that a focused emphasis on the formal structure and content of Christine de Pizan's philosophical arguments about the concept of woman will contribute a complementary perspective to the research that has been recently published by historians and scholars of literature. The first analysis below will set the context in which Christine influenced and was influenced by the four communities of discourse identified in this book, namely academics, religious writers, humanists, and satirists.[5]

---

4. Several of Christine de Pizan's works are not yet available in English. At the same time, a considerable number of them have been partially or wholly translated and printed in English within the last ten years and often with different renderings of their titles. Where available, printed English-language translations have been used in this text. However, in order to have a greater consistency in the development of the argument, in this chapter most titles are given in French.

5. While a summary of some of the salient points will be given in the first part of this chapter, readers may be referred to Charity Canon Willard's biography *Christine de Pizan: Her Life and Works* for more complete details. See also Régine Pernoud, *Christine de Pisan* (Paris: Calmann-Lévy, 1982).

CHRISTINE DE PIZAN'S LIFE AND RELATION TO COMMUNITIES OF DISCOURSE

Academic Community of Discourse

Christine de Pizan was born in Venice in 1363. Her father, Thomas da Pizzano, was a physician who received his medical degree from the University of Bologna, and he held a chair in Astrology there from 1344 to 1356.[6] It can be safely assumed that through her father and his library, Christine had access to various medical texts on generation including those of the Hippocratians, Galen, Avicenna, and later possibly even Albert the Great and Giles of Rome, as well as Aristotelian and Ptolemaic works in astronomy. Her father, a peer of Dante, Petrarch, and Boccaccio, lived in Venice and admired Italian humanism. It is likely that Christine had access to the works of these early Italian humanists through her father's library as well.

In the following extract from her autobiographical work *L'Avision-Christine (Christine's Vision)*, she questions the idea that the female is a malformed male — a manifestation of the gender polarity principle. Christine tells us that her being born as a female was due to a direct choice of nature rather than a defect in the form:

> When [the crowned lady] had put all the molded material into the oven, she took my spirit and exactly as she was accustomed to do to give human bodies form, mixed it all together and left me to cook for a certain period of time until a small human shape was made for me. I was given the feminine sex, however, because she who had cast it wished it to be so rather than because of the mold.[7]

At the age of five Christine and her mother moved to Paris, where her father had been hired as a physician and astronomer for Charles V, King of France. In *Le Livre des faits et bonnes moeurs du sage roi Charles V (The Book of Deeds and Good Customs of the Wise King Charles)* Christine spoke admiringly of her father as "the greatest of astronomers, in the speculative sciences."[8] In her text *Le Livre de la cité des dames (The Book of the City of Ladies)*, Christine notes that her "father, who was a great scientist and philosopher, did not believe that women were worth less by knowing science; rather . . . he took great pleasure from seeing [her] inclination to learning."[9]

In another of her autobiographical texts, entitled *Le Livre du chemin de long*

---

6. Christine de Pizan, *Christine's Vision* (New York and London: Garland Publishing, 1993), pp. i-xii.

7. Christine de Pizan, *Christine's Vision*, I.3, 13. The text also refers to three different kinds of "mothers": Part I, the lady of the crown — mother of France; Part II, the lady of opinion — mother of academics; and Part III, the lady philosophy — mother of wisdom and happiness.

8. See *Le Livre des fais et bonnes moeurs du roi Charles V le Sage* (Paris: Stock, 1997). A selected translation into English can be found in "The Book of the Deeds and Good Character of King Charles V, the Wise," in *The Writings of Christine de Pizan*, ed. Charity Canon Willard (New York: Persea Books, 1994), pp. 235 and 241. See also Christine de Pizan, *Christine's Vision*, III.17, 127-28.

9. Christine de Pizan, *The Book of the City of Ladies* (New York: Persea Press, 1983), II.36, 154. She adds that her mother did not share this same value in educating her daughter in the sciences.

estude (The Book of the Long Road of Learning), Christine also included her father among the list of philosophers who drew from the fountain of wisdom. In the following passage, a Sibyl reveals to Christine the road of long study that she needs to undertake:

> That is where the prince of learning used to live, on that high hill, where he used to fill himself with the fountain's water: this was the philosopher Aristotle. And you see the beautiful and gracious places all around where the other philosophers used to live, on the heights. You see the beautiful, pure places which Socrates and Plato, Democritus and Diogenes used to frequent. The great philosopher Hermes used to delight in these spots. If you raise your eyes you will see where Anaxagoras used to be; Empedocles and Heraclitus often used to enjoy themselves there. Dioscorides the observer, Seneca, Tully, Ptolemy used to come to this beloved school beside the rippling water. The geometrician Hippocrates, Galen, Avicenna, and many other great philosophers used to gather together around the fountain where they equipped themselves with knowledge. They all used to pass through here. Your father knew this place very well, and he certainly should have, because he often spent time here, and carried away great learning.[10]

The list of philosophers is significant because it indicates particular men who directly influenced Christine's education. She elaborates on the particular contributions of several of these philosophers in Book II of L'Avision-Christine. Here Christine follows the same order of reference found in St. Thomas Aquinas's Commentary on Book I of Aristotle's Metaphysics. She describes Aristotle's observations on the early materialist Presocratic philosophers Thales, Diogenes, Anaximenes, Anaximander, Heraclitus, Pythagoras, and Democritus, who isolated water, air, fire, or numbers as the material or efficient causes of all things.[11]

Christine also discusses Aristotle's critique of the opinions of these philosophers as he establishes the foundation for his scientific theory of causes. In particular, she mentions Aristotle texts On the Soul (II.8, 11), Physics (II.8, 9, and 10) and Metaphysics (II.13). To conclude her reflections on the metaphysical theories of ancient philosophers in L'Avision-Christine, through the voice of her narrator, she directs her reader to the original work of Aristotle himself as follows:

> I could tell you much more about what I was [like] in various cases within the ancient philosophers, both in this matter discussed at length above and in the explanations of Aristotle, the true dialectician and wise master. Whoever wants to know more about this subject should seek out the philosopher in his Metaphysics; but as this material is quite obscure, this much must suffice.[12]

---

10. Christine de Pizan, "The Path of Long Study," in The Selected Writings of Christine de Pizan, ed. Renate Blumenfeld-Kosinski and Kevin Brownlee (New York and London: W. W. Norton, 1997), p. 73. A new modern French version of the original text is available as Le Chemin de longue étude (Paris: Librairie Générale Française, 1998).

11. Christine de Pizan, Christine's Vision, II.6-13, 65-76.

12. Christine de Pizan, Christine's Vision, II.13, 76.

Before continuing this analysis of Christine de Pizan's knowledge of philosophical sources, it will be helpful to introduce some more biographical information. At the age of fifteen, Christine married Etienne du Castel, a brilliant young French humanist whom she described in *L'Avision-Christine* affectionately as combining both "great learning and good character."[13] In *Le Chemin de long estude* Christine reflected further on her husband: "In my opinion, he was without equal in the world; I could not have wished for anyone more wise, prudent, handsome and good than he was, in all respects. . . . Our love and our two hearts were completely in accord, much more than between brothers and sisters; our two wills were one, whether it was a question of joy or of sorrow."[14]

Etienne du Castel's position as secretary to King Charles V brought him into contact with scientists and intellectuals whom Charles had gathered in and near his court. In addition, the King had amassed the second largest library in Europe in a tower of his palace, the Louvre.[15] While the King had a very close relation to the University of Paris, he also wanted to establish a center of learning that had some independence from the academic setting. His great desire was to make the more traditional academic texts available to educated laymen. Thus, King Charles V hired translators for many ancient texts from the original Greek, Latin, and Arabic into French. Several of Aristotle's works were translated for the first time into vernacular French, illustrated, indexed, and prepared in manuscript form easily accessible to selected non-academics.[16] In addition, King Charles V also established a center for producing books (before the printing press), occupying copyists (possibly both male and female), illuminators, binders, and booksellers. It was in this extraordinary environment that Christine received the more advanced portions of her higher education in philosophy. It was also in this context that she translated portions of Thomas Aquinas's *Commentary on Aristotle's Metaphysics* from Latin into French.[17] Her work of translation is thought to be "the first known vernacular [French] commentary on Aristotle's *Metaphysics*."[18]

Christine's familiarity with Aristotle's *Metaphysics* and with Thomas Aquinas's *Commentary* is important: both works could have served as a model for dialectical and demonstrative argumentation. Her awareness of the contents of Book I of Thomas's *Commentary* alone would have given her a great deal of information about how a philosopher argues. In particular, Thomas notes that for Aristotle knowledge of universals and causes is superior to knowledge of particulars, that

13. Christine de Pizan, *Christine's Vision,* III.4, 110.

14. Christine de Pizan, "The Path of Long Study," in *The Selected Writings of Christine de Pizan,* from lines 61-104, p. 62.

15. Willard, *Christine de Pizan: Her Life and Works,* pp. 28 and 30.

16. Christine de Pizan identifies the texts in her history of the life of Charles V, *Le Livre des fais et bonnes moeurs du roi Charles V le Sage;* see especially III, i-xv, 195-223. See also Clare Richter Sherman, *Imaging Aristotle: Verbal and Visual Representation in Fourteenth-Century France* (Berkeley/ Los Angeles/London: University of California Press, 1995), esp. pp. 9 and 306-7.

17. Thelma Fenster, "'Perdre son Latin': Christine de Pizan and Vernacular Humanism," in *Christine de Pizan and the Categories of Difference,* ed. Marilynn Desmond. Medieval Cultures, vol. 14 (Minneapolis and London: University of Minnesota Press, 1998), ch. 5, pp. 91-107, 92-93.

18. Christine de Pizan, *Christine's Vision,* 93, note 2 and Book III, 141-43.

knowledge of causes allows one to teach others true wisdom, and that scientific knowledge of causes through demonstration and syllogistic reasoning is superior to opinion, experience, and belief.[19] She concludes: "[t]he more a man attains to a knowledge of the cause, the wiser he is."[20]

Her familiarity with the content of one of Aristotle's texts is demonstrated in Books II and III of *L'Avision-Christine,* where she places all learning in the context of St. Thomas's Commentary on Book I of Aristotle's *Metaphysics.* Christine introduces the goal of study as learning about first causes in true Physics, about common and particular goods in true Ethics, about demonstration and dialectic in true Logic, and about justice and a virtuous life in true Politics. In her several works on woman's identity, she incorporates fundamental principles of Aristotle's ethics and politics while seeking to overturn some of the negative consequences for women of traditional gender polarity.

The translation of portions of Thomas's *Commentary* on Book I of Aristotle's *Metaphysics* may have led Christine de Pizan to reflect on the relation of opinions and truth in the debates of academic communities of discourse. Thomas echoes Aristotle's claim that "those who philosophize seek an end to escape from ignorance."[21] He stresses that opinions are only the first step in an investigation that leads to a true science.[22] Thomas characterizes Aristotle's method as subjecting the opinions of past philosophers to criticism in order to reach the truth of science.[23] He summarizes: "Having stated the opinions which the philosophers held about the principles of things, Aristotle begins here to criticize them. . . ."[24] This is exactly the model that Christine de Pizan follows in her arguments about the concept of woman: she states common opinions about woman's identity and then criticizes them.

Christine de Pizan's biography of King Charles V contains a written record of over thirty different works translated into French at the King's behest. She directly mentions Augustine's *City of God* and Aristotle's *Ethics* and *Politics* among several other texts.[25] Most notable for our purposes was the work of the main translator, Nicole Oresme. Between 1360 and 1390 he translated and supervised the illustration of the complete texts of Aristotle's *Nicomachean Ethics, Politics* and the spurious *Economics.*[26] In addition, he created glossaries of difficult terms, sought to give careful précis as to the meaning of the original texts, along with the medieval scholarly commentaries on them.[27] Oresme had been trained in the academic setting, and had previously taught as a Master of Arts and a Master of Theology. His collaboration with King Charles helped to eliminate some of the boundaries be-

19. St. Thomas Aquinas, *Commentary on the Metaphysics of Aristotle* (Chicago: Henry Regnery Company, 1961), vol. 1, #12-13, 24, 26, and 29.

20. St. Thomas Aquinas, *Commentary on the Metaphysics of Aristotle,* #35.

21. St. Thomas Aquinas, *Commentary on the Metaphysics of Aristotle,* #53.

22. St. Thomas Aquinas, *Commentary on the Metaphysics of Aristotle,* #72.

23. St. Thomas Aquinas, *Commentary on the Metaphysics of Aristotle,* #69.

24. St. Thomas Aquinas, *Commentary on the Metaphysics of Aristotle,* #181.

25. Christine de Pizan, *Le Livre des fais et bonne moeurs du roi Charles V le Sage,* III, xii, 216-18.

26. Sherman, *Imaging Aristotle,* pp. xxi-xxiv.

27. Sherman, *Imaging Aristotle,* pp. 23-33.

tween the academic and intelligent lay communities of discourse. In this way, women such as Christine de Pizan had access to the resources that would help form their minds in higher education. Christine was well acquainted with Aristotle's *Ethics, Politics, Metaphysics, On the Heavens,* and *Rhetoric.*

Happily married for ten years, Christine de Pizan gave birth to three children and had little time for her intellectual studies. Three tragedies occurring within a nine-year period, however, radically altered her circumstances. King Charles V died in 1380 — an event that left her father and husband in a weakened financial position. Around 1387 her father died and in 1390 her husband died in an epidemic. At the age of twenty-five Christine de Pizan was suddenly widowed, left with no means of financial support, and immersed, for the next fourteen years, in lawsuits with unscrupulous men who sought to rob her of financial resources. She had to take care of herself, three children, her mother, and another relative; this desperate situation led her to the decision to become a professional writer.

A fortuitous circumstance provided the educational setting that Christine needed for her intellectual development and professional work. Likely through Jean Gerson (1363-1429), the Chancellor of the University of Paris, and Gilles Malet, the Royal Librarian at the Louvre, Christine was given access to the most up-to-date library sources.[28] Often portraits, such as the one included on the next page, depict Christine sitting in an alcove in a private study or in a library either reading or writing.

In this fertile intellectual environment, Christine learned about science, metaphysics, history, logic, ethics, and politics as they had been taught in academic circles. The suggestion by some historians that she may have worked as a copyist in the King's library or for booksellers in the early years of her bereavement would provide part of the explanation about how she came to learn so much about academic sources.

In Book II of *L'Avision-Christine* she gives a wonderful analogical description of her experiences in the libraries. Taken on a tour as a foreigner, she is being led everywhere in the labyrinth of corridors at the University of Paris, and shown all the libraries. She offers an imaginary vision to describe ways in which academic debates were full of "shadows" of opinion all vying for dominance.

> . . . suddenly I came upon the schools. Delighted to have arrived at such a noble university, eager for my mind profitably to drink in their erudition, I was pausing among scholars of the various learned faculties disputing and debating various questions together, when, just as I pricked up my ears to listen, my sight over-

---

28. Jean Gerson was a great spiritual author of over sixty-six works; in addition, he promoted practical reform of the political structure of society, of universities, and of the Church. See James Connolly, *Jean Gerson: Reformer and Mystic* (St. Louis: B. Herder Book Co., 1928). Gerson was initially interested in Ockhamism and nominalism, but he later came to prefer realism. As we mentioned in Chapter 2, nominalism appeared to be more associated with a gender unity position and realism with a gender polarity position. However, Gerson and Christine de Pizan created a new example of gender complementarity, both in their relation with one another and in their writings about gender. See D. Catherine Brown, *Pastor and Laity in the Theology of Jean Gerson* (Cambridge: Cambridge University Press, 1982), esp. pp. 223-24. For information on Gilles Malet, see also Willard, p. 42.

Christine de Pizan Writing in Her Study in Paris

came my hearing. Lifting my eyes, I saw a great, feminine, bodiless shadow — a spiritual thing quite bizarre in nature — flying among them. Experience proved her to be preternatural; for this substance I saw was a single shadow, yet more than a hundred thousand million (indeed innumerable) parts — some large, others small, others smaller still — did she create from herself. . . .

I saw that all the clerks disputing in these schools were surrounded by these groups of shadows flying through the air. And before the one who wished to propose his question might speak, one of these shadows came to whisper in his ear, as if to advise him what to say. Afterwards, when another wished to respond or reply, another shadow also went to whisper in his ear, so no disputant was thus without one, two, three, four, or even more [shadows] around his head, all giving him advice.[29]

Christine is well aware that, although this academic form of debate could lead to a greater understanding of truth, it also often deteriorated into argument and even sometimes into violence. She notes: "The matter was so arranged that these shadows seemed to cause their discords and debates, which sometimes grew so between them that they made angry ones go *de verbis ad verbera* [from words to blows]."[30] Drawing upon the Aristotelian tradition of dialectical debate, Christine points out that the different shadows or opinions serve two purposes, somewhat akin to hypotheses. Opinions, once tested, can become a starting point that leads to the truth; but if they are left untested by reason, their potential falsity can remain forever undetected.

Christine introduces a variety of ways of evaluating opinions of others. Again, her pattern follows those previously used by Aristotle and elaborated by St. Thomas. For example, in Thomas's commentary on Book I of Aristotle's *Metaphysics,* Aquinas notes that Aristotle proves his point, first by argument and then by example.[31] One method of criticism Aquinas calls "dialectical" because it shows how the opinion fails in relation to its own argument or by another position of the philosopher who has proposed it.[32] Another method of criticism Aquinas calls "disputational" because it shows how the opinion fails in relation to Aristotle's own principles and arguments.[33]

It is interesting that Christine de Pizan rarely, if ever, addresses Aristotle's arguments about the concept of woman or his development of the metaphysical, natural, epistemological, and ethical principles of gender polarity directly. Possibly, what Christine does not advert to here is more significant than what she does refer to. One is inclined to speculate about the significance of this somewhat startling omission. Perhaps this avoidance is due to the great esteem for Aristotle in the academic world. It may be that she includes Aristotle in the broader category that frequently appears

29. Christine de Pizan, *Christine's Vision,* II.1-2, 59-60.

30. Christine de Pizan, *Christine's Vision,* II.2, 60.

31. St. Thomas Aquinas, *Commentary on the Metaphysics of Aristotle,* #52.

32. St. Thomas Aquinas, *Commentary on the Metaphysics of Aristotle,* #185, 201, 210, 239, and 268.

33. St. Thomas Aquinas, *Commentary on the Metaphysics of Aristotle,* #208.

in her writings of "all or most philosophers." Even though she generally avoids direct engagement with Aristotle's own theory of sex and gender polarity, she argues against the more exaggerated, satirized versions of it.[34] Cleverly, she puts to use Aristotle's logical and ethical principles when arguing against satirists who espouse an Aristotelian-type gender polarity theory. She demonstrates, using the Aristotelian logic and ethics much admired by her, that the common good will be supported by a truer understanding of woman's nature and conditions.[35]

Other academic sources, apparently familiar to Christine, were the ideas of Cicero, Seneca, and Pseudo-Plutarch, based upon passages from Vincent of Beauvais's *Speculum historiale*. Beauvais (c. 1190-1264) was a Dominican encyclopedist whose massive encyclopedia provided scholars with access to a wide range of information. The French translation of his first volume, *Speculum historiale*, was the most popular of these works. A second volume was entitled *Speculum naturale* and a third, *Speculum doctrinale*. A spurious fourth volume, composed between 1310 and 1325, called *Speculum morale* was modeled on Thomistic ethics. A separate text (on the education of noble children) contained several pages about the education of girls.[36]

In the area of political and moral philosophy Christine de Pizan also drew upon Giles of Rome's *De regimine principium*. This text, as well as St. Thomas Aquinas's *Commentary on the Metaphysics of Aristotle*, became a primary source for her *Livre des faits et bonnes moeurs du sage roi Charles V*.[37] Further, Christine de

---

34. See Astrid L. Gabriel's opening statement in her seminal article "The Educational Ideas of Christine de Pisan," *Journal of the History of Ideas* 16, no. 1 (1955): 3-21. The statement needs to be interpreted with care: "The life problem of Christine de Pisan was to refute the false conception of Aristotelian anti-feminism, that woman is nothing else than defective man, a *mutilated male (vir occasionatus)* and to show that the compliment given to her by Gerson, *femina ista virilis,* is applicable to her sex" (p. 3).

35. In one of the early classic studies of Christine de Pizan, Alice Kemp-Welch states: "Her master was Aristotle, and she made his ethics her gospel" ("A Fifteenth-Century Feminist, Christine de Pisan," in *Of Six Mediæval Women* [London: Macmillan, 1913], pp. 116-45, esp. 122).

36. See Vincent Beauvais [Vincentius Bellovacensis], *Speculum historiale* (Graz, Austria: Akademischer der Druck, 1965); *Speculum naturale* (Graz, Austria; Akademischer der Druck, 1964), esp. XVI: 1239-1249, XXIII: 1651-1669, XXX, XXXI for references to generation; and *Speculum doctrinale* (Graz, Akademischer der Druck, 1965). See also *Speculum morale* (Graz, Austria: Akademischer der Druck, 1964), and Arpad Steiner, *De Eruditione Filiorum Nobilium of Vincent of Beauvais* (Cambridge, Mass.: Harvard University Press, 1939). For a discussion of Christine de Pizan's relation to this aspect of his work see Rosemary Barton Tobin, "Vincent of Beauvais on the Education of Women," *Journal of the History of Ideas* 35 (July-September 1974): 479-83; and Patricia A. Phillippy, "Establishing Authority: Boccaccio's *De Claris Mulieribus* and Christine de Pizan's *Le Livre de la cité des dames,*" in *The Selected Writings of Christine de Pizan*, p. 333.

37. See Suzanne Solente's introduction to *Le Livre des faits et bonnes moeurs du sage roy Charles V* (Paris: Champion, 1936-40). See also Roberta Krueger, "Christine's Anxious Lessons: Gender, Morality, and the Social Order from the *Enseignements* to the *Avision*," in *Christine de Pizan and the Categories of Difference,* ed. Marilynn Desmond, p. 26. See also Charity Canon Willard, *Christine de Pizan: Her Life and Works,* p. 116; and Earl Jeffrey Richards, "Rejecting Essentialism and Gendered Writing in Christine de Pizan," in *Gender and Text in the Later Middle Ages,* ed. Jane Chance (Gainesville, Fla.: University Press of Florida, 1996), p. 101. Richards also reflects on various aspects of relatedness between Christine de Pizan and Thomas Aquinas, pp. 101-6.

Pizan's *Le Livre du corps de policie* "is based upon John of Salisbury's *Policraticus,* and follows that text's conception of the organic metaphor [of a body politic] closely, while adapting its tenets to the situation of France at the time of Christine's composition."[38] In addition, Christine's *Le Livre des faits d'armes et de chevalerie* was a creative adaptation and translation of Vegetius's *Epitoma rei militaris* and relied as well on Honoré Bouvet's *Arbre des batailles.*[39]

Another important secondary source that Christine used very often was a 1400 French-language summary of classical philosophers called *Dits moraux des philosophes.*[40] The first compilation of sayings of philosophers was done around 1053 in Arabic and entitled *Mokhtâ el-Hiḳam.* It was translated into Spanish between 1200 and 1250 and from 1250 to 1300 into Latin as *Liber philosophorum moralium antiquorum.* Towards 1400 the ancient collection of sayings of philosophers was translated into French and entitled *Dits moraux.* The translator was Guillaume de Tignonville, provost of the City of Paris, Chamberlain to the King, and later correspondent with Christine de Pizan in the public debate about *Le Roman de la rose.* De Tignonville's translation is the likely source for Christine's acquaintance with the text.

The *Dits moraux* offers summaries of some views about many topics including women thought to have been held by ancient philosophers. It is an accurate source of information for Christine when, in her *L'Avision-Christine,* following Aristotle's *Metaphysics,* she describes the Pythagoreans as follows: "They call the even numbers feminine and the odd masculine because finitude signified form, which pertains to active power, while infinite referred to matter, which pertains to passivity."[41] Plato is mentioned as well, and Christine does manifest some awareness of his views in *Epistre de la prison de vie humaine (A Letter concerning the Prison of Human Life),* where she describes Plato's *Phaedo* as containing a demonstration of life of the soul after death.[42] The *Dits moraux* was not always an accurate source. For instance, one example incorrectly cites Socrates saying: ". . . women are snares arrayed and stretched out to capture men for whom they set them. . . ."[43] Another gender-related

---

38. Patricia A. Phillippy, "Establishing Authority," p. 334. See also Enid McLeod, *The Order of the Rose: The Life and Ideas of Christine de Pizan* (London: Chatto and Windus, 1976), pp. 29 and 78.

39. See Charity Canon Willard, "Christine de Pizan on the Art of Warfare," in *Christine de Pizan and the Categories of Difference,* ed. Marilynn Desmond, pp. 3-15, and "Pilfering Vegetius? Christine de Pizan's *Faits d'Armes et de Chevalerie,*" in *Women, the Book and the Worldly,* Selected Proceedings of the St. Hilda's Conference, 1993, ed. Lesley Smith and Jane H. M. Taylor (Suffolk, U.K.: D. S. Brewer, 1995), pp. 31-37.

40. Guillaume de Tignonville, *The Dicts and Sayings of the Philosophers,* trans. Stephen Scrope and ed. Curt F. Bühler (London: Oxford University Press, 1941), p. x.

41. *Christine's Vision,* II.9, 72.

42. Christine de Pizan, *The Epistle of the Prison of Human Life* (New York and London: Garland Library of Medieval Literature, 1984), pp. 61-63. See also Part II of *L'Avision-Christine,* which has some Neoplatonic elements as well.

43. See Tignonville, *The Dicts,* p. 100 (my rendering in modern English). For an excellent history of the different English translations made between 1450 and 1490, see also Curt F. Bühler, *Early Books and Manuscripts: Forty Years of Research* (New York: The Grolier Club — Pierpont Morgan Library, 1973). In Section B1, *"The Dictes and Sayings of the Philosophers,"* he states: "Caxton's first edition of it is the first book printed in England not only giving the place of printing but also the year of is-

example from the *Sayings of Philosophers* argues that it is shameful for a man to be overcome by a woman in battle: ". . . as Alexander fought, women came upon the battle against him, and he withdrew himself immediately and said to his people: if we overcome yonder men there where the women are, we shall never be named for the more worth; and if they overcome us, it should be to our everlasting defaming; wherefore I will not fight with them while the women are there."[44]

While this example concerns military warfare, it is relevant to the question of public intergender dialogue because the medieval universities were created as a kind of intellectual knighthood.[45] As we will see later in this chapter, Christine will enter with full force into a public intellectual battle about woman's identity, and in the context of one debate she will refer to this example of the humiliation of a man who is defeated by a woman.

This brief introduction has revealed Christine de Pizan's remarkable relation to the academic community of discourse. We will turn now to the second community of discourse relevant to Christine de Pizan's life work.

Religious Community of Discourse

Noticeably absent from Christine de Pizan's writings are references to original texts written by women religious such as Roswitha, Herrad, or Hildegard, or Julian of Norwich and Catherine of Siena, nearly contemporary with Christine. These latter two religious women authors, who demonstrated the most sophisticated analogical thinking, did not appear to have a direct influence on her development. Given Christine's propensity to search for examples of wise women, it is likely that she would have used them as direct sources had she been directly acquainted with their works. Perhaps this parallel yet independent development in women's way of thinking occurred as a result of their common experience of Christianity, which itself was grounded in analogical thinking through various Patristic authors. Certainly St. Augustine, whose works abounded in analogies, was a common source. The writings of Christine de Pizan most certainly contained horizontal, vertical, and transcendental analogies and the affirmation of the value of reason in developing self-determination and self-governance.

It is also important to note that Christine de Pizan, though well aware of her existence, did not refer to Heloise. One reason suggested for her omission of Heloise may have been Christine's desire to distance herself from Jean de Meun's admiration of Heloise in *Le Roman de la rose,* and particularly from his suggestion that, as soon as Heloise became knowledgeable through her study in the male community of discourse, she was "alienated from her female nature."[46] Another may

---

sue" (p. 3). The popularity of the text in English is attested by the first edition in 1477, a second edition in 1479-80, and a third edition published in 1489. It is also interesting to note that Scrope was also at work on an English translation of Christine de Pizan's *Letter of Othea,* p. lx.

44. Tignonville, *The Dicts,* p. 22.

45. Hastings Rashdall, *The Universities of Europe in the Middle Ages* (London: Oxford University Press, 1958), vol. 1, p. 287.

46. Earl Jeffrey Richards, "Rejecting Essentialism," p. 96.

have been the desire to distance herself from the sexual history of Heloise. There was also Heloise's extreme hostility to marriage, when, for Christine, marriage was a great gift and joy in her life.[47] One scholar even argues that Christine "was already reading Heloise through misogynist lenses."[48] In any event, it seems that Christine de Pizan made a conscious choice not to include reference to Heloise in her works, despite the wide availability of the story of Heloise and Abelard and their correspondence in France.

Christine de Pizan may have become familiar with traditional religious works through her relationship with her daughter. In *Dit de Poissy* (The Tale of Poissy), Christine describes her love for her daughter who entered a Dominican convent: "It happened once/that I had a desire/To go out to play, so I wished to go see/A daughter that I have, to speak truly, beautiful and refined, young and well schooled, And gracious, As everyone says; she is a religious/At an abbey rich and precious,/Noble, royal, and most delicious,/And the site is/Six leagues from Paris. . . ."[49] Christine herself is believed to have lived in this Dominican Abbey during the last ten years of her life when she fled from the political upheaval in Paris. If this is so, then it is very likely that she would have had access to some of the written texts in the convent library.

While the academic community of discourse has, in this book, been distinguished from the religious community of discourse for the purposes of analysis, it is important to be reminded that in some respects this distinction should not be made too rigid. For there were, no doubt, common texts in the libraries of both institutional structures. Two particular authors come to mind: Augustine and Boethius. Each of these authors had a profound effect on the intellectual and personal formation of Christine de Pizan. The religious orientations of these two early medieval writers offered to her a model of thinking about life. Augustine influenced Christine's method of applying analogical thinking for the purpose of reforming society to become more just; Boethius influenced her determination to use the guidance of philosophy and reason to deal properly with strong human passions.

In *L'Avision-Christine* Augustine is directly introduced, primarily as a religious author, where she draws from his commentaries on Scripture and his homilies. More importantly, in her *Le Livre de la cité des dames* she uses Augustine's *City of God* as a model. Earl Jeffrey Richards, the translator of *Le Livre de la cité des dames* into contemporary English, argues that Christine de Pizan's development of a city of ladies modeled on Augustine's city of God is actually an ironic application of the gender polarity view, namely, that male and female are contraries. Since Augustine states that the City of God is in opposition to the City of Man, Richards argues that by the law of contraries the City of Man cannot be the City of Woman, then the City of Woman must be the City of God. Thus woman becomes the ge-

47. Monica H. Green, "'Traittié tout de mençonges': The *Secrés des dames,* 'Trotula,' and Attitudes . . . toward Women's Medicine in Fourteenth- and Early Fifteenth-Century France," in *Christine de Pizan and the Categories of Difference,* ed. Marilynn Desmond, p. 167.

48. See also Barbara Newman, "Authority, Authenticity, and the Repression of Heloise," *Journal of Medieval and Renaissance Studies* 22 (1992): 121-57, 149.

49. Christine de Pizan, "The Tale of Poissy," in *The Writings of Christine de Pizan,* #39-49, 62.

neric representative of all men and women who live by the higher standards of a virtuous Christian life.[50] Richards's observations point to the seriousness with which Christine de Pizan sought to integrate the theories of her religious and philosophical predecessors.

The use of woman as a generic human being is a concrete application of the theory of horizontal analogy. A particular woman is like another woman or a man in sharing a particular aspect of character (wisdom or virtue), and the generic model is different because she lives at a different time and place, and the circumstances of her life are somewhat different. As will be seen, Christine de Pizan introduces dozens of different generic models of wisdom and virtue in her allegorical city of ladies. In addition, she introduces several vertical analogies to compare an ideal world with the actual world, the ideal justice in a court of pagan gods and the lack of justice in France and Italy, the ideal love between imaginary couples with actual love in the world, and so forth. Finally, Christine de Pizan introduces transcendental analogies in which one set of analogates has to be revealed through faith, while the other comes from actual human experience in the world. These transcendental analogies are most evident when she appeals to saints, to the Blessed Virgin Mary, and to the Christian God and then relates them to particular human situations and character. In addition, Christine de Pizan demonstrates over and over again the intellectual capacity to develop a root analogy throughout an entire text that itself may contain other analogies within it. She is the first female author to have accomplished such a complex way of thinking and writing. This accomplishment, rather than any other particular image or idea, is her real inheritance from the religious authors, Augustine and Boethius.

In a religious text she wrote around 1420, entitled *Heures de contemplacion sur la Passion de Nostre Seigneur (The Hours of Contemplation on the Passion of Our Lord),* Christine introduces herself as the author by first name: "Christine, having taken pity on and felt compassion for ladies and young women especially, but on all women in general who are grieved by troubles past and present, in order to instruct and encourage them. . . ."[51] She then tells her readers: "So I have, through pity and concern for you, translated from Latin into French, and put into the form of the reading of the Hours, according to the texts of Sacred History and the words of several holy doctors, arranged in such a way that they can be the themes of meditation."[52] This simple note would indicate that she drew upon religious sources for her writing, that she was able to read sources in Latin, and that she continued her aim of making texts available in the French vernacular. In 1409, Christine also wrote allegorical meditations on the psalms entitled *Les sept Psaumes allegorisés.*

Perhaps drawing an analogy with the experience of her daughter's Dominican convent school, in *L'Avision-Christine* Christine describes herself being led

50. Earl Jeffrey Richards, "Rejecting Essentialism." Richards notes that Christine de Pizan ". . . took her cue for a universal City of Ladies from Augustine's *City of God,* and her City of Ladies, with the Virgin Mary as its queen, representing allegorically the City of God" (p. 124).

51. Christine de Pizan, "The Hours of Contemplation on the Passion of Our Lord," in *The Writings of Christine de Pizan,* p. 346.

52. Christine de Pizan, "The Hours of Contemplation on the Passion of Our Lord," in *The Writings of Christine de Pizan,* p. 347.

through the corridors of the University of Paris by the "sacristine of Philosophy, the abbess and mother superior of this convent, or school and college of learning."[53] The Abbess invites her to take whatever books she ever wanted to read. Christine offers a self-reflective comment about her identity as a woman: ". . . but since they were too heavy for my weak and feminine body, I carried away very little by the measure of my great desire. . . ."[54] Some scholars interpret this remark as implying that the content of the texts was too weighty for her uneducated female mind or even her naturally weak mind to understand, according to the epistemological principle of gender polarity. However, since Christine did in fact read a great many of these texts, understood them, and evaluated them, she may mean here (possibly in a self-deprecating way) that her desire to improve herself intellectually far outweighed her physical capacity to do so.

We will now turn to consider briefly Christine de Pizan's relation to Boethius's *The Consolation of Philosophy*.[55] This particular text was written in the early sixth century by the Stoic Christian Boethius as a personal reflection on his situation of grief; he had lost his position as a senator, was exiled far from his family, his property had been confiscated, and he was given the death sentence because of false accusations against him during a period of political corruption. This text introduced a vertical analogy in the Platonic tradition of the allegory of the cave and divided line, which moved from false opinions ultimately to insight, true conclusions, and correct choices of the will about the nature of happiness and the good. *The Consolation of Philosophy* was extremely popular among monastic and religious readers during the Medieval and Renaissance periods. It is not surprising that Christine de Pizan found it personally helpful when facing the painful grief and difficult circumstances of her own widowhood. She often mentions in her works that this book of Boethius had brought about a conversion in her attitudes. She uses Boethius in *L'Avision-Christine, Mutacion de fortune, Le Chemin de long estude, Le Livre des faits et bonnes moeurs du sage roi Charles V, Le Livre de la paix,* and *L'Epistre de la prison de vie humaine.*[56]

One of the main goals of Boethius's reflections was to demonstrate how the study of philosophy can help a person overcome painful reversals of fortune. In his text, he introduced a feminine personification of wisdom, Lady Philosophy, who, analogously to a physician, diagnosed his problem and led him to understand the rational steps he needed to take to cure himself. In *The Concept of Woman: The Aristotelian Revolution (750 BC–1250 AD),* I suggested that Boethius offered a model of complementarity when he introduced the feminine figure of Lady Philosophy who entered into dialogue with him, a male philosopher, in such a way as to lead him to develop his own rational powers to overcome the emotional upheavals of grief.[57] In addition, I also suggested that Boethius's imaginary figure of Lady Philosophy served as an analogous model for wisdom in a woman who was able to explain the

---

53. *Christine's Vision,* III.1, 105.
54. *Christine's Vision,* III.1, 105.
55. Boethius, *The Consolation of Philosophy* (Indianapolis: Bobbs-Merrill, 1978).
56. See also Glenda McLeod, notes to *Christine's Vision,* note 6 to ch. 3, p. 144.
57. Allen, *The Concept of Woman: The Aristotelian Revolution,* pp. 236-40.

reasons behind her choices and who could teach the science of philosophy to a man. Thus, Boethius's imaginary model could help women to actually become wise philosophers.[58] Christine de Pizan is a prime example of such a woman. She was deeply influenced by this work of Boethius, and by integrating some of its advice, as well as developing her own literary persona as a wise woman capable of teaching others discursively about human wisdom, Christine de Pizan herself became a philosopher. In Book I of *L'Avision-Christine*, Lady Wisdom is introduced as a venerable goddess who orders things.[59] In Book II, the shadowy figure of Dame Opinion is introduced as accompanying academic philosophers in their dialectical debates, and in Book III, the wise Lady Philosophy leads Christine, often directly speaking of Boethius's *Consolation of Philosophy*, to understand the true meaning of her own life.[60]

In *L'Avision-Christine* Lady Philosophy accuses her of acting like a woman (in the gender polarity model): "You most certainly complain without cause then, for you know not that tribulations are propitious and in this reveal you are a weak, frail, and impatient woman who little understands herself. I will prove this to you by the following reasoning."[61] Then Lady Philosophy offers many different reasons to explain that bad fortune was really best for Christine (this is a double irony, because Christine is writing the book herself): (1) look around; others are worse off; (2) blessed are the poor; (3) God is a Doctor, as St. Augustine says; (4) Fortune actually advantaged you by giving you (a) virtuous parents, including a father who was a philosopher and a good teacher to you, (b) good health, (c) beauty and intelligence, (d) beautiful and good children; (5) tribulations developed your understanding and wisdom; (6) riches do not lead to happiness but to false felicity; and (7) the goal of life, happiness, is beatitude and the beatific vision.[62]

For Christine de Pizan, the move from philosophy to theology was a conscious one. Though Christine was inspired by Boethius, she also surpassed his model in creating her own Lady Philosophy. In the following passage Christine makes her allusion to Boethius's Lady Philosophy clear, but also introduces religious analogies to John the Baptist and Jesus Christ, and to the outsider who begged to be allowed scraps from Jesus' table:

> Oh, most glorious Wisdom, on whom all understanding depends: what a good heart, I thank God and you, who have kindly made me worthy of your acquaintance and have not hated me, an ignorant woman, unworthy to undo the laces of your shoes. Indeed, you have summoned me like a most loving mistress, a courtesy that assures me you will not refuse your handmaiden the small scraps of your comfort that are sufficient for her nourishment. For since you fed your said beloved son Boethius, who so loved and honored you, with the milk of your breasts and your own precious dishes, and since you forgot him not in the time of

58. Allen, *The Concept of Woman: The Aristotelian Revolution*, pp. 245-46.
59. Christine de Pizan, *Christine's Vision*, I.11, 19.
60. Christine de Pizan, *Christine's Vision*, III.6, 114; III.23, 136-37; III.24, 138-39; and III.26, 140.
61. *Christine's Vision*, III.15, 125. She also complains that people mostly liked her work because of the novelty that it was done by a woman. III.11 and III.12, 120-21.
62. Christine de Pizan, *Christine's Vision*, III.16-26, 126-41.

his great need nor likewise several of your other children, I believe you similarly will not forget me, your humble servant, whom you have fed from the scraps of the great dishes of your tables. You will cure me instead, comforting the wounds of my unfortunate adversities.[63]

Christine thus offers a Christianized analogical application of Boethius's *Consolation of Philosophy* to explain her own conversion of attitude about what she had thought was bad fortune. Boethius, on the other hand, always kept his text *The Consolation of Philosophy* within the framework of Stoic and Neoplatonic philosophy, even though he wrote theological tractates that carried important value for the history of the concept of person. That Christine re-creates Lady Philosophy as a theologian is made explicitly clear in the final chapter of *L'Avision-Christine*. Christine's words to her mentor are as follows:

> Then the reverend lady fell silent, and I began to speak: "Oh Philosophy, the repository and substance of all the other sciences, which are your appendages; you, most supreme dispenser of nourishment and medicinal restorative, who not only heal the invalid wounded by sorrow but also give her life, strength, and vigor through the sweet ointment and liquor of your comfort! I see that what they say about you is true. For just as Saint Augustine relates, you are all sciences, and you show yourself to those you love in whatever guise you please, depending on how they wish to search for you. To me, a simple woman, you have shown yourself by your noble grace in the form of Holy Theology to nourish my ignorant spirit most wholesomely for my salvation.[64]

Then Christine takes each field in philosophy and shows how it is integrated into theology: true physics becomes the theology of God as primary cause, ethics leads to the good life in God, logic demonstrates the light and truth of the just soul, and political philosophy is rooted in the common good in a city of people inspired by faith. As Benjamin Semple notes: "[i]n her narrative response to Boethius, Christine shows us how fully she has mastered that art, because she does not simply repeat Boethius, but recognises that to transmit her story a new narrative is necessary."[65]

Before concluding this section on Christine de Pizan's relation to the religious community of discourse, it is important to mention the remarkable text she wrote in praise of Joan of Arc shortly after she won the battle of Orleans in 1429. As the reader may recall from the previous chapter, Jean Gerson, the Chancellor at the University of Paris who had opened doors there for Christine de Pizan, had also entered into exile during the period of political upheaval. Both Christine de Pizan and Jean Gerson supported the claim of the Dauphin to the throne of France. Gerson had written the text, *De quadam puella,* as a positive judgment on Joan's two-month ex-

---

63. Christine de Pizan, *Christine's Vision*, III.2, 107.
64. Christine de Pizan, *Christine's Vision*, III.27, 142.
65. Benjamin Semple, "The Consolation of a Woman Writer: Christine de Pizan's Use of Boethius in *L'Avision-Christine*," in *Women, the Book and the Worldly,* ed. Lesley Smith and Jane Taylor, p. 48.

amination by clerks in exile near Poitiers. In it he defended Joan's integrity before she led the battle at Orleans, and he drew an analogy between Joan of Arc and the female biblical heroines Esther, Judith, and Deborah.[66] Christine de Pizan indicates that she had perhaps seen a copy of Gerson's document before she wrote her own *Dittié sur Jeanne d'Arc.* She gathers a community of women religious leaders, incorporates a philosophical principle, and reflects on Joan's examination before clerks:

> I have learned about Esther, Judith, Deborah, worthy ladies, through whom God restored His people which was so oppressed, and I also learned about many others who were brave, but there was none through whom He has performed a greater miracle than through the Maid.
>
> She was sent by divine command, guided by God's angel to the king, in his support. Her deeds are not illusions, for she was well tested in a council (we conclude that a thing is proved by its effect), and before one wanted to believe her, and before it became known that God sent her to the king she was led before clerks and wise men and was well examined to see whether she spoke the truth.[67]

This text in praise of Joan of Arc was the final text written by Christine de Pizan, and it was the only poem in praise of Joan circulated during Joan's life.[68] Once again we find Christine de Pizan immersing herself in a community of discourse, this time combining political and religious goals; and she led a traditional community of discourse in directions that strengthened the dignity of woman.

Jean Gerson promoted a renewal in theology that highly valued the faith of simple persons against the sterile and pedantic approach taken by many academic theologians.[69] In a text that Gerson had composed in 1397 for his sisters, *Montaigne de Contemplation,* he gave a greater value to the affective wisdom of a simple person than to the intellectual speculation of academic theologians. Christine de Pizan in-

---

66. See Jean Gerson, *De quadam puella,* as translated in Anne Llewellyn Barstow, *Joan of Arc: Heretic, Mystic, Shaman* (Lewiston/Queenston: Edwin Mellen Press, 1986), pp. 133-41. The passage in question is from Gerson's Fourth Proposition: "It is consonant with sacred scripture that through the frail sex and innocent youth joyful salvation has been revealed by God to people and to kingdoms./ This proposition is clear because, as the Apostle is our witness, God chooses the weak things of the world that He may confound the strong [1 Cor. 1:27], whoever they may be. Hence, proceeding by way of examples, one reads that through Deborah, Esther, and Judith deliverance was attained for God's people . . ." (p. 137).

67. Christine de Pizan, "The Tale of Joan of Arc," in *The Selected Writings of Christine de Pizan,* #28-30, 256-57. The editor Renate Blumenfeld-Kosinski writes in note 6, 256, that Angus J. Kennedy and Kenneth Varty mention the connection between Christine and Jean Gerson on this point in their edition of *Ditié de Jehanne d'Arc* (Oxford: Society for the Study of Mediaeval Literatures and Language, 1977).

68. In *Le Ditié de Jehanne D'Arc* (1429) Christine uses a feminine metaphor to describe Joan's relation to France: Joan "suckles France upon her milk of peace, the sweet nourishment, to overthrow the rebel host . . ." ("The Miracle of Joan of Arc," in *The Writings of Christine de Pizan,* pp. 189-91 and 356). See also Deborah A. Fraïoli, *Joan of Arc: The Early Debate* (Woodbridge: The Boydell Press, 2000), for a discussion of both Christine de Pizan's and Jean Gerson's writings on Joan of Arc.

69. Benjamin M. Semple, "Critique of Knowledge as Power: The Limits of Philosophy and Theology in Christine de Pizan," in *Christine de Pizan and the Categories of Difference,* pp. 116-19.

corporated several of Gerson's themes in her *L'Avision-Christine,* and it would seem that their shared support of Joan of Arc may have had roots in a shared recognition of the value of a sincere faith often found in women.

Humanist Community of Discourse

Humanism had a particular interest in returning to ancient sources to glean new insights into wisdom, virtue, and human love, and an emphasis on the theme that true nobility consisted in virtue rather than inherited bloodlines. Throughout her literary career, Christine integrated many of the core humanist themes, transforming them for her own purposes. Around 1399-1400, Christine wrote a prose work of advice, *Les Enseignements moraux [et] Proverbes moraux* (Moral Teachings and Moral Proverbs) for her son Jean, who assumed an educational posting as a clerk to the Earl of Salisbury in England. In this work she reflects on gender identity in advising him: "Never believe all the false blame/of women that some books proclaim,/ For women can be good and sweet;/May it be your fortune such to meet."[70] This early text draws upon ancient texts and principles to state simple moral teachings.

Another text written about the same time returns to ancient myths to establish moral values. The *Epistre d'Othéa à Hector* was addressed to her fifteen-year-old son Hector.[71] The text drew its moral from stories in mythology by integrating sayings from an ancient philosopher, poet, theologian, or spiritual writer.[72] In this text Christine also appealed to the authority of the philosophers Pythagoras, Socrates, Plato, and Aristotle to teach her son about various forms of prudence or practical wisdom.[73] Various scholars have recently emphasized the way in which Christine depicted women as strong educators of men.[74] Thus, Christine, as a Renaissance humanist, reinterpreted classical models in the contemporary context of educating her son.[75]

70. Christine de Pizan, "Christine's Teachings for Her Son, Jean du Castel," in *The Writings of Christine de Pizan,* p. 60.

71. Christine de Pizan, *Letter of Othea to Hector,* trans. Jane Chance (Newburyport, Mass.: Rice University, 1990), p. xii.

72. Charity Willard notes its influence in "Antoine de la Sale, Reader of Christine de Pizan," in *The Reception of Christine de Pizan from the Fifteenth through the Nineteenth Centuries,* ed. Glenda K. McLeod (Lewiston/Queenston: Edwin Mellen Press, 1992), pp. 3-4 and 7-8. Jane Chance describes Christine's contributions in a positive light as ". . . the first female mythographer (interpreter of classical myths), and first female literary theorist" (Christine de Pizan, *Letter of Othea,* intro., p. 1). For a different view see Susan Schibanoff, "Taking the Gold Out of Egypt: The Art of Reading as a Woman," in *Gender and Reading: Essays on Readers, Texts and Contexts,* ed. Elizabeth A. Flynn and Patrocinio P. Schweickart (Baltimore and London: Johns Hopkins University Press, 1986), pp. 83-106. Schibanoff claims: "In the *Othea* Christine schooled herself in the art of reading as a man or, more accurately, a patristic exegete" (p. 91).

73. The presence of so many academic references led Stephen Scrope, the first translator of the text into English, to conclude that "doctors at the University of Paris" rather than Christine had composed it. See Chance's introduction to the *Letter of Othea,* p. 5.

74. See, for example, Roberta Krueger, "Christine's Anxious Lessons," in *Christine de Pizan and the Categories of Difference,* pp. 19-21; and Christine de Pizan, *Letter of Othea to Hector,* pp. 121-33.

75. Roberta Krueger gives this interpretive description of the text: "Through its complex layer-

Christine de Pizan Instructing Four Men

The *Epistre d'Othéa à Hector* was widely circulated. The great popularity of this text among both French and English readers is supported by the number of extant French manuscripts (forty-three) and printings (1499, 1519, 1522, 1540), and the fact that it was translated into English by the mid-fifteenth century. Christine de Pizan demonstrated early in her literary career the ability to appeal to a wide audience.

ing of image, text, gloss, and allegory, the *Epistre Othea* dramatizes the problematic transmission and reception of moral doctrine. . . . The *Epistre Othea* is a multilayered, hermaphrodited text that yokes together classical and French imperial history, popularized mythology, patristic exegesis, and female prophetic visions" ("Christine's Anxious Lessons," p. 21).

Another characteristic of early Renaissance Humanism was its focus on the true identity of love as articulated in poetry in the vernacular. In the beginning of her literary career Christine wrote mostly poetry.[76] In 1399 she wrote a long poem entitled the *Epistre au dieu d'amours (Letter to the God of Love)*, which set the background for the debate about *Le Roman de la rose* of Guillaume de Lorris and Jean de Meun.[77] *Le Roman de la rose* was a vertical analogical poem that operated on two levels: capturing a rose within a walled castle and deflowering a virginal woman who was within a walled castle. Christine de Pizan's response (discussed in detail in the second part of this chapter) was to create a larger vertical analogy of true justice in a court of pagan deities, one that encloses and captures the false justice among those who wrote and read *Le Roman de la rose*.

Christine's talent, in the poetic genre as in so many others, was extraordinary. Claire Nouvet summarizes it as follows: "Christine de Pizan's *Epistre au dieu d'amours* opens with the narrative of a momentous event: the creation of a feminine community bound by a common and painful experience, the experience of defamation . . . this feminine collectivity decides to speak *as a collectivity*. . . . A new and as yet unheard voice is born: the voice of the feminine 'we'."[78] Christine creates a female community of discourse engaged in intergender dialogue about a new kind of theme, the concept of woman, in the traditional genre of poetry.[79]

In her next composition *Dit de la Rose (Tale of the Rose)*, Christine describes the foundation of an Order of the Rose whose purpose was to protect women. There is no clear evidence about whether or not any such order actually existed, but her poem, which creates a horizontal order analogous to other similar orders, again contributes to intergender discourse about the concept of woman in a novel way.[80]

Three poems written in the early 1400s have recently been gathered together by Barbara Altmann under the category of *The Love Debate Poems of Christine de Pizan: Le Livre du debat de deux amants (The Debate of Two Lovers), Le Livre des trois jugements (The Book of Three Judgments)*, and *Le Livre du dit de Poissy (The Tale of Poissy)*.[81] Each poem depicts debates among a variety of characters about the true nature of love. They echo the original question posed in early Renaissance

---

76. For a consideration of the place of dialogue in her early poems see Charity Canon Willard, "Lover's Dialogues in Christine de Pizan's Lyric Poetry from the *Cent ballades* to the *Cent ballades d'amant et de dame*," in *Fifteenth-Century Studies*, ed. Guy R. Mermier and Edelgard E. Dubruck (Ann Arbor: Consortium for Medieval and Early Modern Studies, 1981), pp. 167-80.

77. See Thelma Fenster's Introduction to *Poems of Cupid, God of Love* (Leiden and New York: E. J. Brill, 1990), p. 3.

78. Claire Nouvet, "Writing (in) Fear," in *Gender and Text in the Later Middle Ages*, pp. 279-80.

79. The *Epistre au dieu d'amours* was translated and transformed in 1402 into English by Thomas Hoccleve and titled *Letter of Cupid*. In this English text Hoccleve liberally added his own reflections on Christine's original lines which are "sympathetic towards women, and often provide additional ammunition for Christine's arguments" according to Thelma Fenster in Introduction, Christine de Pizan, *Poems of Cupid, God of Love*, pp. 159-74, 161.

80. Thelma Fenster in Introduction, Christine de Pizan, *Poems of Cupid, God of Love*, pp. 16-18.

81. *The Love Debate Poems of Christine de Pizan: Le Livre du Debat de deux amans, Le Livre des Trois jugemens*, and *Le Livre du Dit de Poissy*, ed. Barbara K. Altmann (Gainesville, Fla.: University Press of Florida, 1998). The spelling of the titles here follows the title of Altmann's book.

Humanism by a lady in Guido Cavalcanti's "Donna me prega." Here, as well as in the earlier work, the nature and value of human love are being explored. Christine de Pizan provides new answers to the old question and new participants to the old debate. Instead of the man Guido Cavalcanti answering to a woman, the woman author Christine de Pizan has several men and women debate the meaning of love from a variety of perspectives. Barbara Altmann summarizes this contribution as follows: "Christine de Pizan's three debate poems show her in mid-career, an accomplished dialectician on the topic of love and a master at manipulating the conventional literary forms and *topoi* in which such discussion was couched."[82] In the third of the three debate poems, *Le Livre de Poissy,* we find Christine drawing a link between the religious and the humanist community of discourse. The debate takes place among women and men in the context of a visit to her daughter's convent at Poissy. The world of religious men and women and the world of humanist concern about love become integrated in a traditional literary framework.

As early as 1404, Christine de Pizan had firmly established herself as a popular author of courtly love poetry, when she wrote *Le Livre du duc des vrais amants (The Book of the Duke of True Lovers).* Here again, she challenged the literary tradition upheld by male poets, i.e., that adulterous love either ruined a man or was good for a man. Christine argues that adulterous love is bad both for a woman and for a man and that both ought to reject it. According to Sandra Hindman and Stephen Perkinson, Christine's critique of adulterous love not only served as a transformation of the courtly love tradition, but perhaps even as a "rebuttal of the *Rose* as the quintessential misogynistic romance."[83]

In *Le Livre du duc des vrais amants* a mature Duchess, Dame de la Tour, teaches a younger woman how to avoid deceivers: ". . . let her neither believe nor trust flatterers, male or female, learning to recognize them instead and chasing them from her . . . "; and "If I advise you on how to confound/Deceivers, trust me. . . ."[84] The young woman, encouraged by the Duchess, writes a letter to the man who has been propositioning her, claiming: "But this wise Lady has opened my eyes to reason and to considering my situation; and if I failed to do that, I would be ruined and dishonored."[85] In this way Christine appeals to reason as the way for a woman to modify her passions and to make virtuous choices. Another aspect of *Le Livre du duc des vrais amants* germane to our topic of the history of the concept

---

82. Barbara Altmann, Introduction to *The Love Debate Poems of Christine de Pizan,* p. 6.

83. Sandra Hindman/Stephen Perkinson, "Insurgent Voices: Illuminated Versions of Christine de Pizan's *Le Livre du Duc des vrais amants,*" in *The City of Scholars: New Approaches to Christine de Pizan,* ed. Margarete Zimmermann and Dina De Rentiis (Berlin and New York: Walter de Gruyter, 1994), p. 228.

84. Christine de Pizan, *The Book of the Duke of True Lovers,* trans. Thelma S. Fenster and Nadia Margolis (New York: Persea Books, 1991).

85. Christine de Pizan, *The Book of the Duke of True Lovers,* p. 122. Madam de la Tour reappears as the wise woman in *Le Livre des Trois Vertus.* Earl Jeffrey Richards notes Christine's skill in using the dictaminal model in this letter which follows the standard of *salutatio, exordium, narratio, petitio,* and *conclusio* in perfect form. See "'Seulette à part' — The 'Little Woman on the Sidelines' Takes Up Her Pen," in The Letters of Christine de Pizan, *Dear Sister: Medieval Women and the Epistolary Genre,* ed. Karen Cherewatuk and Ulrike Wiethaus (Philadelphia: University of Pennsylvania Press, 1993), p. 161.

of woman has recently been developed by Kevin Brownlee in a study of the grammar Christine uses in her text. Again she reveals her extraordinary talent to enter into and transform a particular historical tradition of authorship. As Brownlee summarizes it, referring to Christine's use of the first person I *(je):* "What I am particularly interested in is how Christine exploits these tensions [between the first person author and the first person male protagonist] to effect a critique of the courtly discursive system, and of the romance genre."[86]

An interplay in Christine de Pizan's texts between male and female identity in language and in image is a frequent occurrence. One of the most intriguing of these is the way Christine introduces the theme of a widowed woman mutating into a man to struggle for survival in her *Le Livre de la mutacion de fortune (The Book of the Mutation of Fortune).* In this text, written around 1403, the widow wishes that God had made her a male or that she could be mutated into a male to defend herself better.[87] It is important to note that Christine does not support a general rejection of female identity, for she explicitly states that being a woman is more pleasant. The mutation of the widow into a man simply would allow her more freedom, greater mobility, and greater strength, all of which were essential to her mission in search for knowledge.[88] The exact meaning of Christine's proposal of mutation is controversial, and will, no doubt, continue to draw the attention of scholars. It is important not to conclude too quickly that by it Christine de Pizan espouses an androgyny theory or that she suggests that sex and gender characteristics are simply accidental.[89]

Christine incorporated previous sources into the *Livre de la mutacion de fortune,* including Ovid's *Metamorphoses,* Boethius's *Consolation of Philosophy,* Guillaume de Lorris and Jean de Meun's *Le Roman de la rose,* Brunetto Latini's *Tresor,* and Dante's *Divine Comedy.*[90] Christine de Pizan was the first author to write about Dante in French,[91] and she wrote about him in extremely favorable terms.[92]

---

86. Kevin Brownlee, "Rewriting Romance: Courtly Discourse and Auto-Citation in Christine de Pizan," in *Gender and Text in the Later Middle Ages,* ed. Jane Chance, p. 173. He offers a careful analysis of the text and also of its place ". . . as part of Christine de Pizan's extended literary and ideological polemic with the *Rose,* a polemic whose sheer complexity cannot be overemphasized" (p. 175).

87. See Christine de Pisan, *Le Livre de la mutacion de fortune* (Paris: A. and J. Picard, 1959), ed. Suzanne Solente, vol. 1, pp. 140-56; vol. 2, p. 12. For other views of the role of the father and mother in generating see Andrea Tarnowski, "Maternity and Paternity in *La Mutacion de fortune,"* in *The City of Scholars,* pp. 116-26. See also Nadia Margolis, "The Poetics of History: An Analysis of Christine de Pisan's *Livre de la mutacion de fortune,"* Ph.D. Diss., Stanford University, May 1977, esp. pp. 36-38 and 95-97.

88. See the summary of *Mutacion,* lines 1398-99, in Margolis, "The Poetics of History," pp. 142ff.

89. Earl Richards considers this interpretation in "Rejecting Essentialism and Gendered Writing in Christine de Pizan," when he states: "In other words, by attributing her change of gender to Fortune, Christine situates gender as an accidental quality, a differentiating form within the human species" (p. 108).

90. Suzanne Solente, Introduction to *Le Livre de la mutacion de fortune,* vol. 1, pp. xxx-xcviii.

91. Patricia Phillippy suggests that Christine may have been following Dante's own arguments in *De Vulgari Eloquentia* on the superiority of the vernacular for communication. See "Establishing Authority," pp. 335-37.

92. See Richards, "Rejecting Essentialism," pp. 99-101.

Dante's model was also integrated and transformed by Christine in her *Chemin de long estude*. Kevin Brownlee states that "Christine's *Chemin de long estude* is the first serious reading — the first *rifacimento* of Dante's *Commedia* in French literature."[93] The personas of Christine's father Thomas da Pizano and Dante are intermingled, and Dante's work is contrasted with the satirical content of *Le Roman de la rose*. Brownlee states:

> The first part of Christine's journey in the *Chemin* is explicitly and programmatically modeled on Dante's *Commedia*. . . . First, Christine's initial encounter with the Sibyl (vv. 451-712); second, their journey together to Mt. Parnassus (vv. 714-1170), . . . [and third,] the celestial voyage to the Fifth Heaven and back (vv. 1569-2044). In all three of these passages the Dantean model functions through a process of textual reminiscence and citation that involves simultaneously authority and difference. That is, Christine programmatically evokes Dante both to authorize her self-representation and to differentiate herself from him.[94]

The three-part structure of *L'Avision-Christine* is modeled on the three-part structure of Dante's *Divine Comedy*.[95] There is a similarity in the dreamlike sequences of the two works, which both begin with a descent (into hell for Dante and into the world of vice for Christine), present an intelligent and critical analysis of why things are they way they are (purgatory for Dante and the consideration of the opinions of academic philosophers for Christine), to conclude with the discovery of ultimate truth (paradise for Dante and the affirmation of theology for Christine).[96]

Christine also appears to have borrowed from Dante in *Le Livre de la cité des dames* where she invokes three feminine figures to help lead her out of her state of misery, just as Dante had invoked the three feminine figures of the Blessed Virgin Mary, Beatrice, and Lucy to offer him succour.[97] Christine's three personifications are more philosophically elaborated than Dante's personifications of Reason, Rectitude, and Justice. In both cases, the authors are eventually led to the Virgin Mary,

93. Kevin Brownlee, "Literary Genealogy and the Problem of the Father: Christine de Pizan and Dante," in *Dante Now: Current Trends in Dante Studies,* ed. Theodore J. Cachey, Jr. (Notre Dame and London: University of Notre Dame Press, 1995), p. 206.

94. Brownlee, "Christine de Pizan and Dante," in *Dante Now,* p. 211.

95. Sylvia Huot, "Seduction and Sublimation: Christine de Pizan, Jean de Meun, and Dante," *Romance Notes* 25, no. 3 (Spring, 1985): 361-73. "*L'avision* in turn serves to associate Christine more closely than ever with the great poet of her homeland. The tripartite structure of *L'avision,* moving from political through intellectual history to Christine's own spiritual development, echoes the hierarchical structure of the *Commedia,* while its opening line — 'J'ai pass avoyé la moitié du chemin de mon pèlerinage' — establishes a parallelism between her vision and that of Dante" (p. 368). For another example, see Maureen Quilligan, "The Allegory of Female Authority: Christine de Pizan and Canon Formation," in *Displacements: Women, Tradition, Literatures in French,* ed. Joan DeJean and Nancy K. Miller (Baltimore and London: Johns Hopkins University Press, 1990), pp. 126-43.

96. See Glenda McLeod's Introduction and notes to *Christine's Vision,* p. xlii.

97. Anna Slerca, "Dante, Boccace, et le *Livre de la Cité des Dames,*" in *Une Femme de Lettres au Moyen Age: Études autour de Christine de Pizan,* ed. L. Culac and B. Ribémont (Orléans: Paradigme, 1995), pp. 221-22.

Queen of Heaven, and as narrators they evolve from weakness and timidity to confidence. Personages from history are encountered throughout both journeys, and judgments are made about the contribution and quality of their lives. Grand communities of discourse are invoked with the mutual goal of discerning the truth about the human characters. I argued in Chapter 4 that the introduction of imaginary female personifications of virtue and wisdom could have a positive effect on women readers. Dante, Petrarch, and Boccaccio all introduced female personifications of wisdom and virtue in their texts. Christine de Pizan integrated their models and re-created them for her own purposes.

Earl Jeffrey Richards notes that a new interest in Petrarch provoked a lively activity in Paris in the late fourteenth century through a revaluation of ancient authors, and he suggests further that it was precisely this climate that drew Christine de Pizan into the public dialogue about woman's identity.[98] Christine drew upon Petrarch's works for both content and style. For content, Christine borrowed from Petrarch's *De viris illustribus* women who could serve as models for all men and women in her *Le Livre de la cité des dames*. She may also have used Petrarch's *Secretum* as a literary model for overcoming her personal grief.[99] In addition, Christine's letter to Deschamps, *Epistre à Eustache Morel* (1404), is thought to have been modeled after the moral letters of Petrarch.[100]

Christine is credited with having made Boccaccio's work *De claris mulieribus (On Famous Women)* first known in France through her extensive translations and paraphrasing of its ideas in her *Le Livre de la cité des dames*. She also integrated parts of Boccaccio's *Genealogy of the Gods* in her *L'Epistre d'Othéa à Hector*. Patricia Phillippy summarizes Christine's skill as follows: "Thus while she uses Boccaccio as a source and invokes him by name as a witness in support of her claims, she is equally involved in a revision and correction of his views on women and their capabilities."[101] Christine reorganized the text from its original chronological pattern into a thematic pattern suited to enhance woman's identity. She used fourteen different female models from Boccaccio's text in her *L'Epistre d'Othéa* and sixty-six in her *Le Livre de la cité des dames*.[102] She enriched the original male humanist community of discourse by the inclusion of females in an intergender community of dialogue about the concept of woman.

---

98. Earl Jeffrey Richards, "Rejecting Essentialism," p. 113-14. In particular, the debate in 1397 in Paris focused on Ovid, Virgil, Cicero, Petrarch, and Jean de Meun, p. 116.

99. See Earl Jeffrey Richards, "Christine, Courtly Diction and Italian Humanism," in *Reinterpreting Christine de Pizan,* ed. Earl Jeffrey Richards et al. (Athens, Ga. and London: University of Georgia Press, 1992), p. 261.

100. See Richards's persuasive arguments for Petrarch's influence in *"Seulette à part,"* pp. 154-59. See also Richards, "Christine, Courtly Diction, and Italian Humanism," pp. 250-71. "Christine used Petrarch in the Cité des Dames in two highly prominent ways . . . in compilation as a method of writing and in the interpretation of the story of Griselda" (p. 258).

101. Patricia A. Phillippy, "Establishing Authority," p. 330.

102. Anna Slerca, "Dante, Boccace, et le *Livre de la Cité des Dames,"* in *Une Femme de Lettres au Moyen Age,* pp. 222-23.

Satirical Community of Discourse

As before, we begin our discussion with Christine's omission. This time the omission concerns two authors whose works, other than their satires, were frequently commented on by her. The first is the infamous satire *Corbaccio* authored by Giovanni Boccaccio. It seems odd that Christine de Pizan drew so freely on several other of Boccaccio's works, and yet, she never even mentioned his *Corbaccio*, written in the general tradition of satires as well as appearing to be itself a satire of satires about women. Could it be that Christine was not familiar with the *Corbaccio*? She may have simply chosen to focus more on Boccaccio's positive contributions to women's identity.

The second satirical text that Christine did not mention is the *Miroir de mariage* authored by Eustache Deschamps. Christine corresponded with Eustache Deschamps, exchanged poems with him, and used his model of poetry for her own.[103] She referred to him as her mentor and friend.[104] While she asked him to not despise her female sense in her famous *Epistre à Eustache Morel* (1404), there is no mention of the satirical *Miroir de mariage*.[105] In a letter, Christine invited Deschamps to exchange ideas about the corruption in France. He encouraged her to keep working as a writer, but did not respond to the topics she raised.[106] Christine then wrote the *Mutacion de fortune* as her own analysis of the situation. In addition, it is also thought that "Christine's *Dit de la Rose* constitutes a corrective response directed towards her 'master' and literary father, Eustache Deschamps."[107]

It is interesting to reflect once again on her avoidance of certain works by authors she admired in many ways. A similar pattern was observed in her relation with the works of Aristotle. In general Christine chose to avoid direct criticism of these authors who wrote in the gender polarity tradition. If she was acquainted with their works that devalued woman's identity, a conscious decision to ignore them may have left her free to emphasize their contributions. A direct confrontation with Aristotle's philosophy of woman or Boccaccio's satire about women would have to wait until the work of later writers such as Isotta Nogarola (1418-1466), Baldasar Castiglione (1478-1529), or Lucrezia Marinelli (1571-1653).

Two satirical texts that Christine studied carefully in the French original were Guillaume de Lorris and Jean de Meun's *Le Roman de la rose* and *Le livre de Mathéolus*. Christine used these satires as the focus of her critique against the tradition of gender polarity and its multifaceted devaluation of woman. Her analysis of

---

103. Deschamps actually instructed Christine in ways of writing poetry. See Willard, *Christine de Pizan: Her Life and Works,* p. 28.

104. Richards demonstrates how Christine used Deschamps's poetry as a model for her own, and analyzes the significance of her claim that as Dante was the disciple of Virgil, she is the disciple of Deschamps, *"Seulette à part,"* pp. 150-54.

105. See Christine de Pisan, "Letter to Eustache Morel," line 29, in *Oeuvres poétiques de Christine de Pisan* (Paris: Firmin Didot, 1886-96; reprinted, New York: Johnson, 1985), vol. 2, pp. 295-301.

106. McLeod, *The Order of the Rose,* p. 108.

107. Lori Waters, "Fathers and Daughters: Christine de Pizan as Reader of the Male Tradition of Clergie in the *Dit de la Rose,*" in *Reinterpreting Christine de Pizan,* ed. Earl Jeffrey Richards, pp. 63-76, esp. 71.

the *Rose* set off the first public debate about women in French literature, and her critique of *Mathéolus* begins her major work on woman's identity, *Le Livre de la cité des dames*. A detailed analysis of her critique of these satires on women will follow in the next two parts of this chapter.

A further source of the satirical gender polarity tradition, Theophrastus' *Liber aureolus de nuptiis,* as paraphrased by St. Jerome in *Adversus Jovinianum,* was inserted into Book VIII, chapter 11 of John of Salisbury's *Policraticus.* As mentioned previously, Christine made extensive use of a French translation of Salisbury's text located in the library of King Charles.[108] In addition, her knowledge of the works of Ovid, which also contained passages devaluing woman's identity, came from the French translation of the *Metamorphoses,* revised, purified, and retitled as *Ovide moralisé.*

This introduction attempted to show Christine de Pizan's unique role as the person to initiate an early humanist reformation in the concept of woman. In the next two sections of this chapter Christine de Pizan's contributions to the philosophy of the concept of woman are discussed in greater detail. Her skill in dialectic and discursive reasoning that enabled her to provide a new philosophical foundation for gender complementarity is demonstrated with respect to the public intergender debate in the *Querelle de la rose* and the imaginary dialogue captured in *Le Livre de la cité des dames.*

CHRISTINE DE PIZAN'S PART IN THE *QUERELLE DE LA ROSE*

Five of Christine de Pizan's texts have the identity of woman as a central theme. Christine develops arguments to challenge authors' views she considers false, and she provides other arguments to elaborate what she understands as a true description of women's nature and condition.

The first two texts, *Epistre au dieu d'amours* (1399) and *Dit de la rose* (1401), are poetic works that place the question of woman's identity in the broader context of courtly love and make a rational appeal for justice.[109] The third work, participating more formally in the *Querelle de la rose,* is a collection of prose letters and treatises written among disputants about the meaning of the poem *Le Roman de la rose.* The selection of these letters gathered together by Christine in *Epistres sur le Roman de la rose* (1401-3) and put into a format suitable for a wider audience than the original respondents, constituted the beginning of participation in a public dialogue about women. The last two works in this series of five texts on woman's identity, *Le*

108. Eric Hicks, "A Mirror for Misogynists: John of Salisbury's *Policraticus* (8.11) in the Translation of Denis Foulechat (1372)," in *Reinterpreting Christine de Pizan,* ed. Earl Jeffrey Richards, pp. 77-107. Hicks also points out that Salisbury was a disciple of Abelard, and that Heloise also used Jerome's text in her correspondence with Abelard to justify her decision against marriage, p. 78.

109. A poetic translation of the two texts may be found in *Poems of Cupid, God of Love: Christine de Pizan's "Epistre au dieu d'amours" and "Dit de la Rose," and Thomas Hoccleve's "The Letter of Cupid."* A prose selection of the first text is found in Christine de Pisan, *La Querelle de la rose: Letters and Documents* (Chapel Hill: North Carolina Studies in the Romance Languages and Literatures, 1978), pp. 35-38.

Livre de la cité des dames (1405) and *Le Livre des trois vertus* (1405), are prose texts that return to the realm of imaginary dialogue.

Rational Appeal for Justice

Christine de Pizan's writings about women's identity have two foundations: (1) an appeal to rational arguments to defend her claims and (2) the positioning of her arguments about woman's identity in the context of justice. The first foundation is consistent with Aristotle's theory in the *Nicomachean Ethics,* namely, that the virtuous person is one who exercises his reason well; the second with Aristotle's theory both in the *Nicomachean Ethics* and the *Politics,* namely, that the proper context of ethics is found in the political life of a community that aims to serve the common good of all its members. It is the obligation of the ruler of a political community to work for true justice in all circumstances. These principles shape all of Christine de Pizan's arguments about woman's identity. It is important to consider how she might have become familiar with them.

Nicole Oresme is believed to have translated the *Nicomachean Ethics* around 1370 into French from the Latin translation of Robert Grosseteste that had been made a century before. In addition to the summaries of each book provided by Grosseteste, Oresme used the commentaries of Albert the Great and St. Thomas Aquinas to enhance his own understanding. Oresme's translation of the *Politics* likely used William of Moerbeke's Latin text also dating from the previous century.[110] Even though these translations were twice removed from the original Greek, they appear to be fairly accurate, and contain indexes and glossaries to help the readers' understanding. Oresme was an academic, having taught as a Master in the Faculty of Arts and of Theology, and was appointed Rector of the College of Navarre in Paris. He thus possessed a solid understanding of the philosophical and theological issues of the texts with which he was working. It was these translations that Christine de Pizan would have used just three decades later to understand fundamental ethical and political concepts.

Justice is one of the central themes both in Aristotle's *Nicomachean Ethics* and *Politics.* In chapter 5 of the *Ethics* Aristotle focuses on the kinds of actions justice is concerned with and how justice functions as a mean between two extremes. The significance of justice as a mean between extremes is emphasized in Oresme's translation of the *Ethics* by the numerous miniatures that accompany the text. Claire Sherman notes in her analysis of these miniatures in Oresme's translations of Aristotle's text, that even the figure of justice (usually a feminine personification) is presented in the center of the illustration, representing the mean, instead of being set apart by the largeness of size.[111]

Aristotle considers three kinds of justice in Book V of the *Ethics* and Book II of the *Politics:* general justice, which is oriented towards the proper balance of all virtues as a whole, and two types of particular justice. The first kind of particular

---

110. Sherman, *Imaging Aristotle,* p. 25.
111. Sherman, *Imaging Aristotle,* ch. 9: "The Centrality of Justice (Book V)," pp. 93-116.

justice concerns the proper and fair distribution of goods; the second kind of particular justice concerns rectifying injustice or unfair practices. While in her later works Christine de Pizan can be seen as considering the broader issue of the distribution of the good of positions of responsibility in society, in her earlier essays she focuses on the redressing of injustice towards women. She shows that the slander against women is unjust and unfair because it partakes of the extremes in generalizing about all women. Though Christine de Pizan is a true disciple of Aristotle, she also seeks to correct extreme gender polarity views, some of which were supported by Aristotle's philosophy. She presents her claims about justice for women in the context of a good ruler directing the legal structures of human law in a manner consistent with the ultimately just structure of divine law. We will now turn to the first two of her five written works dedicated to woman's identity. Beginning with pagan deities and personages, through a discussion of the unjust treatment of women, she leads the reader to the ultimate goal of a true Christian understanding of justice.

Christine de Pizan's *Epistre au dieu d'amours (Letter to the God of Love)* is an imaginary dialogue in which Cupid, the God of Love, presents to the gods and goddesses a letter that he had addressed to women in France in response to their complaints of having been unjustly slandered by men. Drawing upon the chivalrous notion that men should protect women and not defame them, writing in the eloquent style of courtly love poetry, the author masterfully places into the mouth of the God of Love her own arguments against the gender polarity themes that abound in academic and satirical texts.

Christine de Pizan juxtaposes the suffering of women who are deceived by men, and the men who make a game of betraying women. In the following passage, two arguments are presented: men should not slander but protect women because women generally are good to men; and, even if some women treat men poorly, this should not lead to a generalization of defaming all women:

> Good God, what gossips! God, what gatherings,
> At which a lady's honor's stripped away!
> And where, in slander, is the profit for
> The very men who ought to arm themselves
> To guard the ladies and defend their name?
> For every man must have a tender heart
> Towards woman, she who is his mother dear,
> Who's never wicked, pitiless toward him,
> But rather, she is pleasant, gentle, sweet;
> When he's in need, she understands and helps.
> She's done and does so many services
> For him; how right her ministrations are
> Gently to serve the creature needs of man.
> At birth, in life, and at his time of death
> Women, always willing, help and assist,
> Compassionate and kind, obliging him.
> The man who slanders them is merciless,

An ingrate, lacking any thought of thanks.
So I repeat: that man too much distorts
His nature who rehearses ugly slurs,
Or blames a woman, thus reproaching her,
Whether it's one, or two, or womankind.
Now if some women are the foolish kind,
Brimming with sin of every stamp and type,
And lacking faith and love and loyalty,
Or puffed-up, evil, filled with cruelty,
Inconstant, loose and low and fickle types,
Or scheming, false, or practising deceit —
Must we, because of that, imprison all,
And testify that none deserves respect?[112]

In addition to her critique of the opinions of individual men, Christine de Pizan also notes ways in which principles of gender polarity were becoming institutionalized and transmitted in textbooks used by young boys in schools. Again in the voice of Cupid she writes:

The ladies mentioned here above complain
Of many clerks who lay much blame to them,
Composing tales in rhyme, in prose, in verse,
In which they scorn their ways with words diverse;
They give these texts out to their youngest lads,
To schoolboys who are young and new in class,
Examples given to indoctrinate
so they'll retain such doctrine when they're grown.
  Thus, "Adam, David, Samson, Solomon,"
They say in verse, "a score of other men,
Were all deceived by women morn and night;
So who will be the man who can escape?"
"They're treacherous," another clerk opines,
"And false and cunning; they're no good at all."
  "They're dreadful liars," other men pronounce,
"They're faithless, fickle, they are low and loose."
Of many other wrongs they stand accused
And blamed, in nothing can they be excused.
And that's what clerks are up to noon and night,
With verses now in Latin, now in French,
They base their words on I don't know what books
Which tell more lies than any drunkard does.
Now Ovid, in a book he wrote, sets down
Profuse affronts; I say that he did wrong.
He titled it *The Remedy for Love,*

112. Christine de Pizan, *Poems of Cupid, God of Love,* l. 163-92, 43.

And there he lays to women nasty ways,
Repulsive, sordid, filled with wickedness.
That women have such vices I deny;
I take my arms up in defense of them
Against all those who'd throw the challenge down.[113]

After the announcement that Cupid, the God of Love, will act as a just judge and take up the challenge of defending women against false accusations, Christine's poem enters into particular judgments about particular men. She argues that Ovid's motivations for writing what he did about women were suspect, possibly because of personal impotency and the motive of envy. Further, Ovid's tendency to generalize from particular examples to all women was criticized as irrational and extreme. Next, Ovid's argument that all women deceive is deemed fallacious. His own text *The Art of Love,* offering advice to men on how to deceive women, is renamed by Christine as *The Art of Great Deceit, of False Appearances.*

It is important to reflect on Christine de Pizan's use of discursive reasoning in her efforts to lay out her argument. Her own experience as a happily married woman is surely drawn upon as she reflects on the nature of love. In addition, however, she analyzes both the medium and the matter of the text under consideration to develop her point; it is not all women, but some men who intentionally use deception in an intergender context for the purposes of domination and fulfilling of lust.

Now Christine turns to *Le Roman de la rose,* and she uses irony to make her case against academics, or clerks, who develop elaborate means of deception to conquer a young girl. Christine raises the question: if all women are as weak as men say they are, then why do they need to be deceived by such elaborate means; or contrarily, if men need to use such elaborate means to deceive women, then this may imply that not all women are weak after all.

But now, if women are such easy marks,
If they're the fickle, foolish, faithless lot
That certain clerks maintain they are, then why
Must men pursuing them resort to schemes,
To clever subterfuge and trickery?
And why don't women yield more readily,
Without the need for guile to capture them?
A castle taken needs no further war,
And surely not from such a learnèd bard
As Ovid, later exiled from his land.
    And Jean de Meun's *The Romance of the Rose,*
Oh what a long affair! How difficult!
The erudition clear and murky both
That he put there, with those great escapades!
So many people called upon, implored,
So many efforts made and ruses found

113. Christine de Pizan, *Poems of Cupid, God of Love,* l. 259-88, 47-49.

To trick a virgin — that, and nothing more!
And that's the aim of it, through fraud and schemes!
A great assault for such a feeble place?
How can one leap so far so near the mark?
I can't imagine or make sense of it,
Such force applied against so frail a place,
Such ingenuity and subtlety.
Then necessarily it must be thus:
Since craft is needed, cleverness and toil,
To gull a peasant or a noble born,
Then women mustn't have such fickle wills
As some declare, nor waver in their deeds.[114]

It is important to grasp the complexity of Christine de Pizan's argument here in or-der to avoid misunderstanding her approach by concluding that she actually be-lieves that any women at all are fickle, foolish, faithless — in other words, weak. If the argument is viewed in its full context, it is evident that she is intentionally as-suming what she wants to disprove. Her argument takes the *modus tollens* form in which the first premise is a universal statement: If all women are weak, then it is not necessary for men to use such complicated means to capture them. The second premise provides a factual statement that negates the consequent: the *Romance of the Rose* demonstrates that men use very complicated means to capture women. The conclusion then negates the antecedent: Thus, all women cannot be weak.[115] By distinguishing universals from particulars, she is able to reach this conclusion. The truth must lie in the mean between the two extremes of all women or no women: that is, some (but not all) women are weak.

The next part of Christine's argument points to the inherently biased nature of evidence used by satirists against women: such evidence is invariably derived from men's works that intentionally devalued women. Christine points out that if women had entered into the dialogue about woman's identity, then some different perspectives would have been given:

Should it be said that books are filled with tales
Of just such women (I deplore that charge!),
To this I say that books were not composed
By women, nor did they record the things
That we may read against them and their ways.
Yet men write on, quite to their heart's content,
The ones who plead their case without debate.
They give no quarter, take the winner's part
Themselves, for readily do quarrelers
Attack all those who don't defend themselves.

114. Christine de Pizan, *Poems of Cupid, God of Love,* l. 379-406, 53.
115. For descriptions of various argument forms, see David Kelley, *The Art of Reasoning* (New York: W. W. Norton, 1988), pp. 224-27.

If women, though, had written all these books,
I know that they would read quite differently,
For well do women know the blame is wrong.
The parts are not apportioned equally,
Because the strongest take the largest cut
And he who slices it can keep the best.
   And still the nasty scandalmongers say,
Who go about disdaining women thus,
That all are false, have been, and will always be;
Never have any had much loyalty;
And suitors find, who try the ladies out,
That all are false, no matter who they are.
For every reason women are accused;
No matter who's done wrong, women are blamed.
   How wrong that is! It's just the opposite,
For when it comes to matters of the heart,
So many women have been true in love;
They are and will be so, despite those times
They may have had to suffer many lies,
Along with ruses, faking, trickery.[116]

Christine prefers a different dynamic, one that, characteristically for a truly intergender dialogue, faithfully represents the perspectives of both participants. She suggests that an accurate depiction of fidelity and loyalty, deception and truthfulness, would end up with an "even sharing" among both men and women. That is, some men and some women would be truthful and loyal while other men and other women would be false and deceitful. Christine de Pizan diagnoses one of the sources of overgeneralization about women: because the dialogue about women's deception was historically based only in male communities of discourse, there were an imbalance and aggression that distorted the conclusions and skewed them towards extreme, false generalizations.

Her analysis of the theme of deception is continued in the *Epistre au dieu d'amours* where it is extended into the theological arena. Biblical accounts of the Creation and the Fall had often been a source of reflections for theories of sex and gender identity. In *The Concept of Woman: The Aristotelian Revolution (750 BC– 1250 AD)* we considered how interpretations of these accounts were used to support sex polarity, sex unity, and sex complementarity theories.

In this light it is interesting to consider Christine de Pizan's introduction of these themes through the voice of Cupid, the God of Love. In her analysis of the

116. Christine de Pizan, *Poems of Cupid, God of Love,* l. 408-36, 55. See also Sydney E. Smith, *The Opposing Voice: Christine de Pisan's Criticism of Courtly Love* (Stanford, Calif.: Honors Essay in Humanities XXXIV, 1990), who notes that for Christine, "the most serious obstacle to true courtly love lies in men's attitudes towards women — attitudes that are perpetrated by male authors. She recognizes that the basis of these attitudes is the male author's ignorance about women's experiences. In response to this recognition, Christine assigns to herself the task of combatting this ignorance" (pp. 44-45).

Creation of woman she suggests a theological foundation for the reverse gender polarity theory soon to be articulated by Italian humanists and the German humanist Henry Cornelius Agrippa in his text on the natural superiority of woman.[117] Christine argues that the first woman was created in the image of God in her intellectual life and that her body was made from a more noble material than man's, which was taken from mud:

> Now God created her resembling Him;
> He gave to her intelligence and skill
> To save her soul, and judgment and good sense.
> When God created her He gave her form
> Majestic, made of very noble stuff:
> For not from earthly mud was she derived,
> But made uniquely from the rib of man,
> Whose body was already, summing up,
> Among the things of earth the noblest one.[118]

With respect to the Fall, Christine argues that Eve did not deceive Adam in offering him the fruit from the tree of the knowledge of good and evil: her motives for her actions were sincere rather than based on the desire to deceive.

> . . . Now as to the deceitful act
> For which our mother Eve is brought to blame,
> Upon which followed God's harsh punishment,
> I say she never did play Adam false,
> In innocence she took the enemy's
> Assertion, which he gave her to believe.
> Accepting it as true, sincerely said,
> She went to tell her mate what she had heard.
> No fraudulence was there, no planned deceit,
> For guilelessness, which has no hidden spite,
> Must not be labeled as deceptiveness.
>
> For none deceives without intending to,
> Or else that isn't really called deceit.[119]

This theme of evaluating the relative blame of Eve for the act of offering Adam the fruit was one that captivated many medieval and humanist authors. In Chapter 10 of this book, we will examine an in-depth dialogue between Isotta Nogarola and a male friend on many aspects of this theme.[120] At this point, it is im-

---

117. Henry Cornelius Agrippa, *On the Superiority of Woman over Man* (New York: American News Company, 1873).

118. Christine de Pizan, *Poems of Cupid, God of Love,* l. 590-99, 63.

119. Christine de Pizan, *Poems of Cupid, God of Love,* l. 604-16, 63-65.

120. See also Thelma Fenster, "*Simplece* et sagesse: Christine de Pizan et Isotta Nogarola sur la

portant simply to note that Christine de Pizan also ventured into this theological arena armed with arguments to redress what she perceived as an imbalance of past interpretation.

In the next phase of her argument, Christine anticipates the method that will soon be followed by Lucrezia Marinelli to prove that women's virtues are better than men's virtues and men's vices are worse than women's vices.[121] She begins her argument by suggesting that she does not want to make comparisons because "[c]omparisons, at times, just cause more hate."[122] Nonetheless she does just that, by the particular examples she introduces. In a repeated appeal to justice, with reference to some autobiographical material from her struggle with those trying to cheat her out of her inheritance, she says:

> Let each be judge,
> And heeding truth, adjudicate the case.
> He'll find, if he will try it honestly,
> Her greatest fault can cause but little harm.
> She doesn't kill or wound or mutilate,
> Or foster any treasonous misdeeds;
> Or dispossess another; set afire;
> Or poison; pilfer silver, steal one's gold;
> Or cheat of wealth or one's inheritance
> Through bogus contracts; nor does she bring harm
> To empires or to duchies or to realms.[123]

Christine then elaborates on the argument that it is no virtue for women to abstain from the acts just listed; because of her nature, she, unlike man, has no inclination to commit those sorts of deeds. When a man, on the other hand, resists such inclinations, against his nature, he is being truly virtuous. She agrees with the argument, but extends it further:

> I quite agree, indeed, that women's hearts
> Are not so made, disposed towards wickedness!
> For woman's nature is but sweet and mild,
> Compassionate and fearful, timorous
> And humble, gentle, sweet, and generous,
> And pleasant, pious, meek in time of peace,
> Afraid of war, religious, plain at heart.
> When angry, quickly she allays her ire,
> Nor can she bear to see brutality

---

culpabilité d'Ève," in *Une Femme de Lettres au Moyen Age, Études autour de Christine de Pizan* (Orléans: Paradigme, 1995), pp. 481-93.

121. Lucrezia Marinelli, *La Nobilità et l'eccelenza delle Donne Co'Diffetti et Mancamenti De gli Huomini* (Venice: Gio Batista Ciotti Sanese, 1601).

122. Christine de Pizan, *Poems of Cupid, God of Love*, l. 630, 65.

123. Christine de Pizan, *Poems of Cupid, God of Love*, l. 637-47, 65.

Or suffering. It's clear those qualities
By nature make a woman's character.[124]

Her conclusion is contrary to the gender polarity ethical principle that in woman, the rational soul is without authority over her irrational nature.

In fact, the overall direction of the entire *Epistre au dieu d'amours* is to reinforce the view that woman's nature is highly intelligent and refined. She is given intelligence by being created in the image of God, she does not use her intelligence to deceive, and her actions towards men deserve gratitude rather than ridicule, blame, or slander. In the end, Cupid even draws a conclusion as if from a demonstrative argument:

It's my conclusion, and I want to prove,
That women do so very much to be
Applauded, and therefore I recommend
Their traits, which show no inclination towards
Vices that scathe the human character
And bring to human beings pain and woe.
So through these just, veracious arguments
I demonstrate that reasonable men
Should value women, love and cherish them;
Nor should they have a mind to deprecate
The female sex, from whom each man is born.
Let none return them evil for their good,
For woman rightly is that single soul
Whom man loves deeply through the natural law.[125]

Since the speech of Cupid, the God of Love, is placed in the context of justice, he ends the poem with a proclamation that those who blame or set out to deceive women as a group will be punished, and banished from the court of love. In an analogy with a court of law, Christine de Pizan emphasizes the overall goal of remedial justice in particular acts. Those who are responsible for unjust or unfair acts that contravene law should be brought to account and punished by the court. Furthermore, divine law, natural law, and human law should be in complete harmony, and when they are, the truly just and virtuous ruler will have achieved the purpose of law in establishing the common good.

Christine de Pizan's poem *Epistre au dieu d'amours* was immediately popular in France and soon after in England.[126] More recently some questions have arisen concerning whether or not she borrowed many of her arguments from other authors in this work. Because this issue touches upon the larger question of Christine

---

124. Christine de Pizan, *Poems of Cupid, God of Love*, l. 666-76, 67.
125. Christine de Pizan, *Poems of Cupid, God of Love*, l. 711-24, 69.
126. Willard, *The Writings of Christine de Pizan*, p. ix. It was loosely translated as early as 1402 into English by Chaucer's disciple Thomas Hoccleve and named *Letter of Cupid*. For the complete text and notes see *Poems of Cupid, God of Love*, pp. 160-215.

de Pizan's originality as a thinker and writer, it is important to consider it before passing on to the next stage of argument in the public quarrel about the rose. To begin, Thelma Fenster notes several similarities between Christine de Pizan's arguments and those found in Jehan Le Fèvre's *Livre de Leesce,* which was attached to his translation of *Le Livre de Mathéolus.* Fenster mentions particularly the criticism of generalizing from the actions of a few women to all women and the particular list of evils that are included as those women do not incline towards. While there is a similarity between Christine de Pizan's list and Le Fèvre's list, both lists also contain the same components as the list found in Book 5 of Aristotle's *Nicomachean Ethics.* Christine de Pizan lists: kill, wound, mutilate, treasonous misdeeds, dispossessing another, setting fire, poisoning, pilfering silver, stealing gold, cheating of wealth or inheritance through bogus contracts, and bringing harm to empires.[127] Le Fèvre lists: "murder, theft, pillage, arson, bearing false witness, adultery, enchantments, poisoning, falseness, treason, and other crimes" (l. 1186-95).[128] Aristotle lists: "theft, adultery, poisoning, procuring, enticement of slaves, assassination, false witness . . . assault, imprisonment, murder, robbery with violence, mutilation, abuse, insult."[129] Thus, while it is very possible that Christine de Pizan borrowed from Jehan Le Fèvre's text, as she admits to reading the French version of Mathéolus's text, it is also possible that both she and Le Fèvre used Aristotle as their common source. In either case, Christine de Pizan personalizes her list by including the malicious act that she directly experienced, namely, of men trying to cheat her out of her own inheritance.

Helen Solterer argues that Le Fèvre's text was so convoluted that it is difficult to reach any definitive conclusions about his own theory.[130] Le Fèvre claimed that he was distancing himself from the theories of Mathéolus, which he nonetheless helped to transmit through his translation. While Le Fèvre sought to defend women in several different ways, his translating of *Mathéolus* from Latin into French so that its arguments could be readily available for a wider audience seems hypocritical. Thus, while Christine de Pizan may have borrowed some ideas from parts of Le Fèvre's text, her own work was the first to focus exclusively on the question of correcting mistaken and slanderous claims about women's identity. Her work consistently pursues this goal. It has an internal unity, and it is situated in the broader Aristotelian model of seeking redress for particular injustices. Christine de Pizan's originality lies in her way of serving a philosophical purpose by writing in the eloquent style of courtly love poetry with a characteristically humanist appeal to pagan deities and personages.

Thelma Fenster also notes that Christine de Pizan might have borrowed this idea — that women would have written very different books than men — from Chaucer's Wife of Bath, who made a similar observation.[131] Again, while it may be

---

127. Christine de Pizan, *Epistre au dieu d'amours,* l. 641-47.

128. See Fenster, *Poems of Cupid, God of Love,* Introduction, p. 14.

129. Aristotle, *Nicomachean Ethics,* Book V, ch. 2, 1131a6-10.

130. Helen Solterer, *The Master and Minerva: Disputing Women in French Medieval Culture* (Berkeley/Los Angeles/London: University of California Press, 1995), ch. 5, "Defamation and the *Livre de leesce,*" pp. 131-50.

131. Thelma Fenster, Introduction to Christine de Pizan, *Poems of Cupid, God of Love,* p. 15. Her

true that Christine de Pizan gathered ideas for her arguments from a variety of sources, what makes her contribution to the history of the concept of woman unique is that she concentrated five complete works primarily on this topic, rather than simply introduce a few sentences here and there. Christine's decision to dedicate complete texts to the concept of woman, and to argue directly with others about what she perceived to be erroneous views in past claims, moved the dialogue about women into a different level of philosophical discourse in the public domain.

On this point, Helen Solterer makes a keen observation in "Christine's Way: The *Querelle du Roman de la rose* and the Ethics of a Political Response": by raising a public complaint against the defamation of women in the *Epistre au dieu d'amours,* Christine has also drawn upon Augustine's view of "defamatory language as a potential threat to the commonweal . . . [in that] [s]landering any single member violates the polis."[132] Her act of public accusation, her request for a just judgment from the God of Love, criminalizes the offenders, in this case Ovid and Jean de Meun, two authors admired and even revered by the academic, humanist, and satirical communities of discourse — a shocking act. Further, as noted above, Christine makes Cupid, the God of Love, the judge of the claim of defamation, and Cupid judges in favor of the women who made the complaint. Thus, Christine de Pizan, as author, is both the initiator of the public accusation and the judge who single-handedly reverses the popular order in which the satirical texts had previously reigned unchallenged.

In *Dit de la rose (Tale of the Rose),* her second text dedicated primarily to woman's identity, Christine de Pizan again offers a context of justice within which to present her arguments. On St. Valentine's Day 1401, a formal Court had been founded in Paris to judge amorous cases in which women had been wrongly treated. Among the six hundred men who were members of the Court, mostly Burgundians, were her foes in the *Querelle de la rose,* Jean de Montreuil, Gontier Col, and Pierre Col. In response, Christine in her *Dit de la Rose* creates on St. Valentine's Day 1402 an imaginary Order of the Rose, which had all its members chosen by women.[133] In this text, the God of Love grieves because of the "tiresome habit" of slander that "dishonors scores of women, wrongly, senselessly, and many worthy men as well, more so now than ever before."[134] While no evidence exists

---

observation also extends to Christine's remark about Ovid's motivation being his impotency, a problem he supposedly had in common with Chaucer.

132. Solterer, *The Master and Minerva,* pp. 152-53.

133. See McLeod, *The Order of the Rose,* pp. 74-75. In her work, the God of Love himself appears through the Goddess of Loyalty to institute the new order that will protect women from slander. Apparently, however, this imaginary Court or Order never became real. See also Willard, ed., *The Writings of Christine,* p. 165. Finally, see Kevin Brownlee, "Discourses of the Self," *Romantic Review* 79, no. 1 (January 1988), for his observations that in the *Dit* Christine transforms the Rose from its meaning in Jean de Meun, in Part I by founding the Order of the Rose for the "intra-textual public" and in Part II by redefining and expanding it to include the "extra-textual public" (pp. 206-7 and 212).

134. Christine de Pizan, "The Tale of the Rose," in Willard, ed., *The Writings of Christine,* p. 165. Slander "brings a double death" to the one who aims it, and the one at whom it is aimed. Christine makes it clear that she is opposed to both men and women who slander. "And when I say a man, I mean a woman, too, should she spread gossip and untruth; for nothing is more poisonous, nor should

concerning whether or not there was such an Order of the Rose, there certainly were other similar kinds of organizations that attracted noblemen.

A Goddess of Love, Loyalty, is sent by the God of Love to introduce an Order of the Rose and to invite members to join. Christine develops the point, which had been so commonly argued by the earlier humanists, Dante, Petrarch, and Boccaccio, that true nobility consisted in a virtuous life and not in a bloodline. Following this principle, the goddess states:

> The god desires that no one here consent
> To have the dear and lovely rose bestowed
> Unless he swears he never will assent
> To any kind of blame or word that's low
> Of Woman, and he keeps her honor close.
> And so, for that, to you he sends me thus;
> All swear that with your strong and forthright vow
> The honor of all ladies is your trust.[135]

Christine's introduction of the Rose as the name of the order is once again a brilliant inversion of the use of the rose by Jean de Meun. In *Le Roman de la rose,* the flower symbolized the simple virgin who was seduced after much plotting. Here, Christine has the members of the Order of the Rose vow to defend every woman's personal honor and to be sure that the name of every woman is not defamed.

In the *Dit de la rose,* Christine has a further development of her own role in the public defense of women. In addition to the noble knights who are sworn into this Order of the Rose, she has a visit from the Goddess of Love, who "called me her Sister in sensibility."[136] The goddess appears to her in a dream, and tells her that she has disturbed her sleep to report a command of the God of Love. This command is based upon an observation that many are losing their proper nobility because they commit acts of slander:

> That tiresome habit is the cause,
> By which so many people lose
> Their honor — it's slandering
> (God curse it!) which dishonors scores
> Of women, wrongly, senselessly,
> And many worthy men as well,
> More so now than ever before.[137]

Christine does not identify men as the only slanderers, for she explicitly states that

---

be less beloved than an evil woman's wagging tongue, which slurs, insults, or ridicules, in fun or with intent to harm" (pp. 165-66).

135. Christine de Pizan, *Dit de la rose,* in *Poems of Cupid, God of Love,* l. 160-68, 101.
136. Christine de Pizan, *Dit de la rose,* in *Poems of Cupid, God of Love,* l. 272-73, 107.
137. Christine de Pizan, *Dit de la rose,* in *Poems of Cupid, God of Love,* l. 405-11, 113.

women as well as men slander, and she calls them equally, both men and women, to conversion from this bad habit.

Then Christine de Pizan is given a mission or charge as part of a covenant with the God of Love, to spread the word about the Order of the Rose, and to call all men and women everywhere in the world to cease slandering others. This charge is sealed with a bull and integrated with the Passion of Christ: "May the God who knew the passion now/Sustain you at that studying/Which brings great learning in its wake."[138] By this mandate sealed with the bull from Heaven, Christine gives herself authority not only to study, but also to write against slander wherever it appears. Towards the end of her tale, she tells her readers that she will act:

> The sight of it, the thought that I
> Was charted with it, delighted me.
> I scarcely merit it at all —
> Still, I'm eager that no one fail.
> And since the charge is placed with me
> To act, I mustn't be remiss
> At doing what I should; that way,
> I'll not be blamed for careless work.[139]

Thus Christine de Pizan is poised to enter full force into a public debate on the topic of slander against woman's identity. Let us now turn to the arguments of the persons who actually participated in this phase of the *Querelle de la rose*.

Dialogue with Jean de Montreuil

In this next phase of the public discourse about the concept of woman, Christine de Pizan shifted from imaginary arenas of discourse to actual exchange of letters with prominent men and women. Secondly, she shifted her language of communication from poetry to prose in order to enter directly into the male humanist community of discourse with its own tradition of prose writing. Thirdly, Christine shifted the ground of the humanist community of Latin discourse right from the start by writing in vernacular French prose instead of the more formal Latin. Thelma Fenster claims that Christine de Pizan played an important role in the attempt to legitimize French vernacular texts; by writing in French, and by trying to raise the level of written French using Latin syntax and grammar, "Christine's writing marks an important evolutionary step in the social history of the French language."[140] For the purposes of this book, it is all the more significant that this first public dialogue in French focused on the concept of woman.

A humanist literary circle existed in the court of King Charles VI, and one of

138. Christine de Pizan, *Dit de la rose*, in *Poems of Cupid, God of Love*, l. 548-50, 119.
139. Christine de Pizan, *Dit de la rose*, in *Poems of Cupid, God of Love*, l. 595-602, 121.
140. Thelma Fenster, "'Perdre son Latin': Christine de Pizan and Vernacular Humanism," in *Christine de Pizan and the Categories of Difference*, ed. Marilynn Desmond, p. 104.

its aims was the promotion of high-quality literary works. In this particular male humanist community of discourse Jean de Meun and Guillaume de Lorris's *Le Roman de la rose (The Romance of the Rose)* held a place of great honor. Christine de Pizan's critique of this revered text came to the attention of this literary circle, for within a year or so Jean de Montreuil, secretary to the King, leading French humanist, and member of the court, wrote a treatise in support of *Le Roman de la rose.* He sent a copy to Christine de Pizan, probably in response to her previous writings, which had charged Jean de Meun with injustice towards women.

While Jean de Montreuil's treatise is now lost, it appears to have made the argument that *Le Roman de la rose* was a work of Christian wisdom and virtue, written in the form of an allegory in which characters presented a variety of different views. He concluded that the authors should not be held responsible for the views of a particular character within the work.[141] Jean de Montreuil also appears to have been offended that a woman, i.e., Christine de Pizan, would have dared to criticize so important a poet and to enter into the male community of humanist discourse in such a challenging way.

This accusation of Jean de Montreuil is the first of many that will seek to draw Christine de Pizan into an emotional response. In light of this dynamic, it is important to digress for a moment and describe how Christine avoided this danger by immersing herself in Aristotle's guidelines for practical wisdom in the *Nicomachean Ethics.* Just as she had taken his theory of justice as the goal or end of her arguments in the *Querelle de la rose,* so also she takes his description of human virtue as the means for achieving this end. More specifically, in the *Ethics* Aristotle develops the claim that the way of virtue or excellence is determined by considering the unique function of something. In the case of human beings, the unique function concerns the exercise of the reason. Thus, he concludes that a virtuous person will be one who uses the reason well. Christine de Pizan will seek to reason well about women's identity in the midst of many factors that could have drawn her away into emotional arguments or personal appeals. As will be seen in the subsequent analysis, she always invited her respondent to agree with her position because of the reasons offered in her arguments and not because of any other factor. In using this consistent method in her public discourse, Christine de Pizan embodies the Aristotelian model of a person with practical wisdom.

In early 1401, Christine wrote a letter directly in response to Jean de Montreuil, a letter that many consider as the official beginning of the dialogue or debate about the meaning of *Le Roman de la rose.*[142] With this letter, Christine shifts from the imaginary dialogue she had described in her use of the figure of Cupid in the *Epistre au dieu d'amours* to a dialogue with the real human being Jean de Montreuil. She directly challenges his interpretation of Jean de Meun's poem and asks for his conversion. To show the intensity of Christine's response we will begin this summary with a short segment towards the ending of her letter in which she

---

141. For original sources of the debate in French and Latin, see Charles Frederick Ward, "The Epistles on the Romance of the Rose," Ph.D. Diss., University of Chicago, 1911.

142. See Jillian M. L. Hill, *The Medieval Debate on Jean de Meung's Roman de la Rose: Morality Versus Art* (Lewiston/Queenston/Lampeter: Edwin Mellen Press, 1991).

states a hope that after Montreuil listens to her arguments he would accept her point of view:

> . . . then you would be more receptive to truth and thus would make a different judgment of the *Rose;* perhaps you would wish that you had never seen it. So much suffices. And may it not be imputed to me as folly, arrogance, or presumption, that I, a woman, should dare to reproach and call into question so subtle an author, and to diminish the stature of his work, when he alone, a man, has dared to undertake to defame and blame without exception an entire sex.[143]

Once again, Christine addresses the tendency of an author to generalize his conclusions in such an extreme way that all women are devalued. She suggests that Jean de Montreuil wrongly recommends *Le Roman de la rose* because even though it may have some good in it, it is very harmful to the reader, and damaging precisely because the good is intermingled with evil.

The letter opens an intergender dialogue on several themes: it appears to be the first formal letter in Western thought that considers arguments about woman's identity in a systematic way. It includes specific references to the satirical views about women of Theophrastus, Walter Map, and Juvenal. In addition, it is also the first text that consistently includes a reflective element about the gendered perspective of the writer as a woman or as a man. For these reasons alone it would be significant, even if Christine's contribution to dialogue about the concept of woman rested here. However, her contribution went much further. Before describing Christine's arguments in more detail, a few reflections on the broader context of the debate would be helpful for those readers who are not familiar with the historical context of this public quarrel about women.

The broader debate about *Le Roman de la rose* incorporated many different themes: the relation between allegory and moral teaching, the value of providing explicit descriptions of sexual organs and activity, the proper purpose and practice of marriage, and accounts of the respective identities of women and men. Some of the specific questions raised include the following: (1) Should sexual organs and activity be directly named and described in a work of literature? (2) Can or should men and women remain faithful to one another in marriage? (3) How should the reader understand the meaning of the ending of a story in which a passive woman (symbolized by a rose) is deceived, seduced, and "deflowered" by a man? and (4) Does this work of literature lead a person towards or away from a life of wisdom and virtue?

The first letter of Christine de Pizan to Jean de Montreuil begins with a comparison of their different educational backgrounds. Given the rather careful way in which she crafts her argument in the text of the letter, it would be reasonable to assume that this passage contains some ironic self-deprecation:

> Reverence, honor, and due respect to you, Lord Provost of Lisle, esteemed Master, sage in morals, lover of knowledge, steeped in learning, and expert in rheto-

---

143. Christine de Pizan to Jean de Montreuil, *La Querelle de la rose: Letters and Documents,* #VI, 56.

ric; from me, Christine de Pizan, a woman weak in understanding and inadequate in learning — for which things may your sagacity not hold in scorn the smallness of my reasons; rather may it take into account my feminine weakness.[144]

Christine mentions that she read the original treatise of Jean de Montreuil, considered it within the limits of her ability, understood it, and disagreed with its conclusions. Her own response was an attempt to describe the grave error present in Jean de Montreuil's thinking.

Christine's analysis of *Le Roman de la rose* focuses on its detachment from the search for truth, its subsequent deterioration in differentiating evil and good, and its ultimate negative effect on the moral life of its readers. She points out that Reason, one of the main personified characters in *Le Roman de la rose,* is false to its heavenly origin and its relation to ultimate truth when it argues in favor of the use of deception. Next, she says that the Old Woman who is presented as the source of information about women provides "reprehensible teachings" and fails to distinguish good from evil or evil from good.[145]

However, it is the characters of the Jealous Man (often referred to as the Jealous Husband) and his mentor Genius who receive Christine's most sustained critique with respect to woman's identity. Below we see Christine using the *modus tollens* form of argumentation that we encountered above in her *Epistre au dieu d'amours:*

And again, for God's sake, let us look a little further to see what profit there can possibly be in his excessive, impetuous, and most untruthful criticism and denigration of women as exceedingly wicked creatures! He declares that their conduct is filled with all manner of perversity, with which condemnations, even with all the give and take among his characters, he cannot fully gorge himself. For if you wish to tell me that the Jealous Man does this as a man overcome by passion, I fail to see how he fulfils the teaching of Genius, for Genius so fully recommends and exhorts men to bed them and to perform the act that he praises so highly. And this Genius, more than any of the characters, makes great attacks on women, saying, in fact, "Flee, flee, flee from the deadly serpent." Then he declares that men would pursue them unremittingly. Here is a glaring contradiction, evilly intended: to order men to flee what he wishes them to pursue, and to pursue what he wishes them to flee. But since women are so perverse, he ought not to command men to approach them at all. For he who fears a problem ought to eschew it.[146]

144. Christine de Pizan to Jean de Montreuil, *La Querelle de la rose: Letters and Documents,* #VI, 46.

145. Christine de Pizan to Jean de Montreuil, *La Querelle de la rose: Letters and Documents,* #VI, 49.

146. Christine de Pizan to Jean de Montreuil, *La Querelle de la rose: Letters and Documents,* #VI, 51.

THE BEGINNING OF PUBLIC DIALOGUE ABOUT GENDER

To summarize her argument form, she begins with a hypothesis: If all women are perverse, then men ought to avoid them. The negation of the consequent is stated: But men pursue women. The conclusion is then reached: Since it is not the case that men try to avoid all women, then all women cannot be perverse.

It is interesting to note in passing that Christine de Pizan playfully inverts the above remarks of Genius about fleeing from women at the end of *The Book of the City of Ladies,* when she, speaking in the voice of the narrator, addresses her audience:

> Oh my ladies, flee, flee the foolish love they urge on you! Flee it, for God's sake, flee! For no good can come to you from it. Rather, rest assured that however deceptive their lures, their end is always to your detriment. And do not believe the contrary, for it cannot be otherwise. Remember, dear ladies, how these men call you frail, unserious, and easily influenced but yet try hard, using all kinds of strange and deceptive tricks, to catch you, just as one lays traps for wild animals. Flee, flee, my ladies, and avoid their company — under these smiles are hidden deadly and painful poisons.[147]

In this way she continued to participate in the *Querelle de la rose* even after the official exchange of letters had been completed.

The view that woman was dangerous and deceptive is also directly challenged by Christine in her letter to Jean de Montreuil. In her next argument, Christine asks what evidence the Jealous Man offers for his claim that no woman can be trusted with a secret. The philosophical underpinning of this view, which is so common to satires, is that woman cannot control her speech. In her argument about woman's nature and activities, Christine draws Jean de Montreuil back to her argument from the earlier poem she had written:

> And it is for this reason that he so strongly forbids a man to tell his secret to a woman, who is so eager to know it (as he records), although I simply do not know where the devil he found so much nonsense and so many useless words, which are there laid out by a long process. But I pray all those who truly hold this teaching authentic and put so much faith in it, that they kindly tell me how many men have been accused, killed, hanged, and publicly rebuked by the accusations of their women? I think you will find them few and far between. . . .
>
> As I have said previously on this subject in my work called "L'Epistre au dieu d'amours," where are those countries and kingdoms that have been ruined by the great evils of women? If it be not presumptuous, let us speak of the great crimes that one can attribute to even the worst and most deceitful of women. What do they do? In what ways do they deceive you?[148]

Once again, it is helpful to open up the argument form that she uses in her letter and bring its structure into the light. Christine takes a general principle of *Le Ro-*

---

147. Christine de Pizan, *The Book of the City of Ladies,* III.19.6, 256.

148. Christine de Pizan to Jean de Montreuil, *La Querelle de la rose: Letters and Documents,* #VI, 51-52.

man de la rose and seeks to show that particular examples contradict it. This **indirect** argument defeats the general principle by a counterexample. Then Christine de Pizan offers a **direct** counterargument against the universal generalizations that the satirist presented in his work:

> But truly since he blamed all women in general, I am constrained to believe that he never had acquaintance of, or regular contact with, any honorable or virtuous woman. But by having resort to many dissolute women of evil life (as lechers commonly do), he thought, or feigned to know, that all women were of that kind; for he had known no others. And if he had blamed only the dishonorable ones and counseled men to flee them, it would have been a good and just teaching. But no, without exception he accuses them all. But if, beyond all the bounds of reason, the author took it upon himself to accuse or judge them without justification, the ones accused ought not to be blamed for it. Rather, he should be blamed who carried his argument to the point where it was simply not true, since the contrary is so obvious.[149]

Christine de Pizan consistently argues that satirical universal judgments against all women are contrary to the evidence; and she concludes, therefore, that the premises and conclusions of the Jealous Man in *Le Roman de la rose* are not true. It is important to recall that the Jealous Man in Jean de Meun's text based his views directly upon the "wise authors of antiquity" whom he identified as including Theophrastus (Aristotle's disciple), Walter Map, and Juvenal. So the views expressed by the Jealous Man could not be dismissed as just a single character's misconceptions; they were the usual historical litany of derogatory claims about woman's identity.

Christine introduces further evidence to support her argument that the universal judgments about women are false. Not only does the man make a hasty generalization from a few isolated, distorted examples of women, he also does not have any knowledge of virtuous women.

> For if he and all his henchmen had sworn it in this matter (let no one take offense), there have been, there are, and there will be more virtuous women, more honorable, better bred, and even more learned, and from whom more great good has come forth into the world than ever did from his person. Similarly, there have been women well schooled in worldly conduct and virtuous morals, and many who have effected a reconciliation with their husbands and have borne their concerns and their secrets and their passions calmly and discreetly, despite the fact that their husbands were crude and brutish toward them. One finds proof enough of this in the Bible and in other ancient histories. . . .[150]

149. Christine de Pizan to Jean de Montreuil, *La Querelle de la rose: Letters and Documents,* #VI, 52.
150. Christine de Pizan to Jean de Montreuil, *La Querelle de la rose: Letters and Documents,* #VI, 52-53.

She then lists several names from the Bible and from other sources of Western history. In this phase of her argument, Christine is giving multiple counterexamples to the universal judgments offered in *Le Roman de la rose*. These examples attempt to prove that not only are all women not deceitful, but some women are direct and forthcoming even when they have been badly treated by others.

Finally, Christine invokes her own experience to provide further evidence for the falsity of the universal premise she is trying to overturn. In the following passage, she also demonstrates an awareness of the difference between a subjective bias and genuine empirical evidence that a particular person may have:

> And do not believe or let anyone else think, dear Sir, that I have written this defense, out of feminine bias, merely because I am a woman. For, assuredly, my motive is simply to uphold the pure truth, since I know by experience that the truth is completely contrary to those things I am denying. And it is precisely because I am a woman that I can speak better in this matter than one who has not had the experience, since he speaks only by conjecture and by chance.[151]

Christine's contribution to intergender dialogue here is extremely important, because she enters a second-order level of reflection in her consideration of whether her own perspective is biased. By offering evidence that is available to others for verification, she transcends individual and group bias, and moves closer to truth. She explains what method ought to be used to verify whether or not the judgment that all women deceive is true or false; and her conclusion is that it is manifestly false.

To summarize: this first letter in the *Querelle de la rose* has initiated an intergender dialogue about woman's identity that includes a second-order reflection on the gender of the participants in the dialogue, and develops several arguments including those of the *modus tollens* form to reject false generalizations about woman.

Dialogue with Gontier Col

Christine's initiative led to contacts with other participants. In September of 1401, Gontier Col, Secretary to King Charles VI, wrote to her requesting a copy of the above letter she had previously sent to Jean de Montreuil.[152] Gontier Col addressed Christine as "Woman of high and exalted understanding" and said that he had heard that she had written an "invective" against Jean de Meun's *Roman de la rose,* which was regarded by many as "a remarkably well-designed argument."[153]

151. Christine de Pizan to Jean de Montreuil, *La Querelle de la rose: Letters and Documents,* #VI, 53. Christine was determined to compare "false literary" views of women with the actual experience of women. See Katharine M. Wilson, "Figmenta vs. Veritas: Dame Alice and the Medieval Literary Depiction of Women by Women," *Tulsa Studies in Women's Literature* 4, no. 1 (Spring 1985): 17-32.

152. See also Hill, "The Royal Secretaries" and "The Debate: Part One, The Royal Secretaries versus Christine de Pizan," in *The Medieval Debate,* chapters 5 and 6, pp. 143-208.

153. Gontier Col to Christine de Pizan, *La Querelle de la rose: Letters and Documents,* #VII, 57-58.

He then told her that he wished to defend his beloved master Jean de Meun, who was "a most profound and excellent philosopher," against her criticisms, bring her back "to the real truth," and help her "to know and understand the works of the said Meun better. . . ."[154]

At this point in the communication, the intergender dialogue seems to be progressing in a direct and open fashion. However, Gontier Col then suggests that Christine was simply led by other critics of Jean de Meun, who ". . . wanted to use you as their cloak, to imply that they knew more about the matter than a woman . . ."; and he concluded with the rather strong pronouncements that ". . . you have chosen, nay dared, to accuse him, correct him, and criticize him."[155] Christine immediately sent him a copy of her work, and two days later she received from him a short letter of bitter reproach.

What began as a simple intergender dialogue has now shifted into the more antagonistic form of dialectical argument that included judgment and reproach. After stating that a person in error should be corrected, first privately and then publicly, Col issued the following proclamation:

> Therefore, since I love you sincerely for your virtues and merits, I have first by my letter (which I sent to you day before yesterday) exhorted, advised, and begged you to correct and amend your manifest error, folly, or excessive wilfulness which has risen in you, a woman impassioned in this matter, out of presumption or arrogance — may it not displease you if I speak the truth. Thus following the holy commandment and having compassion for you by charitable love, I pray, counsel, and require you a second time by this little note of mine please to correct, retract, and amend your aforementioned error with regard to that very excellent and irreproachable doctor of holy divine Scripture, high philosopher, and most learned clerk in all the seven liberal arts. It is astonishing that you have dared and presumed to correct and criticize him detrimentally, as well as his true and loyal disciples: Monsieur the Provost of Lisle and me and others. Confess your error, and we will have pity on you, will grant mercy to you, and will give you salutary penance.[156]

The substance of Gontier Col's appeal consists of a comparison of different levels of education of those who are engaged in dialogue, Christine and Jean de Meun, as well as Christine and Jean's disciples. Instead of a well-designed argument to counter those given by Christine, the academic credentials themselves appear to be a guarantor of truth.

Christine de Pizan's response to Gontier Col was written a few weeks later in October 1401. In her response, she directly identified and attempted to counteract some of the key elements in the gender polarity theory as expressed in Col's letter.

---

154. Gontier Col to Christine de Pizan, *La Querelle de la rose: Letters and Documents,* #VII, 57-58.

155. Gontier Col to Christine de Pizan, *La Querelle de la rose: Letters and Documents,* #VII, 58.

156. Gontier Col to Christine de Pizan, *La Querelle de la rose: Letters and Documents,* #VIII, 60-61.

Her analysis focused on the following points: (1) The recognition that woman was considered "impassioned by nature," (2) the ironic fact that it was Col himself who had acted in an impassioned manner "in a fit of impatience" while Christine herself had proceeded in an orderly way to present her "true opinion, honestly arrived at," (3) the further claim that Col gave more weight to academic credentials than to the careful examination of individual arguments about particular passages, (4) the recognition that Col's argument about woman's impassioned nature was based on a deeper claim of "the inadequacy of my [woman's] faculties"; (5) her own judgment that many women have demonstrated adequate and even outstanding use of their faculties in the practice of virtue, and (6) the claim that she identifies with or prefers to "resemble" them than to have the "goods of fortune," which included presumably among other things the male privilege of academic credentials.

These arguments in Christine's letter demonstrate a real capacity to engage in serious intergender dialogue with a man who has had academic training. Her letter includes four basic parts: a description of the process of their dialogue to the present time, a defense against what she perceives as his attack on her because of her identity as a woman (an *"ad feminam"* version of the *ad hominem*), her reflection on the potential value of her own argument, and a summary restatement of the conclusion of her argument in the original letter to Jean de Montreuil.

The significance of this particular letter of Christine de Pizan to Gontier Col has been noted by Earl Jeffrey Richards, who demonstrates that Christine reveals her expert humanist epistolary art in this letter by the way she chose a single topic, women's identity, as the focus of the letter, refused to get caught in reducing her point of view to a particular perspective of gender or poetic rubrics, and sought to "restore the universality of letters to its own ideals."[157] Because Christine de Pizan's response is a cogent and original example of early humanist intergender dialogue about the concept of woman, each part of the letter will be described below.

In the first part, Christine contrasts the academic credentials of some learned men (including Gontier Col, the Secretary to the King), with her own participation in the general dialogue about the value of *Le Roman de la rose*.

> O wise clerk of philosophic mind, knowledgeable, and accomplished in polished rhetoric and poetic subtlety, please do not willfully choose to reproach and reprove my true opinion, honestly arrived at, just because it is not to your pleasure. I learned from your first letter that you desire to have a copy of a little epistolary treatise which I had previously sent to the worthy clerk, Monseigneur the Provost of Lisle. In this treatise I discussed at length (within the limitations of my small wit) my views, which differ so greatly from the praise which he lavished on the *Roman de la Rose,* expressed, so I discovered, in a letter to a friend of his, a wise and learned clerk. This praise was completely contrary to the opinion of his friend, with whom I agreed. And so in order to meet your wishes, I sent the letter requested.[158]

157. See Richards, *"Seulette à part,"* pp. 158-59.
158. Christine de Pizan to Gontier Col, *La Querelle de la rose: Letters and Documents,* #IX, 62.

In the first sentence, we find Christine giving credit to Col's academic credentials in philosophy, rhetoric, and poetic literature. She places herself in an intermediate level of true opinion, below philosophical knowledge, but above the emotional appeal of rhetoric and the eloquence of poetry. She adds that she had hoped that from Gontier she would have been given the respect due a participant in a common dialogue even though she is limited in wit and intellectual education.

However, the tone of Gontier's reply was hostile and biased towards Christine as a woman. So in the next part of her letter, she directly addresses this problem of bias:

> Whereupon, after you had read and thoroughly scrutinized my letter, wherein your error was punctured by truth, you wrote in a fit of impatience your second, more offensive letter, reproaching my feminine sex, which you describe as impassioned by nature. Thus you accuse me, a woman, of folly and presumption in daring to correct and reproach a teacher as exalted, well-qualified, and worthy as you claim the author of that book to be. Hence you earnestly exhort me to recant and repent. Whereupon, you say, generous mercy will still be extended to me, but that, if not, I shall be treated as a publican, etc. Ha! Man of ingenious understanding! Look rightly according to the most sovereign theological way, and, far from condemning what I have written, you will ask yourself whether one ought to praise those particular passages I have condemned. And, furthermore, note everywhere carefully which things I condemn and which I do not. And if you despise my reasons so much because of the inadequacy of my faculties, which you criticize by your words, "a woman impassioned," etc., rest assured that I do not feel any sting in such criticism, thanks to the comfort I find in the knowledge that there are, and have been, vast numbers of excellent praiseworthy women, schooled in all the virtues — whom I would rather resemble than to be enriched with all the goods of fortune.[159]

In this brief passage Christine set forth her own reasoning against the whole gender polarity tradition that had begun two thousand years before, first with the Presocratics and then developed in great detail by Aristotle. This gender polarity tradition held that woman, because of her natural imperfection, had a weak or inferior development of the faculty of intellect, and as a consequence it concluded that woman's rational soul was without authority over her irrational soul. In a way, we can be grateful that the quarrel about *Le Roman de la rose* elicited the comments from Gontier Col that led Christine de Pizan to respond in the above manner. In this way the dialogue itself, situated in a context of the search for truth about the concept of woman, could develop a new aspect, previously unexpressed in Western thought.

Christine de Pizan's response to Col did not stop here, for she directly addressed his attempt to intimidate her by his letter:

> But, further, if you seek in every way to minimize my firm beliefs by your antifeminist attacks, please recall that a small dagger or knife point can pierce a great,

159. Christine de Pizan to Gontier Col, *La Querelle de la rose: Letters and Documents,* #IX, 62-63.

bulging sack and that a small fly can attack a great lion and speedily put him to flight. So, although by speaking evil of me you seek to threaten me with your subtle reasoning, which is commonly a source of fear to the faint-hearted, do not imagine me so moved or carried away by flightiness that I can be quickly defeated.[160]

We see the manner in which Christine de Pizan uses the same mode of argumentation as her opponent. Since Gontier Col attacked her, she provided a metaphor of attack as a response. At the same time, however, she keeps calling the dialogue back to a basis of rational discourse. As we mentioned at the outset of this section on Gontier Col, Christine's deeper argument turned back on Col his own use of the epistemological principle of gender polarity against her, that her rational soul was without authority over her passions. She also exercised her rational powers by arguing that he should pay more attention to the argument itself than the academic credentials of the persons arguing. She called him to recall the importance of virtue and the fact that many women have led virtuous lives and, in this context, to situate her argument again in the framework of justice and the common good.

Christine de Pizan concludes her argument by reasserting her main theses in straightforward terms:

> Therefore, so that you may retain in brief what I have at other times written at length, I say again and repeat and repeat again as many times as you wish my condemnation of the work entitled the *Roman de la Rose*. I say that it can be a source of wicked and perverse encouragement to disgusting conduct, although it does contain some good things (the more authentic the good, the greater the evil, as I said before), because mankind is naturally inclined to evil. This book can be, for many people, a supporter of the dissolute life; a doctrine full of deceit; the road to damnation; a public defamer; a source of suspicion, mistrust, shame, and, perhaps, of heresy. And in several places a most loathsome book! All this I choose and dare to hold and maintain everywhere and before everyone, and I can prove it by reference to the book itself.[161]

Her conclusions with special relevance to the concept of woman are the following: *Le Roman de la rose* reduces women to sex objects; it criticizes women's alleged deceptiveness, while at the same time it suggests deception as a method for man to conquer woman, and hence it prescribes a double standard; and it defames woman by the satire that depicts vice in a humorous way, rendering it attractive to the readers, while causing embarrassment to its target, women.

---

160. Christine de Pizan to Gontier Col, *La Querelle de la rose: Letters and Documents*, #IX, 63. As the original French in the quotation indicates, the translator has taken license in using the phrase 'anti-feminist attacks.' For the original see the published version of Ward, *The Epistles on the Romance of the Rose and Other Documents in the Debate*, Letter VI, line 40-41, 33.

161. Christine de Pizan to Gontier Col, *La Querelle de la rose: Letters and Documents*, #IX, 63-64.

Dialogues with Queen Isabeau, Provost Guillaume de Tignonville, and Chancellor Jean Gerson

At this point, Christine de Pizan attempted to bring others into the dialogue. She wrote first to two different people, a woman — the Queen of France; and a man — the Provost of Paris. In both cases, she included copies of all the previous relevant texts in the *Querelle* along with her letter, gathering them into a kind of book. Christine modeled herself in this action on the Italian humanists, and particularly Petrarch, who gathered together letters on a literary topic into manuscripts that were then circulated to a wider audience.[162] The significance of Christine's actions in extending the public dialogue by making an epistolary manuscript is further noted by Kevin Brownlee:

> What I shall be focusing on is the "second level" of the *Débat's* historical existence, in the dossier that Christine created by rearranging and recontextualizing a strategically chosen selection of the original documents; by in effect transforming the *Débat* into a "book" of which she was the author. The act of making this book was itself a polemical, public gesture that functioned as part of the ongoing *Débat*. It was also an extraordinary gesture of appropriation, of control on Christine's part, with important implications for the authority of her public voice.[163]

In her letter of February 1402 to Isabeau of Bavaria, after salutary remarks in which she praises the queen's virtue and noble understanding and places herself as the queen's simple, ignorant, and humble servant, Christine attempts to invoke her support as a political figure, potential patron, and as a woman in the intergender context within which woman is being devalued:

> In these letters, my awesome Lady, if you deign to honor me by listening to them, you can understand my diligence, desire, and wish to resist by true defenses, as far as my small power extends, some false opinions denigrating the honor and fair name of women, which many men — clerks and others — have striven to diminish by their writings. This is a thing not to be permitted, suffered, or supported. Although I am weak to lead the attack against such subtle masters, nonetheless my small wit has chosen and now chooses to employ itself in disputing those who attack and accuse women, for, being moved by the truth, I am firmly convinced that the feminine cause is worthy of defence. This I do here and have done in my other works. Thus, your worthy Highness, I petition humbly that you accept my argument, although I cannot express it in as fine a language as another might, and permit me to enlarge upon it, if, in the future, I am able to. May all this be done under your wise and benign correction.[164]

162. Richards, *"Seulette à part,"* p. 158.
163. Kevin Brownlee, "Discourses of the Self: Christine de Pizan and the *Rose,*" *Romantic Review* 79, no. 1 (January 1988): 200-221, 213.
164. Christine de Pizan to the Queen of France, *La Querelle de la rose: Letters and Documents,*

Even though it is clear that Christine is hoping to interest the queen in becoming her patron by financing further writing on this topic, she also appeals to the queen as a woman in this debate about woman's identity. This letter may be the first example in the West of a woman asking another woman to support her in a dialogue with men about some aspects of woman's identity.

However, it is very important to note that Christine asks the queen not just to agree with her because of their common base in being women, but to "accept my argument." So Christine de Pizan appeals to the Queen's reason, rather than female solidarity, in inviting her into the dialogue. She seeks support for her philosophical approaches to the dialogue, which include finding "true defenses" against "false opinions" about women, by using her "small wit" against "subtle masters" to defend the "feminine cause" as seen in the above quotation. So just as she argued against the attacks of Gontier Col by an appeal to reason, so she also argues that the queen should support her because of the reasons for her position. Thus, even in the manner in which Christine de Pizan seeks patrons, she challenged the gender polarity epistemological principle that devalued women's capacity for the authoritative exercise of her rational soul.

A second example of Christine's attempt to dialogue with the Queen of France is found in the letter entitled *Lamentation sur les maux de la France (de la guerre civile du 23 Aout, 1410)*. "Ah, Queen of France, are you asleep? What prevents you from trying to check and make this deadly undertaking cease? Don't you see the heritage of your noble children threatened? Mighty princess, mother of the noble heirs of France, who but you can act? Who would disobey your power and authority, if you truly wished to establish peace?"[165]

A third example is described in detail by Deborah McGrady in a study of Christine's frequent recopying and changing of her manuscripts to offer to different patrons:

> Around 1411, Christine de Pizan presented the queen of France, Isabeau of Bavaria, with an exquisite manuscript copy of her courtly and didactic works [British Library, Harley 4431]. Containing thirty texts and decorated with 130 miniatures, this anthology constitutes the most complete extant collection of Christine's works.[166]

McGrady offers much evidence to demonstrate that Christine de Pizan redefined the relation between author and patron by the way she went about redirecting manuscripts, bartering them for future services, and shifting the purpose from entertainment to education. In this context, she mentions particularly that the relation between Christine de Pizan and Queen Isabeau of France ended with Chris-

---

#X, 65-66. This letter is dated in the text as 1401, but that would not be possible if it included copies of the other letters written in 1401.

165. Christine de Pizan, "Lamentation on the Woes of France," in *The Writings of Christine de Pizan,* pp. 305-6.

166. Deborah McGrady, "What Is a Patron? Benefactors and Authorship in Harley 4431, Christine de Pizan's Collected Works," in *Christine de Pizan and the Categories of Difference,* ed. Marilynn Desmond, p. 195.

tine actually becoming the Queen's teacher, especially through her didactic works. Thus, the initial letter attempting to draw the Queen into the public dialogue about woman's identity ultimately succeeded in early efforts to establish a woman's community of discourse about topics of mutual concern.

When we turn to the second patron that Christine had hoped to invite into the public dialogue about *Le Roman de la rose,* we find her turning to an old friend, Guillaume de Tignonville, the Provost of Paris. Guillaume played a significant role in Christine's life in three other key moments: he translated the *Dits,* which she used in her research about early philosophers; he was the person who finally enabled her to settle her court cases and get free of debts as a widow; and later in life he would also take care of the body of King Louis, Christine's patron, and direct the search for those who brutally assassinated him.[167]

In her letter to Guillaume de Tignonville, she asks that he publicly support her position because it is part of his office as Provost of Paris to "support in all cases the weakest part, insofar as its cause is just."[168] However, again she adds the provision that his support should not come simply from friendship or even because she is the weakest person in the *Querelle,* but from his "giving a hearing to the facts of our debate," "the discreet exercise of your wisdom," and that "he consider and rightly choose the cause which I favour."[169] Once again, Christine places reason as the ultimate arbiter of truth.

At the beginning of her letter Christine refers to the dialogue as a "good-humoured debate stimulated by a difference of opinion among worthy persons," and she identifies the participants.[170] This would seem to imply that she counts herself as one of the worthy persons in the public dialogue. However, at the end of her letter she describes it as "the war undertaken against the aforesaid powerful and strong men."[171] Christine characterizes the deterioration of what had begun as a genuine dialogue about a serious subject but had degenerated by Gontier Col's personal attack on her. Indeed, she directly notes that Gontier Col "became angry with her" because of what she had written against *Le Roman de la rose.*[172] Even in this shift from good-humored debate to war, Christine still identifies herself as a willing partner to continue the discussion.

At this point, the intensity of debate increased significantly. Jean de Montreuil, the person who had in some respects been the originating cause for the contention about the meaning of *Le Roman de la rose* in the first place, wrote three further letters defending it against an anonymous critic of the text, and one letter to a person

---

167. See *Christine's Vision,* 119, note 3; and McLeod, *The Order of the Rose,* pp. 140-42.

168. Christine de Pizan to Guillaume de Tignonville, *La Querelle de la rose: Letters and Documents,* #XI, 68.

169. Christine de Pizan to Guillaume de Tignonville, *La Querelle de la rose: Letters and Documents,* #XI, 67-68.

170. Christine de Pizan to Guillaume de Tignonville, *La Querelle de la rose: Letters and Documents,* #XI, 67.

171. Christine de Pizan to Guillaume de Tignonville, *La Querelle de la rose: Letters and Documents,* #XI, 68.

172. Christine de Pizan to Guillaume de Tignonville, *La Querelle de la rose: Letters and Documents,* #XI, 69.

who admired the text. Then in May 1402 Jean Gerson (1363-1429) entered the debate. As Chancellor of the University, Jean Gerson was expected to speak out on all contemporary issues. It is not surprising then that he would have been willing to engage in the debate about satirical works that he thought contributed to the basic corruption of society and of the institution of marriage. In addition, as mentioned earlier, Jean Gerson had befriended Christine de Pizan when she was first widowed and had given her access to resources from the University of Paris.

Gerson was a complex figure when it came to his view of woman's identity. In 1423 in the context of female visionaries, he argued in *De examinatione doctrinarum,* that "women are especially forbidden to teach men more learned than themselves."[173] However, as mentioned earlier in this chapter as well as in the previous one, in 1429 Gerson wrote of Joan of Arc in *De quadam puella* that her mission was just; she herself was devout; she was urging others to righteousness; and it was alright for her to wear men's clothes. So it is difficult to know with certainty what he thought about women who entered public areas of activity to teach and to lead men. In any event, Gerson decided to enter into the *Querelle de la rose,* and he completed a several-page treatise in Latin that was translated into French as *Le Traité contre le Roman de la rose (Treatise against the Romance of the Rose).* While this text does not directly focus on the question of woman's identity, it does consider ways in which the original treatise devalues married love and the practice of chastity.[174] Thus it serves as an indirect defense of Christine de Pizan, who was publicly criticizing *Le Roman de la rose* on similar grounds. As a theologian with particular interest in spiritual and practical concerns, Gerson believed that *Le Roman de la rose* undermined the relation between men and women by distorting both. In his more indirect manner, Gerson can be considered as a defender of both Christine de Pizan and of woman's identity.

Gerson's text once again establishes the context as one of justice. A feminine personification, "Lady Justice," presides over a court with help from a male personification, "Sound Judgment, chief and chancellor, joined in a firm companionship with Lady Reason."[175] The promoter of lawsuits, a female personification, "Conscience," began to evaluate *Le Roman de la rose.* Gerson's feminine personification of the promoter of a lawsuit against the text reminds the reader of Christine de Pizan's earlier appeals to the court of justice. Gerson indirectly supports this association when he adds as the reason for his choice, "there is nothing that she does not know and report."[176] Conscience picks one lawsuit, by a feminine personification, "Chastity," and eight articles are read out to the court. Within these articles, the key personifications of the original text of *Le Roman de la rose* are identified: the

---

173. Brown, *Pastor and Laity in the Theology of Jean Gerson,* pp. 223-24.

174. For a consideration of Gerson's several works on this topic see Hill, "Jean Gerson," in *The Medieval Debate,* ch. 4, pp. 105-31.

175. The Treatise of Gerson against the *Roman de la rose,* in *La Querelle de la rose: Letters and Documents,* #XII, 70-71. He also introduces "true daughters" of God and Free Will, or Divine Love, Fortitude, Temperance, and Humility, and the "secretaries" of Sound Judgment (presumably male personifications), or Prudence and Knowledge. There were others listed whose gendered personification was not explicitly stated.

176. The Treatise of Gerson, *La Querelle de la rose: Letters and Documents,* #XII, 71.

"accursed Old Woman . . . who encourages men to deceive in order to gain sexual favors from young women," the "evil-minded Jealous Man" who condemns marriage through his own and through others' words, and "Lady Reason" who is slandered and who is used to "war against the virtues."[177]

However, the "Foolish Lover" is the defendant against whom most of the argument is waged by the figure "Theological Eloquence." Jean Gerson gives a masculine personification of "Theological Eloquence" in his original text, as an Advocate of the Christian Court. Since Gerson's focus is the virtue of chastity and faithful married love, the "Foolish Lover" is criticized for encouraging the opposite.[178] In this context there are a few passing defenses of women in particular. One example is the criticism: "He encourages all men to make sport of women, virgins or not, and to do just as they please. And — what is the height of evil — he says that such things are sanctuaries, sacred and estimable acts."[179] In a second example, Jean de Meun is criticized for having "Lady Reason" say to the "Foolish Lover," "such follies — shameful, obscene, and impure words, as well as a thorough condemnation of women. . . ."[180] In conclusion, this treatise of Jean Gerson, while infrequently taking up the defense of women *per se,* nonetheless supports Christine de Pizan's general concerns that *Le Roman de la rose* may interfere with the development of wisdom and virtue in its readers.

Jean Gerson will enter the debate more directly in support of Christine de Pizan once again a little later. However, first the *Querelle* again increased in intensity and tone when Pierre Col entered the public dialogue to defend and augment the position of his brother Gontier Col.

Dialogue with Pierre Col

In September 1402, Pierre Col, also Secretary to the King, addresses a letter of several pages to Christine de Pizan. In it he debates both with her and with the arguments (although not directly by name) contained in Jean Gerson's treatise.[181] First of all, Col attacks Christine directly through first praising and then condemning her intellect. However, instead of engaging with her reasoning, Col begins by questioning whether she was motivated by hatred.

> After I had heard people speak of your high understanding, your clear intellect, and of your melodious eloquence, I desired very greatly to see your letters and

177. The Treatise of Gerson, *La Querelle de la rose: Letters and Documents,* articles 1, 2, and 5, #XII, 70-72.

178. It is also interesting to note that the Foolish Lover represents persons of both sexes: "Then, behold, there arose innumerable men and a great multitude, young and old, of all sexes and ages, who, without preserving order, strove haphazardly, one to excuse, another to protect, another to praise him" ("The Treatise of Gerson," *La Querelle de la rose: Letters and Documents,* #XII, 74).

179. The Treatise of Gerson, *La Querelle de la rose: Letters and Documents,* #XII, 85.

180. The Treatise of Gerson, *La Querelle de la rose: Letters and Documents,* #XII, 89.

181. See Hill, "The Debate: Part Two, Pierre Col versus Jean Gerson," in *The Medieval Debate,* ch. 7, pp. 209-60.

other small things of like kind. Thus after great care in seeking them, there has come into my hand a certain letter of yours. . . . In this letter you make an effort to reproach the very devout Catholic and very excellent theologian, the most divine orator and poet and most perfect philosopher, Master Jean de Meun, in some particular parts of his book of the *Rose*. Yet I myself scarcely dare to open my mouth in praise of this book, lest I should set my foot into an abyss. For as we read of Herod, he did more good to the Innocents through hatred by having them killed than he could possibly have done through love. Perhaps it will be the same for you and others who strive with you to impugn this most novel writer Master Jean de Meun.[182]

At the end of the letter he repeats his personal attack in similar language. Reflecting on the fact that this criticism of *Le Roman de la rose* was produced more than a hundred years after it was originally written, Pierre Col suggests that envy is Christine's motivation for the critique.

If he were contemporary with you who blame him, I would say that you have particular hatred for him personally, but you have never so much as seen him. Thus I cannot imagine whence this comes, save that the very loftiness of the book invites the winds of Envy. . . . Yet I pray you, woman of high intellect, that you preserve the honor you have won for the depth of your understanding and elegant style; and if men have praised you for having, as it were, fired a shot over the towers of Notre Dame, do not attempt to hit the moon with a cannon ball. Take care not to be like the crow who, because someone praised his song, began to sing louder than usual and let his mouthful fall.[183]

In other places in the letter Col also compares Christine with someone who bites another person;[184] and with a pelican who self-destructs by feeding on it-

---

182. Pierre Col to Christine de Pizan, *La Querelle de la rose: Letters and Documents,* #XIII, 92. It is interesting to note that Pierre Col copied the letters of Heloise and Abelard previously translated by Jean de Meun, author of the *Rose,* from Latin to French, and they became very popular in Paris at the time. His colleagues used these letters to support their negative claims for marriage as well as to suggest that a woman could be an intellectual only if she denies her sexuality. For an excellent discussion of this see Richards, *"Seulette à part,"* pp. 141-42 and 159. He notes Christine's "conspicuous absence" of reference to Heloise with the exception of one letter in which she accuses Pierre Col of resembling Heloise in her preference to be a prostitute rather than a married woman or queen.

183. Pierre Col to Christine de Pizan, *La Querelle de la rose: Letters and Documents,* #XIII, 112.

184. See the following passage from the middle of the letter: "But let us go further. You and Lady Eloquence have exclaimed over the dishonorableness to be found in this chapter of the Old Woman, where, you say, one finds nothing but filth, and similarly in the chapter of Jealousy; and you say that you would really like to find someone capable of justifying it for you. 'What end is served by the many dishonorable words which this book contains?' 'But,' you say, 'I do not condemn the author in all places in the aforementioned book,' as if you wish to say that you condemn him in this particular place, and therefore set yourself up as a judge although you have spoken out of prejudice and outrageous presumption. Oh excessively foolish pride! Oh opinion uttered too quickly and thoughtlessly by the mouth of a woman! A woman who condemns a man of high understanding and educated study, a man who, by great labor and deliberation, has made the very noble book of the *Rose,* which surpasses

self.[185] These *ad hominem* attacks (in the *"ad feminam"* form) consistently appear to shift the ground of criticism from the intellectual content of the argument itself to an irrational motivation for Christine's analysis. One could say that they express a particular instance of the universal claim that women's reason is without authority over her emotions. Yet it is Col himself who has reverted to emotions in his critique rather than remain on the level of rational argument.

Pierre Col then attempts to defend the words of the "Foolish Lover," the "Old Woman," and the "Jealous Man" in *Le Roman de la rose* against the arguments of "Theological Eloquence" who had criticized them in Jean Gerson's *Treatise*. In his analysis Jean Gerson's original male personification, "Theological Eloquence," and Christine de Pizan merge into a single female personage of "Lady Theological Eloquence."

Repeating his brother's previous argument to Christine, Col states that words spoken by characters in a literary work mean only what the particular characters represent; they do not offer generalities or the author's views. With respect to the satirical comments about women, then, the reader should not assume anything further than a single perspective represented by the characters.

> I answer Lady Eloquence and you by the same means, and I say that Master Jean de Meun in his book introduced characters, and made each character speak according to his nature, that is, the Jealous Man as a jealous man, the Old Woman as an old woman, and similarly with the others. And it is wrong-headed to say that the author believes women to be as evil as the Jealous Man, in accordance with his character, declares. This is clearly not true of the author. He merely recites what any jealous man says about women invariably, and Meun does this in order to demonstrate and correct the enormous irrationality and disordered passion of jealous men. A jealous man is moved to say so much evil of women in general, and not just of his own, because, I believe, normally a married man, before he becomes jealous, thinks that he has the best wife in the world, or at least as good as any alive.[186]

This argument of Col has merit on the surface, for if a text is simply a work of literature with a variety of characters' views represented, then the reader would be wrong to impute any general weight to a particular set of statements by a single character. To strengthen this approach to the subject, Pierre Col invokes the authority of Aristotle to demonstrate by analogy that a person who is driven by an emotional response tends to universalize judgments. It would follow that a jealous

---

all others that ever were written in French . . . and I suspect it is because Meun spoke the truth that you wish to bite him. But I advise you to keep your teeth to yourself" (Pierre Col to Christine de Pizan, *La Querelle de la rose: Letters and Documents*, #XIII, 103, and for the reference to the pelican, 94).

185. See a later reference of Christine to the pelican image in "The Seven Allegorized Psalms" (1409-1410): "The pelican, Lord, sacrifices itself for its young, and gives its blood to revive them, but Thou, Lord, art the true Pelican, who willingly exposed Thy body on the cross, obedient unto death, in order for Thy young (that is, Thy people) to be saved" (*The Writings of Christine de Pizan*, p. 327).

186. Pierre Col to Christine de Pizan, *La Querelle de la rose: Letters and Documents*, #XIII, 103-4.

man would inevitably think that all women are deceitful, not just that the woman he loves is deceitful. Pierre Col concludes that Jean de Meun is more critical of men than of women in his text. "Yet he speaks more against men than against women. . . . In God's name, this is no attack on the whole feminine sex."[187]

At this point, Pierre Col considers the book as a whole. In this context it is helpful to recall that *Le Roman de la rose* is an allegory about attacking and defending a castle, and plucking a rose within its inner sanctuary. The language of the text makes it clear that the analogy is drawn between the castle and a woman's sexual anatomy.[188] Christine de Pizan and Jean Gerson had argued that the poetic description of a successful attack, conquering, and plucking of the rose is demeaning to women represented by the rose as a passive sexual object throughout the text. Pierre Col argues that a book describing this conquest helps the defenders of the castle to better guard it against similar attacks in the future. Next, he produces the example of a friend who had been converted away from being a "Foolish Lover" by reading the book.[189]

Pierre Col's final argument in support of the whole book places the blame for the satirical comments it contains on the historical texts rather than on the author:

> If his book contains very bawdy words which degrade the feminine sex, it is simply because he quotes other authors who use them, for, as he said, he does nothing more than quote. Thus, it seems to me that one ought to blame the authors rather than those who quote them, as I said before. But you will say to me: "Why does he quote them?" I say that he did it in order to teach more effectively how gatekeepers should guard the castle. Besides, these words are appropriate here. For his purpose was to continue the subject initiated by Guillaume de Lorris, and in so doing to speak of all matters according to their hierarchical rank for the good of the human creature, in both body and soul.[190]

187. Pierre Col to Christine de Pizan, *La Querelle de la rose: Letters and Documents,* #XIII, 106. He adds the following details: "Does he not condemn, in the chapter on Nature, twenty-six vices with which men are corrupted? And in innumerable other places which I pass over."

188. Pierre Col directly affirms this allegorical meaning: "And when Master Jean de Meun calls the secret members of women 'Sanctuaries' and 'relics,' he does so in order to show the great folly that is in the Foolish Lover. For a foolish lover thinks only of this little rosebud, and it is his god and he honors it as his god. . . . He [Meun], in fact, chooses his words very well when he calls a woman's secret members sanctuaries, for the gates and walls of a city are by law called holy . . ." (Pierre Col to Christine de Pizan, *La Querelle de la rose: Letters and Documents,* #XIII, 97).

189. The issue of whether Christine was rejecting *La Roman de la rose* out of a prudish response to its vocabulary and message rather than from a well-considered concern about its effects on people still rages. For example, Sheila Delany in "Mothers to Think Back Through: The Ambiguous Example of Christine de Pizan," in *Medieval Texts and Contemporary Readers,* ed. Laurie A. Finke and Martin B. Shichtman (Ithaca and London: Cornell University Press, 1987), pp. 177-97, argues that "Her main complaint against the *Roman* is that its author talks dirty" (p. 191). In contrast to this negative evaluation, Susan Schibanoff in "Taking the Gold" argues as follows: "Christine did not concern herself with the question of how the *Romance* ought to be read, but how, in her opinion, the work *would* be read by different readers. Basically, she argued that readers would interpret the *Romance* according to their own lights" (p. 93).

190. Pierre Col to Christine de Pizan, *La Querelle de la rose: Letters and Documents,* #XIII, 109-

The substance of this letter is included here, because it provides an important participation in the developing dialogue about woman's identity. The fundamental issues are raised in the context of this debate in a clear and unambiguous way. Once again, this lengthy set of arguments by a man offered Christine de Pizan the opportunity to respond in equal length and depth. Intergender dialogue about gender continued to evolve.

In a further intensification of *Le Querelle de la rose,* Christine responds within one month of receiving the above letter, debating every point made by Pierre Col. Her reply follows the two-leveled approach already seen: an analysis of the dynamics of the intergender dialogue itself, and an analysis of the implications of the text *Le Roman de la rose* for issues about sex and gender. We will consider each of these themes in turn.

At the very beginning of her lengthy letter, Christine reflects on the general dynamics of a dialogue. She introduces the Aristotelian distinction between dialectic based on common opinions and rhetoric that appeals to emotions to convince, and demonstration, which seeks knowledge based on true principles. She suggests that Col's arguments fall into the first category, while her purpose is to argue in the second category. Thus she concludes that Col's arguments are unable to effect damage in her own position:

> Because human understanding cannot attain to a perfect knowledge of absolute truth and cannot comprehend mysteries on account of the gross, terrestrial darkness which impedes and obstructs true light, so that men draw conclusions from opinion rather than from certain knowledge — for these reasons, debates often arise among even the wisest of men because of differing opinions, each one striving to show by his reasoning that his particular opinion is the true one. That this is true can be seen from our present debate. Therefore, O wise clerk, whose keen feeling and facility in expressing your opinions are impeded by no ignorance, I wish to inform you that, although your reasons are well laid out for your purpose, they are contrary to my belief. For despite your beautiful rhetoric, you do not move my heart at all or make me wish to change what I have previously written.[191]

Even though Christine claims in her introduction that she "is no logician," her letter contains a multitude of arguments whose form is drawn from the logical writings of Aristotle to rebut Pierre Col's arguments. Some of these are in single-sentence form, while others involve an elaborate set of premises with clear discursive reasoning to reach their conclusions.

In each stage of the argument Christine chooses to mirror in her rebuttal the tone originally used by Pierre Col. For example, in response to his passage in which

---

10. In the context of his argument he added that Ovid wrote in *The Art of Love* only about how to attack the castle, because he wrote in Latin, which women could not read; Jean de Meun, in contrast, wrote about both attacking and defending the castle because he wrote in French, which both men and women could read, p. 108.

191. Christine de Pizan to Pierre Col, *La Querelle de la rose: Letters and Documents,* #XIV, 116.

he refers to her outrageous presumption, excessively foolish pride, quick opinion, and thoughtless speech, Christine states:

> My answer. Oh man deceived by wilful opinion! I could assuredly answer but I prefer not to do it with insult, although, groundlessly, you yourself slander me with ugly accusations. Oh darkened understanding! Oh perverted knowledge blinded by self will, which judges grievous poison to be restoration from death; perverse doctrine to be healthful example; bile to be sweet honey; horrible filthiness to be satisfying beauty. A simple little housewife sustained by the doctrine of Holy Church could criticize your error! Flee and eschew the perverse doctrine which could lead you to damnation. When God has once enlightened you with true knowledge, you will be horrified by it, when you turn around and look back down the dangerous path you travelled.[192]

In the above passage we can see again Christine's awareness of different foundations for argument. She identifies Col with basing his judgments on willful opinions, darkened understanding, and perverted knowledge, and she contrasts these poor foundations for demonstration with the true knowledge that will be revealed to him by God. In addition, she argues that even someone with the small amount of education that she, a housewife, has, can see the difference between the two. Finally, she offers the opinion that the basis of his errors lies in his will, rather than in his reason, and that it is chosen ignorance, and therefore he will be held responsible for it in the ultimate tribunal after death. In venturing this opinion, Christine engages in judgment and a warning matching what she had already received from Col.

In another passage, Christine completely turns around a sharp criticism of Col, namely that she has responded with biting hatred to the truth of others' arguments. She agrees that her criticism has been biting but that its source is not a passion of the soul. It is rather the love of truth that seeks to bite deep enough to reach the roots of falsehood:

> You say in order to reprove me that truth engenders hatred and flattery friends, as Terence says. And on account of this, you suspect that I wish to bite him, and counsel me to watch my teeth. Know this for a certainty, that you lack somewhat in your thinking there (saving your reverence), for because there are so many deceiving lies and lack of truth in the book, I wish not only to bite, but to pull up by the roots the very great fallacious lies which it contains.[193]

Even though she is willing to discuss the emotional dynamics of the dialogue as above, she uses argument to bring the dialogue back to the real issue, that is, of the meaning and value of the book itself.

Christine also states directly that she is aware of Col's conflation of Jean Gerson's personification of "Lady Theological Elegance" and herself in the cri-

---

192. Christine de Pizan to Pierre Col, *La Querelle de la rose: Letters and Documents,* #XIV, 129-30.

193. Christine de Pizan to Pierre Col, *La Querelle de la rose: Letters and Documents,* #XIV, 130.

tique of *Le Roman de la rose,* and of his argument that a literary character does not necessarily represent the views of the author of a literary work. Her response presses the counterargument further with respect to the derogatory words about woman's identity:

> You respond to Lady Eloquence and me that Master Jean de Meun introduced characters in his book, and made each one speak fittingly, according to what pertained to him. I readily admit that the proper equipment is necessary for any particular game, but the will of the player manipulates such equipment to his own purpose. And it is clearly true (may it not displease you) that he was at fault in attributing to some of his characters functions that do not properly belong to them: as with his priest he calls Genius, who insistently commands men to bed the ladies and to continue the work of nature without leaving off. And yet he then has Genius say that one ought to flee women above all things, accusing them of as much evil and villainy as possible. I do not understand how it pertains to his office or even to the function of many other characters who say the same. You say that it is the role of the Jealous Man to speak in such a way; my reply is that never, in all his characters, can Meun resist the temptation to slander women viciously.[194]

Her argument here involves the counterclaim that although any individual character may not represent an author's views, if the same attitude is found in almost all of them, there is stronger evidence for the conclusion that the author indeed holds that opinion.

Even further, Christine argues that because the book's ending — the seduction of the Rose — particularly degrades women, it proves that the overall intention of the author was not a positive one with respect to women.

> And I dare to say that if Master Jean de Meun had spoken throughout his book of the inclinations and evil conduct of human nature but had concluded in favour of the moral way of life, then you would have had a greater reason for saying that he did it for a good purpose. For you know that if a writer wishes to use rhetoric properly, he first announces his premises and afterward moves from point to point, touching subjects as he chooses, but then always returns, in his conclusion, to the purpose of his narrative. And in this case the author certainly did not fail in any of this in the said book, for its fault is not ignorance. But you will tell me that de Lorris caused this. My answer. I consider the work as a single entity, a fact which is sufficient answer in this regard, although you say many things to suit your purpose, which I pass over, for the whole work comes to a single purpose in the conclusion, interpret as you will.
>
> You have said before that he does not blame women, but rather speaks well of them. But I am waiting for the proof.[195]

---

194. Christine de Pizan to Pierre Col, *La Querelle de la rose: Letters and Documents,* #XIV, 130.
195. Christine de Pizan to Pierre Col, *Le Querelle de la rose: Letters and Documents,* #XIV, 132.

Again Christine de Pizan brings the focus of the discussion back to a proper logic. In this passage she restates the steps that a person takes to develop an argument in the rhetorical tradition: i.e., announcing premises, moving in an ordered sequence from point to point, and then returning in the conclusion to the main purpose of the argument.

Next, she considers the tendency of men to blame women for their own poor choices. In this discussion, she charges Col with distorting a statement of St. Ambrose to imply that the feminine sex "is a sex accustomed to deceive." Christine argues that Ambrose was "blaming only vice" and not woman because she is the occasion for a man deceiving himself and not the cause. ". . . [I]t is the feminine sex through which man frequently deceived his own soul. . . ."[196] The deception, if it occurs, does so through the exercise of the man's free will and so he, not woman, is responsible.

Christine de Pizan charges Pierre Col with distorting the meaning of her argument in other places as well. When she had criticized *Le Roman de la rose* on the grounds that it would make women (including the Queen) blush if it were read out loud in their presence, Col had concluded incorrectly that the reason for the blush was that the women were ashamed of having done the unvirtuous deeds being discussed in the poem. Christine de Pizan, on the other hand, corrects this distorted reading of her view and reiterates that the blush was due to the unseemly satirical words of the character "Jealous man" which simply would embarrass the women.[197]

There is another passage in which de Meun actually recommends deception as a weapon to be used against women. In it, de Meun is appealing to Ovid's *Art of Love,* and Christine criticizes Pierre Col for defending de Meun:

> Ha! *Art of Love!* a book badly named! for of love there is nothing. It could well be called the art of falsely and maliciously deceiving women. This is a beautiful doctrine! Is then everything gained by deceiving women well? Who are women? Who are they? Are they serpents, wolves, lions, dragons, monsters, or ravishing, devouring beasts and enemies to human nature that it is necessary to make an art of deceiving and capturing them? Read then the *Art.* Learn then how to make traps, capture the forts, deceive them, condemn them, attack this castle, take care that no woman escape from you men, and let everything be given over to shame! And, by God! these are your mothers, your sisters, your daughters, your wives, and your sweethearts: they are you yourselves and you yourselves are they. Now deceive them fully, for it is "much better, dear master, to deceive . . . ," etc.[198]

This quotation is from the character Reason in *Le Roman de la rose,* and it was frequently mentioned in the *Querelle de la rose.* The whole sentence is: "It is better to

---

196. Christine de Pizan to Pierre Col, *La Querelle de la rose: Letters and Documents,* #XIV, 133.

197. Christine de Pizan to Pierre Col, *La Querelle de la rose: Letters and Documents,* #XIV, 132-33.

198. Christine de Pizan to Pierre Col, *La Querelle de la rose: Letters and Documents,* #XIV, 135-36.

deceive than to be deceived." The suggestion in *Le Roman de la rose* that it is much better to deceive than to be deceived is one that rankles Christine de Pizan's ethical sensibilities. While deception is always something to be avoided, doing the act is more culpable than being the innocent victim of its plotting. Ultimately Christine de Pizan argues that *Le Roman de la rose* itself is a major deception, for it purports to be about wisdom, virtue, and the praise of women, but in fact it is about false opinion, vice, and deceptive domination of women. To Pierre Col's claim that it brought a false lover to conversion, Christine gives the counterexample in which the book gave a man an excuse to beat his wife.[199]

In a very detailed and lengthy conclusion that includes the recapitulation of many arguments plus the development of a few more, Christine de Pizan turns to the relation between Jean de Meun's text and the satirical work of previous writers. She argues that even though there is a connection among all these works, each author is responsible for the particular concept of woman contained within his own work:

> You say that if he in any way denigrates or defames the feminine sex in the work, he is merely quoting other authors. My answer. I know well that he is not the first to have denigrated women, but he augments what he quotes. You say that this was in order to teach how to guard the castle better. My answer. One should not suppose that to encourage and praise evil is to teach one to guard himself against it. You say that he did it also in order to continue the work of Guillaume de Lorris. My answer. He who chooses to follow a man who has lost his way can hardly be excused if he himself goes astray.[200]

Once again, we see Christine de Pizan arguing point by point against her adversary. In addition to indicating where Col's arguments are weak or fallacious, she also recommends other authors who much more effectively support wisdom and virtue: i.e., Boethius, Augustine, and Dante. In this appeal Christine de Pizan once again inserts herself into the strong line of ethical writers in medieval philosophy, and she draws upon them for support against the distorted thinking of some humanists.

Her lengthy critical letter to Pierre Col concludes with a query about the value of any further dialogue about the topic: "I do not know why we are debating these questions so fully, for I do not believe that we will be able to change each other's opinions."[201] In fact, after this particular letter, Christine withdrew from di-

---

199. "This was an extremely jealous man, who, whenever in the grip of passion, would go and find the book and read it to his wife; then he would become violent and strike her. . . . Thus it seems clear to me that whatever other people think of this book, this poor woman pays too high a price for it" (Christine de Pizan to Pierre Col, *La Querelle de la rose: Letters and Documents*, #XIV, 136).

200. Christine de Pizan to Pierre Col, *La Querelle de la rose: Letters and Documents*, #XIV, 137. In the passage directly preceding this one, Christine again takes up the theme of the deception in *Le Roman de la rose* in the particular voice of the Old Woman. "My answer. God have mercy! how malicious is this manner of deceiving — to show that whatever one does or says, however evil, is to a good cause!" (137).

201. Christine de Pizan to Pierre Col, *La Querelle de la rose: Letters and Documents*, #XIV, 140.

rect intergender dialogue with real persons about the concept of woman. Instead, she turned towards writing books in which dialogue occurred between herself and imaginary figures about the relation between historical texts and personages and her own contemporary experience. In this way, Christine de Pizan created an intellectual and spiritual city in which genuine dialogue could continue to take place, and within which she could provide a further amplification of the truth as she understood it.

In Christine's reply to Col's demeaning analogy that in her writing she was trying to hit the moon with a cannon ball or that was like a crow, singing so loud that she dropped her food, she states: "My answer. Nothing gives one so much authority as one's own experience. Hence, in this case I can speak the truth from certain knowledge."[202] Christine adds that she loves a solitary life of study, and it was not her intention that when this debate about Le Roman de la rose began "accidentally and not deliberately," it would have later become so public. Christine adds that she hopes she can continue to "speak the truth according to my conscience without its being turned against me," and that her small efforts might function like the small point of a needle that cures a great boil.[203]

There is no doubt that Christine de Pizan's contributions to this first public intergender dialogue about gender are astounding both for the initiative she took and for the consistently high quality of her responses. We can only regret that the persons engaged in the dialogue were not receptive enough to her contribution for the dialogue to move continually forward among the real participants in constructive and complementary ways.

Even though the above letter was Christine de Pizan's final contribution to this particular debate, there are some further contributions made by different men. Pierre Col wrote a response to her letter in December in which he noted her decision "to write no more harsh criticism of the Roman de la Rose." Again distorting her motives, Col appears to attribute her decision to not wanting "to persist in sin," while she had clearly indicated that her decision came from the realization that the dialogue was not one that could lead any of the participants to change their views.[204]

In an interesting way, Christine had given Pierre Col an easy way out of the dialogue, by suggesting to him at the end of her letter that he would gain no honor by winning an argument with her, a woman. This harkens back to the passage in the Sayings of Philosophers about Alexander, who claimed that to win a battle with a woman would be no honor for a man, and that to lose would be a humiliation. In any event, Pierre Col keeps arguing:

> What you say a little before the end of your letter may indeed be true, that there is no honor at all in hanging a fool, that is, in attacking you who are the weakest

---

202. Christine de Pizan to Pierre Col, *La Querelle de la rose: Letters and Documents,* #XIV, 142-43.

203. Christine de Pizan to Pierre Col, *La Querelle de la rose: Letters and Documents,* #XIV, 143-44.

204. Pierre Col to Christine de Pizan, *La Querelle de la rose: Letters and Documents,* #XIX, 160. Only a fragment of this letter exists.

part. Seeing that there are many wise teachers, great princes of the realm, and knights who are of your opinion, one ought rather, you say, to break down the great trunk and not concern himself with the small branches. And yet, I have known of no person who blamed him before or after you, save only he who composed the Complaint of Lady Eloquence.[205]

The Reentry of Jean Gerson and Jean de Montreuil

Jean Gerson, the creator of the argument of "Theological Eloquence," reentered the debate by writing a personal response to Pierre Col. His letter, written in Latin towards the end of 1402, directly supported Christine de Pizan's arguments. Gerson states first that his professional occupation as Chancellor of the University of Paris obliges him to argue against error and vice. Then he reasserts his judgment of the negative value of *Le Roman de la rose*. Next, he directly answers Pierre Col's attack of his own *Treatise* against *Le Roman de la rose* which had been indirectly given through the letter Col wrote to Christine de Pizan. Particularly noteworthy about this response is that Gerson finally takes a clear position publicly identifying himself with Christine de Pizan's ability to argue her position well:

> In your attack on my little book, you placed me alongside a remarkable lady, to whom your work is ostensibly addressed, but so chaotically that you jump from her to Theological Eloquence and just as quickly back again. Yet since it was dedicated to her, I ask you if that heroine argued this erroneous thing set in a proverb: "It is better to deceive than to be deceived"? Did she not, rather, refute it and rightly so? The very anxiety and ingenuity of your evasiveness show that the woman had you hard pressed with the sharpness of her reasoning.[206]

Gerson reaffirms that Christine de Pizan won her argument against Pierre Col because of the "sharpness of her reasoning," while Col behaved irrationally by evasion and chaotic reasoning.

Jean Gerson concluded his short letter with the observation that even though he had read all of the sources of *Le Roman de la rose,* including the writings of Juvenal, Ovid, Boethius, Abelard, and Heloise, he would rather recommend authors such as Bonaventure or Augustine. Taking his criticism of Col and the other humanists supporting the text of Jean de Meun, Gerson also preached a public sermon on Christmas Eve 1402 against *Le Roman de la rose*. In this sermon he suggested that the work contained heresy, and that it ought to be burned.[207]

In December of the same year, Jean de Montreuil, who had started the origi-

---

205. Pierre Col to Christine de Pizan, *La Querelle de la rose: Letters and Documents,* #XIX, 161.
206. Jean Gerson to Pierre Col, *La Querelle de la rose: Letters and Documents,* #XV, 148.
207. Jean Gerson, *La Querelle de la rose: Letters and Documents,* #XX, 162. "The *Roman de la Rose* says that the sin by which a woman's body is sullied is the least of sins. This! the cause of her abandoning herself to all the other evils! Beware of those who steer women into error in order to abuse them and make heretics of them. Repent!"

nal dialogue by his public support of Jean de Meun's text, wrote a letter about Christine de Pizan to an unidentified addressee. In this letter he openly named and attacked Christine de Pizan by drawing an analogy between her critique of *Le Roman de la rose* and an ancient critique of Aristotle's disciple, Theophrastus, who had written a satire about women:

> O famous man, you will see and hear, in one of my writings in the vernacular, how unfairly, unjustly, and arrogantly some people have accused and attacked the most excellent Master Jean de Meun. I speak especially of a certain woman named Christine, who has just recently published her writings, and who, within feminine limitations, is not, admittedly, lacking in intelligence, but who, nevertheless, sounds to me like "Leontium the Greek whore," as Cicero says, "who dared to criticize the great philosopher Theophrastus."[208]

This demeaning comparison of Christine de Pizan with Cicero's description of Leontium is not answered in the letters of the *Querelle,* as Christine had made her decision to withdraw from the public debate. However, she will reinterpret more positively the significance of Leontium in *Le Livre de la cité des dames:* "I could tell you a great deal about women of great learning. Leontium was a Greek woman and also such a great philosopher that she dared, **for impartial and serious reasons,** to correct and attack the philosopher Theophrastus, who was quite famous in her time."[209] Again we see Christine calling her readers to the virtue of exercising the reason well, even when she had been attacked. Leontium and Christine criticized what they thought were false positions and arguments, with the passion of daring, and for the impartial and serious reasons of seeking to defend the truth.

Jean de Montreuil repeated the position held previously by Col, i.e., that a difference in opinion about the true nature of satire is the fundamental source of disagreement among the participants in the *Querelle.* He argues that de Meun, as a satirist, is permitted to say many things that would not be allowed another kind of writer. While Christine de Pizan does not enter the dialogue again, her previous position on this point was well stated, namely that when a particular position is stated by most or all of the characters, then it must be presumed to be held by the author of the work as well.

Finally, also in December 1402, Jean de Montreuil sent a letter in French to Gontier Col, in which he reaffirmed his admiration of *Le Roman de la rose.* In this letter, the supporter of the work gave some evidence of his fear of being condemned for heresy because of his love of the poetical work of Jean de Meun. After again trying to justify to others the work as a literary text in which different characters present a variety of opinions, he added that "[i]mmediately they break in and interrupt

---

208. Jean de Montreuil to (possibly) Laurent de Premierfait, *La Querelle de la rose: Letters and Documents,* #XVI, 153. The letter is in Latin and the reference is to Cicero's *De natura deorum,* I.93.

209. Christine de Pizan, *The Book of the City of Ladies,* I.30.3, 68 (emphasis mine). See also Schibanoff, "Taking the Gold." Schibanoff notes that in this transformation of Leontium, Christine is also transforming Boccaccio, whose text she used as a source, to transform herself from a weak to a strong woman reader of texts written by men (pp. 99-100).

my words, so that I scarcely dare to move my lips, lest they threaten me with the disgrace of anathema and firmly judge me worthy of death."[210] So it would appear that the combined efforts of Christine de Pizan and Jean Gerson, as the Chancellor of the University of Paris, had actually effected a change in the climate of public discussion about *Le Roman de la rose*. Poets were to be held responsible for the moral content and tone of their works. While the reasons for considering Jean de Meun's text as potentially heretical focused more on the broader issues of models of virtue and vice, indirectly they included reference to the concept of woman and the place of deception in intergender sexual relations.

Summary of the Arguments in *Querelle de la rose*

The variety and number of arguments to counter traditional gender polarity that Christine introduces in the public debate about *Le Roman de la rose* are extraordinary. As will be demonstrated in the next part of this chapter, the remaining arguments that Christine de Pizan develops in later works develop in greater detail the argument forms already articulated in this public quarrel. Christine de Pizan seeks continually to draw her readers into a more accurate rational understanding of woman's identity and condition. In her creation of the Order of the Rose, she stated that she hoped to encounter reasonable men rather than slanderers and to persuade the latter to reconsider their faulty opinions in the light of philosophical demonstrations.

Because Christine de Pizan's participation in the public debate about women is based so extensively on philosophical arguments, it will be helpful to summarize some of the argument forms that she uses. Even though her arguments may be repeated in different works, in the table on pages 606-9 each instance of her basic argument will be summarized with its intended target and source.

It is not really possible to give a precise individuation of types, but this summary does reveal certain preferred patterns of argument Christine uses to defend her positions. As described below, some of her arguments refer to the internal content of a book, some to the possible remote external effects of a book, some to the prejudices of the author derived from external past events, some to the external prejudices of society at large, and some to the internal technical structure of real argument types.[211]

Most of the arguments below were developed in the specific context of intergender dialogue. As will be seen, many of these same arguments will appear again, but with greater elaboration in subsequent texts. Christine de Pizan will also extend the range of the historical sources she draws upon for access to traditional gender polarity themes as well as to counterarguments and counterexamples that she could use to defend her own views about woman's identity. In effect, she becomes

---

210. Jean de Montreuil to (possibly) Gontier Col, *La Querelle de la rose: Letters and Documents*, #XXI, 166.

211. I am very grateful to Beata Gallay for her help and suggestions about how to sort through these different argument forms in Christine de Pizan's works.

	Structure of Christine's Arguments about *Le Roman de la rose*		
Kind of Argument	**Summary of Argument**	**Target of Argument**	**Source**
Fallacy of gener-alization	1. It is a fallacy to go from the premise that some women are lust-ful to the conclusion that all women are lustful.	Ovid	*Epistre au dieu d'amours*
Modus tollens (ne-gating the conse-quent)	2. If women are so weak, fickle, or unpredictable, then why do men describe such elaborate means to conquer them?	Jean de Meun	*Epistre au dieu d'amours*
"	3. If women are perverse, then why do men pursue them and not avoid them?	Jean de Meun	Letter to Jean de Montreuil
Appeal to author-ity	4. Eve did not deceive Adam out of natural weakness or out of rational calculation, for she was created in the image of God out of more re-fined matter than man, and she acted sincerely and truthfully.	theolo-gians	*Epistre au dieu d'amours*
Use of counter-example to a uni-versal claim	5. For purposes of sexual seduc-tion, women do not deceive men, but men deceive women.	Ovid	Letter to Jean de Montreuil
"	6. Provides examples of virtuous women from her own experience to counter the claim that women are unvirtuous.	Jean de Meun	Letter to Jean de Montreuil
"	7. Provides historical literary exam-ples of virtuous women to counter the claim that women are unvirtu-ous.	Jean de Meun	Letter to Jean de Montreuil
"	8. Argues that if a man claims that women are unvirtuous, it proves only that he did not meet any vir-tuous women.	Jean de Meun	Letter to Jean de Montreuil

Structure of Christine's Arguments about *Le Roman de la rose* (cont.)			
Kind of Argument	Summary of Argument	Target of Argument	Source
"	9. Argues that women have adequate faculties and a well-ordered identity by appealing to historical examples of virtuous women.	Pierre Col	Letter to Pierre Col
"	10. Argues that only men slander women; women authors would not reach the same conclusions about women.	satirists in general	*Epistre au dieu d'amours*
"	11. Reflects on the possible bias of her own perspective as a woman, but provides reasons for distinguishing the truth from the false.	herself	Letter to Jean de Montreuil
"	12. Counters one example in which a book brought about a conversion to a moral life in a male reader by providing another example in which the same book was used by a man for the immoral purpose of beating his wife.	Jean de Meun	Second Letter to Pierre Col
Argues for conclusions of reasonable demonstration	13. Argues that another woman ought to accept her arguments not through gender solidarity but because they are reasonable.	herself	Letter to Isabeau, Queen of France
"	14. Argues that it is not one's academic credentials, but one's reasons (arguments) that should be used for praise or blame.	Pierre Col	First Letter to Pierre Col
"	15. Argues against the claim that she is a "woman impassioned because of the inadequacy of her faculties" by appealing to her reasons (arguments) against it.	Pierre Col	First Letter to Pierre Col

Structure of Christine's Arguments about *Le Roman de la rose* (cont.)			
Kind of Argument	**Summary of Argument**	**Target of Argument**	**Source**
Argument by clarification	16. Distinguishes a direct from an indirect cause of deception, in claiming that women do not deceive men, but men deceive themselves on the occasion of relating to a woman through the free exercise of their own wills.	Jean de Meun	Second Letter to Pierre Col
"	17. Argues that an author who quotes previous satirical authors against women is still responsible for the views he quotes; and if he augments the previous arguments, he is even more responsible.	Jean de Meun	Second Letter to Pierre Col
"	18. Argues against an analogical description of women as like animals to be trapped, and for the claim that women are more like men's mothers, sisters, daughters, and wives to be defended and protected.	Ovid	Second Letter to Pierre Col
Argument about relation of whole and parts	19. Argues that while a single literary character who expresses derogatory views about women may not be identified with an author's own views, when all the characters in a literary work devalue women, one can conclude that the author holds the same views.	Jean de Meun	Second Letter to Pierre Col
"	20. Argues that the whole structure of a book which in an orderly way works towards an ending that devalues women by deceit and seduction gives more evidence about the author's views than does any single character in the book.	Jean de Meun	Second Letter to Pierre Col

Structure of Christine's Arguments about *Le Roman de la rose* (cont.)			
Kind of Argument	Summary of Argument	Target of Argument	Source
Argument about relation of cause to remote effect	21. Argues that a book which contains many immoral passages that reduce woman to a thing (Rose) to be taken by a man, can have a destructive effect on the reader of undermining the dignity of married love.	Jean de Meun	First Letter to Pierre Col
"	22. Argues that a book which describes evil in great detail does not help the reader to defend against evil, but rather tends to praise evil and to encourage the reader to practice it.	Jean de Meun	Second Letter to Pierre Col

more and more educated about the philosophy of sex and gender as she continues to study, think, and write about this topic.

It is interesting to note that in a self-reflective dialogue included in her *L'Avision-Christine,* written in 1405, just three years after the conclusion of the *Querelle,* Christine actually considers the quality of arguments in the public debate. She refers again to a fundamental belief that opinion is the proper starting point for dialogue, but she reiterates that opinion must be tested by reason and experience before it can be accepted as containing true judgments. In the following passage, Christine discusses her previous work with Lady Opinion, the great shadow that "floated around" the University of Paris giving advice:

[Lady Opinion]: Was I not the one responsible for the controversy between you and the clerks — disciples of Jean de Meun as they call themselves — concerning the compilation of the *Romance of the Rose,* which you wrote each other about from opposite positions, each maintaining his or her arguments, just as it appears in the small book that was made about it? . . .

[Christine]: Lady, since the first invention of human deeds — good or bad, crude or subtle — comes from you, as you have said, according to the inclination of the mind, please assure me if I have erred in the matters you engendered within me, things which, through study and such learning and understanding as I possess, are expressed to the best of my ability in my volumes and compilations. . . .

[Lady Opinion]: Dear Friend, be at peace, for I tell you no . . . there is no fault in your works, even though because of me, many people variously argue about them. For some say that students or monks forged them for you and that they could not come from the judgment of a woman. But those who say this are ignorant, for they do not know the written accounts that mention so many valiant and educated women of the past — wiser than you — . . .

. . . I advise you then to continue your work, for it is valid, and do not suspect yourself of failing because of me. When I am based on law, reason, and true judgment in you, you will not err in the foundations of your work in the matters which seem most truthful, for all the various judgments [that come], some from me and others basely from Envy. . . . When Envy directs me, I am dangerous.

[Christine]: . . . because of man's ignorance the world is governed more by you [Lady Opinion] than by great learning.[212]

In this remarkable passage, Christine de Pizan not only raises the point that others think her letters in the *Querelle de la rose* could not have been written by a woman because of their quality of judgment, but she authors a further mission for herself to continue the work she has started. In this way, she answers accusations once again with the appeal to reason, and in this case it is Lady Opinion herself who validates Christine de Pizan's method when she says that when argument is based on law, reason, and true judgment, then it will lead to truth. Lady Opinion takes her on the tour of the great labyrinth of corridors and libraries to lead her to the treasures of knowledge contained in the books of learning to begin her mandate to continue her work.

CHRISTINE DE PIZAN'S *LIVRE DE LA CITÉ DES DAMES*

Christine's goals in *Le Livre de la cité des dames (The Book of the City of Ladies)*, written in 1405,[213] are to confront the bias about women in its many different forms and to present well-reasoned arguments for what she believed was the truth about woman's identity. Here, Christine indirectly continued the intergender dialogue with other historical authors, rather than with those men who were her contemporaries. The Paris Master who illustrated the manuscript depicted Christine throughout in a royal blue dress and white peaked head covering. In the famous illustration on page 611 she is seen writing with her little dog at her feet.

As mentioned in the introduction to Christine's relation with previous religious authors, she demonstrates in *Le Livre de la cité des dames* a very sophisticated ability to use analogical thinking in its horizontal, vertical, and transcendental

212. *Christine's Vision,* II.21, 86; II.22, 86-87, 88. I have changed the style of the quoted passage to draw out the nature of the dialogue.

213. This text, entitled in French *Le Livre de la cité des dames,* was extremely popular in manuscript form. There are still twenty-seven different manuscripts in existence. See McLeod, *The Order of the Rose,* p. 133. This text was first translated into English in 1521 as *The Boke of the Cyte of Ladyes.* For a discussion of the historical context and significance of this translation see Constance Jordan, *Renaissance Feminism: Literary Texts and Political Models* (Ithaca and London: Cornell University Press, 1990), pp. 105-16.

Christine de Pizan Writing *Le Livre de la cité des dames*

forms. The entire text on the construction of a city of ladies is a sustained analogy that operates simultaneously on three different levels. The first level is the literal building of a city with stones, mortar, and other construction materials. Christine refers to her pen as the mortar that holds together the stones. The next level, drawing out a vertical analogy, is the literary construction of the text about the city, and here historical female personages are used as the "stones" out of which the city is constructed. This second level is actually a "reconstruction" of history.[214] The third level, drawing out a transcendental analogy, is spiritual. *Le Livre de la cité des dames* is imbued with Christian meaning: the book begins with a prayer, the three female personifications are called "daughters of God," the Queen of the city is the Blessed Virgin Mary, Mother of God, and the virtuous women who inhabit the towers include many Christians who gave their lives for their Christian faith. There is a constant flux between past and present, time and eternity, in the cast of characters who come to inhabit the city in union with one another and with God.

It is in the second, or middle level, of the analogy that Christine uses philosophical arguments against satirists and gender polarity theorists who had for centuries devalued women. Christine is aware that she is the first person to write an extensive treatise against such arguments, and she organizes her text very carefully so that it addresses all the major aspects of the concept of woman that have so far been elaborated by previous thinkers.[215] The analogical structure of a walled city itself parodies the castle in *Le Roman de la rose*. Christine's development completely inverts the model of Jean de Meun, for instead of having a passive Rose waiting to be plucked at the center of the city, she presents a city full of actively virtuous women who have earned their way to a new nobility by the quality of their lives. At the center of this new city is Mary, Mother of God, often represented as the mystical rose or by white, red, and gold roses in the prayer of the rosary, which had been made popular by St. Dominic and the Dominican Order. As will be seen, the women in Christine de Pizan's city are not characterized as passive in any way; they possess full self-knowledge and self-governance, and they perform virtuous (frequently public) action. They are citizens participating in the just distribution of the goods of all honors and responsibilities.

While Christine de Pizan's direct argument is with the specific satirists she mentions, her indirect argument refers to all members of the following categories

---

214. See Sylvia Huot, "Seduction and Sublimation," for a comparison of the two different ways of generation in *The Rose* and *The City*. "In Jean de Meun's treatment, the central metaphor of generation informs a poetics of desire, a quest for possession and consummation. Christine's feminized version subordinates the role of desire and informs a movement leading not to possession but to production. This recasting of the creative act suggests a shift of focus from the surface artifice of the text, to its underlying message. It is not a sensual engagement with the text that is at issue in Christine's model of reading, but rather the subsequent fruition engendered in the mind of the reader" (p. 367).

215. For one example of classification of traditional arguments against woman, see Glenda McLeod/Katharina Wilson, "A Clerk in Name Only — A Clerk in All But Name: The Misogamous Tradition and 'La Cité des Dames,'" in *The City of Scholars: New Approaches to Christine de Pizan*, ed. Margarete Zimmermann and Dina De Rentiis, pp. 67-76. The authors identify three different kinds: ascetic misogamy (Saint Jerome), philosophic misogamy (Theophrastus), and general, comic, or ironic misogamy (Juvenal, *Quinze joies*, Mathéolus), pp. 68-69.

of men who supported gender polarity principles: "learned men," "many different men," "all men," and "all philosophers and poets." Christine de Pizan's constructed dialogue about sex and gender identity, in the context of an imaginary female community of discourse, sketches significant beginnings for a genuine intergender dialogue about gender. In fact, it is the first example of such an extensive imaginary dialogue about gender in Western thought. While other humanists such as Pietro Bembo (1470-1547), Baldasar Castiglione (1478-1529), and Lucrezia Marinelli (1571-1653) aimed their arguments about gender identity more directly at Aristotle's particular roots of gender polarity, Christine de Pizan was the first to offer extensive critiques of the branches of gender polarity as they spread out in more popular satirical and poetic literature.

The particular approach that will be taken in this critical analysis of Christine's de Pizan's book on the city of ladies is to elaborate in a step-by-step process some of the arguments she offers about women's identity. Other scholars have analyzed her innovative use of sources for this text and the way she uses language to constitute and reconstitute herself as an author.[216] What I hope to add is a demonstration that Christine de Pizan used here, as she did previously in her participation in the *Querelle de la rose,* several different forms of philosophical argument to prove her theses about women's identity. To my knowledge she is not only the first woman to do so, but also the first person to develop such extensive arguments against previous gender polarity views about women. As will be seen, Christine used Aristotelian-based rhetoric, dialectic, and demonstration to disprove gender polarity principles, many of which have their root and support in Aristotelian biology, metaphysics, ethics, and politics. At the end of this section particular argument forms will be summarized. Then, at the end of the chapter, a summary chart of Christine de Pizan's counterarguments to gender polarity will be provided.

Christine de Pizan may have drawn upon two different sources in the history of philosophy for the idea to construct an ideal city as a model for her contemporaries: Aristotle's *Politics* and Augustine's *City of God.* Both of these important texts had been translated into French by King Charles V's far-reaching commission, and it is very likely that Christine had easy access to their arguments. The relevant aspects of each of these two sources will now be briefly described.

Aristotle claims at the beginning of Book I of the *Politics* that the city is the most important kind of community:

> Clearly, then, while all communities aim at some good, the community that aims most of all at the good — at the good that most of all controls all the other goods — is the one that most of all controls and includes the others; and this is the one called the city, the political community.[217]

Since human beings have a natural desire to share the goods of human life, they

216. See especially Maureen Quilligan, *The Allegory of Female Authority: Christine de Pizan's Cité des Dames* (Ithaca and London: Cornell University Press, 1991).

217. Aristotle, *Politics,* in *Aristotle Selections* (Indianapolis/Cambridge: Hackett Publishing Co., 1995), 1252a, 450.

gather together in cities, where they can mutually work towards living a good life. Different individuals fulfill different functions for the good of the whole. Education becomes a central obligation of the city, so that it can pass beyond the simple task of supporting the preservation of its members. There is a mixed kind of rule through which the full flowering of virtue of each person in the city is the ultimate goal. Christine de Pizan's *Livre de la cité des dames* is definitely situated within this Aristotelian understanding of the nature of the city.

Christine's city is a celestial city. This notion participates in Augustine's division of people into two kinds of cities: a city of God and a city of man. Augustine, in his *City of God,* describes the differentiation of citizens as due to the conflict between spirit and flesh. In Christine de Pizan's text, women are identified as members of a city of the spirit. Each woman becomes a generic 'she' that represents all human beings who aspire for a life directed towards wisdom and virtue.[218]

Although the female members of the city serve a generic function, they also retain their distinct identity as women. This is an important point to consider, for it means that Christine de Pizan is not proposing a unisex model of humanity, nor is she proposing a reverse gender polarity model. In other words, in choosing to populate her city only with women, Christine de Pizan is neither arguing that there is no significant difference between women and men, nor that women are better than men.[219] Instead, she is attempting to prove that women, as well as men, are capable of the highest degree of wisdom and of virtue, and that each one, *qua woman,* can provide a good model for both women and men who desire to live more virtuous lives.

Christine de Pizan is developing a new foundation for the complementarity of genders, for her entire text is written in dialogue with texts authored by men, yet she is reinterpreting them for an audience of both women and men. Dante's *Divine Comedy* provides not only a further model for the three-part, hierarchical structure of the celestial city, but also some particular background for some of its inhabitants. Boccaccio's *Concerning Famous Women* provides the greatest number of models for the city's inhabitants, Petrarch's *Concerning Famous Men* and Plutarch's *Lives of Famous Men* contribute their part as well, and throughout the book satirists' texts

218. Earl Jeffrey Richards argues, in "Rejecting Essentialism," that Christine follows Augustine to a unisex model in the *City of Ladies.* Richards claims that Augustine states that all human differences are transcended in the celestial city. However, the passages he cites do not support this conclusion. Augustine refers to transcending manners, laws, and institutions, but we know from his other works that Augustine believes that sex and gender identity continue in heaven, and that they are part of the perfection of woman and man, and not an imperfection to be overcome. See Allen, *The Concept of Woman: The Aristotelian Revolution,* pp. 219-22.

219. Again I would differ with Earl Jeffrey Richard's interpretation of Christine de Pizan's purpose here. He suggests as before that she is proposing a unisex model, and he offers as support her statement that a higher place in the city is given to the person with greater virtue, and not according to the sex. See Richards, "Rejecting Essentialism," p. 125. However, I would argue that her reference is to Aristotle's natural and ethical principles of gender polarity rather than to the irrelevance of sex differentiation. Sex and gender differentiation do have an important place in her schema, but they are not the determining factor in the level of virtue in a particular person. In other words, the male is not naturally superior to the female in the range of possible virtues.

and other gender polarity texts provide a foil against which the city of ladies is constructed to promote the common good.

The construction of *Le Livre de la cité des dames* is directed by three imaginary female personifications: the daughters of God: Lady Reason, Lady Rectitude, and Lady Justice.[220] Christine might have used Boethius, Vincent of Beauvais, and Philippe de Mézières as sources for these figures.[221] Even so, Christine de Pizan also developed the functions of these female personifications in creative new ways: i.e., they provide numerous arguments to prove that derogatory concepts of women are false, they identify women who may serve as models of virtue and wisdom, and they construct a city in which women offer many different contributions to the common good. Christine used the same three figures in *L'Avision-Christine,* where Lady Reason held up the mirror of self-knowledge, Lady Rectitude was depicted as ill with a scale and a measuring cup tipped over, and Lady Justice fully armed lay dishonorably asleep on the ground.[222] While in *L'Avision-Christine* Lady Reason, Lady Rectitude, and Lady Justice were weak and limited, in *Le Livre de la cité des dames* they are the active formative figures of the entire work. In addition, the three Ladies also reappear in *Le Trésor de la cité des dames: Le Livre des trois vertus,* where they continue to act in full moral force, chiding a depleted Christine de Pizan to get back to the work of writing.[223]

First Dialogue with Lady Justice

The entire *Livre de la cité des dames,* as with so many of her other texts, is situated in the overall context of searching for true justice. As mentioned previously, the work of building the city of ladies is done through the guidance of three female personifications, Lady Reason, Lady Rectitude, and Lady Justice. The most central of the three is Lady Justice, who states that all the other virtues are based on her. At the beginning of the text she identifies herself: "My duty is to judge, to decide, and to dispense according to each man's just deserts."[224] After identifying herself as one

---

220. See Judith L. Kellogg, "Christine de Pizan and Boccaccio: Rewriting Classical Mythic Tradition," in *Comparative Literature East and West: Traditions and Trends,* ed. Cornelia N. Moore and Raymond A. Moody (Honolulu: University of Hawaii Press, 1989), pp. 124-31. She delineates the functions of the three figures as follows: "Reason presents the text, the literal story, describing women as they were originally created by Nature, who herself is an active partner of the other allegorical ladies. . . . Rectitude glosses women morally, and finds them superbly able to make proper ethical choices. . . . Justice reveals women's potential for salvation and blessedness through their fierce and loving essential piety," p. 129.

221. Willard, *Christine de Pizan: Her Life and Works.* Willard particularly mentions the appearance of Lady Rectitude in Philippe de Mézière's *Songe du vieil pèlerin (The Dream of the Old Pilgrim),* which had been written in 1397, p. 137.

222. She also introduces other negative female personifications such as Lady Lust and Dame Fraud. See *Christine's Vision,* I.15-16, 23-25.

223. Christine de Pisan, *The Treasure of the City of Ladies, or, The Book of the Three Virtues* (Harmondsworth: Penguin Books, 1985), pp. 31-32.

224. Christine de Pizan, *The City of Ladies,* I.6.1, 14.

with God, Lady Justice then offers a further description of her functions in building the city:

> I teach men and women of sound mind who want to believe in me to chastise, know, and correct themselves, and to do to others what they wish to have done to themselves, to distribute wealth without favor, to speak the truth, to flee and hate lies, to reject all viciousness.[225]

Justice involves having particular knowledge, being free from error, and performing good actions, particularly in the distribution of all levels of goods in the society.

In addition, Christine de Pizan argues, as did Thomas Aquinas, that reason, rectitude, and justice have an intricate connection with each other.[226] Lady Justice continues her speech as follows:

> . . . I have a special place among the Virtues, for they are all based on me. And of the three noble ladies whom you see here, we are as one and the same, we could not exist without one another; and what the first disposes, the second orders and initiates, and then I, the third, finish and terminate it.[227]

To repeat the key argument: reason disposes, rectitude orders and initiates, and justice finishes and terminates. Although Thomas Aquinas uses rectitude to characterize both rightly ordered reason and rightly ordered will, Christine de Pizan appears to associate rectitude mostly with the right ordering of the will and particular choices of the will. She suggests by her personifications that reason begins the process by disposing the mind towards truth, rectitude continues the process by ordering the will towards the truth previously identified and initiating particular acts of will in accord with reason's conclusions, and justice completes the process by providing the proper end and fulfillment or actualization.

The question that follows then is: What is it that reason, rectitude, and justice are working together on here? The answer is found in the conclusion of the construction of the city of ladies. Christine de Pizan carefully presents both the obstacles that inhibit and the achievements that contribute to the destiny of human beings for union with one another and with God. Thus, in this unfolding of the full meaning of justice she goes beyond the simple redressing of wrongs against women that characterized her earlier appeals to divine justice, and now sets forth a concept of justice as right ordering of a whole society based on the dignity of the human person and ruled by divine law. The women in her city represent all persons of virtue, and they dwell in harmony with one another and with God. Lady Justice invites Mary to serve as Queen of this just city. Her conclusion accords with Thomas Aquinas's description of justice in question 58 (II-II) from the *Summa Theologica*:

---

225. Christine de Pizan, *The City of Ladies,* I.6.1, 14.
226. St. Thomas Aquinas, *Summa Theologica* (Westminster, Md.: Christian Classics, 1981), II-II, Q. 58.
227. Christine de Pizan, *The City of Ladies,* I.6.1, 14.

And if anyone would reduce it to the proper form of a definition, he might say that *justice is a habit whereby a man renders to each one his due by a constant and perpetual will* . . . [and reply obj. 6] Just as love of God includes love of our neighbor, . . . so too the service of God includes rendering to each one his due.[228]

Le Livre de la cité des dames is based upon an extended vertical analogy that structures the entire text. The sense base for the analogy is divided into three stages of construction of a city. In the first stage, led by Lady Reason Christine excavates the ground and builds the foundations and exterior walls; in the second stage, led by Lady Rectitude she builds the walls of the palaces and houses inside the exterior walls, and invites some of the residents into the city; and in the third stage, led by Lady Justice she builds the roofs and towers, and invites the rest of the residents and the Queen into the city. Following the model suggested in Aristotle's *Politics,* the different residents of the city have different functions that all contribute to the common good and to the good of each person individually, and there is a mixed rule of the city, which includes both a monarch and virtuous citizens. Also, following the early humanist tradition, all the residents of the city are characterized by their nobility, which consists, not in blood or inheritance, but by degree of virtue.

Christine de Pizan begins *Le Livre de la cité des dames* with an interior dialogue about the satirist Mathéolus's ethical principle of gender polarity. This principle holds that women's virtues are less good than men's virtues, and that women's vices are worse than men's vices. In her introductory reflection, exaggerated claims of the satirical text *Le Livre de Mathéolus* initiate Christine's thinking of "lies" about women and the "lack of integrity" these judgments contained.[229] In her opinion, the satirical book echoed similar gender polarity arguments in other works by philosophers, poets, and orators:

> But just the sight of this book, even though it was of no authority, made me wonder how it happened that so many different men — and learned men among them — have been and are so inclined to express both in speaking and in their treatises and writings so many wicked insults about women and their behavior. Not only one or two and not even just this Mathéolus (for this book had a bad name anyway and was intended as a satire) but, more generally, judging from the treatises of all philosophers and poets and from all the orators — it would take too long to mention their names — it seems that they all speak from one and the same mouth. They all concur in one conclusion: that the behavior of women is inclined to and full of every vice.[230]

---

228. Thomas Aquinas, *Summa Theologica,* II-II, Q. 58 and Reply Obj. 6.

229. Christine de Pizan, *The City of Ladies,* 1.1, 3. There is some debate among scholars concerning whether Christine's source for *Mathéolus* was the text itself as translated by Jean LeFèvre, or a second text entitled *Le Livre de Leesce,* which was an answer to *Mathéolus* by LeFèvre. For different sides of the controversy see Karen Pratt, "Analogy or Logic: Authority or Experience? Rhetorical Strategies for and Against Women," in *Literary Aspects of Courtly Culture,* ed. Donald Maddox and Sara Sturm-Maddox (Cambridge: D. S. Brewer, 1992), pp. 57-66.

230. Christine de Pizan, *The City of Ladies,* 1.1, 3-4.

After stating the difficulty as a premise of her argument, Christine de Pizan then sets out the basic steps of her argument, which ultimately establishes grounds for a *reductio ad absurdum* rejection of the above premise. By using the *reductio ad absurdum* form, she has to prove that the acceptance of the main premise in the argument leads to such absurd conclusions that it must not be true.

The argument is divided into three phases. In the first phase, Christine considers the traditional form of argument, the introduction of a counterexample to defeat a universal generalization:

1. Mathéolus, all learned men, philosophers, poets, and scholars claim that "Woman is inclined to and full of every vice."
2. An appeal to the evidence of her own character and conduct as a woman, and to the character and conduct of other women she knows, provides contrary evidence to the above generalization. Therefore, the claim in premise 1 that "Woman is inclined to and full of every vice" is false.
3. However, if premise 1 is false, then all the famous learned men, philosophers, poets, and scholars, who possess such a great and deep understanding, and who have all written chapters or sections of their work supporting the premise, would have spoken falsely about women.
4. It seems impossible that all these famous learned men could have spoken falsely.
5. Therefore, the contrary example in premise 2, which was provided by her own experience and intellect, must be false, and premise 1, that "Woman is inclined to and full of every vice," must be true.

At this point in her interior dialogue, Christine de Pizan uses the conclusion of this first argument as the first premise in a second argument. She considers what must follow as corollaries from the conclusion that woman is inclined to and full of every vice. Where does this inclination come from, especially if it is a universal characteristic of all women? How does it become part of the nature of woman if not put there by the creator of all nature, or God?

The steps of the second phase of Christine de Pizan's arguments in the introduction to her *Le Livre de la cité des dames* can now be summarized as follows:

6. Assume that the claim that "Woman is inclined to and full of every vice" is true.
7. Then women must be created as monstrosities of nature.
8. But all things in nature are good because they are created by God who is all good.
9. If God is perfectly good He cannot go wrong in anything.
10. But so many men judge, decide, and conclude that so many abominations abound in the female sex and that she has a nature inclined to and full of every vice.
11. And God also says that where two or three witnesses give testimony it must be true.

12. Thus the claims of these witnesses that woman is inclined to and full of every vice must be true.
13. And it must be true that God went wrong in creating woman.
14. And this is a *reductio ad absurdum* conclusion, that the good God created woman as a kind of being whose nature is inclined to and full of every vice.

This introductory argument of Christine de Pizan attempted to demonstrate that acceptance of the main premise as true, namely that woman is by nature full of every vice, leads to the absurd conclusion that God, who is all good, created a being whose nature is not good but evil.

In addition to appealing to the rational form of the argument, Christine also shares with her audience an emotional response as a woman to some of the premises of the argument itself. She notes her emotional response in words that harken to the Aristotelian tradition, namely that women are imperfect creatures: "As I was thinking this, a great unhappiness and sadness welled up in my heart, for I detested myself and the entire feminine sex, as though we were monstrosities in nature."[231] Then she shared her personal response in the form of a prayer: "Oh, God, how can this be? For unless I stray from my faith, I must never believe that your infinite wisdom and most perfect goodness ever created anything which was not good."[232]

Having brought the reader to the *reductio ad absurdum* conclusion that a good God must have created the not-good creature woman, Christine de Pizan moves into the third phase of her introductory argument. It is this third phase of the argument that sets up the context for the rest of her book on the city of ladies. Once again she begins by asserting, as the first premise, the conclusion of the previous argument:

15. The good God created woman as a kind of being whose nature is inclined to and filled with every vice.
16. And by implication the good God created man as a kind of being whose nature is inclined to perfection and virtue.
17. If 15 and 16 are true, then why was Christine not born as a man so that she could be perfect?
18. But she was born a woman, imperfect by nature.
19. Therefore, Christine is most unfortunate because God made her inhabit a female body in the world.

At this point, her argument ends with an open question to be resolved by *Le Livre de la cité des dames*. The book itself will be the refutation of the premises of this argument, for it will demonstrate that women have a nature that is inclined to perfection and virtue. Christine's question of why she was not born a man is one that she had posed in different ways in other works. It was couched in the terms of the natural principle of gender polarity, i.e., the natural perfection of man combined with the natural imperfection of woman. For example, in *The Mutation of*

---

231. Christine de Pizan, *The City of Ladies,* 1.1, 4-5.
232. Christine de Pizan, *The City of Ladies,* 1.1, 5.

Fortune, she describes: "How I, a woman, became a man/by a flick of Fortune's hand/How she changed my body's form/To the perfect masculine norm."[233] One critic argues that Christine takes on a derogatory devaluation of woman as a surrogate man.[234] Another suggests that she "presents herself as an essentially masculine being."[235] I would argue to the contrary, that Christine is not adopting a male identification in her writings. Instead, she is restating the gender polarity principles for the sake of establishing premises that can be refuted by argument. She restates the satirists' exaggerated claim that women are by nature inclined to and full of every evil, and she restates the academic natural principle of gender polarity that the female is an imperfect male.

Thus, it is important to realize that Christine's statements in her introductory first chapter of *Le Livre de la cité des dames* are simply setting the context for the main argument of her book. She will produce massive numbers of contrary witnesses and examples to overwhelm and overturn the testimony of the academic, poetic, and satirical authors she has previously cited. If Christine de Pizan can prove by counterexample that the claims of the authors are wrong, then she can refute the false premises of the argument by the testimony of her witnesses. In addition, she will demonstrate which premises are false in the argument that leads to the fallacious *reductio ad absurdum* conclusion — that a good God creates the not-good creatures women. So both by counterexample and logical argument, Christine will demonstrate that God made no error in creating women, and that women can be as good if not better than men if they work towards developing their character with human wisdom and virtue.

Dialogue with Lady Reason

Lady Reason begins by challenging Christine de Pizan about the conclusion she reached in the argument in the introduction, namely that she was most unfortunate to have been born a woman. A summary of Lady Reason's argument follows:

1. You have accepted the majority opinions of men about woman's identity, rather than your own experience and reason.
2. You need to do more thinking about this to get closer to the truth.
3. Since the greatest philosophers like Plato, Aristotle, and Augustine engage in

233. Christine de Pizan, "The Mutation of Fortune," *Writings,* III.143-44, 112.

234. See, for example, Kathleen Casey, "The Cheshire Cat: Reconstructing the Experience of Medieval Women," in *Liberating Women's History: Theoretical and Critical Essays,* ed. Berenice A. Carroll (Urbana/Chicago/London: University of Illinois Press, 1976), pp. 224-49. "A woman who actually, in true Renaissance mode, exerted an audacious will to challenge fate without scruple was dubbed a *virago,* literally, a surrogate male, as if an alternative were unthinkable" (p. 245).

235. See Lynne Huffer, "Christine de Pisan: Speaking Like a Woman/Speaking Like a Man," in *New Images of Medieval Women: Essays Toward a Cultural Anthropology,* ed. Edelgard E. Dubruck (Lewiston/Queenston: Edwin Mellen Press, 1989), pp. 61-71. Huffer argues that Christine also develops a feminine voice, but that the *City of Ladies* begins in this masculine voice.

debate about contrary opinions, not every opinion of a philosopher can be true.

4. Poets, perhaps including Mathéolus and Jean de Meun, the author of the *Rose,* sometimes have their characters say the opposite of what is true. For example, their claim that wives rule husbands is manifestly contrary to experience.

5. Therefore, reject their absurd claims, reject your superficial conclusions, "recover your senses," and think further for yourself.[236]

Just as in *The Consolation of Philosophy* Lady Philosophy woke up Boethius from his self-pity due to the unfortunate circumstances of his life and challenged him to think through the important questions he had posed, so Lady Reason attempts to wake up Christine from her self-pity at woman's situation and challenges her to think through the important questions she has posed.

Furthermore, in this dialogue in *Le Livre de la cité des dames,* Lady Reason situates Christine in the tradition of the philosophers, Plato, Aristotle, and Augustine, who are not afraid to enter into serious debate about different opinions in order to get closer to the truth. Thus Christine will now begin to analyze various conflicting opinions about woman's identity, in order to present her own synthesis of the proper understanding of woman. This move from the imaginary dialogue with the figure of Lady Reason to the consideration of examples of real women will occur frequently throughout the text, and it constantly serves as the main methodological tool for helping the conversion of her readers from bias to closer approximation of truth.

Lady Reason actually sees this activity as a main part of her role:

> Thus it is my duty to straighten out men and women when they go astray and to put them back on the right path. And when they stray, if they have enough understanding to see me, I come to them quietly in spirit and preach to them, showing them their error and how they have failed, I assign them the causes, and then I teach them what to do and what to avoid. And since I serve to demonstrate clearly and to show both in thought and deed to each man and woman his or her own special qualities and faults, you see me holding this shiny mirror . . . no one can look into this mirror, no matter what kind of creature, without achieving clear self-knowledge . . . thanks to this mirror, the essences, qualities, proportions, and measures of all things are known, nor can anything be done well without it.[237]

The mirror of self-knowledge uncovers error and demonstrates causes, essences, qualities, proportions, and measures. Like Boethius's Lady Philosophy, Christine's Lady Reason will lead the reader to a philosophical understanding through a dialogue about particular things. However, even more than this, she, with her sisters Lady Rectitude and Lady Justice, will console Christine and reward her for her

236. Christine de Pizan, *The City of Ladies,* I.2, 6-8.
237. Christine de Pizan, *The City of Ladies,* I.3, 9.

"great love of investigating the truth through long and continual study," will construct with her for all women "a refuge and defense against the various assailants" who have been at war with them, and will set these previously defenseless women free from "Pharaoh's hands" and lead them into a promised land, an eternal city constructed only for noble women of wisdom and virtue.[238]

If we consider for a moment the three key characteristics of wisdom and virtue that we have previously identified in the writings of women religious authors, we will see a certain similarity with the three key areas previously identified as self-knowledge, self-governance, and public action. Lady Reason focuses on self-knowledge and knowledge of causes, Lady Rectitude focuses on self-governance and the measure of right order in private and public action, and Lady Justice focuses on recompense for good or evil actions. The invitation from these three imaginary Ladies, to join with them to construct a city to protect and reward wise and virtuous women, is received by Christine as an invitation from God. This seems to harken again to her model in Augustine's *City of God;* this city is celestial, not earthly, and it will provide the proper measure for the earthly city. Christine responds to this divine initiative by recognizing the limited strength of her "weak feminine body," but she "happily accepts" the invitation, reflecting that "nothing is impossible for God."[239]

We can see, then, that even in this introductory phase of her work, Christine de Pizan has remarkably brought together in one project the four different communities of discourse that had been operating separately in her culture: the religious, satirical, academic, and humanist communities of discourse. They are all implicated in her project, which is situated in the struggle for justice and truth about woman and man. Her work will continue to integrate these four communities of discourse as it builds itself up stone by stone.

In the first stage of construction, Lady Reason and Christine excavate by digging the "field of letters" or historical texts written by men who attack women. The tool Christine uses is "the pick of cross-examination." Using this brilliant methodology of vertical analogy, Christine first excavates the ground, second, constructs the foundation, and third, builds the exterior walls. Lady Reason marks the place for the questions and then carries away the earth or provides the stones for the foundation and exterior walls by her answers to the questions. This method of question and answer resembles the scholastic method of debate by posing a question, and then introducing a *contra* and a *pro* answer to the question.

Bearing in mind that in the Aristotelian tradition wisdom is the science of causes, Christine sets up the dialogue by posing the first question to Lady Reason as follows:

1. [Christine]: What is the cause of the negativity of different authors against women? Is the cause nature, hatred, or some other source?

238. Christine de Pizan, *The City of Ladies,* I.3-4, 9-11.
239. Christine de Pizan, *The City of Ladies,* I.7, 15-16. In her acceptance, Christine paraphrases the response of the Virgin Mary to the Angel Gabriel at the Annunciation: "Command and I will obey, and may it be unto me according to your words." The Mother of God has a central place in this text, for she is at the beginning and the end of it, initiating the activity and confirming the results.

2. [Lady Reason]: The bond of love which God places between man and woman is the strongest bond in nature; therefore the cause is not nature.

   The causes are varied: For example, some men attack women from the good intention of protecting men from particular evil women, but they wrongly make a universal generalization from some evil women to all women in general.

3. [Christine]: If their intention is good, does the end justify the means?

4. [Lady Reason]: No. Ignorance is never an excuse. To attack all women for the behavior of some women is like attacking fire because someone gets burned.[240]

At this point Lady Reason reflects on Christine de Pizan's previous work as an author: ". . . and you yourself have touched on this point quite well elsewhere in your writings."[241] This likely refers to Christine's argument against the fallacy of hasty generalization made by Ovid and referred to in the *Querelle de la rose*.

Reason continues her observations by claiming that those who generalize from particular examples "formulate their arguments loosely." Their arguments exploit the rights of others, and incorrectly blame women, rather than the choices made by men, as the cause of evil. Here we also find a repeat of an earlier argument of Christine against Jean de Meun in the *Querelle de la rose*. Lady Reason then directs Christine to "throw these "black, dirty, uneven stones" away rather than use them in her construction.[242]

Lady Reason then introduces another set of answers to Christine de Pizan's original question about why different authors speak against women in their books. She offers seven further possible causes for men's attacks on women:

5.(A) Because of good intention, but with faulty reasoning

  (B) Because of a man's own vices

     e.g., Mathéolus, who was dissolute in his youth and then attacked women when he was old to make them less attractive to other men, and Ovid in *Ars amatoria* and *Remedia amoris,* who attacked women because of his own promiscuity.

  (C) Because of hatred of women

     e.g., Cecco d'Ascoli, who tried to get all men to hate and detest all women.

  (D) Because of a defect in some men's bodies

     e.g., Ovid again, who attacked women because of his exile, castration, and deformity, but also any man who avenges the pain of his own defect by attacking women who bring pleasure to others.

  (E) Because of jealousy

     e.g., the author of *De philosophia,* and others who attacked women out of jealousy of the greater understanding and greater nobility that some women have.

---

240. Christine de Pizan, *The City of Ladies,* I.8, 16-17.
241. Christine de Pizan, *The City of Ladies,* 1.8, 17.
242. Christine de Pizan, *The City of Ladies,* 1.8, 18.

(F) Because of some men's natural tendency to slander
     e.g., [Presumably Juvenal and] those men who slander everyone so that
     they slander women also.
(G) Because of some men's desires to show off their knowledge of other authors
     e.g., [Presumably Mathéolus and Jean de Meun], who quote the views of
     previous satirists who attack women.[243]

It is important to note that Christine is careful here not to presume that **all** men
have the same motive or reason for attacking women. There are a variety of causes
depending on the different circumstances and background of the male author as
well as the evil actions of some women. This fifth step in the argument can be summarized more clearly as follows:

> [Lady Reason]: Men are the cause of negative attacks on women through the
> following various causes:
> A. faulty reasoning
> B. their own vice
> C. hatred
> D. defect of their body
> E. jealousy
> F. tendency to slander
> G. desire to show off.

At this point Christine de Pizan shifts the focus from an analysis of the
causes to some of the **contents** of the attacks that male authors have lodged against
women. Following her symbolic building of a city, she has finished excavating the
grounds, and is moving towards constructing the foundations. Here Christine introduces into her dialogue with Lady Reason a popular text spuriously attributed to
both Aristotle and Albert the Great. Significantly, in comparing the text with what
she knows of Aristotle's philosophy, Christine (in the voice of Lady Reason) recognizes that it cannot be a genuine text of the philosopher. In addition, she also
makes an important distinction between false claims made in written texts and
those claims supported by a woman's own intelligence and experience as well as by
the deposit of faith:

> [Christine]: I know another small book in Latin, my Lady called the *Secreta
> mulierum, The Secrets of Women,* which discusses the constitution of their natural
> bodies and especially their great defects.

> [Lady Reason]: . . . Although some say that it was written by Aristotle, it is not be-
> lievable that such a philosopher should be charged with such contrived lies. For
> since women can clearly know with proof that certain things which he treats are

---

243. Christine de Pizan, *The City of Ladies,* I.8-9, 16-22. The examples for these causes are
given when stated, and put in [ ] when presumed.

not at all true, but pure fabrications, they can also conclude that the other details which he handles are outright lies. . . .

[Christine]: My Lady, I recall that among other things, after he discussed the impotence and weakness which cause the formation of a feminine body in the womb of the mother, he says that Nature is completely ashamed when she sees that she has formed such a body, as though it were something imperfect.

[Lady Reason]: But, sweet friend, don't you see the overweening madness, the irrational blindness which prompt such observations? Is Nature, the chambermaid of God, a greater mistress than her master, almighty God from whom comes such authority. . . . If the Supreme Craftsman was not ashamed to create and form the feminine body, would Nature have been ashamed? It is the height of folly to say this! . . . But some men are foolish enough to think, when they hear that God made man in His image, that this refers to the material body. This was not the case, for God had not yet taken a human body. The soul is meant, the intellectual spirit which lasts eternally just like the Deity. God created the soul and placed wholly similar souls, equally good and noble in the feminine and in the masculine bodies.[244]

The integration of the philosophical argument about the natural weakness of women's bodies with the theological argument about the equality of women's and men's souls is an important aspect of Christine de Pizan's comprehensive view of woman's identity. Reason and woman's experience are tested out with revelation and the deposit of faith.

As she completes this phase of her argument, Christine anticipates the later development of a humanist argument by Henry Cornelius Agrippa (1490-1536), namely that woman's material creation by God is superior, not inferior to that of man because while Adam was created from mud Eve was created from the more refined bone of man. However, while Agrippa used this theological reflection to argue for the natural superiority of woman over man, Christine de Pizan does not draw this reverse gender polarity conclusion from the same premise. Instead, she holds to the claim that it is the quality of the soul, not the quality of the body, that determines superiority of a woman or a man.

[Lady Reason]: Now, to turn to the question of the creation of the body, woman was made by the Supreme Craftsman. In what place was she created? In the Terrestrial Paradise. From what substance? Was it vile matter? No, it was the noblest substance which had ever been created: it was from the body of man that God made woman.

[Christine]: My lady, according to what I understand from you, woman is a most

---

244. Christine de Pizan, *The City of Ladies*, I.9, 22-23. Christine was correct in her judgment that it was not written by Aristotle. See Allen, *The Concept of Woman: The Aristotelian Revolution*, p. 455.

noble creature. But even so, Cicero says that a man should never serve any woman and that he who does so debases himself, for no man should ever serve anyone lower than him.

[Lady Reason]: The man or the woman in whom resides greater virtue is the higher; neither the loftiness nor the lowliness of a person lies in the body accord- ing to the sex, but in the perfection of conduct and virtues. And surely he is happy who serves the Virgin, who is above all the angels.[245]

The nobility of wisdom and virtue is a nobility of soul, not of body or inherited bloodlines. Given this criterion of nobility, Lady Reason concludes that Mary, the Virgin Mother of God, is the most noble human being, either man or woman, who has ever lived.

Next, Christine de Pizan offers a playful consideration of one of the ethical gender polarity principles, i.e., that a woman's virtue is silence, and its exaggerated inverted satirical form, i.e., that a woman can never keep silent. She considers the place of woman's speech in spreading the news of the resurrection. Mentioning an attack of some preachers that Jesus first appeared to women at the Resurrection be- cause women did not know how to keep quiet and would therefore spread the news of the Resurrection more rapidly, Lady Reason claims that it would be a contradic- tion to suggest that Christ would choose to reveal such a great perfection as the Resurrection to the world through a vice.[246] The dialogue supports the more rea- sonable claim that the faculty of speech is a divine gift for women, as well as men, and that they are expected to develop it virtuously in the public arena.

The text now turns to another major question which, after the activity of ex- cavating the old stones in the field of letters has been completed, helps to build the new foundation for the city of ladies. Christine's next question and response begin the process of introducing the figures of individual women who will serve as partic- ular stones for the walls of the new city:

[Christine]: Why are women not in the seats of legal counsel, pleading law cases in courts of justice, and handing down judgments? Is it because some men have argued that some woman has governed unwisely in the past?

[Lady Reason]: If these legal functions demand also the enforcement of law through force of arms, then men, who have greater physical strength, would be better at this than women and the tasks should be distinguished according to sex; but if it is a question of ability to learn and understand law, or of having a natural sense of politics and government, then women are as able as men to do these things.[247]

245. Christine de Pizan, *The City of Ladies*, I.9, 23-24.
246. The whole discussion of women's speech is filled with irony and humor, but reaches the conclusion that "God has demonstrated that He has truly placed language in women's mouths so that He might be thereby served" (Christine de Pizan, *The City of Ladies*, I.10, 28-30).
247. Christine de Pizan, *The City of Ladies*, I.11, 30-32. In the preliminary part of her answer

Christine's view that the only natural weakness in women is a lesser physical strength than man, and that this is not the main concern of law and government, is amply supported by the next several sections of Part I of the text. Here Lady Reason introduces counterexamples contemporary with Christine de Pizan, by describing in some detail several women who governed well. A large majority of her examples are drawn from Boccaccio's *Concerning Famous Women*.[248] Each of the women mentioned, with the justification of their virtuous qualities, becomes a further stone in the foundation of the city of ladies. The list of women includes the following 'foundation stones': (1) Nicaula, empress of Ethiopia, (2) Fredegund, Queen of France, (3) Queen Blanche, mother of Saint Louis, (4) Queen Jeanne, widow of King Charles IV; (5) the daughter of Queen Jeanne, (6) Queen Blanche, wife of King John, (7) the Duchess of Anjou, (8) wife of the second older brother of King Charles of France, (9) the Countess of La Marche, (10) and the many women, from upper, middle, and lower classes, who governed their dominions well during the absence of their husbands.[249] The virtues described in relation to these women include governing with prudence, wisdom, and wise counsel, the capacity for negotiation, and good judgment.

At this point Christine asks Lady Reason how to respond to the link between the Aristotelian natural principles and ethical principles of gender polarity, namely that the formation of a weak body in woman leads to weakness in her virtue or excellence:

> [Christine]: Is it true as men [in the Aristotelian tradition] say that the more imperfect a body, the lesser is its virtue?

> [Lady Reason]: On the contrary, Nature makes up the difference for weakness in body by a greater gift in another area. For example (ironically), Aristotle had a very ugly body, with physical deformities, of eyes and face, but Nature gave him a spectacularly retentive mind and great sense.

> In addition, the defect of weakness in women excuses women from committing horrible crimes that take place through the greater strength of men, and it protects women from the severe punishments of soul that follow such crimes in this world and the next.

> Further, there are many counterexamples of the thesis of women's natural weakness, that is, of women who do demonstrate great physical strength and boldness.[250]

Lady Reason then produces another long series of descriptions of women

---

Christine mentions Aristotle's spurious *Problemata*, which argues for the natural inferiority of women, and Aristotle's *Categoriae*.

248. See Kellogg, "Christine de Pizan and Boccaccio," for discussion of this source: "In fact, three fourths of her examples can be traced to his *Concerning Famous Women . . .*" (p. 125). In addition, Quilligan, in *The Allegory of Female Authority*, discusses extensively throughout her text Christine de Pizan's use of Boccaccio's particular examples of famous women.

249. Christine de Pizan, *The City of Ladies*, I.12-13, 32-36.

250. Christine de Pizan, *The City of Ladies*, I.14, 36-38.

who demonstrate virtues related to physical strength, courage, and wisdom in battle. These women serve as further foundation stones for the city of ladies:
(1) Semiramis, (2) Amazons, such as (a) Lampheto, (b) Marpasia, (c) Synoppe,
(d) Thamiris, (e) Orithyia, (f) Menalippe, (g) Hippolyta, (h) Penthesilea,
(3) Zenobia, Queen of Palmyrenes, (4) Artemisia, Queen of Caria, (5) Lilia,
(6) Fredegund, Queen of France, (7) Camilla, (8) Berenice, Queen of Cappadocia,
and (9) Cloelia.[251]

In the midst of these descriptions of public action of women, Lady Reason reaffirms that these same points have been previously made in two of Christine de
Pizan's other works: *Livre de la mutacion de fortune* and *Epistre d'Othéa*.[252] In making this linkage, she is creating a broader community of discourse between these
different texts. In addition, Christine frequently suggests that these are significant
acts of virtue that involve self-willed overcoming of natural "feminine fear"
through boldness, daring, political prudence, wise governance, strong discipline, or
brave taking up of arms. Through these arguments, Christine affirms her view of
the appropriate place for women in public activity, and even in discussing or participating in military action. Drawing upon a variety of historical sources, in 1410
Christine de Pizan also wrote an entire text on precise details of strategy in military
warfare both on land and on sea entitled *Le Livre des faits d'armes et de chevalerie.*
As noted previously, this latter text proved so popular that it was used on the battlefield by kings and soldiers, including one of Napoleon's commandants and even
the king of England.[253]

In *Le Livre de la cité des dames,* by the integration of examples from Scripture,
classical sources, and contemporary Christian history, Christine demonstrates how
well she practices the common methodology of early humanism: "[t]his interweaving of Hebrew, classical and Christian history was a hallmark of humanism. . . ."[254]
In one particular example, Christine borrowed from Boccaccio the story of
Zenobia which had emphasized her virtue of chastity. She then rewrote the story
emphasizing Zenobia's ability to govern well. Later Sir Thomas Elyot, following
Christine's example, developed the theme of Zenobia's philosophical wisdom.[255]

251. Christine de Pizan, *The City of Ladies,* 1.15-26, 38-62. For a contemporary controversy
about the inclusion of Semiramis (who committed incest with her son) as a foundation stone for the
city see Sheila Delany, "Mothers to Think Back Through," in *Medieval Texts and Contemporary
Readers,* pp. 177-200; Quilligan, *The Allegory of Female Authority,* pp. 69-85; and Christine M. Reno,
"Christine de Pizan: At Best a Contradictory Figure?" in *Politics, Gender, and Genre: The Political
Thought of Christine de Pizan,* ed. Margaret Brabant (Boulder/San Francisco/Oxford: Westview Press,
1992), pp. 171-91, esp. 185 note 2.

252. In *Le Livre de la mutacion de fortune* (1400-1403), Christine describes in Part VI the physical feats of the kingdom of women warriors or Amazons.

253. See Willard, *Christine de Pizan,* pp. 183-93 for a discussion of the sources and goals of this
work. For an extract of the text in English see also "The Book of the Deeds of Arms and of Chivalry," in
The Writings of Christine de Pizan, pp. 292-304.

254. Richards, *"Seulette à part," Dear Sister,* p. 163. For a detailed discussion of Christine's use of
sources see the entire text of Quilligan, *The Allegory of Female Authority: Christine de Pizan's Cité des
Dames.*

255. See Dennis J. O. Brien, "Warrior Queen: The Character of Zenobia According to
Giovanni Boccaccio, Christine de Pizan, and Sir Thomas Elyot," *Medieval Perspectives* 8 (1993): 53-68;

Christine's building of the city nearly always included a rebuilding of the sources she used by arrangement, content, and emphasis.

When the building of the foundation of the city was completed, the text moved to begin construction of the exterior walls. At this point Christine posed another set of fundamental questions to Lady Reason. In this context the role of formal education in developing women's minds is considered:

[Christine]: Do women have clever enough minds to develop the virtue of high understanding and learning of sciences (or theoretical wisdom)? Or are the men correct who maintain that women's minds are limited?

[Lady Reason]: The contrary of the men's opinion is true as many examples will demonstrate.

If daughters were taught the natural sciences at schools as sons are, they would learn and understand as thoroughly as sons the arts and sciences.

Further, women have more delicate bodies than men, but they have freer and sharper minds to whatever they apply themselves.

[Christine]: How can you explain why men believe that men know more than women do?

[Lady Reason]: Women do not exercise their minds and experience different things as reasonable creatures, because they stay at home and simply run the household.

[Christine]: If women's minds conceive and learn like men's why don't women learn more?

[Lady Reason]: The public does not require women to learn more, and their lack of performance of the mind means that they usually know less than men, and this habit of learning less makes their capacity for understanding less, just like men who live in the country and are not challenged to learn.

However, Nature does give women the same qualities of body and mind as the wisest and most learned men, and unless they fail to learn, they will possess great learning and understanding as the following examples will demonstrate.[256]

Thus Christine argues that women have as good or better natural competence as men when they apply themselves to learning, but their performance is generally poorer than men because they are not challenged or allowed to develop their skills through adequate education. While in the next chapter in this book various arguments about appropriate formal education for women will be considered, it is im-

---

and Valerie Wayne, "Zenobia in Medieval and Renaissance Literature," in *Ambiguous Realities: Women in the Middle Ages and Renaissance,* ed. Carole Levin and Jeanie Watson (Detroit: Wayne State University Press, 1987), pp. 48-65.

256. Christine de Pizan, *The City of Ladies,* I.27, 63-64.

portant to note that Christine de Pizan already anticipates some of the early humanist claims that women's weaker intellectual skill is due to poor education and not to a natural inability and that therefore women should be given better formal education.

At this point in *Le Livre de la cité des dames* Christine de Pizan introduces another series of descriptions of women who, in this case, have the virtue of theoretical wisdom, and who serve as building stones for the exterior walls of the city of ladies: (1) Cornificia, (2) Proba, (3) Sappho, (4) Leontium, (5) Manto, (6) Medea, and (7) Circe.[257] The virtues emphasized here include being a brilliant poet, teaching perfect philosophy, having beautiful minds, being devoted to study, knowing Virgil's poems by heart, masterfully arranging verses, being expert in several arts and sciences including Grammar, Logic, Rhetoric, Geometry, and Arithmetic, and knowing the powers of herbs and fire.

In the context of this discussion of women of learning, Christine de Pizan also appeals to two incidents concerning Ancient Greek philosophers. First, in an appeal to male authority she notes a legend that Plato, Aristotle's teacher, died with a book of Sappho's poems under his pillow. Second, in a rejection of male authority in order to elevate woman's own authority, she notes that Leontium "was such a great philosopher that she dared, **for impartial and serious reasons**, to correct and attack the philosopher Theophrastus," Aristotle's disciple who wrote a satire against women.[258] As we noted previously in this chapter, her positive description of Leontium is especially significant because Jean de Montreuil, a disputant in the *Querelle de la rose,* had referred to Christine in a derogatory manner as attacking him like Leontium who had dared to criticize the great philosopher Theophrastus.[259]

Not content to rest with examples of learned women, Christine then poses a more difficult question, which we summarize as: Have any women discovered any new arts or necessary sciences that have profited the world? The answer Lady Reason gives consists of examples that freely combine legend and fact: (1) Nicostrata, also called Carmentis, who discovered Roman law and invented the Latin alphabet and the science of grammar; (2) Minerva, also called Pallas, who invented a shorthand Greek script and certain arts of making wool, oil, armor, and wind instruments; (3) Ceres, who invented the tools for cultivation and the construction of cities; and (4) Isis, who invented law and a shorthand script for the Egyptians.[260] Christine, in translating and adapting the stories of these women from Boccaccio's Italian to French, wrongly believed that she was transmitting factual information about the contributions of actual women to Western history and civilization. Today, of course, we know that many of them are legends rather than actual descriptions of historical personages.

In a humorous way Christine draws the Aristotelian gender polarity theory

257. Christine de Pizan, *The City of Ladies,* I.27-32, 62-70.
258. Christine de Pizan, *The City of Ladies,* I.30, 68. My emphasis of the philosophical basis for her description.
259. See the longer text in footnote 208.
260. Christine de Pizan, *The City of Ladies,* I.33-38, 71-80.

into a direct confrontation with this evidence by again making a playful inversion on his dictum from the *Politics,* that "a woman's virtue is silence." First, Christine argues that men ought to keep silent about women:

> Henceforth, let all writers be silent who speak badly about women, let all of them be silent — those who have attacked women and who still attack them in their books and poems, and all their accomplices and supporters too — let all of them lower their eyes, ashamed for having dared to speak so badly, in view of the truth which runs counter to their poems. . . .[261]

Next, Christine directly refers to Aristotle and concludes that the women and their contributions are equal to if not better than those of all philosophers.

> It seems to me that neither in the teaching of Aristotle, which has been of great profit to human intelligence and which is so highly esteemed and with good reason, nor in that of all the other philosophers who have ever lived, could an equal benefit for the world be found as that which has been accrued and still accrues through the works accomplished by virtue of the knowledge possessed by these ladies.[262]

Lady Reason then adds to the list of contribution of ladies the following names and activities: (1) Arachne and dyeing wool cloth, (2) Ceres and breadmaking, (3) Pamphile and weaving silk, (4) Thamaris and painting, (5) Irene and painting, (6) Marcia and painting, (7) Anastasia and painting manuscripts, and (8) Sempronia and perfect knowledge of Latin and Greek.

The final question that Christine asks in the first part of the Book concerns the relation of women to practical wisdom, or prudence, i.e., the ability to know how to do the right thing at the right time, with the right instrument, in the right manner, and to the right person. Prudence is the ability to use a syllogism that ends with a correct choice of action rather than a simple theoretical truth to be known. The discussion of this virtue or practical wisdom, which ends the section of Lady Reason, is very important as a transition into the areas of practical action considered by Rectitude and Justice. Again we will summarize the question and argument as follows:

> [Christine]: Do women exhibit a natural or an acquired virtue of prudence; that is, are they able to reflect on what they ought to do and avoid, learn from the past, manage affairs in the present well, and predict the future? Why do some men who are eminent scholars and who have theoretical knowledge about virtue demonstrate so little prudence in their morals and conduct in the world?

> [Lady Reason]: Prudence is a combination of natural sensibility and acquired knowledge. Acquired knowledge of prudence when written (as with Aristotle

261. Christine de Pizan, *The City of Ladies,* I.38, 80.
262. Christine de Pizan, *The City of Ladies,* I.38, 81.

[and presumably Christine]) is more valuable because it lasts beyond the death of the person.

Many women exhibit both the natural and acquired virtues of prudence, as the following examples indicate.[263]

Lady Reason then describes (1) the good wife in the Book of Solomon, (2) Queen Gaia Cirilla, (3) Dido, (4) Ops, Queen of Crete, and (5) Lavinia, Queen of Laurentines as examples of women of practical wisdom, or prudence. Christine concludes her section with the observation that she has provided "sufficient proof . . . through reasoning and example, that God has never held, nor now holds, the feminine sex — nor that of men — in reproach."[264] In this balanced conclusion, Christine completes the multiple and complex construction of the foundations and exterior walls of her city of ladies. She has attempted to overcome bias against women by the combined use of imagination and discursive reason, frequently integrating historical male authors' examples of famous women with arguments about gender identity in her dialogue within a female community of discourse.

Dialogue with Lady Rectitude

In Part II of the construction of the City of Ladies, Christine de Pizan introduces another aspect of the analogy between constructing a city and writing a text. Her guide in this stage of the process of construction, or reconstruction, is Lady Rectitude, who tells her the following: "Now take your tools and come with me, and go ahead, mix the mortar in your ink bottle so that you can fortify the City with your tempered pen, for I will supply you with plenty of mortar. . . ."[265] The mortar of ink begins to place together new stones, or ladies of wisdom and virtue, to build the inner mansions and palaces for those who reside within the City. Christine again draws upon many different sources for her examples, including again the works from humanists like Boccaccio, poets like Virgil, and the Sacred Scriptures. She Christianizes pagan models of wisdom, the ten Sibyls, whose names signify an office that means "knowing the thinking of God."[266] The new Sibyls include Eruthrea, Almathea, Deborah, Elizabeth, the Queen of Sheba, Nicostrata, Cassandra, Queen Basine, and Antonia. Then a new question is raised:

---

263. Christine de Pizan, *The City of Ladies,* I.43, 86-89.

264. Christine de Pizan, *The City of Ladies,* I.48. The examples are taken from sections I.44-48, 89-97.

265. Christine de Pizan, *The City of Ladies,* II.1, 99.

266. Christine de Pizan, *The City of Ladies,* II.1, 100; II.1-11.6, 100-110. For a discussion of Christine presenting herself as a new kind of literary Sibyl, who prophetically describes Joan of Arc as a new kind of Christian, military, and political hero, see Kevin Brownlee, "Structures of Authority in Christine de Pizan's 'Ditié de Jehanne d'Arc,'" in *Discourses of Authority in Medieval and Renaissance Literature,* eds. Kevin Brownlee and Walter Stephens (Hanover, N. H.: University Press of New England, 1989), pp. 131-50, esp. 137 and 146.

[Christine]: If women have been so wise, then why is it that men and women are unhappy when a female child rather than a male child is born?

[Lady Rectitude]: There are a variety of reasons — (1) excessive simplemindedness, (2) ignorance, (3) the fear of the cost of a dowry to give the daughters in marriage, and (4) the fear that the naivety of their daughters may lead them to be deceived.

In response to these reasons — The naivety of daughters can be overcome with education; daughters actually are not a financial liability, but a financial benefit, and generally daughters are more loving of their parents than are sons. These theoretical claims can all be supported by examples of women.[267]

Her examples are drawn from humanist writers and particularly from Petrarch's rewritten description of the story of Griselda originally found in Boccaccio. Other examples include Drypetina, Hypsipyle, Claudine, and the mother of a Roman woman. The construction of the inner city of mansions and houses has now been completed, and Lady Rectitude is ready to choose its noble citizens, that is, women of good and virtuous character.

At this very crucial point in her text, Christine raises another question concerning the content of satires against women. Directly mentioning the satires of Theophrastus and Walter Map, Christine asks the following:

But could you please confirm for me whether what men claim, and what so many authors testify is true — a topic about which I am thinking very deeply — that life within the institution of marriage is filled and occupied with such great unhappiness for men because of women's faults and impetuosity, and because of their rancorous ill-humor, as is written in so many books? Many assert that these women care so little for their husbands and their company that nothing else annoys them as much. For this reason, in order to escape and avoid such inconveniences, many authorities have advised wise men not to marry, affirming that no women — or very few — are loyal to their mates. Valerius wrote to Rufus along similar lines, and Theophrastus remarked in his book that no wise man should take a wife, because there are too many worries with women, too little love, and too much gossip, and that if a man marries in order to be better taken care of and nursed in sickness, a loyal servant could better and more loyally care for him and serve him and would not cost him nearly as much, and that if the wife becomes sick, the languishing husband does not dare budge from her side.[268]

Lady Rectitude then answers Christine's question, first by referring her back to the real debate about these issues in the *Querelle de la rose* where Christine noted that satirists have never had anyone to argue publicly with them before about the truth or falsity of their testimony. "Certainly, friend," she replied, "just as you yourself once said regarding this question, whoever goes to court without an opponent

267. Christine de Pizan, *The City of Ladies,* II.7-11, 110-16.
268. Christine de Pizan, *The City of Ladies,* II.13, 118.

pleads very much at his ease. I assure you that women have never done what these books say."[269]

The demonstration of Lady Rectitude goes further than simple denial, however. She proceeds first by invoking a contrary set of examples, i.e., of men who have treated their wives badly: "How many harsh beatings — without cause and without reason — how many injuries, how many cruelties, insults, humiliations, and outrages have so many upright women suffered, none of whom cried out for help?"[270] After Christine confirms the affirmative answer to this question with examples drawn from her own experience, Lady Rectitude does not dwell on this kind of argument, which defends women by attacking men. Instead, she balances this view by the different claim that although there have been many bad husbands, there also have been many good ones; and Christine confirms this claim from her own experience of her husband and her marriage. In addition, this more positive direction of argumentation is supported by several examples of women who had been good wives. She describes Hypsicratea, Triaria, Artemisia, Argia, and Agrippina. In her description, Christine also directly mentions Boccaccio, and she links her example with direct statements of the philosopher satirist Theophrastus.[271]

In the middle of her argument, Christine, again with ironic humor against the gender polarity principle that a woman's virtue is to be silent, suggests that Mathéolus himself should be silent. Then she raises a further question about the satirist's claim that because women do not respect scholarship, a scholar should not marry:

> Let Mathéolus and all the other prattlers who have spoken against women with such envy and falsehood go to sleep and stay quiet. But, my lady, I still recall that the philosopher Theophrastus, whom I spoke of above, said that women hate their husbands when they are old and also that women do not love men of learning or scholars, for he claims that the duties entailed in the upkeep of women are totally incompatible with the study of books![272]

Once again, Christine is the first woman to directly raise questions about the arguments of satirists about the relation of marriage and scholarship for a woman. She was also the first to name particular authors, such as Mathéolus and Theophrastus, who held these views. Lady Rectitude answers her questions by providing several counterexamples to the satirists' claims: (1) Julia, the daughter of Julius Caesar, (2) Cornelia, the wife of Julius Caesar, (3) Tertia Amelia, the wife of Scipio Africanus, (4) Xanthippe, the wife of Socrates, (5) Pompeia Paulina, the wife of Seneca, (6) Jeanne de Laval, the wife of Bertrand du Guesclin, (7) Sulpitia, and (8) women who remained faithful to husbands who became lepers, (9) women who remained faithful to husbands who beat and ill-treated them, and (10) women who saved their husbands from death.[273]

---

269. Christine de Pizan, *The City of Ladies,* II.13, 118.
270. Christine de Pizan, *The City of Ladies,* II.13, 119.
271. Christine de Pizan, *The City of Ladies,* II.13-18, 120-27.
272. Christine de Pizan, *The City of Ladies,* II.19, 127-28.
273. Christine de Pizan, *The City of Ladies,* II.14-24, 120-34.

Then Christine de Pizan mentions directly Jean de Meun and the gender polarity satirical theme that women do not know how to keep silent:

> My Lady, now I know for certain what I had suspected earlier, that many women have shown, and show, great love and faith toward their husbands. For this reason I am amazed at the opinion which circulates quite commonly among men — even Master Jean de Meung [Meun] argues strongly (too strongly in fact!) in his *Romance of the Rose,* along with other authors as well — that a man should not tell his wife anything which he wishes to conceal and that women are unable to be silent.[274]

Lady Rectitude's response is measured, in that she qualifies the usual satirical generalization about all women, to suggest that only some women and some men are wise. Therefore, a man needs to know his wife and whether or not he should be able to trust her. In order to support her rejection of the satirist's claim, Lady Rectitude introduces counterexamples of some trustworthy women: Portia, Lady Curia, Nero's wife, and "an endless number of examples" are cited.[275]

At this point Christine moves the argument to a deeper level, for she asks about the ridicule that follows men who have trusted their wives: ". . . I am surprised that several authors claim that men who believe or lend credence to their wives' advice are despicable and foolish."[276] Once again Lady Rectitude meets this argument by a whole series of counterexamples that include what bad things happen to men who do not listen to the wise advice of their wives: (1) Portia, the wife of Brutus, (2) Julia, the wife of Pompey, (3) Andromache, the wife of Hector, (4) Antonia, the wife of Belisarius, and (5) the wife of King Alexander.[277] Next, Christine provides evidence of the good things that women have done for men in the world. She offers the examples of: (1) Mary, who "opened the door to Paradise," (2) Thermutis, the daughter of Pharaoh who saved the life of Moses, (3) Judith, who saved her people by cutting off the head of Holophernes, (4) Esther, who saved her people from extinction by risking her own life, (5) the Sabine women who saved Rome by risking their lives, (6) Ventura, (7) Clotilda, (8) various martyrs, (9) Catulla, and (10) Saint Genevieve.[278]

---

274. Christine de Pisan, *The City of Ladies,* II.25, 134. Christine plays with this concept in her other writings too. See her ironic inversion: "If it is possible for virtue to grow from vice, it pleases me well in this part to have the feelings of a woman. Since many men claim that women do not know how to keep quiet or restrain the abundance of their spirits, let me now come forth boldly and show by several streams the source and inexhaustible fountain of my spirit, which cannot staunch its desire for virtue" ("The Book of Policy, I," in *The Writings of Christine de Pizan,* p. 275).

275. Christine de Pizan, *The City of Ladies,* II.25-27, 134-37.

276. Christine de Pizan, *The City of Ladies,* II.28, 137.

277. Christine de Pizan, *The City of Ladies,* II.27-29, 137-42.

278. Christine de Pizan, *The City of Ladies,* II.30-35, 147-53. In *L'avision,* in a discussion of the Sabine war, she described the women who made peace by stepping between the battle lines of the sides of men fighting for Romulus or Remus: "Rather, their feminine voices, which made their loved ones make peace even on the field of battle, were spared by respect and heart with tenderness" (*Christine's Vision,* I, 14, 22). She argues later, however, that Joan of Arc did more than most of these women: "But

Christine questions why it is that some men do not want their own wives or daughters educated in fear of their morals being ruined. Lady Rectitude argues with direct irony: "Here you can clearly see that not all opinions of men are based on reason and that these men are wrong."[279] In fact, the contrary is true, i.e., that education about virtue ought to help women become more moral in their action. Then, as usual, Lady Rectitude introduces many counterexamples to the men's claims. Among the examples are (1) Hortensia, the daughter of Hortensius, and (2) Novella, the daughter of Giovanni Andrea, a law professor in Bologna. According to legend Novella actually lectured for her father, but behind a curtain.[280] Most significant about this section, however, is Christine's example of herself. "Your father, who was a great scientist and philosopher, did not believe that women were worth less by knowing science; rather, as you know, he took great pleasure from seeing your inclination to learning."[281]

Christine's new question is: "Where does the opinion, that there are so few chaste women, come from?" After providing several Biblical examples of chaste women (Susanna, Sarah, Rebecca, and Ruth) as well as pagan examples (Penelope, Marianne, Antonia, and Sulpitia), her question is further supported by the reflection that in Christine's day, more than any other time, there seem to be "so many men inclined to slander women without reason."[282] To provide an example Christine brings up the theory of some men who argue that women "want to be raped," and she argues to the contrary that it is "the greatest sorrow" for a woman to be raped.[283] Again she provides examples, perhaps borrowed directly from Augustine's *City of God,* which include Lucretia, Hyppo, many married women, virgins, as well as a clever ruse used by women to divert a potential rape. Augustine had argued that no woman raped against her will should be blamed. Christine's argument attempts to demonstrate the blind bias of men who do not pay attention to the experience of women when they make their judgment.

Christine then turns to the satirists' claim based on the gender polarity principle that women are naturally inconstant. She asks first whether the men who accuse women of inconstancy are constant themselves:

Men, especially writing in books, vociferously and unanimously claim that women in particular are fickle and inconstant, changeable and flighty, weak-hearted, compliant like children, and lacking all stamina. Are the men who ac-

---

through the Maid He's done much more than Esther, Judith, and Deborah" ("The Miracle of Joan of Arc," *The Writings of Christine de Pizan,* pp. 218-24 and 357).

279. Christine de Pizan, *The City of Ladies,* II.36, 153.

280. Christine de Pizan, *The City of Ladies,* II.36, 154.

281. Christine de Pizan, *The City of Ladies,* II.36, 154-55. She adds that her mother, however, did not share this opinion. "The feminine opinion of your mother, however, who wished to keep you busy with spinning and silly girlishness, following the common custom of women, was the major obstacle to your being more involved in the sciences." See also McLeod and Wilson, "The Misogamous Tradition," pp. 72-73. Finally, see also Christine de Pizan, *Mutacion de fortune,* for more reflections on the different contributions of her father and her mother to her education, l. 376-400, 95-97.

282. Christine de Pizan, *The City of Ladies,* II.37-43, 155-60.

283. Christine de Pizan, *The City of Ladies,* II.44-46, 160-64.

cuse women of so much changeableness and inconstancy themselves so unwavering that change for them lies outside the realm of custom or common occurrence?[284]

Lady Rectitude's response is in the form of *modus tollens*. She also refers directly to Christine de Pizan's earlier use of this argument in her *Epistre au dieu d'amours*. Basically, she argues that if women are more fragile than men by nature, men should be even more tolerant of women's weaknesses. However, men seem to demand more constancy from women than they do from themselves. Therefore, women cannot be more fragile than men by nature. In addition, although Christine recognizes that many men are strong and consistent, she enumerates several examples of men's inconsistencies.[285] Her examples include the Emperors Claudius, Tiberius, Nero, Galba, Otho, and Vitellius.

At this point, Lady Rectitude suggests a fundamental principle of self-governance for all men and women:

> And to define exactly inconstancy and changeableness, they are nothing but acting against the commands of Reason, for it exhorts every reasonable creature to act well. When a man or a woman allows regard for Reason to be conquered by sensuality, this is frailty or inconstancy, and the deeper one falls into error and sin, the greater the weakness is, the more one is removed from regard for Reason. Therefore, it turns out, according to what the histories recount — and I believe experience does not contradict this — that, regardless of what philosophers and other authors may say about the changeableness of women, you will never find such perversion in women as you encounter in a great number of men.[286]

Her argument continues by listing examples of evil women (Athalia, Jezebel, and Brunhilde) and evil men (Judas Iscariot, Julian the Apostate, Denis, and the categories of evil kings, disloyal emperors, heretical popes, and unbelieving prelates). Then, drawing further on the works of Boccaccio and Petrarch, she gives the opposite examples of good women who are strong, constant, and endure adversity in testing: (1) Griselda, (2) Florence the empress of Rome, and (3) the wife of Barnabo the Genovan.[287]

After her extensive discussions aimed towards increasing self-knowledge and self-governance in men and women, Christine returns again to the issue of the mutual attraction and deception between women and men. She asks Lady Rectitude to explain to her why it is that men insist that women are inconstant, deceptive, and fickle, and why they conclude that women are to be avoided like dangerous snakes hidden in the grass. Linking these two sections together, i.e., the common good with men's judgments about women, Lady Rectitude again offers an argument in the *modus tollens* form:

284. Christine de Pizan, *The City of Ladies*, II.47, 164.
285. Christine de Pizan, *The City of Ladies*, II.47-49, 165-69.
286. Christine de Pizan, *The City of Ladies*, II.49, 169-70.
287. Christine de Pizan, *The City of Ladies*, II.49-52, 170-84.

1. If men were interested in the common good, they would write about both male and female members of the human species who deceived the other.
2. However, men write only about women who deceive men; they never write about men who deceive women.
3. In addition, men often do deceive women.
4. Moreover, good women who do not deceive are as much a part of the human species as good men are.
5. Therefore, men are not interested in the common good.

She ends her argument: "Therefore, I conclude that if these men had acted in the public good — that is, for both parties — they should also have addressed themselves to women and warned them to beware of men's tricks just as they warned men to be careful about women."[288] In her argument against the claim that women are deceitful, Lady Rectitude also recalls that Christine "had adequately handled the subject, answering Ovid and the others in your *Epistre au dieu d'amours* and your *Epistres sur le Roman de la rose*."[289] Once again she reconstitutes her authorship and reaffirms her capacity to reuse sound philosophical arguments in the defense of women.

In conclusion, Christine's argument moves from the range of self-knowledge and self-governance to public action with respect to the common good.[290] In fact, she proves by her own work as a public writer that she is even more concerned with virtuous public action than were the male satirical writers who preceded her, precisely because she defends the common good for all men and women. In fact, in her work *Le Livre du corps de policie*, written around 1406-7, Christine argues that a person who neglects the common good is a tyrant: ". . . he must singularly love the common good and the increase of it more than his own, according to the doctrine of Aristotle in his book of *Politics*, who said that tyranny is when the prince seeks his own profit more than the common good. . . ."[291]

The second part of *Le Livre de la cité des dames* concludes with a series of qualifications about women who had good measure in their love and those who did not. She describes women whose love was so strong that it led to death, women who were not virtuous but were famous, women who attracted men because of their beauty or integrity, and some contemporary women who should be invited to live in the city. The examples are again drawn from humanist texts. The foolish lovers include Dido, Medea, Thisbe, Hero, Ghismonda, Lisabetta, Dame de Fayel,

288. Christine de Pizan, *The City of Ladies*, II.54, 188.
289. Christine de Pizan, *The City of Ladies*, II.54, 187.
290. Christine de Pizan, "The Book of Policy," *The Writings of Christine de Pizan*, IX, 287.
291. A theme that Christine develops in several of her other writings is the role of women in securing public peace. See her integration of this theme in her appeal "Lamentation on the Woes of France": "Princes, open your eyes through knowledge./Ladies, maidens, and other women of France, . . . weep,/O Sabine women, there is need for you in this case, for wasn't the peril even greater and the quarrel already existing among your relatives when with great prudence you played your part in establishing peace, when you rushed dishevelled in great swarms to the battlefield, your infants in your arms, crying out: Have mercy on our dear friends and relatives, make peace!" (*The Writings of Christine de Pizan*, pp. 305-6).

Dame de Vergi, Iseut, and Deianeira. The famous women include Juno, Europa, Jocasta, Medusa, Helen, and Polyxena. The women attractive to men include Claudia Quinta, Lucretia, Queen Blanche, Paulina, and Marguerite. The contemporary women include the Duchess of Berry, Valentina Visconti, the Duchess of Burgundy, the Countess of Clermont, the Duchess of Holland, the Duchess of Bourbon, the Countess of Saint-Pol, Anne, the daughter of the Count of La Marche, and a variety of other noble ladies from all classes.[292] In the midst of this discussion of so many examples of women, Christine repeats her often stated theme (and the theme of humanists like Dante, Petrarch, and Boccaccio before her): "And what is nobility except virtue? It never comes from flesh or blood."[293]

Through her dialogue with Lady Rectitude, the walls of her city of ladies have been rightly constructed, and those women who have led virtuous lives are gathered within it. Their virtue was the result of a rectitude of will, a right ordering of life's choices, based on truths discovered through reason. The city has indeed been fortified with Christine de Pizan's tempered pen filled with the mortar of ink that Lady Rectitude provided at the beginning of her dialogue with the author. The city is now ready for the final stage of construction, the completion and fulfillment predicted by Lady Justice, when she first introduced herself to Christine. Lady Reason has disposed, Lady Rectitude has ordered and initiated, and Lady Justice will now finish and terminate the construction of the city of ladies.

Second Dialogue with Lady Justice and the Virgin Mary

In the third and final part of *Le Livre de la cité des dames,* Lady Justice leads the construction of its roofs and towers and rightly orders its government. In many ways, this phase of construction moves from a philosophical towards a transcendental religious realm of discourse. It is analogous in some ways to Book X of Plato's *Republic,* in which the theme of justice is considered from the perspective of myth and ultimate judgment; it is also analogous in some ways to Book III of Dante's *Divine Comedy,* or *Paradise.* Finally, it is analogous to St. Augustine's *City of God,* as the author herself reveals in the following reflections of Lady Justice after having completed her mission:

> I do not know what more I could tell you, Christine, my friend. I could tell of countless ladies of different social backgrounds, maidens, married women, and widows, in whom God manifested His virtues with amazing force and constancy. But let this suffice for you, for it seems to me that I have acquitted myself well in completing the high roofs of your City and in populating it with outstanding ladies, just as I promised. These last examples will serve as the doorways and gates into our City. And even though I have not named all the holy ladies who have lived, who are living, and who will live — for I could name only a handful! — they can all be included in this City of Ladies. Of it may be said, *"Gloriosa dicta*

292. Christine de Pizan, *The City of Ladies,* II.55-69, 188-215.
293. Christine de Pizan, *The City of Ladies,* II.59, 197.

Christine de Pizan Dialogues with Lady Reason, Lady Rectitude, and Lady Justice

Enlargement of Constructing the Wall of the City with Lady Rectitude

sunt de te, civitas Dei" [Glorious things are said of you, city of God]. So I turn it over to you, finished perfectly and well enclosed, just as I promised. Farewell and may the peace of the Lord be always with you.[294]

The phrase, *Glorious things are said of you, O City of God,* echoes a line in Psalm 87, which is sung at every celebration of the Blessed Virgin Mary. Is Christine de Pizan counting on her reader being aware of this connection? If so, there are two aspects of the psalm that open up the deeper transcendental meaning of this reflection of Lady Justice: that Christine's city of ladies is a representation of the Church, and that it is also a transcendental mother of men and women. A selection from Psalm 87 may help to introduce these possibilities of interpretation:

> On the holy mountain is his city
> cherished by the Lord.
> The Lord prefers the gates of Zion
> to all Jacob's dwellings.
> Of you are told glorious things,
> O city of God.
>
> . . .
>
> and Zion shall be called 'Mother'
> for all shall be her children.
>
> It is he, the Lord Most High,
> who gives each his place.
> In the register of peoples he writes:
> "These are her children,"
> and while they dance they will sing:
> "In you all find their home."[295]

In identifying the city of ladies with the city of God, Christine demonstrates that her city of ladies is generic for all humanity. Each 'she' represents men and women whose lives are full of wisdom and virtue, and who live in a society dedicated to the common good. In addition, the city portrayed in Christine's text also acts like a spiritual mother of all men and women who find their home there.

The city of Zion is often referred to by Christian authors as the city of Mary. Thus, it is not surprising that the Virgin Mary, Mother of God, is introduced in Christine's text as Queen of the City. Her function is to "rule and govern the City . . . [and] to have ministry and dominion over all created powers after the only Son whom she conceived with the Holy Spirit and carried and who is the Son of God the Father."[296] Mary personifies the characteristics of a mother and a ruling Queen

---

294. Christine de Pizan, *The City of Ladies,* III.18.5, 253-54.

295. Psalm 87, *The Liturgy of Hours* (New York: Catholic Book Publishing Co., 1975), Common of the Blessed Virgin Mary, vol. 3, 1618.

296. Christine de Pizan, *The City of Ladies,* III.1.1, 217.

in active governing and exercising dominion over those under her care. After giving a litany of praises to Mary, the following dialogue takes place:

> [Lady Justice]: My Lady, what man is so brazen to dare think or say that the feminine sex is vile in beholding your dignity? . . .

> [The Virgin Mary]: O Justice, greatly beloved by my Son, I will live and abide most happily among my sisters and friends, for Reason, Rectitude and you, as well as Nature, urge me to do so. They serve, praise, and honor me unceasingly, for I am and will always be the head of the feminine sex.[297]

In this little exchange, Christine de Pizan is arguing that the universal claims of the gender polarity theorists and satirists concerning the natural inferiority or imperfection of all women could not be true because Mary, who is the most perfect human being, is a woman.[298] Mary, as the new Eve, recapitulates all women and gives them a new ennobled human life. She gathers and summarizes all women who lived before or live after her, and restores them, through Christ, to new life and communion.[299] Mary rules the city of ladies as a human being, not as divine, but

297. Christine de Pizan, *The City of Ladies,* III.1, 218.

298. Towards the end of her life, Christine wrote several deeply spiritual works. In her "Prayers to Our Lady," she refers to Mary as "predestined pure and perfect" and "mirror of all virtue," *The Writings of Christine de Pizan,* pp. 323-23. She also interweaves her prayers to Mary with those to the Trinity and to Christ. At the beginning of *The City of Ladies* (I.9.3) Lady Reason introduces the following comparison between Eve and Mary: "And if anyone would say that man was banished because of Lady Eve, I tell you that he gained more through Mary than he lost through Eve when humanity was conjoined to the Godhead, which would never have taken place if Eve's misdeed had not occurred. Thus man and woman should be glad for this sin through which such an honor has come about. For as low as human nature fell through this creature woman, was human nature lifted higher by this same creature" (p. 24). See also extracts in "The Seven Allegorized Psalms," *The Writings of Christine de Pizan,* pp. 325-37; and "The Hours of Contemplation of the Passion of Our Lord," *The Writings of Christine de Pizan,* pp. 346-47. In the latter text, she addresses herself directly to women who have suffered grief and translates for them from Latin to French some texts of previous Doctors of the Church.

299. For a consideration of the theme of recapitulation of the human race in Christ as the new Adam and Mary as the new Eve, see Irenaeus, "Similarly, the Word, recapitulating Adam in Himself, very fittingly received from Mary, who was still a virgin, the birth which made recapitulation possible . . ." (III 21, 10); and "Just as Eve, by disobeying, became the cause of death for herself and the whole human race, so Mary, betrothed to a predestined man and yet a virgin, by obeying, became the cause of salvation for herself and the whole human race. . . . What was bound could not be untied without a reversal of the process of entanglement. The first bonds had to be untied by the second, so that the second might set free the first" (III 22, 4 in *The Scandal of the Incarnation: Irenaeus Against the Heresies,* ed. Hans Urs von Balthasar [San Francisco: Ignatius Press, 1990], pp. 60-61); and Irenaeus, "And just as it was through a virgin who disobeyed that man was stricken and fell and died, so too it was through the Virgin, who obeyed the word of God, that man resuscitated by life received life . . . and therefore He did not become some other formation, but He likewise of her that was descended from Adam, preserved the likeness of formation; for Adam had necessarily to be restored in Christ, that mortality be absorbed in immortality, and Eve in Mary . . ." (33, in *Proof of the Apostolic Preaching* [Westminster, Md.: Newman Press, 1952], p. 69). For general discussions of the theory of recapitulation, see Angelo Di Berardino and Basil Studer, eds., *History of Theology,* vol. I, *The Patristic Period* (Collegeville, Minn.: Liturgical Press, 1997), pp. 132-37; and J. N. D. Kelly, *Early Christian Doctrines*

she is commissioned by God for this function. Thus, it is significant that Mary mentions Nature as well as Reason, Rectitude, and Justice as recognizing her entitlement to the role as Queen of the City of Ladies.

In the *City of Ladies* Mary governs by perfect distributive justice sharing the goods of the society with all who live within it. Christine de Pizan's vision of this perfect city has a radical element of reform inherent within it, for by the suggestion that women are capable of governing at every level of society, she accuses the structure of French society of being inherently unjust by its exclusion of women from most offices and honors. Sometimes it is argued that Christine de Pizan was primarily apolitical or utopian in her political views. However, if the reader accepts Aristotle's claim that the most important goods a ruler can distribute are those associated with positions of honor, the obvious evidence contained in Christine's vision of the perfect city of ladies is that women are capable of sharing in these goods distributed by the most just ruler. Those who would measure the practices in society against this situation of perfect justice would have to conclude that their form of society was inherently unjust, and that some radical reforms needed to occur to bring it in line with true distributive justice.[300]

Once the order of just government is established under the dominion of the Virgin Mary, then Christine (through Lady Justice) introduces several examples of women who gave evidence of heroic virtue in their lives. Most of the examples were drawn from the traditional martyrology and from Vincent of Beauvais's *Speculum historiale,* which was available to Christine in a French translation.[301] The entire body of this third part of the book consists in descriptions of the communion of saints and blessed who inhabit the higher regions of the city. These include Saint Catherine of Alexandria, Saint Margaret, Saint Lucy, Blessed Martina, Saint Justine, Saint Macra, Saint Fida, Saint Marcianna, Saint Eufemia, Blessed Theodosina, Saint Barbara, Saint Dorothy, Saint Christine, Blessed Felicia, Blessed Blandina, Saint Marina, Blessed Euphrosyna, Blessed Anastasia, Blessed Theodata, and many others.[302] A few selected passages will be given to demonstrate how Christine uses these models as counterexamples to the traditional gender polarity principles already so well identified by her writings.

(San Francisco: Harper and Row, 1978), pp. 170-74. In the passage cited by Christine de Pizan in which Mary describes herself as the head of the feminine sex a particular aspect of recapitulation is emphasized, namely, that in Mary all women before and after her overcome the limitations of Eve in an ennobling of the human race through her who gave Jesus Christ his human nature. Jesus' indebtedness to Mary and to no other human being for his human body is discussed by Thomas Aquinas in *Summa Theologica,* III, Q. 31, arts. 4-6. It is in this sense that she mediates the recapitulation of the whole human race.

300. I am very grateful to John Hittinger for bringing this aspect of Christine de Pizan's argument about distributive justice to my attention.

301. Christine identifies this source herself in *The City of Ladies,* II.9.4, 234. For more discussion of its significance, see Kevin Brownlee, "Martyrdom and the Female Voice," in *Discourses of Authority,* ed. Kevin Brownlee and Walter Stephens. "[Vincent de Beauvais's] *Speculum historiale* (cited [in the story of Saint Christine] — and most likely consulted by Christine — in the French translation of Jean de Vignay) contains all the stories that appear in part 3 of the *Cité des dames,* for which it serves as the primary source" (pp. 115-35, esp. 117).

302. Christine de Pizan, *The City of Ladies,* III.1-18, 218-54.

Mary, Queen of the City of Ladies, Is Welcomed
by Lady Justice and Lady Christine

Saint Catherine of Alexandria is acclaimed for being "a well-lettered woman, versed in various branches of knowledge, . . . [and able] to prove on the basis of philosophical arguments that there is but one God, Creator of all things, and He alone should be worshipped and no other."[303] Significantly, Saint Catherine's capacity to demonstrate by philosophical argumentation is highlighted, and further that her arguments were so successful they overwhelmed her adversaries, confounded them, and left them unable to answer her. In this particular description, the counter opinion that a woman's reason is weak is refuted.

Saint Margaret is described as so physically agile and brave that she pinned a man down and held him there by putting her foot on his throat. This example refutes claims of women's weakness. Many examples cite the physical and emotional strength of women under torture, noting their "constancy during martyrdom" and their "extraordinary firmness and strength."[304] These examples refute the gender polarity principle that women are inconstant and weak. Christine de Pizan then introduces the martyr Saint Christine, whose torturers attempted to reduce her to silence by the extraction of her tongue, but were foiled as "she spoke even better and more clearly than before." Christine de Pizan continues her mission for Saint Christine through the inspiration of her patron, who gives her own voice authority.[305] This example of a resurrected Christine overcomes the polarity principle that a woman's virtue is silence.

Then, so that the reader will not miss her point of argumentation, Christine has Lady Justice summarize the conclusions of the comparison of examples from the lives of the blessed and saints with claims from authors in the gender polarity tradition as follows:

> What more do you want me to tell you, my fair friend, Christine? I could recall other similar examples to you without stop. But because I see that you are surprised — for you said earlier, that every classical author attacked women — I tell you that, in spite of what you may have found in the writings of pagan authors on the subject of criticizing women, you will find little said against them in the holy legends of Jesus Christ and His Apostles . . . [and] in the histories of all the saints. . . .[306]

The counterexamples provided from these religious sources amply defeat the generalized principles of the classical authors. The argument has been proven by the book itself.

303. Christine de Pizan, *The City of Ladies,* III.3.2, 220.

304. Christine de Pizan, *The City of Ladies,* III.9.4, 234 and III.18.1, 252.

305. For a full development of this argument, see Kevin Brownlee, "Martyrdom and the Female Voice," in *Discourses of Authority,* ed. Kevin Brownlee and Walter Stephens. "For this saint functions as a privileged empowering model for the author of the *Cité des dames:* it is Saint Christine who authorizes the voice of Christine de Pizan as *auctor* [author]" (pp. 117ff).

306. Christine de Pizan, *The City of Ladies,* III.17.1, 251-52.

Summary of Arguments in *Le Livre de la Cité des dames*

In the conclusion of the book, Christine herself addresses all the noble ladies assembled and presumably all her readers. After reiterating that the new city is a refuge for all virtuous women, she invites them to find themselves mirrored in it. Then she warns them not to understand this city as a source of a kind of reverse gender polarity in which women are thought to be better than men: "[a]nd my dear ladies, do not misuse this new inheritance like the arrogant who turn proud when their prosperity grows and their wealth multiplies. . . ."[307] She concludes by encouraging the women to prove the satirists wrong by their own actions, to flee foolish love, to be clear about deceptions, to cultivate virtue, and to act well.

In this extraordinary text, Christine de Pizan has set forth a strong defense of women against nearly all of the gender polarity arguments present in the history of philosophy and in satirical arguments up to the fifteenth century. To help review the many different arguments of Christine de Pizan in *Le Livre de la cité des dames,* the chart on pages 647-49 is offered.

Concluding Reflections on Virtue

As suggested by the above summary, Christine de Pizan often repeats particular themes in several of her works. At the end of *Le Livre de la cité des dames* she had addressed her appeal for living a life of virtue to "all women — whether noble, bourgeois, or lower-class."[308] She immediately took up the theme of particular virtues that women ought to practice in her next book, *Le Trésor de la cité des dames: Le Livre des trois vertus (The Treasure of the City of Ladies: or The Book of the Three Virtues).* In 1405, the manuscript text was given the title with reference to the Three Virtues, while the printed version after 1497 was given the title with reference to the city of ladies.[309] This book was written as a guide for women in all levels of society who might live in the city of ladies; it directly addressed different clusters of women, such as princesses, nuns, widows, prostitutes, unmarried women, and married women.[310] It is also worth noting that Christine has her three guides iden-

---

307. Christine de Pizan, *The City of Ladies,* III.19, 254.

308. Christine de Pizan, *The City of Ladies,* III.19.6, 256.

309. For a consideration of its historical context, see Quilligan, *The Allegory of Female Authority,* pp. 246-60. This book was translated into Portuguese by 1518. While it was well known during her lifetime, by the seventeenth century it had become obscure. See Glenda K. McLeod, ed., *The Reception of Christine de Pizan from the Fifteenth Through the Nineteenth Centuries: Visitors to the City,* especially Charity Canon Willard, "Antoine de la Sale, Reader of Christine de Pizan," ch. 1, pp. 1-10; and Robert B. Bernard, "The Intellectual Circle of Isabel of Portugal, Duchess of Burgundy and the Portuguese Translation of *Le Livre des Trois Vertus,*" ch. 4, pp. 43-58.

310. Sheila Delany notes, however, the absence of addressing the emerging class of professional women who worked in guilds, etc. See "Mothers to Think Back Through," in *Medieval Texts and Contemporary Readers,* ed. Laurie A. Finke and Martin B. Shichtman, p. 189. Perhaps this period in history was too early for women to be defined with respect to their work, rather than their married state.

Structure of Christine's Arguments in *La Cité des dames*			
Kind of argument	**Summary of Argument**	**Against Whom**	**Where repeated**
Part I: Lady Reason *Reductio ad absurdum* (RAA) and *modus tollens*	1. To disprove: that the behavior of women is inclined to and full of every vice (a) if true, then God is not perfect (b) if true, then Christine should have been born a man.	Mathéolus	*Mutacion* in a variation
Appeal to: (a) legitimate authority (b) experience	2. To disprove: that opinions of men about women should be accepted instead of experience and debate avoided (a) debate is a proper philosophical method used by Aristotle and others (b) experience shows that the opinion that wives rule their husbands is false.	Christine's ironic pose	*Le Livre du corps de policie*
Argument by division	3. To prove that there is not one, but several causes of men's opinions about women: (a) ignorance, (b) sexual vice, (c) hatred, (d) revenge for defect, (e) jealousy, (f) slander, and (g) showing off knowledge.	Ovid, Mathéolus, Cesso d'Ascoli, the author of *De philosophia* (and presumably Juvenal and Jean de Meun)	Querelle de la rose
Argument by classification	4. To prove that women are not imperfect because their souls are equally made in the image of God and nature generates bodies according to God's pattern.	*Secreta mulierum* (spuriously attributed to Aristotle)	*Le Livre du chemin de long estude*
Argument by classification	5. To prove that nobility is not characteristic of body, nor of gender, but of virtue and that a man may serve a more noble (more virtuous) woman, e.g., the Virgin Mary.	Cicero	*Le Livre des trois vertus* *Le Livre du corps de policie*

Structure of Christine's Arguments in *La Cité des dames* (cont.)			
Kind of argument	**Summary of Argument**	**Against Whom**	**Where repeated**
Argument by classification and appeal to evidence of women	6. To prove that if a person can practice law because of intelligence, and not body, then women are as equally capable of practicing law as are men.		
Ironic *ad hominem* and appeal to evidence of women	7. To prove that if a person has a physically weak body, then the strength of mind will compensate for it by using the examples of Aristotle who had a weak body and brilliant mind, and of many women who had intelligent minds.		*Mutacion de Fortune; L'Epistre d'Othéa à Hector*
Argument by division and appeal to nurture, not nature	8. To prove that the opinion that women are not intelligent enough to learn the science of wisdom is the result of: (a) lack of education, (b) lack of exercise of the mind, and (c) low expectations for women by society.		*Le Livre du chemin de long estude; Le Livre du corps de policie*
Ironic *ad hominem* and appeal to evidence of women	9. To prove that women have both a natural and an acquired virtue of prudence — men who have theoretical knowledge of virtue demonstrate little prudence, while many women demonstrate prudence.		
Part II: Lady Rectitude Appeal to evidence of women	10. To prove that parents ought not be sad at the birth of a daughter, she argues (a) that education can overcome the limitations of women, (b) that daughters are a financial benefit, and (c) that daughters are more loving of their parents than are sons.		*Le Livre des trois vertus*

| \multicolumn{4}{c}{Structure of Christine's Arguments in *La Cité des dames* (cont.)} |
Kind of argument	Summary of Argument	Against Whom	Where repeated
Appeal to evidence of women, and *reductio ad absurdum*	11. To disprove the arguments of satirists that women cause men unhappiness in marriage for *fifteen* different reasons, she introduces counterarguments and counterexamples to refute each reason: (a) impetuosity, (b) moodiness, (c) disloyalty, (d) lack of love of learning, (e) cannot be silent, (f) cannot be trusted with secrets, (g) cannot give good advice, (h) not chaste (like to be raped and use deception to catch men), (i) fickle, (j) inconstant, (k) changeable, (l) flighty, (m) weak-headed, (n) act like children, and (o) fragile.	Theophrastus, Walter Map, Mathéolus, Jean de Meun	Querelle de la rose, *L'Avision-Christine* (her father); *L'Epistre au dieu d'amours; Le Livre des trois vertus*
Ad hominem against men	12. To prove that women are not more inconsistent than men, she (a) enumerates examples of inconsistent men and (b) argues that more men than women have disregard for the regulation of reason.		
Modus tollens	13. To prove that men are not interested in the common good, she argues that if they were, they would give equal attention to deception by both men and women.		
Part III: Lady Justice Appeal to religious authority	14. To disprove that woman is imperfect, Mary, who is the perfect human being and head of the feminine sex, is recognized Queen of the City of Ladies.		
Appeal to religious authority	15. To disprove the views of pagan authors against women (physically and emotionally weak, inconstant, unable to reason well), counterexamples from lives of the saints are introduced.	All pagan authors who attacked women	

tify the City as a "feminine college," and they hope that the "syllabus of our school may be valuable to all."[311] Christine explicitly stated that *Le Livre des trois vertus* was written for all women. "As we have already mentioned several times before, we intend everything that we have laid down for other ladies and young women concerning both virtues and the management of one's life to apply to every woman of whatever class she may be. It is said as much for one woman as for another, so each one can take whatever part that she sees pertains to her."[312] The entire work, which is placed in the theological context of a love of God, is oriented towards the practical education or practice of a virtuous life.

While Christine describes many of the traditional virtues associated with women, such as patience, compassion, peacemaking, kindness, chastity, and benevolence, she also develops others as well. They include more basic human virtues as well as many traditional virtues associated with men. For example, she challenges princesses who are driven by the vices of pride, vengeance, or desire to dominate others by the strength of their will: "Have you forgotten who you really are?"[313] After describing several aspects of developing the virtue of self-government and practical wisdom or prudence, Christine describes the manner in which a woman ought to develop the virtue of holding authority and governing others.[314] In fact, she directly criticizes men who will not allow women to exercise the particular virtues associated with establishing a good order:

> Any man is extremely foolish, of whatever class he may happen to be, if he sees that he has a good and wise wife, yet does not give her authority to govern in an emergency. There are many men who are so churlish and so ignorant that they do not know how to see or recognize goodness and common sense. They cherish the opinion that women are not sensible enough to have much administrative ability, although we often see the opposite of this.[315]

Further, a woman should learn how to "protect and defend her rights boldly by law and reason."[316] These examples of excursion of the practice of virtue into the public

---

311. Christine de Pizan, *The Treasure of the City of Ladies, or The Book of Three Virtues*, trans. Sarah Lawson (London: Penguin Books, 1985), p. 32.

312. Christine de Pizan, *The Book of Three Virtues*, III, 1, 145.

313. Christine de Pizan, *The Book of Three Virtues*, I, 37.

314. "She will conscientiously hear the proposals that are put forward and listen to everyone's opinion. She will be so attentive that she will grasp the principal points and conclusions of matters and will note carefully which of her counsellors speak better and with the best deliberation and advice, and which seem to her the most prudent and intelligent. And she will also note, in the diversity of opinions, which causes and which reasons most stir the speakers. In this way she will attend to everything, and when someone comes to her to speak on a subject or to reply, according to the circumstances, so wisely will she consider the matter that she cannot be thought simple or ignorant" (Christine de Pizan, *The Book of Three Virtues*, I, 60).

315. Christine de Pizan, *The Book of Three Virtues*, I, 80. In this governing, Christine mentions various capacities such as to oversee teaching the children Latin and the sciences and having detailed knowledge of finances, revenues, and expenses.

316. Christine de Pizan, *The Book of Three Virtues*, I, 82. This claim is developed several times in the text. "It is proper for such a lady or young woman to be thoroughly knowledgeable about the

realm are augmented by an argument that some women need to develop the virtues associated with military action.[317] So in this text Christine de Pizan offers practical advice for a wide range of virtues that women can practice to become truly noble by cultivating traditional feminine virtues, human virtues, and traditional masculine virtues.[318]

That Christine perceived herself personally as a teacher of women in this text, Le Livre des trois vertus, is clearly indicated by the manner in which she identifies herself as its author both in the prologue and in the conclusion. We noted at the beginning of our chapter on Christine de Pizan that she chose to write about herself as an author in the first person, often using the expression "I Christine" to emphasize her own identity in the text. She began Le Livre des trois vertus with the words "After I built the City of Ladies with the help and by the commandment of the three Ladies of Virtue, Reason, Rectitude and Justice. . . ."[319] Then after describing how, in spite of her exhaustion at having completed this task, the three ladies of virtue challenged her to not stop in the middle of her work, she responded with her famous phrase: "Then I, Christine, hearing the soft voices of my very reverend mentors, filled with joy and trembling, immediately roused myself. . . ."[320]

The result of Christine's renewed effort was to write down the book that the three ladies of virtue dictated to her. Then to impress once again her unique identity as author, at the conclusion of the book she introduces her famous phrase of self-identification once more: "With that the three ladies stopped speaking and suddenly disappeared, and I, Christine, remained, almost exhausted from writing for so long, but very happy looking at the beautiful work of their worthy lessons, which I have recapitulated."[321] Christine then states that she will distribute her book far and wide, especially to women of authority. One such person turned out to be the Duchess of Valentino, in whose household Christine's old friend, the Royal Librarian Gilles Malet, now served.[322]

Christine de Pizan does not write about virtue for women only. She also wrote several texts on public virtue directly oriented towards the male reader. While

laws relating to fiefs, sub-fiefs, quit rents, *champarts,* taxes for various causes . . . so that no one can deceive her about them" (II, 130).

317. "We have also said that she ought to have the heart of a man, that is, she ought to know how to use weapons and be familiar with everything that pertains to them, so that she may be ready to command her men if the need arises. She would know how to launch an attack or to defend against one, if the situation calls for it" (Christine de Pizan, *The Book of Three Virtues,* II, 129).

318. Again Christine repeats the often heard humanist refrain that nobility consists not in bloodline, but in virtue: "If you argue that your nobility impels and leads you to desire such honours, let us inform you that no one is noble if he does not have other noble qualities, virtues and good manners. If you do not have these qualities in you, no matter who you are, you are not noble. And if you think you are, you are deceiving yourself" (*The Book of Three Virtues,* II, 137). Note that Christine quotes as her source for this view St. Augustine, not Dante, and a common proverb: "He who is good, prudent, and wise smells sweet as a rose." Could this be a veiled inversion of the satirical use of the image of a Rose?

319. Christine de Pizan, *The Book of Three Virtues,* 31.

320. Christine de Pizan, *The Book of Three Virtues,* 32.

321. Christine de Pizan, *The Book of Three Virtues,* conclusion.

322. Willard, *Christine de Pizan: Her Life and Works,* p. 166.

many of these texts have been identified previously in this chapter, more direct mention will be made of their significance. Christine de Pizan is moving women's speech into increasingly broader areas of public activity. As early as 1404, Christine wrote a text entitled *Prod'hommie de l'homme (On Human Integrity)*. Around 1406, she rewrote the text with a new title, *Le Livre de prudence*. As Charity Canon Willard summarizes it:

> Her principal subject was the duties and responsibilities of any prince or ruler who wished to cultivate virtue, an ideal that was stressed by a number of political writers of Christine's day and even earlier. She was making her first contribution to the great body of medieval literature on the "perfect prince," and it seems evident that she wanted Louis of Orleans in particular to take heed.[323]

Willard suggests that Christine defends her action in her autobiographical *Chemin de long estude (The Long Road of Learning)* in which she indicates that an educated woman such as herself has not only a right, but a duty to speak to those in public leadership about justice and other comparable virtues. Therefore, she was again redefining the range and obligation of a woman's virtue.

During the next fifteen years, Christine wrote several political works. In fact, it could be said that this concern with public forms of virtue was her main preoccupation during this middle to late period of her life. In 1407 she wrote a text for the education of princes, and particularly for Louis of Guyenne, entitled *Le Livre du corps de policie* (The Book of the Body Politic). This text, modeled in part on the Bishop of Chartres, John of Salisbury's *Policraticus* (or Statesman), was well known and available to Christine in the library of Charles V.[324] Kate Langdon Forhan points out that Christine did not simply borrow from the original text, but rather used certain of its concepts to support responsible political action, while adapting it to the very different historical context of a society in political turmoil because of weak leadership.[325]

In an ironic way Christine inserts into the first paragraph of the first chapter a statement that reflects on her unique place as a woman who chooses to enter into public discussion about men's virtues:

> If it is possible for vice to give birth to virtue, it pleases me in this part to be as passionate as a woman, since many men assume that the female sex does not know how to silence the abundance of their spirits. Come boldly, then, and be shown

---

323. Charity Canon Willard, "Christine de Pizan: From Poet to Political Commentator," in *Politics, Gender, and Genre: The Political Thought of Christine de Pizan,* ed. Margaret Brabant, p. 23.

324. For an excellent comparison of the two works see Kate Langdon Forhan, "Polycracy, Obligation, and Revolt: The Body Politic in John of Salisbury and Christine de Pizan," in *Politics, Gender, and Genre,* pp. 33-52. Selections from the original text can be found in English in *The Statesman's Book of John of Salisbury* (Being the Fourth, Fifth, and Sixth books, and Selections from the Seventh and Eight Books, of the *Policraticus*) (New York: Russell and Russell, 1963).

325. Forhan, "Polycracy, Obligation, and Revolt," in *Politics, Gender, and Genre: The Political Thought of Christine de Pizan,* ed. Margaret Brabant, p. 49.

the many inexhaustible springs and fountains of my courage, which cannot be stanched when it expresses the desire for virtue.[326]

This little introductory passage once again reveals Christine de Pizan's ability to engage directly and humorously with traditional stereotypes. She inverts a stereotype of the vice of woman as unable to control her passions and to be silent, into the virtue of a particular woman who passionately and courageously speaks publicly about the need for men to practice virtue.

Perhaps even more surprising was the fact that Christine wrote in 1409-1410 a military manual entitled *Le Livre des faits d'armes et de chevalerie* (The Book of the Feats of Arms and Chivalry). It is surprising for two reasons: first of all that a woman should write a book on such a traditionally masculine subject, and second, that the book should have been so well written as to have become very popular. As mentioned previously it was translated into English by 1489, and it was used on both English and French battlefields.[327] The book basically compiled the common expertise of several different authors on successful battle strategy in an accessible manner. In addition to this compilation, Christine also set guidelines for just wars, for outlawing particularly vengeful motives or means of fighting, and for establishing appropriate conditions for battle.[328]

In 1410 she also wrote a work to the people of France, by addressing the leaders of both sides of a conflict (the Duc de Berri and Isabeau de Bavière) and begging them to avoid civil war. The *Lamentation sur les maux de la guerre civile de la France* (*Lamentation over the harms of the civil war of France*) again gives evidence of her incursion into public realms of action, and particularly into government, which had been traditionally a male domain. Margarete Zimmermann notes the unusual aspect of this action:

> Christine's *Lamentation* is initially presented as a long and impassioned fictional speech, inspired by a feeling of outrage and pain but also by the intention to effect a fundamental change. The appearance of a woman as speaker is unusual, contradicting all rules of conduct formulated in medieval domestic and educational guides. . . .[329]

A further surprising aspect of the work is that it does not appeal just to men to refrain from war, but again specifically to all women from the different classes of society in France to move to a political form of war. Zimmermann cites this action as a "step toward the creation of female group consciousness" that complements the prior step towards her own consciousness as a female author speaking and acting decisively at a specific moment in French history, with a purpose to influence and

---

326. Christine de Pizan, *The Book of the Body Politic* (Cambridge: Cambridge University Press, 1994), p. 3.

327. See *The Book of Fayttes of Armes and of Chyvalrie* (Millwood, N.Y.: Kraus Reprint, 1988).

328. Yenal, *Christine de Pisan: A Bibliography,* #37, 52. Yenal notes that a 1488 French printed version by Antoine Vénard deleted Christine's name and changed the narrator to a male author, p. 53.

329. Margarete Zimmermann, "Vox Femina, Vox Politica," in *Politics, Gender, and Genre: The Political Thought of Christine de Pizan,* ed. Margaret Brabant, p. 119.

change the direction of public events.[330] Unfortunately for Christine and for the people of France, civil war broke out the following year.

From that time on Christine still wrote texts for particular individuals, for example, the *Livre de la paix (The Book of Peace)*, which in 1412-1413 offered guidelines to the Dauphin about how to govern well. In 1416-1418 she wrote *Epistre de la prison de vie humaine (Letter Concerning the Prison of Human Life)*, a letter of consolation for women, especially for those who had lost family members in battle against the English at Agincourt. This text is a passionate account of the suffering of grief along with careful advice about how to move beyond self-pity into a life of responsible and virtuous action.

Because of political events in Paris and the dangers of civil war, Christine de Pizan is presumed to have spent the last ten years or so of her life in retirement in the Dominican Convent of Poissy. While living there Christine wrote meditations on the Passion of Christ, and then in 1429, after Joan of Arc's military victory over the English at Orleans, Christine wrote the poem in her honor entitled *Le Dittié sur Jeanne d'Arc (The Tale of Joan of Arc)*. To recall the significance of this text, which has already been discussed earlier in this chapter as well as in the previous one, it is important simply to note here that in it Christine heralds the fact that a young maid was able to accomplish something that many political men were unable to do. Even in this final text written during her life, Christine de Pizan was pushing the limits of appropriate virtue for women outwards into wider ranges and newer possibilities.

CHRISTINE DE PIZAN'S HUMANIST FOUNDATIONS FOR GENDER THEORY

In this chapter we have demonstrated several different ways in which Christine de Pizan serves as an extraordinary center of integration of previously isolated communities of discourse. Christine, more than any other early humanist writer, advanced the philosophy of gender: in particular, she was the first to articulate a series of arguments about the nature and identity of woman, arguments that challenged traditional gender polarity theory and began to lay a groundwork for a philosophy of gender complementarity.

We have seen ways in which Christine herself was familiar with some texts from the previously isolated communities of discourse we loosely identified as religious (specifically Christian), academic (including Arts, Medicine, Law, and Theology), satirical (in both poetry and prose), and humanist (including Italian and French) communities. In addition, Christine de Pizan interfaced arguments from within these different communities of discourse both within herself and in the broader public arena. She achieved this interfacing through effective philosophical and literary skill expressed in dialogues of poetic and prose forms, and in didactic essays and letters. By various means, Christine shifted previous approaches toward

330. Zimmermann, "Vox Femina, Vox Politica," in *Politics, Gender, and Genre: The Political Thought of Christine de Pizan,* ed. Margaret Brabant, p. 123.

gender identity into new ranges of dialogue. At first her dialogue was based on real, intergender, and public exchanges through the *Querelle de la rose,* and later her dialogue was continued through an imaginary construction of a city of ladies.

In addition to shifting the ground and method of discourse about gender, Christine also contributed to the development of Renaissance Humanism itself by her extraordinary skills in writing and organizing material. She contributed to the acceptance and promotion of classical sources in the development of woman's history. She both used and transformed courtly love poetry, and she became a true woman of letters, seeking to effect change in her readers by the persuasive force of dialectical arguments. Finally, Christine mediated between Italian and French Humanism, and she joined the early Renaissance Humanist movement towards extensive writing in the vernacular. When we consider the ways in which Christine de Pizan challenged traditional gender polarity, we can divide our consideration into two categories: **method** and **content**.

First, her method of **direct** arguments about gender were aimed at particularly selected satirical writers such as Theophrastus (Aristotle's disciple), Ovid, Jean de Meun, Mathéolus, and Walter Map. More particularly, her method consisted in selecting direct quotations from their works, and then introducing a series of philosophical arguments to prove them fallacious or unsound. We sought in this chapter to give precise descriptions of the many ways in which Christine used philosophical arguments such as *reductio ad absurdum* and *modus tollens,* appeal to experience (especially women's experience) and authoritative historical texts for counterexamples, and arguments by clarification of terms — by division, by classification, by relating the whole to parts, and cause to effect. Occasionally, Christine would engage in *ad hominem* attacks, especially when she had been attacked by this same method previously; but for the most part, she avoided fallacious reasoning or rhetorical devices to prove a point.

Second, her method of **indirect** critique of the gender polarity principles common to the Aristotelian tradition usually did not directly attack Aristotle's concept of woman, but rather attacked some exemplary satirical writers who came out of the polarity tradition. It is difficult to know whether avoidance of attacking Aristotle directly is due to her lack of knowledge of many of Aristotle's metaphysical and natural gender polarity positions about woman's identity, or whether Christine deliberately chose to avoid confronting the philosopher whose works had only a century before become fundamental to the curriculum of most universities in Western Europe. Christine de Pizan also avoided directly commenting on gender theory found in Aristotelian philosophers such as Albert the Great or Thomas Aquinas. At the same time, she would invoke Aristotelian or Thomistic principles where they proved useful to her own theories.

When we examined the content of her arguments in detail, we found that Christine countered every one of the themes that devalued woman's identity in the gender polarity tradition. Since it is useful to consider her gender theory positions as a whole, Christine de Pizan's varied arguments against traditional gender polarity are summarized:

Christine de Pizan's Counterarguments to Gender Polarity		
Category	Gender Polarity	Christine's Counterargument
Wisdom	1. Woman as naturally passive	**Self-knowledge** 1. Multiple examples of active women.
	2. Woman as naturally weak	2. If women weak, why are there such elaborate means to deceive them? Plus multiple examples of strong women.
	3. Women wise through true opinion only	3. Women wise through appeal to evidence plus careful reasoning to and with universal judgments, or syllogistic reasoning.
	4. Women's virtue is silence	4. Women wise in oral and written form. Ironic use of dictum about women's inability to keep silence to speak about public issues.
	5. No understanding of a history of women	5. Women wise through appropriating the history of women's past achievements.

Virtue	6. Women have little or no control over their emotions; they are therefore full of:
	    greed
	    lust
	    anger
	    inconstancy
		Self-governance
		6. Women have control over their emotions through the practice of virtue of self-governance. Many examples are given of women who are generous, chaste, self-controlled, and constant in their promises.

	7. God created women as lacking self-governance and prone to vice	7. A good God could not create women as naturally unvirtuous.
	8. Women's virtues ought to be limited to the private sphere of activity.	**Public action** 8. Multiple examples of virtuous women acting in the public sphere with boldness, prudence, daring, strong discipline, and even taking up of arms.
	9. Women seek to deceive men.	9. Women rarely deceive men, while the opposite is a common occurrence.
	10. Women either blindly obey or else dominate men.	10. Multiple examples of women demonstrating wise governance of men and women.

On one level, the preceding chart simply gives a broad sweep of Christine de Pizan's counterarguments to the epistemological and ethical principles of the gender polarity tradition. In so doing, it helps to indicate the ways in which she approached nearly every kind of judgment that devalued women in relation to men. The content of her theory was always oriented towards challenging the universal judgments which claimed that women in general were not as capable of wisdom and virtue as were men.

On another level, Christine de Pizan's direct arguments against the gender polarity theory bore witness to each and every one of the themes that she articulated in her own writings. She demonstrated her own capacity for wisdom and self-knowledge by incorporating autobiographical material into her works, by her love of study and learning, by her active search for truth, by her skillful use of discursive reasoning and dialectic, and by her dedication to the dispersion of her knowledge and wisdom in her writings and public interaction. In addition, Christine's practice of virtue was aptly demonstrated in her self-governance as a woman of high moral character, Christian commitment, and dedicated professional excellence over many years. Finally, by her own bold, prudent, public action and her frequent attempts to build a common good in the French society of her time, she demonstrated the true nobility that was associated with a virtuous life.

In her writings and by her own choices, Christine de Pizan demonstrated belief in a fundamental equality of dignity and worth of women and men. This characteristic provides half of the basis for a genuine complementarity between the genders. The other half is also present in Christine's writings and witness, namely, belief in a significant differentiation of women and men. She argued that if women had written in the past, they would have written somewhat differently from men, because their experience was different. She demonstrated in her own writing this appeal to women's experience, inserting a different perspective into the satirical tradition that devalued women, glamorized war, and did not uphold the true dignity of faithful love between women and men. Throughout her works Christine demonstrated a consciousness of her identity as a woman, without letting this perspective either distort another's view or be distorted by another. In some of her works, she even experimented with transmutation from a woman's to a man's perspective and with the difference in masculine and feminine characteristics when they occur in a male or in a female human being.

Christine de Pizan based her arguments on the common exchange of reason available to all men and women. She was respectful of the many particular contributions of men, especially of male humanist writers such as Dante, Petrarch, and Boccaccio, and she often borrowed and transformed their contributions to provide the humanist foundations for her own writings. She drew extensively from the works of Aristotle, Augustine, Boethius, and St. Thomas Aquinas, to provide fundamental philosophical and religious principles for her thought. She also appealed to Mary as the head of all women, one who gathered individual women throughout history into a collective model of regenerated, ennobled humanity, building a new community based on the common good.

Christine de Pizan demonstrated an active spirit of complementarity that sought to stand alongside and face-to-face with men, while also proclaiming a genuine woman's perspective on a particular theme. We found a similar kind of spirit in the works of Hildegard of Bingen, who sought to articulate by text and example a medieval foundation for gender complementarity. Because of the thoroughness with which Hildegard articulated her theory, we called her "the foundress of the philosophy of sex complementarity." Christine de Pizan did not engage in discussion about the more scientific and metaphysical foundations of sex complementarity by considering theories of generation and categories of opposites, as did her predecessor. However, in the categories of wisdom and virtue, in many ways she went much further. So while Hildegard of Bingen can be considered as foundress of gender complementarity, Christine de Pizan is "the early humanist reformer of gender complementarity."[331]

Both women had the advantage of a context within which men and women interacted on a regular basis, and in which libraries provided important resources to draw upon. Hildegard was situated in the double monastery of the Benedictine monastic tradition while Christine had access to the Royal library and academic community in Paris, but within a social context of humanists who met outside of the academic classes. Both women had extensive correspondence with educated men. Both women engaged also in public dialogue with men and women. These two extraordinary examples support the tentative hypothesis that where there is an environment of genuine complementarity, in which intergender dialogue can occur in natural and ongoing ways, then a philosophical theory of complementarity tends to emerge.

---

331. See Jean Bethke Elshtain's introduction to *Politics, Gender, and Genre: The Political Thought of Christine de Pizan*, ed. Margaret Brabant. "Christine's position, which is not without its own special entourage of nagging troubles, is best seen as sex complementarity" (p. 4).

CHAPTER 8

THE EARLY HUMANIST REFORMATION IN EDUCATION FOR WOMEN

I n 1471, one of the first texts published in Venice was given the Latin title *Decor puellarum* (On the Customs of Girls).[1] The 240-page text *Decor puellarum* was addressed directly to young women; its chapter headings identify the following subjects:

> ... the suitable and necessary goodness of the wise and most prudent maiden, ... the virtues which are proper for you, ... the order of life which you must preserve, ... the manner of beautiful dress, ... with good physical exercises, ... honest loves and holy desires, [and] ... lofty thoughts and devoted recommendations and contemplations beginning with the creation of the world until the point of the final judgement.[2]

The *Decor puellarum* was not the first book printed in Venice; Johannes of Speyer had begun publishing there as early as 1469.[3] Speyer's printing company also pub-

---

1. The full title is: *Decor puellarum: Questa sie una opera la quale si chiama Decor puellarum: zoe honore de le donzelle: la quale da regola forma e modo al stato de le honeste donzelle* (Venice: Per magistrum Nicolaum Ienson hoc opus quod puellarum decor dicitur feliciter impressum est, 1461). The printing date is incorrectly registered on the text as 1461, perhaps as an effort to make a claim for the first book printed in Italy. The printer was the Parisian Nicolas Jenson, who went to Mainz in 1458 to learn the printing trade, returned to Paris in 1461, moved to Venice by 1465, and established his own printing business there after 1470. See George Haven Putnam, *Books and Their Makers During the Middle Ages* (New York: Hillary House Publishers Ltd., 1962), vol. 1, pp. 407-9.

2. Jenson, pub., *Decor puellarum*, 1-3, UCLA Special Collections BL87, 1-3. Translated by Professor Ezio Gallicet, University of Turin and Nicoletta Mackenzie. The printer Nicolas Jenson provided no author's name for this popular and famous text. Given its lengthy volume and wide popularity, it is intriguing that its authorship is still unidentified. In view of the fact that Jenson appears to have offered an incorrect date of publication as well, it would be interesting to trace the sources for the content of the text itself. Two earlier manuscripts on the education of woman that will be considered in this chapter bear careful comparison with the *Decor puellarum*, namely the thirteenth-century Latin text by Vincent of Beauvais and the early fourteenth-century Tuscan text by Francesco Barberino. Since Jenson lived in Paris he likely knew of Beauvais's work, and since he was living in northern Italy at the time of his printing adventures, he may have known of Barberino's work as well. Since tracing these connections went beyond the possible time boundaries for completing the present work, I have not been able to come to a conclusion about this mystery of authorship and sources.

3. Leonardas Vytautas Gerulaitis, *Printing and Publishing in Fifteenth-Century Venice* (Chicago: American Library Association, 1976), pp. 20-23.

lished Augustine's *De civitate Dei (The City of God)* before the end of 1470; and this text has the significant teaching that it is a woman's will that determines the quality of her soul, and not her body or position in society.

In the fifteenth century the invention of the printing press brought about an explosive diffusion of Aristotelian thought and method of argumentation. The first printed Latin editions of Aristotle appeared in 1470, Greek editions appeared in 1495-98 in Venice, and frequent bilingual editions after 1560.[4] These translations, using more recent philological techniques, generated a new interest in the careful study of Aristotle. Further, this period included a great revival of commentaries on Aristotle.

The most important printer to aid the diffusion of original Greek texts was an Italian, Aldus Manutius, who was born around 1450. Although between 1484 and 1486 three Greek books were printed in Venice by other printers, by 1495 Aldus provided a new Greek font that made it possible for the works of Aristotle, Plato, Plutarch, Demosthenes, and others to be printed in the original alongside Latin and/or Italian texts. Aldus had learned Greek from Guarino of Verona, an important humanist educator, and he determined to make original Greek texts available to scholars in Italy, Germany, France, England, Poland, and all over Europe.[5] Eighteen of the twenty-seven books in Greek printed in Venice in the fifteenth century were done by Aldus Manutius, and nearly all of the works in philosophy were by or about Aristotle.[6] The excitement generated by Aldus's Greek texts had the secondary effect that all of Aristotle's arguments in support of gender polarity gained a new vigor and intensity by virtue of their being read in the original. In addition, philosophers who turned to these sources did not have the moderating effect of Christian scholastic philosophers who had introduced in their interpretations of Aristotle other theological arguments for gender complementarity.

In Chapter 4 the contributions of Cavalcanti, Dante, Petrarch, and Boccaccio were analyzed. Particular aspects of the relation of wisdom and virtue to women's identity remain in the background, ready to be drawn upon or contested by subsequent authors. Generally, women were presented as full of self-discipline and engaging actively in the development of virtue, and also willing and able to lead men to greater heights of wisdom and virtue as well. This early humanist view is in direct contrast with academic gender polarity principles derived from the works of Aristotle and with satirical exaggerations or inversions of polarity models. The humanist views are more in keeping with the actual practice of women in religious communities of discourse. It is not surprising, then, that this period of further humanist arguments should be filled with dynamic tensions drawn from all these different sources of discourse about the concept of woman as well as from the personal experience of different authors.

---

4. Charles B. Schmitt, *Aristotle and the Renaissance* (Cambridge, Mass.: Harvard University Press, 1983), p. 36. See also F. Edward Cranz, *A Bibliography of Aristotle Editions: 1501-1600,* Second Edition with addend and revisions by Charles B. Schmitt (Baden-Baden: Verlag Valentin Koerner, 1984).

5. Martin Lowry, *The World of Aldus Manutius* (Ithaca, N.Y.: Cornell University Press, 1979), "The Great Diffusion," ch. 7.

6. Gerulaitis, *Printing and Publishing in Fifteenth-Century Venice,* pp. 89-91.

The previous chapter on Christine de Pizan demonstrated her personal integration of material from all four communities of discourse. In the present chapter no one person begins to accomplish what this author achieved. However, instead of gathering together material from several different sources into a common framework, there is a scattering of discussions about women in many different authors. Instead of an integration into a cohesive view of gender identity, there are a dispersion of ideas and inconsistency of arguments. Early humanist authors during the period 1430-1500 are predominantly located in different cities in northern Italy and Germany, and there appears to be little influence from dynamic French humanists to the concept of woman in other authors of different nationalities. In a certain sense, Italian humanists had to rediscover all over again what Christine de Pizan had learned nearly a century before. The Italians would build their own discoveries on the same Italian foundations that Christine de Pizan had used: the works of Dante, Petrarch, and Boccaccio and the return to classical sources which these authors recommended. In addition, the traditionally Christian works of Augustine and Boethius also provided part of the initial point of departure.

A significant philosophical development during this end of the fifteenth century will be the introduction of the works of Plato, both in their original Greek and in Latin translations. Plato's arguments for the fundamental equality and non-differentiation of men and women will become important to new theories about women's identity. Yet the ancient Greek philosopher's radical unisex arguments in his utopian *Republic* and *Laws* will also be modified by Christian theology, which emphasizes the central importance of the body for human identity.

The second half of the fifteenth century is a very dynamic period during which there is much human suffering from the effects of the plague, war, and widespread anxiety about the relation of women to various kinds of evils. At the same time, there are considerable advances in the proposals for the education of women in philosophy and in the quality of public dialogue about the concept of woman. In this chapter a brief introduction to the history of educating women in philosophy from the ancient Greek Pythagoreans up to the twelfth century is presented. Then a short summary is given of the contents of texts by two twelfth- to thirteenth-century authors, Vincent of Beauvais and Francesco Barberino, on education of girls and women. Next, we will consider the relation between the two great fourteenth- to fifteenth-century founders of humanist schools, Vittorino of Feltre and Guarino of Verona, and women humanists who begin to be educated in philosophy. Finally, the educational theories of three humanist authors, Leonardo Bruni, Francesco Barbaro, and Albrecht von Eyb will be examined with specific reference to their influence on early Renaissance Humanist women.

WOMEN'S EDUCATION IN PHILOSOPHY THROUGH THE FOURTEENTH CENTURY

In *The Concept of Woman: The Aristotelian Revolution (750 BC–1250 AD)* different theories and practices about the education of women in philosophy were described in some detail. A brief summary will be given of this important aspect of women's history, and readers who would like the relevant references may be directed to the preceding volume.

In the fifth century B.C. Aspasia is thought to have been a disciple of Anaxagoras. Then, according to Plato, Socrates described himself as having been a student of Diotima in the same century. There are no extant texts by either woman, which makes claims about their education as philosophers impossible to prove. The Pythagoreans, who were gathered into religious communities, appeared to have educated women in philosophy. Records suggest that sixteen out of 118 disciples of Pythagoras were women. Both men and women were the educators and the recipients of the education, and fragments remain by female authors who wrote between 400 and 100 B.C. Scholars identify these authors by the names of Perictione I, Theano, Phyntis, Perictione II, Aesara, Myia, and Theano II.

Plato's arguments in the *Republic* and *Laws,* that women ought to be as well educated as men to become philosophers, are well known. Thus it is not surprising that the names of two women, Lastheneia and Axiothea, were recorded by Diogenes Laertius as being educated in the Academy in the fourth century B.C. even after Plato's death. Their names, and the fact that one of them wore men's clothes, were often repeated by humanist philosophers. Diogenes Laertius also described Crates' wife Hipparchia as a serious philosopher who belonged to the Cynic School in the fourth century B.C. The Epicurean School apparently had several women in attendance, and the names of three were recorded: Themisto, Leontium, and Theophilia.

The absence of women in Aristotle's Peripatetic School is particularly notable in view of the acceptance of women by other ancient Greek philosophers into their educational programs. In *The Concept of Woman: The Aristotelian Revolution: 750 BC–1250 AD),* it was suggested that in ancient Greek and medieval philosophy, there was a direct correlation between the concept of woman proposed by a particular philosopher and the presence or absence of women in his school of philosophy. Without going through the details of the argument to defend this claim here, the same phenomenon will be seen in fourteenth- and fifteenth-century philosophy. Women will directly benefit from programs of education set forth within humanist schools while they will still be excluded from participation in academic philosophy, which was still dominated by Aristotelian-based forms of gender polarity. When a woman does become educated in philosophy in relation to the new humanist education, she may begin to manifest an ability in philosophy in her own right. Written documentation of precisely this development in women's ability in philosophy will be seen in some of the authors considered in this chapter.

In Stoic schools male philosophers began to directly discuss the issue of whether women ought to study philosophy. Seneca, living in the first century A.D., addressed essays to two women, Helvia and Marcia, in which he argued that a woman ought never to excuse herself from the search for wisdom and virtue because of her sex. In addition, he offered the practical advice that the study of philosophy will enable them to overcome the extreme passions of grief over the death of a son. Furthermore, the second-century Roman Stoic Musonius Rufus directly argued that women ought to be educated to lead a philosophical life because they have the same reason as men. In *Predications* Musonius Rufus not only invoked

Platonic arguments to prove that men and women have the same fundamental identity. Following Plato's line of argument in the *Republic* and *Laws,* he also argued against those who would claim that women ought to have a different education and different virtues from men. Musonius Rufus concluded that since men's and women's natures were the same, they ought to be given the same education, and to practice the same virtues. Then in the sixth century, the Stoic Christian Boethius in his *Consolation of Philosophy* presented his well-developed feminine model of Lady Philosophy, who taught him everything he needed to learn about life.

Among the Neoplatonists, Plutarch in the first century A.D. popularized Plato's views in many areas, although he did not accept the Greek philosopher's suggestions for the abolition of the family. On the contrary, Plutarch had a great devotion to family life, and his treatise *On the Education of Children* suggested many ways that mothers and fathers ought to cooperate in the education of their children. In addition he suggested that mothers become literate in order to better teach their own children. He also recommended the study of philosophy to women. In the third century the Neoplatonist Porphyry more directly argued, in a letter to his wife Marcella, that she should hold firm to philosophy as her guide. By the fifth century the Neoplatonic school in Alexandria was actually directed by the woman philosopher Hypatia. Her special area of interest was mathematics, in which she worked on the revision of Ptolemy's texts and wrote commentaries on other philosophers' works.

One of the interesting themes in the present chapter will be to trace the influence of Platonism and Neoplatonism on theories about the concept of woman. There were no radically new developments in the Neoplatonic thinking about the relation of women to philosophy until the renewal of Neoplatonism in the fifteenth century. Some of the particular aspects of this later Neoplatonic approach to the concept of woman will be considered along with the earlier prompting to change views about women as a result of the discovery of Plato's arguments about gender identity.

Before turning to specific authors in the humanist tradition, the last part of the history of the education of women in philosophy that needs to be mentioned concerns Christian schools of philosophy. The earliest record of a Christian woman educated in philosophy is found in the Cappadocian tradition. Macrina the Younger (c. 327–c. 379), sister of Saints Basil and Gregory of Nyssa, is recognized in two extant works in Greek by Gregory, *Life of Saint Macrina* and *On the Soul and the Resurrection.*[7] Jaroslav Pelikan states that ". . . at the death of their parents she became the educator of the entire family, and that in both Christianity and Classical culture. Through her philosophy and theology, Macrina was even the teacher of

---

7. Gregory of Nyssa, *A Letter from Gregory, Bishop of Nyssa, On the Life of Macrina,* in *Handmaids of the Lord: Contemporary Descriptions of Feminine Asceticism in the First Six Christian Centuries* (Kalamazoo, Mich.: Cistercian Publications, 1996), #143, pp. 51-86. See also Gregory, Bishop of Nyssa, *The Life of Saint Macrina* (Toronto: Peregrina Publishing Co., 1998). Gregory of Nyssa, *On the Soul and the Resurrection* in *A Select Library of Nicene and Post-Nicene Fathers of the Christian Church,* vol. 5: Gregory of Nyssa (Grand Rapids: Eerdmans, 1979), pp. 430-68. I am extremely grateful to Prof. R. J. Schoeck and Rev. Chrysostom Frank for introducing me to the importance of Saint Macrina.

both of her brothers, who were bishops and theologians. . . ."[8] Macrina integrated Greek philosophy and rhetoric with Christian revelation to provide a model which her brothers followed. Their family home at Annisa (now located in Turkey) served as a kind of informal monastic school divided into three residences, one for men, another for women, and one a hermitage.[9] Those participating in this educational community included also Gregory of Nazianzus. Macrina was widely known for her capacity as a teacher in this "School of Virtue" which drew people continually to the "ideal of philosophy."[10]

Gregory's dialogue *On the Soul and the Resurrection* placed Macrina in the role of "The Teacher," paralleling Socrates' position in Plato's *Phaedo*. Writing in 380, shortly after Macrina's death, Gregory defends the Christian doctrine of the resurrection of the body against different pagan theories, and he places the most important arguments in Macrina's words. Since Macrina was not discussed in the first volume, *The Concept of Woman: The Aristotelian Revolution (750 BC–1250 AD)*, a brief description of her philosophical ability will be offered here.

Macrina poses her methodology in the dialogue: "Well, replied the Teacher, we must seek where we may get a beginning for our discussion upon this point; and if you please, let the defence of the opposing views be undertaken by yourself. . . . Then, after the conflicting belief has been stated, we shall be able to look for the truth."[11] She also directly links the objections to Greek philosophical positions: "The Teacher sighed gently at these words of mine, and then said: Maybe these were the objections, or such as these, that the Stoics and Epicureans collected at Athens made in answer to the Apostle. I hear that Epicurus carried his theories in this very direction."[12] Next, she elaborates Epicurus' theory using traditional philosophical vocabulary and arguments:

> . . . he thought that human life was like a bubble, existing only as long as the breath within was held in by the enveloping substance, inasmuch as our body was a mere membrane, as it were, encompassing a breath; and that on the collapse of the inflation the imprisoned essence was extinguished. To him the visible was the limit of existence; he made our senses the only means of our apprehension of things; he completely closed the eyes of his soul and was incapable of seeing anything in the intelligible and immaterial world, just as a man whose walls and roof obstruct the view outside, remains without a glimpse of all the wonders of the sky.[13]

As the dialogue progresses, Macrina introduces the Neoplatonic theory of man as a microcosm of the universe when she states: "It has been said by wise men that man is a little world in himself and contains all the elements which go to complete the

---

8. Jaroslav Pelikan, *Christianity and Classical Culture: The Metamorphosis of Natural Theology in the Christian Encounter with Hellenism* (New Haven and London: Yale University Press, 1993), p. 8.

9. Joan Peterson, introduction to *The Life of Macrina* in *Handmaids of the Lord*, pp. 42-43.

10. Gregory of Nyssa, *The Life of Saint Macrina* in *Handmaids of the Lord*, pp. 80 and 56.

11. Gregory, *On the Soul and the Resurrection*, p. 431.

12. Gregory, *On the Soul and the Resurrection*, p. 432.

13. Gregory, *On the Soul and the Resurrection*, p. 432.

universe. If this view is a true one (and so it seems), we perhaps shall need no other ally than it to establish the truth of our conception of the soul."[14] Macrina offers her definition of the soul, which is challenged by Gregory, and further refined to reach a common consensus. The complex dialogue weaves its way through sophisticated logical arguments and metaphysical theories until ultimately Macrina solves all the philosophical difficulties encountered. The Teacher, as she was identified by Gregory, truly led the reader as an astute philosopher and guide. A similar early Christian example of a woman educated in philosophy is that of Monica, as depicted by Augustine in his early dialogues *De ordine* and *De beata vita*. Again the dialogue takes place in the context of a small school in which issues of importance are discussed among Christians. In this same time-frame of fourth to fifth century A.D. the two idealized models of women philosophers, Boethius's Lady Philosophy in *The Consolation of Philosophy* and the legend of St. Catherine of Alexandria, add to the notion that women can both be educated in and teach others fundamental philosophical theory.

Between the ninth and eleventh centuries especially, education of women in philosophy occurred mostly in Benedictine monasteries, which were established throughout Europe. One text that most clearly documents the education of woman during this period is the *Hortus Deliciarum* or *Garden of Delights* composed in the twelfth century by Herrad of Landsberg. This large text was an extensive encyclopedia written for religious women. It not only compiled the general knowledge of the age, but it also drew directly upon the writings of philosophers such as Augustine, Boethius, and Anselm to guide students to understand basic philosophical and theological theories. In addition, it included references to the thought of Socrates, Plato, and Aristotle as described in secondary sources. Furthermore, the Augustinian three-part division of soul into memory, understanding, and will was described as well as the philosophical relation of soul to body. Finally, the *Hortus Deliciarum* divided philosophy into the three basic categories of physics, logic, and ethics, and described the subject matter of the seven liberal arts — grammar, rhetoric, dialectic, music, arithmetic, geometry, and astronomy. Using female models to illustrate various virtues, Herrad provided an engendered text and method for women to learn the foundations of western knowledge.

The Benedictine Age marks a high point in the education of women in philosophy for many centuries to come. As has been mentioned frequently in this book, a radical shift in the center of higher education occurred in the thirteenth century. Even though medicine had been taught in Salerno since the eleventh century and law in Bologna since the twelfth, the foundation of four-faculty universities in Paris and Oxford in the thirteenth century began a movement away from the Benedictine monastic centers of education and towards the new urban centers. Within the next two centuries dozens of universities were founded by the union of bishops and royal patrons, and these universities were patterned on the model established by Paris: philosophy was required in the Faculty of Arts, and then Theology, Medicine, or Law followed as graduate faculties. In addition, these new universities were established only for male students, and thus women were *de facto*

14. Gregory, *On the Soul and the Resurrection*, p. 438.

excluded from the academic study of philosophy in a Faculty of Arts. However, women were not completely cut off from higher education, because many Dominican friars, with an academic education, took upon themselves the task of educating and forming Dominican religious women. Thus, many women continued to receive a second-hand academic education through this route.

By the fifteenth century, two hundred years had passed since the historical revolution in institutional education that had limited academic philosophy to the male gender alone. Thus, the whole situation of women's access to education in philosophy had to begin again from the beginning. In addition, as also mentioned often in the present text, simultaneous with the exclusion of women from the new form of higher education, Aristotle's gender polarity rationale for women's inferior intellect and weaker will was inserted into the heart of the philosophical principles studied in Faculties of Arts everywhere. An overriding impression was formed that women were not capable of being educated as philosophers. So the question of women's access to philosophical formation had to overcome two hurdles simultaneously: one was the lack of access to philosophical sources and teachers; the other was the prevailing belief that women were not capable of learning philosophy well.

In the previous chapter we discovered how Christine de Pizan managed to work away at both of these hurdles, first by gaining access to library sources in Paris, and second by engaging directly with the prejudice about women's ability to learn philosophy. Soon we will see how men and women together began to work away at the same hurdles in various cities in Italy. The work of overcoming bias and closed institutional structures had to be done all over again, by different people, and in different situations.

Christine de Pizan, who was born in Venice but lived most of her life near Paris, may also have partly built her own understanding of the education of women on works of previous educational theorists. Two such authors were likely Vincent of Beauvais and Francesco Barberino. Since the present chapter is on women's education in philosophy, each of these theorists of women's education will now be briefly discussed.

Vincent of Beauvais (1190-1264)

In Chapter 7 it was mentioned several times that Christine de Pizan used Vincent of Beauvais's Encyclopedia, *Speculum maius,* to prepare many of her manuscripts. Beauvais claimed in one of the texts included in the general encyclopedia, the *Speculum doctrinale,* that "constant instruction and effective education" in the study of philosophy was the best way to overcome the limitations of ignorance and disordered passions due to the results of the Fall.[15] Beauvais suggested several categories of education for young men: grammar, logic, rhetoric, poetics, moral philosophy, economics (household management), political science (including criminal and civil jurisprudence), military science, medical science, and math-

15. Astrid L. Gabriel, *The Educational Ideas of Vincent of Beauvais* (Notre Dame: University of Notre Dame Press, 1962), pp. 9-10.

ematics.[16] His analysis generally summarized what had already been written on the subject rather than introduced any new theories of education. In philosophical areas such as moral philosophy, Vincent of Beauvais and his disciples summarized the teachings of previous authorities rather than engaged directly in philosophical argument about a particular moral problem.[17]

However, Beauvais was original in the choice of some of the subjects included in his encyclopedic gathering of information about education. For example, in Book 12, chapter 31 of this text he considered practical issues such as how to feed and bathe an infant and how to balance study and physical exercise. It is important to note that Vincent of Beauvais, a Dominican, was not himself a teacher of children, and so his approach to the subject was theoretical rather than practical. St. Louis, King of France, had asked Vincent to compose an encyclopedia of the sciences taught in the universities at the time to be used to educate his sons. Thus Beauvais worked together with the teacher of the children of King Louis of France, providing him with the information needed for the actual education to occur. He composed a treatise, *De eruditione filiorum nobilium (On the education and instruction of noble children),* which was attached to his larger work.[18] In this text Beauvais wrote about the choice of an educational master, qualities of good students, proper discipline, arts of reading, writing, and note-taking, guidelines for making writing public, development of memorization, skills of disputation aimed at developing arguments aimed towards the truth, and development of a moral life and proper friendship.

The last ten chapters (42 to 51) of *De eruditione filiorum nobilium* attended particularly to the education of noble girls. The entire text had been dedicated to Queen Marguerite. One suggestion is that the queen asked the Dominican to write a text to help educate her son Louis (1244-60) and her daughter Isabelle (1242-71);[19] but another is that Beauvais's text on the education of women is actually a homily, on *Ecclesiasticus* 7:25-26, added to the original document rather than a properly constituted appendix.[20]

In any event, the text itself assumes that girls have a reading ability in both French and Latin and the skill to write long passages in either language into notebooks. Beauvais aims at developing both the intellect and will, with particular emphasis on developing a habit of virtuous works and actions. His text is practical in orientation, and seeks to develop in the girls the usual virtues of self-knowledge and self-governance. The text is focused on Biblical exegesis of texts that defend the guarding and segregation of girls from public dangers to their chastity, and it places a prohibition on them to "learn . . . not to run around in strange houses, not to loiter in the streets, nor to get involved in public conversa-

16. Vincent of Beauvais, *Speculum Doctrinale* (Graz, Austria: Akademische Buch-u.-Verlagsanstalt, 1965). See also Gabriel, *The Educational Ideas of Vincent of Beauvais,* pp. 13-15.

17. Gabriel, *The Educational Ideas of Vincent of Beauvais,* p. 19.

18. Vincent of Beauvais, *De eruditione filiorum nobilium,* edited by Arpad Steiner (Cambridge, Mass.: Medieval Academy of America, 1938).

19. Gabriel, *The Educational Ideas of Vincent of Beauvais,* p. 20.

20. Rosemary Barton Tobin, in "Vincent of Beauvais on the Education of Women," *Journal of the History of Ideas* 35 (July-September, 1994): 485-89, 486.

tions. . . ."[21] At the same time, Beauvais also argues that girls should be well educated: "Meanwhile, however, while well brought up girls are kept safe in the above-mentioned way in the care of their parents, it is correct to instruct them in letters and morals."[22]

Even though Beauvais suggests that the primary goal of education is a girl's self-governance over her thoughts and actions, he also offers concrete suggestions that encourage her to learn. In the following passage he paraphrases the advice of St. Jerome in a letter to a woman named Laeta on how to educate her daughter:

> [L]et her have a set of letters made of boxwood or ivory . . . and let her play with them, and let the playing be a road to learning. . . . Let her also have companions in her studies with whom she can engage in rivalry, and by whose praise she would be spurred on. She should not be scolded if she is a little slow, but her mind must be sharpened by praise, so that she may rejoice when she has succeeded and sorry when she has failed. . . .[23]

Although Vincent of Beauvais includes instruction in the usual skills of women's work of weaving and sewing, he also states clearly that girls should be educated in the same areas as boys: "Further to what was said above about boys, the same thing should be done in the youth of girls, that is, they should be instructed in morals and good behavior."[24] Then he stipulates the four virtues that they need to be taught: modesty, humility, silence, and maturity of behavior and gesture. The rest of his text focuses on the need for girls to learn how to subdue their external appearance.

It has been noted that Christine de Pizan "utilized all the authorities introduced by Vincent of Beauvais" in her discussion of the education of women in *Le Trésor de la cité des dames: Le Livre des trois vertus.*[25] At the same time, Beauvais's instruction on the education of girls emphasizes more traditional values associated with single females in the noble class, while Christine de Pizan's text on education of women moved far beyond this previous source. She identifies principles for women of many different classes and situations seeking to develop a program of education useful to all women.

Francesco Barberino (1264-1346)

The second author who may have influenced Christine de Pizan's theories about women's education was born the year that Vincent Beauvais died, 1264. Francesco Barberino, a Tuscan, was trained in both moral philosophy and law. He was best known for his *Documenti d'amore,* which followed the form of a public de-

---

21. Vincent of Beauvais, *De eruditione filiorum nobilium,* XLII. Translated by Andrea Jarmei, as are all passages from this work.

22. Vincent of Beauvais, *De eruditione filiorum nobilium,* XLIII.

23. Vincent of Beauvais, *De eruditione filiorum nobilium,* XLIII.

24. Vincent of Beauvais, *De eruditione filiorum nobilium,* XLIII.

25. Astrid Gabriel, "The Educational Ideas of Christine de Pisan," *Journal of the History of Ideas* 16 (1955): 10; and Gabriel, *The Educational Ideas of Vincent of Beauvais,* p. 44.

fense of several questions concerning the nature of love.[26] The *Documenti d'amore* was a text written primarily for men about the love for women. More significant for the purposes of this chapter was the fact that between 1318 and 1320 Barberino wrote a separate text directly for women entitled *Del reggimento e costumi di donna (On the Regimens and Customs of Women).*[27] This text of over four hundred pages is written in the common language of Tuscany in a simple style accessible to literate women. Perhaps because of its intended audience and subject matter, the *Del reggimento* remained relatively unknown in comparison to the very popular *Documenti d'amore* until it was rediscovered and printed in 1667.

A recent scholar has suggested that Barberino's text *Del Reggimento* bears striking resemblances to Christine de Pizan's *Livre des trois vertus* in structure and content of instruction, especially to bereaved women. In particular it invites women to think about their identities and activities, and practical ways to improvement where possible.[28] In addition, it introduces a feminine personification of wisdom who calls the author to write as a specific mission, as Christine was given the mission to write by her feminine personifications of virtue. Another parallel is seen in that just as Christine referred to herself in her text in the first person "I Christine" so Barberino refers to himself in the first person: "I am Francis" and "Young ladies, I am actually one who is putting together a book."[29] While it is not proven that Christine de Pizan directly took these structural models from Francesco Barberino, she could have read the text in its original language of Tuscan because of her own Italian background. The similarities between them are notable, particularly because of their focus on educating women and on pushing the author into a first-person role in this effort of education. However, the content of the texts differs, and it is to this subject our analysis will now turn.

Barberino writes this text for women within the context of an imaginary intergender dialogue. He opens a dialogue between himself as a male author and women readers by creating an imaginary dialogue between himself and a female figure, Madonna, who challenges him to write not just for men but for women:

> In this story, Francesco, I speak with honesty, and entreat many other women with my lament; and I say that there are many who have written books on the elaborate customs of men, but not of women.[30]

---

26. Francesco Barberino, *Documenti d'amore* (Rome, 1640). The date of composition is given variously as sometime between 1290 and 1314. It was immediately popular in manuscript form and appeared in libraries all over Europe. However, it was not printed until 1640.

27. Francesco Barberino, *Del reggimento e costumi de donna* (Bologna, 1875).

28. See Lilian Dulac, "Mystical Inspiration and Political Knowledge: Advice to Widows from Francesco da Barberino and Christine de Pizan," trans. Thelma Fenster, in *Upon My Husband's Death: Widows in the Literature and Histories of Medieval Europe,* ed. Louise Mirrer (Ann Arbor: University of Michigan Press, 1992), ch. 10, pp. 223-58.

29. Repeated from *Del reggimento* (213, 1.14, 19), in Dulac, "Mystical Inspiration," in *Upon My Husband's Death,* p. 249.

30. Barberino, *Del reggimento,* Proemo 1, 1-8, 3. Translated by Dominique Deslandres, as are all other passages from this text unless otherwise noted.

Barberino is aware of the novelty of his attempting to write this book about women for women, and he places the responsibility for the initiative of this movement in the request of the imaginary female character, Madonna.[31]

In *Del reggimento* Barberino seriously addresses the need to provide an education for women. While Barberino's text is written within the context of traditional European society, it nonetheless considers women's wisdom and virtue to be important topics. In its content and its language *Del reggimento* signals a change from the devaluation of woman common to the polarity tradition; it invites women directly to consider principles related to their respective ways of life. However, the text does not go into details of particular theories of philosophers that could be helpful to women in achieving these goals. So it is more like the treatise on education by Vincent of Beauvais, which indicated that it would be good for girls to be educated in self-governance and the practice of virtues, but did not suggest particular philosophical theories they should study.

Addressing himself to a much larger female audience than did Beauvais, Barberino divided his book into twenty sections, considering twenty different stages in a woman's life. The first section focuses on the beginning of an ethical sense of the difference between right and wrong in a young girl; sections two through seven reflect on issues in marriage; eight through ten consider various religious options for women; eleven through fourteen study different kinds of service in the household; the fifteenth considers children; the sixteenth studies women's general knowledge, adornments, and adventures; the seventeenth studies women's consolations; the eighteenth focuses on love; the nineteenth considers forms of dialogue between women and men; and the twentieth describes women's discourses.[32] The wide range of educational issues for women in this early humanist work is impressive.

In the text itself, female personifications of the various virtues such as industry, eloquence, prudence, and justice are mentioned. However, Madonna points out that while virtues may inform an individual, none of them are able to write a book. Only Francesco, a living human being, can accomplish that. The use of the imagination in this way is an excellent intermediate step that raises in the mind of the female reader the possibility that she might embody some of the characteristics of the imaginary character herself or even that she may become an author. This possibility may have occurred to Christine de Pizan too, had she read Barberino's text. That Francesco Barberino wanted his book to be read by many women is evident from the following exchange, which occurred after he agreed to take on the activity of writing this book for women. When the imaginary Madonna sends her author to meet the female personification of various virtues, Honesty directs Eloquence to help Francesco as follows:

31. Lilian Dulac notes the importance of the interaction of Barberino with the figure of Madonna: "Madonna, protectress of the writer, along with the personified virtues that she delegates to his side, are, with the author himself, the actors in scenes that introduce or interrupt the narrative, as if the text were being written before the reader's eyes" ("Mystical Inspiration," in *Upon My Husband's Death,* p. 224).

32. Barberino, *Del reggimento,* Proemo 11.22–14.130, 18-23.

And here I send you Industry and you, Eloquence, to tell him all of my intentions; and then you will go with him, and both of you remain with him until the work will be finished.

Listen to me, Eloquence, and understand what I say. Your treatise will be on the customs pertinent to women, which I will present in such a way that men will be able to draw upon their fruits. However, this information will be given by Industry. I do not want it to be your obscure speech. So that every woman can easily remember what is written you will speak in rhyme.[33]

This brief introduction to Francesco Barberino's early humanist text on women's education was written within a common theological, philosophical, and political understanding of women's place in the world at the time.[34] Nonetheless it has a style and purpose that opened up new possibilities for women through its forms of intergender dialogue about issues of gender and education.[35] It remains for later humanist authors to open up new dimensions of wisdom and virtue for women and to aid the progress of the reformation of women's education in philosophy.

FIFTEENTH-CENTURY FOUNDERS OF HUMANISTIC SCHOOLS

Turning now from authors who preceded the work of Christine de Pizan to those who were actually contemporary with her, it is important to note two different men who had an impact on the history of the education of women: Guarino of Verona and Vittorino of Feltre. An intellectual and institutional reform of education forms the broader context of their contributions. Previous to this reform, education of young men and women had occurred primarily through religious men and women in monastic communities. Young boys and girls would enter monastic schools, usually as an early vocation to religious life, and if they demonstrated the talent for intellectual work their education followed as a matter of course. The content of their education followed at first a Benedictine model, and later a scholastic model associated with schools and universities educating men for the clerical state, the practice of medicine, or the practice of law. As mentioned previously, men of the Dominican order had a special place in educating women in religious communities during this latter period, and then educated religious women would in turn educate young girls.

---

33. Barberino, *Del reggimento,* Proemo 6, 13-28, 14-15.

34. Dulac, "The perils against which the widow is warned to be on her guard are of a moral order especially. She does not personally have to confront events that thrust her onto the stage of a social or political life in which her role might compare with that of a man. Such an eventuality is not envisaged by Barberino, not even for the widow of high rank, whose sphere of activity will remain very limited. Scarcely anything is asked of her but to put herself wisely in the hands of officials who will act for her" ("Mystical Inspiration," in *Upon My Husband's Death,* p. 240).

35. Dulac notes that Christine de Pizan moves beyond Barberino in her direct appeal to middle-class widows to "take matters into their own hands for their own protection" ("Mystical Inspiration," in *Upon My Husband's Death,* p. 253).

With reformation of educational structures initiated by the early Italian humanists, there was a radical shift in purpose and content of education of boys and girls. Instead of the education being oriented towards a religious or clerical state, or even towards the practice of medicine and law, these fifteenth-century humanists sought to educate their students towards general participation in civic life. They did this by emphasizing classical principles of rhetoric, ethics, and politics. This new orientation signaled a shift away from logic, natural philosophy, and metaphysics. Women were affected by this shift as well as men; and specific ways in which the concept of woman was changed by this early humanist reformation will be traced throughout this chapter.

Boys and girls started to be able to receive an education outside of a monastery or school run by religious. Two early humanists stand out for having founded schools of classical studies: Vittorino of Feltre and Guarino of Verona. These schools offered an alternative place of intellectual and moral formation, especially for young men who were being formed for participation in civic life. At the same time, selected young women also benefited from these schools either by being able to attend them directly or by receiving a parallel education directed by their founders. These small schools had the flexibility of new educational units, which the larger institutional structures associated with universities and monasteries did not have. Thus, new educational opportunities began to open up for women in this period of reform of education for men. In the subsequent analysis of Guarino and Vittorino, because of the interrelation of their educational innovations, material concerning both educators will be found in the section focusing on each one separately. The distinction between them is useful, however, for separating their particular contributions to the history of the concept of woman.

Guarino of Verona (1370-1460)

A few reflections on the academic background of the new humanist educators will be given before turning again more directly to the theme of women's education in philosophy. Both Vittorino and Guarino received their own education in similar ways from traditional academic educations. They were fellow students at the University of Padua at the end of the fourteenth century, when the university was filled with students from England, France, Germany, Hungary, and Italy. A great intellectual vitality among professors attracted the minds of these young humanists, while a general decadence among the lives of many students repelled them.[36] Vittorino lived in Padua as a student and teacher of rhetoric and mathematics between the years 1396 and 1415. Because of a situation of financial poverty, he began to take students into his own home and to tutor them in philosophy and mathematics. In this practical development Vittorino also was able to protect these students from the more general decadent practices found in student life in general.

---

36. William Harrison Woodward, *Vittorino da Feltre and Other Humanist Educators* (New York: Columbia University Bureau of Publications, 1963), pp. 5-15.

Therefore, this situation of financial necessity helped to develop a new model of a private residential school that continued to evolve among the humanist educators.

Another important formative factor for Guarino and Vittorino also occurred during this same time period. Manuel Chrysoloras (1350-1413), a Greek scholar from Constantinople, was invited to the first Chair of Greek Letters in the Studium of Florence. He taught Greek language and literature in Florence from 1397 to 1400 and then in Pavia from 1400 to 1403. Guarino followed Chrysoloras, living in his home in Constantinople between 1403 and 1408.[37] During this time Guarino carried on a correspondence with Francesco Barbaro, who was living in Venice. As will be seen shortly in this chapter, Barbaro wrote an important treatise on women's identity that Guarino likely collaborated on. As James Hankins states it: ". . . Guarino [may have] read the *Republic* with a particular purpose in mind, *viz.* to help his student and life-long friend Francesco Barbaro in the composition of the latter's famous treatise *De re uxoria*. There is a good deal of circumstantial evidence that this was the case."[38] Barbaro was "all his life intimately attached to Guarino" as a friend and fellow humanist, and they both encouraged women's growth and development through education.[39]

A further factor in the quality of Guarino's friendships with other humanists and significant contributions to the history of the concept of woman may also be seen in Guarino's friendship with Leonardo Bruni, another humanist he met in 1410 on his return to Venice and subsequent sojourn in Bologna. As Woodward describes it: "At the instance of Bruni he was at once invited to Florence, where for the first time he found his true calling as a teacher of Graeco-Roman antiquity."[40] Guarino opened a private school in the humanities and began to participate in the humanistic discourse of the Florentines. As will be demonstrated later in this chapter, Leonardo Bruni, just fourteen years later, wrote the first major treatise on women's humanistic education. Thus, two close friends of Guarino, Barbaro and Bruni, both seriously explored central aspects of the concept of woman.

Guarino also edited a manual of the Greek language from Chrysoloras's lectures. This opened the possibility for Italian scholars to begin to read the philosophical works of Plato, Aristotle, and Plutarch in their original language. There is evidence that in Guarino's schools the ethical writings of Plato and Aristotle were given special attention.[41] In 1430 Guarino wrote a *Life of Plato,* a text that emphasized Plato's views on moral and political life and left out all his substantial views in most areas of philosophy, including those related to the concept of woman. As

---

37. William Harrison Woodward, *Studies in Education during the Age of the Renaissance, 1400-1600* (New York: Teachers College Press, 1967). Woodward notes that "[f]or two years he worked incessantly at Greek; the son of Chrysoloras, the young Johannes, a teacher of literature to the noble youth of Constantinople acted as Guarino's master" (p. 28).

38. See James Hankins, "A Manuscript of Plato's *Republic* in the Translation of Chrysoloras and Uberto Decembrio with Annotations of Guarino Veronese," in *Supplementum Festivum: Studies in Honor of Paul Oskar Kristeller,* ed. James Hankins, John Monfasani, and Frederick Purnell, Jr. (Binghamton, N.Y.: Medieval and Renaissance Texts and Studies, 1987), pp. 149-88, 173.

39. Woodward, *Education during the Age of the Renaissance,* p. 29.

40. Woodward, *Education during the Age of the Renaissance,* p. 29.

41. Woodward, *Education during the Age of the Renaissance,* p. 45.

James Hankins summarizes it: "Plato's doctrine of the community of women, children and goods, notorious from Aristotle's *Politics,* is passed over in silence, and of Plato's dialectic, metaphysics, epistemology, and natural philosophy there is no mention at all."[42] This omission is remarkable in view of the fact that Guarino had carefully read and annotated a Latin version of Plato's *Republic.* Hankins, who identified the annotated manuscript as Guarino's in 1983, notes that:

> Guarino has annotated the passages of the *Republic* describing the foundation of the city, the education of the guardians, the censorship of the poets, the tripartite soul and the nature of the four virtues, the community of women, children and goods, the philosopher-kings, and the distinction between knowledge and opinion.[43]

This recent discovery that Guarino had carefully read Plato's *Republic* is significant for the history of the concept of woman because it indicates that one of the early humanist educators, who contributed significantly to the development of education for women, was well aware of Plato's gender unity principles. Even though Guarino chose not to write about them in his *Life of Plato* he did advert to their philosophical significance in relation to Aristotle's principles. Hankins summarizes it as follows: "Guarino was evidently familiar with the *Politics* and *Economics,* for he remarks two instances where Aristotle's doctrine diverges from Plato's (457a6 and 457c10) with respect to female dress and the community of women and children."[44] Although Guarino was interested in other issues than gender identity, he did foster an interest in humanistic education in such a way that supported the education of women, especially by his own disciples who became tutors of women. In addition, he translated Neoplatonic texts that directly mentioned women's education.

Guarino's translation in 1411 from Greek to Latin of Plutarch's *On the Education of Children* is credited with having first forged a new sense of what it is to be an educated human being.[45] Guarino's translation of Plutarch's text on education has also been cited as an extremely important development that gave a very workable ancient model of education to the new humanists.[46] Plutarch (46-125), a Neoplatonist philosopher, was educated in Athens, but spent most of his life teaching in Rome. Plutarch's text on education, the first book of his collected writings entitled *Moralia,* contains interesting teachings about woman's identity. Most notable for our purpose is the final two paragraphs of his treatise *On the Education of Children,* where he introduces the model of a mother who decided to educate herself in literary skills in order to be able to educate her children:

42. Hankins, "A Manuscript of Plato's *Republic,*" in *Supplementum Festivum,* p. 167.

43. Hankins, "A Manuscript of Plato's *Republic,*" in *Supplementum Festivum,* pp. 171 and 151, note 4.

44. Hankins, "A Manuscript of Plato's *Republic,*" in *Supplementum Festivum,* p. 172.

45. Woodward, *Vittorino da Feltre and Other Humanist Educators,* p. 25.

46. Edward J. Power, *Main Currents in the History of Education* (New York/San Francisco/Toronto/London: McGraw-Hill, 1962), pp. 278-79.

We must endeavour, therefore, to employ every proper device for the discipline of our children, emulating the example of Eurydice, who, although she was an Illyrian and an utter barbarian, yet late in life took up education in the interest of her children's studies. The inscription which she dedicated to the Muses sufficiently attests her love for her children:

> Eurydice of Hierapolis
> Made to the Muses this her offering
> When she had gained her soul's desire to learn.
> Mother of young and lusty sons was she,
> And by her diligence attained to learn
> Letters, wherein lies buried all our lore.[47]

Plutarch's model of an educated mother is not to be considered an exception or oddity. He insists in the final words of his treatise that his goals are achievable. In addition, although he recognizes at the beginning of the work on education that nature is important, he emphasizes the greater role of reason, or the act of learning, and habit, or constant practice. He then concludes that the combination of nature, reason, and habit is perfected in Pythagoras, Socrates, and Plato, and that they ought to be a model for others. In fact, Plutarch states directly that "it is necessary to make philosophy as it were the head and front of all education."[48] Plutarch also argued in other books of his *Moralia* that women ought to be educated in philosophy. In his "Advice to Bride and Groom," he invoked the model of the Pythagorean woman philosopher Theano and suggested that both husband and wife study philosophy together; and in "Dinner of Seven Wise Men," he introduced with admiration another female philosopher, Eumetis, who also contributed her advice to civic government.[49]

In other parts of the essay on the education of children Plutarch speaks about the biological aspect of motherhood in breeding and nursing the child. Here, he introduces the value of a mother nursing her own child: "Mothers ought, I should say, themselves to feed their infants and nurse them themselves. For they will feed them with a livelier affection and greater care, as loving them inwardly, and, according to the proverb, to their finger-tips."[50] In an interesting appeal to authority, Plutarch introduces Plato to support the claim that the earliest education of a child is important: "Plato, that remarkable man, quite properly advises nurses, even in telling stories to children, not to choose at random, lest haply their minds be filled at the outset with foolishness and corruption."[51]

Finally, Plutarch in *On the Education of Children* sets forth a principle that is central to the humanist educational reform, namely the gathering of texts written by ancient authors:

47. Plutarch, *The Education of Children,* in *Plutarch's Moralia,* 14 vols. (Cambridge, Mass.: Harvard University Press, 1959), vol. 1 (#14), pp. 67-69.

48. Plutarch, *The Education of Children,* in *Plutarch's Moralia,* vol. 1 (#7), 35.

49. Plutarch, *Moralia,* II. 138B-154B, 337-93. For a consideration of the relation between Plutarch's theory of women's education in philosophy and other aspects of his gender theory see Allen, *The Concept of Woman: The Aristotelian Revolution (750 BC–1250 AD),* pp. 195-201.

50. Plutarch, *The Education of Children,* in *Plutarch's Moralia,* vol. 1 (#3), 13-15.

51. Plutarch, *The Education of Children,* in *Plutarch's Moralia,* vol. 1 (#5), 17.

In regard to education I do not know why it is necessary to take the time to say more; but in addition to the foregoing, it is useful, or rather it is necessary, not to be indifferent about acquiring the works of earlier writers, but to make a collection of these, like a set of tools in farming. For the corresponding tool of education is the use of books, and by their means it has come to pass that we are able to study knowledge at its source.[52]

Following Plutarch's lead, Guarino of Verona put into practice many of the Neoplatonist's suggestions. In particular, Guarino focused on the education of children who would be formed for public life in relation to extended households.

In 1414, just three years after translating Plutarch's work *On the Education of Children,* Francesco Barbaro visited Florence and encouraged Guarino to leave the city, presumably because of political tensions, and to reestablish himself in Venice. Guarino accordingly opened a small school in Venice, and in 1415 Vittorino of Feltre joined him there.[53] During the next year and a half Guarino taught Vittorino Greek while Vittorino taught Guarino Latin, and the two men established a close friendship that lasted the rest of their lives. In addition Guarino married in 1418, and eventually had a large family of over twelve children, most of whom appear to have been educated by humanistic principles.[54]

The two humanists, Guarino of Verona and Vittorino of Feltre, worked together for a few years until Guarino moved to Verona to continue his school for humanistic education there. Sometime after 1421 Guarino became a Master of Rhetoric for the City of Verona. The school of Guarino was widely respected and its influence spread beyond the borders of the city. "So great was the honor in which the famous teacher Guarino Guarini of Verona was held, for example, that he was given the task in 1443 of delivering the inaugural lecture of the new-founded University of Ferrara."[55] In fact, the University of Ferrara grew out of the humanist school Guarino had established with the financial help of the Marquis Leonello d'Este, who had been his student as a young boy. Guarino's reputation was so important to learned men and women that Isotta Nogarola, a humanist author in her own right, sought hard to win his approbation. At the same time, however, there is no evidence that girls or women were directly educated in Guarino's schools as they were in the schools of his friend Vittorino.[56]

---

52. Plutarch, *The Education of Children,* in *Plutarch's Moralia,* vol. 1 (#10), 37.

53. Woodward, *Vittorino da Feltre and Other Humanist Educators,* pp. 16-17. See also Woodward, *Education during the Age of the Renaissance,* p. 31.

54. Woodward, *Education during the Age of the Renaissance,* p. 32.

55. Gordon Griffiths, James Hankins, and David Thompson, eds. and trans., *The Humanism of Leonardo Bruni: Selected Texts* (Binghamton, N.Y.: Medieval and Renaissance Texts and Studies, 1987), p. 8.

56. Woodward, *Education during the Age of the Renaissance,* p. 34. One of Vittorino's female pupils, Margherita Gonzaga, later married the Marquis Leonello d'Este, p. 36.

Vittorino of Feltre (1378-1446) and the Gonzaga Household

While Guarino became established as a humanistic educator in Verona, Vittorino moved back to Padua and began to take in student boarders. Both men had periods of teaching in Chairs of Rhetoric at universities in their respective localities at the same time that they worked with younger students in their new school curriculums. In 1422 Vittorino accepted a Chair of Rhetoric at the University of Padua, but because of the poor state of discipline and the decadent student lifestyle in the university town, he decided to leave the University of Padua. He resigned his Chair and moved back to Venice.

Then, in 1423-24, Vittorino accepted an invitation of Gianfrancesco and his wife Paola de Malatesta Gonzaga to move to Mantua and open an official school of humanities under their patronage. This school, set aside on private grounds, with both faculty and student boarders, functioned with great success for the next twenty-three years. It was open not only to children of the nobility but also to intelligent boys whose families were in less solvent financial situations. Vittorino "has thrown open his school to ability without distinction of rank and provided an education free of all charges to many deserving boys. He treated all on one and the same footing and had no higher interest than their success."[57] In addition, Vittorino accepted students of very different ages, adapting his educational program to meet the needs of each one according to ability and situation in life.

Vittorino based his educational program on the *Institutio Oratoria* of Quintilian (35–c. 100).[58] Vittorino and Guarino had studied Quintilian together during their time in Venice, and they had both determined to put his program of education into practice in their new humanistic schools.[59] Quintilian was nearly contemporary with Plutarch, but he had been born and educated first in Spain before coming to Rome to live and to teach. His *Institutio Oratorio,* written towards the end of his life after many years of teaching, outlined an extensive program of education for boys from the first moments of their lives, and focused much attention on the place of the family in this program of education. Quintilian stated:

> My aim, then, is the education of the perfect orator, . . . [l]et our ideal orator then be such as to have a genuine title to the name of philosopher: it is not sufficient that he should be blameless in point of character . . . : he must also be a thorough master of the science and the art of speaking, to an extent that perhaps no orator has yet attained. . . . Perfect eloquence is assuredly a reality, which is not beyond the reach of human intellect.[60]

In sum, then, a good orator according to Quintilian needs to have a good character, be a philosopher, and have perfect eloquence by mastering the science and art of

---

57. Woodward, *Vittorino da Feltre and Other Humanist Educators,* p. 79.
58. Quintilian, *The Institutio Oratoria of Quintilian,* 4 vols. (Cambridge, Mass.: Harvard University Press, 1953).
59. Woodward, *Studies in Education during the Age of the Renaissance,* pp. 15 and 31.
60. Quintilian, *Institutio Oratoria,* Pr. I, 9 and 18-20.

speaking. Quintilian later added the art of writing to this list of characteristics as well.

The first stage of education described by Quintilian is that of the nurse who takes care of an infant as soon as he or she is born. It is here that the classical author directly refers to woman's identity:

> Above all see that the child's nurse speaks correctly. The ideal, according to Chrysippus, would be that she should be a philosopher: failing that he desired that the best should be chosen, as far as possible. No doubt the most important point is that they should be of good character: but they should speak correctly as well. It is the nurse that the child first hears, and her words that he will first attempt to imitate.[61]

Quintilian accepts the advice of the Stoic philosopher Chrysippus and offers even more supportive evidence in support of the claim that the nurse should be as highly educated as possible as well as having a good character. In addition, he argues that the mother of the child should have the same standards:

> As regards parents, I should like to see them as highly educated as possible, and I do not restrict this remark to fathers alone. We are told that the eloquence of the Gracchi owed much to their mother Cornelia, whose letters even to-day testify to the cultivation of her style. Laelia, the daughter of Gaius Laelius, is said to have reproduced the elegance of her father's language in her own speech, while the oration delivered before the triumvirs by Hortensia, the daughter of Quintus Hortensius, is still read and not merely as a compliment to her sex.[62]

These reflections on the place of education in women's identity occur at the very beginning of Quintilian's *Institutio Oratoria,* in contrast to Plutarch's reflections, which occurred at the end of his *Moralia.* In both cases, however, the classical authors make a clear argument that women ought to be educated primarily for the higher quality of service they will be able to give to the boys who will be educated in their care. At the same time, however, Quintilian does offer the examples cited above of women who used their oratorical powers in more public contexts. As will be seen in the following descriptions of the women who were educated by Vittorino, they did go far beyond their own household in exercising their educated oratorical skills.

We now turn directly to our topic of the education of women in humanistic schools. Vittorino did accept female students into his school at Mantua. Cecilia Gonzaga (1425-1451) was the most prominent of his students. Margherita Gonzaga, who married Leonello d'Este, also studied there, as did Barbara von Hohenzollern, a princess from Brandenburg who later married Ludovico Gonzaga and continued sponsoring the humanist school directed by Vittorino. Girls and

---

61. Quintilian, *Institutio Oratoria,* I.i. 4-5.
62. Quintilian, *Institutio Oratoria,* I.i. 6.

women were beginning to receive a new form of education directly from one of the great humanist founders of the new schools.

As will be seen, young women who had received the benefits of a new form of humanistic education often had difficulty sustaining the intellectual life in a public context after their formal education ended. This is not a surprising phenomenon, since new possibilities were also just being forged for men. Careers in civil life for married or single men, not in the clerical state, were just opening up for humanists. The model offered by Christine de Pizan of a woman who could earn her living as a professional writer did not yet penetrate into the Italian context. Just as Christine was completing her literary career, and living in seclusion during the political turmoil in France, these new humanistic schools and programs of education were opening for women in Italy.

A short description is in order of the curriculum Vittorino offered to his male and female students. Greek and Latin skills were developed together right from the beginning. "Cecilia Gonzaga was already learning the grammar at the age of seven, and rapidly became proficient; and possibly her brother Gianlucido had begun even earlier."[63] There is also evidence that at the age of six Cecilia had been given two Latin manuals for instruction and in 1432 at the age of seven she received a copy of the four Gospels in Greek.[64] Reading aloud, memorization, and recitation in Latin and Greek were daily exercises for Vittorino's students. "Whole orations of Cicero or Demosthenes, books of Livy and Sallust, besides large portions of Vergil and Homer, were recited with accuracy and taste by boys or girls of less than fourteen years of age. And this art of Recitation was regarded as of the greatest importance by Vittorino, as evidence of intelligent appreciation of the matter and form of classical reading."[65]

It is significant to note in passing that the language of education was not the vernacular that had been developing among earlier humanists such as Dante, Petrarch, and Boccaccio in Italy and Christine de Pizan in France. Instead, the turn to the Renaissance of ancient Greek and Latin texts by the Italian humanist educators shifted the focus back to Greek and a dynamic new Ciceronian type of Latin as the proper language for educated men and women. However, since many girls were learning the languages along with the boys, the question of language no longer barred their access to important texts. Consequently, educated women outside of monasteries and convents soon were writing in Latin as well as men.

Other subjects taught in Vittorino's school were natural philosophy, mathematics, music, grammar with composition, history, literature, and ethics. Vittorino developed a large library of sources, including Plato's dialogues, Aristotle's writings, and works of the Stoics. Significantly, the study of logic and especially dialectical disputation was not emphasized in humanist schools. Following Petrarch's earlier rejection of the use of clever arguments in public disputations without regard for the search for truth, other Italian humanists tended to temper instruction in logic in their schools. In this way, logic was used as a means to clarity, proper rea-

---

63. Woodward, *Vittorino da Feltre and Other Humanist Educators,* pp. 50-51.
64. Woodward, *Vittorino da Feltre and Other Humanist Educators,* p. 70.
65. Woodward, *Vittorino da Feltre and Other Humanist Educators,* p. 40.

soning, and the detection of fallacies rather than as an end in itself. Vittorino lived to the age of sixty-eight, and his directions and example for the new education were respected all over Italy. As will be seen shortly in the consideration of a text on women's education by Leonardo Bruni, the basic orientations practiced in Vittorino's school were passed on as particularly useful to men and women who wanted to become educated humanists in the new Italian Renaissance tradition.

There is a notable similarity between Christine de Pizan's situation in France and that of several women humanists in Italy. These women who were breaking new ground in the concept of woman by their own education and example were often supported by the more stable institutional models for women's education, i.e., religious communities. There is a continual movement back and forth, in and out of women's religious communities, and in and out of participation in public forms of oration and dialogue. The solid practices for a life of wisdom and virtue, which had been forged for centuries by women's religious communities, provided a foundation on which humanist women could begin to forge new models of wisdom and virtue. Examples of this phenomenon are found in the lives of Cecilia Gonzaga, who after having received her humanistic education from Vittorino entered religious life in 1444, and Laura Cereta (1469-1499) who, at the age of seven spent two years in a convent being educated in reading and writing, and who then returned home to be educated in humanistic studies by her father.[66]

While educating the mind to higher knowledge of self and of the world, and disciplining the will towards greater self-governance, were common goals for both religious and humanistic education, there is one important difference that needs to be noted. The content of the texts studied varied significantly. Generally speaking, religious communities did not accept secular poetry or classical pagan essays as part of their curriculum. Thus the enthusiasm for the Renaissance revival of ancient Greek and Latin secular texts would not have been shared by women's religious communities. A particular example of this phenomenon may suffice to demonstrate this point. Cecilia Gonzaga wanted to enter a religious community against the wishes of her father, Francesco Gonzaga, who had founded the school headed by Vittorino da Feltre in Mantua. He wanted his daughter, who was well educated in humanistic studies, to remain in the world. Both Cecilia's mother and Vittorino supported Cecilia's desires for a consecrated life, but she was not able to go against her father's wishes until he died in 1444. Then, both Cecilia and her widowed mother Paola Gonzaga entered this same religious community which she had founded.

In a letter written by Gregorio Correr (1409-64) to Cecilia during the interim period, when she was considering whether to remain in the world as a humanist or to enter religious life, a stark contrast is drawn between the books she should study in the convent and those available to her in the world of humanistic studies. Gregorio Correr had studied in Vittorino's school and since that time he had been ordained as a priest and was in service to the Pope. Vittorino had asked Gregorio

---

66. See the introduction to *Her Immaculate Hand: Selected Works By and About the Women Humanists of Quattrocento Italy,* ed. Margaret L. King and Albert Rabil, Jr. (Binghamton, N.Y.: Medieval and Renaissance Texts and Studies, 1983), especially pp. 17-25.

Correr to write to Cecilia to offer his own opinion about her situation in the hopes that it would also persuade her father to allow her to fulfill her wishes. The letter primarily identifies difficulties Cecilia would face if she were to stay in the world of courtly life while at the same time attempting to live in celibacy and to continue her studies. However, it also offers concrete suggestions about what she should study as a way to prepare to leave her household and enter religious life:

> There remains [something to be said about your studies]. I forbid utterly the reading of secular literature, particularly the works of the poets. For how can I believe that you have renounced the world if you love the things which are of the world? What does it matter what form your love for the world takes? Certainly you love the world if you love worldly literature. Laymen can be forgiven if, having at least given up indecent writers, they continue to study others. [But] a bride of Christ may read only sacred books and ecclesiastical writers. So you must put aside your beloved Virgil, with Vittorino's pardon. Take up instead the Psalter [and], instead of Cicero, the Gospel.[67]

This passage is very instructive, for in it the author reveals that he is even going against the general educational program of Vittorino by suggesting to Cecilia that she refrain from studying Virgil and Cicero. The strong use of the word 'forbid' by Gregorio Correr suggests that he may have been given some authority as a spiritual director by Cecilia's mother, Paola, and perhaps during the personal meeting that precipitated the writing of the letter in the first place. It is also important to note that his directives would not necessarily be followed in a convent, which would be under another line of authority, or the directives of the Prioress. However, they do indicate a certain differentiation of secular from Christian works, and support the conclusion that at this early period of the humanistic reformation secular works were not valued in the same way as classical Christian texts.

In the following passage from his letter Gregorio Correr emphasizes the separation of secular and Christian works, while still encouraging Cecilia to engage in the highest level of study.

> Believe me, I speak from experience: even if secular literature causes no harm beyond this, it leads the mind away from divine reading. You have in ecclesiastical writers, if you require it, the highest eloquence. Turn to the books of Lactantius, Cyprian, Hilary, Jerome, Ambrose, Augustine, Gregory, Leo, Cassian, Sulpitius, Bernard, and Salvianus also, whose books *On the Providence of God* I brought back with me from German dungeons to Italy on my return from the Council of Basel. Is there not found here such eloquence that there is no need to seek from the heathen words which delight and persuade?[68]

It is also important to note that Gregorio Correr is not differentiating a woman's

---

67. Gregorio Correr, "Letter to the virgin Cecilia, on Fleeing this worldly life," in *Her Immaculate Hand,* pp. 102-3.
68. Gregorio Correr, "Letter to the virgin Cecilia," p. 103.

list of books to study from those appropriate for a man in similar circumstances. The clue that he is suggesting these guidelines for anyone wanting to live a serious Christian life is the phrase "Believe me, I speak from experience. . . ." He had been a student of Vittorino's and had loved the new humanistic studies. In fact, Gregorio Correr is known for having written at the age of eighteen a tragedy called *Progne,* which received great approbation from Vittorino. He shared with Cecilia his own intense fascination with humanistic studies: "But immersed as a youth in secular studies, I was overcome by an enormous and frenzied love of the poets. I could not live a day without Virgil. I composed several verses each day in imitation of him. Vittorino hoped I would become, as it were, another Virgil."[69]

Gregorio Correr also notes in his letter to Cecilia that he had written a satire about the education of boys while he was in Vittorino's school at Mantua and that he had written six other satires and a lyric poem. He also noted that he was driven by competition with another student who wrote poetry more eloquently than he did. His turn to satire as a form of literary creation may indicate further how often the medium of exaggeration can be used as a kind of weapon, not so much to express fundamental truths about reality as to establish a reputation for cleverness by ridiculing someone or something else. In any event, Gregorio Correr vulnerably shares with Cecilia Gonzaga his own past experience with humanistic studies, and concludes from it that his advice would be worthwhile for her as well. He adds: "Why do I speak at such length about myself? So that you may understand that I have passed through the thorns and brambles of secular letters, from which I now dissuade you with such concern, and from which, having barely escaped with rent shirt and full of wounds, I flee to the healing power of divine studies."[70]

In this remarkable letter, Gregorio Correr speaks with Cecilia from his personal experience and encourages her to make a decision similar to his own. We have no written response, nor do we know what texts she continued to study in her life, but as mentioned above, Cecilia Gonzaga did enter a convent with her mother, Paola de Malatesta Gonzaga, after the death of her father, Gianfrancesco Gonzaga. Other women humanists will carry on a tradition of study of humanistic texts in the world, and they will relate to Cecilia Gonzaga as one of the original models for this choice. Costanza Varano, related by blood to Cecilia Gonzaga through the Malatesta line, will write to her during this same period.

Our analysis now turns to the consideration of more substantial written contributions by three humanist philosophers: Leonardo Bruni, Francesco Barbaro, and Albrecht von Eyb. The text of each philosopher will be regarded with specific reference to the particular philosophy of gender incorporated. While each philosopher wrote specifically on some aspect of the concept of woman, each introduced something innovative into the discourse about woman's identity in relation to man.

69. Gregorio Correr, "Letter to the virgin Cecilia," p. 104.
70. Gregorio Correr, "Letter to the virgin Cecilia," p. 105.

LEONARDO BRUNI (1369-1444)

Before turning to a direct analysis of the contents of Leonard Bruni d'Arezzo's (or Aretinus's) important essay on women's education, some introductory reflections need to be made about Bruni's life and about his place in the history of humanistic studies with respect to the work of previous philosophers. Leonardo Bruni, who came from a poor family background as the son of a grain dealer in Arezzo, was informally adopted after his father's death by Coluccio Salutati, the Chancellor of Florence. Then, while studying law in Florence he converted to the study of Greek literature when Chrysoloras arrived in Florence. As mentioned previously, Bruni became friends with Guarino of Verona, and prevailed upon him to move to Florence and open the school in humanistic studies there. In 1412 Guarino replaced Chrysoloras in the Civic Florentine Chair of Greek Studies.[71] Later on, Bruni became a Secretary in the Papal Court and then married a wealthy woman named Tommasa. Finally, Bruni was appointed to the widely respected position of Chancellor of Florence for the last seventeen years of his life.[72] The elegance of Bruni's tomb attests to his economic status at the end of his life, and to the fact that within humanistic Florence a man's nobility was determined not by his blood but by his civic virtue.

Just these facts of Bruni's humble origins and later position of great importance testify to the way in which humanistic education empowered a man on the basis of ability, rather than of nobility or wealth, to flourish in the public life of an important city. Bruni is considered "the most distinguished of that first generation of Italian humanists to learn Greek under Manuel Chrysoloras."[73] In his *Commentarius* Bruni describes his own decision to leave the study of law at the University of Florence for the study of Greek:

> For seven hundred years now, no one in Italy has been able to read Greek, and yet we admit that it is from the Greeks that we get all our systems of knowledge. . . . There are plenty of teachers of the Civil Law, so you will always be able to study that, but this is the one and only teacher of Greek; if he should disappear, there would then be nobody from whom you could learn.
>
> Overcome by such arguments, I took myself to Chrysoloras, with such an ardor to study that what I learned in my waking hours during the day, I would be working over at night even in my sleep.[74]

Leonardo Bruni's skill in language led him to become a well-known translator of classical Greek texts into Latin. Bruni first translated Plato's *Phaedo* (1403-5), *Apology, Crito, Gorgias* (1405-9), *Phaedrus* (1424), and *Letters* (1426). Then in 1426-27 he published a collection of translations of Plato's *Phaedo, Gorgias, Crito,*

---

71. Woodward, *Education during the Age of the Renaissance,* p. 30.

72. For details about Bruni's career and family see Lauro Martines, *The Social World of the Florentine Humanists: 1360-1460* (Princeton: Princeton University Press, 1963), pp. 165-76 and 199ff.

73. Griffiths et al., *The Humanism of Leonardo Bruni,* p. 23.

74. Cited in Griffiths et al., *The Humanism of Leonard Bruni,* pp. 23-24.

The Wealth of the Tomb of Leonardo Bruni

Apology, Phaedrus, and *Letters.* He also translated Xenophon's *Apology* (1407) and *Oeconomicus* (1420), which had been mistakenly ascribed to Aristotle.

The humanist community of discourse rose up initially around Manuel Chrysoloras and his love for significant texts. This community of discourse, begun in private conversations in a particular household, soon spread to numerous cities in Italy. As Margaret King has well documented: "Venetians engaged with non-Venetians in the circulation of important texts. Leonardo Bruni asked Pietro Miani to give to Chrysoloras Bruni's copy of [Augustine's] *The City of God,* and to request that scholar to bring to the curia any interesting Greek manuscripts."[75] Later, Bernardo Bembo's transcribed and annotated copy of Bruni's translation of Plato's *Phaedo* was donated to the Vatican library. Greek and Latin texts traveled back and forth among the various humanists and their libraries, creating an intellectual union — in Plutarch's analogy — of tools for education.

During the years 1404-1409, very early in his career, Bruni translated several works of Plutarch. A century would pass before Plutarch's several-volume *Moralia* would be published, in 1509, by Aldus Manutius in the original Greek.[76] Also, Bruni's translations preceded by two years Guarino of Verona's popular translation of the first book of the *Moralia, On the Education of Children.* Thus, Bruni was a central figure in making Plutarch's theories available to the Italian humanists.

Plutarch is an important transitional figure for woman's identity in several ways. He was trained in the Academy in Athens, and integrated many Platonic and Aristotelian themes of gender identity. Since his theories are considered in some detail in *The Concept of Woman: The Aristotelian Revolution (750 BC–1250 AD),* only a few reflections will be offered here. Although Plutarch incorporated several of Aristotle's gender polarity principles in the areas of opposites and generation, he chose a radically different direction in the areas of wisdom and virtue. Plutarch had a great devotion to family life and a great reverence for the capacities of women to excel in wisdom and virtue. Drawing upon the Platonic tradition that men and women have the same virtues, he wrote treatises *On the Bravery of Women* and *On Sayings of Spartan Women* that demonstrated multiple examples of women's bravery, intelligence, and capacity for virtue. He described women philosophers, wives and husbands who worked together in governing the household, and men and women who worked together in the public domain as well. Thus, Plutarch provided a model for Bruni of a theory of gender that corrected both the extreme present in Plato's unisex theory and that in Aristotle's gender polarity theory. In addition, he provided a model of an educated man who chose to marry and live in a household and who was devoted to philosophy, to great works of literature, to poetry, and to a life of civic virtue. While Plutarch's model was no doubt extremely useful to Bruni, at the same time it did not enter into the deeper philosophical foundations of theories of gender identity, as had Plato or Aristotle before him. Thus, further philosophical work had to be accomplished before a new foundation for the concept of woman in relation to man could be articulated.

75. Margaret King, *Venetian Humanism in an Age of Patrician Dominance* (Princeton: Princeton University Press, 1986), p. 6.
76. Lowry, *The World of Aldus Manutius,* p. 151.

Civic Humanism and Gender Identity

Bruni's work in translation and his text *On Correct Translation* (1424-26) are considered foundational for the emerging field of literary criticism.[77] Attempting to convey the spirit of an author's thought rather than a literal accounting, Bruni offered an elegant account of an important text, but he also made errors of interpretation. This dual aspect of elegance and errors sparked several academic debates and controversies; Bruni's work was compared with previous scholastic versions of the same texts, versions that were usually inelegant but accurate. However, in spite of his errors Bruni's versions became immediately popular outside of academia and remained so for centuries.[78]

Leonardo Bruni's insistence on the value of the vernacular language, especially when it was integrated with eloquent translations of classical texts and applied to contemporary Florentine life, started a movement called "civic humanism."[79] In the 1430s Bruni argued that every language has its own perfection, and he brought to the life of Florence a renewed vitality, following the earlier literary contributions of Dante, Petrarch, and Boccaccio. In addition, since all the ancient languages such as Greek, Latin, and Hebrew were originally vernacular languages, the hope was that Florentine Italian would in time evolve to the eloquence of these others languages. Thus, it became a duty of a civic humanist to work for this goal by writing eloquently in the vernacular. As Hans Baron summarizes it:

> By engendering a new type of Humanism — *civic Humanism* — the transition about 1400 in the early Quattrocento even transcended in significance the history of Florence and of Renaissance Italy. Civic Humanism, as it emerged from the challenge of the crisis, exhibited . . . several diverse facets. There was the new philosophy of political engagement and active life, developed in opposition to ideals of scholarly withdrawal. There was the new historical interpretation of Rome and the *Imperium Romanum* from the vantage-point of contemporary political experience. And finally, there was the fresh approach to a vernacular Humanism and a defence of the moderns against the ancients — the still inconsistent, but already unmistakable demand that in the present-day world, in dealing with one's own state, language, and literature, one should act as the ancients acted in dealing with *their* states, languages, and literatures.[80]

---

77. For dates of translations, see James Hankins, *Plato in the Italian Renaissance,* 2 vols. (Leiden/New York: E. J. Brill, 1990). See also Walter Ullmann, *Medieval Foundations of Renaissance Humanism* (London: Paul Elek, 1977), esp. pp. 172ff. Ullmann notes the development within humanism of reflective study of language, identification of authorship, concern with style.

78. See the note to Bruni's translation of the *Economics,* in which it is stated that from the fifteenth century there were 219 copies of Bruni's text in contrast to only 13 of Alberti's treatise "On the Family," *The Humanism of Leonardo Bruni,* p. 302.

79. Hans Baron, *The Crisis of the Early Italian Renaissance* (Princeton: Princeton University Press, 1966), p. 338.

80. Baron, *The Crisis of the Early Italian Renaissance,* pp. 459-60.

The last of the three goals of civic humanism was particularly relevant for the history of women in education. Since several respected ancient philosophers argued that women ought to be educated in philosophy, language, and literature, it followed that the perfect contemporary state would do the same.

Without entering into the controversies about when Leonardo Bruni wrote his famous *Laudatio* of the City of Florence, it is thought that this particular oration along with his extensive *History of the Florentine People* provided the historical foundation for the birth of civic humanism.[81] The aim of these compositions was to form in the minds of Florentines a deep admiration for their proper identity, and to awaken within them the desire to make Florence into a new Athens or a new Rome. This appeal to the highest glory for the city of Florence provided the background for the development of humanist education for men as well as for women.

As we turn to the philosophical aspects of the new civic humanism and the concept of woman, the central question of the importance of Plato's and Aristotle's ethical and political philosophy must be considered. Leonardo Bruni had a central role in this aspect of the new developments as well, for he made a new translation of Aristotle's *Ethics* (1416-17) and *Politics*. These translations, along with a translation of the pseudo-Aristotelian (Xenophon's) *Economics,* presented the Greek philosopher as an eloquent writer and thinker. Thus Bruni's translations of Aristotle became extremely popular in humanistic circles, which considered literary eloquence as having the highest value. In addition, in 1429 he wrote a popular *Life of Aristotle* to give a general description of the Greek philosopher's main contributions to rhetoric, ethics, logic, and natural philosophy.

The translations done by Bruni also grappled with the problem of how to make the pagan Greek philosophers acceptable to Christian readers, especially on topics such as reincarnation and the natural immortality of the soul, whether Socrates' death was a suicide or martyrdom, how to interpret erotic sexual behavior in Plato's dialogues, and how to explain Plato's theories about women and the family. In some situations, Bruni simply avoided or obscured controversial passages, and in others he actually changed their meaning.[82]

Of particular note for the history of the concept of woman, Bruni refused to retranslate the *Republic*. A 1402 translation of Plato's *Republic* had been done by Manuel Chrysoloras, Bruni's Greek teacher, and Uberto Decembrio (ca. 1370-1427).[83] The translation appears to have happened in two phases, Chrysoloras translated from Greek to a literal Latin, and Decembrio, not referring to the Greek original, rewrote the Latin to make it more elegant. As a result of this two-phased

81. See Baron, who devotes several chapters of his *The Crisis of the Early Italian Renaissance* to this topic, chapters 9-12.

82. Hankins has traced several of these distortions in his text *Plato in the Italian Renaissance*. He notes that in his translation of the *Phaedrus* Bruni changes suggestions of homoerotic love into chaste Platonic love; in his translation of Plato's *Letters* he represents Plato as a lover of liberty and supporter of oligarchical government like the city of Florence; and in a translation of Alcibiades' speech from the *Symposium* he changes the meaning of Alcibiades' attempted sexual seduction of Socrates into a pursuit of Socrates' wisdom, p. 80.

83. Hankins, *Plato in the Italian Renaissance,* pp. 108-10.

translation, the first Latin version of the *Republic* had many errors and omissions in relation to Plato's ontological theories.

There was also a difficulty for the translators concerning Book V of the *Republic* where in the original text Plato suggested a community of wives, the abolition of private property and family, and the equality of women and men fighting in wars and in governing the republic. Plato had offered principles of gender unity (unisex) to support these claims, namely, that the identity of a person resided only in the soul, that the soul could be born in various reincarnations in male or female (or even animal) bodies, and therefore that there are no significant differences between the two sexes. Women and men should be educated for the same things and be allowed to serve the same functions in the republic if the nature of their soul is similar. The ancient Greek philosopher allowed for some weakness in women that would mandate a slightly longer period of education, but otherwise there were to be no differences between the sexes. Chrysoloras and Uberto Decembrio's translation of Book V of the *Republic* was misleading, and in a subsequent commentary on the text by Decembrio, *De republic,* he actually took things out of context or even made Plato say things opposite to what he actually said.[84]

Leonardo Bruni simply refused to retranslate the *Republic* in 1441 when requested to do so because of some of its controversial contents: "There are many things in those books repugnant to our customs; things which, for the sake of Plato's honor, it would be preferable to remain silent about than to publicize."[85] As early as 1429, however, Bruni voiced his opposition to Plato's theory of gender. He appears to have accepted Aristotle's criticisms of Plato as expressed in the second book of the *Politics,* and in the *Life of Aristotle* his reservations are expressed as follows:

> In establishing his ideal state he expressed some opinions utterly abhorrent to our customs and ways of living. He believed, for instance, that all wives should be held in common — one can hardly imagine why — with the result that no one could tell his own children from those of a perfect stranger. He would do away with the laws of inheritance and have all things held in common. Aristotle opposed these and similar notions, and it was when he hit upon plausible counterarguments to them that he began to find followers, even though Plato was still alive. Plato's doctrine was, moreover, inconsistent and unclear; Socrates wandered to and fro wherever he was led with no order to his teaching, and did whatever he pleased. In disputation he seems not so much to be giving his own views as to be refuting the views and statements of others. Aristotle, on the other hand, was both more cautious in his teaching (he never commenced a subject unless he could offer proof), and more moderate in his opinions. As a result, he gave support to normal usages and ways of life, instead of imagining strange, abhorrent, and unprofitable ones.[86]

84. Hankins, *Plato in the Italian Renaissance,* p. 117.

85. Bruni, Letter to Niccolò Ceva who had requested the translation, in Hankins, *Plato in the Italian Renaissance,* p. 66.

86. Bruni, "Life of Aristotle," in *The Humanism of Leonardo Bruni,* pp. 288-89.

On this particular issue, Bruni developed the contrast between Plato and Aristotle, while in most others he followed Cicero's example of finding the common ground between them.[87] Thus, while Bruni was the medium through which Platonic and Aristotelian principles of gender polarity were transmitted, he also forged an independent relation to his cherished ancient authors. Thus, Bruni did not fall into the Platonic gender unity tradition, nor into the Aristotelian gender polarity tradition. He carved out a new territory in the concept of woman by providing concrete particular directions about woman's identity, especially in the two categories of wisdom and virtue.

His early (1401) *Dialogues for Pier Paolo Vergerio* are considered one of the "first masterworks of humanist letters," in which the relation of antiquity and humanism is evaluated by an intense series of dialogues.[88] The three most significant philosophers in Bruni's philosophical formation were Plato, Aristotle, and Cicero. When this fact is assessed with respect to an expectation that he might adopt a particular approach to the concept of woman, a difficulty is encountered. Specifically, Plato, who founded the gender unity position, argued that there are no significant differences between women and men, because individual identity resides in a sexless soul that uses instrumentally different bodies during a series of reincarnations. Thus for Plato, the function and education of women would be the same as for men, with the exception that the education might take a little longer because of the weaker physical nature of a woman. In contrast with this view of Plato, Aristotle, who founded the gender polarity position, argued that a human being's soul and body are a hylomorphic unity, that there are significant differences between women and men, and that men are by nature superior to women. The gender polarity principles that followed from Aristotle's position have been thoroughly articulated in this book, particularly in Chapter 2. They imply that women and men have different functions and that they ought to be educated in very different ways. Especially significant for our purposes are the gender polarity principle of separation of public and private spheres for men's and women's virtuous activities and the relation of public forms of speech to gender differentiation. For Aristotle, a woman's virtue is to remain silent in public and to undertake activities of governing only in the private sphere.

The question that naturally arises when Bruni's relation to Plato and Aristotle's concept of woman is considered is which view did he adopt, gender unity or gender polarity? As will be seen, he was a critical evaluator of both Plato's and Aristotle's concept of woman, and he forged a new synthesis drawn from several of their arguments. In this area, Bruni was similar to Cicero, who sought to present a unification of the two Greek authors in his own writing. However, Bruni differed from Cicero in one important way: he appears to have been absorbed in Plato up to the age of fifty. Then, in 1419, he turned away from Plato towards Aristotle. It appears that at least part of the reason for this conversion was a revulsion for certain aspects of Plato's views in the *Republic* about the community of woman.[89] In addi-

87. Hankins, *Plato in the Italian Renaissance,* p. 63.

88. See David Quint, "Humanism and Modernity: A Reconsideration of Bruni's *Dialogues,*" *Renaissance Quarterly* 38, no. 3 (Autumn 1985): 423-45, esp. 425.

89. Griffiths et al., *The Humanism of Leonardo Bruni.* ". . . the tones of the convert as perhaps

tion, Bruni was completely taken by Aristotle's thoroughness, his breadth of knowledge, his emphasis on virtue in the ethical and political life, and his eloquence in writing. The latter category often surprises contemporary readers because in comparison with Plato, Aristotle's writings appear often to be stilted. Bruni translated Aristotle's works in such a way that a beauty of composition became more evident. He claimed: "[i]n Aristotle, all is perfection. Indeed no one was his equal for taking care in composition."[90]

At the same time, however, Leonardo Bruni's preference of Aristotle over Plato was not complete. As James Hankins so well points out, Bruni's careful republication in 1426-27 of his collection of Plato's dialogues was used to justify certain themes popular to those in power in Florence.[91] First of all, he presented Plato as a support for the republican government in Florence, which would be ruled by a noble prince open to help from enlightened commoners such as Bruni. In the 1427 dedication of his translations of Plato's *Letters* to Cosimo de' Medici, and in the letters themselves, Bruni emphasized the value of the oligarchical form of government in the line of wealthy families, who at the same time valued philosophy.[92]

Second, Bruni uses Socrates and Plato to reinforce the view that in the afterlife a person is judged according to the moral value of his or her life in the world. Third, he also invokes their authority to support the value of poetry. The latter two views were developed in his 1424 translation of the *Phaedrus,* which was completed in the same year as his letter on education addressed to a woman. His 1424 text *De studiis et literis (On the Study of Literature)* is the first in the West to give a detailed set of instructions for the content of a woman's humanistic education. Bruni argues there that it is worth studying poetry even when immoral behavior is recounted within it because great poetry can lead the reader to an understanding of the good. In his letter, he appealed to the Greek authorities: "Plato and Aristotle studied them [the great poets], and I refused to allow that they yield to you [a Christian critic] either in moral seriousness or in practical understanding."[93]

Bruni then goes on to make an important distinction between different kinds of poetical works that contain passages describing immoral behavior. This distinction is very important with respect to the *Querelle de la rose* discussed in the previous chapter.

> But I don't insist; I am perfectly willing to abandon a little of my ground, especially given that I am addressing a woman. I admit that, just as there are distinc-

---

recognizable in Bruni's horror at Plato's doctrine of the community of women and of goods . . . ," introduction to chapter six, p. 261.

90. Bruni, "Life of Aristotle," in *The Humanism of Leonardo Bruni,* p. 291.

91. Hankins, *Plato in the Italian Renaissance,* pp. 66ff.

92. Hankins summarizes Bruni's use of Plato at this later stage in his life in *Plato in the Italian Renaissance,* as follows: "In his translation of the *Letters,* then, Bruni has made Plato the mouthpiece of his political convictions in much the same way as in the [translation of the] *Phaedrus* Socrates is employed to promote Bruni's cultural values. And in dedicating the volume to Cosimo de Medici, Bruni may well have seen himself as a new Plato, giving the Dio of Florence the benefit of his profound moral wisdom" (p. 80).

93. Bruni, "On the Study of Literature," in *The Humanism of Leonardo Bruni,* p. 249.

tions between nobles and commoners, so too among the poets there are certain grades of respectability. If somewhere a comic poet has made his theme too explicit, if a satirist excoriates vice a little too frankly, let her avert her gaze and not read them. For these are the plebeian poets. The aristocrats of poesy, Vergil, I mean, and Seneca and Statius and the others of their sort, must be read if she is not to do without the greatest ornaments of literature.[94]

Bruni wisely separates satirists from poets in general. In a passage from the same text he clearly states what he believes to be the value of poetry in humanistic education: ". . . that it is to poetry, more than to any other branch of letters, that nature attracts us; that it possesses utility, pleasure, and nobility; and that the man who has no knowledge of it can by no means be said to be liberally educated."[95] With his civic humanism that attempts to create an ideal republic based on the classical models of the ancients, education holds a central place and he includes women in his category of "liberally educated man." It is to this theme that our analysis will now turn.

The Household of Battista Malatesta

Leonardo Bruni took a direct role in the education of a woman, Battista Malatesta of Montefeltro (ca. 1384-1447), the daughter of Antonio, Count of Urbino. The date of an intergender exchange between Bruni and Lady Battista *On the study of literature* has been given as early as 1405 and as late as 1429.[96] Depending on which dates are selected, Battista was either a young woman just married to Duke Galeazzo Malatesta, or else she was a mother and mature woman who sought to continue developing her humanist education. The most likely date, 1424, is suggested by James Hankins, because of the mention of Bruni's translation of the *Phaedrus*, which was done in the same year.[97] This would place Battista's age at forty.

Bruni's initiative both with respect to the sex of his correspondent and to the serious content of the letter constitutes a reform in the history of the concept of woman. This text is the earliest known example of a humanist intergender dialogue about woman's education.[98] Bruni begins his treatise by indicating that he

94. Bruni, "On the Study of Literature," p. 250.
95. Bruni, "On the Study of Literature," p. 249.
96. Various dates have been given for Bruni's text. Luiso and Baron date it between 1422 and 1429 while Grittiths et al. estimate that it was written in 1424. See Griffiths et al., *The Humanism of Leonardo Bruni*, pp. 376, note 1 and 240. On the other hand William Woodward, *Vittorino da Feltre and Other Humanist Educators*, dates it at 1405, pp. 199-120. Margaret King follows Woodward's dating. See *Her Immaculate Hand*, p. 13. There are also differences of opinion about the dates of Battista's life. King suggests the dates 1369-1444, and Woodward states that she was 31 in 1405, which would place her birth date at 1374 and her death at 1450. Since I am placing this text in the context of Bruni's works, I will follow Griffiths's conclusions.
97. Hankins, *Plato in the Italian Renaissance*, pp. 69-70.
98. William Harrison Woodward states that it is "probably the earliest humanist tract upon education expressly dedicated to a lady." *Vittorino da Feltre and Other Humanist Educators*, p. 119.

had heard of Battista's "wonderful virtues" and that he wanted to encourage in her "the perfect development of those innate powers of which I have heard so much that is excellent."[99] Then Bruni lists the names of past women philosophers such as Cornelia, Sappho, and Aspasia to indicate that the study of philosophy was not uncommon among women, and he draws upon their renown by gathering Battista into a common history of women philosophers: "Be encouraged and elevated by their excellence!"[100]

Just as significant perhaps is the fact that Bruni also gathers Battista into the collective history of male philosophers. He states the importance of studying works of the Greek philosophers Plato and Aristotle, the Stoics Cicero and Seneca, and the Christian philosophers Boethius and Augustine. Bruni encourages his student Battista in two particular ways: first when he states that she has the ability for the highest intellectual endeavor, and second when he begs her to undertake the new kind of literary studies:

> It is not fitting that such understanding and intellectual power as you possess were given you in vain, not fitting that you should be satisfied with mediocrity; such gifts expect and encourage the highest excellence. And your glory will be all the brighter, for those other women flourished in ages when there was an abundance of learned persons whose very number decreases the estimation in which we must hold them, while you live in these times when learning has so far decayed that it is regarded as positively miraculous to meet a learned man, let alone a woman. By learning, however, I do not mean that confused and vulgar sort such as is possessed by those who nowadays profess theology, but a legitimate and liberal kind which joins literary skill with factual knowledge, a learning Lactantius possessed, and Augustine, and Jerome, all of whom were finished men of letters as well as great theologians.[101]

True learning, then, demands attention to knowledge of facts and literary skill; it demands the study of history, poetry, letters, and philosophy. The goals of a humanist education for Battista are described as a movement away from what Bruni considers to be the deterioration of scholastic education.

Then, in a most delicate way the letter suggests that Bruni is not simply setting down goals for Battista as would a master for a student, but rather sharing with her his own thoughts about the subject so that she might understand him. "Let me rather pursue our discourse, not for you to be instructed by me (for of that I imagine you have no need), but for you to understand my views on the subject of literary study."[102] A slightly different translation by Woodward of this same passage better illuminates Bruni's views on this subject:

99. Leonardo Bruni, "On the Study of Literature," p. 240. This passage is translated somewhat differently in Woodward's translation in *Vittorino da Feltre and Other Humanist Educators*. "I offer it, partly as an expression of my homage to distinction already attained, partly as an encouragement to further effort" (p. 123).

100. Bruni, "On the Study of Literature," p. 240.

101. Bruni, "On the Study of Literature," p. 240.

102. Bruni, "On the Study of Literature," pp. 240-41.

This leads me to press home this truth — though in your case it is unnecessary — that the foundations of all true learning must be laid in the sound and thorough knowledge of Latin, which implies study marked by a broad spirit, accurate scholarship, and careful attention to details. Unless this solid basis be secured it is useless to attempt to rear an enduring edifice. Without it the great monuments of literature are unintelligible, and the art of composition impossible. To attain this essential knowledge we must never relax our careful attention to the grammar of the language, but perpetually confirm and extend our acquaintance with it until it is thoroughly our own.[103]

We mentioned previously that Christine de Pizan appeared to know some Latin, but she preferred to read and write in the vernacular French. Obviously Battista understood Latin, as Bruni chose to write his treatise to her in the classical language, and he notes above that she did not have to be told about its importance. However, it is interesting that Bruni encourages her to perfect her language skills in order to become professionally literate, that is, to have a thorough knowledge. This challenge to a woman overturns the satirical image of her as a dilettante incapable of doing scholarly work as well as the previously expressed conviction of Bruni that even the work of most male scholars had deteriorated in his present age.

Leonardo Bruni offers some practical suggestions to help a person become a better educated humanist: to study only the best literary works, to practice reading out loud in order to grasp the meaning of the passage as well as to learn the language's beautiful cadences, and to ponder critically the reasons for the relative placing of words and phrases. He identifies particular authors who best serve these purposes:

> Hence a woman who enjoys sacred literature and who wishes to observe stylistic propriety will take up Augustine and Jerome and any authors she finds similar to them, such as Ambrose and Cyprian . . . Lactantius Firmianus . . . Gregory Nazianzen, John Chrysostom, or St. Basil the Great, the Greek Doctors of the Church. I would advise you to read them, too — so long as you read them in good Latin translations, not perversions. A woman, on the other hand, who enjoys secular literature will choose Cicero, a man — Good God! — so eloquent! so rich in expression! so polished! so unique in every *genus* of glory! Next will be Vergil, the delight and ornament of our literature, then Livy and Sallust and the other poets and writers in their order. With them she will train and strengthen her taste, and she will be careful, when she is obliged to say or write something, to use no word she has not first met in one of these authors.[104]

It is clear in this passage that Bruni not only expects Battista to be able to immerse herself intelligently in the great classical writers, but also to understand them and use them as an educated man would in normal conversation and writing. She

---

103. Bruni, "Concerning the Study of Literature," in Woodward, *Vittorino da Feltre and Other Humanist Educators,* p. 124.
104. Bruni, "On the Study of Literature," p. 242.

would become a true woman of letters by following these methods of critical immersion in the best authors available to her.

Bruni encouraged Battista to study the Greek Doctors of the Church. This advice raises the question of whether the philosophical model of Macrina, sister of Basil and Gregory of Nyssa and friend of Gregory Nazianzen, would have been known by Bruni, who had immersed himself in Greek manuscripts. Gregorio Correr had also recommended Gregory (without identifying which one of the Greek Fathers) to Cecilia Gonzaga. Gregory of Nyssa's *Life of Macrina* was first translated from Greek into Latin in Venice in 1553, and *On the Soul* was translated into Latin in Paris in 1557.[105] Since none of the authors on women's intellectual history who wrote in the fourteenth and fifteenth centuries, i.e., Giovanni Boccaccio, Christine de Pizan, and Albrecht von Eyb, include reference to Macrina, it seems likely that she became known to the Latin West only after the sixteenth century.

It is in the broader context of becoming a knowledgeable person, which surpasses the development of literary skill *per se,* that Bruni specifically invites Battista to consider questions in ethics, to study the major philosophers of antiquity, and to integrate Christian and pagan approaches to knowledge. In short, he opens up the field of philosophical inquiry to her:

> What, then, do I encourage her, when do I spur her on? Just when she devotes herself to divinity and moral philosophy. It is there I would beg her to spread her wings, there to apply her mind, there to spend her vigils. First, let the Christian woman desire for herself a knowledge of sacred letters. What better advice could I give? Let her search much, weigh much, acquire much in this branch of study. . . .
>
> Nor would I have her rest content with a knowledge of sacred literature; let her broaden her interests into the secular studies as well. Let her know what the most excellent minds among the philosophers have taught about moral philosophy, what their doctrines are concerning continence, temperance, modesty, justice, courage, liberality. She should understand their beliefs about happiness: whether virtue is in itself sufficient for happiness, or whether torture, poverty, exile, or prison can affect it. . . . Whether human felicity consists in pleasure and the absence of pain, as Epicurus would have it, or in moral worth, as Zeno believed, or in the exercise of virtue, which was Aristotle's view. Believe me, such subjects as these are beautiful and intellectually rewarding. They are valuable not only for the guidance they give in life, but they also supply us with a marvelous stock of knowledge which can be used in every variety of oral and written expression.[106]

In this encouragement to Battista to study different theories of ethics, Bruni is setting a direction that he repeats for male humanists as well. Drawing upon Cicero's

---

105. My source for the translation of *The Life of Macrina* is Professor Ezio Gallicet, University of Turin, who adds that the translation was commissioned by the Bishop of Vicenza, Aloysius Limomanus, and that Pietro Francesco Zini was the translator. *On the Soul* is listed in the Prolegomena, ch. 5, Mss. and editions, Schaff and Wace, eds., *Gregory of Nyssa,* p. 32.

106. Bruni, "On the Study of Literature," pp. 244-45.

summary of different philosophical schools as well as the works of Plato and Aristotle, he argues that a person ought to understand the different claims made by philosophers and the reasons why Aristotle's theory of virtue is to be preferred to them all. For instance, in *An Isagogue of Moral Philosophy* he tells Galeotto Ricasoli, "What, indeed, could be more seemly for a nobleman outstanding for his intellectual qualities and by nature a lover of the virtues, than to acquire a science through which he may cease to live at random, and by whose aid he may decide for himself on his course and his actions?"[107] Then, in the *Isagogue* Bruni goes on to distinguish the Stoics and Epicureans from the Peripatetics with respect to the different goals of their ethics.

Bruni's method of education goes far beyond a simple memorization of *Sayings of Philosophers* as he seeks to educate the student to become a philosopher by understanding the reasoning as well as the conclusions reached. In a letter to Lauro Quirini, written some seventeen years after his essay to Lady Battista Malatesta, Bruni clarifies Aristotle's goals in ethics, and he emphasizes, following Aristotle, that knowledge is not enough to become a virtuous person, but that virtues have to be brought to perfection by training, practice, and habit.[108] Thus Bruni sets forth a program of study for his female correspondent in the area of ethics that is very similar to the one he set forth for his male correspondent. As will be seen later in this section, there are some significant differences in his advice to men and to women in some areas of his program, but in the one just discussed the differences are minimal.

Next, Bruni argues that a woman ought to study history. This is particularly significant in view of the fact that Bruni is considered by many scholars to have been the founder of modern historiography.[109] Two of his seminal works in developing the new civic humanism, *De Militia (On Knighthood)* and *Historiae Florentini Populi (History of the Florentine People),* are considered to be early examples of modern historical texts.[110] In particular, Walter Ullmann notes that Bruni's "new historiography reflected man's active participation in the historical process."[111] With this attitude towards history, it is not surprising that Bruni would place so much emphasis on education in general and on the importance for women to have access to a formal education in particular.

Using a wide number of Greek and Latin sources, Bruni established a critical method that enabled him to begin to separate out legends from facts. Bruni's 1415 text *The New Cicero* was a turning point in his development of a critical historical method. He used a variety of different sources to check the accuracy of historical

---

107. See Bruni, "An Isagogue of Moral Philosophy" for Galeotto Ricasoli, in *The Humanism of Leonardo Bruni,* p. 267.

108. Bruni, "A Letter to Lauro Quirini," in *The Humanism of Leonardo Bruni,* p. 298.

109. Griffiths et al., General Introduction to *The New Humanism of Leonardo Bruni,* pp. 13-14.

110. See for example, Giuseppe Bisaccia, "Past/Present: Leonardo Bruni's *History of Florence,*" *Renaissance and Reformation* 9, no. 1 or old series, 21, no. 1 (1985): 1-18. For a detailed account of Bruni's "civic humanism" see Hans Baron, *The Crisis of the Early Italian Renaissance: Civic Humanism and Republican Liberty in an Age of Classicism and Tyranny* (Princeton: Princeton University Press, 1966), chapters 9-17.

111. Ullmann, *Medieval Foundations,* p. 174.

accounts, to argue that Cicero should be given a most important recognition as the father of Latin speech, letters, and the infusion of Greek philosophy into Italian life. As we saw in our previous discussions of authors such as Plutarch, Boccaccio, and Christine de Pizan, there was a lack of distinction between legend and facts in historical accounts of the lives of famous women. This mixing of real and unreal counterexamples to reject distorted accounts of women's identity weakens the ultimate effectiveness of their arguments. Thus, Bruni's introduction of a critical historical methodology would eventually be very helpful to women's history.

Up to this point in time history had been generally understood as the simple compilation of persons and events. However, Bruni claims that it is important for the development of both an identity as well as good moral judgment to examine critically one's own particular history:

> It is true that the marvel of human excellence, that excellence which raises a name to genuine celebrity, is the direct result of a wide and various knowledge; and it is true, too, that we should read much and learn much, selecting, acquiring, weighing, and examining all things from all points of view, from which we derive great benefit for our studies. Yet at the same time we should choose carefully and consider thoughtfully the time at our disposal in order to give first place to those things that are most important and most useful.
>
> To the aforesaid subjects there should first be joined, in my view, a knowledge of history, which is a subject no scholar should neglect. It is a fit and seemly thing to be familiar with the origins and progress of one's own nature, and with the deeds in peace and in war of great kings and free peoples. Knowledge of the past gives guidance to our counsels and our practical judgment, and the consequences of similar undertakings (in the past) will encourage or deter us according to our circumstances in the present.[112]

Bruni encourages woman to think also about the public sphere of activity, to learn its facts, and to penetrate through the facts to the general moral principles they reveal. In this way the woman student becomes able to use her powers of reflection and her discursive reasoning to enter into a dialogue with history in order to gain a "foresight" into contemporary public affairs.

Detailed consideration of other areas of education is also given. Oratory should be studied because it teaches distinctions between various emotions, lends elegant expressions for literary compositions, and improves vocabulary and style of writing. As will be seen in subsequent sections of this chapter, women humanists began to excel in the art of oratory, which gave them a way of participating in a highly respected form of public speech. Bruni's exact encouragement to Battista to study the art of oratory is as follows:

> I would further urge her not to neglect the orators. Where else is virtue praised with such passion, and vice condemned with such ferocity? It is the orators who teach us to praise the good deed and to hate the bad; it is they who teach us how

112. Bruni, "On the Study of Literature," pp. 245-46.

to soothe, encourage, stimulate, or deter. All these things the philosophers do, it is true, but in some special way anger, mercy and the arousal and pacification of the mind are completely within the power of the orator. Then, too, those figures of speech and thought, which like stars or torches illuminate our diction and give it distinction, are the proper tools of the orators which we borrow from them when we speak or write, and turn to use as the occasion demands. In sum, all the richness, power, and polish in our expression, its lifeblood, as it were, we derive from the orators.[113]

Bruni himself gave significant public orations. One was written in 1427 when he became the Chancellor of the city of Florence. The occasion for the oration was the funeral of a military man of some importance to the city. In his oration, after recognizing the importance of the figure being eulogized, Bruni praised the city of Florence itself for its liberty and equality of all the citizens who may hold public office if they have talent, virtue, and probity rather than simply royal blood. In addition, in his oration Bruni praised the city of Florence for reviving Latin and Greek and . . . "humanistic studies themselves, which are the best and most distinguished branches of learning and the most appropriate to humankind, being essential to private as well as to public life, [which] were embellished by our native literary erudition and came, with the support of our city, to spread throughout Italy."[114]

Bruni's support of humanistic education was often juxtaposed to his critique of traditional academic or scholastic education. In order to evaluate his suggestion to Battista that she avoid certain kinds of learning, it is important to consider similar arguments he made to his male humanist correspondents. In his *Isagogue of Moral Philosophy* Bruni writes to Galeotto Ricasoli criticizing the younger man's past love of natural philosophy:

> Now of course I have not forgotten how devoted you have been to philosophy from your earliest years, but your devotion is to that branch of philosophy which deals with the investigation of nature. Such philosophy is sublime and excellent, to be sure, but is still less useful in life than moral philosophy, which descends to the level of human mores and virtues. Unless, perchance, you think yourself better instructed in the Good Life for having learned all about ice, snow, and the colors of the rainbow, or that your behavior is improved by a knowledge of aureoles and whirlwinds! The rest of what one learns in natural philosophy is the same. It is very impressive to possess such knowledge, no doubt, but it is of no practical use.[115]

For a woman humanist too, meticulous attention to arithmetic, geometry, and astrology is to be avoided although some proficiency in these subjects is valued.

113. Bruni, "On the Study of Literature," p. 246.
114. Bruni, "Oration for the Funeral of Nanni Strozzi," in *The Humanism of Leonardo Bruni*, pp. 124-26.
115. Bruni, "An Isagogue of Moral Philosophy," in *The Humanism of Leonardo Bruni*, p. 268.

Disciplines there are, of whose rudiments some knowledge is fitting, yet whereof to obtain the mastery is a thing by no means glorious. In geometry and arithmetic, for example, if she waste a great deal of time worrying their subtle obscurities, I should seize her and tear her away from them. I should do the same in astrology, and even, perhaps, in the art of rhetoric.[116]

Bruni's main preoccupation for both men and women humanists was that they not waste their time on subjects that have no practical moral value. It is unfortunate that some contemporary critics isolate Bruni's claims in his letter to Battista and conclude that he is making a particular judgment about woman's identity.[117] The fact is that while Bruni did limit some subjects of study and certain kinds of public debate for women, he also did not want men to be totally taken up with these subjects either.

The one area in which he seems to have been a little more specific in limiting a woman's participation than a man's is in the study of rhetoric. What the study of rhetoric involves can be seen by the detailed description Bruni gives, dialectical argumentation and intellectual warfare common to academic and law courts, and he does not see a value for women to participate in it.

For why should the subtleties of the *status,* the *epicheirmata,* and the *krinomena,* and a thousand other rhetorical conundrums consume the powers of a woman, who never sees the forum? The art of delivery, which the Greeks call *hypocrisis* and we call *pronunciatio,* and which Demosthenes said was the first, the second, and the third most important acquirement of the orator, so far is that from being the concern of a woman that if she should gesture energetically with her arms as she spoke and shout with violent emphasis, she would probably be thought mad and put under restraint. The contests of the forum, like those of warfare and battle, are the sphere of men. Hers is not the task of learning to speak for and against witnesses, for and against torture, for and against reputation; she will not practice the commonplaces, the syllogisms, the sly anticipation of an opponent's arguments. She will, in a word, leave the rough-and-tumble of the forum entirely to men.[118]

Bruni tells his correspondent that he has "some hesitation" in limiting women's participation in the study of rhetoric because he has himself given considerable attention to it. In addition, it is important to note again that Bruni also cautions his male students against the aggressive kind of argumentation that takes place in legal

116. Bruni, "On the Study of Literature," p. 244.

117. See Melinda K. Blade, *Education of Italian Renaissance Women* (Mesquite: Ide House, 1983): "Although Bruni approved of history in curriculum development for girls, he considered astronomy, arithmetic and geometry as unfeminine topics and, thereby, rendered them unsuitable and unwholesome for girls and women" (p. 35). She also notes that, "In opposition to the Bruni opinion, [Matteo] Palmieri felt that geometry and music trained 'the voice and the mind,' and that Vittorino da Feltre, too, was a staunch supporter of the value of music as a suitable subject to be included in a curriculum for girls" (p. 35).

118. Bruni, "On the Study of Literature," p. 244.

battles or in highly speculative academic debate. He considered these developments to be a deterioration in which the focus was simply on winning an argument. In an early dialogue Bruni ridiculed the "barbarism," "absurdity," and "frivolity" that occurred in British dialectical arguments, and he even mentioned Ockham as an example to be avoided.[119] He sought to reinstate rhetoric in its original intent of helping people to live a more virtuous life. Thus, the public display of rhetorical skill for the sake of winning an argument was generally repulsive to him.[120]

Unfortunately, some contemporary scholars seem to select the above passage prohibiting woman's participation in rhetoric and emphasize it as Bruni's main contribution to the philosophy of woman.[121] It is certainly true that Bruni argued that a woman would not be able to apply the results of a careful study of rhetoric in public life in dialectical argument or legal battles. In this belief, he did not foresee even what Christine de Pizan had already accomplished in France in both of these areas. Yet, as previously mentioned, Bruni also cautioned male humanists about spending too much time on these pursuits as well. Bruni's letter to Niccolo Strozzi is instructive here. In this letter, written between 1431 and 1434, Bruni situates his first set of recommendations to study philosophers, poets, orators, and historians in the context of his previous letter to Battista: "I do not linger over this much, since I know you have read my little book *On the Study of Literature* where I set out, or at least implied, a program of learning."[122] Thus he uses his program of studies laid out for a female humanist as a model for a young male humanist. In addition, however, Bruni argues strongly in favor of the study of humanities and against the study of law. After arguing that particular law varies from city to city and focuses on "the mercenary business of quarrels and litigation," Bruni concludes: ". . . to study the civil law is sheer boredom, which is why the ancients, with perfect truth, named it the 'yawning science.'"[123] It would seem, then, that he does not recommend the skill in public rhetorical debate as a very suitable subject for humanist men or women to undertake.

Instead, educated talents in writing and general conversation were to be the focus of his humanistic program of study. In the conclusion of his letter to Battista, Bruni summarizes the different areas of education that a woman ought to have, and he emphasizes the fact that she ought to be able to express herself in writing in addition to absorbing information through study.

---

119. Bruni, "The Dialogues," in *The Humanism of Leonardo Bruni*, p. 69.

120. This conclusion is supported by an oration of Bruni. See Bruni in Bisaccia, *History of Florence*, "Please, let's put aside such pompous rhetoric; let's get, as I said, to the *substance* of the matter!" (p. 10).

121. See Margaret L. King, "Book-Lined Cells: Women and Humanism in the Early Italian Renaissance," in *Beyond Their Sex: Learned Women of the European Past*, ed. Patricia H. Labalme (New York and London: New York University Press, 1980). "Leonardo Bruni, in outlining . . . a program of humane studies, cautioned against the study of rhetoric — the one discipline the knowledge of which would enable a woman to participate publicly in intellectual discourse . . ." (p. 77).

122. Bruni, "A Letter to Niccolo Strozzi," in *The Humanism of Leonardo Bruni*, p. 252.

123. Bruni, "A Letter to Niccolo Strozzi," in *The Humanism of Leonardo Bruni*, pp. 252-53.

In sum, then, the excellence I speak of comes only from a wide and various knowledge. It is needful to read and comprehend a great deal, and to bestow great pains on the philosophers, the poets, the orators and historians and all the other writers. For thus comes that full and sufficient knowledge we need to appear eloquent, well-rounded, refined, and widely cultivated. Needed too is a well-developed and respectable literary skill of our own. For the two together reinforce each other and are mutually beneficial. Literary skill without knowledge is useless and sterile; and knowledge, however extensive, fades into the shadows without the glorious lamp of literature. Of what advantage is it to know many fine things if one has neither the ability to talk of them with distinction or write of them with praise? And so, literary skill and factual knowledge are in a manner of speaking wedded to each other. It was the two joined together that advanced the glory and fame of those ancients whose memory we venerate: Plato, Democritus, Aristotle, Theophrastus, Varro, Cicero, Seneca, Augustine, Lactantius, Jerome, with all of whom we can scarce decide whether it is their knowledge or their literary power that is the greater.[124]

It is clear that Bruni believes that if a woman can communicate eloquently through private dialogue and writing of letters or essays, this would constitute a more important aspect of her education than simply learning what others have said. Perfection of this "double capacity" is the goal of education. In conclusion, it is clear that Bruni generally rejected epistemological gender polarity principles. He did not believe that a woman's intelligence was naturally weak in comparison with a man's, nor did he argue that a woman ought to remain silent and that a man ought to speak. Instead, he encouraged women to develop their intelligence and to educate their speech in ways common to all humanists.

However, there are two areas in which Bruni did appear to accept ethical gender polarity principles: in the gender differentiation of particular virtues and in the engendered separation of public and private spheres of virtue. Each of these areas will be considered briefly in turn. In his *Isagogue of Moral Philosophy* Bruni writes about the relation of the particular virtue, fortitude, to military activity. He identifies fortitude as a particularly male virtue, and further he explains how the meaning of virtue and fortitude came to mean almost the same thing in Latin.

Yet occasions do arise when a wise man will prefer an honorable death to a disgraced life, when suffering physical harm for the sake of glory is better than being healthy but despised. For such occasions that marvelous virtue fortitude was brought into being. It is without doubt the fairest of the virtues, the theme of orators, the virtue so esteemed among men that we commonly see the statues of the dead dressed in military garb, as though to win military distinction in one's life were specially admirable. It is indeed quite common for fortitude to appropriate the term 'virtue' for its own. And this is not entirely unwarranted. The word 'virtue' is, after all, derived from 'man' *(vir)*, and 'man' seems to designate something steadfast and martial. From there it is an easy step to the saying 'if you are

124. Bruni, "On the Study of Literature," p. 251.

men,' meaning 'if you are brave.' Caesar harangued his troops saying he did not so much want virtue in a soldier as restraint — using, obviously, the word virtue in the sense of fortitude. In this matter, as in so many others, the Greeks put it more clearly than we do: they call fortitude *andreia,* which means, literally, 'manliness.'[125]

The particular limitation of fortitude with the military courage of males is significant in Bruni as well as his citing Greek thought as its origin. Bruni even suggested that military activity should be obligatory for citizens instead of the practice of hiring militias. This suggestion, if accepted, would have completely excluded women from citizenship. In his essay *On Knighthood (De militia)* Bruni refers often to Plato as a source for the origin of the idea of a military of citizens to defend a city. He even identifies Plato's *Republic* as setting aside a class of guardians who would bear arms: "He [Plato] said that they should be stern soldiers and fierce in the face of the enemy, but benign and gentle toward their fellow citizens."[126] Yet, Bruni fails to mention that Plato argued forcefully that the military should include women as well as men, and that courage, and thus fortitude, would be the appropriate virtue for members of either gender who were soldier guardians of the republic. This omission is a good example of Bruni's selective transmissions, and even distortions, of Plato's philosophical positions.

In addition, in Aristotle's *Ethics* there is no suggestion that the particular virtue of fortitude ought to be restricted to men, even military men. Instead, Aristotle usually argued that women had a lesser measure of most virtues than men, not different virtues. Thus, Bruni's limitation of the virtue of fortitude to men, and his subsequent repetition of a more popular conflation of fortitude with virtue, are not derived from the two Greek philosophers he so often respects. It is interesting to think about how Bruni might have considered, had he known about them, the actions of Catherine of Siena boldly facing the soldiers who came to her home or Joan of Arc's bravery and fortitude in leading military forces in France. Would they have provided sufficiently strong counterexamples for him to question a gender polarity approach to ethics as he had previously questioned gender polarity approaches to women's education and pursuit of wisdom?

The second area in which Leonard Bruni appears to support a traditional gender polarity view concerns the proper sphere of governing activity for women. Bruni believed that there were three different areas within which the virtue of good governance could and should be practiced: the first was self-governance, the second, governance in a household, and the third, governance in a city. Bruni often appealed to three different texts he believed to have been authored by Aristotle to define the particular range of virtues appropriate to each sphere of activity: *The Nicomachean Ethics* for self-governance, the pseudo-Aristotelian (Xenophon's) *Economics* for governance of the household, and the *Politics* for governance of a city. Bruni argued that women have just as much obligation to excel as men in the first category of personal virtue, but that women have no place to excel in the third cate-

125. Bruni, "An Isagogue of Moral Philosophy," in *The Humanism of Leonardo Bruni,* p. 275.
126. Bruni, "On Knighthood," in *The Humanism of Leonardo Bruni,* pp. 129-30.

gory of civic virtue. Indeed, in the latter category he argued that it had only been a recent opportunity for most men to develop the virtue needed to help rule a city. Bruni sent several copies of his new translation of Aristotle's *Politics* to leaders who he believed would benefit from learning from the ancient Greek philosopher about virtues useful for governing a city-state.[127] He did the same with his 1416 translation of Aristotle's *Ethics*.[128]

It is the second category of the virtue, or household governance, that is particularly relevant to the present topic. The *Economics* was not written by Aristotle but rather was based on a text of Xenophon, *Oeconomicus,* which was translated into Latin at the end of the thirteenth century and included as part of Aristotle's *Politics,* receiving commentaries by Averroes and Thomas Aquinas.[129] Significantly, the spurious work modified some of the gender polarity principles in the original *Politics* of Aristotle, and so Bruni and others, who believed it to be an authentic work of the Greek philosopher, absorbed some new principles through it. For example, in the *Politics* Aristotle had argued that a woman (wife) could only be an unequal friend of man, while in the *Economics* it is argued that a wife and a husband could have a friendship of equality. Bruni also repeats the views from the *Economics* that a wife is not a property of the husband and that, following from a principle of justice, he ought not to physically injure her when they are together and should remain faithful to her when they are separated.[130]

In the area of governing the household Bruni argues that "the man is the head of the household, the king, so to speak, of his own house, . . ." and further that "[i]t is the role of one to nourish and of the other to give learned instruction. For training *(educatio)* is by the mother, as [the author of the *Economics*] said above, while *eruditio* is by the father, and so it can be said that each makes a contribution to the common benefit."[131] In this commentary on the *Economics* Bruni appears to divide the sphere of the virtues along gender lines. Certainly Bruni does, as a general rule, identify the man as the *paterfamilias,* the single ruler of the household. For example, in his notes to Book I, Chapter 1 of the *Economics* he elaborates on the meaning of the original text: ". . . [i]n the commonwealth, then, there are many rulers; in the family, however, only the *paterfamilias.* For he has the power to give orders and directions in the family, and his commands one must obey."[132]

However, in one very revealing letter written on the occasion of the death of Nicola di Vieri de Medici's mother, we find Bruni giving a remarkable testimony to

---

127. See Bruni's letters on the *Politics* of Aristotle to Humphrey, Duke of Gloucester (1434 and 1437), to Pope Eugenius IV (1437), in *The Humanism of Leonardo Bruni,* pp. 154-74, and to the King of Aragon, where he refers to the *Politics* as "a *summa* of the whole science of ruling and governing people . . ." (p. 168).

128. Bruni sent a copy to Pope Martin V. See *The Humanism of Leonardo Bruni,* pp. 201 and 213-17.

129. See Aristotle (Spurious), *Economique* (Paris: Les Belles Lettres, 1968), Introduction by B. A. van Groningen, pp. xi-xxviii; and *The Politics and Economics of Aristotle* (London: Henry G. Bohm, 1853).

130. Bruni, "Notes on the *Economics,*" in *The Humanism of Leonardo Bruni,* pp. 310-15.
131. Bruni, "Notes on the *Economics,*" in *The Humanism of Leonardo Bruni,* pp. 313-15.
132. Bruni, "Notes on the *Economics,*" in *The Humanism of Leonardo Bruni,* p. 307.

a woman who both governed and educated her family. After Bruni describes how Bice de Medici (1359-1433) exemplified all the ordinary qualities that make a woman excellent, such as family background, appearance, children, wealth, virtue, and a good reputation, he then gives testimony to those qualities that made her an especially excellent woman:

> Yet the gifts most visible in this woman were the gifts of her mind: her marvelous uprightness, her signal humanity, her nobility, her outstanding liberality, and most of all a lofty spirit attuned to the seemly and the good. What should I say of her wonderful kindness, her charity towards her own, her affection to all — in sum, her singular goodness, whose like, I can honestly affirm, I have found in no other woman? The greatness of her prudence can be estimated from the way she governed a very large household, a large crowd of clients, a vast and diversified business enterprise for more than thirty years after the death of her husband. So great were her powers of administration that no one felt the loss of her husband's advice and prudence, and there was no falling-off in the regulation of morals, or the discipline and standards of integrity and honor.[133]

Nowhere in this letter did Bruni even suggest that these virtues found in Bice were not appropriate to her as a woman. Thus, we can conclude that since a governing and educating authority in the household was proper to a woman in the state of widowhood, it was not a universally engendered characteristic reserved only to men. If a woman's husband was still alive, then she would educate and govern with him, by sharing different tasks, but if he was absent, then the woman was perfectly capable of assuming the complete authority.

Before concluding this section on the contribution of Leonardo Bruni to the history of the concept of woman, it is helpful to consider what further factors may have helped Bruni to come to the conclusion that a woman ought to be educated in humanist principles and sources. In other words, how was it possible for Bruni not only to conclude that women were as capable as men of the highest humanistic education, but to actually initiate a curriculum that a woman could follow in the context of the new emerging educational environment of the household? In addition to the classical arguments about women's education in Quintilian, Plutarch, and stories of various Platonist and Pythagorean women philosophers, there are perhaps two different sources that may have served as genuine counterexamples to the academic gender polarity model and even to satirical views of women's intellectual weakness: namely, first, the pervasive presence of religious institutions in which women were already being educated, and second, the model of feminine personifications of wisdom in the works of the earliest humanists, i.e., Dante, Petrarch, and Boccaccio.

Bruni often heralded the ancestors of Florentine culture, and these three writers formed the core of his cultural inheritance. Bruni was so interested in his predecessors that he wrote both a "Life of Dante" and a "Life of Petrarch" in which

---

133. Bruni, "Consolation for the Death of Mother to Nicola di Vieri de Medici," in *The Humanism of Leonardo Bruni*, p. 338.

he merged his reflections on the historical authors with his own hopes for the future of Florence. While Bruni's direct interests focused on language, literature, and history, it is likely that he would have been influenced by the early humanists' imaginary projections of the intelligent women Beatrice, Laura, and Fiammetta. When literary possibilities raised by these authors for women's wisdom were added to the actual situation of numerous women's religious communities in which education was taught as a matter of course, it was not a difficult step to begin a new application of these principles to women who were actually living in households in the world. What Bruni did was to offer a new application of fundamental principles of humanist education to women in a different situation. His model was shared by other humanist educators such as Vittorino da Feltre and Guarino Veronese during the same period of the early fifteenth century.

However, as mentioned previously, there were no structures external to the household or convent in which women could continue to develop their intellectual skills by teaching others or engaging in the collegial discussions common to a small educational institution. In fact, teaching in humanist schools was a profession just opening up for men. Thus, even though Bruni's contributions, as well as those of Vittorino and Guarino, provided clear advances for women, they did not yet provide a sufficient foundation for the full participation of women in the other areas of civic life. So women were able to develop skills in two of the three key humanist areas of responsibility, individual virtue, and household virtue, but not in public or civic virtue. In this latter area, there were neither sufficient literary nor worldly counterexamples to provide models strong enough to break open the gender polarity distinction that excluded the sphere of woman's virtuous activity from the public world.

The intermediate world of the household was becoming established as a new institutional structure for the education of women in the higher sense, and this important base will be given further attention by the three subsequent authors to be considered in this chapter. Before turning to them, however, it is illuminating to consider briefly what happened to Lady Battista di Montefeltro, the woman to whom Bruni addressed his text *On the Study of Literature*. As mentioned previously, she had developed a genuine interest in being educated in the new method and texts of the humanists. Her father-in-law apparently shared this interest with her, and they exchanged canzoni and letters that are still extant.[134] Thus Battista's extended household served as an informal school of continuing education in the humanities, which began with her father-in-law and eventually included her own daughter and granddaughter, Costanza Varano.

Battista's marriage ended in widowhood in 1431 after her husband, a reputedly cruel lord of Pesaro, was murdered by his subjects. A public oration that Battista gave to King Sigismund of Hungary when he was on his way to Rome to be crowned Holy Roman Emperor reveals some of the skill she had learned from Bruni about the power of oration. Bruni had written to her about the power of oratory to touch the human passions. In her oration, Battista communicates her deep personal suffering from the effects of a violent civil war in Pesaro:

134. Woodward, *Vittorino da Feltre and Other Humanist Educators*, p. 120, note 1.

Do not suppose, triumphant prince, that this happened to them because of any cruelty toward their subjects or any oppression of them or any kind of cause; rather it happened because of the prideful violence of a few arrogant citizens who would not condescend even a little to bend their necks to a sweet-tempered lord, to the yoke of merciful rule, and treacherously turned the city of Pesaro to rebellion. On this account an unhappy populace, lacerated by intestine *[sic]* war and domestic strife, has been lured into great chaos. For many were sentenced to exile, others were despoiled of all their goods, others tortured in prisons, others were hanged, suffering death's sting. Thus depopulated, the city suffered in the end such damage that the elegant tongue of Demosthenes would falter in describing it.[135]

In her oration Battista places herself in the line of the great Greek orator Demosthenes, and she draws her audience into the depth of the suffering felt by the citizens of the city of Pesaro at this unjust situation. In her introduction, Battista tries to influence future public events by appealing for the Emperor's intercession to bring about a new justice. In this way, she practiced a civic virtue in the public sphere just by delivering this oration.

At the same time, Battista also addresses injustices insofar as they affected her own household. First, she describes how the rebellion affected her personally in relation to her ancestry; and second, she describes how it has affected her daughter by imprisoning her husband, murdering his brother, and leaving her children (Battista's grandchildren) poverty-stricken:

> I could briefly mention the violated tomb of my lord and father, and the remains of orthodox princes savagely mutilated. But yet I cannot go further; for tears would erupt ahead of my words; my throat is choked by indignation and pain alike. . . .
>
> Finally, something exceedingly, overwhelmingly bitter (which, when I reflect upon it, causes enormous disturbance of mind) recently happened, Serene Prince, to your devoted son and dedicated servant Pier Gentile da Camerino, the husband of my only daughter . . . you are aware of the horrible crime, the violent and tragic murder of his brother. I add the unexpected capture of my son. For you know, most clement of princes, he is held in prison, bound in fetters, by the governor of the Marches. . . .
>
> Among the nearly innumerable blows which afflict my unhappy lord is the thought of his wife, left alone, an unfortunate girl with four small children despoiled of all her fortune and wealth, with not even a robe left her, except the one alone which she was wearing when captured. And at present the castle in which she is confined is guarded by mercenaries who favor her brother and persecute her innocent child.[136]

---

135. "Oration of Battista da Montefeltro Malatesta to the Emperor Sigismund," in *Her Immaculate Hand,* p. 37.

136. "Oration of Battista da Montefeltro Malatesta to the Emperor Sigismund," in *Her Immaculate Hand,* pp. 37-38.

Battista requests of the Emperor that he intervene with those who may be able to free her son-in-law and return him to her daughter and family. In closing her oration, Battista invokes the image of the good character of the Emperor with the words "a monarch decorated with a wondrous radiance of virtues. . . ."[137]

Unfortunately, Pier Gentile da Camerino was killed in prison before he could be rescued. After this event, Battista's daughter was able to return to Pesaro and educate her children in the humanist tradition, with her mother's guidance. It is thought that after many years of living widowed at home, Battista, late in life, entered a Franciscan women's religious community of Saint Claire.[138] If this information is correct, it suggests again an interconnection between an educated female humanist and a woman's religious community of discourse in the extended context of learning.

The granddaughter of Battista da Montefeltro Malatesta, Costanza Varano, also achieved public prominence as a humanist. A few of her orations are extant, and they seem to imitate the style of Battista herself in both their structure and content. In fact, Costanza invokes the presence of her grandmother Battista in the public audience of one of her orations whose content will be considered below. This evidence of the direct continuity of the tradition of humanist education in an extended household that had undergone great trial and suffering indicates strongly that a new institutional structure for higher education of women was beginning to take shape.

In the following two orations given in the year 1444 by Costanza Varano, attention is again given to the subject of justice. In the first oration, a petition to redress an injustice is addressed to her future sister-in-law, Bianca Maria Visconti, whose husband, Francesco Sforza, ruled the very territory that her father Pier Gentile had been ruling before his death in prison. The oration begins with the usual form of praise to the person to whom it is addressed; Costanza also places herself in the historical tradition of great orators as her grandmother Battista had done before her:

> For what oratorical flair, what richness of speech can I muster from my jumbled store of words so little suited to the task, [to praise] your nobility, wisdom, dignity, piety, most kind generosity, and other virtues? In such a matter, not only would a plain, uncultivated and girlish speech be insufficient, but even the spirits of the wisest men and most brilliant orators would flag; and, what is more, even the unvanquished and lush oratory of the most eloquent Cicero would collapse and fail. What, therefore, can I do, an ignorant, rough, and inexperienced girl? Even though I tremble both in mind and body, and a blush stops my mouth from speaking freely, [still], may I say, the stones of this palace will proclaim your praise. But enough![139]

137. "Oration of Battista da Montefeltro Malatesta to the Emperor Sigismund," in *Her Immaculate Hand,* p. 38.

138. King and Rabil, eds., *Her Immaculate Hand,* introduction, p. 16.

139. "Oration of Costanza Varano to Bianca Maria Visconti," in *Her Immaculate Hand,* pp. 39-40.

Latin scholars point out the irony in Costanza's self-deprecating characterization of herself as uncultivated. For example, in another oration with a similar set of self-deprecating comments, the style itself is heralded as an example of Costanza's high level of skill as a humanist: ". . . the excuses themselves are offered in the most florid Latin, certainly intended to demonstrate the opposite of what the letter actually asserts. . . ."[140] Thus, it is not surprising that Costanza continues her oration with a whole paragraph of poetic praises of the woman to whom she has just addressed her hesitations.

After completing her introductions of praise Costanza turns to her petition, which is placed clearly in the context of justice. Her own father lost his life in prison and with it his title to rule the city of Camerino because of his support for Bianca Maria Visconti's father. In addition, Costanza's brother Rodolfo was placed in the care of Bianca Maria Visconti's father, the Duke of Milan. Thus, it follows in Costanza's mind that the title to rule should be restored to her brother by Bianca's husband, who now holds the title to rule Camerino among many others. Costanza's oration is developed as follows:

> You indeed, I know, are aware that the magnificent and honorable father of my only brother Rodolfo, your servant, came from the Varano family. He ruled so virtuously and earnestly and was joined by such love and by the bond of charity to your illustrious and most powerful father that [the latter's] praises always flowed from the [former's] sweet speech. For that reason he, though innocent, suffered the torment of an undeserved and atrocious death. Whence it happened that we were at once orphaned of our noble father and expelled from our kingdom; and shortly before he fell asleep in the Lord, [our father] bequeathed to that same most excellent prince, your father, the Duke of Milan, his aforenamed son, so that he might bestow upon one whom he loved in life a precious treasure in death. For this reason, I, a suppliant, plead for your clemency and ask you to favor — which is the most easy for your Excellence to do — your servant Rodolfo Varano, who suffers the burdens of exile as a result of dutiful devotion, and moreover, has lost an honorable parent.[141]

Costanza then turns in her conclusion to a series of praises of Francesco Sforza, drawing upon many Ciceronian images of military might and victory. Thus Costanza indicates to her audience once again her knowledge of classical literature and ability to apply its lessons analogically to contemporary situations of virtue. Then, giving a more original direction to her oration, Costanza describes the fully human character of Francesco Sforza: "[h]e possesses, however, something [still] more excellent, that is, qualities of soul which neither the mutability of fortune nor human strength has the power to weaken: humanity and clemency."[142]

---

140. King and Rabil, eds., *Her Immaculate Hand,* Introduction to an Oration of Costanza Varano to Lady Cecilia Gonzaga, p. 53.

141. "Oration of Costanza Varano to Bianca Maria Visconti," in *Her Immaculate Hand,* pp. 40-41.

142. "Oration of Costanza Varano to Bianca Maria Visconti," in *Her Immaculate Hand,* p. 41.

As it turned out, Costanza's petition was fulfilled, and Francesco Sforza returned the rule of Camerino to her brother Rodolfo. The significance of Costanza's oration lies not so much in the fact that it was fulfilled as she had hoped, for her grandmother Battista's oration, which was equally significant, had the opposite result. Yet both of these orations are important because in them a woman humanist attempted to do her part to contribute to the public dialogue about appropriately just acts. Thus, even though there was self-interest in the petitions, and even though they led to different results because of other persons and events in the public domain, these two orations mark the beginning of a new form of participation of women in acts of virtue through public forms of speech. They are clear counterexamples of the gender polarity principles that a woman's virtue ought to be silence in public and that her proper sphere of activity is not in building up the common good in civic life. Granted that the high social status of their household had an extension into the public realm, and that their petitions sought to strengthen their households, Battista and Costanza still entered into new ranges of virtuous activity for women. They did this by placing themselves within the newly evolving humanist culture of oratorical arguments and citations.

With a second oration Costanza Varano furthers the development of women's participation in public life. She gives a public oration directly to the people of Camerino after its rule was returned to her brother Rodolfo. Again Costanza begins her oration with the usual combination of simultaneous ironic self-deprecation and self-insertion into the tradition of great orators:

> I have never yearned so much with all my soul and strength for knowledge of letters and a refined eloquence of speech as I do at this moment, illustrious citizens and excellent fathers. For now we see that day made so glorious by your magnanimity, wisdom and humanity, that day so unimaginable, so long-awaited, one which I would like to have not my slight speaking skill, but that superlative and almost divine eloquence of Demosthenes, so that I could convey to all posterity with worthy praise and elegant words your abundant merits, and the dignity, glory and triumph of this famed city which has surpassed all the cities of Italy in mercy, kindness and clemency. Yet I quake and tremble not a little, and grow irritated at myself, for I realize that I, ignorant and inexperienced, am in no way adequate for so serious and important a task: for my meagre intellect is weak, and I have scarcely begun my studies of letters and eloquence.[143]

The ironic reference to herself as having hardly begun studies of letters and eloquence is increased when Costanza proceeds to draw upon Aristotle to enhance the political situation in which the city of Camerino will now be ruled by a person of noble lineage. Summarizing Aristotle's theory of different forms of rule as elaborated in his *Nicomachean Ethics,* Costanza offers the following argument to her public audience as she compares Camerino with Constantinople for its willingness to adopt a particular form of government:

---

143. Costanza Varano, "Oration to the people of Camerino," in *Her Immaculate Hand,* p. 42.

Now, Aristotle, the prince of philosophers, records in his book of *Ethics* (which you even when asleep know better than I when awake) that there are three forms of rule [found] in the world. [Of these] surely the least satisfactory is rule by the people; the second is rule by many citizens outstanding in virtue; the best, however, and far more worthy than all others, as Aristotle shows, is rule of kings and princes — that form of rule which, when it had been lost through adverse fortune, you, with one will and heart, by your skill and wisdom, reestablished.[144]

Clearly, Costanza uses the philosopher Aristotle to self-justify the continuity of her own family line of authority. She may indeed have truly believed that it is the best possible form of government, given that rule by the people had in the recent past ended in rebellion and unjust acts of torture and murder, and that she had perhaps not had experience of rule by many virtuous citizens. What is significant to our topic is not so much the particular conclusion that Costanza reached, but that she sought to articulate a position in public on the issue of civic government, and that she knew enough about Aristotle's theory to invoke him as an authority to support her own position. Her interpretation of Aristotle could be debated, however, for he seems to have preferred a mixed rule rather than simply one form. However, Costanza had studied about the Greek author's views and she was aware of one part of his main line of argument.

In bringing her oration to a conclusion, Costanza invokes ". . . the ornament of all ladies, and our sweet [grandmother], Lady Battista . . ."[145] along with other members of her family to thank the citizens of Camerino for their decision to accept the return of their rule. This invocation reveals a continuity of humanist discourse by women in the extended household of Battista's three-generation family. Costanza next extols the virtues of the people of Camerino and promises that her family will attempt to fulfill all their just wishes. The Varano family did continue their rule successfully in Camerino for nearly fifty years.

The female community of humanist discourse included a wider membership than already mentioned, for Costanza Varano entered into correspondence with two other women humanists. First, there is a letter written to Cecilia Gonzaga who had studied in Vittorino da Feltre's school but who decided, as indicated above, to enter a religious convent after the death of her father, Gianfrancesco. Second, there is a letter written around the same time to Isotta Nogarola who had corresponded with Guarino, the important early humanist educator.[146] These letters are instructive about the intellectual background of their author and recipients. In her letter to Cecilia Gonzaga, even though Costanza used her usual content of literary self-deprecation joined with perfect style in Latin, the particular phrases she introduces are significant. For example, she states: "[b]ut embarrassed by my own ignorance and clumsiness, and [aware] of your indescribable virtue and great knowledge of rhetoric, I did not write more

144. Costanza Varano, "Oration to the people of Camerino," in *Her Immaculate Hand,* p. 43.
145. Costanza Varano, "Oration to the people of Camerino," in *Her Immaculate Hand,* pp. 43-44.
146. For these two letters see King and Rabil, eds., *Her Immaculate Hand,* pp. 53-56.

quickly, and a considerable delay was occasioned."[147] Costanza was clearly aware of the education that Cecilia Gonzaga had received in the special humanist school established by her parents, and in particular the knowledge of rhetoric that her correspondent had received. Although Costanza's letter did not contain any rhetorical arguments, her concern about this particular quality of Cecilia is interesting in two ways: first, in its appeal to a woman's learning, and second, in her inclusion of praise of her great knowledge of rhetoric. Given that Bruni had expressly stated in his text *On the Study of Literature* to Battista, Costanza's grandmother, model, and teacher, that rhetoric was a subject not suitable for a woman, the praise of a woman's knowledge of rhetoric by the third generation of women humanists stands out as noteworthy.

The second letter of Costanza Varano written to Isotta Nogarola is even more instructive concerning the respect that one humanist had for another in this emerging new community of discourse. In the tenth chapter it will be argued that Isotta Nogarola was one of the most intellectually sophisticated of all the Italian women humanists, at least from the perspective of philosophical argumentation. In this letter Costanza, a contemporary of Isotta Nogarola, indicates a similar judgment about the qualities of her correspondent. Significantly, Costanza knows about Isotta not just through reputation, but by the study of her letters, which had circulated within various humanist circles. In the first part of her letter she begins with the usual set of self-deprecations and praises:

> After I had read repeatedly your elegant letters, most learned Isotta, letters redolent of that ancient dignity of the Romans, letters in which the embellishments are as suited to the thoughts as to the words, I became aware of how much I am affected with love for you, [and I was] moved by your eloquence to tell you so in my letter, although my words are unpolished, partly because of the poverty of my mind and partly because of the inadequacy of my training in eloquence.[148]

Then, once again, Costanza brings forth her own erudition to develop an argument addressed to the need for women to develop the mind instead of the body. Costanza places herself in communion with Isotta and in the line of classical authors:

> Hence I congratulate you, for you have advanced to the highest peaks, to the great splendor and glory of your name. For nothing could be more expedient and fruitful for women than to forget the needs of the body and to reach out strenuously for those goods which fortune cannot destroy. You have obeyed from earliest infancy that injunction of Lactantius Firmianus, not the least among theologians. Those who neglect the goods of the soul and desire those of the body, he says, spend their lives in shadows and death. This statement from our Cicero's words *On Duties* you have also respected. For we are all drawn and led to the de-

147. Costanza Varano, "To the magnificent and glorious Lady Cecilia Gonzaga," in *Her Immaculate Hand,* p. 54.

148. "Costanza Varano sends greetings to Isotta Nogarola," in *Her Immaculate Hand,* pp. 55-56.

sire for knowledge and science, in which we think it fine to excel, but [consider it] shameful and base to falter, wander, be deceived and ignorant. This does not escape that shrewd orator Quintilian in his *Oratoria institutio:* For just as birds are born for flight, horses for the race, wild beasts for savagery, so to us is distinctive a certain vitality and swiftness of mind.[149]

In the conclusion of this part of her letter, Costanza has included herself with Isotta in the collective community of discourse of us who have "a certain vitality and swiftness of mind." Those formed in the new humanist education, who know Cicero, Quintilian, ancient Christian writers, and who live by their precepts, are included in this fortunate category of persons whose desires are filled with knowledge and science.

Costanza Varano further specifies the category of learned humanists to include learned women. At the close of her letter, she gathers herself and Isotta into this historical tradition of women who have learned principles from the past and made them their own guide in the present:

> All these maxims you have gathered to your breast always and guarded diligently. This being so you must be judged the equal of those most excellent learned women of whom in antiquity there was no small multitude. Such were Aspasia, Cornelia, Scipio's daughter, Elphe, and others of whom this is not the place to speak. Indeed you, who for some considerable time now have excelled in studies, know this far better than I. I cannot express in words how much I admire you; [whatever I say] falls short of what is in my mind. And please believe that there is nothing which contributes to the sum of your merit which, I promise, I shall not willingly undertake with all my strength to perform.[150]

Thus, Costanza not only admires Isotta but she also initiates entering into dialogue with her and includes herself in a common historical women's humanist circle of discourse.

The above orations and letters of Costanza appear to have been written in the early to mid-1440s, around the time of her brother's return to rule Camerino and her own marriage in 1444 to Allesandro Sforza, Lord of Pesaro. Costanza's life ended within a few short years as she died shortly after giving birth to her second child. Thus, she was not able to continue the humanistic dialogues and orations that had been so eagerly initiated in her youth. However, as will be seen later in this chapter, other humanists engaged in new ways of articulating the concept of woman. The educational environment of the extended household became the main institutional structure that fostered these new dialogues.

Before concluding this section on the relation of Leonardo Bruni to the history of the concept of woman, a few closing remarks need to be offered concerning his impact on subsequent philosophical studies. James Hankins has pointed out in his monumental work *Plato in the Italian Renaissance* that "Bruni was the best-

---

149. "Costanza Varano sends greetings to Isotta Nogarola," in *Her Immaculate Hand,* p. 56.
150. "Costanza Varano sends greetings to Isotta Nogarola," in *Her Immaculate Hand,* p. 56.

selling author (at least in manuscripts) of the fifteenth century and his Platonic translations, which survive in over 250 codices, were about as popular as his other works for whose diffusion there is good information."[151] In particular, Bruni's translations of Aristotle's *Ethics* and *Politics* remained extremely popular. Bruni's Platonic dialogues were printed only in 1470 and 1474, because Marsilio Ficino's translations soon became the standard printing source. Manuscript copies of Bruni's translations were nevertheless dispersed to other countries: England, Castile, and Germany. In addition, an Italian translation of Bruni's *Letters* of Plato was also made available in 1441. Bruni's manuscript versions of Plato's dialogues were found mostly in monastic libraries or in the private libraries of wealthy humanists. None appear to have been lectured on in universities. Thus, Hankins concludes that there is no evidence that academic scholars were interested in Plato's own philosophical foundations. In addition, educated members of the populace adopted a utilitarian approach to Plato's philosophy by selecting passages from his works to support their own interests, especially in the areas of government or culture.[152] From the perspective of the history of the concept of woman, this means that there were still not yet any new philosophical foundations either from which to critically evaluate the solidly Aristotelian-based foundations for gender polarity fundamental to academic education or upon which to build a new philosophy of gender identity.

FRANCESCO BARBARO (1390-1454)

When Francesco Barbaro was just seven years old, Chrysoloras began teaching the Greek language in Florence. By the spring of 1400, when Barbaro was ten, Chrysoloras was drawn away to teach Greek in Milan, a city that was presently at war with Florence. Within two years of this move Chrysoloras and Uberto Decembrio (ca. 1370-1427) made a translation of Plato's *Republic*. This is significant here because Francesco Barbaro and Guarino of Verona apparently read together privately this translation of the *Republic*.[153] In addition, it would appear that Barbaro used Guarino's annotated version of Plato's *Republic* in composing his text *On Wifely Matters*. According to James Hankins:

> Guarino's annotations cover approximately the same range of subjects dealt with in the *De re uxoria*. Finally, Guarino addresses him ["Nota, Francise"] by name in one of the marginal glosses, and several passages from the *Republic* appear in the *De re uxoria* that display verbal affinities with the translation of Chrysoloras and Decembrio.[154]

---

151. Hankins, *Plato in the Italian Renaissance,* p. 95.
152. Hankins, *Plato in the Italian Renaissance,* pp. 98-99.
153. See Hankins, *Plato in the Italian Renaissance,* p. 98, note 176; and Hankins, "A Manuscript of Plato's *Republic,*" in *Supplementum Festivum,* pp. 173ff.
154. Hankins, "A Manuscript of Plato's" in *Republic, Supplementum Festivum,* p. 174.

As previously mentioned, this 1402 first Latin edition of Plato's *Republic* contained many errors and distortions. These errors crossed over into the area of the history of the concept of woman, for Uberto Decembrio, as had Leonardo Bruni before him, rejected Plato's arguments in Book V for the community of women. In Uberto Decembrio's commentary *De republic,* Plato's views are often misrepresented, mistranslated, taken out of context, and inverted to say the opposite of what the Greek author actually said.[155] As a result, readers of Chrysoloras and Uberto Decembrio's translation of the *Republic* would not have been exposed to the actual claims that Plato made in Book V for the equality of men and women in an ideal society. Thus, Barbaro would have gleaned something of Plato's approach to the concept of woman through his reading of the distorted 1402 translation of the *Republic*. However, he would not have been exposed to Plato's foundations for the theory of gender unity.

Francesco Barbaro did his academic studies at the University of Padua, receiving a doctorate from the Faculty of Arts in 1412.[156] The University of Padua was one of the centers of Aristotelian-based scholastic philosophy, and so he would have been exposed to Aristotle's gender polarity arguments in his studies in the Faculty of Arts.[157] During 1414-1419, when Barbaro was in his mid-twenties, Guarino of Verona was running a humanistic school in Venice; and he was trained under Guarino in the developing Renaissance Humanism. It was in this educational context that the two read Plato's *Republic* privately together. It is also likely that Barbaro would have read Guarino's translation of Plutarch's *Education of Children* as well. Vittorino da Feltre joined Guarino in Venice briefly in 1415, left for Padua, and then returned to Venice from 1422 to 1423. So after completing his academic training in traditional scholastic philosophy at the University of Padua, Barbaro was exposed to the thinking and educational guidelines of both of the two great founders of humanism. Barbaro was part of the upper class Venetian society, and he, with others, became very interested in developments in humanism.

Gender and the Household

Francesco Barbaro spent the summer of 1415 in Florence in the home of the Medici family making acquaintance with Florentine humanists and rooting himself in the aura of the birthplace of humanism. Being a wealthy patrician, Francesco Barbaro apparently also bought manuscripts for Vittorino's library.[158] After returning to Venice in 1415, Barbaro composed *De re uxoria (On Wifely Matters)*[159] and dedicated it to Lorenzo de Medici, who was about to marry Ginevra

155. Hankins, *Plato in the Italian Renaissance,* p. 117.

156. King, *Venetian Humanism in an Age of Patrician Dominance,* p. 325.

157. For the development of the University of Padua with its Aristotelian base see Schmitt, *Aristotle and the Renaissance,* p. 10.

158. Woodward, *Vittorino da Feltre and Other Humanist Educators,* p. 69.

159. King and Rabil, eds., *Her Immaculate Hand.* Barbaro's relation to the early humanist educators is summarized as follows: "Francesco studied under three well-known teachers of his time: Giovanni Conversini da Ravella, Gasparino Barzizza, and Guarino da Verona. He learned Greek

Cavalcanti.[160] *De re uxoria* has also been translated as *On Marriage*.[161] The topic of Barbaro's treatise indicates how much attention was being given to woman and to marriage during this initial phase of early humanism. It also follows a tradition first begun by Plutarch to foster the development of wisdom and virtue within a family household. *On Wifely Matters* was an extremely popular work, written in Italian and later translated and printed in Latin, French, and English.[162]

The early humanists quickly became aware of new texts, and they often commented on one another's works, much as contemporary scholars do in book reviews, articles, and professional conferences. The awareness of important new humanist initiatives went far beyond the borders of a particular city. Margaret King describes the response to Barbaro's work as follows:

> Some works by Venetians received high acclaim from the audience beyond the lagoons. Andrea Giuliani's oration for Chrysoloras circulated widely — a sign of favor — and was praised enthusiastically by Gasparino Barzizza, Poggio Bracciolini, and Buarino Veronese. Francesco Barbaro's *On Marriage* was even more of a success. Extant in a multitude of contemporary manuscripts, it was celebrated by Ambrogio Traversari and Pier Paolo Vergerio.[163]

The broad purpose of *De re uxoria* was to help noblemen select a proper wife and then to guide them in the upbringing of children who would be able to carry on the rule of the nobility. A more particular purpose of the text was to argue for certain wifely duties towards husband, children, and household government. Barbaro elaborated a set of virtues appropriate for ordering a household. This topic is thus situated between discussions of individual virtues, on the one hand, and virtues of those who take part in civic life, on the other hand. As will be seen in the subsequent analysis, many of Barbaro's arguments reaffirm traditional gender polarity principles, while several others move into new ranges, especially in the area of husband and wife relations. Barbaro also appealed to the authority of Aristotle and to Plato to defend certain of his positions.

It has been pointed out by Ernst Cassirer that the Renaissance is an abstract phrase that "expresses 'a unity of *direction*' not a unity of *actualization* [or, of actual particulars]. The particulars *belong together*, not because they are alike or resemble each other, but because they are *co-operating* in a *common task*, which in contrast to

---

thoroughly and in 1415, still a young man, astonished humanist circles with a treatise *On Marriage*" (p. 19).

160. King, *Venetian Humanism in an Age of Patrician Dominance*, p. 92. See also Woodward, who places the date of *De re uxoria* as late as 1428. *Vittorino da Feltre and Other Humanist Educators*, p. 180.

161. Francesco Barbaro, *Directions for Love and Marriage* (London: John Leigh, 1677). For a modern translation of selections see Barbaro, "On Wifely Duties," in *The Earthly Republic: Italian Humanists on Government and Society*, ed. Benjamin G. Kohl et al. (Philadelphia: University of Pennsylvania Press, 1978).

162. It was printed in Latin in Amsterdam in 1639, in French in Paris in 1667, and in English in London in 1677.

163. King, *Venetian Humanism*, p. 10.

the Middle Ages, we perceive to be new. . . . We perceive them [i.e., the individuals] to be not only different, but even opposed."[164] Cassirer's analysis continues by pointing out that in spite of, or even because of, the opposition of different positions on a topic that is perceived to be new, these works contribute to the spirit of a new humanist Renaissance. This view of Cassirer has application to the relation of Francesco Barbaro to other authors such as Christine de Pizan or Leonardo Bruni on the topic of the concept of woman. For the common topic is woman's range and type of virtue in the household, but there are differences of opinion about in what these virtues consist, at least in some important areas.

Francesco Barbaro married Maria di Pietro Loredan in 1419, and in time they had a family of six children, five of whom were daughters. Three of his daughters entered religious life even though their father had given great attention to woman's important place within an extended household. At the end of the analysis of *De re uxoria* in this chapter, the question of the relation of Francesco Barbaro and his daughters will be considered again with respect to the theme of whether his concept of woman may have discouraged his daughters from considering the vocation to be a wife in the world.

The Barbaro household in Venice was a center of humanistic discourse. His own father, Candiano Barbaro, had begun this tradition right at the beginning of interest in the new humanistic education by inviting another great humanist educator, Gasparino Barzizza, to stay often in his home. During these periods the young Francesco was able to experience the excitement of other young men seeking to learn from a great teacher. Then, when his own home was established in Venice, "Filippo Morandi da Rimini described the crowds of learned who met in Francesco Barbaro's house, and with whom Barbaro himself, 'transformed into a humble philosopher,' conversed."[165]

The Venetian households worked as educational centers in complement with early humanist schools that had been founded, as previously mentioned, by Guarino of Verona and Vittorino da Feltre. Two other educators, Gasparino Barzizza and Pier Paolo Vergerio, also taught near Venice. This particular city fostered institutional structures of education in a remarkable way. Margaret King has traced those humanists who attended the newly formed public schools of Venice and noted the remarkable phenomenon that these schools were founded in 1403 by an "ardent Aristotelian" and affirmed by Senate decrees.[166]

Barbaro was primarily a man of civic action, and during the over thirty-year period following his composition of this text, 1422-1454, he held offices in Treviso, Vicenza, and Verona, ending as Proconsul of San Marco.[167] In addition, he served as ambassador at various times to Rome, Florence, Ferrara, Bologna, and Milan. The latter posting came after he led a military victory against Milan, which had

164. Mario Domandi, translator's introduction to Ernst Cassirer, *The Individual and the Cosmos in Renaissance Philosophy* (New York: Barnes and Noble, 1963), p. viii.

165. King, *Venetian Humanism*, p. 15.

166. King, *Venetian Humanism*, p. 19.

167. Barbaro worked tirelessly for a stable and lasting peace in which the Italian people could live in freedom. For a description of his work in this area see Baron, *The Crisis of the Early Italian Renaissance*, pp. 394-99.

been besieging Brescia.[168] Throughout his public career, Barbaro always continued his love of humanism. For example, in 1426, while serving as Ambassador from Venice to the papal curia, he discovered a valuable manuscript. Margaret King describes the event and subsequent communication between Francesco Barbaro and Guarino of Verona as follows:

> [Barbaro] one day strayed from his path and stumbled upon a treasure in a dismal warehouse attached to the monastery of Santa Maria di Frascati. Amid barrels of wine lay Greek books, beautifully written, worthy of the library of a Varro or a Ptolemy, neglected and unread. Barbaro described his triumph to his friend and mentor Guarino Veronese "that you may know that in this age the good fortune and diligence of one 'barbarian' (Barbaro) unearthed near Rome these treasures of Greek learning which the Roman people allowed to be hidden and buried in squalor and dirt."[169]

Humanists gained a reputation for raiding monastic libraries and buying or taking texts that had previously been part of the monastic educational tradition. Since so many humanists were also from wealthy households, they were able to buy manuscripts to build up their own private libraries.

Barbaro seems to have frequently tried to integrate his civic responsibilities with humanism. He frequently exhorted his political colleagues to study the humanities. For example, he wrote a letter to Santo Venier, governor of the Venetian Republic, arguing that the leaders ought to undertake study of ancient Latin and Greek texts. Margaret King summarizes Barbaro's plan in *Venetian Humanism*:

> The ancients have bestowed upon us, through their writings, models of virtue, "which if our citizens hold before themselves in administering the republic, by that reflection upon illustrious men, they shall become more prudent and capable." To illustrate this point, Barbaro sent Venier with his letter, "so that I might serve myself and you and the city itself," Cicero's letter to his brother Quintus on the administration of public office. . . . The texts of the ancients are seen here, and described as such to a man in the center of power by another destined for that position, not merely as tools for the development of the mind, but as handbooks of effective management.[170]

As will be described latter in this chapter, Barbaro also dispersed among the patricians Latin translations of Greek texts, such as George of Trebizond's translation of Plato's *Laws,* which he felt would be immediately applicable to government in Venice.

Before entering into a more detailed description of Barbaro's text *De re uxoria,* it will be helpful to reflect briefly on the particular circumstances of Venetian humanism, which differed greatly from those already seen in Florence, Man-

168. King, *Venetian Humanism in an Age of Patrician Dominance*, p. 324.
169. King, *Venetian Humanism*, p. 6.
170. King, *Venetian Humanism*, pp. 42-43.

tua, or other cities that supported the early birth of humanistic studies. The Venetian government at the beginning of the fifteenth century had two characteristics that directly impacted upon the citizens who lived there: by 1406 it was aggressively territorial, taking over the neighboring cities of Padua, Vicenza, Verona, and Treviso, and it was governed by the nobility alone rather than opening itself to men of lower-class backgrounds as had occurred in Florence. Thus, there was not in Venice the same willingness to integrate some of the newer humanistic ideas that had been more prevalent in Florence, such as that true nobility lay not in bloodlines but rather in virtuous quality of life. In addition, Venetian intellectual life was influenced by Aristotelian philosophy as taught at the University of Padua and the University of Paris.[171] As Margaret King puts it: "Indeed, the Venetian conquest of Padua early in the century led to the Paduan 'conquest' of Venice, an enthusiastic Aristotelianism that penetrated every outpost of the culture. The launching of patrician humanism coincided with the intensification of a tradition of Aristotelian philosophy."[172] Consistent with this phenomenon, Barbaro's concept of woman manifests this strange combination of humanism and traditional Aristotelian-based academic gender polarity theory common to Venetian culture at the time.

In the context of a discussion of virgins who marry, Barbaro appears to repeat the Aristotelian theory of generation:

> For those . . . who enquire exquisitely into the hidden causes of things, that nature herself intends that which is best, and that when she cannot produce a male, she conceives a female, which is ennobled and perfected by the union of the male; and therefore that women love those most to whom they are joined in the first congress.[173]

At the same time, Barbaro does not suggest that the female is defective in transmitting the material body of the child in generation. In fact, he appears to suggest the opposite, namely, that the quality of body and mind of the mother determines the quality of the child. This supports the value given to intermarriage among the nobility, which would emphasize the importance of a woman's as well as a man's biological background.

In the following passage Barbaro compares human generation analogically with grafting or planting, and concludes with a strong suggestion that the female may even determine the gender of procreation:

> Seeds are reduced into their proper origins, and we find that those are the best crops which are produced by the most excellent corn; and we know that very many, and those the best sorts of berries, nuts and shrubs, will not grow but in their proper and fertile soils; and if they be transplanted to a more barren soil

---

171. Margaret L. King, "Humanism in Venice," in *Renaissance Humanism,* ed. Albert Rabil, Jr., 3 vols. (Philadelphia: University of Pennsylvania Press, 1988), vol. 1, p. 211.

172. King, "Humanism in Venice," in *Renaissance Humanism,* vol. 1, p. 214.

173. Barbaro, *Directions for Love and Marriage,* p. 19. The quotations from this text have been rendered into more modern English by the author.

they lose their natural virtue, as apples losing their former juice degenerate: also excellent strains if they be ingrafted in bad stocks, bear worse fruits. Which is also incident to men themselves, that they expect more illustrious children from noble women. Hence chiefly we discern in them the representations of their mother's bodies and minds (as we see in most children) and it is certain that a woman is of great concern in the generation of children. For some judicious physicians assert, that a female is briefly procreated by the woman![174]

Barbaro thought that higher and lower qualities of things could effect dynamic interactive change. So just as good seed in bad soil produced a third kind of something that would be of lesser quality than the combination of good seed and good soil, or good branch grafted onto a bad stock would produce a new tree of lesser quality than a good branch grafted onto good stock; thus a good seed, when deposited by a male in a noble female, would potentially generate children of superior qualities. Plutarch had made a similar argument at the beginning of *On the Education of Children* when he advised men to cohabit only with the "well born."[175]

Also following the line of argument in Plutarch, Francesco Barbaro further added the idea that the milk provided by a mother or wet nurse could affect the quality of the child being fed. He concluded that a noble woman should sometimes nurse the children of her servants, and that neither slaves nor strangers should nurse a woman's children. Barbaro amplifies this theme by introducing the suggestion that the contribution of a mother's milk to the properties of mind and body of the child is "almost equivalent" to that of the male seed. Barbaro understood a mother's milk to be a highly refined state of blood, similar to the male seed in Aristotelian biology. This followed his study of Aristotelian natural philosophy and the view that both the milk in a female and the seed in a male are highly refined forms of blood:

> For no nourishment seems more fit, none more wholesome than that the same aliment, which is endowed with much heat and vigour, and which is a known and familiar food, should be given to the children; whose efficacy is such that in the forming of the properties of the body and mind it is almost equivalent to the virtue of the spermatick faculty; this is evidently perceived in many things.[176]

A recent commentary on the work of Francesco Barbaro, *De re uxoria,* has emphasized its discussions of woman as the property of man in securing the continuity of a noble line through marriage.[177] It is certainly true that Barbaro did em-

174. Barbaro, *Directions for Love and Marriage,* pp. 24-25.
175. Plutarch, *On the Education of Children* in *Moralia,* vol. 1 (#2), 5.
176. Barbaro, *On Love and Marriage,* p. 116.
177. See for example, Constance Jordan, *Renaissance Feminism: Literary Texts and Political Models* (Ithaca and London: Cornell University Press, 1990). "Barbaro describes the best means of ensuring dynastic integrity . . . and insists on the importance of women as property and property holders" (p. 41). See also Margaret King, "Caldiera and the Barbaros on Marriage and the Family: Humanist Reflections of Venetian Realities," *Journal of Medieval and Renaissance Studies* 6, no. 1 (Spring 1976): 19-50, "The primary end of marriage for Francesco Barbaro is thus the procreation of noble descendants capable of bettering and ruling society" (35).

phasize this theme and in so doing often simply perpetuated a gender polarity attitude. At the same time, he also introduced some new dynamics between men and women that signal a slight movement away from polarity and towards complementarity. Thus, Barbaro is a transitional figure in the early humanist reformation. A recent study of wills of married women in Venice during the years 1305-1450, exactly the time Francesco Barbaro had written his text on woman's identity, indicates that women were not simply considered to be the property of men. Stanley Chojnacki has demonstrated that married women in fifteenth-century Venice had power to determine their own bequests, and that they often divided their inheritances evenly among the families of their birth and those of their marriage.[178] He argues that women themselves often determined by personal preference, rather than biological lines, whom to favor with their wealthy property distributions after their death. This sociological evidence supports a broader understanding of woman's identity as wife or mother during this period in Venetian history than simply seeing her as the property of man.

It is important to note also that Francesco Barbaro does not simply reduce the influence of women on children to a bodily efficacy. He often states that both body and mind ought to be considered. So it would be superficial to conclude that Barbaro perceives woman as simply a physical material possession of man for the purposes of propagation. He argues that woman has a crucial role to play in the education of children as well:

> Neither does the nobleness of the mother avail only to the procreation, but much to the education of the children: who is so ignorant that he does not perceive that this matter is of great importance to them that are born? For the choicest seeds being sown (that we may use an analogy of the same kind), unless the field be tilled with great care and industry, the corn will be obnoxious to many hazards. Nobody can doubt that anything is more esteemed by renowned women than that the honour of the parents may be more and more illustrated by the splendor of the children.[179]

Many key elements are listed as central to the education of children: to instill a sense of duty to God, country, and parents, to defer to those who are superior to them, to be affable with those who are their equals and courteous to those who are their inferiors, to learn the art of conversation, and to develop the virtue of temperance. Mothers should actively correct bad habits such as ridiculing the poor, giving in to anger, avarice, concupiscence, and swearing. In short, the mother is responsible for developing the character of the child.[180]

Barbaro argues further that the education of young men ought to differ from that of women in two significant ways. First, only men are to be taught the foundations of the humanities: "generous young men should be instructed and taught ex-

---

178. Stanley Chojnacki, "Patrician Women in Venice," *Studies in the Renaissance,* vol. 21 (New York: The Renaissance Society of America, 1974), pp. 176-203, esp. p. 181.

179. Barbaro, *Directions for Love and Marriage,* p. 26.

180. Barbaro, *Directions for Love and Marriage,* pp. 118-22.

cellent studies and arts."[181] In this directive, Barbaro takes a distinctly different path from his contemporaries Leonardo Bruni and Christine de Pizan. This decision may also have had an impact on the three of his daughters who decided to enter religious life, where advanced study was commonplace. Second, Barbaro argued that only men should be taught how to engage in public speech. Here Barbaro takes the same position as Leonardo Bruni but a different one from Christine de Pizan.

Barbaro argued that women should be allowed to move in some ways into the public realm: "For they are not to be confined in their bedchamber, as in prisons; but they should go abroad, that this liberty which we allow them may be an evidence of their virtue and chastity."[182] However, he added the qualification that women's outings should be in the company of their husbands: "I would have them be seen in the presence of their husbands, but in their absence they should be retired at home."[183] So we find here a limited moderation of the strict division of the public and private spheres; woman may participate in the public sphere with men, but not on their own.

The adoption of the gender polarity principle of different and lesser virtues for women than for men is also seen in an entire chapter in *Directions for Love and Marriage* entitled "Concerning the speech and silence of women." A man's virtue is to speak well in civic life, while a woman's virtue is to remain silent in public. Barbaro invokes many classical authors to support his views. For example, he appeals to the Roman Marcus Cato to suggest that public speech is against woman's nature:

> Marcus Cato the elder, when he observed the Roman women, contrary to the order of nature, and the modesty of the female sex, sometimes to be conversant in the courts of judicature, and ambitiously to pursue honour, and to discourse with strangers, he inveighed against, reproved and restrained them, as the honour of that most grave citizen and of that empire required.[184]

Then, citing an initiation rite of the Pythagoreans, he concluded that women ought to be perpetually silent in public:

> We know that the Pythagoreans were commanded to be silent for no less a time than two years at their first entrance.... But we appoint to wives a perpetual time and space of silence, wheresoever any access to levity, dishonesty, and impudence shall appear; being spoken to, they should answer most modestly to their familiar friends, and make them civil salutations, and they should so briefly dispatch those things which place and occasion shall offer, that they may rather be thought to be provoked to, than to provoke public discourse; they should also endeavour to be rather praised for a discreet brevity than an eloquent prolixity of speech.[185]

181. Barbaro, *Directions for Love and Marriage*, p. 39.
182. Barbaro, *Directions for Love and Marriage*, p. 82.
183. Barbaro, *Directions for Love and Marriage*, p. 82.
184. Barbaro, *Directions for Love and Marriage*, pp. 83-84.
185. Barbaro, *Directions for Love and Marriage*, p. 84.

Of course, this obligation of all new members of the Pythagoreans to be silent for two years, which was lifted after that time only for men, is a rather forced command in application to Italian Renaissance women who, as was demonstrated in the preceding section of this chapter, engaged in various forms of public oration. It is as if Barbaro's arguments were attempting to stem a tide that was just beginning to rise. Barbaro draws together many ancient sources to support his claim that a woman's virtue is silence. In the following passage he uses the words of Theano, a Pythagorean woman, to defend his claim:

> Theano, when she put forth her hand to take her mantle, a certain young man turning to his companions, said, how handsome is that arm! To whom she answered, it is not a common one. Wherefore it is expedient, that not only the arms, but indeed the discourses of a woman should not be common; for the speech of such a woman is not less to be feared, than the nakedness of the body.[186]

Of course, the irony of this particular quotation is that Theano is speaking publicly about women's virtue of remaining silent.

In contrast to his admonition to women to be silent, Barbaro extols public speech in men and the tongue that nature has given them, which "produces the best and most pleasant fruits."[187] Men must be taught how to be selective and cautious in their speech. Then, Barbaro wittily ends his discussion by reflecting on his own propensity to talkativeness; he reasserts a differentiation between the two genders with respect to public speech and silence:

> For if I should grant . . . that it were sometimes expedient for men, yet I should judge it, for the most part, repugnant to the modesty, gravity, and stability of a wife; wherefore Sophocles . . . hath termed silence a singular ornament in women; therefore they should think that they shall obtain the glory of eloquence, if they adorn themselves with the famous ornament of silence; for neither the praise of a declamatory play, nor the applause and flattery of an oration, but an eloquent, and well behaved, and grave silence is required of them. But what do I do? I must take heed, especially since I treat of silence, lest perchance I seem to thee too talkative.[188]

The passage referring to Sophocles could have been drawn from Aristotle's *Politics* where it is said: "All classes must be deemed to have their special attributes; as the poet says of women, 'Silence is a woman's glory;' but this is not equally the glory of man."[189] The fact that Barbaro is self-conscious about his own claims about the dif-

---

186. Barbaro, *Directions for Love and Marriage*, pp. 84-85. Peter Stallybrass argues that for Barbaro, "Silence, the closed mouth, is made a sign of chastity. And silence and chastity are, in turn, homologous to woman's enclosure within the house" ("Patriarchal Territories: The Body Enclosed," in *Rewriting the Renaissance: The Discourses of Sexual Difference in Early Modern Europe*, ed. Margaret W. Ferguson et al. [Chicago and London: University of Chicago Press, 1986], p. 127).

187. Barbaro, *Directions for Love and Marriage*, p. 85.

188. Barbaro, *Directions for Love and Marriage*, p. 86.

189. Aristotle, *Politics* 1260b 28-31.

ference between a man's virtue of 'elegant speech' and a woman's virtue of 'grave silence' is significant here. It is also interesting that he addresses himself to his woman readers in this text *On Wifely Duties*. Barbaro is aware of a disparity when he worries "lest perchance I seem to thee too talkative." There is a certain discomfort expressed in his gender polarity principle with its extreme division between the virtues of a man and of a woman with respect to speech in public.

Perhaps this disparity is also obvious to Barbaro because he strongly encouraged private dialogue between a husband and wife. He describes an open and perfect kind of communication between man and woman in the mutual sharing of concerns:

> Whatsoever things are troublesome to them (so that they be worthy to be told to a prudent person) let them mutually impart, let them feign nothing, let them dissemble nothing, let them conceal nothing; oftentimes sorrow and trouble of mind is mitigated by counsel and discourse (which ought to be most pleasant with her husband).[190]

Therefore, even though Barbaro differentiates between the genders with respect to public dialogue, he does not make the same distinction with respect to private dialogue. In fact, he encourages intergender dialogue within marriage itself. In the next part of the chapter, this view will be sharply contrasted with that of another Italian Renaissance author, Leon Battista Alberti, who prohibited even serious private intergender dialogue.

Barbaro describes the relation of husband and wife as one of the highest forms of friendship: "Now let us speak of conjugal love, the great efficacy and dignity whereof (as worthy men assure us), in a manner expressing the pattern of a perfect friendship...."[191] In this friendship, nourished by honest and open dialogue, husband and wife should grow towards a union of mind. "Finally I would that wives should so live with their husbands, that in a manner they might be of one mind, and if it could be done (as Pythagoras would have it in friendship) that the two should become one."[192] This humanist appeal to a Pythagorean model of intergender friendship in a marriage is opposed to the unequal friendship of man and woman described in Aristotle's *Nicomachean Ethics,* but it is consistent with that proposed in the pseudo-Aristotelian *Economics* and with Thomas Aquinas.

The dignity of the friendship between husband and wife is based on a mutual pursuit of a life of virtue. While Barbaro does claim that the wife's virtue includes obedience and following the will of her husband, he does not include any of the strong statements against disobedient women found in other authors.[193] Instead, Barbaro seems more concerned with developing woman's capacity to rule the household well in complement with her husband who rules in his public affairs.

190. Barbaro, *Directions for Love and Marriage,* pp. 69-70.
191. Barbaro, *Directions for Love and Marriage,* p. 68.
192. Barbaro, *Directions for Love and Marriage,* p. 70.
193. Barbaro, *Directions for Love and Marriage,* pp. 48-49 and 62-63.

Barbaro seeks to develop in her the virtue of prudence, or practical wisdom, commensurate with her husband's, a virtue that would enable both of them to bring a harmony and order into their proper sphere of activity.

In the following passage Barbaro cites Plato to support his claim that virtue is the most important quality in a wife. Note that Plato is not identified in any way with the abolition of private property or family in this passage. Instead, he is presented as the supreme authority for rule by those who have wisdom, that is, the man in the commonwealth and the woman in the family:

> What composes, regulates, and renders commendable the family affairs, but chiefly the diligence, frugality, and dignity of the wife? As a prince shall not well govern a city unless he be expert in the common law, the customs of his ancestors, and the public affairs, neither can a pilot, which is ignorant of the marine art, reduce a ship into the haven out of a cruel storm. Neither shall a charioteer which is unskillful in his employment be rewarded. So neither can domestic affairs be rightly managed, unless the excellence of the mistress of the family be a singular example to the rest. . . .
>
> Plato, that most grave philosopher, in those books which he has excellently written concerning the commonwealth, had instituted that magistracies should be bestowed on the most excellent, not the most ambitious citizens. . . . Wherefore he proposed a public reward to the magistrates, lest the damage which may accrue to their private affairs, should impede the public duties of the commonwealth; for we should so greatly esteem prudence in a wife (that if our fortunes will permit) we should even neglect a wife's portion, or willingly be content with very little, that we may obtain domestic praise and peace.[194]

In a metaphor borrowed from the pseudo-Aristotelian *Economics,* the wise and virtuous wife is compared to a Queen Bee who sends men and women servants here and there from the home, to do what is advantageous for the home, while remaining at the center of the activity.[195] She is also compared to a master musician who tunes all the strings of the harps so that everyone and all activities are brought into a perfect harmony that increases and confirms the dignity of the family.[196]

Because of the great value attributed by Barbaro to the governing activity of the wife in a marriage, it is not surprising that he emphasizes that a husband should ". . . not so much esteem portion, extraction, and beauty, as virtue and agreeableness of disposition in a wife. . . ."[197] In other words, a woman's virtuous character is more important in building a marriage than her physical characteristics, blood, or wealth. Barbaro concludes that marriage is a value both for the purpose of generation and also for the purpose of the friendship and union of love between the husband and wife:

194. Barbaro, *Directions for Love and Marriage,* pp. 15-16.
195. Barbaro, *Directions for Love and Marriage,* p. 105.
196. Barbaro, *Directions for Love and Marriage,* p. 111.
197. Barbaro, *Directions for Love and Marriage,* p. 49.

We pursue wisdom, friendship, and health for themselves: we desire wit, learning, knowledge, and a comely agreeableness of manners, conjugal embraces, meat, drink, and sleep, as necessary for the other. Therefore, we believe marriages to be good, both for the sake of issue and the society of both sexes.[198]

Barbaro's humanism seemed to balance in some ways the more formal gender polarity principles about women's identity that would have been acquired in his study in the Faculty of Arts at Padua. In addition, his view of woman's role in marriage goes far beyond a simple exchange of a woman for the extension of property. It opens up into a beginning theory of union of minds and hearts in private dialogical interaction about matters of substance.

Barbaro's Daughters

At the beginning of this section, we noted that three of Francesco Barbaro's daughters entered religious life. They were all in the same Convent of the Angels, and it is clear that their father, Francesco, maintained a close and affectionate relation with them. Evidence for this fact comes from a letter he wrote to his daughter Costanza Barbaro in 1447. By considering what Francesco says to his daughter, on the occasion of the death of her cousin Luchina Miani, who had lived in Padua, we can glean three different aspects of their relationship that have particular relevance to the concept of woman.

The first notable thing about this letter are the extensive references to sources common in humanist communities of dialogue. Francesco invokes classical authors in a natural and free manner in conversation with his daughter Costanza. This indicates both that he recognized their value in the serious context of a letter of consolation and that he expected his daughter to be well acquainted with them as well. This reveals that Francesco Barbaro did not, as did Gregorio Correr in his letter to Cecilia Gonzaga written just four years previously, think that once a woman entered a convent, she should turn her mind away from all pagan authors and think only of classical Christian authors.[199] The following passage from Barbaro's letter will support this claim:

But I shall not presume, as would perhaps be allowed, to make up a speech in praise of her according to the custom and precedent of our ancestors; nor should I be faulted if in the matter of adorning and glorifying [my] daughter I think more about what I should than what I could do, especially since from my youth I have determined to seek models of counsel and behavior from the deeds of outstanding men. Thus Q. Fabius Maximus, a man illustrious in war and peace, and G. Caesar praised from the pulpit their dead sons, and the tears of the Roman populace, we read, did not shake their composure. We have also learned through

---

198. Barbaro, *Directions for Love and Marriage,* pp. 6-7.
199. "Gregorio Correr: 'Letter to the virgin Cecilia, on Fleeing this worldly life,'" in *Her Immaculate Hand,* pp. 91-105. This letter is discussed above in the section on Leonardo Bruni.

our father's memory that Robert, King of Sicily, did the same, which we both admire and praise. I say nothing of Caesar who, when he heard, as he marched through Britain, of the death of his daughter, quickly, as he says, conquered sorrow, just as he was accustomed [to conquer] all things. Books, antiquity, history, sparkle with examples as numerous as the stars, of those whose virtue was no less in facing the death of their loved ones than in bearing arms. But why do I look to antiquity?[200]

The sources for these references have been identified by Margaret King and Albert Rabil, Jr., as Plutarch's *Life of Fabius,* Petrarch's *Seniles,* and Boccaccio's *Concerning Famous Women.*[201] Thus, Barbaro shares with his daughter Costanza references to three highly important historical authors in the humanist community of discourse.

These references lead to the second point of interest in this letter of Francesco to his daughter, namely that they promote the view that women as well as men are called to practice the virtue of self-governance. Significantly, in this shared view we discover an intersection of values shared in both the religious and humanist communities of discourse. In the following passage, after listing various contemporary examples to complement his previous examples from ancient sources, Francesco integrates both Christian and pagan practices with respect to the value of reason governing the passions:

> But I am not asking you to do what they did, which you willingly do [in any case] — assuage your sorrow with reason — for though she was a worthy sister to you, you also knew that she was mortal, and you are now longing for her as though she were absent, not dead, so that you seem to await her, not to have lost her. For the disciples of Christ, as Jerome holds, should do better than the philosophers of the world. And yet, peoples who did not know God and did not hope for resurrection, have so bravely and firmly borne the death of sons that they can provide a great example to Christians of the truth that the death of good men should be little mourned. Both your name and your duty to your convent, if I may say so, require that you preserve with dignity a grave manner.[202]

Again King and Rabil point out that Francesco's reference to philosophers who did not have Christian faith, yet who understood that the death of a good man should not be mourned, was introducing the figure of Socrates. In Plato's *Apology,* Socrates had argued before the jury at Athens who had condemned him to death: "You too, gentlemen of the jury, must look forward to death with confidence, and fix your minds on this one belief, which is certain — that nothing can harm a good man either in life or after death. . . ."[203]

From the above letter, it might be concluded that Francesco Barbaro was imposing a burden on his daughter that was attached to her name, implying that she

---

200. "Francesco Barbaro to his Daughter Costanza," in *Her Immaculate Hand,* pp. 106-7.
201. King and Rabil, eds., *Her Immaculate Hand,* p. 147, notes 2, 3, and 4.
202. "Francesco Barbaro to his Daughter Costanza," in *Her Immaculate Hand,* p. 107.
203. Plato, *Apology,* 41c-d. See also King and Rabil, eds., *Her Immaculate Hand,* p. 147, note 7.

is simply an extension of his own identity. In other words, she is required to preserve her dignity in grief because otherwise it would degrade the name of the Barbaro family. It is interesting to note that Francesco Barbaro uses a similar appeal in a letter to his son Zaccaria. In the context of a discussion about his son's attitude towards education, Francesco says: "If [your teacher] Lorenzo Casano is there, work hard to cultivate your mind with his knowledge and virtue, lest you allow those seeds of virtue given you by God and nature to perish — while if you permit them to mature, you will recognize yourself as born for the honor of your country and for the glory and amplification of our family."[204] This attitude of duty to the family, then, applies equally to Francesco's daughter and son.

There seems to be no reason to doubt that Francesco Barbaro is writing to his daughter Costanza within the context of a Christian humanist community of discourse, and he presumes an education commensurate to the references that are being invoked. It is also very possible that within a convent that housed three sisters from the same family, one sister who received a letter from their father on a matter of such importance as the death of a cousin would be prone to share it with the other sisters. Therefore, it may be presumed that not only Costanza, but also her siblings had not been discouraged from reading humanist or pagan philosophical sources in religious life. Rather to the contrary, the letter implies a positive attitude towards humanistic education and its particular application to practical situations in the world.

There is one final issue the content of Francesco's letter raises with respect to the history of the concept of woman. This issue concerns his theory of gender identity and the presence of elements of gender unity or unisex themes. The historical roots of such themes, as has been already pointed out, can be found in Plato's theory that the soul is an asexual entity that uses a body. Another historical root for this theme can also be found in Augustine's philosophy, which absorbed Platonic and Neoplatonic tendencies. In particular, Augustine argued that women who turned their total attention towards spiritual life, moved from a gender-specified worldly identity towards a kind of sexless spiritual identity where there is neither male nor female. Augustine described nuns as doing this, as well as his mother Monica, in some of his earlier philosophical dialogues.[205] In any event, in Francesco's description of the life of his niece, Luchina Miani, there are similar themes of gender unity expressed. After a detailed description of Luchina's character as a married woman Barbaro begins to describe her in the period of her last illness:

> Luchina's husband, Francesco Miani, who, without her, it seemed, either wished to die or was unable to live, as well as others who were present there, she so bravely consoled that she showed that **virtue should be measured not by sex** but by loftiness of soul. She only complained about her discomfort when [her pain] was intense and [then she spoke] with restraint. Of her children and other dear ones she so spoke, looking up into heaven, that she overcame her love for the

204. In King, *Venetian Humanism*, p. 25.
205. For a detailed account of these themes see Allen, *The Concept of Woman: The Aristotelian Revolution (750 BC–1250 AD)*, the chapters on Plato and on Augustine, pp. 57-81 and 218-35.

children by her greater love of God, and **she forgot that she was a mother,** as it is written, in order to remember that she was the handmaiden of Christ. The lesson of her death then was: "Be unwilling to love the world and those things in the world, but give a gift, and hope in the Lord."

What need is there of more? Even before she had despaired of her life **she put aside womanly softness,** so composed her soul, and so spoke of God with mixed joy and tears that one could perceive that she did not fear death but piously hoped for it.[206]

In the three phrases highlighted for emphasis in the above passage, a tendency towards a unisex model of virtue for spiritual women is revealed. Barbaro suggests traditional gender polarity principles usually applied to married women in the world: (1) virtue measured by sex differentiation; (2) identity of a woman defined as being a mother; and (3) woman's nature characterized by softness or weakness. Then he indicates that Luchina's character rejected the world and resided instead in the highest ranges of her soul where she was no longer characterized by an engendered woman's identity; her virtue had no relation to her sex, she forgot that she was a mother, and she transcended her feminine identity. Nowhere in this letter of Francesco is there any indication of a gender complementarity theory of the human person, namely, that Luchina, as a woman and a mother, reached a profound level of spiritual development in the acceptance of her suffering and death. In other words, Francesco appears to have expressed a duality for woman: either gender polarity in the world or gender unity in the soul. This combination of an Aristotelian-based and a Platonic-based view of woman's identity does not yet reach the point of integration of gender identity and personal identity towards which ultimately Christian philosophy aims. Yet, there is a step forward in the building of complementarity in the kind of discourse indicated by Francesco's letter to his daughter Costanza. It could be said, then, that the practice of complementarity in early humanist discourse precedes in some ways the theory of complementarity that has yet to be articulated from a philosophical and theological foundation.

Early Translations of Plato and Gender Identity

The relation of Barbaro to Platonic thought has already been considered briefly above with respect to Guarino's annotated copy of Decembrio and Chrysoloras's distorted 1402 translation of Plato's *Republic*. We know that around 1414, Barbaro spent time in Florence where Chrysoloras taught Greek and Bruni had already translated Plato's *Phaedo, Apology,* and *Crito.* Barbaro was introduced to some Latin versions of the Greek philosopher's view about the immortality of the soul, and perhaps even through his knowledge of Greek, Plato's suggestions of a unisex identity of the soul found in his discussions of different reincarnations of the soul in either male or female bodies. We also noted that Barbaro wrote his text

---

206. "Francesco Barbaro to his Daughter Costanza," in *Her Immaculate Hand*, p. 109. My emphasis.

On Wifely Duties in 1415, shortly after this period in Florence, and that Bruni likely did not write his text *On the Study of Literature* for Lady Battista Malatesta until ten years later in 1424, the same year he translated Plato's *Phaedrus*.

The drama of the accuracy and integrity of various translations of Plato's *Republic* continued during the fifteenth century. Even though Barbaro did study Greek, it is likely that Latin translations of Plato's dialogues had their influence on his thinking as well as on that of other Italian humanists. For instance, in 1437-39 the son of Uberto Decembrio, Pier Candido Decembrio (1399-1477), made still another translation of Plato's *Republic*. Pier Decembrio, in contrast with both his father and with Bruni, translated the ancient text literally. At the same time, he was also uncomfortable with Plato's arguments about the equality of women and men in an ideal republic. So Pier Candido Decembrio introduced a collection of strategies to succeed in a more accurate translation of Plato's *Republic* while at the same time defeating Plato's arguments about women's identity in the text. First of all, he considered Aristotle's criticism (in Book II of the *Politics*) of Plato's views in Book V of the *Republic,* and decided that it provided a distorted understanding of Plato's own views. This criticism of Aristotle escalated his disagreement with Leonard Bruni, who had just recently translated the *Politics*. At the same time, however, Decembrio did not himself accept all of Plato's views about woman, and so, as he worked on his translation of the *Republic,* he also introduced a framework of sub-headings, summaries, and commentaries for interpretation of each section. James Hankins summarizes Decembrio's strategy as follows: "The effect of this apparatus of prefaces, letters, arguments, rubrics and marginalia was to produce a sort of frame to regulate the reader's perception of the text."[207]

In addition, like Bruni, Chrysoloras, and his father before him, Pier Candido Decembrio chose to distort several passages concerning women's identity and passages suggesting immoral behavior by mistranslating them or rendering them obscure so as not to offend his readers. Again Hankins is precise in his description of this manipulation of Plato by the translator: "Passages suggesting the equality of the sexes [in Plato] are obscurely translated, surrounded with marginalia such as those reading (455b ff.), 'Natural differences'; 'Women's work'; 'Woman is weaker than man in all things'; 'Women's natures are different,' etc."[208] This strategy of Decembrio emphasizes the passage in which Plato modifies his sex unity theory by a kind of gender polarity. Even though Plato argued that the soul is an asexual entity that could be reincarnated in either male or female bodies, he also believed that female embodiment was a weaker state of human existence. Thus, his metaphysical foundations for gender unity were modified somewhat by a gender polarity theory about the actual states of men and women in the world. Specifically, Plato suggests that as a punishment for a man who lived a cowardly or immoral life a soul may be reincarnated in a female body. In this state he would begin the next stage of existence in a weakened female form as a kind of punishment for the poor ethical quality of the previous life. Decembrio focuses in his comments on Plato's view of this aspect of a woman's existence, on the differences or weaknesses found in

207. Hankins, *Plato in the Italian Renaissance,* p. 133.
208. Hankins, *Plato in the Italian Renaissance,* p. 138, note 62.

women in the world, and the subsequent imbalanced differentiation of functions and work of men and women as actually found in ordinary society.

At the same time, however, Plato argues in both the *Republic* and the *Laws* that women ought to be educated the same as men so that they can presumably escape these cycles of reincarnation. In addition, he suggests that structures in society be changed to allow women freedom to acquire such an education. This is one pragmatic root for Plato's theory of the community of women and children. The only qualification he makes is that women's education may take somewhat longer because of their inherited weakness, but otherwise girls are to be treated the same as boys and women are to be treated the same as men. It is this argument of Plato that orients the reader of his dialogues towards the metaphysical foundations for the underlying sex unity claim instead of towards observations about how men and women live in human society. Therefore, Decembrio's strategies to neutralize Plato's teachings about woman's identity distorted the original philosopher's claims to fit a gender polarity view of society. However, even with his attempts to veil original recommendations of Plato about how society should be restructured to allow both women and men to achieve the greatest possible intellectual growth through education, and how their work should not be determined by sex differentiation as much as by natural talent and inclination, the fact that more of the *Republic* was accurately translated in this 1437-39 version than had previously been done made it possible for more of Plato's arguments to become widely known.

That the question of woman's identity was seriously debated among fifteenth-century Italian humanists is indisputable. In *Dialogi in Lactantium,* written in 1443 by Antonio da Rho, a dialogue is recounted as having taken place among three humanists: defenders of Plato Pier Candido Decembrio and Antonio da Rho, and a defender of Aristotle Niccolò Arcimboldi. James Hankins describes how the dialogue begins with an exaggerated distortion of Plato's views:

> The discussion begins with Arcimboldi reading aloud to the assembled scholars an entire chapter from the third book of Lactantius' *Divine Institutes,* a chapter in which the apologist had caricatured Plato's teachings in *Republic V* as a plan to turn the female sex into Amazonian prostitutes. "This commune of men and women is nothing but non-stop sex and adultery."[209]

This interpretation neglects to mention Plato's differentiation of classes of women and his regulation in the ideal republic of sexual intercourse among men and women.

However, the debate continued and at a certain point, after the argument got more intense: "Niccolò and Pier Candido pull out their texts of the *Politics* and the *Republic* with the air of knightly champions drawing their trusty blades. Niccolò proceeds to read out the entirety of *Politics* II.ii, the passage containing Aristotle's attack on the doctrine of *Republic* V, in Bruni's Latin translation. . . ."[210] Some members present then criticize Bruni's inaccurate translation, and then Pier

209. Hankins, *Plato in the Italian Renaissance,* p. 150.
210. Hankins, *Plato in the Italian Renaissance,* pp. 150-51.

Candido Decembrio explains how Aristotle misunderstood Plato. In the dialogue, Decembrio is presented as rationalizing away all the points of disagreement between Plato and Christian Milanese culture. For example, Plato's advocacy of common property is compared with the vow of poverty in religious life, and it is pointed out that this would apply only to an elite class of guardians; arrangement of marriages is compared with present practices of arrangement of marriages in the society of Milan, and so forth. "He admits that Plato conceived of women as taking part in warfare and politics, but dismisses this (citing a passage in Augustine's *City of God*) as an aberration stemming from the social idiosyncrasies of ancient Athens."[211] Thus the dialogue ends with Pier Candido Decembrio making Plato perfectly compatible with his humanist audience in Milan. While the goal of translation at this early part of the fifteenth century is still far from presenting an accurate account of the deeper thinking of the ancient Greek philosophers Plato and Aristotle about women's identity, it must be noted that philosophical arguments about woman's identity was a topic that generated a considerable amount of interest in humanist circles. It was taken as a serious and important issue for discussion.

The next phase of translation finally found a translator who was willing to offer a more accurate rendering of the original Greek text. Antonio Cassarino insisted that "the translator should avoid meddling in any way with the text, whether to make it more appealing to patrons or for any other reason."[212] Cassarino made a new translation of Plato's *Republic* sometime between 1439 and his death in 1447. His superior version of the *Republic* avoided many of the earlier distortions about woman's identity found in the two previous versions. In fact, Antonio Cassarino directly addressed his personal orientation to translating Plato in his *Isagogicon:*

> It does not much bother me, nor do I think it is any of my business, what I have heard certain persons say, that Plato was a madman to have thought women and children should be held in common — as though I should think it my duty here to defend Plato's opinions, or that indeed it were any of the translators' business [to do so]; or as though Plato's authority were not so great that it ought to be held of more account than the ignorance of certain glib babblers.[213]

This more enlightened approach to translating a historical text, namely, to allow the text to stand by itself without having to defend the views of the author, is an important development in the history of philosophy. Therefore, by the middle of the fifteenth century humanist philosophers, having access to Latin translations of original Greek sources, began to probe more deeply into the philosophical inheritance they had received from the Greeks.

At this point in the discussion, Francesco Barbaro once more became directly involved in the whole dynamic of the translation of texts. He particularly supported another translator, George of Trebizond (1396–c. 1472), who provided a new translation of Plato's *Laws* in 1450-51. George had first worked as a Greek scribe for

211. Hankins, *Plato in the Italian Renaissance,* p. 151.
212. Hankins, *Plato in the Italian Renaissance,* p. 156.
213. Antonio Cassarino, *Isagogicon,* in Hankins, *Plato in the Italian Renaissance,* pp. 156-57.

Barbaro when he was a young man who had just immigrated to Venice from Crete. While there, George also studied Latin under Guarino, with whom he later came into conflict. George was a man who always seemed in the midst of controversies and as a result he entered into conflict wherever he went, moving at various times to Vicenza, Venice, and Rome. His conflicts also came into the intellectual realm, for between 1426 and 1433 he began new translations of Aristotle's works on natural philosophy and at the same time he started to both attack Plato's philosophy and to translate more of Plato's dialogues than any other translator up to Marsilio Ficino. In his annotations to the *Laws,* George remarks, for example: "In the same book [V], see; he thinks his first state [that of the *Republic,* mentioned at *Leg.* V, 739B 8f], where all things are held in common, even women, will be immortal! . . . Look at his impossible customs!"[214] Again we have the situation where the translator at least provides a more accurate rendering of a text while stating his reservations to what he translates.

George of Trebizond's cantankerous personality also made it difficult for him to find patrons to help finance his translations. However, through Francesco Barbaro's intercession, George found a patron in Venice for a copy of his translation of Plato's *Laws.* Barbaro, among other Venetian patricians, used George's version of Plato's *Laws* to help defend Venice's form of government. In his preface to the *Laws,* "George claims that the mixed constitution recommended by Plato in his *Laws* was the exemplar of the most perfect constitution the world had ever seen, namely that of the present-day Venetian state."[215] This pattern of appeal to Plato or Aristotle to defend the particular form of civic government in Venice, Florence, Milan, and even other smaller cities like Camerino was followed so often that it not only distorted the original philosophers' views but also reduced their value as legitimate authorities.[216] In any event, Plato's *Laws* did provide a further source for gender unity arguments: that both men and women ought to be citizens whose excellence resides in virtues of the soul (770d), that there should be a common table for men and women (781a-b), and that girls must be trained exactly as boys (804e). However, it did modify the rejection of the family and the community of women suggested in *Republic* V, by allowing for private homes and families in more than just the laboring class (776a and 930b-c). As a result, Plato's *Laws* continued to provide further arguments against the gender polarity traditions that differentiated both the education and virtues of men and women.

In the next section of this chapter, humanist arguments about the identity of woman will begin to move out from Italy and into Germany through a focus on the work of Albrecht von Eyb.

---

214. Hankins, *Plato in the Italian Renaissance,* p. 181, note 30.
215. Hankins, *Plato in the Italian Renaissance,* pp. 181-82.
216. See Hankins for a thorough discussion of these themes, *Plato in the Italian Renaissance,* pp. 140-43.

ALBRECHT VON EYB (1420-1475)

Just as in Italy, the first movement of humanism in Germany occurred in a reformation of education and founding of new institutional structures or schools. Because of the importance of the Brethren of the Common Life for the development of humanism in Germany, some introductory reflections will be given on its founder and structure. Gerhard Groote (1340-1384), who had studied in the Faculties of Arts and Law at the University of Paris and in Prague, went through a personal conversion after leading a dissolute life.[217] Filled with zeal after his conversion, Groote set out to reform the Church by introducing a new religious movement, *Devotio Moderna,* which emphasized simple acts of devotion and shunned academic theological studies. "He carried on an active campaign against the dying scholasticism of his day. 'Why should we indulge in those endless disputes,' he would say, 'such as are held at the universities, and that about subjects of no moral value whatsoever?'"[218] Thus, Groote's reform had an undermining effect on Aristotelian-based foundations for gender polarity by its generalized turning away from scholasticism.

In 1379 Gerhard Groote founded a lay community called "Sisters of the Common Life." These women worked in common, shared expenses, and performed particular tasks in varying enterprises. Groote had given the women their first home, from his own considerable wealth, and then drew up constitutions for their association. This little group became a model for the more widely known "Brethren of the Common Life."[219] This community had groups of priests and lay men and women who provided houses in which young boys and girls could be educated separately in the Catholic faith. In some cities the Brethren actually taught the young, while in others they provided a place for the young to live and be taught by others. The first main locations of houses for the Brothers and Sisters of the Common Life were in Deventer (1383), Zwolle (1386-87), and Windesheim (1394-95), basically in the low countries of the Netherlands and in northern Germany. After Groote's death his successor, Florens Radedijns (1350-1400), led the Brothers and Sisters of the Common Life in expanding brother-houses and sister-houses into other areas of Germany, the Rhineland, and the Netherlands.[220]

Several of the Brothers and Sisters of the Common Life were teachers. While many of them did not have a high level of either theological or humanist education, some did educate the lay youth in both classical pagan and Christian literature, including the subjects of rhetoric, grammar, philosophy, mathematics, logic, and the-

---

217. Albert Hyma, *The Brethren of the Common Life* (Grand Rapids: Eerdmans, 1950), pp. 18-21.

218. Hyma, *The Brethren of the Common Life,* p. 30.

219. Hyma, *The Brethren of the Common Life,* pp. 49-51; and Power, *Main Currents in the History of Education,* p. 291.

220. Steven Ozment, *The Age of Reform, 1250-1550: An Intellectual and Religious History of Late Medieval and Reformation Europe* (New Haven and London: Yale University Press, 1980), pp. 96-97. See also R. J. Schoeck, *Erasmus of Europe: The Making of a Humanist (1467-1500)* (Savage, Md.: Barnes and Noble, 1990), Appendix B: "The *Devotio Moderna* and Brethren of the Common Life," pp. 264-71.

ology.[221] Schools in which the Brethren taught were opened in several places in Germany, teaching in both Latin and the vernacular. Discussions open to the public in the vernacular were held on a wide range of topics. Being both religious and intellectual, they provided a foundation for a new kind of community of discourse between strictly religious communities and strictly academic communities. The members of the Brethren of the Common Life produced a new intellectual elite in Germany and the Netherlands. The rapid expansion of the number of houses of the Brothers was extraordinary: 1400 in Münster, 1410 in Osterberg, 1415 in Osnabrück, 1417 in Cologne, 1428 in Herford, 1436 in Wesel, and 1440 in Hildesheim. There were houses in several other cities in Germany and the lowlands as well. In addition, the Sisters of the Common Life also founded many houses: in Deventer five, in Zwolle six, in Zutphen three, in Duisburg two, in Utrecht two, and so on.[222] The size of the schools was also an important factor in the reform of education. For example, the Deventer school under the leadership of Alexander Hegius at the end of the fifteenth century had up to 2200 students.[223] Many poorer students were given both housing and education, so education became not so much associated with upper-class status as with natural intelligence and eagerness to learn.

The curriculum in these schools at the beginning of the German Renaissance, and especially the one in Deventer, modeled that which had already been developed in the new Italian humanist schools. In addition to there being a similar content of education in the new German and Italian humanist schools, there was also a common pedagogy of "combining a sound religious instruction with a well-selected list of studies . . . [which] sought to inculcate a love for individual research by letting pupils delve among the classics rather than confine themselves to textbooks, and taught the boys the use of their vernacular as well."[224] The students and others associated with the Brethren often earned their living by copying ancient manuscripts, and later by printing them. Printing began in Deventer as early as 1476 and in Zwolle in 1478.[225] The claim that the particular school in Deventer was a center of intellectual humanism is supported by the fact that there were "450 classical works . . . printed by the Deventer presses before 1500."[226] By comparison with other centers of printing, "[d]uring the 1490's . . . more classical texts came from the presses of Deventer than from Paris."[227]

Men and women associated with the Brethren were immersed in classical texts of ancient Latin and German culture. As a result they helped educate scholars outside of the strictly academic tradition. Not only did Nicholas of Cusa study

---

221. For a good discussion of the controversies surrounding both education and the role of the Brethren in schools, see R. J. Schoeck, "The *Devotio Moderna* and Brethren of the Common Life," in *Erasmus of Europe: The Making of a Humanist (1467-1500)*, Appendix B, pp. 264ff.

222. Hyma, *The Brethren of the Common Life*, pp. 106-7.

223. Hyma, *The Brethren of the Common Life*, p. 119.

224. Hyma, *The Brethren of the Common Life*, p. 123.

225. Schoeck, *Erasmus of Europe: The Making of a Humanist (1467-1500)*, p. 11.

226. Power, *Main Currents in the History of Education*, p. 292. See also Hyma, *The Brethren of the Common Life*, p. 121.

227. Schoeck, *Erasmus of Europe: The Making of a Humanist (1467-1500)*, p. 47.

there, but Thomas à Kempis and Erasmus did as well. Erasmus studied from the age of eight to sixteen (1475-1483) at Deventer, where some of the Brethren of the Common Life were teaching, where he met Rudolf Agricola, and while the school was being transformed by the printing press. The famous educator Alexander Hegius moved to Deventer in 1483, but Erasmus left during a period of the return of plague in 1484, and so he did not benefit much from this relation.

In addition to humanist influences on the schools associated with the Brethren of the Common Life, Neoplatonism also played an important role. Ernst Cassirer, in *The Individual and the Cosmos in Renaissance Philosophy,* notes the significant influence of Meister Eckhart on the founder Gerhard Groote and in particular on the Neoplatonic directions of his thought. More specifically, the Brethren emphasized the theme of the birth of God in the individual soul, and they adopted a Platonist epistemology to correspond to this belief.[228] Eckhart also considered the theme of the reconciliation of opposites. In addition, the mystical writer Jan van Ruusbroec was a personal friend of Groote as well, and he had been partly responsible for the promotion of the writings of women religious authors. As noted in earlier chapters these two men, Eckhart and Ruusbroec, communicated a respect for woman's identity in ways not common to academic gender polarity. By their relationships with women and their own writings, they offered some models for developing gender complementarity. At the same time, however, they were influenced by Neoplatonism with its tendencies towards a unisex model of human identity.

We will now turn to consider the work of a popular German author, Albrecht von Eyb, who directly engaged with arguments about the inferiority of woman. After returning from a humanist and academic education in Italy, Eyb released an important book about the concept of woman and addressed it to the German public, who welcomed his writings.

Book about Marriage

The earliest direct infusion of Italian Renaissance thinking about the concept of woman into the humanist reform of Germany took place primarily through the work of Albrecht von Eyb, who was born in a castle in eastern Bavaria in the town of Eschenbach. Eyb's lengthy 1471 text was entitled *Ehebüchlein: Ob einem manne sey zunemen ein eelichs weyb oder nicht (Little Book of Marriage: Whether a Man Should Marry an Honorable Wife or Not).*[229] This was one of the first texts in the German language to focus directly on several aspects of woman's identity, drawing upon the traditional humanist sources of both pagan and Christian authors.

The Eyb family was from the lower nobility, and education was valued by his parents. His oldest brother Georg, a priest, died young. His next brother, Ludwig, took over the duties of head of the family after his father died in 1438 and dedicated his life to diplomacy and politics. Albrecht's youngest brother Wilhelm died in a

228. Cassirer, *The Individual and the Cosmos in Renaissance Philosophy,* p. 33.
229. See Joseph Anthony Hiller, *Albrecht von Eyb: Medieval Moralist.* Ph.D. Diss., Catholic University of America, Washington D.C., 1939. (Carthagena, Ohio: Messenger Press, 1939).

military battle, leaving Ludwig and Albrecht as the two to carry on the Eyb heritage. One personal factor that appeared to influence Albrecht Eyb's decision to defend both women and marriage was his close relationship with his own mother, Margaret von Wolmershausen. Her great love of literature was a strong part of his life until her untimely death when he was only twelve. In his introduction to an early text on rhetoric and grammar entitled *Margarita poetica,* Albrecht von Eyb explains why he names his book after his mother: "Not without good reason, glorious work, take up for yourself the name of my worthiest mother, Lady Margaret of Wolmershausen, a most eminent woman, from whom I derived the first elements as well as the best of literature."[230] This relationship is worth noting, because, in contrast to the more usual humanist trend of a father educating his daughter, here we discover a mother educating her son. In addition, the personal example of his own mother's love of learning could have provided the crucial evidence about a woman's identity that enabled Albrecht to write a major text supporting the dignity of woman against the contrary views of satirists such as Juvenal and Theophrastus and against the common opinion that a woman would lead a man away from intellectual study.

Eyb's *Margarita poetica* and *Little Book of Marriage* were both very successful in Germany. Since he was not the first German humanist intellectual who imported Italian Renaissance thinking into Germany, the broader interest in humanist ideas that already existed in Germany at the time of the publication of Eyb's works, in part because of the houses of the Brothers and Sisters of the Common Life, may have partly accounted for their immediate success.

Albrecht von Eyb studied in Italy in the Faculty of Arts at the University of Pavia from 1444 to 1447 after having learned classical Latin in Rothenburg from 1439 to 1443 and beginning the studies of Law at the University of Erfurt, Germany. It was during this period in Pavia that Eyb was first exposed to a curriculum including logic, metaphysics, and rhetoric.[231] The official program of graduate studies that Eyb followed was in the complement fields of Canon Law and Roman Civil Law. He studied Law at universities in Bologna and Padua, and graduated with a Doctorate in Roman Law from the University of Pavia in 1459.

At the University of Pavia Eyb had also come into contact with Manuel Chrysoloras, the famous teacher of Greek, who was now influencing Italian humanists in Milan. Eyb was also apparently influenced by Guarino of Verona to study ancient Greek and classical Latin authors. During the fifteen-year period that Eyb spent in Italy, 1444-1459, the new schools of Guarino and Vittorino were flourishing and Italian humanism was the attractive new field for intellectuals. Albrecht von Eyb took advantage of this new humanist approach to education while he was studying for his official degrees in Law. There is evidence that Eyb, right from the beginning of his studies in Italy, developed an early interest in tracts about women's identity and particularly those that focused on the topic of marriage. Guarino, who was married by 1418, had written some orations in support of marriage. Other texts that have already been considered in this book, and with which Eyb was familiar, include the treatise supporting marriage by Francesco

---

230. Hiller, *Albrecht von Eyb,* p. 3. Translated from the Latin by Michael Woodward.
231. Hiller, *Albrecht von Eyb,* pp. 7-9.

Barbaro, *On Wifely Duties*. In addition, Eyb kept a notebook of citations from ancient Greek philosophers and classical Latin poets, and "a large number of these 'dicta' deal directly with marriage and woman."[232] Eyb's personal library of classical manuscripts was so large that it was considered one of the best in Europe.[233] Thus, Eyb would have also been familiar with Plutarch's suggestion, perhaps in Guarino's Latin translation of *On the Education of Children*, that mothers ought to take up the study of letters in order to better educate their own children.

In addition, Theophrastus' satirical treatise against marriage, *Liber de nuptiis*, included in St. Jerome, *Adversus Jovianum*, was well known by Eyb, and according to Hiller, "The *Ehebuch* is a refutation of that book, so widely read in the fifteenth century."[234] Theophrastus had argued that no wise man should marry because a wife would inevitably distract him from his philosophical pursuits. It is interesting to consider what other factors than simple exposure to Italian humanists would have led Albrecht von Eyb to have dedicated so much attention to the theme of woman's identity, and especially to a defense of marriage. It is especially significant that Eyb chose to do so in the light of his own vocation as a celibate cleric in minor orders. In other words, Eyb was not married himself, and remained celibate in service of the Church, yet without being ordained as a priest.

Eyb's study of law, and particularly the Roman legal system, and his subsequent appointment as an ecclesiastical lawyer on his return to Germany placed him in a position to consider the legal situation of women. As Hiller summarizes it, Eyb wrote many opinions for cases on which he was consulted: "The subject matter is: last wills, contracts, benefices and above all marriage cases. The last named was not only Eyb's preferred field in general, but as a spiritual judge, he also took up cases in defence of women in particular."[235]

At the time of Albrecht von Eyb's work, Germany was divided into regional administrative units, led by princes and magnates. In the pattern of civic humanism, he addressed his major text, *Das Ehebüchlein*, or *Little Book on Marriage*, directly to the Imperial City of Nuremberg, to its council, and to its community. His purpose was to educate men about women and particularly about the value of marriage, drawing upon the model of the ancients. It has recently been noted:

> [I]f any German city can be said to approximate the Italian republican models of Venice or Florence, it was Nuremberg, dubbed by one of its citizens, Christoph Scheurl, the 'German Venice.' . . . In Nuremberg culture was valued only if it was demonstrably useful and practical and if it added material value or enjoyment of life. . . . Further contributors to this intellectual climate before Willibald Pirckheimer came upon the scene were the author of the *Pearl of Poetry*, Albrecht von Eyb. . . .[236]

232. Hiller, *Albrecht von Eyb*, p. 115.
233. Rado L. Lencek, "Humanism in the Slavic Cultural Tradition with Special Reference to the Czech Lands," in *Renaissance Humanism*, vol. 2, *Humanism Beyond Italy*, p. 357.
234. Hiller, *Albrecht von Eyb*, p. 115.
235. Hiller, *Albrecht von Eyb*, p. 29.
236. Noel L. Brann, "Humanism in Germany," in *Renaissance Humanism*, vol. 2, *Humanism Beyond Italy*, p. 128.

As Eyb's doctorate was in Roman Law, he hoped to encourage the adoption of Roman jurisprudence in Germany. This was the practical aim that complemented his humanist interest in the subject of woman's identity in marriage. It is perhaps significant that Nuremberg did change its marriage laws and officially adopted Roman Law in 1479, just seven years after the publication of Eyb's *Little Book on Marriage*.[237] In addition, in the 1500s after the Protestant Reformation, the government of the Lutheran City of Nuremberg placed all marriage law under civic, rather than religious, jurisdiction.[238]

The particular problem that Eyb considered in his *Ehebüchlein* is whether or not a man should marry. This problem, as previously discussed in this book, was often addressed by satirists, male religious authors, and academics in such a way as to argue that a man ought not to marry because of a devalued account of woman's identity, i.e., woman would lead a man away from higher studies, she would dangerously tempt him to vice, or she might even rule him like some animal. Eyb demonstrates in his works that he is thoroughly familiar with the satirical literature against women. His goal was to write a refutation of the views associated with Theophrastus, Juvenal, and others that a man ought not to marry. Eyb states his purpose directly in his introduction to *Ehebüchlein*:

> The natural masters posed and disputed a fine common question in their exercises and schools: Whether a man should marry or not. Although these same masters disposed of this question in a few words, I, Albrecht von Eyb, doctor of both laws, archdeacon of Würzburg and Cathedral canon of Bamberg and Eichstätt, have nevertheless decided to write about this question for the praiseworthy imperial city of Nuremberg and its honourable, wise, and prudent council and its entire community out of special love, good will, and affection, and from friendly neighbourliness, which I especially have towards them, for the praise, honour, and strengthening of their policy and government.[239]

The "natural masters [who] posed and disputed" this question refers to professors of natural philosophy in Faculties of Arts.

It was in his capacity as a practicing lawyer that Eyb, in his preface to the *Ehebüchlein* above, suggested that his goal in writing the text was to strengthen the policy and government of his neighboring city of Nuremberg concerning marriage. In other words, Eyb not only had a theoretical interest in the concept of woman, but he also had a pragmatic interest in how to change laws to protect women and to support the institution of marriage. Eyb's *Little Book on Marriage* was immediately popular. In it he translated many Latin sources into German, so that the general public could grasp his main line of argument. Thus Eyb not only defended mar-

---

237. Hiller, *Albrecht von Eyb*, p. 119.

238. Steven Ozment, *When Fathers Ruled: Family Life in Reformation Europe* (Cambridge, Mass. and London: Harvard University Press, 1983), pp. 30-31.

239. Albrecht von Eyb, *Das Ehebüchlein: Ob einem manne sey zunemen ein eelichs weyb oder nicht*, Deutsche Schriften (Berlin: Weidmann, 1890), p. 4. Translated by Robert Sullivan, as are all other passages from this text.

riage and women against their detractors, but he also introduced his reading audience to some of the dominant themes in ancient literature and philosophy about marriage and women's identity.

Eyb's *Little Book on Marriage,* a text of around one hundred pages, was divided into three parts: The First Part posed the question, Whether a man should marry or not?, and offered some counterarguments to satirists and others who had answered it in the negative. The Second Part developed Eyb's positive answer to the question and ended with a section that praised both marriage and women. The Third Part considered some practical aspects of the married state. Throughout the text, Eyb appealed to a cluster of ancient theorists to support his claims. His references were usually anecdotal and drawn from a wide range of sources. They were often quoted second-hand, which meant that passages were taken out of context, and sometimes even falsely attributed. Our analysis of Eyb's citation of sources will be divided into two sections: first, we will consider directly Eyb's own thinking about the concept of woman; and second, we will consider Eyb's use of humanistic sources to defend his views. It is in the first section that Eyb's contributions to the history of the concept of woman are most noteworthy.

First of all, Eyb, in a chapter entitled "In Praise of Women," credits woman for inventing and developing the art of writing.

> To praise the worth and superiority of women, to which I am especially inclined, is no easy task for me. But in so far as I can know and do so, I shall attempt it. First, I shall consider the praise which comes from the wisdom, skills, and writings of women. For we read that nothing is greater, more worthy, and more useful to the human race than the art of writing. Through this skill we are taught to do right towards ourselves and others, to promote the commonweal, and to lead a pious and blessed life. No one can be rightly called wise, who is ignorant of and lacking the art of writing, for such a person errs, is deceived, and easily makes mistakes in little things, all of which could not be more disagreeable to a wise man.
>
> So it is plain that all knowledge of divine and human things and all wisdom is contained in the art of writing. Who revealed to us the utility and use of writing, who was its inventor and teacher? Women.[240]

After this introduction to his theme, which argues both that the skill of writing is the most useful thing for a wise man and that women were the ones who invented and taught this precious skill, Albrecht von Eyb then provides proof for the strong claim. He translates into the German language examples drawn from traditional humanist authors, including especially Boccaccio's Latin text, *Concerning Famous Women:*

> Isis, a woman, not only invented the first letters in Egypt, but also discovered how to cultivate the earth, and the use of flax. Nicostrata, who is also called Clementis, invented Latin letters and taught how to put them together. Sappho

240. Eyb, *Das Ehebüchlein,* p. 69.

wrote many books on poetry which the Greeks hold and preserve in honour on account of their own special meaning, eloquence, and art. Cornelia composed and wrote many Latin letters and epistles which were still used after her death. Aspasia was such a highly educated and eloquent woman that Socrates was not ashamed to learn many skills from her.

Centona took and used many passages from the poet Virgil on the old and new marriage and in praise of God. Amesia, who had a man's spirit, Gaia Afrania, Calpurnia, and Tanaquil spoke and worked inwardly and outwardly in the law courts before the powerful in Rome and freed many from guilt.

Augeriona restored many a person to health and freed him from the bonds of death through the art of beneficial medicine. When men still took their nourishment from acorns just like animals, Ceres discovered how to cultivate the earth, to gather fruits, to grind wheat, and to bake bread. And Minerva found how to use and weave wool, discovered numbers and their representation, oil, and the methods and order of disputation.[241]

This listing of women's accomplishments, which mixed actual historical women with goddesses, was common among the early humanists. Eyb, however, is conscious of this odd clustering, and he notes that the pagans tended to consider women they honored for "art, wisdom, and virtue" among their goddesses. Eyb appears to have thought that all of the women had actually existed, and he continues to offer evidence for his claim by introducing contemporary women who also give evidence of similar characteristics. Eyb's argument continues as follows:

> It is not necessary to relate the art, wisdom, and virtue of women of our time since they show themselves in all lands every day. But for the honour and praise of the German tongue, I shall mention the illustrious and noble princess, Lady Barbara Margravine in Mantua, born von Brandenburg, who knows four languages and speaks them powerfully: German, her native language, Italian, Latin, and Greek. She is also educated in the writings of the poets and natural masters which she acquired through her great observation and wisdom and for which, along with many other virtues, God has gifted her, she cannot be rightly praised enough.[242]

Mantua, it should be recalled, was the site in Italy at which the Gonzaga family invited Vittorino da Feltre to establish his first institutional structure for humanistic education. From Eyb's description it would appear that the tradition of encouraging women's education, begun there with Cecilia Gonzaga, was continuing with Lady Barbara Margravine.

In this short argument in praise of women, Eyb overturned the dictum of most satirists that a woman would lead a man away from intellectual studies. Instead he suggests that women will lead men to a greater appreciation of literature through their own literary skills, wisdom, and virtue. It follows from his argument

241. Eyb, *Das Ehebüchlein,* pp. 69-70.
242. Eyb, *Das Ehebüchlein,* p. 70.

that a man could marry without harming his intellectual life. Eyb's direct arguments "In Praise of Marriage" go further than simply sharing a love of literature and intellectual life. He situates his argument in the theological framework of the creation of the two sexes by God.[243] Then he suggests that nature also plants a desire in men and women to have children, but adds that a woman's will as well as a man's will should be engaged in the marital union. Then, after stating that marriage is useful both for individuals and for society Eyb concludes with a strong endorsement of the joy and friendship that marriage offers to a man and woman:

> And marriage is a joyful, pleasant, and sweet thing; for what could be more joyful and sweet than the name of father, mother, or children who need their parents' assistance and receive many a sweet kiss from them? If both married man and woman have such love, will, and friendship towards each other, then what one wants, the other wants, and what one says to the other is kept silent as if the person had said it to himself. If good and evil are shared by both, the good is that much more joyful and the unpleasant that much more tolerable. These and more reasons, which were related above, praise and laud holy, worthy marriage and answer the question, which we posed: A man should marry. With this I have concluded and finished with it.[244]

The conclusion that comes at the end of Part II of Eyb's *Little Book on Marriage* is that marriage is an aid to a man to grow in wisdom, in virtue, and the joy of friendship.

There is no doubt that Albrecht von Eyb is one of the first men to defend publicly the dignity of woman in marriage. He is not completely consistent on this theme, in contrast to Christine de Pizan and in line with other men who have written about married women. Yet, Eyb certainly affirms the dignity of woman in a new way. His arguments, however, do not appear to participate in the theme of recapitulation that played a role in Christine de Pizan's defense of woman's dignity. Instead, he seems to base his arguments on natural desires of woman and man in the state of nature and on the transforming action of the sacramental bond of marriage itself.

Our consideration will now turn to the second aspect of our analysis, or Eyb's use of sources. At the beginning of this same part of the text, Eyb introduced his reader to the methodology he would follow to prove his point. After mentioning that he would follow the theological guidance of Lactantius, Eyb then adds: "for it is my intention to fill this little book with the teaching and mastery of the poets, the natural masters, orators, and philosophers, although I would also use the teachers and masters of Holy Scripture, of civil and canon law, and medicine."[245] In these categories of authority Eyb has invoked all the usual sources of humanism as well

---

243. Eyb, *Das Ehebüchlein*, pp. 68-69. Eyb's argument follows the Augustinian line that man alone is created in the image of God and woman is created in the image of man: "He first created man in His divine image and then woman in the image of man so that there would be two sexes . . ." (p. 68).

244. Eyb, *Das Ehebüchlein*, p. 69.

245. Eyb, *Das Ehebüchlein*, p. 38.

as those of the four Faculties in academia: Arts, Theology, Law, and Medicine. We will now consider some examples of Eyb's citation of sources to consider how effectively he has introduced these authorities to prove his point that a woman's wisdom and virtue are an aid to a man, and therefore a man should be willing to marry.

Among the Greek philosophers Eyb mentions are Empedocles, Socrates, Gorgias, Xenophon, Xenocrates, Hippocrates, and various Stoics and Epicureans. These references are sprinkled throughout his hundred-page text without any one author receiving a larger amount of attention than another. Eyb appears to have gleaned his information about the Presocratic and Socratic philosophers from secondary sources, for nowhere is there any indication that he read the works of Greek philosophers in the original Greek or even in the Latin translations that had recently become available of Plato's dialogues. While it is possible that Eyb had read some accounts of them in Aristotelian texts studied perhaps during his undergraduate years in Arts at the University of Pavia, there are no passages included in his *Ehebüchlein* that would indicate familiarity with more detailed theories of opposites, generation, wisdom, or virtue as argued by the ancient Greek philosophers.

Consequently, Eyb's appeal to these philosophers is more anecdotal than systematic and the particular passages he chooses often contain false information about the previous philosophers. For example, in the very first sentence of the text after the preface, the authority of Socrates is introduced, yet the words of the Greek philosopher do not come from the more serious dialogues about him, but rather from a story:

> The philosopher Socrates, a natural master in Athens at the time of King Ahasuerus, was asked by a young man whether he should marry or not. The master answered him and said: "Whatever you do, you will regret it. For if you marry, you will always have cares and fears. You will be in constant war with the woman, with in-laws, with her friends, with the settlement of the dowry and in uncertainty of the children. However, if you remain without a wife, then you will worry and suffer by living alone without a wife's love and comfort, robbed of children, and awaiting the decline of your family and a foreign uncertain heir." Thus, with two extremes, Socrates gave no joyful, desirable answer to the young man's question whether to marry or not.[246]

Socrates is also quoted as saying, "No woman is so good that she has no fault."[247] Eyb even has Socrates married simultaneously to two women who were continually fighting over him![248] Nowhere is there any consideration of Socrates' arguments in Book V of the *Republic* about the equality of women and men or any references to the debate in Italy about the propriety of the community of women or any of Plato's gender unity themes. Thus, even though Eyb appeals to the authority of Socrates to frame the whole purpose of his text, namely, to expound on the question of whether a man should marry or not, yet he does not consider Socrates' own

246. Eyb, *Das Ehebüchlein*, p. 5.
247. Eyb, *Das Ehebüchlein*, p. 8.
248. Eyb, *Das Ehebüchlein*, p. 50.

arguments about the concept of woman, as portrayed in some depth by Plato or another philosopher.

In a similar way, Eyb mentions but dismisses the ancient Greek philosophers who had supported a gender polarity theory. The Sophist Gorgias, who had argued that male and female ought to have separate virtues, is simply identified as hypocritical because he speaks about unanimity in public when he has none at home: "[Gorgias] commands us to be unanimous although he himself cannot live in unity with his wife and maid, three in a house. He is daily burdened by war with his wife."[249] The most surprising omission concerns Aristotle, whose philosophical views must have been known to Eyb since they were still taught in Faculties of Arts and Theology in both Germany and Italy. In the following passage that considers the mortality of human life, Eyb almost seems to dismiss the ancient Greek philosopher:

> Where [are] the great King Alexander and the learned Aristotle? They have all been swept away like the leaves of a tree in a fast wind. The tree is bare. They were all like the night or a dream, and at dawn none are seen. They were a shadow and have disappeared; like smoke that has been blown away; like a spider's web that has been ripped aside.[250]

It may be that Albrecht von Eyb associates Aristotle's concept of woman with the views of his disciple Theophrastus, whose antagonism to women and to marriage the *Ehebüchlein* is trying to overcome. In the following passage Eyb clearly associates Aristotle with Theophrastus, and he demonstrates the duplicity in Theophrastus' views that a man can marry if he finds the right kind of woman, but a philosopher or wise man can never find that right kind of woman:

> Theophrastus, who was a student of Aristotle, writes on this question in the book of weddings and says: If she is pretty and has good morals, is born of honourable parents and is fertile, and if she is healthy and rich, then a wise man can marry a woman. But since these things seldom occur simultaneously, a wise man should not marry. For a woman hinders book learning and wisdom and no one can serve the arts and woman, wisdom and a bed.[251]

Although Eyb does not directly confront Aristotle's theories of gender polarity, his argument against Theophrastus indirectly confronts the hidden presumptions that a woman is not wise or good in the same way as a man, and that woman hinders a man's search for wisdom and virtue as well.

Turning from Greek authors to classical Latin authors, Eyb demonstrates that he had read several of them in the original. Those authors he refers to most include Cicero, Seneca, Juvenal, Valerius Maximus, Plutarch, Ovid, Terence, and

---

249. Eyb, *Das Ehebüchlein*, p. 7.
250. Eyb, *Das Ehebüchlein*, p. 86.
251. Eyb, *Das Ehebüchlein*, p. 6. As mentioned previously, this reference to Theophrastus' text *Liber de nuptiis* was transmitted through St. Jerome's *Adversus Jovianum*.

Plautus. Among them Cicero stands out as having the most significant place in Eyb's analysis, and Juvenal stands as a close second. The others are mentioned only in a cursory fashion. Both Cicero and Juvenal are used as authorities for the negative answer as to whether or not a man should marry. Copies of Cicero's letters and orations as well as Juvenal's satires were in Albrecht von Eyb's library, so he had close access to their arguments.[252] Cicero is invoked to defend the exaggerated satirical claim that a man who marries becomes a slave to his wife: "And if you place the entire house in her command, everyone has to serve her. But if you retain something in your power, then she says you don't trust her. She will hate you and become angry, will scold you and curse you, and perhaps she will plan to kill you."[253] Juvenal is invoked along with his traditionally exaggerated view of woman as unable to control her self. Eyb states:

> In a married couple's bed there is rarely good rest, for there is lust, war, and no peace. Juvenal writes: women want to fight about everything and always want to be right. They imagine that everything is permitted to them and they can do no wrong. Who can endure a woman who wants to know and do everything? He continues by saying that nothing is worse and more insufferable than a rich woman, and a gentle, kind woman is a rare bird and comparable to a black swan or a white crow.[254]

Juvenal's example of a black swan or white crow comes from Aristotle's logic. Those familiar with the use of the example will recognize that Juvenal is claiming that while it is a logical possibility that a woman could be kind to a man, it is an empirical impossibility, just as it is a logical possibility that a swan could be black or a crow white, but an actual occurrence has never been empirically observed.

Now, as mentioned at the beginning of this section of analysis of arguments about the concept of woman in his *Little Book of Marriage*, Eyb introduces many examples of negative answers to the question of whether a man should marry or not before giving his own argument in support of an affirmative answer. Eyb's appeal to the two great early Italian humanists Petrarch and Boccaccio needs to be considered. Both of these authors are used to provide support for both the affirmative and the negative answer to the question about the value of marriage. In other words, Eyb uses stories contained in the works of these authors, who may either defend or attack women's character. Petrarch had been known in Germany since the time he visited Charles IV in Prague in 1356.[255] Eyb's text *Das Ehebüchlein* contains more references to Petrarch than to any other philosopher; and most of his references concentrate on a man's need to develop a virtuous character. However, in a somewhat surprising way, Eyb introduces quotations from Petrarch to devalue

---

252. Hiller, *Albrecht von Eyb*, p. 21. For a more complete description of his library holdings see pp. 13-21.

253. Eyb, *Das Ehebüchlein*, p. 6.

254. Eyb, *Das Ehebüchlein*, pp. 8-9.

255. Hiller, *Albrecht von Eyb*, p. vii. For a discussion of the broader concept of woman in the early fifteenth century in Prague see John Klassen, "Women and Religious Reform in Late Medieval Bohemia," *Renaissance and Reformation* 5, no. 4 (1981): 203-21.

woman. The reason this is surprising is that an in-depth analysis of Petrarch's concept of woman, as attempted for example in Chapter 4 of this book, reveals that he had a generally positive view of woman's identity, especially in the categories of wisdom and virtue. A few examples of Eyb's inclusion of Petrarch will suffice to make this point.

In one passage Eyb invokes Petrarch to suggest that a married man will be completely miserable. In fact he introduces the claim that a woman is a dangerous deceiver of man:

> If you imagine that you have married a pleasant wife, then you are deceived and mistaken, for she has taken and captured you. As Petrarch writes: For a long time you have lived freely and for yourself. Now you belong to your wife. To you has come your wife and master; for your stepchildren, if you have any, a torturer; an enemy to relatives; to the servants a heavy burden and yoke; for the kitchen daily work; for the cellar a burden; a drain on the chests and money; an ornament for the window and a constant watchman; by day a busybody; by night a matchmaker; a heavy weight on your back; and a hard slipper for your feet and hands. She is not a guest for a day, but for as long as you live. No one but death can release you from her. If you have celebrated a wedding with a woman, then you have parted with peace and burdened your rest with eternal misery.[256]

In still another passage in which Eyb discusses chastity in daughters, he introduces Petrarch as first noting that "[w]omen are inconstant and fickle. As constancy is rare in all things, so no constancy can be seen in women."[257] Albrecht von Eyb, however, also states that men should hold themselves to the same standards of chastity as they do women. In other words, there should be no double standard.

Although some scholars suggest that the source of the story was indirectly through Leonardo Bruni, Boccaccio is directly referred to in one of the longest stories included in *The Little Book of Marriage*.[258] The story is about a prince Tancredus and his daughter Sigismunda, and it concerns the question of the right time for a man to marry a woman. In the tragic love affair Sigismunda met secretly with Guiscardus, a man of lower station, because her father would not let her remarry after being widowed as a young wife. Her father Tancredus discovers this subterfuge, executes Guiscardus, and Sigismunda commits suicide after confronting her father with the injustice of his actions. Eyb concludes that the father, who had made a serious error in trying to keep his widowed daughter from remarrying, had to be taught by his daughter about the integration of the passions in human nature. As mentioned at the beginning of this analysis of Eyb's text, Boccaccio's example of women who excelled in writing and other intellectual pursuits was offered as the evidential support for the positive conclusion that a man ought to marry.

Before concluding this analysis of the contribution of Albrecht von Eyb to the history of the concept of woman, some attention should be given to other works

256. Eyb, *Das Ehebüchlein*, p. 7.
257. Eyb, *Das Ehebüchlein*, pp. 9-10.
258. Hiller, *Albrecht von Eyb*, p. 150.

written by him. All of the following works were private in their circulation, and in many ways they were preparatory for his larger text *Das Ehebüchlein*. The significant number of Eyb's texts that focused on the concept of woman reveals how important he considered this subject to be. Between the years 1441 and 1453 Eyb wrote four Latin treatises, two of which were directly concerned with woman's identity: *Tractatus de speciositate Barbare puelle* and *Appellacio mulierum Bamberfensium*. The first text is a description of the beauty of a woman named Barbara, and it calls to mind the descriptions by Dante of Beatrice, by Petrarch of Laura, and in some works by Boccaccio of Fiammetta. The second work is a satire on the immorality of the women of Bamberg that uses Leonardo Bruni's *Oratio Heliogabilis* to develop its line of thinking. It also calls to mind parts of Boccaccio's *Decameron* or even his satirical *Corbaccio*. In addition, according to Hermann, Eyb's library contained codices with various works collected by him from 1452 and organized by headings that include areas such as praise of women, philosophy of women, chastity, marriage, children, and so forth.

In addition, one of the codices also contained three Latin treatises of Eyb that considered some aspect of the concept of woman. The *Clarissimarum feminarum laudacio*, written in 1459, the year Eyb completed his doctorate in Pavia, recalls Boccaccio's *Concerning Famous Women*, and it praises women's accomplishments in science, art, and religion. The second text, *Invectiva in lenam*, condemns evil qualities in women. It was also written in 1459, but at the request of the Canons of Eichstätt who thought that Eyb's first text, *Clarissimarum feminarum laudacio*, was too positive an account of woman's identity. The third text, *An viro sapienti uxor sit ducenda*, written a few years later, praised marriage. It appears to be an outline for the more detailed *Ehebüchlein*, which was completed in 1472.[259] In Eyb's private collection there was also a poem in praise of women simply entitled *Laus mulieris*. All this information from Eyb's private library simply supports the contention that he was concerned over a long period of time about the whole topic of woman's identity, and that he took several years to prepare his major text on the subject.

Between 1451 and 1464 Eyb wrote a textbook of rhetoric, *Margarita Poetica*, including the oration entitled "Ad laudem et commendationem clarissimarum oracio," which had the following praise of women in marriage:

> There is nothing more joyful, than to seek a chaste and honest woman in marriage. A woman who in time of fortune and misfortune will be your companion, your wife and your all. She will be with you in youth and will not desert you in old age. She will be at your side at night, accompany you on your travels, assist you in your toils. Labor she will not despise nor dangers fear. It (marriage) is a sacrament in which not only righteousness and (social) utility but also the greatest fame and happiness go hand in hand.[260]

This early text of Eyb's already sets the direction for his later thought. For example,

---

259. Max Hermann, *Albrecht von Eyb und die Frühzeit des Deutschen Humanismus* (Berlin, 1893), pp. 156-57 and 266, as cited in Hiller, *Albrecht von Eyb*, p. 22. See also pp. 59-64.

260. Eyb, translated in Hiller, *Albrecht von Eyb*, p. 109.

the theme that a wife would risk all danger to be with her husband is developed in the *Ehebüchlein* in the following description:

> Hypsicratea, the queen, put aside a woman's clothing and figure out of love for her husband Mithridates and took a man's clothing, weapons, armour, and horses. She followed him with a shaven head through all enemies and battles until he was defeated. Such love and fidelity from a woman was a great joy to the man and happy delight in the midst of difficulty.[261]

This positive description of a woman who would take on even a military persona to fulfill a mission brings a memory of the feats of Joan of Arc only some thirty years previous. Yet Eyb does not condemn these women for their actions, which imitate those of men, but rather he praises their courage and love, and argues that they would bring a man great happiness.

It should be noted that Eyb followed the more common practice of early Italian humanist writers, who distinguished masculine and feminine characteristics from simple male and female identity. In other words, a masculine and a feminine characteristic could be attributed to either a man or a woman. This development manifests an awakening of consciousness that something more occurs in gender identity than simply male or female biological identity. At the same time, also following Italian practices before him, Eyb usually gave a positive valuation to a masculine characteristic and a negative one to a feminine characteristic, no matter whether it was attributed to a man or a woman. In his final text, the *Spiegel der Sitten,* written in 1474, Eyb mentions directly that the association of masculine with strength leads to the word *man,* i.e., *vir* from *virtus,* meaning power and strength: "Man is so called precisely for the virtues of firmness, steadiness, thrift and piety."[262]

In the passage from the *Margarita Poetica* cited above, where a woman was praised for assuming a man's attire to follow her husband in dangerous situations, Eyb followed the general tradition that identified courage as a positive masculine characteristic or virtue. Generally, he associates masculinity with strength and courage and femininity with weakness. A few examples will suffice to demonstrate this point. In describing the story of Lucretia, who committed suicide because she was raped, Eyb stated that: "When Lucretia had finished this lament, with manly spirit, she took a knife and stabbed her chaste breast."[263] In another passage, after stating that "many women had a powerful and masculine temper," Eyb described Queen Semiramis's decision to take back in a military action a city that had been defeated and thus to avenge the death of her husband. Eyb stated: "She was moved with a man's anger and would not have the second [braid] braided until she had — in her own person, with unkempt and flowing hair — regained the city of Babylon and made it obedient and subservient to her."[264]

261. Eyb, *Das Ehebüchlein,* p. 9.
262. Eyb, *Spiegel der Sitten* in Hiller, *Albrecht von Eyb,* p. 185.
263. Eyb, *Das Ehebüchlein,* p. 15.
264. Eyb, *Das Ehebüchlein,* pp. 30-31.

Not only did Eyb portray a masculine spirit as a virtue for women, it was also a virtue for man, and inversely, femininity is considered a sign of weakness.

> Homer, therefore, spoke wisely when he said that the earth bears nothing weaker than man. Nevertheless, men should have a strong, masculine spirit in sickness and suffering and not a womanly one, writes Cicero. Pain should yield to reason and moderation.[265]

In the story of Sigismunda and Guiscardus, Eyb describes a dramatic scene of confrontation:

> Her heart was burdened with woe and pain and she could hardly refrain from weeping and crying. But her great spirit overcame feminine weakness and she answered her father with steady face and raised head.[266]

In an opposite attribution of a feminine characteristic to a man, Eyb states: "Avarice causes much unpleasantness for men and makes a manly body and disposition effeminate."[267] Thus, for Eyb, although so-called feminine characteristics of weakness and masculine characteristics of strength were given negative and positive valuations generally, Eyb did not conclude that women and men themselves had these clearly different valuations. It was up to the individual man or woman to develop a particular kind of character. In the praise of woman included with his *Margarita Poetica* and other works, Eyb generally described woman's character in very positive terms.

The *Margarita Poetica* was printed in Germany, Italy, and France at least fifteen times between 1472 and 1503. It not only introduced its readers to the important thinkers in the new humanism, such as Leonardo Bruni, Virgil, Seneca, Socrates, Plato, Petrarch, and Plautus, but it also linked together the rhetorical aims of humanism with the praise of women and the value of married life for the male scholar.[268]

In the more mature *Ehebüchlein,* Eyb also forwarded views that had been current in the works of the very earliest humanists, Dante, Petrarch, and Boccaccio, particularly that true beauty and nobility consist in virtue. For example, he inserts the following passage:

> Now at this point I should explain what is meant by a beautiful woman according to the flesh in so far as it is seemly for men. Plautus writes that a pretty, naked woman is more beautiful than one clothed in purple. And no matter how well a woman is clothed, if she does not have good morals, she cannot be called pretty: for pretty clothes and evil morals are like a pig in the mud.[269]

265. Eyb, *Das Ehebüchlein,* pp. 83-84.
266. Eyb, *Das Ehebüchlein,* p. 55.
267. Eyb, *Das Ehebüchlein,* p. 33.
268. Hiller, *Albrecht von Eyb,* p. 69.
269. Eyb, *Das Ehebüchlein,* p. 17.

Eyb also appeals to Cicero to support the same thesis, as applied not only to nobility, but also to recently acquired wealth:

> True eternal wealth is seen in virtues and not in much gold, silver, and the pleasures of the flesh. For virtues cannot be taken, or stolen, or burnt, or drowned and they cannot be changed or seized by the storms or misery of time. Only the virtuous are rich, for they have and possess fruitful and eternal things, namely virtues which never decay.[270]

Eyb so develops this point that he offers various examples of wealthy or noble men who chose to marry women without dowries simply because their character was so virtuous. In these examples, Eyb applies new humanist principles to a woman's situation in such a way as to encourage her to actively seek to grow in wisdom and virtue.

Another theme from the earliest humanists that Eyb also transmits is the view that a woman has natural passions as much as a man, and that she ought to be allowed to express them appropriately. Eyb follows Boccaccio's example in the *Decameron* by offering stories of what happens to a woman who is not allowed by her father to marry at the proper time. In his retelling of Boccaccio's story of Sigismunda and Guiscardus, Eyb concludes that a woman was harmed by her father's refusal to give her in marriage when she was ready. All women and men ought to order their passions in appropriate ways, avoiding both excess and defect.

By translating Latin stories and morals into the German language, and making them available to the German literate public, Eyb brought similar dimensions to the concept of woman in Northern Europe as had previously been expressed in Italy. In 1893, Max Hermann argued that Eyb was the first thoroughgoing German humanist.[271] There is no doubt that Eyb understood himself, much as Christine de Pizan saw herself before him, as a mediator from Latin works of the Italian humanists into the vernacular. Christine de Pizan rephrased Boccaccio's stories about women into French while Eyb rephrased Boccaccio's stories into German. In relation to one of Boccaccio's stories, Eyb says: "I will interpret this story and shorten it, if possible"; and in another he says: "I shall shorten it and translate from Latin into German, just as I have translated and arranged many parts of this little book from Latin."[272]

Albrecht von Eyb translated the dramas of Plautus from Latin into German. These dramas, with many aspects that accented immoral behavior, had a strong impact on the early Renaissance Humanists. In 1429, during the humanist gatherings at the Council of Basil, Nicholas of Cusa sold to Cardinal Orsini a manuscript containing sixteen dramas of Plautus. In 1430, this manuscript was copied by three great supporters of humanism in northern Italy: Filippo Maria of Milan, Leonello d'Este of Ferrara, and Lorenzo de Medici of Florence.[273] Eyb copied this manu-

---

270. Eyb, *Das Ehebüchlein,* p. 35.

271. Hiller, *Albrecht von Eyb,* pp. xi-xii. Hermann's text entitled *Albrecht von Eyb und die Frühzeit des Deutchen Humanismus* brought Eyb to the attention of the scholarly world in a new way.

272. Eyb, *Das Ehebüchlein,* pp. 54 and 59.

273. Hiller, *Albrecht von Eyb,* pp. 33-34.

script and translated the plays from it into German around 1451. Although the dramas of Plautus had been well received when they were still in the Latin manuscript form, when Eyb published his German versions in 1511 as *Spiegel der Sitten* he radically changed their structure and content for moral rather than dramatic purposes. Eyb translated so freely that he gave new German names to old Roman characters, edited out parts of the pagan stories that he found offensive, and also moralized their conclusions. Thus, Eyb perceived himself as more than a translator. He was an interpreter and defender of a particular set of values that were supported by selected passages from classical Latin texts. The whole advent of printing transformed the cultural situation within which texts with reference to gender identity were being distributed and read.

Conrad Celtis and the Roswitha Manuscripts

Before the end of the fifteenth century other new developments in German humanism occurred. One of particular relevance for the history of the concept of woman was the discovery in 1493 by Conrad Celtis (1459-1508) of the codex containing the works of Roswitha of Gandersheim (c. 935–1002). Glenda Wall, in "Hrotsvit and the German Humanists," describes the impact of this discovery as follows:

> The discovery caused a sensation. The newly found writer was not only Christian Europe's first known playwright, she was also the first Saxon poet, and the first known woman to write a German history. She was also, however, something of a personal triumph for Celtis and his humanist friends, who had long decried the neglect by German scholars of the rare manuscripts stored in their own monastic libraries. . . .
>
> He had unearthed a unique text. One of the principal monuments of medieval drama, it was also an illustrious example of Germany's past and the work of a forgotten writer whose learning and rhetorical polish could be placed on a level with those of the writers of antiquity.[274]

Significantly, Roswitha was compared with Virgil, Horace, Terence, and Sappho, the great Latin and Greek writers so revered by the early humanists.[275] It was Roswitha's style rather than the particular content of her writing that brought so much delight to the humanists. In *The Concept of Woman: The Aristotelian Revolution (750 BC–1250 AD)*, philosophical aspects of Roswitha's plays were considered with respect to what they revealed about woman's identity. This information will not be repeated here except to mention that Roswitha presented several examples of wise and virtuous women in her works, and she included in dialogues female characters who used mathematical and philosophical arguments to defend their views.

---

274. Glenda Wall, "Hrosvit and the German Humanists," in *Hrotsvit of Gandersheim: Rara Avis in Saconia?* ed. Katherina M. Wilson (Ann Arbor, Mich.: Marc Publishing Co., 1987), p. 253.

275. Wall, "Hrotsvit and the German Humanists," in *Hrotsvit of Gandersheim,* p. 255.

It should be noted again, however, that the early humanists were not as much interested in the philosophical content of her dramas as they were in the fact that they were composed in Latin, self-consciously imitated Terence, and followed perfectly the classical models of good literature. Another example of Celtis's publications that sought to support German humanism was his choice of Nicholas of Cusa's *De li non aliud,* or the famous text on the not-other (which will be discussed in the next chapter).[276]

Conrad Celtis was a man who left a mixed legacy. He first received a Bachelor of Arts at the University of Cologne before moving to Heidelberg, where he discovered humanism.[277] Celtis developed a passion for classical texts studied by Renaissance Humanists and a loathing for the scholastic method. Pursuing his interests Celtis traveled around Europe, spending time in Padua, Florence, Rome, Venice, Croatia, Hungary, and Poland before returning to Germany to support the continuing development of humanism. Celtis also had gained a reputation for an immoral and irresponsible lifestyle, wandering from university to school, living with different mistresses, casually teaching rhetoric, missing classes, taking manuscripts without returning them, and so forth.[278]

At the same time, Celtis kept pressing forward in helping to found small study groups of humanists. A German community of humanists was established in 1495 by an organization called *Sodalitas Rhenana* or *Societas litteraria Rhenana.* Conrad Celtis was one of the founders of this organization. The group was called an "Academia Platonica," especially because it was dedicated to following up some of the central principles of Florentine Neoplatonism.[279] The society was devoted to printing books after the invention of printing in 1450, and it developed strong nationalist flavor by praising all things German. Celtis encouraged the foundation of literary sodalities in many German regions, the original one in the Rhineland, then others in the Danube region of Vienna and Linz, the Vistula in Poland, and in the Baltics. After his death more sodalities were founded in cities throughout Germany. "Besides such standard humanist preoccupations as the searching for codices, copying inscriptions, collecting antiques, and the like, the most important function of the sodality was, Celtis believed, to publish the classic authors and contemporary humanist writings, especially his own."[280]

When Celtis discovered the Roswitha manuscripts in the Benedictine monastery of St. Emmeran in Regensburg, he was delighted to find that a German

---

276. Lewis W. Spitz, *Conrad Celtis: The German Arch-Humanist* (Cambridge, Mass.: Harvard University Press, 1957), p. 67.

277. Spitz, *Conrad Celtis: The German Arch-Humanist,* pp. 1-3.

278. For example, Spitz describes Celtis's relation to the Roswitha manuscript as follows: "What a find! Here was a playwright and a woman who in the Middle Ages held aloft the light of classic learning and writing in the manner of Terence. Celtis was elated. He borrowed the codex from the prior, Laurentius Aicher, promising through Friedrich Rosenritter, an honorable citizen of Nuremberg, to return it, which, of course, he never did." Celtis even wrote his own comments into the manuscript and had no reverence for the original text, *Conrad Celtis: The German Arch-Humanist,* p. 42.

279. Lowry, *The World of Aldus Manutius,* p. 264. See also Spitz, *Conrad Celtis: The German Arch-Humanist,* pp. 46-52.

280. Spitz, *Conrad Celtis: The German Arch-Humanist,* p. 61.

woman had, as early as the tenth to eleventh centuries, written such erudite Latin texts. This feat situated Roswitha four hundred years earlier than the Italian Renaissance, and it suddenly established German humanists as no longer peripheral to this new movement in western Europe. For Celtis, Roswitha's German identity was much more important than her identity as a woman. Consequently, the *Sodalitas Rhenana* decided to publish Roswitha's works; "(f)or Celtis and his friends, she seemed the Renaissance ideal incarnate. . . ."[281] Her works were published in 1501 by John Trithemius, the Abbot of Spannheim, with a beautiful woodcut by Albrecht Dürer portraying Roswitha offering her book to both the Abbess of Gandersheim and the Emperor Otto I.[282] Celtis organized the work into three books, dividing them by literary form: eight legends, six plays, and two historical epics. In this way he took charge of the structure and presentation of Roswitha's writings.

In addition, Conrad Celtis dedicated his publication of Roswitha's works to Charitas Pirckheimer, Abbess of the Franciscan Convent of St. Clare. "From one of the leading families of [Nuremberg] . . . reputed for its learning, [Charitas] was the most famous of the Pirckheimer circle of seven sisters and five daughters, all of whom received a serious education."[283] At the age of twelve Charitas Pirckheimer had entered religious life and as an adult she educated herself in the new humanist direction of education. She and her sisters became fluent in reading and writing Latin letters and thus represented, once again, the development of wisdom in women who had been exposed to both religious and humanistic education. Willibald Pirckheimer, the brother of Charitas, was a close friend of Celtis and a member of the Nuremberg humanist circle. Celtis knew of Charitas's humanist interests, and he considered her as a new Roswitha capable of the highest erudition in both German and Latin.

When the Abbess Charitas received the book, she wrote a response that emphasized more Roswitha's gender identity than her German identity. It also introduced a direct challenge to Celtis concerning man/woman relationships. A part of her response to Celtis is as follows:

A few days ago I received the beloved writings of the learned virgin Roswitha which your lordship sent to me in my insufficiency without deserving it in the least. For this I rejoice that the Benefactor of the Soul grants deep wisdom not only to right thinking and learned men, but also does not deny to the weaker sex and the retarded creature a few crumbs which fall from the tables of the richly learned. The word of the apostle proved to be true in the case of that young vir-

281. Wall, "Hrotsvit and the German Humanists" in *Hrotsvit of Gandersheim,* p. 258.

282. For a reproduction see *The Plays of Roswitha* (New York: Cooper Square Publishers, 1966), frontispiece. Spitz argues that Dürer contributed only the preparatory sketches for the Roswitha woodcuts, *Conrad Celtis: The German Arch-Humanist,* p. 89. Dürer was a close member of the Nuremberg humanist group with Willibald Pirckheimer and Conrad Celtis. He also discovered perspective in art when he traveled in Italy and came across Leon Battista Alberti's text *On Painting.* See Noel L. Brann, "Humanism in Germany," in *Renaissance Humanism,* vol. 2, *Humanism Beyond Italy,* pp. 143-44.

283. Margaret L. King, *Women of the Renaissance* (Chicago: University of Chicago Press, 1991), p. 204.

gin: "What the world thought weak God chose to shame the mighty." Praiseworthy indeed is the grace of the Holy Ghost who ornamented and decorated this virgin talent with such brilliance of knowledge and industry. Your care in publishing the writings and poems of a woman without despising the weaker sex and the humble position of a little nun is also to be praised and lauded.[284]

Although a certain amount of self-deprecation was common to correspondents, it is quite interesting that Charitas chose to emphasize so much the gender differentiation between Roswitha and learned men.

Conrad Celtis's response to Charitas Pirckheimer's letter sought on the one hand to reduce her to her German identity, and on the other hand, if she chose to reflect on themes of gender identity, to reduce man/woman relations to those of erotic love. The former consisted in an ode in which he connected Charitas with the glory of Germany, and the latter in sending her a copy of a collection of erotic poems, *Amores,* which he had just published. Celtis's erotic poems were consistent with an Epicurean attitude towards woman, a kind that was articulated by Lorenzo Valla in his book (which will be discussed in the next chapter) *On Pleasure: De voluptate.*

In the *Amores* Celtis described four different lovers in the four corners of Germany based on the character of four different mistresses he had. In addition, the female characters in his *Amores* shared many qualities of those found in traditional satires about women's identity. One scholar summarizes it this way:

> Celtis, like Ovid, seems to have been created for writing love poems. He knew all the joys and sorrows of sensual love. He was experienced in all the artful devices of womankind — deceitful tears, angry looks, feigned sobs, deceptive actions. The female heart is never constant; what it spurns it seeks and what it hates it desires.[285]

It is relevant to note that these views were common among Celtis's friends. For example, as Lewis Spitz points out, when Celtis had considered whether or not to marry one of his friends, a physician Dietrich Ulsenius advised him not to because marriage was like a nest of baby chickens in which those who are in the nest want to crawl out, and those that are outside the nest want to crawl in. Another friend from Nuremberg, Sebald Schreyer, also told Celtis that if he married he would be tormented by his wife day and night and be enslaved by her.[286] It was precisely these attitudes that Eyb had attempted to overcome by his work on marriage. However, Celtis chose to accept the advice of his friends and not marry.

The Abbess Charitas responded to the humanist's gifts of an ode in her honor and his work *Amores* by challenging Conrad Celtis in three ways. First, she asked him not to compare her with the earthly fatherland of Germany but rather the heavenly homeland of the new Jerusalem. Second, she warned him that he

---

284. In Spitz, *Conrad Celtis: The German Arch-Humanist,* p. 85.
285. Spitz, *Conrad Celtis: The German Arch-Humanist,* p. 87.
286. Spitz, *Conrad Celtis: The German Arch-Humanist,* p. 53.

should prepare for his death by acts of virtue and not by emphasizing earthly love. Third, she admonished him for turning to tales of pagan goddesses rather than focusing on Christian verities. The relation between the Abbess and the humanists remained ambivalent, for she continued to study and excel in reading and writing Latin until, after the Protestant Reformation, the German humanists became more directly associated with the reform.[287]

Although Roswitha's works were published in Germany eight years after their discovery in 1493, as early as 1497 Celtis and Aldus Manutius, the greatest of the Venetian publishers, were in communication about texts that the German humanists wanted to purchase from the Italian printer in both Greek and Latin.[288] Celtis soon moved to Vienna, and apparently sought to establish a literary link between the Venetian publisher and a newly established Viennese circle of German humanists, called the *Sodalitas litteria Collegii Viennensis*. It is noteworthy that Aldus Manutius himself founded in Venice an *Aldine Academy* entitled *Neo-academia Nostra* and modeled on the Florentine Academy of Marsilio Ficino. Aldus had lived during the years of 1482-84 at the home of Giovanni Pico della Mirandola, whose sister, the Princess of Capri, funded not only his printing business in Venice in 1495, but also his Academy.[289] The Aldine Academy, whose first president was Aldus Manutius himself, selected Greek texts for publication and engaged in dialogue about their significance. Its members were drawn from Venice, Padua, Rome, Bologna, and the low countries, and included such important humanists as Erasmus.

Even the illustrator Albrecht Dürer visited Aldus and the Venetian printing company to study new techniques for woodcuts for printing. Venice had established itself as the main publishing center in Europe early in the mid-1470s due to the ready availability of capital, paper production, and trade routes.[290] However, because of an overpublication of classical Latin texts and weakening of the financial status of publishers, German printing companies entered into partnerships with Italian printers. Significant for the history of the concept of woman is that German businesswomen and men together worked in the publishing and printing business in cooperation with Italians. One of the largest Italian printing concerns was run by a German businesswoman, Paula, who after being widowed married successive German business partners. She became directly involved in the printing business in Venice.[291]

---

287. Charitas Pirckheimer continued to choose an independent path during all the turbulence of the Reformation. According to King, she "guided a community of about sixty women, managed considerable property, dealt directly with city officials, enhanced the convent library, and ran its Latin school for girls. Her *Denkwürdigkeiten,* or *Memoirs,* of 1524-28 recorded her heroic defense of the convent during those years, when Nuremberg underwent the process of reform," *Women of the Renaissance,* p. 99. In another passage in the same text, it is suggested that Charitas was requested by her religious community, the Sisters of St. Clare, to cease writing in Latin, a request to which she submitted although she kept reading classical texts in the ancient language, pp. 204-5.

288. Lowry, *The World of Aldus Manutius,* pp. 264-65.

289. Putnam, *Books and Their Makers During the Middle Ages,* vol. 1, pp. 417-23.

290. Gerulaitis, *Printing and Publishing in Fifteenth-Century Venice,* pp. 20-23.

291. A recent study has actually demonstrated that the first printers in Venice, between 1469

In spite of the enthusiasm of German humanists for the printing of Roswitha's works and the attempts to draw close connections between the Italian printers and German humanists, most of the books published in Venice in the fifteenth century were those of more traditional academic interest. These served as texts at the Universities of Padua, Pavia, Bologna, and Ferrara. Consequently, the printing press in Italy likely did more to support initially the transmission of academic gender polarity than a new humanist view of the respective identities of men and women. A careful analysis of texts published in Venice in the fifteenth century reveals the central place held by the works of Aristotle and Aristotelian commentaries, Thomas Aquinas, Duns Scotus, and Leonardo Bruni's paraphrase of Aristotle in his *Isogogicon*.[292] At the same time, however, the printers did produce central texts, especially in the vernacular, of the three early Italian humanists Dante, Petrarch, and Boccaccio.[293]

Texts from the separate communities of discourse — academic, humanist, and religious — were being published by the same printers and dispersed into libraries and homes in such a way that they were becoming accessible to a wider audience of readers. These readers became exposed to a variety of different ways of considering the concept of woman. For example, the early printing lists (1470s) from Lyons, France, included traditional satirical texts by authors such as Juvenal, Ovid, and Theophrastus. Putnam points out that in France the first printed books were done in Lyons, where the printers were free from the censorship of the University of Paris's faculty. When the titles of publications are examined, it is evident that satires against women abound. "The early Lyons lists of the fifteenth century included indeed a series of quite frivolous publications, in the vernacular, such as *Le Roman de la Rose, La Farce de Pathelie, Les Quinze Joies de Mariage, Le Champion des Dames*, and a French version of the *Facetiae* of Poggio."[294] William Caxton learned about the printing trade from the Brethren of Common Life in Cologne (1470-71) and learned a specific printing type and process at Lyons before returning to England in 1474 to produce numerous printed works. He also published satires on women's identity. In addition, Caxton became an important source for works by Christine de Pizan and for the translation into English of many more serious works in French and Latin such as the *Dictes and Sayings of the Philosophers*.[295] It is worth noting that Caxton's work in printing was financially supported by Princess Margaret of England, the sister of King Edward IV and wife of Charles the Bold, Duke of Burgundy. The connection between the financial support of wealthy women for printing businesses and the publication of texts that support a theory of the dignity of woman occurred not only in France and England but also in Italy and Germany.

For example, a portion of the letters of Catherine of Siena had been previously published as early as 1492 in Bologna, and a German businesswoman, Margarita Ugelheimer, a widow of a German publisher who had been a partner in

---

and 1474, were mostly Germans, but that by 1481 the presses were mostly owned by Italians. See Gerulaitis, *Printing and Publishing in Fifteenth-Century Venice*, p. 30.

292. Gerulaitis, *Printing and Publishing in Fifteenth-Century Venice*, pp. 67-68, 98, and 89.

293. Gerulaitis, *Printing and Publishing in Fifteenth-Century Venice*, p. 117.

294. Putnam, *Books and Their Makers During the Middle Ages*, vol. 2 (1500-1709), p. 111.

295. Putnam, *Books and Their Makers During the Middle Ages*, vol. 2 (1500-1709), pp. 102-11.

a Venetian publishing company, was the actual publisher who contracted with Aldus Manutius to print the complete collection of letters of St. Catherine of Siena in 1500.[296] Women as well as men were the publishers, the authors, and also the readers of these printed texts. In this way of dispersion of printed texts, the boundaries between the different communities of discourse were rapidly opening up. Eventually, gender polarity theories about the concept of woman articulated in academic and satirical texts were challenged in new and dramatic ways by other views. Thus, the printing press and publishing business offered a further avenue for new forms of education about woman's identity.

In Germany, where in 1450 printing had first begun in the city of Mainz, a slightly different configuration of texts was being published. While in Italy the greatest numbers fell into the category of academic texts, in Germany the greatest number were religious. Steven Ozment notes that: "By the end of the fifteenth century printing presses existed [in Germany] in over two hundred cities and towns. An estimated six million books had been printed and half of the thirty thousand titles were on religious subjects. More books were printed in the forty years between 1460 and 1500 than had been produced by scribes and monks throughout the entire Middle Ages."[297] This dramatic change in access to various texts expanded the range of men and women who could become educated about a variety of subjects. No longer was education for women restricted to monasteries, homes of wealthy patrons of libraries, or even formal schools. "It has been estimated that 3 to 4 percent of Germany's population, about 400,000 people, could read by 1500."[298] If the literate population in France, Italy, England, the Netherlands, Czechoslovakia, and Spain are added to this number, then among them would have been many who became educated about past and present theories of the concept of woman. In this context of growing literacy they could have been exposed to both Aristotelian and Platonic roots for the theories of gender polarity and gender unity, as well as other arguments in support of an emerging philosophy of gender complementarity.

EDUCATION OF WOMEN TO THE THIRD GENERATION

Now that we have completed this analysis of texts written by early humanists, particularly on educational aspects of gender identity, it is possible to summarize some of the main points of their contributions to the history of the concept of woman. An aspect of the reform in educational structures that was noted early on concerned the direct inclusion of female students in humanist schools, Vittorino's school in Italy, and the Sisters and Brothers of Common Life in Germany. Another aspect was the frequent occurrence of men who had been trained in humanist schools and then worked as second-generation humanists tutoring women in the third generation. Students of Guarino often fell into this category. In the following summary chart some of these relationships are noted:

296. Gerulaitis, *Printing and Publishing in Fifteenth-Century Venice*, pp. 43-44.
297. Ozment, *The Age of Reform, 1250-1500*, p. 199.
298. Ozment, *The Age of Reform, 1250-1500*, p. 201.

Humanist Educators and the Concept of Woman			
Name	Contribution	Models Emphasized	Persons Influenced
Vincent of Beauvais 1190-1264	*De Eruditione filiorum nobilium (On the Education and Instruction of Noble Children)* with last 9 chapters on the education of noble girls	Girls to read and write Latin and French, learn philosophy, self-knowledge and self-governance Laeta in St. Jerome	King Louis and Queen Marguerite of France, their sons and daughter Christine de Pizan
Francesco Barberino 1264-1348	*Del Reggimento e costumi di donna (On the Regimens and Customs of Women)* — 400 pages on the customs of women	Imaginary inter-gender dialogue form First person "I — Francesco" write to women, in Tuscan, encouraging self-knowledge and self-governance	Christine de Pizan
Manuel Chrysoloras 1350-1413	First to teach Greek to many humanists from Chair of Greek Letters in Florence, Pavia, and in Milan First translation from Greek to Latin of Plato's *Republic*	A modified version of Plato's theory of gender identity	Guarino of Verona Leonardo Bruni

Humanist Educators and the Concept of Woman (cont.)			
Name	Contribution	Models Emphasized	Persons Influenced
Vittorino da Feltre 1378-1446	First Chair of Greek and Latin at University of Padua Opened humanist school for Gonzaga family and others of all classes in Mantua Established library of Greek and Latin classical sources	Especially Quintilian's treatise on education to encourage women to read and write philosophy, to educate their children, and to become true orators through studying in the family and in small schools Modified Platonism, Stoicism, and women Pythagoreans	Gregorio Correr Cecilia Gonzaga Margherita Gonzaga Paola Gonzaga Barbara von Hohenzollern
Guarino of Verona 1370-1460	Opened humanist schools in Venice and in Verona Translated first book of Plutarch's *Moralia, On the Education of Children,* from Greek to Latin Wrote orations on marriage	Especially Plutarch and Quintilian's treatises on education to encourage women to read and write, and educate their children in the family and in small schools Modified Platonism and Stoicism and the woman philosopher Eurydice	Francesco Barbaro George of Trebizond Isotta Nogarola His son Battista Guarini who taught Isabella d'Este and Aldus Manutius, the printer

Having completed this chapter on the early humanist educators, it is important now to summarize some of the main points of their various contributions to the history of the concept of woman. In the twelfth and thirteenth centuries two texts were written that directly addressed the education of girls. In the fourteenth to fifteenth centuries three men provided the means for a new transmission of classical Greek and Latin texts. This opened the way for the renaissance of Platonic arguments that recognized an equal capacity in women and men for the study of philosophy. Some women began to be directly influenced by these new developments, and undertook a serious study of philosophy; and in some situations they actually turned the method of this discipline towards a consideration of their own identity *qua* woman. Consequently, these early humanist educators played an important transitional role in the history of the concept of woman.

The chart on pages 759 and 760 summarizes the specific written contributions to the history of the concept of woman, the models of philosophers that these texts emphasize, and some of the particular persons influenced by these works. Again the effect to the third generation may be well noted.

In the next chapter our analysis will turn to a consideration of the development of new theories of gender identity and the frequent association of this theoretical reformation with dialogues about the concept of woman. The focus will shift from the question of how women ought to be educated in philosophy to the question of how dialogue functioned to reform theories about the concept of woman. In addition, the infusion of Platonic and Epicurean arguments will introduce new theoretical foundations for arguments about gender identity in the works of Nicholas of Cusa, Leon Battista Alberti, Lorenzo Valla, Marsilio Ficino, and Giovanni Pico della Mirandola.

Educational Treatises on Woman's Education and Identity			
Name	Contribution	Models Emphasized	Persons Influenced
Leonardo Bruni	Wrote *De studiis et literis (On the Study of Literature)* (1424) addressed to a woman Translated from Greek to Latin: Plato's *Phaedrus, Phaedo* Aristotle's *Ethics, Politics* Xenophon's *Oeconomicus* Plutarch's *Moralia* Wrote *Life of Aristotle* vs. aspects of Plato, *Life of Dante* and *Life of Petrarch*	Plato, Aristotle, Cicero, Virgil, Demosthenes, Cornelia, Sappho, and Aspasia Emphasized moral philosophy, history, poetry, and oration for women with knowledge of literature, self-governance, and shared governance of household	Battista Malatesta of Montefeltro who gave a public oration (1433) Costanza Varano who gave public orations (1444) on political issues and corresponded with Isotta Nogarola and Cecilia Gonzaga
Francesco Barbaro	*De re uxoria (On Wifely Matters)* (1415) Addressed to noblemen Dispersed translations of Plato's *Laws*	Pythagoreans Plutarch Aristotle Plato Emphasized woman's role biologically and intellectually in the formation of children, woman's speech at home but silence in public, and women's self-government and virtues A mixed Neoplatonic and Aristotelian view of gender identity	Costanza Barbaro

Educational Treatises on Woman's Education and Identity (cont.)			
Name	Contribution	Models Emphasized	Persons Influenced
Albrecht von Eyb	*Ehebüchlein (Little Book of Marriage)* (1471) Addressed to men on the council and city of Nuremberg Wrote *Margarita Poetica* (1451-64) dedicated to his mother and including an oration that praised women in marriage	To refute satirists Juvenal, Theophrastus, and Golias vs. marriage Refers to Empedocles, Socrates, Gorgias, Xenophon, Hippocrates, Stoics, Epicureans, Plutarch, Aristotle, Cicero, Seneca, Valerius Maximus, Virgil, Terence, Plautus, Petrarch Use of Boccaccio to praise literate and articulate women: Isis, Nicostrata, Sappho, Cornelia, Aspasia, Centona, Gaia Afrania, Calpurnia, Tanaquil, and Minerva Praises the linguistic ability of Lady Barbara Margravine Praises his mother Lady Margaret of Wolmershausen's love of literature	The council of the city of Nuremberg to change marriage laws Protection of women in marriage-law cases The development of German humanism

CHAPTER 9

THE EARLY HUMANIST REFORMATION
IN THEORY ABOUT GENDER

O ne of the most striking aspects of Renaissance Humanism is its concern with interpersonal interaction. Humanists come to know, write letters, exchange visits, send their essays and writings to each other for comment and dispersion, and they study texts together in one another's homes. These interactions often take place through various forms of dialogue. Recently it has been suggested that "dialogue is the new name for charity . . . [as] it helps us to see the true implications of problems and allows them to be addressed with greater hope of success."[1] This observation has application to all contexts in which dialogue takes place among people who know one another. When dialogue fails to achieve this ideal of charity, it deteriorates into polemic and hostile exchange of opinions. When dialogue becomes charity, it draws upon intelligent observations of persons who may offer different perspectives on a common issue. The goal of genuine dialogue is to achieve a greater degree of truth about the issue under discussion.

Dialogue constituted a central philosophical method right from the beginning of humanism. We already noted at the earliest period of the development of Italian humanism that Cavalcanti, Dante, Petrarch, and Boccaccio associated dialogue about woman's identity with the theme of love. Although their dialogues were extended in literary works, they were all rooted initially in an interpersonal relationship between the author and a particular woman. Thus, we may conclude that the slogan 'dialogue is the new name for charity' had some of its historical antecedents in Italian humanism as well as in religious communities.

In addition, through the discovery of classical Greek and Latin texts, the humanists sought to enter into a kind of dialogue with an ancient author through reading his text in the original Greek and then applying its principles to problems or issues current at their time. Texts by Plato and Xenophon also included the dialogical form of argumentation, which further enhanced the value of this form of communication. This practice helped Boccaccio develop the concept of woman as wise and virtuous when he introduced content from Plutarch. Christine de Pizan also used it for the same purpose when she introduced content from Boccaccio into her own texts. However, the same practice could be harmful to the concept of

---

1. Pope John Paul II, *Vita Consecrata* (Boston: Pauline Books and Media, 1996), #74, pp. 121-22.

woman when it was used to restate views of satirists such as Theophrastus and Juvenal.

In humanism there is a notable shift of focus in philosophical argumentation from principles to persons. One consequence of this shift is that the rather neat categories that characterized the academic and Aristotelian approach towards the concept of woman were replaced by less precise principles and frequently inconsistent attitudes towards woman's identity. By the end of the fifteenth century the works of Plato will be translated from Greek into Latin. The infusion of Plato's arguments about gender identity will bring another dimension into the dialogue about the concept of woman. These texts contain substantial arguments for the theory of gender unity (unisex). However, Plato's arguments underwent a transformation because of the Christian culture into which they were integrated. While Plato promoted a unisex theory, Christian culture contained mixed elements of gender complementarity, gender polarity, gender unity, and gender neutrality.

The dignity of a human person who is responsible for determining his or her unique identity in cooperation with the creative action of God will be recognized in this period. The approach to the human being as self-defining opens new possibilities for women and men beyond obligations for gaining self-knowledge and self-governance previously articulated in the traditional ways already noted.

Finally, there will be a new dimension of reflection on the meaning of masculine and feminine. Several philosophers will consider different ways a man or a woman integrates both masculine and feminine characteristics, i.e., the engendered aspects of masculine or feminine qualities, along with male and female qualities, will be philosophically analyzed. Gender will be interpreted on several different levels of being: animal, human, and cosmic. Valuations will be given to the relative importance of gendered identity at these different levels. Thus, not only are 'masculine' and 'feminine' identified as aspects of gender identity, they are also evaluated in relation to other aspects of human identity.

In this chapter, the theoretical foundations for the philosophy of woman will be considered in five philosophers, each of whom contributed something different to the discourse about gender identity: Nicholas of Cusa, Leon Battista Alberti, Lorenzo Valla, Marsilio Ficino, and Giovanni Pico della Mirandola. Each philosopher struggled to reform the concept of woman in different ways. Some were more successful than others, but all of them contributed something to the history of the concept of woman.

NICHOLAS OF CUSA (1401-1464)

The works of the philosopher Nicholas of Cusa, also known as Cusanus, abound in metaphysical speculation; they are extremely abstract, often employ geometrical and mathematical models, and are not directed either towards the general public, a small humanist community, or even an individual woman. For the most part, Cusanus wrote highly speculative treatises on philosophy and natural theology for the development of his own thinking, which he then shared with others upon request. He began to develop an original approach to the topic of gender identity, an approach that combined Neoplatonic, scholastic, humanist, and Christian elements. Cusanus also spoke in many public contexts as a Roman Catholic bishop and later cardinal, and he was actively engaged in the fifteenth-century attempt at Church reform.

At the beginning of *On the Summit of Contemplation,* an essay written shortly before his death as a dialogue between himself and Peter of Erkelenz, a Canon in Aachen, Cusanus notes: "... already for fourteen years you have heard me say many things, publicly and privately, about what I discovered in my studies. ..."[2] In this latter capacity, it is possible that some of Nicholas of Cusa's ideas about the feminine and the masculine were shared with men and women in church congregations. Cusanus was driven by a deep desire to reconcile opposites. He worked untiringly to reconcile the Byzantine Greek and Roman Catholic Latin churches; he also tried to find points of reconciliation between the Koran and Scripture, between Islam and Christianity. It will be seen that Cusanus also sought to bring about a reconciliation of masculine and feminine identity in his metaphysical system. Cusa sought to elevate the position of the educated layman, and in so doing, he extended the sphere of influence of discussions about fundamental issues in philosophy of gender beyond the academic and religious settings in which they had been found in the past.

Nicholas of Cusa's contributions to the history of the concept of woman may be divided into two categories: (1) his **direct** arguments about gender identity; and (2) his other arguments that **indirectly** influenced subsequent developments in gender theory. Cusanus has often been described as the most original thinker of the fifteenth century.[3] This characterization also holds true of his contributions to gender theory. Cusanus introduced several new approaches to a consideration of the identity of woman in relation to man, and some of these introductions helped pave the way for the eventual overturning of Aristotelian grounds for gender polarity. A description of the core elements in Nicholas of Cusa's theory of gender will be given below after providing a preliminary description of how he came to be educated as a humanist. A list of his major works with relevance for the history of the concept of woman runs as follows:

1440	*De docta ignorantia (On Learned Ignorance)*
1440-44	*De coniecturis (On Conjectures)*
1449	*Apologia doctae ignorantiae*
1450	*Idiota de sapientia (The Layman: About Knowledge)*
1450	*Idiota de mente (The Layman: About Mind)*

2. Nicholas of Cusa, "On the Summit of Contemplation," in *Nicholas of Cusa: Selected Spiritual Writings* (New York and Mahwah, N.J.: Paulist Press, 1997), p. 293.

3. The classic author who makes this claim is Ernst Cassirer, who in *The Individual and the Cosmos in Renaissance Philosophy* devotes two chapters to the work of Nicholas Cusanus, as a point of departure for all attempts to systematize the philosophy of the Renaissance (trans. Mario Domandi [New York: Barnes and Noble, 1963], p. 7). See also Pamela O. Long, "Humanism and Science," in *Renaissance Humanism,* vol. 3, *Humanism and the Disciplines,* ed. Albert Rabil, Jr. (Philadelphia: University of Pennsylvania Press, 1988), where she describes Cusanus as "one of the most original philosophers of the fifteenth century" (p. 501); and Louis Dupré, "Introduction," *American Catholic Philosophical Quarterly: Special Issue, Nicholas of Cusa* 64, no. 1 (1990): 1.

1453	*De visione dei (On the Vision of God)*
1458	*De Beryllo (On Beryllus)*
1460	*Trialogus de possest*
1462	*De li non aliud (On the Not-Other)*
1464	*Compendium (Compendium)*
1464	*De apice theoriae (The Summit of Contemplation)*[4]

Before analyzing the contents of his works a few reflections will be given on Nicholas of Cusa's background and intellectual formation. He was born in Kues, Germany, and educated as a young man by the Brethren of the Common Life in Deventer. Following upon the practice of copying ancient texts and translating them into German, "Cusa left the school at Deventer well equipped with a knowledge of the classics" and with an awakened "desire for the new learning that was sweeping Europe."[5] Nicholas of Cusa's attachment to this school of his youth was so strong that before his death he used part of his inheritance to establish a *Bursa Cusana* for twenty poor students at Deventer.[6]

In 1416 Nicholas of Cusa received an undergraduate scholastic education that included an exposure to nominalism at the Faculty of Arts at the University of Heidelberg, where he discovered a partial affinity with the works of William of Ockham and Jean Gerson. At the same time, however, Cusanus always preserved a fundamental realism in his epistemology that enabled him to avoid the relativism that plagued some nominalist theories. Next, Cusanus traveled to Italy to study at the University of Padua from 1417 to 1423 for his Doctorate in Canon Law. Cassirer describes an effect of this experience on Cusanus: "At Padua he dips into the stream of humanistic culture. He learns Greek, enabling him to study Plato more deeply and also to study Archimedes and the basic problems of Greek mathematics."[7] The University of Padua was also at that time "the leading scientific school of Europe," and Cusanus became immersed in the study of mathematics and science.[8] From then on he sought to develop a complete philosophy and theology that was unified and illustrated by mathematical structures of thought.

In addition to his immersion in Greek language, science, mathematics, and law in Padua, Nicholas of Cusa also "befriended Paolo Toscanelli and the humanist educators Guarino of Verona and Vittorino da Feltre."[9] While we have already

---

4. A more complete listing of Cusanus's philosophical and theological works may be found in Louis Dupré's introduction to the special issue on Nicholas of Cusa, *American Catholic Philosophical Quarterly* 64, no. 1 (1990): 5.

5. John Patrick Dolan, introduction to *Unity and Reform: Selected Writings of Nicholas de Cusa* (South Bend, Ind.: University of Notre Dame Press, 1962), pp. 10-11.

6. H. Lawrence Bond, introduction to *Nicholas of Cusa: Selected Spiritual Writings*, p. 13.

7. Cassirer, *The Individual and the Cosmos in Renaissance Philosophy*, p. 35.

8. Dolan, ed., *Unity and Reform: Selected Writings of Nicholas de Cusa*, p. 18. Bond notes that at this time Cusa became a close friend with the mathematician Paolo del Pozzo Toscanelli, who twenty years later sent him a copy of Pseudo-Dionysius' *The Mystical Theology*, introduction to *Nicholas of Cusa: The Spiritual Writings*, p. 4.

9. Pamela O. Long, "Humanism and Science," in *Renaissance Humanism*, vol. 3, *Humanism and the Disciplines*, p. 501.

noted the significance of Guarino and Vittorino for the history of the philosophy of gender, it is worth noting that Toscanelli, a mathematician and physicist, is credited with having influenced Christopher Columbus in the 1480s by providing him with "a map and the scientific information required for . . . a voyage" to the New World.[10] Cusanus developed a lifelong love for the acquisition and study of classical Greek and Latin texts, and at his death he left a large collection of around three hundred manuscripts to the library at the hospice he founded in Kues.[11] Through these various educational roots Nicholas of Cusa was formed in all the fundamental humanist principles and practices. Throughout his learning, Nicholas of Cusa was also deeply attracted to basic Neoplatonist texts such as Proclus's *Elements of Theology* and commentary on Plato's *Parmenides,* works of Pseudo-Dionysius, and Plotinus. He was also interested in the dramas of Plautus, which he sold to Cardinal Orsini at the Council of Ferrara-Florence in 1429.

When Cusanus returned to Germany in 1425, he gave a certain credibility in ecclesiastical circles to the new humanist theories. He also enrolled in the University of Cologne, and there became acquainted with some of the central thoughts of the medieval Christian philosophers John Scotus Erigena, Albert the Great, and Thomas Aquinas.[12] From this particular heritage, Cusanus continued to adopt a philosophy that gave a heightened role to the intellect.[13] As will also be seen, he adopted various theories of gender identity as well. From the tradition of Albert and Thomas he inherited strong foundations for gender polarity based on an Aristotelian biology and metaphysics. From the Platonic tradition (also found in Erigena), he adopted a preference for mathematical (and mainly geometrical) principles to explain fundamental metaphysical axioms. This tradition also tended towards an exclusion of gender identity at the highest levels, a defense of gender unity at the intermediate level, and an introduction of gender polarity at various points within the broader theory. For example, John Scotus Erigena claimed that God created a unisex human being, which after the Fall was differentiated as man and woman, and will at the end of time become once again unisex.[14] As will be seen, Nicholas of Cusa's philosophy of gender identity contains all three of these aspects. Yet it also contains some remarkable innovations, new to the history of philosophy, in its systematic approach to the presence of masculine and feminine aspects within a man or a woman. In addition, it promotes a resolution of the opposition of masculine and feminine with a theory of the coincidence of opposites.

Ordained as a priest sometime between 1436 and 1440, Cusanus worked as

10. William F. Wertz, Jr., Introduction, *Toward a New Council of Florence, 'On the Peace of Faith' and Other Works by Nicolaus of Cusa* (Washington, D.C.: Schiller Institute, Inc., 1993), p. 14.

11. Bond, introduction to *Nicholas of Cusa: Selected Spiritual Writings,* p. 13.

12. Cusanus's Thomistic teacher in Cologne was Hymeric Von den Velde, also known as Heymericus de Campo. See John Patrick Dolan, introduction to *Unity and Reform: Selected Writings of Nicholas de Cusa,* p. 21.

13. Donald F. Duclow, "Mystical Theology and Intellect in Nicholas of Cusa," *American Catholic Philosophical Quarterly* 64, no. 1 (Winter 1990): 127-28.

14. See Allen, *The Concept of Woman: The Aristotelian Revolution (750 BC–1250 AD),* pp. 240-42. See also John Scotus Erigena, *Periphyseon: De Divisione Naturae,* Book 2, pp. 532-41, and Book 5, p. 20.

secretary to the humanist Cardinal Giordano Orsini, who further introduced him to more of the leading humanists in Europe. Later, he worked directly for Pope Eugenius IV, and was named a bishop and cardinal. Cusanus worked tirelessly in support of efforts to reform the Catholic Church at the same time that he wrote numerous philosophical and theological texts. His public actions for the reform are well known; two are particularly interesting for our purposes. First, Cusanus worked hard for "the strict enclosure of convents."[15] While the goal of this action was the reform of immoral sexual behavior, another effect was the further isolation of women from dynamic occasions for engaging in public discourse on issues of interest in higher education.

Second, during the Ferrara-Florence Council, which occurred during 1438-39 for the purpose of reuniting the Roman Catholic Church and the Byzantine Greek Church, Cusanus spent much time in discussion with other humanists. "At this council . . . the Greek scholars in attendance conducted a kind of continual 'seminar' in Hellenic studies for the Latins. . . . The number of Latin scholars present at the council is remarkable, including many celebrated humanists, for example Bruni . . . , Lorenzo Valla, Leon Battista Alberti, and the philosopher Nicholas of Cusa. Opportunities for intellectual exchange were frequent."[16] Many of these men wrote about the concept of woman: Leonardo Bruni's theory has already been discussed, Lorenzo Valla and Leon Battista Alberti will be discussed in this chapter, and Nicholas of Cusa's theory will now be considered in more detail.

Direct Schema of Gender Identity

Nicholas of Cusa's works carried forward Neoplatonic themes that he had discovered early on in his intellectual life. He was deeply influenced by the mathematical aspect of Platonic theory; he was convinced that the world was ordered according to mathematical ratios and principles. Thus, for Cusanus, the intellect grasped truth not so much by empirical observation as by mathematical reasoning. Generally speaking, an emphasis on mathematical reasoning tended to be consistent with a gender neutrality or gender unity position. For example, the Neoplatonist Hypatia appears to have exemplified gender neutrality while the Neoplatonist Porphyry argued for gender unity. Cusanus, on the other hand, elaborated a complex combination of gender polarity and gender complementarity. Thus, even though mathematical principles are neutral with respect to gender differentiation, Cusanus added other elements to them within his own schema.

Nicholas of Cusa reached further back than Plato into the Pythagorean table of opposites to articulate fundamental categories of thought. In the Pythagorean model, mathematical principles were combined with a theory of the polarity of opposites, including specifically the opposites of male and female. In 1437, just before

15. Bond, introduction to *Nicholas of Cusa: Selected Spiritual Writings*, p. 8.

16. Deno J. Geanakoplos, "Italian Humanism and Byzantine Émigré Scholars," in *Renaissance Humanism*, vol. 1, *Humanism in Italy*, p. 356.

the Council of Ferrara-Florence, Cusanus traveled to Constantinople to meet with Church leaders there, and during his two-month return trip he had an intuition about a theory that included reference to "the coincidence of opposites." This theory, along with its axioms and consequences, ruminated in Nicholas of Cusa's mind during the dynamic Council that took place during the following two years, 1438 and 1439. By 1440 Cusanus had completed his best-known work *De docta ignorantia (On Learned Ignorance)* and soon after a companion text *De coniecturis (On Conjectures)*. It is in the latter text that Nicholas writes directly about the coincidence of the opposites: masculine and feminine.

Cusanus first introduces a relation of masculinity and femininity as one in a series of pairs of opposites that are located within the two extreme categories: unity and otherness. His introductory statement is as follows:

> If, therefore, you direct your view to Figure P, then you will see through the descent of unity into otherness and the regression of otherness into unity, how in the supreme heaven, everything that there is of otherness, advances to unity itself: divisibility to indivisibility, darkness to light, grossness to subtlety, the composite to the simple, the mortal to the immortal, the mutable to the immutable, the feminine to the masculine, the potential to the actual, the imperfect of the part to the whole, etc. It is to the contrary in the lowest world, where indivisibility degenerates to divisibility. For the unity of indivisible form follows divisible nature, so that every part of water is water, every part of earth is earth. Stability is here in instability, immortality in mortality, actuality in potentiality, masculinity in femininity, etc. In the middle world, however, the habitude is median.[17]

If we conjoin the pairs of opposites directly mentioned by Cusanus with his model in Figure P, it will look something like the horizontal intersection of two triangles as follows:

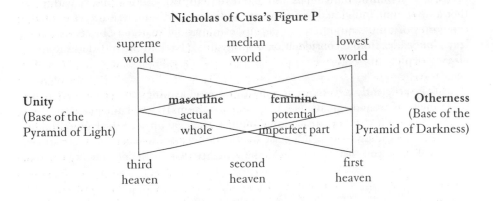

Nicholas of Cusa's Figure P

17. Nicholas of Cusa, "On Conjectures," in *Toward a New Council of Florence: 'On the Peace of Faith' and Other Works by Nicolas of Cusa* (Washington, D.C.: Schiller Institute, Inc., 1993), I, xii, 77-78.

Two aspects of this model of Nicholas of Cusa should be noted: (1) there is a suggestion of gender polarity in the association of the masculine with the actual, with light, with wholeness, and of the feminine with the potential, with darkness, and with the imperfect part, and (2) there is a resemblance to the Pythagorean table of opposites with some of these categories. The second point will be developed before returning to the first one.

In *Metaphysics* Aristotle had recorded a table of ten opposites attributed to the Pythagoreans: limit and the absence of limit, one and many, male and female, odd and even, right and left, rest and motion, straight and curved, good and bad, light and dark, and square and oblong.[18] There is no doubt that Cusanus had a great interest in many aspects of Pythagorean theory. In *On Learned Ignorance,* Cusanus referred several times to his indebtedness to the Pythagorean theory of numbers and the place of mathematics in apprehending truths.[19] There is also evidence that Cusanus had his copy of Aristotle's *Metaphysics* corrected by Bessarion, the Archbishop of Nicaea, who shared his voyage by ship from Constantinople to Venice in 1438.[20] Thus, Cusanus would have been familiar with the Pythagorean table of opposites as recorded by Aristotle in *Metaphysics,* and when he formulated his theory of the coincidence of opposites, it is likely that several of these pairs were in his mind. In any event, Cusanus explicitly associates the masculine with light, actuality, and wholeness; and the feminine with darkness, potentiality, and imperfect division into parts. Nicholas of Cusa's theory of the coincidence of opposites introduces a factor of the perspective of opposites when compared with infinity. Pythagoras had also considered the relation of the unlimited to the limited in his system of drawing numbers by the relation of dots to spaces, but for Pythagoras the male was associated with limit and the female with the unlimited. For Cusanus, the opposites, masculine and feminine, are reconciled and harmonized in infinity.[21]

In Part II: Section VIII of *On Conjectures,* which is titled "On the Difference of Individual Things," Cusanus elaborates a theory both about the relation of masculine and feminine individuals and about masculinity and femininity within either a masculine individual or a feminine individual. His analysis draws upon the categories of unity and otherness and upon individual material objects. Cusanus leads his reader from a consideration of individuals back to the broader categories already depicted in Figure P:

It is sufficiently well known to you that in sensible things the seeds and similarly the trees are individuals. You see also that in animals, which are like trees, some are masculine, others are feminine. Therefore, if you imagine the Figure P, where the descending light signifies actuality and the shadow potentiality, the species will show you that in the species the actuality absorbs the potentiality and vice

18. Aristotle, *Metaphysics,* 986a22-25.
19. Nicholas of Cusa, "On Learned Ignorance," in *Nicholas of Cusa: Selected Spiritual Writings,* pp. 95-96, 98, and 101.
20. Bond, introduction to *Nicholas of Cusa: Selected Spiritual Writings,* p. 5.
21. For an excellent discussion of the different meanings of the coincidence of opposites see Bond, introduction to *Nicholas of Cusa: Selected Spiritual Writings,* pp. 19-36.

versa, and that accordingly the individuals participate in its nature. If, in order to be more specific, the actuality is resolved into Figure P, then the light will be the masculinity of actuality, and the shadow its femininity; it is likewise in regard to potentiality.[22]

Presumably the analogy with potentiality that Cusanus suggested at the end of this paragraph would read something like the following: if the potentiality is resolved into Figure P, then the darkness will be the femininity of potentiality, and the light its masculinity. Once again, this association of masculinity with actuality and light, and femininity with potentiality and darkness seems to suggest a devaluation of the feminine in relation to the masculine. However, as Cusanus further develops his concrete understanding of how masculine and feminine individuals constitute their respective identities, he introduces a balancing factor that reduces somewhat this devaluation of the feminine.

In the following passage Cusanus introduces the principle that in individual things (sensible living objects) that are masculine, the masculinity absorbs femininity, and in individual things that are feminine, the femininity absorbs masculinity. In addition, no masculine individuals are identically masculine, and no feminine individuals are identically feminine:

> However, it is necessary to differentiate both the masculine as well as feminine. For no masculine individual can be found which agrees precisely in its masculinity with another, and there can also be none that is the maximum masculine. Therefore, in all masculinity femininity is absorbed in different ways. Hence, we also see, that in masculine animals, feminine characteristics, for example the indications of breasts, appear. Likewise seeds also act in a contrary manner. Every individual absorbs the other in its singular individualization, as in your individual masculinity femininity is absorbed; just as the seed, from which a being of masculine seed came into actuality, has overcome femininity, so femininity in its manner absorbs masculinity. The masculine seed contracts the feminine in itself and in its potentiality embraces the actual masculine and feminine. It is the opposite in regard to the feminine seed.[23]

In this remarkable passage Cusanus anticipates the development of a theory of unique and unrepeatable personalities. He also suggests a complementarity of value in masculine and feminine components of individual identity. Finally, in his observation that none can be the maximum masculine, he indicates that the masculine never occurs without some feminine and vice-versa. In addition, he limits the range of masculinity and femininity to living non-Divine individuals. The God/man Jesus Christ is called the maximum human, but not the maximum masculine, in Nicholas of Cusa's schema.

In order to help the reader follow this very abstract manner of expression, Cusanus offers a concrete example in which he associates the masculine identity

---

22. Nicholas of Cusa, "On Conjectures," in *Towards a New Council of Florence,* II, viii, 112.
23. Nicholas of Cusa, "On Conjectures," in *Towards a New Council of Florence,* II, viii, 112.

more with a tree and the feminine identity more with a seed. Nicholas of Cusa's theory introduces a hierarchical understanding of nobility, or value, that at times appears to invert the traditional gender polarity valuation. In the less noble species, the feminine turns out to be superior to the masculine, while in the more noble species, the masculine remains consistently superior to the feminine.

> We know that these individuals participate in the species in varied ways. Some participate more perfectly in the species as seeds, some as trees. The more ignoble and potential a species is, the more perfectly the seeds participate in its nature. The more noble and perfect, formal and actual a species is, the more do the trees participate in its nature, and where the trees participate in it more perfectly, that species is more perfect which is more masculine, and where the seeds participate more perfectly, that species is more perfect which is more feminine. Hence the pear tree is more noble than the pear and the masculine lion more noble than the lioness and the seed of the lion. It is the reverse, however, with wheat, where the seed is better than the chaff, etc.[24]

Thus, Cusanus allows in some individuals a superiority of the seed over the rest of the plant, i.e., when during reproduction the plant dies while the seed remains. In this case, e.g., in wheat, since the seed is considered as feminine and the stalk as masculine, Cusanus says that the feminine is more noble or superior to the masculine. However, in higher forms of life, where the individual survives and is able to produce more seeds, the individual, e.g., pear tree, lion, and human being, is superior to the seed, and thus the masculine member of the species is more noble or superior to the feminine.

Since the latter case concerns higher forms of life, it would apply to the analysis of man and woman. Therefore, in this aspect of Nicholas of Cusa's schema, man is considered more noble and superior to the woman. Cusanus continues his analysis as follows:

> Where the tree participates more in the conditions of the incorruptible species, since it produces the fruit from itself and nevertheless retains the power to produce further fruits, the tree participates more in the perfection of the species. However, where the seed contracts the nature of the incorruptible species more, and the power of the tree is exhausted with its production, because it has passed over entirely into the seed, as with grains of wheat, white wheat, oats and the like, the grain of the seed is more perfect, and indeed so much the more noble, the more feminine. No seed, however, can be found, which is so feminine and so much in potentiality, that it could not be more in potentiality; likewise no tree is in such perfect actuality, that it could not be still more so.[25]

To summarize this dual-level argument about different categories of nobility the following linear depiction may be helpful:

24. Nicholas of Cusa, "On Conjectures," in *Towards a New Council of Florence,* II, viii, 112-13.
25. Nicholas of Cusa, "On Conjectures," in *Towards a New Council of Florence,* II, viii, 113.

Relative Nobility of Masculine and Feminine Species

More noble species	Less noble species
masculine more noble than feminine	feminine more noble than masculine
humans lions pear tree	wheat
individual exists longer than the seeds	seeds exist longer than the individual

The analogy between masculine identity and a tree, and feminine identity and a seed, has many rich aspects in Nicholas of Cusa's thought. It inverts the usual identification of seed only with the father's contribution to generation. Instead, it suggests that the mother's identity is connected with fertility. While it would be tempting to conclude from this that Cusanus intuitively suggests a double-seed theory of gender identity, there is no further evidence to support this conclusion. In fact, in a passage on the role of the Virgin Mary in the conception of Jesus, it seems as though he repeats the commonly held Aristotelian-scholastic view that the mother provides only passive matter to generation, while the father provides the formal seed in cooperation with God. Cusanus describes Jesus as the "maximum human," by which he means the most perfect human nature:

> And because the maximum human is the highest begotten being and is most immediately united to the beginning, this beginning, from which this maximum most immediately exists, is as one who creates and begets, as a father, and the human beginning is as a passive beginning, providing receptive matter. Hence, this maximum human is from a mother without male seed. . . .
>
> As speech is formed from our breath, so it is as if this Spirit, by breathing into, fashioned the animal body from pure and fruitful virginal blood. And the Spirit added reason so that this would be a human being. . . .
>
> No one, however, should doubt that this mother, who was so full of virtue and provided the material, surpassed all virgins in the complete perfection of virtue and received a more excellent blessing than all other fertile women.[26]

It is clear from this passage that Cusanus accepted the traditional account of woman's contribution to generation; namely, in the Aristotelian model, she provides the material, and the father (with God) provides the form.

In a work written in 1453, *De Visione Dei (On the Vision of God)*, Cusanus introduces again the metaphor of a seed and a tree, without directly mentioning its association with gender identity. This non-advertence to gender identity is due to the fact that his example focuses on non-material seeds, or rational ideas in the mind of God. Nonetheless, his comments are instructive, for Cusanus introduces a new dynamic in his analysis of the respective value of actuality and potentiality. As will be seen later in this analysis, towards the end of his life, at the highest level of contemplation, Cusanus suggests that infinite potentiality has a kind of priority over actuality. As Peter Casarella summarizes it: "Consequently, he leaves behind the Aristotelian-Scholastic tradition which begins with the claim that actuality is

---

26. Nicholas of Cusa, "On Learned Ignorance," in *Nicholas of Cusa: Selected Spiritual Writings,* vol. 5, pp. 208-12, 181-82.

the end of all possibility."[27] This shift in metaphysical priorities has a transcendental application to the gender polarity theory, which had associated the male more
with the properties of act and the female more with properties of potentiality. It introduces a difference in valuation of actuality and potentiality that in turn may
have a spill-over effect on the valuation of man and woman as well.

The context of one discussion about the value of power or potentiality of rational seeds concerns a reflection on the face of Jesus Christ:

> For since you, O Lord, are that power of principle from which all things come
> and since your face is that power or principle from which all faces are what they
> are, I then turn myself towards this great and lofty nut-tree and seek to perceive
> its principle. With my sensible eye I see it as tall and wide, colored, and heavy
> with branches, leaves, and nuts. And then with the eyes of the mind I perceive
> that this tree existed in the seed, not as I look at it now, but virtually. I study with
> care the wonderful power of this seed, in which existed this entire tree and all its
> nuts and all their seminal power, and all trees existed in the seminal power of the
> nuts. I also see how this power can never at any time be fully unfolded by the
> movement of the heavens. But this power of the seed, although not able to be
> completely unfolded, is nevertheless contracted, because it has power only in this
> one species of nuts. Consequently, although I see the tree in the seed, I still see it
> only in a contracted power. Then, O Lord, I consider the power of the seeds of all
> the different species of trees, a power that is contracted to the species of each, and
> in these seeds I see the trees in their potential.[28]

Cusanus is drawing upon Augustine's theory that the exemplars of the seeds of all
things are in God at the time of creation. These seeds are non-material or rational
seeds that contain the potential power for any particular species. When Cusanus
introduces the concept of power that is contracted, he specifies a particular seed to a
particular kind of thing, a species.

Cusanus also describes a particular individual as a contracted member of a
species. In this case, there is a sensible or material thing, and seeds flowing from it
are also material. Cusanus makes distinctions between different levels of being
ranging from the sensible, through the rational, to the intellectual. The masculine
and feminine duality play a dynamic role through all three levels. In *On Conjectures,* bringing the reader back once more to his Figure P, Cusanus offers the following description of masculinity and femininity in a consideration of the relation of
nature and art:

> If you want to investigate the differences of nature and art and the connection of
> both, then return to the frequently revealed guidance of the figure. Nature in-
> deed consists of masculine unity and feminine otherness. In intellectual mascu-

27. Peter J. Casarella, "Nicholas of Cusa and the Power of the Possible," *American Catholic
Philosophical Quarterly* 64, no. 1 (Winter 1990): 32.
28. Nicholas of Cusa, "On the Vision of God," in *Nicholas of Cusa: Selected Spiritual Writings,*
7.22, 245.

linity femininity is absorbed. It is therefore fertilized unitively in itself. In vegetative femininity otherness determines the masculine nature in itself; hence it fructifies unfoldedly. The nature of animals distinguishes the sexes; the man generates in the woman, the woman gives birth externally. In intelligent beings nature engenders intellectual fruit, in animals animal fruit, in vegetation vegetative fruit. The sensible nature obeys the rational, the rational the intellectual, the intellectual the divine. The sensibly formable thing obeys the rational art, the rational the intellectual, the intellectual the divine. As all nature is contracted sensibly in a sensible thing, so the formability is also contracted sensibly in a sensible thing, rationally in a rational thing.[29]

Once again we see the masculine associated with the more noble category of unity, and the feminine with the less noble category of otherness in a kind of metaphysical gender polarity. In the chapter that precedes this particular description, Cusanus stated, again referring to figure P, "let unity be the soul, but otherness, the body."[30] However, he also suggests that any differentiation of individuals demands a differentiation of both soul and body, and a dynamic downward movement of the spirituality into the corporeality and an upward movement of the corporeality into the spirituality.

At the same time, Cusanus elaborates further what he means by the phrase in the above longer quotation, that intellectual masculinity absorbs femininity and fertilizes itself. Of the three regions, intellectual, rational, and sensible, "The intellectual region, which absorbs the alterable darknesses in itself, is of the masculine, subtle, most unified, and most noble nature."[31] Cusanus describes a dynamic Neoplatonic hierarchy of regions descending from the Divine, intellectual, rational, and sensible, or ascending in reverse order. From the perspective of the highest, or the Divine, the intellect represents otherness, from the perspective of intellect the rational represents otherness, and from the perspective of the rational, the sensible represents otherness. In reverse order, the higher region represents the unity of the lower region. It is through this dynamic enfolding of the lower by the higher, or unfolding of the lower from the higher, that Cusanus introduces his theory of the coincidence of opposites.

In *On the Vision of God* Nicholas of Cusa frequently elaborates the way in which God remains beyond a wall of the coincidence of opposites, and a human being may come up to the wall and pass beyond it and return. What is significant for the purposes of the history of the philosophy of gender is Nicholas of Cusa's claim that from the perspective of the Divine, the opposites become equal, and neither is superior to the other. In other words, if the feminine had been perceived previously as less noble than the masculine, because of its association with otherness, division, darkness, potentiality, and the unfolding of generation, from the perspective of the Divine, the opposites coincide and all valuation of superiority and inferiority disappears, even while each opposite keeps its proper identity:

29. Nicholas of Cusa, "On Conjectures," in *Towards a New Council of Florence,* II, xii, 122.
30. Nicholas of Cusa, "On Conjectures," in *Towards a New Council of Florence,* II, x, 116.
31. Nicholas of Cusa, "On Conjectures," in *Towards a New Council of Florence,* II, xiii, 123.

Trusting in your help, O Lord, I return again in order to find you beyond the wall of the coincidence of enfolding and unfolding. When at the same time I go in and go out through this door of your word and concept, I discover the sweetest nourishment. I enter when I find you as a power that enfolds all things. I go out when I find you as a power that unfolds. I both go in and go out when I find you as a power that both enfolds and unfolds. I go in proceeding from creatures to you, the Creator, from the effects to the cause; I go out from you, the Creator, from the cause to the effects. I go in and go out simultaneously when I see how to go out is to go in and to go in is simultaneously to go out. In the same way one who is counting unfolds and enfolds alike; as one counts one unfolds the power of unity and enfolds number in unity. For the creature's going forth from you is its entering into you, and to unfold is to enfold. When I see you, O God, in paradise, which this wall of the coincidence of opposites surrounds, I see that you neither enfold nor unfold, whether disjunctively or together. For disjunction and conjunction alike are the wall of coincidence beyond which are you, absolute from all that can be spoke or thought.[32]

Thus the enfolding, which had been associated more with the masculinity of unity, and the unfolding, which had been associated more with the femininity of otherness, appear to hold an equal position just inside the wall of coincidence of opposites, from the perspective beyond the wall itself. In other words, Cusanus seems to suggest that the superior evaluation given to those things associated with masculinity, from someone using human rationality or intelligence, falls away at the higher level of apprehension, closest to the Divine.

In the following discussion of the relation of unity and otherness, a similar dynamic is expressed:

You, Lord, tell me that just as in unity otherness is without otherness because it is unity, so in infinity contradiction is without contradiction because it is infinity. Infinity is simplicity itself of all that are spoken; contradiction does not exist without otherness. Yet in simplicity otherness exists without otherness because it is simplicity itself. For all that can be said of absolute simplicity coincides with it, because in absolute simplicity having is being. The opposition of opposites is an opposition without opposition, just as the end of finite things is an end without an end. You are, therefore, O God, the opposition of opposites, because you are infinite, and because you are infinite, you are infinity itself. In infinity the opposition of opposites is without opposition.[33]

While much in Nicholas of Cusa's descriptions seems similar to other Neoplatonic philosophers, or religious writers such as Marguerite Porete or Meister Eckhart, Cusanus seems to argue that the identity of individuals is not ultimately lost in this

32. Nicholas of Cusa, "On the Vision of God," in *Nicholas of Cusa: Selected Spiritual Writings,* 11.46, 255-56.
33. Nicholas of Cusa, "On the Vision of God," in *Nicholas of Cusa: Selected Spiritual Writings,* 12.54, 259.

theory of the coincidence of opposites. This is an important consideration for the history of the concept of woman, for in other Neoplatonic theories, a human person seemed to lose his or her proper identity.

Sometimes, however, Cusanus appears to follow the usual Neoplatonic direction of loss of human identity in union with God. For example, in *The Vision of God,* he says from the perspective of infinity that otherness is a kind of non-being, a statement of something that is not another thing, and thus he concludes: "Otherness, therefore, is not anything."[34] This would seem to imply, if we presume as was stated previously that otherness is associated with the feminine, that the feminine is not anything, and perhaps, by extension, woman is not anything. This seems to support the conclusion that Cusanus failed to avoid the same difficulties encountered in other Neoplatonists, namely the problem of how to maintain the unique and unrepeatable identity of the human person in union with the Divine. However, Cusanus guards against this kind of interpretation in four different ways, all of which are sketched out, but not fully developed in his consideration of (1) the identity of Socrates, (2) the face of Jesus, (3) the identity of the Virgin Mary, and (4) dialectical perspectives on unity and otherness in relation to the Divine. Each of these examples will be briefly described below.

In the section of *On the Vision of God* entitled "How Without Otherness God Enfolds All Things," Cusanus considers the simple identity of Socrates, who represents any individual human being, man or woman. He states:

> For example, the essence of Socrates embraces all Socratic being, and in the simple Socratic being there is no otherness or diversity. For the being of Socrates is the individual unity of all that is in Socrates. And so in this single being is enfolded the being of all that exists in Socrates, namely, in the individual simplicity where nothing other or diverse is found.[35]

Cusanus includes in his category of all Socratic being, the various parts of Socrates' body, such as the hand or arm, which if extended, would certainly include sexual differentiation. At the same time, Cusanus insists on the unique and unrepeatable aspect of a particular contracted Socratic being, or Socrates as a human person. He concludes: "And thus I see, because you illumine me, O Lord, that the simple Socratic being is utterly incommunicable and cannot in any way be contracted to the being of any one member."[36] It would seem to follow from Nicholas of Cusa's argument not only that Socrates' unique identity cannot be contracted into any one member of his body, but also that Socrates' identity remains in some simple and unified way present in God.

A second possible guard against Neoplatonic loss of individual identity may

---

34. Nicholas of Cusa, "On the Vision of God," in *Nicholas of Cusa: Selected Spiritual Writings,* 14.58, 261.

35. Nicholas of Cusa, "On the Vision of God," in *Nicholas of Cusa: Selected Spiritual Writings,* 14.59, 261.

36. Nicholas of Cusa, "On the Vision of God," in *Nicholas of Cusa: Selected Spiritual Writings,* 14.59, 262.

be found in Nicholas of Cusa's reflections on an iconographic painting of the face of Jesus Christ. In this reflection, Cusanus draws a transcendental analogy in which aspects of a human face, especially the eyes and the expression, take on transcendental characteristics of the Divine Being. The sense-base for the icon is specified, but it changes in its aspect depending on who is looking at the face and from what angle the perception occurs. Thus, the face is always specified; it does not lose identity altogether, but it changes its appearance depending upon the perspective of the one who views it.

> Therefore, while I look at this painted face from the east, it likewise appears that it looks at me in the east, and when I look at it from the west or from the south it also appears to look at me in the west or south. In whatever direction I turn my face, its face seems turned towards me. Thus, too, your face is turned to all faces which look on you. Your vision, Lord, is your face. Consequently, whoever looks on you with a loving face will find only your face looking on oneself with love. And the more one strives to look on you with greater love, the more loving will one find your face. Whoever looks on you with anger will likewise find your face angry. Whoever looks on you with joy will also find your face joyous, just as is the face of the one who looks on you. So indeed the eye of flesh, while peering through a red glass, judges that everything it sees is red or if through a green glass, that everything is green. In the same way, the eye of the mind, wrapped up in contraction and passivity, judges you, who are the object of the mind, according to the nature of the contraction and passivity.[37]

In his analysis of the human vision of Jesus' face, or of the Divine vision of a particular human face, Cusanus introduces the theme of darkness and light once more. Remembering that in his metaphysical schema darkness is associated with the feminine and light with the masculine, it is interesting to note that even at the highest levels of intellectual activity, the perspectives of darkness and light interplay.

> In all faces the face of faces is seen veiled and in enigma. It is not seen unveiled so long as one does not enter into a certain secret and hidden silence beyond all faces where there is no knowledge or concept of a face. This cloud, mist, darkness, or ignorance into which whoever seeks your face enters when one leaps beyond every knowledge and concept is such that below it your face cannot be found except veiled. . . . Whoever, therefore, has to leap beyond every light must enter into that which lacks visible light and thus is darkness to the eye.[38]

Again, just as we noted Cusanus's revaluing the traditional superiority of actuality over potentiality, we find him transcendentally revaluing the superiority of light over darkness. Given his previously identified association of the feminine with

37. Nicholas of Cusa, "On the Vision of God," in *Nicholas of Cusa: Selected Spiritual Writings,* 6.19, 243.
38. Nicholas of Cusa, "On the Vision of God," in *Nicholas of Cusa: Selected Spiritual Writings,* 6.22, 244-45.

darkness, it is interesting to reflect on the indirect way in which darkness has emerged as a higher experience of the Divine than those associated with light.

In other sections of *On the Vision of God,* Nicholas of Cusa refers to God as "rational receivable Light" and "Bridegroom" of the soul. In these two appellations the human being is plunged into darkness in relation to the rational receivable light and is characterized as a feminine bride in relation to the Divine Bridegroom.

> By your love that loves, you have betrothed every rational soul, but not every bride loves you, her Bridegroom, but very often clings to another. But how, my God, could your bride, the human soul, attain her end if you were not lovable so that thus by loving you, the lovable, she could attain to the happiest bond and union?[39]

While Cusanus does introduce other metaphors to characterize the relation of the union of the human person and God, such as adopted son and Father, they all maintain a distinct identity of the Divine Being and the human being who are in union.

The final example of possible ways Cusanus avoids difficulties common to Neoplatonism concerns the relation between God and the Virgin Mary. While the passage describing the conception of Christ in the Virgin Mary was previously quoted in relation to the place of woman in generation, it is helpful to consider a different consequence of Nicholas of Cusa's description here. It is the hypostatic union of the Divine and human nature in Jesus Christ, by the cooperation of the Holy Spirit and the Virgin Mary, that Cusanus emphasizes; and it is the central identity of Jesus Christ as both God and man that enables Cusanus to overcome the tendency within Neoplatonism towards the disappearance of unique personal identity. He argues that Jesus' human soul and body were resurrected, and this is the significant fact that determines the ultimate differentiation between God and all human beings:

> There is, however, only one indivisible humanity and essence of species of all humans, and through it all individuals are numerically distinct beings. Consequently, there is the same humanity in Christ and all human beings, yet the numerical distinction of individuals remains unconfused. Hence, it is clear that the humanity of all human beings, who temporally, either before or after Christ, existed or will exist, has in Christ put on immortality. The conclusion is evident: Because Christ the human arose, all human beings will rise through him after all motion of temporal corruptibility will have ceased, so that they will be forever incorruptible.[40]

For a more thorough analysis of Nicholas of Cusa's philosophy of gender, it would be necessary to consider his theology in some depth. Since these themes go

---

39. Nicholas of Cusa, "On the Vision of God," in *Nicholas of Cusa: Selected Spiritual Writings,* 18, 80-81, 271.

40. Nicholas of Cusa, "On Learned Ignorance," in *Nicholas of Cusa: Selected Spiritual Writings,* 8, 227, 189.

beyond the limits of our analysis in this book, we will have to rest with the general outline of his views as sketched above. There is no doubt that Cusanus opened up a richness of speculation about the meaning of masculine and feminine and their relation both to major metaphysical categories and to individual men and women. As noted previously Nicholas of Cusa's schema of gender identity can be divided into two parts: direct arguments about masculinity and femininity in male and female beings in the world, and indirect arguments against traditional positions that provided the foundation for traditional gender polarity. Accordingly, we will provide two summary charts, one for the direct arguments (pp. 778-79) and one for the indirect arguments (pp. 787-88).

Nicholas of Cusa's Direct Schema of Gender Identity		
Level of Identity	Masculinity	Femininity
Intellectual Level: actuality and potentiality	The masculine is the actuality of femininity.	The feminine is the potentiality of masculinity.
whole and part	The masculine is like the whole.	The feminine is like the part.
light and dark	The masculine is closer to light. The light is the masculinity of femininity. The light is the masculinity of darkness.	The feminine is closer to darkness. The shadow is the femininity of masculinity. The darkness is the femininity of light.
unity and otherness	The masculine is unity in nature.	The feminine is otherness in nature.
enfolding and unfolding	Enfolding is the masculinity of unity.	Unfolding is the femininity of otherness.
noble and ignoble	The intellectual region is of masculine, subtle, most unified, most noble nature. In intellectual masculinity, femininity is absorbed and the masculine is fertilized unitively in itself.	

Nicholas of Cusa's Direct Schema of Gender Identity (cont.)		
Level of Identity	Masculinity	Femininity
The Sensible Level: male and female bodies	Masculinity absorbs femininity in different ways: e.g., in masculine animals there is an indication of breasts.	Femininity absorbs masculinity in different ways.
masculine and feminine seeds	Beings coming from masculine seeds have overcome femininity. The masculine seed contracts the feminine in itself.	Beings coming from feminine seeds have overcome masculinity. The feminine seed contracts the masculine in itself.
masculine and feminine members of species	The masculine, as actual, is more like a tree. In more noble species, the masculine is superior to the feminine, e.g., pears, lions, humans.	The feminine, as potential, is more like a seed. In less noble species the feminine is superior to the masculine, e.g., wheat.
man and woman in human generation	In animals, male generates in female.	In animals, female provides only the material for generation. In animals, female gives birth externally.
		In vegetative femininity, otherness determines the masculine nature in itself, and it fructifies unfoldedly.

The above chart indicates how many traditional gender polarity categories Cusanus incorporated into his analysis, in the valuation of the masculine as more noble than the feminine. At the same time, however, he also brought about a greater balance than is common to traditional gender polarity theories by his identification of the feminine with the fertility of seeds, even though the seeds were of lower or less noble species. Cusanus also introduced a dynamism of interaction of the masculine and feminine through his categories of enfolding and unfolding and eventually through his development of the theory of the coincidence of opposites. In this aspect of his thought, the feminine is no longer associated with passivity, but rather with a dynamic potentiality or fertility.

Indirect Arguments about the Concept of Woman

An area worth examining in this respect is the revaluation of the priority of actuality and possibility that Cusanus continues throughout his explorations. In other words, since he identified the concept of woman (through a predominance of femininity) more with potentiality and the concept of man (through a predominance of masculinity) more with actuality, the respective valuations of these two metaphysical categories are significant for the valuation of gender differentiation. More precisely, in the Aristotelian tradition actuality is prior to potentiality, and it associates the male with actuality, the more perfect development of the human form, and the female with the potentiality of matter, especially in generation, but also, by association, in wisdom and virtue. It follows that if Cusanus makes possibility prior to actuality, then he rejects one of the fundamental metaphysical principles of traditional gender polarity. A summary of Cusa's thinking about this topic will now be given.

There appear to be three stages in the development of Cusanus's thought about the relation of actuality and potentiality. The first stage has already been described in his early work, *On Conjectures* and *On Learned Ignorance*, in which the masculine is associated with the more noble actuality and femininity with the less noble potentiality, yet the two are in dynamic relation by the dialectic of unfolding and enfolding. In a second stage, Cusanus introduces a category of the *"posse"* or the "can-is," which seems to unify the potential and the actual.[41] In this stage, in a text entitled *De Possest,* absolute possibility and actuality are joined in a coeternal union.[42] In the third stage, Cusanus appears to argue that possibility itself is the highest priority. In his 1464 text *De apice theoriae (On the Summit of Contemplation),* possibility itself is described as that "than which nothing can be more powerful or prior or better. . . ."[43] As Peter Casarella points out, Cusanus in defending this thesis "achieves an outright reversal of the Aristotelian-Thomistic priority of God's actuality . . . once it is maintained that in God possibility is itself prior to actuality."[44]

It is important to note that there is a difference between infinite possibility, which Cusanus identifies as being fundamental to the Divine Identity, and a specified potentiality, which he had previously associated with female identity. The for-

---

41. See Nicholas of Cusa, "On the Summit of Contemplation," in *Nicholas of Cusa: Selected Spiritual Writings,* pp. 293-303, and Casarella, "Nicholas of Cusa and the Power of the Possible," *American Catholic Philosophical Quarterly* 64, no. 1 (Winter 1990): 7-34.

42. See Casarella, "Nicholas of Cusa and the Power of the Possible," *American Catholic Philosophical Quarterly* 64, no. 1 (Winter 1990): 18-26.

43. Nicholas of Cusa, "On the Summit of Contemplation," in *Nicholas of Cusa: Selected Spiritual Writings,* 5, 295.

44. Casarella, "Nicholas of Cusa and the Power of the Possible," *American Catholic Philosophical Quarterly* 64, no. 1 (Winter 1990): 27.

mer is the possibility of all possibilities, infinite in extension, and ontologically prior to all specified potentiality. The latter is a particular finite potentiality in the world, which has a specified capacity for a particular kind of actualization. Thus, it is not possible to argue that Nicholas of Cusa's revaluation of the Aristotelian priority of actuality over potentiality, by his assertion that possibility itself is prior to actuality in the Divine, has direct consequences for the concept of woman. On the other hand, to the extent to which he places in question the absolute priority of actuality, it could be argued that Cusanus may have raised some doubts about some premises of Aristotelian metaphysics, and that these doubts could encourage the questioning of other aspects of the Aristotelian schema. From my perspective, however, it would be more accurate to maintain the original Aristotelian-scholastic thesis of the priority of actuality over potentiality, and to elevate the concept of woman to include more kinship to actuality, than to devaluate actuality and elevate possibility or potentiality as a way of enhancing woman's identity.[45]

There are several other, more accurate, ways in which the philosophy of Nicholas of Cusa prepared the way for the eventual overturning of Aristotelian metaphysical, natural, and epistemological principles of gender polarity. In fact, it is likely that his indirect arguments had more long-term effects on the history of the concept of woman than did his direct schema of masculinity and femininity. Aristotle had argued that the earth was the heavy, static center of the world, and since the earth was cosmically identified as "mother," this physics of the macrocosm contributed to the devaluation of woman's identity. Nicholas of Cusa challenged two aspects of Aristotle's view: he argued that the earth was in motion, and that it was not at the center of the world. In *On Learned Ignorance,* Cusanus summarizes his position as follows:

> The earth, which cannot be the center, cannot lack all motion. In fact, it is even necessary that it be moved in such a way that it could be moved infinitely less. Therefore, just as the earth is not the center of the world, so the sphere of fixed stars is not its circumference, even though, by comparison of earth with the sky, the earth itself seems nearer the center and the sky nearer the circumference. . . . For even if at some distance from the center the earth were revolving on an axis through the poles of the sphere in such a way that one part of the earth would face upward towards one pole of the sphere and the other part downward toward the other pole, then, clearly, only half the sphere would be visible to those on the earth, who would stand at as great a distance from the poles as the horizon is extended. Furthermore, the very center of the world is not more within the world than outside it; nor does this earth or any sphere even have a center. Because the center is a point equidistant from the circumference and because it is impossible for there to be a sphere or a circle so perfectly true that a truer one could not be

---

45. A similar argument could be made against some process theorists who make a similar move to Cusa's in suggesting that a pantheistic approach demands the devaluation of the notion that the Divine can only be pure act. For a consideration of some aspects of this topic see Dermot Moran, "Pantheism from John Scotus Erigena to Nicholas of Cusa," *American Catholic Philosophical Quarterly* 64, no. 1 (1990): 131-52.

given, it is evident that to any given center an even truer and more precise center could always be given. Precise equidistance to different points cannot be found outside God, for God alone is infinite equality.[46]

Nicholas of Cusa's argument for the motion of the earth rests on his mathematical understanding of the perfect structure of the world. He rejects Aristotle's empirical approach in favor of a mathematical calculation of the perfect center of the world, which will in time be able to be empirically tested. In the process, the earth is revitalized from its previously heavy, passive characterization by Aristotle. Cusanus repeats himself to be certain that his readers understand his conclusion: "It is clear from what has been stated that the earth is moved."[47]

At this point in his argument Cusanus introduces a theory of the relativity of perspective in a person's consideration of the earth that explodes traditional ways of understanding. His argument anticipates not only the Copernican revolution,[48] but also aspects of the contemporary theory of relativity:

> If, therefore, in light of what has just been said you wish truly to understand something about the motion of the universe, you must make use of your imagination as much as possible and enfold the center with the poles. Suppose one observer were situated on the earth and underneath the northern pole and another on the pole itself; just as to the one on the earth the pole would seem to be at the zenith so to the other on the pole the center would appear at the zenith. Just as the antipodes have the sky above, as we have, so to those at either of the two poles the earth would appear to be at the zenith, and wherever a person finds oneself, one will believe one is at the center. Therefore, enfold these different images, so that the center is the zenith and vice versa, and then by means of your intellect, which is aided only by learned ignorance, you come to see that the world and its motion and shape cannot be grasped, for it will appear as a wheel in a wheel and a sphere in a sphere, nowhere having a center or a circumference, as we said.[49]

By appealing to the reader to use the imagination, and then the intellect, Cusanus has opened new possibilities for understanding the identity of the earth. He does not leave it at this mental experiment, however, but states its consequences several times: "The earth's shape, therefore, is noble and spherical, and its motion circular, but it could be more perfect"; and "The earth, therefore, is a noble star, which has light, heat, and influence. . . ."[50]

46. Nicholas of Cusa, "On Learned Ignorance," in *Nicholas of Cusa: Selected Spiritual Writings,* II.11.157, 158.

47. Nicholas of Cusa, "On Learned Ignorance," in *Nicholas of Cusa: Selected Spiritual Writings,* II.11.159, 159.

48. See Prudence Allen, "Mother Earth and Father Sun in Copernicus and Galileo," *Lonergan Review* 3 (1994): 271-88.

49. Nicholas of Cusa, "On Learned Ignorance," in *Nicholas of Cusa: Selected Spiritual Writings,* II.11.160, 160.

50. Nicholas of Cusa, "On Learned Ignorance," in *Nicholas of Cusa: Selected Spiritual Writings,* II.12.164 and 166, 161-62.

In Aristotelian cosmology, the four elements fire, air, water, and earth, were arranged in a hierarchical schema leading up to the unmoved mover as pure nonmaterial act, with the most superior being like fire and the inferior like earth. This hierarchical valuation also occurred in Aristotle's description of the sun and the higher planets as partaking most of the nature of fire. Since the qualities of the sun were associated more with the male, and the qualities of the earth more with the female, they were given a gender polarity valuation as well. However, in Nicholas of Cusa's schema, there is no hierarchical ordering of elements or of the universe *per se* because the Divine is equally close to every point, since God is both center and circumference of the universe. Thus the Aristotelian gender polarity valuation, present throughout the whole cosmos, is overturned by Nicholas of Cusa's new cosmology.

Cusanus thus argues that when the earth is compared with the sun there is no reason to conclude that the earth is inferior. His argument unfolds in several parts:

> The fact that the earth is smaller than the sun and is under its influence is no reason to say that the earth is inferior, for the entire region of the earth, which stretches to the circumference of fire, is great. . . .
>
> In addition, the influence that the earth receives is no evidence of its imperfection. For as a star it perhaps equally influences the sun and its region, as was stated. . . .
>
> Not even the fact that the things of earth perish, as we know from experience, is an effective argument that the earth is ignoble.[51]

Cusanus still includes some aspects of traditional Aristotelian valuations. For example, while considering the possibility of different inhabitants on the sun, the moon, and the earth he suggests characteristics for the sun that are similar to those he also identified with masculinity and for the earth that are similar to those he also identified with femininity:

> We surmise that in the sun's region the inhabitants are more solar, bright, illuminated, and intellectual, even more spiritual than those on the moon, who are more lunar, and than those on the earth, who are more material and more weighty. We also presume that these solar intellectual natures are mostly actual and only a little potential, while the earthly natures are more potential and a little actual and the lunar natures fluctuate in between.[52]

In addition, Cusanus also considers possible ways in which, when a member of a particular species dies, it dissolves into its components, and the body seems to descend towards the center of the earth while the soul or form ascends to the circumference. In this context he reflects on Platonist views as well as directly gives the earth the feminine appellation of "mother earth":

51. Nicholas of Cusa, "On Learned Ignorance," in *Nicholas of Cusa: Selected Spiritual Writings,* II.12.167, 168, and 172, 162-64.

52. Nicholas of Cusa, "On Learned Ignorance," in *Nicholas of Cusa: Selected Spiritual Writings,* II.12.172, 164.

> Or who can know whether only the form returns to the exemplar or soul of the world, as the Platonists maintain, or whether only the form returns to its own star from which the species received actual being on mother earth and matter returns to possibility, while the spirit that unites them remains in the motion of the stars?[53]

It seems from the manner of expression that Cusanus is not simply repeating the Platonic description of earth as a mother, but that he is metaphorically describing the earth with a cosmic feminine description as well.

Returning to the more fundamental contribution of Nicholas of Cusa to a critique of Aristotelian cosmology, namely to his suggestions that the earth is in motion and that it is not the center of the universe, a recent commentator on the relation of humanism to science has noted the significance of Cusanus's cosmological theories for the discoveries of Copernicus, Kepler, and Galileo in the following century. "They lived at a time when an alternative to the Aristotelian/Ptolemaic cosmos had been elaborated and widely disseminated. It was for them to provide the scientific basis for that alternative."[54] Thus Cusanus can be understood as being one of the voices that had provided an alternative to Aristotelian cosmology and its devaluation of the cosmic feminine through a vertical analogy of characteristics of human mothers and of mother earth.

The final indirect contribution of Nicholas of Cusa to the history of the concept of woman is the perspectival epistemological theory that he proposed. Early in this chapter we noted his reflections on looking at the face of Christ, and how from a different perspective the face would take on a different appearance. Cusanus often compares a human with a Divine vision, and in this comparison points out perspectival aspects of knowledge and of ignorance. At the same time, however, he also introduces the theme of perspectival vision of different human beings towards things on the earth. Anticipating a Kantian theory in which the perceiver is an active participant in perception, Cusanus offers the following description in *On Learned Ignorance:*

> The ancients did not attain the truths that we have just stated, for they lacked learned ignorance. It is already clear to us that the earth, in truth, is moved, yet it may not appear this way to us, since we detect motion only by a comparison to a fixed point. How would a passenger know that one's ship was being moved, if one did not know that the water was flowing past and if the shores were not visible from the ship in the middle of the water? Since it always appears to every observer, whether on the earth, the sun, or another star, that one is as if at an immovable center of things and that all else is being moved, one will always select different poles in relation to oneself, whether one is on the sun, the earth, the moon, Mars, and so forth. Therefore, the world machine will have, one might

---

53. Nicholas of Cusa, "On Learned Ignorance," in *Nicholas of Cusa: Selected Spiritual Writings,* II.12.173, 165.

54. Pamela Long, "Humanism and Science," in *Renaissance Humanism,* vol. 3, *Humanism and the Disciplines,* p. 504.

say, its center everywhere and its circumference nowhere, for its circumference and center is God, who is everywhere and nowhere.[55]

Although the theory of perception is situated in the midst of cosmological arguments, it is remarkable and opens indirectly a new way to approach the issue of gender identity. As we noted in earlier communities of discourse that stressed the importance of dialogue among participants with different points of view, there is no doubt that early humanism also offered an epistemology of dialogue as well.

Let us apply the principles of the above paragraph to the history of the concept of woman in order to demonstrate this point. Cusanus criticized the ancients who had argued that the earth was the passive center of the universe; and he criticized them for lacking learned ignorance. Put in an inverse manner, he argued that they proposed dogmatic assertions beyond adequate foundations for knowledge. In a similar manner one could criticize ancient foundations for gender polarity, namely, that woman's nature could be explained by an appeal to the principle of contrariety and that the female was the privation of the male. In fact, Cusanus openly criticized Aristotle's theory of contrariety in a 1458 essay, *On Beryllus:*

> If Aristotle had understood the principle, which he named privation, so that this privation is the principle which establishes coincidence of opposites and is thus deprived of contrariety, because it precedes the duality which is necessary in opposites, then he would have seen correctly. The timidity, however, to acknowledge that opposites are simultaneously in the same, restrained him before the truth of this principle.[56]

Aristotle chose male identity as the ideal stable point, and he then described female identity as a derived or inferior kind of being in relation to that fixed point. However, the discovery that a woman could bring a new perspective into any discourse about sex and gender identity offers an analogous example to Cusanus's ship, which one may or may not take as the stable point of observation. The observer may consider the self to be the stable point, and therefore, the center of the world will be wherever there is an observer, a man or a woman.

Again, it would go beyond the limits of the purpose of the present text to consider in more depth the issues of Nicholas of Cusa's perspectival epistemology. Others have already begun this important work.[57] It is important to note only that this view has implications for the revaluation of a woman's perspectives on her own identity in relation to a man's perspectives. It offers a rationale for philosophy being undertaken in the form of a dialogue among different persons. Dialogue becomes an experience of another as well as an experience of truth; it opens a real experience

---

55. Nicholas of Cusa, "On Learned Ignorance," in *Nicholas of Cusa: Selected Spiritual Writings,* II.12.162, 160.

56. Nicholas of Cusa, "On Beryllus," in *Towards a New Council of Florence,* XXV, 322.

57. Clyde Lee Miller, "Perception, Conjecture, and Dialectic in Nicholas of Cusa," *American Catholic Philosophical Quarterly* 64, no. 1 (Winter 1990): 35-54.

of a coincidence of opposites, in this case of a man's and a woman's way of perceiving woman's identity and man's identity.[58] Thus, one could say that just as Cusanus opened up a metaphysical and cosmological foundation for the active movement of 'mother' earth, so he also opened up an epistemological foundation for the active movement of woman as an observer and participant in dialogue about gender identity.

We are now in the position to offer a summary chart of Nicholas of Cusa's indirect contributions to the concept of woman.

Cusanus's Indirect Arguments about the Concept of Woman				
Principles	Aristotelian View	Relation to Traditional Gender Polarity	Cusanus's View	Possible Implications
Metaphysical Principles	Actuality prior to Potentiality	Man's identity more akin to actuality; woman's identity more akin to potentiality	Possibility itself prior to actuality Masculine more akin to actuality; feminine more akin to specified potentiality	Raising doubts about certitude of Aristotelian schema
	In two contraries one is always the privation of the other.	The female is the contrary privation of the male.	Masculine and feminine opposites enfold and unfold into one another and ultimately coincide. Neither is the absolute privation of the other.	The female and the feminine are shifted from a position of contrary privation to equal opposites moving towards complements.

58. For the theological foundations of Cusanus's theory of the relation of dialogue and coincidence of opposites, see Bond, introduction to *Nicholas of Cusa: Selected Spiritual Writings*, pp. 43-50.

Cusanus's Indirect Arguments about the Concept of Woman (cont.)				
Principles	Aristotelian View	Relation to Traditional Gender Polarity	Cusanus's View	Possible Implications
Principles of Natural Philosophy	The earth is the heavy, passive center of the universe.	Mother earth as cosmic feminine is heavy, passive, and ignoble.	The earth moves and is the center of the universe.	Prepares the way for Kepler, Galileo, and the Copernican Revolution Mother earth is no longer passive but active.
	The earth is less noble than the sun.		The earth is as noble as the sun.	The cosmic feminine and cosmic masculine are revalued from a relation of polarity to one moving towards complementarity.
	Generation occurs by the union of the active formal contribution and the passive material contribution.	The male contribution of seed to generation is associated with form; the female contribution of no seed or infertile seed is associated with matter.	Accepts the Aristotelian view of generation, but also associates the feminine with fertile seed	Imaginary association of the feminine with fertile seed raises possibilities for later discovery of women's contribution of fertile seed to generation.

Cusanus's Indirect Arguments about the Concept of Woman (cont.)				
Principles	Aristotelian View	Relation to Traditional Gender Polarity	Cusanus's View	Possible Implications
Epistemological Principle	There is one prime model, man's, of the exercise of speculative and practical reason to achieve knowledge; all other ways are derived.	Man may exercise his rational faculty to gain knowledge and wisdom; woman has the rational faculty, but it is without authority. The virtue of a woman's rational faculty is limited to true opinion.	Introduces the argument that perception, judgment, and knowledge are perspectival	Offers an epistemological schema that is consistent with the need for dialogue Implies that a woman's and a man's perspective would be different and both helpful in determining knowledge about the human being

In terms of the ultimate influence on the history of the concept of woman, most important of all of these indirect arguments was Nicholas of Cusa's scientific approach to Aristotelian theory of the respective positions and nature of earth and sun. Cusanus's argument that the earth was not the heavy passive center of the universe, but was in motion played a part in preparing the way for the Copernican revolution and the overturning of Aristotelian and Ptolemaic astronomy. With the historical metaphorical association of the concept of woman with mother earth, this contribution also helped overcome traditional gender polarity.

Nicholas of Cusa, cardinal, philosopher, and church reformer was a brilliant and complex thinker. The invention of the printing press helped considerably the dispersion of his writings. His complete works were published in 1488 in Strasbourg, 1502 in Italy, 1514 in Paris, and 1565 in Basel.[59] Yet, perhaps because of the mathematical and abstract manner of his expression, Cusanus did not be-

---

59. Bond, introduction to *Nicholas of Cusa: Selected Spiritual Writings,* p. 77, note 70.

come a popular writer. Nevertheless, for the history of the concept of woman he stands as a most significant theorist, who genuinely sought to articulate a new theory of the relation of masculinity to femininity even though his works did not have a direct or immediate influence on other authors interested in the same theme.

LEON BATTISTA ALBERTI (1404-1472)

Jacob Burckhardt in his classic study, *The Civilisation of the Renaissance in Italy* characterizes Leon Battista Alberti as a man filled with zeal for dialogue with anyone about anything:

> Under the pressure of poverty, he studied both civil and canonical law for many years, till exhaustion brought on a severe illness. In his twenty-fourth year, finding his memory for words weakened, but his sense of facts unimpaired, he set to work at physics and mathematics. And all the while he acquired every sort of accomplishment and dexterity, cross-examining artists, scholars, and artisans of all descriptions, down to the cobblers, about the secrets and peculiarities of their craft.[60]

Alberti excelled in a number of areas: athletics, painting, sculpture, architecture, music, mathematics, literature, law, and philosophy.[61] He is also credited with having written a grammar of the Tuscan language thought to be, together with Dante's *De vulgari eloquentia,* one of the first grammars of a living European language. Two particular characteristics are often identified with Alberti's approach to any subject: (1) combining the old with the new, and (2) introducing perspective. The pattern of combining a classical form with contemporary content was common to Alberti's contributions in a number of areas. His great success as a Renaissance man was due to his ability to forge this union of the old with the new.[62] As mentioned earlier in the introduction to this text, Alberti was also the first to articulate laws of perspective in painting and architecture. With his love of communication and the use of the dialogue form, Alberti sought both to identify different perspectives in a common painted scene and also to introduce different perspectives into a discussion about a common theme. These characteristics are applied to his concept of woman as well.

While Alberti introduced perspective into his dialogues about the identity of man and the family, he also maintained a consistent approach to the concept of woman. Alberti reasserted a gender polarity position within humanist discourse for

---

60. Jacob Burckhardt, *The Civilisation of the Renaissance in Italy,* trans. S. G. C. Middlemore (New York: The Macmillan Co., 1921), pp. 136-37.

61. See Joan Kelly Gadol, *Leon Battista Alberti: Universal Man of the Early Renaissance* (Chicago: University of Chicago Press, 1969); William Harrison Woodward, *Studies in Education during the Age of the Renaissance, 1400-1600* (New York: Columbia University Press, 1967), ch. 3, pp. 48-64; and Burckhardt, *The Civilisation of the Renaissance in Italy,* p. 136.

62. Gadol, *Leon Battista Alberti: Universal Man of the Early Renaissance,* pp. 215-18.

a more fundamental dignity of women and men. Elements of his gender polarity theory can be seen in categories of opposites, generation, wisdom, and virtue. Alberti argues that women and men are in opposition by their desire to control one another, that generation of male heirs and maintenance of order in the household are woman's tasks in marriage, that woman should not be highly educated or allowed access to libraries, and that woman is virtuous by silence, obeying her husband, and ruling within the private sphere of the household, while man is virtuous by participation in public speech and works, by ruling others, and participating in true friendships with other men.

Alberti was the illegitimate son of a noble father, Lorenzo Alberti, an exiled merchant banker from Florence, and Bianca di Carol Fieschi, a widowed aristocratic mother.[63] His mother died just two years after Leon Battista was born, and his father died when he was seventeen. His childhood was marked by much traveling and moving among different cities: Genoa, Venice, and Bologna.[64] Alberti studied in Bologna and in Padua, earning a Doctorate in Civil Law in 1428. As noted in the first part of this chapter, the Faculty of Arts at the University of Padua was a staunch defender of Aristotelian philosophy, and it was thus a prime location for the transmission of an academic foundation for gender polarity. However, Padua was also the city in which humanism was developing, and Alberti imbibed through his association with the school of Gasparino Barzizza humanistic attitudes, especially towards language, literature, and mathematics.[65] Alberti was well versed in Latin, Greek, the Tuscan dialect of the Italian language, and basic principles of mathematics and natural science.

Leon Battista Alberti was ordained a priest and spent his life in service of the Church, first in Bologna, Rome, and Mantua before 1434, when he came to Florence, the city of his exiled youth, but now in the employment of the papal chancery. This was an extraordinary opportunity for Alberti as Leonardo Bruni was the Chancellor of Florence, and Italian humanism was flourishing there under his leadership. "Florence, Eugenius IV's haven during his exile from the Eternal City, thus provided residence for nearly all the leading humanists of the day, and Alberti, like other humanists, benefited from this stimulus."[66] In addition to drawing inspiration from the humanism that was already present in Florence, Alberti introduced into the civic humanist community of discourse an interest in natural science. He also incorporated artists into the same community by his treatise *On Painting*. In these ways Alberti extended the range of persons to be incorporated into humanist communities of discourse from its previous base of historians, educators, poets, orators, and politicians, to include scientists, visual artists, and architects as well.

63. Charles L. Stinger, "Humanism in Florence," in *Renaissance Humanism,* vol. 1, *Humanism in Italy,* p. 190. See also Cecil Grayson, "The Humanism of Alberti," *Italian Studies* 12 (1957): 37-56, 38.

64. Woodward, *Studies in Education,* p. 49.

65. Renée Neu Watkins, introduction to Leon Battista Alberti, *The Family in Renaissance Florence* (Columbia, S.C.: University of South Carolina Press, 1969), p. 5.

66. Stinger, "Humanism in Florence," in *Renaissance Humanism,* vol. 1, *Humanism in Italy,* p. 190.

It is also worth recalling that during the years 1438-39 Alberti took part in the famous Church Council at Ferrara-Florence along with Leonardo Bruni, Nicholas of Cusa, and Lorenzo Valla. During the Council the humanists had a running seminar, or community of discourse with one another, about common areas of interest. According to Ernst Cassirer, the bond between Cusanus and Alberti strengthened over time, and "[a]side from their personal relationship, there are the references in Alberti's main theoretical works to Cusanus' mathematical and philosophical speculation, especially to his studies in method relative to the problem of squaring a circle."[67]

Describing a sequence of events connecting humanism and science in Florence, Pamela Long suggests that Manuel Chrysoloras in 1400 brought a copy of the Greek text of Ptolemy's *Cosmographia* when he introduced the teaching of Greek into Florence. Ptolemy describes in his text a method of projection that introduced the notion of linear perspective. That Alberti wrote his treatise on perspective in painting just one year after arriving in Florence in 1434 attests to the creative environment of the city at the time. Ptolemy's text probably influenced (together with Filippo Brunelleschi and Cenvino Cennini) Alberti's own development of a theory of perspective in two areas: painting and cartography:

> In his treatise *De pictura (On Painting)* (1435), Alberti transformed painting into a humanist discipline. He conceived it as a mathematical subject by virtue of its new tool of geometric perspective. He also gave it a rhetorical component; through its *istoria,* the painting should move the soul of the viewer. . . .
>
> Alberti's interest in practice extended to scientific subjects. He was a cartographer who made the most accurate map of Rome of its time, and he wrote a treatise on practical measurement (*Ludi matematici,* c. 1450). . . .[68]

Long suggests that this work of Alberti's may have also been partly responsible, along with Toscanelli's works, for the development of maps that enabled Christopher Columbus to discover the New World in 1492.

With this introduction to Leon Battista Alberti's general areas of interest, it is obvious that consideration of the concept of woman is simply one theme among many in his illustrious career as a true Renaissance man. At the same time, however, Alberti wrote at least six works that include direct reflections on woman's identity in relation to man. These works, all written in the vernacular Tuscan, can be dated approximately as follows:[69]

67. Cassirer, *The Individual and the Cosmos in Renaissance Philosophy,* pp. 50-51.

68. Pamela O. Long, "Humanism and Science," in *Renaissance Humanism,* vol. 3, *Humanism and the Disciplines,* p. 493. See also Leon Battista Alberti, *On Painting,* ed. and trans. J. R. Spencer (New Haven: Yale University Press, 1956).

69. It is worth noting that a fifteenth-century edition of Leon Battista Alberti's *Hecatomphila sive de amore* was published in Venice; and slightly later an *Opera nonnulla* was published in Florence. See Leonardas Vytautas Gerulaitis, *Printing and Publishing in Fifteenth-Century Venice* (Chicago: American Library Association, 1976), pp. 86 and 134.

Before 1428	*Deifira*
	Ecatonfila
1432-37	*Della famiglia*
1432-34	Parts I-III
1437	Part IV
Around 1437	*De amore*
	Sofrona
After 1437	*Momus*

The concept of woman was something that held the interest of Alberti for much of his adult life. The first two dialogues were written by Alberti before he completed his doctoral studies in Padua, Parts I-III of *Della famiglia* were written while he was in Rome, and Part IV was written after he moved to Florence. The last three dialogues, all satires, were written while he was living in Florence.

Alberti's legacy with respect to the concept of woman has been controversial. On the one hand, he is credited, and rightly so, with having given serious attention to the interior structure of marriage and governing of a large household. In this context, he focused on the position of woman, and brought the whole question of the intimate relation of husband and wife into the forefront of philosophical discourse. This contribution to the history of the concept of woman is noteworthy and, like Albrecht von Eyb, Alberti begins to correct the situation in which issues central to the family were often excluded from academic communities of discourse.

At the same time, however, when the content of Alberti's concept of woman is carefully analyzed, it reveals rather extreme gender polarity principles. Therefore, paradoxically an effect of Alberti's focus on the place of women in the family was to offer a renewed version of traditional devaluation of woman's identity. The one exception to this general pattern was his development of the theory that a woman ought to govern her household of children and servants in a good and proper order, through the authority delegated to her by her husband. In this particular aspect, Alberti suggests that a woman is capable of ruling both herself and others. Alberti also attempted, but unsuccessfully it seems, to Christianize a utilitarian approach to conjugal relations. His utilitarian approach will be both described and evaluated according to humanistic principles.

Generally speaking, Alberti views women as dangerous and controlling of men and suggests that they share this characteristic with the feminine personification of fortune. A man, therefore, has to wrest control from both fortune and women by exercising his reason and will, and also by carefully setting boundaries to what women can or cannot do in their lives. Consequently, Alberti subordinates women's development as persons within his conception of the needs of a man and his family. While men are encouraged to develop all their intellectual capacities and to exercise these in civic society, in friendship with other men, women are to be kept from being educated and are also to be separated from the task of educating boys, including even their own sons. Alberti's perceptions offer what could be described as a regressive view of women's educative role in the family. For Alberti, the development of boys and of men demands the repression of the intellectual development of girls and women.

There is another paradoxical area of Alberti's legacy that needs to be noted. Alberti emerges as among one of the first authors to articulate a conscious awareness that others (and especially women) will not agree with his conclusions, and in a remarkable way, he allows both female and male characters in his dialogues to express reservations about his claims. This indicates that he was able to entertain a perspective of opposition to his own gender polarity views. However, in the end, other characters in his dialogues always reassert the original position, which generally devalues women's identity. The overall effect is that his texts offer an even stronger argument for his gender polarity position, which views a man and a woman in struggle for control over one another. As a consequence, Alberti rejects an engendered relationship based on passionate sexual love and suggests instead a relationship based only on a friendship of utility and unequal virtues.

Our analysis of Alberti's works will focus on: first, his earliest dialogues, *Deifira* and *Ecatonfila;* second, his most well-known dialogue, *Della famiglia;* and third, two of his later dialogues, *De amore* and *Sofrona.* By using a chronological approach, it is possible to demonstrate the consistency of Alberti's concept of woman. Because he is such an important and controversial figure, many of the passages that directly concern the concept of woman will be included. Texts from the early and later dialogues are translated into English for the first time, and those from the middle dialogue on the family are put into a systematic ordering. Summary charts of Alberti's conclusions are presented after each of the three stages of this analysis.

Early Concept of Woman

In one of his earliest dialogues entitled *Deifira,* Alberti states a theme that will continue through all his works: that a woman seeks to enslave a man by love. This theme echoes Cavalcanti's claim that love destroys the lover because the intensity of passions interferes with the exercise of reason and will. This negative view of love and its identification of woman as its cause was somewhat modified by later humanist arguments of Dante and Petrarch. Alberti, however, seems to adopt the earlier view when he portrays a dialogue between a young man, Pallimacro, who is suffering from the effects of his love for Deifira, and an advisor, Filarco, who seeks to free him from this suffering. There are four general steps in the argument:

1. Love for a woman destroys a man's capacity to reason and to will, and it makes a man a slave of woman;
2. Woman is an unworthy object for this love because of her natural inconstancy (which she shares with Fortune).
3. Therefore, the object of the love, woman, should be rejected;
4. Friendship between men should be embraced instead.

Because of the fact that Alberti repeats this general structural argument throughout all his works on women's identity, each of the steps will be described in further detail.

In *Deifira*, Pallimacro often states the effects that love has had upon him; one such example is as follows:

> **Pallimacro:** I did not intentionally want to become a slave, and fall victim, to love. However, one sometimes loses control of his desires and chases what is harmful to him. I affirm that I was forced to love. I loved, against my volition. I wanted that which I hated and I hated that which I said and did continually. I did not wish to follow the Fortune which has led me in this misery. But what man so cold could abstain from loving someone who gives him love, as I have been given?[70]

After Pallimacro described his enslavement to Deifira, Filarco then advised: "Oh crazy Pallimacro! Is this how little you value your freedom? Were you so foolish as to become a woman's servant?"[71] Pallimacro, for his part, confesses: "Even though I have tried to stop myself by appealing to my senses, I could not escape from love's fervour."[72] His reason and his will are captive to the woman he loves, and he feels incapable of making a different decision.

Filarco moves into the second stage of the argument and here seeks to demonstrate that woman is an unworthy object of a man's love.

> **Filarco:** At this point, I wish to explain something of women's nature to you naive lovers who quickly become slave to her. As everyone can see, it is in woman's nature to oppose and dominate. This is where that old proverb stems from: "She wants not that which you do, she wants that which you do not."[73]

The theme of women's inconstancy, which had been so prominent in the gender polarity literature, reappears in *Deifira*:

> **Filarco:** Pallimacro, everything in life has an end. Do not be surprised if this feminine and fickle soul does not reach to you as she once did. It is foolish to think that they [women] are constant. Certainly, there is an end to your love as well. . . . More frequently than men, women become suspicious and hold grudges without reason. No other enemy but a woman could be so cold as not to feel any sorrow for her lover's pain. But if you wish not to fall in love, realize the pain involved in loving.[74]

---

70. Leon Battista Alberti, "Deifira," in *Opera Volgari,* ed. Cecil Grayson (Bari: Laterza, 1960), vol. III, pp. 224-46, esp. p. 230. All passages are translated by Clelia Giangrande.

71. Alberti, "Deifira," in *Opera Volgari,* III, 232.

72. Alberti, "Deifira," in *Opera Volgari,* III, 233.

73. Alberti, "Deifira," in *Opera Volgari,* III, 233.

74. Alberti, "Deifira," in *Opera Volgari,* III, 236.

The thought that the woman he loves could be his enemy is difficult for Pallimacro to accept. He addresses his thought to the absent Deifira, but Filarco presses his own argument to its conclusion:

> **Pallimacro**: Alas, my sweet Deifira, how could I ever believe you to be my enemy? I have done nothing but praise you. Perhaps you have been annoyed that I loved you too much and that I have been patient with you? What do you want from me, Deifira, what do you want?
>
> **Filarco**: I shall tell you. She wishes that you are consumed in your abundant love for her. And I shall remind you, Pallimacro, that women know either how to love or how to hate. The sooner a woman's heart sparks with love, the earlier it inflames with spite; she is not constant in anything other than bearing grudges. . . .
>
> **Pallimacro**: There could never be enough animosity to destroy my love for you, Deifira, or to consider you an enemy. And what will my life without you be like? Miserable and painful.
>
> **Filarco**: Instead it will be free of worry. Deifira's life, on the other hand, will be miserable because her spite will consume her with rage.
>
> **Pallimacro**: And how could I stay without loving you, Deifira?
>
> **Filarco**: But you could never know without trying.[75]

At this point in the argument Filarco returns to his original claim, introduced at the beginning of the dialogue, that woman is an unworthy object of love. Since he has not been successful in convincing Pallimacro to come to a new decision in his relationship with Deifira, he tries one further action to bring about a change:

> **Filarco**: But since you have not made it possible to give an easy remedy to your predicament, there is only one thing left. Flee far away from her, from her family and from anything that reminds you of her. The further you go, the more love will tire in pursuing you. Love that is unnourished, perishes.
>
> **Pallimacro**: Poor Pallimacro! You shall flee from your country, friends and family. Perhaps it is a just punishment for having loved too much. . . .[76]

In the context of the dialogue, Filarco had shared with Pallimacro the fact that he, too, had suffered in the past from this intense kind of love for a woman. In his earlier dialogue, *Ecatonfila*, Alberti revealed that Ecatonfila was his own first love.[77] Using her voice throughout the dialogue Alberti has her describe characteristics in

---

75. Alberti, "Deifira," in *Opera Volgari*, III, 242.
76. Alberti, "Deifira," in *Opera Volgari*, III, 243-44.
77. Leon Battista Alberti, "Ecatonfila," in *Opera Volgari*, III, 199-219.

an ideal man to love, characteristics that appear to fit some aspects of Alberti's own self-description: not too old, not too young, not too rich (he was rich), not too handsome (he was handsome), not too famous (he was famous), but with prudence, modesty, virtue, and intelligence. Finally, he suggests through Ecatonfila that when a woman finds this kind of man, she should esteem him highly, not be suspicious, and remain faithful or constant in her love for him. This early essay, then, offers a description of woman's nature in contrast to those found in Alberti's other writings about woman. It is almost the mirror image of his usual claims about woman's identity. This could be understood then as an ideal to which women should aim, but which, by nature, most fail to reach.

To return to our consideration of the *Deifira:* Filarco places his discussion in the context of the friendship between Pallimacro and himself. It is here that the fourth step of his argument can be reviewed. Filarco claims that he can help Pallimacro overcome his unhappy situation because of their friendship, but it demands that Pallimarco be willing to share the causes of his suffering with him:

> Filarco: But what is this that cannot be communicated to someone who loves you? Is this secret that cannot be shared so devious? Careful, if you demonstrate little trust in me, I could no longer consider you a true friend. He who does not trust, fears betrayal; and one cannot love someone who thinks him to be perfidious. Love has always been the seed of friendship and friendship blossoms when love is exchanged. Friendship dictates trust and merit. If you place trust in me, I will prove my worth to you.[78]

The comparison of friendship between men with love between a man and a woman is a theme that Alberti returns to time and again. In the above example we also see the secondary theme of the inconstancy of women and the constancy of men. A third theme is the polarized dynamic of control and freedom that operates in love in contrast to an equality of sharing that is found in friendship. Again at the beginning of the *Deifira* Filarco describes the dynamics of friendship among the two men:

> Filarco: My dear Pallimacro, I cannot but be surprised to see you in such a state. I wish to discover what reasons caused this unhappiness in you — you, a young, rich, beautiful, virtuous, prudent and studious man whom so many others admire. Since I know how you consider me to be one of your most admirable friends, I felt it my right and duty to ask that you confide your burden to me. Having been moved by your anguish, I truly wish to help rid you of this pain. It is not only useful to one's soul, but it is also a virtue to do so. If I seem bothersome to you, just remember that together, two can accomplish that which one cannot. Therefore, I can either help you overcome your pain or share it with you.[79]

78. Alberti, "Deifira," *Opera Volgari,* III, 227.
79. Alberti, "Deifira," in *Opera Volgari,* III, 225.

When this beautiful description of the potential of the friendship of equals is compared with the polarized dynamic of control and enslavement of unequal persons that seems to mark the relations of man and woman, the difference is remarkable. As will be seen in the subsequent analysis of both Alberti's major work *Della famiglia* and his later dialogues, this contrast is a constant feature of his philosophy.

Characteristics associated with the concept of woman in Alberti's early dialogue *Deifira* are summarized as follows:

Alberti's Early Concept of Woman		
Category of Relation	Pallimacro	Filarco
Love of a man for a woman	Love enslaved Pallimacro to Deifira.	It is foolish for a man to be enslaved to a woman. A woman is an unworthy object of love: a. woman's nature is to dominate man. b. woman is fickle. c. woman is always inconstant. d. woman is suspicious. e. women hold grudges without reason.
	Cannot believe that Deifira is his enemy	Woman is man's enemy: a. woman either hates or loves. b. if she loves, she then turns to spite and to rage.
	Cannot govern his passion of love by his reason or will	If man does accept that woman is unworthy object of love, then the remedy is to flee far away from relation with woman.
Friendship between two men	Sees Filarco as his admirable friend: a. he shares his story of enslavement to love. b. he accepts Filarco's advice and decides to flee Deifira.	Man can be a constant and trusted friend of man: a. a friend can share a burden through communication. b. a friend can offer advice.

Middle Concept of Woman

In Alberti's most extensive work on the family, the concept of woman remains consistently within the gender polarity tradition. Alberti's decision to write about the family in the Tuscan dialect of the Italian language likely explains its immense success among the broader population. Alberti's first major vernacular dialogue, *Della famiglia* (The Family), was so popular that it "circulated as a handbook among the bourgeois families of fifteenth-century Florence."[80] Given Alberti's illegitimate background, his mother's early death, and his difficult life of exile from his father's home city of Florence, it is significant that he chose as the topic of this most notable work the importance of stability and education in a family. Woodward summarizes the broad intentions of Alberti as follows:

> Alberti then took the Family, its life, its common interests, its continuity, its sanctions to self-denial, its scope for corporate and personal fame, as the *milieu* within which personality could be most fitly developed, and as the end to which each member of it must devote all that he is and has. . . . The personality of the individual is the adornment of the family. The fuller, the wider his individual gifts, the greater the service rendered by the son of the house to the unity of which he is a part. In the same way the special excellence of the family — its distinction, its peculiar genius — is the contribution which that family makes to the State or City.[81]

Alberti's emphasis on the development of personality was focused only on the sons and not on the daughters of the family, and in civic humanism; the gift to the city-state of the developed talents of the family member held true only for husbands, not for wives. Thus, even though Alberti supported the importance of education within a family, he did not extend this orientation to women. Alberti is considered a prime representative of this attitude typical of civic humanism.[82]

In this text, in English often referred to as *The Family in Renaissance Florence,* Alberti considers many themes in relation to women's identity: a prescriptive narrowing of women's education in the context of other humanist suggestions that it be broadened, a prescriptive separation of the private and public spheres with respect to women's and men's virtue, and a stereotyped development of meanings and gender polarity valuation for masculine and feminine characteristics. Alberti's discussion of gender in *Della famiglia* is divided into four chapters: (1) bringing up children, (2) marrying a wife and conceiving children, (3) household management, and (4) love and friendship.

The text on the family is constructed as a dialogue among several men with different perspectives. The characters in the dialogue are patterned on male mem-

---

80. Gadol, *Leon Battista Alberti,* p. 215.
81. Woodward, *Studies in Education during the Age of the Renaissance, 1400-1600,* p. 53.
82. For an excellent introduction to the general aspects of this new emphasis on men actively working to improve the city see Albert Rabil, Jr., "The Significance of 'Civic Humanism' in the Interpretation of the Italian Renaissance," in *Renaissance Humanism,* vol. 1, *Humanism in Italy,* pp. 141-74.

bers of Alberti's family: "Alberti's own family was both subject and object of *Della Famiglia*."[83] The dialogue is situated on the day of the death in 1421 of Lorenzo Alberti, Leon Battista's father. In the dialogue, the character of Battista represents the seventeen-year-old student Leon Battista Alberti himself. His brother Carlo is also present. Other older relatives include Adovardo, a forty-five-year-old married man with three daughters and a son; Lionardo Alberti, a twenty-nine-year-old bachelor, and Giannozzo, a distant sixty-four-year-old relative of Leon's great-grandfather. Finally, Piero and an older servant of the Alberti family named Buto complete the list of those who engage in the dialogue about family life in renaissance Florence.

Although these male characters express with greater and lesser degree of vehemence many different opinions about a man's proper identity in this context, they tend to echo the same views about women's identity. All of them argue for a type of gender polarity in which the woman is devalued in relation to the man. For this reason it is helpful to consider briefly the ancient sources that Alberti integrates into his *Della famiglia*. The most important is the Socratic philosopher Xenophon (c. 430-357 B.C.). Alberti directly tells the reader in his own voice in the Prologue to Book III that "I have done my best to imitate the charming and delightful Greek writer Xenophon."[84] In fact, Alberti's purpose was to take the principles of the Greek author and to incarnate them in a villa in Florence. Xenophon's *Oeconomicus*, on estate management, was one of the earliest texts to defend gender polarity. Leonardo Bruni's translation in 1420 of Xenophon's treatise could have been available to Alberti. It provided a foundation for the separation and attribution of unequal virtues for husband and wife. For the purposes of this analysis it is helpful to summarize Xenophon's gender polarity principles:[85]

XENOPHON'S PRINCIPLES OF GENDER IDENTITY

Xenophon's Natural Principles of Gender Identity

Woman's nature is suited to indoor tasks:
    as her body is less capable of endurance
    as she is more fearful and prone to protect stores.

Man's nature is suited to outdoor tasks:
    as his body and mind are more capable of enduring cold and heat,
    journeys and campaigns, and
    as he is more courageous and able to defend against wrongdoing.

---

83. Renée Neu Watkins, introduction to Leon Battista Alberti, *The Family in Renaissance Florence*, trans. Renée Neu Watkins (Columbia, S.C.: University of South Carolina Press, 1969), p. 4.

84. Alberti, *The Family*, III, 154.

85. Xenophon, *Memorabilia and Oeconomicus* (New York and London: G. P. Putnam's Sons and William Heinemann, 1923). See also Allen, *The Concept of Woman: The Aristotelian Revolution (750 BC–1250 AD)*, pp. 53-57 and 449-52.

Xenophon's Epistemological Principles of Gender Identity

Men and women have equal share of memory and attention.

A woman may have a 'masculine' mind with a high level of reasoning.

Xenophon's Ethical Principles of Gender Identity

Men and women have equal powers of self-control.

It is woman's duty to remain indoors
and it is man's duty to work outdoors.

It is woman's duty to obey her husband
by allowing him to determine how she governs the household
by allowing him to determine how she governs herself — including
even directives not to wear cosmetics.

Xenophon's principles, while including some elements of gender unity with respect to capacities for memory, attention, and self-control, generally distinguish separate and unequal virtues based on the premise of different natures. Alberti will incorporate all of Xenophon's gender polarity principles without giving much attention to any of the gender unity principles.

An appeal to ancient Greek philosophers was also given by Lionardo in Book II in a context in which he recommended that others study their works:

> You would do better, in fact, to explore the realm of erudition for yourselves. Take better guides and higher authorities. Among the Greeks you have Plato, Aristotle, Plutarch, Theophrastus, Demosthenes, and Basil. Among the Latins you have Cicero, Varro, Cato, Columella, Pliny, and Seneca, and there are many others. With these guides you could more successfully reach the high ground where the fruits are rich and beautiful.[86]

Lionardo and Adovardo are the only two characters in the dialogue *Della famiglia* who actually integrate these ancient philosophers into their arguments. They refer to stories or illustrations of principles rather than to arguments themselves. For example, Lionardo mentions philosophical banquets described by Plato, Xenophon, and Plutarch, and he invokes Plato to describe a man who is caught with pleasure as being like a fish on a hook. It is possible here that Alberti used Bruni's 1405-9 translation of Plato's *Apology* for his references to philosophical banquets and to views of Alcibiades. Adovardo identifies Plato as the prince of philosophers, notes that Plato and Xenophon were enemies, and mentions some correspondence between Plato and the tyrant Dion. Here again, Bruni's 1426 translation of Plato's *Letters* would have been a useful source for Plato's correspondence with the tyrant.

86. Alberti, *The Family*, II, 108.

Finally, Adovardo mentions a few views of Aristotle on friendship and a story about his refusal to choose his successor.[87] Aristotle's view of the three kinds of friendship, based on virtue, utility, and pleasure, plays a significant role in *Della famiglia,* and so it is very possible that Bruni's 1416-17 translation of Aristotle's *Nicomachean Ethics* would have served as a basis for these reflections. Still, it would seem that Alberti's gender theory must be attributed directly to his own thought and to his integration of principles derived from Xenophon, Plato, and Aristotle, as Christianized and applied to fifteenth-century Florence.

The following analysis of Alberti's *Della famiglia* will demonstrate the consistency of the concept of woman shared by the different characters in the dialogue. For greater ease of identification of those participating in this discourse on the family, each longer passage quoted will begin with the name of the speaker.

In Book II, Lionardo reveals an awareness of humanist interest in educated women as identified in classical texts. Yet, while revealing this awareness, he also dismisses it as impossible in Renaissance Florence. Alberti situates the discussion in the context of characteristics a man should look for in a wife:

> **Lionardo**: For yes, it is as you say: all marriages cannot be as I wish. Nor can all wives be like that Cornelia, the daughter of Metellus Scipio, who was married to Publius Crassus, a woman who was beautiful, well educated, skilled in music, geometry, and philosophy, and most praiseworthy of all in a woman of such abilities and virtue, not at all haughty or aloof or demanding. But let us take the advice of the slave girl, Birria, in Terence: "If you can't do what you want, then want what you can do."[88]

There is no indication in the text of why Lionardo, who is not married, cannot find the educated woman he wants as a wife. Nor is there any appeal to offer formal humanist education to women as Guarino, Vittorino, or Leonardo Bruni did. This is surprising in view of the fact that Alberti was a close friend of Ludovico Gonzaga, and had often spent time with him in Mantua, where Vittorino had established his humanist school in which Ludovico's own sister Cecilia and Barbara von Hohenzollern had flourished.[89] Instead, Lionardo limits his desires to settle for a wife "mainly to have children by her."[90] This utilitarian approach to the wife is Alberti's central view of woman's identity and purpose. There is no indication of the value of encouraging a woman to develop her intellectual capacities simply because it is a good thing to do, as Bruni had suggested, or as Ludovico Gonzaga had certainly experienced in Vittorino's school in Mantua. Thus, we can conclude that Alberti's choices concerning the concept of woman were made not out of ignorance but with full knowledge of other alternatives, and sprang, perhaps in part, from his own merchant, bourgeois upbringing.

---

87. Alberti, *The Family* (Lionardo) I, 57; IV, 271; and (Adovardo) I, 57; IV, 300, 310 and 314; and IV, 267, 310, and 315.

88. Alberti, *The Family,* II, 118-19.

89. Woodward, *Studies in Education during the Renaissance, 1400-1600,* pp. 20-21 and 24.

90. Alberti, *The Family,* II, 119.

In an earlier discussion about education of children in Book I there is a total neglect of girls' education, and a strong preoccupation with the education of sons. In this context, we see the beginning of an association of women's actions with vice and men's with virtue:

> Lionardo: Young boys should, from the first day of life, be accustomed to life among men. There they can learn virtue rather than vice.
> From early childhood on they can be made virile by activities as noble and grand as are possible for their age. They should be segregated from all feminine activities and habits.[91]

This theme of the separation of boys from feminine activities and habits is developed throughout Alberti's text so that we find him offering a very simplistic association of men with masculinity and women with femininity. In addition, with a subsequent devaluation of all that is female and feminine women become associated with vice and men with virtue.

In addition to strengthening a boy's masculinity through education, Alberti also argued that boys should be protected from girls' femininity, and men should be protected from women's femininity. Again in Book III, in the context of a discussion of the relation of a man to governing the affairs of a household the following reflections are inserted:

> Lionardo: No doubt of it, therefore, Giannozzo, those idle creatures who stay all day among the little females or who keep their minds occupied with little feminine trifles certainly lack a masculine and glorious spirit. They are contemptible in their apparent inclination to play the part of women rather than that of men. A man demonstrates his love of high achievements by the pride he takes in his own. But if he does not shun trifling occupations, clearly he does not mind being regarded as effeminate. It seems to me, then, that you are entirely right to leave the care of minor matters to your wife and to take upon yourself, as I have always seen you do, all manly and honorable concerns.[92]

It could be argued that Lionardo is concerned here only with a few boys who seem inclined to adopt women as a model for their development rather than with the education of all boys. However, his conclusion also seems to suggest that there is something harmful in the association with women, something that could inhibit the development of masculinity in a boy.

Using his own voice in the prologue to *Della famiglia,* Leon Battista Alberti offers another kind of argument that tends to the conclusion that men ought to acquire only masculine characteristics. He invokes the classic identification of fortune as a feminine force engaged in a battle with a man's reason. In the following passage from the Prologue, Alberti directly reveals what he thinks about man's struggle:

91. Alberti, *The Family,* I, 62-63.
92. Alberti, *The Family,* III, 208.

Shall we consider subject to fortune's fickle and arbitrary will these standards which men, with mature wisdom and with hard and painful efforts, set up for themselves? How can we say that fortune with her equivocal ways and her inconstancy, can ruin and destroy the very works which we most want to subordinate to our own watchfulness and reason, and not to another's whim? How shall we admit that what we fervently and laboriously strive to maintain belongs to fortune rather than to us? It is not in fortune's power, it is not as easy as some foolish people believe, to conquer one who really does not want to be conquered. Fortune has in her hand only the man who submits to her.[93]

This passage clearly shows Alberti's polarized view of a man-woman relation. Either man wins the battle with the exercise of his reason and will, or the feminine fortune wins it with her fickle and arbitrary power. He describes in a similar way the battle between a man's passions and a woman as object of his love. Either the man wins the battle by the exercise of his reason and will or the woman wins by a fickle and arbitrary power over him.

Alberti's bitter comments about fortune may have in part been due to his own suffering, through his own illegitimate birth, the death of his mother when he was only two, and his destitute poverty at the age of seventeen after the death of his father. He believed, again as part of the emerging understanding of humanism, that an individual was responsible for determining the quality of his own life. The association of a feminine personification of Fortune with inconstancy and whims carries with it the legacy of the gender polarity principle of a woman's natural inconstancy. In this context, a man's reason, on the other hand, is "more powerful than fortune" and can conquer it (or her).[94]

It is interesting to note in passing that Boethius had also argued in his *Consolation of Philosophy* that a man ought to use his reason to fight against a feminine personification of fortune, but Boethius had also introduced a feminine personification of human reason, Lady Philosophy, who led the philosopher to the appropriate conclusions. In contrast to this, Alberti has no other feminine personification than fortune, and so the development of his argument polarizes into a masculine-feminine conflict. Machiavelli will follow Alberti's lead in this development when he advises political men to fight and subdue the feminine personification of fortune.[95]

In a very interesting differentiation between a man's and a woman's ways of fighting an enemy Alberti repeats a pattern he had introduced in his earlier dialogue *Deifira*. There, Filarco had advised Pallimacro to flee his enemy, the woman who held him enslaved to love, after it became evident that he was not able or willing to withdraw his affections in her presence. Giannozzo offers similar advice to his wife in Book III of *Della famiglia*:

Now, there are only two ways of dealing with enemies, my dear. One is to defeat

93. Alberti, *The Family,* Prologue, 27-28.
94. Alberti, *The Family,* Prologue, 30.
95. See, for example, Hannah Fenichel Pitkin, *Fortune Is a Woman: Gender and Politics in the Thought of Niccolo Machiavelli* (Berkeley, Los Angeles, London: University of California Press, 1984).

them in open fight; the other is flight, if one is weak. Men ought if possible to fight and win, but women have no alternative but flight for their safety. Flee, therefore, and do not let your eye rest on any enemy of ours.[96]

It seems clear from the context that Alberti is thinking of enemies here who might engage in military combat. However, the principle underlying his reflections, when combined with other writings on facing one's enemy, implies that weakness is a characteristic of a person who flees, whether it be of a man or a woman.

Alberti views fortune primarily as a destructive force or enemy operating within a limited range. In the voice of Adovardo, in Book I of *Della famiglia,* the limitations of fortune are considered with respect to the value of human character and education above that of wealth or nobility: "Fortune cannot take all from us, I do see, not all, I admit. She cannot give us certain things either — character, virtue, letters, or any skill. All these depend on our diligence, our interest."[97] However, while it might seem as though a well-educated and virtuous humanist man could achieve a certain kind of security and confidence in the face of fortune, Lionardo in Book III implies that fortune is always lurking to destroy a man: "Our cruel fortune casts us hither and thither from day to day and never gives us peace. We are her victims, and she is ever on our trail, ever wounding, ever overwhelming us with new calamities more terrible than the old."[98] Lionardo does not despair, however, because every new attack of fortune offers the opportunity for the man to conquer bad fortune and adversity through the exercise of the mind and the cultivation of virtue. Man needs to rule fortune through his masculine strength of mind and will.

The polarization of ruling and obedience and their connection with masculine and feminine identity through association with reason and fortune are the presumed foundation for the argument that men should rule over women in *Della famiglia*. In the following passage from Book III, this dynamic is described:

> **Giannozzo**: All wives are thus obedient, if their husbands know how to be husbands. But some I see quite unwisely suppose that they can win obedience and respect from a wife to whom they openly and abjectly subject themselves. If they show by word and gesture that their spirit is all too deeply lascivious and feminine, they certainly make their wives no less unfaithful than rebellious. Never, at any moment, did I choose to show in word or action even the least bit of self-surrender in front of my wife. I did not imagine for a moment that I could hope to win obedience from one to whom I had confessed myself a slave. Always, therefore, I showed myself virile and a real man.[99]

According to this polarized view, a 'real' man, or a masculine man, never surrenders to a feminine (lascivious) spirit in a woman, just as a masculine man never surrenders to fortune.

96. Alberti, *The Family,* III, 229.
97. Alberti, *The Family,* I, 89.
98. Alberti, *The Family,* III, 183.
99. Alberti, *The Family,* III, 216-17.

When Giannozzo's general principles for relationship with his wife are first articulated, he seems to offer a very cooperative model of mutual companionship and service. His words even imply a relation of equality that substantially changes a polarity model of the wife's natural inferiority. Again, following Xenophon, Alberti introduces a military metaphor to describe the way that husband and wife share responsibility for guarding home and family:

> **Giannozzo:** We shall imitate those who stand guard on the walls of the city; if one of them, by chance, falls asleep, he does not take it amiss for his companion to wake him up that he may do his duty for his country. Likewise, my dear wife, if you ever see any fault in me, I shall be very grateful to you for letting me know. In that way I shall know that our honor and our welfare and the good of our children are dear to your heart. Likewise be not displeased if I awaken you where there is need. Where I am lacking, you shall make it good, and so together we shall try to surpass each other in love and in zeal.
>
> This property, this family, and the children to be born to us will belong to us both, to you as much as to me, to me as much as to you. It behooves us, therefore, not to think how much each of us has brought into our marriage, but how we can best maintain all that belongs to both of us. I shall try to obtain outside what you need inside the house; you must see that none of it is wasted.[100]

In spite of the extremely open and cooperative model proposed by Giannozzo here, when the specifics of the relationship are delineated, it becomes clear that there is very little complementarity or equality present. The husband decides in all areas, even to the minutest details concerning the inside of the house and the personal details of dress and manner of the wife. The woman's only role is to carry out the orders of the man, and to put into practice all the dictates he offers.

When particular ways are specified concerning how a wife should rule over the household, we find a strict delineation of ruler from the one who obeys:

> **Lionardo:** Did you teach your wife how to handle rough and uncouth persons, therefore, and how to make them obey her?
>
> **Giannozzo:** The fact is that servants are as obedient as masters are skilled in commanding. . . . I find that the best way to make the impression of a real master is to do what I told my wife to do, talk as little as possible with her maid and even less with other servants. Too much familiarity kills respect. I also told her to give her orders in detail and at frequent intervals.[101]

Neither relation of the wife to members of the household, nor relation of the husband to the wife offers any example of complementary dialogue. Instead, discourse in these relations consists in orders presented from ruler to the ruled. The ruler is

---

100. Alberti, *The Family,* III, 211.
101. Alberti, *The Family,* III, 218-19.

guarded and keeps a distance from the ruled. Giannozzo stipulated for his wife all the details of household management. One of his instructions follows below:

> **Giannozzo**: After my wife had been settled in my house a few days, and after her first pangs of longing for her mother and family had begun to fade, I took her by the hand and showed her around the whole house. I explained that the loft was the place for grain and that the stores of wine and wood were kept in the cellar. I showed her where things needed for the table were kept, and so on, through the whole house. At the end there were no household goods of which my wife had not learned both the place and the purpose.[102]

Giannozzo's instructions were so detailed that he stipulated how she should sew, clean silverware, and rotate storage for summer and winter items. As the text unfolds, it would appear as though the wife had come into her marriage with no knowledge at all of how to take care of a home. All the details of her sphere of governing activity were supplied by her husband, and her role was reduced to one of simple maintenance of the order previously established by Giannozzo. It is almost as though the husband offers the form of every decision, and the wife provides only the matter with which to carry it out.

In another example, taken almost directly from Xenophon, Giannozzo describes how he rules over his wife's gestures, expressions, clothes, and cosmetics. The tone of voice of a selection of just one of these rulings of Giannozzo reveals the extent to which he expects his wife to obey him in all matters of her person. The husband begins each of his pronouncements with the phrase "my dear wife":

> **Giannozzo**: You will disdain, first of all, those vanities which some females imagine will please men. All made up and plastered and painted and dressed in lascivious and improper clothing, they suppose they are more attractive to men than when adorned with pure simplicity and true virtue. Vain and foolish women are these who imagine that when they appear in makeup and look far from virtuous they will be praised by those who see them. They do not realize that they are provoking disapproval and harming themselves. Nor do they realize, in their petty vanity, that their immodest appearance excites numerous lustful men. . . .[103]

Then Giannozzo told about an actual situation in which his wife had appeared to wear cosmetics. After he drew an analogy between her face and a statue that had been painted and scraped off several times, he introduced an example of a woman who was poisoned by the makeup she wore. Finally, Giannozzo described to Lionardo a conversation he had with his wife after an occasion when she disobeyed his orders to not wear cosmetics:

> **Lionardo**: Yet I imagine you must have been troubled if in this matter your wife failed to obey you as she should have.

102. Alberti, *The Family*, III, 208.
103. Alberti, *The Family*, III, 213.

Giannozzo: Yes, yes, true enough. But I did not, for all that, show her that I was troubled.

Lionardo: Didn't you scold her?

Giannozzo: Ha, ha, yes, in the right way . . . it is much better to reprimand a woman temperately and gently than with any sort of harsh severity. . . .

Lionardo: How did you reprimand her?

Giannozzo: I waited until we were alone. Then I smiled at her and said, "Oh dear, how did your face get dirty? Did you by any chance bump into a pan? Go and wash yourself, quick, before these people begin to make fun of you. The lady and mother of a household must always be neat and clean if she wants the rest of the family to learn good conduct and modest demeanor."

She understood me and at once began to cry. I let her go wash off both tears and makeup. After that I never had to tell her again.

Lionardo: What a perfect wife. I can well believe that such a woman, so obedient to your word and so modest by her own nature, could elicit respect and good behavior in the rest of the household.[104]

With Alberti's description of the family, especially as voiced by Giannozzo in *Della famiglia,* there often seems to be a sense of danger or disorder lurking in the subservient member of the relationship. This was also the view of the younger Alberti, as we saw in his early work *Deifira.* There the themes that women seek to control men and that a man should not be enslaved to a woman were first introduced.[105] Thus, either a man is enslaved by a woman or he rules her. This is the constant choice that Alberti offers his reader.

The older and more traditional character, Giannozzo argues consistently for rigid distinctions between husband and wife in the home. In Book III of *Della famiglia,* when considering woman's possible access to his library we find him intentionally hiding books from his wife:

Giannozzo: Only my books and records and those of my ancestors did I determine to keep well sealed both then and thereafter. These my wife not only could not read, she would not even lay hands on them. I kept my records at all times not in the sleeves of my dress, but locked up and arranged in order in my study, almost like sacred and religious objects. I never gave my wife permission to enter that place, with me or alone. I also ordered her, if she ever came across any writing of mine, to give it over to my keeping at once. To take away any taste she might have for looking at my notes or prying into my private affairs, I often used

---

104. Alberti, *The Family,* III, 216.
105. See Evelyn Rivers Wilbanks, "The Changing Images of Women in the World of Petrarch, Boccaccio, Alberti, and Castiglione," Ph.D. Diss., University of Chicago, 1977, pp. 108-13.

to express my disapproval of bold and forward females who try too hard to know about things outside the house and about the concerns of their husband and of men in general.[106]

As Giannozzo further elaborates reasons for his policy of excluding his wife from reading or even seeing written texts, woman is clearly barred from her own educational development. In Alberti's model of utilitarian friendship between husband and wife, woman is prohibited from having access to great works of literature in philosophy, history, or theology that presumably could offer her continual sources of personal enrichment.

Her husband limits their dialogue with one another as well. Not only is there no place for intergender dialogue about philosophy, history, literature as written and shared within their culture, but there is also no place for intergender dialogue about personal matters of importance in the family:

Giannozzo: I always tried to make sure, first that she could not, and second that she did not wish to, know more of my secrets than I cared to impart. One should never, in fact, tell a secret, even a trivial one, to one's wife or any woman. I am greatly displeased with those husbands who take counsel with their wives and don't know how to confine any kind of secret to their own breast. They are madmen if they think true prudence or good counsel lies in the female brain, and still more clearly mad if they suppose that a wife will be more constant in silence concerning her husband's business than he himself has proved. Stupid husbands blab to their wives and forget that women themselves can do anything sooner than keep quiet! For this very reason I have always tried carefully not to let any secret of mine be known to a woman.[107]

At this point, the reader may be tempted to dismiss these thoughts as simply belonging to the old character Giannozzo and not representative of Alberti himself. However, in the very next sentence we find Lionardo exclaiming at the end of Giannozzo's argument: "An excellent lesson."[108] In addition, no other character offers rebuttal to these positions. Thus, it seems safe to conclude that these are Alberti's views. He is defending an extreme gender polarity position with its satirical exaggerations that women are inconstant, cannot keep silent, and cannot be trusted.

In another exchange in the dialogue, Alberti also appears to accept the epistemological principle of gender polarity that women's minds are weaker by nature than men's minds. In Book III, Lionardo refers to historical claims about women's intellectual identity: "They used to say that men are by nature of a more elevated mind than women. . . ." Putting this statement in the past tense might imply that Aristotle or some other ancient philosopher held this view, but that Lionardo did not hold it in contemporary society. However, Giannozzo soon offers a contemporary support for the same view: "Yes, you see that's my long-standing

106. Alberti, *The Family*, III, 209.
107. Alberti, *The Family*, III, 210.
108. Alberti, *The Family*, III, 210.

conviction."[109] In addition, Alberti again does not introduce any counterarguments to support a different position, so the reader is left with the conclusion that this is Alberti's view about gender identity as well. It is worth noting here that this view of the weakness of woman's mind is not shared by Xenophon, who had argued partly in support of an epistemological gender unity principle.

In another area of gender identity, the *Della famiglia* gives considerable attention to the details of the wife's duties and to the effects of her governance on the household. In the following passage we see a clear distinction between the public sphere (of the husband's range of activity) and the private sphere (of the wife's range of activity) and a linking of this distinction to differences in nature between men and women:

> **Lionardo:** The character of men is stronger than that of women and can bear the attacks of enemies better, can stand strain longer, is more constant under stress. Therefore men have the freedom to travel with honor in foreign lands, acquiring and gathering the goods of fortune. Women, on the other hand, are almost all timid by nature, soft, slow, and therefore more useful when they sit still and watch over our things. It is as though nature thus provided for our well-being, arranging for men to bring things home and for women to guard them. The woman, as she remains locked up at home, should watch over things by staying at her post, by diligent care and watchfulness. The man should guard the woman, the house, and his family and country, but not by sitting still. He should exercise his spirit and his hands in brave enterprise, even at the cost of sweat and blood.[110]

This structure and rigid distinction between women's and men's activities are repeated later by Giannozzo in a description of a conversation he had with his own wife: "It does not befit a woman like you to carry a sword, nor to do other manly things that men do."[111]

Just as the above argument repeats Xenophon's, so does the following one, where men and women are separated not only with respect to bearing arms and traveling, but also strictly separated with respect to financial aspects of daily living. Applying with exactitude Xenophon's gender polarity principle here, Alberti argues that neither men nor women ought to enter the proper domain of the other:

> **Giannozzo:** Let the father of the family follow my example. Since I find it no easy matter to deal with the needs of the household when I must often be engaged outside with other men in arranging matters of wider consequence, I have found it wise to set aside a certain amount for outside use, for investments and purchases. The rest, which takes care of all the smaller household affairs, I leave to my wife's care. I have done it this way, for, to tell the truth, it would hardly win us respect if our wife busied herself among the men in the marketplace, out in

109. Alberti, *The Family*, III, 207-8.
110. Alberti, *The Family*, III, 207-8.
111. Alberti, *The Family*, III, 226.

the public eye. It also seems somewhat demeaning to me to remain shut up in the house among women when I have manly things to do among men, fellow citizens and worthy and distinguished foreigners.[112]

Once again we perceive a devaluation of the woman with respect to the man when the author states that it is demeaning for a man to be "shut up in the house among women," and brings disrespect to a man and woman for her to busy herself "among the men in the marketplace, out in the public eye."

An important theme in *Della famiglia* is the nature of friendship. Aristotle had devoted Books VIII and IX of the *Nicomachean Ethics* to the theme of friendship, and he had argued that there are three different foundations for friendship: pleasure, utility, and virtue. A summary of Aristotle's views is important for the subsequent analysis:

> There are therefore three kinds of friendship, equal in number to the things that are loveable. . . . Now those who love each other for their utility do not love each other for themselves but in virtue of some good which they get from each other. So too with those who love for the sake of pleasure. . . . Therefore, those who love for the sake of utility love for the sake of what is good for *themselves,* and not in so far as the other is the person loved but in so far as he is useful. And thus these friendships are only incidental; for it is not as being the man he is that the loved person is loved, but as providing some good or pleasure. . . .
>
> Perfect friendship is the friendship of men who are good, and alike in virtue; for these wish well alike to each other *qua* good, and they are good in themselves. Now those who wish well to their friends for their sake are most truly friends; for they do this by reason of their own nature and not incidentally. . . .[113]

In addition, Aristotle had argued that husband and wife were unequal friends because of inequality in their natures. Again the original passage is an important reference point for Alberti's analysis:

> But there is another kind of friendship, viz. that which involves an inequality between the parties, e.g., that of father to son and in general of elder to younger, that of man to wife and in general that of ruler to subject.[114]

Alberti considers the possibility of and grounds for friendship between husband and wife and comes to the following conclusions:

1. Friendship is a better basis for relationship between husband and wife than is love;
2. The kind of friendship which a husband and wife may have is a friendship of inequality based on utility;

112. Alberti, *The Family,* III, 207.
113. Aristotle, *Nicomachean Ethics* 1156a 7-20 and 1156b 6-11. Aristotle's emphasis.
114. Aristotle, *Nicomachean Ethics,* 1158b 12-15.

3. It may be that women are even incapable of friendships of utility.

To defend the first point, that love is not a good basis for relation, Alberti has his own voice, or that of the young Battista, recall an argument previously made in *Deifira* and *De amore,* namely that love for a woman has great dangers for a man as it renders his reason and will incapable of functioning well. In *Della famiglia* the same view is presented through the words of Battista. Referring to the figure of Alcibiades from Plato's *Symposium,* Battista argues that love makes a man like a beast who is driven to fulfill his insatiable natural appetite. He then concludes:

> **Battista:** I have observed, in fact, that by its own or nature's law, or through some defect in man, love has always had the power to conquer and to govern mortal man. I do not think that among ancient historians there is any mention of someone, however virtuous he might have been and worthy of every sort of special praise, in whom love did not fully illustrate her power. It overcame not only young men, who might seem to have had their fill and to have outlived their capacity for amorous delights. . . .
>
> Other men, too, and not a few of them, have been overcome in spite of lofty rank, high office, great dignity, and extensive reputation. They have surrendered to love's power great careers and high renown. . . .[115]

Not only have men's reputations and careers been governed by the power of love for a woman, but also the very interior structure of their personalities. Battista continues:

> Surely love, then, would appear to be a force greater and more powerful than merely human strength. It is obvious that spirits pierced by the divine arrow, with which the powers say that Cupid strikes and wounds the human heart, are too completely subjugated and enslaved to be able to desire or to pursue anything other than what they think desired and loved by their beloved. It is truly astonishing to see how their labors, their words, their thoughts, their whole mind and soul, stand constantly ready and dedicated solely to obey the will of one to whom love has subjected them. Our very limbs are not more obedient and serviceable to us than is the lover to the one to whom he has entirely dedicated himself.[116]

Battista fills his dialogue with multiple examples of men from all positions in life who had become enslaved to a woman out of love.

In the middle of the context of this discussion of the destructive qualities of love Battista introduces a new argument that shifts the meaning of love between husband and wife from a bond of destructive force to one of friendship.[117] Battista

---

115. Alberti, *The Family,* II, 97.

116. Alberti, *The Family,* II, 99.

117. Alberti, *The Family,* II, 98ff. See Constance Jordan, *Renaissance Feminism: Literary Texts and Political Models* (Ithaca, N.Y.: Cornell University Press, 1990), for a discussion of his argument, pp. 48ff.

offers an ideal view of married love that includes the three Aristotelian grounds for friendship: virtue, pleasure, and utility:

> **Battista:** We may consider the love of husband and wife greatest of all. If pleasure generates benevolence, marriage gives an abundance of all sorts of pleasure and delight: if intimacy increases good will, no one has so close a continued familiarity with anyone as with his wife; if close bonds and a united will arise through the revelation and communication of your feelings and desires, there is no one to whom you have more opportunity to communicate fully and reveal your mind than to your own wife, your constant companion; if, finally, an honorable alliance leads to friendship, no relationship more entirely commands your reverence than the sacred tie of marriage.[118]

Two aspects of this well-known passage of Alberti on conjugal love need to be noted. The first is that it is expressed in a hypothetical form, "If pleasure . . . if intimacy . . . if close bonds . . . and if an honorable relationship, . . . then marriage commands your reverence." However, nowhere does Alberti actually argue that the hypothetical "if clauses" are fulfilled. The second aspect is that while Battista presents an ideal view of spousal love, much like Giannozzo had proclaimed to his wife, it turns out that when the details of the relationship are articulated, it no longer manifests a friendship based on equality of companionship, communication, and friendship but rather a friendship based almost completely on utility of how useful the wife is to the husband.

This emphasis on the utilitarian dimension of marriage causes Battista to be blind as to why many women do not accept his reasoning:

> **Battista:** Add to all this that every moment brings further ties of pleasure and utility, confirming the benevolence filling our hearts. Children are born, and it would take a long time to expound the mutual and mighty bond which these provide. They surely ally their parents' minds in a union of will and thought. This is a union, indeed, which one may well call true friendship. I will not lengthen my discourse by describing all the advantages stemming from this conjugal friendship and solidarity. After all, it preserves the home, maintains the family, rules and governs the whole economy. It governs areas of life so vital to women that almost anyone would suppose nothing for them could be more sacred and constant than conjugal love. Yet somehow, I do not know why, it happens not infrequently that a woman prefers a lover to her own husband.[119]

It is at this point in the analysis that Alberti begins to specify that a primary utilitarian basis of the friendship between husband and wife is the bearing of male children. The secondary utilitarian bases of preserving the home, governing the economy, and maintaining the family he sees as having their foundation in the ability of the woman to produce male heirs.

118. Alberti, *The Family,* II, 98.
119. Alberti, *The Family,* II, 98.

To support this utilitarian basis for conjugal love and friendship, Alberti draws on other characters in his dialogue *Della famiglia*. First of all, Lionardo considers the basis for judging the beauty of a prospective wife: "I think that beauty in a woman, likewise, must be judged not only by the charm and refinement of her face, but still more by the grace of her person and her aptitude for bearing and giving birth to many fine children."[120] Then, following the humanist propensity, he refers the reader back to classical texts:

> **Lionardo**: In her body he must seek not only loveliness, grace, and charm but must also choose a woman who is well made for bearing children, with the kind of constitution that promises to make them strong and big. There's an old proverb, "When you pick your wife, you choose your children." All her virtues will in fact shine brighter still in beautiful children. It is a well-known saying among poets: "Beautiful character dwells in a beautiful body." The natural philosophers require that a woman be neither thin nor fat. . . . They find that a woman is most suited to bear children if she is fairly big and has limbs of ample length.[121]

Battista pauses to summarize his older relative Lionardo's advice and chooses very pointedly to emphasize the significance of male children:

> **Battista**: I would not interrupt your rapid exposition, if you had not yourself given me leave to do it. But it would help to stop a moment and let me turn my head to fix in my memory what you have traversed to this point, if I can remember it rightly. You have said, I gather, that one should select a virtuous woman of good parentage, one well dowered and suited to bear a fair number of sons. All these things are very difficult. Lionardo, do you think one could easily find them all combined in one woman, let alone in as many as a large family like ours requires?[122]

In response to the question posed by Battista, Lionardo invokes the example of an ancient Greek philosopher to ensure that the wife will produce: ". . . the first thing you ought to do is as Xenophon has the good husband say to Socrates: pray to God that he graciously grant that your bride will be fertile, and that you may always have peace and honor in your house."[123] Then he repeats this advice just to be certain that his younger relative grasps its point: "Many should be the prayers addressed to God, therefore, that he may grant the young husband a wife who will prove good, peaceful, honorable, and, as we have said, prolific."[124]

Battista then raises an important issue, which indicates that Alberti recognizes that the views he is expressing through Lionardo may be somewhat controversial. Battista suggests that Lionardo has doubts about women's character. A de-

120. Alberti, *The Family*, II, 115.
121. Alberti, *The Family*, II, 116.
122. Alberti, *The Family*, II, 118.
123. Alberti, *The Family*, II, 119-20.
124. Alberti, *The Family*, II, 120.

fensive response is offered by the older mentor: "Quiet, Battista, don't do me any injustice; don't misinterpret my words to make it seem that I rail against feminine character and conduct. It's just that I believe in calling on the help of God in every undertaking, be it an easy or a difficult one."[125]

The dialogue *Della famiglia* proceeds to offer detailed directions on how best to conceive a healthy child. The directions were common to gynecological texts of the time. They note the weather conditions, state of the father's health, and the timing of sexual intercourse to help parents conceive a healthy child. Alberti goes on to consider the option of adoption for those unable to conceive. Once again he draws examples from ancient texts, and then reasserts the utilitarian aim of producing male children in Lionardo's conclusion: ". . . to avoid leaving a barren solitude, to prevent the decline of the family into emptiness and sadness one should legitimately adopt a son."[126]

As mentioned previously, in *Della famiglia* Alberti devotes much attention to the theme of friendship among men. He encourages the development of friendships based on virtue and utility. While passionate love destroys all the power of reason, true friendship and love of the family overcome irrational passion and allow a man to live an honorable life. Thus a man ought to seek and build up true friendships. A man is able to do this by exercising his reason to distinguish good things from bad, and by using his will to develop a virtuous character through his acts.

Alberti argues that a man ought to develop all his capacities. Lionardo suggests that a man who remains idle and passive is hardly alive. He asks: ". . . what man, however poorly endowed, would want to pass through life without making use of his mind, his body, and all his capacities?"[127] Then he goes further by arguing that even a life of contemplation is opposed to the full development of a man's capacities:

Lionardo: Intelligence, intellect, judgment, memory, appetite, anger, reason, and discretion — who would unreasonably deny that these divine forces, by which a man outdoes all other animals in strength, in speed, in ferocity, are capacities given to us to be amply used? I must object, therefore, to the saying of Epicurus the philosopher, who teaches that the highest happiness of God consists in doing nothing. . . . The Stoics taught that man was by nature constituted the observer and the manager of things. . . . Chrysippus thought everything on earth was born only to serve man, while man was meant to preserve the friendship and society of men. . . . Plato, in a letter to Archytas of Tarentum, declared that men were born to serve their fellow men, and that we owe a part of ourselves to our country, a part to our kinsmen, and a part to our friends. But it would take long to tell all the teachings of the ancient philosophers on this question. . . . These have occurred to me for now, and, as you see, all of them think that man should live not in idleness and repose but in works and deeds.[128]

125. Alberti, *The Family*, II, 120.
126. Alberti, *The Family*, II, 129.
127. Alberti, *The Family*, II, 132.
128. Alberti, *The Family*, II, 134.

Aristotle and scholastic philosophers had argued that friendships based on virtue, or deeds supporting the good of the friend, were the best form. Those based simply on utility or pleasure were not only of lesser value, but also endured for only short periods of time, i.e., as long as the pleasure or usefulness persisted. In Book IV of *Della famiglia,* Alberti questions the value of an Aristotelian and scholastic theoretical approach to friendship:

> **Adovardo:** Really, what is the practical use of being able to argue in debate that only friendship based on virtue is strong and enduring while friendships for utility and pleasure are transitory? . . .
>
> I don't deny that the scholastic definitions and descriptions composed by learned men in their sheltered leisure are useful as a kind of preparation, like jousting for the use of arms. You have to live in the world, however, and deal with the actual ways and habits of men. If all you know is whether it is the mother or the father who naturally loves the children more . . . , I'm afraid you end up like poor Formius, the peripatetic. He gave a long discourse on military affairs in the presence of Hannibal, who after hearing him out, remarked that he had seen a good deal, but nothing sillier than this fellow who apparently believed that one could do on the field in the presence of an enemy just what one could think of while arguing in the schools. . . .
>
> **Lionardo:** . . . But I also find it hard to believe that you are displeased with the ancient writers for setting out according to their own principles and methods, that true friendship is nothing but a combining together of all our human and divine concerns, reaching agreement and loving one another with entire good will and perfect charity.[129]

After considering the basic foundation for friendships among men, the question is raised as to whether or not a woman is capable of a friendship of equality with her husband. The answer to this question had to be for Battista that a husband and wife could have a friendship based on virtue, but it would be the virtue of unequals. Men's virtues and women's virtues are different, as has been amply demonstrated by the passages cited above: a man's virtue is to rule, and woman's to obey, and the public realm is the sphere of a man's virtuous activity while the private realm is the sphere of a woman's virtuous activity. Thus, following the Aristotelian tradition, a husband and wife participate in a friendship of inequality. While Alberti seems to accept this position, the stronger one seems to be that the friendship of husband and wife is primarily one of utility — the wife bears the husband sons, and she protects the order and the goods of his household.

It is at this point in the argument that a further suggestion about woman's incapacity for friendship with man is introduced. This argument is offered by the old servant of the Alberti family:

> **Buto:** They said, for one thing, that good friendship requires the union of two

129. Alberti, *The Family,* IV, 266-67.

persons so that they become one. For that you need more salt than I can tell. I assure you I loved my wife a lot better when she was still a virgin than later, when I had married her and made her mine. It was an evil hour when we were joined in matrimony, for as long as she was with me in this life, I never enjoyed a half hour of sitting near her without a barrage of shouting and attacks of scolding. Perhaps the wise men who wrote those pretty things about friendship cared little about making friends with women, or perhaps they thought everyone knew you could never have a true friendship with a woman. As for me, I have grown wiser now and don't blame women anymore for the annoyance they certainly do give when, lord in heaven what a pain, they won't ever be quiet.[130]

If Buto's argument is accepted then even true friendship based on the virtue and utility of equals in Alberti's *Della famiglia* appears to be reserved for men alone. This kind of mixed friendship of virtue and utility was both useful and long-standing because the families endured in a common city-state over a long period of time. However, the love and friendship between husband and wife was devalued, and the bond between men and women reduced primarily to a material bond of generating and overseeing the goods of a particular household.

At this point, it is important to pause and summarize the positions of each of the interlocutors used by Alberti in his *Della famiglia* to support his utilitarian bases for conjugal love and friendship. This summary is presented in chart form below on pages 817-19.

Later Concept of Woman

Our analysis will now turn to two of the later dialogues of Leon Battista Alberti that are paired together as satires about women. The first text, *De amore*, is in the form of a letter written to Paolo Codagnello to discourage him from giving in to love for a woman. Alberti's argument follows the line of Theophrastus, Walter Map, and Golias on why a man should not marry. He also uses images common to Juvenal and other early satirists. Just as we saw in the early dialogue *Deifira*, the *De amore* tries to convince Paolo to reject love by ridiculing woman as the object of love. At the end of this letter to Paolo, Alberti directly states his awareness that if women read his letter they would lose respect for him: "Truthfully, if this discussion has helped you realize that a woman consists of hypocrisy and perversity, I do not mind losing women's respect for me."[131] Then Alberti warns Paolo: "Once you feel these letters have helped you, destroy them, for they could fall into the wrong hands."[132]

The second text, *Sofrona*, is a dialogue sent subsequently to comfort Paolo, who was grieving for the death on September 9, 1437, of his uncle Lucido Conte.

---

130. Alberti, *The Family*, IV, 247.
131. Leon Battista Alberti, "De Amore," in *Opere Volgari* (Bari: Laterza, 1960), III, pp. 249-53. All passages from this text are translated by Clelia Giangrande.
132. Alberti, "De Amore," in *Opere Volgari*, III, p. 264.

Alberti's Middle Concept of Woman		
Interlocutor in *Della famiglia*	Description of Man	Description of Woman
Alberti (Prologue)	Man should use reason and will to resist being conquered by Fortune.	Fortune (she) is inconstant, equivocal, destructive, and a dangerous power, which wants to make a man submit.
Battista	Love for a woman ruins many men's careers and reputations. Love enslaves men.	The greatest love is between husband and wife in marriage: a. communication b. companionship c. friendship of utility; but many women prefer love to friendship.
Lionardo	Boys' education should be segregated from the effeminate influence of girls and women. Boys' masculinity should be strengthened by avoiding being around women. Man can conquer fortune by exercise of virtue. Men's minds are stronger than women's minds. Men are by nature strong, able to withstand stress, and constant. A man should develop all his intellectual capacities by works and deeds.	It is not possible to find a well-educated wife. Choose a woman to be wife who can be fertile, prolific, and bear sons. Fortune victimizes men. Women's minds are weaker than men's minds. Woman is by nature soft and slow.

Alberti's Middle Concept of Woman (cont.)		
Interlocutor in *Della famiglia*	Description of Man	Description of Woman
Adovardo	Men can develop character, virtue, and letters by their own skill and diligence.	Fortune cannot take away character, virtue, and skill in letters.
	Men's minds are stronger than women's minds.	Women's minds are weaker than men's minds.
	A man needs practical experience, not theoretical study, to form good friendships.	
Giannozzo	A real man rules with virility.	A wife is obedient if her husband knows how to rule her.
	A husband governs the whole household and delegates some areas of governing to his wife.	A wife governs the children and servants in the household under the authority of her husband.
	A husband governs the expressions, clothing, and cosmetics of his wife.	A wife ought to obey her husband's dictates concerning her personal appearance and behavior.
	Only the husband reads and writes.	A wife is kept from the household's library and records.
	A good husband speaks well in public.	A good wife keeps silent in public and speaks little in the home.
	A man communicates the needs of the household in the public arena.	Only bold and forward women seek to know what is going on in the marketplace.
	It is demeaning for a man to be shut up in the house with women.	The wife takes care of the smaller household affairs.

Alberti's Middle Concept of Woman (cont.)		
Interlocutor in *Della famiglia*	Description of Man	Description of Woman
Buto	Men are capable of friendships — which are useful to them.	Women are not capable of friendship. Women are never silent. Women are always attacking.

In the introduction Alberti indicates that the first letter to Paolo had fallen into the hands of a woman named Sofrona, and that it was read aloud and commented on by a group of women together.[133] In this remarkable text Alberti describes an intergender dialogue between Battista and Sofrona about main points in the satirical letter to Paolo. The sequence of these two texts seems to indicate that Alberti had intended them to be joined together from their conception. They also raise the possibility that Alberti was introducing the satire against women in order to undermine it by a satire of the satire. We suggested in Chapter 5 that Boccaccio may have done a similar thing in his *Corbaccio*. However, in contrast to Boccaccio, there are no other texts of Alberti that suggest a different concept of woman than the traditional gender polarity satirical model. Therefore, it is unlikely that Alberti was in these two short texts introducing a reversal of the direction of the rest of his thought about woman. Our analysis will now turn directly to the texts for verification of this hypothesis.

In *De amore* Alberti describes how love "is harmful and useless to scholars," how it creates a servitude in the lover, and how it torments and weakens him every day.[134] He invokes the example of his friend described in the earlier text *Deifira,* who was ruined by his unrequited love for a woman: "Poor Pallimacro! Now he cries his ill fortune. He had to abandon his studies and is now ruined for having loved that proud, stubborn, cruel, unstable and perverse-minded woman called Deifira."[135] This linkage with the early text implies that Alberti still accepts the argument put forward by Filarco in the *Deifira.* In fact, the *De Amore* will go even further in developing the same argument, particularly in the part that sought to demonstrate that woman is an unworthy object of love. While Filarco had generally limited himself to trying to prove that Deifira was an unworthy object of love, in the *De amore* Alberti himself generalizes about all women. This shift in voice from imaginary character to Alberti himself and from reference to a particular woman Deifira to all women implies a hardening of Alberti's gender polarity theory.

133. Alberti, "Sofrona," in *Opere Volgari,* III, pp. 267-71.
134. Alberti, "De Amore," in *Opere Volgari,* III, p. 249.
135. Alberti, "De Amore," in *Opere Volgari,* III, p. 255.

Following the usual satirical method of universal generalizations, Alberti shifts from describing a particular incident of failed love to making a generalization about all women:

> Furthermore, what pleasure could an unlearned (which all women are), insipid, inept and foolish woman ever give a scholarly and dignified man such as your- self? In public you see her with head held high but in a more familiar surround- ing, her head dangles as if she had no collarbone. Indeed, in such a context, she would hardly converse with you.[136]

Continuing the traditional satirical inversion of appearance and reality, Alberti ar- gues that while a woman may appear to be beautiful, in reality she is ugly:

> If you look at a woman, you will find that her eyes are feeble and her forehead and cheeks are freckled and that her teeth are dirty and dingy. It is miraculous if this is not so. You could always see her dirty nails, though I wonder why they are so discolored. . . . Despite this you still serve her.[137]

The author goes further than simply ridicule the surface appearance of a woman when he satirically generalizes about women's intentions. "How foolish we men are in believing and loving them! We forget that as soon as they are born they vow to be immodest, vain, deceitful, and to never reveal their true feelings."[138] The theme of intentional deception by women is developed in great detail; Alberti argues that a woman pretends to love one man, but in fact loves many different ones, that she enjoys tormenting men, and particularly uses deceit to catch them. Furthermore, woman takes great care to change her appearance:

> Now just think about the way women disguise their appearance. Nature has not given them the light silvered hair which you see, for that hair which you see be- longed to another girl who has long since been buried. Her real face, before it is beautifully made up, is pale and wrinkled. Her lips and cheeks are not rosy. Moreover, she presents herself taller than she really is. Maybe you think a certain woman to be well-built and warm but in reality she is skinny and cold-hearted. Indeed, you will never find anything authentic about a woman. In fact, a woman who one day seems clean and well-groomed is hardly recognizable in her own home, where she is transformed into a dirty and vulgar creature.[139]

Alberti's generalizations about woman extend beyond intentional deception by changing her physical appearance to include other kinds of actions and thoughts. He gives many different examples of the various forms of deception a woman uses to catch a man. While they are similar in some respects to those exam-

136. Alberti, "De Amore," in *Opere Volgari,* III, p. 255.
137. Alberti, "De Amore," in *Opere Volgari,* III, p. 256.
138. Alberti, "De Amore," in *Opere Volgari,* III, p. 257.
139. Alberti, "De Amore," in *Opere Volgari,* III, pp. 259-60.

ples of satires previously studied in this book, Alberti adds some new dimensions to them:

> Just as a woman's physical appearance is deceiving so too are her actions and thoughts — as I hope you realize. That which you think to be worthy in her is to be scorned. A woman will use someone else's name and the fame which goes with it because she is proud, insolent, quarrelsome, brutish and intolerable. . . . She has many friends and acquaintances so that she only bothers them and imposes herself on them. She knows only how to spend someone's wealth. Furthermore, you can observe such vile women constantly going out under religious pretexts in order to accomplish their immodest tasks. Paolo, do not ever doubt that if a woman were to do something diligently it is because she is motivated by her desires and vices.[140]

And as if to excuse women for their actions, Alberti appeals to the gender polarity principle that woman is naturally inconstant:

> As you know, her inconstancy does not permit her to hold on to something for very long. Also, she uses her intelligence and ingenuity either to destroy the peace within a family or to indulge her lust. Surely, if she possessed true intelligence she would not be so quick to change her opinions and run to seek advice. I only observe that women foster evil doings. She is empty-headed with respect to any other matter. All these observations seem to prove that she is anything but worthy of praise. Having, therefore, demonstrated the harm women bring to themselves and to man, how can one not hate their foolishness?[141]

The letter to Paolo concludes with some reflections by Alberti concerning why he decided to write the letter in the first place. Alberti claims that he has done this to help Paolo realize that "a woman consists of hypocrisy and perversity" and that she only pretends to love him. If Paolo would just realize this truth, then he would be rid of the chains of love. Alberti adds that if and when this happens the two men could continue their studies together and achieve the fame that is denied those "blinded by love." These themes of being enslaved by love for a woman and freed when this love is overcome are repeated frequently by Alberti in his letter to Paolo. Then, as mentioned at the outset, Alberti warns Paolo to destroy the letter so that it would not fall into the wrong hands.

The second text, *Sofrona*, begins with a rather extraordinary description of Sofrona, widowed after three different marriages to a doctor, a jurist, and an attorney, and now purportedly seeking advice from Alberti. Her request for advice takes place in a public setting in the presence of a group of women who have all read Alberti's original letter to Paolo.

The dialogue itself is filled with *ad hominem* attacks from both of its main participants: Alberti and Sofrona. The older woman begins: "And you, Battista,

---

140. Alberti, "De Amore," in *Opere Volgari*, III, p. 260.
141. Alberti, "De Amore," in *Opere Volgari*, III, p. 261.

what foolishness prompted you to write such infamous things about us women in your letters to Paolo? You are not worthy of the grace that women have bestowed upon you!"[142] She accuses him of being motivated by revenge for having been rejected by a woman he loved. This attack focuses on Alberti's motivations rather than on his arguments. Sofrona concludes: "You have therefore made women into your enemies and me, their leader."[143]

Alberti suggests in response that all the women are motivated by a personal hatred of him. The dialogue continues as follows:

Alberti: Sofrona, I cannot believe that you, most prudent woman, consider me to be too foolish or undeserving of your praise and that of these other women, whose honor I have never offended. In my letters to Paolo I never intended to criticize any one of you. I am confident that you, Sofrona, will set an excellent example for these women by not being quarrelsome. And I am sure that these women, in turn, will help teach you how to benefit from your lover. . . . I pray that you, merciful woman, do not turn against me without first examining my merits.

Sofrona: And what are these merits? Still, who would not consider you blameworthy? Oh, what a burden these learned men are! Each wants to ridicule women, as if he were flawless. You men all wish to be considered erudite and eloquent by proving us unlearned. Ironically, you very men praise women all day long. And I know that you, Battista, were the first, among the other men, to love. We heard of your relationship and your eclogues; you loved a stubborn market woman![144]

This part of the dialogue is remarkable because it demonstrates that Alberti not only consciously devalued women, but he also understood that some women perceived him making unfounded generalizations about them. It also introduces the theme of tensions between educated men who make these generalized satirical claims and uneducated women, who are nonetheless able to recognize fallacies in another person's arguments about their own identity.

The argument by Sofrona continues with the claim that Alberti is primarily motivated by revenge for having been spurned by an unlearned woman. Alberti does not deny that he had fallen in love with a woman, but he suggests that it was the woman's fault for first captivating his love and then for being inconstant in it. A long discussion ensues between Alberti and Sofrona concerning who is more responsible for this state of affairs. Alberti argues that women particularly deceive educated and virtuous men, but prefer to remain with other men who are more vile. Sofrona argues that women choose to be with men who really enjoy their company, not men who take pride in conquering a woman. She adds: "You are ostentatious in believing you are wanted by all."[145]

142. Alberti, "Sofrona," in *Opere Volgari,* III, p. 267.
143. Alberti, "Sofrona," in *Opere Volgari,* III, p. 267.
144. Alberti, "Sofrona," in *Opere Volgari,* III, pp. 267-68.
145. Alberti, "Sofrona," in *Opere Volgari,* III, p. 269.

The gender polarity principle of woman's inconstancy pervades the dialogue. Sofrona claims that what Alberti perceives as fickleness in a woman is actually a sign of her prudent virtue when she withdraws from a man's amorous advances. The dialogue continues with the following interaction focusing on the issue of constancy and inconstancy:

> **Battista**: I praise your judgment, Sofrona, but I cannot clearly understand why women allure men with whom they do not wish to have a serious relationship. If you take pleasure in giving others displeasure then I do not praise you.

> **Sofrona**: You speak as though you were slow to realize that before a woman meets the right man she must first encounter many unfit ones. Do you truly believe that our greatest joy comes from burdening you, honourable men, all night long with things which we never think of so that you may later write letters to sorrowful lovers? Oh silly silly men! The more astute you are, the more inept you are. You think it clever, in hopes of understanding us, to scrutinize our every word and gesture, but you only waste your time in vain. Is there any greater insanity than that of someone who continually thinks about a woman's instability? And how much more prudent we women are than all you men; only when we are among you do we think of you, and in this sense we scoff at you.[146]

Sofrona continues her argument by criticizing the ethical gender polarity principle that a woman's actions ought to remain within the private sphere while a man's virtue is practiced in the public sphere. This distinction, she claims, is imposed on women:

> And if it were permitted, do you think we would stay at home in the dark rather than go among other people? Oh God! How incredible and marvelous our prudence is! Indeed as inexperienced as we may be still, we surpass you. But you continue to confine us within the solitary walls of our homes. Even so you cannot say that we are senseless. . . . And how prudent you must esteem us to be for you maintain that through our ingenuity and shrewdness we control our husbands and other men as well.[147]

In this passage Alberti again demonstrates that he is aware of the paradoxical situation in which a man argues that women ought to remain at home and he imposes this limited sphere of virtue on them, while at the same time he claims that women control their husbands. Yet, he does not resolve this paradox by removing one of its two contradictory claims. Instead, he attacks Sofrona. He responds that he never doubted that Sofrona was astute, but he did not believe that a woman could pursue her ambitions consistently over a period of time. In conclusion, Sofrona calls Alberti an "unfit scholar!" and asks him to "remove from your mind that we are fickle. Enough about constancy!"[148]

146. Alberti, "Sofrona," in *Opere Volgari,* III, p. 270.
147. Alberti, "Sofrona," in *Opere Volgari,* III, p. 270.
148. Alberti, "Sofrona," in *Opere Volgari,* III, pp. 270-71.

As can be seen by this brief summary of the main line of argument in the *Sofrona,* the dialogue remains primarily on a superficial level, and yet it contains within it many of the deeper gender polarity principles traditionally used to devalue women. Even though Alberti sometimes makes himself appear foolish in his articulation of criticisms women make of him, the tone of the satire generally mocks women's way of reasoning more than it does a man's. Alberti ends the dialogue by claiming that he told the women that their discussion helped him and that he would accuse himself of having erred. This might make it appear that Alberti had come to a new insight about gender identity, and that he wrote this satire as a reversal of his earlier gender polarity position. However, right after making the observation that the women helped him, he adds the following rider to Paolo: "I praised them even if they did not merit it much."[149] This sarcastic addendum would indicate that the whole exercise was a satire in the traditional gender polarity model.

The chart on page 825 summarizes the main aspects of the concept of woman articulated by Alberti in his two late dialogues. As stated previously, Alberti articulated many of these positions in his own voice rather than through the voice of a fictional character created by him to act as his foil.

Alberti wrote one more satirical text late in his life entitled *Momus.* Grayson characterizes this text as "a mordant satire on princes and courtiers, women and philosophers, in which no human values and idols are spared and the hero is a beggar with no cares and responsibilities."[150] It is difficult to know whether Alberti actually changed his views about the concept of woman later in his life. There seems to be no evidence contrary to the claims that he consistently made from his early dialogues to his late ones. The only difference appears to be an increasing awareness that women do not accept his arguments.

Drawing now upon all of his dialogues, the basic gender polarity principles that Leon Battista Alberti offers with respect to his concept of woman are summarized in the chart on page 826.

This chart shows clearly that Alberti's approach to the concept of woman reasserted traditional gender polarity principles in the four categories of opposites, generation, wisdom, and virtue. Even though he had been exposed to some humanist principles, Alberti did not adopt them in any way with respect to gender identity. Instead, he restated traditional gender polarity arguments both in his serious dialogue on the family and in his satirical letter and the dialogues. The fact that manuscripts of *Della famiglia* abounded and that the text was written in the vernacular Tuscan meant that Alberti's incarnation of gender polarity arguments in a fifteenth-century Italian family was dispersed far beyond the confines of academia. This text received considerable notoriety because, as Jacob Burckhardt noted in *The Civilisation of the Renaissance in Italy,* it "is the first complete programme of a developed private life."[151]

149. Alberti, "Sofrona," in *Opere Volgari,* III, p. 271.

150. Grayson, "The Humanism of Alberti," *Italian Studies* 12 (1957): 52.

151. Burckhardt, *The Civilisation of the Renaissance in Italy,* p. 132. Burckhardt notes the recent discovery by Fr. Palermo that this text, previously attributed to Pandolfini, was actually written by Alberti, p. 132, n. 1.

Alberti's Later Concept of Woman		
In satires De amore and Sofrona	Alberti's position to Paolo	Sofrona's response to Alberti
Generalized claims:	All women are: unlearned, insipid, inept, foolish, dirty and vulgar, disguise their appearance, proud, quarrelsome, brutish, intolerable, motivated by desires and vices, inconstant, empty-headed, allure men and take pleasure in giving displeasure to men.	Learned men are: a burden ridicule women wish to be considered erudite, eloquent, and flawless, but are silly, inept, insane for continually thinking about women's inconstancy, imprudent and contradictory as they both confine women and say that women control men.
Particularized claims:		Battista Alberti is: foolish, inventing lies about women, motivated by revenge, spurned by a market woman, made women his enemies, blameworthy, ostentatious, an unfit scholar.

Alberti's arguments effectively undermined the beginning movement in humanism towards a new theory of gender identity that incorporated some gender complementarity and gender unity principles. At the same time Alberti brought the topic of woman and the family into the center of philosophical discourse. Thus he leaves a paradoxical legacy for the history of the concept of woman. One side of the paradoxical legacy is an affirmation of Alberti's interest in and attention to woman and the family. This affirmative evaluation of his contribution may be seen in Jacob Burckhardt's description of a later version of Book III of *Della famiglia* that was mistakenly published in 1734 as *Il trattato del governo della famiglia* (The treatise on the governing of the family) and falsely attributed to Agnolo Pandolfini (d.

Alberti's Categories of Gender Polarity		
Category	**Men**	**Women**
Opposites	Men are in constant battle for control over women and fortune.	Women and fortune are in constant battle for control over men.
	Love for woman enslaves man's reason and will.	Fortune and woman are inconstant and dangerous.
	Boys ought to be only masculine (and not do effeminate things).	Girls ought to be only feminine (and not do manly things).
Wisdom	Use reason with manly will Elevated mind Stronger by nature Study reading and writing Develop counsel	Weaker will, inconstant Mind focused on trivial matters Mind weaker by nature
	Be educated separately from girls and women.	Kept away from books and study
	Engage in public and private speech.	Not able to keep secrets or give counsel to men
		Speak only and briefly to children, servants, and husband.
Virtue	Self-governance	Overcome fickle, changeable, deceptive tendencies
	Public sphere of activity Rule outside home Rule wife	Private sphere of activity Rule children and servants Obey husband
	Rejection of the passion of love	Rejection of the passion of love
	Friendships with men based on virtue and utility	Friendship with husband (if possible) based on utility and unequal virtues.
Generation	Man should seek to generate sons.	Woman chosen as wife should be fertile, prolific, and generate well-formed sons.

1446).[152] Burckhardt's description of Pandolfini's version of Alberti's text on household management is as follows:

> He represents a father speaking to his grown-up sons, and initiating them into his method of administration. We are introduced into a large and wealthy household, which if governed with moderation and reasonable economy, promises happiness and prosperity for generations to come. . . . Nothing is considered of so much importance as education, which the head of the house gives not only to the children, but to the whole household. He first develops his wife from a shy girl, brought up in careful seclusion, to the true woman of the house, capable of commanding and guiding the servants. . . .[153]

Clearly Burckhardt interprets the orientation of the text as moving towards a genuine complementarity in which the wife rules with strength in complement with her husband. Pandolfini's version of Book III of Alberti's *Della famiglia* was extremely popular; it was used as a practical manual to guide wealthy Florentines in the government of their wealthy villas in the countryside surrounding the city.

Apparently a descendent of Pandolfini discovered the *Della famiglia* in his library, with the names of participants in the dialogue changed to include Agnolo Pandolfini and his five sons rather than the looser family cluster found in the original text by Alberti, and he published the first printed version. The confusion about authorship lasted around one hundred years. For our purposes it is important primarily to note that the participants in the dialogue about the family and women in both cases included only men. Whether the participants in the text were Alberti's Lionardo, Battista, Giannozzo, and Buto or Pandolfini and his sons, the gender polarity positions communicated were the same in both instances even though some critics, such as Burckhardt, interpreted the dialogue as being more favorable to woman's identity.

The other side of the paradoxical legacy of Alberti, or the devaluation of woman contained in his work on the family, is offered by Constance Jordan in *Renaissance Feminism*. Comparing the model of wife in Francesco Barbaro and Leon Alberti she concludes:

> The Alberti wife's part in restoring her family to prosperity is clear and crucial: she is to maintain domestic order by conserving what her husband has acquired. If she fails to do so, she not only hurts her family but also affects the financial stability of the state. For goods that are kept within a family do not enter the marketplace; conversely, those that are lost or sold are put back into competitive play. In excessive quantities, goods in the process of being exchanged can cause men to feel greed, ambition, and an indifference to law. Rather than define her value as that of an object exchanged between men, as Barbaro does, Alberti sees a woman as one who by conserving property *limits* the number of (real) objects to be ex-

---

152. Agnolo Pandolfini, *Trattato del governo della famiglia,* preface by Giuseppe Ripamonti Carpano (Milan: 1805).

153. Burckhardt, *The Civilisation of the Renaissance in Italy,* pp. 402-3.

changed among men, and thereby prevents rapid shifts in the fortunes of her family and, by extension, of those of others. His disorderly wife stands for a systematic confusion that threatens the well-being of the state itself.[154]

Jordan emphasizes the economic role and value of women in a patriarchal society. In this, she perceives woman primarily as an object of use to man, for the enhancement of his own status and security in broader society.

While there is a certain line of truth in both sides of the paradox emphasized by Burckhardt and Jordan, I would like to offer a third approach to the evaluation of Alberti's legacy. Alberti sought to offer new humanist principles for relation of husband and wife that contained within them many arguments about the concept of woman in relation to man. However, he failed to recognize the radical demands of a full Christian-based humanism for dynamics guiding conjugal love and friendship. Thus, while Alberti began the important process of bringing woman's identity in the family to the forefront of philosophical discourse, he was unable to draw the conclusions consistent with his Christian-based humanism. When he differentiated man and woman, he did so at the expense of woman by introducing a polarization and devaluation of woman in relation to man.

The full development of a Christian humanism has only occurred in the twentieth century, but some of the Christian-based principles had already begun to be identified in the fourteenth to sixteenth centuries. These fundamental principles are identified and each one is now discussed with an indication of which Christian humanist was among the first to articulate the particular principles under consideration:

The Principle of Equality

Alberti did not view men and women as having equal dignity and worth nor as having equal rights. The principle that a woman and man have an equal dignity and worth was informally indicated by Christine de Pizan and by Laura Cereta, and formally articulated only later by Marie de Gournay Le Jars (1566-1645) in her text *Egalité des hommes et des femmes (Equality of men and women),* published in 1622.[155] Appealing to the classical philosophers, Socrates and Plato, de Gournay argued for the principle of the fundamental equality of identity and rights of women and men.

The Principle of Personalism

Alberti did not understand the unique and unrepeatable identity of each person, man or woman. He especially implied that a woman was simply a female hu-

---

154. Jordan, *Renaissance Feminism,* pp. 47-48.
155. Marie de Gournay, "Egalité des hommes et des femmes," in *La Fille d'Alliance de Montaigne: Marie de Gournay* (Paris: Librairie Honoré Champion, 1910).

man being whose value was determined by her usefulness to her husband and extended family. She was a something — a fertile, productive wife and mother who governed the household as determined by her husband, rather than a unique someone worthy of love. Giovanni Pico della Mirandola was the first humanist to begin to articulate the principle of personalism, of unique personal identity. His theory will be described later in this chapter. Emmanuel Mounier was the first humanist to formally state the application of this principle to woman's identity in his 1936 article, "Le femme aussi est une personne" ("Woman is also a person").[156]

Flowing from the principle of personalism is the personalist norm. This norm, drawing from Immanuel Kant's second version of the categorical imperative, states that a person should always be treated as an end in himself or herself, and never as a means. Another version of the personalist norm is that a person should always be treated as a someone and never as a something. Within the Jewish humanist tradition Martin Buber began to articulate this principle in drafts of his 1919 text *I and Thou*.[157] More recently, Karol Wojtyla, better known as Pope John Paul II, has drawn out the explicit conclusions for the ethical dimension of personalism and the personalistic norm in "Analysis of the Verb 'To Use'" in his text entitled *Love and Responsibility*.[158] Wojtyla demonstrates the limitations of the utilitarian view that understands woman primarily in terms of her usefulness to man.

The Principle of the Person and the Common Good

This principle identifies the goal of all communities, including the family. Specifically, it states that each member of a community should work both for the common good of the community as well as for the fulfillment of the individual good of each person in that community. This dual goal of the common good is also called the "principle of solidarity." It characterizes the perfect development of all Christian humanism. The principle was first articulated by Jacques Maritain in *The Person and the Common Good* and in *True Humanism*.[159] It has been developed in more detail by Karol Wojtyla in "Intersubjectivity by Participation," from *The Acting Person*.[160] Although this principle was informally projected by both Christine de Pizan and Laura Cereta and their respective husbands, it was not understood by Alberti, as is evidenced in his perception that the husband bears no commitment to

---

156. Emmanuel Mounier, *Esprit* (June 1936): pp. 292-97.

157. Martin Buber, *I and Thou* (New York: Scribner's, 1970).

158. Karol Wojtyla, *Love and Responsibility* (San Francisco: Ignatius Press, 1981), pp. 21-34. Translated by H. T. Willetts from the 1960 Polish version. See also Karol Wojtyla, "Personalism and Naturalism." Part III: Marriage and the Family, in *Person and Community: Selected Essays* (New York: Peter Lang, 1993), pp. 284-91. Translated by Teresa Sandok from a 1965 article in Polish.

159. Jacques Maritain, *The Person and the Common Good* (Notre Dame: Notre Dame Press, 1985), p. 103, originally published in 1947; and *True Humanism* (New York: Charles Scribner's Sons, 1938), pp. 127ff.

160. Karol Wojtyla, *The Acting Person* (Boston: D. Reidel Publishing Company, 1979), pp. 276-300. Translated by Anna-Teresa Tymieniecka from the 1969 Polish edition.

his wife's full development as a person. Furthermore, this was particularly reinforced by stating that women and girls were not allowed access to literacy or to education either inside or outside the household. Thus, Alberti made it clear that women were not able to develop their intellectual capacities. At the same time, however, women were expected to help boys and men have an environment supportive of the full development of their education.

Edith Stein has recently articulated the fundamental principles of the relation of education to the formation and development of personality in "Fundamental Principles of Women's Education" and "Problems of Women's Education."[161] Many earlier humanists also considered the need of women to be educated, but Stein is to be credited for articulating the principles in a clear and concise manner.

Another area of limitation in Alberti's principles with respect to the common good is a lack of understanding of the principle of subsidiarity. This principle involves the recognition that each level of management has its own obligations and rights, and that higher levels should not interfere with the proper functioning of lower levels. Thus, when Alberti delegated to his wife the obligation for governing the household, including servants, children, possessions, and storerooms, according to the principle of subsidiarity he should have allowed her the freedom to determine how best to achieve this area of responsibility. Instead, however, the husband entered into the minutest details of household management, telling her what to do and how to act. This violation of the principle of subsidiarity went even to the extent of his determining the details of her own appearance and expressions. Such intervention and control by the husband further indicate the lack of understanding of woman as a person in her own right, able to enter into dialogue and consultation.

In conclusion, it is important to note that Leon Battista Alberti's legacy was helpful to the concept of woman in one respect, namely, in bringing the dynamics of conjugal love and friendship into the forefront of philosophical consideration. However, his legacy was severely limiting in that Alberti did not introduce the fundamental principles required to establish the family as a true community of persons. Consequently, the household as elaborated by Alberti was a structure primarily for the good of man, while the woman was reduced to a lesser being defined by her utility to the men and boys within the family.

LORENZO VALLA (1407-1457)

Our analysis moves now from a philosopher who attempted to Christianize utility to one who attempted to Christianize pleasure as the basis for relationship. Lorenzo Valla argued forcefully throughout his life that pleasure and self-love are the motivation for all human action. From this position he argued against Aristotle's claim that pleasure was the lowest form of the three motivations for friendship, and against Aristotle's view as elaborated by the Stoics, that virtue, love of the good of another, and disinterested love were higher values. While promoting an

---

161. Edith Stein, *Essays on Women*, 2nd rev. ed. (Washington, D.C.: ICS Publications, 1996), chapters 4 and 5, pp. 129-236.

ethics of pleasure, Valla also delineated his own understanding of the identity of pleasure from that common to Epicurean philosophy. Valla's approach to the highest good was so different from anyone who preceded him, and even those who followed him, that it is not surprising that he also introduced some different themes into the history of the concept of woman. Accordingly, woman not only was viewed as an object of pleasure for man, but was seen as someone motivated by seeking pleasure as her highest good. Before describing Valla's philosophy of gender in more detail, a few important aspects of his life and academic formation will be offered here to help understand his ethics of pleasure as the basis of relationship.

So far our analysis of humanist approaches to the concept of woman has focused primarily on authors who were educated in northern Italy. With Lorenzo Valla educational formation shifts to the south. Valla was born in Rome into a wealthy family well established in legal work for the Curia.[162] He was educated by a tutor at home and became fluent in Greek and Latin. In the fifteenth century, Latin was the common language among scholars of various nationalities who came to work at the Curia and who often shared a common interest in the new humanist attention to ancient Latin texts. Lorenzo Valla became fascinated with the works of Cicero and Quintilian, and he decided to develop his skills particularly in the areas of grammar, rhetoric, and oration.

Even though Valla did not have a formal academic education he was well enough educated in ancient Greek and Latin philosophy to enter into public arguments about the highest good or goal of life. Leonardo Bruni came to Rome during these early years of Valla's intellectual formation, and the young Lorenzo was deeply influenced by Bruni's approach to philosophical knowledge and the beauty of rhetorical language. They also shared a common dislike for formal scholastic disputation. Valla was well acquainted with Bruni's translations of Plato's *Gorgias, Phaedrus,* and *Letters* and of Aristotle's *Nicomachean Ethics.* He was also familiar with Decembrio's distorted translation of Plato's *Republic,* which he drew upon to quote or paraphrase Plato in his own works. Consequently, some of Valla's literary characters expressed inaccurate opinions about Plato's views.

Women, Pleasure, and the Good

Valla's relevant text for the history of the concept of woman is given the double title in English translation — *On Pleasure: De voluptate.*[163] It was written in the form of a dialogue occurring in Latin between an Epicurean, a Stoic, and a Christian in a dynamic context of a discussion among several male humanists who gathered in Rome about the question of the highest good. Valla's earliest journal version of the di-

162. John F. D'Amico, *Renaissance Humanism in Papal Rome: Humanists and Churchmen on the Eve of the Reformation* (Baltimore and London: Johns Hopkins University Press, 1983), pp. 7, 62, and 69.

163. Lorenzo Valla, *On Pleasure: De voluptate* (New York: Abaris Books, Inc., 1977). Translated by A. Kent Hieatt and Maristella Lorch from the critical edition of M. Lorch of *De Vero Falsoque Bono* (Bari: Adriatica Editrice, 1970).

alogue (1431) was situated in the Roman Curia. Leonardo Bruni, who had arrived in Rome in 1427, was selected as the key person who introduced the topic of discussion. According to Maristella Lorch, giving Bruni the initiative established Valla in the line of humanists reaching back to Petrarch who had attempted to place philosophy on a new anti-scholastic foundation.[164] In addition, Valla shared with Petrarch an admiration for the Roman understanding of "virtue which is not seen simply as a moral quality but as evidence of a strong will, energy, *vis,* to achieve one's potential. . . ."[165]

On Pleasure: De voluptate went through several revisions in location, changes of names of the key participants in the dialogue, and titles until it became known in 1433 as *De vero falsoque bono (On the True and False Good)* and was situated on the porch of a church in Pavia near Milan. In this version, the scholars are no longer from Rome, but from Lombardy.[166] A third revision and retitling as *De vero bono (The True Good)* occurred in the city of Naples between 1444 and 1449. The context for these revisions was in part due to Valla's being questioned for heresy by the Inquisition in 1444 on charges partly related to the degree to which his work appeared to espouse an Epicurean approach to love for the highest good.[167] Valla did change his orientation to progressively Christianize his intrigue with the nature of pleasure, both for motives of self-protection and seemingly out of a genuine interest in trying to revitalize Christianity with a new humanist approach.

An in-depth study of this progressive transformation of the several different versions of his dialogue on pleasure is given by Maristella de Panizza Lorch in *A Defense of Life: Lorenzo Valla's Theory of Pleasure.* Her remarkable commentary enters the internal dynamic of Valla's search for the highest good in a way that anticipates an almost Nietzschean approach to the tensions of self-actualization. Since her analysis goes far beyond the goals of the present study of the history of the concept of woman, it will be used as a background for our discussion rather than as an object of study itself. The actual version of the dialogue that will be used in our study is the middle or 1433 version that is given in Lorch's translation the title of the earliest version, namely, *On Pleasure: De voluptate.*

Valla was a highly polemical writer and orator who seemed almost to precipitate public conflicts with many different persons throughout his career. Maristella Lorch characterizes his method of writing as follows: "In every document written during his life. . . . Lorenzo Valla *fought* for his ideas using the *words* as a sword (a metaphor he employs often) in proud awareness of his innovative approach to language."[168] After his early education in Rome, and his initial failure to be appointed

---

164. Maristella de Panizza Lorch, *A Defense of Life: Lorenzo Valla's Theory of Pleasure* (Munich: Wilhelm Fink Verlag, 1985), p. 39.

165. Lorch, *A Defense of Life: Lorenzo Valla's Theory of Pleasure,* p. 13.

166. The dates of revision are given as 1433, 1439, and 1444-1449. See Brian Vickers, "Valla's Ambivalent Praise of Pleasure: Rhetoric in the Service of Christianity," *Viator: Medieval and Renaissance Studies* 17 (1986): 271-319. Vickers argues that the change was due to a misunderstanding of Valla's rhetorical technique. See also Lorch, *A Defense of Life: Lorenzo Valla's Theory of Pleasure,* p. 5.

167. For a description of the particular charges and their relation to Valla see Maristella Lorch, "Italy's Leading Humanist: Lorenzo Valla," in *Renaissance Humanism,* vol. I, *Humanism in Italy,* pp. 332-49.

168. Lorch, *A Defense of Life: Lorenzo Valla's Theory of Pleasure,* p. 15.

as a papal secretary, Valla taught at the *studium* in Pavia from 1431 to 1432. Then, because his life was threatened, he left Pavia and went to Milan. From 1435 to 1444, he worked as a secretary to the court of Alfonso of Aragon in Naples. During this time Valla wrote *Elegantiae linguae latinae (Elegances of the Latin Language)* and *Disputationes Dialecticae (Dialectical Disputations).* These texts provided brilliant foundations for the rhetorical use of eloquent Latin and hostile attacks on what Valla considered to be the crude Latin used by scholastic philosophers and judges.

Valla also wrote a *Declamatio* or *De falsa Constantini Donatione,* a discourse revealing the forgery of the alleged donation of the Roman Empire by Emperor Constantine to the Roman Catholic Church. He directly attacked the Papacy's claim for temporal authority, a text that directly influenced Luther's attitude towards the Church. Valla's style has been characterized as "invective as genre" in such a way that "publicizes a private quarrel" and draws the audience into the dialogue in various communities of accomplices.[169] Perhaps it is not surprising, then, that Valla was called before the Inquisition in Rome in 1444 to defend his positions. He was freed, and nearly retried in 1446, but then left Rome for Naples to write an *Apologia* to defend himself from further accusations.

In 1448 Valla's fortunes changed, in part through the patronage of Nicholas of Cusa, who was now a cardinal. Nicholas appointed Valla as a writer of the Pope's letters and engaged him and others in a project of translating all the major Greek works into Latin. From 1450 Valla was appointed to a chair of Greek studies at the Roman *studium,* beating out George of Trebizond, the translator of Plato's *Laws* who had been supported by Francesco Barbaro. During this period in Rome Valla was able to continue his scholarly work. His earlier text *Elegantiae linguae latinae* had become extremely popular, and he worked on a second edition. In 1455 Valla was elevated in the Curia by an appointment as secretary to Pope Calixtus III, and he soon gave an *Oratio in principio sui studii* as an inaugural lecture for the University of Rome. His oration was a praise of the study of liberal arts and humanistic studies. Valla's purpose was to establish the Curia in Rome as a center of humanism. He envisioned the Latin language and culture, instead of the ownership of land and temporal political power, as a new foundation for the Roman Empire. His goal was to provide an intellectual framework within which a dynamic union of Christian values and classical culture and language could flourish.[170]

As mentioned previously the dialogue *On Pleasure: De voluptate* takes place among three different men, each of whom represents a different way of looking at the highest good.[171] The first section of the dialogue tries to prove that pleasure is

---

169. Nancy Streuver, "Lorenzo Valla: Humanist Rhetoric and the Critique of the Classical Languages of Morality," in *Renaissance Eloquence: Studies in the Theory and Practice of Renaissance Rhetoric,* ed. James J. Murphy (Berkeley/Los Angeles/London: University of California Press, 1983), pp. 191-220, esp. 198-201. The quote in full states: "The invective dialogue, after all, publicizes a private quarrel; the arguments, which concern social usage, inevitably pertain to communities, groups; and the extent to which the audience as community is accomplice in the adversary role is left imprecise, unclear in an unsettling manner" (p. 201).

170. D'Amico, *Renaissance Humanism in Papal Rome,* pp. 118-19.

171. For a detailed description of the development of the three different characters and their re-

good, the second section that virtue is not the highest good, and the third section that pleasure is the true and highest good. Part of the purpose of the dialogue is to establish a new meaning for pleasure or *voluptas*. It is not simply a feeling or experience, but has an ontological dimension as well. It seeks to capture an exultation, delight, or joy in union with forces of nature that aim towards self-actualization.[172] Basically Valla will argue that other ethical norms inhibit this energetic good.

The concept of woman appears throughout Valla's dialogue on pleasure. In other words, while Valla identifies in his dialogue the Epicureans, Stoics, and Christians, another group called 'woman' also emerges alongside of or within the three-part division. Our analysis will reflect on ways in which Valla presents various views of woman's identity while he describes three very different kinds of men. Thus, it will approach Lorenzo Valla's theory of gender from the perspective of woman's identity within it.

Among the characters represented in the conversation about the highest good are some previously named in our discussion of women's education: Pier Candido Decembrio, a translator and defender of Plato, and Guarino of Verona, the humanist educator. Lorenzo Valla often used the names of real persons for the characters in his dialogues. He would usually identify the individual with a particular kind of philosophy, but then put words and arguments into his mouth that went beyond or even contradicted his actual claims. As a result of this method of incorporation and transformation of actual men, Valla became involved in controversy with those people whose names he chose to represent by characters. For example, in the first version of *On Pleasure: De voluptate,* the Epicurean was represented by Antonio Beccadelli (1394-1471), also called Panormita, a humanist poet who had published in 1425 a text of erotic epigrams and poems entitled *Hermaphroditus.* Valla had become an associate of Panormita during the early period of his life in Rome, and it would appear that Panormita was actually the initiator of the idea of the dialogue itself.[173]

Panormita was a professor at the *studium* in Pavia and a poet to the court of Milan. Because Panormita also lived a very dissolute life, Valla's use of his name to represent the Epicurean position in his dialogue led readers to conclude that Valla was supporting some aspects of this position. In addition, Panormita, who had invited Valla to move to Pavia, suddenly turned against him, and so in a second version of the dialogue Valla changed the name of the Epicurean character from Panormita to 'Veggio' after Maffeo Veggio (1407-1458), who also was a member of the *studium* at Pavia.[174] Although the character Veggio argued the Epicurean position the man Veggio actually lived a chaste life, and was widely respected in Pavia. In fact, Veggio chose to leave his teaching position at Pavia because of the immoral behavior of the students in that town. The views of a Ciceronian Stoic position in

---

lation to actual people Valla knew, see Maristella de Panizza Lorch, in her introduction to *On Pleasure (De voluptate)* (New York: Abaris Books, Inc., 1977), pp. 7-26.

172. Lorch, *A Defense of Life: Lorenzo Valla's Theory of Pleasure,* pp. 27 and 113-14.

173. Lorch, *A Defense of Life: Lorenzo Valla's Theory of Pleasure,* p. 40.

174. Albert Rabil, Jr., "Humanism in Milan," in *Renaissance Humanism,* vol. 1, *Humanism in Italy,* p. 246.

the dialogue were represented no longer by Leonardo Bruni, but by Catone Sacco, a jurist and humanist from Valla's circle. Again Valla chose as his character a Lombard of impeccable reputation, even though Sacco disagreed with the positions taken. Valla infuriated the Faculty of Law at Pavia by writing a letter to Catone Sacco that attacked a text by another jurist. Valla's life was put in danger and Panormita protected him in his own home until he could leave Pavia for Milan.[175] In addition, following his usual pattern of polemical relationships Valla and Panormita became enemies as well.[176] He also alienated his old mentor Bruni by writing a public attack on Bruni's oration on the city of Florence, and also by identifying Bruni with an Aristotelian virtue-based approach to the highest good, an approach Valla strongly rejected.

The Christian character was represented by a Franciscan friar, Antonio Raudense (1398-1450/53), also known as da Rho. Raudense was a professor of rhetoric at the University of Milan and well trained in both humanism and Christian theology.[177] However, in real life Antonio da Rho presented an ambivalent model for Christian virtue because he had written in 1425 a text of erotic poetry consistent with an Epicurean view, and he also appeared to follow Cicero's way of thinking. Thus, Valla's cast of characters presents a consistently ambivalent perspective on the topic; if they were men of good reputation like Veggio or Sacco, they represented views they did not hold to in real life; or if like Raudense their reputation was somewhat tarnished, their presented views appear to be Christian. This ambivalent means of communication creates a constant tension about what is a false good and what is a true good. Thus, Valla forces his readers to enter into these tensions; he uses tension as a rhetorical device the reader is invited to overcome in order to come to new insights about the true good.[178] Our analysis will now enter into the text to determine to what extent these tensions affect his concept of woman.

The Stoic position is first articulated by Catone Sacco, who draws upon the tradition of "Pythagoras, Socrates, Plato, Aristotle, Theophrastus, Zeno, Cleanthes, Chrysippus" and others including Boethius for his theory of virtue.[179] Catone introduces an engendered distinction when he explains his rejection of Epicurean theory and his adoption of Stoic teaching about virtue as the only good:

> But to what purpose is all this? Simply to make it clear that the Vergilian, or better the Epicurean, farmers ought not to be excluded from the ranks of fools and sinners. Things being thus, it is certainly right for me to wonder with amazement why the human mind, which we mean to be divine, should be so perversely misled as to embrace so quickly what is frivolous, vain, useless, futile, and, in a word, evil, and then to hold it firmly, instead of grasping the true and solid virtue

---

175. Rabil, "Humanism in Milan," in *Renaissance Humanism*, vol. 1, *Humanism in Italy*, p. 248.

176. Lorch, "Italy's Leading Humanist: Lorenzo Valla," in *Renaissance Humanism*, vol. 1, *Humanism in Italy*, p. 333.

177. See Rabil, "Humanism in Milan," in *Renaissance Humanism*, vol. 1, *Humanism in Italy*, for details about Antonio da Rho's life and polemics with both Panormita and Valla, pp. 246-47. It should be noted that Rho is also referred to as Raudensis.

178. Lorch, *A Defense of Life: Lorenzo Valla's Theory of Pleasure*, pp. 31-32.

179. Valla, *On Pleasure: De voluptate*, I, 57.

by which alone we come close to the gods and, if it is permissible to say so, become gods. In the teaching of this virtue, the Stoics seem to be the most famous, since they say that the only good is rightful behaviour; I am accustomed to admire them more than all others. Our Seneca rightly and wittily desired them to be considered, among the rest of the philosophers, as males among females.[180]

The use of feminine and female to represent the soft, weak, frivolous, vain, useless, futile, and irrational side of life and masculine and male to represent the hard, strong, serious, productive, and rational side of life was a key to Valla's depiction of the Stoic view. Men, he claims, need to develop a strong will in the virtuous pursuit of good. In that context women are identified with the weaker part of man's personality: "But let us observe what is surely another virtue: gravity. Who, however, could be called serious, rather than sad, strict, and austere, or on the contrary, lax, soft, and womanish (effeminatus)?"[181] What is womanish or feminine is soft and lax, or the opposite of the character of a rational and virtuous Stoic. Later in the dialogue, almost echoing this view, Veggio teases Catone when he says: "And, to quote something from your Stoic and manly (masculo) Seneca. . . ."[182]

Catone also develops a negative metaphorical feminine association when he interprets Nature as like a cruel stepmother who needs to be fought against from within the mind and will of the virtuous man:

> Who will ever doubt that Nature has acted very unjustly toward us, not as a mother but (if it is permissible to say so) as a stepmother, imposing upon us laws more cruel than those Lycurgus inflicted upon the Spartans, and exacting from us tributes and revenues greater than those one could require from stepchildren, from slaves, from prisoners? Never has a subjection to the cruellest tyrants compared in seriousness to this: that we should live according to the rules of virtue only with much fatigue and pain. Nor did I say what I did in order to bewail the vicissitudes of your fate or even mind, since, with labor and vigils greater than human reason seems capable of, we have managed to swim to shore. But I pity the condition of those not endowed with so much diligence and with, so to speak, the art of swimming; and you know how great is the throng we not unjustly call by that already familiar name, "the ignorant multitude."[183]

Catone's metaphorical identification of Nature with a cruel stepmother who tyrannizes her children, and his suggestion that only a few men are able to live, or swim to the shore of virtue, relegate all women to the category of 'the ignorant multitude.'

The Epicurean Veggio challenges Catone's negative view of Nature as a wicked stepmother, by arguing that even though at times Nature sends difficult things, it is better to view Nature more like a kind mother who sends pleasures:

180. Valla, *On Pleasure: De voluptate,* I, 59.
181. Valla, *On Pleasure: De voluptate,* I, 61.
182. Valla, *On Pleasure: De voluptate,* I, 83.
183. Valla, *On Pleasure: De voluptate,* I, 63.

Nature, as I said, did not create many vices, nor did she allow the vices to rage against us, as is believed by Stoics, the most simpleminded and foolish among men, who grow pale and flee from eels as though they were serpents. We, instead, not only do not flee from eels, but with the greatest relish prepare them as food, and if there were no other seasoning, we should certainly not lack the chance while feasting of making fun of Stoic rusticity and foolishness. . . .

When you see that Nature has placed before you pleasures and at the same time has bestowed upon you and given you a soul favorably disposed toward them, will you still not be grateful to her? I do not know what illness or insanity (for thus it must be called) causes you to choose a solitary, sad life, and (to make the offense complete) causes you to assail Nature, under whom, as under the rule of a most indulgent mother, you might live very happily if you had a little good sense.[184]

The contrasting views of Epicurean and Stoic concerning the metaphorically feminine Nature as an indulgent mother or a cruel stepmother respectively are matched by their approach to women as well. The Epicurean places considerable attention on women as being able to give pleasure (and therefore good) to man; while the Stoic tries to push away woman as a danger to a man who rationally seeks the good. The Stoic defines himself over and against the metaphorically feminine Nature so that woman for him is simply a challenge to be overcome or an example of weakness and failure from the perspective of a rationally constructed ethics.

One of Catone's arguments reflects on the story of Lucretia, who committed suicide because she had been raped by an enemy of her husband. This classical story repeated by Augustine in *The City of God* captivated humanists.[185] In Roman culture, suicide was often considered a heroic act, and Lucretia had been admired by the ancients for her action. Augustine, who had criticized her decision, still treated her with compassion. Augustine's argument contained two significant aspects: first, if a woman is raped against her will, there is no culpability or even loss of purity for her, and second, suicide is always wrong because it usurps God's place to determine life and death. Catone's purpose in introducing the story of Lucretia was to use her as an example to support his main claim that "virtue is the sole good, and vice the only evil."[186] Catone attempts to explain why it is that human nature is so cruel as to seek to ruin people's attempts to lead virtuous lives:

Why should we delight so in defiling women who are chaste, virginal, pure and respectable; and why are we more quickly inflamed by the desire to dishonor them than to possess prostituted, depraved, lascivious, and base women, even when these are more beautiful? Certainly, Sextus Tarquinius was induced to ravish Lucretia not so much by her beauty (for he had seen her several times before) as by her austere way of life, of which he had been previously ignorant. It seems

184. Valla, *On Pleasure:De voluptate,* I, 81.
185. Augustine, *The City of God* (New York: Modern Library, 1950), book 1, 19-23.
186. Valla, *On Pleasure: De voluptate,* I, 65.

clear that in so doing he was influenced by the sole desire to sin and to defile virtue.[187]

It is at this point that Catone's defense of the Stoic argument begins to unravel. He portrays the feminine personification of 'stepmother Nature' as so cruel that either a person can never achieve a life of virtue, or if he does, he is miserable. Catone reflects: "I wish we did not have so many examples — Anaxagoras, Theramenes, Socrates, Callisthenes, Zeno, Scipio, Rutilius, Cicero, Seneca, and others — whom, to use the words of Quintilian, 'the possession of virtues made miserable.'"[188] So Catone concludes that virtue is such a divine quality that Mother Nature allows only a few miserable persons to possess it and deprives all others. This means that the Stoic position of the true good is unavailable to the vast majority of humanity; it serves only a few rare individuals.

Veggio then accuses Catone of not only poorly defending the Stoic position but also misrepresenting Nature as a cruel and harsh stepmother, who makes most people miserable, instead of as a kind mother who generously responds to humanity:

> When you see that Nature has placed before you pleasures and at the same time has bestowed upon you and given you a soul favorably disposed toward them, will you still not be grateful to her? I do not know what illness or insanity (for thus it must be called) causes you to choose a solitary, sad life, and (to make the offense complete) causes you to assail Nature, under whom, as under the rule of a most indulgent mother, you might live very happily if you had a little good sense.[189]

The dialogue has a complex structure of half truths, distortion of truths, and combination of invective along with the integration of historical sources about women or feminine personifications to support these different positions. Furthermore, Valla uses a technique in his dialogue of having disputants self-destruct through the very structure of their argument. As Brian Vickers points out, "his *personae* must undermine themselves by their own arguments. Their speeches ostensibly argue the Stoic or Epicurean case, but in fact negate it."[190] So the force of the conclusion of the dialogue comes not so much from direct arguments for the Christian position, as from the incoherence of the arguments maintaining the Epicurean and Stoic positions. We will now turn to consider directly the concept of woman as described by Veggio, who defends the Epicurean position for purposes of argument.

Where Veggio presents an Epicurean view of the pleasures of the five external senses in *On Pleasure: De voluptate,* woman is described as an attractive sexual object for man's enjoyment. Veggio analyzes the positive effects of various aspects of her body on men's senses.

---

187. Valla, *On Pleasure: De voluptate,* I, 65.
188. Valla, *On Pleasure: De voluptate,* I, 67.
189. Valla, *On Pleasure: De voluptate,* I, 81.
190. Vickers, "Valla's Ambivalent Praise of Pleasure," *Viator: Medieval and Renaissance Studies,* p. 297.

Let us move forward, speaking now of the other sex. Nature, the mother of all things, gave many women a face, as Terence says, "beautiful and generous." . . .

Nor are women graced only with beautiful faces, but also with beautiful hair, which Homer praises so highly in Helen and many others, with beautiful breasts, with beautiful thighs, and indeed with beauties of all the body, whether they be tall, white of complexion, luscious, or well proportioned. . . . If we allow certain women who have beautiful hair, beautiful faces, and beautiful breasts to go with those parts uncovered, why should we be unjust to those who lack these beauties but have other parts that are beautiful?[191]

Following a law of nature, Veggio suggests that all women and men have a natural desire to take pleasure in the beauty of one another's bodies. Thus, woman too perceives a man as a sexual object to be possessed:

The same kind of thing happens with men. For as we do with women, so also do women pursue with the most ardent glances those of us who are most handsome to behold. And will anyone deny that men and women are born beautiful and especially prone to mutual affection for the one purpose of receiving delight by observing each other, by dwelling together, and by passing their lives together?[192]

Veggio suggests that since women and men both choose to relate to one another primarily as objects of physical attraction they ought to be able to be united by these natural desires simply if they want to. Thus Valla combines a theory of pleasure and utility: the beauty of a woman's body and the energy this brings to a man who is inspired by it, are useful to a man when sexual union occurs. The same theory applies analogously to woman. The senses are heightened by the perfection of physical beauty, and this offers a strong experience of pleasure to the one sensing.

Thus, Valla provides a critical framework for situations in which the senses are offended by ugliness. The Epicurean argument does not refer only to positive effects woman has on a man's senses, but also, in considering the sense of smell, introduces some negative effects produced by both men and women:

. . . [N]othing seems to be more despicable than those men of whom Horace remarks: "Rufillus smells of mouth lozenges; Gorgonius smells like a billy goat."

Why need we say more? Ugly wives, wives who cannot speak or who speak inharmoniously, wives, finally, who are far gone in sickness, cannot be repudiated; those who smell, can be. And how much more is this condition to be reproached in us men who live in the forum, in the Senate, in public office, especially if we arouse others' repugnance by a fault that is not of the body, as with women, but of the soul, as with Rufillus and Gorgonius?[193]

Thus, the person who chooses pleasure as the highest good will do all he can to

191. Valla, *On Pleasure: De voluptate,* I, 97-99.
192. Valla, *On Pleasure: De voluptate,* I, 99.
193. Valla, *On Pleasure: De voluptate,* I, 111.

avoid offending through the senses. In the above passage, while Veggio appears to give an equal admonition to women and to men, there is an undercurrent of devaluation of woman's identity through the implication that she cannot help smelling because of her body, while a man could, if he chose, avoid this consequence. This pattern of suggesting an equality of men and women, while actually drawing out a differentiation that devalues women more than men is common to Veggio's arguments. He presents a kind of qualified gender polarity attitude, drawing upon Plato's principles to justify his views.

Use of Plato's Principles of Gender

The Epicurean position is then summarized as a reformulation, i.e., distortion, of the scholastic description of cardinal virtues: prudence is "knowing how to procure advantages to yourself and avoid what is disagreeable, . . . [c]ontinence consists in limiting yourself to one pleasure so as to enjoy greater pleasures, and more of them, . . . [and j]ustice consists in procuring goodwill, favor, and advantages for yourself among mortals."[194] Temperance becomes trying to avoid offending others by "uncouth" manners or appearance. Pleasure is the "mistress" that guides all actions. By these distortions Valla creates tensions in his reader concerning the value of ethics as traditionally taught by Thomists. In the following developments the tensions increase even more.

Anticipating a moralist's criticism of his views, Veggio introduces a linguistic argument to prove that free sexual association between a man and a woman who please one another is good:

> "What if you commit adultery?" What a hateful word! Why should we assail adulterers, if it pleases us to look at Nature? There is absolutely no difference between a woman's going to bed with her husband or with her lover. . . . And what else does *maritus* [husband] mean if not *mas* [male]? Isn't the adulterous man also a male? Be careful lest occasionally he is, perhaps, more masculine than the marital partner.[195]

In the above grammatical point, Veggio appears to be supporting women's desires as much as men's. However, in the following addition, he refers to women as property of men or of the state, in an appeal to the common (erroneous) understanding of the community of women in Plato's *Republic*:

> However, if it were possible to live according to the Platonic formula, those charming women would not belong to particular private persons, or tyrants, as I might almost say, but to the state itself, that is, to all the people; we and they would be permitted to enjoy each other's kindliness indiscriminately. And thus there would be one city, one government, one marriage, and, nearly, one home

194. Valla, *On Pleasure: De voluptate,* I, 115.
195. Valla, *On Pleasure: De voluptate,* I, 119.

and one family. . . . It would be perfectly just that the first favors of a virgin would go to the first who gained her goodwill and who obtained this reward by her own free choice. Might we only submit to this Platonic law instead of the Julian law!

But why do I say Platonic? I should say, rather, the law of Nature. That Julian Law was written; this one is innate.[196]

Anyone actually familiar with the original text of Plato would be aware that Veggio is distorting some key components of the Greek philosopher's suggestions. Plato argued that only in the guardian class should there be abolition of private marriage, and in this class sexual relations occurred only once a year for purposes of propagation. While the warrior class was allowed access to women as reward for their military successes, women did not belong to the state or to all the people. It is also difficult to know whether Valla implied by his argument that Epicureans tended to interpret Plato as supporting these exaggerated claims, or whether Valla himself believed that Plato held these views. As we noted earlier in this chapter, the first translations of Plato's *Republic* either avoided or distorted elements that appeared to be immoral to the Christian culture. Even though Valla could read Greek, he was likely using Decembrio's early Latin translations of Plato's works, which would have led him to draw this erroneous conclusion.[197] He may also have been basing his conclusions on Bruni's translation of Aristotle's *Politics,* which also distorted somewhat Plato's original positions.

It is clear that Valla does understand one important aspect of Plato's arguments about gender identity in the *Republic* and *Laws,* namely that women should share with men the political guardianship of an ideal society. He introduces this concept, while at the same time distorts its significance, in his continuation of the defense of Epicurean views. In the following passage Veggio has a female character, a Vestal Virgin, address a "Platonic Senate composed of women and men":

. . . [b]ecause I am a patron of women (young ones, not old ones), it is my pleasure to chastise and reprehend our ancestors, who were not scrupulous about everything. I shall not speak as a man in arguing the case, but in the role of one of those women who has been forced into the priesthood against her will and who now, in a Platonic Senate composed of men and women, speaks as follows: "What, Senators, do you intend by this harshness against us, most unhappy of maidens, by which you force us to drag out our lives in a way contrary to the nature of all animate beings and even of the gods themselves? Nothing in human affairs is a more intolerable torment than virginity."[198]

Veggio mocks Plato's arguments even as he uses them to defend the more common understanding of Plato as supporting immoral behavior. Veggio's paraphrase of a

---

196. Valla, *On Pleasure: De voluptate,* I, 119.

197. Rabil, "Humanism in Milan," in *Renaissance Humanism,* vol. 1, *Humanism in Italy.* Rabil notes in relation to a discussion of Valla and Plato's *Republic* that "Plato's *Republic* circulated freely in the Pavia-Milan circle in Decembrio's translation" (p. 248).

198. Valla, *On Pleasure: De voluptate,* I, 123-25.

discontented Vestal Virgin's plea is developed over several pages of the dialogue. It includes a wide range of invectives against forced celibacy for women. After a hypothetical appeal to the Senators and their wives to remember their own experience, Veggio's female voice argues that celibacy outside of marriage is an impossible goal and that in marriage there is a double standard in which only men, and not women, are allowed lovers. She exclaims: "O harsh conditions of our sex!"[199]

Lamenting the forcing of women into perpetual virginity while men may marry, Veggio's Vestal Virgin reflects on Plato's suggestion in the *Laws* that bachelors be doubly fined and encouraged to procreate. She adds:

> I ask you, noble Senators, why is this pious custom not correspondingly applied to women? Unless, perhaps, you males alone are human beings! We women are as useful as men to the procreation of mankind! Do you not see, O wisest of men, what a disaster humankind would suffer if all were as we are? Truly the race would be finished.[200]

In this short sequence within the longer argument, we can see Veggio's fallacious conclusion. Just because some people practice celibacy, it does not follow that the race would end. So Veggio's very form of argument destructs itself.

As the Vestal Virgin develops further examples to support her contention that it is both impossible and undesirable for there to be some women chosen to live as virgins, she introduces an ironic play on the concept of man as the stronger sex and woman as the weaker sex:

> And if the stronger sex is not strong enough to preserve chastity, let your conscience be your guide as to how the weaker sex can do it! For fear that I may seem to be pronouncing judgment on you rashly, I point out that you yourselves show your opinion of yourselves with one circumstance: no men are forced to endure this condition, exception by castration or by being rendered impotent with some potion. . . .
>
> Moreover, I implore all you mothers; I implore all you women, in the people's name; and I summon all you, most unhappy virgins, more than those whose legal status is at stake: flock together in one spot, grasp their hands, and put your arms around the necks of these very men, and cry aloud to them, entreat them, or do them violence! Believe me, no one will harm us, no one will drive us away. All the young men, who are strongest, will give us help against these old ones. Let us persist and struggle until this vile law is annulled.[201]

The Epicurean point of view expressed by Veggio consistently attempts to reorganize society to affirm the value of pleasure, and particularly sexual pleasure. Borrowing from the tradition in which women did belong to Epicurean schools, he uses a woman's voice to defend his own interests. He is, as he told his listener, a pa-

---

199. Valla, *On Pleasure: De voluptate*, I, 125.
200. Valla, *On Pleasure: De voluptate*, I, 125.
201. Valla, *On Pleasure: De voluptate*, I, 127-29.

tron of young women who are attractive to his senses. These young women with the help of young men will break down the constraints of old law.

Veggio also directly attacks the Stoic position of Catone who had previously introduced the example of Lucretia. Valla's Epicurean tries to prove that Lucretia did not act out of love of virtue as the highest good, but rather from other motives. Veggio's argument is drawn out in shrill tones:

> Concerning you, Lucretia, what am I to say? Although I know that you were strict, I daresay that you had not even heard what virtue was. Pythagoras, the first swallow of philosophers, had not yet taken flight to Italy, had not yet been seen or heard. Then who taught you chastity, especially of so severe a kind? Had you heard about Dido, founder of Carthage? I do not think so; it was not her glory that you envied. Then what motive impelled you, precipitated you, flung you, into so rash a deed? I have the answer: it was shame before other women! If the matter were to become known in any way, you feared that some filthy gossip would be spread about you, and that the original splendor in which, sublime and erect, you used to go forth would be turned into a foul story.[202]

While Augustine had introduced the motive of shame in his description of Lucretia's act of suicide, Veggio goes even further to ridicule the Stoic position, by suggesting that Lucretia would not actually be deceiving her husband if she chose to remain silent about the incident, or even, more absurdly, if she continued to meet with the man who raped her out of desire for sexual pleasure. His rationale for this argument is that no husband remains faithful, and therefore wives would not necessarily have to remain faithful as long as their husbands did not learn about it. Valla ridicules the Stoic position even more when he condemns Lucretia most of all not because she may have been motivated by shame, not because she did not choose to become deceitful to her husband, but because she broke her marriage contract to a man:

> Is it part of the fidelity due to marriage to kill yourself when by so doing you have ruined and destroyed the entire marriage and all your conjugal fidelity? Mad woman, why do you persecute yourself as if you were to blame? Why do you pay the penalty, to your own injury? Why do you reopen with your own hands the wound you have received, so that your own guilt is now greater than that of Sextus? He did violence to another; you abused yourself as an enemy. He used you as a wife; you abused yourself as an enemy. He used no instrument of iron but his own body; you turned a sword, unnatural for women, not against him but against yourself. He did not hurt your body in any way; you killed yourself. Savage, cruel woman, do you punish so small a fault with so great a punishment?[203]

He trivializes Lucretia's decision by comparing her with a woman who accidentally broke an urn by bumping into someone she passed by, and then decided to

---

202. Valla, *On Pleasure: De voluptate,* II, 145-47.
203. Valla, *On Pleasure: De voluptate,* II, 147.

drown herself in the well where she had drawn water. In this move Valla has Veggio take the practice of a particular virtue to an absurd extreme. Lucretia's crime, for the Epicurean, is that she broke her promise of fidelity to her husband by killing herself. It was not, as it was for Augustine, that it is God's and not a woman's prerogative to determine the time and mode of death. Instead, for Veggio, the rape is relegated to a simple accident, like breaking an urn, while the suicide is elevated to a major contravention of marriage. In this way the Epicurean undermined the Stoic's claim that Lucretia acted out of virtue.

Veggio completes his argument against Catone's position by returning to the sources of a virtue-based theory, and reinterpreting their views. It is helpful to quote a short passage simply to indicate the way in which ancient Greek philosophers were now being integrated into humanist theories about the goal of philosophy:

> Your own Aristotle established that there are three goods that ought to be desired. He says (we use here the words of our friend Leonardo Aretina [Bruni], who recently translated the *Ethics* into a rich and clear Latin): "We desire honor and pleasure and all comprehension and all virtue, for their own sake and for the sake of happiness." He had indicated this earlier in other words, dividing life into the sensitive, the civic, and the contemplative, which follow Plato's establishment of three ends or goals in *The Republic:* knowledge, honor, and wealth, which were derived from Homer's well-known figure of the three goddesses, Juno, Minerva, and Venus — but this does not concern our subject. Aristotle spoke unlearnedly and tastelessly when he said that those three things should be desired both for themselves and for happiness, as if happiness itself were something different from those three.[204]

Following his usual pattern, the Epicurean distorts the meaning of Plato and Aristotle for his own purposes of making pleasure the highest good. He does this not only in his treatment of the concept of woman, as demonstrated above, but also for all fundamental categories in philosophy. This conclusion to Book II of *On Pleasure: De voluptate* sets up the context in which Valla can introduce, in Book III, a transformed Christian argument about the nature of the highest good.

The position of the Christian philosopher is represented in the dialogue by Antonio Raudense. He rejects both the Epicurean premise that simple pleasure is the highest good and the Stoic premise that a rational basis for virtue is the highest good. Instead, Raudense argues that the highest good *and* greatest source of pleasure and virtue is God. Raudense defends the main thesis of Valla's work, namely that a person loves God not for God himself, but because it gives him the greatest pleasure and personal fulfillment to do so. In this way, the Christian character in the dialogue offers a new way of understanding the goal of Christianity, a way that rejects both the Aristotelian and scholastic argument that good ought to be loved for its own sake and not because it gives pleasure. Raudense indicates clearly that he prefers Plato to Aristotle as his authority for a Christian philosophy: ". . . we

---

204. Valla, *On Pleasure: De voluptate,* II, 197.

have not only the authority of Aristotle but, what is more, that of Plato, which in my opinion has always been, and ought to be, of greater value."[205] However, he adds that he prefers most of all not depending on any authority, but rather to examine each position on its own merit. Raudense then proceeds to offer a scathing attack on Aristotle's theory of virtue.

His argument against Aristotle has two parts: to disprove first, Aristotle's view that virtue resides in the mean between two extremes, and second, that virtue is the only good. Valla, through Raudense, creates an incredible tension in the scholastical listener by arguing for the direct opposite of Aristotle's views, namely that extremes are often virtuous and the mean is often vicious. According to Raudense: "As it happens, I do not understand why it is necessary to speak of the mean and the extremes, which later Aristotle calls excess and defect, as if whatever is a mean is good and whatever is an extreme is excessive or deficient. I myself sometimes notice that this very mean is vicious and the extreme is right, as in speaking."[206] Raudense then introduces examples from rhetoric to prove his thesis. He concludes that a systematic and quantitative ranking of virtues and vices simply does not match reality. Valla's exaggerated account of the mean and extreme in Aristotle's ethics leaves out the middle part of his definition of virtue, namely the "mean relative to us." Aristotle does not offer an objective common mean for any virtue. However, Valla has identified a sense in which Christian ethics at times argues that an extreme action is the right one, and that a moderated one is inappropriate. So the Christian's critique of Aristotle's ethics has some merit.

The second argument of Raudense against Aristotle is actually more of an argument against scholastic ethics as well. Basically, he claims that virtue cannot be the only good because a good is recognized by its contrary, and human beings share with animals a seeking for pleasure and avoidance of displeasure. Thus, pleasure, implanted by Nature, is the good they seek. Pleasure is actually the inner dynamic through which a human being seeks to fulfill its earthly desires in an upward movement towards love of God.

In the context of this kind of argument, woman is viewed as someone who may pull man away from his supreme good. Thus, even though Valla seeks to redefine the goal of Christian ethics, he nonetheless depicts woman as the indirect and dangerous cause of a man's downfall:

> With great danger (it is hoped without damage) I have learned what I shall repeatedly advise and warn you of: nothing draws youth more strongly from right studies and every virtue than the love of beauty, either another's or one's own. . . . When I speak of another's beauty, I think mainly of the beauty of women; the desire for all things is more temperate, but for women, truly mad. I want the same to be understood of the ardor for man by which women are inflamed. In all my discourse I mention only our sex because I am talking with males, and all I say can easily be changed to fit the other sex.[207]

205. Valla, *On Pleasure: De voluptate,* III, 237.
206. Valla, *On Pleasure: De voluptate,* III, 245-47.
207. Valla, *On Pleasure: De voluptate,* III, 293.

Antonio Raudense is self-conscious that his words are addressed in this dialogue to men alone, but insists that his argument can be applied inversely to women as well. This would imply that he is not devaluing women *per se,* but rather love of women based solely on attraction for physical beauty.

One aspect of Raudense's argument may seem to reinforce a polarity position that women cause men's downfall: i.e., his use of examples of men who were captivated by beauty: Samson's violent destruction by Delilah and David's adultery with Bathsheba and homicide of her husband. However, the Christian character is careful not to blame women directly for men's distractions from the pursuit of their highest good. Instead, he argues that it is self-love, or a form of narcissism in the man, that is the direct cause of this consequence. Raudense claims that a man who is transfixed by his own handsome looks will not remain faithful to higher goals: "As long as we abandon ourselves to such thoughts, we cannot maintain either our mental or our physical stability. We imagine that we are falling in love with every woman, and we think that every woman should fall in love with us."[208] However, when Raudense implies that the fault lies with man, he does state that a person who gets caught this way is like a "weak and effeminate *(effeminata)* youth."[209] Thus, the Christian character, while generally avoiding a devaluation of individual women and placing the direct blame on men, nonetheless associates weakness with a negative feminine characteristic in a man, or effeminateness.

Raudense offers a solution to a man who gets caught in this difficulty of choosing temporal over eternal goods, namely to carefully exercise his imagination:

> What I have said relates to this: every time you are moved by the beauty of a woman or your own good looks, which, I have explained, amount to very little, don't let go or be softened, but invoke all the arms of hope and remember that you must abstain from the love of earthly beauty if you wish to possess the heavenly kind, as I desire and hope that you will desire to do. Always reflect what a trifling thing you are pursuing in a woman. . . . But in the place of looking at women, substitute, as I have said, angels (who are neither male nor female) and all the other sanctified men and women. . . . You already are afraid of losing your looks; you are pained if they are lost or diminished; you are never sure of the very girlfriend in whose beauty and its praise you take delight; you are afraid that she will prefer someone to you, that another will join you in loving her. But in heaven there will be none of these absurdities and troubles.[210]

By substituting imaginary images of saints and angels for the sense images of actual women, Raudense suggests that a man develop the habit of turning towards a greater eternal good and thus detach himself from preoccupation with temporal goods that do not last. It is significant that his suggestion does not take the usual route of satires that attempt to associate women with animals or suggest that external beauty is a false appearance of the state of her real character.

208. Valla, *On Pleasure: De voluptate,* III, 295.
209. Valla, *On Pleasure: De voluptate,* III, 295.
210. Valla, *On Pleasure: De voluptate,* III, 295-97.

However, it is worth noting that Valla devalues a traditional Stoic model for woman as wise teacher of man. While he allows female saints to fill the imagination, through Raudense he banishes the feminine personification of Philosophy, a model used both by Plato as Diotima in the *Symposium* and by Boethius as the physician Lady Philosophy in his *Consolation of Philosophy*. Again Valla's harsh words create a tension in the listener:

> But to return to the argument, listen to how, supporting myself on the authority of faith, I shall make my reply much better and more briefly than the Lady Philosophy of Boethius could do. . . . Farewell, then, farewell to Philosophy, and let her, as though she were a loose woman of the stage, remove her foot from the sacred temple, and cease to sing, or to prate, like a sweet siren drawing men to their deaths; since she herself is afflicted with foul diseases and many wounds, let her leave it to another physician to cure and care for the sick.
>
> Which physician? I. How? Surely by speaking in this way: "Why do you weep, why do you groan, O invalid, why do you accuse God? If you look for eternal goods, why do you feel the need for earthly ones? . . ." With this rebuke all those who complain of Fortune and God should be scourged; idle-talking Philosophy could never do so, for she did not love God and worship him when she knew him or could have known him, choosing rather to fornicate with lovers of the earth.[211]

In this rejection of the Stoic Lady Philosophy who leads only by the direction of reason, Valla opens again the way to consider pleasure as a good that leads the human being ultimately to God. Antonio Raudense continues the upward climb of his argument:

> However, let me return to the subject. We were saying that the good is twofold: one kind of that which receives; the other, of that which is received. Yet what is rightly called the good is generated from both of them and is called pleasure. As this is received from creatures so is it also, but much more strongly, from the Creator. He is the source of the good, but because this good of joy is manifold, let us say that he is the source of goods. Therefore, if we have loved him from whom we have received so many goods, then certainly we have attained all virtue and its very sister, the principle of honorable and rightful action.[212]

It is important to note that the Christian Antonio Raudense is not rejecting relations with real women by his methodology for overcoming forms of addiction to the pleasure of self-love or attraction to others. His worldview emphasizes very strongly a communal structuring of society. In a consideration of the meaning of the creation of man and woman in *Genesis* Raudense states:

> As God says in the Pentateuch: "It is not well that man should be alone. Let us

211. Valla, *On Pleasure: De voluptate*, III, 273.
212. Valla, *On Pleasure: De voluptate*, III, 277.

make him a helpmeet, like unto him." Although this was said of woman, it should be understood for man as well. As the wife is the helpmate of the husband, so is the husband of the wife; and all other men are helpmeets to each other, in which consists the true sense of charity.[213]

The Epicurean man wants women to be objects of his own pleasure in a radical egotism; the Stoic defines himself away from women and relates to them through rational principles. The Christian, on the other hand, relates to women and men as helpmates, cooperating in the building of a new society of men and women saints persisting into the next world. Raudense describes this new society as being led humanly by the Virgin Mary "[w]ith the company of all the sanctified women, whose number is equal to that of the blessed who are men."[214] This conclusion appears to suggest a movement towards a gender complementarity, which posits a fundamental equality of dignity in both men and women, along with a significant differentiation. Members of the two genders remain separately identified, as men and as women, but they work together for the common good.

Raudense elaborates his view that love of the beauty of heaven is a greater joy than love of beauty on earth by describing particular female saints:

> Who could report or indeed who could conceive the beauty and adornment of Mary Magdalene and of her sister Martha? Or of Mary Cleophas, of Mary Salome, of Mary, mother of James, of Anne, grandmother of our Lord, of Anne the Prophetess, or Anne, mother of Samuel, of Catherine, or Agnes, and of the other chief ones?[215]

Valla encourages both men and women to contemplate this higher form of beauty and the joy awaiting those persons who will come into union with these saints, with Mary, and the Divine Persons of the Holy Trinity in the heavenly Jerusalem. In this way, Valla engenders his theoretical argument that love of God is the highest good because it offers the greatest pleasure. As Lorch summarizes Valla's conclusion: "That God should not be loved per se, but as the creator of the good that makes our life possible, indicates what Valla actually meant by true theology. . . ."[216] This conclusion radically overturns scholastic theology and the fundamental claim of Thomistic metaphysics that the highest good must be loved for itself, in a disinterested love, which is founded on authentic charity.

In the text *On Pleasure: De voluptate* Valla next has Guarino of Verona, a character named after the humanist educator, reductively summarize the views already presented in the dialogue. Guarino declines to comment on the Stoic posi-

213. Valla, *On Pleasure: De voluptate,* III, 283. Brian Vickers reflects on the meaning of this passage in the context of Valla's dialogue: "There the Ciceronian concept of human society as a series of bonds, deriving from the prime institution of marriage, is united with a Christian view, both set against the antisocial tendency of Epicurus" ("Valla's Ambivalent Praise," *Viator: Medieval and Renaissance Studies,* p. 315).

214. Valla, *On Pleasure: De voluptate,* III, 315.

215. Valla, *On Pleasure: De voluptate,* III, 315.

216. Lorch, *A Defense of Life: Lorenzo Valla's Theory of Pleasure,* p. 281.

tion of Catone because he is staying in his home. He does, however, compare Veggio, the Epicurean defender, to a swallow, whose voice is heard by many in cities, and Raudense, the Christian defender, to a nightingale who sings in the countryside where no one dwells. By implication, Valla suggests that the Epicurean position is widely held and the Christian view not adhered to at all. The overall aim of Valla's dialogue *On Pleasure: De voluptate* was to reject a Christian adaptation of Stoic foundations for love of God as a love of virtue for the sake of the good itself. These Stoic foundations were first articulated in Plato and Aristotle, and then built upon by Boethius and Thomas Aquinas. Thus, Valla's purpose was to undermine fundamental scholastic teachings about the true good, and to introduce instead an argument to support a neo-Epicurean position that the good should be loved because it gives the highest pleasure. To accomplish this goal, Valla had to distinguish a so-called "Christian" approach to pleasure from the Epicurean approach to pleasure. He did this by polarizing the two theories and identifying Epicureanism with lower sensual pleasures and Christianity with higher intellectual and personal pleasures. However, in both cases, self-love is the prime motive for love of the good and love of God.

It is important to note as well, that Valla's argument against a virtue theory approach to the highest good was also a rejection of the philosophy of Leonardo Bruni, who had emphasized the value of virtue, built upon the philosophy of Aristotle and the Stoics Cicero and Boethius. Thus Valla sought to influence the direction of humanist thought in ethics as well as to simply reject scholasticism. Perhaps it is not surprising that since he differed so much from Bruni's approach to ethics, he also differed from Bruni's approach to woman's identity. While Bruni emphasized the dignity of woman and especially her possibilities for receiving and flourishing with a humanist education, Valla emphasized woman's lower passions and offered polarized engendered characterizations of the feminine.

The concept of woman is a thread running throughout Valla's dialogue *On Pleasure: De voluptate*. He introduces a gender polarity theory of woman, particularly in its Epicurean and Stoic versions. He also opens some possibility for equality and differentiation in a Christian theory while seeming to suggest that no one follows this theory. The dialogue *On Pleasure: De voluptate* also includes a derogatory understanding of the feminine and effeminate as including reference to weakness, softness, and tending towards evil. So we find within Valla's Renaissance Humanism that the cluster 'woman and feminine and masculine' is differentiated from 'man and feminine and masculine,' with the former cluster given a valuation inferior to the latter.

In the chart on page 850 the views of the three different characters in Valla's dialogue are summarized.

Another important aspect of Valla's thought that is summarized here is his use of Plato's philosophy to introduce and defend certain arguments about the concept of woman. In the dialogue *On Pleasure: De voluptate* several principles of gender identity were introduced as Platonic. Some are accurate while others are distorted or false. Most, however, are used to argue for a gender unity position, but some suggest gender polarity.

Valla's Categories of Gender Identity and Relation		
Character and Position	**Man's Identity**	**Woman's Identity**
Veggio: Epicurean Pleasures are good. Gender polarity Commonly held view in cities	Sexual pleasure higher good than marital fidelity Law of nature greater than Julian law (Roman law of marriage contract) The stronger sex, yet not able to live in chastity Man benefits from Mother Nature.	Attractive sexual object to men Platonic law of community of women in *Republic* is natural law. The weaker sex cannot and ought not to live in virginity. Nature is a kind mother who sends many pleasures.
Catone: Stoic Pleasures are evil. Virtue the highest good Gender polarity	A virtuous man needs to be strong. Stoics are "males." Man has to fight nature to become virtuous.	Women are weak, soft, effeminate. Epicureans are "females." Nature is a cruel stepmother.
Raudense: Christian Self-love motivates a development from earthly pleasures to heavenly pleasures. Love of God the highest good as giving the greatest pleasure Gender complementarity Exists in heaven, but hardly on earth	Love of a woman's physical beauty can lead to a man's downfall, e.g., Samson and David. Love of woman is due to man's fault — to his weakness and self-love. A man is capable by exercise of the imagination to think about higher beings, angels and saints. A man who does not do this is weak and "effeminate." Goal is for men to help women build up a society with pleasure-based common good in union with the communion of saints and Mary.	Love of a man's physical beauty can lead to a woman's downfall. An analogous process for women A rejection of the feminine personification of Lady Philosophy by comparing her with a harlot in union with those seeking earthly love Goal is for woman to help man build up a society with pleasure-based common good in union with the communion of saints led by Mary.

Valla's 'Platonic Law' from the *Republic:*
1. Women and men have the same natural desires for sexual union;
2. Society should be structured to allow natural sexual unions to occur at will among women and men "like Plato's community of women." Platonic law follows natural law;
3. In this practice women are property of the state;
4. Both men and women participate in civic debate in a Platonic governing body or senate.

Valla's 'Platonic practice' from the *Laws:*
5. If bachelors are fined for not being married at a particular age, so should un-married women or virgins be fined if not married by a certain age.

Seeking to defend a new humanism drawing upon ancient Greek and Latin sources, Valla also publicly attacked the institutional structures imbued with scholasticism. Just before his death in 1457 Valla gave another oration, this time in honor of St. Thomas Aquinas. Though he praised the medieval philosopher's holiness of life and his intelligence, Valla directly attacked Thomas's dependence on a dialectical method, his metaphysics, and his approach to theology. "These criticisms struck at the very foundation of Scholastic thought and provided a rationale for constructing a new base for theology."[217] Before including some of Valla's own words on this critique of scholasticism, it should be noted that at the beginning of his oration on St. Thomas, Valla introduced a gender distinction that contained a devaluation of the concept of woman. The bases for these devaluations are similar to those he used in *On Pleasure: De voluptate.*

> For whoever invokes the gods does so to ask them to protect truth and justice, and this is something that evil men would not want. It was abandoned by the defenders of good causes, partly because they wanted to show they trusted in their own justice independently of the protection of the gods, partly because they thought they would appear more distinguished and more manly if they did not act like women and at the very outset resort to calling on the gods. For in those times there seemed to be something womanish, not manly, about invoking the help of divine powers; so it is that, as Sallust tells us, Cato says: "It is not by vows and womanish supplications that the aid of the gods is procured."[218]

Here we have the generalized claim that women's weakness led them to pray to God and that a man should avoid similar actions for fear of being considered weak or womanish. However, Valla inverts the claim by arguing that this generalization held only for the worship of false gods, and that since he believed in the true God, it was not only permissible but also appropriate for Valla to invoke Mary's intercession on the occasion of his oration and thus reintroduce a pious and honorable practice.

217. D'Amico, *Renaissance Humanism in Papal Rome,* p. 146.
218. Valla, "In Praise of Saint Thomas Aquinas," in *Renaissance Philosophy: New Translations,* ed. Leonard A. Kennedy (The Hague, Paris: Mouton and Co., 1973), p. 17.

Valla continues his oration by listing several virtues of St. Thomas and by comparing him with other great saints. After praising him in various ways, he then creates his usual rhetorical tension by offering a polemic against Thomas's metaphysical approach:

> But as for these things which are called metaphysics and modes of signification and other things of that sort, which the new theologians marvel at as if they were a new sphere lately discovered, or the epicycles of the planets, I for my part do not find them so wonderful at all, and I do not think it matters so much whether one knows about them or not — things that perhaps are better not known because they are obstacles in the way of better kinds of knowledge.[219]

Valla argues that one can be a good theologian without knowing metaphysics, dialectic, or other traditional areas required by scholastic theologians and philosophers. This particular point will turn out, in time, to have an impact on the history of the concept of woman. As mentioned previously, academic foundations for gender polarity were grounded in Aristotelian natural philosophy and metaphysics of contraries, and extended into his ethics and politics. The attack on various aspects of scholastic philosophy ultimately led to a situation in which revised Aristotelian theory no longer served as the sole academic framework for understanding woman's identity.

In reading Valla's critiques of Thomas Aquinas it often seems as though he is more polemical against the effects of Aquinas's philosophy on subsequent scholastic thought than against the fundamental arguments of Thomas himself. Valla despised the disputational method of doing philosophy and the abstract claims it seemed to produce. He wanted philosophy to concern itself with real flesh-and-blood issues. As a consequence, Valla appeared to disregard the basic function of the faculty of intellect, and to emphasize instead the lower operations of the senses and the human passions, especially the passion of pleasure. However, if Valla had immersed himself in Part I-II, Questions 22-35 of the *Summa Theologica* he would have discovered a rich consideration of the passions of the soul, of the relation of good and evil in the passions, and the morality of pleasures. Valla would have discovered that Thomas came to the same conclusion as he did about the Stoic and Epicurean theories of pleasure. For example, Thomas states: "While some of the Stoics maintained that all pleasures are evil, the Epicureans held that pleasure is good in itself, and that consequently all pleasures are good. They seem to have thus erred through not discriminating between that which is good simply, and that which is good in respect to a particular individual."[220]

At the same time, however, Thomas stresses that the intellect has an important function in determining which goods are true goods. Valla, by rejecting the role of the intellect because of its overemphasis by the Stoics and later scholastic philosophers, ended up with a theory of pleasure that was unable to offer any concrete criteria for determining when a pleasure leads a person away from a true good

---

219. Valla, "In Praise of Saint Thomas Aquinas," in *Renaissance Philosophy,* p. 23.
220. Thomas Aquinas, *Summa Theologica,* Pt. I-II, Q. 34, art. 2.

and when it leads a person towards a true good. Being directed towards love of God is not enough. The challenge is found in *how* a person is directed towards the love of God. A similar difficulty is present in love of other persons. The question is how one's love is directed towards another person. Without the presence of the intellect making careful determinations in individual situations, Valla's theory of pleasure can end in self-delusion and exploitation of others.

In this context it is useful to turn towards contemporary principles of Christian humanism to offer a further evaluation of Valla's contribution to the history of the concept of woman. On the one hand, Valla rightly brings the human passions into the forefront of human relations. As Boccaccio had attempted to do before him, Valla argues correctly that women as well as men have the full range of human passions, and further that any theory of human identity has to incorporate an appropriate value for the operation of the passions. To disregard the passions or to view them as evil as did many Stoics is an error in philosophical anthropology. Thus, Valla's analysis does attempt to bring about a gender unity, at least in respect to the active presence of passions, and especially of the passion of pleasure. In so doing, Valla presents woman not so much as a dangerous threat for a man, as a source of continual pleasure. The contrary is true for woman; i.e., man is not so much a ruler or rational principle who orders her irrational desires as a source of continual pleasure for her. Thus, Valla overturns some aspects of traditional gender polarity for a new dynamic theory of gender complementarity founded on the role of pleasure as motivation for all actions.

However, this new theory has the serious difficulty of failing to conform to the personalist norm, namely, of always treating another person as an end and never as a means. To be more specific, Valla's theory leads to the consequence that a man and a woman mutually use one another for the purpose of gaining the greatest pleasure. The following critique of this position by Karol Wojtyla contains the core elements of personalist humanism:

> Egoism will remain egoism in this type of harmony, the only difference being that these two egoisms, the man's and the woman's, will match each other and be mutually advantageous. The moment they cease to match and to be of advantage to each other, nothing at all is left of the harmony. Love will be no more, in either of the persons or between them; it will not be an objective reality, for there is no objective good to ensure its existence. 'Love' in this utilitarian conception is a union of egoisms, which can hold together only on condition that they confront each other with nothing unpleasant, nothing to conflict with their mutual pleasure. Therefore love so understood is self-evidently merely a pretense which has to be carefully cultivated to keep the underlying reality hidden: the reality of egoism, and the greediest kind of egoism at that, exploiting another person to obtain for itself its own 'maximum pleasure.' In such circumstances the other person is and remains only a means to an end, as Kant rightly observed in his critique of utilitarianism.[221]

221. Wojtyla, *Love and Responsibility*, p. 39.

Therefore, if we compare Valla's concept of woman with Alberti's concept of woman we find some interesting parallels. Both philosophers sought to correct the marginalization of woman's identity within philosophical discourse. This was an important move for the history of gender theory. Alberti concentrated on woman in the household and Valla on the relation of woman to pleasure. However, both philosophers ended up with a utilitarian approach to man-woman relationships. Alberti's theory used women for the purposes of the work of reproduction and maintaining order in a household. Valla's theory used women for the purposes of mutually sharing pleasures with men. In both theories woman becomes a thing of use by a man, a means to an end; and in both theories man may easily become a thing of use by a woman, a means to an end. Consequently, neither of these early Renaissance Humanists arrived at the fullness of a philosophy of intergender relations, even though both attempted to include woman's identity in serious philosophical discourse. Therefore, they leave a mixed legacy for the history of the concept of woman.

Before concluding this section on the work of Lorenzo Valla, it is important to note the direct influence he had on the development of humanism. Desiderius Erasmus is without doubt one author who was deeply influenced by Valla. In 1488 Erasmus wrote a summary or epitome of Valla's *Elegance of the Latin Language,* which had been published since 1471, and he wrote a text on a similar topic entitled *Against the Barbarians,* begun in 1487 and revised in 1494-95. In addition, he also modeled his own 1489 dialogue *On the Contempt of the World* on Valla's text *On Pleasure: De voluptate.*[222] While Erasmus argued for some different conclusions from Valla, he publicly defended his Italian mentor and insisted on his value for the future of humanism, especially in the area of clarity of expression and in the rejection of the scholastic method of philosophy.[223] Through the works of Erasmus, humanism moved out of Italy into the Low Countries and eventually into England and into the home of St. Thomas More. We turn now to consider the effect of the translation of Plato's dialogues in providing new Neoplatonist foundations for theories of gender identity.

MARSILIO FICINO (1433-1499)

Through his role in reviving and transforming Platonism and Neoplatonism, Marsilio Ficino dramatically changed the philosophical basis for valuations of woman's identity. Ficino's contributions can be divided into two different categories: (1) his accurate translations of the complete works of Plato; and (2) his interpretations and commentaries on the Platonic corpus. Ficino greatly desired to in-

222. Albert Rabil, Jr., "Desiderius Erasmus," in *Renaissance Humanism,* vol. II, *Humanism Beyond Italy,* pp. 218-22.

223. See R. J. Schoeck's description of Erasmus' admiration for Valla in *Erasmus of Europe: The Making of a Humanist (1467-1500)* (Savage, Md.: Barnes and Noble Books, 1990). "For many years, then, Valla remained Erasmus' model *par excellence* for scholarship and style; and for perhaps a dozen years this was largely on the grounds of the *Elegantiae* alone; but he then began to read and assimilate more of Valla's writings" (p. 155).

troduce Plato to the West in such a way that the ancient Greek philosopher would provide a dynamic new foundation for Christian thought. Nicholas of Cusa had previously attempted this integration of Plato in his own work, but he did not produce translations of Plato's works to help others reach a similar goal.[224] Ficino's complete and accurate translations from the original Greek texts of Plato allowed Latin readers for the first time to come to their own decisions regarding the meaning of Plato's arguments about gender identity. Before elaborating the rich contribution of Ficino to the history of the concept of woman, some background information about his life and the intellectual context of his work will be introduced.

Marsilio Ficino lived in and near the city of Florence. His father Diotifeci Ficino was a successful physician and surgeon who served, among others, the family of Prince Cosimo de Medici.[225] His mother Sandra was a devout woman with intuitive and clairvoyant powers. Marsilio appears to have had two brothers, Daniele and Arcangelo, and a sister, Beatrice. In 1445, the young Ficino went to Florence to study humanities and logic before turning to the study of Aristotelian philosophy in a small *studio* in Florence from 1451 to 1458. During this latter time period, he was introduced to the natural philosophy of Aristotle, Hippocrates, Galen, and Avicenna as part of an education towards becoming a physician like his father.[226] In addition, Ficino began to educate himself in the field of astrology, an interest that lasted his entire life.

During this time of study Marsilio Ficino decided not to continue in the field of medicine, but instead to perfect his knowledge of Greek and devote himself to philosophy. Scholars have identified as an important factor in Ficino's decision the experience he had of Florentine culture. As James Hankins describes it: "This is the world of the religious confraternity, the *scuola* or *compagnia,* where lay persons, humanists and scholastics mixed freely with priests and religious in common pursuit of a richer spiritual wisdom and a deeper commitment to the Christian life."[227] In this city of the birthplace of humanism the ideas of Dante, Petrarch, Boccaccio, and Bruni were imbibed along with academic and religious authors.

In this dynamic context Ficino also discovered Plato through Bruni's and Decembrio's translations. By the year 1456, while still in his early twenties, Ficino even wrote his own version of a systematic account of Plato's thought drawn from

---

224. Paul Oskar Kristeller says that he sees "no direct evidence" of Ficino's dependence on Cusanus in "The Platonic Academy of Florence," *Renaissance Thought II: Papers on Humanism and the Arts* (New York/Evanston/London: Harper Torchbooks, 1965), p. 94. While there appear to be many similar aspects to the thought of these two Neoplatonists, the controversies surrounding the question of direct influence go beyond the boundaries of this book. For a comparison of Ficino and Cusanus see Maurice de Gandillac, "Neoplatonism and Christian Thought in the Fifteenth Century (Nicholas of Cusa and Marsilio Ficino)," in *Neoplatonism and Christian Thought,* ed. Dominic J. O. O'Meara (Norfolk, Va.: International Society for Neoplatonic Studies, 1982), pp. 143-68.

225. For notarized documents of payments to Diotifeci as a physician and other matters related to his mother Sandra, sister Beatrice, and two brothers Daniele and Arcangelo see Paul Oskar Kristeller, *Marsilio Ficino and His Work After Five Hundred Years* (Florence: Leo S. Olschki, 1987), pp. 195-96.

226. James Hankins, *Plato in the Italian Renaissance* (Leiden: Brill Academic Publishers, 1991), vol. 1, pp. 269-71.

227. Hankins, *Plato in the Italian Renaissance,* vol. 1, p. 276.

the rather meager sources available at the time.[228] Ficino's knowledge of and interest in Plato were seriously limited by two factors: (1) previous translations of Plato's dialogues had often distorted the Greek philosopher's views, and (2) a polarized conflict between the Florentine scholar Georgius Gemistus Pletho (1355-1450) and the Byzantine scholar George of Trebizond (1396-1484) had created a polarization between a Christianized Aristotle and a corrupt Plato. They had bitterly attacked one another concerning relative merits of Plato and Aristotle and had also drawn many members of the Church hierarchy into this public conflict.

In his *De Platonicae atque Aristotelicae Philosophiae Differentia* Pletho supported Plato and attacked Aristotle, while Trebizond argued that Plato was a dangerous philosopher for Christian Italy. Cardinal Bressarion offered a scathing attack on George's translation of Plato's *Laws* and then published in 1468 his own text *In Calumniatorem Platonis.*[229] This public debate posed a problem for the young Ficino, who was both a committed Christian and personally drawn to Plato's philosophy. Cardinal Bressarion defended Plato as a legitimate source compatible with the Christian faith.

In a peripheral way, the concept of woman was also drawn into the public controversy. George argued, for example, in the third book of his *Comparatio Platonis et Aristotelis* that Plato "tried to disturb the normal bonds of matrimony by advocating (in the *Republic*) the universal prostitution of the female sex (III.3) . . ." and "had wanted men and women to take exercise together naked (see *Rep.* 452B) in order to make them too effeminate for military service (III.10)."[230] There was also a highly charged claim that Plato lived an immoral life of promiscuous homosexual relations while Aristotle lived the moral life of a married heterosexual. Thus, it appeared dangerous in Christian culture to admit to admiring Plato rather than Aristotle, and even further to publicly argue that Plato could provide a good foundation for a new Christian philosophy. Cardinal Bressarion in his *In Calumniatorem Platonis* defended the moral quality of Plato's life, and he also argued that "[v]iews such as those on the relations of the sexes in the *Republic* are explained as familiar to the age and country of [Plato], and are confronted with examples from actual life."[231]

Even though many Aristotelian concepts and forms of argument remained in his writings, Ficino determined to defend Plato as a new and better foundation than Aristotle for Christian thought and life.[232] He did this in two ways: by making accurate translations of all the works of Plato so that the public could read accurate versions of the ancient Greek philosopher's works, and by offering an interpreta-

---

228. The title of this no longer extant work was *Institutiones Platonicae disciplinae.* See Hankins, *Plato in the Italian Renaissance,* vol. 1, p. 279.

229. Nesca A. Robb, *Neoplatonism in the Italian Renaissance* (London: George Allen and Unwin, Ltd., 1935), pp. 48-51.

230. As summarized by Hankins, *Plato in the Italian Renaissance,* vol. 1, p. 240.

231. Robb, *Neoplatonism in the Italian Renaissance,* p. 53.

232. Although as Paul Kristeller notes, Ficino also borrowed many Thomistic and Augustinian concepts and arguments. "Many metaphysical statements and arguments show a close relationship to Thomas, especially to his *Summa Contra Gentiles.* Even more profound is the influence of Augustine, from whose works Ficino quotes entire passages" ("Platonic Academy," pp. 14-15).

tion of the dialogues in commentaries that would explain in a manner consistent with fundamental principles how Plato's philosophy and way of life were not only compatible with Christianity but also highly favorable to it. These two goals that were achieved during Ficino's life had two very different consequences for the history of the concept of woman, and therefore our consideration of Ficino's contributions to the topic will be divided into two corresponding sections. However, first a few more details about Ficino's life and the historical context of his work need to be highlighted.

In 1457 Ficino wrote a treatise on pleasure entitled *De voluptate*. This treatise came out of his fascination with the problem of hedonism and the role of different levels of pleasure in the human being.[233] This fascination led Ficino to transcribe in 1460 the Greek text of Plotinus's *Enneads*, and he wrote many notes in its margins, especially in Book III, chapter 5, "On Love."[234] Both Plotinus and St. Augustine had appealed to Plato as a great philosopher of love, and these two sources helped Ficino to formulate one of the main themes of his own philosophical preoccupations, namely, the true nature of love of God and how it affects love and friendships among men and between men and women. In "On Love" Plato's dialogues, *Symposium, Philebus,* and *Phaedrus,* were given a Neoplatonic rendering by Plotinus, and several of the opinions introduced there were integrated into Ficino's own subsequent analysis. At the same time, however, Ficino differentiated his own analysis from many aspects of Plotinus's theory. For example, Ficino followed Augustine and Thomas Aquinas and emphasized the role of desire and the will in the upward movement of love. With respect to the body, Ficino gave it a more positive interpretation than is often found in Platonic and Neoplatonic texts.[235]

In September 1462, Cosimo de Medici (1389-1464) gave Ficino a manuscript containing the complete dialogues of Plato in Greek. At the same time, Ficino also received from another patron a second Greek manuscript of Plato's dialogues.[236] Using these two manuscripts, Ficino's preliminary work in Greek translation and Latin teaching began on a solid foundation. In 1463 Cosimo gave Marsilio Ficino the use of a villa on his property at Careggi, near Florence, to devote himself to his translations and studies and to begin a new form of Platonic Academy.[237]

Just two years later, during the final week of Cosimo de Medici's life, Marsilio Ficino was invited to read to the ruler on his deathbed Latin translations of Xenocrates' treatise *On Death* and Plato's dialogues *Parmenides* and *Philebus,* on

---

233. Michael J. B. Allen, *The Platonism of Marsilio Ficino: A Study of his "Phaedrus" Commentary, Its Sources and Genesis* (Berkeley/Los Angeles/London: University of California Press, 1984), pp. 205-7.

234. Plotinus, "On Love," *Enneads,* trans. A. H. Armstrong (Cambridge, Mass.: Harvard University Press, 1967), vol. 3, 3.5, pp. 167-209.

235. For a more detailed analysis of these points see Laura Westra, "Love and Beauty in Ficino and Plotinus," in *Ficino and Renaissance Neoplatonism,* ed. Konrad Eisenbichler and Olga Zorzi Pugliese (Ottawa: Dovehouse Editions, 1986), pp. 175-87.

236. Hankins, *Plato in the Italian Renaissance,* p. 300.

237. Ficino claims that it was the controversial philosopher Pletho who gave Cosimo de Medici the idea of beginning a new form of Platonic Academy in Florence. See Charles Stinger, "Humanism in Florence," in *Renaissance Humanism,* vol. 1, *Humanism in Italy,* p. 194.

the subjects of the one principle of the highest good. James Hankins notes how remarkable was this fact of inviting Ficino to use Plato to prepare someone for death when in the past more traditional Christian devotional sources would have been used.[238] It indicates that Ficino had at this early time already been successful in redefining Plato's value for Christian society. Recent evidence has indicated that Ficino was hired in 1466 by the *Ufficiali dello Studio* of Florence to teach philosophy.[239] This was the same school at which Ficino had previously studied from 1451 to 1462. Neither the particular subject Ficino lectured on nor the exact location of his lectures is known, but the contract and payment indicate that Ficino was accepted as a professional philosopher at this time in his career in Florence.

The reinterpretation of Plato as compatible with Christianity appears to have enabled Ficino to resolve the earlier conflict that he had experienced between Christianity and Platonism, and in 1473 Ficino was ordained a priest. In 1474 Ficino published a major work entitled *Theologia Platonica* and achieved sudden widespread fame.

By 1487 Ficino was appointed canon of the Cathedral of Florence. Even so, he kept running the Academy until his death, with the support of the Medici family which had donated large resources including Greek Platonic and Neoplatonic manuscripts.[240] After the death of Cosimo de Medici, first his son Piero, and then his grandson Lorenzo continued to support Ficino both financially and personally. The personal support can be seen in Lorenzo's defense of Ficino in a conflict with the poet Luigi Pulci, who publicly attacked the Platonic Academy's contemplative orientation in his poem *Morgante*.[241] Controversy was not an uncommon element in Ficino's life. Towards the end of his life he published a work that brought him into conflict with the Church hierarchy itself. In 1489 Ficino published a text entitled *Liber de Vita (The Book of Life)*, which combined three different shorter texts: a 1480 tract "On Caring for the Health of Students or Those Working in Letters," and two 1489 texts "On How to Prolong Your Life" and "On Making Your Life Agree with the Heavens."[242] He was reported to Pope Innocent VIII for writing about magic and astrology, but managed by 1490 to defend himself with an *Apology* and the intervention of the humanist Ermolao Barbaro. The predominant meaning of this text has turned out to be its healing aspects and the development of a systematic approach to "astrological medicine," which emphasized the active role of the human being in determining an attitude towards a disease. Raymond Klibansky, for example, praised Ficino's work in analyzing the relation between Saturn and Melancholy.[243]

238. Hankins, *Plato in the Italian Renaissance,* vol. 1, p. 268.

239. Jonathan Davies, "Marsilio Ficino: Lecturer at the Studio Fiorentino," *Renaissance Quarterly* 45, no. 4 (Winter 1992): 785-90.

240. Paul Oskar Kristeller, *The Philosophy of Marsilio Ficino* (Gloucester, Mass.: Peter Smith, 1964), pp. 12-17.

241. Constance Jordan, *Pulci's "Morgante": Poetry and History in Fifteenth-Century Florence* (Washington, D.C.: Folger Books, 1986), pp. 31-42.

242. See *Marsilio Ficino: The Book of Life* (Woodstock, Conn.: Spring Publications, 1996). See also Marsilio Ficino, *Three Books on Life* (Binghamton, N.Y.: Medieval and Renaissance Texts and Studies, 1989).

243. Raymond Klibansky, Erwin Panofsky, and Fritz Saxl, *Saturn and Melancholy: Studies in the*

Marsilio Ficino with Pico, Poliziano, and Others

Then in 1494 the French army invaded Florence. "Ficino . . . survived long enough to cast an eye over the Aldine text of some of his translations, but his single letter to the printer is haunted by references to ill health, famine, and books scattered abroad in a city to which he dared not return for fear of plague and violence."[244] His two friends and associates Ermolao Barbaro and Giovanni Pico della Mirandola had both died the preceding year, and his benefactors, the Medici family, had been exiled. Thus, the Florentine Platonic Academy had come to a sudden end. In 1497, after the closing of the Platonic Academy, Marsilio Ficino purchased a house in Florence, presumably for his mother's and his own use.

Ficino's Neoplatonic legacy survived through the transmission of printed editions of his works, and the history of the philosophy had been changed defini-

---

History of Natural Philosophy, Religion, and Art (London: Thomas Nelson and Sons Ltd., 1964), pp. 366ff.

244. Martin Lowry, *The World of Aldus Manutius* (Ithaca, N.Y.: Cornell University Press, 1979), p. 193.

tively by the insertion of the Platonic corpus into higher education. In an analysis of books published in Florence in the fifteenth century, there were seventeen editions in philosophy, four of which were Aristotelian, five of which were Marsilio Ficino's Latin translations of Plato and Plotinus and his own texts *Theologia Platonica, De vita,* and *De sole.* By the middle of the next century, two of five philosophical editions came from Ficino, namely his *Commentaria in Platonem* and translation of Pseudo-Dionysius and the other from his friend Pico della Mirandola, the *Heptaplus.*[245] In addition, collections of Ficino's Letters were printed in 1495 in Venice and then reprinted soon after in Nuremberg.[246]

We turn to a more direct consideration of the legacy of Ficino's translations of Plato's dialogues and of the particular ways he interpreted Plato's philosophy as applied to the history of the concept of woman. From the perspective of our focus on dialogue as a way of philosophizing, it must be noted that Ficino was a master who used many different forms of dialogue in his work. First of all, by his translations of Plato's dialogues he introduced the Socratic model of dialogue into the heart of fifteenth-century philosophical debate. Second, by his commentaries on Plato's dialogues he brought his own voice into the discourse about the opinions and truths that Plato was seeking to differentiate. Third, in his Florentine Platonic Academy Ficino initiated through his own teaching and example a context of continual philosophical dialogue about issues of fundamental importance. Finally, by his extensive correspondence Ficino engaged in written dialogue with a number of persons on a wide range of philosophical and religious issues. In addition, Ficino sought to uncover what has been called a single line of truth throughout history by all these various means of dialogue. Thus, the different voices that entered into his discourses had the common goal of identifying and claiming the components in that line of truth.

Marsilio Ficino had more effect on subsequent theory about gender identity than did any other philosopher writing in this period of the early humanist reformation. He effectively changed the valuation of Aristotelian foundations for Christian philosophy and brought about a new synthesis of Platonism and Christian philosophy that significantly altered the entrenchment of gender polarity principles so closely identified with Aristotelian foundations. However, the two ways in which Ficino effected this change were not exactly compatible: the first was by making available Plato's own theories of gender identity, and the second was by offering interpretations of Plato's theories that altered in some significant ways the grounds for Plato's conclusions.

Gender Identity Themes Transmitted through Plato's Dialogues

The decade between 1460 and 1470 was extremely important in Ficino's formation as a careful translator of philosophical texts from Greek to Latin. In 1463 he completed a translation of the *Corpus Hermeticum.* By summer of 1464 when

245. Gerulaitis, *Printing and Publishing in Fifteenth-Century Venice,* p. 135.
246. Gerulaitis, *Printing and Publishing in Fifteenth-Century Venice,* pp. 87 and 153.

Cosimo de Medici died, Ficino had translated ten dialogues of Plato, which he dedicated to his first patron. During the next two years he translated another thirteen dialogues, and it is believed that by 1468-69 he had completed preliminary translations of the entire thirty-six dialogues of Plato as well as personal commentaries on several of them. Ficino kept revising his translations over the next several years before he published them. He worked with the Latin translations of the *Republic* by Chrysoloras and Decembrio and the *Laws* by Bruni and George Trebizond. Ficino borrowed extensively for his own translations where he agreed with the earlier versions and made his own translations where the other translators had erred. He even used the Dominican scholastic source, William of Moerbeke, for his translation of the *Parmenides.* Ficino worked as a true scholar, comparing multiple translations with the original sources and then consulting with other experts on the meaning of certain terms, phrases, or sentences.

Ficino's first publication, *De Amore,* occurred in 1469. This text was an extremely popular *Commentary on Plato's Symposium,* which included many references to Plotinus's "On Love," from the *Enneads,* Book III, chapter 5.[247] Then, he completed in 1474 and published in 1482 the lengthy *Theologia Platonica,* which included many references to Plotinus's *Enneads,* Book III, chapter 5, as well as indicated how Platonic philosophy could provide a suitable foundation for Christian theology. In that same year Ficino also wrote another religious text, *De christiana religione,* and in 1476 he wrote a treatise on *Five Questions Concerning the Mind.*[248]

At this point Ficino published the complete corpus of Plato's dialogues. In a way he had already prepared the Christian culture of Florence for an acceptance of Plato's original arguments. Ficino's systematic commentaries and arguments that Plato was a suitable philosopher with whom to begin a dramatic renewal of the Christian faith had been successfully received by many persons. Ficino believed that there were phases of illumination and then interpretation in the development of the Christian faith and that he had been chosen to herald in a new era of illumination.[249]

Consequently, the 1484 publication of Ficino's complete translation of Plato's dialogues at a Dominican Convent outside of Florence was a remarkable event in both the history of philosophy and Christian intellectual thought. In his 1484 collection Ficino also added a *Life of Plato* and complete commentaries on the *Symposium* and the *Timaeus.* Ficino's commentary on the *Timaeus* was the only "full commentary on the *Timaeus* in the fifteenth century . . . [and it became] the definitive Renaissance interpretation and subsequently the one that held the stage until superseded by the accounts of the nineteenth and twentieth centuries. . . ."[250]

---

247. Al Wolters, "Ficino and Plotinus' Treatise 'On Eros,'" in Eisenbichler and Pugliese, eds., *Ficino and Renaissance Neoplatonism,* p. 192.

248. This treatise can be found in *The Renaissance Philosophy of Man,* ed. Ernst Cassirer, Paul Oskar Kristeller, and John Herman Randall, Jr. (Chicago: University of Chicago Press, 1963), pp. 193-222.

249. Hankins, *Plato in the Italian Renaissance,* vol. 1, pp. 282-87.

250. Michael J. B. Allen, "Marsilio Ficino's Interpretation of Plato's *Timaeus,*" in *Supplementum Festivum,* ed. James Hankins et al. (Binghamton, N. Y.: Medieval and Renaissance Texts and Studies, 1987), p. 403.

Ficino's decisions about which dialogues to include as authentic and which to exclude established a framework within which Plato's works were studied for the next several centuries. Ficino's translations, which sought to articulate the author's original intentions, opened up a new way of approaching ancient texts within humanism. Instead of simply borrowing an idea that could be used by the fifteenth-century author, Ficino seriously attempted to convey to the reader the content of the complete arguments that either Plato or one of the interlocutors in his dialogues made. Ficino's abilities to understand subtle distinctions in the Greek language and to provide accurate translations of both words and sentences from Plato's original texts are still recognized.[251]

A similar judgment is made about Ficino's translations of Plotinus, namely, that contemporary scholars still use them because of their fidelity to the arguments and concepts of the original Greek text.[252] Finally, Ficino sought to present the Platonic writings as a unified whole and Plato as an original and profound thinker about the truth, beauty, oneness, and goodness of God and the natural desire of human beings to be brought into union with God. These multifaceted contributions of Ficino's translations have implications for the history of the concept of woman as will be seen shortly in our consideration of gender identity.

By 1489 Ficino had completed translating texts by Porphyry and Proclus, and by 1492 translations of Dionysius. Also in 1492 Ficino published a second translation and commentary on Plotinus's *Enneads* based on his early translation of 1484-86. In 1496 he published a collection of his commentaries, textual summaries, and notes on Platonic works entitled *Commentaria in Platonem*. This text contained commentaries on and summaries of the *Parmenides*, *Timaeus*, *Phaedrus*, *Philebus*, and Book VIII of the *Republic*. Absent from this collection were commentaries on the key sections of dialogues concerned with the concept of woman, namely Book V of the *Republic* and sections of the *Laws*. Ficino had intended to publish extensive commentaries on all of Plato's dialogues, but the death of Lorenzo de Medici in 1492 made it necessary for him to publish smaller amounts of his work than originally planned.

The insertion of the accurate translation of thirty-six Platonic dialogues into the fifteenth-century humanist discourse about woman's identity had an effect on the concept of woman. Ficino's accurate translations made Plato's claims in support of a gender unity theory (unisex) available to the educated Latin reader. Plato had argued that there are no philosophically significant differences between

251. Hankins summarizes it this way: "From the time of Erasmus nearly every scholar who has had occasion to study in detail Ficino's translation of Plato has come away impressed by its accuracy, completeness, and philosophical penetration. . . . Ficino's translation retained its reputation well into the nineteenth century, despite the efforts of other translators and revisers to displace. Modern students of Ficino's *Platonis opera omnia* have mostly concurred with the traditional judgment" (*Plato in the Italian Renaissance*, vol. 1, p. 311).

252. Al Wolters, "Ficino and Plotinus' Treatise 'On Eros,'" in *Ficino and Renaissance Platonism*. Even though Ficino took only the two years between 1484 and 1486 to make his translation of the complete works of Plotinus, he seems to have pondered carefully Plotinus's text, writing notes in the margins at different periods in his life, for over thirty years. It is believed that this careful time of study is precisely what enabled him to make the translation in such a short period of time (pp. 192-94).

women and men in an ideal society. These philosophical arguments for equal identity, education, and roles of men and women were now available to counteract the more common arguments found in gender polarity (which combined the devaluation of the female with significant differences) and gender complementarity (which combined equality with significant differences).

However, Ficino's translations also allowed for some of the secondary cosmic gender polarity views of Plato's *Timaeus* to be accessible as well (i.e., that the female was the reincarnation of a cowardly or immoral male). Plato had suggested that the soul was a sexless entity that could be born through reincarnation in either a male or a female body.[253] He also introduced other gender polarity distinctions in various dialogues. However, since the main innovations in Plato's philosophy of woman were his arguments in support of gender unity (unisex), Ficino's translations offered new metaphysical and political foundations for reform of gender polarity theory. In order to see at a glance Plato's different arguments about gender identity, the following summary is provided. A fuller account of Plato's philosophy of woman's identity is found in *The Concept of Woman: The Aristotelian Revolution (750 BC–1250 AD)*.[254] In the summary below, the dialogue is listed with its paragraph and line number and the theory of gender identity is identified with a brief summary of its content:

GENDER IDENTITY THEMES IN PLATO'S DIALOGUES

Symposium

189e-191e: Gender polarity — in Aristophanes' myth of the origin of love — as man-man/man-woman/woman-woman split in hierarchical ordering.

201c-212b: Gender unity — in Socrates presenting Diotima as a wise woman who taught him about the true nature of love.

Meno

71e-73b: Gender unity — Socrates argues against what is presumed to be Gorgias' view of separate spheres of virtue for a man (managing a city's affairs well) and a woman (to be a good housewife, careful with her stores, and obedient to her husband).

Socrates wants virtues applied equally to both genders — justice and temperance.

---

253. For a fuller development of Plato's and Plotinus's concept of woman see Allen, *The Concept of Woman: The Aristotelian Revolution (750 BC–1250 AD)*, pp. 57-75, 79-81, and 193-213.

254. Allen, *The Concept of Woman: The Aristotelian Revolution (750 BC–1250 AD)*, ch. 1, pp. 57-82.

Republic

Book V
453a-454e: Gender unity — Men and women with same natures should have the same tasks, i.e., philosophers, soldiers, or workers.

Identity comes from the soul which is sexless, not the body, which either begets or bears children.

455c-456a: Modified gender polarity–gender unity — Natural capacities are distributed alike among men and women, but women are generally weaker than men. Men generally surpass women, yet some women are better than many men in many things.

Both men and women have the same nature to be guardians, but woman is weaker and man stronger.

456b: Gender unity — To the same natures give the same pursuits.

457b-458c: Gender unity — Women and children should be common to all men.

No parent should know the offspring nor child its parent.

There should be a common table and no private possessions.

Book VIII
543a: Gender unity — All education and pursuits of men and women must be the same in peace and war.

546a-e: Dates for conception and generation of children should be determined by proportional numbers for best eugenic results.

Laws

770d: Gender unity — Males and females are both citizens whose excellence resides in virtues of the soul.

780e-781b: Gender unity — There should be a common table and common laws for men and women.

Gender polarity — It harms the state to leave woman isolated and without education as her nature is weak and inferior.

783d-785b: Gender unity — Regulation of procreation by years and dates with same penalties for men and women who do not obey.

Modified gender unity — Variation in ages for men and women, but equal appointments to rule and for military service.

804e and 834a: Gender unity — Girls must be trained exactly as the boys.

776a and 930b-c: Modifies the *Republic* by allowing private homes and families.

838e-841e: Gender unity — Equal sanctions against unregulated sexual intercourse, homosexuality, and promiscuity for both men and women.

Timaeus

18c: Gender unity — Women's and men's natures are the same. Women and

men should receive the same training, and be assigned the same pursuits in war and in ordinary life.

50c-51b: Gender polarity — "Mother" receptacle passively receives the active
Forms.

69e-70a: Implied gender polarity — There is an analogy between, on one
hand, superior and inferior parts of the mind and, on the other, the
men's and women's apartments in a household.

90e-92b: Gender polarity — Men who were cowards or immoral are changed
into women in second generation (reincarnation).

Phaedrus

Gender neutrality — There is no mention of gender differentiation in his description of reincarnation.

Phaedo

Gender neutrality — There is no mention of gender differentiation in his descriptions of the immortality of the soul.

59e: Implied gender polarity — in the contrast between Xanthippe and Socrates' self-control over passions.

Theaetetus

149a-150b: Implied gender polarity — Socrates as midwife brings to birth in
men, not women, true philosophy from the soul, not the body.

Epinomis

(Apocryphal Platonic dialogue attached to the end of the *Laws*)

992d: Implied gender unity — The Athenian says that everyone should re-
vere gods of either sex, but he places worship of the Olympian deities
under the higher study of astronomy and relations of numbers as a necessary precondition for acquiring wisdom.

When the themes associated with Aristotelian-based gender polarity were
analyzed in respect to their integration into academia, we divided them into four
categories corresponding to the distinctions: opposites, generation, wisdom, and
virtue. The four categories were called: metaphysical principles, natural principles,
epistemological principles, and ethical principles of gender polarity. A similar kind
of summary can be provided for Plato's arguments for gender unity (unisex). It is
useful to do so because it helps demonstrate the radically new foundation that
Plato's dialogues offered for arguments about woman's identity.

First, to recall **the four principles of Aristotelian-based gender polarity:**

- **Metaphysical principle**: The female is the contrary privation of the male.
- **Natural principle**: The female is generated as a deformed male.
- **Epistemological principle**: A woman's rational faculty is without authority.
- **Ethical principle**: A woman has a lesser measure of virtue than does a man.

Second, to summarize:

The Four Platonic-Based Principles for Gender Unity

- **Metaphysical principle**: Human identity comes from the soul, which is an eternal sexless entity.
- **Natural principle**: Men and women are generated when a sexless soul transmigrates (reincarnates) into a male or a female body.
- **Epistemological principle**: A man and a woman have the same rational faculty.
- **Ethical principle**: A man and a woman ought to have the same functions, education, and virtues.

These four principles for gender unity establish the framework within which Plato's arguments for equal education and role of women and men in an ideal society occur. Men and women humanist authors in the coming generations will appeal especially to the Platonic epistemological and ethical principles of gender unity to argue for reforms in education and social and political structure of society. Porphyry was the one early Neoplatonist who adopted all four of Plato's gender unity principles without qualification. Later humanist authors who appeal to them and to Plato and Socrates by name include, for instance, Marguerite of Navarre (1492-1549) and Marie de Gournay (1566-1645).[255]

In Plato's dialogues, as the themes identified above indicate, each fundamental principle of gender unity was modified by a gender polarity qualification. Some of these modifications were transmitted in the Neoplatonic evaluations of Plato's views, by Plotinus and by Ficino, for example. Therefore, it is important to identify the qualifications or amplifications that accompany each of the principles. The table on pages 867-68 offers a summary of the principles and qualifications of Plato's gender identity principles.

Even without Ficino's transmission of his interpretation of Plato's arguments, it is clear that the Platonic legacy for the history of the concept of woman is mixed. Still, the radical proposals of Plato in the *Republic, Laws,* and at the beginning of the *Timaeus,* namely, that women have the same mind, and should have the same education, pursuits, and virtues as men, when added to the appeal of Socrates

---

255. See, for example, Robert W. Bernard, "A Mirror for Renaissance Education and Feminism — Marguerite de Navarre (1492-1549)," *Vitae Scholasticae* 2, no. 1 (Spring 1983): 19-32; Marguerite de Navarre, *L'Heptaméron,* ed. Michel François (Paris: Gernier, 1964); Frank Jones, "Equality of Men and Women by Marie de Gournay," *The French-American Review* 2, no. 3 (1978): 121-28; and Marie de Gournay, "Égalité des hommes et des femmes," ed. Mario Schiff (Paris: Librairie Honoré Champion, 1910), pp. 61ff.

Plato's Gender Unity Principles and Gender Polarity Qualifications		
Principles	Qualifications/men	Qualifications/women
Metaphysical: Sexless souls exist in heaven of Forms.	The Forms are active like a father.	The receptacle of the Forms is passive 'matter' like a mother.
Natural: Souls fall into male or female bodies.	Male bodies are given to souls that lived a good past life.	Female bodies are given to souls that lived a cowardly or immoral past life.
Dates for conception should be regulated by numbers.	Men should have sexual intercourse with women only at specified ages and times for the best eugenic results.	Women should have sexual intercourse with men only at specified ages and times for the best eugenic results.
Epistemological: A man's soul and a woman's soul have the same capacity to know the Forms.	The superior part of the mind is analogous to men's apartments in a household.	The inferior part of the mind is analogous to women's apartments in a household.
Diotima was the wise teacher of Socrates.	A boy and a man can learn faster, and thus need fewer years of education.	A girl and women take longer to learn, and thus need more years of education.
Socrates acts like a midwife in bringing ideas to birth in men's souls.		
Both men and women can reach perfect wisdom and escape the cycles of reincarnation by union of the soul with the Forms.		

Plato's Gender Unity Principles and Gender Polarity Qualifications (cont.)		
Principles	Qualifications/men	Qualifications/women
Ethical: The same virtues for men and women — justice, wisdom, and temperance Men and women should both be philosophers, guardians, and soldiers.	Men are generally stronger.	Women are generally weaker, predisposed to secrecy and craft, inferior, and they become harmful to the state when left isolated from laws and a common table.
There should be a common table, common wives, common children, no private property.	Aristophanes' myth of male/male sexual relations as superior.	Aristophanes' myth of male/female or female/female sexual relations as inferior.
	Socrates portrayed as always in control of his emotions.	Xanthippe, Socrates' wife, portrayed as unable to control her emotions.

to his woman teacher Diotima in the *Symposium,* introduce strong gender unity elements into a society saturated by academic and satirical gender polarity arguments to the contrary.

To demonstrate the accuracy of Ficino's translations of Plato's *Timaeus* two passages concerning the concept of women are presented here. The first is from *Timaeus* 18c: "And concerning women we have also said that, having been compared to the likeness of men in nature, they should be joined with them also in all business, both of war and of the rest of life, that should be shared by all."[256] Clearly this passage transmits directly Plato's gender unity principle. The second passage is from *Timaeus* 90e-91a: "So then concerning this let such an account be made: of those who had been born men, whoever had been lazy and unjust throughout life, just as probably reason shows, being born again with changed nature, they were born women."[257] This passage translates directly Plato's gender polarity principle. Consequently, Plotinus transmitted the complex combination of gender unity and gender polarity that was evident in the original Greek text. Ficino's translation of Plato's dialogues alone was an enormous contribution to discourse about women's identity. Suddenly there were arguments of some quality that could offer some other philosophical foundation than the Aristotelian and scholastic models of women's identity that had dominated western thinking for so long.

256. *Platonis Opera, Greek and Latin,* trans. Plotinus, ed. C. E. Ch. Schneider (Paris: Didot, 1883). Translated into English by Michael Woodward, vol. 2, *Timaeus* 18c.
257. *Platonis Opera,* trans. Michael Woodward, vol. 2, *Timaeus* 90e-91a.

It was also noted that Ficino translated the complete works of Plotinus. The question that naturally occurs is: How did Plotinus's concept of woman add to or detract from that articulated in Plato's dialogues? The significance of Ficino's translation of the works of Plotinus for the history of the concept of woman does not come so much from his direct transmission of Plotinus's concept of woman as from the Plotinian interpretation of Plato's works. Plotinus's own concept of woman is not very original or rich; he simply combines various aspects of Plato's and Aristotle's theories, especially in his discussions of matter, form, and generation, and while he certainly notes with approval women who are philosophers, he does not put forward any gender unity arguments that women ought to become philosophers, or that women's and men's virtues ought to be the same.

Instead, in Book III, chapter 5 of the *Enneads,* Plotinus's interpretation of the nature of love, as a Platonic desire for union with absolute beauty, is amplified by Ficino. This particular theory of love as seeking union with the Idea of Beauty informs Ficino's concept of woman and offers a new perspective on the ideal nature of man/woman friendship and love. Thus, we could say that Ficino influences the history of the concept of woman by the indirect route of using and then transforming Plotinus's understanding of Plato's theory of love. Plotinus's understanding of Plato, however, was also interpretative, and so both the ancient and the Renaissance authors introduced a modification of Plato's concept of woman. Ficino's contribution to the history of the concept of women by interpreting Plato's philosophy for Christian Florence will now be the focus of our consideration. As will be seen, while accepting certain Platonic principles, he also rejected some of Plato's fundamental principles of gender identity. In addition, Ficino attempted to reconcile certain views of Plato with especially Aristotle's *Ethics.* Thus he sought to introduce a new harmony between the two ancient Greek schools of philosophy. The artist Raphael depicted this harmony in his portrait of the School of Athens with Aristotle carrying his *Ethics* and Plato his *Timaeus.*

Reinterpretation of Plato's Philosophy of Gender

Ficino's attempt to render Plato's philosophy more consistent with Christian thought and life affected the concept of woman in several different ways. Basically, he chose to separate out those elements in the dialogues that were contrary to Christian views, and then to associate them with some other philosophers such as Pythagoras, Socrates, or with general Athenian culture. Thus, he argued that reincarnation was Pythagorean, that radical communism was Socrates' way of bringing a corrective into an imbalanced cultural situation, and that homosexuality was simply a cultural phenomenon that Plato strongly opposed. Ficino concluded, for example, that the arguments in the *Republic* were mostly Pythagorean and Socratic, while those in the *Laws* were more authentically Platonic.[258] In these ways, Ficino distilled a pure line of Platonic thought that could become a new metaphysical and epistemological foundation for Christianity. Most scholars suggest that

---

258. Hankins, *Plato in the Italian Renaissance,* pp. 53-56.

Plato and Aristotle at the School of Athens

Ficino did not hypocritically manipulate Plato's dialogues the way previous translators did, to hide or distort his claims, but rather he truly came to believe that certain views present in the dialogues were not actually Plato's own.[259]

Given that Ficino also provided Plato's original dialogues, there seems to be some merit to the hypothesis that he did not intend to deceive his audience about Plato's true philosophy. On the other hand, certain of Ficino's conclusions do appear to the contemporary reader to be unsound interpretations of the ancient Greek philosopher. Since our present purpose is to trace the history of the concept of woman between 1250 and 1500 rather than to enter into specialized debate about particular interpretations of Platonic texts, we will refrain from giving too much attention to this complex issue. However, notice will be taken when a particular interpretation has a direct effect on the gender theory being proposed.

Four principles identified above as part of Plato's philosophy of woman and subsequently reinterpreted by Ficino are: (1) reincarnation of sexless souls into male or female bodies; (2) the upward movement of an educated soul towards union with the highest good; (3) the possibility of women philosophers; and (4) the question of the equality or polarity valuation of engendered rationality, functions, and virtues. In this section of the chapter on Ficino's concept of woman, each of these four topics will be considered in turn under the four headings of (1) Gender and the Soul/Body Relation, (2) Platonic Love and Friendship, (3) Women Philosophers, and (4) Engendered Virtues.

Gender and the Soul/Body Relation

Ficino frequently offers an epistemological explanation for what appeared to be a different kind of observation in Plato's dialogues. James Hankins describes his method this way:

> In his version of the *Meno,* for instance, Ficino has done his best, without grossly altering the text, to discourage the reader from finding the doctrine of transmigration in Plato's words. Ficino always denied that Plato had held such a doctrine (in one place he scolds Plotinus for so interpreting him), and hence renders the Platonic doctrine of recollection so as to suggest that recollection should be understood as a higher mental state than a memory of a previous existence.[260]

Ficino's claim that Plato did not support a theory of reincarnation or transmigration directly undermines the metaphysical and natural principles of gender unity. Indeed, it undermines half of the theoretical foundation of Plato's argument for why women should be educated the same as men, namely, since their souls were the same, they should be given the same opportunities to be educated in wisdom and virtue so that they could finally escape the cycles of reincarnation. The other half of Plato's argument, that it is better for the state if women are educated, still stands.

259. See, for example, Hankins, *Plato in the Italian Renaissance,* vol. 1, pp. 313-14.
260. Hankins, *Plato in the Italian Renaissance,* vol. 1, p. 213.

Ficino had a strong metaphysical interest in arguments for the immortality of the soul, and he devoted his important work *Theologia Platonica de immortalitate animorum* to this topic. His purpose was to argue against three opposing views: the Averroists, who held that there was one intellect; the radical Aristotelians, who denied proof for the immortality of the soul; and those ancient philosophers such as the Pythagoreans, who supported a theory of reincarnation.[261] In addition, he wanted to prove that philosophy reveals a desire for God in every human act and aspiration, that the immortality of the soul means that this desire will be fulfilled in life after death, and that life on earth is filled with the presence of God drawing man towards union.[262] Ficino set out to prove, drawing upon Plato's and Thomas Aquinas's arguments, that the individual human soul, because of its non-material identity, was capable of union with God, with eternal Forms or Ideas in the mind of God, and of continued existence after the death of the body.[263]

In his *Five Questions Concerning the Mind,* Ficino argued that the highest part of the soul, or the mind, has a natural desire for union with infinite truth and goodness. Furthermore, he held that the intellect, more than the senses, has an affinity with the highest form of truth and goodness, and is able, even in this life, to move towards union with the highest good, or God. Among the principles needed for this movement, Ficino includes that of separation "from the passions of matter and the condition of corporeal forms."[264] This effort of the will to achieve the proper separation from earthly things in order to move towards contemplative union is difficult, given the situation of a human being in the world. Ficino appeals to the "Pythagoreans and Platonists . . . [who] say that the soul is manifestly afflicted in the sensible world by so many ills because, seduced by an excessive desire for sensible goods, it has imprudently lost the goods of the intelligible world."[265] Ficino concludes his argument by linking the immortality of the soul with the resurrection of the body:

> The natural end itself, moreover, seems to exist only in a natural condition. The condition of the everlasting soul which seems to be in the highest degree natural is that it should continue to live in its own body made everlasting. Therefore, it is concluded by necessary reasoning that the immortality and brightness of the soul can and must at some time shine forth into its own body and that, in this condition alone, the highest blessedness of man is indeed perfected. Certainly, this

261. See Paul Oskar Kristeller, "The Immortality of the Soul," in *Renaissance Concepts of Man and Other Essays* (New York: Harper and Row, 1972), pp. 22-42.

262. Ardis B. Collins, *The Secular Is Sacred: Platonism and Thomism in Marsilio Ficino's "Platonic Theology"* (The Hague: Martinus Nijhoff, 1974), p. 7.

263. For a detailed account of the use by Ficino of Thomas Aquinas's arguments especially in the *Summa Contra Gentiles* for immortality of the soul, and his use of Thomas's distinction between essence and being see Collins, *The Secular Is Sacred,* pp. 68ff.

264. Ficino, "Five Questions Concerning the Mind," in *Renaissance Philosophy of Man,* ed. Cassirer et al., p. 206.

265. Ficino, "Five Questions Concerning the Mind," in *Renaissance Philosophy of Man,* ed. Cassirer et al., pp. 209-10.

doctrine of the prophets and theologians is confirmed by the Persian wise men and by the Hermetic and the Platonic philosophers.[266]

By this argument Ficino has solved two historical problems at once. First, the past tendency of Neoplatonic philosophers to lose individual, personal, and gender identity by union of the soul with God is remedied by Ficino's insistence on the unique identity of the individual person through union with a particular, engendered body, even after death. Second, the natural desire for union with God can occur through contemplation even while a person lives on earth before death, and the Platonists have prepared a foundation for how this can occur by the union of the highest part of the mind with truth, beauty, and goodness.

Ficino often described the soul as left with a desire after the death of the body to return to the same body. This gave a philosophical explanation for the Christian belief in the resurrection of the body. He argued further in his treatise on the immortality of the soul that this desire ought to be fulfilled:

> Since one natural compound is made out of the Soul and the human body, and since the Soul is endowed with a natural inclination toward the body, the Soul evidently is bound to the body not only according to the order of the universe but also according to the order of its own nature, and consequently it is contrary to the universal as well as to its own nature that the Soul remain separated from the body. But the Souls remain eternal after the destruction of the body. Since that which is contrary to nature cannot be eternal, it results that the Souls will again receive their bodies at some time.[267]

The resurrection of the body implies that women will be eternally differentiated from men. In other words, a specific soul desiring to be united to its own body will be sexually differentiated by that object of its desire. Thus, Ficino avoids falling into a gender unity theory of sexless souls existing either after death, or, as in Plato's own dialogues, existing by ignoring the body during life.

In his commentary on Plato's *Phaedrus,* Ficino closely links the metaphysical theory of the immortality of the soul with an epistemological theory of how an individual soul may come into union with the highest good by motion of the intellect and ultimately by love. He argues that the soul is active, or self-moving, once it has been put into motion by God. Ficino concludes that as a principle of motion the soul has perpetual motion or eternal life.[268] It is important to note that Ficino distinguishes between the higher rational soul, which is the principle of motion, and a lower irrational soul, which is passive and only mirrors the higher rational soul more or less accurately. The rational soul, he concludes, was not generated and

266. Ficino, "Five Questions Concerning the Mind," in *Renaissance Philosophy of Man,* ed. Cassirer et al., pp. 211-12.

267. Marsilio Ficino, *De Immort. Ani.,* translated in Kristeller, *The Philosophy of Marsilio Ficino,* p. 195.

268. See Allen, *The Platonism of Marsilio Ficino,* for detailed descriptions of the relevant arguments, especially chapter 3: "Immortality Proofs," pp. 68-85.

cannot be destroyed; only particulars in the sensible world come into being and pass away. The soul is able to move by reason, intellect, and love to contemplation of the Divine, or it may fall, descend, or be dragged down towards the world of sensible particulars. The choice is up to the individual human being who determines a particular life path.

Ficino also accepted the Platonic principle of the need to develop a strong and healthy body to support the vigor of the soul. In the Apology attached to his *De Vita,* Ficino states the principle explicitly: "There can be no question that the most magnificent service of all, one that is very necessary, one that is most sought by humanity, is the work that gives mankind a healthy mind in a healthy body. And even we can be good at this, if we join medicine to the priesthood."[269] In this claim, Ficino challenges two hundred years of separation of academic study for the priesthood and for medicine. By practice and by canon law men had been prohibited from combining study for the priesthood and medicine since the end of the thirteenth century when the faculties and curriculum at the University of Paris became the model for all new universities being formed in Europe.[270] Thus, Ficino's boldness in writing *De Vita* was his attempt — based, he claims, in charity — to reform the practice of the fragmentation of the disciplines. He also stated that he wrote this book for his own physician father and because the careful practice of healthy eating and living had cured his own tendencies towards depression, or melancholia.

The medical writings of Ficino have implication for the history of the concept of woman in two distinct but related ways: first, in prescriptions about sexual intercourse; and second, in their association of certain characteristics with masculine and feminine deities. Noticeably absent from his considerations are the traditional gender polarity analyses of male and female identity. His treatises on medicine are written for a male audience of students and scholars, and they encourage celibacy. The judgments are based upon the balance of humors, and the relation between various herbs, foods, and drinks.[271] In addition, Ficino considers the effects of the stars and planets on temperaments and decisions. Perhaps because of the controversial nature of his claims Ficino frequently appeals to authority to defend his choice of subject and his method of approach. For example, he refers to Albert the Great, Thomas Aquinas, Ptolemy, and Avicenna, as well as Porphyry, Plotinus, Plato, and Socrates.[272]

---

269. "The Apology of Marsilio Ficino," in *The Book of Life,* p. 185. He is well aware that this is a radical stance: "Someone, for example, will say, 'Is not Marsilio a priest? He certainly is. Well what do priests have to do with medicine? And furthermore, what business of his is astrology?'" (p. 184).

270. See Allen, *The Concept of Woman: The Aristotelian Revolution (750 BC–1250 AD)* for a description of the original separation of Theology and Medicine, pp. 435-36.

271. While Ficino drew upon common interpretations of the effects of humors, it is interesting to note that he associates black bile with depression in scholars while Hildegard of Bingen associates black bile with violence in men who physically attack women during intercourse. For an excellent introduction to the *De vita* see Carol V. Kaske and John R. Clark's Introduction and Notes to Marsilio Ficino, *Three Books on Life,* pp. 3-90.

272. Marsilio Ficino, "On Making Your Life Agree with the Heavens," in *De Vita*. For Albert the Great see ch. 12, p. 126; ch. 18, p. 149; and ch. 25, p. 175. For Thomas Aquinas he says: ". . . I would not be saying anything that Thomas Aquinas did not already say . . ." (ch. 8, p. 110). For a second refer-

To return to the first theme of soul/body relation and gender identity in Ficino's *De Vita,* we discover the common view that sexual intercourse depletes a man's energy for study and contemplation. To set up his claim, Ficino first draws upon Plato to describe how the mind of the philosopher, which so often contemplates immaterial realities, seems to depart, separate itself, and flee from the body. He then identifies five principal enemies of students: phlegm, black bile, coitus, overeating, and sleeping late. To be more precise he adds: "The first of these monsters is the coitus of Venus, for even if it is only a little excessive, it suddenly exhausts the spirits. It weakens the brain and attacks the stomach and the heart, troubles which could not possibly be more adverse to thought."[273] He also warns that too much coitus dries out a man's body and leaves him vulnerable to black bile. This kind of warning is often repeated in his writings. Ficino describes an opposition between the bodily activity of sexual intercourse and the mental activity of contemplation. He concludes: . . . "there is nothing more harmful to the business of being contemplative or curious than Venereal activity, and nothing more contrary to Venereal activity than careful contemplation."[274] He argues that the fire of a mind engaged in intellectual life is "blown out by the Venereal" or suffocated by melancholia. Ficino considers this point to be so important that he refuses to work with men who do not accept his advice. He concludes that, "A man, therefore, should know which way he is, and be his own self-regulator. A man should be his own doctor. Let those who plan to live in a state of constant coitus consult somebody else!"[275]

In his analysis of the powers of the deities Ficino warns his readers against the tricks of Venus, who takes the life away from a man and gives it instead to his offspring. Venus is in control of a man during the first of five stages, namely when he is either totally under the sway of the senses or more attracted by the senses than by reason. Mercury, on the other hand, oversees a man when he moves to the three higher stages of development, namely when he alternates between his senses and reason, when he is led more by reason than by senses, and when he is ruled entirely by his reason. After establishing this hierarchy over the student of a feminine goddess, Venus, and a masculine god, Mercury, Ficino then introduces an almost satirical rendering of Venus's deceptive and dangerous activities:

> If we may return to Venus for a moment: if you have ever seen Venus you saw her as young, dolled-up in finery and makeup as if she were a prostitute. She who is always new always wants the new, and she hates the old. She destroys what she had made of the old in order to make new all over again. Again, if I may say so, she is like a prostitute who is not content with one man but loves everybody, and,

ence to Thomas's *Summa Contra Gentiles* see ch. 18, p. 150, and for his book *On Fate* see ch. 25, p. 177. For Socrates and Pythagoras see ch. 12, p. 125. For Plato see ch. 11, p. 117. For Galen see ch. 10, p. 115. For Porphyry and Proclus see ch. 13, p. 127.

273. Ficino, "On Caring for the Health of Men of Letters," in *The Book of Life,* ch. 7, p. 12.
274. Ficino, "How to Prolong Your Life," in *The Book of Life,* ch. 16, p. 69.
275. Ficino, "How to Prolong Your Life," in *The Book of Life,* ch. 16, p. 70.

if I can speak dialectically here, she promiscuously favors the species rather than the individual.

She doesn't just knock you out with a touch — oh no, she deceives you daily with the taste, too, and those who are deceived by her she then destroys.[276]

This feminine stereotype of the dangerous woman is further specified in its application to physical generation in contrast to mental generation, which Ficino associates with Saturn. Ficino specifies: "Venus fertilizes the body, and stimulates fertility. Saturn presses the mind, pregnant by his seed, to give birth."[277] Ficino does not want to insist that Venus and Saturn are contrary enemies of each other, but rather he suggests that they differ as to their effects on human beings. Venus draws a man to pleasures in external things, while Saturn draws a man towards the interior pleasures of the mind. Excess of either kind of pleasure can destroy someone. Thus, a balanced man has a healthy balance in his soul/body relation.

For Ficino the world has a dynamic of masculine and feminine interaction on all its many levels. The macrocosm, with its interaction of masculine and feminine planets, is mirrored in an analogous masculine and feminine dynamic in the microcosm of the individual soul. The key for Ficino is at what level a man or woman wants to participate in this dynamic. If it is at the lower level of physical intercourse, then it seems to limit a capacity for participation at a higher level. Ficino summarizes it this way:

> Orpheus called this nature of the world, and Jove's world, both masculine and feminine. It is so because the world is everywhere hot to make love to its own mutual parts. Everywhere it is mixed between the masculine and feminine sex, as the order of signs declares, where, in perpetual order, the masculine goes first, the feminine follows. The trees and herbs prove this too, which have both sexes the same as animals.
>
> I will pass over the fact that fire goes to air, and water goes to earth, like man to woman, because there is nothing surprising in the fact that the world's limbs, among themselves and all its parts, lust for copulation with each other. The planets are in accord with this too, part of them being masculine, part of them, in fact, feminine, and Mercury in particular is both masculine and feminine, as the father of Hermaphroditus.[278]

The philosopher chooses an intellectual form of conception rather than a physical form. The higher level draws into it all the dynamics of the lower levels. Thus, the body of a student or scholar needs to be healthy and totally oriented towards the intellectual conception of the mind as it moves towards chaste union with God.

Before turning to consider intellectual conception *per se,* it is important to consider in this section on gender and the soul/body relation a text Ficino wrote to-

276. Ficino, "How to Prolong Your Life," in *The Book of Life,* ch. 15, p. 66.
277. Ficino, "How to Prolong Your Life," in *The Book of Life,* ch. 15, p. 67.
278. Ficino, "On Making Your Life Agree with the Heavens," in *The Book of Life,* ch. 26, p. 179.

wards the end of his life. The only extensive commentary he wrote on Plato's *Republic* was a commentary on Book VIII, written in the 1490s and published in 1496 under the title *De Numero Fatali (The Fatal Number)*.[279] The context of Ficino's commentary was a concern to understand Socrates' claim in the *Republic* that even the best eugenic results can degenerate during a particular temporal cycle in which the "fatal number" presides, astrologically. Earlier scholars, such as Boethius, had struggled to discover the number hinted at in *Republic* Book VIII 546a ff. Ficino decided to enter the debate full force in his commentary, and in his reflections several aspects of gender identity were articulated.

Ficino believed with Plato and Pythagoras that there existed a realm of numbers intermediate between the human being and the highest reality. These numbers were in relations of proportions and had a generative dynamic that influenced not only the planets and stars but also human life. He came to believe that it was the specific work of a philosopher to gain as much understanding as possible of the numeric structure of the world, and to use this knowledge to help plan human societies and interactions.

Before describing Ficino's claims in his commentary, descriptions of three different kinds of numbers need to be understood:[280]

1. **Male and female numbers**: Following the Pythagorean table of opposites, odd numbers are male and even numbers are female, e.g., 1 is male, 2 is female, 3 is male, 4 is female, etc. Giving an allegorical interpretation of Plato's description of the fall of the male into a female body in subsequent generations, Ficino suggests that the male number is indivisible, while the female is a kind of first fall from the number 1.

2. **Spousal or nuptial numbers**: Again following the Pythagorean tradition, the product of the multiplication of two adjacent numbers, a male odd number and a female even number, is a spousal or nuptial number, e.g., 6 (2 × 3), 12 (3 × 4), etc. According to Plato spousal or nuptial numbers "signal the best opportunities for marriage and begetting in a state that wants to resist a decline before its fatal time." (*Republic* 546b3)

3. **Perfect numbers**: Numbers identical with the sum of their factors, e.g., 6 (1 + 2 + 3), 28 (14 + 7 + 4 + 2 + 1), 496, 8128, etc. According to Plato the perfect numbers "contain the circuit itself of divine generation" — "as rare as is the perfection, so rare is the divine progeny that proceeds." (*Republic* 546b3)

4. **The fatal number**: Ficino argued that 1728 is the fatal number. It is 12 raised to the third power, and contains "a discordant concord" that contains both obvious and hidden ratios that are both proportional and geometric. According to Plato, Iamblichus, and Plutarch, the state should beware of the fatal

---

279. The entire text with extensive commentary has recently been published in English by Michael J. B. Allen, *Nuptial Arithmetic: Marsilio Ficino's Commentary on the Fatal Number in Book VIII of Plato's "Republic"* (Berkeley/Los Angeles/London: University of California Press, 1994).

280. These descriptions are based on Michael Allen's summaries, *Nuptial Arithmetic*, pp. 48-52.

number when planning mass weddings, as children born under the fatal number will lead to the decline of the state ahead of its time.[281]

From the perspective of gender identity, it is interesting to note that Ficino does not suggest that either the male or the female is always superior to the other. The male numbers are given one kind of priority, in that the even female number 2 is described as a fall from the primary male number 1. However, the even female number 6 is a perfect number. Even the Pythagorean perfect number 10 is an even number. The fatal number is also a female even number, and it had its roots closely connected with the perfect number 6. There is no absolutely perfect valuation of engendered numbers, but all occurs in a dynamic of relations at times moving towards perfect generation and other times towards degeneration.

More significant than either male or female numbers is the dynamic of their interaction. For Ficino all generativity is the result of proportional relations. Equal numbers have no generativity. Thus, it can be argued that his numerology supports neither a gender polarity nor a gender unity view. Instead, it contains the principles of gender complementarity, or equal dignity and worth along with significant differentiation.

Early in his text *De Numero Fatali* Ficino invokes Plato's authority to emphasize the importance of the number 12, which is also highly favored in Judaism and Christianity:

> But Plato venerates the number 12 not only secretly here but also openly in the *Laws,* the *Phaedo,* the *Timaeus,* the *Phaedrus,* and the *Critias.* . . . Wherefore Plato judges this number twelve to be the governor of the universal world form, of the human form, and of the form of the state. He judges it to accord most with the propagation or mutation of things, since, as we will show later, it is the first of the increasing and abundant numbers. Twelve is made from the number six twinned, from six the perfect number as we call it. In other words, twelve is more than perfect.[282]

The concept of a fertile or abundant number is carefully explained by Ficino. A number is considered fertile if its factors add up to a larger number than itself; it is considered deficient when its factors add up to a smaller number than itself. For example, 12 is an abundant number because its factors — 6, 4, 3, 2, and 1 — add up to 16, while 8 is a deficient number because its factors — 4, 2, and 1 — add up to 7. Ficino concludes:

> Therefore twelve accords most with the universe and signifies fertility and increase, especially because it is the first and the prince of the abundant numbers. Furthermore, the Pythagoreans called 6 the spousal number, because in its conception a male joins with a female, that is, an odd [number] with an even — 2 ×

---

281. For the complicated mathematical derivation of the fatal number see Michael Allen, *Nuptial Arithmetic,* pp. 71-80.

282. Ficino, "De Numero Fatali" III, i.40-57, in Michael Allen, *Nuptial Arithmetic,* pp. 178-80.

3. But 6 is the first of the spousal numbers and 12 is the second (in the twelve's conception 3 mingles itself with 4 — 3 × 4 = 12). But where even and odd are distanced by intermediary numbers, they do not seem to unite as spouses.[283]

After establishing the principle of spousal or nuptial numbers, Ficino then enters into an analysis of the male and female components. It is here that we see his dynamic of seeking a complementary evaluation of male and female yet also promoting a modified gender polarity. First, from the perspective of multiplication the feminine even number has the capacity to change an odd number into an even when they are multiplied. So if an even is in the root, when it multiples an odd or the reverse, it makes it an even, as 2 × 3 = 6, 3 × 4 = 12; likewise 3 × 6 = 18. Second, from the perspective of division the masculine odd number is given a higher priority:

> The odd numbers naturally excel the even, however; for the even seem to be like corporeal and divisible things, but the odd like incorporeal and indivisible things. Again, the first even, namely 2, is the first division and diversity, and the first fall from the 1. But the first odd, that is 3, is as it were the return to the one and to [its] principle; it abounds in the one more than the even [2] does, and on account of this obvious copiousness it is called masculine. But the even [2], on account of [its] dearth, partition, and fall, appears as it were to be feminine. The human and moral praise is given to the even numbers insofar as there is a just distribution in their partition on both sides. But the more sacred and divine praise is extended to the odd numbers, since in the even number justice has been broken up as it were and has no hinge on which it might depend. But in the odd number there is always the one: it is the mean between the number's even parts on either side. It is as it were the center and the god by whom equal distribution is governed and to which it is referred as to its end.[284]

Ficino ultimately places the superior valuation of the male in more direct relation to the incorporeal and divine and the female in more direct relation with the corporeal and human. Thus his initial complementarity is modified by a mathematical polarity that draws upon the ancient association of the female with matter and the male with form.

This polarity association is also found in Ficino's analysis of the effects of addition. Here the male number exhibits the active properties of form and the female number the passive properties of matter. Significantly, Ficino appeals to a lost Aristotelian work for his defense of this argument:

> This Aristotle says in the *Pythagorean,* although the Pythagoreans [themselves] were more willing to call the one an odd. For it is proper for an even number not to change the number it is added to: if it is added to an even, it preserves it as an even; if to an odd, it preserves it as an odd. When the one meets an even number,

283. Ficino, "De Numero Fatali" IV, in Michael Allen, *Nuptial Arithmetic,* pp. 184-86.
284. Ficino, "De Numero Fatali" VI, 74-87, in Michael Allen, *Nuptial Arithmetic,* pp. 192-94.

on the other hand, it makes it an odd; and when it meets an odd, it makes it an even. In the same way, the odd number — as the male and effective number — changes the number it meets: out of an even number it makes an odd, out of an odd it makes an even. However, the even number — as the female — does not change; rather it is itself changed and itself suffers.[285]

Ficino also appeals to Plato's discussion of the proper age for a man and a woman to conceive in *Laws* and *Republic* to introduce a further rationale for female inferiority. After noting the differences in ages for a man (25 or 30 to 55) and for a woman (20 to 40) for optimal conception and associating these differences with mathematical principles, he concludes: "But the age for a woman begins from the unequilateral [20], and the interval of [her] conceiving similarly spans the unequilateral, namely 20 years. For the female is inferior herself and is deemed inferior in the office of generating."[286]

Ficino's numerical gender polarity is rooted also in the Pythagorean table of opposites that had been recorded in Aristotle's *Metaphysics*. He introduces a dynamic of ratios that basically changes the relation of masculine and feminine numbers as ratios themselves change. While the polarized identification of superior and inferior is still associated with the male and female respectively, the polarized gender identification of odd and even changes:

> The Pythagorean and Platonic view is that from two good parents is born an entirely good offspring, from two bad an utterly bad; from a bad and good together an offspring that is not wholly bad indeed, but never good. Likewise the view is that the odd numbers are in the order of the good and should be called males and bridegrooms and fathers (especially because of the strength which they possess in their middle knot, namely the one); but that the even numbers, when compared with the odd, are in the class of the bad and should be called females and brides and mothers — if, that is, they are joined to the odd numbers. For within each class too numbers can be called in a way grooms or brides, since a more outstanding even number can be called groom for an inferior even number, and an inferior odd number can be called bride for a superior one.[287]

This introduction of a hierarchical progression of masculine and feminine, with the feminine always being identified as the inferior one, shifts the foundation of the engendered metaphor from identification with a concrete particular to identification with a ratio. Ficino notes that Plato speaks "of both kinds of fertility, that is, of bodies and of souls," and he describes the relative identities of understanding/reason/irascible appetites/concupiscible appetites in an ascending order.[288]

Ficino's use of ratios extends through many aspects of life: the relation of the planets, the powers of the mind, the elements in nutrition. Thus, ratios become a

285. Ficino, "De Numero Fatali" VIII, 28-35, in Michael Allen, *Nuptial Arithmetic,* p. 198.
286. Ficino, "De Numero Fatali" XVI, 58-61, in Michael Allen, *Nuptial Arithmetic,* p. 224.
287. Ficino, "De Numero Fatali" XIII, i-xiii, in Michael Allen, *Nuptial Arithmetic,* pp. 210-12.
288. Ficino, "De Numero Fatali" XIV, 65, in Michael Allen, *Nuptial Arithmetic,* p. 216.

common element in levels of being of soul/body and cosmos/elements. Given the association of male with odd and female with even as well as the second-level association of bridegroom and husband with superior and bride and mother with inferior, Ficino's numerology or *Nuptial Arithmetic* contains much that is significant for the history of the concept of woman. The core elements in Ficino's use of ratios are summarized in the chart below:

Ficino's Engendered Ratios				
Ratio	Planets (Macrocosm)	Powers of Mind (Microcosm)	Elements	Values
4:3	Favorable ratio on us of Jupiter:Venus Masculine: feminine	In rulers — ratio of understanding: reason In soldiers — ratio of reason: understanding	ratio of air:fire ratio of heat:wet	Even:odd = female:male Superior: inferior = bridegroom and father: bride and mother
3:2	Favorable ratio on us of Venus:Sun Feminine: masculine	In rulers — ratio of reason: irascible power	ratio of fire:water ratio of wet:dry	Odd:even = male:female Superior: inferior = bridegroom and father: bride and mother
2:1	Favorable ratio on us of Sun:Moon Masculine: Feminine	In rulers — ratio of irascible power: concupiscible power	ratio of water:earth ratio of heat:cold	Even:odd = female:male Superior: inferior = bridegroom and father: bride and mother

Ficino's meticulous analysis of numbers and ratios is in the first case oriented towards interpreting Plato's concern for proper breeding and eugenics and in the second case towards conditions that are conducive to the building up of harmony in the state. As he faced the coming of the semimillennial year 1500, Ficino was also eager to determine all the various factors that were helpful for the growth or the decline of a civilization. He concludes his summary of ideal ratios as applied to Plato's Book VIII with a return to the fatal number:

> As long as all proportions and harmonies of this kind prevail among mankind, then a good habit endures in bodies, spirits, souls, and states. But when they fail, that habit also becomes exhausted, and at length the republic changes for the worse. Discipline can do much, but the fatal order seems to determine that when the number 12 — the number in which the said proportions and harmonies are first unfolded and which has been destined for the universe — has been changed into its plane [i.e., its share] of 144, then among men a great mutation occurs, which is for the better if our discipline endures; but that when 12 arrives at its solid [i.e., its cube] of 1728, as at its highest end, then the republic, the state itself — if the discipline has endured thus far — also attains to its highest end; and that thereafter gradually it declines by the fatal law to a worse condition, even as the discipline by the same fate also degenerates little by little. However, before these limits have been reached, if the discipline fails through our negligence or infelicity, then the public form totters that much earlier, brought low not only by a particular fate but also by our imprudence.[289]

Ficino's experiences of the expulsion of the Medici from Florence, the end of his Platonic Academy, the early death of Pico della Mirandola, and the violent death of Savonarola were interpreted as signs of the degeneration of his own society. At the same time, Ficino's commentary on Plato's Book VIII of the *Republic* also indicates that there were also elite men who would arise, and it is likely that Ficino included himself among their number. In the final paragraph of his commentary he states: "Finally, Plato seems as it were to have prophesied that in those ages and times which arrive at, or return to, the perfect number, certain divine men will arise; and to them the ends of those ages will be known."[290] Ficino's belief that he had been given access to divine secrets formed a key part of his epistemological theory and of his teaching about the relation between love and knowledge of ultimate truth, goodness, and beauty. In this area as in all others, gender identity has its proper place.

The place of mathematics in Ficino's philosophy cannot be overestimated. Michael Allen points out in his *Nuptial Arithmetic* that in the entrance to the original Platonic Academy hung the saying: "Let no one enter here who is not adept in geometry," and that Ficino added a gloss that again emphasized the place of mathematics in both body and soul: "Understand that Plato was intending this to apply not only to the proper measurement of lines but also of [our] passions."[291] Mathe-

---

289. Ficino, "De Numero Fatali" XII, 49-64, in Michael Allen, *Nuptial Arithmetic*, pp. 208-10.
290. Ficino, "De Numero Fatali" XVII, 103-5, in Michael Allen, *Nuptial Arithmetic*, p. 232.
291. Allen, *Nuptial Arithmetic*, 97, note 46.

matical ratios formed the structure within which the souls and bodies of men and women either generated, lived in harmony, or declined into disorder and conflict. We will now turn more directly to consider the steps that Ficino suggested for educating humanity towards the better goal.

Platonic Love and Friendship

Kristeller states that Ficino's description of Platonic love in a letter to Almanno Donati is the first time in the history of philosophy and of literature that the phrase "Platonic love" is introduced.[292] In a contemporary sense, Platonic love usually refers to a relationship between a man and a woman that is chaste or celibate, and that has the intensity of a deep personal friendship. It is contrasted with sexually expressed or erotic relations between a man and a woman. Ficino's use of the phrase "Platonic love" also incorporates man/woman relations, but it is more closely rooted in the original Platonic context of homosexual relations among men and boys. Ficino seeks to elaborate the sequence of arguments that Socrates offered in Plato's dialogue *Symposium* and to persuade his listeners to move from a focus on the particular beauty of an individual beautiful object of sexual love to a contemplation of the Form of Beauty and the Highest Good. In this context the individual human being, who was the original object of physical attraction, is a step on the way to love of the Good. The man/man relation then is purified of its particularized erotic elements, and the two become "Platonic Lovers" or "Chaste Friends" together helping one another on the path to the highest contemplation.

Ficino takes great effort to develop this theme throughout several of his works. In his extensive commentary on Plato's *Philebus*, Ficino constantly repeats Socrates' argument that desire for union with the highest good is a greater value than pleasure. In Plato's original dialogue Socrates summarizes the argument as follows:

> **Socrates:** Well, Philebus says that the good for all animate beings consists in enjoyment, pleasure, delight, and whatever can be classed as consonant therewith, whereas our contention is that the good is not that, but that thought, intelligence, memory, and things akin to these, right opinion and true reasoning, prove better and more valuable than pleasure for all such beings as can participate in them, and that for all these, whether now living or yet to be born, nothing in the world is more profitable than so to participate. That, I think, Philebus, is the substance of our respective theories, is it not?[293]

Ficino's elaboration of Plato's argument allows for a radical rejection of the Epicurean principle that had been articulated by Lorenzo Valla and others. Since not pleasure, but rather the exercise of the highest activities of the mind is the good to be sought after, the relations among men and women become transformed by their proper goal.

In a letter Marsilio Ficino addressed to his friends, Ficino links love for either

292. Kristeller, *The Philosophy of Marsilio Ficino*, p. 286.
293. Plato, *Philebus* 11b-c.

a beautiful female or male body to this process of progressive elevation of the soul of one who is drawn to particular beauty. Ficino is drawing an analogy between love of Virtue and love of a beautiful body. The letter begins with a pronouncement by Ficino on methodology:

> It is pointless for you to praise a maiden to the ears of a young man and describe her in words in order to inflict upon him pangs of love, when you can bring her beautiful form before his eyes. Point, if you can, to her beautiful form; then you have no further need of words. For it is impossible to say how much more easily and powerfully Beauty herself calls forth love than do words.
>
> Therefore, if we bring into the view of men the marvellous sight of Virtue herself, there will be no further need for our persuading words: the vision itself will persuade more quickly than can be conceived.[294]

Next, in order to make the leap from sensation to interior apprehension of form better understood, Ficino goes step by step through his ladder of Platonic love. Following a Platonic method, he begins with the beautiful body of a man and then moves to an analogous beautiful structure of soul:

> Picture a man endowed with the most . . . acute faculties, a strong body, good health, a handsome form, well-proportioned limbs and a noble stature. Picture this man moving with alacrity and skill, speaking elegantly, singing sweetly, laughing graciously: you will love no one anywhere, you will admire no one, if you do not love and admire such a man as soon as you see him.
>
> Now, in order to reflect more easily upon the divine aspect of the mind from the corresponding likeness of the beautiful body, refer each aspect of the body to an aspect of mind. For the body is the shadow of the soul; the form of the body, as best it can, represents the form of the soul; thus liveliness and acuteness of perception in the body represent, in a measure, the wisdom and far-sightedness of the mind; strength of body represents strength of mind; health of body, which consists in the tempering of the humours, signifies a temperate mind. Beauty, which is determined by the proportions of the body and a becoming complexion, shows us the harmony and splendour of justice; also, size shows us liberality and nobility; and stature, magnanimity; in the same way dexterity indicates to us civility and courteousness; fine speaking, oratory; sweet singing, the power of poetry. Finally, gracious laughter represents serene happiness in life and perfect joy, which Virtue herself showers upon us.[295]

In the third stage of his methodology, Ficino then gathers different lower forms into an apprehension of the single form of Virtue, and calls his correspondents to contemplation of the beauty of Virtue itself:

> Now bring into one whole each single part and attribute of Virtue, which we

294. Ficino, *The Letters of Marsilio Ficino* (London: Shepherd-Walwyn, 1975-88), vol. 4, #51, 66.
295. Ficino, *The Letters of Marsilio Ficino*, vol. 4, #51, 66-67.

have mentioned; you will at once see clearly a spectacle to be admired and vener-
ated. How worthy of love, how worthy of admiration, is this form of the soul,
whose shadow is the form of the body so loved and admired by everyone. But just
as Virtue, when she is seen, instantly draws each man to herself by her lovely
form so, without doubt, will Vice, if clearly seen, immediately terrify by his deformity and drive everyone away.

Come, friends. Let us always hold before our eyes the divine idea and form of
Virtue. She will at once draw us to herself by the grace of her splendour, unceas-
ingly delight us with the sweetness of her proportion and harmony, and completely fill us with an abundance of all that is good.[296]

While the particular sensory base for this analogy was a young man, the same
methodology would hold for the movement from physical beauty to love of virtue
in the case of a young woman. Thus, Ficino offers a different model of relationship
than had been proposed by either Epicureans or Stoics, or Christians who had been
directly influenced by these two philosophical trends.

While for the Epicureans woman was the object of the highest pleasure, for
the Stoics woman was a dangerous force that drew men away from their proper
end. Often in western gender polarity and particularly in the Stoic and satirical traditions, woman's beauty had been portrayed as an obstacle to a man's purpose and
end because it interrupted his studies and rendered him weak and ineffective. In
contrast to this, Ficino argues that a woman's beauty is a positive intermediate step
in a man's movement towards God. As Paul Kristeller notes: "For Ficino the love
for a person . . . is a simple preparation, more-or-less conscious, for the love of
God. . . . Since this love always has beauty as its object, it is not sensual, but limited
to eye, ear, and thought."[297]

Ficino did a similar interpretive transmission of another central Renaissance
Humanist text on the concept of woman. Guido Cavalcanti's "Donna me prega,"
or "A Lady Asked Me," had proposed that love for a woman could lead to the
downfall of a man, when his passions were too intense. It could also lead the man
towards love of an abstract ideal woman as well. At the beginning of Chapter 4 we
noted that this text held a seminal place in the history of early humanism. It provided a source for numerous commentaries, and spawned a continual analysis of
the nature and causes of love between a man and a woman. Marsilio Ficino introduced Guido Cavalcanti's "Donna me prega" in his *Commentary on Plato's Symposium*.[298] "Ficino's brief chapter on Cavalcanti not only went against every previous
and contemporary opinion on 'Donna me prega,' but it also exerted a profound influence on later interpretations of the *Canzone*."[299] Specifically, Ficino ignored the

---

296. Ficino, *The Letters of Marsilio Ficino*, vol. 4, #51, 67.

297. Kristeller, *The Philosophy of Marsilio Ficino*, p. 276.

298. Kristeller notes in *The Philosophy of Ficino* that "In his concept of love he combines the will
of St. Augustine, the charity of St. Paul, the friendship of Aristotle, and the Stoics with love in Plato's
sense of the term into a new and fertile idea. Moreover, Ficino's speculation on love was foreshadowed
. . . by the old Provençal and Tuscan lyric to which he himself consciously refers" (p. 287).

299. Massimo Ciavella, "Ficino's Interpretation of 'Donna me prega,'" in *Ficino and Renaissance Neoplatonism*, ed. Eisenbichler and Pugliese, p. 43.

negative effects of erotic love for a woman on a man, and instead emphasized the value she provided for the progressive elevation of an object of love moving towards union with absolute beauty. Ficino turned Cavalcanti into a Neoplatonic philosopher of love, and even into an original source for the development of his theory of Platonic love.

Since scholars have demonstrated that Ficino was among the most careful readers and translators of ancient texts, it is not possible to claim that he did not understand Plato, Plotinus, or Cavalcanti when he offered his Neoplatonic interpretations of their views about the nature, causes, and effects of love between a man and a woman. Instead it must be admitted that Ficino purposefully used the ancient texts in his commentaries to elaborate his own theory about how man/woman relations ought to be.

In a similar way, Ficino both used and transformed Diotima's arguments in his commentary on Plato's *Symposium*. Ficino referred to Diotima as a "Sibyl" who revealed to Socrates the secrets of the art "ascending from sensible to moral to intellectual to intelligible beauty."[300] Her art involved coming to discover the beauty of God as well as God's goodness by disciplining the power of exterior and then interior sight. Following Plato's use of the metaphors of sight and light, Ficino elaborates the process of ascent in the *Phaedrus*. As Michael Allen summarizes it: "From being subordinate to hearing, seeing has become the supremely intellectual act, the act of the unitary man in love with the Divine Being."[301]

In his commentary *De amore*, Ficino often considers love as a kind of divine force that binds all things together rather than a direct relation between two persons.[302] Diotima's conclusions about love drew upon and at the same time transformed aspects of the argument of one of those present at the banquet. In one example, Ficino summarizes the argument of Pausanias, who had introduced a distinction between two different sources of love, or two Venuses corresponding to a higher and a lower kind of love respectively. The names of the gods and goddesses were changed by Ficino from the Greek, Aphrodite and Zeus, to the Roman, Venus and Jupiter:

> The first Venus, which is in the Angelic Mind, is said to have been born of Uranus "of no mother," because for the natural philosophers, *mother* means *matter*, and the Angelic Mind is completely foreign to any relationship with corporeal matter.
>
> The second Venus, which is in the World-Soul, was born of Jupiter and Dione: born of Jupiter, that is, of that faculty of the World-Soul which moves the heavens. She it was who created the power which generates these lower forms. The philosophers attribute a mother as well as a father to this Venus because she

---

300. Ficino refers to Diotima as a Sibyl both in his commentary *De Amore* 6.1 and in his commentary on *Philebus* 1.5. See Allen, *The Platonism of Marsilio Ficino,* p. 56.

301. Allen, *The Platonism of Marsilio Ficino,* p. 83.

302. Michael J. B. Allen, "Marsilio Ficino's Interpretation of Plato's *Timaeus* and Its Myth of the Demiurge," in *Supplementum Festivum: Studies in Honor of Paul Oskar Kristeller,* ed. James Hankins, John Monfasini, Frederick Purnell, Jr. (Binghamton, N.Y.: Medieval and Renaissance Texts and Studies, 1987), vol. 49, pp. 399-439.

is thought to be related to matter, since she is incorporated in the matter of the world. To sum it all up, Venus is two-fold: one is clearly that intelligence which we said was in the Angelic Mind; the other is the power of generation with which the World-Soul is endowed. Each has as consort a similar Love.[303]

When Ficino both uses and embellishes Plato's views he takes Pausanias's identification of matter with the cosmic mother receptacle of the world and argues that the presence of matter implies a Venus of lower value than a Venus with no matter at all. The conflation of matter with mother is used to describe the higher Venus as being born from a Father only, while the lower Venus has the presence of both parents. Ficino suggests that by analogy the soul has two powers as well:

> The soul also has two powers. It certainly has the power of comprehension, and it has the power of generation. These two powers in us are the two Venuses which are accompanied by their twin Loves. . . .
>
> Of what, therefore, does Pausanias disapprove in love? I shall tell you. If a man is too eager for procreation and gives up contemplation, or is immoderately desirous of copulation with women, or consorts unnaturally with men, or prefers the beauty of the body to that of the soul, insofar he abuses the dignity of love.[304]

Ficino often quotes Diotima's words from Plato's *Symposium* while he develops further his own interpretation of their significance. He extends the two powers of soul identified by Pausanias to five and elaborates Diotima's classification of loves to include daemons or gods:

> But now let us return to Diotima. After she had shown that love, for the reasons we have mentioned, is included among the number of the daemons, she described to Socrates the origin of Love, in this way: "On the birthday of Venus, while the Gods were feasting, Porus, the son of Thought, drunk with a draught of nectar, lay with Penia in the garden of Jove, and from this union was born Love."
>
> "On the birthday of Venus," that is, when the Angelic Mind, and the World-Soul, which for the reason we have mentioned elsewhere, we have called Venuses, were born from the supreme majesty of God. . . .
>
> These twin Venuses and their twin loves are not only in the World-Soul, but also in the souls of the spheres, the stars, daemons, and men. . . .
>
> But in us, there are found not two only, but five loves. The two extreme ones are daemons, of course, the three median ones are not simple daemons, but desires. Now, in the mind of man there is an eternal love for seeing the divine beauty: thanks to it we pursue the study of philosophy and the practices of justice and piety. There is also in the power of generation a certain mysterious stimulus for propagating offspring. . . .

303. *Marsilio Ficino's Commentary on Plato's Symposium,* trans. Sears Reynolds Jayne (Columbia, Mo.: University of Missouri Press, 1944), p. 142.

304. *Ficino's Commentary on Plato's Symposium,* p. 143.

Between these two extremes, there are three loves in us which, however, since they are not in the soul in the same way as those two most firmly established ones, but begin, grow, decrease, and cease, will better be called emotions or passions than daemons. Of these, one is equidistant from the two extreme ones; the other two lie between the mid-point and either extreme.

And so all love begins with sight. But the love of the contemplative man ascends from sight to the mind; that of the voluptuous man descends from sight into touch, and that of the practical man remains in the form of sight. Love of the first is attracted to the highest daemon rather than to the lowest, that of the second is drawn to the lowest rather than to the highest, and that of the last remains an equal distance from both. These three loves have three names: love of the contemplative man is called divine; that of the practical man human; and that of the voluptuous man, animal.[305]

In a detailed analysis of Ficino's four different methods of "allegorizing the pagan Gods 'Platonically,'"[306] Michael Allen indicates the vital and serious ways in which gods and goddesses serve as divine forces either helping or hindering the ascent of the soul to union with the Highest Good. In addition to different Venuses, the goddesses Diana, Vesta, and Pallas Athena also have a role to play. Notable for our purposes, however, is the general place that female beauty has in helping men to know and to love perfect beauty and goodness.

Different dialogues of Plato identify different stages in the soul's ascent. The *Parmenides* focuses on the ascent of the mind to the One, while the *Phaedrus* indicates how an individual intellectual soul can reach a vision of the intelligible forms. At the same time, Ficino is also concerned with those who do not cooperate with the ascent through the proper stages of Platonic love. Others, as mentioned above, tend to choose, not the divine, nor even the human, but rather the animal mode of existence. Their souls, instead of ascending to higher realms of beauty, truth, and goodness, descend. In this case a human being's intellectual powers are weakened and the lower passions with the imagination and biological powers are intensified. With this theoretical background Ficino suggests that those who relate to others primarily as particular objects of pleasure are in an intellectually weakened state. Michael Allen notes that Ficino's translation in *Phaedrus* 248 D 1-2 of Plato's suggestion of the reincarnation of this kind of soul in a beast or animal in a subsequent life, shifts the meaning to imply that the soul is condemned to associate with beasts or animals, not to become one.[307] As will be seen in the section on engendered virtues, Ficino considers similar negative effects on a man who associates with women and girls.

In the following passage from his commentary on the *Symposium*, Ficino considers those who descend to the lower kind of loves:

305. *Ficino's Commentary on Plato's Symposium*, pp. 192-93.
306. Allen, *The Platonism of Marsilio Ficino*, p. 137.
307. Allen, *The Platonism of Marsilio Ficino*, "Plato's operative phrase at 248D1-2: 'The soul shall not be implanted in her first birth in any brute beast,' Ficino translates as *in aliquam brutalem ire naturam*. By choosing *natura*, he can skirt around the possibility that the human soul might subsequently enter into a brute soul absolutely" (p. 174).

According to Plato, the soul is as pregnant as the body, and they are both aroused to procreation by the stimuli of love. But some men, either on account of their nature or their training, are better equipped for offspring of the soul than for those of the body. Others, and certainly the majority of them, are the opposite. The former pursue heavenly love, the latter earthly. The former, therefore, naturally love men more than women and those nearly adults rather than children, because the first two are much stronger in mental keenness, and this because of its higher beauty is most essential to knowledge, which they naturally wish to generate. But the others are just the opposite, because of their passion for the physical union of love, and the sensuous effect of bodily generation. But, since that genital force of the soul has no power of cognition, it makes no discrimination between the sexes: but is naturally aroused for generation whenever we see any beautiful object, and it consequently happens that those who associate with males have intercourse with them in order to satisfy the urge of their genital parts.[308]

Beauty may be a source of ascent as well as of descent, and it is to this important point that Ficino's theory of Platonic love most forcibly returns. Beauty approximates the truth the more it moves towards a unity from a context of several particulars. Thus, it moves from the sensation of sense particulars of sensible individuals by abstraction to a single sensible form of beauty, and then it moves from the rational comparison of several intellectual particulars of higher forms of beauty to intellectual contemplation of the one true and beautiful good.

In the following passage from his commentary on Plato's *Symposium*, Ficino suggests that Platonic love is most effective among those who have a masculine intellectual capacity that has been purified of lower particularities:

Perhaps someone may ask by whom especially and by what means lovers are entrapped, and how they are freed. Women indeed snare men easily, but those do it most easily who assume a masculine nature; and men do it as much more easily than women as they are more like men, and they have blood and spirit that is clearer, warmer, and thinner; for of this Cupid's net consists. Among men, those attract men and women most strongly who are predominantly sanguine and somewhat choleric, and have large, blue, shining eyes, especially if they live chastely, and have not stained their bodies by exhausting their clear spirits in coitus.[309]

Platonic love remains chaste among men or between men and women and is bound by the intensity of a true friendship oriented towards the love of God.[310] As

308. *Marsilio Ficino's Commentary on Plato's Symposium*, pp. 155-56.

309. *Marsilio Ficino's Commentary on Plato's Symposium*, p. 207.

310. Concerning the question of whether Ficino's theory of Platonic love was actually a sublimated male homosexual model of love see two opposing views. Reginald Hyatte, "A Poetics of Ficino's Socratic Love: Medieval Discursive Models of Amor in Marsilio Ficino's and Lorenzo de' Medici's Amatory Epistles," in *Fifteenth-Century Studies* 20 (1993): 99-117, ed. Edelgard E. Dubruck and William C. McDonald, supports the position that it is analogous to male homosexual lovers, while Paul

Kristeller summarizes it: "Thus Ficino could say that friendship was the bond that linked the members of his Academy with each other, or that a true friendship always required three partners, two friends and God, the common ground of their friendship."[311]

Our analysis now needs to turn to consider the relation between women and higher intellectual activity. If what is attractive to men is engaging in philosophical discourse, does this imply that women who do philosophy "assume a masculine nature" as Ficino suggests above? If so, this would undermine a complementarity approach in which men and women both engage in philosophical thinking, but neither is considered particularly masculine for so doing. In order to address this issue, we turn directly to the question of the relation of Marsilio Ficino and women philosophers.

Women Philosophers

The first question that should be asked is whether or not there were any women in Ficino's Platonic Academy in Florence. An affirmative answer would be given in the Platonic and Neoplatonic traditions. Ficino was aware that Plato had women disciples, for in a letter in which he discusses the disciples of Plato he mentions "several others, among them two women, Lastheneia of Mantinea and Axiothea of Phlius, who both wore men's clothes."[312] Ficino's statement that both women wore men's clothes is an addition to the more generally accepted view that only one of them wore men's clothes. However, it is consistent with the fundamental model of the male philosopher as being in love with the Heavenly Venus.

The women who publicly supported Ficino's Academy included members of the Medici family. However, these benefactors may have simply offered financial and personal support rather than being themselves disciples or professional colleagues of Ficino. In addition, Ficino left a list of persons who were his close friends. This list identified sixty-seven men and no women.[313] Should we conclude then that no women studied philosophy with Ficino? No. There is an alternate source of information that indicates that women were included both in meetings of the Academy and in correspondence with members of the Academy. Letters from the well-known member of the Florentine Academy, Angelo Poliziano, to Cassandra Fedele and to Lorenzo de Medici indicate that Allesandra Scala participated in performances and discussions of Greek dramas with Ficino, Pico della Mirandola, and Poliziano. In addition, this same correspondence invited Cassandra Fedele to be incorporated in some ways into the Florentine humanist community of discourse. Since the details of this incorporation will be discussed in Chapter 10, the

Oskar Kristeller "absolutely excludes such an interpretation" and argues that this is a misleading "erotic" coloring of Ficino's philosophy and letters of correspondence (*The Philosophy of Marsilio Ficino,* pp. 282-83).

311. Kristeller, "The Platonic Academy of Florence," in *Renaissance Thought II,* p. 96. See also Kristeller, *The Philosophy of Marsilio Ficino,* p. 286.

312. *The Letters of Marsilio Ficino,* vol. 3, p. 38.

313. Hankins, *Plato in the Renaissance,* vol. 1, p. 298.

phenomenon of the acceptance of some women into the new Platonic Academy will just be mentioned here.[314]

Another piece of information about his Academy is worth considering. Ficino's Platonic Academy was not set up like an official school with academic courses. Kristeller describes its activities as follows:

> The chief activities of the Academy were closely linked with Ficino himself: improvised conversations with friends or visitors; organized banquets and discussions such as the famous celebration on Plato's birthday; speeches or declamations delivered by Ficino; public courses given by Ficino in the church of S. Maria degli Angeli on Plato, on Plotinus, on St. Paul; also a certain amount of private instruction, based on the reading of Plato and perhaps of other authors. These activities of the Academy must be added to the writings and correspondence of Ficino and his friends if we wish to understand the vogue and prestige attained by the Academy during the more than thirty years of its life and in the course of subsequent centuries.[315]

In this enumeration of activities, there is one that may have had a direct effect on women, namely the public lectures that Ficino gave in the church of S. Maria degli Angeli. In fact, it is believed that Ficino gave lectures during certain periods every day at this church.[316] This assumption is based on a letter from a Camaldolese General who wrote to the Prior of the Church and complained: "Entering thus the House of Angels, I was astonished to see what is customarily the house of God practically filled with a chorus of lay persons on benches, an oratory changed into a gymnasium; the seat by the altar . . . betrayed to a philosopher. . . ."[317] In this public location, it is very possible, if not likely, that some women would be present who would have directly benefited from Ficino's observations on Plato and Plotinus, among other authors. In addition, Ficino also offered discourses in private homes and villas around Florence. Women may also have been present in some of these information classes. Thus, a few women may possibly have grown to love philosophy as Ficino taught it. However, without extant written records of female disciples of Ficino it is not possible to assess this point further.

There are two written records of Ficino himself that illuminate his concept of woman in relation to philosophy: the description of Diotima in his *Commentary on Plato's Symposium* and various comments in his letters about the feminine personification of philosophy. It is to these two sources that we will now turn. Ficino describes Socrates as claiming that he had received his knowledge not from the natu-

---

314. See Anthony Grafton and Lisa Jardine, *From Humanism to the Humanities: Education and the Liberal Arts in Fifteenth- and Sixteenth-Century Europe* (Cambridge, Mass.: Harvard University Press, 1986), pp. 49 and 53-54. See also Margaret King and Albert Rabil, Jr., eds., *Her Immaculate Hand: Selected Works By and About the Women Humanists* (Binghamton, N.Y.: Medieval and Renaissance Texts and Studies, 1983), pp. 87-88 and 127.

315. Paul Oskar Kristeller, "The Platonic Academy of Florence," in *Renaissance Thought II*, pp. 89-101, 93.

316. Hankins, *Plato in the Italian Renaissance,* vol. 1, p. 299.

317. Hankins, *Plato in the Italian Renaissance,* vol. 1, p. 348.

ral philosophers, rhetoricians, or Aspasia, but from Diotima. Socrates introduces Diotima as "a woman who was deeply versed in this and many other fields of knowledge . . . [and he concluded] . . . it was she who taught me the philosophy of Love."[318] In this light, Diotima's views are therefore well worth considering. In continuing the Socratic tradition of invoking Diotima as the supreme authority for the philosophy of love, Ficino conveyed an identification of the female with wisdom. Diotima was portrayed as a wise philosopher and adept teacher of philosophy. Diotima's speech in Plato's original version of the *Symposium* described a progressive ladder of love ascending from love of a physically beautiful body, moving to the love of physically beautiful bodies in general, to a discovery that the most beautiful thing is a beautiful soul and to love of interior beauty of soul or goodness, and finally to love of the Form of the Good itself as the highest object of human love. In the original dialogue, different characters attending a banquet offer their versions of the origin and nature of love according to popular opinion. Socrates interacts with each character, and critically evaluates every opinion in order to distill the one element of truth contained within it. Socrates next shares with those present at the banquet Diotima's philosophy of love. He also attributes learning his "Socratic method" of question and answer to her as well.

Boethius had previously invoked Lady Philosophy as his guide, Dante his Beatrice, Petrarch his Laura, and occasionally Boccaccio his Fiammetta. So there were examples in medieval philosophy and early humanism of female personifications of wisdom as well. Still, even with these historical examples in the Platonic, medieval Stoic, and Italian Humanist traditions, Ficino went further than his predecessors.

In a letter to Bernardo Bembo, Ficino responded to a request to praise philosophy by developing a long and detailed description of the way in which Philosophy is "our mother and nurse."[319] In a section on the "Oratorical Praise of Philosophy" Ficino stated:

> Oh Philosophy, guide of life, seeker of virtue, scourge of vice! What would we be, what would the life of men be, without you? You have begotten cities, called scattered men into the fellowship of life, brought them together first within dwellings, then in marriage, then in communion of tongue and letters. You were the inventress of laws, mistress of men's conduct and discipline.[320]

Then in the next section, entitled the "Moral Praise of Philosophy," Ficino draws out the analogy of the marriage of the philosopher with the female personification of philosophy for the purpose of intellectual conception:

> If the properties of words derive partly from the properties of things and partly from those of ideas, as Plato, Aristotle, Varro and Saint Augustine have shown in great detail, then certainly Philosophy, the explorer and discoverer of the concep-

318. Plato, *Symposium*, 201d 1-2 and 4-5.
319. *The Letters of Marsilio Ficino*, vol. 1, p. 186.
320. *The Letters of Marsilio Ficino*, p. 187.

tion of things, brought forth Grammar, the measure of correct speech and writing. . . .

Philosophy endowed states with souls when she made human laws on earth reflect the divine laws of heaven. She brought forth the body of the state and made it grow by providing agriculture, architecture, medicine, military skill and every other art which gives nourishment, elegance or protection to a state.[321]

It is in the third section of the letter entitled the "Dialectal [sic] and Theological Praise of Philosophy" that Ficino describes philosophy as teacher of a step-by-step process through which the philosopher comes to full illumination. In this part of the analogy Ficino emphasizes more the nursing aspect of the female personification:

> Philosophy uses the tools of dialectic, created by her own hand, to discover the truth in things through contemplation, the virtue in them through use, and the goodness in them through both. . . . Of the many things she teaches I shall mention one in particular. The end is superior to those things that are related to it, just as a master is superior to his servants; so it is quite right that external, mortal and bodily things should serve the body, the body should serve the soul, the senses should serve reason, active reason should serve contemplative reason, and contemplation should serve God.[322]

This hierarchy of relations within the body and soul along with the orientation of the soul itself is ordered through the effective teaching of philosophy. In the following passage Ficino describes in even more detail this nurse-educative function of philosophy:

> The divine Plato considers that the heavenly and immortal soul in a sense dies on entering the earthly and mortal body and lives again when it leaves it. But before the soul leaves the body by the law of nature, it may do so by the diligent practice of meditation, when Philosophy, the medicine of human ills, purges the sickly little soul, buried under the pestilent filth of vice, and enlivens it with her medicine of moral conduct. Then by certain natural instruments she raises the soul from the depths, through all that is compounded of the four elements, and guides it through the elements themselves to heaven. Then step by step on the ladder of mathematics the soul accomplishes the sublime ascent to the topmost orbs of Heaven.[323]

The ultimate goal of the teaching of philosophy is union with God or, as Ficino sometimes says, becoming God.

> That the soul, with the help of Philosophy, can one day become God, we conclude from this: with Philosophy as its guide, the soul gradually comes to com-

321. *The Letters of Marsilio Ficino*, pp. 187-88.
322. *The Letters of Marsilio Ficino*, p. 188.
323. *The Letters of Marsilio Ficino*, p. 189.

prehend with its intelligence the natures of all things, and entirely assumes their forms; also through its will it both delights in and governs particular forms; therefore, in a sense, it becomes all things. Having become all things through this principle, step by step it is transformed into God, who is the fount and Lord of them all. . . . The mind of the truly philosophic man, like God, also conceives within itself the true and eternal causes of all things.[324]

Finally, Marsilio Ficino closes his letter with a stream of intercessions to the female personification of philosophy:

Oh most wonderful intelligence of the heavenly architect! Oh eternal wisdom, born only from the head of highest Jove! Oh infinite truth and goodness of creation, sole queen of the whole universe! Oh, true and bountiful light of intelligence! Oh healing warmth of the will! Oh generous flame of our heart! Illumine us, we beg, shed your light on us and fire us, so that we inwardly blaze with the love of Your light, that is, of truth and wisdom. This alone, Almighty God, is to truly know You. . . .

My Bernardo, I think that your Marsilio has already written as much as a letter can bear. So farewell, and fare fortunately, patron of philosophers; and as you have done hitherto, live continually in the blessed arms of holy Philosophy.[325]

The image of wisdom as springing from the head of Jove recalls the ancient myth of Athena as the female personification of wisdom springing from the head of Zeus. Ficino frequently invokes this metaphor in his works. In his essay entitled "Five Questions Concerning the Mind," he states:

Wisdom, sprung from the crown of the head of Jove, creator of all, warns her philosophical lovers that if they truly desire ever to gain possession of their beloved, they should always seek the highest summits of things rather than the lowest places; for Pallas, the divine offspring sent down from the high heavens, herself frequents the high citadels which she has established. She shows, furthermore, that we cannot reach the highest summits of things unless, first, taking less account of the inferior parts of the soul, we ascend to the highest part, the mind. She promises, finally, that if we have concentrated our powers in this most fruitful part of the soul, then without doubt by means of this highest part itself, that is, by means of mind, we shall ourselves have the power of creating mind; mind which, I say, is the companion of Minerva herself and the foster-child of highest Jove.[326]

The male philosopher unites with the female personification of philosophy to "cre-

---

324. *The Letters of Marsilio Ficino,* p. 190.
325. *The Letters of Marsilio Ficino,* p. 190.
326. Marsilio Ficino, "Five Questions Concerning the Mind," in *The Renaissance Philosophy of Man,* ed. Ernst Cassirer, Paul Oskar Kristeller, and John Herman Randall, Jr. (Chicago and London: University of Chicago Press, 1963), pp. 193-94.

ate" mind. The function of the female personification of philosophy is to elevate the thinking of the male philosopher from the lower to the higher functions of soul. Thus true philosophy occurs with conception between a male philosopher and a female personification of wisdom.

As Ficino's theory of wisdom and virtue is unfolded further, the engendered aspects of particular virtues and vices make it more evident that men and women have a different relation to discursive reasoning and what are usually identified as the philosophical operations of the mind. It is in this engenderment that we begin to see how far Ficino has moved from a Platonic theory of gender unity, especially in its arguments that women as well as men could be philosopher rulers of society.

Engendered Virtues

Before entering into a discussion of Ficino's association of gender with particular virtues, it is necessary to state that Ficino fundamentally reoriented philosophy away from a previous humanistic concern with virtues in civic life. Instead, all of Ficino's ethical theory concentrated first on virtues needed for the contemplative life. Ficino believed that contemplative knowledge of the true good would lead men to live more just lives. Therefore, he placed contemplation first and public action second.[327]

Since contemplation was the first goal of intellectual life, Ficino did not make the radical distinction between public and private spheres of activity for men and for women that we saw in Bruni or Alberti. Still, he did introduce some hierarchical engendered distinctions among virtues proper to men and women along with common intellectual virtues for contemplative union with God. His analysis did not simply promote either the gender unity of Plato or the gender polarity of Aristotle, but rather drew out a mixture of some aspects of both theories.

Ficino's most popular ethical text is his commentary on the *Symposium*. The structure of the original dialogue of Plato's *Symposium* involves, first, a consideration of a variety of popular (mostly false, but partly true) views of love; second, a description of love that combines the partly true aspects of previous views; and third, a description of Diotima's teaching about the true nature of love for the beautiful and the good. Ficino's comments on the first part of the *Symposium* reinterpret epistemologically some of the ancient mythical stories about the origin and nature of love. Whereas Aristophanes had introduced a concept of three different double sexes — male-male, male-female, and female-female — to explain a hierarchically valued theory of sexual orientation, Ficino uses it to explain the integration of mind and will in the development of three different virtues in the soul. Ficino states his understanding of Plato's views as follows:

> *Human beings had three sexes, Masculine, Feminine, and Bi-Sexual. They were offspring respectively of the Sun, the Earth, and the Moon, and they were whole. But because of their insolence, when they aspired to equal God, they were cut in two; if they*

---

327. See Hankins, *Plato in the Renaissance*, vol. 1, p. 294.

are insolent again, they are to be split again. Once this split is made, each half is drawn by love to the other half, so that their unity may be restored; and when this has been completed, the race of men will have found bliss.

The gist of our interpretation will be this: *Men* (that is, the souls of men) *originally* (that is, when they were created by God) *were whole* and equipped with two lights, one natural and the other supernatural; by the natural light they beheld inferior and co-equal things; and by the supernatural light, superior things. *They aspired to equal God;* they reverted to the natural light alone. Hereupon *they were divided,* and lost their supernatural light, were reduced to the natural light alone, and fell immediately into bodies. *If they become too proud, they will again be divided,* that is, if they trust too much to natural ability, that innate and natural light which remains to them will be also extinguished in the same way.

They had three sexes: Males born from the sun, Females from the earth, and Bisexuals from the moon. The first type received the glow of God as Bravery, which is masculine; others as Temperance, which is feminine; others as Justice, which is Bi-sexual. These three virtues in us are the offspring of another three which God possesses. In God these three are called Sun, Moon, and Earth, but in us, Male, Bi-sexual, and Female.[328]

In this interesting passage Ficino goes far beyond the original myth as expressed by Aristophanes by shifting the focus from sexual orientation to the epistemological virtues of the soul. In the following table these innovations of Ficino are summarized:

Ficino's Association of the Platonic Division of the Soul with Gender Identity			
Plato		Ficino	
Parts of Soul	Virtue	Gender	Cosmology
Reason	Wisdom (Prudence)	Like mother or father depending on object	
Will	Courage	Male (masculine)	Sun
Emotions	Temperance	Female (feminine)	Earth
Harmony in the soul	Justice	Bi-sexual (mixed)	Moon

328. Jayne, trans., *Marsilio Ficino's Commentary on Plato's Symposium,* pp. 155-56. For a more recent translation see Marsilio Ficino, *Commentary on Plato's Symposium on Love,* trans. Sears Jayne (Dallas: Spring Publications, 1985), p. 73.

The engenderment of the three categories of virtue as male, female, or mixed is developed even further. As his analysis of the myth of Aristophanes continues, Ficino states that there is a natural desire for union with God, moving the soul towards all the virtues:

> To that bliss we are led by four virtues: Prudence, Courage, Justice, and Temperance. Prudence first shows bliss to us. The other three virtues, like three paths, lead us to bliss. . . .
>
> Courage in men because of their strength and bravery is called Masculine. Temperance is called Feminine because of a certain relaxed and cooler nature of Woman's passions and her gentle disposition. Justice is called Bi-sexual: Feminine inasmuch as because of its inherent innocence it does no one any wrong, but Masculine inasmuch as it allows no harm to be brought to others.[329]

This interesting description of Ficino implies that all of the virtues, masculine as well as feminine, are found in man's soul. In addition, using a common historical identification he identifies the feminine with the lower part of the soul, or the ordering of the emotions. At the same time, however, he positively values feminine virtues by arguing that women's cooler and more relaxed passions enable her to have a gentle disposition. This description echoes the Hippocratian and Aristotelian identification of the female as cooler than the male by nature, and also Hildegard's claim that the female nature is more gentle than the male. This runs counter to the Aristotelian and Albertan argument that woman is less able to control her emotions because of the weakness of her intellect.

Ficino continues his analysis of engendered virtues as follows:

> And since it is the function of the male to give and the female to receive, for that reason, the sun, which receives light from none and furnishes it to all, we call Male; the moon, which receives light from the sun and gives it to the elements, we call Bi-Sexual, since it both gives and receives; the earth, since it indeed receives from everything and gives to nothing, we call Female. Wherefore the Sun, Moon, and Earth, or Courage, Justice, and Temperance, are rightly designated by the terms Male, Bi-Sexual, and Female. In order to provide worthier titles for God, in Him we call these virtues Sun, Moon, and Earth: in ourselves, we call them the Male, Bi-Sexual, and Female sex. Those who have been endowed at birth with divine light from the divine sun accompanied by a desire for Courage, we say have been granted a Masculine light; those in whom the light from the divine moon with the desire for Justice was infused, we say have been given a Bi-Sexual light, and those in whom the light from divine earth with the desire for Temperance was infused, a Feminine light. . . .
>
> In short, each one seeks his own other half as he first received it from God: some, through the masculine light of God, once lost but now recovered, wish to enjoy the masculine courage of God; others through the bi-sexual light similarly

329. *Marsilio Ficino's Commentary on Plato's Symposium*, pp. 77-78.

desire to enjoy the bi-sexual virtue, and others through the feminine in the same way.[330]

In the above passages there does not appear to be much devaluation of the feminine in relation to the masculine. The virtues of courage, justice, and temperance appear to be important to the philosopher. So the philosopher is encouraged to be united (or reunited) with masculine, feminine, and mixed virtues. Since a specific virtue is infused by God into the soul there does not appear to be any moral culpability about being more courageous than temperate, etc. One should simply achieve one's own proper virtue. Prudence, or practical wisdom, channels the desires towards their proper end.

It could be argued that the descriptions of the masculine virtues themselves appear to be given a higher valuation than the feminine virtues, so that giving is better than receiving and strength better than gentleness. Supporting this hypothesis is the fact that in other works of Ficino a slightly derogatory tone is given to a man who has feminine characteristics. In his commentary on Plato's *Symposium,* Ficino uses "effeminate" in order to devalue a man in the following passage:

> They clearly give themselves up so much to their loved ones that they try to transform themselves into them in nature and imitate them in themselves with words and deeds. Who does not become effeminate and childish with the constant imitation of boys and girls?[331]

It is this particular passage that seems to offer a basis for the reinterpretation of Plato's theory that it is a kind of punishment for men to be condemned to associate with women, children, or beasts. Thus men who descend from union with God live bestial or effeminate lives. In addition, in a letter that considers various kinds of duty Ficino states: "A man should beware of being effeminate in any way. A woman should strive to have the spirit of a man in some measure, but above all to be modest. As being magnanimous becomes a man, so modesty becomes a woman."[332]

Without stipulating what he means by effeminate, we could suppose that it includes vices that correspond to the feminine virtue, or the vices associated with temperance such as weakness, sloth, etc. Contrarily, in a passage from another letter Ficino appears to suggest that there are masculine characteristics that tend to vice as well as feminine: "If you wonder why I give Niccolo Michelozzi the special title of true man, I reply it is because in him I find nothing effeminate, nothing brutish and nothing deceitful. Both outwardly and within himself he reveals nothing that is not virtuous."[333] If we consider brutishness to be a masculine type of vice and deception as either masculine or feminine, then we could conclude that according to Ficino, a 'true man' has only masculine and feminine virtues, and not either "macho" or "effeminate" vices. So the 'true man' incorporates the golden

---

330. *Marsilio Ficino's Commentary on Plato's Symposium,* pp. 160-61.
331. *Marsilio Ficino's Commentary on Plato's Symposium,* p. 196.
332. Ficino, Letter to Cerubino Quarquagli, in *The Letters of Marsilio Ficino,* vol. 2 #34, 67.
333. Ficino, Letter to Bartolomeo della Fonte and Alessandro Braccesi, vol. 1, #54, 100.

mean, while avoiding the extremes of masculine and feminine characteristics. An important contribution of Marsilio Ficino (and Nicholas of Cusa as well) to the history of the concept of gender is this beginning reflection on what could be called masculine and feminine characteristics within the individual soul of a man, even though the particular characteristics he identified as masculine or feminine may be seriously questioned.

If we move from our consideration of Ficino's engenderment of interior virtues of mind and soul, to exteriorly oriented virtues of private and public forms of activity, we find him drawing an analogy between particular virtues in the mind and in the world. In the same letter just referred to above, Ficino describes the different duties of the members of the household:

> The duty of the master is to serve law and reason, so that he can rule his servants lawfully and reasonably; to consider the servant to be a man as much as the master, and always to combine humanity with authority. The servant's duty is to regard his own life as his master's and his master's interest as his own; the husband's to love his wife as his own body and faculty of perception, and most carefully to lead her; the wife's to honour her prudent husband as if he were her mind and reason, and to follow him most willingly.[334]

In this amplification of the dictum of St. Paul for a husband to love his wife as his own body, Ficino adds the phrase "faculty of perception." It is this faculty that is so central to Ficino's consideration of sight as the middle faculty of the soul. So Ficino has broadened the theological dictum with a philosophical category to reinforce the degree to which the husband should love his wife. That is, she should mean more than the body, namely the middle faculty of soul. In a similar way, he states that the wife should submit herself to her husband as to the higher faculties of the soul, the mind and reason. So the husband and wife follow the proper ordering of the soul as follows:

Faculty	Virtue	Person
Reason	Authority of Ruling	Husband
Perception	Obedience	Wife

Although Ficino referred to Plato's chastity and he himself did not marry, he nonetheless praised marriage in a letter to Antonio Pelotti:

> By matrimony, man, as if divine, continually preserves the human race through succession. . . . Like a true and generous sculptor he carves in his offspring a living image of himself. Moreover, it is only, or principally, through these means that he obtains loving companionship for life and faithful guardianship of his af-

334. *The Letters of Marsilio Ficino*, vol. 3, p. 66.

fairs. He also has a domestic republic, in the governing of which he may exercise the powers of prudence and all the virtues.[335]

The view of the family as the ideal setting in which to practice governing is repeated throughout Ficino's letter. "Surely, just as the state consists of households, so skill in state affairs consists of the judicious handling of family affairs. He who has not learnt to govern his household will never know how to rule the state."[336] Ficino carries the concept of the family as the training ground for the virtues far beyond the simple relation of governing for the man:

> Anyone who is not occupied in family matters will each day become more neglectful and degenerate through idleness and license. He will never know how to love anyone truly and steadfastly if he does not experience the true and imperishable love of wife and children. He will never learn to endure the world, and by enduring to conquer, if he has not had a family to teach him patience. He will not learn to feel compassion for men if he has never experienced a weeping wife or child, for indeed, if the mind is not unacquainted with misfortune, it learns how to succour the afflicted.[337]

In the context of several satires discouraging men from marrying because it would distract them from the study of philosophy Ficino argues: "The powerful have always respected it and the wise have not disdained it, having seen that it is conducive to the ordering of society and does not hinder learning, provided one lives temperately and spends one's time carefully."[338]

Ficino even invoked Socrates, who had a reputation for being married to a difficult wife, as a support for marriage:

> At the same time, he provides the greatest protection for his old age, which he may spend more serenely in the bosom of a beloved wife, or in the arms of sons or grandsons, or in the care of relatives by marriage. Finally, a wife and family offer us sweet solace from our labours, or at least the strongest incentive towards more philosophy: wherefore Socrates used to confess that he had learnt much more moral philosophy from his wives than natural philosophy from Anaxagoras or Archelaus.[339]

Ficino, then, followed the general trend of the humanist movement by supporting marriage and the regular interaction of men and women.

Ficino's theory of gender identity is complex because of all the different historical theories he attempted to integrate. In the following summary chart some central patterns in his theory are identified:

335. *The Letters of Marsilio Ficino*, vol. 3, p. 69.
336. *The Letters of Marsilio Ficino*, vol. 3, p. 70.
337. *The Letters of Marsilio Ficino*, vol. 3, p. 71.
338. *The Letters of Marsilio Ficino*, vol. 3, p. 69.
339. *The Letters of Marsilio Ficino*, vol. 3, p. 69.

Summary of Ficino's Theory of Gender Identity			
Category	Man	Woman	Both Genders

Opposites	Masculine sex like the sun
	
	Male is:
	    active
	    hotter
	    like an odd
	    number
		Feminine sex like the earth
		
		female is:
		    passive
		    colder
		    like an even
		    number
			Bi-sexual like the moon

Generation	Father generates by union with earthly Venus. Soul "fathers" body. Male has purer blood for generating.	Mother means 'matter.' Lower part of the soul "mothers" the body.	
Wisdom	Male philosopher intellectually generates by union with heavenly Venus. e.g., Socrates, Plato, Plotinus, and Ficino	Philosophy is the 'bride' of the philosopher. Philosophy is the 'mother' of dialectic, speech, writing, grammar, and the disciplines. Philosophy is a 'nurse.' Diotima is the wise teacher of Socrates.	Theoretically capable of philosophy, e.g., Plato's women and men disciples Wisdom moves from intellectual apprehension of beauty of a particular body to the Form of beauty and goodness itself in union with Divine.

Summary of Ficino's Theory of Gender Identity (cont.)			
Category	Man	Woman	Both Genders
Virtue	Masculine virtues in soul: wisdom or prudence — of reason; courage or bravery — of will	Feminine virtues in soul: temperance — of emotions	Harmony of masculine and feminine virtues in soul: justice
	Man's separate virtues: husband rules wife — as reason rules perception	Woman's separate virtues: wife obeys husband as perception obeys reason	Both men and women ought to have all masculine and feminine virtues in soul.
	Magnanimity	Modesty	Both men and women are called to will "Platonic Love" ascending to love of Beauty, Truth, One, Good.

How should Ficino's legacy for the history of the concept of woman be evaluated? If we simply considered his effect on women living during his lifetime, it would seem as though he had a strong influence on men, especially through the revaluation of the place of women's beauty in helping to lead men to the contemplation of absolute Beauty. By this measure, his influence on women would be negligible. However, if a longer time frame is selected, it would seem as though Ficino had an important influence on women becoming philosophers. Two of his most famous disciples wrote texts that brought innovations into the history of the concept of woman.[340] Pietro Bembo's (1470-1547) *Gli Asolani* recorded the first actual dialogue in which three living women participated with three men in the context of a humanist community of discourse. Baldassare Castiglione's *Il Cortegiano (The Courtier)* contains the first direct arguments against Aristotle's foundations for the gender polarity theory. It also describes a woman at a court where "Neoplatonist doctrines of love are much in evidence . . . and justify the presence of women at court, both because of their beauty and because of their virtue."[341] Leon Hebreo (1470-1530), one of the first Jewish humanists, also known as Judah Leo

340. A good general introduction to the two following authors is found in Christine Raffina, *Marsilio Ficino, Pietro Bembo, Baldassare Castiglione: Philosophical, Aesthetic, and Political Approaches in Renaissance Platonism* (New York/Washington/Baltimore/Boston: Peter Lang, 1998).

341. Ian Maclean, *The Renaissance Notion of Woman: A Study in the Fortunes of Scholasticism and Medical Science in European Intellectual Life* (Cambridge/London/New York: Cambridge University Press, 1980), p. 64.

Abrabanel, wrote *Dialoghi de Amore (Dialogues of Love)* between a wise female personification of wisdom, Sophia, and a young student, Philo. Finally, Marguerite of Navarre discovered Plato through Ficino's translations of his dialogues, which from 1500 on "appeared almost yearly" in France along with an extremely popular publication of Ficino's commentary on Plato's *Symposium,* which appeared in Paris and Rouen around 1489.[342] Marguerite was very enthusiastic about Plato's arguments for the equality of men and women and about Ficino's theory of Platonic love and friendship, and she integrated these themes into her major work *Heptaméron.*

In evaluating Ficino's philosophy of gender there are two aspects that ought to be particularly noted: first, the odd mixture of Platonic and Aristotelian elements it contains, and second, the way in which it seems to have a hidden utilitarian approach in its interpersonal relationships. In all categories, except perhaps that of wisdom, Ficino adopts Aristotelian gender polarity foundations in his explanation of the relations of men and women. In the category of opposites, he associates the male with heat and activity and the female with cold and passivity. In the category of generation he associates the father with purer blood and the capacity of formation, and the mother with matter. In the category of ethics, he supports separate and unequal spheres of activity for man and woman as well as the traditional virtue of ruling for husband and obeying for wife. At the same time, however, in the category of wisdom Ficino follows Plato in at least identifying the highest wisdom with a female character (Diotima), and he also argues that men and women ought to cultivate in their souls both the masculine virtues of wisdom and courage and the feminine virtue of temperance. In addition, in the whole area of the elaboration of Platonic love and friendship, Ficino elevates human relations from either the pleasure-based or external, utilitarian-motivated (i.e., sharing governing a household) relations that had been so evident in the work of previous humanists such as Valla and Alberti.

However, when Ficino's Platonic friendships and love are examined further the question does arise as to whether or not he succeeded in avoiding all utilitarian dynamics in his philosophy. In other words, does Ficino end up with a philosophy of using another person's beauty simply as a stepping stone to love of Beauty itself and ultimately to contemplating the Beauty of God? If the answer is affirmative, then he did not succeed in establishing grounds for an integral complementarity among men and women. Ficino appears to have attempted to establish a philosophy of the genuine autonomy of the human being, along with a view that the particular body of a woman or man is an integral part of that identity. However, for Ficino human dignity was derived from the immortality of the soul rather than from the dignity of human life on earth. Even so, Charles Trinkaus argues that Ficino ". . . developed the fullest and most far-reaching exposition of the ideal of human autonomy in the Renaissance. . . ."[343] Trinkaus bases his claim on Ficino's

---

342. L. Clark Keating, *Studies on the Literary Salon in France (1500-1615)* (Cambridge, Mass.: Harvard University Press, 1941), pp. 14-15.

343. Charles Trinkaus, "Marsilio Ficino and the Ideal of Human Autonomy," in *Ficino and Renaissance Neoplatonism,* ed. Eisenbichler and Pugliese, pp. 141-53, 142.

descriptions of the function of human intelligence and will to transform the world of nature relating to, but not determined by, the forces of the stars and planets. Whether Ficino succeeded or not is open to question. For example, Kristeller concludes that "[f]or Ficino, man is identical with his rational soul, and his excellence consists in the role played by this soul as the center and bond of the universe. . . ."[344] Even though the gender differentiation of the macrocosm is reflected in the microcosm of the human soul, Ficino argues that human perfection involves passing beyond gender differentiation. Thus, while Ficino seems to want to avoid the loss of personal and gender identity that plagued so many previous Neoplatonists, he seems to end up as did Plato with a sexless soul as the center of human identity.

Kristeller argues further that sexual differences disappear in Ficino's description of Platonic love and friendship.[345] This disappearance of sex identity suggests that Ficino proposes a unisex theory of human identity. So, the question remains as to whether or not he succeeded in supporting the full development of each person as a woman or as a man in his epistemological and ethical theory. This may be one of the reasons why particular women philosophers did not flourish under his leadership of the reformation of Christian philosophy through the Platonic Academy he established in Florence. However, many men did flourish as philosophers under the same set of circumstances. So we are left with an open question about why Ficino's efforts at reform directly affected only men during his lifetime.

If a man's work may be judged by its fruits, it could be said that Ficino's actual writings and his transmission of Plato's dialogues changed the ground for philosophical discourse about woman's identity in relation to man. Thus, even though he did not seem to have notable female disciples during his life, his legacy included both men and women who gave considerable attention to the early humanist reform of the previous concept of woman.

It is to another important disciple that our analysis now turns. Giovanni Pico della Mirandola, perhaps Ficino's most famous associate, contributed an important new emphasis to the history of gender identity when he argued in support of a significant autonomy of the human being. Indeed, it will be this factor — the discovery of a genuine autonomy of the individual human person — that finally enabled several women to become creative and independent philosophers.

GIOVANNI PICO DELLA MIRANDOLA (1463-1494)

Although living for only thirty-one years Giovanni Pico della Mirandola influenced the history of the concept of woman in two significant ways: first, he articulated a principle of the dignity of human self-determination; and second, he adopted a stance of intentional non-advertence to sex and gender differentiation for a new foundation for gender neutrality. Neither of these contributions sprang up in a void, as the cultural discoveries of the proper autonomy of the human person and the neutrality perspectives had been provided by philosophers in the rich

---

344. Ficino, "The Platonic Academy of Florence," in *Renaissance Thought II,* p. 97.
345. Kristeller, *The Philosophy of Marsilio Ficino,* p. 277.

historical past. Nevertheless, Pico offered a new articulation in both of these areas. Since both of these contributions are directly related to the history of the concept of woman, they merit our attention. However, first — some background on Pico's life.

Giovanni Pico della Mirandola, the third son of the Prince of Mirandola, was a child prodigy. From his early childhood he received an intense education in the classics from his mother, Giulia Boiurdo Pico, whose own family excelled in poetic gifts. Pico's nephew, Giovanni Francesco Pico (1469-1533), wrote in his famous posthumous biography *Life of Giovanni Pico* a detailed description of the mother-son educational relationship that his uncle enjoyed:

> Under the rule and governance of his mother he was set to matters and to learning: where with such an ardent mind he labored at the studies of the humanities: that within a short while he was (and not without a cause) accounted among the chief orators and poets of that time: in learning marvellously quick and of such a ready wit, that the verses which he heard once read he would again rehearse forward and backward to the great wonder of the hearers, and over that would hold it in perfect remembrance.[346]

Giovanni Pico's prodigious memory helped him to excel in learning to such a degree that by the age of fourteen he attended the University of Bologna for the year 1477-1478. Again Pico's mother played an important role in the direction of his education:

> In the fourteenth year of his age by the commandment of his mother (who longed very much to have him become a priest) he departed to Bologna to study in the laws of the Church, which when he had two years tasted, perceiving that the faculty leaned to nothing but only merry traditions and ordinances, his mind fell from it: Yet lost he not his time there, for in that two years, yet being a child, he compiled a breviary or summary of all the decretals.[347]

Leaving Canon Law at Bologna, Giovanni Pico then went to study philosophy and theology, first in 1478-1479 at the University of Ferrara, one of the centers of Italian humanism, and then at the University of Padua, the center of Italian scholasticism, from 1480 to 1482. While the sixteen-year-old Pico was immersed in academic studies, he developed a great interest in foreign languages, both classical and modern. In addition, he grew fascinated with Jewish philosophy and especially with the mysteries of the Cabala. Pico subsequently went to Perugia to study Hebrew and Jewish philosophy in greater depth, and he visited many other schools in Italy such as the University of Pavia. It was in Padua in 1480 that Pico met Elijah

---

346. Giovanni Francesco Pico, *Giovanni Pico della Mirandola: His Life* (London: David Nutt, 1890), p. 8. See also the more recent translation in *The Complete Works of St. Thomas More,* ed. Anthony Edwards, Katherine Gardiner Rodgers, and Clarence H. Miller (New Haven and London: Yale University Press, 1997), vol. 1, pp. 51-127.

347. Giovanni Francesco Pico, *Giovanni Pico della Mirandola: His Life,* p. 9.

Giovanni Pico della Mirandola on a Medallion

Delmedigo, an important Jewish philosopher who worked with the Islamic texts of Averroes. They developed a close personal relationship, and Pico commissioned Delmedigo to translate Averroes's commentary on Plato's *Republic* as well as to explain to him fundamental concepts of the Cabala.[348] As will be seen later, Pico's adaptation of the ten levels in the *sefirot* will have applications to the history of the concept of woman.

Pico's eagerness to understand the secrets of the Jewish Cabala led him around 1481 to associate with a Jewish convert to Christianity named Flavius Mithridates. As David Ruderman describes it: ". . . he joined Pico and proceeded over the course of the following years to translate for him some forty kabbalistic

348. David B. Ruderman, "Italian Renaissance and Jewish Thought," in *Renaissance Humanism,* vol. 1, *Humanism in Italy,* p. 387.

[cabalistic] and other works, still extant in some 3,500 folio pages. The massive undertaking included translations of almost all the major cabalistic works available to Pico's contemporaries and those which most decisively influenced the course of Pico's thinking."[349] The intensity of the relations among Pico and Jewish philosophers is captured in a letter Marsilio Ficino wrote to Domenico Benivieni "describing a series of disputations at Pico's home between two Jews, Elijah Delmedigo and another named Abraham, against Flavius Mithridates."[350]

In 1482 Aldus Manutius came to live for two years with Pico della Mirandola and he became tutor of the sons of Pico's sister, the Princess of Capri. This connection between Aldus and the Pico family bore fruit in two very important ways. First, when Aldus opened his printing office in Venice in 1494-95, the funds were provided by the Princess of Capri, her sons, and Pico himself. This fact once again reveals the important cooperation of women with humanists in the financing of the printing business. It also suggests that Giulia Boiurdo Pico communicated to both her daughter and son a lively interest in education in the new humanism. Second, as early as 1497 Aldus printed a Greek and Latin dictionary, in 1502 a Latin and Hebrew grammar, and by 1515 a grammar in Greek.[351] The strong interest in the Hebrew language first introduced by Pico della Mirandola was institutionalized in the printing work of the Aldine press. So the informal humanist circle in Pico della Mirandola's home radiated its influence outwards through the extraordinary success of the printing business of Aldus Manutius.

Pico spent the year 1484-1485 in Florence, where he made the acquaintance of Girolamo Savonarola (1452-1498) and participated in Marsilio Ficino's Florentine Academy of humanist scholars. Pico continued to deepen his knowledge of Jewish philosophy. In Florence he met another great Jewish scholar and medical doctor, Yohanan Alemanno, who was also deeply interested in the new humanism. Pico commissioned Alemanno to write a *Commentary on the Song of Songs* that integrated Jewish and humanistic themes.[352]

Giovanni Pico della Mirandola then studied in France at the University of Paris from 1485 to 1486 to continue his efforts to become expert in Greek, Latin, Arabic, Hebrew, French, and Italian. While in Paris he developed a further admiration for the scholastic method of debating, an admiration he never lost from his first exposure to it at the University of Padua. More important than even Pico's phenomenal ability at languages was his desire to read and understand all the philosophers of the past. Pico's intellectual goal was to bring about a syncretist union of all philosophers and theologians. He mentions that he has given considerable attention among others to the philosophers Heraclitus, Empedocles, the Pythagoreans, Plato, Aristotle, the Neoplatonists, Lucretius, Seneca, Augustine, Boethius,

349. Ruderman, "Italian Renaissance and Jewish Thought," in *Renaissance Humanism*, vol. 1, *Humanism in Italy*, p. 401.

350. Ruderman, "Italian Renaissance and Jewish Thought," in *Renaissance Humanism*, vol. 1, *Humanism in Italy*, p. 406.

351. George Haven Putnam, *Books and Their Makers During the Middle Ages, Vol. I (476-1600)* (New York: Hilary House Publishers Ltd., 1962), pp. 417-19.

352. Ruderman, "Italian Renaissance and Jewish Thought," in *Renaissance Humanism*, vol. 1, *Humanism in Italy*, pp. 394-95.

Averroes, Albert, Thomas, Scotus, Giles of Rome, and Roger Bacon.[353] In this process of study Pico evaluated particular philosophers differently than did most of his contemporaries. He sought to bring about a concord among all philosophers. Thus, instead of either setting up or remaining within an isolated community of discourse, Pico actively plunged into all philosophies, crossing academic, religious, and humanist boundaries. The only areas of discourse he appears to have not entered were those of women religious writers and satirists.

Like Ficino before him, Giovanni Pico became convinced that there is a single line of truth that can be traced in all historical periods. The philosopher's task was to bring this single line of truth into the light so that it can be seen and understood by others.[354] Consequently, all major (male) philosophers and religious writers were worth studying. None should be ignored. In 1485 Ermolao Barbaro (1453-1493) wrote to Pico complaining that the study of the scholastic philosophers was a waste of his time. Pico responded with vehemence and irony, defending the scholastics as worth his efforts:

> By Hercules! When I read this I was thunderstruck! Overwhelmed by bitterness, how I regretted all the effort I had expended in study — six whole years of my time and energies on so worthless an enterprise. Fruitless, the hours spent in studying Thomas, Scotus, Albert, and Averroes! Misspent, the best years of my life![355]

Barbaro had been arguing from the perspective of rhetoric, which valued the beauty of expression, and from this perspective he had suggested that the scholastics were a waste of time. Pico responded by arguing that philosophy is more important than rhetoric because it seeks true knowledge rather than rhetorical persuasion, which has to introduce elements of deception.[356] Pico appears to be defending himself as a philosopher rather than a rhetorician at this point in his life.[357] At the same time, however, Pico also wants to differentiate himself from a narrow academic understanding of philosophy. Quirinus Breen summarizes Pico's stance: "As to a doctrine of man he seems to hold that it is proper to be *humanus*, i.e., to be a humanist, not a barbarian; but one must also be *homo*, that is, a complete human being. If the former is attained by polite letters, the latter is achieved

353. See Giovanni Pico della Mirandola, "Letter to Ermolao Barbaro" and "Oration on the Dignity of Man," in *The Italian Philosophers: Selected Readings from Petrarch to Bruno*, vol. 1, *Renaissance Philosophy*, ed. Arturo B. Fallico and Herman Shapiro (New York: Modern Library, 1967), pp. 106, 111-13, 116-17, 144, 152, 155, 162-63, 165, 167, 169, and 171.

354. See Ruderman's description of Ficino's original articulation of this theme in "Italian Renaissance and Jewish Thought," in *Renaissance Humanism*, vol. 1, *Humanism in Italy*, p. 397.

355. Pico, "Letter to Ermolao Barbaro," in *The Italian Philosophers*, ed. Fallico and Shapiro, vol. 1, p. 106.

356. Quirinus Breen, "Giovanni Pico della Mirandola and Ermolao Barbaro," in *Christianity and Humanism: Studies in the History of Ideas*, ed. Nelson Peter Ross (Grand Rapids: Eerdmans, 1968), pp. 3ff.

357. See William G. Craven's convincing argument to this effect, *Giovanni Pico della Mirandola: Symbol of His Age, Modern Interpretations of a Renaissance Philosopher* (Geneva: Librairie Droz, 1981), pp. 38-42.

through philosophy."[358] Pico, in sum, wanted to rehabilitate philosophy and make it the center of human life.

By the very next year, Pico indicated in his *Oration on the Dignity of Man* that he consciously chose not to follow any particular philosopher, but rather to be an independent thinker:

> Those who are disciples of one or another of the philosophers — of Thomas or Scotus, for example, who today have the widest following — can indeed make trial of their particular doctrines with a few questions. I, by contrast, have trained myself so that I am the disciple of no one man. I have examined all the masters of philosophy; perused all their works; become acquainted with all schools.[359]

In this intellectual independence Pico's attitude towards a new form of gender neutrality is set. He will follow neither the gender polarity of the Aristotelian, scholastic, and Jewish traditions, nor the gender unity of the Platonic and Islamic religious traditions, nor even the occasional gender complementarity of the Augustinian, Christian monastic, and earliest humanist traditions. Nor will he assume the position of the logicians who simply ignore sex and gender differentiations as irrelevant to "higher" philosophical considerations of species rather than accidents. Instead, he chooses to pass through and beyond gender differentiations because of his theory of the hierarchy of being and of knowledge. Because Pico immerses himself in many different philosophical traditions, his stance of gender-neutrality must be understood as a clearly chosen position.

Gender Theory in the Nine Hundred Theses

In an extraordinarily bold move in 1486 at the age of twenty-three, the young Count Giovanni Pico della Mirandola posted a list of nine hundred theses in various parts of the city of Rome. These theses comprised all the basic tenets in philosophy and theology that Pico wanted to defend, and he invited scholars from all over Europe to come to Rome at Pico's own expense to engage in public debate with him on any thesis of their choice. The exact words of his invitation are as follows:

> THE CONCLUSIONS will not be disputed until after the Epiphany. In the meantime they will be published in all Italian universities. And if any philosopher or theologian, even from the ends of Italy, wishes to come to Rome for the sake of debating, his Lord the disputer promises to pay the travel expenses from his own funds.[360]

---

358. Quirinus Breen, *Christianity and Humanism,* p. 8.

359. Pico, "Oration on the Dignity of Man," in *The Italian Philosophers,* ed. Fallico and Shapiro, vol. 1, p. 106.

360. *Pico's 900 Theses,* ed. Stephen Alan Farmer, *Syncretism in the West: Pico's 900 Theses (1486): The Evolution of Traditional Religious and Philosophical Systems* (Binghamton, N.Y.: Medieval and Renaissance Texts and Studies, 1998). ·

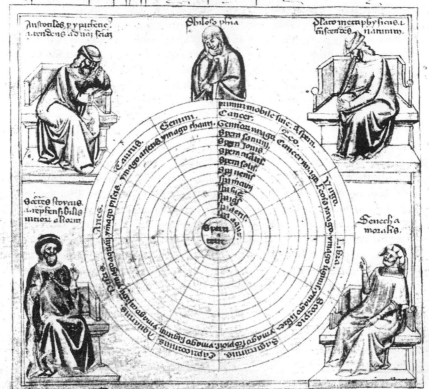

Philosophia Contemplating the Universe among Plato,
Aristotle, Cicero, and Seneca

Giovanni Pico, Count of Mirandola had moved his entire household to Rome in anticipation of the public debate, and he had projected that it would be held in the Vatican itself before the college of Cardinals with Pope Innocent VIII acting as the supreme judge. His great hope was to bring about a council of reconciliation, especially of Christianity, Islam, and Judaism through this public demonstration of how philosophy can offer a model of reconciliation of seemingly opposing views.

The stir that this bold action caused led some scholars to report the theses as possibly heretical to Pope Innocent VIII. After appointing a commission to examine the theses, thirteen of them were "placed under the ban of the Church and Pico was obliged to take refuge in France."[361] The Pope intervened to forbid the public debate. Pico published an *Apology* that directly attacked the Papacy and the Dominicans, including Thomas Aquinas and the Dominican vicar-general, and thus further exacerbated the situation. Then, in what is thought to be the first official banning of a printed work, Pope Innocent VIII had a bull "read at Mass in every city and diocese in the Christian world," forbidding "anyone presuming 'to read, to copy, to print; or to have read, copied, or printed; or to hear others reading it in whatever fashion' Pico's text."[362] Giovanni Pico was himself captured, excommunicated, and imprisoned in France until Lorenzo de Medici intervened, and he was offered a provisional release, only to escape to Florence.[363]

Only seven years later in 1493 did Pope Alexander VI absolve Pico of any heresy. The nine hundred theses were published after Pico's early death in 1494 under the title *Conclusiones philosophicae, cabalisticae, et theologicae.*[364] While in Florence, Pico lived and worked in close proximity with Marsilio Ficino. During this period he wrote several texts: *Heptaplus, Commentary on the Psalms, On Being and the One, On the True Computation of the Ages, Concord of Plato and Aristotle,* and *Disputations against Divinatory Astrology* (1494) among other works.[365] In his final work, Pico took a different direction from his colleague Ficino, for Pico came to believe that astrology interfered with the dignity of free will in the human being. However, in seeking a harmony of Plato and Aristotle Pico followed Ficino's line of thinking, and the painter Raphael captured this important innovation of the Neoplatonist school in the famous fresco of Plato holding his *Timaeus* and pointing heavenward while Aristotle holds his *Nicomachean Ethics* and points out towards the world. In this concord, natural science and ethics are brought together, along with the contemplative and active life of a philosopher.

Pico died of unknown causes in 1494 on the very day the French army of Charles VIII conquered Florence.[366] Recent scholarship has suggested that Pico may have been poisoned by his secretary Cristoforo de Casale for personal gain and to win approval from the Medicis, who rejected Pico for his support of

361. Robb, *Neoplatonism in the Italian Renaissance,* p. 60, note 1.

362. Farmer in *Pico's 900 Theses,* p. 16.

363. Farmer in *Pico's 900 Theses,* pp. 1 and 48, note 48.

364. Giovanni Pico della Mirandola, *Conclusiones philosophicae, cabalisticae, et theologicae* (Rome, 1486) (reprinted Geneva: Librairie Droz, 1973).

365. Farmer in *Pico's 900 Theses,* p. 138.

366. Robb, *Neoplatonism in the Italian Renaissance,* p. 60, note 1. See also Farmer in *Pico's 900 Theses,* where it is stated that the French King sent two physicians to help Pico, p. 137, note 11.

Savonarola.[367] The French invaders sent two physicians to attempt to cure him on behalf of King Charles, who remembered Pico from his sojourn in France. Pico was informally buried in a Dominican habit because of his ties with Savonarola, but he did not officially enter the Dominican Order. Pico's nephew, Giovanni Francesco, sought control of his uncle's manuscripts immediately following his death, and he not only changed the content of several of them, he also plagiarized sections for his own writings. At the end of this section we will return to this topic and consider the contributions of Pico's nephew to the history of the concept of woman. Now our analysis will turn directly to consider the significance of the elder Pico's nine hundred theses for the philosophy of gender.

When the theses are examined from the perspective of the history of the concept of woman, certain methodological approaches of Pico to the history of philosophy begin to emerge. It is necessary to keep in mind that Pico's main goal in the debate, and indeed in all his writing, was to bring about a concord or harmony among what appeared to be conflicting opinions. Thus, he sought to construct a single worldview that incorporated the insights of all previous philosophers, theologians, and religious writers from the Jewish, Islamic, and Christian traditions. As might be imagined, this goal took great ingenuity on Pico's part, especially where fundamental disagreements had occurred in the past. Stephen Farmer has identified ten different methodological strategies that Pico used in his nine hundred theses to achieve a harmony.[368] The one particular strategy he used most often in relation to *prima facie* conflicting views of gender identity is called "Hierarchical or correlative distinctions," and it functions by placing different views about gender on different levels of reality and analysis. Thus, conflicts are resolved by separating out components of direct contradictions on the same level to different levels of meaning and interpretation.

Particularly relevant to the present study is Pico's method of reconciling Aristotle's and Plato's concepts of woman. As has been pointed out repeatedly in this book and in the preceding volume of *The Concept of Woman,* Plato generally supported gender unity and Aristotle gender polarity. While there are some inconsistencies in Plato's philosophy, with his inclusion of modified gender polarity principles, Aristotle was completely consistent in his set of principles and arguments for gender polarity. The question then was, how could Pico reconcile these two authors? Basically, Pico placed Aristotle's epistemological theories on a level below that of Plato's, so Aristotle's claims were accurate concerning nature, but Plato's were accurate on a supernatural or Divine level. Pico studiously avoids entering into the direct arguments of either Plato or Aristotle about gender identity. Instead, he simply states their conclusions in a hierarchical order. Thus, at certain levels gender polarity is introduced, but for the most part Pico consistently presents a gender-neutral stance, namely, he does not advert to sex and gender differentiation at all. Since his pronouncements are placed in the context of his total immersion in the texts of the historical authors, we have to conclude that the gender neutrality stance is consciously chosen as the higher view.

---

367. Farmer in *Pico's 900 Theses,* p. 177, especially note 126. Apparently Cristoforo confessed this under torture by Savonarola, but no other evidence exists at present to support his claim.

368. Farmer in *Pico's 900 Theses,* pp. 59-73.

The nine hundred theses are divided into numerical groupings by author and subject content. Again Pico's own words in the preface to his theses reveal the extraordinary breadth of his purpose:

> The following nine hundred Dialectical, Moral, Physical, Mathematical, Metaphysical, Theological, Magical, and Cabalistic opinions, including his own and those of the wise Chaldeans, Arabs, Hebrews, Greeks, Egyptians, and Latins, will be disputed publicly by Giovanni Pico of Mirandola, the Count of Concord. In reciting these opinions, he has not imitated the splendor of the Roman language, but the style of speaking of the most celebrated Parisian disputers, since this is used by almost all philosophers of our time. The doctrines to be debated are proposed separately by nations and their sect leaders, but in common in respect to the parts of philosophy — as though in a medley, everything mixed together.[369]

Pico begins with the scholastic philosophers, several of whom have been studied in this text with respect to their views on the concept of woman: Albert the Great, Thomas Aquinas, John Duns Scotus, and Giles of Rome, among others. Most of these philosophers had promoted gender polarity on the level of nature, with some gender complementarity on the level of grace. In Pico's sixteen theses according to Albert (1.1–1.16), in forty-five conclusions according to Thomas (2.1–2.45), in twenty-two conclusions according to John Scotus (4.1–4.22), and in eleven conclusions according to Giles of Rome (6.1–6.11) there are no references to sex or gender differentiation. In fact the first 115 theses provide a gender-neutral approach.

Pico turns next to consider theses from the Islamic philosophers who claim to follow Aristotle. Again we find a similar result. Even though several of these philosophers had directly adverted to Plato's gender unity arguments and/or Aristotle's gender polarity arguments, Pico's theses take a completely gender-neutral stance towards forty-one conclusions of Averroes (7.1–7.44), twelve conclusions of Avicenna (8.1.–8.12), eleven conclusions of Al-Farabi (9.1–9.11), and three conclusions of Moses Maimonides (12.1–12.3). In his direct consideration of philosophers in Aristotle's school, the Peripatetics, Pico takes the same stance of gender polarity. Perhaps most notable is his four conclusions according to Theophrastus (15.1–15.4), whose satire devaluing woman had become well-known.

It is only in the next section, on Platonists, that the introduction of gender differentiation first occurs. The first-mentioned Platonist still provides a gender-neutral position: i.e., fifteen conclusions of Plotinus (20.1–20.15). In the Platonic theses, the concept of reincarnation is introduced (20.4 and 21.8), but with no mention of gender differentiation. The first engendered thesis occurs among the twelve conclusions of Porphyry (22.1–22.12). He states at 22.1: "By the father in Plato we should understand the cause which from itself produces every effect; by the maker that which receives matter from the other."[370] This thesis is numbered 250, and it is

---

369. Pico, *Pico's 900 Theses,* first preface, p. 211.
370. Pico, "Conclusions," *Pico's 900 Theses,* p. 307.

taken by Porphyry from Proclus's commentary on Plato's *Timaeus*. In fact in the forty-five conclusions according to Proclus, there are several engendered theses focusing on intellectual realities or on the deities. Pico's conclusions according to Proclus are listed below:

24.1: What in intelligibles is limit and infinite, in intellectuals is male and female; in supermundanes identity and otherness, similitude and dissimilitude; in the soul the revolution of the same and the revolution of the other. (271) . . .

24.5: In intelligibles number does not exist but multitude, and the paternal and maternal cause of numbers; but in intellectuals number exists according to essence and multitude communicatively. (275) . . .

24.12: Between the extreme paternal gods, Saturn and Jove, Rhea necessarily mediates through the property of fertile life. (282) . . .

24.16: The same thing that is called Rhea as it coexists at its summit with Saturn, as it produces Jove, and with Jove the total and partial orders of the gods, is called Ceres. (286) . . .

24.18: Just as the paternal property exists only in intelligibles, so the productive or formative property exists only in the new gods; the paternal and productive property simultaneously in the intelligible exemplar; the productive and paternal property in the demiurge. (288) . . .

24.30: Although the whole second trinity of supermundane gods is called Proserpina, its first unity among the Greeks is called Diana, the second Persephone, the third Minerva; but among the barbarians [Chaldeans], the first is called Hecate, the second is called soul, the third, virtue. (300) . . .[371]

Three aspects of Pico's introduction of gender differentiation in his discussion of Proclus are interesting. First, he incorporates the traditional Pythagorean association of male with limit and female with the unlimited. Second, he integrates cross-religious cosmic allegorical gender characteristics in discussions of the gods and goddesses, with respect to fertility, the nature of the soul, and virtue. Third, Pico takes an ironic stance with respect to gender in relation to the Aristotelians and the Platonists. He inverts the traditional association of gender differentiation with Aristotelian and Peripatetic philosophers and of no gender differentiation with Plato and Platonist philosophers and instead assumes no gender differentiation when describing the Aristotelians and an invoked gender differentiation with the Platonists.

Next, in his fourteen conclusions according to the mathematics of Pythagoras (25.1–25.14), Pico introduces cosmic feminine associations:

371. Pico, "Conclusions," *Pico's 900 Theses,* pp. 315-33.

25.5: In one, three, and seven, we recognize in Pallas [Athena] the unification of divided things, and the causative and beautifying power of the intellect. (330)

25.6: The three kinds of proportion — arithmetic, geometric, and harmonic — indicate to us the three daughters of Themis, existing as symbols of judgment, justice, and peace. (331)[372]

In the analogical realm, the cosmic feminine is associated with the highest values of intellect, judgment, justice, and peace as well as fertility, soul, and virtue (as per Proclus, above). For Ficino, Pallas Athena is also represented by the number 7, as the virgin after the perfect number 6. In Pico's use of Pythagoras, Athena is given an active unifying power in the intellect of the philosopher, enabling him to achieve the highest levels of illumination and contemplation.

The next section of *Pico's 900 Theses* to introduce engendered distinctions is found in his forty-seven conclusions of the Hebrew Cabalist Wisemen (28.1–28.47). Pico came to believe, in his serious study of the Jewish Cabala, that he too could benefit from the secret signs and symbols of the ancient Hebrew scholars; intelligence applied to the secrets of the Cabala was able to unlock ultimate truths and predictions about the future. The following reflections focus on the levels of *sefirot,* or practical science, to which the soul's activities or functions are adapted.[373] Pico's explicit engendered theses are as follows:

28.17: Every place in Scriptures that the love of a male and female is mentioned designates to us mystically the conjunction of *Tiferet* [6th *sefirot* = Beauty] and *Keneset Israel* [10th *sefirot* = Kingdom], or of *Bet* [3rd *sefirot* = Intelligence] and *Tiferet* [6th *sefirot* = Beauty].[374] (372) . . .

28.32: Circumcision occurs on the eighth day [9th *sefirot* = Foundation], because it is superior to the universalized bride [10th *sefirot* = Kingdom]. (387) . . .

28.45: After prophecy through the spirit ceased, the wisemen of Israel prophesied through the daughter of the voice. (400) . . .[375]

In the first two conclusions Pico uses feminine identity allegorically each time to represent the lower of the two levels of union, of female with male, of beauty with the kingdom, and of the intellect with beauty, of the universalized bride with foundation. In the third conclusion, the feminine daughter of the voice is a lower kind of prophecy that falls out of the higher level of spirit. So while there is a male/female dynamic, the female symbolically represents the inferior partner in the conjunction.

372. Pico, "Conclusions," *Pico's 900 Theses,* pp. 335-37.
373. See Pico, "Conclusions," *Pico's 900 Theses,* p. 549.
374. See especially Farmer's explanatory notes, *Pico's 900 Theses,* p. 353, note 28.17, and p. 351, 28.10.
375. Pico, "Conclusions," *Pico's 900 Theses,* pp. 345-63.

In the second half of Pico's theses, he moves from simply restating conclusions he agrees with in previous thinkers, to presenting "Five hundred conclusions according to his own opinions which are divided in ten sections into Physical, Theological, Mathematical, Paradoxical Dogmatizing, Paradoxical Reconciliative, Chaldaic, Orphic, Magical, and Cabalistic conclusions."[376] In his first section reconciling Aristotle and Plato (1.1–1.18) there are no references to gender identity, and in the second section of eighty conclusions (2.1–2.80), which differ from common philosophy but not from common philosophical methods, Pico introduces no reflections about gender even though he discusses themes such as relation, substance, and accident, and indicates that he has read Aristotle's works on generation, all of which would have provided the context within which to introduce issues of gender identity. Even in his subsequent sections on Theology and his own reflections on paradoxical conclusions on new philosophy there are no reflections on gender. Altogether Pico makes over two hundred conclusions in this second section of his theses before introducing any concepts of gender identity.

It is only when he turns to his sixty-two conclusions about Plato (5.1–5.62) that gender is introduced again. He begins again with cosmic feminine and masculine deities:

5.5: By the intelligible sphere extended from Venus, Empedocles meant nothing but the archetypal world extended from the order of first providence, which dwells in itself. (604) . . .

5.9: Speaking Platonically of the soul, I say that the soul lives a contemplative life with Saturn, with Jove a political and practical life, with Mars an irascible and ambitious life, with Venus a sensual and voluptuous life, with Mercury a vegetative life with the dull senses. (608) . . .

5.11: The first seventh of human life exists under Mercury, the second under Venus, the third under Mars, the fourth under Jupiter, the fifth under Saturn, and the remaining sevenths under whatever dominated in the preceding. (610) . . .

5.14: When we hear Plato calling Pallas [Athena] and Love [Eros] philosopher gods, we should understand him this way: that Love is a philosopher by reason of the means, Pallas by reason of the end. (613) . . .

5.21: When Plato says that Love was born from the union of Poverty and Plenty in the garden of Jove, on the birthday of Venus while the gods feasted, he means only this, that then the first love, that is, the desire of beauty, was born in the angelic mind when in it the splendor of ideas, though imperfectly, began to shine. (620) . . .

5.23: By two Venuses in Plato's *Symposium* we should understand nothing but two kinds of beauty, sensible and intelligible. (622)[377]

---

376. Pico, "Conclusions," *Pico's 900 Theses*, p. 365.
377. Pico, "Conclusions," *Pico's 900 Theses*, pp. 437-59.

Although Pico began with the names of feminine and masculine cosmic deities, he ended his reflections with a depersonalization of the deities, and an analogical application of their identities to activities of the soul. In this reinterpretation of Plato's conclusions we find Pico beginning to move towards his own philosophy of gender neutrality. Male and female differences, masculine and feminine differences, man and woman differences simply disappear from his analysis. It is only the gender-neutral philosopher moving towards union with the eternal forms and with God.

In particular, Venus is interpreted as representing at one time the intelligible world of forms, the angelic world, intelligible beauty, and at another time sensual and voluptuous life, sensible beauty, and the dominant feature of youth. Pallas Athena represents the philosopher who is using the intellect to contemplate ends rather than means. Thus, the concept of woman represents supernatural qualities of the world and important qualities of the soul, but ultimately it is submerged in the identity of the soul of the philosopher to become gender neutral. This early pattern of Pico with respect to ultimately advocating a gender neutrality stance will be repeated in his later writings as well.

Among the remaining over two hundred theses of Pico a similar pattern is discovered. The final sections of his massive work introduce several different subjects, numbers, natural magic, Orphic hymns, and the relation of Cabalism to Christianity. A few of Pico's reflections on gender in this diverse collection of conclusions are included in the following sample:

> 10.8: Anyone who profoundly and intellectually understands the division of the unity of Venus into the trinity of Graces [the beauty of the intellectual nature and its correspondents on lower levels of reality] . . . will perceive the method of duly proceeding in Orphic theology. (805) . . .

> 10.19: Anyone who does not attract Vesta [principle of unity and stability found on different levels of reality] will possess nothing firm in his work. (816) . . .

> 10.31: Whoever carefully notes the words of Aristotle in his exposition of the definition of the soul will see why Orpheus attributes wakefulness to Pallas [intellect] and Venus [will]. (828) . . .[378]

The final selections reveal the same pattern as seen above, namely, the association of cosmic feminine deities with qualities of the human soul. We will now turn to consider other aspects of Pico's philosophy of gender before returning to consider how in his later writings he manifested the same pattern of argumentation as seen above in his nine hundred theses.

---

378. Pico, "Conclusions," *Pico's 900 Theses*, pp. 461-553. The information in the [ ] is supplied by Farmer in notes to each passage.

Human Dignity

Pico's famous introduction to the projected public debate about his *Conclusions* came to be known as "Oration on the Dignity of Man" even though it was originally untitled, and appeared to be more of an oration in praise of philosophy.[379] It was common practice to give an oration in praise of one's own academic field at the beginning of an academic session, and Pico's oration was in line with this ancient tradition.[380] Since the debate was forbidden, the oration was never given as intended. However, it was published in a posthumous collection of Pico's works by his nephew Giovanni Francesco Pico della Mirandola. It was also translated and shortened into English by Sir Thomas More. Because of the oration's later title emphasizing the dignity of man, and its simplicity and elegance of expression, it has become a symbolic piece representing the aspirations of the early humanist movement.

"The Oration on the Dignity of Man" states clearly that each human being is responsible for freely choosing how to develop his or her own moral identity. Pico articulates this mandate through the voice of God, the Creator, who tells Adam, the first human being:

> All other creatures have their natures defined and limited by laws which We have established; you, by contrast, unimpeded by any such limits, may, by your own free choice, to whose custody We have assigned you, establish the features of your own nature. We have made you a creature neither of heaven nor of earth, neither mortal nor immortal, so that you may freely and proudly make yourself in the form which you wish. It will be in the orbit of your power to descend to the inferior and brutish form of life, just as it will be within your power to rise, through your own choice, to the superior orders of divine life.[381]

Pico does not project the fuller meaning of individual self-determination that will evolve from his proclamation of the dignity of a human being created with freedom to determine his or her own particular identity. The personalist meaning of unique and particular self-definition will take several centuries of further elaboration before being unfolded. It will also take a few centuries before others in the Enlightenment will jettison the religious context within which Pico proclaims the dignity of self-determination to suggest that the human being does this free determining of a particular self-identity against God rather than in cooperation with God.

For Giovanni Pico della Mirandola the dignity and freedom of the human being are set within pre-established levels of being, in a hierarchy or chain of beings in ascending relation with God. In the following passage Pico continues to explain his own meaning:

---

379. Farmer notes that the oration was mistitled in a later publication. Its original title, if any, was meant to be something like "Oration in praise of philosophy" (*Pico's 900 Theses*, p. 18, note 50).

380. Craven, *Giovanni Pico della Mirandola: Symbol of His Age*, p. 37.

381. Pico, "Oration on the Dignity of Man," in *The Italian Philosophers*, ed. Fallico and Shapiro, pp. 143-44.

It was to man alone, at the moment of his creation, that God bequeathed seeds laden with all potentialities — the germs of every form of life. Whichsoever of these a man cultivates will mature and bear fruit within him; if vegetative, he will become a plant; if sensitive, a brute; if rational, he will discover himself a heavenly being; if intellectual, he will be an angel and the son of God.[382]

Thus, a human being has to choose at which level he or she wants to live: vegetative, animal, rational, or intellectual/angelic. Paul Oskar Kristeller offers the following comparison of Ficino's and Pico's attitude towards the dignity of the human being. His summary is instructive for it offers a way to understand the two humanists' views of gender identity as well:

> . . . Ficino gives a metaphysical basis to the doctrine of the excellence and dignity of man that had been dear to the earlier humanists and was so close to their cultural and educational program, the *studia humanitatis*. For Ficino, man is identical with his rational soul, and his excellence consists in the role played by this soul as the center and bond of the universe, in its infinite capacity of thinking and willing, knowing and loving, of identifying itself with all other things. This important idea received a further development by Pico in his famous oration. For him, man and his soul are no longer a part, even a privileged central part, of the universal hierarchy; man is not outside the hierarchy, he is a world for himself and has no fixed place in the order of things but rather determines his place and nature through his own individual choice, since he is able to live all lives, those of the animals as well as those of the angels and even of God.[383]

Scholars have noted the bold challenge that Pico offered to the human being, namely to determine to proceed up a hierarchical structure past all the angels even to reach God.[384] In fact, there is an irony in Pico's challenge to men and women to choose their own identities, for in the ultimate choice of angelic or divine being, they lose, in a certain sense, their own human identity. This point will be developed in further detail with reference to issues of gender identity later in this section.

At present, it is important only to note that the choices of individual men or women are directed only to what level or form of life he or she wants to live. Pico repeats often in different texts a view of a hierarchy of forms of life and of the human being's placement within these forms. In the *Heptaplus,* or his commentary on the first seven days of Creation in *Genesis,* Pico elaborates the ways in which each of these levels was brought into being by God:

> This is enough about the three worlds [intelligible, celestial, and sublunar] about which it must be especially observed — a fact on which my intention almost

---

382. Pico, "Oration on the Dignity of Man," in *The Italian Philosophers,* ed. Fallico and Shapiro, p. 144.

383. Kristeller, "The Platonic Academy of Florence," in *Renaissance Thought II,* pp. 97-98.

384. William Kerrigan and Gordon Braden, "Pico della Mirandola and Renaissance Ambition," in *The Idea of the Renaissance* (Toronto: University of Toronto Press, 1993), ch. 7, pp. 117-33.

wholly depends — that the three worlds are only one, not solely because all are related by a single beginning and to the same end, or because, regulated by defined laws, they are connected to each other by a harmonious natural bond and by an ordinary series of steps; but because whatever is in all of the worlds is at the same time also contained in each of the others. If I understand him correctly, this, I believe, was the opinion of Anaxagoras — also expressed by the Pythagoreans and by the Platonists. Therefore, whatever is in the lower worlds is also in the higher ones, but in a more refined (superior) form; similarly, what is found in the higher worlds can be seen also in the lower ones, but in a deteriorated condition and with a somewhat adulterated nature, so to speak.[385]

This principle of the parallels among the different levels is filled out with respect to the various levels of presence of gender differentiation in the universe. Integrating references to Plato's *Phaedrus, Timaeus, Alcibiades,* and *Republic,* Aristotle's *Physics, Metaphysics, Posterior Analytics, De caelo,* and *De anima,* and Plotinus's *Enneads,* Pico analyzes Moses' account of the seven days of creation in *Genesis* and transforms it into an analysis of the different forms of life within a particular human being.

The creation of man and woman in *Genesis* is given an allegorical interpretation:

> Similarly, it is not without mystery why God created man male and female. It is, in fact, the prerogative of the celestial souls to undertake simultaneously both the function of contemplating and dominating the bodies, and the latter cannot be an obstacle or an impediment to the former nor the former an obstacle to the latter. Especially among the ancient people, it was the custom, as we observe in the Orphic hymns, to designate by the terms "male" and "female" these two powers in the same substance, one of which contemplates while the other rules the body.[386]

Although the order would be inverted in the above passage, it would seem that the male function is to rule the body while the female function is to contemplate. Obviously Pico is arguing that the same human being, a man or a woman, may exercise both functions in the soul. In this way, he interprets the *Genesis* account of the Creation of man and woman as an allegory about the nature of the human being.

In his *Disputationes adversus astrologiam divinatricem* Pico also reflects upon celestial engendered characteristics, and he concludes that there are so many differing opinions about the meaning of masculine and feminine in the celestial sphere that the terms become meaningless. In the following passage several different ancient sources are considered with respect to the masculine and feminine nature of different planets:

> Now come those matters to be discussed which they pass down absolutely concerning those degrees, that some [planets] are luminous, others dark, others of

---

385. Pico della Mirandola, *Heptaplus or Discourse on the Seven Days of Creation,* trans. Jessie Brewer McGaw (New York: Philosophical Library, 1977), pp. 23-24.
386. Pico, *Heptaplus,* p. 48.

good fortune; some, they say, are for spring water, others health, which they call alzemena; some are masculine, others feminine. But this was largely covered above; now we should add this, that Ptolemy also rejected all of these degrees, whose translator, Avenroda, seems to concede to me only that people might follow these things if they discovered that the truth of experience was in them. But what confidence in experience will there be when six opinions are brought forth concerning the masculine and feminine degrees? Those conditions are described one way by Firmicus, another way by Albumasar, another way by Avenroda, another way in Achabitius; Abraam says various things in many places; then others differ completely from all these when they make the twelfth part of each sign masculine, or feminine alternatively, determining the first parts from the kind of sign. I omit those who place twelve degrees out of thirty in the sex of the sign, following just as many in the opposite sex, then dividing the remaining six equally into each sex.[387]

Pico's theory of the hierarchy of worlds allows him to conclude that at the highest levels differences that appear important on lower levels cease to have meaning. This is the ultimate result of his preference for gender neutrality as the most refined understanding of human identity. It is the great dignity of the human being to choose whether to interpret life from the perspective of the adulterated lower levels of existence or from the refined highest levels.

What is remarkable about Pico's relation to his historical sources is that he always avoids either incorporating or rejecting direct arguments in this text for gender polarity or for gender unity. Pico's gender neutrality stance allows him to borrow and redefine Plato's theory of reincarnation and Aristotle's metaphysical and epistemological principles without becoming enmeshed in either gender unity or gender polarity. When Pico writes about the dignity of man, he means the dignity of all men and women. He simply assumes that reference to man is neutral with respect to gender issues, and thus he does not argue it either way.

In the following passage from the *Heptaplus,* philosophy and Jewish heritage are integrated with the forms of life among which a man has to choose:

> So much for the cognitive powers of the soul. Now Moses shifts to those whose function is to desire, the seats of anger and wantonness, or lust. These he represents by the beasts and the irrational sort of living things, since they are common to us and the beasts, and what is worse, often drive us to a brutish life. Hence comes that saying of the Chaldeans: 'The beasts of the earth dwell in your body.' And in Plato's *Republic* we learn that we have various kinds of brutes dwelling within us, so that it is not hard, if it is properly understood, to believe the paradox of the Pythagoreans that wicked men turn into brutes. The brutes are within our bowels, so that we do not have to travel far to pass into them.[388]

387. Giovanni Pico della Mirandola, *Disputationes adversus astrologiam divinatricem, books vi-xii,* ed. Eugenio Garin (Florence: Vallecchi Editore, 1946), ch. 17, pp. 130-31. Translated from Latin to English by Michael Woodward.

388. Pico, "Heptaplus," in *On the Dignity of Man/On Being and the One/Heptaplus* (Indianapolis: Library of Liberal Arts, 1965), 4.5, 123.

Not only has Pico agreed with Ficino, namely, that the theory of reincarnation in Plato's *Republic* is Pythagorean rather than Platonic, he has also followed Ficino in transforming the reincarnation thesis from a theory of the transmigration of souls to an epistemological and ethical theory about levels of decision-making and behavior in the human being. The individual human being has to choose whether to live like a beast, like a man, or like an angel. With his gender neutrality stance, there is no mention of Plato's suggestion about the reincarnation of immoral or cowardly men as women in the next generation, nor is there the introduction of an epistemological principle analogous to this Pythagorean metaphysical principle. Pico also adds, drawing upon the theme of recapitulation, that because of the original sin of Adam human beings tend to be "degenerated into beasts, disgracing the form of man and that [i]n the newest Adam, . . . Jesus Christ, . . . we are reformed by grace and regenerated. . . ."[389] Pico concludes his text *Heptaplus* with a reflection on the different levels of happiness or felicity that correspond to the different levels of being.

Giovanni Pico della Mirandola was not writing about these issues solely from an intellectual point of view. He had experienced in his short life consequences of different choices himself. As a youth, the young Count had been involved in different intimate relations with women, and he had written erotic poetry in Latin and Italian. Pico never married, but his nephew described a possible conversion he had a year before his death at age thirty-one:

> Before this he had been both desirous of glory and kindled in vain love and holden in voluptuous use of women. The comeliness of his body and the lovely features of his visage, and therewith all his marvellous fame, his excellent learning, great riches, and noble kindred, that many women were on fire for him, from the desire of whom he not abhorring (the way of life set aside) was from that fallen into wantonness. But after that he was once with this variance wakened he drew back his mind flowing in riot and turned it to Christ. Women's blandishments he changed into the desire of heavenly joys, and despising the blast of vainglory, which he before desired not with all his mind, he began to seek the glory and profit of Christ's church.[390]

While there is some controversy about whether or not Pico actually went through a conversion to the extent that he destroyed his earlier erotic writings, there seems to be no doubt that he did adopt a more ascetic lifestyle after meeting Savonarola.[391] There are also two notable aspects of Pico's attitudes and his analysis of how free self-determination may participate in selection of higher or lower forms of life. The first is that Pico never seems to present woman as an obstacle for a good choice or as a source of blame for a lesser choice. For example, in *Heptaplus* in the context in which Adam's sins were noted, Eve is not considered at all. Moreover, in his other works, to my knowledge there is no mention at all of a blame

389. Pico, *Heptaplus,* 4.6, 125-26.

390. Giovanni Francesco Pico, *Giovanni Pico della Mirandola: His Life* (London: David Nutt, 1890), p. 12.

391. Farmer contests Gianfrancesco Pico's account of this event. See *Pico's 900 Theses,* p. 155.

or a devaluation of woman in relation to man. This factor is quite remarkable given the intense immersion that Pico had in traditional gender polarity literature. The second notable aspect of Pico's philosophy is that it consistently presents a gender-neutral stance in that it does not advert to gender differentiation.

Giovanni Pico della Mirandola, therefore, offers a unique approach in early humanism as a promoter of gender neutrality. His independence from either gender polarity or gender unity is remarkable. Pico even distances himself from Ficino's gender theories in his interpretation of masculine and feminine epistemological dynamics and from any references to gender polarity, unity, or complementarity within the Christian tradition. Pico also differs from the Neoplatonist schema of masculine and feminine identity found in Nicholas of Cusa's *De conjecturis*.[392] As one commentator expresses it, while Nicholas of Cusa made an individual human being independent of the particular location in space, Pico Mirandola made the individual human being independent of a particular location in time.[393] The question of how much women can determine the dignity of their own particular identity is left as open as it is for man. It is simply up to an individual to make moral decisions concerning whether or not to live more like a vegetative, animal, human, or angelic being.

Gender Neutrality in Love and Beauty

One important text written by Giovanni Pico and not yet considered in this chapter needs some analysis, as it seems to run counter to the above hypothesis of Pico's intentional gender neutrality stance and his independence from all past philosophers. In a work written between 1486 and 1490 and entitled *A Platonic Discourse Upon Love,* Pico offers his own thinking about the nature of love and comments on the work of Girolamo Benivieni, who had summarized Marsilio Ficino's philosophy of love in a popular treatise.[394] The text was reputedly abandoned by Pico with Ficino's concurrence as it appeared to be "too pagan" and not appropriate for Christian readers.[395] These pagan elements can be seen in the hints about the Platonic doctrine of recollection and the emphasis upon union with Forms rather than interpersonal communion with God and the communion of saints. However,

---

392. In this light it is interesting that later Neoplatonists try to make a link between the two authors. See Pauline Moffitt Watts, "Pseudo-Dionysus the Areopagite and Three Renaissance Neoplatonists: Cusanus, Ficino, and Pico on Mind and Cosmos," in *Supplementum Festivum: Studies in Honor of Paul Oskar Kristeller,* ed. James Hankins et al., where she observes: ". . . Cusanus's cosmogram of the *De coniecturis* appears in a French translation of Pico della Mirandola's *Heptaplus* by Nicolas Le Fèvre de la Boderie, published in Paris in 1579" (p. 285).

393. Craven, *Giovanni Pico della Mirandola: Symbol of His Age,* p. 23.

394. Pico della Mirandola, *A Platonick Discourse Upon Love* (Boston: Merrymount Press, 1914). In the printed title the 'k' is added in this edition by Gardner. Since it is not the usual way of spelling Platonic, in the text the 'k' will be eliminated. For a more recent translation see Giovanni Pico della Mirandola, *Commentary on a Poem of Platonic Love,* trans. Douglas Carmichael (Lanham, Md./New York/London: University Press of America, 1986).

395. Robb, *Neoplatonism in the Italian Renaissance,* p. 118.

after Pico's death it was published, with Benivieni's permitted inclusion of his own text, in the collection of Pico's works. It turned out to be as popular as Ficino's own *Commentary on Plato's Symposium* among later Neoplatonists, and these two texts established the direction of Christian Neoplatonism for centuries to come. From the perspective of our study of the concept of woman in particular, when Pico describes another philosopher's views he does repeat their gender associations, and this could lead a reader to imply that he accepts them as well. However, when all the evidence of Pico's text is weighed it would appear that he intentionally does not use gender distinctions himself but rather keeps to his stance of gender neutrality.

In Book I of *A Platonic Discourse Upon Love,* Pico describes a Neoplatonic world that includes levels of different kinds of beings. God created a first mind, from which all other things are generated. Then Pico adds that this first mind is given a feminine personification of Daughter by some authors:

> We conclude, therefore, that no creature but this first mind proceeds immediately from God: for of all other effects issuing from this mind, and all other second causes, God is only the mediate efficient. This by Plato, Hermes, and Zoroaster is called the Daughter of God, the Mind, Wisdom, Divine Reason, by some interpreted the Word: not meaning (with our Divines) the Son of God, he not being a creature, but one essence coequal with the Creator.[396]

Pico then elaborates a view of the levels of being contained in the microcosm created by God: the first level is that of stones and metals both in the world and in the heavens, the second level is that of plants, the third of beasts or animals, the fourth of rational souls, the fifth of angelic minds, and "above these is God, their origin."[397] He concludes Book I with the Neoplatonic theory that love is the way a being can ascend to union with a higher form of life. "Their only means of release from this bondage is the amatory life; which by sensible beauties, exciting in the soul a remembrance of the intellectual, raises her from this earthly life to the eternal; by the flame of love refined into an Angel."[398]

In Book II the passions of the soul are introduced with their proper object. "Love is a species of desire; Beauty of good."[399] Next, Pico claims that desire follows knowledge, and then he offers his three-leveled powers of the soul: sense, reason, and intellect. He concludes, as usual, that the reason is the median power that can incline either towards the senses or towards the heights of intellect. It is up to the human being to choose.

To elaborate this human choice Pico introduces Empedocles' principle that all beauty arises from the union of contraries. In this context he invokes "the fiction" of cosmic male and female identification in the interaction of the gods and goddesses as described by poets:

396. Pico, *A Platonick Discourse Upon Love,* I, iv, 6.
397. Pico, *A Platonick Discourse Upon Love,* I, xi, 15.
398. Pico, *A Platonick Discourse Upon Love,* I, xii, 17. The text is rendered into modern English by the author.
399. Pico, *A Platonick Discourse Upon Love,* II, i, 21.

Thus in the Fictions of Poets, Venus loves Mars: this Beauty cannot subsist without contrariety; she curbs and moderates him; this temperament allays the strife betwixt these contraries. And in Astrology, Venus is plac'd next to Mars, to check his destructive influence; as Jupiter next Saturn, to abate his malignancy. If Mars were always subject to Venus (the contrariety of principles to their due temper), nothing would ever be dissolved.[400]

Pico does not draw out any conclusions for gender identity from these poetical and astrological views. Instead, he moves directly to Plato's views, and repeats the view that was first stated in the *Symposium* and then repeated in Ficino's commentary *De amore,* namely that there are two Venuses, the celestial Venus which is the object of the intellect, and the vulgar Venus which is the object of the senses. He concludes that beauty is the material cause of love by being the object of love, but the soul is the efficient cause of love. The human being, by virtue of a free rational power in the soul, must make the choice of which object to love. Then, invoking one residue of the natural principle of gender polarity common to Neoplatonist authors, he associates the material cause with the concept of woman and the efficient cause with the concept of man: "For in Philosophy the efficient is assimilated to the Father, the material to the Mother."[401]

Pico does not rest here in his analysis, but presses the source of beauty further to conclude, following Plato, that the Divine Ideas precede the birth of Venus. The goal of human life is to return to the higher union of intellect with the Divine, and the way is through the ladder of love:

When the species of sensible Beauty flow into the eye there springs a twofold appetite of union with that whence this beauty is derived, one sensual, the other rational: the principles of bestial and human love. If we follow sense, we judge the body, wherein we behold this beauty, to be its fountain; whence proceeds a desire of coition, the most intimate union with it. This is the love of irrational creatures. But reason knows that the body is so far from being its original, that it is destructive to it, and the more it is sever'd from the body, the more it enjoys its own nature and dignity: we must not fix with the species of sense, in the body; but refine that species from all relics of corporeal infection.[402]

There are several aspects of the above passage that need noting. First, Pico reasserts the unique nature and dignity of the human species. Second, he devalues the body and suggests that corporeal aspects of human identity need to be purified as if they were like the remnants of an infectious disease. Third, the human being must use the reason and will to take responsibility for ascending from love for sensual beauty to love for a purely rational beauty.

It is not surprising that Pico again does not advert to the sex or gender dynamics of sensual love that seeks union by coition. Instead, he explains the process

400. Pico, *A Platonick Discourse Upon Love,* II, v, 26.
401. Pico, *A Platonick Discourse Upon Love,* II, viii, 29.
402. Pico, *A Platonick Discourse Upon Love,* II, xx, 43.

by which the human mind is able to abstract the form of beauty from the individually beautiful human being and move towards an intellectual union with pure Beauty.

> Thus in our soul . . . there may be three loves; one in the intellect, angelical; the second human; the third sensual. The two latter are conversant about the same object, corporeal beauty; the sensual fixes its intention wholly on it; the human separates it from matter. The greater part of mankind go no further than these two; but they whose understandings are purified by philosophy, knowing sensible beauty to be but the image of another more perfect, leave it, and desire to see the celestial, of which they have already a taste in their remembrance; if they persevere in this mental elevation, they finally obtain it; and recover that which, though in them from the beginning, yet they were not sensible of, being diverted by other objects.[403]

In the above passage Pico hints at a theme that will preoccupy him for many years, namely that a few select individuals are able to plumb the secrets of the world, while most human beings live at a lower level of knowledge. The persons with elite knowledge have such a high degree of union of intellect with Divine truth that they have become "angelic," leaving behind the material condition of their human life. Pico states clearly in Book II that "man ariseth from one perfection to another, till his soul (wholly united to the intellect) is made an angel."[404]

With this emphasis on angelic life as the goal of human reason we can begin to understand a fundamental reason why Pico adopted a gender neutrality stance. Angels have no gender, being purely spiritual beings. Pico emphasizes over and again that a human being ought to use the reason and will to choose to focus on the same objects of intelligence that angels do. Only if the reason and will choose to focus on the same objects of sensibility as animals do will sex and gender differentiation become part of the human being's object of love.

In Book III of *A Platonic Discourse Upon Love* Pico directly analyzes a sonnet by Benivieni on the nature of love. The sonnet uses the traditional feminine personification of both the celestial and earthly Venus, and it seeks to evoke in the reader a desire to become united with the Divine through a movement away from earthly love to heavenly love. Pico begins the book by de-personalizing the poet's account and philosophizing its content: "To treat of both Loves belongs to different sciences; Vulgar Love to Natural or Moral Philosophy; Divine, to Theology or Metaphysics."[405] Then the first sentence in Stanza I of Pico's commentary on the sonnet introduces a hierarchical ordering of governing within the world:

> The chief order established by divine Wisdom in created things is, that every inferior nature be immediately governed by the superior; whom while it obeys, it is guarded from all ill, and led without any obstruction to its determinate felicity;

403. Pico, *A Platonick Discourse Upon Love*, II, xxii, 47.
404. Pico, *A Platonick Discourse Upon Love*, II, xx, 44.
405. Pico, *A Platonick Discourse Upon Love*, III, intro., 63.

but if through too much affection of its own liberty, and desire to prefer the licentious life before the profitable, it rebels from the superior nature, it falls into a double inconvenience. First, like a ship given over by the pilot, it lights sometimes on one rock, sometimes on another, without hope of reaching the port. Secondly, it loses the command it had over the natures subjected to it, as it has deprived its superior of his. Irrational nature is ruled by another, unfit for its imperfection to rule any. God who by his ineffable excellence provides for every thing, himself needs not the providence of any other: betwixt the two extremes, God and brutes, are angels and rational souls, governing others, and govern'd by others.[406]

In his elaboration of this hierarchical ordering Pico describes how God enlightens the first hierarchy of angels, who in turn enlighten Plato's daemons or the Hebrew guardian angels, who also in turn enlighten human beings especially with ideas of intellectual beauty.

Then, in the typical fashion of Ficino, Pico argues that the same metaphysical order that occurs in the macrocosm also occurs in the microcosm, or the interior structure of each man's soul:

> The same order is in the lesser world, our soul: the inferior faculties are directed by the superior, whom following they err not. The imaginative corrects the mistakes of the outward sense: reason is illuminated by the intellect, nor do we at any time miscarry, but when the imaginative will not give credit to reason, or reason confident of itself, resists the intellect. In the desiderative the appetite is govern'd by the rational, the rational by the intellectual, which our poet implies, saying,

> "Love whose hand guides my heart's strict reins."

> The cognitive powers are seated in the head, the desiderative in the heart. In every well order'd soul the appetite is govern'd by intellectual love; implied by the metaphor of reins borrowed from Plato in his "Phaedrus."

> "Love to advance my flight, will lend the wings by which he did descend into my heart — "

> When any superior virtue is said to descend, we imply not that it leaves its own height to come down to us, but draws us up to itself: its descending to us, is our ascending to it: otherwise such conjunction would be the imperfection of the virtue, not the perfection of him who receives it.[407]

Two aspects of this passage are significant for our purposes. The first is that Pico avoids making any gender association with higher or lower functions of the soul. He simply offers a gender-neutral description of the activities involved in self-governing. The second is that he clearly states that the human being is drawn upwards in this ladder of love by the higher nature. This would imply that for Pico

406. Pico, *A Platonick Discourse Upon Love,* III, i, 64.
407. Pico, *A Platonick Discourse Upon Love,* III, i, 65-66.

the angelic gender neutrality stance follows from being drawn into a higher kind of intellectual ordering.

Towards the end of Book III he describes a six-degree process of ascending that incorporates the engendered models of the poet Benivieni and philosophers Ficino, Plotinus, and Plato along with some aspects of the Thomistic theory of abstraction and knowledge. With this passage our analysis of Pico's *A Platonick Discourse Upon Love* will conclude. The enumeration is Pico's:

1. From material beauty we ascend to the first fountain by six degrees: the soul through the sight represents to herself the beauty of some particular person, inclines to it, is pleased with it, and while she rests here, is in the first, the most imperfect material degree.

2. She reforms by her imagination the image she has received, making it more perfect as more spiritual; and separating it from matter, brings it a little nearer ideal beauty.

3. By the light of the agent intellect abstracting this form from all singularity, she considers the universal nature of corporeal beauty by itself: this is the highest degree the soul can reach while she goes no further than sense.

4. Reflecting upon her own operation, the knowledge of universal Beauty, and considering that everything founded in pattern is particular, she concludes this universality proceeds not from the outward object, but her intrinsic power: and reasons thus: If in the dim glass of material phantasms this Beauty is represented by virtue of my light, it follows that, beholding it in the clear mirror of my substance divested of those clouds, it will appear more perspicuous: thus turning into her self, she finds the image of Ideal Beauty communicated to her by the Intellect, the Object of Celestial Love.

5. She ascends from this Idea in herself, to the place where Celestial Venus is, in her proper form: who in fullness of her Beauty not being comprehensible, by any particular intellect, she, as much as in her lies, endeavours to be united to the first Mind, the chiefest of Creatures, and general habitation of Ideal Beauty.

(6.) Obtaining this, she terminates, and fixes her journey; this is the sixth and last degree. They are all imply'd in the 6th, 7th, and 8th stanzas:

"Form'd by th' eternal Look, etc."[408]

Even though the soul, *anima,* is given its traditional feminine personification, the genders of the human beings who are the objects of love and of the lover are left out

---

408. Pico, *A Platonick Discourse Upon Love,* III, vi, vii, and viii, 73-74. The linear separation of each numbered stage was done by this author for ease of reading, while in the original text they are in sequence in a single paragraph.

of the description. While originally Platonic love was developed as a description of chaste love and friendship among men, in time the object of love and lover shifted to a heterosexual context. In a chapter entitled "The 'Trattato D'Amore,'" in *Neoplatonism of the Italian Renaissance,* Nesca Robb traces the shifting of the engendered aspects of fifteenth- and sixteenth-century treatises on love from the original focus of male friendships to the man/woman relations of Christian Italy.[409] Nearly all of these treatises based themselves on Ficino's *De Amore* and/or Pico's *A Platonic Discourse Upon Love.* Many of them introduced new questions with gender identity at their core. However, since they go beyond the time-frame established for the present study, we will return to concluding reflections on Giovanni Pico della Mirandola's contribution to the concept of woman.

At the beginning of this section we suggested that Pico made two contributions to the history of the philosophy of gender. The first contribution was his identification of the great dignity of the human being to whom God gives the responsibility to "by your own free choice . . . establish the features of your own nature" and "freely and proudly make yourself in the form which you wish."[410] Second, in Pico's own independent manner of not being the disciple of any one man, he consciously chose a gender neutrality stance in the manner in which philosophers had continually invoked both gender polarity and gender unity arguments. In our subsequent analysis of his writings, it became clear that the free choice a human being was given to determine his or her own nature was delineated as a choice among various levels of being, especially animal and angelic, and that the human reason was limited to choosing between an animal-like sensible nature and an angelic-like intelligent nature. In addition, it also became clear that Pico's gender neutrality stance was informed by his admiration for the angelic level of being, and his belief that the corporeal or material aspects of human identity had to be purified or refined out of one's identity.

With these general outlines of Pico's approach to the philosophy of gender the chart on the following page may be offered as a summary of his position.

If the human level of being is considered in further depth, Pico's contribution to the history of the concept of woman must be viewed in two contrary ways: first, he opened a pathway towards the future of humanism by his declaration in the "Oration on the Dignity of Man" that God has given the human being a unique and remarkable gift of free choice of his or her own identity, of giving form to a human life by particular choices. However, when the particular choices that Pico delineates are considered further it is obvious that the human level of being turns out to be almost akin to an empty function or formula in mathematics. In other words, the choices of a human being, according to Pico, consist in moving to either a higher or a lower level of being, to the angelic or the animal. There is no sense in Pico that the human being chooses itself as a level appropriate to its own way of being. Thus, Pico ends up rejecting the very human existence that provides him with the ground of choice, and in so doing he rejects a woman choosing herself *qua* woman or a man choosing himself *qua* man.

409. Robb, *Neoplatonism in the Italian Renaissance,* pp. 176-211. See also the previous chapter on "The Medici Circle," pp. 135-75.

410. Pico, "Oration on the Dignity of Man," in *The Italian Philosophers,* pp. 143-44.

Pico della Mirandola's Gender-Neutral Stance			
Levels of Being	Epistemological Corollary	Object of Love	Gender Aspect
Divine	Mind	God	
Angelic	Intelligence	Poetic: Celestial Venus Philosophical: Ideal Beauty	Gender neutral
Human	Reason	Six steps of as-cending or de-scending objects of love	If angelic level is chosen, then gen-der neutral
	Free Will	Must choose proper level of self-governing	If animal level is chosen, then en-gendered
Animal Vegetable	Sensation	Poetic: Earthly Venus Philosophical: Beauty of a partic-ular body	Engendered as male and female

In Pico's rejection of the human body and materiality in general, he not only provides the rationale for his goal of gender neutrality in imitation of angelic exis-tence, he also undermines the very ground for his own philosophy. For the body is the very territory in which a human person can act to determine his or her own unique identity. Rather than being like a residue of an infectious disease that inter-feres with ideal choices, the human body is the gift that enables a person to truly become self-governing.[411] It is odd, in a way, that Pico's philosophy ended up in re-jecting an engendered material aspect of human identity because he accepted Thomas Aquinas's argument that the essence of man involves both soul and body.[412] Yet, when his epistemological theory is traced from beginning to end, it is

411. See Wojtyla, *The Acting Person,* for an excellent analysis of this point. See "It is generally recognized that the human body is in its visible dynamism the territory where, or in a way even the medium whereby, the person expresses himself. Strictly speaking, the personal structure of self-governance and self-possession may be thought of as 'traversing' the body and being expressed by the body" (p. 204).

412. See Pico, *Pico's 900 Theses,* 2.31, 229. See also the excellent discussion of this point in Avery Dulles, *Princeps Concordiae: Pico della Mirandola and the Scholastic Tradition* (Cambridge, Mass.: Har-vard University Press, 1941), p. 114.

clear that the Neoplatonist move towards intellectual union demands a rejection of the material condition of the knower.

Finally, Pico's philosophy does not provide any place for interpersonal communion on earth. In essence, it falls back into a utilitarian model similar to Ficino's, in which one person is valuable to another only in so far as his or her beauty awakens in the other a desire for ascending to union with God, as a step through which to come to love Ideal Beauty. Therefore, while Giovanni Pico della Mirandola contributed to the development of understanding of the great dignity of a human person freely able to determine his or her own existence, he did not offer a foundation for a genuine integral complementarity among different human persons. With regard to this matter, the significance of Giovanni Pico della Mirandola's nephew, Gianfrancesco Pico della Mirandola, referred to earlier in this chapter, needs clarification. Some earlier reflections have already been offered regarding Gianfrancesco's use and abuse of his uncle's texts. James Farmer has carefully delineated the "evidence of posthumous tampering in Pico's works by Gianfrancesco Pico, Savonarola, and their associates," so his conclusions do not need to be repeated here.[413] Gianfrancesco's father was Galeotto I Pico, the eldest brother of Giovanni, and his mother was Bianca Maria d'Este, the illegitimate daughter of Niccolò III d'Este.[414] Right after Giovanni Pico's death, Gianfrancesco rushed to take control of Pico's unpublished papers, and within a year they were turned over to Savonarola and the Dominicans in Florence. In 1496, Gianfrancesco published in Bologna a somewhat revised and edited version of his uncle's collected works. In 1498, Pico's papers were moved to Rome where they had been bought by a Cardinal. However, it was the 1496 published version that provided scholars with access to what they thought was Pico's philosophy. His nephew, Gianfrancesco, had not only distorted some of the actual texts written by Pico, but he also wrote a biography that cast his uncle in a different light than historians now believe to be true.[415]

From the perspective of the history of the concept of woman there are two particular aspects of Gianfrancesco's decisions that need to be noted. The first is that he held back from publication all of Giovanni's poems in Latin and Tuscan, and he suggested that his uncle had destroyed them in a moment of conversion. There is no evidence to support this conclusion of conversion. Second, he published a dialogue in 1523 entitled in Latin *Strix* and translated into Italian as *La strega* in 1524 and 1555. This dialogue is described as "a remarkable example of the mixture of magic and (critiques of) eroticism," and it became extremely popular.[416] In an extraordinary way the dialogue introduces into Italy the content of the *Malleus maleficarum* and the gender polarity exaggerations it contains. Gianfrancesco even included reference to the Bull of Innocent VIII that was in-

---

413. Farmer, *Pico's 900 Theses*, pp. 151-79.

414. Charles B. Schmitt, *Gianfrancesco Pico della Mirandola (1469-1533) and His Critique of Aristotle* (The Hague: Martinus Nijhoff, 1967), p. 11; and Farmer, *Pico's 900 Theses*, p. 153.

415. See Farmer's summary of Gianfrancesco's textual adulterations in *Pico's 900 Theses*, pp. 170ff.

416. Gustavo Costa, "Love and Witchcraft in Gianfrancesco Pico della Mirandola: *La Strega* Between the Sublime and the Grotesque," *Italica* 67, no. 4 (Winter 1990): 427-39.

cluded as an introduction to the *Malleus* and gave a vivid portrayal of the evil acts of witches. "Indeed, Pico's dialogue is a transposition of the content of the *Malleus maleficarum* by Heinrich Kramer and Jacob Sprenger into artistic terms to render it more palatable to Italian readers."[417]

In his own work on witchcraft Gianfrancesco differed radically from his uncle Giovanni. The nephew attacked witchcraft and associated women's identity anew with its worst characteristics; the uncle distinguished between two kinds of witchcraft: one associated with evil and the other associated simply with natural science. Giovanni Pico della Mirandola sought above all to defend the value of natural magic or witchcraft as something positive for society. Giovanni Pico, through his study of the Cabala and in his *Apologia,* and Ficino, through his study of hermeticism and in his translation of Trismegistus and writing of *Pimander, De amore,* and the third section of *De vita,* supported the development of a new attitude towards natural magic.[418]

In this discourse between humanists, on the one hand, and scholastic and popular interest in the relation between women's identity and witchcraft we find a new intensity emerging. For the humanists, Ficino and Pico, witchcraft is depersonalized and moved from its past associations with the demonic towards an interest in the powers of nature, of health, and natural science. For scholastic writers and for Gianfrancesco witchcraft is personalized once again and reasserted in its connection both with the demonic and with woman's identity. In addition, the intense attack that had been previously initiated in Germany by the Dominicans Kramer and Sprenger with the support of Pope Innocent VIII and the Faculty of the University of Cologne is now introduced into Italy by the nephew of the man whose nine hundred theses Pope Innocent VIII condemned. While it is not possible to draw any definitive conclusions from these events, there does seem to be a connection once again between certain attitudes towards gender and the attraction to extreme positions that devalue woman's identity.[419]

In spite of the distortions that Gianfrancesco Pico della Mirandola introduced into Giovanni Pico della Mirandola's *Opera* and *Vita,* his publication of the works of his uncle turned out to be an important historical event. They were reprinted in Lyons by 1498, in Venice in 1498, in Strasbourg in 1504, in Reggio in 1506, in extracted French translations in 1509, and in Thomas More's English translation in Oxford in 1510.[420] More's translation edited even further the previ-

---

417. Costa, "Love and Witchcraft in Gianfrancesco Pico della Mirandola," *Italica* 67, no. 4 (Winter 1990): 428.

418. See Paola Zambelli's discussion of this in "Scholastic and Humanist Views of Hermeticism and Witchcraft," in *Hermeticism and the Renaissance: Intellectual History and the Occult in Early Modern Europe,* ed. Ingrid Merkel and Allen G. Dubus (Washington, D.C.: Folger Books, 1988), ch. 6, pp. 125-53, esp. 127-29.

419. The one differing factor here is that Gianfrancesco offered a serious critique of the philosophy of Aristotle. See Schmitt, *Gianfrancesco Pico della Mirandola (1469-1533) and His Critique of Aristotle.*

420. Anthony S. G. Edwards, ed., *The Complete Works of St. Thomas More* (New Haven and London: Yale University Press, 1997), vol. 1, pp. xlii and xxxix. More's translation came from the 1504 Strasbourg edition of the *Opera omnia,* p. xliv.

ously contrived *Vita*. For example, he deleted information connecting Pico with magic, with the Cabala, and with mathematical and scientific arguments. Instead, More emphasizes Pico's contemplative life and his affirmation of the dignity of the human being. His *Life of Pico* became very popular, and it was reprinted around 1525. Thomas More is an important figure for the next phase of the history of the concept of woman because of the model he offered for the humanist education of his daughters. The redefinition of Pico as a good model for Christians had been so successful that when Thomas More was in the Tower of London awaiting his execution, Thomas Elyot translated a work by Pico entitled "Rules of Christian Life," to send to More as a devotional text.

Before concluding this consideration of Gianfrancesco Pico della Mirandola, one further aspect of his own work needs to be noted. In *Gianfrancesco Pico Della Mirandola and His Critique of Aristotle* Charles Schmitt has given a thorough critique of the several different ways that Gianfrancesco Pico sought to attack Aristotle's approach to philosophy.[421] Significant for the history of the concept of woman was Pico's consistent attack on Aristotle's scientific method and conclusions. Pico argued that Aristotle's approach was contradictory and false, and it produced nothing but opinions. In spite of the hostility that Pico evidenced towards Aristotle's empirical approach to knowledge, and even in spite of Pico's own skepticism, his work did contribute to the eventual overturning of Aristotelian grounds for gender polarity in his theories of generation and of cosmology. Thus, inadvertently Gianfrancesco Pico della Mirandola aided the philosophy of gender by raising doubts about the absolute veracity of Aristotle's metaphysical and natural principles of gender polarity. In this way, he contributed to the ongoing reform of the concept of woman.

THE STRUGGLE TO REFORM THE THEORY OF GENDER IDENTITY

In this chapter several different attempts were provided by philosophers to reform the Aristotelian gender-polarity theory. The period was filled with intense struggle by individual philosophers who embarked in new directions of thought about woman's identity. Even though the concept of woman was merely a part of a broader scope of renewal by each of these philosophers, it nonetheless benefited by very significant attempts at new orientations of thought. Since each philosopher's theory has been carefully summarized in the particular section in which it was considered, these conclusions will not be repeated here. Instead, the general directions of their efforts at reform will be restated.

First of all, the meaning of masculine and feminine was elevated from a past limited association with male and female identity. No longer was a man simply defined by what is male or a woman by what is female. Instead, a man could have masculine and feminine characteristics and a woman could have feminine and masculine characteristics. Exactly what was meant by "masculine" and "feminine"

---

421. Schmitt, *Gianfrancesco Pico della Mirandola,* chapters 2-5.

often included traditional gender-polarity categories divided as active-passive, actual-potential, light-dark, rule-obey, and so forth. Yet, even with the gender-polarity contents remaining unchanged, there were still an elevation of category, and an introduction of a new dimension to engendered human existence.

Secondly, the human being was seen as capable of choosing a perspective with respect to space and to time, and even a perspective with respect to self-determination within pre-set levels of moral existence. This also elevated the dignity of the human being beyond mere existence controlled by external factors. The implications of this innovation will be felt in generations to come by both men and women.

Thirdly, woman was redefined more explicitly by some philosophers as an object of pleasure or an object of use. These Epicurean and utilitarian approaches to the concept of woman, while innovative, were seen to be severely limiting to the dignity of woman and to the need for her to grow to her full potential as a human being with intellect and free will.

Fourthly, the whole question of the relation between cosmic masculine and feminine dimensions and engendered human life was raised and evaluated by several philosophers. Astrological, astronomical, and mathematical theories of engenderment drew upon ancient Cabalist, Pythagorean, and Orphic texts. While some philosophers adopted a theory of cosmic engenderment, others viewed it as superficial and lacking meaning for higher philosophical speculation.

Fifthly, the introduction of translations of Plato's dialogues was seen to have had a long and controversial history. Frequently those passages that directly concerned Plato's concept of woman were distorted or ignored, until finally Ficino's accurate translations brought a new clarity into the history of gender theory. As a result, the principle especially of equality of soul, reason, and will was introduced by the humanist reform. This principle will become foundational for the next phases of the humanist reformation in the concept of woman.

Our analysis will now turn to consider the first woman humanists of Italy who wrote texts with considerable depth of argument. Isotta Nogarola penned a sustained argument between a female and male humanist on the topic of gender identity. Laura Cereta provided an important augmentation in the history of the concept of woman in a series of short texts revealing multiple communications among female and male members of humanist communities of discourse.

CHAPTER 10

THE EARLY HUMANIST REFORMATION
BY WOMEN PHILOSOPHERS

Theoretical reformation of the concept of woman was accompanied by an increased access of women humanists to institutional structures of higher education and to the development of intellectual friendships of men and women. In Chapter 8 we noted the "third generation" effect of humanist education on women, i.e., the first generation of educators were the founders, Chrysoloras, Guarino, Vittorino; the second generation were usually male, but occasionally female students, taught by the first generation; and the third generation were female students of the second generation, who gave public orations and wrote eloquent letters as part of their participation in the early Renaissance Humanism. In the present chapter, we will demonstrate the cultural effect of this "third generation" phenomenon. As humanist founders aged and their leadership was replaced by humanist institutions of schools for young persons and academies for adults, women educated in these schools formed intellectual relationships with men and were invited to participate in humanist life and practices. Soon these women began to explore in earnest the concept of woman and woman's actual situation in society.

While the formal academic world remained mostly closed to women students, some exceptions occurred. For example, the University of Bologna had a long tradition of individual women teaching law there, going back to the twelfth century, and it continued to the fourteenth century with Novella d'Andrea as one of their instructors. According to university records, during the Renaissance Bettina Sangiogi and Teodora Crisola taught Greek and Giovanna Bianchetti Latin. There was a female student who attended lectures among the male students at Bologna, and whose lectures and writings were well known in the fifteenth century.[1] She may have collaborated with Francesco Filelfo, the husband of Teodora Crisola, on a speech she gave to the humanist Cardinal Bessarion.

In addition, women often engaged in dialogue with men in informal academies at private homes. Many recent scholars have described the achievements of women humanists in these situations.[2] The "third generation" effect is notable in

---

1. Albert Rabil, Jr., *Laura Cereta: Quattrocento Humanist* (Binghamton, N.Y.: Center for Medieval and Early Renaissance Studies, 1981), p. 31, note 10.
2. See, for example, Margaret King, *Women of the Renaissance* (Chicago and London: Univer-

this context as well. In the 1440s Lauro Quirini (1420–c. 1480), a student of Guarino of Verona with an Arts and Law degree from the University of Padua, corresponded with Isotta Nogarola after reading "with great pleasure" several of her texts.[3] In response to a request from her brother, Quirini outlined for Isotta his own version of a detailed study program for philosophy that included Boethius, Aristotle's logic, ethics, natural philosophy, and metaphysics, Averroes, and Thomas Aquinas. During the years 1451-1453, Isotta wrote her most sophisticated philosophical work, incorporating many of Aristotle's dialectical tools while at the same time undermining his gender polarity theory. The philosophical aspects of this work are detailed in the next part of this chapter.

In a second example, during the 1450s, Laura Cereta participated with her brother in an informal humanist group at the monastery in Chiara and possibly in a "Mondella Academy" in Brescia.[4] The academy was reputably held in the home of the physician Aloysii Mundellae, who, like Pico della Mirandola, was well versed in Hebrew, Arabic, Latin, and Greek languages. In the second section of this chapter several of Laura Cereta's letters about gender to other humanists associated with the different centers of study will be considered in detail.

In a third example, Cassandra Fedele (1465-1558) initiated a correspondence with Giovanni Pico della Mirandola in 1489 after reading one of his texts:

> But after your *Lucubrationes,* most rich in words and ideas, had been brought to me recently by that best of men, Salviatus, and I had often read them avidly, and had become acquainted with your intellectual skill and singular learning from them, I feared lest I might be reproved by many unless I celebrated your unheard-of gifts to the best of my feeble ability to all men, by whom you are held to be a miracle, you are praised and you are revered, especially as a result of the dissemination of your works. Because in those works are contained fine phrasing, most serious meaning, brilliance, divine sublimity of interpretation, and finally, all things cohere harmoniously by divine influence.[5]

In 1491 Pico, along with the well-known humanist professor of poetry and rhetoric in Florence, Angelo Poliziano (1454-94), also known as Politian, made a personal visit to the home of Cassandra Fedele during a trip to Venice.

---

sity of Chicago Press, 1991); Margaret King and Albert Rabil, Jr., eds., *Her Immaculate Hand: Selected Works By and About the Women Humanists* (Binghamton, N.Y.: Medieval and Renaissance Texts and Studies, 1983); Rinaldina Russell, ed., *Italian Women Writers: A Bio-Bibliographical Sourcebook* (Westport, Conn. and London: Greenwood Press, 1994); and Constance Jordan, *Renaissance Feminism: Literary Texts and Political Models* (Ithaca and London: Cornell University Press, 1990).

3. Lauro Quirini to Isotta Nogarola, in *Her Immaculate Hand,* ed. King and Rabil, p. 112.

4. Rabil, *Laura Cereta: Quattrocento Humanist,* pp. 30-31.

5. Fedele to Pico, in Anthony Grafton and Lisa Jardine, *From Humanism to the Humanities: Education and the Liberal Arts in Fifteenth- and Sixteenth-Century Europe* (Cambridge, Mass.: Harvard University Press, 1986), p. 46. The complete works of Cassandra Fedele will be published in a translation by Diana Robin entitled: Cassandra Fedele, *Humanist Letters and Public Orations* (Chicago: University of Chicago Press, 2000). I regret that they were not available at the time of this publication.

Poliziano wrote about this meeting with the woman humanist to Lorenzo de Medici, whose children he had tutored:

> Yesterday evening I visited that learned Cassandra Fedele, and I greeted her, Excellency, on your part. She is a miraculous phenomenon, Lorenzo, whether in the vernacular or in Latin; most modest, and to my eyes also beautiful. I departed stupefied. She is a great admirer of yours, and speaks of you most knowledgeably, as if she knew you intimately. She will come to Florence one day, in any case, to see you; so prepare yourself to honour her.[6]

Apparently, mediated by Pico and Poliziano, Cassandra Fedele was invited to become a member of the Academy and Court circle of Florence. She corresponded with Poliziano, and was compared by him to philosophers of the past, to the Pythagoreans, Diotima, and Aspasia. He held her up as a counterexample to Aristotelian-based gender polarity: "Now we know, truly by this [your written texts] we know, that your sex has not after all been condemned to slowness and stupidity."[7] In the same letter, he introduces the concept of beauty and perfection, so integrated with the Florentine Neoplatonists, while comparing Fedele with Pico:

> Neither Thracian Orpheus nor Linus would conquer me with songs [as you could by your words] even though Calliopea, the mother of Orpheus, be at his side, and Apollo, the father of Linus, at his. Indeed, I used to marvel at Pico della Mirandola, than whom no other mortal is more beautiful or more outstanding (I believe) in all branches of learning. Now behold, Cassandra, I have begun to venerate you next after Pico, perhaps also along with him.[8]

Cassandra Fedele next received a letter from another woman scholar in Florence who had heard about her from the circle of humanists around the Medici Court. Alessandra Scala wrote on October 6, 1492:

> Whoever comes to [Florence] from [Venice] celebrates your virtue, so that now your name is revered here as much as there. Admirable and almost incredible things are told us about your intellect, learning, and manners. For this reason I congratulate you and give thanks, because you have made illustrious not only our sex but also this age.[9]

Yet, Scala had previously written to Fedele asking her advice about whether or not to marry. Fedele's response (February 15, 1492) bears repeating here for two reasons. It incorrectly attributes to Plato a view of Thomas Aquinas, that something is perceived according to the mode of the receiver:

6. Poliziano to Lorenzo de Medici, in Grafton and Jardine, *From Humanism to the Humanities,* p. 47.

7. Poliziano to Fedele, in *From Humanism to the Humanities,* p. 49.

8. Poliziano to Cassandra Fedele, in *Her Immaculate Hand,* ed. King and Rabil, p. 127.

9. Alessandra Scala to Cassandra Fedele, in *Her Immaculate Hand,* ed. King and Rabil, p. 87.

Angelo Poliziano

Ætatis An. XVI.

CASSANDRA FIDELIS VENETA LITERIS CLARISSIMA.

Cassandra Fedele

And so, my Alessandra, you are of two minds, whether you should give yourself to the Muses or to a man. In this matter I think you must choose that to which nature more inclines you. For Plato states that all advice which is received, is received in proportion to the readiness of the receiver. You must certainly be prepared to make a sound judgment and not act impetuously.[10]

The response also reveals that Fedele has accepted the view amply defended by Alberti and deeply ingrained in society, that a woman must choose between the intellectual life or the married life, that is, between developing her mind or offering her utility in domestic service.

By 1493 Poliziano writes to Cassandra Fedele about Alessandra Scala. He took Fedele's letters to her and had "Scala read them aloud to the assembled company. Bartolomeo Scala, Marsilio Ficino, and Pico della Mirandola praised their accomplishment."[11] This description provides solid evidence that the Florentine Academy was open to the participation of women and that some of its members actually took much interest in women's participation. Meetings at the Scala home appeared to be a regular event, for Poliziano also mentions an occasion on which Sophocles' tragedy *Electra* was performed in Greek, with Alessandra in the main role of Electra demonstrating exceptional talent and the ability to communicate with "her gestures everywhere so prompt and effective, so appropriate to the argument, so covering the range of the various feelings, that they added greatly to the truth and believableness of their fiction."[12]

We observed the fathers of early Renaissance Humanism, Guarino of Verona, Marsilio Ficino, and Pico della Mirandola being involved in some aspects of the intergender discourse. Although more often it was their disciples who engaged with women humanists, in general we can assert that in fifteenth-century Italy — in Florence, Brescia, Venice, and elsewhere — the educational and intellectual culture was receptive to women's participation. Women humanists were beginning to become philosophers in their own right. In the present chapter the works of two women humanists, Isotta Nogarola and Laura Cereta, will be analyzed. A large number of sources are available for studying the depth of original thinking in these authors. Before that, two small orations of Cassandra Fedele that bear upon the theme of the concept of woman will be briefly introduced.

In 1487 Cassandra Fedele gave a public oration in front of the governing body, faculty, and students of the University of Padua, on the occasion of her young relative Bertucio Lamberto graduating with a Degree in Liberal Arts. The oration, while not displaying originality, is nonetheless important to our study because it offers a perfectly integrated summary of central humanist ideals common to her culture. At the age of twenty-two Cassandra Fedele states publicly that she, ". . . too young to be learned, ignoring my sex and exceeding my talent, [proposes] to speak before such a body of learned men, and especially in this city where today

---

10. Fedele to Scala, in Grafton and Jardine, *From Humanism to the Humanities*, pp. 87-88.
11. Grafton and Jardine, *From Humanism to the Humanities*, p. 53.
12. Poliziano to Fedele, in Grafton and Jardine, *From Humanism to the Humanities*, pp. 53-54.

(as once in Athens) the study of liberal arts flourishes . . . dare[s] to advance to speak."[13]

Following the pattern of Ficino and Pico, who sought to reconcile Plato and Aristotle in the one line of truth, Cassandra Fedele then adds:

> I have chosen as the subject of my praise the threefold tradition of Cicero, Plato, and the Peripatetics, who believed that men derived true honor from the goods of the soul, the goods of the body, and from those goods which some prominent philosophers ascribed to fortune. Therefore, I beseech you, illustrious gentlemen, to pay close attention, although I know that you expect no profound insights from me. Lest you think that I speak ostentatiously (which I am striving particularly not to do), I shall use humble, everyday words, which I am sure will please you. However brilliant one's origin, it is granted highest praise, as you know, only when the record of one's virtues achieves the level of one's nobility.[14]

Here she unifies Plato, Aristotle, and Cicero, asserts her preference for simple but eloquent language, and reasserts the general view that virtue is the only true nobility. Fedele notes the value of speech in human identity even further when she reflects: "For it is in speech that men excel beasts."[15] Yet, her simple phrase "although I know that you expect no profound insights from me" betrays the sting of traditional bias about women's ability or about her own particular talent that she must have experienced. Still, Fedele clings to the humanist principle established by the early humanists Dante, Petrarch, and Boccaccio, that the value of a person consists in virtue, not in any form of inherited status.

Next, Cassandra Fedele reflects on Petrarch's humanist praise that philosophy makes a person more human:

> Certainly for this reason this part of philosophy has laid claim for itself to the sweet name of "humanity," since those who are rough by nature become by these studies more civil and mild-mannered. But I am here to praise the youth [Bertucio], pursuing the study of philosophy, which [branch of] knowledge has always been thought divine among the wisest men, and rightly so. For the other disciplines deal with matters related to man; this one teaches clearly what man himself is, what he must strive for, what he must flee. There is no understanding of life, no outstanding principle, and finally, nothing which pertains to living well and happily, which does not result from the study of philosophy. Has anyone ever plunged into error who was imbued with philosophy? These studies refine the mind, intensify and strengthen the force of reason. . . . What [contributes] more to dignity, what more happily to righteous pleasure, or more aptly to the glory of cities than the branches of philosophy? For this reason Plato, a man almost divine, wrote that republics are blessed when their administrators have

13. Fedele, Oration for Bertucio Lamberto, in *Her Immaculate Hand,* ed. King and Rabil, p. 70.

14. Fedele, Oration for Bertucio Lamberto, in *Her Immaculate Hand,* ed. King and Rabil, pp. 70-71.

15. Fedele, Oration for Bertucio Lamberto, in *Her Immaculate Hand,* ed. King and Rabil, p. 72.

been trained in philosophy, or when men trained in philosophy have undertaken to administer them.[16]

Ficino's translation of Plato's *Republic* would have been available for three years prior to this oration, so it is possible that she read the text in Latin. The notion that the rulers of Venice or Padua should be educated akin to Plato's philosopher guardians had been 'in the air' for several years. In any event, Cassandra does not directly advert to Plato's view but promotes the value of equal education for all:

> Happy, therefore, are you, Cassandra, that you happened to be born into these times! Happy this age and this excellent city of Padua, overbrimming with so many learned men. Now let everyone cease, cease, I say, to marvel at the ancients! The highest and greatest God has wished the studies of all peoples to flourish in this place, and to be commended and consecrated to eternity.[17]

In a second *Oration in Praise of Letters* Fedele continues to reflect on humanist studies as an enhancement of human identity, and in particular, on woman's possibilities in humanism. There is a sense of unease in her words describing women's search for meaning and purpose in their studies:

> Giorgio Valla, that great orator and philosopher, who found me worthy of his attention, most serene Prince, Senators, and learned men, encouraged and exhorted me — as I considered how women could profit from assiduous study — thereby to seek immortality. Aware of the weakness of my sex and the paucity of my talent, blushing, I decided to honor and obey him inasmuch as he was demanding [something] honorable, in order that the common crowd may be ashamed of itself and stop being offensive to me, devoted as I am to the liberal arts.[18]

Clearly, Fedele was taunted by the "common crowd" for her devotion to study of the liberal arts. Fedele concludes with an ironic and oblique reference to another Valla (Lorenzo), who wrote several versions of *De voluptate* (On Pleasure and On the True Good) in the 1440s, that the goal of studies or the highest good for women has to be intellectual pleasure:

> Of these fruits I myself have tasted a little and [have esteemed myself in that enterprise] more than abject and hopeless; and, armed with distaff and needle — woman's weapons — I march forth [to defend] the belief that even though the study of letters promises and offers no reward for women and no dignity, every woman ought to seek and embrace these studies for that pleasure and delight alone that [comes] from them.[19]

---

16. Fedele, Oration for Bertucio Lamberto, in *Her Immaculate Hand,* ed. King and Rabil, p. 72.
17. Fedele, Oration for Bertucio Lamberto, in *Her Immaculate Hand,* ed. King and Rabil, p. 73.
18. Fedele, Oration in Praise of Letters, in *Her Immaculate Hand,* ed. King and Rabil, p. 74.
19. Fedele, Oration in Praise of Letters, in *Her Immaculate Hand,* ed. King and Rabil, p. 77.

Again the polarization of women intellectuals and women engaged in domestic service is raised. The latter is identified with the distaff and needle as women's weapons. The intellectual weapons, i.e., a refined intellect and eloquent powers of speech, clearly do not match the domestic ones. The oration presents a series of contrasting pairs: pain versus pleasure, domestic service versus intellectual activity, contemplative humanism versus civic humanism. Laura Cereta will be able to resolve these contrasts of women's everyday life. Cassandra Fedele managed only to identify them.

In her oration Cassandra repeats many of the themes of the previous one, that, according to Plato, philosophers make the best administrators of a republic, that the study of philosophy frees the mind from anxiety and being under the control of fortune, that the study of literature "polishes intelligence, illuminates and shapes the force of reason," and perfects the endowments of the soul and adds beauty to the body. As an example she mentions Alexander the Great, who was educated by the philosopher Aristotle.[20]

These two orations of Cassandra Fedele were given when she was a young woman in her early twenties. They demonstrate a strength of character and a mind able to grasp the fundamental principles of humanism. Cassandra Fedele's fame as a young woman was widespread, and she was invited to spend time at the Court of Queen Isabella of Spain, probably through the mediation of her relative, who was a cleric assigned there by the Vatican. Fedele did not accept the offer, for reasons that are unclear but seem to include the turmoil of war and the desire of the governors of Venice to keep her there.

Fedele, who believed that a woman must choose between a life of intellect and marriage, chose marriage to the physician, Gian-Maria Mapelli.[21] Her husband's untimely death twenty-two years later in a shipwreck rendered her impoverished and in desperate search for financial support. At the end of her life, at the age of ninety-one, Cassandra Fedele was invited by the Senate of Venice to give another public oration, this time to Francesco Vernier, the Ruler of Venice, on the arrival of the Queen of Poland. Fedele, following Boccaccio's *Concerning Famous Women,* praised her "singular prudence in governing your peoples, and your wonderful fortitude of mind in the disturbances of wars (in which you easily outstrip Thamyris, Queen of the Scythians, or Hypsicratea of Pontus). . . ."[22] Although Cassandra Fedele engaged in dialogue with many different persons about a wide variety of issues, we have no extant copies of any works with philosophical depth.[23]

20. Fedele, Oration in Praise of Letters, in *Her Immaculate Hand,* ed. King and Rabil, pp. 76-77.

21. See Diana Robin, "Cassandra Fedele's *Epistolae* (1488-1521): Biography as Ef-facement," *The Rhetorics of Life-Writing in Early Modern Europe: Forms of Biography from Cassandra Fedele to Louis XIV,* ed. Thomas F. Mayer and D. R. Woolf (Ann Arbor: University of Michigan Press, 1995), pp. 187-203.

22. Fedele, Oration on the arrival of the Queen of Poland, in *Her Immaculate Hand,* ed. King and Rabil, pp. 49-50.

23. Diana Robin's article, "Cassandra Fedele's *Epistolae* . . .," in Mayer, ed., *The Rhetorics of Life-Writing in Early Modern Europe,* begins to evaluate some themes related to Fedele's self-concept as a writer. See the subtopics, 'Writing, Femininity, and Chastity,' 'The Shrinkage of the Female Self,' 'The Female Body as "Corpus Debile,"' 'Hermaphroditic Themes,' and 'Ef-facement,' pp. 191-99.

Our analysis will turn now to the two women humanist authors who have left a considerable legacy of their works, Isotta Nogarola and Laura Cereta. They, like Fedele, had to fight prejudice attaching to their intellectual talents. They searched for a meaning as women humanists that eluded Cassandra Fedele. Nogarola found it in scholarship and Cereta in teaching, but they both had to suffer considerably for these achievements. By their writings and their lives they countered the Aristotelian model of gender polarity, the Epicurean model of relating to women for pleasure, and the Alberti model of relation for utility. By contrast, these women humanists proposed the higher ideal of relation for the sake of virtue in all circumstances, for the good of the other and the good of self.

ISOTTA NOGAROLA (1418-1466) AND LUDOVICO FOSCARINI

Half a century after the flourishing of Christine de Pizan, Isotta Nogarola follows a similar pattern to her predecessor with respect to intergender dialogue. She dialogues with men and women humanists about issues of gender identity; with Ludovico Foscarini, Doctor of Arts, of Canon Law and Civil Law, she is the co-author of a sophisticated tri-level dialogue about gender identity. Like her predecessor, Isotta uses rhetoric and logic very effectively to make her point. There are, however, some significant differences between the two women philosophers: Isotta, unlike Christine, modeled actual intergender dialogues in her writing and introduced references to Aristotle's concept of woman. However, unlike Christine, Isotta was unable to find meaning in her life by becoming a professional writer.

Isotta Nogarola, a member of a well-known aristocratic family in Verona, was educated in humanist studies at her mother's insistence along with her two sisters, Angela and Ginerva, by the tutor Martino Rizzoni, who had been taught by Guarino of Verona.[24] The school of Guarino had by now produced many humanists, and even though he did not have women in his school, his graduates, acting as tutors, opened up the field of humanist education for women.[25] Isotta became fluent in Latin and knowledgeable in classical philosophy and rhetoric as well as in the study of Scriptures and Theology. She chose to live a celibate life as a private scholar in the home of her mother.[26]

---

24. Margaret L. King, "Book-lined Cells: Women and Humanism in the Early Italian Renaissance," in Albert Rabil, Jr., ed., *Renaissance Humanism* (Philadelphia: University of Pennsylvania Press, 1988), vol. 1, pp. 434-53, esp. 435.

25. Rizzoni is officially categorized as one of Guarino's pupils. See Grafton and Jardine, *From Humanism to the Humanities,* p. 34, note 12.

26. Unfortunately, Margaret King's frequent references to Isotta's choice of "religious life" vs. marriage are very misleading. Religious life in the Catholic tradition involves three core aspects that were missing in Isotta's life: the public profession of the vows of chastity, poverty, and obedience; the following of a rule approved by the Church, and living a life in common with other religious. While Isotta lived a private practice of the vow of celibacy, she cannot be accurately described as choosing religious life. King did qualify her use of "religious life" but then continued to use it incorrectly. See Margaret King, "Thwarted Ambitions: Six Learned Women of the Italian Renaissance," *Soundings: An Interdisciplinary Journal* 59, no. 3 (Fall 1976): 280-304, esp. 285.

Contrary to the method used in this book, we will at this juncture first analyze Isotta Nogarola's works and then reflect on the significance of certain aspects of her life and legacy. In particular we wish to emphasize the remarkable sustained dialogue she had with Ludovico Foscarini.[27] This dialogue, more than any other aspect of her life and writings, marks a new level of gender complementarity in the history of the concept of woman. Isotta and Ludovico participated in the dialogue as equals while they held significantly different engendered perspectives. They were able to sustain the dialogue without degenerating into antagonistic disputation. With the support and encouragement of Ludovico, Isotta wrote a manuscript version of the dialogue in Latin for circulation among other humanist scholars. Their encounter offers a new model of gender complementarity.

The Tri-level Dialogue about Adam and Eve

St. Augustine in Book XII of his *De Genesi ad litteram* had concluded that Adam and Eve had sinned equally according to pride, but unequally according to sex.[28] According to this, Eve was more guilty than Adam for the fall of humanity from union with God. In her correspondence with Ludovico Foscarini in the early 1450s, Isotta Nogarola challenged this view. Ludovico purposively took the part of a man's perspective in defending Adam, and Isotta deliberately took the part of a woman's perspective in defending Eve.[29] Sometime after the exchange of letters, Isotta decided, with Ludovico's agreement, to write a literary work capturing their previous discourse. Although the dialogue is rooted in part on Augustine's Commentary on *Genesis,* its articulation by Isotta and Ludovico is original.

The dialogue *De pari aut impari Evae atque Adame peccato* (1451-53) has its long English title *Of the Equal or Unequal Sin of Adam and Eve: An Honorable Disputation Between the Illustrious Lord Ludovico Foscarini, Venetian Doctor of Arts and Both Laws, and the Noble and Learned and Divine Lady Isotta Nogarola of Verona, Regarding this Judgment of Aurelius Augustine: They Sinned Unequally According to Sex, But Equally According to Pride.*[30] This dialogue is a work of the mature (thirty-three- to thirty-five-year-old) Isotta, incorporating many philosophical and theo-

---

27. Ludovico is characterized with these three professional degrees in the title of the dialogue. See King and Rabil, eds., *Her Immaculate Hand,* p. 51.

28. Augustine, *De Genesis ad Litteram* in *Oeuvres* (Paris: Desclée, De Brouwer, 1936), XII, 11.35.

29. See Margaret L. King, "The contention that Isotta and Ludovico argued from male and female vantage points is supported by Ludovico's statement that, if he had not been born a man, he would have argued differently" ("The Religious Retreat of Isotta Nogarola (1418-1466): Sexism and Its Consequences in the Fifteenth Century," *Signs: Journal of Women in Culture and Society* 3, no. 4 [1978]: 807-22, esp. 818, note 52).

30. The text of dialogue can be found translated by Margaret King, in *Her Immaculate Hand,* pp. 59-69. The original is found in *Isotta Nogarola, Opera,* II, 187-216. I am very grateful to Joseph T. Moller, who translated this dialogue from Latin to English for me before the published translation became available. King suggests 1453 or later as the date in "Thwarted Ambitions," *Soundings* 59, no. 3 (Fall 1976): 288, and 1451 as the date in "The Religious Retreat," *Signs* 3, no. 4 (1978): 818.

logical premises. It also considers consequences of two fundamental gender polarity claims about women's identity: weakness of intellect and inconstancy.

The dialogue shares a common generalization in which, paradigmatically, Adam represents all men and Eve all women. Whether man or woman has the greater guilt for sin refers not only to the theory of Original Sin, but to the broader context of men's and women's responsibility for the condition of evil in the world. Rather than quote at length, I have summarized the main points of emphasis in the dialogue. The speaker's name is placed in brackets, direct quotations in quotation marks, and my summaries appear without quotation marks.

The first part of the argument may be summarized as follows:

[**Ludovico**]: Eve's sin was worse than Adam's because (1) its effect, her punishment was worse, (2) the cause of her sin was the unforgivable act against the Holy Spirit of believing she was like God, and (3) she caused, by her suggestion, Adam's sin, but he did not cause hers.

[**Isotta**]: "But I see things — since you moved me to reply — from quite another and contrary viewpoint." Eve must be judged less guilty than Adam. "For where there is less intellect and less constancy, there is less sin; and Eve [lacked sense and constancy] and therefore sinned less."

Adam must be judged more guilty than Eve because God commanded him (not them) not to eat the fruit, and he, in greater contempt, broke this command.[31]

Further, Eve ate the fruit not because she believed she was like God, but because of her weakness and attraction to pleasure.

In addition, if Eve alone had sinned, it would have only affected her but had no effects on the human race, but Adam's sin affected all future generations, so the man's sin had a greater effect than the woman's.[32]

Finally, it is wrong to conclude that Eve's punishment was worse than Adam's because although she was condemned to pain in bringing forth children, longing for her husband, and being under his dominion, Adam was condemned to toil in his work, and to eventually die (returning to dust). Since death is the most terrible punishment that can be received, Adam's punishment was worse than Eve's.[33]

Isotta employs an ironic appeal to gender polarity that devalues women (i.e., woman's weakness, inconstancy, attraction to pleasure) to prove her conclusion

31. Isotta's claims are consistently backed up by quotations from the relevant passages in Scripture, especially from *Genesis*.

32. Although Isotta refers to Scripture (a letter of St. Paul) to defend this claim, it was a common understanding of the effect of Aristotelian theory of generation, that the soul is provided in generation by the father alone, and scholastic integration of this teaching into the theological claim that original sin is passed down from generation to generation through the soul and not through the body.

33. Nogarola, "Of the Equal or Unequal," in *Her Immaculate Hand*, ed. King and Rabil, pp. 59-60. Isotta argues that the language of Scripture supports her claims: "notice that God appears to have admonished Adam alone [using the singular form of 'you'] and not Eve." . . . "For God said to Adam: 'to dust you shall return,' and not to Eve . . ." (p. 60).

that woman's sin was less reprehensible than man's. Conversely, gender polarity extolling man's superiority (i.e., greater intelligence and constancy) ascribes greater responsibility to man. She hints that because the devil knew man was more constant, he avoided testing him (and so woman became the scapegoat), and because man was more intelligent, God gave him the command (and so woman did not know it directly). Both of these subsidiary claims lead to the conclusion that woman was less culpable.

The global structure of the above argument is that one cannot both claim that woman is weaker by nature and that woman is more culpable for Original Sin. Therefore, by a *reductio ad absurdum* argument woman's weakness may be disproved. In other words, Ludovico claims that Eve's blame for the causes and effects of sin is greater than Adam's. This conclusion is doubly ironic as it inverts Augustine's original premise that Adam and Eve sinned unequally according to sex, and that the woman's sin was worse than the man's. In Isotta's argument, man and woman's alleged inequality ends with a greater responsibility on man's part.

Isotta adds a short ironic disclaimer that suggests an awareness that she is entering into the traditionally male domain of discursive reasoning and debate, but also invites a response: "I have written this because you wished me to. Yet I have done so fearfully, since this is not a woman's task. But you are kind, and if you find any part of my writing clumsy you will correct it."[34] Her partner, Ludovico, responds with the humorous reflection that he would accept her argument on its own basis, except for the fact that he is a man (and presumably does not like the conclusions it leads to), and so he will try to attack the foundations she used to build her case. This passage indicates that both Isotta and Ludovico were aware of their engendered identity and its role in lending perspective to a dialogue about gender identity.

> [**Ludovico**]: You defend the cause of Eve most subtly, and indeed defend it so [well] that, if I had not been born a man, you would have made me your champion. But sticking fast to the truth, which is attached by very strong roots, I have set out [here] to assault your fortress with your own weapons. I shall begin by attacking its foundations, which can be destroyed by the testimony of Sacred Scripture, so that there will be no lack of material for my refutation.[35]

The second part argues that weakness of character is no excuse. Again, I summarize with direct quotations delineated by quotation marks:

> [**Ludovico**]: You argue that because Eve is ignorant and inconstant her sin is less culpable. But ignorance is no excuse. Just as Aristotle, who teaches true philosophy in the *Ethics*, argued that a drunk and ignorant person is doubly to blame.
>
> Inconstancy is also no excuse, and it is even more blameworthy than ignorance. Evil acts issuing from inconstancy, which is also an evil, are doubly to blame.

---

34. Isotta Nogarola, "Of the Equal and Unequal," in *Her Immaculate Hand,* ed. King and Rabil, p. 61.

35. Nogarola, "Of the Equal and Unequal," in *Her Immaculate Hand,* ed. King and Rabil, p. 61.

"Also, woman's fragility was not the cause of sin, as you write, but her pride," for she acted because she was promised new knowledge. In fact, Augustine tells us: "The first impulse [of sin], therefore, was an inordinate appetite for seeking that which was not suited to its own nature," for Eve was tempted when the serpent offered her to "be like God, knowing good and evil." Her sin was so bad that I may even, jokingly, be allowed to say that it might not have warranted, like the fallen angels, the Redemption of Christ. Fortunately, Adam's sin did.

In addition, your claim that the effect of sin was worse for Adam, who was condemned to death, does not take into account the fact that Eve, and all women, also suffer this effect of death. In fact, woman suffers all the effects of man plus the pains of giving birth. Therefore her punishment and her sin are worse.[36]

Ludovico rejects the gender polarity starting point, with its devaluation of woman, as an excuse for bad actions. He states that it was not woman's natural weakness of intellect, inconstancy, or her fragility that caused her to make a bad choice, but rather her inordinate appetite or pride, which flowed from a free choice to be like God.

The dialogue continues with Ludovico attempting to put forward new support for the greater culpability of Eve. A summary of his ensuing arguments of the third phase of the dialogue is offered below again with direct quotations placed inside quotation marks:

[**Ludovico**]: Aristotle states in *Posterior Analytics* that "the cause of a cause is the cause of that which is caused. Indeed, every prior cause influences an outcome more than a secondary cause." Since the cause of Adam's sin was Eve's prior choice, Eve sinned much more than Adam.

Further, "Just as it is better to treat others well than to be well-treated, so it is worse to persuade another person to do something evil than to be persuaded to do evil by someone else." Since Eve persuaded Adam by her prior example, Eve sinned much more than Adam.

In addition, if we assume that Eve is inferior by nature to Adam, and that they both thought they were "worthy of the same glory" by choosing to eat the fruit, then Eve departed further from the mean by her choice than did Adam, and so Eve sinned much more than Adam.

Moreover, Eve took advantage of Adam's vulnerability and love for her to deceive him, while the serpent, who had no such relation with her, deceived her just the same. So Eve sinned much more than Adam.

Even the fact that Eve sinned for a longer time, beginning first, than did Adam contributes to the conclusion that Eve sinned much more than Adam.

Finally, because Eve was the cause, and example of the sin of betrayal for Adam, Eve sinned much more than Adam.[37]

---

36. Nogarola, "Of the Equal and Unequal," in *Her Immaculate Hand,* ed. King and Rabil, pp. 61-62.

37. Nogarola, "Of the Equal and Unequal," in *Her Immaculate Hand,* ed. King and Rabil, pp. 62-63.

In this set of arguments we find Ludovico introducing new themes related to woman as cause of deception, persuasion, and seducing man away from his true end. He also invokes ideas from Aristotle's *Prior Analytics* and *Ethics* to support his gender-specific claims. Isotta Nogarola demonstrates a real understanding of these concepts. She understands that according to Aristotle's *Ethics* the mean is the ethical measure of virtue between two extremes. Since the mean is supposed to be measured relative to an individual, she argues, if woman were naturally inferior, then the choice of knowledge appropriate for the higher glory of God would be the choice of an even greater extreme, and therefore not a good choice.

In the next part of the dialogue Ludovico says that, although his conclusions are consistent with most Christian theorists, Isotta should not be afraid to contradict him: "Farewell, and do not fear, but dare to do much, because you have excellently understood so much and write so learnedly."[38] Isotta fears that the dialogue is turning into an assault rather than a discussion, but she persists in developing her side of the argument. Once again, their awareness of their gender as participants in a dialogue about gender is remarkable:

> [**Isotta**]: "I had decided that I would not enter further into a contest with you because, as you say, you assault my fortress with my own weapons. [The propositions] you have presented me were so perfectly and diligently defended that it would be difficult not merely for me, but for the most learned men, to oppose them. But since I recognize that this contest is useful for me, I have decided to obey your honest wish. Even though I know I struggle in vain, yet I will earn the highest praise if I am defeated by so mighty a man as you."[39]

A summary of Isotta's arguments in the beginning of the fourth phase of the dialogue is as follows:

> [**Isotta**]: Your claim that ignorance and inconstancy are no excuse does not work because Eve's ignorance and inconstancy were innate, and implanted by nature, and not the result of character and past bad actions.
>
> The same argument holds for her imperfection. Man [male human beings] was created perfect in understanding, knowledge of truth, and wisdom. Woman was created for man's consolation. Therefore, since more was given to man, his sin was greater.
>
> Your argument that woman's pride, not her fragility, was the cause of her sin is not accurate. Aristotle tells us in the *Metaphysics* that all men [human beings] naturally desire to know, and woman sinned through the desire to know the difference between good and evil. Man, on the other hand, went directly against a commandment of God, and transgressions of commandments are caused by

---

38. Nogarola, "Of the Equal and Unequal," in *Her Immaculate Hand,* ed. King and Rabil, p. 63.

39. Nogarola, "Of the Equal and Unequal," in *Her Immaculate Hand,* ed. King and Rabil, p. 63.

pride. So man, and not woman, sinned through pride, and man, not woman, had the greater sin.

In response to your joke that woman's sin was so bad that it did not merit redemption, we can take two [equally humorous] options. First, we could argue that because woman was made from Adam's flesh and bone, when Adam was redeemed, she was too. Second, we could argue that if she was not redeemed, it was because God thought that her sin was so negligible that she did not need redemption. Further, the angels, being intellectual beings, sinned from desire for power, but woman, being rational, sinned only from the desire for knowledge. So the analogy does not work.

Also the "severity of the punishment is proportional to the severity of the sin." Christ's free choice of crucifixion on the cross was the most severe punishment that could be because in his suffering he took upon himself all the suffering of women and men ("on the cross he endured in general every kind of suffering by type"). Augustine tells us that Christ restored what Adam ("and he does not say Eve") lost, so Adam's sin was the greatest possible sin.[40]

In all of her examples, we find Isotta using traditional gender polarity texts or theories (which begin with the premise of some kind of inferiority of woman) to prove that man was more culpable than woman. She consistently undermines the logic of the classical theological texts by introducing philosophical distinctions and theological reflections on Scriptures and writings of the Church Fathers. Again, she places before Ludovico the uncomfortable paradox, namely, that if woman is inferior by nature, then she ought not to be blamed more than man for evil in the world.

In the fifth phase of the dialogue, Isotta again makes ironic use of the gender polarity themes of woman's natural inferiority to prove man's moral inferiority:

[Isotta]: Your use of Aristotle's theory that "whatever is the cause of the cause is the cause of the thing caused" to prove that Eve caused Adam's sin does not work in the argument, because Aristotle is referring to the first principle, or God who is perfect, while you were referring to Eve who is not a first cause, and who is imperfect. Furthermore, if Adam did not have free will, then he did not sin; and if he had free will, he could not be forced to sin by Eve. "Yet only something that is superior to something else can force it, but Eve was inferior to Adam, therefore she was not herself the cause of sin."[41]

In response to your argument that woman could more easily deceive man than the serpent deceive the woman, I answer that Eve sinned less by listening to the "wise" serpent than did Adam by listening to the persuasive voice of the "imperfect" woman.

In addition, your argument that woman is more culpable because she sinned longer is fallacious because it depends upon the presumption that "the two sins

40. Nogarola, "Of the Equal and Unequal," in *Her Immaculate Hand,* ed. King and Rabil, pp. 63-65.

41. In her analysis Isotta also argues that man appeared to accuse God as the cause of his sin since he blamed him for actions of the woman whom God had placed at his side.

are equal, and in the same person or in two similar persons. But Adam and Eve were not equals, because Adam was a perfect animal and Eve imperfect and ignorant." Therefore, the time of their sins is not comparable.

Finally, Christ condemned sins not because they were first, but because they had malicious or vicious motives and were done as betrayals by people whom he loved.[42]

Ludovico cannot hold both the gender polarity theory, which devalues woman by nature, and a gender polarity theory in moral theology, which holds woman as the greater sinner.

Isotta ironically remarks: "Let these words be enough for me, an unarmed and poor little woman."[43] She is hardly "unarmed," and she is hardly a "poor little woman." Despite her irony, the tone of the dialogue is always civil between the two participants. It never slides into the *ad hominem* forms we previously saw in Christine de Pizan's *Querelle de la rose* or in satires and witchcraft interrogations. Isotta has carefully crafted a dialogue, based on real letters exchanged in an intergender relationship, ready to be shared by others within an emerging intergender humanist culture.

In the conclusion of her argument "Of the Equal or Unequal Sin of Adam and Eve", a new kind of balance is brought about in the conversation. She gives Ludovico the final word, but it is developed by her in an interesting way; namely, his arguments nearly all fail to meet the core of her argument — they fail by side-stepping the issues. After Ludovico's praise for the quality of her arguments, which seem to him to be divinely inspired and not open to contradiction, he responds to her invitation to continue: "Yet, lest you be cheated of the utility [you say you have begun to receive from this debate], attend to these brief arguments which can be posed for the opposite view, that you may sow the honey-sweet seeds of paradise which will delight readers and surround you with glory."[44] Again we perceive the mutual respect that, at the same time, allows for serious disagreement about the issue at hand.

Ludovico's final arguments are as follows:

[**Ludovico**]: Any ignorance that Eve had was due to her own actions, and therefore it cannot be used to excuse her sin. In fact, her choice to follow the advice of the serpent rather than the dictates of God was extremely stupid.

Further any inconstancy Eve had was not due to nature but to habit. "Actually, woman's nature was excellent and concordant with reason, genus and time. For just as teeth were given to wild beasts, horns to oxen, feathers to birds for their survival, to the woman mental capacity was given sufficient for the preservation and pursuit of the health of her soul."

42. Nogarola, "Of Equal and Unequal," in *Her Immaculate Hand,* ed. King and Rabil, pp. 66-67.

43. Nogarola, "Of the Equal and Unequal," in *Her Immaculate Hand,* ed. King and Rabil, p. 67.

44. Nogarola, "Of the Equal and Unequal," in *Her Immaculate Hand,* ed. King and Rabil, p. 67.

In addition, if you argue that woman was created for man's consolation, then it follows that woman acted against her nature when she brought him great sorrow. In fact, her harming another person deserves greater punishment in line with human law in which the more that seizing another person's goods harms that person, the more serious the punishment ought to be.

Also, you cannot accuse man and acquit woman of the transgression of God's commandments, because she did not keep them either.[45]

There is not enough space to respond to your argument which uses a distinction between the intelligence of angels and the reason of women to conclude that Eve's sin was less serious, although "it is a huge issue . . . [and it] provides worthy food for your brilliant mind."[46]

I cannot understand how you can claim that the greater punishments (death, childbearing, and subjection to man) are given by God to those who have sinned less, because that would be incompatible with understanding God as being the principle of the highest goodness.[47]

In addition, you too strictly limit what Aristotle says about first causes, for every cause of a cause is a cause of a thing caused. And because Adam had free will, I do not make him immune to committing wrong; and although I attributed every fault of Adam in some degree to Eve, nevertheless Eve was not the complete cause in every respect.[48]

I agree with you about free will and the goodness of human nature. And I, because you are a woman, will avoid speaking about the deceitfulness of the female sex, although an ancient proverb attests to the fact that an enemy in the family is like the most harmful plague. And Eve, the first mother, set a wild fire, which is still not put out, and which is filled with diseases of the soul.[49]

In his conclusion, Ludovico invites Isotta who is "most learned," "most brilliant," and who has "great goodness," to revise his clumsy arguments in order to make them "very evident and clear" to other readers. Once again we perceive the cooperative nature of their intergender dialogue when we read Ludovico's analogy with military battle in the final lines of the text:

45. This argument misses the point of Isotta, because she claimed that Eve was not given the commandments in the first place; they were given only to Adam.

46. Again Ludovico slips past the argument here without a counterargument.

47. Ludovico does not understand Isotta's argument here. It is complex in that it involves two separate phases: first that Christ took on himself atonement for all the suffering due to punishment for sin of all women as well as all men, and that Scripture argues that Christ did this because of Adam's sin. Second, without this transformation of sin through the redemptive suffering of Christ, there would be a problem in claiming that woman, who sinned less, was condemned by God to suffer more.

48. Translation of this passage is by Joseph Moller, as it heightens the distinctions being made. Note that Ludovico does not answer Isotta's argument here either. Isotta argued that because of Adam's free will, Eve is not the cause of his actions in any respect.

49. Here Ludovico sidesteps the issue of whether woman is naturally deceitful, but he concludes by blaming Eve for subsequent diseases of the soul. This image of woman infecting like the plague, or setting on fire, has echoes of the witchcraft trials and punishments studied in chapter 6. He concludes his argument by linking it back to Augustine's original claim. The whole of his argument is found in Nogarola, "Of the Unequal and Equal," in *Her Immaculate Hand,* ed. King and Rabil, pp. 67-68.

[**Ludovico**]: "For you march forward to new battles to the sound of sacred eloquence (as do soldiers to the clamor of trumpets), always more learned and more ready. And you march forward against me, who has applied the whole sum of my thinking to my reading, all at the same time, and to my writing, that I might present my case and defend myself against yours, although the many storms and floods of my obligations toss me about at whim."[50]

At this point it is fairly obvious to the attentive reader that while Isotta allows Ludovico to have the last word in the dialogue, it is actually her own views that prevail precisely through the structure of the argument. For her main theme has been consistently this: if woman is weak, inconstant, fragile, etc. then she does not hold the greater culpability for Original Sin. In addition, Ludovico claims that if (1) woman has rational powers, (2) error is due to bad habit, not nature, (3) women as well as men have free will, and (4) nature is good, then it follows that Eve is equal to Adam and women equal to men in terms of culpability for sin in the world.

Recently, Margaret King has come to a different conclusion about the meaning of Isotta Nogarola and Ludovico Foscarini's dialogue. She argues that: "Ludovico emerges the victor," or "Ludovico clearly won" the debate.[51] King's argument is based on the observations that Ludovico opens the debate, has the last word, and that Isotta develops her defense of Eve "paradoxically, on the weakness of female nature."[52] I would like to suggest a different set of conclusions, which indicate that if there is to be a victor at all, it ought to be only on the first level of the debate that Ludovico wins the argument. However, there are two further levels of the debate in which Isotta emerges as the clear winner. These levels involve a complex disjunctive argument and the counterexample to the original premises of the argument provided by Isotta herself. After all, she is the author of the dialogue, and she chose exactly the opening and closing of the text. Furthermore, the unfolding of the argument avoided the pitfalls of all forms of *ad hominem* attacks that we have seen in previous examples of intergender dialogue about gender. Therefore, it would be better to consider Ludovico and Isotta as joint winners because they were able to engage in fruitful complement dialogue about gender with one another.

In order to help demonstrate the claims just made above, the chart on the following page traces the three different levels of argument in the dialogue with respect to woman's identity.

We can see by this analysis that to conclude that Ludovico is the winner of the dialogue is to limit the analysis to the woman's part of the first level and the man's part of the second level instead of recognizing the third level of the argu-

50. Nogarola, "Of the Equal and Unequal," in *Her Immaculate Hand,* ed. King and Rabil, p. 69.

51. King, "The Religious Retreat," *Signs* 3, no. 4 (1978): 820; and *Her Immaculate Hand,* ed. King and Rabil, p. 59.

52. This attitude that Isotta Nogarola accepted a gender polarity view of women's weaknesses is found in King, "Book-lined Cells," in *Renaissance Humanism,* ed. Rabil, vol. 1, p. 438; and "Thwarted Ambitions," *Soundings* 59, no. 3 (Fall 1976): 288. See also "The Religious Retreat," *Signs* 3, no. 4 (1978): 820.

Isotta Nogarola's Levels of Argument in the Dialogue about Adam and Eve			
	Proponent of the argument	Logical Form of the argument	Gender-Related Content in the argument
First level	**Tradition:** Augustine/ Aristotle	**Conjunction:** Woman (Eve) is imperfect and more to blame for sin than is Adam.	Variations: Woman's imperfection includes: ignorance, inconstancy, fragility, weakness, deceptiveness, lack of control of emotions, the cause of man's downfall, full of pride.
Second level: woman's part	Isotta in the intergender dialogue	**Hypothetical:** If woman is imperfect, then she is not the more blameworthy one.	If woman has the above imperfections placed in her innately by nature, she cannot be held responsible for what she causes through them.
Second level: man's part	Ludovico in the intergender dialogue	**Denial of one conjunct:** Woman is not imperfect, therefore she is still the more blameworthy one.	Woman does not have the above imperfections by nature, but by bad habit, and so she can be held responsible for them. Woman's nature is good and perfect, but by poor use of her reason and free will she sins and she causes others to sin.
Third level: woman's and man's complementary parts	Isotta as author of dialogue	**Counterexample:** The dialogue itself demonstrates by example that woman is not imperfect and that she is not to blame.	Isotta as author is perfect, knowledgeable, constant, agile, strong, truthful, in control of her emotions, the help for man's enlightenment, and humble. The dynamics of the dialogue has no sin in it, as it is a balanced exchange in true friendship.

ment, or the careful crafting of the argument as a written dialogue. It also means to ignore that Isotta assumes the traditional position in order to prove it wrong by a form of the *reductio ad absurdum* argument. Her consistent claim is that both premises cannot be true, namely, that woman is imperfect by nature, and that she holds the greater blame for sin. Ludovico accepts that much of the structure of her argument and chooses to argue that woman is not imperfect by nature, she is only imperfect through bad choices and bad habits. Counterexamples of women without bad habits only refute the generalization that all women have bad habits. However, Ludovico still argues that woman has the greater blame, which certainly suggests a universal generalization. Isotta as the author of the dialogue challenges his universal generalization. The dialogue is a medium through which the ancients are defeated and the conclusion reached that neither man nor woman has the greater blame *per se,* but they both are called to a life of wisdom and virtue, and in complement they may help one another achieve these goals.

The quality of the intergender dialogue itself between Ludovico and Isotta is a significant counterargument to its ironically proposed claim that woman is weak, inconstant, imperfect, fragile, etc. Isotta demonstrates a strength in forcefully making a point, a constancy in considering the specific issues at hand, a successful integration of scholarly sources, and an alacrity in responding to different challenges by her opponent. The dialogue demonstrates the virtues of friendship, moderation, courage, temperance, and both practical and theoretical wisdom. We suggest that this friendship involves all three levels identified by Aristotle: pleasure, utility, and concern for the good of the other. Furthermore, friendship is based on equality rather than inequality despite the gender difference between the two participants. Isotta Nogarola is significant for being the first person in western history to portray an intergender dialogue about gender that contains real disagreements about gender identity defended by a man and a woman, and that demonstrates a genuine complementarity of interaction.

A Woman Humanist's Search for Meaning

We are told that when Isotta was only 18, she initiated intergender dialogue with many different men from political, religious, and humanist contexts.[53] In a letter written in 1434 to the Protonotario Barbaro, Isotta demonstrates a sense of humor about the historical satirical association of talkativeness with the concept of women, knowledge of classical sources, and the humanist epistolary or oratorical skill:

Peter, the judge, evidently a most learned man, was seen to laugh well and truly at some men, who, though mute and tongueless themselves, were the critics of

---

53. King, "Thwarted Ambitions," *Soundings* 59, no. 3 (Fall 1976): 283. Margaret King has done outstanding work in providing excellent bibliographies about Isotta Nogarola. I am extremely grateful for her pioneering work in bringing Nogarola's writings and their historical context to the attention of English-speaking readers.

others and thought themselves born of Minerva while they listened to an oration of Cicero or some verses of Virgil. He said this after someone had woven a verse into meter and arranged the subtle sense of the words into a rhetorical frame, and thus thought himself to have immediately arrived on the Helicon mountain. I am afraid that the same thing will befall me, Most Reverend Father, when I dare to come into the public with these humanist studies, which I have not yet touched upon with my voice, and do not hesitate to publish my writings or rather my absurdities which will be examined by critics, and most of all [I do not hesitate] to write to you, a man who is in a position of honour, and is justly endowed with modesty, humanity, seriousness, excellence in eloquence, and knowledge of Pontifical Law. But among many, my own sex will be sufficient to excuse me in this regard, since it is very difficult to find a mute woman, as our satirist says. . . .

[Isotta then gives an oration of praise to Barbaro, and she concludes by returning to the concept of speech in a woman.]

So that truly I do not seem to you, with my words, to be too talkative even if your praise asks for an overabundant oration, I will put an end to my writing, so that it cannot be deservedly said against me what Aristotle said to some verbose man, who, when he joined in a gathering of men, the others ran away, so that the words could produce no feeling of repugnance. When he complained of this very thing to Aristotle, Aristotle said: I wonder even that those who have feet wait for you. So, you have a verbose letter as a testament of my love for you, which, if it is not unpleasant, I shall be pleased that I have not uselessly taken up this trouble of writing. Farewell.[54]

In this example we can see Isotta ironically using both the satirical claim that a woman cannot keep silent and an Aristotelian observation that people run away from a talkative person. Her irony is developed with wit when she expresses her purpose to write an oration of praise for a worthy man and, thus, it is permissible for her, a woman, to speak. Because her speech is put in the proper form of an eloquent oration, it is appropriate.

In another letter, written to Antonio Bonromco in 1436-37, during this early period in Isotta's life, we see her confronting the bias of men who disregard the contributions of women to the study of wisdom and virtue. In this letter, Isotta includes herself among ancient models of wise women, including Plato's disciples. She also offers some of her letters to Bonromco, whom she hopes will provide her with funds to purchase books. She states:

I had determined many times to give you my uncultivated and common letters, but when I thought it over by myself, about how many men there were, if they can be called men, who say that letters written by females are a disease and a

54. Isotta Nogarola to the Protonotario Barbaro, S.P.D. (1434), in *Isotae Nogarolae Veronensis Opera Quae Supersunt Omnia* (Vindobonae: Gerold et Socios, 1886), vol. 1, pp. 6-12. Translated by Joseph Moller, as are all other passages from this text unless otherwise noted.

public plague, I deterred myself right from the beginning. Truly, as it seems to me, they are a plague of men suffering under someone else's praise, who think that nothing is correct except that which they do or think; for this comes about from perversity and ignorance of mind. For I certainly know that they do not read what illustrious and outstanding women write, with well-deserved praise, women who spend all their time, effort, care, and study in virtue. The Muses themselves were women and taught and made great men and inspired famous poets. Certainly there was no disgrace to Maro [Virgil] who calling forth their deeds sang. . . .

In Plato it is certain that women had time for divine philosophy; I mean, of course, Lastheneia, Mantinea, and Axiothea Philasia, who they say put on men's clothes for the purpose of dialogue. In how many verses is Cornelia, the mother of the Gracchi, sung about? Our ancestors relate with deserved and everlasting fame that Christiana, the wife of Adelphus, a woman of outstanding quality and religion, was so educated that she is said to have held the entire poem of Virgil in her memory and wrote about the New Testament beautifully and distinctly. Since this is so, do letters [written] by females stand out as the cause and foundation of all evils, do they deprive females of their dignity? Or [do they] increase their admiration, since women surpass not only females in excellence, but also men.[55]

Isotta found a patron enabling her to continue to study by purchasing for her an important text of Livy that had recently come up for sale. In addition, Isotta invited him to compare biased public views against the writings of women with actual works she had composed. Thus, Isotta Nogarola initiated an intergender dialogue about gender in the context of broader humanist issues. In this early phase of her search for affirmation as a scholar and writer, she succeeded in establishing herself because her work was financially supported by Antonio Bonromco.

In 1436 the humanist Jacopo Foscari sent copies of some of Isotta's and some of Ginerva Nogarola's writings to Guarino of Verona. The following extract of a letter from Guarino to Foscari indicates the older humanist educator's considered response both to the humanist qualities of the writing as well as to the nationalist value of their contributions:

On this above all I bestow my admiration: such is the likeness of each sister's expression, such the similarity of style, such the sisterhood of writing and indeed the splendour of both their parts, that if you were to remove the names Ginerva and Isotta you would not easily be able to judge which name you should place before which; so that anyone who is acquainted with either knows both together. Thus they are not simply sisters in birth and nobility of stock, but also in style and readiness of speech.

Oh the glory indeed of our State and our Age! Of how rare a bird on earth, like nothing so much as a black swan! If earlier ages had honoured these proven virgins, with how many verses would their praises have been sung, how many de-

55. Isotta Nogarola, *Opera,* I, 42-44.

served praises from truly unstinting authors would have consigned them to immortality![56]

Guarino likens educated women to the black swan, a favorite example of logic texts
about something that is logically possible, but is never empirically observable.
Thus, Guarino reveals his complete and utter lack of acquaintance with educated
women.

Guarino decided to send copies of Isotta's and Ginevra's compositions to
Leonello d'Este and promote them in letters to other humanists. As a result of this
public recognition, the nineteen-year-old Isotta initiated a correspondence with the
sixty-three-year-old founder of the humanist school in Verona. Her first letter went
unanswered simply because Guarino was otherwise occupied at the time. However, the men and women in Verona interpreted this fact in a derogatory manner,
consistent with gender stereotypes. Consequently, Isotta wrote a second letter in
which she directly addressed the place of gender in the situation:

> There are already so many women in the world! Why then was I born a woman,
> to be scorned by men in words and deeds? I ask myself this question in solitude. I
> do not dare to ask it of you, who have made me the butt of everyone's jokes. Your
> unfairness in not writing to me has caused me the greatest suffering.
> . . . I was happy when I wrote you that letter. I even thought you would praise
> me, since you yourself had said that there was no goal I could not achieve. But
> now that nothing has turned out as it should have, my joy has given way to sor-
> row. You might have cared for me more if I had never been born. For they jeer at
> me throughout the city, the women mock me. [I, a woman, in turning to you, a
> man, am like a donkey yoked to an ox; when I fall in the mud, as I must, when
> dragged by so strong a beast, neither my own kind, nor yours, will have anything
> to do with me.] I cannot find a quiet stable to hide in, and the donkeys tear me
> with their teeth, the oxen stab me with their horns.[57]

Isotta Nogarola's intensely emotional response, with its derogatory animal metaphors, bitterness towards other women's attitudes, accusations of lack of fairness,
imputation of a motive of scorn in Guarino, and self-pity about the worth of her
life, betray the depth of insecurity about her value as a writer and humanist. Her
search for affirmation by the renowned educator Guarino appears desperate in this
letter.

Guarino of Verona did respond to this letter and, always the educator, he clarified where Isotta made hasty judgments and where she was accurate. His response
reveals also another kind of bias, namely that a woman who develops virtue is developing "the man in the woman." We see the rough give-and-take of correction
and challenge between an older man and a younger woman who both are not yet
free of gender polarity presumptions.

56. Guarino, translated in Grafton and Jardine, eds., *From Humanism to Humanities,* 35.
57. Isotta Nogarola ad Guarinum Veronensem (c. April 1437), *Opera,* I, 79-83. See also King,
"Thwarted Ambitions," *Soundings* 59, no. 3 (Fall 1976): 285.

Guarino, in line with Plato in the *Republic,* challenges Isotta to perceive her female identity simply as a weaker starting point of nature, but not as in any way ultimately limiting. Instead of blaming nature, she should have worked towards her own perfection.

> Because you were born a female, you complain and therefore feel and show your-self to be unfortunate, when you ought to have conducted yourself in the oppo-site fashion, so that you should ascribe sex, on the one hand, to nature, and a loft-iness of mind, to virtue. This kind of declaration, these studies or the imitation of outstanding persons guarantee, [and] which history, the teacher of life, sows for you like a most fertile field. . . .
>
> The self-same knowledge and correct recollection of deeds must make you happy, cheerful, smiling, high-spirited, resolute, and a man in a woman, what-ever happens when you are laughed at, as you say, and even when your own class mocks you and asses taunt you by biting, and bulls taunt you with their horns.[58]

This line about becoming a man in a woman, taken by itself, seems to imply that Guarino was suggesting that Isotta deny her sex altogether. However, when the let-ter is studied as a whole, it appears that the older humanist is also open to a new understanding of woman's virtue while he gropes for a way to express what was commonly considered a masculine virtue.[59]

Guarino asks Isotta to stop battling against him, as she had in her accusatory second letter. Instead, she should join the battle with him against her real enemies. In an intriguing way Guarino suggests that her female nature is not naturally un-disciplined but rather governed and moderate. He suggests that they may shift from a master-and-student relationship (or worse, from one devalued into the ani-mal-like nature of ox and donkey) into one of fellow soldiers, and in doing so, he links Isotta with previous positive models of women.

> Well then Isotta, most steadfast female warrior, call yourself back and now sound the signal for retreat, and prepare to bring out the battle line on the other side with me against your enemies, using me as your leader or finally as a fellow sol-dier. With you, because you were born a woman, moderation is in control; Dido was clearly a most chaste female, [and] Cornelia, the mother of the Gracchi, what more? Finally the Muses call to mind that they were themselves females, who instructed, taught, and made famous great men and divine poets.[60]

---

58. From Guarinus of Verona to Isotta (1437), I, 84-85. King translates "class" by "sex" ("Thwarted Ambitions," *Soundings* 59, no. 3 [Fall 1976]: 285).

59. My interpretation of this exchange is thus different from that of Margaret King, who argues that Guarino "must have conveyed to Isotta that because she was a woman, she was at fault, and that she could only succeed in setting her sex aside . . ." ("Thwarted Ambitions," 285). I would argue that this is only part of the message: the deeper challenge he gave was to become a strong and virtuous woman, and to stop feeling sorry for herself, or blaming others by hiding behind a perceived weakness of her nature as female.

60. Guarino to Isotta, *Opera,* I, 88.

We could say that at this point, the decision as to direction of intergender dialogue is left in Isotta's hands.

In the following year (1438) Isotta Nogarola became the innocent victim of a malicious attack on her character. A male humanist writer from Verona, using the satirical pseudonym "Pliny," wrote a public letter to another satirist "Ovid" accusing Isotta of promiscuity and incest with her brother.[61] The accusation included suggestions of sexual improprieties of other men and women as well. The content of this letter of false accusation draws upon traditional satirical views of woman's identity and applies them directly, with full weight of scandal, to the individual woman, Isotta Nogarola. It made two direct biased claims: that woman in general has no control over her passions, and that "an eloquent woman" or a woman "who dares to engage so deeply in the finest literary studies" in particular "is never chaste" and "sets no limit in this filthy lust." One can only imagine the suffering this must have caused to Isotta.

The accusations were seen to be maliciously false, and they were at the time publicly rejected by Niccolò Barbo and other writers. However, many other local persons believed them, and they created an atmosphere of ridicule for Isotta just as she was attempting to gain confidence in her identity as a woman humanist. Because of this impact of the slander it is important to repeat the false accusations here:

> Let us cease to wonder at all these things, when that second unmarried sister, who has won such praise for her eloquence, does things which little befit her erudition and reputation — although this saying of many wise men I hold to be true: that an eloquent woman is never chaste; and the behavior of many learned women also confirms its truth. . . . But lest you approve even slightly this excessively foul and obscene crime, let me explain that before she made her body generally available for promiscuous intercourse, she had first permitted — and indeed even earnestly desired — that the seal of her virginity be broke by none other than her brother, so that by this tie she might be more tightly bound to him. Alas for God in whom men trust, who does not mingle heaven with earth nor the sea with heaven, when she, who sets herself no limit in this filthy lust, dares to engage so deeply in the finest literary studies.[62]

The satirical qualities of the letter are most obvious — that learning increases lack of self-governance rather than the opposite, i.e., that learning helps develop self-knowledge and self-governance as both the religious and humanist writers have so consistently argued. It would appear that even if it was meant as satirical humor, it had a deep effect on Isotta, for she withdrew and moved to Venice. She lived there for about three years, until Venice was caught in war and an outbreak of the plague occurred. She returned to Verona in 1441 with a decision to live a single, reclusive, celibate life, and to devote herself quietly to a life of study.

61. King and Rabil, eds., *Her Immaculate Hand*, introduction, p. 17.
62. The relevant passage is translated by Margaret King, in "The Religious Retreat of Isotta Nogarola (1418-1466): Sexism and Its Consequences in the Fifteenth Century," *Signs: Journal of Women in Culture and Society* 3, no. 4 (1978): 807-22, esp. 809.

During the next several years we discover the maturing of the humanist writer and thinker. At this point Isotta's brother intervened to support his sister's education, by writing to Lauro Quirini, another student of Guarino of Verona. Quirini responded:

> Your brother, Leonardo . . . asked me some time ago if I would write something to you, seeing that at this time you are devoting extremely zealous study (as he terms it) to dialectic and philosophy. He was anxious for me to impress upon you, in most solid and friendly fashion, which masters above all you ought to follow in these higher disciplines.[63]

Most important for our study is the phrase "you are devoting extremely zealous study to dialectic and philosophy." This indicates that Isotta was already struggling on her own to learn the structure of disputation and fundamental components in the history of philosophy. Thus it is not surprising that she was able to enter into the sophisticated tri-level argument analyzed in the previous section of this chapter.

The humanist Quirini, however, offers even more helpful guidelines for Isotta's continued growth in relation to philosophy. He suggests that she go back to the original sources rather than read contemporary examples of scholastic debate:

> I absolutely insist, and I place the weight of my authority behind this, that you avoid and shun the new philosophers and new dialecticians as men minimally schooled in true philosophy and true dialectic, and that furthermore you harden your heart against all their writings. For they do not teach the approach to the old tried and tested discipline of dialectic, but obscure the clear and lucid path of this study with goodness knows what childish quibbles, inextricable circuities and pedantic ambiguities. And while seeming to know a great deal, they distort the most readily intelligible matters with a kind of futile subtlety. . . . On which account, having been diverted by these obstacles, they are unable to aspire to the true philosophy, in which indeed, although they wish to seem sagacious debaters, they let slip the truth, as the old saying goes, with excessive cross-examination.[64]

The distinction between dialectic used for the pursuit of truth and used for simply winning an argument is well made by Quirini. In addition, he points out a value distinction between the humanist approach and the academic approach to the study of philosophy.

Next, Quirini lists the names of the philosophers along with some texts that he would recommend Isotta "should follow [and] [r]ead studiously."[65] They in-

---

63. Quirini, translated in Grafton and Jardine, *From Humanism to the Humanities,* pp. 29-30. The original sources are cited as *Lauro Quirini umanista,* ed. Branca (Florence, 1977), and Eugenius Abel, *Isotae Nogarolae veronensis opera quae supersunt omnia, accedunt Angelae et Zeneverae Nogarolae epistolae et carmina,* 2 vols. (Vienna: apud Gerold et socios; Budapest: apud Fridericum Kilian, 1886).

64. Quirini, translated by Grafton and Jardine, *From Humanism to the Humanities,* p. 30.

65. Quirini, translated by Grafton and Jardine, *From Humanism to the Humanities,* p. 31.

clude Boethius's Latin translations of Aristotle's *Categories* and *De interpretatione,* direct translations of Aristotle's natural philosophy, metaphysics, and ethics, Averroes, and Avicenna's commentaries on Aristotle's philosophy, and works of Thomas Aquinas. In addition, she should also study the moral texts of the Roman writers. Quirini concludes his letter with praise of the value of philosophy and a clear mandate to Isotta to become a true scholar of the humanities:

> For nothing is more seemly than philosophy, nothing more lovely, nothing more beautiful, as our Cicero was wont to say; and I may perhaps add, more properly, nothing more divine in matters human. For this is the single, most sacred discipline, which teaches true wisdom and instructs in the right manner of living. Whence it comes about that to be ignorant of philosophy is not simply to go through life basely, but also ruinously. Accordingly, throw yourself wholeheartedly, as they say, into this one matter. For I wish you to be not semi-learned, but skilled in all the liberal arts, that is, to be schooled in the art of discourse, and in the study of right debating, and in the science of things divine and human.[66]

In this remarkable letter we find another example of the effect of the second generation of Guarino's students on the history of the concept of woman. Isotta's first tutor, Martino Rizzoni, and her second tutor, Lauro Quirini, were both students of Guarino. While the master Guarino himself thought of an educated women as rare as a black swan, his own students had a different orientation. They appeared to consider educating women as worthwhile and not particularly unusual, and the effect of their efforts as teachers was to help produce a woman who was "not semi-learned, but skilled in all the liberal arts . . . and schooled in the art of discourse . . . and right debating. . . ."

A network of educated women was established. Costanza Varano, the granddaughter of Battista de Malatesta, who had received Leonardo Bruni's famous letter on humanist studies, wrote to Isotta in 1443-44.[67] In this letter we discovered evidence of an emerging collective female consciousness of women's history. Costanza's relationship with Isotta was that of a student to a master, but her master was one of the growing group of male humanist authors and female learned women.

Costanza Varano clearly admired Isotta Nogarola for her humanist erudition and for her simple living and ascetical practices. Margaret King suggests that "the learned women [of the Renaissance, including Isotta] conquered from within, capitulated and withdrew from battle" into "book-lined cells."[68] King's

---

66. Quirini, translated by Grafton and Jardine, *From Humanism to the Humanities,* pp. 31-32.

67. "Costanza sends greetings to Isotta Nogarola," in *Her Immaculate Hand,* ed. King and Rabil, pp. 55-56.

68. King, "Book-lined Cells," in *Renaissance Humanism,* ed. Rabil, vol. 2, p. 440. The quotation continues: "They withdrew from study altogether, into marriage or into grief. They withdrew to convents and to good works and to silence. They withdrew from secular studies, where men excelled, and took up sacred studies, appropriate for women, and formed cloisters of their minds. They withdrew from friendships, from the life of their cities, from public view, to small corners of the world where they worked in solitude: to self-constructed prisons, lined with books — to book-lined cells — which may serve as a symbol for the condition of the learned women of this age" (p. 440).

negative interpretation of Isotta's decision to live as a private scholar neglects the extremely important place of intergender dialogue through letters, in addition to regularly occurring private meetings. The humanist epistolary form of interaction generated a great deal of intellectual development and exchange. The most significant intergender dialogue in Isotta Nogarola's letters took place with Ludovico Foscarini over several years of Isotta's mature life.[69] In these letters we discover both personal and intellectual considerations with relevance for the concept of woman. Ludovico was a well-known Venetian diplomat who was appointed as governor of Verona well before 1453 and again in 1456. Extant letters between Isotta and Ludovico begin in 1453 and extend to 1466. Thus, they cover a period of almost fifteen years of continued friendship. There is little doubt that this experience of intellectual and personal complementarity between Isotta and Ludovico was highly formative of Isotta's identity as a humanist and religious scholar.

In one letter, written around 1453, Ludovico reflects on ways that Isotta has overcome her nature by the voluntary practice of "obedience" to her mother, by her choice of "voluntary poverty" in rejecting her familial wealth, and her choice of virginity for the sake of study.[70] He describes Isotta's zeal as being equal to the "diligence of the greediest merchants in your business of letters and Christian life."[71] Ludovico emphasizes that Isotta integrates both Christian and secular learning, that she adorns her soul by learning "in the cultivation of the liberal arts in studies."[72] In one important passage, he places her in the line of humanists and notes her excellence in the study of history and rhetoric as preparation for her serious study of Scripture and Theology.

> When Geno asked how he could best live, Apollo advised him with a famous reply: by revering the dead. Heeding such admonitions, you have always wisely been engaged in letters, in those . . . which, I say, render you learned and good. And though you heard the poets in your youth from learned teachers, you have wished . . . to master those disciplines by which your soul can best be nourished; and more zealously than the Epicureans were said to have pursued the delights of the body you were delighted by rhetoric, in which you greatly excel. . . . Thereafter you turned to sacred volumes. Not with a superficial learning, but by diligent and acute study, you have omitted nothing at all that you knew pertained to the best mode of leading the present life and to future glory.[73]

Isotta's serious study of Christian theology, when added to her knowledge of classical texts, places her in the line of a Petrarchian Christian humanism.

69. See Isotta Nogarola, *Opera,* II, 28-183.

70. Ludovico Foscarini to Isotta Nogarola, trans. Margaret King, in *Her Immaculate Hand,* pp. 117-19. The original is in Isotta Nogarola, *Opera,* II, 39-51. Ludovico emphasizes that Isotta is freely living these traditional Christian vows, and not under necessity. He also adds a list of Christian virtues, modesty, temperance, and humility ("you never insist on your own glory") (p. 119).

71. Ludovico, in *Her Immaculate Hand,* ed. King and Rabil, p. 119.

72. Ludovico, in *Her Immaculate Hand,* ed. King and Rabil, p. 119.

73. Ludovico, in *Her Immaculate Hand,* ed. King and Rabil, p. 119.

Her friendship with Ludovico made him aware of the developing culture of female scholars and humanists. Ludovico explicitly reveals this knowledge in his letter:

> I often peruse the histories of the most outstanding women. Ancient Rome, which extended its empire to the ends of the earth and its spirit as high as Olympus, produced none equal to you. Your writings from as long ago as your adolescence and an even younger age exist, which manifest a rare mind and not ordinary knowledge. . . . The ancient learned men who sang songs to Sempronia and Cornificia would have extolled you to heaven with praise, since you have rendered poetry and every kind of human study in speaking and disputing most familiar to you. Equipped to read sweetly and write easily in all the liberal disciplines, you surpass learned men in pronunciation, bookish men in celerity and elegance. I have often seen you, as you know, speak extemporaneously with such glory that I suspect there was nothing ever more worthy and sweet. What can be more glorious, what more magnificent, than to hear you pleading in a way most worthy of majesty, gracious with noble modesty, bright with distinction, severe with authority, in teaching dignified and in diligence most sound? What woman therefore was ever more learned than you or could be, who from the school of childhood up to this age, by learning and teaching, have committed to memory more books than many learned men have seen? What kind of liberal learning is there in which you are not versed? Oratory, poetry, philosophy, theology declare that there is nothing that can adorn the mortal mind which you have neglected.[74]

Ludovico mentions Sappho and the Queen of Sheba as former female models of wisdom. He does not seem to be aware, however, of Christine de Pizan, who had written in French rather than Italian or Latin. Ludovico also notes Isotta's great love of Cicero, Virgil, Jerome, and Augustine. Then he reflects on the admiration of some contemporary men for her work.

In this context we again find reference to the public intergender dialogue that was constantly taking place through the exchange of letters. A contemporary analogy for this kind of dialogue might be found in professional meetings and journals through which scholars exchange their ideas and challenge one another's perspectives.

> The letters of learned men which are delivered to you from various and diverse places, have increased your authority, and your responses are awaited and circulated more avidly than once the counsels of the Sibyls. Cardinal [Giuliano] Cesarini judged nothing more worthy in his whole long journey than meeting you, and concluded that nature, virtue, and learning were at your command. For that reason, you may rejoice in the Lord, since you so greatly excel by birth, are outstanding in majesty, flourish in letters, are conspicuous in virtue — which

---

74. Ludovico, in *Her Immaculate Hand,* ed. King and Rabil, pp. 119-20. He also includes frequent reference to Isotta's openness to the Holy Spirit, and to the way in which she is also taught by the Spirit, so that her intellect leads others both through the results of study and the effects of prayer.

should be praised in every sex, but in a woman much more, because it rarely occurs and thus is judged more worthy and admirable.[75]

The only characteristics in the above list that would be considered rare for a woman would be learning and flourishing in letters, for the other characteristics would have been common to many Christian saints, well known by then. So in these areas, and in her regular participation in intergender dialogue, both in oral and written forms, Isotta Nogarola advanced the concept of woman by her own example.

In the practice of particular areas such as rhetoric and learning of language, literature, philosophy, and theology in which she excelled, Isotta raised women's contribution to a more professional level than had been previously seen in western culture. For even though Christine de Pizan wrote extensively about gender issues as well as broader humanist concerns, she did not know well how to work in the academic language of Latin, although she appears to have been able to translate from Latin to French. Isotta, on the other hand, not only trained herself in the classical language, she immersed herself in the scholarly texts of many different fields and integrated the material to such an extent that she was able to communicate professionally with others. Isotta can be identified as the first woman scholar who participated in Renaissance professional intergender dialogues.

However, it should also be noted that Isotta was not able to sustain her humanist scholarly career in institutional structures beyond those allowed by epistolary exchange. She had no teaching position, no public office, and no way to engage directly with many humanists. Aside from her one relationship of note, with Ludovico Foscarini, Isotta did not appear to have any sustained humanist exchange with other scholars. Thus, in spite of her significant contribution to the history of the concept of woman through the multi-leveled dialogue about Adam and Eve, Isotta Nogarola's search for meaning was limited by the circumstances of her life.

Before concluding this part of the chapter, we will briefly consider some of the later recognition of Isotta Nogarola's contribution to western thought. The first example is taken from a letter of Laura Cereta to Augustinus Aemilius, written in 1487. The letter concludes with a reiteration of part of the second level of Isotta's argument:

> For [woman's] nature is not immune to sin; nature produced our mother [Eve], not from rock, but from Adam's humanity. . . . We are quite an imperfect animal. . . . [But] you great men, wielding such authority, commanding such success. . . . For where there is greater wisdom, there lies greater guilt.[76]

Although Laura Cereta does not directly mention Isotta Nogarola here, it is presumed by scholars that she took this argument from her colleague.[77] In another let-

---

75. Ludovico, in *Her Immaculate Hand,* ed. King and Rabil, p. 121.

76. Laura Cereta, in *Her Immaculate Hand,* ed. King and Rabil, p. 80. See also Albert Rabil, Jr., *Laura Cereta: Quattrocento Humanist* (Binghamton, N.Y.: Medieval and Renaissance Texts, 1981), pp. 82-83.

77. Margaret King concludes concerning Cereta's knowledge of the dialogue authored by Isotta

ter, Cereta includes Isotta in a long line of intellectual women as a contemporary who had reached "the heights of knowledge."[78]

In 1563 Isotta Nogarola's dialogue about Adam and Eve was published in Venice in a revised form.[79] In this slightly changed version, Ludovico is dropped from the conversation, and two other participants, Naugerio and Pronotarius, are inserted. The substance of the argument is the same as it was in Isotta's original version. However, the context is reversed so that the two men imply that they are writing up their experience of speaking with Isotta, rather than the other way around. This pedagogical change effectively drops the third level of the above analysis, for it does not allow Isotta's text to serve as a counterexample to the presuppositions about women's inferiority. However, another device somewhat mitigates this inversion, namely, that the dialogue opens with a depiction of Isotta filled with happiness outdoors in a garden, analogous to paradise.[80] Isotta may be playing a similar role to Dante's Beatrice or Petrarch's Laura, who speaks to men on earth from the perspective of heaven.

The character Pronotarius then suggests that this original happiness was lost because of the fault of one man and one woman. At this point Isotta initiates the contentious part of the dialogue:

> [Isotta]: See, however, to which of these parents the fault is more to be attributed; for I have always thought that Adam is the one to be blamed.

> [Naugerio]: But on the contrary, if you were a man, you would accuse Eve.

> [Isotta]: Rather, if the choice of either sex were to be given me by nature, still I would rather be a woman, so that I might be as far as possible from the sin of Adam.

> [Pronotarius]: Of course we are slipping by degrees into a discussion of that question which, as I recall, Isotta has thought about for a long time and she has prepared for herself the most beautiful weapons for dispute. For that reason, we who are perhaps unprepared should not undertake this battle rashly.

> [Naugerio]: This place and this conversation hold the greatest attraction for me

---

Nogarola: "This last paragraph is surely a reference to Isotta Nogarola's Dialogue on Adam and Eve. Cereta appears to be backing down from her defense of women, but she is doing so satirically, turning the tables on Aemilius, so to speak, and putting him on the defensive" (*Her Immaculate Hand,* p. 141, note 11).

78. Laura Cereta to Bibulus Sempronius, "Defense of the Liberal Instruction of Women," in *Her Immaculate Hand,* p. 83.

79. Isotta Nogarola, *Opera,* II, 222-57. All passages from this version are translated by James Moller. Margaret King suggests that this version was "plagiarized" by Francesco Nogarola.

80. After Isotta describes the beauties of the countryside (including ironically "fish fighting with each other"), Naugerio responds: "What delights you tell of, what delights I see! Not other than these could have been the delights of those happy fields which the first age called paradise" (*Opera,* II, 224).

and offer us a subject which, though it has too often been treated narrowly and confusingly by theologians and patrons of women, I have long wanted discussed by a woman herself. Besides, whom from the ranks of women shall I find more apt to this task than you, Isotta? Wherefore, while the leisure of midday and the amenity of this place invite us, speak, debate, as an emissary in this contest: by what laws do you think that Adam is more to be blamed than Eve? For myself, in whatever way I can, I will not desert Adam, and I trust that Pronotarius will do the same; for he, though joined to you by close family ties, is more closely joined to me in the nobility of our sex.[81]

In this dialogue the author situates the discussion once again in the domain of purposefully engendered arguments. The woman, Isotta, who happily chooses her identity as a woman, will defend the part of Eve; while the men who choose to identify more with gender than family will defend the part of Adam.

In the next phase of the dialogue, the rules of debate are established:

[**Isotta**]: You want greater things from me than an unarmed woman can proffer against strong men. Still, I will expound what I do not deny having been thinking about for some time, though I prepared not for the subtleties of questions but thought to establish the judgment of truth. Nonetheless, fairness of procedure demands that you, brother, who have rushed to the accusation, also begin to speak in the first place; I will then answer whether by rebuttal or by exposition whatever little argument a slight strength of intelligence and memory will supply.

[**Pronotarius**]: I will begin with you nevertheless forewarned, in case you readily suspect the arguments as contentious personal reproof. I will propound to uphold the truth in regard to your sex. Speech between us should be well spoken and polite.

[**Isotta**]: You should certainly take the same care; for I will return like for like.[82]

Isotta ironically refers to her weaker intelligence and memory, but she warns her opponent that she will use the same method as he does.

The dialogue contains many of the same arguments that are found in the original document by Isotta. However, the arguments both in method and content are amplified by making their logic more evident and by inserting the names of authoritative scholars in fields other than Theology or Scripture. Observe the following:

[**Pronotarius**]: If the seriousness of any sin can be greater than another, who does not see that Eve was more culpable in that she was condemned by a just judge with a harsher punishment? For a punishment is required so that the inequality of an injustice which has been committed may be restored to equality. . . .

81. Nogarola, *Opera*, II, 225-26.
82. Nogarola, *Opera*, II, 226-27.

[**Isotta**]: Now you may learn that an opinion, however firm, can be drawn into an opposite conclusion. Where there is less sense and less constancy, there is less sin; and that indeed is true of Eve; therefore, her sin was the less serious one. Woman in the state of innocence was more imperfect than man, and not only with respect to body but also to soul, and in so far as I have learned from theologians, I understand that in women there is not sufficient strength of mind to resist concupiscence. . . . Aristotle also asserts that woman is more easily deceived than man, which we understand happens on account of her weakness. . . .

Moreover, if Adam had not sinned, sin would not have gone farther. For if the woman alone had sinned, posterity, if any had been born, would have received corporal deficiencies and the capacity for suffering, but they would not have been born subject to original sin. Nor would they have experienced those deficiencies which derive from the soul, since the body, according to Aristotle, comes from the woman, while the soul from the man. This is so, not because the rational soul is transmitted from the semen but because in the semen is the formative strength, through which in the other animals the sensible soul is induced, but in man the body organized and prepared for the reception of the rational soul. . . .

Since, therefore, Eve injured herself alone and not posterity, her sin, in that it was damning to the sinner alone, is thought to be less serious. On the other hand, the man, Adam, brought destruction on himself and all his progeny and standing as the agent of those to come was the first occasion of perdition.[83]

It is significant that the author of this revision of the dialogue presents Isotta as directly appealing to Aristotle in her argument, because in the original dialogue she never does. The only two direct references to Aristotle were found in the voice of Ludovico with respect to the passage from the *Ethics* about ignorance being no excuse for women's actions and from the *Metaphysics* concerning woman's culpability as a cause of a cause of a cause. In the revision, however, Isotta directly refers to Aristotle three times in her argument. While one of these references simply repeats a theory of cause through the voice of Pronotarius, the other two references are original. As shown in the above quotation, they include reference to "woman's weakness" as a general Aristotelian principle and reference to the differing contributions of soul and body by the man and woman to generation. So Isotta is presented to the readers as a scholar of Aristotle as well as of Scripture and Theology.

Pronotarius introduces two new Aristotelian references. He uses the distinction between parts and wholes from the *Posterior Analytics* to argue that Eve, who was created from part of Adam, holds greater responsibility for harm, and a distinction between accidental and essential qualities to argue that woman's inconstancy is accidental while her intelligent exercise of reason is essential to her identity. Again, the dialogue serves as a counterexample to the original claims of gender polarity theorists.

Before concluding this section of the chapter, we will make brief mention of the fact that Isotta Nogarola appears to have been well known within certain intellectual circles right from the time she lived. Margaret King, who has done so much

83. Nogarola, *Opera,* II, 227-32.

to make her life and texts available to contemporary English scholars, states: "Isotta's fame seems to have been established in her own century, and the historiographical tradition has not neglected her from her own day to ours."[84] Isotta was known by Cardinal Bessarion, Pope Nicholas V, and Pope Pius II.[85] In addition, Paoli Maffei, Matteo Bosso, and Ermolao Barbaro the elder all mentioned her name in their works.[86]

The two texts of Isotta that received the most attention were her correspondence with Guarino of Verona and her dialogue about Adam and Eve. Her complete works were published in Latin in Vienna and Budapest by Eugenius Abel in 1886. This publication became a source of study for many scholars in subsequent decades. Margaret King has traced in some detail the trail of scholarship on Isotta Nogarola.[87] She was a true scholar who dedicated her life to study, to dialogue, and to writing short letters and tracts, and the quality of her scholarship continues to be admired and evaluated.

From the perspective of the history of the concept of woman, Isotta Nogarola contributed her sustained dialogue in complementary discourse with a male discussant. She did this in a context in which her scholarship and personal life had been subjected to ridicule and slander. Her acute experience of the direct effects of evil did not deter her from being able to enter into a sustained argument about whether man or woman is more to blame for the presence of evil in the world. Perhaps in part due to her positive experience of friendship with Ludovico, Isotta was able to achieve a philosophical insight into fundamental questions of meaning in her life.

As our analysis turns now to the final figure to be considered in this study of early humanism, we observe a mounting pressure to change certain structures limiting for women. Isotta Nogarola lived quietly at home, but Laura Cereta sought to participate actively in her contemporary life. She also unleashed strong passions of righteous anger in her effort to bring about a more integral situation for women humanists.

LAURA CERETA (1469-1499)

It is appropriate that this study of *The Concept of Woman: The Early Humanist Reformation (1250-1500)* should end with a consideration of the philosophical contribution of a young woman from Brescia who, in her short life of thirty years, did more personally in terms of offering a new humanist model for woman's identity than any woman before her. This is a strong claim in the context of the works of Christine de Pizan and of Isotta Nogarola. Yet, when the content of her writings is evaluated, it becomes clear that Laura Cereta truly entered into a reform of the concept of woman in an even more personal manner than her predecessors. She

84. King, "The Religious Retreat," *Signs* 3, no. 4 (1978): Appendix, 822.
85. King, "The Religious Retreat," *Signs* 3, no. 4 (1978): 813, note 26.
86. King, "The Religious Retreat," *Signs* 3, no. 4 (1978): 813, note 25.
87. King, "The Religious Retreat," *Signs* 3, no. 4 (1978): 820-22.

also demonstrated forms of original philosophical thinking about gender identity. Our analysis of Laura Cereta will be divided into the following five sections: (1) Philosophical Autobiography, (2) Gender and Self-knowledge, (3) Interpersonal Dialogue about Self-governance, (4) Public Action in Building the Common Good, and (5) Integral Gender Complementarity.

Laura Cereta's philosophy concentrates on the full development of the human person. She writes about the need for a high level of integration of the passions, intellect, and will with a relentless drive for the truth in human discourse and support for the common good in public action. While other women, especially women religious, have held similar goals, Cereta is the only one who defended them by constant appeal to humanist sources and philosophical arguments. In these ways she offers a new model of a woman who defends self-knowledge, self-governance, and public action as a humanist philosopher, and she does this, not in general, but one-on-one with each and every man and woman with whom she enters into dialogue. Nearly all of her extant writings consist of letters and public discourses. Over one-third of her correspondence was with women whom she befriended. These women were not wealthy patrons but ordinary women who were struggling to articulate their own identities in various ways. The quality of Cereta's writings with respect to the values identified above makes her a remarkable contributor to the history of the concept of woman.

Laura Cereta was born as the eldest of six siblings to Silvestro Cereta, an attorney and humanist, and Veronica di Leno from an old Brescian family.[88] She was educated in a convent school.[89] She participated with her brother in small discussion groups of humanists meeting at a monastery in Chiara and possibly in the home of the humanist physician, Luigi Mondella, that reputedly followed the tradition of the Platonic Academy in Florence, calling themselves "the Mondella Academy."[90] At 15 Laura Cereta married a young merchant, Pietro Serina, but was widowed within a year and a half. She described this rapid transition in a letter to Emilio Augustino as follows: "Thus one unspeakable year saw me a girl, a bride, a widow, and bereft of all the goods of fortune."[91] She continued to study and write even in her grief, and in 1488, at the age of nineteen, released a manuscript of eighty-four collected letters and addresses.[92]

After this major set of writings Cereta did not contribute to posterity any other organized publications. Reasons offered for her literary silence during the

---

88. Albert Rabil, Jr., ed., *Laura Cereta: Quattrocento Humanist* (Binghamton, N.Y.: Center for Medieval and Early Renaissance Studies, 1981); and *Italian Women Writers: A Bio-Bibliographical Sourcebook,* ed. Rinaldina Russell (Westport, Conn. and London: Greenwood Press, 1994), pp. 67-75.

89. Diana Robin, ed., *Laura Cereta: Collected Letters of a Renaissance Feminist* (Chicago and London: University of Chicago Press, 1997).

90. Rabil, *Laura Cereta: Quattrocento Humanist,* p. 8.

91. Cereta (February 12, 1487), *Laura Cereta: Collected Letters,* p. 82.

92. Two manuscripts are extant: One in the Vatican Library, Vat. lat. 3176, and another in the Biblioteca Nazionale Marciana in Venice, Marc lat. 4186. A printed version is entitled *Laurae Ceretae Brisiensis Feminae Clarissimae Epistolae iam primum e MS in lucem productae,* ed. Jacopo Filippo Tomasini (Padua: Sebastiano Sardi, 1640). For the number of the letters at eighty-four for the Vatican manuscript see Rabil, *Laura Cereta: Quattrocento Humanist,* p. 30, note 7.

LAVRA CERETA BRIXIENSIS
LITERIS ORNATISSIMA

Laura Cereta

last eleven years of her life vary from a religious conversion, a preoccupation with teaching rather than writing, or simply being worn out from her previous efforts in scholarly activities. It is also worth pondering some other events that may have played a role: Pico della Mirandola's famous posting of his nine hundred theses in 1486, the reading of the condemnation of his work in every Church in Italy, his subsequent flight and arrest, and his being absolved of heresy in 1493. Another event was Marsilio Ficino's publishing of the *Book of Life* in 1489 and his being reported for possible heresy. During the years 1486-89 the religious reformer Savonarola visited Brescia twice, and his public sermons often attacked humanistic studies. It was widely believed and later reported by Lucrezia Marinelli that "A noble Brescian named Laura wrote many elegant letters to Brother Girolamo Savonarola."[93] Savonarola was burned to death for heresy just one year before Laura Cereta's own death in 1499.

This was also a period of wars. The French had entered Florence in 1494 and the Germans were attempting to conquer Venice. Laura Cereta's spiritual counselor, a Dominican priest named Thomas from Milan, wrote to her that it was "dangerous" for her to continue to write as she had done before. Cereta's response is telling:

> I have abandoned my plan to seek fame through human letters, lest my mind, bereft, unhappy, and unaware of the future should seek happiness through diligence. What is more, since too great a concern for knowledge raises the suspicion that one leads a prodigal life, our all-night sessions of study ought not to continue, as if we were born solely for the sake of literature.
>
> We may, however, indulge our inclinations thus: orations must be delivered about a topic, and God must be honoured with the gift of service. . . .
>
> Therefore, this first part of my "Familiar Letters" is concluded — arranged in a lame and faulty order summarily and by headings — and I have removed my pen. What remains for me now is to begin to make notes worthy of what I have written so that I may obtain **without danger** both lasting fame for this sinful and small soul of mine and also the reward of a higher good without illness.[94]

The danger may simply refer to ruining her health and being misunderstood in her vigorous approach to night study, or it may perhaps include a concern about the heresy and witchcraft accusations that women had been facing in northern Europe, especially since the 1448 release of the *Malleus maleficarum*. As a Dominican, Brother Thomas would have been well aware of events occurring north of Italy in France and Germany at the time.

It is disputed whether Cereta actually taught publicly beyond the letters and orations referred to above. Albert Rabil, Jr., who published the critical Latin text of her writings, has researched this question and discovered a controversy. He notes that Ortensio Lando, in *Forcianae quaestiones* published in 1536, includes the name of "Laura bresciana" in a list of female philosophers.[95] Ottavio Rossi, author of

---

93. In Rabil, *Laura Cereta: Quattrocento Humanist,* p. 30, note 5.

94. Cereta (February 4, 1488/December 11, 1487), *Laura Cereta: Collected Letters,* pp. 112-13.

95. Rabil, *Laura Cereta: Quattrocento Humanist,* p. 29, note 5.

Elogi istorici de Bresciani illustri published in 1620, records that Laura Cereta "defended theses in philosophy at the age of eighteen [1487] and taught philosophy publicly for seven years from the age of twenty [1489-1497] [and that] Tomasini, Calzavacca, Cozzando, and Chiaramonte repeat this assertion."[96] Certainly the view that Cereta began teaching publicly in 1487 would be consistent with the strength of convictions that her writings reveal at that time. Since her collected works were released in several manuscripts in 1488, it is also possible that besides publicly defending particular philosophical theses she taught some of the classical humanistic sources she used. Her Latin was fluent, and she knew some Greek as well. Thus it would have been possible for her to have taught a few students on a regular basis.

However, as Rabil points out, there is no corroboration for this initial assertion of Rossi or its subsequent repetition even in city records from Brescia at the time.[97] In fact, Rabil prefers another thesis, namely that after her father's death in 1488 Cereta turned away from her vocation as a "humanist intellectual" because she had lost the primary person who supported her in this endeavor. My own view is that Cereta was more of a caregiver of her father than a support-receiver, and that it would be very consistent with her personality for her to have continued to teach in an educational setting in Brescia. If she did, then it would be the first example of a laywoman, aside from possibly Aspasia and Hypatia, to teach philosophy. In any event, in 1499 at the early age of thirty Laura Cereta died suddenly of unknown causes. She was given a public funeral and honored with great festivities by the people of Brescia. Fortunately, Laura Cereta left a considerable legacy in her published work.

While the several hundred pages of texts written by Cereta are extremely rich from many different perspectives, we will concentrate only on her philosophy of gender, which focuses on the equal dignity of man and woman along with significant areas of gender differentiation. We have included lengthy passages of her works, which were translated into English only a few years ago. Without them, her wonderful lively style of discourse would otherwise be lost from view.

Philosophical Autobiography

Laura Cereta often reflected on the significance of her first name "Laura." Petrarch had immortalized this name in his writings, as representing a woman of great wisdom and virtue. In Chapter 4 we suggested that Petrarch's positive concept of woman might in the future entice women to exercise the qualities he had identified. The model for a most perfectly developed woman was found in Petrarch's figure of "Laura," who represented both the literary development of a woman he had loved and also the laurel crown that he wore as poet laureate. "Laura," because she had all the perfect qualities of wisdom and virtue, was able to lead Petrarch, and through him, other men to the perfection of their own nature and identity as man.

---

96. Rabil, *Laura Cereta: Quattrocento Humanist,* p. 29, note 5.
97. Rabil, *Laura Cereta: Quattrocento Humanist,* p. 23.

Laura Cereta was conscious of the meaning of her name, and she reflected on its significance in her response to Sister Nazaria Olympia's request that she write a narrative of her life:

> It is well established from our family records that I was born in the fourth month before the coming of the seventieth year in the century one thousand four-hundred of our Savior. Our laurel tree, which shaded with its bold branches a polished and burgeoning garden, had grown shriveled and dry in the wake of the icy frost that followed a brutal storm. I myself kept the name with which this tree was endowed. And thus, the whole house rang constantly with this sweet appellation, and I, who was carried around alternately in each of their arms, became for my adoring parents their most precious source of delight, for parents usually favor their firstborn child.[98]

In another letter to her uncle, Lodovico di Leno, she invokes Petrarch's Laura and explains that her ancestral coat of arms with its symbolic moon and star awakened a love of astronomy in her:

> This was the live spark that first set my mind afire with a burning desire to know the courses of the heavens and the spheres of the planets. This fire was like a sense of purpose that stood over me sentinel-like in the night. This being my guide, my schooling first opened up new doors to me so that I could trample the leisure I had reaped. Nor should you think that, in return for such sweet labor, I promised myself the rewards for literary studies of an Augustus or a Maecenas [the patrons of Horace and Virgil]. I took on all this work myself so that the name of Laura, so wondrously celebrated by Petrarch, might be preserved in a second and quite new immortality — in me.[99]

Cereta's fame had indeed begun to spread, and she admitted to her uncle that "public acclaim has built a solid enough foundation for my immortality, and in this way an initial reservoir for my glory has been established: I, for example, who was a young girl to the wonderment and perturbation of everyone until now, may perhaps emerge as an exceptional woman."[100]

Still, there were many difficult situations ahead of her, and at times Laura also reflected on the passing value of fame, her own inadequacies in seeking immortality through her writing, and the relation of her name to these struggles. In a letter to another sister, Martha Marcella, known in religion as Deodata di Leno, Cereta offers a strong defense of Epicurus, following the argument of Lorenzo Valla,[101] and again reflects on her first name:

---

98. Cereta (November 5, 1486), *Laura Cereta: Collected Letters,* p. 24. It is presumed, but not proven, that the recipient of this letter was a nun, Robin, p. 22.

99. Cereta (July 16, 1485), *Laura Cereta: Collected Letters,* p. 49. See also note 83.

100. Cereta, *Laura Cereta: Collected Letters,* p. 49.

101. Cereta (December 12, 1487), *Laura Cereta: Collected Letters,* pp. 120-21.

And although I am not yet called Laura in the place where you dwell, sister — that would be to put a skylark next to a phoenix — still, out of the kindness of your heart, you will not cast me out of the purview of your love. For the magpie did not think the nightingale unworthy of her; nor did the peacock always show disdain for the hoopoe. For you will come up with a fair plan, I do not doubt, if you reflect how anxiety-ridden this time of ours is, for it draws all things born in this world, in an irrevocable course, to one end.[102]

The horizontal analogies comparing herself with a skylark, nightingale, and hoopoe, and Sister Deodata with a phoenix, magpie, and peacock drew their references from Pliny's texts on the history of animals.

Turning from autobiographical reflections on her name of Laura to two examples of letters to her parents, we find Cereta experimenting with different literary forms to make her point. Diana Robin, editor and translator into English of her collected letters, notes that in a letter to her mother, Veronica di Leno, Cereta imitates the work of the Roman authors Persius and Martial in wanting to offer her mother a special token of a beautiful day they had spent together. Robin also notes that "Cereta's positioning of the story of the crippled female poet at the center of her letter suggests a relationship between herself and the child, between poetry and lack, and between writing and wounding."[103] The letter is a beautiful lyrical description of the day Laura and her mother spent in the country together.

> We gazed at the meadows blooming with flowers and glistening with small stones and winding streams, and we felt full of contentment. . . .
>
> In the middle of the garden stood a makeshift tent where a humpbacked girl sang, sweetening old tales she learned at her father's knee with her own melodies. . . .
>
> There was a pleasant grove of white willows, whose leafy boughs offered us coolness, and there was a bower for Idalian Venus, so that the lovely nymphs — the Dryads, the Nyads, and the Napaeae — could enjoy the pleasures of the shade.[104]

In the following example of a letter written to her father, Silvestro Cereta, Laura Cereta reveals a shared understanding of their common intellectual life. She asks her father, an attorney, to judge a disagreement she has encountered with some humanists from Chiari. In the letter we see the seething rage that Cereta often expresses, as well as the freedom she felt to speak openly to her trusted intellectual companion:

> I had only just recently moved to Chiari because the ignorant public and other certain men who had suddenly got learning of some sort or other came to me, since they were stricken with the sickness of jealousy of my literary knowledge

---

102. Cereta, *Laura Cereta: Collected Letters,* p. 121.
103. Robin, ed., *Laura Cereta: Collected Letters,* p. 35, note 43.
104. Cereta (September 5, 1485), *Laura Cereta: Collected Letters,* pp. 35-36.

(and how slight that knowledge really is). Although their sputtering bile sometimes made me so angry that I was sick, I am not such a country bumpkin that I believed I should reject them as opponents in a literary exchange, even though they had challenged me — disadvantaged though I was by an unsteady hand — to an epistolary contest.

I know they are jealous, since, having received, in addition to my pledge, something greater and more hallowed by time from me, they have no more challenging a game than to boast about their quickness of mind, by which these cowards could preempt my letters quickly with their own epistles to me, as though they believed that an error composed in haste would have more authority than a well-conceived correctness.

These men, just as certain others, find fault with the slowness that immortalized the mature verses of Euripides' *Alcestis*. . . . Moreover, these empty little teachers of rhetoric are irked because it shames them that their motivation for speaking comes from me, with the result that they rightly consider that their own empty hostility cannot be compared with the thought of the orators. Accordingly, puffed up with tumorous swelling they wallow in a succession of excuses, and like firebrands they proclaim their poisonous maledictions. But the ignorant ones who are more careful secretly withdraw in unseen treachery.

Nor is it characteristic of my nature to hide in meadows that have been mown down with a sickle. You yourself have seen most of the writings they've sent. Consider, in your role as judge, this two-day epistle which you yourself might compare, in response to their bragging, to the epistle I wrote in an hour, so that literary moderation can more clearly assert itself in opposition to these ignoramuses.[105]

This letter indicates that Cereta was truly part of a humanist community of discourse in Chiari and that they challenged one another to epistolary contests. There is no previous evidence of women who regularly participated in a community of discourse. The expression "unsteady hand" in the phrase, "they had challenged me — disadvantaged though I was by an unsteady hand — to an epistolary contest," refers to the hand of grief, for her husband had just died suddenly a few months previously. Cereta went through a period of shock and mourning, the philosophical aspects of which we will consider in the next section on self-knowledge.

Concerning Cereta's reflections about the level of her knowledge and ability, "how slight that knowledge is," it is worthwhile to consider exactly what she knew and how she learned it. In her letter to Sister Nazaria Olympia, Laura describes exactly what she learned at the age of seven in the convent where she lived for two years:

During this period, as soon as I had scarcely learned for the first time to use the letters of the alphabet to form syllables, I was entrusted to a woman highly esteemed both for her counsel and sanctity, whose learning, habits, and discipline I, who was to be educated, intently absorbed.

She kept me constantly at her side in the inner chambers of the convent, the

---

105. Cereta (February 1, 1486), *Laura Cereta: Collected Letters*, p. 62.

doors to which were opened and shut with a hundred locks. She was the first to teach me to find a passage through my nights of insomnia by using an embroidery needle to draw pictures. My hand, obedient enough after a brief period of time, committed the rudiments of my new learning to thread and fabric. There was in fact no embroidery stitch so elegant or difficult that I could not master it, once I discerned its fine points through delicate and gentle probings. In this way a mind quite helpless and quite deficient in knowledge was able to raise itself up, once it was inspired, to those gentle breezes of hope.[106]

Although learning how to read, write, and embroider was common for young girls in convent schools, the way that Laura Cereta later integrated these skills was unusual. She often invoked metaphors of threads and weaving into her letters and addresses. The whole process of weaving threads together became a model for the intellectual life as Laura wove humanist, Christian, and gender issues into a single work of art. She never thought of the different strands of history, knowledge, or literature as impossible to be integrated. She rejected the mentality of contrasting women's needlework to intellectual work so evident in Cassandra Fedele. Instead, she worked towards a new unity of truth that both Ficino and Pico had articulated as a goal for the new philosophy.

After she returned home at the age of nine, her father became concerned that she was losing her intellectual abilities, and so he sent her back to school as noted in her letter to Sister Nazaria Olympia:

My father, however, the more purposeful figure in the family in his role as our governor and, above all, a man of temperate counsel, soon sent me back to my instructress in liberal studies since I had already begun to be bored with childish pursuits and he feared that at my age I might slip into indolent habits and grow dull from the free time I would have. With all the vigor of my genius depending on her, my teacher, I immersed myself night and day, blinking back my fatigue, in long vigils of study. Then in my eleventh year, after I had entered into this dry diet, I was removed from the discipline of the rod; for by this time I had already digested all the necessary elements in the obligatory paradigms of grammar.

At home, as though starving for knowledge, I diligently studied the eloquence of the tragic stage and the polish of Tully [Cicero] insofar as I was able. But when scarcely a year had gone by, I assumed the responsibility for almost all of the household duties myself. Thus it was my lot to grow old when I was not far from childhood. Even so, I attended lectures on mathematics during the days I had free from toil, and I did not neglect those profitable occasions when, unable to sleep, I devoured the mellifluous-voiced prophets of the Old Testament and figures from the New Testament too. Even then, when I was only a girl, I saw my father occupy three external magistracies, happy in my studies and full of the pleasure of peace and tranquillity.[107]

106. Cereta (November 5, 1486), *Laura Cereta: Collected Letters*, pp. 25-26.
107. Cereta (November 5, 1486), *Laura Cereta: Collected Letters*, pp. 27-28.

Once again Cereta combines intellectual fields that were often placed in juxtaposition or even conflict with one another and domestic service in the care of her brothers, father, and household, with the demands of study in mathematics, philosophy, and theology. Her study expanded to include astronomy. During the "night vigils," as she called them, Cereta would measure the distance between planets and stars in undertaking her own astronomical experiments. In a letter to Brother Thomas, a Dominican priest from Milan, their common love for astronomy is revealed:

> So I can respond to both of your letters now, I have postponed for a little while my late-night sessions of fairly rigorous study, which I had begun, patiently and because it was my desire to do so, to make measurements of the earth. For by proposing hypotheses, I have tried to pursue this subject more deeply, to investigate it, and to unravel the mystery of its causes. My curiosity has been heartened, and I am indebted to you, because by treating this subject at length in your letters, you have opened the doors to a mind whose light and energy, previously dulled by vertigo, lay inert in darkness.[108]

The "vertigo" and "darkness" are allusions to her struggle with grief, which her studies have helped to overcome. Laura Cereta's interest in astronomy was not limited to empirical studies and measurements. She also seemed to understand its theory as developed by Aristotle, Ptolemy, and others who sought to add corrections to their hypotheses of perfect circular motion of the planets. For example, in a letter to Agostino Emilio, another intellectual friend, she reveals her knowledge of "wandering planets" that do not fit the Ptolemaic hypothesis:

> I had devoted myself to the temple of Minerva and I had surrendered my whole mind to the Muses, so that I could observe the wandering, falling planets and those bodies which sometimes move in a retrograde position, sometimes in a descending course, and at other times with more velocity under the continual revolutions of the rising and sinking stars, since I was trying to find out, using rigorous proofs, whether the stars remained fixed while the heavens were descending, or whether they were propelled in a circular orbit away from us, equidistantly in a vast orbit. And I was as patient an observer as I could be, so that I might come to understand what higher causes, emanating from a lofty boundary, sprinkle the evil we experience with a certain celestial dew. Because of this, I dared to castigate those corrupt philosophical sects who predict the movements of the moon beneath the earth, spreading of the sun's rays through the clouds, the gathering and dispelling of the rains, the wars and clashing of the winds, and the day on which these things will occur.[109]

Cereta clearly identifies with astronomers and against astrologers on the basis of an understanding of the differences between the two approaches to the plan-

108. Cereta (December 11, 1487; February 4, 1488), *Laura Cereta: Collected Letters*, p. 110.
109. Cereta (February 6, 1487), *Laura Cereta: Collected Letters*, pp. 100-101.

ets and stars. She demonstrates knowledge of astrology in a letter to Pietro Fecchi, who was to be married:

> The ascent of the planet Venus on your birthday is connected with the second appearance of Pisces, while the power of Venus rising in the house of good fortune is a benefit to your marriage bonds; for it is Venus and Pisces who control the process of procreation. But a fortunate wife will be given to you as a bride when Jupiter appears, and by her you will receive a grandson from a happy son. The discordant Great Bear moves towards the influences of these heavenly bodies, whose eightfold pairs of rays had begun to rise with you at the first darkness of the night. And although Chance might cause you to be deceived in a prior promise of marriage, still you will be consoled: in opposition to Fortune, you will soon evade the enemy and two hearts joined together under the law of chastity will enjoy themselves in an indissoluble knot of love for a long time to come.[110]

In spite of this use of astrology, Laura Cereta rejects it as a means of predicting the future in favor of a more metaphysical and religious approach to events. In her letter to Sister Nazaria Olympia, Laura invokes an Aristotelian-scholastic principle of the relation of the first cause (the unmoved mover or God) and secondary causes (the motions of the stars and planets):

> I myself used to enjoy these studies; now because I imitate the first cause, I consider of lesser importance secondary causes, because of their instability. Owing to this, I would prefer to be ignorant rather than to know what the fates have in store for me. In any case, among those who believe in Christ, fate — once linked to the cause of things — now has no meaning. For God is one and the same everlasting and omnipotent being, who moves and rules us in harmony with the arching vault of heaven. Because of this, I myself believe that to investigate God's judgment regarding the future is the mark of foolish curiosity rather than of a heart that is faithful. The quick, fleeting speed of the stars eludes the buried intelligences of human minds, however subtle the genius. I beg you, now that you have tasted the vanity of foolish ignorance, not to long for the certainty of promised events. . . . On [God] surely the guiding principle behind every sidereal body and all the orbiting planets depends. He causes the glacial horror of frozen snows to grow warm, the intense heat of the blazing sun to boil, and the moon to move nearer the planets. Nor is he far from the sight and slanting movements of the constellations.[111]

One reason for this scientific curiosity may be that Laura Cereta was part of a community of scientists who shared their studies with one another. These informal communications among astronomers helped prepare the way for the Copernican Revolution and the eventual overturning of the Aristotelian cosmology. The participants in this early Renaissance Humanist community of discourse had a serious

110. Cereta (February 3, 1486), *Laura Cereta: Collected Letters*, pp. 65-66.
111. Cereta (November 5, 1486), *Laura Cereta: Collected Letters*, p. 29.

interest not only in mathematics and science, but also in philosophy, literature, history, and art. This phenomenon had already occurred in Florence at the time of Alberti, but to discover it recurring in smaller locations like Brescia and Chiara is an indication of how much humanistic preferences changed the fragmentation of the disciplines in academic institutions.

Cereta's love of literature, history, and the artistic craft of embroidery is reflected in a letter to her cousin, Bernardino di Leno:

> And so, because my mother bore me to be a sister to you, my heart chafes and swells with a burning desire for fame; in this way my noble hopes of becoming an exemplum for posterity are fed. Since the Amazons' name is now extinct, and those women who bore arms have returned their weapons and bows to the temple of Bellona, I have completely transferred my passion for feminine things to the love of literature. . . . [A]s I began to mature, greater interest in learning also grew in me, and little by little it became so important that the desire for learning and cultivation left me thirsting for more. For certainly the work of study comes very easily to minds naturally suited to it. I spent seven years so that I would be able to purchase this priceless dowry for myself, for who would not go into debt to buy this most luxurious jewel?
>
> Time is not something that belongs to us; it depends instead on the nature of the sun's journey. Thus, after the fruits of my study ripened and the golden grain fell from the stalk, I began to gather the harvest with my rustic pen, so that it could safely and quickly be transported to faraway peoples of the world. And although this ordinary knowledge that I have (whatever it is) may amount to nothing since I have not yet mastered, for example, the more obscure and knotty examples, still, I shall write an elegant enough work about the things that I do know. And with you as my judge, this work can win a place for me, a woman writer, among the most highly praised of our ancestors.[112]

The themes of hard work, study, writing, desire for fame are constantly interwoven with the mention of specific intellectual objects of her devotion. As Laura Cereta plunges more deeply into the vast field of intellectual sources, she settles upon philosophy as the one that draws her the most. In the Dedication of her *Collected Letters* to Cardinal Ascanio Maria Sforza, Laura Cereta describes her intellectual journey as follows:

> My love of reading caused me to sample different kinds of subjects, and only in study did I feel a sense of inner contentment. And, although I remained ill-equipped for the task despite my passion for learning, I reached a decision that awakened in me a desire for fame and honor, as though my mind were challenging itself to scale new heights.
>
> As my eagerness for knowledge grew, so did the capacity of my mind, and in the course of this growth, the fruitfulness and the fertility of my pen caused me to

112. Cereta (February 26, 1486), *Laura Cereta: Collected Letters,* pp. 51-52.

prefer philosophy over all other studies, just as fruit would have given me more pleasure than leaves.[113]

Philosophy is the "fruit" that Laura Cereta sought above all other fields. She decided to publish her works, not only to grow in study but also to serve society through becoming a writer. She ultimately became a teacher *par excellence*. Cereta used philosophical sources, the usual ones for oration and rhetoric — Demosthenes and Quintilian — to support her position. For example, in her allegorical "Dialogue on the Death of an Ass," which drew heavily upon the *Golden Ass* of Apuleius, Philonacus says to the character with her name:

> You, Laura, give us a distinguished speech with the majesty of Demosthenes. . . . With a more compassionate pen say those things that can elegantly and with lucid reason thrash the deadly wound of regret that lies in wait to trap us. Take now the rotating podium for speakers where, filled with the spirit of the age and its volatility, even if I was imbued with neither the classical authors, nor authority, nor guided by the look or appearance of polish, still I poured out, in whatever way I could, a flood of words and tall tales more trifling than trash.
>
> But you, a girl born to true eloquence, who are called to this field for funeral assemblies and meetings of the mourners' senate, it is your turn to speak. Remember now, I beg you, that your memorial should have enough happiness for a kingdom. Now, scatter from your virgin's lips the balm of Quintilian's nectar, dripping with purity and modesty like a crystalline spring. Clothe the rest of your speech with this balm because you must arouse your audience's piety.[114]

All the core elements of proper rhetoric are captured here: speaking "elegantly and with lucid reason," using "classical authors" and "authority," for the purpose of arousing the passion of "piety."

In a letter to a pseudonym, "Europa solitaria," Cereta critiques the tendency of some philosophers to choose a contemplative rather than an active lifestyle:

> You are deceived, dearest Europa, by this empty restfulness; and while you live in tranquil seclusion, you are uprooting every bit of serenity from the good fortune that is yours. In this I will not imitate your plans which, following in the footsteps of noble men, emulate the stories of the past that are celebrated in schools. You believe, I think, that you, because of the nobility of our mind, are patterning yourself on Camillus and the Curii, Metellus, Publius Scipio, Quinctus Cincinnatus, and Sulla and, from among the Greeks, Pittacus, Anaxagoras, Euripides, Myson, Heraclitus, and Parmenides.[115]

---

113. Cereta (March 1488), *Laura Cereta: Collected Letters,* pp. 37-38.

114. Cereta, *Laura Cereta: Collected Letters,* p. 196. For a comparison of Cereta's version with the original Latin of Apuleius' *Metamorphoses* see Robin's introduction, pp. 180-81.

115. Cereta (February 29, 1487/88), *Laura Cereta: Collected Letters,* p. 125.

In contrast, she invokes the Presocratic poet Sappho in a positive manner in the following passage from a letter to Brother Lodovico de la Turre:

> Read the complicated lyric poetry that Sappho sings and the centos of Proba. But I also want to add that I have not woven together these exempla from the ancients in order that I, who am neither their equal nor have the capacity to be so, would want my mind to be compared in any way with that of those extraordinary women. But neither have I done injury to this capacity, since the passion and thirst for knowledge that I've had for a decade of my young life have roused this moral righteousness in me against envy, and this has so liberated my mind from a life of sloth and purposelessness and freed it from every care and duty that I can study furiously and for long stretches of time. . . .[116]

Homer is integrated in a letter to Brother Thomas: "Surely I am a person who can steer a ship safely past the bewitching songs of the Sirens, with Ulysses unharmed. For I have reason, which can subvert passion, in my arsenal, and because virtue, not pleasure, is my mainstay."[117]

More important to our study is Laura Cereta's knowledge and use of the Greek philosophers Socrates, Plato, and Aristotle.[118] For example, in a letter to Clemenzo Longolio, teacher of rhetoric, she notes: "Cato and the Socratic Xenophon both proposed a rule that people should think before they speak so that their tongues should not outpace their thoughts. Therefore I have shown you what is being said about you, speaking not in figurative or allegorical terms or in anger, but openly and out of friendship. . . ."[119] In another allusion to Plato's *Apology* where Socrates shares his experience of the Delphic oracle, Laura Cereta writes to Cardinal Ascanio Maria Sforza: "The excellence of your mind and your erudition, worthy of the Athenian Stoa, is astounding. Through your lips, Socrates and Plato utter their oracles and the virginal Muses of the Helicon speak, making themselves known to us even without thunderbolts."[120] There is also a statement that Plato, Socrates, and Aristotle rejected the goddess Fortune.[121]

An interesting pattern occurs in Laura Cereta's references to Aristotle, which refer primarily to his philosophy of logic and to first cause in the *Physics* and *Metaphysics*. In one of her letters to Brother Thomas, she clearly admires the ancient Greek philosopher:

---

116. Cereta (August 25, 1485), *Laura Cereta: Collected Letters*, pp. 176-77.

117. Cereta (November 11, 1487), *Laura Cereta: Collected Letters*, p. 109.

118. In addition to these three classical philosophers, she refers to the philosophers Xenocrates, Chrysippus, Epicurus, Cicero, and Seneca, the poets Horace, Apuleius, and Virgil, the historians Pliny, Valerius Maximus, and Diogenes Laertius, and the satirists Ovid and Juvenal. Christian models, such as Eve, Rebecca, Mary, Elizabeth, Boethius, and Augustine appear in her letters along with the Neoplatonists, Porphyry, and Plutarch. In all of these references Cereta appropriately invokes a particular philosopher or philosophy as part of a larger argument.

119. Cereta (October 31, 1485), *Laura Cereta: Collected Letters*, p. 177.

120. Cereta (February 28, 1488), *Laura Cereta: Collected Letters*, p. 45.

121. Cereta (undated), *Laura Cereta: Collected Letters*, p. 157.

You have, however, a clear affinity with Aristotle, after whom no one has come who is greater than you. You, who are the equal of the inventors of argumentation, have fully exposed the most specious ambiguities among sophistries, which the puzzling subtlety of the dialectic entangles even more confusingly. I would say confidently that to hold a discourse on the arcane divinity of the trinity without regard for the envy of the theologians is unique — and this is my guess — in you, who explain this most present and immediate plane by an investigation that relies not only on the seeing but also the feeling intellect. Nor should you think on this account, I hope, that I believe that God is demonstrable matter — a machine made of clay. Rather, among the most preeminent of causes, he is the most powerful. This cause, as if the overseer and guardian over us, inhabits minds which have not been taken over by passions in human ways.[122]

In her "Dialogue on the Death of an Ass" Laura Cereta introduces Plato by name in the context of a consideration of reincarnation:

> In addition, Plato seems to have thought that the souls of men who devoted themselves to shameful pursuits for the sake of sensual pleasure were changed into their opposites after they departed from this life. What else? By naming the two small autumnal stars shining in the head and claw of the constellation, Cancer, the "Little Asses," the religion of a prior era taught (as if it knew) that these asses had been elevated from a life of great punishment on earth to one of caring for human suffering in heaven.[123]

It seems clear from the context that Cereta means by the phrase "changed into their opposites" a change from one realm (earthly) to another realm (heavenly). This would follow Plato's description in the *Laws* where Plato describes those who are "transported to live in the opposite realm."[124] It would also follow Ficino's and Pico's Neoplatonic theory of a hierarchy of levels of being, although their theories have more levels than two opposites would cover. However, Cereta's manner of expression seems to imply that the souls themselves are changed into their opposites, not that the same soul is moved into a different realm. This more precise description recalls Plato's description in *Timaeus*: "[o]f the men who came into the world, those who were cowards or led unrighteous lives may with reason be supposed to have changed into the nature of women in the second generation."[125] In Aristotelian terminology, the female is the opposite of the male, which would accord with this latter interpretation. Since the oration on the funeral of the ass is an allegory, it is not possible to give a definite interpretation of Cereta's meaning here. What is clear, however, is that she understands Plato's philosophy to include a theory of reincarnation.

There is another passage in Cereta's writings that raises a possible echo of Plato. At the end of a letter to Bibolo Semproni she introduces a notion of a "repub-

---

122. Cereta (December 11, 1487), *Laura Cereta: Collected Letters,* p. 111.
123. Cereta (undated), *Laura Cereta: Collected Letters,* p. 198.
124. Plato, *Laws* 904e.
125. Plato, *Timaeus* 90e-91a.

lic of women." Cereta's remarks are in a context in which her work had been attacked because of her sex identity:

> I am a scholar and a pupil who has been lulled to sleep by the meager fire of a mind too humble. I have been too much burned, and my injured mind has accumulated too much passion; for tormenting itself with the defending of our sex, my mind sighs, conscious of its obligation. For all things — those deeply rooted inside us as well as those outside us — are being laid at the door of our sex.
>
> In addition, I, who have always held virtue in high esteem and considered private things as secondary in importance, shall wear down and exhaust my pen writing against those men who are garrulous and puffed up with false pride. I shall not fail to obstruct tenaciously their treacherous snares. And I shall strive in a war of vengeance against the notorious abuse of those who fill everything with noise, since armed with such abuse, certain insane and infamous men bark and bare their teeth in vicious wrath at the **republic of women, so worthy of veneration.**[126]

The translator of Laura Cereta's letters into English, Diana Robin, states that she is not aware of the expression "republic of women" elsewhere, although it does occur in a letter replete with references to Boccaccio's *Concerning Famous Women*. Thus, it is possible that Cereta gave a general term to gather together the women Boccaccio described. A more remote possibility is that Cereta was aware of Christine de Pizan's *Book of the City of Ladies,* which drew upon Boccaccio's descriptions of women. With this interpretation, the expression "republic of women" refers to the republic or gathering of women of letters. Diana Robin argues that this is the appropriate translation of the phrase, given the original Latin, *muliebris respublica.*[127]

I would like, however, to raise another possibility, namely that the phrase "republic of women" also harkens to Plato's theory of educated women philosopher-guardians in his utopian *Republic*. My reasons for this suggestion are as follows. First, increasingly more accurate versions of Plato's *Republic* were made available to Italian readers of Latin by various translators (in 1402 by Chrysoloras and Uberto Decembrio, in 1437-39 by Pier Candido Decembrio, in 1439-47 by Antonio Cessarino, and in 1484 by Marsilio Ficino). Second, Plato's community of women in the *Republic* had received considerable notoriety for its moral, intellectual, and political suggestions about women. Third, for ten years preceding January 13, 1488, when Laura Cereta wrote her letter addressed to Bibolo Semproni, Cardinal Bessarion and Marsilio Ficino had attempted to redefine Plato as morally compatible with Christian life. Fourth, Laura Cereta had already proven herself willing to use controversial classical phrases and concepts when it suited her own purposes. Fifth, through her humanistic communities of discourse in Brescia, modeled in part on Ficino's Florentine Academy, Laura Cereta may have been well aware of Plato's suggestion that women were capable of the highest intellectual develop-

---

126. Cereta (January 13, 1488), *Laura Cereta: Collected Letters,* p. 80. My emphasis.

127. In a private conversation about this passage Robin remains convinced that *Muliebris respublica* refers generally to a republic of women of letters and that it has no association with Plato.

ment in an ideal republic. Therefore, it is possible that she was raising an echo of women's place in Plato's *Republic* in her phrase *"muliebris respublica"* even as she was describing ill treatment of a general republic of women of letters.

Of women philosophers contemporary with Cereta, there are three who stand out as important to her: Nicolosa of Bologna, Isotta of Verona, and Cassandra of Venice. In addition, she notes with appreciation four male philosophers — Petrarch, Boccaccio, Valla, and Ficino. Cereta integrated particular aspects of each of these authors into her own philosophy of personal and gender identity. She desired to be immortalized as a second version of Petrarch's Laura, and she positioned herself in a historical context of many wise and virtuous women identified in Boccaccio's *Concerning Famous Women*. Petrarch served as an inspiration to her, but Boccaccio provided historical records with which she could ground her identity as a woman intellectual. In the impassioned letter to Bibolo Semproni mentioned above, Cereta draws upon Boccaccio to defend herself and other scholarly women against the scorn of learned men who do not accept their talents. She states that the accusations against her as a woman scholar are false and unjust:

> Your complaints are hurting my ears, for you say publicly and quite openly that you are not only surprised but pained that I am said to show this extraordinary intellect — of the sort one would have thought nature would give to the most learned men — as if you had reached the conclusion, on the facts of the case, that a similar girl had seldom been seen among the peoples of the world. You are wrong on both counts, Semproni, and now that you've abandoned the truth, you are going to spread information abroad that is clearly false.[128]

Laura Cereta illuminates her accusers' motives: bad will, lazy mind, violent words, and dim intelligence. Bibolo Semproni, whose name may be a "fictional creation and vehicle for her polemic," becomes the one criticized, but with truthful and just accusations:

> I think you should be deeply pained — no, you should actually be blushing — you who are no longer now a man full of animus but instead a stone animated by the scorn you have for the studies that make us wise, while you grow weak with the sickness of debilitating leisure. And thus in your case, it is not nature that goes astray but the mind, for which the path from the appearance of virtue to villainy is a fairly easy one. In this manner, you appear to be flattering a susceptible young girl because of the glory that has accrued to her — my — name. But that snare of flattery is seductive, for you who have always set traps for the sex that has been revered all throughout history have been ensnared yourself. And duped by your own madness, you are trying, by running back and forth, to trample me underfoot and smash me to the ground with your fists. Sly mockery is concealed here, and it is typical of the lowborn, plebeian mind to think that one can blind Medusa with a few drops of olive oil. You would have done better to have crept up

---

128. Cereta (January 13, 1488), *Laura Cereta: Collected Letters*, pp. 74-75.

on a mole than a wolf, since the former, being shrouded in darkness, would see nothing clearly, while the latter's eyes radiate light in the dark.[129]

Cereta then turns to her own motivations. Using a Neoplatonic description of the path of the intellect, she explains that reason makes her aware of her own anger and desire for revenge due to centuries of attack on the female sex:

> In case you don't know, the philosopher sees with her mind; she furnishes paths with a window of reason through which she can ascend to a state of awareness. For Providence, the knower of the future, conquers marauding evil, trampling it with feet that have eyes. I would remain silent, believe me, if you, with your long-standing hostile and envious attitude towards me, had learned to attack me alone; after all, a ray of Phoebus' can't be shamed by being surrounded by mud. But I am angry and my disgust overflows. Why should the condition of our sex be shamed by your little attacks? Because of this, a mind thirsting for revenge is set afire; because of this, a sleeping pen is wakened for insomniac writing; because of this, red-hot anger lays bare a heart and mind long muzzled by silence.[130]

Next, Cereta demonstrates that women together have a legitimate line of inheritance of literacy and virtue. Diana Robin, the translator of her works, points out that Laura uses "terms common in property and inheritance law: *legitima, hereditatis, possessio,* here applied to the intellectual and cultural legacy of generations of learned women."[131]

> My cause itself is worthy: I am impelled to show what great glory that noble lineage which I carry in my own breast has won for virtue and literature — a lineage that knowledge, the bearer of honors, has exalted in every age. For the possession of this lineage is legitimate and sure, and it has come all the way down to me from the perpetual continuance of a more enduring race.[132]

The reference to "the perpetual continuance of a more enduring race" is somewhat puzzling. While it has been suggested by Robin that Cereta is claiming that women, as a race, are more enduring than men, this seems unlikely to me in view of other claims she makes, even in the same letter, about the equality of the two genders.[133] With further clarification from Robin, it seems as though Cereta was implying that women are more enduring than one might think women would be, rather than as men are. Along this line of thought Cereta goes on to show that women's contributions to literature and virtue existed temporarily before men's.

129. Cereta (January 13, 1488), *Laura Cereta: Collected Letters,* p. 75.
130. Cereta (January 13, 1488), *Laura Cereta: Collected Writings,* p. 75.
131. Robin, ed., *Laura Cereta: Collected Letters,* p. 76, note 40.
132. Cereta (January 13, 1488), *Laura Cereta: Collected Letters,* p. 75.
133. Robin, ed., *Laura Cereta: Collected Letters,* p. 76, note 40. Robin's words are: "Here again Cereta expresses the notion of women as a collectivity, as a race, breed, or generation 'more enduring' than that of males."

This thesis of temporal priority of contribution would fit with her introduction, to support her claims, of examples from Boccaccio's *Concerning Famous Women* of women who helped men. A condensed version of her references to Boccaccio will be offered with the chapter from *Concerning Famous Women* placed in brackets:

> We have read that the breast of Ethiopian Sabba, imbued with divinity, solved the prophetic riddles of the Egyptian king Solomon [*CFW,* 41]. The first writers believed that Amalthea, a woman erudite in the knowledge of the future . . . [*CFW,* 24]. Thus, the Babylon prophetess Eriphila, looking into the future with her divine mind far removed . . . [*CFW,* 19]. Nicostrata, too, the mother of Evander and very learned in prophecy as well as literature, attained such genius that she was the first to show the alphabet to the first Latins in sixteen figures [*CFW,* 25]. The enduring fame of Inachan Isis will flourish, for she alone of the Argive goddesses revealed to the Egyptians her own alphabet for reading [*CFW,* 8]. But Zenobia, an Egyptian woman of noble erudition, became so learned not only in Egyptian but also in Latin and Greek literature that she wrote histories of barbarian and foreign peoples [*CFW,* 98].
>
> Shall we attribute illiteracy to Theban Manto . . . , who was full of those Chaldaean arts . . . [*CFW,* 28]? Where did all the great wisdom of Tritonian Pallas come from, which enabled her to educate so many Athenians in the arts . . . [*CFW,* 6]? Those little Greek women Phyliasia and Lasthenia were wonderful sources of light in the world of letters and they filled me with new life because they ridiculed the students of Plato, who frequently tied themselves in knots over the snare-filled sophistries of their arguments [Diogenes Laertius, *Lives of the Philosophers*].
>
> Lesbian Sappho serenaded the stony heart of her lover with tearful poems . . . [*CFW,* 45]. Soon the Greek tongue of Leontium, full of the Muses, emerged, and she, who had made herself agreeable with the liveliness of her writing, dared to make a bitter attack on the divine words of Theophrastus [*CFW,* 58]. Nor would I omit here Proba, noted both for her exceptional tongue and her knowledge; for she wove together and composed histories of the Old Testament with fragments from Homer and Virgil [*CFW,* 95].
>
> The majesty of the Roman state deemed worthy a little Greek woman Semiramis, for she spoke her mind about the laws in a court of law and about kings in the senate [*CFW,* 2]. Pregnant with virtue, Rome bore Sempronia, who, forceful in her eloquent poetry, spoke in public assemblies and filled the minds of her audiences with persuasive orations [*CFW,* 77]. Hortensia, the daughter of Hortensius, and also an orator, was celebrated at a public meeting with equal elegance . . . [*CFW,* 82]. Add also Cornificia . . . who wrote epigrams in which every phrase was graced with Heliconian flowers [*CFW,* 84]. I will not mention here Cicero's daughter Tulliola or Terentia or Cornelia, Roman women who reached the pinnacle of fame for their learning; and accompanying them in the shimmering light of silence will be Nicolosa of Bologna, Isotta of Verona, and Cassandra of Venice.[134]

134. Cereta (January 13, 1488) and Diana Robin's identification of sources, *Laura Cereta: Col-*

Laura Cereta organizes her sources chronologically: various goddesses or ancient religious holy women, followed by women philosophers in the Pythagorean, Platonic, and Stoic traditions, then Roman women of law, rhetoric, poetry, and politics. Finally, contemporary women scholars from three cities in northern Italy provide counterexamples to the argument that the above-mentioned contributions of women were simply a thing of the past. She states the fundamental principle of equality:

> All history is full of such examples. My point is that your mouth has grown foul because you keep it sealed so that no arguments can come out of it that might enable you to admit that nature imparts one freedom to all human beings equally — to learn.[135]

This principle undermines the principle of polarity that Bibolo had asserted at the beginning, namely, that it is contrary to nature for a woman to excel in study. Let us recap her steps in the argument:

1. Restates the false and unjust claims made against woman's identity.
2. Illuminates the motives (including passions) of the accuser.
3. Considers her own motives (including passions) for self-defense.
4. Establishes woman's right of inheritance to a particular engendered history.
5. Provides historical counterexamples to the false claim from Boccaccio's *Concerning Famous Women*.
   a. goddesses and holy women
   b. women philosophers
   c. Roman women of law, rhetoric, poetry, and politics
6. Provides counterexamples of contemporary Italian women humanist scholars.
7. Concludes with principles of freedom and equality to learn for all men and women.

As to her other methods of philosophical argumentation, Cereta was well aware of the difference between demonstration and dialectic, the former method aiming for certainty and the latter for probability. Cereta was also aware of the goal of rhetoric to persuade by an appeal to human passions as well as to human reason. Cereta also used the contrasting of different positions in subsequent letters in the form of a dialogue about a common theme, or a triptych that does the same for three different positions. Diana Robin has demonstrated her ways of doing this in imitation of Lorenzo Valla's dialogue *De voluptate* and elsewhere. Robin notes: "Taken together as a diptych, Cereta's letters to Deodata di Leno and Europa solitaria exemplify — as though they were the speeches of two different interlocu-

---

lected Letters, pp. 76-78 and notes 41-57. Because we are considering Cereta's use of sources here and Cereta extends her description of them over four long paragraphs, and because these sources have been carefully identified by Robin, we are condensing the selection.

135. Cereta (January 13, 1488), *Laura Cereta: Collected Letters,* p. 78.

tors in a dialogue — the humanist ideal of *in utramque partem*, the arguing of both sides of a question."[136]

Cereta made use of the three different kinds of analogy — horizontal, vertical, and transcendental — as a fundamental tool of her philosophical methodology. Analogies are woven throughout all of her writings, in simple metaphors, in sustained arguments, and in developed allegories. In her letter to Sister Deodata di Leno, we see all of these analogies employed for the purpose of defending a kind of Christian Epicurean philosophy. Here is an example of horizontal analogies between a philosopher and a bird, a wrestler, and a traveler:

> The subtlety of your question has opened my mind to more important roads to understanding. But I am not the person to defend the argument at hand, since empty air does not support wings that have no feathers [a reference, perhaps, to one of Aristotle's definitions of man as a "featherless biped"]. I have no desire to enter into an academic wrestling match with you since I have acquired only a shadow of learning, and this outside the academy and without any study of the fine points of logic. You asked about our departure point and the sequence of places on our itinerary. The story would be plain enough, but the difficulty lies wholly in our destinations, for you tacitly impugn pleasure when you attack our delight in Epicurus. Still, I would not so easily attribute pleasure to vice, since the philosopher locates this pleasure not in the delights of the senses but in the sating of the mind. But more on this later. Now to what you ask.[137]

The two most frequent foundations for horizontal analogies in Cereta's writings were images taken from embroidery or jurisprudence. In the following passage from the same letter she reflects on her own methodology:

> Let us awaken our souls from sleep, dear sister. Let those of us who are reclining and who are cowardly rise to greater illuminations of the faith. Let us put away the cares of this age from the threshold of anxiety and let us tear the slender threads of arrogance from falsehood and deception.[138]

The particular phrase "tear the threads of arrogance from falsehood and deception" will become manifested repeatedly in Cereta's manner of engaging in philosophical dialogue with her correspondents. She pulls out these destructive threads of falsehood and deception from the woven material of her opponents' positions, seeking all the while to illuminate the true and integral communication.

Cereta's knowledge of the legal process likely came through her father, who was an attorney and magistrate. However, her application of it to uncover truth about human nature and gender identity is uniquely her own. In a letter addressed to her husband, Pietro Ferino, she responds to his complaints that she did not write to him often enough:

---

136. Robin, ed., *Laura Cereta: Collected Letters,* p. 115.
137. Cereta (December 12, 1487), *Laura Cereta: Collected Letters,* p. 116.
138. Cereta (December 12, 1487), *Laura Cereta: Collected Letters,* p. 119.

You charge me with laziness and attack me for my long silence as though I were a defendant in court. You act as if I were the sort of person who would write to strangers and only neglect you, as though I were forgetful of you when in fact I accord you a place of honor above that of other learned men. And although I might boast that I have received whatever learning I have from you for the sake of your honor, still I won't offer further epistolary flattery in place of an excuse in any hope that there could be impunity for one who has committed an offense; for the hunger of false friendships uses flattery to set up her nets. Consequently, my innocence alone will be the tinder for your forgiveness of me.

But really, the motive separates innocent from the guilty. And I should not be summoned to a court without a judge by a plaintiff who is absent, since the alleged offence seems to have been committed against him who is absent. . . . And so, your accusation requires the mounting of an indictment against the accused. But no confirmation of witnesses or arguments of proof are necessary in this case. I am not going to deny the charge that I have been silent, provided that the one who accuses me, the plaintiff himself, appears.

This legal inquiry should not be protracted any longer. Some might well take the case from the benches to the highest tribunal; we ourselves will agree with the first verdict we receive, especially since the judge will be our common father. He, who is as just as the members of the Athenian Aeropagus, will adjudicate the case not for his own family but for everyone.[139]

The horizontal analogy between Pietro and a Plaintiff, Laura and a Defendant, and her father and a Judge is sustained through the entire letter.

Most of Laura Cereta's vertical analogies compare nature-based sense analogates with a state of soul or moral identity of a human being. In a letter to Lucilia Vernacula, Laura Cereta reflects on vicious attacks by women on herself and other female scholars:

Besides, these women, being idle with time on their hands and no interests of their own, occupy themselves with keeping watch over other people's business, and, like scarecrows hung up in the garden to get rid of sparrows, they shoot poison from the bows of their tongues at those who cross their paths. What after all is the purpose of honor if I were to believe that the barking roars of these sharp-tongued women were worth tolerating, when decent and cultivated women always extol me with honorable words? . . . Nor would I want, because of my speaking out, someone to criticize me for intolerance; even dogs are allowed to protect themselves from more aggressive fleas by crushing them, with their nails. An infected sheep must always be isolated from the healthy flock.[140]

Cereta often reflects on the behavior of animals to distinguish morally acceptable or unacceptable actions. Returning to Laura's letter to Sister Deodata di Leno, we find a lyrical description of a country scene in which a frightened "scapegoat" just

---

139. Cereta (July 14, 1485), *Laura Cereta: Collected Letters*, pp. 88-89.
140. Cereta (November 1, 1487), *Laura Cereta: Collected Letters*, pp. 81-82.

barely escapes death. A vertical analogy between the goat and herself as a writer often attacked at the summit of an intellectual mountain is strongly suggested:

> Finally, taking diverse routes, once we had reached the mountain top and the highest point of its summit, we launched a cascade of rocks which rolled headlong down into the depths of the valley. Then, roused by the racket, rabbits flew down the slopes ahead of us. Dogs, keen-scented and well-trained for the hunt, accompanied us. Next, right in front of our eyes, a small trembling goat began to grow agitated at the sound of their yelping, and while the dogs followed his scent and trail with aggressive intent, he, with the violent dogs at his heels, chose flight by leaping down from the jutting ridges.[141]

The notion of an innocent scapegoat is carried over into a sustained allegory, "Dialogue on the Death of an Ass." In this mock funeral oration, modeled on the classic tale of *The Golden Ass* by Apuleius, Cereta introduces both a vertical analogy and a transcendental analogy. In the vertical analogy she compares a classical funeral oration for a human dignitary and this unique funeral oration for a donkey. Cereta seems to be mocking the dignity of human death and grief by her dialogue, which caused much scorn on the part of others. Obviously, the human funeral and oration have a higher dignity than a funeral and oration for an animal. Yet, given what Laura Cereta had suffered over the death of her own husband, it was unlikely that she would demean or ridicule funerals.

As to the transcendental dimension of her analogy, many hints suggest that in some ways the little donkey paralleled the primordial scapegoat, Jesus Christ. Another component in the transcendental analogy is the figure of Laura Cereta herself, who acts as an intermediary between the animal and Christ. Thus, in the extended analogy three levels of being are interwoven in a single story:

> **Philonacus:** But anyway this miller's ass of ours, who was outstanding in the sweat and hard work he devoted to his duties, always rose to the challenge of his tasks and frequently offered his tired neck to the pulling of carriages . . . he learned to submit his proud neck to the halter and to cross the more secure roadways leading away from the noisy city's menacing assault. . . . Brescia is his witness. . . . What could be more gentle or more submissive than this animal, who, covered with a tapestry of many colors, straightened his legs gently first on one side and then the other and thus carried my sister to her wedding, her hair arranged in a little tower with garlands braided in between her curls?
>
> Nor should I fail to mention that he, though he was innocent of evil himself, learned to protect me from getting caught for my crime when I would cut the crops with a sharp scythe and steal them from the fields at night. Certainly he was so compliant that he never bore either stings from insects or blasts from the wind with an ill temper. Still, I shall confess an act that needs expiation, and whose villainy distresses me every time I recall it, namely that I, angry scoundrel that I was, punished him by whipping him with sticks when he did not want to

---

141. Cereta (December 12, 1487), *Laura Cereta: Collected Letters,* p. 118.

soak himself in the river in order to wash away the filth from the mange he had on his coat. After this he showed his sadness, looking only at the ground with glassy eyes. He refused to eat for three nights in a row nor did he rise to his feet for those three days.[142]

Philonacus had committed "this one unspeakable crime, this one terrible arrogance, this one savage and unavenged cruelty that has caused me, a perpetrator of despicable vile, so merciless, so fierce, and so barbarous, to prey upon an innocent creature."[143] Laura Cereta suggests uncontrolled passion as a motive for this crime of harming an innocent being. Philonacus says: "I admit that I should be seized, stripped, and beaten with a whip because, inflamed with the sin of rage, I inflicted punishment on one who was innocent. Should this ass, your refuge from us who were the rogues in your household, have been so bitterly and cruelly tortured?"[144]

The character, Laura, offers the final judgment. The poor innocent animal, brutally murdered, serves as an innocent scapegoat for the people:

> Let us consider ourselves what anger would fill our hearts or what bitterness would cause our minds to seethe if we were to think that he, who with his continuing labors carried help, protection, and extra supplies to us in our affairs, had been ill-treated with beatings or verbal abuse. Certainly if we were to review the life and exploits of this swift-footed creature of ours, there was never a time when the townspeople had reason to abuse him.[145]

She reflects on Plato's theory of the transmigration of souls and the possibility that the little donkey had been changed into a heavenly constellation, and moved from suffering on earth to caring for human suffering in heaven, and concludes: "But these are matters of faith."[146] The perspective of faith is another clue that her analogy is transcendental; it goes beyond human senses and reason alone. Finally, Cereta quotes Pliny concerning the healing power of an ass's milk, blood, dung, ashes, hooves, liver, hide, genitals, and lungs. She concludes with a ringing tribute to this particular immortal donkey who heals all aspects of human life:

> Asellus[, who] himself was superior to other asses and did many things that learned men will celebrate and hand down to posterity[,] counsels us to lift all the cares and baggage from our minds. Therefore, father Soldus, it will be gratifying to your reputation that so many writers will commend the glorious deeds of this animal to the immortality of letters.[147]

Laura counsels Soldus, the bereaved owner of the ass:

142. Cereta, *Laura Cereta: Collected Letters,* pp. 192-94.
143. Cereta, *Laura Cereta: Collected Letters,* p. 195.
144. Cereta, *Laura Cereta: Collected Letters,* p. 196.
145. Cereta, *Laura Cereta: Collected Letters,* pp. 197-98.
146. Cereta, *Laura Cereta: Collected Letters,* p. 199.
147. Cereta, *Laura Cereta: Collected Letters,* p. 200.

Now, using reason, rise above the circumstances owing to which your humanity has overwhelmed you with emotion.

Look, I have persuaded everyone; they are returning to their senses. I alone, who came here for the purpose of consoling others, must now be consoled together with you. I beg you, take my advice seriously.[148]

Laura Cereta's use of three different kinds of analogies can be summarized as follows:

Horizontal analogies

- Embroidery and philosophical method: weaving the one line of truth
- Legal system and philosophical method: uncovering false judgments by trial and evidence

Vertical analogies

- State of nature and state of soul
- Some women like scarecrows who watch others
- Dogs crush fleas as Laura fights poisoned tongues
- Small trembling goat chased by dogs like Laura chased by slanderers
- Oration for funeral of an ass like oration for funeral of an innocent person (Laura)

Transcendental analogies

- Ass and Laura as scapegoats like Christ as scapegoat
- Those who torture and murder the scapegoat like those who tortured and murdered Christ

While Laura Cereta used many other analogies, the few included above indicate the teaching method she used to lead her reader to a philosophical or theological insight.

Gender and Self-Knowledge

In the history of philosophy, Socrates is credited with the dictum "know yourself," but Augustine and Boethius were the first two philosophers who left a written legacy of the dynamic struggle to come to self-knowledge in a set of particular circumstances. Laura Cereta continued this process. She came to understand the dynamic structure of the human person with such facility that she could use it to interpret different aspects of her own and other's identity and actions; and, she

---

148. Cereta, *Laura Cereta: Collected Letters,* p. 201.

brought into self-knowledge an acute awareness of herself as a woman, widow, scholar, and teacher.

Cereta may also have been influenced by St. Thomas Aquinas's analysis of the passions of the soul in the *Summa theologica* through her spiritual advisor, the Dominican Brother Thomas from Milan.[149] Thomas Aquinas delineated eleven fundamental passions of the soul: the six concupiscible passions of love and hate, desire and aversion, pleasure (delight) and pain (sorrow), and the five irascible passions of hope and despair, fear and daring, and anger. Cereta, very much in union with Thomas's analysis, demonstrated the relation between the passions of the soul, intellect, and will in her philosophy of the human person. She discussed how particular concupiscible and irascible passions may either help or hinder the development of virtue. She agreed with Thomas that Truth was the proper object of the intellect and that Good was the proper object of the will. She delineated the steps for the proper ordering of human passions by reason and will, act and habit, for the greater development of truth, justice, and the common good:

1. Awareness of the passions and situations surrounding human acts.
2. Judgment of reason about the relative value of particular passions in particular circumstances.
3. Make a better choice.
4. Constant vigilance and working towards greater virtue.

In her autobiographical narrative to Sister Nazaria Olympia, Laura Cereta describes her problems after the death of her husband:

> Surely my husband's spirit lies now among the shades; and now unspeakable marble kisses his limbs. Now that ashy dust sighs in my ears, now one cave awaits me who lives among the living. For the dead, this life is a dream, whose course hangs over all humans like a brief watch in the night. And so, if I thought that it was completely unclear how the events of my life would proceed and in what order, and if you cared about these things, I would describe them more fully and at greater length — **if my mind should ever become conscious of itself.**[150]

One year later, in a letter written to Brother Thomas, Cereta explains that she wants to gain a true knowledge of herself:

> Shall I — and I see myself as a girl who aspires to neither of these occupations — penetrate either with the eyes of my mind or the shining beacon of truth those eternal dwelling places, gazing up at which, as though under a prodigious weight, Thomas, Dionysius, and so many of our celebrated ancestors spent their days and nights? . . .
> The sea of knowledge about celestial things is vast, and its immensity sur-

149. Thomas Aquinas, *Summa theologica* (Westminster, Md.: Christian Classics, 1981), II,II Q. 22-48.

150. Cereta (November 5, 1486), *Laura Cereta: Collected Letters,* p. 28. My emphasis.

rounds the minds of humans, continuing on forever and disappearing into the distance. An eagle can fly above the clouds, soaring beyond the inaccessible tops of mountain crags. I, content with a lowlier path, shall follow the teaching of our Savior in the gospel. There is one law, one word of God, and one true virtue, which should be disseminated in the temple of our hearts in its purest form so that he may fill us with his love amid the vicissitudes of human fragility. . . .

We miserable women, being nothing in ourselves as long as we are alive, are together overcoming the confused and turbulent passions of the mind by obedience to the law, to the extent that we can. . . .

All posterity learns from the story which teaches that great is the heady power of knowing, which — like the sweet smell of imminent exaltation — enabled the serpent to fool Eve in spite of God's false hopes. **Best of all the things that are knowable is the true knowledge of oneself.**[151]

Two years later, in an introduction to the manuscript of her collected letters to Cardinal Ascanio Maria Sforza, Cereta explains that this self-knowledge goes further than just gathering particular data. It involves coming to a knowledge of the causes of virtue and of things that interfere with the active pursuit of virtue:

Still, this was not the home of happiness or pleasure that I sought, though it was adorned with a beautiful understanding of things. For I was ignorant of the causes that would lead me to virtue; moreover, too great a diversity of studies disturbed my natural abilities. Yet the decision I had made remained more firmly entrenched than ever to proceeding with the study of sacred literature so that I might see if such writings had more nobility in them. This **inward-looking path to knowledge played so important a role in my life** that I devoted whole nights to this study without stopping to rest, and all other desire for relaxation eluded me like a thief and vanished.[152]

The first aspect of self-knowledge that she comes to understand is the gift and the limits of her own talent. In the same letter to Cardinal Sforza, Cereta concludes that she is most effective as a writer when she uses her own reason to write in a simple style about a modest topic related to the theme of virtue:

There is, however, one humble style that can give pleasure in all letters: this style should not astonish, even if it is adorned with very few, though living, colors. For what profit can there be in a brilliant oration framed by curving vine tendrils entwined with an elaborate foliage of words? . . . [C]ertainly educated readers respect a modestly written oration more than one that is not so: superfluous effort is exerted for superfluous elegance.

No one should expect me to possess a rarefied way of speaking that has come down to me from the age of Phoenix. This native literature of ours will be enough for everyone, though no Greek Amphion has ever burst into harmonious

151. Cereta (September 10, 1486), *Laura Cereta: Collected Letters*, p. 105. My emphasis.
152. Cereta (March 1988), *Laura Cereta: Collected Letters*, p. 38. My emphasis.

song, and no Demosthenes, no Theophrastus have made speeches; nor do these pages of mine, which are illuminated with pictures, represent Aesop as more esteemed than Virgil. From all the maxims of antiquity, my mind distils figures that are alive and fresh. Because of this, I may not express the opinion that the vulture is a more noble creature than the silvery little sparrow. For virtue does not inhabit the first living seeds of things — but what precious thing in the ancient maxims could be more precious than virtue?

And so I, who have hardly acquired even the first rudiments of learning, am a small chattering woodpecker among poetic swans. **Each should display her own particular gifts for study. For no one is safe who strives beyond her abilities; and thus it is safer to trust in reason than in men's opinions.** The road to fame that is everlasting runs along the precipices and is difficult and narrow. I can boast, I admit, about the intellectual gifts the Omnipotent Lord has given me since rare is the girl in any age who writes books with painstaking grace and brilliance. I have spent on the liberal arts whatever the river of time has allotted me; yet all my strength of mind has composed only these few cold and lifeless letters with a short and inadequate pen.[153]

This trust in reason will become a rallying cry in all of her correspondence. Reason is the arbiter not only of men's opinions but also of the dynamic life of the passions within the soul. Reason leads her to true self-knowledge and knowledge of the human person. The goal of the intellect is truth, the object of all of Laura Cereta's study and reflection. In order to demonstrate how she unfolds the inner dynamism of the human person we will consider her self-knowledge in the phases of grief that followed upon her husband's sudden death.

The earliest mention of grief in Laura Cereta's letters is found in a challenging letter of July 17, 1486 to her husband Pietro Serina. In this letter she assumes a position similar to Seneca's in his letters "On Consolation to Marcia" and "On Consolation to Helvia," where he encourages his correspondents to become aware of their extreme responses in the face of human mortality.[154] Laura Cereta does the same with her husband:

> You bear your bereavement over the untimely death of Nicolai with unending tears, as though you yourself had died, and in such a way that you seem to have banished all hope of living from your mind. Have you forgotten, most mindful and brave among men, that nature has so ordained dying for all men and that only the good die well? And even if he had survived vile death, would you not be induced to tear your hair, cry out, and beat your breast at another man's funeral? Should I, poor thing, believe that you would lose sight of that magnanimity of mind that has enabled you to watch your own family struggling through years of death when it fell victim to the pestilent plague?

153. Cereta (March 1988), *Laura Cereta: Collected Letters,* pp. 40-41. My emphasis.

154. Seneca, "To Marcia on Consolation" and "To Helvia on Consolation" in *Moral Essays* (New York and London: C. P. Putnam's and Sons and William Heinemann Ltd., 1928-32), VI, 3-49 and 425-77.

I myself would like you, and I do beg you now because it is time, to return to your former self, since you have a greater duty towards me than you do towards the dead: for a man and his wife must so mutually love one another that they will not turn aside from that love at any time. Get a hold of yourself, then, and control this weeping of yours that has affected you so bitterly and harshly, lest you seem either to be at war with yourself, or, by the Julian law, to have launched a campaign against the gods who steal men's souls.

You ought to remember that even if the fates were to give you to Nicolai, you would still be far more precious to me than to him, since we are now, and always will be, two souls belonging to a single being.[155]

This letter is significant for several reasons. It indicates a certain judgmental attitude toward her husband, who experienced great bereavement over the death of his brother. She is critical of his extreme response and concerned that his passions have become disordered. The letter also reveals her view of their marriage as "two souls belonging to a single being." This reference is interesting as it keeps a certain distinction, by the differentiation of separate souls, while also preserving a unity, through the view that by marriage they have become a "single being." Finally, it reveals a tension as Pietro appears to be more emotionally identified with a member of his family than with his wife. This ambivalence in their relationship as husband and wife is a constant factor in their correspondence.

A few short weeks later, Laura Cereta herself was stricken with grief when Pietro suddenly died, possibly of the same pestilence as his brother. After only eighteen months of marriage she was a widow at the age of seventeen. She described her own suffering in great detail.

In the earliest letter dated August 5, 1486, to the attorney Alberto degli Alberti, Cereta describes vividly her grief, numbness, and overwhelming sorrow:

Your letters, flowing with milky liquor in the perfect image of loyalty and respect, strive to comfort me with persuasion in my affliction; but the weakness of an injured mind has become so frozen inside me that I can no longer be restored by exhortations or advice; for my sorrow torments me and I am mute. Nor can I fail to be suffocated by a fortune without hope. I shall confess this, nor will shame stand in my way. Although many may call me a fool, I do not know whether life is dearer to me than death. How fortunate are those infants whose luck it is to die in a mother's lap! I myself have survived, but my weeping is reborn; and I have washed with unending tears the pale face of an adolescence soon to be gone.[156]

She states a longing to become a pagan so that she can end her suffering by suicide, as expressed in reference to Ovid's *Metamorphoses,*

I would surely consider the Atlantides more fortunate than I, for people believe that, after mourning for their mutilated brother Hyas, they were changed into a

155. Cerete (July 17, 1486), *Laura Cereta: Collected Letters,* p. 92.
156. Cereta (August 5, 1486), *Laura Cereta: Collected Writings,* p. 96.

constellation. No less fortunate is Halcyon, who on account of her weeping for Eeyx after he drowned, changed into a bird. Likewise the grieving Heliades were able to relieve their sorrow, when, after Phaeton's fall, they grew into leafy poplars on the Po. You too being scorned, Phyllis, were changed into an almond tree because of Demophoon's delay. You, Scylla, saw well enough how passions dissolve, when you hid yourself from your lover Glaucus under the sharp Sicilian rocks. Thus Cyane's tears disappeared from her eyes, when because of the rape of her friend Proserpina, she melted into a spring. Thus Hecuba was metamorphosed into a dog to relieve her wretched weeping after losing her king and realm. And thus Niobe was finally turned to stone, owing to the equal pity the gods took on her after her long period of mourning for her sons, whom Diana had impaled on a rock.

Ah me, battered by disconsolate lamentation, for whom death, though hoped for, still waits in the wings: life, cruel and inexorable, does not withdraw. O that I might at least die a pagan, since it is not possible according to Christian dogma to elect not to live. Would that those changers of forms, the gods, now summoned so sorrowfully and humbly, might help me in my misfortune.[157]

Five days later a letter to the physician Felicio Tadino shows her grief deepening and moving from her "injured mind" to her "embattled heart." Cereta expresses anxiety, anger, and fear, and switches from classical references to visions springing up in her imagination:

Your letter has been a comfort to me, though I drenched it with tears before I read it: such is the tenderness of an embattled heart and so great the grief that wells up in an anxious breast. I had scarcely come to the middle of the letter in my short-lived reading of it when it prompted a fresh flow of tears for my mourning from eyes already bleary. Thus weeping evoked more weeping; and the floodgates were loosed in these two eyes of mine.

And so, in this overflow of mourning, winged death flooded my spirit deep within with monstrous horror. For, swathed in the tattered cloak of death and carrying arrows spread out in her right hand and a menacing bow, she showed me her snarling, wan face, as she alternately ground and gnashed her teeth at me. I looked over at this underworld Fury, who barely clung to her filthy bones; and when the light caught her, garlanded with coils of snakes and brandishing a scythe and a grindstone, she hurled herself at me. Frightened at the sudden attack of the approaching apparition, I was paralyzed with fear to the depths of my being.[158]

In another letter written during the same week to the physician Michel da Carrara, she states that: "[f]or a long time now my all-night bouts of writing have been less important to me, the one labor that remains for me is that of griev-

---

157. Cereta (August 5, 1486), *Laura Cereta: Collected Letters*, pp. 96-97.
158. Cereta (August 10, 1486), *Laura Cereta: Collected Letters*, p. 94.

ing. . . ."[159] This "labor of grieving" interferes with her ability to write. Her concentration and eloquence are fragmented:

> Now, so much sorrow is left in me that every effort at eloquence runs clumsily aground among the reefs and at sea. You, however, amid the copiousness of my style will not think ill of this letter, woven as it is of rather tiny pieces, and worn away for so long a time now by the corrosive sobbings of a young girl's pen.[160]

The difficulty in concentrating is mentioned in a letter written one month later to her spiritual advisor, the Dominican Brother Thomas. Here Cereta considers, but rejects, the possibility of entering a religious vocation:

> For the premature death of my husband has brought me such grief that, crushed and in turmoil, my mind floats, storm-tossed amid the tears and depression of a heart in mourning. But alas, that thought, which my irrevocable loss reproves, is too late and surely too extreme: the solace of the convent, for which the recurring pain in my heart often longs, is no stranger to me.[161]

Although Laura Cereta seems depressed, she continues her "labor of grief." In fact, a month later on October, 6, 1486 she consoles another widowed woman, Martha Marcella. First, she focuses on the other person's grief, but soon turns to her own suffering. Her visit to the underworld is similar to Virgil's, to Dante's visit to *Inferno* and *Purgatorio,* and to the visit from the underworld figure of death that Laura had previously described to Felicio Tandino:

> Why, dear sister, do you weep with bitter sorrow for one who is dead? Do you think the kings of the underworld care about human tears? I remember that last year I was seized and dragged through the perpetual ice of Orcus, the intense flames of the Phlegethon, and the ashy chasms of the Acheron. And though I believe I saw the realms of Tartarus with my own eyes, I might lie to myself in my dreams. Still, my trembling imagination did see men being cast down and thrown into the furnace of Hades, drowning in eternal night. At that time, in the most profound state of terror, I was seized by grief and fear. I tore my hair and scratched at my pale cheeks, making myself unsightly; I mourned my husband with disconsolate weeping, and I showed the incurable wound in my heart, which felt lacerated and eaten away.
>
> But in the end it was all for nothing. Cruel fate, ever more hostile, stood in my path, while gluttonous Pluto, standing in front of me and leading the way, threatened me with instant death and exile from my home. Shouting hoarsely with a loud voice that was strangled and broken, he said, "Girl, watch where you go before the coming of your time, lest a locked gate make a mockery of all your bold-

---

159. Cereta (August 13, 1486), *Laura Cereta: Collected Letters,* p. 95.
160. Cereta (August 13, 1486), *Laura Cereta: Collected Letters,* p. 95.
161. Cereta (October 21, 1486/September 10, 1486), *Laura Cereta: Collected Letters,* p. 106.

ness, for once the inexorable procession of the fates leads one thus, all capacity to return is removed."[162]

Laura Cereta then tells about her descent into the levels of hell. She mentions classical figures such as the boatman Charon and the dog Cerberus, and that she did not find her dead husband "in the entire realm of Dis." She overcame her own temptation to suicide by the sure knowledge that if she chose to end her life "before the coming of her time," she would not be able to return to those she loved on earth.

The dream of searching for her dead husband in the underworld also appears six months later in a correspondence with the twenty-two-year-old Cassandra Fedele, to whom she shows off her literary knowledge of Virgil's journey in the *Aeneid*:

> From here, I was taken across the boiling shallow waters to the cave where the Cyclopes and Vulcan, the frightening craftsman, were laboring at forging lightning for the gods with constant hammering, din, and the metallic clashing of elements. From this place where thunderbolts were being cut out and beaten, I descended to the gate of horn, next to which Tiresias, who was mounted on a dragon, sang oracles to those who came to consult him. I approached, though quivering with fear of the monster, and I asked sorrowfully, in the manner of a suppliant, where my dead husband was. He said, "Your husband is far from this place; seek him in other realms. His blessed shade already inhabits the Elysian Fields." When the seer uttered these responses, his wandering and fluid mind began to enjoy the pleasure of divination. Indeed, after his prophecy, when I sought the difficult ascent on the left, being ignorant of the path, I became confused at its precipitousness, after which, roused by my terror, I awoke.[163]

Laura Cereta renders herself vulnerable to Cassandra Fedele in mentioning the passion of terror combined with personal confusion. In a move of self-defense, in the next paragraph she distances herself from it:

> Therefore, although these hackneyed stories may seem to be inventions smelling of the poets who arbitrarily make up silly tales, promising gods and demons and whatever else they wish to invent, still I myself would not dare to improve on nature regarding the content of a dream. In any case, I will not deny the things about the underworld on which there is nearly complete consensus. For I myself profess sometimes the distinctions of the three-bodied Peripatetic, and at other times the uncertain probabilities of the Academy. It is my goal to ask questions, not to settle them or make the rules about great philosophical issues such as these. Let others who are more desirous of great glory decide these questions. For me the one thing ordained is my wish to search out the Isles of the Blessed, where I may find the Fates and destined resting place of my faithful spouse, to whom mutual affection of a most tender love beyond the vows of human love has joined me.[164]

---

162. Cereta (October 8, 1486), *Laura Cereta: Collected Letters,* pp. 129-30.
163. Cereta (April 14, 1487), *Laura Cereta: Collected Letters,* p. 143.
164. Cereta (April 13, 1487), *Laura Cereta: Collected Letters,* pp. 143-44.

Cereta's purpose in writing is not simply to show off her knowledge of Virgil. She also wants to become friends with Cassandra Fedele:

> These are the things I thought I should write to you, Cassandra, whether or not I meant to consult with you as a Venetian prophet or oracle. Nor is it really the case that I have more interest in the dream than I have in you. On the contrary, I have written to you for the purpose of engaging the fineness and precision of your mind in thinking about an issue that requires those particular qualities. And although the miserly character of mother nature has produced in our sex minds that are petty [small-minded, stinting, or miserly], still you will rouse that brilliant and seasoned mind of yours for unravelling the enigmas of causes in nature, because of which I visited the underworld as I did.
>
> I know you will consider this first gift worthy enough so I won't think that you've rejected me or turned your back on my work.[165]

It is worth noting that in her very first letter to Cassandra Fedele she raises Aristotle's theory of the natural inferiority of women's minds, no doubt ironically: she says that since Cassandra Fedele's mind is "capable and seasoned," it can unravel "the enigmas of causes in nature," which according to Aristotle is the characteristic of a man who has the highest degree of wisdom as the science of causes.

Turning back again to the letter to Martha Marcella, Cereta demonstrates her awareness of the Epicurean philosophy, and recognizes that the higher pleasure of virtue is one remedy for the opposite passion of pain. She also reflects on the place of a virtuous friendship in the "labor of grief":

> I work on, I am restless, and I cannot stand myself because I lost so quickly my companion, the most beloved and precious part of me. But it is dangerous to grieve in this way. For the Epicureans believe that the wise man finds contentment in himself, that virtue is sweeter than any friend, and that our happiness proceeds not from any pleasure, or husband, or wealth, but from virtue. What good is a pleasure which is tangled and woven with passion? The allurements of the senses are the traps of birdlime, which the burning hour of death turns to ash. . . . Friendship doesn't look either for what brings advantage or what follows from it.[166]

Cereta has become repulsed by her overindulgence in sorrow, and she seeks to distance herself from extreme feelings "which are all for nothing" or "are dangerous." At the same time, she determines to seek virtue from within herself because it is good in itself, and not because it brings some utilitarian or pleasurable value along with it. She offers to Martha a challenge that reaffirms her belief in God:

---

165. Laura Cereta (April 13, 1487), *Laura Cereta: Collected Letters,* p. 144. See also Robin's note 70 for the translation of *avara* as petty, small-minded, stinting, or miserly.

166. Cereta (October 6, 1486), *Laura Cereta: Collected Letters,* p. 132.

> Do you believe that God is unjust in his divine and everlasting judgment? He has given the blessed a home in heaven, where the just rest secure in undisturbed tranquillity and wondrous peace. There our companions and husbands reside, bound by duty and concern for us.[167]

No longer does Cereta want to be metamorphosed into a pagan; she is firmly rooted in her faith as a devoted Christian. She also introduces the Neoplatonic theme of immortality of soul. Here, the reference, following Plato, Porphyry, Proclus, and Ficino, is to the immortal nature of the soul itself. For example, in "Dialogue on the Death of an Ass" the character Laura says to Soldus, who is grieving, "[t]he body ages, but the soul, which has been given the gift of immortality, does not."[168] Since the soul does not age, she implies that it does not die. The body, which ages and dies, has need to be resurrected in order to be rejoined to a particular man's or woman's soul in the afterlife. According to Neoplatonic Christians, while resurrection is a matter of faith, immortality is a matter of reason.

Laura Cereta returns to humanist themes of developing strength of mind and steadfastness of heart. She and Martha, as two friends, should exercise their wills by rowing together with "stronger oars":

> Adversity always fosters courage and, at the end of the play, constancy carries the day. But whenever strength of mind goes into the middle of a storm, though its sail may be torn, its ship may be damaged by perilous hail, and the din of the whirlwinds may resonate everywhere, with still greater steadfastness of heart it will not fear the yawning holes in the vessel.
>
> Come, therefore, let us struggle in this deep sea of adversity with stronger oars, and let us raise ourselves up in the midst of danger with steadfast hearts. For wherever the danger is greater, there is more glory to attain and more palms. For the roads to death lead men in many different directions, thus the ultimate end is unequal and uncertain for each.
>
> In the meantime, if fortune should take away any of the things it has granted us, let us bear it with an unwounded mind.[169]

The wound of grief that afflicted her mind is healing.

On November 30, 1486 Laura Cereta gives a funeral eulogy on the death of a child to Giuliano Trosoli. In this remarkable oration, apart from the usual observations about the "unforeseen mortality" of life, the "unutterable wound of bereavement," "[d]eath draws everything headlong in its train . . . [and] it has been decreed in heaven," and "there is nothing more sacred to virtue than adversity," she also reflects on the meaning of a child.[170] She invokes the Neoplatonic reverence for beauty and its relation to goodness. After describing the circumstances of the young baby girl's birth she concludes: "Thus the highest promise of goodness inno-

---

167. Cereta (October 8, 1486), *Laura Cereta: Collected Letters*, p. 132.
168. Cereta, "Dialogue on the Death of an Ass," *Laura Cereta: Collected Letters*, p. 190.
169. Cereta (October 8, 1486), *Laura Cereta: Collected Letters*, p. 133.
170. Cereta (November 30, 1486), *Laura Cereta: Collected Letters*, pp. 159-60.

cently revealed itself to us, and each of her individual features contributed to a total impression of beauty."[171]

Cereta appeals to other parents to share their own experience of this kind of loss and grief. She stresses that, while she has known grief from her own experience, she does not know how it feels from a mother's perspective:

> Now let those parents whose excellent sons and daughters have met the day of their death speak themselves of the causes of tears. I, childless and wretched, will feel your terrible sorrow, though I sense not the toils of your suffering in my inmost being. Alas, this is a parent's love; ponder these things in your heart, and may you who survive your children have compassion; intractable fate has snatched from you the sweet promise of your lineage.[172]

The phrase, "ponder these things in your heart," would naturally evoke the memory of Mary, Mother of Jesus Christ, who "pondered in her heart" the birth of her son and finding him again in the temple after he had been lost (*Luke* 2:19 and 2:51). She concludes with another phrase that would evoke the memory of Christ's offering: "I, who am filled with pain and anxiety with you in your grief, would willingly choose to die if I could bring back your daughter."[173] Her offer to die is not caused now by a desire to get rid of her own pain and sorrow, but by her compassion for others.

In spite of Laura Cereta's eagerness to complete her "labor of grief," she still has a long road of suffering to follow. In a letter of February 6, 1487 to Agostino Emilio, Laura admits that the wound of death has brought a blow to her mind and that she has stopped her astronomical investigations, her reading, and her writing. She has fallen into a period of anger and depression. She portrays her experience as a young girl in battle with Fortune:

> But O unhappy day, through the everlasting death of my husband, I have come to the road of mourning, common to all men, and on it I have left the glory of a wife's fidelity: my ululation and my torn hair. Ah, the uncertain lot of humans, ah, the unpredictability of things, and o mortality, unfriendly to greening minds. Shameless Fortune is jealous of a mind at peace. In her anger at me, she has hurled the darts of her own instability at the heart of an innocent girl. And with this wound of death, she has thrown the serenity of my study into confusion and she has redirected my investigations into the subtleties of heavenly things to grim mourning — all so that she, who bore arms, could go to war against an unarmed girl. Thus, pained by this bitter laceration and this grievous blow to my mind, I abandoned every nourishment that I delighted in and that my love of active study used to relish. What wonder is it then, if I have abandoned my sweet night vigils of reading and my search for the causes of things, with the pressure I feel from my husband's dying?[174]

171. Cereta (November 30, 1486), *Laura Cereta: Collected Letters,* p. 159.
172. Cereta (November 30, 1486), *Laura Cereta: Collected Letters,* p. 159.
173. Cereta (November 30, 1486), *Laura Cereta: Collected Letters,* p. 160.
174. Cereta (February 6, 1487), *Laura Cereta: Collected Letters,* p. 101.

She recognizes that the poor quality of her work is caused by the emotion of turmoil in her grief:

> But this is the turmoil and confusion of a mind that is roiling amid the tinder of my emotions. You yourself should consider what intellectual pleasure of delight in the pen there could possibly be for me now — whom blood exuding from a still beating heart has wet. You have expected, I am sure, that my poor little letters would radiate with genius and the lamp of eloquence. Your opinion has deceived you in this and your trust was elicited under false pretences — whether you were influenced by your love of me or my reputation. For while I have a lot of knowledge about desire, I know little about how to find a well for a pen that has gone dry. For it is not possible to do great things with small means.[175]

Her experience of emptiness, of an inkwell gone dry, continues for several more months. Cereta describes how she has been able to recover her external self-control in conversations with others, but her internal suffering and confusion continue unabated. Her turmoil has turned to bitterness in the following letter of May 1, 1487 to the physician Felicio:

> In the losing through death of the man I most longed for, death has taken everything from me. The pain draws tears to my eyes. Unconscious of bitterness, I have spurned my misfortune. I have spent a long time weeping, and even iron hearts have wept with me, but my wounded mind could not be healed with sobbing; for reason, not lamentation, removes sorrow. Still, I have returned at last and I have striven, insofar as I could, to remove the sting of inner pain from the wound of a mind in turmoil.
>
> After a short time I put aside tears but not the deeper, inner sighing. And thus, the face smiled because it was restrained, while the spirit within was afflicted, so much so that an uncertain confusion developed in me between reason and feeling. For though the mutilated body of Hippolytus could be restored to life, the lacerated mind of Apollo could not be healed; for the wound that love inflicts is more deadly than that of sorrow. But he who was designated for me in marriage was the one most desired; he was the one hoped for beyond all others who have lived, and when he loved me in return, all other desire in my heart lost its fire.[176]

In another letter written shortly after the one above, to Alberto degli Alberti, Cereta compares her emptiness to the fate of women who threw themselves on the funeral pyres of their husbands and died with their death:

> But misfortune occurred, alas, which was unexpected and hard to bear; and thus the seeds were sown that heaped up a harvest of funerary lamentations for me, in accord with the obligation of widowhood. For recently my beloved husband, whom I scarcely knew, perished under my very gaze, leaving my life though not

175. Cereta (February 6, 1487), *Laura Cereta: Collected Letters*, p. 102.
176. Cereta, *Laura Cereta: Collected Letters*, pp. 98-99.

my heart. . . . An inner pain beset me; and I had no hope left in my heart, which, being unarmed and incautious, was nearly pierced through and through by despair. I, like a sacrificial victim at a funeral service, seemed to die with the dead man, propelled toward death by the strange phenomenon of his dying. After this, a cry of grief, an attack of mournful weeping, launched by the siege engines of my mind, rose up suddenly and turned against the wall of bitterness inside me.[177]

Once again, we discover the strength of Laura Cereta's mind and will, to attend to her experience and be critical of it at the same time. Her grief still weighs too heavily:

> And so, although I wrote to you tearfully on the occasion of your departure, and although filial obligation [concerns for her father] moves me to write you again, still I myself, because I have been distracted from my studies, am neither distinguishing myself among the Muses [for literary inspiration], nor am pulled in a different direction by Apollo [for philosophical reflection]. Lamentation alone is left for me to cultivate. Thus my pen, cut down in the bloom of its eloquence, has dried up, and my accustomed thoughts have dissolved into tears.
>
> Under these circumstances, it will not be a difficult thing to make the accusation that my poor little gift of an inept tongue has fallen victim to the confused groaning deep inside me. For who can involve a mind which is strained by a siege of sorrows in the pleasure of a polished oration? Since I must therefore occupy myself with reflection for the time being rather than with writing, I beg you, who are so steeped in the tropes of eloquence, to allow the thin ramblings of a letter sterile and discordant, which concerns the unhappiness of a wounded heart, to excuse me in your eyes.[178]

Recovery did eventually come for Laura Cereta. Within two years of the death of her husband she had completed her manuscript of *Collected Letters,* including her composition "Dialogue on the Death of an Ass." By this time Laura had sufficiently recovered from her own grief to offer advice to another: "Do not remain suspended wholly in grief";[179] and a method for eventually overcoming grief: "Now, using reason, rise above the circumstances owing to which your humanity has overwhelmed you with emotion."[180] Reason, however, needs the exercise of will to accomplish the self-governance that the intellect perceives as a higher value than succumbing to the blind direction of the passions.

Her general principles, applied to her analysis of her own "labor of grief," are as follows:

1. **Become aware** of the data of self-consciousness (mind becomes conscious of itself in an inward journey):

177. Cereta (May 7, 1487), *Laura Cereta: Collected Letters,* p. 99.
178. Cereta (May 7, 1487), *Laura Cereta: Collected Letters,* p. 100.
179. Cereta, "Dialogue on the Death of an Ass," *Laura Cereta: Collected Letters,* p. 186.
180. Cereta, "Dialogue on the Death of an Ass," *Laura Cereta: Collected Letters,* p. 201.

    a. Gather data

        [numbness, desire to die by suicide, reject God, pining, searching for the dead person, terrifying dreams, uncontrollable weeping, anger, fear, sorrow, pain, bitterness, depression, and so forth].

    b. Recognize the strength and weaknesses of one's own nature, talents, and situations

        [past genius not able to function in writing or reading, mind floats, roiling mind, injured mind, battled heart, tinder of emotions, well for pen gone dry].

2. **Use reason** to analyze the data:

    a. Trust in reason, not in men's opinions

        [apply fundamental principle of humanism to this difficult situation].

    b. Draw upon analogies with experience of others

        [Virgil's and Dante's visit to the underworld like her dream of seeking her dead husband; Boethius's consolation of philosophy].

    c. Come to a knowledge of causes by reason and prayer

        [A good God's providence and not a cruel goddess Fortuna leads events; persons have the ability to respond to the events by the powers of their reason and will].

    d. Seek friendships with others

        [Martha Marcella — two oars in one boat; Cassandra Fedele — shared interest in humanism; write to physicians, attorneys, and spiritual advisors].

    e. Give self time and space to heal

        [ponder things in the heart; let mind rest by not writing for a while and giving up night vigils; focus on helping others who have suffered losses by death; continue the labor of grief].

    f. Come to insight

        [adversity strengthens virtue; reason, not lamentation, removes sorrow; God lost His Son through suffering and death too].

    g. Share insights with others

        [move to publish writings in a complete manuscript as a way of contributing to the common good].

Her meticulous account of her own grief and process of coming to self-knowledge is a concrete application of the principles of early Renaissance Humanist philosophy, and its vivid eloquence invites the reader to follow a similar path of self-discovery. There is, however, another phase of the process, namely the exercise of the will in developing self-governance. Insight is not enough, for it has to become integrated into personal actions, habits, and virtues before the transformation of human character can fully occur.

Interpersonal Dialogue about Self-Governance

    In her words of advice to the grieving Soldus, Laura describes the process of developing a new habit of will: "[m]odulate little by little the whispering phrases [of sorrow], and cutting these short, interrupt them, bending them to your will with your voice."[181] The will has the power to make choices in relation to the passions, to accept or to reject them, to order them according to a hierarchy of values grasped by the intellect. In a letter to Sister Deodata di Leno, Laura Cereta explains the Epicurean and scholastic principles relevant to the subject of will. Following the neo-Epicurean philosophy of Lorenzo Valla, Cereta states:

> Virtue alone finds the road to true peace of mind. False, sister, are the painted enticements that Epicurus was accustomed to scorn as ephemeral and transitory pleasures. For he, since he was a man of great moderation and temperance, spurned these casual diversions among the quieting forms of relaxation, and not rashly so. For just as the inclination of our emotions draws us towards those things which appear shining and beautiful on the surface, so the appetite becomes sated to the point of nausea once our desires have been requited. Epicurus thought that the pleasure which is born in us is constantly reborn in a more vigorous form through the agency of the freedom that comes from a pure heart and mind. For the mind that emulates the gods in its pursuit of happiness is full and contented. All other joys, because they grow old, torment us cruelly, with a sense of burning.
>
> The great blessedness of virtue ought to be admired. Thus that man Epicurus, full of moral fiber and wisdom, believed that all short-lived sweetness, all imaginary petty devices, all erroneous efforts to achieve true serenity would be punished. We, whom this foolish satiety in sweet things rightfully exhausts, should satisfy our hearts more delightfully with God's love and we should chart a course for a virtue unviolated in this fleeting life, with the sail of our hearts pulled taut.[182]

Cereta later introduces the scholastic claim that "[n]ature has taught us always to incline our hearts freely and deliberately towards the good. . . ."[183] The suggestion to "incline our hearts freely and deliberately" invokes the presumption of a free human that is able to act through deliberate choice. The object of this choice is "the good," the ultimate value presented to the human will. The first step to distinguish between false and true goods is to learn the hierarchy of values through a study of moral and religious texts. In a letter to Lucilia Vernacula she states:

> Human error causes us to be ashamed and disgusted that those women who are themselves caught in a tangle of doubt have given up hope of attaining knowledge of the humane arts, when they could easily acquire such knowledge with skill and virtue. For an education is neither bequeathed to us as a legacy, nor does some fate or other give it to us as a gift. Virtue is something that we ourselves acquire; nor can those women who become dull-witted through laziness and the

---

181. Cereta, "Dialogue on the Death of an Ass," *Laura Cereta: Collected Letters*, p. 186.
182. Cereta (December 2, 1487), *Laura Cereta: Collected Letters*, p. 120.
183. Cereta (December 12, 1487), *Laura Cereta: Collected Letters*, p. 121.

sludge of low pleasures ascend to the understanding of difficult things. But for those women who believe that study, hard work, and vigilance will bring them sure praise, the road to attaining knowledge is broad.[184]

The second tool for distinguishing among false and true goods is a sensitivity to the guidance of one's own conscience, or the evaluation of the moral quality of an act through a judgment of reason. This occurs in the depths of the soul of a person where he or she meets the absolute Good, or God.[185] In the following letter to "Europa solitaria" Cereta describes how her conscience told her it would be a lesser good to live a solitary life in the country than to participate in an active life with others: "Once I myself crossed the plains and mountains in the company of our mothers, but my mind was profoundly covered with shame that tortured my soul through the secret witness of my conscience."[186] In a letter to her spiritual advisor Brother Thomas, Cereta states that ultimately her own conscience will be the guide for what she will do for the rest of her life:

> I have opened the ears of my conscience to the precepts in your letters. And since she is always with me, I always am my own conscience, and thus I have one companion in temperance, and one simultaneous course that leads to God once human affairs are put aside. On account of this, whether there will be a plan after this to feed the mind with more active studies that prepare those who are already knowledgeable for greater things, or whether, by putting away my pen, I will show myself to God after a period of recovery and tranquil rest, still, I shall not be able to keep myself from gathering together, at least mentally, information regarding hypotheses about the heavens. Nor does labor, the brother of virtue, allow the noble mind to be at rest.[187]

The remarkable phrase, "I always am my own conscience" reveals the great dignity of the human being who has access to the guidance of ultimate truth and goodness in a particular circumstance regarding a human decision. In a passage from another letter, Cereta describes to Brother Thomas how she came to a conversion of will about the priority of values with respect to her gift as a philosopher:

> There is one conversion of the will to God which surpasses all others, and this consists in the remembering of, and meditation on, the judgment and the resur-

---

184. Cereta (November 1, 1487), *Laura Cereta: Collected Letters,* p. 82.

185. *The Catechism of the Catholic Church,* #1777: "Moral conscience, present at the heart of a person, enjoins him at the appropriate moment to do good and to avoid evil. It also judges particular choices, approving those that are good and denouncing those that are evil. It bears witness to the authority of truth in reference to the supreme Good to which the human person is drawn, and it welcomes the commandments. When he listens to his conscience, the prudent man can hear God speaking." See also #1778: "Conscience is a judgment of reason whereby the human person recognizes the moral quality of a concrete act that he is going to perform, is in the process of performing, or has already completed." (New York: Image Doubleday, 1994), p. 490.

186. Cereta (February 29, 1487/1488), *Laura Cereta: Collected Letters,* p. 128.

187. Cereta (February 4, 1488/December 11, 1487), *Laura Cereta: Collected Letters,* p. 113.

rection. Therefore, since this mortal life of ours will live on after death, I have renounced — for it is holier to do so — that glory, transitory and slipping, which being full of the contrariness of earthly beings, separates from the true religion of pious faith, and embroils us in hybristic displays of greater intelligence.[188]

Laura Cereta's belief in the resurrection of her body and that she will live on in some glorified state is a matter of faith. Yet, she had to exert her will to renounce the transitory glory of "hybristic displays of greater intelligence." Her act of will to choose a greater good followed the apprehension of a greater truth by the intellect.

The third tool that Cereta uses in her pursuit of self-governance is interaction with others, or dialogue with friends. This involves listening to the criticism of friends as well as offering critique when necessary. Laura Cereta's correspondence offers a remarkable record of forthright interaction in the service of calling persons to greater virtue. In a letter to Santa Pelegrina, Cereta offers an impassioned defense of true friendship in a context in which their friendship had faltered. She appeals to historical writings about friendship:

> Those men who have written about friendship [Cicero] have one thought: they see it as a bond that is both extraordinary and by law itself lifelong, since it springs from the very font of honor. And no wonder, for ethics is that state of being useful which is also honorable. The thing all men seek, however, is that which is useful. And so friendship, though extraordinary in its ethical dimensions and lifelong in its physical aspect, is disregarded among human desires. Since this is the case, a certain torpor of thought sets in, and all of the esteem we have for friends ebbs and flows back to the place whence it originally came. Thus, though the seed of mutual love that was sown between us had already grown strong from a deep root of honor, it suddenly died, as if sucked dry in ground without water: it was as though this seed were stubborn enough to flee by itself from both nature and humankind.[189]

Cereta argues that when nobility ceases to be a goal and is replaced by utility alone the friendship naturally degenerates. Her own friendship with "Santa Pelegrina" has suffered this consequence. She levels a serious accusation against her former friend:

> The problem and its solution look to you to say why there has been an interruption in so important a cultivation. Am I to believe that you think that the divine law of friendship is about the exchange of flattery and gifts? What did you really think you would achieve with so long a silence, though not one on my part? Still if I can be accepted as an arbiter in this situation, I would refuse both flattery and gifts, because both are false tokens, since virtue can neither be counterfeited nor bought. What is more, it is close to impossible to divert virtue from its course.[190]

188. Cereta (October 21, 1486/September 10, 1486), *Laura Cereta: Collected Letters*, p. 105.
189. Cereta (February 26, 1486), *Laura Cereta: Collected Letters*, pp. 136-37.
190. Cereta (February 26, 1486), *Laura Cereta: Collected Letters*, p. 137.

Cereta requests clarification as to what happened:

> But if you have anything to say that would refute my complaints, I am asking you, trusting in your wisdom, to write it in a long and elaborate letter. Still, I want this whole matter to be put to rest, and I want this plea of mine to succeed. Only the truth should be taken into consideration, since in our situation it is the case that each one of us would aim to teach, not to defeat the other. For what can it mean for a friend to be victorious over her friend?[191]

In this remarkable distinction between teaching and battling, Cereta reveals her genuine motives in the interpersonal dialogue. She wants an honest exchange aimed at a virtuous goal, and ordered with self-governance.

Laura Cereta invokes classical sources:

> There is no place for us to hold a debate, as Carneades did when, taking dubious and inextricable positions in the gymnasium, he argued first on the side of the Stoics and then against them. The question you raise has to be debated, not mocked or belittled, so that the sacred pledge of our loyalty and respect for one another, though now beaten and broken, can be healed, and so that everything — once the sickness in our thoughts about one another has been medicated — may soon be right again between us.[192]

Disordered passions and distorted thoughts need to heal before the proper kind of debate about the truth of their friendship can occur. The letter concludes that issues between the two ex-friends must not be reduced to simple differences of opinion. Since there is an objective truth about the situation that needs to be discovered and, hopefully, agreed upon, each person has to become aware of and admit to her own weakness in the relationship and to forgive the weakness of the other. This involves an act of will:

> I am so concerned about you that nothing is more precious to me than my being loved by you, who are the most beloved of friends. If you were ever to catch me in some wrongdoing, I have no doubt at all, since you are a person of the utmost kindness, that you would be compassionate and forgiving. After all, this is the hallmark of one's humanity: the ability to recognize one's own weakness. Therefore dismiss the thought of a quarrel as the result of our difference of opinion. Nor should less lenience be reckoned as due the wrongdoer than her wrong. After all, which of us would inflict a punishment on the other, when she might not know the other's heart equally, and when there could be a mutual exchange between pure minds that are inextricably connected in every way?[193]

---

191. Cereta (February 26, 1486), *Laura Cereta: Collected Letters*, p. 137.

192. Cereta (February 26, 1486), *Laura Cereta: Collected Letters*, p. 137. Robin includes in her note the information that: "Carneades (213-128 B.C.) was known as the founder of the Athenian Third Academy. He is known for arguing both sides of a question with equal rhetorical skill" (p. 137, note 57).

193. Cereta (February 26, 1486), *Laura Cereta: Collected Letters*, p. 138.

This model of "a mutual exchange of pure minds" is Cereta's standard for self-governance in the mutual support of two friends working hard to achieve wisdom and virtue.

Let us see two other examples in which she speaks about order in the other person and calls her correspondent to a greater self-governance. In one, she admonishes her younger sister Diana Cereta for addressing her (Laura's) accomplishments in too grandiose terms:

> Yesterday and the day before yesterday I received first the one and then, with more anticipation and longing, your other letter. But a little reading has brought me only a modest amount of pleasure after so much hope. For in these letters first you envision me as a laurel putting out leaves, and then you call me a sister of Apollo, when I'm a small and very fragile tree growing up among the choicest trees, and can hardly even be called an Apollinian magpie among the Muses. So please tell me, how can there be such a happy endowment of genius in me? And from what evidence are you making up these stories? Tall tales (and you know this) are not taken very seriously by learned men, who always delight in testing the truth for the sake of greater wisdom. . . .
>
> You yourself know, and I'm sure about this, that if I'm falsely believed to like your praises of me, then the motivation behind your mistake can backfire against me. Our minds are very badly deceived when they are dragged headlong, like a chariot without a driver, towards corrupt thoughts. I beg you, sister, not to be in such a hurry for honors. Things of greater weight rise slowly rather than too quickly. For speed can never be praised without the tempering effect of diligence. Those who enjoy the sweetest praises from men, whether they are cheated by the stain of false virtue or broken by adverse fortune, often incur shameful ridicule for their failure to live up to their reputations. The delight in study should not come from the reward of being praised, but should be exercised for the sake of virtue. I think it is enough that those who embark upon the road to learning are the winners of their own wisdom and glory.[194]

The lack of self-governance in her sister is caused by the youthful desire for praise, fame, and glory, and results in flattering phrases. Because her passions were not tempered by the will, they dragged the younger sister, "like a wild chariot without a driver," into distorted thinking.

In another example, Laura Cereta pinpoints the imagination as the potential cause of disorder when she warns Veneranda, the new Abbess of Santa Chiara, not to become enamored with the power of her office and to keep in mind the final judgment that will be given to her actions: "Remember that the smoke from burning incense must be dedicated to God; and see to it that your altars do not smoke for you, in some empty fantasy of domination."[195]

In many of her letters Cereta suggests that there is an area of life that one cannot govern by mind and will. Fortune can hold power over a person and render

---

194. Cereta (July 1, 1486), *Laura Cereta: Collected Letters,* pp. 148-49.
195. Cereta (August 13, 1487), *Laura Cereta: Collected Letters,* p. 150.

the mind and will useless. In a letter to Barbara Alberti she notes its threatening nature: "Fortune always threatens us more when our happiness is most perfect."[196] In
her "Dialogue on the Death of an Ass," Laura Cereta reflects that no one escapes
fortune's power: "[a]ll of us are born to know the frequent calamities of fickle fortune."[197] In a letter to Sister Deodata di Leno she describes the effects of destroying
self-governance that fortune often causes: "Look, the iniquity of raging Fortune
carries us and all other things away, and all grounds for arrogance fly upwards
when the spirit has fled the body. But surely our mind is too often bereft of judgment, clouded by blind hope and the false promise of flimsy pleasure."[198]

In a public lecture addressed to Francesco Fontana, Laura Cereta offers her
philosophy on how we may overcome bad fortune, in the framework of a battle between Christians and the goddess Fortuna.

> There is no reason, moreover, why all of us should not be prepared to mock and
> jeer at Fortuna. For she is our adversary, inflicting us with evils she herself would
> not tolerate with the profound scowl of her malice. Nonetheless, those who have
> turned away from God have made her their goddess; but there are men, who hav-
> ing suffered worse things, believed that injuries of both a fleeting and long-
> lasting sort would befall us as the result of her avenging wrath. It is a different
> matter, however, for those who examine, explore, test the truth, and reweave rea-
> sons which allow it to be known that this very goddess is simply the outcome of
> things, who — given the inclination of fate — sometimes alters events with the
> gentlest of winds and at other times meets them head-on with a hostile attack.
> Such unpredictable changes are caused by something which is uncertain and
> empty, which enfolds the world in doubt and ambiguity, and which is surely im-
> pelled by the force we call Fortuna.[199]

In *Consolation of Philosophy*, Boethius moves from self-pity at the devastating loss
of his family, reputation, library, and position on the Senate through false charges,
to a confident understanding of the true nature of events. Cereta follows Boethius's
moving from a belief in the works of a cruel goddess Fortune, through a struggle
with fate, eventually to a belief in Divine Providence.[200]

One important difference between Boethius and Cereta is that Lady Philosophy taught Boethius to move from rebellion against Fortune and Fate to acceptance
of Divine Providence, while Laura Cereta, having learned herself how to accomplish this, teaches others. Thus, the imaginary feminine personification of wisdom's teacher in the early medieval text is replaced by a real woman in the early
humanist text. In both cases the human being undergoing the transformation has
to exercise his or her reason and will. In this process of shifting of beliefs Cereta

196. Cereta (November 21, 1486), *Laura Cereta: Collected Letters*, p. 134.
197. Cereta, *Laura Cereta: Collected Letters*, p. 190.
198. Cereta (December 12, 1487), *Laura Cereta: Collected Letters*, p. 121.
199. Cereta (Ides of April), *Laura Cereta: Collected Letters*, pp. 153-54.
200. Boethius, *The Consolation of Philosophy* (London: Penguin Books, 1969), especially Books
II and IV.

demonstrates how the person has to work hard "to examine, explore, test the truth and reweave reasons" to overcome the initial shock of the experience of bad fortune. Cereta offers examples from classical sources, gleaned from Cicero and Valerius Maximus, of events that seemed to be due to the fickle and cruel goddess Fortuna. She describes situations of historical figures such as Hannibal, Regulus, Xanthippus, Scipio, Hasdrubal, Sempronius, Semilius, Philip, Pausanias, Alexander, Caesar, Alcibiades, Conon, Carius, and Cyrus. She explores the meaning of these events in a larger perspective, trying to move her listener from a belief in a pagan divinity to become a dispassionate observer of historical events. She introduces an Aristotelian notion of "accidental disposition of events":

> Who of these men, fortunate in his own time, did not remain in the end without glory? Who could adequately consider the madness of those men who are not afraid to worship this slaughterer of the frail human race, against whom no accusation can be too harsh? My campaign against this blood-thirsty idol exhausts and irks me because she continues to contribute to the pollution and degradation of everything shameful. It should seem enough to argue that it is not Fortuna who angers us but rather contingency, for which neither nature nor God is responsible beyond the accidental disposition of events. But really what we ourselves call Fortuna is nothing other than the image of empty terror about which the pagans have taught us. But as long as we struggle with hatred, as long as we enter into hostile paths and are subjected to misfortunes and immersed in perils, these terrible oscillations and shifts will proceed one after another, because of which fear is born in times of sorrow as is religion in times of fear.[201]

Once again Cereta adverts to passions, hatred (hostility and anger) and fear (terror) and sorrow, and to the effects that these passions, when left disordered, can have on a person.

Next, Laura Cereta mentions "the thief Cacus, the inebriated Bacchus, and those impudent women, Venus, Flora, and Acca."[202] Her argument follows that of the early Presocratics, Plato, and Aristotle in its attack on the immorality of the Olympian and later Roman deities:

> Vain is the worship of pagans who believed that insensible and inert things, demons, and corrupt men were elevated to the heavens. But much worse still is our credulity, which pays homage to Fortuna — an imaginary personage — as though she were its own undisputed divinity. Fortuna is, after all, nothing whatsoever and there cannot be anything more worthless than nothing. All the schools of theologians have addressed her; yet she has followed a downward course from the contempt she deserves to the oblivion of philosophy. And although the enormity of Epicurus' and Euripides' being silenced can be laid to their own error — namely, while denying that the care of the world belongs to God, they affirm that all things happen by chance or by some sort of contingency

201. Cereta (Ides of April), *Laura Cereta: Collected Letters,* p. 156.
202. Cereta (Ides of April), *Laura Cereta: Collected Letters,* p. 157.

— still all the rest of the philosophers have spat on Fortuna. Aristotle never admitted Fortuna into his philosophy. Socrates denied her, and Plato showed disdain for her. Therefore those men who seek this goddess among the empty deities profane themselves with the direst perjury and they have no god at all.[203]

Finally, Cereta offers an existential observation of how she, a woman, overcame bad fortune. She introduces the metaphor of healing so central to Boethius's consolation, augments her analysis with an introduction of the relation of God to the suffering of Jesus Christ, the Son, and then completes it with a reminder that the true value of life rests in the human decision to build a life of virtue:

> By meditating on these things peacefully by myself, after a little while I managed to moderate the tearful laments which the intense ardor of my sad bereavement had kindled. Therefore I have seemed to be healed by sorrows, particularly when I consider that in this mortal realm I am a woman. For it shouldn't be much to be saddened with misfortune when nothing among human affairs considers itself stable. A mortal husband was given to me but he gave back his spirit to God before his day. I can have pity and overcome misfortune with my mind, but I cannot accuse God of any harm since the life of the one who is dead and his day belonged to God. If he, however, who is forever omnipotent on his throne of everlasting divinity, did not spare his only begotten son, what causes us to think he would spare us poor beings?
>
> Every age loses its flowers, and death is the common fortune of all men: there is but one end for the good man who is fortunate. Fortuna therefore neither curses nor blesses the just, and every outcome in death depends on virtue or vice.[204]

Cereta's argument against believing in the goddess Fortune can be summarized as follows:

1. Begin with the opinion that events are caused by the cruel whim of the goddess Fortuna.
2. Work hard to examine, explore, test the truth and reveal reasons.
3. Bring forward examples from history of people who believed in the goddess Fortuna.
4. Argue against these examples by invoking Aristotle's theory of the accidental disposition of events.
5. Attack the immorality of the Olympian and Roman deities.
6. Invoke the authority of Socrates, Plato, and Aristotle, who rejected the goddess Fortuna.
7. Offer an existential description of her own overcoming of bad fortune by faith in God who sacrificed his own Son.

---

203. Cereta (Ides of April), *Laura Cereta: Collected Letters,* p. 157.
204. Cereta (Ides of April), *Laura Cereta: Collected Letters,* pp. 157-58.

Laura Cereta's philosophy of the will and its role in self-governance contains the following general guidelines:

1. The will should learn how to make choices according to reason in relation to the passions.
2. Following Epicurus' example, the choice of a higher pleasure (i.e., study) can counter pain (i.e., grief).
3. The will is the rudder that leads to virtue.
   a. By choosing to study moral texts to learn theoretical principles of virtue (how to discern between true and false goods in general)
   b. Sensitivity to the guidance of one's own conscience concerning the morality of a particular act
   c. Conversion of the will to choose the greater good in a particular situation
   d. Develop friendship with good persons based on virtue and a shared understanding of objective truth (mutual exchange of pure minds)
4. Orientation of the will towards helping others
   a. To discover disordered choices
   b. Correct false views of the imagination
   c. Limit exercise of power over others, yet recognize the power of one's own will.

In the next section of this chapter, we will consider how Laura Cereta went about doing good in both the private and public spheres of activity. Here, as in other areas of her life, she engaged in new areas of activity, truly affecting an early Humanist Reformation in the concept of woman.

Public Action Building the Common Good

Laura Cereta excelled in levels of action for the common good: (1) of the family and particularly her siblings, husband, and father, (2) of persons involved in humanistic studies and education, and (3) of Church and society. She extended her sphere of action into ranges not previously encountered by women, and she attempted to further the good of the persons involved. Her guiding principles were: moral integrity, knowledge of letters, and love of human beings.

In early Renaissance Humanism, women's responsibilities in the household were most often presented as having primarily a utilitarian value for man. In the extreme case of Alberti, woman was not allowed to read or offer advice in the public realm, and she was discouraged even from educating her own sons. Laura Cereta challenges all these ascribed roles of woman. Her life was dedicated to various forms of domestic service and she extended this service into the public realm. She accomplished in practice what Pico and Cusanus theoretically posed, namely that a person in the fifteenth century was capable of introducing a new perspective to the traditional categories that had previously determined human life and activity.

Laura Cereta's formation in domestic service had begun at the early age of nine when she was called back home from her convent school to help care for her brothers. There is no indication of why this occurred, and after a period at home she returned to her intellectual studies. In 1485, when her father, an attorney and magistrate, was banished, the fifteen-year-old Laura took over the responsibility for two of her brothers' education. They were attending a school under the tutelage of the humanist teacher, Giovanni Olivieri. In the following letter to her brothers, Ippolito and Basilio, she presents them with a choice: study and work for a virtuous life or dissipate themselves in a life of pleasure:

> Although I had to tell your teacher many things about you by letter, still I knew it was only right and fitting for me to send these letters on to you, lest it should later seem that it was through my doing that your natural talents, which we hope will enable you to arrive at the culmination of your studies in the liberal arts with outstanding results, were prevented from coming to the fore.
>
> For this reason, while some of your schoolmates are fussing with their hair, and others are spending their time grooming themselves — whether they dodge school to play in places where they won't be found, or sit around taking their leisure — while some of your friends waste their nights sleeping and others squander their days babbling and telling idle tales, I urge and implore the two of you to press on with your studies and to be diligent and remain alert. In this way your native intellectual gifts will enable you to obtain knowledge, which is a more lasting possession. In addition to his being of assistance to you, Olivieri is a man of authority and distinction who has taught students in his home, in the fields, and in the streets, just as he has taught in academies. If you obtain his counsel, you will acquire a great deal of knowledge. . . .
>
> Since nature has made it possible for you to surpass the intellectual endowments of many men, light now the torches of the better part of your soul for the sake of learning. This effort is of crucial importance, since either pleasure will separate you from the great men of this city or virtue will distinguish you from the dregs of the populace. The choice between these two roads is, however, yours. Take care lest the precipitous pain of desire should cause you to be afflicted with a still greater wound — that of regret. The quiet serenity of virtue inhabits the loftiest places in the hills.[205]

By stating clearly that "the choice . . . is . . . yours," Laura Cereta reveals her deep respect for the freedom of the human person. She also demonstrates her awareness that the life of virtue is determined by choices. Finally, she speaks directly to her brothers, and not to their teacher, so that they will receive appropriate praise if they make the better choice.

Two extant letters to Giovanni Olivieri are very instructive as to how Cereta extended her realm of action outside the home. They reveal a pattern of response to her initiatives in building the common good. The pattern usually has three phases: first, she engages in public action in a straightforward manner. Then, because such action is so unusual for a woman, the respondent initiates a counteraction of questionable quality. Finally, Cereta responds by confronting the lack of integrity in this response.

205. Cereta (August 3, 1485), *Laura Cereta: Collected Letters,* pp. 55-56.

In her first letter to Giovanni Olivieri, she thanks Giovanni and his wife Elena for their kindness and generosity to feed and protect her two brothers. She asks that Professor Olivieri take particular concern to educate her brothers well because their learning will "be a testimony to your work and your effort . . . [and will] weave a garland of glory for you, as the best of all teachers."[206] In stating that she, Laura Cereta, is "committed to immortalizing your name and I shall always honor this commitment," she anticipates the distribution of a manuscript of her letters a few years later and the achievement of her own literary fame. Next, she introduces her view of the goals of a humanistic education, especially in the area of building the common good:

> My father hopes with me, and so do we all, that the end result will be that, with you as their guide, Ippolito and Basilio will prefer virtue to pleasure. And mind you, there is nothing that will bind my father more tightly to you in his enduring appreciation and mindfulness of your service to him than if you have instilled in his sons **moral integrity, a knowledge of letters, and the conviction that the love of one's fellowmen must always in the most just of worlds be valued above all other things.**[207]

Her letter concludes with the admission that her father, "now banished from the city, looks after his fields and lives the rustic life."[208]

Laura Cereta appears to have sent to Giovanni Olivieri samples of her own writing in Latin asking for his editorial suggestions as colleagues are apt to do. In this move, she placed herself in the vulnerable position of seeking a critical evaluation from a professional in a similar field. Giovanni Olivieri, suspecting that Cereta could not have written this, chose, in a very underhanded manner, to send his wife Elena to catch Cereta in a "deception" by requesting her to write something in Latin on the spot. Cereta's letter to Olivieri captures her anger seething below the surface and expressed in a sarcastic manner:

> Although I have neither consulted the divination of Tages nor the Sybilline books in order to know the future, nor have I been possessed by the god, or guided by auguries, still I had a suspicion that had already caused me to write on another occasion that I thought you'd be rightly amazed that I'd have enough courage — mere woman though I was, untutored in literature, and utterly ignorant — to send you a little epistolary oration, however crude and in need of editing with a scythe it might be.
>
> Anyway, look how conveniently it has worked out that a more prescient mind than mine has provided inspiration from higher places. Your wife has approached me in a friendly manner — and she is very charming and addresses everyone in the right way at the right time. It seemed she wouldn't leave me alone until she asked me to write something on the spur of the moment to you even

206. Cereta (August 1, 1485), *Laura Cereta: Collected Letters,* p. 54.
207. Cereta (August 1, 1485), *Laura Cereta: Collected Letters,* p. 54. My emphasis.
208. Cereta (August 1, 1485), *Laura Cereta: Collected Letters,* p. 54.

though I had nothing in the least worthwhile to say. I don't know if she came over, in the role of a scout or deserter herself, to have a look at the modest education I've had. In any case I do see the nature of these attempts of hers: and they are — if you'll permit me the liberty of saying so — underhanded missions under the guise of which you expect me to get tangled up in the net of my own inexperience, just as you tend to imagine me wandering around on unknown roads, blind without a father's guidance.[209]

In her response Laura Cereta invokes a Neoplatonic theme when she speaks ironically of their "illumination from higher places" and her supposed "blindness," when in fact she is the one who sees what is really going on and they are blind. She also refers to Aristotle's theme of practical wisdom in ironically describing Elena's mission as being done "in the right way and at the right time," when in fact it was done in the wrong way (i.e., deceitfully) and at the wrong time (i.e., when Cereta had nothing to say).

Giovanni Olivieri's unvirtuous action is particularly lamentable since he was professionally dedicated to teaching his students how to be virtuous:

Education is a thing highly esteemed — and this is something learned men certainly know well enough. I've obtained whatever plumage I do have from strong wings — this I don't deny. But finally I progressed beyond the stage of being a chick and my skill at flying has become so good that the great forest of Mt. Ida might find me worthy of adopting. Perhaps in a short time the radiant realm of the sun will receive me, to which, in our own era, the rare phoenix flew.

And now let me refine my argument so that the things I've said in all seriousness won't be taken as merely an attempt to show off my talent — since this could make it seem as though I was starting a war between the lovers of wisdom and philosophy, though surely the truth is that I, your most obedient servant, esteem you for your virtue best of all. This is all for now.[210]

In this approach we see the core element in Cereta's method of working towards building the common good. She poses the ideal of humanism, or moral integrity, then measures an action of the educator against this ideal, and states directly to the person her assessment in the hope that knowledge of the discrepancy will bring about a conversion of mind and will. Thus, even though she expresses her conclusion with irony, she also speaks honestly when she says "the truth is that I . . . esteem you for your virtue best of all."

Laura Cereta's domestic service involved taking care of her husband's business affairs. In the following letter, written in 1485, she offers business advice along with some strong criticism of a previous accusation on his part:

With fear and trembling we have viewed, through your letters, the raging fires on the Rialto, and we have seen the sum total of your business all but thrown into

209. Cereta (October 31, 1487), *Laura Cereta: Collected Letters*, p. 56.
210. Cereta (October 31, 1487), *Laura Cereta: Collected Letters*, p. 57.

the billowing inferno there. And so, we can hope for nothing more than that you sell off piecemeal the tattered remains of your goods and household furnishings to other merchants at the open market, in such a way that the buyer who can offer you the appropriate silver for your goods will seek you out. But as to your writing me that I don't love you very much, I don't know whether you're saying this in earnest or whether I should realize that you're joking with me. Still, what you say disturbs me. You are measuring a very healthy expression of a wife's loyalty by the standard of the insincere flattery of well-worn phrases. But I shall love you, my husband. What does it mean to you that you reassure me with those trivial little compliments? Do you want me to believe that you expect me to comb my hair in a stylish fashion for your homecoming? Or to feign adoring looks with a painted face? Let women without means, who worry and have no confidence in their own virtue, flutter their eyelashes and play games to gain favor with their husbands. This is the adulation of a fox and the birdlime of deceitful bird hunting. I don't want to have to buy you at such a price. I'm not a person who lays more stock in words than duty. I am truly your Laura, whose soul is the same one you in turn had hoped for.[211]

In the private world of husband-wife relations Laura Cereta again chooses virtue over flattery and truth against deception. Confidence in her own financial status and character gives her a strong basis from which to forge a better relation with her husband. She says that her husband uses a poor standard of measure, while her own is a more accurate one. She invites him to discuss the proper standard of measure for spousal love. Thus, she seeks to build the common good in the small community of marriage.

Laura Cereta also engaged in domestic service for her father, especially after his banishment and illness. To the attorney Alberto degli Alberti, Laura draws horizontal analogies with legal situations to beg forgiveness on her father's behalf:

The divine spirit of friendship must instead be given to undoing the wrong that has been cultivated with intense efforts on both your parts — yours, father Alberti, and that of my parent. For when he strives on a daily basis to write to you, tears suddenly flow down from his eyes in great drops. Thus, he often took up the pen he dropped, and then dropped the pen he had taken up, groaning and sighing to himself as he did so, as though he were a man who envied you, desperately and self-destructively. Your mutual tenderness, deeply engraved in his heart, grew so much. Thus did I myself freely, and that man violently, wreak our damage.

Therefore I beg you to want to absolve both my father of the wrong he did you through his silence and his daughter of her sympathy for the wrong, particularly since, once a case has been reviewed, it lies within the jurisdiction of the judge to revoke the penalty, whether in the case of a criminal or civil proceeding. But if you have weighed the case itself clearly and simply, you will become a greater judge in proportion to how forgiving you are. Now will you be welcoming me

211. Cereta, *Laura Cereta: Collected Letters*, p. 91.

back into a friendship from which I never withdrew, but instead you will be pardoning me for the sin of rusticity here in my rustic peasant's hut, even if I have already begun to be sated with the common folk in this village, where every street and narrow alley is filled with trash and piles of dung.[212]

In 1486, when this letter was written, the widowed Cereta had to take care of her depressed father in the country village to which he was banished, a banishment made worse by the lack of written communication. Her concern is to restore the common bond between her father and Alberti. She admits the weakness on her and her father's part and takes responsibility, but asks for a corresponding forgiveness from Alberti. Thus, she acts as an intermediary for the restoration of a broken friendship.

In other correspondence Cereta reflects on the realistic aspects of a woman's place in country life. Her woman friend, "Europa Solitaria," thinks she will find tranquillity by living in the country. Cereta offers a very strong statement that the different states of human life would likely interfere with any idealistic view of tranquil country living:

I have read your long-awaited letters, in the narratives of which you describe the enduring solace of the countryside. I congratulate you on behalf of all of us, and thank you on my account because, by renouncing civic honors for the sake of your peace of mind, you have found — if rest is still to be had — recompense in your own private life. But I fear for your peace of mind. I have written, lest the sweet and gentle serenity of fleeing peace and quiet should elude you. For what tranquillity can be vouchsafed in human affairs when as infants we howl, as children we are oblivious, as teenagers we are sluggish, and as old women we become withered and decrepit in our misery and boredom? We are all stricken by the onslaughts that come our way from the injustices of nature. Only the woman who does not give in to the power of Fortune is a sage. But I also consider that woman wise who does not remove herself from participation in the commonwealth for the sake of the pleasures of solitude but who struggles for the reward of eternal life in the midst of cyclones of evil with a steadfastness that will prevail.[213]

The final sentence reveals Laura Cereta's own struggle in the "midst of cyclones of evil with a steadfastness that will prevail." To engage in the struggle to build up the common good in the midst of domestic service to brothers and sisters, husband, mother, and father, is Laura Cereta's goal.

How would this be possible, when the prevailing view was that a woman had to choose between marriage and scholarly activities? The answer to this question lies in Cereta's remarkable understanding of time. In a letter to Sister Deodata di Leno, Cereta introduces the theme of time:

This living of ours is so uncertain and aimless that time, speeding onward, tightly binds the day of our birth to that of our death. And so, no day should slip,

212. Cereta (February 3, 1486), *Laura Cereta: Collected Letters*, p. 60.
213. Cereta (February 29, 1487/1488), *Laura Cereta: Collected Letters*, p. 124.

for the sake of leisure, through our hands. Let us reclaim the nights with our speeches; let ordered thoughts alone give our minds respite. Let us believe each day that this is our last on earth. . . .[214]

The January 1486 letter to Sigismondo de Bucci, Doctor of laws, shows Cereta's thinking about the nature of time and space:

> Though I came down to my father's magistracy so that I could have some leisure time, I still have not had even the time to catch my breath. It is as though I'm being pulled in opposite directions — I'm torn between my desire to help settle my father's affairs and my responsibilities as a wife. The way things are here, opportunity beckons me to stay, but worry tugs at me to return home. And so I am troubled because I want, alternatively, to be in both places.
>
> I have no leisure time for my own writing and studies unless I use the nights as productively as I can. I sleep very little. Time is a terribly scarce commodity for those of us who spend our skills and labor equally on our families and our own work. But by staying up all night, I become a thief of time, sequestering a space from the rest of the day, so that after working by lamplight for much of the night, I can go back to work in the morning. My point is that the first shadows of the waning day don't ever deprive me of the time to read and write.[215]

Cereta becomes "a thief of time" and "sequesters a space" to do her intellectual work at night while she continues her domestic service to her family during the day. She uses this stolen time and space for two projects: for completing a manuscript of her letters and for an elaborate "linen which I've worked on with a needle and thread of different hues." This artistic piece, described in exquisite detail, took her three months to complete.

Cereta creates a beautiful metaphor, noting the result when this kind of artistic project is not inspired: "such a loss of time is wasteful when time — the necklace of life — is spent on pointless work."[216] The image of time as a "necklace of life" is very insightful. A necklace binds the person in some respects, yet one is able to move around. In other words, time goes as determined by the will of the human being. A necklace is also beautiful, and thus "time — the necklace of life" invokes the Neoplatonic theme of beauty, order, and goodness. It adorns each person with order and beauty, when it is not wasted or misused. It is a particularly feminine philosophical metaphor applied to all persons who live and work in a temporal world.

The following chart is a brief summary of Laura Cereta's acts for the common good as a woman in the family. In each situation she measures the action against a humanist ideal and seeks the conversion of her correspondent:

---

214. Cereta (December 12, 1487), *Laura Cereta: Collected Letters,* p. 121.

215. Cereta (January 1, 1486), *Laura Cereta: Collected Letters,* p. 32.

216. Cereta (January 1, 1486), *Laura Cereta: Collected Letters,* p. 32. I am grateful to Diana Robin for noting in a personal conversation the Neoplatonic associations of this metaphor of time as a necklace of life.

Cereta's Work Towards the Common Good as a Woman in a Family		
Humanist Principle	**Measured Action**	**Aim of Conversion**
Moral Integrity	Sending his wife Elena to sneak proof that Laura could write eloquently in Latin	Her brothers' Professor Olivieri, a humanist educator, to live the virtue he teaches
Expression of love related to quality of virtue in soul, not deceptive physical appearance (pleasure) or financial status (utility)	The statement that Laura does not love her husband enough	Her husband, Pietro, to come to a more virtuous understanding of love as two souls in one being
Friendship as a virtue of constancy and forgiveness in adversity and exile	Not absolving her father from poor decisions and lack of communication in the past	Her father's past friend, Alberto degli Alberti, to renew his friendship
A philosopher should not live a solitary life — but an active one	Statement that a woman will be able to grow as a philosopher only in solitude	Her symbolic friend, "Europa Solitaria," to embrace the active life along with philosophy
A person should determine his or her own relation to time and space	Women deceive themselves who say they have no time for intellectual studies	Sister Deodata di Leno and others need to become thieves of time and sequesterers of space for study

Turning now to a broader participation in the common good, we see Laura Cereta beginning to define her public character as she struggles to bring this work to completion:

This grand volume of epistles, for which the final draft is now being copied out, bears witness, letter by letter, to whatever muses I have managed to muster in the dead of night. I have placed all my hope in my love of literature. Others may cross the seas in pursuit of worldly riches, but I, who am more cowardly, will molder away at home for the sake of a possession that is immortal, with the example of a diligent parent before me. For the possession of virtue fires great minds to pursue the fruits of fame, which are everlasting, though the labor itself is ephemeral.[217]

217. Cereta (January 1, 1486), *Laura Cereta: Collected Letters*, p. 34.

Six years before Columbus sailed to the New World, Cereta is well aware of the exploration for new riches. Still, she finds the meaning of her own life in literature and creation of a "grand volume of epistles" that will travel the world for her. It is clear that Laura Cereta viewed the completion and dispersion of the manuscript of her letters as a way of benefiting others. Her early foray into the public had met with a striking failure, and Cereta admitted that she had made an error in her selection of a particular topic:

> I am happy to have the opportunity to express my opinion about something that may exonerate me from criticism. I preferred to please the crowd rather than myself. Stimulated by the desire for fame, I was drawn into a prodigious error in the course of my writing. Namely, the first thing I wrote was a funeral oration composed to be read over the corpse of a donkey. This one humble oration stirred up the envy of a number of men, who cruelly sharpened the teeth of their spite against me, and as though their mouths had been swords, I was left trembling like a lamb among wolves. Full of their mockery of me, these men did not hesitate to dishonor me with their spittle, while I was hard-pressed by my wounds.[218]

The desire to contribute to the common good of society was very deep in Laura Cereta, and the negative reaction of males in humanist circles, where she too was a member, mattered a great deal to her:

> Since men receive an education in literature and other studies, however, so that they may benefit from the example of their forebears, the most elect men of diverse orders have said publicly that education has been wasted on me because it has benefited only me and not others.[219]

Appealing to Boethius's *Consolation of Philosophy* and its model of total self-governance in the midst of adversity, Laura Cereta decided at first to not respond to the scathing criticisms of the male humanists:

> For a long time I bore all these attacks patiently in order that no one would be able to accuse me of writing about the consolation of philosophy while I indulged the whims of an unstable mind: thus a stern excellence of mind taught me to disdain those slanderers so that threats would not seem to be vying with counter threats as though in a sword fight, or mutual blows parrying with one another. For a self-restraint that is free from earthly passion will triumph in its own simplicity: patience, not turbulence, ought to be exhibited in the face of our troubles. Otherwise, our lives would constantly be wasted in vendettas. For even if injury can indeed be bought, vengeance should still not be sold.[220]

After a while she decided to respond to ward off the increasing damage to her

218. Cereta (March 1488), *Laura Cereta: Collected Letters*, p. 39.
219. Cereta (March 1488), *Laura Cereta: Collected Letters*, p. 39.
220. Cereta (March 1488), *Laura Cereta: Collected Letters*, p. 39.

reputation, and this led to further accusations. Cereta described the situation to Cardinal Sforza:

> But since I became justifiably concerned about protecting my reputation, I could not imagine myself being worth so little that I would not respond in writing — whether I was provoked once or many times. And when I had written back, soon a great crowd of harassers wrote to me. I responded at greater length, and more eloquently than I would have believed. Nonetheless, after persevering for days, during which time a great deal of costly labor was wasted, I managed to extract from the business of writing to those men some residue at least that was suited to my work; for that which is bought at the cost of time is too costly. And so my epistolary commerce grew in both ways.[221]

Angered, she wrote to her father in 1486 about this situation. Several extant letters reveal the ability of Laura Cereta to engage in polemical dialogue without succumbing to counter-polemics. In all cases, she follows her usual method of stating the humanist ideal and then measuring the conduct against this ideal.

In the first example, written to Brother Lodovico de la Turre on August 25, 1485, Cereta says the following:

> When I arrived at Chiari fresh from my visit at the Ursine monastery, I met Giovio Antonio hurrying towards me as though out of breath in his excitement to explain to me the whole nature of the argument about me at your convent. Instead, he explained the various stock paradoxes in your argument, which cause me to become flustered, and I did blush a little as men frequently do when they become red in the face from indignation. And although I would not have thought it bad or inappropriate to the discussion at hand had it come from you, still I was surprised that you who are philosophers were shocked and thunderstruck, as though you regarded it as something miraculous that I, a young girl, should have absorbed not only the precepts which the art of oratory and rhetoric depend on, but also those that concern the place to which the travelling constellations return, as if you had never heard of something that many men who have read a great deal have heard.[222]

Here the ideal is simply the knowledge of letters, rhetoric, and philosophy common to humanists supplemented with interest in contemporary advances in mathematics and astronomy. Laura argues that Brother Lodovico has no grounds for surprise, for she simply does what other humanists have done. His response is disordered and inappropriate.

During this same early period of rejection of Laura Cereta's talents, in another letter she attempts to appeal to the higher qualities of another man hostile to her work. To one of the professors of rhetoric, Clemenzo Longolio, she states:

221. Cereta (March 1488), *Laura Cereta: Collected Letters*, p. 40.
222. Cereta (August 25, 1485), *Laura Cereta: Collected Letters*, p. 176.

... I consider slanderers no less despicable than adulators, since both are equally harmful to those who believe them. But let those who are malicious bruit their nonsense around. I do believe you are a decent person and I regard you as knowledgeable among those educated in the humanities. Do not alter any further the opinion you have of me.[223]

In other words, the ideal rhetorician does not resort to slander to win a point. The measure of decency and love for other human beings needs to be adhered to in rhetoric as in other humanistic studies.

Just one year later Cereta was attacked by Michael Baetus, who accused her of plagiarizing some book on astronomy. She claimed that she learned astronomy from others and became an experimental astronomer. To prove this she provides the description of the motions of the moon and planets dated four days prior to the letter to him. Given the closeness of the date, there is no way the information could have been previously published in a book authored by someone else.[224]

Two years later Cereta had to respond to further accusations. In her appeal to the rhetorician Clemenzo Longolio, all three principles of her humanist approach to principles of the common good are present, i.e., moral integrity, knowledge of letters, and love for human beings:

All the men most zealous about the study of literature at Santa Chiara hurriedly rivaled one another to write to me when I first arrived here. You alone stirred up rival factions against me and without cause. Nor have you ceased to wound me in every way with your arrogant talk and your supercilious manner. And as though a war had been declared, you unfurled your standards and marshaled them against me. Still, I never considered you a stranger because of your reputation. (Though I don't know you by sight, I used to look to you and converse with you through your works, as though you were present.) For the probity of my nature taught me to consider the philosophers important. Nor do I understand what hostility has taught you, who have received an education in the humanities, to speak so inhumanely of a woman who has honoured you, Clement. . . .[225]

Cereta appeals to the humanist education aimed at forming virtuous men, and to the study of philosophy aimed at the pursuit of truth, and she holds these models up as a measure for the actions of the man himself. She attempts to appeal to her correspondent's better nature, but she also reveals her domestic situation and ends with a realistic caution about further interactions:

I have at times attributed my slight hesitation in writing this letter to the general undertaking of my present responsibilities — the kind of thing women are very much involved in — for fear that some awkward discussion of excuses would tarnish my subject. Nor should I fail to mention that it is some pain stemming from

---

223. Cereta (October 31, 1485), *Laura Cereta: Collected Letters,* p. 177.
224. Rabil, *Laura Cereta: Quattrocento Humanist,* pp. 75 and 142-43.
225. Cereta (October 1, 1487), *Laura Cereta: Collected Letters,* p. 178.

anger that impels me to write to you; for a mind that is secure is not disturbed at every storm cloud. But I have done this to win your esteem as though I were going to deliver an essay to an extremely erudite man. For even Philip, the father of Alexander, became intensely preoccupied with the northern peoples of Scythia as though this were his last battle, not because they were people to be looked down upon, but because it was necessary to take extra precautions against them.[226]

Although Cereta displays her proclivity to anger, it is clear that her motivation comes from a higher source, the desire for a more productive communication between them.

On July 1, 1487 she responds to Fronto Carito concerning the false charge that her father authored her letters:

As to your writing me that Eusebio has read my letters and thought they were my father's and not mine, I would not have seen either judgment as being at all offensive. Whether he thinks they are my father's as he asserts, or mine, as he denies, you will come to your own conclusion. In any case, this man's judgment does me great honor, whatever the reasons behind it. Nor do I think it makes much difference whether I am said to be the daughter of an orator thought more eloquent than all others or whether he calls me a stylish and cultivated writer for my tender years.

Eusebio is no more trustworthy on the subject than Orosio, who, though learned on certain small points, is without subtlety and examines minutely the things I have written, going over them letter by letter so that he can contaminate with his monk's hood of envy a single line of my writing that might be sleeping peacefully, oblivious to the incautious slip of a letter. These are the traps of sophistry which the bile of his mind interweaves with threads of envy. Still, the course of his accusation, lambent and furtive, remains unclear to me. Never has my muse concealed herself in a cave. My abilities are obvious to everyone, and the speculation that has surfaced about me, late and unseasonably, serves only to increase not my fear but my diligence. . . .[227]

The mention of "the cave" suggests Plato's image from the *Republic,* and Laura Cereta's response to her accusers indicates a clear understanding of her own worth as a writer. Her purpose goes far beyond grammatical corrections of minute points or misjudgments about authorship; it raises the high standard of the true purpose of grammar and rhetoric, i.e., eloquence, and it measures the petty focus on slips in letters and writing against the higher ideal.

In another letter Cereta takes a different approach. Here she writes an invective against Orestes and Phronicus, accusing them of the lowest sort of writing against her, and she compares their approach to the great classical writers, Cicero, Livy, and likely Ficino's newly articulated restatement of Plato's arguments for the immortality of the soul. Here Laura's humanistic standard is knowledge of letters:

226. Cereta (October 1, 1487), *Laura Cereta: Collected Letters,* pp. 178-79.
227. Cereta (July 1, 1487), *Laura Cereta: Collected Letters,* p. 178.

> We have received the illiterate letters that have come from you and that equally
> uneducated fool [Phronicus], and although they babble idiotic nonsense, still
> these letters should by all means call for a beating rather than a forced politeness.
> But I am quite amazed that you, Orestes, a scarcely human little mannequin,
> without worry that you might be injured, unarmed and totally unfit for war,
> should march out against me when I'm at least shielded by pen if not by a sword.
>
> But do tell us please, you unseeing slanderer, you lowbrow prone to making a
> scene in public places, how and why it is that I have come to deserve your casti-
> gation to the point that you have garrulously excoriated everything in my letters,
> condemning them to the rod, and you have vomited up muddy sentiments on the
> subject of envy? Oh how I wish you had at least heard Cicero making speeches,
> Livy reading aloud, or Plato discoursing on immortality. . . .[228]

Her correspondents measure low in the knowledge of letters with their humanistic
illiteracy and lack of education. Their slander of Laura Cereta not only demonstrates a lack of self-knowledge and integrity, but also shows envy. Finally, their
public displays of hostility reveal disrespect to other human beings. Yet, Cereta calls
them to conversion by way of studying Cicero and Livy, Plato and Neoplatonism.

Laura Cereta accused her opponents of dishonesty regardless of fame or social position. She did not differentiate among persons when she perceived an injustice or discrepancy between the humanist ideals and their actions. In a lengthy and
detailed letter written on August 22, 1487 to Bonifacio Bembo, Cereta comments
on Cassandra Fedele's public statement that Cereta's father authored her letters.
Again she begins with the humanist principle of communication in truth to build a
just society, and then she measures the action against this principle:

> But many voluntarily follow a road of errors; we, in making our preparations
> openly, will pursue truth on the correct path to justice, so that things that contra-
> dict justice may certainly be known. Of course it is alien to sacred law that any-
> one should make an accusation against a person who is not present via a third
> person, especially since no magistrate would hand down a judgment against
> someone who was not called to testify in court. You yourself know that a charge
> brought by an informer is judged on its merit with the defendant present. For
> there is one kind of jurisdiction in the court, another in the bedroom, and still an-
> other in the street. Hadrian proposed a law according to which no one should be
> sentenced without charges being brought and there being a trial.
>
> Cassandra therefore gives grounds for abuse, because she believes that the
> things I have written are not mine but came from the pen of the father who edu-
> cated me. While I was pondering these things myself and my mind was playing
> the intermediary in helping me to get in touch with reason, I was amazed that
> with no evidentiary testimony she should have been moved by what merely had
> the superficial appearance of truth. But this argument from verisimilitude will
> work equally well against her, since the two of us are alike in sex and age, unless
> perchance it should have rained literature in her more intellectually fertile

228. Cereta (July 1, 1487), *Laura Cereta: Collected Letters*, p. 177.

household, in comparison to which my family's house would supposedly have been drier and less cultivated, and thus the place where I grew up would have been at fault, and not Laura. But these things are fictions.[229]

Playing with the Platonic notions of appearance and reality, Cereta argues well that Cassandra Fedele has leapt to a judgment without proper evidence. With irony, Cereta introduces the notion of arguing from similarities of appearances to demonstrate that the original conclusion of Fedele is false.

Laura Cereta's letter discusses the possible motive that led Cassandra Fedele to make such a poor judgment. Her passions interfered with proper reasoning concerning Cereta's knowledge and eloquent writing:

> Cassandra attacks me, though no specific charges have been leveled. Possibly motivated by the sting of envy, she takes pains to poke holes in my knowledge — meagre though it is — with complicated double-talk. And so it would appear that she either has contempt for her peers or heaps more abuse on people who are more knowledgeable than she.
>
> But the appearance of deceptiveness in a person's speech is often the cover for a fearful heart. This woman doesn't impair the firmly rooted trust that my all-night sessions of study have strengthened in the eyes of everyone regarding me, does she? But merciful gods, what has become of love? Where is the trust which cannot be violated? Where does the old compassion for one's fellow humans lie sleeping? No longer is there a show of friendship among people but only darkness. This sister, whom I praised with such reverence so many times, insinuates that I am a person whose learning is specious.[230]

The passions of envy and fear, accompanied by a lack of compassion, love, and constancy in friendship, are identified as the causes of Cassandra Fedele's misjudgment. Cereta offers another explanation, that Fedele was influenced by others' erroneous thoughts:

> I forgive her: she doesn't pursue these baseless thoughts alone. For the minds of individuals are different everywhere, and the entire sky is illuminated by stars whose appearance is in each case different. But little by little, time has so eradicated such suspicions about me that there isn't anyone who doesn't know of my literary gifts (if one can say such a thing). Indeed this is the truer story, which everyone sees with their own eyes. It is not worth being surprised if illiterate grammarians, who are contemptuous of the work of so many celebrated minds, disapprove of my pen — which in any case is covered with mildew [because of her grieving]. The opinions of Eusebius and Orosius are said to be utterly obscure, the philosophical position of the one making incomprehensible that of the other, and thus not only Orestes and Phronicus but also even the common people at-

---

229. Cereta (August 22, 1487), *Laura Cereta: Collected Letters,* pp. 145-46.
230. Cereta (August 22, 1487), *Laura Cereta: Collected Letters,* p. 145.

tack me with laughable arguments. For it is by no means easy for the hot and burning throat of envy to quench its greedy thirst for verbal abuse.[231]

Just as Cassandra Fedele noted the bias of the "common people" towards her intellectual talents, so Laura Cereta is affected by what she calls the "laughable arguments" of the common people. The sting of the false accusations is felt beneath her brave recourse to philosophical and legal arguments to defend herself from slander:

> In any case, suppose that these things were appropriate charges to bring and not merely the execrations of people who have no shame. Once Cassandra has charged me in a court of law, I would be delighted if she — who is the gloss and ornament of virtue — would show and tell where the summons of the plaintiff is for a ruling on the allegation, where the scrutiny is for the indictment of the defendant, where contumacy is, and where the confession. If credence must be given to her charge against me, why has there been no preliminary hearing for me to answer her charge? The opportunity to clear oneself in the case of a false charge must always be provided, lest the defendant be punished on a false allegation before the procedures prescribed by the law have been administered. We have written to Chiari, we have written to Brescia, and the case is being referred to Rome.[232]

In referring to Cassandra Fedele as the "gloss and ornament of virtue" Cereta echoes the phrase used by Angelo Poliziano, *O decus Italiae virgo*.[233]

In the conclusion, Cereta returns to the appropriate use of reason in self-defense aimed at certainty of the kind in Aristotelian demonstration before pronouncing judgment:

> But in my view, Bonifacio, you ought not to grieve or be surprised that I have put myself in the path of so many slanderous swords that I felt were stabbing me. For one is on guard against the ecclesiastical principle to the effect that one who does not take care to clear himself of an accusation may be thought to be admitting his guilt.
>
> Wherever the cause of honor is being undermined, one's hand must always be armed with reason; for small lawsuits are sometimes the consequence of great anger. . . .
>
> Thus I am given the chance to exonerate myself from this underhanded calumny, so that those butchers of literature who have been confused about this wrong will understand how arrogant vanity looks after its own interests. This most distinguished sister of mine should admit that she has been cautioned by a

231. Cereta (August 22, 1487), *Laura Cereta: Collected Letters*, p. 146.
232. Cereta (August 22, 1487), *Laura Cereta: Collected Letters*, p. 146.
233. Robin, ed., in *Laura Cereta: Collected Letters*, p. 147, note 77. See also "Angelo Poliziano to Cassandra Fedele,"in *Her Immaculate Hand,* ed. King and Rabil, pp. 126-27. Finally, see a different interpretation of the value of contributions of women humanists in the article by Lisa Jardine, "'O Decus Italiae Virgo,' or The Myth of the Learned Lady in the Renaissance," *The Historical Journal* 28, no. 4 (1985): 777-818.

sister that one should only speak about what is either demonstrably or inescapably true.[234]

Laura Cereta's final area of contribution to building the common good involves an extension of her activity into society at large. In the 1485 letter to Paolo Zane, Bishop of Brescia, she begins with an ideal measure of those who treat the property they administer with the greatest respect. She then compares the bishop's neglect of a shrine in Brescia with the ideal:

Who is so crazy or so wasteful of money that he would leave his case or clothes or pearls lying around in a public place? Look at how our church, which is half in ruins, languishes under a crumbling roof. No one need call out the guard, for none was commissioned; no one knows that this place is a shrine. No one batters on doors already open, for the entrances lie free and accessible to one and all. The host is protected by no bolt, no barrier, and never by any lock. Today when the holy relics were brought forth from their small hiding place, they cried out: "We pardon you, ungrateful believers. But God does not pardon you, since you take up the Son from such a lowly and undeserved place: the Son, coeternal with the Father, whose flesh and blood any thieving, irreligious member of the human race can steal, sell, violate, and trample. Thus the most divine body of the son of God is now left at the disposal of everyone; thus the sacred preparations of the altar, where the services for the dead are sanctified through expiation, are now the property of magicians and night-wandering sages."[235]

In her challenge to the bishop to live up to his responsibilities for "domestic service" of his Church, Laura is calling for his conversion to proper ordering. At the same time, she is aware of the possible lack of propriety of a simple member of the Church in confronting her bishop with such a strong accusation of lack of moral integrity.[236] In the final paragraph she invites him to correct her opinions:

Although these may not be suitable professions for an unlearned girl who for the most part agrees with what the popes' decrees have sanctified, still her mind does not accede to the notion that the great only-born son of the virgin of Judaea should be left in an open shrine both night and day, freely accessible to the impious. However, if my audacious criticisms are in any way untrue, I beg you, most perfect and honorable proconsul and one most learned in all law, to decide either what I should think on this subject or what I, your little daughter in Christ, should unlearn.[237]

234. Cereta (August 22, 1487), *Laura Cereta: Collected Letters,* pp. 147-48.
235. Cereta (September 22, 1485), *Laura Cereta: Collected Letters,* pp. 47-48.
236. It is not clear whether Laura modeled her letter to the bishop on earlier similar letters of correction by St. Catherine of Siena. It is certainly possible that she would have been aware of the model of intervention of her predecessor. St. Catherine of Siena's letters had been circulating in manuscript for some time, although they were not published until 1492 and 1500. See Leonardas Gerulaitis, *Printing and Publishing in Fifteenth-Century Venice* (Chicago: American Library Association, 1976), pp. 43-44.
237. Cereta (September 22, 1485), *Laura Cereta: Collected Letters,* p. 48.

Laura Cereta's public lectures aimed at bringing persons to insight of mind and conversion of will. In the introduction to the publication of her manuscript she states this goal clearly to Cardinal Sforza:

> Though I was untrained and scarcely exposed to literature, through my own intelligence and natural talents I was able to acquire the beginnings of an education. While my pleasure in embarking on such a journey of the mind and my love of study were strong at the outset, the weak seeds of my small talent have grown to such a degree that I have written speeches for public occasions, and these I embellished grandly, painting pictures with words in order to influence people and stimulate their minds.[238]

The twin goal, "to influence people and stimulate their minds," marks Cereta's orientation as a public lecturer and teacher. As her thinking about the common good continued to grow, she came to understand the difference between dialogue and vendetta and between just war and war from greed or power. As she grew in this awareness, her writings and lectures took on a greater urgency, influencing others to reach a similar conclusion. Cereta addressed the war of words among persons and the military wars among men of different nations.

The best example of Cereta's arguments against warring discourse is found in a letter she wrote to the Dominican, Brother Thomas, who appears to have released publicly a critical evaluation of her writing. She distinguishes between integral philosophical criticism and a philosopher's brawl:

> Your thorny letter is an angry swarm of bees, whose numerous sharpened stings are hidden in so many honey-bearing knees. But this odious poison should touch minds more deserving of blame; I myself have not yet learned to walk the thorny paths of censure, nor do I purchase pens of such virulence that they drip with wormwood. If Plato rejects Parmenides, if Socrates does the same to Anaxagoras, if Philo of the Academy dismisses the Stoics and Diogenes does likewise to Euclid, and finally if Sallust reproves Cicero and Cicero does the same to Marcus Antonius, why should I be interested in those thinkers? This amounts to a brawl and not a discussion among philosophers. The defending of a war of nasty insults held in the public arena is the task of a gladiator, not a critic.[239]

Cereta offers a summary of her self-knowledge as a philosopher, namely that she aims to speak the truth, but is led by passions:

> I am happy rather than sad that the name Laura has become unpopular with everyone, because it is the truth contained in my writings that has caused them to offend the public. You don't believe, do you, that my words have emanated from my highest faculties? For the most part, these words were born in the lower, visceral regions of my being. For it is here that the mind, liberated from restraint, is

---

238. Cereta (March 1488), *Laura Cereta: Collected Letters,* p. 37.
239. Cereta (November 11, 1487), *Laura Cereta: Collected Letters,* p. 107.

free to exercise its own powers and strength. Thus I am explicit with my friends about whatever it is that hurts my mind. My mind always causes me to hesitate, whenever I am persuaded that I should reproach friends to whom I have opened my whole heart. Because of this, through listening to my own counsel and conscience, I have established a life obedient not to other people's opinions but to my own heart. I think it quite unjust that your own criticism, which is itself abrasive, should bemoan my abrasiveness, since you attack me — though I am innocent — in public.[240]

The nature of epistolary exchange in northern Italy among humanists is inflamed by the public knowledge of its accusations and defenses. The common good cannot be served, when public accusations are false. Despite having been publicly and wrongly accused by Brother Thomas, she urges that their communication should follow the ideal of charity or love of human beings:

I respect you both as my instructor and as one well steeped in the readings of the philosophers, since the discipline of philosophy remains a venerable one among all men. But charity, not ill-will or enviousness, is the object of the well-ordered mind, nor can charity, whose hunger for the divine is always great, be fed on smoke. Aimless and empty are the paltry rewards for human glory. . . .

As I prepare a mirror of my mind for death, I always hold up to my mind the teaching of our Savior. And though vain criticism may sometimes cause me to be distracted, still I rise up again from misfortune more determined than before with the help of God. . . .[241]

Cereta will not deny the suffering caused by unjust accusations, yet she calls for the conversion of mind in her correspondent:

But no one is a person of such integrity that he can attain sufficient happiness of the mind without humility. And so I felt the stinging nettles of your letter; this lethal potion caused even the hemlock that grows in brambles to tremble. But let the shining Catos make noise in the Senate, and let them commit those speeches to writing. Let the clamorous academy of logicians entangle you in questions about definitions concerning the physical world. Thus let the school of Porphyry introduce the first *isagogas* demonstrating the logical propositions, let the Peripatetics argue categorial pronouncements, and let Apuleius and Aristotle give birth to Perhiermenian subtleties from the virginities of their minds. Since I, a mere female, inept at literary matters and deficient in talent, cannot cover myself with glory by making public my talent in the arenas of debate, I shall declaim my arguments against you in my small and humble cell, with Christ.

May the various kinds of oppositions, hypothetical and paralogical, which differ among themselves, and may the many and varied kinds of definitions and arguments derived from rhetorical topics remain yours. The hallmark of my speech

240. Cereta (November 11, 1487), *Laura Cereta: Collected Letters,* p. 107.
241. Cereta (November 11, 1487), *Laura Cereta: Collected Letters,* p. 108.

is not contentiousness but grace. Whatever your web weaves too intricately will give me an excuse to maintain silence, and patience will be my beatitude. For more trustworthy are those ears which often interrupt in an indirect manner.[242]

In this remarkable, ironic letter, Cereta shows how to battle using the tools of logic and disputation, but instead of engaging in a public war of arguments she prefers to cease the battle and bear witness to the truth. In so doing, she shares Socrates' fate of accepting the hemlock of her false accusers, but she goes further than her ancient Greek model by facing death to her desire for human glory with Christ, in humility and grace.

With respect to military war, we find Cereta developing a consistent approach to the topic, that searches for the underlying motivations for such extreme violence and destruction. She describes war as "Hell" in a dreamlike study sent to Martha Marcella. After a descent to the underworld Cereta states:

> The last lot one could draw was that of unfortunate war — a lot that burned many of those who pursued it with brands, and drowned many others who had fled through the remote and rough channels that led down to the sulphurous sea. Others were sent plunging down from the steep precipice of a mountain. In this spectacle of divine retribution, clouds of arrows flew through the air everywhere far and wide; there was never a state of peace, armistice, or cease-fire. Everything blazed with truculent rage. No wonder all hope of putting an end to the evils here was in vain. With no hope of any delay intervening, each person's torments were reborn again. Thus the battle lines were rearmed again on each side, and on both sides, the defeated shades groaned at their uncertain fate. They were crowded together, they creaked and rattled, and they gnashed their teeth in anger. And then the crashing of renewed tumult was heard in the form of diabolical war trumpets.[243]

If unrelenting war is the effect of a diabolical or evil force, then how does a person who lives in a time often ravaged with war work towards the common good?

In a letter to Elena di Cesare, Cereta describes the poor motivations of both sides in a war that occurred in 1453 between the Turks and Christians in Constantinople. The Turks are motivated by pride, the Christians in Italy by avarice and hatred. Neither are concerned about the common good. First, her description of the Turks:

> Do you not feel as though you hear the shouting and tumult of the invasion of Constantinople and the destruction of Clalchis and Scutari, which threw heaven and earth into disorder and silence? The bravest leaders were slain there in battle, if you remember; kings were mutilated, kingdoms overturned, captives were killed in pride and rage, and unburied bodies were thrown into the sea. The barbarian showed the vanquished no mercy; he had no respect for virgins, married

---

242. Cereta (November 11, 1487), *Laura Cereta: Collected Letters,* pp. 108-9.
243. Cereta (October 8, 1486), *Laura Cereta: Collected Letters,* p. 131.

women, or nuns; and he evinced no chastity and no religion. The avenging Turk gazed upon the severed heads of Christians with pleasure, he transformed all Greece into one grave and all Pergamon into a conflagration, and he, as victor, surveyed the whole world with unbridled pride.[244]

Then Cereta turns her gaze on Italy and its own moral state:

> But if those clouds of bow-carrying Turks should descend on Italy, what do you think would be a sure guarantee for our defense? What will the wretched nations of peoples do, if that Thracian lion, powerful in arms, should come? Will some cities, unprepared for war, go to others for help? Already spirits weaken, and fondness for compassion withers. The comfort of a place to hide is no longer an option for us. There is no flight to friends and guardians. . . .
>
> Thus we have all been led astray by hope, blinded by hate, and possessed by avarice. No one stands guard over the Christian realm; no one looks to the interest of the common good.[245]

The main point of her argument is that each side is driven by avarice, to gain what it can for itself, with the possible result that all Christian realms fall. Cereta calls her listener(s) to conversion like the inhabitants of Nineveh who, following Jonah's prophecy of the destruction of their city, converted, and the city was spared:

> I am no Cassandra who with lamentation could foretell the destruction of Troy long before it fell. I am a mere simplehearted girl who — if not present myself — can only be inoculated by previous examples of fidelity. For in the mirror of the past, events of the future can be discerned. One founder alone remains in heaven, one law, and in nature one order. We alone, turned away from God, continue to strive; we alone have become lawless and have shaken off every yoke of humanity from our savage minds. Our pardon, however, comes from heaven. Let us be aware, and let us correct the errors of our ways . . . [like] the inhabitants of Nineveh. . . .
>
> Let us therefore renounce fruitless desires; let us reject all the pomp of the age.[246]

In the following letter to Luigi Dandolo, magistrate of Brescia, after saying that she "has insufficient knowledge of military matters," Cereta describes in gruesome detail the outcome of a three-stage battle between Germans and Venetians. The Germans began the war "for the sake of plunder or to avenge themselves in a just war," but they left "without a clear victory."[247] Laura decries the uselessness of this battle among two groups of Christians that left "carnage on both sides" and "corpses now [lying] piled high in carts and being hauled away on

---

244. Cereta (December 20, 1485), *Laura Cereta: Collected Letters*, p. 139.
245. Cereta (December 20, 1485), *Laura Cereta: Collected Letters*, pp. 139-40.
246. Cereta (December 20, 1485), *Laura Cereta: Collected Letters*, p. 140.
247. Cereta (August 29, 1487), *Laura Cereta: Collected Letters*, p. 161.

all sides."[248] Then she asks why the war did not end at this point, why it was not "a time when bloodshed might have touched and softened men's minds."[249] She also makes an appeal "for us simply to reconsider the whole situation, rationally and lucidly."[250]

Cereta describes in detail how the battle goes back and forth until the Italians defeat the Germans, but at a terrible cost.[251] Her description brings attention to the personal side of war, of those suffering the pain of wounds and of loving members of families grieving death:

> On both sides, those who were not yet defeated slaughtered one another in a massacre equal to that at Cannae. The wounded and many who were barely breathing lay on the ground like sacrificial victims whose throats had been cut. Here lay a thousand unburied corpses, over whose bodies no grieving mothers sighed, and none wept over the ashes that were collected. On both sides a tearful lamentation rose up for the soldiers who had left their wives widowed. The horror is still fresh over the many dead, whose bodies were rolled and turned by the Adige, as it ran down in ripples that receded into the foaming shoals of the Po and continued underneath its deep waters all the way to the sea, although still the erupting crests of the waves belched forth many corpses from the swelling waves, pulling them back to the sea over and over again with the tide.[252]

Cereta concludes her appeal to the magistrate of Brescia to join his forces in a common goal of defense with Venice rather than to engage in military conflict with this city. She asks for diplomatic initiatives rather than military ones:

> I believe there has been far too little consultation among these nations, who in the situation that lay ahead did not adequately take into account the constancy of the Venetians and their moral courage honed by adversity, their sound planning at home, their experience in military matters. . . .[253]

In another letter to Lodovico Cendrate Veronese, Cereta places contemporary wars in Italy in a historical context of wars throughout history, i.e., of Africans, Greeks, Romans, Persians, Egyptians, etc. Diana Robin points out that Lodovico was a student of Guarino of Verona and also a correspondent of Isotta Nogarola. Thus, he shares the tendency of early humanists to place all discussions in a context of ancient history.[254]

---

248. Cereta (August 29, 1497), *Laura Cereta: Collected Letters*, p. 161.

249. Cereta, *Laura Cereta: Collected Letters*, p. 161.

250. Cereta (August 19, 1487), *Laura Cereta: Collected Letters*, p. 162.

251. However, because of Italians rising up against one another, the German army returned, another battle ensued, and this time the Germans fled. Cereta notes that the "foreign troops' readiness to flee encouraged the Italians in turn to engage in booty taking. Meanwhile, enemy reinforcements, lying hidden and ready for ambush in a secluded area in the woods, sprang on our soldiers in the midst of their spoils" (Cereta [August 29, 1487], *Laura Cereta: Collected Letters*, p. 162).

252. Cereta, *Laura Cereta: Collected Letters*, p. 163.

253. Cereta (August 29, 1487), *Laura Cereta: Collected Letters*, p. 164.

254. Cereta, *Laura Cereta: Collected Letters*, p. 169.

To Lodovico, Laura Cereta emphasizes the immoral motives that drive generals and soldiers to war. She refers to envy, rage, lust for domination, restless minds, pleasure in taking cities through treachery, and boiling hatred. Then she documents the process of reducing people to weakness out of fear:

> But when those men whose commitment to the war was greatest allowed the soldiers to despoil certain villages which here and there had resisted, frightened regiments of soldiers from the rural areas began to grow weak. The enemy, encouraged by these events, extorted goods from the townspeople in every way, they sent out edicts, they called local citizens to appear before their tribunals, and they posted lists of those proscribed. A sudden siege ringed the town and hemmed it in with ditches and walls. After this, fear on the part of many and the collapse of trust inclined people towards a civil uprising, kindling in them a zeal for rebellion.[255]

In just this short excerpt we see the destruction of the principles of moral integrity or interest in the common good that comes as an effect of war and anarchy.

Laura Cereta's contribution to the common good, by measuring particular acts against the humanist ideal, and by furthering the conversion of her interlocutors, is summarized below:

Laura Cereta's Building Common Good in Society at Large		
Humanist Ideal	Measure of Action or Event	Goal of the Intervention
Appropriate Humanist Dialogue	Particular dialogue against Laura Cereta with: Mock attacks Slander Vendettas	To protect her reputation in general society against the false accusations of men in the humanist circle at the Chiari monastery
Men and women Humanists should draw truthful conclusions from careful consideration of the evidence	Accusation that her father wrote her letters Accusation that she plagiarized material from books in her letters	To call the male humanists Eusebio, Fronto, Canto, and Michael Baetus and the female humanist Cassandra Fedele to a more integral relation to evidence supporting truth To win acceptance that women as well as men can be excellent humanist scholars

255. Cereta (March 15, 1486), *Laura Cereta: Collected Letters,* p. 172.

Laura Cereta's Building Common Good in Society at Large (cont.)		
Humanist Ideal	Measure of Action or Event	Goal of the Intervention
Humanists should have a good knowledge of letters	Illiterate levels of communication against Laura Cereta	To lead the illiterate writers Orestes and Phronicus to study Cicero, Livy, and Plato
Public officials should take proper care of public property	A Church left in disrepair and the sacred objects left unguarded	To call the bishop to be a proper administrator
Philosophers in general should hold appropriate verbal discussions with a charitable witness to the truth	The constant examples of verbal wars, exchange of insults, and ill-will among philosophers	To interrupt the warlike mentality of philosophers and invite them to a genuine experience of humanist discourse aimed towards truth and virtue
Military wars should be undertaken only in self-defense.	Wars are held for reasons of power, avarice, or hatred. Wars cause useless suffering of soldiers, families, and innocent persons. War is hell.	To induce the Brescian government to associate with Venice for self-defense To encourage Italians to engage in self-examination and conversion to lives oriented towards virtue so that war will not come as a punishment for lazy and immoral behavior

As we reach the end of our reflections on Laura Cereta's general theory and practices related to self-knowledge, self-governance, and virtue, we note that in all three areas she demonstrated a new and dynamic way for women to teach others about fundamental principles of human development and integrity. Through letters and public lectures she constantly challenged others to live according to the values they professed and to work always towards a greater moral integrity, knowledge of letters, and love for others.

Integral Gender Complementarity

Although Laura Cereta often expressed her anger and even rage at the unjust treatment of women, she did not propose that women were naturally superior to men; she stayed away from the theory of reverse gender polarity that begins to be formulated at the end of the fifteenth century. Treatises that began to articulate foundations for reverse gender polarity, i.e., that women are naturally superior to men, include the following: Martin Le Franc's *Le Champion des dames* (1442, printed in 1485), Antonio Cornazzano's *De mulieribus admirandis* (1467), Vespasiano da Bisticci's *Il Libro delle lode e commendazione delle donne* (c. 1480), Giovanni Sabadino degli Arienti's *Gynervera de le clare donne* (1483), and Bartolomeo Gogio's *De laudibus mulierum* (1487).[256] These shorter texts led up to the more well-known defense of woman's natural superiority over man written by the German humanist Cornelius Agrippa von Nettesheim, *De Nobilitate et praecellentia foeminei sexus* (On the Nobility and Superiority of the Female Sex) (1509).[257]

Through the influence of Neoplatonism, early Renaissance Humanists such as Petrarch, Boccaccio, and Dante, Cereta came to accept a principle of the natural equality of men and women. This equality extended to the capacities to learn, to develop the virtue of self-governance, and to participate in building the common good. Her fundamental conviction that men and women were of equal dignity and worth armed her against the theory and practice of gender polarity, which gave a natural superiority to men without moving towards a reverse gender polarity that gave a natural superiority to women.

At the same time, Cereta did not adopt a gender unity position. Even though she appeared to accept the Neoplatonic thesis of immortality of the soul, she did not suggest that there are no significant differences between men and women. On the contrary, in many situations Cereta brought forward those areas of woman's identity that had a unique aspect: women's history, women's experience of being female in a particular culture, women's domestic service expanded from the home into society, and most interestingly, particular attention to the development of the human person in all situations. Laura Cereta brought attention to the whole person, to measuring a person's actions against the ideals of human dignity as expressed in a humanist culture. She did this consistently in a concrete and practical manner in all her interactions with both men and women. We will consider her comments on woman's identity in general, on particular groups of women, and on individual women. In this move from the universal to particular it can be shown that Cereta actually articulated rudiments of a theory of integral gender complementarity.

In her letter to Pietro Fecchi on matrimony, Laura Cereta appears at first to claim that women are superior to men. She states that "the powers of maternal authority are great."[258] Then, drawing upon Boccaccio's *Concerning Famous Women,*

---

256. Three excellent descriptions of the contents of these works can be found in Conor Fahy, "Three Early Renaissance Treatises on Women," *Italian Studies* 11 (1956): 30-55; Pamela Benson, "From Praise to Paradox: The First Italian Defenses of Women," in *The Invention of the Renaissance Woman,* (University Park, Pa.: Penn State University Press, 1992), ch. 2, pp. 33-64; and Marc Angenot, *Les Champions des femmes: examen du discours sur la supériorité des femmes 1400-1800* (Montreal: Les Presses de l'Université du Québec, 1977), pp. 16-21.

257. See Henry Cornelius Agrippa, *On the Superiority of Woman over Man* (New York: American News Company, 1873).

258. Cereta (February 3, 1486), *Laura Cereta: Collected Letters,* p. 68.

she lists several historical examples of mothers who saved their sons: Coriolanus's mother, Nero's mother Agrippina, Aenobia, the mother of Hermonianus and Timolaus, and Constance, the mother of the emperor Henry. Next are several examples of "warrior widows" who were victorious over staunch male warriors and of several women, including, of course, Lucretia, who "bravely" committed suicide rather than be vanquished by men's evil acts. Then Cereta says: "If you ponder these things in your mind, and consider them with a keen eye, manfully and with foresight, you will conceive of a surer plan for entering into marriage and you will prepare the kinds of torches you should be lighting at the altar of holy matrimony."[259]

The exaltation of women's qualities continues through a litany of virtues that wives and mothers demonstrate in the ordinary circumstances of married life: "toil and duty, that enables us to rear up children amid wailing and all-night vigils, and . . . guard your treasures and offices with solicitous love for the long duration of your life."[260] Cereta offers a description of a wife as the peacemaker and protector of men:

> And while they preserve the always flourishing and much-cherished unity of holy matrimony women govern themselves by obeying their ancestors and they smooth over all the pain when there is dissension in the household with their own good sense. They mount unheard-of plans in the face of inescapable events; they keep the din of war far from their borders and towns; and, relying both on arms and the bonds of kinship, they protect kings and they pacify realms. And if ever they are summoned to resolve the injuries of their husbands, these women immediately wash the animosity away from the heart that has been bruised, having first dissolved it with their little tears. And, soothing egos with compliments to promote a happy mood, they extinguish noisy shouting when tempers flare.[261]

Then Laura Cereta reverses the theme of women's superiority. Drawing from satirical literature, especially from Pliny, she offers a caricature of woman's obedience to husband and family. Here all the powerful women become ridiculously weak. This seems to apply to all women, rather than to a type of woman:

> You have no need of little sparrows who are accustomed to come to your hand. Wives come to their husbands just to receive their nods of perfect approval, like little girls who depend on their nurse's opinion. Why do you men hold noisy pet dogs in your arms? A woman rolls herself over like a dog begging and, while she longs for a word of praise, she talks about whips.[262]

Laura Cereta's use of the rhetorical device of exaggeration and reversal, common to satirical literature, leads us to conclude that neither of the extreme views may be taken as Cereta's own. She uses, as did Isotta Nogarola before her, the method of philosophical argument that catches the other person in a conflict of two extreme

---

259. Cereta (February 4, 1486), *Laura Cereta: Collected Letters,* pp. 68-70.
260. Cereta (February 3, 1468), *Laura Cereta: Collected Letters,* p. 71.
261. Cereta (February 3, 1486), *Laura Cereta: Collected Letters,* pp. 71-72.
262. Cereta (February 3, 1486), *Laura Cereta: Collected Letters,* p. 72.

positions, both of which are false. Woman is either superior or inferior to man. Neither of the theses being acceptable, one is forced to come to a new point of view. In the language of gender theory, Cereta builds the tension between the two opposing and unacceptable theses: either reverse gender polarity or traditional gender polarity. Since they both must be rejected, the conclusion is that there must be another alternative: integral gender complementarity or gender unity. In both situations men and women have an equal dignity and worth; neither is naturally superior to the other. However, the question still remains as to whether there are philosophically significant differences between them.

Cereta will distinguish between types of women rather than make universal claims about all women being either naturally superior or inferior to men. Her basic claim is that a woman makes choices concerning the kind of woman she will be. The moral choices she makes have a great power to determine the quality of her character. In a passage from her letter to Bibolo Semproni, Laura Cereta identifies all three categories: universal, type, and particular:

> . . . nature imparts one freedom to all human beings equally — to learn. But the question of my exceptionality remains. And here choice alone, since it is the arbiter of character, is the distinguishing factor. For some women worry about the styling of their hair, the elegance of their clothes, and the pearls and other jewelry they wear on their fingers. Others love to say cute little things, to hide their feelings behind a mask of tranquillity, to indulge in dancing, and lead pet dogs around on a leash. For all I care, other women can long for parties with carefully appointed tables, for the peace of mind or sleep, or they can yearn to deface with paint the pretty face they see reflected in their mirrors. But those women for whom the quest for the good represents a higher value restrain their young spirits and ponder better plans. They harden their bodies with sobriety and toil, they control their tongues, they carefully monitor what they hear, they ready their minds for all-night vigils, and they rouse their minds for the contemplation of probity in the case of harmful literature. For knowledge is not given as a gift but by study. For a mind free, keen, and unyielding in the face of hard work always rises to the good, and the desire for learning grows in depth and breadth.
>
> So be it therefore. May we women, then, not be endowed by God the grantor with any giftedness or rare talent through any sanctity of our own. Nature has granted to all enough of her bounty, she opens to all the gates of choice, and through these gates, reason sends legates to the will, for it is through reason that these legates can transmit their desires.[263]

In this remarkable passage Laura Cereta defines her theory of gender: men and women alike have freedom of the will and mind to study, learn, and gain knowledge by hard work. This is not a rare talent bestowed by God on any individual or group, but is the inheritance of all human beings. Some women, like herself, have opened the "gates of choice"; other women have chosen a "lower value" in working only on their physical appearance.

263. Cereta (January 13, 1488), *Laura Cereta: Collected Letters,* pp. 78-79.

Cereta introduces one of her disjunctive tensions between traditional gender polarity and reverse gender polarity:

> I shall make a bold summary of the matter. Yours is the authority, ours is the inborn ability. But instead of manly strength, we women are naturally endowed with cunning; instead of a sense of security, we are suspicious. Down deep we women are content with our lot. But you, enraged and maddened by the anger of the dog from whom you flee, are like someone who has been frightened by the attack of a pack of wolves. The victor does not look for the fugitive; nor does she who desires a ceasefire with the enemy conceal herself. Nor does she set up camp with courage and arms when the conditions are hopeless. Nor does it give the strong any pleasure to pursue one who is already fleeing.[264]

She juxtaposes man's superiority through authority, strength, and security with man's inferiority through rage, fleeing madness, terrifying fear, and cowardliness in the face of woman's intellectual achievements. Woman's inferiority through attitudes of cunning, suspiciousness, and contentment with her lot in life is contrasted with woman's superiority through natural ability, victory over man, desiring a ceasefire, openness, practical judgment in the face of hopelessness, and restrained strength when the enemy flees. Thus, a close reading of Cereta's argument forces the reader to reject her polarized alternatives and seek a more balanced position of gender complementarity. It is particularly striking that she uses material from Juvenal's famous Sixth Satire against women, but changes his universalizations about *all* women to the more qualified category of *some* women or *one* woman. Never does Cereta offer a universal generalization that is derogatory or satirical against all women or all men.

When proposing her own views, too, Cereta qualifies the universals and reduces them to the more distinguished categories of many, some, or one. In one of her strongest letters to Agostino Emilio, she explains why she chooses the long-lasting value of virtue over the shorter-lasting value of physical beauty, and she invites the senators of the city to do the same:

> There are some people who are impressed by the attribute of beauty. I myself would rather see senatorial uncorruptibility rewarded since, as with the physical beauty of youth, so often the stimuli for such attractions burst into flames themselves. But honor, the light of beauty, surpasses all the contrived arts of polishing and all the little flowers of softness. Mark Anthony might delight in the bejeweled Cleopatra; but I myself will imitate the integrity of Rebecca.[265]

Rebecca did not settle for the appearance but chose rather to risk all to defend a deeper choice.[266]

---

264. Cereta (July 13, 1488), *Laura Cereta: Collected Letters*, p. 79.

265. Cereta (February 12, 1487), *Laura Cereta: Collected Letters*, p. 84.

266. For controversial interpretations of the figure of Rebecca, see Christine Allen, "Who Was Rebecca? — On Me Be the Curse, My Son," ch. 10 in *Encounter with the Text: Issues in Hermeneutics with Special Attention to Genesis 25–35*, ed. Martin Buss (Missoula, Mont.: Scholar's Press, 1979), pp. 159-72.

Cereta next makes the claim that men and women in her own city have become caught by emphasizing the exterior physical characteristics of women. She borrows the examples straight from Juvenal. However, she always qualifies each statement so that it is not a universal condemnation of women. To summarize:

- "Some" women sport a knot of someone else's hair
- "Another" woman's hair hangs down
- "Another" puts her blond hair up
- "Some" wind strings of pearls
- "One" walks in a way to attract popularity
- "Another" makes her breasts look larger by a sash
- "Some" trail silken tunics
- "Others" wear strong perfumes and veils
- "Many" try to soften their faces with bread
- "Many" polish their wrinkled skin
- "A few" use white powder
- "Some" wear exotic dresses
- "Certain" women redden their cheeks. . . .[267]

Cereta includes herself among women in the categories of "us," "we," and "our" to emphasize that she has the same set of circumstances as other women within which to choose her own identity as a particular kind of woman. Again her statements will be summarized:

- "How crooked is the weakness of **our** sex in its delights?"
- How do earrings enable **us** to imitate our nobility?
- Our purpose is not to dote on **our** image in a mirror
- As Christian women **we** refuse ostentatiousness
- We should blush at **our** misguided ambition for superior beauty
- **Our** madness is lascivious and arrogant
- **We** have come from ashes
- **Our** desires have caused our sins[268]

She concludes with a direct challenge to every woman: "Let each woman take counsel; let each one heal the injury from which she, being wounded, now languishes."[269] It is up to the individual woman to make the proper choice.

Finally, Cereta introduces the theme that women's tendency to make an improper choice comes in part from original sin. Yet, following Isotta Nogarola's argument on Adam and Eve, Cereta suggests that women were formed from man, not the earth, but from Adam, which lessens female guilt. She concludes that men have the greater blame for the miserable state of society:

267. Cereta (February 12, 1487), *Laura Cereta: Collected Letters,* pp. 84-85.
268. Cereta (February 12, 1487), *Laura Cereta: Collected Letters,* p. 85.
269. Cereta (February 12, 1487), *Laura Cereta: Collected Letters,* p. 85.

Therefore, as many times as you, Agostino, have looked at me and have seen boasts devoid of great splendor, please pardon my age or at least my sex. For Nature, which produced our **foremother** *(genetrix nostra)* not from earth or stone but from the humanity of Adam, is complicit in our guilt. However, humanity always leans towards that which it can either assist or delight in. We are the more imperfect animal, and our few strengths are not effective in wars of courage. You, preeminent men of great authority, on whom the highest matters of state devolve, and who have amongst yourselves, by the right of assembly, so many Brutuses, Curii, Fabii, Catos, and Enylios, be careful to see that we women, being constituted as we are, are not taken in the birdlime of this sort of elegance. For where there is greater deliberation in councils of state, there the greater blame should rest.[270]

Laura Cereta also ironically reasserts the Aristotelian-based natural principle of gender polarity, namely, that woman is by nature weaker than man, and the epistemological principle of gender polarity, namely, that men have a greater capacity for deliberation than do women, and therefore, they have greater responsibility for virtue and greater blame for vice in the state. Men and women have the responsibility to choose virtue over superficial beauty with respect to their own personal values.

Laura Cereta's juxtaposition of gender polarity and reverse gender polarity, as Isotta Nogarola's before her, is a tactic of argumentation, and not a statement of her own theory of gender. If we consolidate the different approaches and arguments that Laura Cereta offered throughout her writings about the concept of woman and gender identity, it is clear that she was working towards a philosophy of integral gender complementarity in all four categories of opposites, generation, wisdom, and virtue. Her approach was primarily practical, but with a theoretical foundation. In the chart on the following page her positions are summarized.

Laura Cereta's theory of complementarity is 'integral' rather than 'fractional' because she emphasized the development of the whole person. Although she did not articulate a theory of integral gender complementarity, in practice she supported its principles. For example, even in her description of marriage, she avoided suggesting the fractional complementarity premise that the mind of the two persons joined to become one mind, with man providing the reason and woman the intuition or sense data. Instead, Cereta stated that in marriage the two souls remained distinct from one another — each with its proper integrity of intellect and will — but joined together in mind and heart to act as one being. Thus, the integrity of the gender differentiation remained intact while the union of hearts and minds served as a goal for relationship. In addition, in all of her correspondence and writing with numerous women and men, Laura Cereta respected the dignity of the other person by calling for a greater integrity of response to the values espoused. She did not determine for others how they were to act or think. Rather, she posed alternatives, hoping for a better choice. Laura Cereta both wrote about and modeled a philosophy of integral gender complementarity.

270. Cereta (February 12, 1487), *Laura Cereta: Collected Letters,* p. 86. See note 80 for the Latin. Diana Robin suggests that this understanding of Eve as women's foremother is a new development in literature.

Laura Cereta's Philosophy of Integral Gender Complementarity		
Category of Gender Identity	**Principle of Equality**	**Principle of Differentiation**
Metaphysical: Opposites	No metaphysical polarization of man as opposite to woman.	No metaphysical polarization of woman as opposite to man.
Natural: Generation	Men and women created equally by God as having a soul that does not die and a body that ages and dies.	Created individually as a woman or as a man. Ironically, man created from earth or stone, woman from man's humanity. The male or female body is resurrected and reunited to the soul in an eternal engendered identity.
Epistemological: Wisdom	Men and women given equal capacity to learn letters, literature, history, philosophy, including demonstrative and rhetorical argumentation. Reason the same in all human beings. Its object is the truth. It places the human being in a perspectival relation to time and space. Self-knowledge is the same goal as central part of wisdom. It demands attention to the passions and their analysis by reason.	Women have a different collective literary and societal history than do men. Women's originating contexts for using reason differ from men's contexts in some ways, i.e., domestic service and governing the republic. Yet women can cross over through letters and orations into the public domain. Women and men need to identify those particular situations that arouse certain passions and lead them to make particular decisions about their respective identities.

Laura Cereta's Philosophy of Integral Gender Complementarity (cont.)		
Category of Gender Identity	Principle of Equality	Principle of Differentiation
Ethical: Virtue	Men and women are equally responsible for exercising the will to choose virtue. Men and women alike should work towards moral integrity. Men and women alike should work towards the common good, being motivated by love for others and love of the truth.	The contexts within which men and women exercise their will are often gender-differentiated. In the particular circumstances of women's experience of being widowed or of excelling in humanistic studies women's domestic service may extend into the broader common good. Women tend to be more concerned with persons-in-relation, personal development, and peacemaking; men tend to be more concerned with the development of thoughts, arguments, and wars.

EARLY HUMANIST WOMEN PHILOSOPHERS' ATTENTION TO PERSON-IN-RELATION

In chapters 8 and 9 we traced ways in which male philosophers contributed to a reform of educational structures and of theories of gender identity. This reform retrieved works by Quintilian, Plutarch, Plato, and various Neoplatonists. A new dynamic of interpersonal relations outside of academia and religious communities also contributed to the development of communities of discourse about identity. Full personal development aided by the study of classical texts on rhetoric, eloquence, wisdom, and virtue was jointly studied and put into practice by men and women.

In Chapter 10 we considered how women philosophers benefited from and contributed to the momentum of early Renaissance Humanism. The works of three women were considered: Cassandra Fedele, Isotta Nogarola, and Laura Cereta. While few original sources are available from Fedele, the latter two women have left a considerable legacy from which to judge their thoughts and actions. Distinct from the contributed texts of those who preceded them, these women each proposed a focus on "person-in-relation." A consistent theme of their orations and letters is that a humanist woman pays attention to the full development — both private and public — of the human person: of oneself and of others. The implication is that a male humanist ought to do the same. Thus, the women humanists not only formulated a principle of care for the development of the person, but also embodied this principle in their interaction with others. This double aspect of their philosophy can be characterized as an orientation towards applied ethics, with specific attention to person-in-relation.

Cassandra Fedele, Isotta Nogarola, and Laura Cereta were highly educated in speech and in writing. They drew upon classical sources in the content and form of their contributions. Their intellectual gifts were of such a nature that they were able to move freely among educated humanist men, speaking and writing in Latin, and at times in Greek, sharing a common culture of discourse based on ancient texts in philosophy, literature, and history. Because of the quality of their intellects and education, they were accepted into active circles of humanists. Laura Cereta also shared a deep interest in new developments in science and mathematics.

A summary of the persons-in-relation to the selected women humanists follows on pages 1047-50.

Fedele, Nogorola, and Cereta proposed a humanist virtue-based model of relation. Consequently, their lives and writings undermined premises of Aristotelian gender polarity that had emphasized women's natural and intellectual weakness, disordered emotions, and limitation to the private sphere of activity. They argued against both the Epicurean pleasure-based model of relation and the Albertian utility-based model of relation.

The breadth of sources studied, principles proclaimed, and identified persons-in-relation clarifies that during the fifteenth century women humanists extended the domain of their studies and influence. Women humanists reoriented intellectual study away from a purely contemplative exercise towards development of each person in commitment to the common good. This was the women humanists' contribution, this was their genius — careful attention to fostering the full development of persons-in-relation.[271]

271. See Pope John Paul II, *The Genius of Women* (Washington, D.C.: United States Catholic Conference, 1997) and *On the Dignity and Vocation of Women* (Boston: St. Paul Books and Media, 1988).

Women Humanists and Persons-in-Relation				
Humanist	Selected Sources	Principles	Women-in-Relation	Men-in-Relation
Cassandra Fedele	Plato, especially the *Republic* Cicero Peripatetics Plutarch Boccaccio's *Concerning Famous Women*	Value of Liberal Arts — especially philosophy Praise for humanity Women's weakness and social structures limit women's goal in study to delight alone, not service to the Republic. Women should either choose an intellectual life or marriage.	Alessandra Scala Laura Cereta Isabella, Queen of Spain	Giovanni Pico della Mirandola and Angelo Poliziano Lorenzo de Medici and the Florentine Academy Learned men from the University of Padua

Women Humanists and Persons-in-Relation (cont.)				
Humanist	Selected Sources	Principles	Women-in-Relation	Men-in-Relation
Isotta Nogarola	Augustine's *De Genesi ad litteram* Aristotle's *Ethics, Posterior Analytics, Metaphysics, Categories, De interpretatione,* and natural philosophy Cicero, Virgil, and classical sources in rhetoric Plato, and his female disciples Boethius Thomas Aquinas Averroes Avicenna's *Commentary on Aristotle*	Woman (Eve) cannot be both weaker and more to blame than man (Adam) for sin. An engaged and sustained dialogue about the truth of woman's and man's identity is a valuable medium of discourse about the true and the good. Silence and withdrawal from slanderous accusations about her by "Pliny" to "Ovid"	Her two sisters, Angela and Ginerva Costanza Varano, the granddaughter of Battista de Malatesta	Her tutor, Martino Rizzoni, student of Guarino of Verona Lauro Quirini, another student of Guarino Ludovico Foscarini, Doctorate in Arts and Law, and Governor of Verona Protonotario Barbaro Antonio Bonromco Jacopo Foscari Guarino of Verona

Women Humanists and Persons-in-Relation (cont.)				
Humanist	Selected Sources	Principles	Women-in-Relation	Men-in-Relation
Laura Cereta	Demosthenes and Quintilian Presocratics Anaxagoras, Heraclitus, Parmenides, Sappho Socrates, Plato, especially the *Republic* Aristotle, especially the logical works, natural philosophy, cosmology, and *Metaphysics* Xenophon, Epicurus Porphyry Plutarch Ptolemy Pliny, especially *History of Animals* Valerius Maximus Diogenes Laertius Virgil, especially the *Aenead* Horace Apuleius	Moral integrity Knowledge of letters Love for common good Self-knowledge (especially role of passions in action) Self-governance (exercise of will to choose one's own relation to time and space, and one's own particular identity as woman or man) Public service to the common good in domestic service (marriage) and intellectual life at the service of society Respond to false accusations by engagement and direct defense of truth	One-third of her correspondents were women she had befriended Sister Nazaria Olympia Sister Martha Marcella, her cousin Deodata di Leno Diana Cereta, her sister Cassandra Fedele Isotta Nogarola Elena di Cesare	Her father Sylvestro and brother Daniel Luigi Mondella, physician, humanist, and founder of the Mondella Academy Lodovico di Leno, her uncle, and Bernardino di Leno, her cousin Pietro Serina, her husband Alberto degli Alberti, attorney Cardinal Ascanio Maria Sforza, her patron Brother Thomas, OP, advisor Clemenzo Longolio and Giovanni Olivieri, professors of rhetoric Bonifacio Bembo

Women Humanists and Persons-in-Relation (cont.)				
Humanist	Selected Sources	Principles	Women-in-Relation	Men-in-Relation
Laura Cereta (cont.)	Cicero Seneca Ovid Juvenal Thomas Aquinas Petrarch Boccaccio, especially *Concerning Famous Women* Lorenzo Valla (indirectly), the *De voluptate*	Method of self-defense: give principle, measure actions, invite to conversion Men and women equally have the talent to learn, as in "republic of women" Hard work determines the results in quality of literacy Most wars should cease		Bibolo Semproni Agostino Emilio Felicio Tadino, physician Francesco Fontana Lodovico Cendrate Veronese Brother Lodovico de la Turre and the Chiari humanist circle including Clemenzo

SECTION II

SUMMARY AND EVALUATION: GENDER AND INTEGRATED COMMUNITIES OF DISCOURSE

The six chapters of Section II traced reforms in the concept of woman. The boundaries, which during 1250 and 1400 had separated the four communities of discourse — academic, women religious, satirical, and early humanist — loosened in 1400 to 1500 to allow integration. Academically trained men (especially Dominican priests) engaged in sustained dialogue with religious women. Women started to draw upon academic and humanist sources for their intellectual formation. Academics studied humanist classical sources, and humanists attended universities for studies in law, medicine, theology, and arts. Humanist schools were established in university towns, allowing some students to be formed concurrently in a university and school of humanities. Women humanists frequently associated with women's religious institutions. Women religious authors developed a capacity for sophisticated reasoning, elaborating lengthy and detailed analogies to explain their perspective on ultimate values in the world. They also began in large numbers to educate young girls in a variety of intellectual and cultural skills.

These developments marked a change from a time in which women had been excluded from higher education, and they marked an improvement in the quality of intergender dialogue and of women's writing about gender identity. The new voice of women, acting as a *sed contra,* disturbed the previous balance of the *status quo,* upheld by the separate communities of discourse. Some male members of society reacted negatively by slandering or defaming women. Women were arrested, put on trial, and even executed for their alleged practice of witchcraft, heretical actions, or words.

In Medieval Europe, Abbesses of monasteries or women of royalty wielded great power over men through ownership of vast lands and armies, and sometimes by political force. When improperly used, their power created an emasculating effect on men and a deep-seated suspicion of women and women's communities holding power. Reactions, including attacking and burning women's monasteries, were not uncommon; new satires against women also appeared. Mass distribution of the satires was facilitated by the invention of the printing press. The heightened emotionality of satires with extreme and vicious exaggerations against women may have been influenced by an increase of fear brought about by recurring episodes of the plague, constant warfare, and even apocalyptic nervousness about the possible end of the world in the year 1500.

Male authors often employed an Aristotelian rationale for women's natural inferiority. The satirists went far beyond the original thought of the Greek philosopher in their exaggerated stereotypes. Elements of the Aristotelian-based gender polarity tradition in their writings were traced in the second section of this book, along with a Neoplatonic application of the distinction between a woman's appearance and reality. A list of the stereotyped uses of philosophical concepts in patterns of satires against women may be found in a table later in this summary.

During the period 1250-1500 reform was needed on many levels of society. Immoral behavior and abuses of power were rampant among men and women who professed to live one way of life but simultaneously indulged in behavior contrary to their professed values. A rupture in the heart of society between God and man, men and women, and within the human intellect, will, and passions had far-reaching effects. Instead of working toward the common good, many men and women were self-focused; instead of cooperative dialogue, many engaged in argumentative disputation and blame; and instead of truthful intergender exchange, many deceived.

In these turbulent times the early Renaissance Humanists began reform partly based on a new interest in the humanity of Jesus Christ. The belief that Jesus Christ was true God and true man, supported by such Christian philosophers as St. Augustine and St. Thomas Aquinas, carried a radical affirmation of the dignity of human identity. The dignity of the intellect, free will, and the human passions took on a new radiance. Religious women authors heralded this new insight about the dignity of the human being. The Renaissance Humanists elaborated its philosophical meaning and practical application in the lives of men and women.

Christine de Pizan confronted satirical and demeaning images of women. She also engaged in epistolary and poetic forms of dialogue with men who disagreed with her theories about humanist literature and woman's identity. Women humanist authors, Christine de Pizan, Cassandra Fedele, Isotta Nogarola, and Laura Cereta, could read Latin, discuss the classical sources with ease, and communicate orally and in writing eloquently with others. Even though at times all four women experienced the negative effects of ruptured relations with some male humanists, their contributions went far beyond the personal suffering these confrontations produced. They each had much to say about human identity and gender identity, not simply as a way of thought, but also as a way of life from a woman's perspective.

Several women in this period remained faithful to their agendas of reform even when they were perceived as challengers of the *status quo*. St. Joan of Arc surely did this in fulfilling her mission. St. Catherine of Siena as a religious and Christine de Pizan and Laura Cereta as humanists are examples of women with plans of reform. They were able to reform society, engage in battle, military or verbal, and fight fearlessly for what they perceived as right, while never failing to respect the dignity of their opponents. Later women humanists revealed similar qualities in vigorously discussing the concept of woman with men, pointing out falsehoods or errors, and appealing to men to improve their ways and work on their personal development. Christine de Pizan did this as a writer, Isotta Nogarola as a scholar, and Laura Cereta as a teacher. Together they provided the foundations for an emerging theory of integral gender complementarity.

Woman's access to philosophical sources was made possible, in great part, because of the reform in education brought about by the early humanist educators who established small schools sponsored by wealthy patrons or cities. They introduced ancient Greek and Latin texts, took a strong stance against exaggerated philosophical practices of disputation taught in universities, and opened their classes to female students. As a result many women studied rhetoric, grammar, literature, history, and philosophy. Several of the early Renaissance Humanists also had an interest in mathematics and scientific experimentation, especially in astronomy, and they began to raise questions about the Aristotelian-Ptolemaic cosmological system. Women educated in this new environment participated in discussions and produced orations and writings.

A new relation to Aristotle began during the years 1250-1500. Leonardo Bruni and others offered eloquent translations of his *Ethics* and *Politics*. Aristotle's ethics and politics were applied to civic humanism and governing of republics. Aristotle was utilized to support a humanistic ideal of building the character of virtuous men and the common good of virtuous states. Isotta Nogarola, Laura Cereta, and Christine de Pizan frequently invoked Aristotelian ethical principles in their writings about gender identity.

Elements of gender polarity from Aristotle's *Ethics* and *Politics* continued to persist in many texts, i.e., the inequality of male/female friendships, the lack of authority of woman's rational soul over her passions, and the dictum that a woman should remain silent in public, along with the severe criticisms of women's identity in Plato's *Republic*. Some gender polarity themes were particularly notable in works by the humanists Leonardo Barbaro and Leon Battista Alberti, who argued that woman primarily serves in a relation of utility to her husband and family. Christine de Pizan chose to ignore Aristotle's arguments on these themes; instead, she attacked satirists who used and exaggerated them. Alberti wrote satires, using principles from both Aristotle and Xenophon, which directly challenged women's new arguments against gender polarity. Later women humanists such as Nogarola and Cereta began to argue directly against the ancient Greek philosophers' views.

Another area of Aristotle's philosophy that remained constant was the application of his *Organon* or logical writings to philosophical discourse. Even though humanists objected to the scholastic propensity towards public debate of the most nuanced point, they nonetheless used Aristotle's structures for rational argument in their own works. This is particularly evident in the arguments about gender identity that women humanists put forward. Christine de Pizan, Isotta Nogarola, and Laura Cereta demonstrated a skill in different forms of argumentation, and they used it very effectively to refute improper or unjust judgments about women's identity in general or their own identity in particular. Even though Aristotle's natural philosophy was eventually overturned by the Copernican Revolution in science, his logic maintained its prominence in philosophical discourse for centuries to come.

Particular developments in the concept of woman with respect to Aristotle's original theory of gender identity are summarized below. Using the same categories of Aristotelian gender polarity as in the chart in the summary to Section I, the following table traces developments occurring in the fifteenth century.

Characteristics of Woman in Communities of Discourse (1250-1500)			
Female Characteristics in Aristotelian Gender Polarity	Exaggerated in Satires and Witchcraft Manuals	Women Religious as Counterexamples	Women Humanists Elaborate Theory of Counterexamples
Rational faculty without authority over passions	Woman as full of lust and greed	Rational faculty seen to have authority over passions	Rational faculty has authority over passions even in the heat of public debate and argument
Wise through true opinion; not through discursive reason	Woman as always a self-deceiver	Exercises discursive reasoning in complex transcendental analogies	Wise through discursive reason; able to engage in rational dialogue and to teach others rational principles
Silence in public	Woman as always a deceiver of others	Engages in many forms of public speech and writing	Dialogues publicly with men and women on many philosophical issues
No self-control: inconstant	Woman's weakness prone to being deceived by evil	Exercises will in self-control; moderates desires; and makes conscious choices	Self-controlled in a wide variety of situations

Characteristics of Woman in Communities of Discourse (1250-1500) (cont.)			
Female Characteristics in Aristotelian Gender Polarity	Exaggerated in Satires and Witchcraft Manuals	Women Religious as Counterexamples	Women Humanists Elaborate Theory of Counterexamples
No self-governance	Woman's weakness prone to being deceived by evil	Overcomes desires; governs senses	Self-governed and virtuous in situations of serious attack and slander
Not able to rule over others; either passive or dominating	Woman as dominating men or passively waiting to be dominated by men	Chooses to rule or obey depending upon the situation	Rules over others where appropriate, especially in domestic situations
Public action not appropriate; virtue in private sphere only		Engaged in many forms of virtuous public action	Public actions aiming towards reform appropriate and praiseworthy
Accidental, imperfect, deformed male	Woman as a monster of nature	Woman's nature good as created by God	Perfectly formed by nature and perfected by grace
Male academic forms of discourse		Engages in dialogue with women religious, with men religious, and with humanists	Engages in dialogue with academically trained males and with other humanists
'He' as paradigm analogously extended to include women		'She' as paradigm analogously extended to include men	Brings a woman's perspective into dialogue as complement to a male perspective

THE BEGINNING OF PUBLIC DIALOGUE ABOUT GENDER

While the above chart summarizes ways in which religious and humanist authors overturned the Aristotelian roots of gender polarity, during this same period new forms of gender polarity were also articulated. Therefore, the challenge to develop a theoretical foundation for gender complementarity had to defeat not only Aristotelian arguments but the arguments of new philosophers as well. In the following table, a summary is offered for the new versions of gender polarity:

New Forms of Gender Polarity (1400-1500)		
Philosopher or Genre	Man	Woman
Satirical Literature: Platonic influence — Distinction between appearance and reality *Miroir de mariage* *Quinze joyes de mariage*	Like animals caught in a trap by woman whose real nature is different from apparent nature	Appears to be beautiful and good, but is in reality deceptive, dangerous, ugly, evil, and like a ferocious animal or an animal trainer

New Forms of Gender Polarity (1400-1500) (cont.)		
Philosopher or Genre	**Man**	**Woman**
Leon Battista Alberti **Xenophon's influence** — Separation of indoor and outdoor spheres of activity Husband rules all aspects of wife's life	Enslaved by love for a woman	An unworthy object of love dominates men, is fickle, inconstant, and man's enemy
Utilitarian model — woman is an object of use to man	Uses reason and will to conquer fortune Enslaved by love for woman	Like fortune — inconstant, equivocal, destructive, dangerous, seeking to rule men
New Development in Male Consciousness — Directly argues against woman's critiques of his theory of gender polarity	Masculinity strengthened by avoiding women Mind stronger than women's minds	Prefers love to friendship with men Not well-educated, minds weaker than men's minds
	Rules the whole household — delegates some authority to his wife	Should be fertile, prolific, and bear sons
	Demeaning to be shut up in the house with women	Should be kept from household library and records
	Capable of friendships with men	Incapable of friendships with men
	Communicates in public	Silent in public
	Characteristics inverted in satire	Characteristics exaggerated in satire

New Forms of Gender Polarity (1400-1500) (cont.)		
Philosopher or Genre	**Man**	**Woman**
Lorenzo Valla		
Epicureanism — the highest good gives the greatest pleasure	The stronger sex, unable to live in chastity	The weaker sex, unable to live in chastity
	Weak in response to sexual pleasures	Attractive sexual object to men
Epicurean Model — woman as an object of pleasure for man and vice-versa	Love for a woman dangerous	Love for a man dangerous
Platonism — support for a community of women with Epicurean focus on natural pleasure	Stoics as "males"	Epicureans as "females"
Stoic Christianity — love for God as the highest pleasure exists only in Heaven		

These new forms of gender polarity refocused the man and woman relationship away from an earlier emphasis on virtue as the highest value. Instead, utility, pleasure, and avoiding dangerous entrapment were portrayed as higher values. The satires demeaning woman or man, and the gender polarity arguments in these new forms, did not succeed in stopping the momentum that was building against gender polarity theory. Further philosophical reforms occurred during early Renaissance Humanism, for example, a deeper relating of the concept of woman to philosophical sources such as Epicurus, Plato, Plutarch, Quintilian, and Cicero. By 1500 all the theoretical foundations were in place for the eventual overturning of the original Aristotelian Revolution and subsidiary developments in the concept of woman.

A new relation to Plato occurred primarily through translations of his works from Greek into Latin. The translations took several attempts by different authors. Especially through the efforts of Ficino, accurate texts were made available and certain Platonic principles about gender identity began to appear. The most frequent of these principles were Plato's theory of the immortality of the soul, of the equal capacity of men and women to be educated, and the claim that philosophers make the best rulers of the republic. Also presented, with some distortion, was the view that Plato's community of women was composed of women and men who engaged in sexual relations without any constraints, and that all children were to be held in common. Humanists understood that Plato and the Platonic Academy offered a principle of equal dignity of women and men, contrary to Aristotle's gender polarity thesis of the natural inferiority of women. The pattern observed in ancient philosophy was repeated: schools associated with Aristotelian philosophy that promoted gender polarity excluded the participation of women, while schools associated with Platonic philosophy allowed access to at least a few women. The Neoplatonic Academy in Florence invited Cassandra Fedele, and the Chiara Academy in Brescia invited regular participation by Laura Cereta.

The introduction of Platonist interest in mathematics and the higher Forms of Beauty, Goodness, and Truth brought about a change in the meaning of the terms 'masculine' and feminine,' especially in the works of Cusanus, Ficino, and Pico. While in the earlier phase of humanism, the masculine or feminine characteristics of individual men or women introduced a new dimension beyond simple male or female identity, several of the Neoplatonists reflected on a cosmic dimension of gender identity. Because this aspect of the integration of Platonism introduces a change in the history of the concept of woman, a summary of their speculations is offered here:

Developments in Consideration of Masculinity and Femininity (1400-1500)		
Philosopher	Meaning of Masculine	Meaning of Feminine
Nicholas of Cusa **Contributions to the concept of woman:** Posits female seed Movement of the earth Introduces perspectives in space Revalues possibility, actuality, and potentiality Moves towards complementarity while maintaining elements of gender polarity	**On the Intellectual Level:** The actuality of femininity Like the whole Closer to light Unity in nature Enfolding of unity Most noble **On the Sensible Level:** In male bodies masculinity absorbs femininity. Masculine seeds contract the feminine in itself.	**On the Intellectual Level:** The potentiality of masculinity Like the part Closer to darkness Otherness in nature Unfolding of otherness Less noble **On the Sensible Level:** In female bodies femininity absorbs masculinity. The feminine seed contracts the masculine in itself.

Developments in Consideration of Masculinity and Femininity (1400-1500)		
Philosopher	Meaning of Masculine	Meaning of Feminine
Nicholas of Cusa (cont.)	In more noble species of animals the masculine is superior to the feminine.	In less noble species the feminine is superior to the masculine.
	In animals, man generates in woman.	In animals, woman gives birth externally.
	In Metaphysical Principles:	**In Metaphysical Principles:**
	Possibility itself is prior to actuality and masculine more akin to actuality.	Feminine is more akin to specified potentiality.
	Masculine and feminine opposites enfold and unfold into one another and ultimately collide.	The female and feminine are not contrary privations of masculine but more like complements.
	In Principles of Natural Philosophy:	**In Principles of Natural Philosophy:**
	The earth moves and is the center of the universe.	The earth is as noble as the sun, no longer passive, but active.

Developments in Consideration of Masculinity and Femininity (1400-1500)		
Philosopher	Meaning of Masculine	Meaning of Feminine
Marsilio Ficino	**Engendered ratios**	**Engendered ratios**
Contributions to the concept of woman:	Male numbers are odd, e.g., 1, 3, 5, 7 . . .	Female numbers are even, e.g., 2, 4, 6, 8 . . .
Neither male nor female number has absolute value.	Male numbers have priority.	Female numbers are a "fall" from a male number.
All generation is the result of proportional relations and contains elements of gender complementarity.	A spousal number is the product of two adjacent numbers (a male number and a female number), e.g., 6 (2 × 3), 12 (3 × 4) . . .	6 is the perfect number (identical with the sum of its factors). 1728 is the fatal number (contains a discordant concord).
In division and addition gender polarity associations of male with form and female with matter are retained.	In hierarchical mathematical progression the masculine is always superior, the female inferior.	In hierarchical mathematical progression, the female is always inferior and the male superior.
Masculine and feminine structure of microcosm, soul, and macrocosm	These ratios are seen in the planets, the mind, and elements where the masculine represents reason in relation to understanding and the irascible in relation to the concupiscible power.	These ratios are seen in the planets, the mind, and elements where the feminine represents understanding in relation to reason and the concupiscible in relation to the irascible powers.
	Masculine virtues in soul: wisdom — of reason courage — of will	**Feminine virtues in soul:** temperance — of emotions

Developments in Consideration of Masculinity and Femininity (1400-1500)		
Philosopher	Meaning of Masculine	Meaning of Feminine
Giovanni Pico della Mirandola **Contributions to the concept of woman:** Goal of the philosopher is to be united with gender neutral Ideal of Beauty through six steps of ascending objects of love. All gender polarity and gender complementarity related to lower animal human life Masculine and feminine distinctions as ideally transcended	Engendered theses: Proclus: male is limited, identity, similitude. Cabala: the masculine represents the higher of two levels in union, of kingdom in relation to beauty and of beauty in relation to intellect. His own view: The male philosopher loves either the heavenly Venus (Ideal Beauty) or the earthly Venus (beauty of a particular body).	Engendered theses: Proclus: female is unlimited, otherness, and dissimilitude. Pythagoras: Athena unifies and causes the beautifying power of the intellect. Cabala: the feminine is the lower of two levels in union, of beauty in relation to kingdom, of intellect in relation to beauty. The feminine represents the heavenly Venus or earthly Venus.

The above summary chart indicates ways in which Cusanus adopted many polarity associations of the masculine with light, actuality, unity, and nobility, and the feminine with darkness, potentiality, otherness, and inferiority. He also argued that the relation of masculine and feminine is not fixed but variable, feminine in one context and masculine in another. Ficino introduced the notion of male and female numbers and nuptial numbers optimum for human generation. In his schema masculine and feminine ratios incorporated gender polarity elements. He also interpreted masculine and feminine ratios as occurring outside the individual man or woman, in the cosmos. Pico's hierarchical understanding of human beings introduces masculine and feminine identities at the level of metals, stones, and animals. He offers a choice of gender neutrality to human beings, a state that is shared with the angelic level of being. By ignoring gender differences a human being can reach a higher level of existence beyond the engenderment of animality. With Ficino there is also a movement towards gender neutrality: one can achieve a loving union with the Form of the Beautiful, rising above the beauty of an individual woman or man. These Neoplatonic developments in the concept of woman accentuated a rejection of embodiment in favor of an abstract model of gender identity.

In general, humanists were caught in a bind between Plato's and Aristotle's concepts of woman with no easy solution. Some, e.g., Pico and Ficino, emphasized the unity between the two philosophers and ignored their incompatible views on the concept of woman. Another path, chosen by several humanists, emphasized the differences between Plato and Aristotle; consequently, they engaged in many public battles over the greater value of one or the other. The concept of woman was caught in the middle of these battles in which Plato's views were often distorted to emphasize the immorality of his positions for a Christian context of marriage and family life. No resolution was reached by the end of the fifteenth century.

Aristotle's authority was beginning to erode in many areas, quite apart from his direct views about the concept of woman. Gianfrancesco Pico della Mirandola criticized Aristotle's scientific method, and most humanists attacked the style of his works as taught in academia. They particularly disliked the scholastic emphasis on disputation. In addition, Nicholas of Cusa introduced a novel idea concerning space, that the observer's point of reference can change, depending on where he or she is located. Further, Giovanni Pico della Mirandola, the uncle of Gianfrancesco, introduced a new relation to time, with a perspectival approach similar to Cusanus's. Neoplatonism offered a different way of understanding the human being's relation to the past and present, and this, too, contributed to the erosion of confidence in Aristotle's philosophy. Laura Cereta argued that a woman needs to determine her own relation to time and to space; she provided an existential application of the more theoretical views of Cusanus and Pico.

In the fifteenth century the tensions between a Platonic-based gender unity or gender neutrality theory and an Aristotelian-based gender polarity theory were combined with a grass-roots movements towards gender complementarity. Complementarity theory drew partly on Christian theological principles of gender complementarity; equal dignity and worth followed from the belief that men and women are created equally in the image of God. Significant differentiation followed from the belief that gender differentiation is "from eternity" in the mind of God when a particular man or woman is generated in his or her individual act of existence and that at the end of time the engendered body will be resurrected for each person belonging to the communion of saints. During the fourteenth and fifteenth centuries there was a broadening experience of complementarity among men and women with shared interests in the identity of the human person and the common good. In religious and humanist communities of discourse, many men and women spoke and wrote at length about issues related to gender identity. Thus, an existential background of complementary relations anticipated future articulations of the theory of integral gender complementarity.

Conducive to supporting a theory of integral complementarity was the appreciation of a human being as an individual responsible for determining his or her own identity. Giovanni Pico della Mirandola's *Oration on the Dignity of Man* is often cited as foundational for this theory, although in his view self-determination was limited to ranges of moral identity akin either to animal-like or angelic-like life. Still, the idea was contained in this oration, and it continued to infiltrate the culture. Laura Cereta frequently chose to assert her own identity in very intense and complicated situations; she fostered personal choice in all of her correspondence whenever she measured particular acts against the humanist ideals. For Pico, Cereta, and others, God was considered as a partner working together with the human being in the activity of self-determination. Their complementarity theory was deeply Christian; it did not suggest the absolute autonomy of the individual, an idea developed only later, in Enlightenment philosophy.

A challenge for early Renaissance Humanists arose in creating a theory of personal identity in the framework of equal dignity for man and woman as a person-in-relation to God and to other human beings. A Platonic theory would be problematic with respect to the engendered identity of the individual. An Aristotelian theory would present other problems as the devaluation of woman is central to its principles as long as contrary privation in the union of form (as the principle of the human species) and matter (as the principle of individuation) is the way to explain differentiation of men and women. Christianity offered a spiritual intuition that would preserve differentiated identities and also the equal dignity and worth of men and women, but philosophers had not yet found a way to articulate it without being enmeshed in Platonic gender unity or Aristotelian gender polarity. Even though men and women were living the reality of integral gender complementarity, they had not yet fully articulated its philosophical principles.

Christine de Pizan, Leonardo Bruni, and Laura Cereta began the momentum towards such an articulation in contribution to the community of discourse of women about gender identity. It would appear that while women made significant contributions to the history of the concept of woman, the *sed contra* of a woman here and there, while very valuable, was not enough to complete the reform in the concept of woman. The questions raised in the early Humanist Reformation had to wait for their answers several more centuries.

CONCLUSION

T he early Renaissance brought a new dimension into the history of the concept of woman. Paralleling the discovery of artistic and architectural perspective, women authors articulated their own observations on gender identity. Prior to the thirteenth century there are few records of women's viewpoints; expression by women flourished between the thirteenth and fifteenth centuries. Most extant theories about women's identity in Ancient and Medieval Philosophy are expressed by men. Male perspectives established the philosophy of gender as a central and important field in philosophy from its earliest origins in Presocratic thought through its sophisticated articulation in Greek and Medieval Platonic and Aristotelian theories. Meanwhile, female philosophy was very weak, although observations are apparent within the Pythagorean, Neoplatonic, and Christian monastic traditions.

This study of philosophical texts about the concept of woman from the mid-thirteenth to the late fifteenth centuries considered four different communities of discourse: religious, academic, satirical, and humanist. Although women authors were absent in the academic and satirical, their representation was quite strong in the religious and humanist communities of discourse.

WOMEN'S CONTRIBUTIONS TO THE
REFORM OF THE CONCEPT OF WOMAN

Women authors acted as counterexamples to the Aristotelian-based gender polarity theory in the areas of wisdom and virtue. They revealed a mature intellect as they utilized reason to express self-knowledge and to search for truth about the world. They exercised will in self-governance and in virtuous activity in private and public spheres. By example as well as by philosophical arguments, women authors demonstrated that the gender polarity premises of women's weak intellect, disordered will, and natural subservience to men were false.

Women authors often relied on their female experience from which to articulate a theory of their own identity. Experiences in the household, in a small village, in marriage, in religious life, in nature, and in the court provided empirical and rational foundations for reflection on woman's identity. Reasoning by way of analo-

CONCLUSION

gies regarding their experience, women strove to articulate fundamental principles of wisdom and virtue when fighting corruption. A shifting focus occurred from medicine and philosophy of nature in Ancient and Medieval Philosophy to law in Renaissance Philosophy. Women often employed legal terms and methods to defend themselves and others against false accusations and other injustices. They worked tirelessly to bring a just order into public structures, events, and actions.

Several women authors argued against injustice by contrasting it with a Christian ideal. Their perspective was born from their faith in a Divine Order missioned by God, experienced in prayer, and described in classical texts such as Augustine's *City of God* and *Confessions,* Boethius's *Consolation of Philosophy,* and Thomas Aquinas's *Summa theologica.* These texts provided theoretical foundations for the mission of the ideal Divine Order to regenerate earthly life. Thomas summarized it: "Thus, mission as regards the one to whom it is sent implies two things, the indwelling of grace, and a certain renewal by grace."[1] Considerations of justice by women authors included reflections on: giving recompense to God, defending justice as a virtue in general, appealing to God to defend women in the context of injustice, and arguing that women should be allowed full leadership roles through the just distribution of goods in society. Concrete appeals by women followed unjust accusations of actions contrary to traditional gender roles; they were based on arguments about the nature of unjust and just actions in Renaissance society. The virtue of justice became deeply loved and integrated by women who built up the common good.

In attempting to understand the sources of renewal that enabled the early humanists to combat injustice, error, and distortions about woman's identity, we need to make mention of a theological mystery of recapitulation. Johannes Quasten offers a short summary of recapitulation as articulated by St. Irenaeus, a second-century Greek Father of the Church:

> Recapitulation is for Irenaeus a taking up in Christ of all since the beginning. God rehabilitates the earlier divine plan for the salvation of mankind which was interrupted by the fall of Adam, and gathers up his entire work from the beginning to renew, to restore, to reorganize it in his incarnate Son, who in this way becomes for us a second Adam. . . . By this recapitulation of the original man, not only Adam personally but the whole human race was renovated and restored. . . .[2]

The mystery of recapitulation of the nature of all human beings in Jesus Christ and in a special way of the nature of woman in Mary goes far beyond the reaches of philosophical thinking. Recapitulation folds back onto philosophy and acts as a leaven in its own search for truth. The recapitulation function attributed to Mary is operative only in and through Christ, who by the act of love in which He died and

---

1. Thomas Aquinas, *Summa theologica* (Westminster, Md.: Christian Classics, 1981), Pt. I, Q. 43, art. 6.
2. Johannes Quasten, *Patrology, Vol. I: The Beginnings of Patristic Literature* (Westminster, Md.: Newman Press, 1950), pp. 295-96.

is risen, in union with the Father, released the Holy Spirit who renews the world. While emphasizing that all renewal is through Christ, Irenaeus accentuates Mary's role in recapitulation. There would have been no Redemption without the Incarnation; Mary becomes "the new mother of mankind . . . [and Irenaeus] speaks of the birth of Christ as 'the pure one opening purely that pure womb which regenerates men unto God.'"[3] The mystery of recapitulation has recently been proposed by Rev. Francis Martin as a key to understanding "feminist theology in the light of Christian tradition."[4] In this conclusion, I will consider its relevance to the philosophy of woman.

The Christian belief in recapitulation, that Christ is the new Adam and Mary is the new Eve, operates in the background of early humanist reform in the concept of woman. Christine de Pizan introduces this notion in her classical *Livre de la cité des dames*. Lady Reason states: "For as low as human nature fell through this creature woman, was human nature lifted higher by this same creature."[5] Recapitulation not only enables Mary to gather in the entire history of women and to offer a new beginning, it also takes the nature of woman *per se* and elevates it to a new dimension of reality. In this way, the appeal to a just order is no longer understood as something simply outside of humanity to which human persons must appeal for redress. It becomes integrated into the very heart of each human person. It is a "field of force" of the Holy Spirit into which a person is freely drawn and given the opportunity for a new beginning.[6]

A similar kind of Christian momentum for reform is seen in the works of three male humanists, all with a knowledge of Greek. Perhaps with some awareness of the theory of recapitulation, Nicholas of Cusa, Marsilio Ficino, and Giovanni Pico della Mirandola initiated a redefinition of masculine and feminine identity to elevate it above a lower level of human nature. They sought to bring about a coincidence of opposites, to discover a single line of truth. They defended the dignity of all men and women to begin anew and to gather together all that is beautiful and good into a unified understanding of higher goals of human life. The content of their theories lacked an embodiment common to theories by women humanists, perhaps because of an undue influence of Neoplatonic principles. They elevated discussion above a focus on the natural weakness or inferiority of women's nature.

Considering in the light of the mystery of recapitulation the various concepts of woman studied during this period of 1250-1500, many authors focused on the nature of the old Eve or on woman outside of the transforming presence of Jesus Christ with Mary. They offered repeated analysis — in academic treatises, satires, and manuals on witchcraft — of what was wrong or weak with woman. Their reflections were on the limitations of woman's nature and often on the dangerous ef-

3. Quasten, *Patrology,* p. 299.

4. Francis Martin, "A Proposal" in Epilogue, in *The Feminist Question: Feminist Theology in the Light of Christian Tradition* (Grand Rapids: Eerdmans, 1994), pp. 415-22. I am grateful to Fr. Martin's insight into this theological mystery and to his encouragement to see its applications to philosophy.

5. Christine de Pizan, *The Book of the City of Ladies* (New York: Persea Books, 1983), I.9.3, 24.

6. J. N. D. Kelly, *Early Christian Doctrines* (San Francisco: Harper and Row, 1978), pp. 170-74.

fect of these limitations upon men. In contrast, the early Christian Renaissance Humanists perceived a redemptive quality in woman's nature that participated in the mystery of recapitulation in Mary, the new Eve. This is present in the literary reflections of Dante, Petrarch, and Boccaccio, who wrote imaginary texts that included dialogue and descriptions of Beatrice, Laura, and Fiammetta, and historical feminine figures that included Mary, the Mother of God. It also occurred directly in the religious writers who addressed prayers to and wrote meditations on Mary.

The dialogue on Adam and Eve by Isotta Nogarola accents a discrepancy in discussions about woman's identity. She asks: If man really believes that woman has a defective nature, why does he blame her for making weak decisions? Christine de Pizan notes a similar discrepancy when she asks men why, if they believe women are so weak and dangerous, they continue to pursue women and to seek union with them? Writing from the perspective of the potentially redemptive identity of woman, these early humanists recognize the error of male authors who limit themselves to writing about the old Eve. More broadly, men who persist in describing women within a gender polarity framework place themselves in a pre-Christian context, with no awareness of the new actualization through Jesus Christ and the active cooperation of the Blessed Virgin Mary. Considering the historical period studied in this book as "a distant mirror" for our own time, we can see how some contemporary women theorists, who describe men in terms of the old Adam's set of weaknesses, also place themselves in a pre- (not post-)Christian mentality in which recapitulation has not yet been discovered. Further study of this phenomenon could be undertaken from the perspective of philosophy, as well as anthropology, sociology, and so forth.

St. Irenaeus offered a helpful metaphor when he first articulated the mystery of recapitulation. He described a "knot" that Eve tied and Mary untied: "What was bound could not be untied without a reversal of the process of entanglement. The first bonds had to be untied by the second, so that the second might set the first free."[7] While there are many strands to this knot, including most critically death and sin, we could also select individual tangled strands related to woman's identity and distinguish what was knotted by Eve and untied by Mary. The texts of academic philosophers and satirists named many characteristics of woman knotted into a tangled net of devaluation: weak, deformed, passive, deceitful, dangerous, driven by inordinate passions, and prone to evil, to name just a few. The reversal of the process of entanglement is seen in early humanist texts that describe woman as strong, beautifully formed, active, truthful, capable of self-governance, drawn to and leading others towards the common good.

The momentum for combating distorted theories of gender identity can be related to the theological mystery of recapitulation. Within Christianity there appears to be an ever present impulse towards a balanced understanding of engendered human nature. Two further examples from 1250 to 1500 may help to demonstrate some philosophical consequences of this theological mystery: defense by

---

7. Irenaeus, *The Scandal of the Incarnation: Irenaeus "Against the Heresies"* (San Francisco: Ignatius Press, 1990), III 22,4, 61.

women authors of the dignity of women in marriage and an emphasis on the value of the whole person-in-relation.

Gender polarity theorists often assaulted woman's identity in marriage. In ancient Aristotelian-based texts, the wife was viewed as the unequal friend of the husband. In Platonic texts, the wife was viewed as potentially her husband's equal, but at the loss of her feminine identity in relation to her own children and household. In satires, these polarity trends were exaggerated so that the wife was perceived as domineering, out of control, unfaithful, and dangerous to her husband. As a consequence, various humanist texts written by men suggested that a woman be kept away from reading, from public life, and from educating her sons. Male humanists, including Alberti, Barbaro, Bruni, Eyb, and Valla, wrote about wives and marriage. While they understood the need to develop a philosophy of marriage and of the household, their suggestions based the husband-wife relation on utilitarian or Epicurean principles. Other authors, on the one hand, supported the dignity of woman's identity and, on the other hand, promulgated a litany of attacks on women's identity. Eyb and Bruni strongly defended woman's dignity with respect to education. Eyb, preceded by Boccaccio, counterbalanced support of woman with satirical views common to the gender polarity tradition. In most texts, woman's identity was associated with the old Eve whose weaknesses were so great that she needed to be controlled by her husband. While some Christian-based philosophies attempted to renew the ancient views, by defending a woman's free-will agreement to a marriage contract or by promoting equal friendships between husband and wife, they fell far from enhancing a full dignity of woman in marriage.

It is only with the entry of several women authors into the dialogue about woman's identity that we begin to discover the consistent elevation of the full dignity of a wife and mother. Women religious authors heralded this new development in their descriptions of the spousal dimension of the Christian union with God. St. Bridget of Sweden, a married mother, introduced rich transcendental analogies about the spiritual life grounded on the division and works within a household. Julian of Norwich elaborated a deep set of transcendental analogies of works of motherhood as experienced in Jesus Christ's economy of salvation. Then early women humanists, several of whom were married and widowed, defended with great vigor the dignity of woman as wife and mother. Christine de Pizan directly took on the attackers in her public debates and in her numerous texts on love and on woman's identity. Laura Cereta, a childless widow, demonstrated personally a new dignity of woman by engaging in frequent dialogues with both men and women. Never before in western history had there been such strong and thoroughly developed arguments in support of this theme. Christine de Pizan and Laura Cereta participated in this dynamic of renewal, revealing good judgments, personal responsibility, and new life for women and men.

Turning to the second example of a philosophical effect of the theory of recapitulation, women authors emphasized human identity as a whole person-in-relation. The theological mystery of recapitulation can be understood only in the context of interpersonal relations, especially of Mary working in and through Jesus Christ. The Incarnation is initiated by the Father in relation to Mary, shared by Mary's relation to Christ's Passion and Resurrection as the new Adam, and activated in the world of history by Mary's relation to the Holy Spirit. It is restorative of the concept of woman by Mary's relation to Eve and to all women born from the beginning of time. Recapitulation is preeminently a mystery of persons-in-relation. The old Eve both helped cause and shared the consequences of a fundamental rupture in human relations: with Adam, with nature, and with God. In this historical context of rupture in human relations, during the period 1250-1500 a new dimension of human relations began to develop; these relations are founded upon intellectual and spiritual friendship. Women humanist authors demonstrated a new initiative in focusing on the human person in relation to all circumstances.

In a context of historical rupture among human relationships, particularly the man-woman set of relations, Christine de Pizan offered towards the end of *Le Livre de la cité des dames* the premise that Mary recapitulates the old Eve. This author described the relation of Mary with the Divine Persons of the Holy Trinity. At the moment of welcoming Mary as Head of the City of Ladies, Lady Justice proposed:

> Now come to us, Heavenly Queen, Temple of God, Cell and Cloister of the Holy Spirit, Vessel of the Trinity, Joy of the Angels, Star and Guide to those who have gone astray, Hope of the True Creation. My Lady, what man is so brazen to dare think or say that the feminine sex is vile in beholding your dignity?[8]

This juxtaposition — the praise of Mary in her relation with the Holy Trinity, and the judgments of men that woman's identity lacks dignity — is crucial. Christine de Pizan repeats this theme again in the next section; this time she places the words directly in Mary's speech: . . . "I am and will always be the head of the feminine sex. This arrangement was present in the mind of God the Father from the start, revealed and ordained previously in the council of the Trinity."[9] The recapitulation of all women in Mary is crucial to Christine's argument; it occurs precisely because of the relations among the Divine Persons and of Mary's relation to Father, Son, and Holy Spirit.

Several women authors during the period 1250-1500 emphasized human identity as person-in-relation. In addition to a transcendental dimension of relation with God, the experience of being a female person-in-relation had a horizontal dimension. Authors demonstrated an awareness of being an integral part of their religious communities, while maintaining autonomy as individual persons. This orientation is especially noted in works in education: the Beguines, the Sisters of the Common Life, and members of religious orders. Institutes educated girls and women, teaching them intellectual skills and habits of study and work modeled after a long line of wise and virtuous women. For the first time in the western world, a collective women's history for mutual inspiration developed. Communities of women prided themselves in being part of a powerful group of women whose talents were nurtured through the study of great women and men spiritual writers, including such classical authors as Boccaccio, Plutarch, and Diogenes Laertius.

8. Christine de Pizan, *The Book of the City of Ladies,* III.1.3, 218.
9. Christine de Pizan, *The Book of the City of Ladies,* III.1.3, 218.

Men and women began to interact in novel ways for their mutual benefit. New institutional structures evolved that fostered relations that had been impossible for centuries within male-only academies. Aristocratic families opened their homes to frequent and serious dialogues among men and women; libraries and humanist academies became available to women students. Fathers made serious efforts to educate their daughters; mothers educated their children and grandchildren; and women's relationships with their male humanist tutors often developed into deep intellectual and personal friendships. Women and their male spiritual directors engaged in ongoing discourse about shared intellectual projects. Some women authors had multiple intellectual friendships with men.

In the table on the following page, some of the more notable of these constructive relations are identified.

Despite fruitful personal exchanges with men, women's relationships with men were far from being consistently positive. Lengthy acerbic public quarrels about women's identity ensued. Beginning with the fourteenth century, women had the education, eloquence, and a sufficient degree of autonomy, self-knowledge, and self-government to meet directly their opponents. Exchanges involved confrontation in an honest and respectful manner, and with the common good as their ultimate goal. The common good involved the acceptance of the other person as autonomous while attempting to change attitudes and apparently unjust structures. In their dialogue, women identified false claims, exposed invalid motives, and presented their opponents with accurate insights. In these actions they contributed to the untying of what was entangled, the setting free of what was knotted. They challenged men and women to a greater integrity in life according to religious and humanist principles.

Two sources for the women humanists' zealous attention to persons-in-relation include, first, the religious inspiration of Mary as the new Eve, actively reversing the bonds of gender entanglement, and second, the humanist inspiration of persons engaged in serious dialogue about fundamental aspects of personal gender identity. By joining these two sources, early women humanists offered a first articulation in western history of a uniquely feminine way of fostering the dignity of the whole person in every circumstance. At this point in the analysis we will now turn away from considering philosophical aspects of the religious mystery of recapitulation in order to return to our summary account of philosophical arguments and theories about woman's identity during this fascinating period of 1250-1500.

NEW RELATION TO SPACE AND TIME

In the fourteenth century a new theory of the relation between human beings and events in space and time was posited. The philosopher Nicholas of Cusa introduced the notion that the observer is in a relative position with respect to space. Giovanni Pico della Mirandola suggested that the observer is in a relative position with respect to time. Previously, a human being usually seemed to be trapped by constraints of observable time and space. These two theoretical insights, formulated by men deeply influenced by Neoplatonism, prepared for the Copernican Revolution.

Women's Attention to Persons-in-Relation	
Women-to-Women Relations	**Men-To-Women Relations**

Spiritual guides:
 	
Two Gertrudes —
   two Mechtilds at Helfta
Julian of Norwich — Margery Kempe
 	
Sister Nazaria Olympia — Laura
Cereta
	Spiritual guides:
	
	Several Confessors and Spiritual Direc-
	tors of
	   — Margery Kempe
	   — Bridget of Sweden
	   — Julian of Norwich
	   — Catherine of Siena
	   — Laura Cereta

Mother and grandmother guides:
 	
Battista Malatesta — Costanza Varano
Giulia Boiurdo Pico — The Princess
of Capri
	Father guides:
	
	Thomas Pizzano —
	   Christine de Pizan
	Francesco Barbaro —
	   Costanza Barbaro
	Sylvestro Cereta —
	   Laura Cereta
	
	Mother guides:
	
	Margaret von Wolsmershausen Eyb —
	   Albrecht von Eyb
	Giulia Boiurdo Pico —
	   Giovanni Pico della Mirandola

Humanist guides: Cassandra Fedele — Allesandra Scala Isotta Nogarola — Costanza Varano	**Humanist guides:** Leonardo Bruni — Battista Malatesta Lauro Quirini — Isotta Nogarola

Personal friendships:
 	
Dominicans at Poissy —
   Christine de Pizan
Deodata di Leno — Laura Cereta
	Personal friendships:
	
	Henry Suso — Elsbeth Stagel
	Jean Gerson — Christine de Pizan
	Ludovico Foscarini —
	   Isotta Nogarola
	Conrad Celtis — Charitas Pirckheimer

Women also began to break out of constraints that had conditioned their activities to very narrow units of space and time. Women began to travel long distances on personal quests. Others successfully directed military and political actions, participated in public debates, studied in small academies of higher learning with men, and gave public orations at universities. Their writings were copied, printed, and dispersed throughout Europe, often with the help of wealthy women who financed printing businesses. Women were no longer silent. Rigid borders between the private and public spheres of activity began to soften. While many men continued to oppose any form of public activity for women, Christine de Pizan earned her living as a professional writer and Laura Cereta wrote of the ability to "steal time" and "sequester space" for her intellectual work of writing and teaching.

During the period of early Renaissance Humanism, people discovered their own relation to time and space. They were able to determine the way they lived as a man or a woman. The dignity of this newly discovered autonomy elevated the human being as a co-creator with God of a unique personal human identity. This dignity rejected dependence on an external force of whimsical fortune, "the goddess Fortuna," and took responsibility for determining actions and attitudes towards one's own life.

For the purposes of thematic analysis contemporary authors were separated into different chapters in the book. This method of division and analysis enabled us to focus more sharply on the differing dynamics within the four distinguished communities of discourse. For purposes of integration and historical continuity, it is useful to offer a chronological account of the authors and events relevant to our topic.

Particular contributions of men and women to the history of the concept of woman during this period of 1250-1500 are summarized below with the titles of many of the works in English. Noting simultaneous events in different places will allow the reader to grasp the evolving concept of woman. Breaking the time-line into fifty-year segments enables us to note the increasing numbers of publications and events concerning women's identity.

TIME-LINE OF CONTRIBUTIONS TO THE CONCEPT OF WOMAN (1250-1500)

From 1200 to 1250 Aristotle's gender polarity arguments are infused with controversy into academia, while women religious authors begin to articulate their self-understanding in religious communities.

c. 1200	There is exclusion of women from universities founded 1200-1400 in France, England, Germany, and most of Italy.
1210-40	Aristotle and Averroes are translated into Latin in Spain.
1210	Some Aristotelian texts are condemned by the University of Paris. The condemnations are repeated in 1231.
1235	Condemnations of Aristotle at the University of Paris are lifted.
c. 1240	Hadewijch completes her writings.

c. 1246   The first translation into Latin of Aristotle's *Ethics* is undertaken by Robert Grosseteste at Oxford and is used by Albert the Great for lectures in Cologne.

From 1250 to 1300 academic and women religious communities exploded with new authors articulating various aspects of the concept of woman. Satirical texts containing exaggerated gender polarity views multiplied. The first short treatises on the education of women in a humanist context are written by men. The first long Neoplatonic treatise is written by a woman.

c. 1250   Beatrice of Nazareth writes *The Seven Stages of the Love of God*.

c. 1250   Vincent of Beauvais composes a text *On the Education of Noble Children*.

c. 1255   Aristotle's works are made required reading at the University of Paris.

1256-59   Thomas Aquinas begins teaching at the University of Paris.

1256   By Papal Order Dominican friars are required to act as spiritual directors to Dominican nuns.

c. 1258   Albert poses gender-related *Questions on Aristotle's Books on Animals* in Cologne.

1259   Albert and Thomas work on a commission to establish philosophy as foundational for Dominican houses in Germany, Italy, and France.

1261-63   Albert finishes commentaries on Aristotle's *Ethics* and *Politics*.

1269-72   Thomas returns to the University of Paris to teach. He dies in 1274.

1272-77   Giles of Rome teaches at the University of Paris. He writes his work on human generation.

1274   Dante meets the young Beatrice.

1275   Satirical *dits* about women begin to appear and continue until 1330.

1277   Several propositions aimed at Thomas Aquinas are condemned at the University of Paris and at Oxford.

1277-84   Eckhart studies at the University of Paris and in Cologne, where he meets Albert the Great.

1278   Jean de Meun completes the popular satire *Le Roman de la rose*.

1278   The Dominican Order mandates the teaching of Thomas Aquinas in all its communities.

1278-85   Giles of Rome is exiled from the Theology Faculty at the University of Paris. He writes his text on the governing of rulers. After a retraction he returns to teach there from 1285 to 1291.

1283   Dante meets Guido Cavalcanti and begins to write poetry about "Beatrice."

1284   Helfta monastery is attacked.

c. 1285   The satirical *Gospel of Women* begins to appear and continues augmentation to 1350.

1285	Mechtild of Magdeburg retires to the Benedictine monastery at Helfta where Gertrude is abbess and writes *The Flowing Light of the Godhead.*
c. 1290	The satirical *Book of Matheolus* is written in Latin.
c. 1290	Marguerite Porete writes the Neoplatonic text *The Mirror of Simple Souls.*
1292	Giles of Rome is now Prior General of the Augustinians and Archbishop of Bourges. His manuscript on generation is used in medical schools in Italy, England, and France. His manuscript on governing is found in multiple versions between 1282 and 1484.
1292	Guido Cavalcanti meets "The Lady" on pilgrimage to Santiago de Compostela in Spain.
1292	Mechtild of Hackeborn shares her religious experiences in *The Book of Special Grace.*
1294	Helfta monastery is attacked and robbed during a war.
1296	Helfta monastery is placed under interdict and closed to the public temporarily.
Before 1302	Gertrude the Great writes *The Herald of Divine Love* and *Exercises.*

From 1300 to 1350 academics and women religious wrote about the concept of woman. Another treatise was written on the education of women, and academically trained Dominican priests intellectually befriended Dominican nuns. This period was filled with different forms of violence, including closing of a university, trials, condemnations, forced exile, burning to death for heresy, and the devastation of the plague. At the same time, gender complementarity in early Renaissance Humanism established a firmer foundation.

1300	Guido Cavalcanti is sent into exile from Florence.
1301	Dante is exiled from Florence.
1301	Duns Scotus and many other Masters are banished from the University of Paris for political activity supporting Pope Boniface VIII and objecting to the King of France's plan to tax Church property to support a war against England.
1301-04	The University of Paris is closed for three years by the Pope in retaliation.
1305	The University of Paris reopens with Duns Scotus and others as Masters again.
1306	Between 1296 and 1306 Marguerite Porete's book *The Mirror of Simple Souls* is condemned and copies are destroyed.
1310	Marguerite Porete is put on trial at the University of Paris for charges of heresy and refusal to stop distributing her book. She is condemned to death by burning.
1311-13	Eckhart writes Latin works in Paris.
1314	Eckhart begins to direct nuns in Strassburg and writes German works.
1318-20	Barberino writes *On the Regimens and Customs of Women.*

1323	Thomas Aquinas is canonized as Saint.
1324-27	Suso studies with Eckhart in Cologne.
1327	Petrarch meets Laura.
1329	Eckhart undergoes trial for his writings in 1326 in Cologne, 1327 in Avignon, and is condemned by Papal Bull.
1336	Boccaccio meets Maria d'Aquino and later characterizes her as "Fiammetta."
1330s-60	Suso works with Elsbeth Stagel on their writings, *The Exemplar* and a *Sister-Book,* which are widely circulated.
1339-47	William of Ockham's nominalist views are condemned at the University of Paris.
1340	Petrarch begins to write about "Laura."
1341	Petrarch receives the laurel crown in Rome.
1342	Helfta monastery is set on fire and its books destroyed.
1344	Bridget of Sweden is widowed and begins to write her *Revelations,* which are completed in 1373.
1347-48	Half of the population of Europe (three quarters of Florence) dies from the plague.

From 1350 to 1400 women religious authors achieve a very deep level of analogical thinking in their writings and a sophisticated range of public action. The Greek language begins to be taught to humanists in Florence. Satires against women increase. Early Renaissance Humanists write on the history of women, and the first woman humanist writes about justice to redress slander against women.

1350	Petrarch and Boccaccio meet in Florence en route to Rome for the Jubilee.
1350	Bridget of Sweden moves to Rome for the Jubilee Year.
1352-65	Boccaccio writes the *Decameron, Concerning Famous Women,* and his satirical *Corbaccio.*
1356	Petrarch visits Charles IV in Prague and his works are promoted in Germany.
c. 1370	Chaucer translates *Le Roman de la rose* into English and satirizes it in his *Wife of Bath Tale.*
1372	Bridget of Sweden takes a pilgrimage to Jerusalem.
1373	Julian of Norwich writes her "Short Text" of *Showings.*
1377	Pope Gregory XI sees Catherine of Siena secretly after she convinced him to move the Papacy from Avignon back to Rome.
1377	Catherine of Siena is appointed by the Pope as ambassador to Florence to resolve a conflict.
1379	Gerhard Groote founds a lay community of Sisters and Brothers of the Common Life in Germany. It expands rapidly with brothers teaching in several schools by 1400.
1380	Chaucer translates into English Boethius's Latin *Consolation of Philosophy.*
1381-1420	*The Mirror of Marriage* is composed.

1390	The popular satirical *Book of Matheolus* is translated into French by Jean le Fèvre.
1390	Christine de Pizan is widowed and defends herself in court.
1393	Julian of Norwich writes the "Long Text" of her *Showings*.
1395	Jean Gerson is appointed Chancellor of the University of Paris until 1409.
1397	Manuel Chrysoloras begins to teach Greek in Florence.
1399	Christine de Pizan writes *Letter to the God of Love*.

From 1400 to 1450 the first public debate among women and men about woman's identity occurs. A woman humanist writes several books about women's identity, religious women travel widely, and one leads military battles. Men and women are burned to death for heresy in England and France. Early Platonist and Neoplatonist works begin to be translated from Greek to Latin and studied by scholars. Humanist schools are formed inclusive of girls and women. Male and female humanists correspond. Women educated in the humanist tradition begin to give public orations on topics of public interest. Male humanists reaffirm gender polarity and explore new theoretical foundations for gender identity.

1400	The *Liber philosophorum moralium antiquorum* is translated into French as *Dits moraulx (Moral Sayings)*.
1401	Christine de Pizan writes *Sayings about the Rose*.
1401	The English statute *De haeretico comburendo* condemns any relapsed heretic to death.
1401-03	Christine de Pizan engages in the *Quarrel about the Rose* with Jean de Montreuil, Gontier and Pierre Col, Guillaume de Tignonville, and Jean Gerson. She disperses the *Letters about the Romance of the Rose* to the general public.
1402	Chrysoloras and Decembrio translate a distorted Plato's *Republic*.
1403	Christine de Pizan writes the *Book about the Mutation of Fortune*.
1403	Bruni translates Plato's *Phaedo, Apology,* and *Letters*.
1405	Christine de Pizan writes *Book of the City of Ladies* and *Book of Three Virtues*.
1410	Bradly the Taylor is burned to death for heresy in Canterbury.
1411	Guarino translates Plutarch's *On the Education of Children*, and in 1412 he replaces Chrysoloras in Chair of Greek Studies in Florence.
1413	William Sawtre, a Lollard, is burned to death in Lynn.
1414	Margery Kempe visits Julian of Norwich.
1414	Francesco Barbaro visits Florence and brings Guarino to open a small humanist school in Venice. Vittorino joins him there in 1415. They study Plato's *Republic* together.
1413-38	Margery Kempe is accused of heresy as she journeys through England and Europe.
1415	Bridget of Sweden is canonized as Saint. Margery Kempe travels to Rome for the canonization.
1415	Francesco Barbaro writes *On Wifely Matters*.

1416	Nicholas of Cusa completes his early schooling with the Brothers of Common Life, attends the University of Heidelberg, and goes to Italy from 1417 to 1423 to study law and humanism.
1417	Lucretius' *On Natural Things* is recovered after being lost since the fourth century.
1420	Bruni translates Xenophon's (Pseudo-Aristotle) *Oeconomicus* (On Household Economy).
1421	Guarino opens a humanist school in Verona.
1423-24	Vittorino opens a humanist school in Mantua for the Gonzaga family and others.
1424	Bruni writes *On the Study of Literature* to Battista Malatesta.
1425	Cusanus returns to Germany and studies scholastic philosophy at the University of Cologne.
1426-33	George of Trebizond translates anew Aristotle's works on natural philosophy.
1428	Leon Battista Alberti writes two dialogues about women — *Deifira* and *Ecatonfila*.
1429	Jean Gerson writes *De quadam puella* in support of Joan of Arc.
1429	Joan of Arc leads the victorious Battle of Orleans.
1429	Christine de Pizan writes *Ditty about Joan of Arc* praising Joan's victory.
1429	Nicholas of Cusa sells a manuscript of Plautus's dramas to Cardinal Orsini at the Council of Basel.
1430	Fillippo Maria of Milan, Leonello d'Este of Ferrara, and Lorenzo de Medici of Florence procure copies of Plautus's dramas.
1431	Joan of Arc is tried for heresy and burned to death.
1431	Battista Malatesta gives a public oration on the effects of war to King Sigismund of Hungary, who is on his way to Rome to become the Holy Roman Emperor.
1431	Lorenzo Valla writes the first version of his dialogue *On Pleasure*.
1432-37	Alberti writes his text *On the Family* and three more satires about women — *On Love, Sofrona,* and *Momus*.
1433	Valla revises his dialogue on pleasure and renames it *On the True and False Good*.
1434	Isotta Nogarola writes to the Protonotario Barbaro.
1436	Jacopo Foscari sends copies of Isotta and Ginerva Nogarola's writings to Guarino of Verona.
1437	Nogarola initiates a correspondence with Guarino.
1437-39	Pier Candido Decembrio makes a second translation of Plato's *Republic*.
1438	"Pliny" writes a satirical letter to "Ovid" slandering Isotta Nogarola. She moves to Venice and does not return to Verona until 1441.
1438-39	At the Council of Ferrara-Florence the humanist circle of Cardinal Orsini, Nicholas of Cusa, Lorenzo Valla, Leonardo Bruni, and Leon Battista Alberti meet frequently.

1440	Nicholas of Cusa writes *On Learned Ignorance* and begins *On Conjectures*.
1440	Lauro Quirini, a student of Guarino, corresponds with Isotta Nogarola.
1441-64	Albrecht von Eyb writes three Latin treatises on women's identity and a textbook on rhetoric.
1442	Martin le Franc writes *The Champion of Women* in defense of women.
1443	Guarino gives the inaugural lecture at new University of Ferrara.
1443	Antonio da Rho writes a dialogue on Plato's views on women.
1444	Costanza Varano (granddaughter of Battista Malatesta) gives two public orations on the theme of justice.
1444-47	Valla is charged by the Inquisition and revises and renames his dialogue as *On the True Good*.
1444	Costanza Varano writes letters to Cecilia Gonzaga and to Isotta Nogarola.
1444-59	Von Eyb travels to Italy to study law and humanism.
1447	Barbaro writes letters to his daughter Costanza.

From 1450 to 1500 the invention of the printing press leads to the dissemination of satires against women and tracts on women's education. Plato's dialogues are printed with gender unity arguments; academic texts are distributed with gender polarity arguments; and texts written by women are also made available. Several men are accused of heresy; some are exiled or condemned to death. Women are burned to death as witches and gender polarity arguments are integrated into a published manual on witchcraft. Several treatises in praise of women are published. The theoretical foundation for the concept of woman moves more widely into the public arena. Women and men humanists develop long-lasting intellectual friendships and women humanists publish sophisticated treatises and letters on gender identity. New foundations for gender complementarity are articulated, especially by women humanists.

1450	The printing press is invented in Mainz, Germany.
1450-56	Joan of Arc's Trial of Rehabilitation occurs and her accusation of heresy is removed.
1450-1500	Fifty "witches" are executed in southwestern Germany
1450's	Laura Cereta and her brother Daniele participate in humanist circles in Brescia.
1450's	Isotta Nogarola and Ludovico Foscarini correspond.
1450	George of Trebizond translates Plato's *Laws*.
1451-53	Isotta Nogarola writes her dialogue on *The Equal or Unequal Sin of Adam and Eve*.
1451	Papal Bulls put forth Thomas Aquinas as the model for truth.
1451	Von Eyb translates Plautus's dramas and "germanizes" them.
1457	Valla gives his critical oration on St. Thomas Aquinas.
1458	Cusanus writes *On Beryllus*.

1462   Cusanus writes *On the Not-Other.*
1463   Ficino begins his translations of Plato and the Platonic Academy in Florence.
1467   Antonio Cornazzano writes *On Admirable Women.*
1469   *Customs of Girls* is one of the first books to be printed in Venice.
1470   Juvenal's satires are printed in Venice, Florence (1472), Ferrara and Milan (1474), Lyons (1485), Paris (1493), Turin (1494), and Nuremberg (1497).
1470-74   Bruni's translation of Plato's dialogues is printed and dispersed in England, Castile, and Germany.
1471   Von Eyb writes his *Little Book of Marriage* addressed to the people of Nuremberg. His textbook on rhetoric with a Latin oration in praise of women is printed fifteen times in Germany from 1472 to 1503.
1474   Ockham's nominalist views are condemned again at the University of Paris.
1474   James Sprenger is appointed Inquisitor in southern Germany and Austria.
1474   Ficino publishes his major work *On Platonic Theology.*
1474-1500   Five Latin versions of Giles of Rome's book on governing are printed.
1478-82   Giovanni Pico della Mirandola studies at various universities in Italy, where he discovers the Cabala.
1479   The City of Nuremberg officially adopts Roman Law in marriage.
1480   Bisticci writes a text *In Praise and Commendation of Women.*
1480-90   The satirical *Fifteen Joys of Marriage* is printed in Lyons.
1481   The Prohibition against Ockham at Paris is lifted permanently.
1482   Aldus Manutius lives with the Pico family and tutors the Princess of Capri's children.
1483   Arienti writes *Gynervera de le clare donne.*
1484   Pope Innocent VIII promulgates a Bull against witchcraft.
1484   Ficino publishes his first translations of Plato's dialogues.
1484   Pico spends the year in Florence with Ficino and meets Girolamo Savonarola. He continues studies at the University of Paris in Greek, Latin, Arabic, and Hebrew.
1485   Laura Cereta corresponds with several men and women.
1485   Martin le Franc's defense of women is printed.
1486   Lucretius' *On Natural Things* is printed in Verona and Venice (1495).
1486   James Sprenger and Heinrich Kramer collaborate on *The Hammer of Witches.*
1486   Pico posts his *900 Theses* in Rome and sends them to all the universities in Italy, inviting philosophers and theologians to enter into debate with him. Pope Innocent forbids the debate as heretical. Pico flees to France, is captured, imprisoned, and later released. Pico escapes to Florence.

1486	Savonarola preaches in Brescia and again in 1489.
1486	Laura Cereta corresponds with several more men and women.
1487	Boccaccio's satirical *Corbaccio* is printed in Italy and in Lyons and in Paris (1496).
1487	*The Hammer of Witches* is approved by the Faculty of Theology of Cologne.
1487	Cassandra Fedele gives a public oration to the University of Padua on the Liberal Arts.
1487	Laura Cereta corresponds with more men and women.
1487	Gogio writes *In Praise of Women*.
1488	Laura Cereta's manuscript of letters and orations is published. She is thought to have retired from writing, but continues to teach.
1489	Ficino publishes *The Book of Life* and is reported to Pope Innocent VIII for possible heresy. He successfully defends himself the following year. He translates texts by Porphyry and Proclus and later Plotinus.
1489	Cassandra Fedele initiates a correspondence with Giovanni Pico della Mirandola.
1491	Angelo Poliziano and Pico visit Cassandra Fedele in her home, and after reporting the visit to Lorenzo de Medici, Cassandra is invited to become an informal member of the Florentine court and Platonic Academy.
1492	Alessandra Scala and Cassandra Fedele correspond.
1492	With the financial help of Isabella of Spain, Christopher Columbus sails to America. Isabella also invites Cassandra Fedele to visit the Spanish Court.
1493	Pico is absolved of heresy and dies under unusual circumstances in 1494. Savonarola gives his funeral oration.
1493	Poliziano writes to Cassandra Fedele about Alessandra Scala's participating in the Florentine humanist community of discourse.
1494	Conrad Celtis discovers Roswitha's manuscripts, to be printed in 1501.
1494	Aldus Manutius opens a printing business in Venice with financial support from Pico's sister, the Princess of Capri.
1495	Aristotle's, Plato's, and Plutarch's works are printed in Greek and Latin in Venice.
1495	The German humanist "Academy Platonica," the *Sodalitas litteraria Rhenana,* is founded by Conrad Celtis and others with a focus on printing texts.
1496	Ficino publishes a collection of his commentaries on Plato's dialogues.
1496	Gianfrancesco Pico publishes an edited version of his uncle Giovanni Pico della Mirandola's works. His *Oration on the Dignity of Man* is very successful. They are printed in Lyons and Venice in 1498.
1497	The satirical *Book of Matheolus* is printed in France.

1499	Savonarola is burned to death for heresy in Florence.
1499	At the age of thirty Laura Cereta dies.
c. 1500	The satirical *On Why Golias Should Not Marry* is printed four times.
1500	The letters of *Catherine of Siena* are printed by Aldus Manutius in Venice.
1500	The Great Jubilee occurs with pilgrimages to Rome and Jerusalem.

What general conclusions can be drawn from this time-line in the early Renaissance? The period begins with a predominance of Aristotelian philosophy coupled with the exclusion of women from universities and ends with the increased importance of Platonic philosophy accompanied by the inclusion of women in humanist communities of discourse. Initially men taught about the concept of woman in all-male academic institutions; subsequently, women were teaching men about the concept of woman in a variety of contexts. Aristotelian philosophy coincided with women's exclusion; Platonic philosophy justified women's inclusion in intellectual life.

Another interesting phenomenon is the religious influence on the concept of woman. Just as the period between 800 and 1100 may be characterized as "The Benedictine Age in the Concept of Woman," so the period between 1250 and 1500 may be characterized as "The Dominican Age in the Concept of Woman." Vincent of Beauvais's early text on the education of children, the scholastic contributions of St. Albert the Great and St. Thomas Aquinas, the innovations of Meister Eckhart, Johannes Tauler, Henry Suso, and Elsbeth Stagel, the Dominicans Kramer and Sprenger's manual on witchcraft, and the role of the Dominicans in Joan of Arc's trials of condemnation and rehabilitation demonstrate a powerful Dominican presence in woman's identity issues. The religious renewal associated with the third-order Dominican Catherine of Siena, Savonarola, and Giovanni Pico della Mirandola, and the spiritual direction of Laura Cereta, demonstrate the influence of the Dominican Order.

Contrary to the earlier Medieval Benedictine writings of Anselm, Herrad, and Hildegard, providing a philosophical foundation of gender complementarity, the Dominicans did not provide a particular theory of gender identity. Rather, the Dominicans articulated **all** the theories. Gender polarity, which devalued woman, was developed and applied by Albert the Great and by Kramer and Sprenger. Gender unity, with a unisex approach, was extended by Eckhart and Tauler. The principles of equal dignity and significant differentiation of man and woman based on gender complementarity were explored in theology by Thomas Aquinas, in literature by Christine de Pizan, and in humanist epistolary discourse by Brother Thomas of Milan. The lives of Catherine of Siena, Henry Suso, and Elsbeth Stagel demonstrated the principles of complementarity in practice. While the Dominicans did not represent a united theory of gender identity, they usually defended individual theories. The willingness of several Dominicans to engage in dialogue with women about human identity eroded the exclusion of women from participation in intellectual discourse. Even with mixed support for gender polarity, gender unity, and gender complementarity, the Dominican Age had an overall positive effect on women's education and their developing capacity for self-articulation.

Another general pattern concerns the relation between culture and philosophical discourse. On the negative side, gender polarity arguments, originally elaborated in academia, hardened and spread ridicule of women by means of satires. The printing press infused these notions into a broader public. For example, the wide dispersion of a manual associating women's weak character with the spread of witchcraft linked academic gender polarity arguments with more public events.

On the positive side of the relation of culture and philosophy, throughout the thirteenth and fourteenth centuries women religious authors and male literary authors heralded a new concept of woman as wise and virtuous. With the use of intuitive analogies and imaginary projections of women these authors proposed models of women capable of leading men to greater wisdom and virtue. This heralding of a concept of women prepared the way for strong, virtuous women to follow. In the fifteenth century, women humanist authors surpassed the projected models by their complex discursive texts; these discourses introduced into western thought original philosophical speculations concerning the concept of woman.

The first phase of the study from 750 B.C.–1250 A.D. demonstrated that philosophical considerations of the respective identities of woman and man began in Greece, and spread through the Mediterranean area to Sicily, Italy, northern Africa, and southern Spain. They then penetrated England, France, and Germany. The second phase of the study, from 1250 to 1500, shows a further expansion northward into the Low Countries and Scandinavia and eastward through Austria and Hungary. The center of scrutiny shifts from Paris and Oxford to northern Italy and Germany.

A general observation of the time-line above reinforces a conclusion reached in the earlier volume of this study of the history of the concept of woman: namely, "that the philosophy of sex (gender) identity was a central aspect of philosophy since its inception in Greece in the sixth century BC."[10] From the original articulation by the Presocratics of four areas of questions (opposites, generation, wisdom, and virtue), through systematic answers to these questions in theories of gender unity, gender polarity, and gender complementarity, the most important philosophers in the West have considered the concept of woman in relation to man. The period 1250-1500 continues this central interest in most, if not all, of its most well-known philosophers. If we limit our list to authors usually taught in academic philosophy programs, the following are included:

- Albert the Great
- Thomas Aquinas
- Giles of Rome
- John Duns Scotus
- William of Ockham

10. Sr. Prudence Allen, R.S.M., *The Concept of Woman: The Aristotelian Revolution (750 BC–1250 AD)* (Grand Rapids: Eerdmans, 1997), p. 474.

- Leonardo Bruni
- Nicholas of Cusa
- Leon Battista Alberti
- Lorenzo Valla
- Marsilio Ficino
- Giovanni Pico della Mirandola

The contemporary view that the philosophy of gender is a recent addition to philosophy is demonstrated to be false.

THEORETICAL CONCLUSIONS ABOUT
THE CONCEPT OF WOMAN (1250-1500)

An overall characterization of these developments is offered on the following page. While these general lines of advancement in the theoretical foundations for the concept of woman are fairly clear, their sources of origin are complex. The Platonic and Neoplatonic emphases on the immortal soul as distinct from the body provided a foundation for the equal dignity and worth of men and women. Integration into humanist schools and some religious communities was often joined with accepting women as intellectual colleagues. The opportunity for higher education gave women intellectual tools with which to examine their own identity and situation.

It would be incorrect to credit Plato's theories and Neoplatonism as the sole impetus for advances in the concept of woman. Aristotle's *Ethics* and *Politics* provided many theoretical foundations that women used to engage in public dialogue about justice, particularly as applied to their own situations. Christian women's religious communities, writings, and educated, virtuous women provided a further foundation for the revaluation of previously limited theories about women's identity.

There is an insistence within complementarity theories on upholding the principle of equal dignity of woman and man while identifying philosophically significant differences. The principle of equal dignity is infused with new vitality through two sources in this period: the Platonic principle of a similar reason present in the human soul and the Christian principle of creation with an intellect and free will in the image and likeness of God. Humanists interested in Neoplatonism incorporated the principle of equality from new Latin translations of Plato's dialogues and the principle of equal education for men and women from Plutarch and Quintilian.

The principle of equality led some Neoplatonists to shift towards a gender unity or gender neutrality position. Even when they considered the importance of gender differentiation, such as in birthing or masculine and feminine characteristics, at the highest levels all reference to gender differentiation ceased and the model of the perfect human moved toward a unisex being, a soul with no gender identity. The Christian Neoplatonists reoriented the object of love away from the Greek male homosexual model to a heterosexual one. While its ultimate goal was

Theoretical Developments in the Concept of Woman (1250-1500)			
Opposites	Generation	Wisdom	Virtue
Moves from: primary focus on male and female characteristics	**Moves from:** primary focus on reproductive biological male and female characteristics	**Moves from:** women excluded from higher education, limited intellectually to opinion, and silence in public	**Moves from:** women excluded from political life, and limited to unequal types of friendship and justice
Moves to: male with masculine/feminine qualities female with feminine/masculine qualities	**Moves to:** metaphorical spiritual generation, analogous to a man or woman giving birth to God in the soul	**Moves to:** women gaining access to academic texts and humanist schools that provide opportunities to develop intellectually through discursive reasoning	**Moves to:** women building common good in public spheres of activity
and: categories of masculine and feminine as relation-determined	**and:** Divine action in the world, analogical to a mother birthing and caring for a child	**and:** women engaging in public debate with men	**and:** women applying categories of justice to redress injustices and to share equitably in redistribution of goods (including governing) of society

the same as Socrates and Plato, namely the beauty of goodness, its original orientation was not a young boy or man, but rather a beautiful woman. The ultimate rejection of the human body, however, was the same in both forms of Platonism, as the original loved object is passed over into a love for the gender-neutral form of beauty.

Sustained intergender communities of discourse were able to reconcile the principle of equal dignity and worth with the principle of differentiation without falling into a unisex model or a gender polarity model, by constant reflection on individual human beings' unique identity. Christine de Pizan and Laura Cereta formulated a basis for integral complementarity in which a woman and a man in relation to another person maintain an autonomous identity. These authors referred to women's history, women's ranges of experience, and a particular attention to fostering the growth of the human person in all actions contributing to the common good.

These new developments towards an integral complementarity theory took place amidst violent ruptures in relations of men and women. These ruptures were manifested in the radical separation of the sexes with respect to higher education and in the proliferation of satires devaluing woman's identity in relation to man. Women who confronted some of the causes for these ruptures were persecuted and slandered. Certainly, the violence of the period was not directed against women only; men also were exiled, imprisoned, and even burned to death, if not destroyed by the ravages of war and pestilence.

The achievement of the common good depended upon the cooperation of both sexes to improve their relationship. This was greatly aided by the Renaissance Humanists. The first men to heal the rupture of radical gender polarity were the founders of humanism: Dante, Petrarch, and Boccaccio. Their innovative use of the imagination to express love and respect for a woman radically transformed the popular view that women were less capable of wisdom and virtue than men. Their imagination paved the way for reality. The texts of Petrarch and Boccaccio, frequently called upon by later humanist writers as evidence for women's historical greatness, allowed women to have a Renaissance.

Later educators, Guarino, Vittorino, and Bruni, helped to heal the rupture of radical gender polarity by building schools, forming communities of discourse, recovering ancient texts that valued women's abilities and contributions, and educating directly or indirectly women interested in the intellectual life of humanistic studies. Several male humanists in small academies welcomed the participation of women, tutored them, and corresponded with women colleagues.

Third, a group of men introduced a new meaning of masculinity and femininity beyond the simple distinction of male and female identity: Leon Battista Alberti, Lorenzo Valla, Nicholas of Cusa, Marsilio Ficino, and Giovanni Pico della Mirandola. While their theories did not achieve a full balance between the two principles of integral gender complementarity, they generated new thinking about the meaning of being a man or a woman within a particular culture.

What can we say about the women who worked directly to heal the rupture of radical gender polarity? Several come to mind: Bridget of Sweden, Julian of Norwich, Catherine of Siena, Christine de Pizan, Joan of Arc, Margery Kempe, Battista Malatesta, Isotta Nogarola, Costanza Varano, Cassandra Fedele, and Laura Cereta. Each woman engaged in public discourse and presented a new model for woman's identity by her questions and actions and by challenging particular men to come to new conclusions about their own engendered identity. To accomplish these goals, they often risked ridicule, danger, and even death.

For the first time in western history, several women integrated and critically used the works of major philosophers. The following table offers a summary of the most notable of these integrations:

Women Authors' Notable Integration of Philosophers	
Woman Author	Philosopher Used
Christine de Pizan	Presocratics Aristotle Augustine Boethius Thomas Aquinas Dante Petrarch Boccaccio
Cassandra Fedele	Plato Cicero Plutarch Petrarch Boccaccio Giovanni Pico della Mirandola
Isotta Nogarola	Aristotle Cicero Augustine Boethius Averroes Avicenna Thomas Aquinas
Laura Cereta	Presocratics Plato Aristotle Epicurus Ptolemy Cicero Seneca Plutarch Boccaccio Thomas Aquinas

Women became serious philosophers in their own right. They entered the collective history of western philosophy by selecting authors upon whom to critically build a new theoretical foundation for their own work. Christine de Pizan, Isotta Nogarola, and Laura Cereta developed original arguments about gender identity that should enter the collective historical discourse for subsequent philosophical work in this area.

Unique Contributions of Women Humanists to the Philosophy of Gender

Christine de Pizan:
- Gender polarity arguments are an example of injustice towards women.
- Several gender polarity arguments contain the fallacy of generalization, unsubstantiated universal claims, and *ad hominem* attacks.
- Gender polarity arguments in literary texts, when extensive, tend to have a destructive effect on the reader.
- Several persons offering gender polarity arguments act contrary to their claims. Their gender polarity arguments have several different causes.
- Gender polarity arguments about the nature of woman are inconsistent with a perfect Divine Creator.
- History and experience provide strong evidence for the equal dignity and worth of women and men.
- Other women are limited in their development by lack of education, lack of exercise of the mind, and low expectations by society.
- Women are capable of participating in all levels of society in building a just and common good.
- Arguments about gender identity ought to be accepted on the basis of their rationality and conformity to true justice and not on gender solidarity.

Isotta Nogarola:
- Gender polarity arguments about woman and man, derived from the account of Adam and Eve, may be demonstrated to be incoherent by a *reductio ad absurdum* argument-form.

Laura Cereta:
- Gender complementarity arguments support the claim that women should steal time and sequester space from domestic service for study of humanist texts, science, and art.
- Gender complementarity arguments indicate that women scholars should situate themselves in both the historical and contemporary communities of discourse built by women and men intellectuals.
- When a humanist lives inconsistently with the humanist values professed, he or she should be measured against the ideal and appropriately corrected.
- Gender complementarity arguments support the principles of equality and differentiation in the categories of generation, wisdom, and virtue in the context of early Renaissance Humanism.
- Integral gender complementarity, oriented towards a woman or towards a man as a whole person, is supported in practice.

These three original women philosophers introduced new principles of equal dignity for men and women without losing significant differentiation of the two sexes or the integrated intellectual/material identity of woman and man. Between 1250 and 1500 these three women philosophers provided new philosophical foundations for integral gender complementarity. They kept an appropriate understanding of the soul/body unity of the human being and integral relations among men and women. While Hildegard of Bingen was identified as the founder of gender complementarity, Christine de Pizan, Isotta Nogarola, and Laura Cereta may be characterized as the "builders of integral gender complementarity." The period 1250-1500 is a period of transition, filled with tensions and insights, aimed at a greater understanding of the purpose of human life and, within this broader context, of the respective identities of women and men.

EVALUATION OF WEAKNESSES AND STRENGTHS

Beginning with the text's weaknesses, it should be noted that the vastness of the period, the sheer number of sources, and the pronounced disagreement among scholars about authors and texts of this period make it difficult to ensure accuracy. Several outstanding critical works published within the last ten years have clarified developments that took place during the period 1250-1500. The history of the concept of woman within this period itself is vast; the effect is a long text. Some of my textual interpretations are preliminary at best. Perhaps these interpretations will serve as an incentive for other scholars to treat areas of controversy more in depth.

The book's strength is that it appears to be one of the first systematic texts to consider the philosophy of gender in early Renaissance Humanism. It therefore includes foundational documents, providing a useful scholarly source. While many arguments were summarized, others have been kept in direct form so that the reader is able to see the author's own manner of articulation. To the best of my ability, all the relevant, available western philosophical sources on this subject are included. Sources, gathered from far and wide, have been translated into English or have been abstracted from religious or literary texts. The material has been made accessible to public scrutiny; this may at times result in conclusions different from my own, thus fostering further discourse on gender identity in the history of philosophy.

The extraordinary work of contemporary scholars of Neoplatonism, Religious Studies, and Renaissance Humanism made my analysis possible. This may be likened to the opportunity opened by the Latin translations of Greek works in the thirteenth century and the vernacular translation of classical Latin and Greek texts in the fourteenth and fifteenth century. Renaissance Latin, Italian, French, and German texts about women's identity are now available in English. Others may evaluate how this extraordinary period serves as a distant mirror to this new millennium.

A deep impulse within Christianity towards integral gender complementarity reappears at different moments in history, especially when distortions have entered into these respective identities. When significant differentiation shifts to the radical devaluation of one gender, an impulse moves towards affirming the equal dignity of man and woman. When equality is interpreted in a unisex model of human identity, the impulse moves towards engendered appropriation of significant differences between women and men. An example exists in Volume I of *The Concept of Woman* in Augustine's original affirmation of the principles of complementarity, i.e., eternally significant differentiation and equal dignity of woman and man, in the face of gender polarity arguments that women would be turned into men at the resurrection of the body. Hildegard offered a systematic analysis of the body/soul complementary identities of women and men; this impulse contributed to an understanding of the human being as a unified spiritual and material entity. In Volume II of *The Concept of Woman,* Christine de Pizan's ardent defense of the significant differentiation and equal dignity of woman and man began another phase of the articulation of this impulse. The collective efforts of several religious and humanist authors accentuated the integral complementarity of men and women building toward a common good.

Renaissance Christian humanist articulations of new foundations for integral gender complementarity occurred in the real context of men and women sharing a highly intellectual, and often religious, community of discourse with one another. Conversely, where polarity theories abounded, the institutional separation of the genders led to isolation, distrust, and hostility. While these contexts were rooted in Christian academic philosophy, they did not appear to contain an impulse of renewal as much as a playing out of old systematic structures of polarity originally articulated by Ancient Greek Aristotelian philosophy.

There are ample sources for exploring the next phase of the development of the Concept of Woman from 1500-2000. The foundations for integral complementarity established by humanist philosophers will be overturned by the infusion of Cartesian arguments in support of gender unity. With the "Cartesian turn to the subject," the human being is characterized as a "thinking thing" with no reference to gender differentiation. The momentum towards a new theory of integral complementarity is stopped, overcome by the "Cartesian Reformation." This radical dominance of a single theory of gender identity is similar to the Aristotelian Revolution of the thirteenth century that overturned the original momentum for gender complementarity initiated by the Benedictine influence. The history of the concept of woman continues its dramatic progress into the rationalism of the eighteenth century, followed by other phases in the nineteenth and twentieth centuries.

BIBLIOGRAPHY

Abel, Elizabeth, ed. *Writing and Sexual Difference.* Chicago: University of Chicago Press, 1982.

Abelard, Peter, and Heloise. *The Letters of Abelard and Heloise.* Translated by Betty Radice. Harmondsworth: Penguin Books, 1974.

Adams, Marilyn McCord. *William of Ockham.* Notre Dame: University of Notre Dame Press, 1987.

Agrippa, Henry Cornelius. *On the Superiority of Woman over Man.* Translated by Amaudin. New York: American News Company, 1873.

Albert the Great, St. *Opera Omnia.* 38 vols. Edited by Augusti Borgnet. Paris: Apud Ludovicum Vives, 1890-1899.

———. *Opera Omnia.* vol. 18. Edited by Bernhardo Creyer. Aschendorff: Westfalorum Monastery, 1955.

———. (Spurious). *De Secretis Mulierum, or the Mystery of Human Generation Fully Revealed.* London: Curil, 1725.

Alberti, Leon Battista. *The Family in Renaissance Florence.* Translated by Renée Neu Watkins. Columbia, S.C.: University of South Carolina Press, 1969.

———. *On Painting.* Edited and translated by J. R. Spencer. New Haven: Yale University Press, 1956.

———. *Opera Volgari.* Edited by Cecil Grayson. Bari: Laterza, 1960.

Alcoff, Linda. "Cultural Feminism versus Post-Structuralism: The Identity Crisis in Feminist Theory." *Signs: Journal of Women in Culture and Society* 13, no. 3 (1988): 405-36.

Allen, Christine. "Christ Our Mother in Julian of Norwich." *Studies in Religion* 10, no. 4 (1981): 421-28.

Allen, Michael J. B. *Nuptial Arithmetic: Marsilio Ficino's Commentary on the Fatal Number in Book VIII of Plato's 'Republic.'* Berkeley and Los Angeles: University of California Press, 1994.

———. *The Platonism of Marsilio Ficino: A Study of His 'Phaedrus' Commentary, Its Sources and Genesis.* Berkeley and Los Angeles: University of California Press, 1984.

Allen, Sister Prudence. "Analogy and Human Community in Lublin Existential Personalism." *Toronto Journal of Theology* 5, no. 2 (Fall 1989): 236-46.

————. "Can Feminism Be a Humanism?" *Études Maritainiennes/Maritain Studies* 14 (1998): 109-40.

————. *The Concept of Woman: The Aristotelian Revolution: 750 BC–1250 AD.* Montreal and London: Eden Press, 1985. 2nd rev. ed. Grand Rapids and Cambridge: Eerdmans, 1997.

————. "Descartes: The Concept of Woman and the French Revolution." In *Revolution, Violence, and Equality,* edited by Yaeger Hudson and Creighton Peden, pp. 61-78. *Studies in Social and Political Theory,* vol. 10: *Social Philosophy Today,* no. 3. Lewiston, N.Y.: Edwin Mellen Press, 1990.

————. "Hildegard of Bingen's Philosophy of Sex Identity." *Thought* 64 (September 1989): 231-41.

————. "The Influence of Plato and Aristotle on the Concept of Woman in Medieval Jewish Philosophy." *Florilegium* 9 (1987): 89-111.

————. "Integral Sex Complementarity and the Theology of Communion." *Communio* 17, no. 4 (Winter 1990): 523-44.

————. "Language and the Invitation to Conversion." *Language and Faith: Proceedings from the Nineteenth Convention of the Fellowship of Catholic Scholars.* St. Louis, Mo. (1997): 93-128.

————. "Metaphysics of Form, Matter, and Gender." *Lonergan Workshop* 12 (1996): 1-26.

————. "Mother Earth and Father Sun in Copernicus and Galileo." *Lonergan Review* 3 (1994): 271-88.

————. "Rationality, Gender, and History." *American Catholic Philosophical Association Quarterly* 68 (1994): 271-88.

————. "Sex Unity, Polarity, or Complementarity?" In *Women and Men: Interdisciplinary Readings on Gender,* edited by Greta Hofman Nemiroff, pp. 3-20. Toronto: Fitzhenry and Whiteside, 1987.

————. "Soul, Body, and Transcendence in St. Teresa of Avila." *Toronto Journal of Theology* 3 (Fall 1987): 252-66.

————. "Two Medieval Views on Women's Identity: Hildegard of Bingen and Thomas Aquinas." *Studies in Religion* 1 (1987): 21-36.

————. "A Woman and a Man as Prime Analogical Beings." *American Catholic Philosophical Quarterly* 66, no. 4 (1992): 465-82.

————, and Filippo Salvatore. "Lucrezia Marinelli and Woman's Identity in Late Italian Renaissance." *Renaissance and Reformation* 16, no. 4 (Fall 1992): 5-39.

Angenot, Marc. *Les Champions des femmes: examen du discours sur la supériorité des femmes 1400-1800.* Montreal: Les Presses de l'Université de Québec, 1977.

Anglo, Sydney, ed. *The Damned Art: Essays in the Literature of Witchcraft.* London, Henley, and Boston: Routledge and Kegan Paul, 1977.

Anscombe, Elizabeth. "Human Essence." Unpublished manuscript available in microfiche. In *Proceedings of the World Congress of Philosophy.* Brighton, U.K., 1988.

Anselm, St. *Monologium, Basic Writings.* Translated by S. W. Deane. LaSalle, Illinois: Open Court Publishing Company, 1962.

————. *The Prayers and Meditations of St. Anselm.* Translated by Benedicta Ward. Harmondsworth: Penguin Books, 1973.

Antonopoulos, Anna. "Writing the Mystic Body: Sexuality and Textuality in the *écriture-féminine* of Saint Catherine of Genoa." *Hypatia* 6, no. 3 (Fall 1991): 185-207.

Arden, Heather M. *The Roman de la Rose: An Annotated Bibliography*. New York: Garland Publishing, 1993.

Aristotle. *Aristotle Selections*. Translated by Terence Irwin and Gail Fine. Indianapolis: Hackett Publishing Company, Inc., 1995.

————. *The Art of Rhetoric*. The Loeb Classical Library. Cambridge, Mass.: Harvard University Press, 1957.

————. *The Basic Works of Aristotle*. Edited by Richard McKeon. New York: Random House, 1941.

————. (Spurious). *Economique*. Paris: Les Belles Lettres, 1968.

————. *Eudemian Ethics*. The Loeb Classical Library. Translated by H. Rackham. Cambridge, Mass.: Harvard University Press, 1935.

————. *Generation of Animals*. The Loeb Classical Library. Translated and edited by A. L. Peck. Cambridge, Mass.: Harvard University Press, 1943.

————. *The Organon*. The Loeb Classical Library. Translated by Harold P. Cooke and Hugh Tredennick. Cambridge, Mass.: Harvard University Press, 1949-50.

————. (Spurious). *The Politics and Economics of Aristotle*. Translated by Edward Walford. London: Henry G. Bohm, 1853.

————. (Spurious). *Problems*. Translated by W. S. Hett. London: William Heinemann, 1937.

————. (Spurious). *Pseudo-Aristotle, Secret of Secrets: Sources and Influences*. Edited by Charles B. Schmitt and W. F. Ryan. London: Warburg Institute, 1982.

————. (Spurious). *The Works of Aristotle, the Famous Philosopher*. Edited by Charles and Carroll Rosenberg. New York: Arno Press, 1974.

Armitage, Angus. *The World of Copernicus*. New York: New American Library, 1963.

Arrothoon, Leigh A., ed. *The Craft of Fiction: Essays in Medieval Poetics*. Rochester, Mich.: Solaris Press, Inc., 1984.

Artz, Frederick B. *Renaissance Humanism: 1300-1550*. Oberlin: Kent State University Press, 1996.

Ashley, Benedict M. *Aristotle's Sluggish Earth: The Problematics of 'De Caelo.'* River Forest, Ill.: Albertus Magnus Lyceum, 1958.

————. *Theologies of the Body: Humanist and Christian*. Braintree, Mass.: The Pope John Center, 1985.

Ashworth, E. J. *Language and Logic in the Post-Medieval Period*. Dordrecht and Boston: D. Reidel Publishing Company, 1974.

————. *The Tradition of Medieval Logic and Speculative Grammar*. Toronto: Pontifical Institute of Mediaeval Studies, 1978.

Atkinson, Clarissa W. *Mystic and Pilgrim: The Book and the World of Margery Kempe*. Ithaca, N.Y.: Cornell University Press, 1983.

Augustine, St. *De beata vita*. Translated by Francis E. Tourscher. Philadelphia: Peter Reilly, 1937.

————. *De ordine.* Translated by Robert P. Russell. New York: Cosmopolitan Science and Art Service Co., Inc., 1942.

————. *Letters.* Vols. 1-5. Translated by Sister Wilfred Parsons. New York: Fathers of the Church, 1951.

————. *Oeuvres.* Paris: Desclée, De Brouwer, 1936.

————. *The City of God.* Translated by Marcus Dods, D.D. New York: Modern Library, 1950.

————. *The City of God Against the Pagans.* 7 vols. Translated by Philip Levine. London: William Heinemann, 1966.

————. *The Soliloquies of St. Augustine.* Translated by Thomas F. Gilligan. New York: Cosmopolitan Science and Art Service, 1943.

Averroes. *On Plato's 'Republic.'* Translated by Ralph Lerner. Ithaca, N.Y.: Cornell University Press, 1974.

Avery, Catherine B., ed. *The New Century Italian Renaissance Encyclopedia.* New York: Appleton-Century-Crofts, 1972.

Avicenna. *A Treatise on the 'Canon of Medicine' of Avicenna, Incorporating a Translation of the First Book.* Translated by O. Cameron Gruner. New York: AMS Press, 1973.

Bacon, Roger. *Opera Hactenus Inedita Rogeri Baconi.* 16 vols. Edited by Robert Steele. Oxford: Clarendon Press, 1909-40.

————. *Opus Majus.* Frankfurt: Minerva Verlag, 1964.

————. *Three Treatments of Universals by Roger Bacon.* Translated by Thomas S. Maloney. Binghamton, N.Y.: Medieval, Renaissance Texts and Studies, vol. 66, 1989.

Balthasar, Hans Urs von. *The Glory of the Lord: A Theological Aesthetics.* Vol. 3. *Studies in Theological Style: Lay Styles.* Translated by Andrew Louth. San Francisco: Ignatius Press, 1986.

Barbaro, Francesco. *Directions for Love and Marriage.* Translated by James Wright. London: John Leigh, 1677.

Barberino, Francesco. *Del reggimento e costumi de donna.* Bologna: G. Romagnoli, 1875.

————. *Documenti d'amore.* Rome: Nella stamperia di Vitale Mascardi, 1640.

[Barbier]. *La defense des femmes contre l'alphabet de leur pretendu malice et imperfection.* Paris, 1617.

Baron, Hans. *The Crisis of the Early Italian Renaissance: Civic Humanism and Republican Liberty in an Age of Classicism and Tyranny.* Princeton: Princeton University Press, 1966.

————. *From Petrarch to Leonardo Bruni: Studies in Humanistic and Political Literature.* Chicago and London: University of Chicago Press, 1968.

Barstow, Anne Llewellyn. "Joan of Arc and Female Mysticism." *Journal of Feminist Studies in Religion* 1, no. 1 (Fall 1985): 29-42.

————. *Joan of Arc: Heretic, Mystic, Shaman.* Lewiston, N.Y.: Edwin Mellen Press, 1985.

————. *Witchcraze: A New History of the European Witch Hunts.* San Francisco: HarperCollins, 1994.

Beal, Rebecca S. "Beatrice in the Sun: A Vision from Apocalypse." *Dante Studies* 103 (1985): 57-78.

Beatrijs van Nazareth. *Seven Manieren Van Minne.* Edited by L. Reypens and J. Van Mierlo. Leven: S. V. de Vlaamsche Boekenhalle, 1926.

Beauvoir, Simone de. *The Second Sex.* Translated by H. M. Parshley. New York: Vintage, 1974.

Bembo, Pietro. *Gli asolani.* Translated by Rudolf Brand Gottfried. Bloomington: Indiana University Press, 1954.

Bennett, H. S. *Six Medieval Men and Women.* Cambridge: Cambridge University Press, 1955.

Bergin, Thomas B. *Boccaccio.* New York: Viking, 1981.

Bernard, Robert W. "A Mirror for Renaissance Education and Feminism — Marguerite de Navarre (1492-1549)." *Vitae Scholasticae* 2, no. 1 (Spring 1983): 19-32.

Bernardo, Aldo. *Petrarch, Laura, and The Triumphs.* Albany: State University of New York Press, 1974.

[Bernier]. *Apologie contre le livre intitulé "Alphabet de la méchanteté des femmes."* Paris, 1618.

Bhattacharya, Rajlukshee Debee. "Because He Is a Man." *Philosophy* 49, no. 187 (January 1974): 49.

Bird, Otto. "Cavalcanti, Guido. 'Canzone D'amore': Medieval Philosophic Thought as Reflected in the 'Canzone D'amore' of Cavalcanti According to the Commentary of Dino Del Garbo: Text and Commentary." Ph.D. Dissertation, University of Toronto, May 1, 1939.

Birgitta of Sweden. *Life and Selected Revelations.* Translated by Albert Ryle Kezel. Edited by Marguerite Jader Harris. New York: Paulist Press, 1990.

———. *The Revelations of Saint Birgitta.* Edited by William Patterson Cumming. London: Oxford University Press, 1929.

Bisaccia, Giuseppe. "Past/Present: Leonardo Bruni's *History of Florence.*" *Renaissance and Reformation* 9, no. 1 or old series, 21, no. 1 (1985): 1-18.

Blackwell, Elizabeth. *Learning for Ladies (1508-1895): A Book Exhibition at the Henry E. Huntington Library.* San Marion: Huntington Library, 1936.

Blade, Melinda K. *Education of Italian Renaissance Women.* Mesquite: Ide House, 1983.

Bloom, Harold, ed. *Dante: Modern Critical Views.* New York: Chelsea House Publishers, 1986.

Blumenfeld-Kosinski, Renate, and Timea Szell, eds. *Images of Sainthood in Medieval Europe.* Ithaca and London: Cornell University Press, 1991.

Boccaccio, Giovanni. *Amorous Fiametta.* Edited by Edward Hutton. Westport, Conn.: Greenwood Press, 1970.

———. *Boccaccio on Poetry: Being the Preface and the Fourteenth and Fifteenth Books of Boccaccio's "Genealogia Gentilium."* Translated and edited by Charles Grosvenor Osgood. Indianapolis and New York: Bobbs-Merrill, 1956.

———. *Concerning Famous Women.* Translated and edited by Guido Aldo. New Brunswick, N.J.: Rutgers University Press, 1963.

————. *Corbaccio.* Urbana: University of Illinois Press, 1975.

————. *Ecologues.* Translated by Janet Levaire Smarr. New York and London: Garland Publishing, 1987.

————. *The Book of Theseus (Teseida delle Nozze d'Emilia).* Translated by Bernadette Marie McCoy. New York: Medieval Text Association, 1974.

————. *The Decameron.* Translated by Mark Musa and Peter Bondanella. New York and Scarborough, Ontario: New American Library/Mentor, 1982.

————. *The Fates of Illustrious Men.* Translated and edited by Louis Brewer Hall. New York: Frederick Ungar Company, 1965.

————. *Thirteen Most Pleasant and Delectable Questions of Love (Filocolo).* Translated by Henry Carter. New York: Clarkson H. Potter, Inc., 1974.

————, and Leonardo Bruni. *The Earliest Lives of Dante.* Translated by Robinson Smith. New York: Frederick Ungar Publishing Co., 1963.

Boethius. *The Consolation of Philosophy.* Translated by Richard Green. Indianapolis: Bobbs-Merrill, 1962.

————. *The Consolation of Philosophy.* Translated by V. E. Watts. London: Penguin Books, 1969.

————. *The Theological Tractates.* Translated by H. F. Steward and E. K. Rand. Cambridge, Mass.: Harvard University Press, 1918.

Boguet, Henry. *An Examen of Witches: Drawn from Various Trials of Many of this Sect in the District of Saint Oyan De Joux Commonly Known as Saint Claude in the County of Burgundy Including the Procedure Necessary to Judge in Trials for Witchcraft.* Translated by E. Allen Ashwin. Edited by Montague Summers. London: John Rodker, 1929.

Borrensen, Kari Elisabeth. "God's Image, Man's Image? Female Metaphors Describing God in the Christian Tradition." *Temenos* 19 (1983): 17-32.

————. "Male-Female, a Critique of Traditional Christian Theology." *Temenos* 13 (1977): 31-42.

Bottomley, Frank. *Attitudes to the Body in Western Christendom.* London: Lepus Books, 1979.

Bouwsma, William J. *The Interpretation of Renaissance Humanism.* 2nd edition. Washington, D.C.: American Historical Association, 1966.

Boxer, Marilyn J., and Jean H. Quataert, eds. *Connecting Spheres: Women in the Western World, 1500 to the Present.* New York: Oxford University Press, 1987.

Boyd, Beverly. "Wyclif, Joan of Arc, and Margery Kempe." *Mystics Quarterly* 12, no. 3 (1986): 113-18.

Boyle, Marjerie O'Rourke. *Petrarch's Genius: Pentimento and Prophecy.* Berkeley, Los Angeles, Oxford: University of California Press, 1991.

Boyle, Patrick. *Perception and Passion in Dante's Comedy.* Cambridge: Cambridge University Press, 1993.

Brabant, Margaret, ed. *Politics, Gender and Genre: The Political Thought of Christine de Pizan.* Boulder, Colo.: Westview Press, 1992.

Bradley, Ritamary. *Julian's Way: A Practical Commentary on Julian of Norwich.* London: Harper Collins, 1992.

————. "Perception of Self in Julian of Norwich's *Showings.*" *The Downside Review* 104, no. 356 (July 1986): 227-39.

Branca, Vittore. *Boccaccio: The Man and His Works.* Translated by Richard Mongres. New York: New York University Press, 1976.

Bridenthal, Renate, and Claudia Koonz, eds. *Becoming Visible: Women in European History.* Boston: Houghton Mifflin, 1977.

Brown, D. Catherine. *Pastor and Laity in the Theology of Jean Gerson.* Cambridge: Cambridge University Press, 1982.

Browne, Sir Thomas. *The Complete Works of Sir Thomas Browne.* Chicago: University of Chicago Press, 1964.

Brownlee, Kevin. "Discourses of the Self: Christine de Pizan and the *Rose.*" *Romantic Review* 79, no. 1 (January 1988): 200-221.

————, and Walter Stephens, eds. *Discourses of Authority in Medieval and Renaissance Literature.* Hanover, N.H.: University Press of New England, 1989.

Buber, Martin. *I and Thou.* New York: Scribner's, 1970.

Bühler, Curt F. *Early Books and Manuscripts: Forty Years of Research.* New York: The Grolier Club — Pierpont Morgan Library, 1973.

Bullitt, John M. *Jonathan Swift and the Anatomy of Satire: A Study of Satiric Technique.* Cambridge, Mass.: Harvard University Press, 1953.

Burckhardt, Jacob. *The Civilisation of the Renaissance in Italy.* Translated by S. G. C. Middlemore. New York: The Macmillan Co., 1921. 2nd edition. Illustrated version. 2 vols. 1958.

Buss, Martin, ed. *Encounter with the Text.* Missoula, Mont.: Scholar's Press, 1979.

Butler, Judith. *Gender Trouble: Feminism and the Subversion of Identity.* New York: Routledge, 1989.

Bynum, Carolyn Walker. *Holy Feast and Holy Fast: The Religious Significance of Food to Medieval Women.* Berkeley and Los Angeles: University of California Press, 1987.

————. *Jesus as Mother: Studies in the Spirituality of the High Middle Ages.* Berkeley and Los Angeles: University of California Press, 1982.

————, Steven Harrell, and Paul Richman, eds. *Gender and Religion: On the Complexity of Symbols.* Boston: Beacon Press, 1986.

Cachey, Theodore J., Jr. *Dante Now: Current Trends in Dante Studies.* Notre Dame and London: University of Notre Dame Press, 1995.

Callahan, Annice, R.S.C.J., ed. *Spiritualities of the Heart: Approaches to Personal Wholeness in Christian Tradition.* New York and Mahwah, N.J.: Paulist Press, 1990.

Capellanus, Andreas. *The Art of Courtly Love.* New York: Frederick Ungar, 1957.

Capone, Cynthia Constance. "The Representation of Women in Boccaccio's *Decameron.*" Ph.D. Diss. Rutgers University, 1992.

Caporello-Szykman, Corradina. *The Boccaccian Novella: Creation and Waning of a Genre.* New York: Peter Lang, 1990.

Carney, Sheila. "Exemplarism in Hadewijch: The Quest for Full-Grownness." *Downside Review* 103, no. 353 (October 1985): 276-95.

Carroll, Berenice A., ed. *Liberating Women's History: Theoretical and Critical Essays.* Urbana: University of Illinois Press, 1976.

Carter, Robert E., ed. *God, the Self and Nothingness: Reflections Eastern and Western.* New York: Paragon House, 1990.

Casarella, Peter J. "Language and *Theologia Sermocinalis.* In Nicholas of Cusa's *Idiota de sapientia. Old and New in the Fifteenth Century. Acta* 17 (1991): 131-42

————."Nicholas of Cusa and the Power of the Possible." *American Catholic Philosophical Quarterly* 64, no. 1 (Winter 1990): 7-34.

Cassirer, Ernst, Paul Oskar Kristeller, and John Herman Randall, Jr., eds. *The Individual and the Cosmos in Renaissance Philosophy.* Translated by Mario Domandi. New York: Barnes and Noble, Inc., 1963.

————. *The Renaissance Philosophy of Man.* Chicago: University of Chicago Press, 1963.

Catechism of the Catholic Church. New York: Doubleday, 1995.

Catherine of Genoa, St. *Purgation and Purgatory: The Spiritual Dialogue.* Translated by Serge Hughes. New York: Paulist Press, 1979.

Catherine of Siena, St. *The Dialogue.* New York: Paulist Press, 1980.

————. *Saint Catherine of Siena as Seen in Her Letters.* Translated and edited by Vida D. Scudder. New York: E. P. Dutton, 1911.

Catholic Encyclopedia. New York: Robert Appleton Company, 1907.

Cereta, Laura. *Collected Letters of a Renaissance Feminist.* Transcribed, translated, and edited by Diana Robin. Chicago and London: University of Chicago Press, 1997.

Chambers, P. Franklin. *Juliana of Norwich: An Appreciation and Anthology.* London: Victor Gollancz, 1955.

Champion, Honoré, ed. *Procès de Condamnation de Jeanne D'Arc: Texte, traduction et notes.* Paris: E. Champion, 1921.

Chance, Jane, ed. *Gender and Text in the Later Middle Ages.* Gainesville, Fla.: University Press of Florida, 1996.

Chaucer, Geoffrey. *The Legend of Good Women.* Translated by Ann McMillan. Houston: Rice University Press, 1987.

————. *The Tales of the Clerk and the Wife of Bath.* Edited by Marion Wynne-Davies. London and New York: Routledge, 1992.

————. Translation of *Boethius "De Consolatione Philosophiae."* Early English Text Society. Edited by Richard Morris. London: Kegan Paul, Trench, Trubner and Co. Ltd., 1868.

Cherewatui, Karen, and Ulriche Wiethaus, eds. *Dear Sister: Medieval Women and the Epistolary Genre.* Philadelphia: University of Pennsylvania Press, 1993.

Chojnacki, Stanley. "Patrician Women in Venice." In *Studies in the Renaissance.* New York: The Renaissance Society of America, 1974.

Cholmeley, Katherine. *Margery Kempe: Genius and Mystic.* London: Catholic Book Club, 1948.

Clark, Andrew. *Register of the University of Oxford.* Oxford: Oxford University Press, 1887.

Clark, Elizabeth A. *Women in the Early Church: Message of the Fathers of the Church.* Wilmington, Del.: Michael Glazier, Inc., 1983.

Clarke, W. Norris. *Person and Being.* Milwaukee: Marquette University Press, 1993.

————. "Person, Being, and St. Thomas." *Communio* 19, no. 4 (Winter 1992): 601-18.

————. "Response to David Schindler's Comments." *Communio* 20 (Fall 1993): 593-98.

Coiner, Nancy. "The *homely* and the *heimliche:* The Hidden, Doubled Self in Julian of Norwich's *Showings.*" *Exemplaria* 5, no. 2 (Fall 1993): 305-23.

Colaneri, John. "Guido Cavalcanti and the *Canzone D'amore.*" Introduction to *Francesco de Vieri: Lezzioni d'Amore.* Munich: Wilhelm Fink Verlag. Humanistiche Bibliothek. Reihe 2. Texte, BD. 6., 1973.

Coleman, T. W. "The Lady Julian." In *English Mystics of the Fourteenth Century.* London: John Murray, 1906.

Collingwood, R. G. *The Idea of Nature.* New York: Oxford University Press, 1960.

Collins, Ardis B. *The Secular Is Sacred: Platonism and Thomism in Marsilio Ficino's Platonic Theology.* The Hague: Martinus Nijhoff, 1974.

Comiskey, Brendan, Bishop of Ferns. "A Story to Make Some of Us Blush." *The Irish Catholic,* Thursday, April 20, 1995.

Compayré, Gabriel. *Abelard and the Origin and Early History of Universities.* New York: Greenwood Press, 1969.

Congar, Yves. *I Believe in the Holy Spirit.* 3 vols. Translated by David Smith. New York: Crossroad, 1997.

Conner, Paul M. "Catherine of Siena and Raymond of Capua: Enduring Friends." *Studia Mystica* 12 (1989): 22-29.

Connolly, James. *Jean Gerson: Reformer and Mystic.* St. Louis, Mo.: B. Herder Book Co., 1928.

Copernicus, Nicholas. *On the Revolutions of the Heavenly Spheres.* Translated and edited by A. M. Duncan. New York: Barnes and Noble, 1976.

Costa, Gustavo. "Love and Witchcraft in Gianfrancesco Pico della Mirandola: *Le Strega* Between the Sublime and the Grotesque." *Italica* 67, no. 4 (Winter 1990): 427-39.

Courtney, Edward. *A Commentary on the Satires of Juvenal.* London: Athlone Press, 1980.

Cranz, F. Edward. *A Bibliography of Aristotle Editions: 1501-1600.* Baden-Baden: Verlag Valentin Koerner, 1984.

Craven, William G. *Giovanni Pico della Mirandola: Symbol of His Age, Modern Interpretations of a Renaissance Philosopher.* Geneva: Librairie Droz, 1981.

Crombie, Alistair Cameron. *Oxford's Contribution to the Origins of Modern Science.* Oxford: Basil Blackwell, 1954.

————. *Robert Grosseteste and the Origins of Experimental Science (1100-1700).* Oxford: Oxford University Press, 1953.

Crowe, S.J., Frederick E. "Complacency and Concern in the Thought of St. Thomas." *Theological Studies* 20 (March 1959): 1-39; (June 1959): 198-230; and (September 1959): 343-95.

Crysdale, Cynthia W. "Horizons That Differ: Women and Men and the Flight from Understanding." *Cross Currents* (Fall 1994): 345-61.

————, ed. *Lonergan and Feminism.* Toronto: University of Toronto Press, 1994.

Cumming, William Patterson, ed. *The Revelations of Saint Brigitta.* London: Oxford University Press, 1929.

Cusa, Nicholas of. *Nicholas of Cusa: Selected Spiritual Writings.* Translated by H. Lawrence Bond. New York and Mahwah, N.J.: Paulist Press, 1997.

———. *Toward a New Council of Florence: 'On the Peace of Faith' and Other Works by Nicolaus of Cusa.* Translated by William F. Wertz, Jr. Washington, D.C.: Schiller Institute, Inc., 1993.

———. *Unity and Reform: Selected Writings of Nicholas de Cusa.* Edited by John Patrick Dolan. South Bend, Ind.: University of Notre Dame Press, 1962.

Czarmach, Paul E., ed. *An Introduction to the Medieval Mystics of Europe.* Albany: State University of New York Press, 1984.

D'Amico, John F. *Renaissance Humanism in Papal Rome: Humanists and Churchmen on the Eve of the Reformation.* Baltimore and London: Johns Hopkins University Press, 1983.

Dante Alighieri. *Dante's Lyric Poetry.* Edited by K. Foster and P. Boyde. Oxford: Clarendon Press, 1967.

———. *"De vulgari eloquentia": Dante's Book of Exile.* Translated by Marianne Shapiro. Lincoln and London: University of Nebraska Press, 1990.

———. *La vita nuova: Poems of Youth.* Translated by Barbara Reynolds. Harmondsworth: Penguin Books, 1969.

———. *The Banquet.* Translated by Christopher Ryan. Stanford French and Italian Studies 61. Saratoga, Calif.: Anima Libri, 1989.

———. *The Divine Comedy. 1: Hell (L'inferno).* Translated by Dorothy L. Sayers. Harmondsworth: Penguin Books, 1983.

———. *The Divine Comedy. 2: Purgatory (Il Purgatorio).* Translated by Dorothy L. Sayers. Harmondsworth: Penguin Books, 1981.

———. *The Divine Comedy. 3: Paradise (Il Paradiso).* Translated by Dorothy L. Sayers and Barbara Reynolds. Harmondsworth: Penguin Books, 1982.

Davies, Jonathan. "Marsilio Ficino: Lecturer at the Studio Fiorentino." *Renaissance Quarterly* 45, no. 4 (Winter 1992): 785-90.

Davies, Paul. *God and the New Physics.* New York: Touchstone, 1983.

Debus, Allen G. *Chemistry, Alchemy and the New Philosophy: 1550-1700.* London: Variorum Reprints, 1985.

———. *The Chemical Philosophy: Paracelsian Science and Medicine in the Sixteenth and Seventeenth Centuries.* New York: Neale Watson Academic Publications, 1977.

De Ganck, Roger. *Towards Unification with God: Beatrice of Nazareth in Her Context, Part Three.* Kalamazoo, Mich.: Cistercian Publications, 1991.

Dejean, Joan, and Nancy K. Miller, eds. *Displacements: Women, Tradition, Literatures in French.* Baltimore and London: Johns Hopkins University Press, 1990.

Denomy, A. J., C.S.B. "The *De Amore* of Andreas Capellanus and the Condemnation of 1277." *Mediaeval Studies* 8 (1946): 107-49.

Derrida, Jacques. *Spurs: Nietzsche's Styles.* Translated by Barbara Harlow. Chicago: University of Chicago Press, 1979.

Descartes, René. *Oeuvres.* Paris: Librairie Philosophique, 1969.

Deschamps, Eustache. *Oeuvres complètes.* Paris: Firmin Didot, 1903.

Desmond, Marilyn, ed. *Christine de Pizan and the Categories of Difference.* Medieval

Cultures, vol. 14. Minneapolis and London: University of Minnesota Press, 1998.

Diamond, Irene, and Lee Quinby, eds. *Feminism and Foucault: Reflections on Resistance.* Boston: Northeastern University Press, 1988.

Di Bernardino, Angelo, and Basil Studer, eds. *History of Theology: I, The Patristic Period.* Collegeville, Minn.: Liturgical Press, 1997.

Dictionary of the Middle Ages. Edited by Joseph Reese Stayer. New York: Scribner's, 1984.

Di Scipio, Giuseppe C. "The Hebrew Women in Dante's Symbolic Rose." *Dante Studies* 101 (1983): 111-21.

Disputatio Perjucunda, qui Anonymus probare nititur Mulieres Homines non esse: Cui opposita est Simonis Gedicci, Defensio Sexus Muliebris, Qua singula Anonymi argumenta distinctis thesibus proposita viriliter enervantur. The Hague, 1541.

Dondaine, Antoine. *Secrétaires de saint Thomas.* Rome: S. Sabina, 1956.

Doran, Robert. *Theology and the Dialectics of History.* Toronto: University of Toronto Press, 1990.

Doughty, Mark. "This Side of the Looking-Glass: Space-Time: An Impossible Universe." *Canadian Catholic Review* (March 1986): 94-97.

———. "Time Transcended: Man the Communicator." *Canadian Catholic Review* (September 1985): 23-25.

Drake, Stillman. *Galileo.* New York: Hill and Wang, 1980.

———. *Galileo at Work: His Scientific Biography.* Chicago: University of Chicago Press, 1978.

Dresden, Sem. *Humanism in the Renaissance.* Verona: Officine Grafiche Arnoldo Mondadori, 1968.

Dronke, Peter. *Women Writers of the Middle Ages.* Cambridge: Cambridge University Press, 1984.

DuBruck, Edelgard E., ed. *New Images of Medieval Women: Essays Towards a Cultural Anthropology.* Lewiston, N.Y.: Edwin Mellen Press, 1989.

Duclow, Donald F. "Mystical Theology and Intellect in Nicholas of Cusa." *The American Catholic Philosophical Quarterly* 64, no. 1 (Winter 1990): 127-28.

Dufournaud-Engel, Monique. "Le miroir de mariage d'Eustache Deschamps: édition critique accompagnée d'une étude littéraire et linguistique." 2 vols. Ph.D. Diss. McGill University, 1975.

Dulac, L., and B. Ribémont, eds. *Une Femme de Lettres au Moyen Age, Études autour de Christine de Pizan.* Orléans: Paradigme, 1995.

Dulles, Avery. *Princeps Concordiae: Pico della Mirandola and the Scholastic Tradition.* Cambridge, Mass.: Harvard University Press, 1941.

Duns Scotus, John. *Duns Scotus on the Will and Morality.* Translated and edited by Allan B. Wolter, O.F.M. Washington, D.C.: Catholic University of America Press, 1986.

———. *God and Creatures: The Quodlibetal Questions.* Translated by Felix Alluntis, O.F.M. and Allan B. Wolter, O.F.M. Princeton: Princeton University Press, 1975.

———. *Opera omnia.* Paris: Apud Ludovicum Vives, 1893-97.

———. *Opera omnia.* Westmead, U.K.: Gregg International, 1969.

————. *Philosophical Writings*. Revised Latin-English edition. Indianapolis: Hackett Publishing Company, 1987.

————. *Summa theologica*. Edited by Girolamo de Montefortino. Rome: Ex Typographia Sallustiana, 1900-03.

Dupré, Louis. Introduction to *Nicholas of Cusa*. Special Issue. *American Catholic Philosophical Quarterly* 64, no. 1 (1990): 1-6.

————. *Passage to Modernity: An Essay in the Hermeneutics of Nature and Culture*. New Haven and London: Yale University Press, 1993.

Easton, Stewart C. *Roger Bacon and His Search for a Universal Science*. New York: Russell and Russell, 1952.

Ebner, Margaret. *Margaret Ebner: Major Works*. Translated by Leonard P. Hindsley. New York and Mahwah, N.J.: Paulist Press, 1993.

Eckhardt, Caroline D. "The Art of Translation in The Romaunt of the Rose." *Studies in the Age of Chaucer* 6 (1984): 41-63.

Eckhart, Meister. *Breakthrough: Meister Eckhart's Creation Spirituality in New Translation*. Translated by Matthew Fox. Garden City, N.Y.: Doubleday, 1978.

————. *Meister Eckhart: The Essential Sermons, Commentaries, Treatises, and Defense*. Edited by Edmund Colledge and Bernard McGinn. New York: Paulist Press, 1981.

Eckstein, Lina. *Women Under Monasticism: Chapters on Saint-Love and Convent Life Between A.D. 500 and A.D. 1500*. New York: Russell and Russell, 1963.

Edwards, Anthony, Katherine Gardiner Rodgers, and Clarence H. Miller, eds. *The Complete Works of St. Thomas More*. New Haven and London: Yale University Press, 1997.

Eggerz-Brownfield, Solveig. "Anti-Feminist Satire in German and English Literature of the Late Middle Ages." Ph.D. Diss. The Catholic University of America, 1981.

Eigo, Francis A., ed. *Dimensions of Contemporary Spirituality*. Villanova: University Press, 1982.

Eileen, Sister Mary. "The Place of Lady Julian of Norwich in English Literature." In *Julian of Norwich: Four Studies to Commemorate the Sixth Centenary of the Revelations of Divine Love*. Fairacres, Oxford: SLG Press, 1976.

————, ed. *Julian of Norwich: Four Studies to Commemorate the Sixth Centenary of the Revelations of Divine Love*. Fairacres, Oxford: SLG Press, 1976.

Eisenbichler, Konrad, and Olga Zorzi Pugliese, eds. *Ficino and Renaissance Neoplatonism*. Ottawa: Dovehouse Editions, 1986.

Eisenstein, Hester, and Alice Jardine, eds. *The Future of Difference*. Boston: G. K. Hall, 1980.

Elkin, P. K. *The Augustan Defence of Satire*. Oxford: Clarendon Press, 1973.

Elliott, Robert C. *The Power of Satire: Magic, Ritual, Art*. Princeton: Princeton University Press, 1960.

Elshtain, Jean Bethke. *Augustine and the Limits of Politics*. Notre Dame: University of Notre Dame Press, 1995.

————. "Christianity and Patriarchy: The Odd Alliance." *Modern Theology* 9, no. 2 (April 1993): 109-22.

————. "Feminist Discourse and Its Discontents: Language, Power, and Meaning." *Signs: Journal of Women in Culture and Society* 7, no. 31 (1982): 603-21.

————. *Politics and the Human Body.* Nashville: Vanderbilt University Press, 1995.

————. *Public Man, Private Woman: Women in Social and Political Thought.* Princeton: Princeton University Press, 1981.

————. *Women and War.* New York: Basic Books, 1987.

Encyclopaedia Britannica. 1945 Edition.

Enders, Jody. "Rhetoric and Dialectic in Guido Cavalcanti's 'Donna me prega.'" *Stanford Italian Review* 5, no. 2 (1985): 161-74.

Erigena, Johannes Scotus. *De Divisione Naturae.* Edited by I. P. Sheldon-Williams. Dublin: The Dublin Institute for Advanced Studies, 1972.

————. *Periphyseon (On the Division of Nature).* Translated by Myra L. Uhlfelder. Indianapolis: Bobbs-Merrill, 1976.

L'Excellence des femmes, avec leur réponse à l'auteur de l'Alphabet, accompagné d'un doite et subtil discours de la Reyne Marguerite sur le même sujet à l'auteur des "Secrets Moraux." Paris, 1618.

Eyb, Albrecht von. *Das Ehebüchlein: Ob einem manne sey zunemen ein eelichs weyb oder nicht.* Deutsche Schriften. Vol 1. Edited by Max Herrman. Berlin: Weidmann, 1890.

Fabricius of Aquapendente. *The Embryological Treatises of Hieronymus Fabricius of Aquapendente.* Edited by Howard B. Adelman. Ithaca, N.Y.: Cornell University Press, 1942.

Fahy, Conor. "Three Early Renaissance Treatises on Women." *Italian Studies* 11 (1956): 30-55.

Fallico, Arturo B., and Herman Shapiro, eds. *The Italian Philosophers: Selected Readings from Petrarch to Bruno, Renaissance Philosophy.* New York: Modern Library, 1967.

Fedele, Cassandra. *Humanist Letters and Public Orations.* Translated and edited by Diana Robin. Chicago: University of Chicago Press, 2000.

Ferguson, Margaret W., Maureen Quilligan, and Nancy J. Vickers., eds. *Rewriting the Renaissance: The Discourses of Sexual Difference in Early Modern Europe.* Chicago and London: University of Chicago Press, 1986.

Ferrante, Joan M. *Woman as Image in Medieval Literature from the Twelfth Century to Dante.* Durham, N.C.: Labyrinth Press, 1985.

Festugière, André Marie. *La Révélation d'Hermès Trimégiste.* Paris: Librairie Lecoffre, 1950.

Ficino, Marsilio. *The Book of Life.* Translated by Charles Boer. Woodstock, Conn.: Spring Publications, 1996.

————. *Marsilio Ficino's Commentary on Plato's Symposium.* Translated by Sears Reynolds Jayne, M.A. Columbia, Mo.: University of Missouri, 1944.

————. *Commentary on Plato's Symposium on Love.* Translated by Sears Jayne. Dallas: Spring Publications, Inc., 1985.

————. *The Letters of Marsilio Ficino.* Vols. 1-4. London: Shepherd-Walwyn, 1975-1988.

————. *Three Books on Life.* A critical edition and translation by Carol V. Kaske and John R. Clark. Binghamton, N.Y.: The Renaissance Society of America, 1989.

Fiero, Gloria J., Wendy Pfeffer, and Allain Marthétrans, eds. *Three Medieval Views of Women: La Contenance des Fames, Le Bien des Fames, Le Blasme des Fames.* New Haven and London: Yale University Press, 1989.

Finke, Laurie A., and Martin B. Shichtman, eds. *Medieval Texts and Contemporary Readers.* Ithaca and London: Cornell University Press, 1987.

Finnegan, O.P., Mary Jeremy. *The Women of Helfta: Scholars and Mystics.* Athens, Ga. and London: University of Georgia Press, 1991.

Fiorini, Pierluigi. "Beatrice, That is, 'On Fidelity'." *Communio: International Catholic Review* 24, no. 1 (Spring 1997): 84-98.

Flax, Jane. "Postmodernism and Gender Relations in Feminist Theory." *Signs: Journal of Women in Culture and Society* 12, no. 4 (1987): 621-43.

Fleming, John V. "Jean de Meun's Reason and Boethius." *Romance Notes* 16 (1975): 678-85.

———. *Reason and the Lover.* Princeton: Princeton University Press, 1984.

Flynn, Elizabeth A., and Patrocinio P. Schweickart, eds. *Gender and Reading: Essays on Readers, Texts, and Contexts.* Baltimore and London: Johns Hopkins University Press, 1986.

Foucault, Michel. *The Archaeology of Knowledge.* London: Tavistock, 1972.

———. *The History of Sexuality: The Use of Pleasure.* New York: Vintage Books, 1986.

Fraioli, Deborah A. *Joan of Arc: The Early Debate.* Woodbridge: The Boydell Press, 2000.

Frank, Robert G. *Harvey and the Oxford Physiologists.* Berkeley and Los Angeles: University of California Press, 1980.

———. "Science, Medicine, and the Universities of Early Modern England: Background and Sources, Part 1." *History of Science* 11 (September 1973): 3-13.

Franklin, James C. *Mystical Transformations: The Imagery of Liquids in the Work of Mechthild von Magdeburg.* Rutherford, N.J.: Fairleigh Dickinson University Press, 1978.

Friedman, Lionel J. "'Jean de Meung,' Antifeminism, and 'Bourgeois Realism'." *Modern Philology* 57 (1959/1960): 13-23.

Fuller, Buckminster. *Critical Path.* New York: St. Martin's Press, 1981.

———. *Synergetics: Explorations in the Geometry of Thinking.* 2 vols. New York: Macmillan, 1982.

Fulton, John, ed. *The Four Hundredth Anniversary Celebration of the De Humani Corporis Fabrica of Andreas Vesalius.* New Haven: Yale University School of Medicine, 1943.

Gabriel, Astrid L. "The Educational Ideas of Christine de Pisan." *Journal of the History of Ideas* 16, no. 1 (1955): 3-21.

———. *The Educational Ideas of Vincent of Beauvais.* Notre Dame: University of Notre Dame Press, 1962.

Gadol, Joan Kelly. *Leon Battista Alberti: Universal Man of the Early Renaissance.* Chicago: University of Chicago Press, 1969.

Galilei, Galileo. *Dialogue Concerning the Two Chief World Systems — Ptolemaic and Copernican*. Berkeley and Los Angeles: University of California Press, 1962.

———. *Dialogues Concerning Two New Sciences*. Translated by Henry Crew and Alfonso de Salvio. New York: Dover Publications, 1954.

———. *Galileo's Early Notebooks: The Physical Questions*. Translated by William A. Wallace. Notre Dame: University of Notre Dame Press, 1977.

Gardner, Edmund G. *Dante and the Mystics*. New York: E. P. Dutton, 1913.

———. "Juliana of Norwich." In *The Catholic Encyclopedia*. New York: Encyclopedia Press, 1913.

Gardner, Judith E. "Women in the Book Trade, 1641-1700: A Preliminary Survey." In *Gutenberg-Jahrbuch*. Mainz: Gutenberg-Gesellschaft, 1978.

Garin, Eugenio. *L'educazione in Europa 1400/1600: Problemi e programmi*. Bari: Editori Laterza, 1966.

———. *Educazione umanistica in Italia*. Bari: Editori Laterza, 1967.

———. *Italian Humanism: Philosophy and the Civic Life in the Renaissance*. Translated by Peter Munz. New York: Harper and Row, 1965.

Gersh, Stephen. *Middle Platonism and Neo Platonism: The Latin Tradition*. Notre Dame: University of Notre Dame Press, 1986.

Gertrude the Great, St. *Oeuvres spirituelles: Le hérault*. Paris: Editions du Cerf, 1968.

———. *Spiritual Exercises*. Translated by Gertrud Jaron Lewis and Jack Lewis. Kalamazoo, Mich.: Cistercian Publications, 1989.

———. *The Exercises of Saint Gertrude*. Translated by a Benedictine Nun of Regina Laudis. Westminster, Md.: Newman Press, 1956.

———. *The Herald of Divine Love*. Translated by Margaret Winkworth. New York and Mahwah, N.J.: Paulist Press, 1993.

Gerulaitis, Leonardas Vytautas. *Printing and Publishing in Fifteenth-Century Venice*. Chicago: American Library Association, 1976.

Gibson, Strickland, ed. *Statuta Antiqua Universitatis Oxoniensis*. Oxford: Clarendon Press, 1931.

Giles of Rome. *LI Livres du Gouvernment des Rois: A XIIth Century French Version of Egidio Colonna's Treatise 'De Regimine Principium.'* Translated and edited by Samuel Paul Molenaer. New York: AMS Press, 1966.

Gilson, Etienne. *Elements of Christian Philosophy*. Garden City, N.Y.: Doubleday, 1960.

———. *History of Christian Philosophy in the Middle Ages*. New York: Random House, 1955.

———, ed. *St. Thomas Aquinas: Commemorative Studies (1274-1974)*. Toronto: Pontifical Institute of Mediaeval Studies, 1974.

Goddu, André. *The Physics of William of Ockham*. Leiden/Köln: E. J. Brill, 1984.

Goldschmidt, Ernest Philip. *Medieval Texts and Their First Appearance in Print*. London and Oxford: University Press, 1943.

Gournay, Marie de. *Égalité des hommes et des femmes*. Edited by Mario Schiff. Paris: Librairie Honoré Champion, 1910.

———. *La Fille d'Alliance de Montaigne: Marie de Gournay*. Paris: Librairie Honoré Champion, 1910.

Govier, Trudy. "Getting Rid of the Big Bad Wolf." *Philosophy* 56 (1981): 258-61.

————."Woman's Place." *Philosophy* 49 (1974): 303-9.

Grafton, Anthony, and Lisa Jardine. *From Humanism to the Humanities: Education and the Liberal Arts in Fifteenth- and Sixteenth-Century Europe.* Cambridge, Mass.: Harvard University Press, 1986.

Grassi, Ernesto. *Heidegger and the Question of Renaissance Humanism: Four Studies.* Binghamton, N.Y.: Medieval and Renaissance Texts and Studies, 1983.

Grayson, Cecil. "The Humanism of Alberti." *Italian Studies* 12 (1957): 37-56.

Green, Judith M. "Aristotle on Necessary Verticality, Body Heat, and Gendered Proper Places in the Polis: A Feminist Critique." *Hypatia* 7, no. 1 (Winter 1992): 70-96.

Gregory of Nyssa, St. *A Letter from Gregory, Bishop of Nyssa, On the Life of Macrina.* In *Handmaids of the Lord: Contemporary Descriptions of Feminine Asceticism in the First Six Christian Centuries,* pp. 51-86. Kalamazoo, Mich.: Cistercian Publications (#143), 1996.

————. *The Life of Saint Macrina.* Translated, with introduction and notes by Kevin Corrigan. Toronto: Peregrina Publishing Co., 1998.

————. *On the Soul and the Resurrection.* In *A Select Library of Nicene and Post-Nicene Fathers of the Christian Church.* Vol. 5: *Gregory of Nyssa,* pp. 430-68. Grand Rapids: Eerdmans, 1979.

Gregson, Vernon, ed. *The Desires of the Human Heart: An Introduction to the Theology of Bernard Lonergan.* New York: Paulist Press, 1988.

Griffin, Susan. *Woman and Nature: The Roaring Inside Her.* New York: Harper Colophon Books, 1980.

Griffiths, Gordon, James Hankins, and David Thompson, eds. *The Humanism of Leonardo Bruni: Selected Texts.* Binghamton, N.Y.: Medieval and Renaissance Texts and Studies, 1987.

Grosseteste, Robert. *Hexaemeron.* Edited by Richard C. Dales and Cervus Gieben. London: Oxford University Press, 1982.

————. "Woman's Place." *Philosophy* 49 (1974): 303-9.

Guerlac, Henry. "Copernicus' and Aristotle's Cosmos." *Journal of the History of Ideas* 29 (January-March 1968): 109-13.

Gunn, Alan M. F. *The Mirror of Love: A Reinterpretation of 'The Romance of the Rose.'* Lubbock, Tex.: Texas Tech Press, 1952.

————. "Teacher and Student in the Roman de la rose: A Study in Archetypal Figures and Patterns." *L'Esprit créateur* 2 (1962): 126-34.

Haack, Susan. "On the Moral Relevance of Sex." *Philosophy* 49 (1974): 90-95.

Hadewijch. *The Complete Works of Hadewijch.* Translated and edited by Mother Colomba Hart, O.S.B. New York: Paulist Press, 1980.

Hadzits, George Depue. *Lucretius and His Influence.* New York: Longmans Green, 1935.

Hainsworth, Peter. *Petrarch the Poet: An Introduction to the 'Rerum vulgarium fragmenta.'* London and New York: Routledge, 1988.

Hall, Joseph. *The Collected Poems of Joseph Hall: Bishop of Exeter and Norwich.* Liverpool: Liverpool University Press, 1949.

————. *The Discovery of a New World*. Cambridge, Mass.: Harvard University Press, 1937.

Hankins, James. *Plato in the Italian Renaissance*. 2 vols. Leiden/New York: E. J. Brill, 1990.

————, John Monfasini, and Frederick Purnell, Jr., eds. *Supplementum Festivum: Studies in Honor of Paul Oskar Kristeller*. Binghamton, N.Y.: Medieval and Renaissance Texts and Studies, 1987.

Hanley, M. Esther, ed. *Renaissance Philosophy: New Translations*. Translated by Leonard A. Kennedy. The Hague/Paris: Mouton and Co., 1973.

Hartel, Joseph Francis. *Femina Ut Imago Dei: In the Integral Feminism of St. Thomas Aquinas*. Rome: Edition Gregorian Pontifical University, 1993.

Hastings, Robert. *Nature and Reason in the Decameron*. Manchester: Manchester University Press, 1975.

Hawking, Stephen. *A Brief History of Time*. New York: Bantam, 1988.

Haywood, Eric, and Barry Jones, eds. *Dante Comparisons: Comparative Studies of Dante and Montle, Foscolo, Tasso, Chaucer, Petrarch, Propertius and Catullus*. Dublin: Irish Academic Press, 1985.

Hecker, Isaac, ed. *Life and Doctrine of Saint Catherine of Genoa*. New York: Catholic Publication Society, 1874.

Heffner, Blake R. "Meister Eckhart and a Millennium with Mary and Martha." *Lutheran Quarterly* 5, no. 2 (Summer 1991): 171-85.

Heinrichs, Katherine. "Lovers' Consolations of Philosophy in Boccaccio, Machaut, and Chaucer." *Studies in the Age of Chaucer* 11 (1989): 93-115.

Hermann, Max. *Albrecht von Eyb und die Frühzeit des Deutschen Humanismus*. Berlin: Weidmannsche, 1893.

Herrad of Hohenbourg. *Hortus Deliciarum: Reconstruction*. Edited by Rosalie Green et al. London: The Warburg Institute and Leiden: E. J. Brill, 1979.

————. *Hortus Deliciarum: Commentary*. Translated and edited by Rosalie Green et al. New Rochelle, N.Y.: Caratzas Brothers Publishers, 1971.

Hesiod. *Theogony*. Translated by Norman Oliver Brown. Indianapolis: Bobbs-Merrill, 1953.

Hester, Marianne. *Lewd Women and Wicked Witches*. London and New York: Routledge, 1992.

Hewson, M. Anthony. *Giles of Rome and the Medieval Theory of Conception: A Study of the De Formatione Corporis Humani in Utero*. London: Athlone Press, 1975.

Highet, Gilbert. *The Anatomy of Satire*. Princeton: Princeton University Press, 1962.

————. *Juvenal the Satirist*. Oxford: Clarendon Press, 1960.

Highmore, Nathaniel. *The History of Generation*. London: John Martin, 1651.

Hildegard of Bingen. *Book of Divine Works with Letters and Songs*. Edited by Matthew Fox. Santa Fe, Calif.: Bear and Company, 1987.

————. *Causae et Curae. Patrologia cursus completus, series latina (1841-1864)*. Vol. 197. Edited by J. P. Migne. Santa Fe, Calif.: Bear and Company, 1987.

————. *Heilkunde: Das Buch von den Grund und Wesen und der Heilung der Krankheiten (Causae et Curae)*. Salzburg: O. Muller Verlag, 1972.

————. *Scivias.* Translated by Bruce Hozeski. Santa Fe, Calif.: Bear and Company, 1987.

————. *Scivias.* Translated by Mother Columba Hart and Jane Bishop. New York: Paulist Press, 1990.

Hill, Jillian M. L. *The Medieval Debate on Jean de Meung's 'Roman de la Rose': Morality Versus Art. Studies in Medieval Literature* 4. Lewiston, N.Y.: Edwin Mellen Press, 1991.

Hiller, Joseph Anthony. "Albrecht von Eyb: Medieval Moralist." Ph.D. Diss. The Catholic University of America, Washington, D.C., 1939. Carthagena, Ohio: Messenger Press, 1939.

Hinnebusch, William A., O.P. *The History of the Dominican Order, Intellectual and Cultural Life to 1500.* New York: Alba House, 1973.

Hirsh, John. "Author and Scribe in The Book of Margery Kempe." *Medium Aevum* 44 (1975): 145-50.

Hocedez, E. "La condamnation de Gilles de Rome." *Recherches de Théologie Ancienne et Médiévale* 4 (1932): 34-58.

Hollander, Robert. *Boccaccio's Two Venuses.* New York: Columbia University Press, 1997.

Holloway, Julia Bolton, Joan Bechtold, and Constance S. Wright, eds. *Equally in God's Image: Women in the Middle Ages.* New York: Peter Lang, 1990.

Howard, Lloyd. "Dino's Interpretation of Donna me prega and Cavalcanti's Canzoniere." *Canadian Journal of Italian Studies* 6, nos. 24-25 (1983): 167-82.

————. "Virgil's Discourse on Love in Purgatorio XVIII and Guido Cavalcanti." *Quaderni d'italianistica* 6, no. 2 (1985): 167-77.

Howell, Samuel. *Logic and Rhetoric in England, 1500-1700.* Princeton: Princeton University Press, 1956.

Huebner, Wayne. "Convention and Innovation in the Satirical Treatment of Women by the Major Satirists of the Early Eighteenth Century." Ph.D. Diss. University of Minnesota, 1964.

Hügel, Friedrich von. *The Mystical Element of Religion as Studied in Saint Catherine of Genoa and Her Friends.* London: James Clarke and James Dent, 1961.

Hult, David F. *Self-fulfilling Prophecies: Readership and Authority in the First 'Roman de la Rose.'* Cambridge: Cambridge University Press, 1986.

Hunt, Felicity. "The London Trade in the Printing and Binding of Books: An Experience in Exclusion, Dilution, and De-Skilling for Women Workers." *Women's Studies International Forum* 6, no. 5 (1983).

Huot, Sylvia. *The 'Romance of the Rose' and Its Medieval Readers: Interpretation, Reception, and Manuscript Transmission.* Cambridge: Cambridge University Press, 1993.

————. "Seduction and Sublimation: Christine de Pizan, Jean de Meun, and Dante." *Romance Notes* 25, no. 3 (Spring, 1985): 361-73.

Hyatte, Reginald. "A Poetics of Ficino's 'Socratic Love': Medieval Discursive Models of Amor in Marsilio Ficino's and Lorenzo de Medici's Amatory Epistles." *Fifteenth-Century Studies* 20 (1993): 99-117.

Hyma, Albert. *The Brethren of the Common Life.* Grand Rapids: Eerdmans, 1950.

Inge, William. "Julian of Norwich." In *English Mystics of the Fourteenth Century.* Edited by T. W. Coleman. London: John Murray, 1906.

Iovino, Angela Maria. "The Decameron and the Corbaccio: Boccaccio's Image of Women and Spiritual Crisis." Ph.D. Diss. Indiana University, 1983.

Irenaeus, St. *Proof of the Apostolic Preaching.* Translated by Joseph P. Smith, S.J. Westminster, Md.: Newman Press, 1952.

————.*The Scandal of the Incarnation: Irenaeus Against the Heresies.* Translated by John Saward. Edited by Hans Urs von Balthasar. San Francisco: Ignatius Press, 1990.

Jacoff, Rachel. "The Tears of Beatrice: Inferno II." *Dante Studies* 100 (1982): 1-12.

————, ed. *The Cambridge Companion to Dante.* Cambridge: Cambridge University Press, 1993.

Jaggar, Alison. "On Sex Equality." *Ethics* 84 (1974): 275-91.

James, Montague Rhodes. *Anecdota Oxoniensia: Texts, Documents, and Extracts Chiefly from Manuscripts in the Bodleian and Other Oxford Libraries, Medieval and Modern Series. Part IV, Walter Map, De Nugis Curialium.* Oxford: Clarendon Press, 1914.

James I. *Demonology.* 1597.

Jantzen, Grace M. *Julian of Norwich: Mystic and Theologian.* New York: Paulist Press, 1988.

Jardine, Lisa. "'O Decus Italiae Virgo', or The Myth of the Learned Lady in the Renaissance." *The Historical Journal* 28, no. 4 (1985): 777-818.

[Jenson, Nicolas, pub.]. *Decor puellarum: Questa sie una opera la quale si chiama Decor puellarum: zoe honore de le donzelle: la quale da regola forma e modo al stato de le honeste donzelle.* Venice, 1461 [i.e., 1471].

Jeremiah, Sister Mary. "Catherinian Imagery of Consecration." *Communio* 17 (Fall 1990): 362-74.

Jerome, St. *Selected Letters of Saint Jerome.* Cambridge, Mass.: Harvard University Press, 1954.

John of Salisbury. *The Statesman's Book of John of Salisbury (Being the Fourth, Fifth, and Sixth Books, and Selections from the Seventh and Eighth Books of the Policraticus).* Translated by John Dickinson. New York: Russell and Russell, 1963.

John Paul II, Pope. *Evangelium Vitae.* Boston: Pauline Books and Media, 1995.

————. *Fides et ratio* (Boston: Pauline Books, 1998).

————. *The Genius of Woman.* Washington, D.C.: United States Catholic Conference, 1997.

————. *Mulieris Dignitatem. On the Dignity and Vocation of Woman.* Boston: St. Paul Editions, 1988.

————. *Original Unity of Man and Woman: Catechesis on the Book of Genesis.* Boston: St. Paul Editions, 1981.

————. *Vita Consecrata.* Boston: Pauline Books and Media, 1996.

Johnson, Anne E. "Before the Renaissance, a Renaissance Woman." *The New York Times* (Sunday, September 29, 1997): pp. 27 and 34.

Johnson, Francis R. *Astronomical Thought in Renaissance England: A Study of the*

English Scientific Writings from 1500 to 1645. New York: Octagon Books, 1968.

Johnson, Penelope D. *Equal in Monastic Profession: Religious Women in Medieval France.* Chicago and London: University of Chicago Press, 1991.

Jones, Cheslyn, et al. *The Study of Spirituality.* New York and Oxford: Oxford University Press, 1986.

Jones, Frank. "Equality of Men and Women by Marie de Gournay." *The French-American Review* 2, no. 3 (1978): 121-28.

Jordan, Constance. *Pulci's 'Morgante': Poetry and History in Fifteenth-Century Florence.* Washington, D.C.: Folger Books, 1986.

————. *Renaissance Feminism: Literary Texts and Political Models.* Ithaca and London: Cornell University Press, 1990.

Jorgensen, Johannes. *Saint Bridget of Sweden.* Translated by Ingeborg Lund. London: Longmans Green, 1954.

Julian of Norwich. *Showings.* Edited by Edmund Colledge and James Walsh. New York: Paulist Press, 1978.

Juvenal. *The Satires of Juvenal.* Bloomington: Indiana University Press, 1958.

Kant, Immanuel. *Critique of Pure Reason.* Translated by Norman Kemp Smith. London: Macmillan, 1963.

Keating, L. Clark. *Studies on the Literary Salon in France (1500-1615).* Cambridge, Mass.: Harvard University Press, 1941.

Keidel, George C. *Les Evangiles aux Femmes: An Old-French Satire on Women.* Baltimore: Friedenwald, 1895.

Kelley, David. *The Art of Reasoning.* New York: W. W. Norton, 1988.

Kelly, J. N. D. *Early Christian Doctrines.* San Francisco: Harper and Row, 1978.

Kelso, Ruth. *Doctrine for the Lady of the Renaissance.* Urbana: University of Illinois Press, 1956.

Kemp-Welch, Alice. *Of Six Mediæval Women.* London: Macmillan and Co., 1913.

Kempe, Margery. *The Book of Margery Kempe: The Autobiography of the Madwoman of God.* Translated by Tony D. Triggs. Liguori, Mo.: Triumph Books, 1995.

————. *The Book of Margery Kempe.* Edited by Sanford Brown Meech and Hope Emily Allen. London: Oxford University Press, 1940.

————. *The Book of Margery Kempe: A Modern Version by W. Butler-Bowdon.* London: Jonathan Cape, 1936.

Kendrick, Laura. "Transgression, Contamination, and Woman in Eustache Deschamps's Miroir de mariage." *Stanford French Review* 14, no. 102 (Spring-Fall 1990): 211-30.

Kennedy, Angus J. *Christine de Pizan: A Bibliographical Guide, Supplement I.* London: Grant and Cutler Ltd., 1994.

Kennedy, Leonard A., ed. *Renaissance Philosophy: New Translations.* Translated by M. Esther Hanley. The Hague/Paris: Mouton and Co., 1973.

Kepler, Johannes. *Kepler's Somnium: The Dream, or Posthumous Work on Lunar Astronomy.* Translated by Edward Rosen. Madison: University of Wisconsin Press, 1967.

————. *Mysterium Cosmographicum: The Secret of the Universe*. New York: Abaris Books, 1981.

King, Margaret L. "Caldiera and the Barbaros on Marriage and the Family: Humanist Reflections of Venetian Realities." *The Journal of Medieval and Renaissance Studies* 6, no. 1 (Spring 1976): 19-50.

————. "The Religious Retreat of Isotta Nogarola (1418-1466): Sexism and Its Consequences in the Fifteenth Century." *Signs: Journal of Women in Culture and Society* 3, no. 4 (1978): 807-22.

————. "Thwarted Ambitions: Six Learned Women of the Italian Renaissance." *Soundings: An Interdisciplinary Journal* 59, no. 3 (Fall 1976): 280-304.

————. *Venetian Humanism in an Age of Patrician Dominance*. Princeton: Princeton University Press, 1986.

————. *Women of the Renaissance*. Chicago and London: University of Chicago Press, 1991.

————, and Albert Rabil, Jr., eds. *Her Immaculate Hand: Selected Works By and About the Women Humanists*. Binghamton, N.Y.: Medieval and Renaissance Texts and Studies, 1983.

King, Ursula, ed. *Religion and Gender*. Oxford: Blackwell, 1995.

King-Farlow, John, and William R. Shea, eds. *Values and the Quality of Life*. New York: Science History Publications, 1976.

Kirkham, Victoria. "A Canon of Women in Dante's Commedia." in *Women's Voices in Italian Literature*. Edited by Rebecca West and Dino S. Cervigni. *Annali D'Italianistica* 7 (1989): 16-41.

Klaits, Joseph. *Servants of Satan: The Age of Witch Hunts*. Bloomington: Indiana University Press, 1985.

Klassen, John. "Women and Religious Reform in Late Medieval Bohemia." *Renaissance and Reformation* 8, no. 4 (1981): 203-21.

Klibansky, Raymond. *The Continuity of the Platonic Tradition During the Middle Ages*. London: The Warburg Institute, 1939.

————, Erwin Panofsky, and Fritz Saxl. *Saturn and Melancholy: Studies in the History of Natural Philosophy, Religion, and Art*. London: Thomas Nelson and Sons, Ltd., 1964.

Koenig, Elisabeth K. J. "Julian of Norwich, Mary Magdalene, and the Drama of Prayer." *Horizons* 20, no. 1 (1993): 23-43.

Koestler, Arthur. *The Sleepwalkers*. New York: Macmillan, 1968.

————. *The Watershed: A Biography of Johannes Kepler*. Garden City, N.Y.: Anchor Books, 1960.

Kohl, Benjamin G. *Renaissance Humanism, 1300-1550: A Bibliography of Materials in English*. New York and London: Garland Publishing, 1985.

————, et al., eds. *The Earthly Republic: Italian Humanists on Government and Society*. Philadelphia: University of Pennsylvania Press, 1978.

Koyré, Alexandre. *The Astronomical Revolution: Copernicus-Kepler-Borelli*. Translated by R. E. W. Maddison. Ithaca, N.Y.: Cornell University Press, 1973.

Kramer, Heinrich, and James Sprenger. *The Malleus maleficarum*. Translated by Montague Summers. New York: Dover Publications, 1971.

Krapiec, M. A. *Metaphysics: An Outline of the History of Being*. New York: Peter Lang, 1991.

Kristeller, Paul Oskar. *The Classics and Renaissance Thought*. Cambridge, Mass.: Harvard University Press, 1955.

————. *Eight Philosophers of the Italian Renaissance*. Stanford, Calif.: Stanford University Press, 1964.

————. *Marsilio Ficino and His Work After Five Hundred Years*. Florence: Leo S. Olschki, 1987.

————. *The Philosophy of Marsilio Ficino*. Gloucester, Mass.: Peter Smith, 1964; originally published New York: Columbia University Press, 1943.

————. *Renaissance Concepts of Man and Other Essays*. New York: Harper and Row, 1972.

————. *Renaissance Thought and Its Sources*. Edited by Michael Mooney. New York: Columbia University Press, 1979.

————. *Renaissance Thought: The Classic, Scholastic, and Humanist Strains*. New York: Harper and Row, 1961.

————. *Renaissance Thought II: Papers on Humanism and the Arts*. New York: Harper Torchbooks, 1965.

———— and Philip P. Wiener, eds. *Renaissance Essays*. New York and Evanston: Harper Torchbooks, 1968.

Kristeva, Julia. "Women's Time." *Signs: Journal of Women in Culture and Society* 7, no. 1 (1981): 13-35.

Krupnick, Mark, ed. *Displacement: Derrida and After*. Bloomington: Indiana University Press, 1983.

Kuhn, Thomas S. *The Copernican Revolution: Planetary Astronomy in the Development of Western Thought*. New York: Random House, 1959.

Kuntz, Marion Leathers, and Paul Grimley Kuntz, eds. *Jacob's Ladder and the Tree of Life: Concepts of Hierarchy and the Great Chain of Being*. New York: Peter Lang, 1987.

Labalme, Patricia H. *Beyond Their Sex: Learned Women of the European Past*. New York and London: New York University Press, 1980.

Langland, William. *Piers Plowman: A New Translation of the B-Text*. Edited by A. V. C. Schmidt. Oxford: Oxford University Press, 1992.

Larner, Christina. *Enemies of God: The Witch-Hunt in Scotland*. London: Chatto and Windus, 1981.

————. *Witchcraft and Religion: The Politics of Popular Belief*. Oxford: Basil Blackwell, 1984.

[La Sale, Antoine de]. *The Fifteen Joys of Marriage*. Translated by Elizabeth Abbott. New York: Orion Press, 1959.

Lea, Henry. *A History of the Inquisition in the Middle Ages*. New York: Russell and Russell, 1958.

Leclerq, Jean, O.S.B. "Liturgy and Mental Prayer in the Life of St. Gertrude." *Sponsa Regis* 31 (1960).

Leff, Gordon. *Paris and Oxford Universities in the Thirteenth and Fourteenth Centuries: An Institutional and Intellectual History*. New York: John Wiley and Sons, 1968.

————. *William of Ockham: The Metamorphosis of Scholastic Discourse.* Manchester: Manchester University Press, 1975.

Leigh, Gertrude. *The Passing of Beatrice: A Study in the Heterodoxy of Dante.* London: Faber and Faber, 1932.

Leo XIII, Pope. "Aeterni Patris: Encyclical Letter on the Restoration of Christian Philosophy." In *One Hundred Years of Thomism: Aeterni Patris and Afterwards, A Symposium.* Edited by Victor B. Brezik, C.S.B. Houston: Center for Thomistic Studies, 1981.

Leonardo da Vinci. *Leonardo da Vinci on the Human Body.* Translated by Charles D. O'Malley and J. B. Saunders. New York: Henry Schuman, 1952.

Levin, Carole, and Jeanie Watson, eds. *Ambiguous Realities: Women in the Middle Ages and Renaissance.* Detroit: Wayne State University Press, 1987.

Lewis, Gertrud Jaron. *By Women, for Women, about Women: The Sister-Books of Fourteenth-Century Germany.* Toronto: Pontifical Institute of Mediaeval Studies, 1996.

Lincoln, Victoria. *Teresa: A Woman.* Albany: State University of New York Press, 1984.

Listerman, R. W. "Saint Teresa de Avila: Reader of German Mystic Johann Tauler?" *The USF Language Quarterly* 24, nos. 1-2 (Fall-Winter 1985): 25-26.

Lloyd, G. E. R. *Polarity and Analogy: Types of Argumentation in Early Greek Philosophy.* Cambridge: Cambridge University Press, 1966.

Lochrie, Karma. *Margery Kempe and Translations of the Flesh.* Philadelphia: University of Pennsylvania Press, 1991.

Lonergan, Bernard. *Insight: A Study of Human Understanding. Collected Works of Bernard Lonergan,* vol. 3. Toronto: University of Toronto Press, 1992.

————. *Method in Theology.* Minneapolis: Seabury Press, 1972.

————. *Understanding and Being. Collected Works of Bernard Lonergan.* Vol. 5. Toronto: University of Toronto Press, 1990.

Lorch, Maristella de Panizza. *A Defense of Life: Lorenzo Valla's Theory of Pleasure.* Munich: Wilhem Fink Verlag, 1985.

————. *De Vero Falsoque Bono.* Bari: Adriatica Editrice, 1970.

Lorris, Guillaume de, and Jean de Meun. *The Romance of the Rose.* Translated by Harry W. Robbins. New York: E. P. Dutton, 1962.

Lovino, Angelo Maria. "The 'Decameron' and the 'Corbaccio': Boccaccio's Image of Women and Spiritual Crisis." Ph.D. Diss. Indiana University, 1983.

Lowry, Martin. *The World of Aldus Manutius: Business and Scholarship in Renaissance Venice.* Ithaca, N.Y.: Cornell University Press, 1979.

Lucas, Elona K. "The Enigmatic, Threatening Margery Kempe." *The Downside Review* (October 1987): 294-305.

————. "Psychological and Spiritual Growth in Hadewijch and Julian of Norwich." *Studia Mystica* 9, no. 3 (1986): 3-20.

Lucas, J. R. "Because You Are a Woman." *Philosophy* 48 (1973): 161-72.

————. "Vive la Différence." *Philosophy* 53 (1978): 363-73.

Lucretius. *The Nature of Things.* New York: W. W. Norton, 1977.

Luzzi, Mondino de. *Anathomia in the Fasciculus Medicinae of Joannes de Ketham.* Milan: R. Lier, 1924.

Maclean, Ian. *The Renaissance Notion of Woman: A Study in the Fortunes of Scholasticism and Medical Science in European Intellectual Life.* Cambridge and New York: Cambridge University Press, 1980.

MacLeish, Andrew, ed. *The Medieval Monastery.* St. Cloud, Minn.: North Star Press, 1988.

———. *Woman Triumphant: Feminism in French Literature, 1610-1652.* Oxford: Clarendon Press, 1977.

Maddox, Donald, and Sara Sturm-Maddox, eds. *Literary Aspects of Courtly Culture.* Cambridge: D. S. Brewer, 1992.

Mahowald, Mary Briody, ed. *Philosophy of Woman: Classical to Current Concepts.* Indianapolis: Hackett, 1978.

Map, Walter. *De Nugis Curialium (Courtiers' Trifles).* Translated by Frederick Tupper and Marbury Dladen Ogle. London: Chatto and Windus, 1924.

Marcil-Lacoste, Louise. *La Raison en Procès: essais sur la philosophie et le sexisme.* Ville Lasalle, Que.: Hurtubise HMH, 1987.

———. *La Thématique Contemporaine de l'Égalité.* Montreal: Les Presses de l'Université de Montréal, 1984.

Margolis, Nadia. "The Poetics of History: An Analysis of Christine de Pisan's *Livre de la mutacion de fortune.*" Ph.D. Diss. Stanford University, 1977.

Marguerite de Navarre. *L'Heptaméron.* Edited by Michel François. Paris: Gernier, 1964.

Marinelli, Lucrezia. *La Nobilità et l'eccelenza delle Donne Co'Diffetti et Mancamenti De gli Huomini.* Venice: Gio Batista Ciotti Sanese, 1601.

Maritain, Jacques. *The Person and the Common Good.* Notre Dame: Notre Dame Press, 1985. Reprint, New York: Charles Scribner's Sons, 1938.

Marrone, Steven. *William of Auvergne and Robert Grosseteste: New Ideas of Truth in the Early Thirteenth Century.* Princeton: Princeton University Press, 1983.

Martin, Rev. Francis. *The Feminist Question: Feminist Theology in the Light of the Christian Tradition.* Grand Rapids: Eerdmans, 1994.

Martines, Lauro. *The Social World of the Florentine Humanists: 1360-1460.* Princeton: Princeton University Press, 1963.

[Mathieu le Bigame]. *Le Livre de Mathéolus.* Translated by Jean le Fèvre. Brussels: A. Mertens et fils, 1846.

Matulka, Barbara. *An Anti-feminist Treatise of Fifteenth Century Spain: Lucena's "Repitición De Amores."* New York: Institute of French Studies, 1931.

———. *The Novels of Juan de Flores and Their European Diffusion.* New York: Comparative Literature Series, 1931.

———. "The Novels of Juan de Flores and Their European Diffusion: A Study in Comparative Literature." Ph.D. Diss., Columbia University, 1931.

Mazzotta, Giuseppe. *Dante's Vision and the Circle of Knowledge.* Princeton: Princeton University Press, 1993.

———. *The World at Play in Boccaccio's "Decameron."* Princeton: Princeton University Press, 1986.

McCool, S.J., Gerald A. "Why St. Thomas Stays Alive." *International Philosophical Quarterly* 30, no. 3 /issue no. 119: 275-87.

McDonnell, Ernest W. *The Beguines and Beghards in Medieval Culture.* New Brunswick, N.J.: Rutgers University Press, 1954.

McGinn, Bernard. *Introduction to Meister Eckhart: The Essential Sermons, Commentaries, Treatises, and Defense.* New York: Paulist Press, 1981.

McLeod, Enid. *The Order of the Rose: The Life and Ideas of Christine de Pizan.* London: Chatto and Windus, 1976.

McLeod, Glenda K., ed. *The Reception of Christine de Pizan from the Fifteenth through the Nineteenth Centuries.* Lewiston, N.Y.: Edwin Mellen Press, 1992.

Meade, Catherine M., C.S.J. *My Nature Is Fire: Saint Catherine of Siena.* New York: Alba House, 1991.

Mechtild of Hackeborn. *Le Livre de la Grace Spéciale: Révélations de Sainte Mechtilde vierge de l'ordre de Saint-Benoit.* Traduites sur l'editions Laine des Pères Bénédictins de Solesmes. Tours: Maison Mame, 1920.

Mechthild of Magdeburg. *Flowing Light of the Divinity.* Translated by Christiane Mesch Galvani. New York and London: Garland Publishing, 1991.

—————. *The Revelations of Mechtild of Magdeburg.* Translated by Lucy Menzies. London: Longmans Green, 1952.

Memory and Reconciliation: The Church and the Faults of the Past. International Theological Commission. Boston: Pauline Books & Media, 2000.

Merchant, Carolyn. *The Death of Nature: Women, Ecology, and the Scientific Revolution.* San Francisco: Harper and Row, 1980.

Merkel, Ingrid, and Allen G. Dubus, eds. *Hermeticism and the Renaissance: Intellectual History and the Occult in Early Modern Europe.* Washington, D.C.: Folger Books, 1988.

Mermier, Guy R., and Edelgard E. Dubruck, eds. *Fifteenth-Century Studies.* Ann Arbor: Consortium for Medieval and Early Modern Studies, 1981.

Meunier, Mario. *Femmes Pythagoriciennes.* Paris: L'Artisan du livre, 1932.

Meyer, Arthur William. *Human Generation: Conclusions of Burdach, Dollinger and von Baer.* Stanford, Calif.: Stanford University Press, 1956.

—————. *The Rise of Embryology.* Stanford, Calif.: Stanford University Press, 1939.

Midelfort, H. C. Erik. *Witch Hunting in Southwestern Germany, 1562-1684: The Social and Intellectual Foundations.* Stanford, Calif.: Stanford University Press, 1972.

Miller, Clyde Lee. "Perception, Conjecture, and Dialectic in Nicholas of Cusa." *American Catholic Philosophical Quarterly* 64, no. 1 (Winter 1990): 35-54.

Mirror, Louise, ed. *Upon My Husband's Death: Widows in the Literature and Histories of Medieval Europe.* Ann Arbor: University of Michigan Press, 1992.

Mobinson, Mary A. *The End of the Middle Ages: Essays and Questions in History.* London: T. Fisher Unwin, 1988.

Moi, Toril. "Feminism, Postmodernism, and Style: Recent Feminist Criticism in the U.S." *Cultural Critique* (Spring 1988): 3-22.

Molinari, Paul. *Julian of Norwich.* Toronto: Longmans Green, 1958.

Mommaers, P., and N. de Paepe, eds. *Jan Van Ruusbroec: The Sources, Content and Sequels of His Mysticism.* Leuven: University Press, 1984.

Monter, E. William, *Enforcing Morality in Early Modern Europe.* London: Variorum Reprints, 1987.

———. *Witchcraft in France and Switzerland: The Borderlands during the Reformation.* Ithaca and London: Cornell University Press, 1976.

Moore, Cornelia N., and Raymond A. Moody, eds. *Comparative Literature East and West: Traditions and Trends.* Honolulu: University of Hawaii Press, 1989.

Moran, Dermot. "Pantheism from John Scotus Erigena to Nicholas of Cusa." *American Catholic Philosophical Quarterly* 64, no. 1 (1990): 131-52.

Morelli, Mark D., and Elizabeth Morelli, eds. *The Lonergan Reader.* Toronto: University of Toronto Press, 1997.

Morgan, Alison. *Dante and the Medieval Other World.* Cambridge and New York: Cambridge University Press, 1990.

Morgan, Robin, ed. *Sisterhood Is Powerful: An Anthology of Writings from the Women's Movement.* New York: Random House, 1970.

Mounier, Emmanuel. "La Femme aussi est une personne." *Esprit* (June 1936): 291-97.

———. *Personalism.* Notre Dame: University of Notre Dame Press, 1952.

Mozans, H. J. *Women in Science.* Cambridge, Mass.: MIT Press, 1974.

Murphy, James J. *Renaissance Eloquence: Studies in the Theory and Practice of Renaissance Rhetoric.* Berkeley and Los Angeles: University of California Press, 1983.

———. *Rhetoric in the Middle Ages: A History of Rhetorical Theory from Saint Augustine to the Renaissance.* Berkeley: University of California Press, 1974.

Murray, T. Douglas, trans. and ed. *Jeanne D'Arc: Maid of Orleans Deliverer of France, Being the Story of Her Life, Her Achievements, and Her Death, as Attested on Oath and Set Forth in the Original Documents.* London: William Heinemann, 1902.

National Union Catalog Pre-1956 Imprints. London: Mansell Information Publishing Ltd., 1968.

Neaman, Judith S. "Potentiation, Elevation, Acceleration: Prerogatives of Women Mystics." *Mystics Quarterly* 14, no. 1 (March 1988): 22-31.

Needham, Joseph. *A History of Embryology.* Cambridge: Cambridge University Press, 1959.

New Catholic Encyclopedia. Prepared by an editorial staff at the Catholic University of America. New York: McGraw-Hill, 1967-79.

Newman, Barbara. "Authority, Authenticity, and the Repression of Heloise." *Journal of Medieval and Renaissance Studies* 22 (1992): 121-57.

———. *Sister of Wisdom: Hildegard's Theology of the Feminine.* Berkeley and Los Angeles: University of California Press, 1987.

———. "Some Medieval Theologians and the Sophia Tradition." *Downside Review* 108, no. 371 (April 1990): 111-30.

Nichols, John A., and M. Thomas Shank, eds. *Medieval Religious Women: Peaceweavers.* Washington, D.C.: Cistercian Publications, 1987.

Nogarola, Isotta. *Isotae Nogarolae veronensis opera quae supersunt omnia, accedunt Angelae et Zeneverae Nogarolae epistolae et carmina.* Edited by Eugenius Abel. 2 vols. Vienna: apud Fridericum Kilian, 1886.

———. *Isotae Nogarolae Veronensis Opera Quae Supersunt Omnia.* Vindobonae: Gerold et Socios, 1886.

Nolan, Michael, Mgr. "The Aristotelian Background to Aquinas' Denial That 'Woman Is a Defective Male.'" *The Thomist* 64 (2000): 21-69.

———. The Defective Male: What Aquinas Really Said." *New Blackfriars* 75, no. 880 (March 1994): 156-66.

———. *Defective Tales: The Story of Three Myths*. Ireland: Printcomp Ltd., 1995.

———. "Passive and Deformed? Did Aristotle Really Say This?" *New Blackfriars* 74, no. 876 (November 1993) and *New Blackfriars* 75, no. 884 (September 1994).

Nye, Andrea. *Words of Power: A Feminist Reading of the History of Logic*. New York and London: Routledge, 1990.

Obelkevich, James, ed. *Religion and the People*. Chapel Hill: University of North Carolina Press, 1979.

O'Brien, Mary. *The Politics of Reproduction*. Boston: Routledge and Kegan Paul, 1981.

Ockham, William of. *Philosophical Writings*. Translated and edited by Philotheus Boehner, OFM. Toronto: Thomas Nelson and Sons, 1959.

———. *Summa Logiae*. Translated by Michael J. Loux. London: University of Notre Dame Press, 1974.

Offen, Karen. "Defining Feminism: A Comparative Historical Approach." *Signs: Journal of Women in Culture and Society* 13, no. 1 (1988): 144-58.

Olsen, Glenn W. "St. Augustine and the Problem of the Medieval Discovery of the Individual." *Word and Spirit* 9 (1987): 129-56.

O'Malley, C. D. *Andreas Vesalius of Brussels (1514-1564)*. Berkeley and Los Angeles: University of California Press, 1964.

O'Meara, Dominic J. O., ed. *Neoplatonism and Christian Thought*. Norfolk, Va.: International Society for Neoplatonic Studies, 1982.

Oury, Dom Guy-Marie. *Marie Gruyart*. Translated by Miriam Thompson. Cincinnati: Specialty Lithographing Company, 1978.

Owen, Dorothy L. *"Piers Plowman": A Comparison with Some Earlier and Contemporary French Allegories*. Folcroft, Pa.: Folcroft Library Editions, 1971.

Owst, G. R. *Literature and Pulpit in Medieval England*. Cambridge: Cambridge University Press, 1933.

———. *Preaching in Medieval England: An Introduction to Sermon MS. of the Period 1350-1450*. New York: Russell and Russell, 1965.

Ozment, Steven. *The Age of Reform, 1250-1550: An Intellectual and Religious History of Late Medieval and Reformation Europe*. New Haven and London: Yale University Press, 1980.

———. *When Fathers Ruled: Family Life in Reformation Europe*. Cambridge, Mass. and London, 1983.

Pagel, Walter. *Paracelsus: An Introduction to Philosophical Medicine in the Era of the Renaissance*. Basel: S. Karger, 1958.

Paglia, Camille. *Sexual Personae: Art and Decadence from Nefertiti to Emily Dickinson*. New Haven: Yale University Press, 1990.

Pandolfini, Agnolo. *Trattato del governo della famiglia*. Milan: Giovanni Silvestri, 1805.

Paolucci, Anne. "The Women in the *Divine Comedy* and *The Faerie Queene*." Ph.D. Diss., Columbia University, 1963.

Pelikan, Jaroslav. *Christianity and Classical Culture: The Metamorphosis of Natural Theology in the Christian Encounter with Hellenism.* New Haven and London: Yale University Press, 1993.

————. *The Christian Tradition: A History of the Development of Doctrine. Vol. 1: The Emergence of the Catholic Tradition (100-600).* Chicago and London: University of Chicago Press, 1973.

————. *Eternal Feminines: Three Theological Allegories in Dante's "Paradiso."* New Brunswick, N.J. and London: Rutgers University Press, 1990.

Pernoud, Régine. *Blanche of Castille.* Paris: Colmann-Lévy, 1982. Translated by Henry Noel. London: Collins, 1975.

————. *Christine de Pisan.* Paris: Colmann-Lévy, 1982.

————. *Héloise et Abélard.* Paris: A. Michel, 1981. Translated by Peter Wiles. New York: Stein and Day, 1973.

————. *Joan of Arc.* Translated by Edward Hyams. London: Macdonald, 1964.

————. *Joan of Arc: By Herself and Her Witnesses.* Translated by Edward Hyams. New York: Stein and Day, 1969.

————. *Lumière du Moyen Âge.* Paris: Éditions Grasset et Fasquelle, 1981.

————. *Pour en finir avec le Moyen Âge.* Paris: Éditions du Seuil, 1977.

————. *The Retrial of Joan of Arc: The Evidence at the Trial for Her Rehabilitation, 1450-1456.* Translated by J. M. Cohen. London: Methuen and Co. Ltd., 1955.

Peter, John. *Complaint and Satire in Early English Literature.* Oxford: Clarendon Press, 1956.

Peters, Brad. "Julian of Norwich and the Internalized Dialogue of Prayer." *Mystics Quarterly* 20, no. 4 (December 1994): 122-29.

Peters, Edward. *Inquisition.* New York: The Free Press, 1988.

————. *The Magician, the Witch, and the Law.* Philadelphia: University of Pennsylvania Press, 1978.

————. *Torture.* Oxford: Blackwell, 1985.

————, ed. *Heresy and Authority in Medieval Europe: Documents in Translation.* Philadelphia: University of Pennsylvania Press, 1980.

Petrarch. *A Dialogue Between Reason and Adversity: A Late Middle English Version of Petrarch's "De remediis," Book II.* Translated by F. N. M. Diekstra. Assen: Van Borcum and Comp., N.V., 1968.

————. *De remediis utrisque fortune, Book I.* Translated by Conrad H. Rawski. Cleveland: The Press of Western Reserve University, 1967.

————. *Letters from Petrarch.* Translated by Morris Bishop. Bloomington and London: Indiana University Press, 1966.

————. *Petrarch's Africa.* Translated by Thomas G. Bergin and Alice S. Wilson. New Haven and London: Yale University Press, 1977.

————. *Petrarch's Book Without a Name.* Translated by Norman P. Zacour. Toronto: The Pontifical Institute of Mediaeval Studies, 1973.

————. *Petrarch's Bucolicum Carmen.* Translated by Thomas G. Bergin. New Haven and London: Yale University Press, 1974.

————. *Petrarch's Letters to Classical Authors.* Translated by Mario Emilio Cosenza. Chicago: University of Chicago Press, 1910.

————. *Petrarch's Lyric Poems: The Rime Sparce and Other Lyrics.* Translated by Robert M. Durcling. Cambridge, Mass. and London: Harvard University Press, 1976.

————. *Petrarch's Secret of the Soul's Conflict with Passion: Three Dialogues Between Himself and St. Augustine.* Translated by William Draper. London: Chatto and Windus, 1911. Reprint, Norwood, Pa.: Norwood Press, 1976.

————. *Rerum familiarium libri I-VIII.* Translated by Aldo S. Bernardo. Albany: State University of New York Press, 1975.

————. *The Triumphs of Petrarch.* Translated by Ernest Hatch Wilkins. Chicago: University of Chicago Press, 1962.

Petroff, Elizabeth Alvilda, trans. and ed. *Medieval Women's Visionary Literature.* New York: Oxford University Press, 1986.

Phillips, Dayton. *Beguines in Medieval Strasbourg.* Stanford, Calif.: Stanford University Press, 1941.

Pico, Giovanni Francesco. *Giovanni Pico della Mirandola: His Life.* Translated by Sir Thomas More. Edited by James Macmullen. London: David Nutt, 1890.

Pico della Mirandola, Giovanni. *Commentary on a Poem of Platonic Love.* Translated by Douglas Carmichael. Lanham, Md. and London: University Press of America, 1986.

————. *Conclusiones philosophicae, cabalisticae, et theologicae.* Rome, 1486; reprinted Geneva: Librairie Droz, 1973.

————. *Disputationes adversus astrologiam divinatricem.* Libri vi-xii. Edited by Eugenio Garin. Florence: Vallecchi Editore, 1946.

————. *Heptaplus or Discourse on the Seven Days of Creation.* Translated by Jessie Brewer McGaw. New York: Philosophical Library, 1977.

————. *On the Dignity of Man/On Being and the One/Heptaplus.* Translated by Douglas Carmichael. Indianapolis: Library of Liberal Arts, 1965.

————. *Pico's 900 Theses.* Edited by Stephen Alan Farmer. *Syncretism in the West: Pico's 900 Theses (1486): The Evolution of Traditional Religious and Philosophical Systems.* Binghamton, N.Y.: Medieval and Renaissance Texts and Studies, 1998.

————. *A Platonick Discourse upon Love.* Edited by Edmund G. Gardner. Boston: Merrymount Press, 1914.

Pitkin, Hannah Fenichel. *Fortune Is a Woman: Gender and Politics in the Thought of Niccolo Machiavelli.* Berkeley and Los Angeles: University of California Press, 1984.

Pitts, Brent A. "Feast and Famine in the *Quinze joyes de mariage.*" *Romance Notes* 26, no. 1 (Fall 1985): 69-73.

Pizan, Christine de. *The Book of the Body Politic.* Translated and edited by Kate Langdon Forhan. Cambridge: Cambridge University Press, 1994.

————. *The Book of the City of Ladies.* Translated by Earl Jeffrey Edwards. New York: Persea Press, 1983.

————. *The Book of the Duke of True Lovers.* Translated by Thelma S. Fenster and Nadia Margolis. New York: Persea Books, 1991.

————. *The Book of Fayttes of Armes and of Chyvalrie.* Millwood, N.Y.: Kraus Reprint, 1988.

————. *Le Chemin de longue estude.* Translated and edited by Andrea Tarnowski. Paris: Librairie Générale Française, 1998.

————. *Christine de Pizan's "Letter of Othea to Hector."* Translated by Jane Chance. Newburyport, Mass.: Rice University, 1990.

————. *Christine's Vision.* Translated by Glenda K. McLeod. New York and London: Garland Publishing, 1993.

————. *Ditié de Jehanne d'Arc.* Edited by Angus J. Kennedy and Kenneth Varty. Oxford: Society for the Study of Mediaeval Languages and Literature, 1977.

————. *The Epistle of the Prison of Human Life with an Epistle to the Queen of France and Lament on the Evils of the Civil War.* Translated and edited by Josette A. Wisman. New York and London: Garland Library of Medieval Literature, 1984.

————. *Le livre de la mutacion de fortune.* 2 vols. Edited by Suzanne Solente. Paris: A. and J. Picard, 1959.

————. *Le Livre des fais et bonnes moeurs du roi Charles V le Sage.* Translated by Eric Hicks and Thérèse Moreau. Paris: Stock, 1997.

————. *Le Livre des fais et bonnes moeurs du sage roy Charles V.* Paris: Champion, 1936-40.

————. *The Love Debate Poems of Christine de Pizan: Le Livre du Debat de deux amans, Le Livre des Trois jugemens,* and *Le Livre du Dit de Poissy.* Edited by Barbara K. Altmann. Gainesville, Fla.: University Press of Florida, 1998.

————. *Oeuvres poétiques de Christine de Pisan.* 3 vols. Edited by Maurice Roy. Paris: Firmin Didot, 1886-96. Reprint, New York: Johnson, 1985.

————. *Poems of Cupid, God of Love.* Translated and edited by Thelma S. Fenster and Mary Carpenter Erler. Leiden and New York: E. J. Brill, 1990.

————. *La Querelle de la rose: Letters and Documents.* Edited by Joseph L. Baird and John R. Kane. Chapel Hill, N.C.: North Carolina Studies in the Romance Languages and Literature, 1978.

————. *The Selected Writings of Christine de Pizan.* Translated by Kevin Brownlee. Edited by Renate Blumenfeld-Kosinski. New York and London: W. W. Norton, 1997.

————. *The Treasure of the City of Ladies, or, The Book of the Three Virtues.* Translated by Sarah Lawson. Harmondsworth: Penguin Books, 1985.

————. *The Writings of Christine de Pizan.* Edited by Charity Canon Willard. New York: Persea Books, 1994.

Plato. *The Collected Dialogues of Plato, Including the Letters.* Edited by Edith Hamilton and Huntington Cairns. New York: Pantheon Books, 1961.

Plotinus. *Enneads.* Translated by A. H. Armstrong. Cambridge, Mass.: Harvard University Press, 1967.

Plummer, Charles, ed. *Elizabethan Oxford Reprints of Rare Tracts.* Oxford: Clarendon Press, 1887.

Plutarch. *Moralia.* Vols. 1-5. Translated by Frank Cole Babbitt. Cambridge, Mass. and London: Harvard University Press and William Heinemann, 1927-37.

————. *The Education of Children,* in *Plutarch's Moralia,* 14 vols. Translated by Frank Cole Babbitt. Cambridge, Mass.: Harvard University Press, 1959.

Polak, Lucie. "Plato, Nature and Jean de Meun." *Reading Medieval Studies* 3 (1977): 80-103.

Popik, Kristin Mary. *The Philosophy of Woman of St. Thomas Aquinas.* Rome: Angelicum, 1979.

Porete, Marguerite. *The Mirror of Simple Souls.* Translated by M. N. Edited by Clare Kirchberger. London: Burns, Oates and Washbourne, Ltd., 1927.

————. *The Mirror of Simple Souls.* Translated by Ellen L. Babinsky. New York: Paulist Press, 1993.

Porphyry. *Isagoge.* London: H. G. Bohn, 1853.

————. *The Philosopher to His Wife, Marcella.* Translated by Alice Zimmern. London: George Redway, 1896. Reprint, Grand Rapids, Mich.: Phanes Press, 1980.

Pothier, R. J., ed. *Pandectae Justinianeae; in novum ordinem digestae, cum legibus, codicis, et novellis.* Paris, 1825.

Potter, Joy Jambuechen. "Woman in the *Decameron.*" In *Studies in the Italian Renaissance: Essays in Memory of Arnolfo B. Ferruolo.* Edited by Fian Paolo Baisin et al. Naples: Società Editrice Napoletana, 1985.

Power, Edward J. *Main Currents in the History of Education.* New York: McGraw-Hill, 1962.

Power, Sir d'Arcy. *The Foundations of Medical History.* Baltimore: Williams and Wilkins, 1931.

Prokes, FSE, Mary Timothy. *Toward a Theology of the Body.* Grand Rapids: Eerdmans, 1996.

Ptolemy. *Almagest.* Translated by G. J. Toomer. New York: Springer-Verlag, 1984.

Putnam, George Haven. *Books and Their Makers During the Middle Ages.* New York: Hillary House Publishers Ltd., 1962.

Quasten, Johannes. *Patrology. Vol. I: The Beginnings of Patristic Literature.* Westminster, Md.: Newman Press, 1950.

Quay, Paul M. "The Theology of Recapitulation: Understanding the Development of Individuals and Cultures." In *The Dynamic Character of Christian Culture: Essays on Dawsonian Themes,* edited by Peter J. Cataldo, pp. 57-95. Lanham, Md.: University Press of America, 1984.

Quilligan, Maureen. *The Allegory of Female Authority: Christine de Pizan's Cité des dames.* Ithaca and London: Cornell University Press, 1991.

Quint, David. "Humanism and Modernity: A Reconsideration of Bruni's *Dialogues.*" *Renaissance Quarterly* 38, no. 3 (Autumn 1985): 423-45.

Quintilian. *The Institutio Oratoria of Quintilian.* Translated by H. E. Butler. 4 vols. Cambridge, Mass.: Harvard University Press, 1953.

Rabil, Jr., Albert. *Laura Cereta: Quattrocento Humanist.* Binghamton, N.Y.: Center for Medieval and Early Renaissance Studies, 1981.

————, ed. *Renaissance Humanism: Foundations, Forms, and Legacy.* 3 vols. Philadelphia: University of Pennsylvania Press, 1988.

Raffina, Christine. *Marsilio Ficino, Pietro Bembo, Baldassare Castiglione: Philosophi-*

cal, Aesthetic, and Political Approaches in Renaissance Platonism. New York: Peter Lang, 1998.

Raitt, Jill, ed. *Christian Spirituality: High Middle Ages and Reformation*. New York: Crossroad, 1987.

Ramsey, Roy Vance. "Tradition and Chaucer's Unfaithful Woman." Ph.D. Diss. University of Oklahoma, 1964.

Randall, John Herman, Jr. *The School of Padua and the Emergence of Modern Science*. Padova: Editrice Antenore, 1961.

Rashdall, Hastings. *The Universities of Europe in the Middle Ages*. London: Oxford University Press, 1958.

Ratzinger, Cardinal Joseph. "Concerning the Notion of Person in Theology." *Communio* 17 (Fall 1990): 439-52.

Raymond of Capua, Blessed. *The Life of St. Catherine of Siena*. New York: P. J. Kennedy and Sons, 1960.

Redpath, Helen Mary Dominic, Sister. *God's Ambassadress: St. Bridget of Sweden*. Milwaukee: Bruce Publishing Co., 1946.

Reed, Gail H. "Chaucer's Women: Commitment and Subversion." Ph.D. Diss. University of Nebraska, 1973.

Reed, Jr., Thomas L. *Middle English Debate Poetry and the Aesthetics of Irresolution*. Columbia, Mo. and London: University of Missouri Press, 1990.

Reiter, Rayna R., ed. *Towards an Anthropology of Woman*. New York: Monthly Review Press, 1975.

Richards, Earl Jeffrey, et al., eds. *Reinterpreting Christine de Pizan*. Athens, Ga. and London: University of Georgia Press, 1992.

Robb, Nesca A. *Neoplatonism of the Italian Renaissance*. London: George Allen and Unwin, Ltd., 1935.

Robinson, Mary. *The End of the Middle Ages: Essays and Questions in History*. London: T. Fisher Unwin, 1889.

Rocca, Gregory Philip. "Analogy as Judgment and Faith in God's Incomprehensibility: A Study in the Theological Epistemology of Thomas Aquinas." Ph.D. Diss. The Catholic University of America, 1989.

―――. "Aquinas on God-Talk: Hovering Over the Abyss." *Theological Studies* 54 (December 1993): 641-61.

―――. "The Distinction between *Res Significata* and *Modus Significandi* in Aquinas' Theological Epistemology." *Thomist* 55 (April 1991): 173-97.

Rodriguez, Otilio. "Saint Teresa of Jesus and Mental Prayer." In *Word and Spirit: A Monastic Review Dedicated to St. Teresa of Avila*. Still River, Mass.: St. Bede's Publications, 1983.

Rogers, Katherine. *The Troublesome Helpmate: A History of Misogyny in Literature*. Seattle: University of Washington Press, 1966.

Rose, Mary Beth, ed. *Women in the Middle Ages and the Renaissance: Literary and Historical Perspectives*. Syracuse, N.Y.: Syracuse University Press, 1986.

Ross, Nelson Peter. *Christianity and Humanism: Studies in the History of Ideas*. Grand Rapids: Eerdmans, 1968.

Roswitha. *The Plays of Roswitha*. Translated by Christopher St. John. New York: Cooper Square Publishers, Inc., 1966.

Rothkrug, Lionel. "Religious Practices and Collective Perceptions: Hidden Homologies in the Renaissance and Reformation." *Historical Reflections/ Réflexions Historiques* 7, no. 1 (Spring 1980): 103-23.

Rousseau, Mary, ed. *The Apple, or Aristotle's Death*. Milwaukee: Marquette University Press, 1968.

———. *Community: The Tie That Binds*. Lanham, Md.: University Press of America, 1991.

Rowland, Beryl, trans. and ed. *Medieval Woman's Guide to Health: The First English Gynecological Handbook*. Kent, Ohio: Kent State University Press, 1981.

Russell, Jeffrey Burton. *Witchcraft in the Middle Ages*. Ithaca and London: Cornell University Press, 1972.

Russell, Rinaldina, ed. *The Feminist Encyclopedia of Italian Literature*. Westport, Conn. and London: Greenwood Press, 1997.

———. *Italian Women Writers: A Bio-Bibliographical Sourcebook*. Westport, Conn. and London: Greenwood Press, 1994.

Ruud, Jay. "Nature and Grace in Julian of Norwich." *Mystics Quarterly* 19, no. 2 (June 1993): 71-81.

Sackville-West, Victoria Mary. *Saint Joan of Arc*. London: Corden-Sanderson, 1936.

Sadler, T. W. *Langman's Medical Embryology*. 5th edition. Baltimore: Williams and Wilkins, 1985.

Salter, Nancy Clark. "Masks and Roles: A Study of Women in Shakespeare's Drama." Ph.D. Diss. University of Connecticut, 1975.

Schindler, David. "Catholic Theology, Gender, and the Future of Western Civilization." *Communio* 20 (Summer 1993): 200-239.

———. "Norris Clarke on Person, Being and St. Thomas." *Communio* 20 (Fall 1993): 580-92.

Schmidt, Robert W., S.J., ed. *The Domain of Logic According to Saint Thomas Aquinas*. The Hague: Martinus Nijhoff, 1966.

Schmitt, Charles B. *Aristotle and the Renaissance*. Cambridge, Mass.: Harvard University Press, 1983.

———. *Gianfrancesco Pico della Mirandola (1469-1533) and His Critique of Aristotle*. The Hague: Martinus Nijhoff, 1967.

———. *John Case and Aristotelianism in Renaissance England*. Montreal: McGill-Queen's University Press, 1983.

———. "Philosophy and Science in Sixteenth Century Universities: Some Preliminary Comments." In *The Cultural Context of Medieval Learning*. Edited by James Edward Murdock and E. D. Sylla. Boston Studies in the Philosophy of Science, vol. 26. Dordrecht: D. Reidel, 1975.

———. "Towards a Reassessment of Renaissance Aristotelianism." *History of Science* 11 (September 1973): 159-93.

Schnapp, Jeffrey T. "Dante's Sexual Solecisms: Gender and Genre in the *Commedia*." *Romantic Review* 79, no. 1 (January 1988): 143-63.

Schoeck, R. J. *Erasmus of Europe: The Making of a Humanist (1467-1500)*. Savage, Md.: Barnes and Noble, 1990.

———. *Erasmus of Europe: The Prince of Humanists (1501-1536)*. Edinburgh: Edinburgh University Press, 1993.

Schroeder, J. H., trans. *Canons and Decrees of the Council of Trent.* St. Louis, Mo.: Herder, 1950.

Schütze, Tobias. *Harmonia macrocosmi cum microcosmo.* Frankfurt am Main: Daniel Reicheln, 1654.

Schwertner, Thomas Maria. *St. Albert the Great.* New York: Bruce Publishing Company, 1932.

Schwoebel, Robert, ed. *Renaissance Men and Ideas.* New York: St. Martin's Press, 1971.

Scot, Reginald. *Scot's Discovery of Witchcraft.* London: Giles Calvert, 1584.

Scott, Karen. "St. Catherine of Siena, 'Apostola'." *Church History* 61, no. 1 (March 1992): 34-46.

Scott, S. P., ed. *The Civil Law.* 17 vols. Cincinnati: Central Trust, 1932.

Seelaus, Vilma. "The Feminine in Prayer in the Interior Castle." *Mystics Quarterly* 13 (December 1987).

Seigel, Jerrold E. *Rhetoric and Philosophy in Renaissance Humanism: The Union of Eloquence and Wisdom, Petrarch to Valla.* Princeton: Princeton University Press, 1968.

Seneca. *Moral Essays,* Loeb Edition. New York and London: C. P. Putnam's Sons and William Heinemann, Ltd., 1925.

Shank, Lillian Thomas, and John A. Nichols. *Distant Echoes: Medieval Religious Women.* Vol. 1. Kalamazoo, Mich.: Cistercian Studies Series #71, 1984.

————. *Peaceweavers: Medieval Religious Women.* Vol. 2. Kalamazoo, Mich.: Cistercian Studies Series #72, 1987.

Shapiro, Marianne. *Women Earthly and Divine in the "Comedy" of Dante.* Lexington: University Press of Kentucky, 1975.

Shapiro, Susan C. "Amazons, Hermaphrodites, and Plain Monsters: The 'Masculine' Woman in English Satire and Social Criticism from 1580-1640." *Atlantis* 13, no. 1 (Fall 1987): 66-76.

————. "Sex, Gender, and Fashion in Medieval and Early Modern Britain." *Journal of Popular Culture* 20, no. 4 (1987): 113-28.

Shea, William R. *Galileo's Intellectual Revolution.* London: Macmillan, 1972.

Sherman, Clare Richter. *Imaging Aristotle: Verbal and Visual Representaiton in Fourteenth-Century France.* Berkeley and Los Angeles: University of California Press, 1995.

Sinnreich-Levi, Deborah M., and Gale Sigal, eds. *Voices in Translation: The Authority of "Olde Bookes" in Medieval Literature* (Essays in Honor of Helaine Newstead). New York: AMS Press, 1992.

Smarr, Janet Levarie. *Boccaccio and Fiammetta: The Narrator as Lover.* Urbana and Chicago: University of Illinois Press, 1986.

Smith, Lesley, and Jane H. M. Taylor, eds. *Women, the Book and the Worldly.* Selected Proceedings of the St. Hilda's Conference, 1993. Reprint, Suffolk, U.K.: D. S. Brewer, 1995.

Smith, Sydney E. *The Opposing Voice: Christine de Pisan's Criticism of Courtly Love.* Stanford, Calif.: Honors Essay in Humanities XXXIV, 1990.

Sokolowski, Robert. *Eucharistic Presence: A Study in the Theology of Disclosure.* Washington, D.C.: Catholic University Press, 1993.

————. *The God of Faith and Reason*. Notre Dame: University of Notre Dame Press, 1982.

Solterer, Helen. *The Master and Minerva: Disputing Women in French Medieval Culture*. Berkeley and Los Angeles: University of California Press, 1995.

Southern, R. W. *Western Society and the Church*. Harmondsworth: Penguin Books, 1982.

Spitz, Lewis W. *Conrad Celtis: The German Arch-Humanist*. Cambridge, Mass.: Harvard University Press, 1957.

Sprung, Andrew. "'We never shall come out of him': Enclosure and Immanence in Julian of Norwich's *Book of Showings*." *Mystics Quarterly* 19, no. 2 (1989): 47-62.

Stakel, Susan. *False Roses: Structures of Duality and Deceit in Jean de Meun's "Roman de la Rose."* Stanford French and Italian Studies 69. Saratoga and Stanford: Anima Libri and Department of French and Italian, Stanford University, 1991.

Stein, Edith. *Essays on Women*. 2nd ed. Washington, D.C.: ICS Publications, 1996.

Steiner, Arpad. *De Eruditione Filiorum Nobilium of Vincent of Beauvais*. Cambridge, Mass.: Harvard University Press, 1939.

Stier, Sister Jane. "The Role of Women Religious Active in Education and Other Apostolates during the Renaissance: An Historical Study." Ph.D. Diss. The Catholic University of America, 1966.

Stocks, John Leofric. *Aristotelianism*. New York: Cooper Square Publishers, 1963.

Sturm-Maddox, Sara. *Petrarch's Laurels*. University Park, Pennsylvania: State University Press, 1992.

————. *Petrarch's Metamorphoses: Text and Subtext in the Rime Sparse*. Columbia: University of Missouri Press, 1985.

Summers, Montague. *The Geography of Witchcraft*. Secaucus, N.J.: Citadel Press, 1973.

Supple, David, O.S.B., ed. *Virgin Wholly Marvelous: Praises of Our Lady by the Popes, Councils, Saints, and Doctors of the Church*. Cambridge: Ravengate Press, 1991.

Suso, Henry. *Henry Suso: The Exemplar, with Two German Sermons*. Translated by Frank Tobin. New York: Paulist Press, 1989.

Sutherland, Ronald. *The Romaunt of the Rose* and *Le Roman de la Rose*: A Parallel-Text Edition. Berkeley and Los Angeles: University of California Press, 1968.

————. "The *Romaunt of the Rose* and Source Manuscripts." *Publications of the Modern Languages Association* 74 (1959): 178-83.

Szarmach, Paul E., ed. *An Introduction to the Medieval Mystics of Europe*. Albany: State University of New York Press, 1984.

Tambling, Jeremy. *Dante and Difference: Writing in the "Commedia."* Cambridge: Cambridge University Press, 1988.

Tauler, Johannes. *Sermons*. Translated and edited by Josef Schmidt. New York: Paulist Press, 1985.

Taylor, Charles. *The Malaise of Modernity*. Concord, Ont.: Canadian Broadcasting Corporation, 1991.

————. *Sources of the Self: The Making of a Modern Identity.* Cambridge, Mass.: Harvard University Press, 1989.

Teresa of Avila, St. *The Collected Works,* 2 vols. Translated by Kieran Kavanaugh, O.C.D. and Otilio Rodriguez, O.C.D. Washington, D.C.: ICS Publications, 1976.

Test, George A. *Satire: Spirit and Art.* Tampa: University of South Florida Press, 1991.

Thomas Aquinas, St. *Commentary on the "Metaphysics" of Aristotle.* 2 vols. Translated by John P. Rowan. Chicago: Henry Regnery, 1961.

————. *Commentary on the 'Nicomachean Ethics.'* Translated by C. I. Litzinger. Chicago: Henry Regnery, 1965.

————. *Disputed Questions on Truth.* Translated by R. W. Schmidt. Chicago: Henry Regnery, 1952.

————. *In Octo Libros Politicorum Aristotelis Expositio seu De Rebus Civilibus.* Quebec City: University of Laval, Tremblay and Dion, 1940.

————. *On the Truth of the Catholic Faith: Summa Contra Gentiles.* Garden City, N.Y.: Image Books, 1956.

————. *Petri Lombardi Sententiarum Libri Quattuor.* Paris: J. P. Migne, 1853.

————. *Summa theologica.* 5 vols. Translated by Fathers of the English Dominican Province. Westminster, Md.: Christian Classics, 1948. Reprint, 1968.

————. *Summa theologiae.* Blackfriars edition. Vols. 1-60. New York: McGraw-Hill, 1964.

Thompson, Bard. *Humanists and Reformers: A History of the Renaissance and Reformation.* Grand Rapids and Cambridge, U.K.: Eerdmans, 1996.

Thwaites, Reuben, and S. R. Mealing, eds. *The Jesuit Relations and Allied Documents.* Toronto: McLelland and Stewart, 1963.

Tignonville, Guillaume de. *The Dicts and Sayings of the Philosophers.* Translated by Stephen Scrope. Edited by Curt F. Bühler. London: Oxford University Press, 1941.

Tillman, Mary Katherine. "Scholastic and Averroistic Influences on the *Roman de la rose.*" *Annuale medievale* 11 (1970): 89-106.

Tobin, Rosemary Barton. "Vincent of Beauvais on the Education of Women." *Journal of the History of Ideas* 35 (July-September 1974): 479-83.

Tomasini, Jacopo Filippo, ed. *Laura Ceretae Brisiensis Feminae Clarissimae Epistolae iam primum e MS in lucem productae.* Padua: Sebastiano Sardi, 1640.

Took, J. F. *Dante: Lyric Poet and Philosopher: An Introduction to the Minor Works.* Oxford: Clarendon Press, 1990.

Tornay, Stephen Chak. *Ockham: Studies and Selections.* Lasalle, Ill.: Open Court, 1938.

Trinkaus, Charles. *The Poet as Philosopher: Petrarch and the Formation of Renaissance Consciousness.* New Haven and London: Yale University Press, 1979.

Tuana, Nancy, ed. *Feminist Interpretations of Plato.* University Park, Pa.: Pennsylvania State University Press, 1994.

Tuchman, Barbara W. *A Distant Mirror: The Calamitous 14th Century.* New York: Ballantine Books, 1978.

Tucker, Samuel Marion. *Verse Satire in England before the Renaissance.* New York: Columbia University Press, 1908.

Twain, Mark. *Personal Recollections of Joan of Arc by the Sieur Louis de Conte (Her Page and Secretary): Freely Translated out of the Ancient French into Modern English from the Original Unpublished Manuscript in the National Archives of France by Jean François Alden.* San Francisco: Ignatius Press, 1989.

Ullmann, Walter. *Medieval Foundations of Renaissance Humanism.* London: Paul Elek, 1977.

Underhill, Evelyn. *The Mystics of the Church.* New York: Schocken Books, 1964.

Undset, Sigrid. *Catherine of Siena.* Translated by Kate Austin-Lund. New York: Sheed and Ward, 1954.

Utley, Francis Lee. *The Crooked Rib: An Analytical Index to the Argument about Women in English and Scots Literature to the End of the Year 1568.* Columbus: Ohio State University Press, 1944.

———. *A Manual of the Writings in Middle English: 1050-1500.* Vols. 1-8. Hamden, Conn.: Archon Books, 1967.

———, ed. *The Forward Movement of the Fourteenth Century.* Columbus: Ohio State University Press, 1961.

Valens, Acidalius. *Paradoxe sur les Femmes où l'on tâche de prouver qu'elles ne sont pas de l'espèce humaine.* Translated by Ch. Chapiès. Paris, 1766.

———. *Problème sur les femmes où l'on essaye prouver que les femmes ne sont point des créatures humaines.* Translated by Meusnier de Querlon. Amsterdam, 1744.

Valla, Lorenzo. *On Pleasure: De voluptate.* Translated by A. Kent Hieatt and Maristella Lorch. New York: Abaris Books, 1977.

Van Dijk-Hemmes, Fokkelien, and Athalya Brenner, eds. *Reflections on Theology and Gender.* Kampen, the Netherlands: Kok Pharos Publishing House, 1994.

Van Hamel, A. G. *Les Lamentations de Matheolus et le livre de Leesce.* 2 vols. Paris: 1892-1905.

Van Kessel, Elisja Schulte, ed. *Women and Men in Spiritual Culture, XIV-XVII Centuries: A Meeting of South and North.* The Hague: Netherlands Government Publishing Office, 1986.

Van Steenberghen, Fernand. *Aristotle in the West: The Origins of Latin Averroism.* Louvain: E. Nauwelaerts and Verlag Herder, 1959.

Vauchez, André. *The Laity in the Middle Ages: Religious Beliefs and Devotional Practices.* Translated by Margery J. Schneider. Edited by Daniel E. Bornstein. Notre Dame and London: University of Notre Dame Press, 1993.

Verminus, Thomas. *Compendiosa Totius Anatomie Delineatio.* London: Dawson's of Pall Mall, 1959.

Vesalius, Andreas. *The Epitome of Andreas Vesalius.* Translated by L. R. Lind. New York: Macmillan, 1949.

———. *The Illustrations from the Works of Andreas Vesalius of Brussels.* Edited by J. B. de C. M. Saunders and Charles D. O'Malley. Cleveland: World Publishing, 1950.

Vickers, Brian. "Valla's Ambivalent Praise of Pleasure: Rhetoric in the Service of Christianity." *Viator: Medieval and Renaissance Studies* 17 (1986): 271-319.

Vincent of Beauvais. *De eruditione filiorum nobilium*. Edited by Arpad Steiner. Cambridge, Mass.: Medieval Academy of America, 1938.

———. *Speculum doctrinale*. Graz, Austria: Akademischer Druck, 1965.

———. *Speculum historiale*. Graz, Austria: Akademischer Druck, 1965.

———. *Speculum morale*. Graz, Austria: Akademischer Druck, 1964.

———. *Speculum naturale*. Graz, Austria: Akademischer Druck, 1964.

Waithe, Mary Ellen, ed. *A History of Women Philosophers: Volume II: Medieval, Renaissance and Enlightenment Women Philosophers: A.D. 500-1600*. Dordrecht: Kluwer, 1989.

Walker, Hugh. *English Satire and Satirists*. New York: Octagon Books, 1972.

Wallace, William A. *Causality and Scientific Explanation. Medieval and Early Classical Science*. Vol. 1. Ann Arbor: University of Michigan Press, 1972.

———. *The Elements of Philosophy: A Compendium for Philosophers and Theologians*. New York: Alba House, 1977.

———. *From a Realist Point of View: Essays on the Philosophy of Science*. 2nd ed. Lanham, Md.: University Press of America, 1983.

Ward, Charles Frederick. "The Epistles on the Romance of the Rose." Ph.D. Diss. University of Chicago, 1911.

Warner, Marina. *Joan of Arc: The Image of Female Heroism*. New York: Vintage, 1981.

Watkins, Renée Neu. "Two Women Visionaries and Death: Catherine of Siena and Julian of Norwich." *Numen: International Review for the History of Religions* 30, fasc. 2: 188.

Watson, Nicholas. "'Classics of Western Spirituality' II: Three Medieval Women Theologians and Their Background." *Kings Theological Review* 12 (1989): 57.

Wayman, Dorothy G. "The Chancellor and Jeanne d'Arc: February-July, A.D. 1429." *Franciscan Studies* 17-18 (1957): 273-305.

Weber, Alison. *Teresa of Avila and the Rhetoric of Femininity*. Princeton: Princeton University Press, 1990.

Weinberg, Steven. *The First Three Minutes: A Modern View of the Origin of the Universe*. New York: Basic Books, 1977.

Weisheipl, O.P., James., ed. *Albertus Magnus and the Sciences: Commemorative Essays 1980*. Toronto: Pontifical Institute of Mediaeval Studies, 1980.

———. *Nature and Motion in the Middle Ages*. Edited by William E. Carroll. In *Studies in Philosophy and the History of Philosophy*. Edited by Jude P. Dougherty. Washington, D.C.: Catholic University of America Press, 1985.

———. "Thomas d'Aquino and Albert His Teacher." *The Etienne Gilson Series 2*. Toronto: Pontifical Institute for Mediaeval Studies, 1980.

Welch, John, O.C. *Spiritual Pilgrims: Carl Jung and Teresa of Avila*. New York: Paulist Press, 1982.

Wemple, Suzanne. *Women in Frankish Society: Marriage and the Cloister 500-900*. Philadelphia: University of Pennsylvania Press, 1981.

Wiesen, David S. *St. Jerome as a Satirist: A Study in Christian Latin Thought and Letters*. Ithaca, N.Y.: Cornell University Press, 1964.

Wilbanks, Evelyn Rivers. "The Changing Images of Women in the World of

Petrarch, Boccaccio, Alberti, and Castiglione." Ph.D. Diss. University of Chicago, 1977.

Wilkins, Ernest Hatch. *A History of Italian Literature*. Cambridge, Mass. and London: Harvard University Press, 1974.

Willard, Charity Canon. *Christine de Pizan: Her Life and Works*. New York: Persea Books, 1984.

Williams, Charles. *The Figure of Beatrice: A Study in Dante*. London: Faber and Faber, 1943.

Wilson, Katharina M. "Figmenta vs. Veritas: Dame Alice and the Medieval Literary Depiction of Women by Women." *Tulsa Studies in Women's Literature* 4, no. 1 (Spring 1985): 17-32.

———, ed. *Hrotsvit of Gandersheim: Rara Avis in Saconia?* Ann Arbor, Mich.: Marc Publishing Co., 1987.

———, ed. *Medieval Women Writers*. Athens, Ga.: University of Georgia Press, 1984.

———, ed. *Women Writers of the Renaissance and the Reformation*. Athens, Ga.: University of Georgia Press, 1987.

Wippel, John F. "The Condemnations of 1270 and 1277 at Paris." *The Journal of Medieval and Renaissance Studies* 7 (1977): 169-201.

Wojtyla, Karol. *The Acting Person*. Boston: D. Reidel, 1979.

———. *Love and Responsibility*. San Francisco: Ignatius Press, 1981. Reprint, 1993.

———. *Person and Community: Selected Essays*. Translated by Theresa Sandok, O.S.M. *Catholic Thought from Lublin*. vol. 4. Edited by Andrew N. Woznicki. New York: Peter Lang, 1993.

Woodward, William Harrison. *Studies in Education during the Age of the Renaissance, 1400-1600*. New York: Columbia University Press, 1967.

———. *Vittorino da Feltre and Other Humanist Educators*. New York: Columbia University Bureau of Publications, 1963.

Woznicki, Andrew Nicholas. *Christian Humanism: Karol Wojtyla's Existential Personalism*. New Britain, Conn.: Mariel Publications, 1980.

Wright, Thomas, ed. *The Latin Poems Commonly Attributed to Walter Mapes*. Hildesheim: George Olms Verlagsbuchhandlung, 1968.

Xenophon. *Memorabilia and Oeconomicus*. New York and London: G. P. Putnam's Sons and William Heinemann, 1923.

Yenal, Edith. *Christine de Pisan: A Bibliography of Writings by Her and about Her*. Metuchen, N.J., and London: Scarecrow Press, 1982.

Yunck, John A. *The Lineage of Lady Meed: The Development of Medieval Venality Satire*. Notre Dame: University of Notre Dame Press, 1963.

Zilboorg, Gregory, M.D. *The Medical Man and the Witch During the Renaissance*. Baltimore: Johns Hopkins University Press, 1935.

Zimmermann, Margarete, and Dina De Rentiis, eds. *The City of Scholars: New Approaches to Christine de Pizan*. Berlin and New York: Walter de Gruyter, 1994.

INDEX

Abel, Eugenius, 961n.63, 969

Abelard, Peter, 32, 68, 71-72, 92, 110, 167, 190, 195, 229, 551, 565, 594, 603

Abraham: the Patriarch, 327; the humanist, 907

Academy: Aldine, 753, 859, 907; Chiara, 936, 970, 980, 1011, 1025, 1059; Florentine, 753, 890, 940, 984; Mondella, 936, 994, 1049; Platonic, in Florence, 855-60, 882, 890-91, 904, 919n.83, 970, 1083, 1080; Platonic, in Germanic regions (Rhineland, Vienna, Linz, Poland, Nuremberg), 750; Platonic, in Greece, 1083

Accident: in academia, 175; in Albert, 118-21, 170; in Aristotle, 12, 75, 77-80, 98-100, 132, 164, 168, 170, 243, 319, 1014, 1055; in Bacon, 86; in Cavalcanti, 234, 236, 243; in Cereta, 1013-14; in Christine de Pizan, 561; in Dante, 243, 258n.138; in Grosseteste, 83; in Joan of Arc, 497; in Julian, 408, 410; in Nogarola, 968; in Ockham, 87; in Pico, 909, 916; in Porphyry, 77-80; in satires about gender, 78-79, 202, 221n.121, 234, 315-16; in Scotus, 160; in Thomas Aquinas, 10, 131, 170, 410; in other contexts, 21, 132, 324, 385n.172, 844

Adam, 145-46, 208, 210, 240, 327, 347-49, 389n.190, 508, 511, 513, 572, 606, 625, 642n.299, 918, 922, 945-53, 954, 965-68, 1043, 1066-70, 1079, 1088

Aemilius, Augustinus, 965, 966n.77

Aesare of Lucania, 31

Agrippa, Henry Cornelius: and reverse gender polarity, 17, 572, 622, 625, 1038

Agrippina, 634, 1039

Albert, brother of Abbess at Helfta, 344

Albert the Great, St.: Aristotle's natural philosophy as basis for gender polarity in, 112-27, 169-70, 172-76, 1074; relation to Christine de Pizan, 541, 566, 624-25; Cusanus, 765; Eckhart, 344-45, 348-49, 435, 1074; Ficino, 874; *Malleus Malificarum,* 504-9, 511, 515; Mechtild, 332-33; Pico, 908, 913; Suso, 365; Mary in, 114; method in, 69-70, 82-84, 122, 154, 169, 1074; person in, 11, 55, 169; *De secretis mulierum,* 126, 624-25; in satires, 511; teacher of Thomas Aquinas on woman, 113-29, 131, 133, 136-39, 145-46, 150, 170, 1074, 1128; theory of gender identity in, 10, 69-70, 113-27, 154, 172-76, 418, 1082-83

Alberti, Alberto degli, 1004, 1022, 1049

Alberti, Barbara, 1012

Alberti, Leon Battista, art in, 751, 789-91; humanist dialogue with, 766, 789-830, 1078; gender polarity in, 322, 417-19, 722, 792, 797, 825-26, 1015, 1053, 1057; masculine and feminine in, 802-4; relation to Ludovico Gonzaga, 801; relation to Valla, 854; relation to Xenophon, 799-800, 1057; satire against feminists in, 817-25, 1053, 1078; utilitarian view of the family in, 686n.78, 792, 798-816, 827-28, 944, 1069

Alcibiades, 76, 687n.82, 800, 811, 920, 1013

Alemanno, Yohanan, 907

Alexander of Aphrodisias, 109, 111

Alexander the Great, 85, 284, 550, 602, 742, 943, 1026

Al-Farabi, 110-11, 913